JavaScript™ Bible

3rd Edition

JavaScript™ Bible
3rd Edition

Danny Goodman
With a foreword by Brendan Eich, JavaScript's creator

IDG Books Worldwide, Inc.
An International Data Group Company

Foster City, CA ✦ Chicago, IL ✦ Indianapolis, IN ✦ Southlake, TX

JavaScript™ Bible, 3rd Edition

Published by

IDG Books Worldwide, Inc.

An International Data Group Company

919 E. Hillsdale Blvd., Suite 400

Foster City, CA 94404

www.idgbooks.com (IDG Books Worldwide Web site)

Library of Congress Catalog Card No.: 97-078208

ISBN: 0-7645-3188-3

Printed in the United States of America

10

3B/SQ/RR/ZY/IN

Distributed in the United States by IDG Books Worldwide, Inc.

Distributed by Macmillan Canada for Canada; by Transworld Publishers Limited in the United Kingdom; by IDG Norge Books for Norway; by IDG Sweden Books for Sweden; by Woodslane Pty. Ltd. for Australia; by Woodslane Enterprises Ltd. for New Zealand; by Longman Singapore Publishers Ltd. for Singapore, Malaysia, Thailand, and Indonesia; by Simron Pty. Ltd. for South Africa; by Toppan Company Ltd. for Japan; by Distribuidora Cuspide for Argentina; by Livraria Cultura for Brazil; by Ediciencia S.A. for Ecuador; by Addison-Wesley Publishing Company for Korea; by Ediciones ZETA S.C.R. Ltda. for Peru; by WS Computer Publishing Corporation, Inc., for the Philippines; by Unalis Corporation for Taiwan; by Contemporanea de Ediciones for Venezuela; by Computer Book & Magazine Store for Puerto Rico; by Express Computer Distributors for the Caribbean and West Indies. Authorized Sales Agent: Anthony Rudkin Associates for the Middle East and North Africa.

For general information on IDG Books Worldwide's books in the U.S., please call our Consumer Customer Service department at 800-762-2974. For reseller information, including discounts and premium sales, please call our Reseller Customer Service department at 800-434-3422.

For information on where to purchase IDG Books Worldwide's books outside the U.S., please contact our International Sales department at 650-655-3200 or fax 650-655-3295.

For information on foreign language translations, please contact our Foreign & Subsidiary Rights department at 650-655-3021 or fax 650-655-3281.

For sales inquiries and special prices for bulk quantities, please contact our Sales department at 650-655-3200 or write to the address above.

For information on using IDG Books Worldwide's books in the classroom or for ordering examination copies, please contact our Educational Sales department at 800-434-2086 or fax 817-251-8174.

For press review copies, author interviews, or other publicity information, please contact our Public Relations department at 650-655-3000 or fax 650-655-3299.

For authorization to photocopy items for corporate, personal, or educational use, please contact Copyright Clearance Center, 222 Rosewood Drive, Danvers, MA 01923, or fax 978-750-4470.

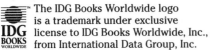

ABOUT IDG BOOKS WORLDWIDE

Welcome to the world of IDG Books Worldwide.

IDG Books Worldwide, Inc., is a subsidiary of International Data Group, the world's largest publisher of computer-related information and the leading global provider of information services on information technology. IDG was founded more than 25 years ago and now employs more than 8,500 people worldwide. IDG publishes more than 275 computer publications in over 75 countries (see listing below). More than 60 million people read one or more IDG publications each month.

Launched in 1990, IDG Books Worldwide is today the #1 publisher of best-selling computer books in the United States. We are proud to have received eight awards from the Computer Press Association in recognition of editorial excellence and three from *Computer Currents'* First Annual Readers' Choice Awards. Our best-selling *...For Dummies*® series has more than 30 million copies in print with translations in 30 languages. IDG Books Worldwide, through a joint venture with IDG's Hi-Tech Beijing, became the first U.S. publisher to publish a computer book in the People's Republic of China. In record time, IDG Books Worldwide has become the first choice for millions of readers around the world who want to learn how to better manage their businesses.

Our mission is simple: Every one of our books is designed to bring extra value and skill-building instructions to the reader. Our books are written by experts who understand and care about our readers. The knowledge base of our editorial staff comes from years of experience in publishing, education, and journalism — experience we use to produce books for the '90s. In short, we care about books, so we attract the best people. We devote special attention to details such as audience, interior design, use of icons, and illustrations. And because we use an efficient process of authoring, editing, and desktop publishing our books electronically, we can spend more time ensuring superior content and spend less time on the technicalities of making books.

You can count on our commitment to deliver high-quality books at competitive prices on topics you want to read about. At IDG Books Worldwide, we continue in the IDG tradition of delivering quality for more than 25 years. You'll find no better book on a subject than one from IDG Books Worldwide.

John Kilcullen
CEO
IDG Books Worldwide, Inc.

Steven Berkowitz
President and Publisher
IDG Books Worldwide, Inc.

Eighth Annual Computer Press Awards ≥ 1992

Ninth Annual Computer Press Awards ≥ 1993

Tenth Annual Computer Press Awards ≥ 1994

Eleventh Annual Computer Press Awards ≥ 1995

Credits

Acquisitions Editor
Michael Roney

Development Editors
Susan Pines
Denise Santoro
Matt Lusher
Laura Brown

Technical Editors
David Wall
Mike Shaver

Copy Editors
Ami Knox
Michael D. Welch

Production Coordinator
Ritchie Durdin

Book Designers
Draper and Liew, Inc.
Catalin Dulfu
Kurt Krames

Graphics and Production Specialists
Jude Levinson
Linda J. Marousek
Hector Mendoza
Maureen Moore
Ed Penslien
Christopher Pimentel
Dina F Quan

Quality Control Specialist
Mick Arellano
Mark Schumann

Proofreader
Christine Sabooni

Indexer
Tech Indexing

About the Author

Danny Goodman is the author of numerous critically acclaimed and best-selling books, including *Danny Goodman's AppleScript Handbook*, *Living at Light Speed*, and *The Complete HyperCard Handbook*, one of the all-time best-selling Macintosh titles with nearly half a million copies in print. He is renowned as an authority and expert teacher of computer scripting languages and writes the "JavaScript Apostle" column for Netscape's *View Source* online developer newsletter. His writing style and pedagogy continue to earn praise from readers and teachers around the world. To help keep his finger on the pulse of real-world programming challenges, Goodman frequently lends his touch as consulting programmer and designer to leading-edge World Wide Web and intranet sites.

Foreword

As JavaScript's creator, I would like to say a few words about where JavaScript has been, where it is going, and how the book you're holding will help you to make the most of JavaScript.

JavaScript was born out of a desire to let HTML authors write scripts directly in their documents. This may seem obvious now, but in the spring of 1995 it was novel and more than a little at odds with both the conventional wisdom (HTML should describe static document structure only) and the Next Big Thing (Java applets, hyped as the one true way to enliven and extend Web pages). Once I got past these contentions, JavaScript grew quickly along the following lines:

+ **"Java-lite" syntax.** Although the "natural language" syntax of HyperTalk was fresh in my mind after a friend lent me *The Complete HyperCard Handbook* by some fellow named Goodman, the Next Big Thing weighed heavier, especially in light of another goal: scripting Java applets. Gratuitous differences would not pay off for those programmers who made the jump from JavaScript to Java. But requiring class and type declarations, or a semicolon after each statement when a new line would do, were out of the question — scripting for most people is about writing short snippets of code, quickly and without fuss.

+ **Events for HTML elements.** Buttons should have onClick event handlers. Documents load and unload from windows, so windows should have onLoad and onUnload handlers. Users and scripts submit forms: onSubmit. Although not yet as flexible as HyperCard's messages (whose handlers inspired the onEvent naming convention), JavaScript events let HTML authors take control from remote servers and respond quickly to user gestures and browser actions.

+ **Objects without classes.** The Self programming language proved this concept with its prototype-based inheritance. For JavaScript, I wanted a single prototype per object (for simplicity and efficiency), based by default on the function called using the new operator (for consonance with Java). To avoid distinguishing constructors from methods from functions, all functions receive the object naming them as the property that was called, in the this parameter. Although prototypes didn't appear until Navigator 3, they were prefigured in Version 2 by quoted text being treated as an object (the String prototype, to which users could attach methods).

+ **Generated HTML.** Embedding JavaScript in HTML gave rise to a thought: Let the script speak HTML, as if the emitted text and markup were loaded in place of the script itself. The possibilities went beyond automating current or last-modified dates, to computing whole trees of tables where all the repeated structure was rolled up in a scripted loop, while the varying contents to be tabulated came in minimal fashion from JavaScript objects forming a catalog or mini-database.

At first, I thought JavaScript would most often find use in validating input to HTML forms. But I was surprised to see many more compelling applications of generated HTML and JavaScript objects, such as Bill Dortch's `http://hidaho.com` pages. It became clear from user demonstration and feedback that significant applications could be built quickly and effectively with just a few images, HTML, and JavaScript. The crucial advantages were the complementary and proportionate means available to the author's end. The key was to let several easy-to-use languages play to their strengths and not require the programming expertise needed to light all pixels and handle all events from one big traditional application.

The primacy of JavaScript on the Web today vindicates our early belief in the value of a scripting language for HTML authors. By keeping the "pixel-lighting" bar low, HTML with images has made Web designers out of millions of people. By keeping the "event-handling" bar low, JavaScript has helped many thousands of those designers become programmers.

JavaScript is also a general language, useful apart from HTML. It has been embedded in servers, authoring tools, and other browsers (for such things as 3D graphical worlds). It is now an international standard, ECMA-262. But compared to languages such as Perl and even Java, it is still quite young. Among its youthful shortcomings, several are worth mentioning, to be aware of now and to fix in a future version:

+ **Lack of decimal arithmetic:** JavaScript uses the IEEE double-precision floating-point standard, but for many "dollars and cents" calculations, the decimal result has no exact binary representation: 70.46 – 39.96 yields 30.499999999999993. This amounts to a drawback for most users; it should be addressed by an optional decimal numeric model.

+ **Event inflexibility:** Users would like to write multiple handlers or "listeners" for an event directed to a given object or a hierarchy of objects. JavaScript 1.2 shows some progress in this area, but much more could be delivered here, as any HyperCard fan can see.

+ **Lack of exceptions and modules.** These "power-programming" features become necessary as one accumulates and reuses sets of functions and scripts. I hope to see thoughtful extensions in these areas developed soon, to be standardized by the ECMA technical committee.

It is clear to me that JavaScript would not have survived without a creative, loyal, and patient community of developers; I owe them each a huge debt of thanks. Those developers who took up the beta releases of Navigator 2, and disseminated vital workarounds and feature requests by e-mail and net-news, are the language's godparents. Developer support and feedback continues to make JavaScript the eclectic, rambunctious success it has been.

The book in your hands compiles thousands of those "developer miles" with the insight of an expert guide and teacher. Danny didn't know at the time how much inspiration I found in his HyperCard book, but it was on my desk throughout the development of JavaScript in 1995. His energy, compassion, and clear prose helped me keep the goal of "a language for all" in mind. It is enormously gratifying to write the foreword to the third edition of this book, which has earned so many "satisfied reader miles."

I highly recommend Danny Goodman's *JavaScript Bible* to anyone who wants to learn JavaScript, and especially to those HTML authors who've so far written only a few scripts or programs—you're in for a lifetime of fun on the "scripting road" with a trusty guide at your side.

—Brendan Eich

Netscape Communications Corporation

Preface

For the past 15 years, I have written the books I wished had already been written to help me learn or use a new technology. Whenever possible, I like to get in at the very beginning of a new authoring or programming environment, feel the growing pains, and share with readers the solutions to my struggles. This third edition of the *JavaScript Bible* represents almost two years — an eon in Web time — of daily work in JavaScript, and a constant monitoring of newsgroups for questions, problems, and challenges facing scripters at all levels. My goal is to help you prevent the same frustration and head scratching I and others have experienced through three generations of scriptable browsers.

Because this book is about JavaScript, and not Microsoft's JScript version of the language, the frame of reference throughout is from Netscape's implementation of the language. In a lot of places I point out the differences between Netscape's and Microsoft's implementations, but you will not read much here about Microsoft-only language and object issues. Most of what you learn here about JavaScript works with full compatibility in Internet Explorer 4.

Organization and Features of This Edition

If you read previous editions of this book, you will see a radical new structure in this edition. In addition to covering the vast amount of new material necessitated by scripting powers of JavaScript 1.2 in Netscape Navigator 4, I believed it was time to rethink the structure and presentation of information to make it easier to learn the language and use the book as a reference later on. The primary changes include a separate tutorial section and a more extensive reference section that provides narrowly targeted chapters organized around an alphabetical treatment of language syntax. Here are some details about the book's new structure.

Part I

Part I of the book begins with a chapter that shows how JavaScript compares to Java and discusses its role within the rest of the World Wide Web. The Web browser and scripting world have undergone significant changes since JavaScript first arrived on the scene. That's why Chapter 2 is devoted to addressing challenges facing scripters who must develop applications for both single- and cross-platform browser audiences amid rapidly changing standards efforts. Chapter 3 provides the first foray into JavaScript, where you get to write your first practical script.

Part II

All of Part II is handed over to a tutorial for newcomers to JavaScript. Nine lessons provide you with a gradual path through browser internals, basic programming skills, and genuine JavaScript scripting. Exercises follow at the end of each lesson to help reinforce what you've just learned and challenge you to use your new knowledge (you'll find answers to the exercises in Appendix C). The goal of the tutorial is to equip you with sufficient experience to start scripting simple pages right away while making it easier for you to understand the in-depth discussions and examples in the rest of the book. By the end of the final lesson, you'll know how to script multiple frame environments and even create the mouse-rollover image swapping effect that is popular in a lot of Web pages these days.

Part III

Part III, the largest section of the book, provides in-depth coverage of the language. Most of the chapters focus on specific objects in documents. But you'll also find complete coverage of other core language facilities, such as control structures, functions, and every other part of the language. With the wide range of language and browser versions encompassing JavaScript, each language entry includes a compatibility chart so you can see which browsers support the term. Chapters 14 through 36 feature guide words in black bars on key pages to help you locate information on JavaScript terminology with ease.

Part IV

In Part IV, I get down to the business of deploying JavaScript. These are the practical aspects of JavaScript, such as Chapter 37's coverage of client-side form data validation and Chapter 38's coverage of blending Java applets into pages. Chapter 39 digs deeply into Navigator 4's new event model, while Chapter 40 goes into great detail about security issues for JavaScript-enabled applications. Dynamic HTML occupies no fewer than three chapters, as I show you how to deploy DHTML applications for Netscape Navigator 4, Internet Explorer 4, and both browsers at the same time. Along the way, I show you the same Dynamic HTML application optimized for each type of deployment. Even though this book's perspective is from Netscape's implementation of JavaScript, you should have an idea of what differences exist with Microsoft's implementation, as covered in Chapter 44. Debugging scripts is the focus of Chapter 45, with tips on understanding error messages, building your own debugging tools, and using Netscape's debugger. A survey of third-party authoring tools rounds out this implementation-heavy part of the book.

Part V

Finally, several appendixes at the end of the book provide helpful reference information. These resources include a Netscape Navigator object road map in Appendix A, a list of JavaScript reserved words in Appendix B, answers to Part II's tutorial exercises in Appendix C, and Internet resources in Appendix D. In Appendix E, you'll also find information on using the CD-ROM that comes with this book.

CD-ROM

The accompanying CD-ROM contains complete HTML documents that serve as examples of most of the JavaScript vocabulary words in Part III. You can run these examples with your JavaScript-enabled browser. I could have provided you with humorous little fragments out of context, but I think that seeing full-fledged HTML documents (simple though they may be) for employing these concepts is important. I intentionally omitted the script listings from the tutorial part (Part II) of this book to encourage you to type the scripts. I believe you learn a lot, even by aping listings from the book, as you get used to the rhythms of typing scripts in documents. You will also find many scripts from Parts I and IV on the CD-ROM.

The bonus applications on the CD-ROM consist of seven full-fledged, JavaScript-enhanced applications. Most of these examples also run on my Web site (http://www.dannyg.com/javascript/), so you can use them from the CD-ROM or see how well they work online from a server. Each application demonstrates important concepts that you will likely want to include in your applications. You will read about each segment of JavaScript code and learn about the implementation decisions I made in designing these applications — the same kinds of decisions you will have to make for your site.

The object road map from Appendix A is in .pdf format on the CD-ROM for you to print out and assemble as a handy reference booklet, if desired. Adobe Acrobat Reader is included on the CD-ROM so you can read this .pdf file. Finally, the text of the book is in a .pdf file on the CD-ROM for easy searching.

Prerequisites to Learning JavaScript

Although this book doesn't demand that you have a great deal of programming experience behind you, the more Web pages you've created with HTML, the easier you will find it to understand how JavaScript interacts with the familiar elements you normally place in your pages. Occasionally, you will need to modify HTML tags to take advantage of scripting. If you are familiar with those tags already, the JavaScript enhancements will be simple to digest.

Forms and their elements (text fields, buttons, and selection lists) play an especially important role in much of typical JavaScript work. You should be familiar with these elements and their HTML attributes. Fortunately, you won't need to know about CGI scripting or passing information from a form to a server. The focus here is on client-side scripting, which operates independently of the server after the JavaScript-enhanced HTML page is fully loaded into the browser.

The full vocabulary of the current HTML standard and Netscape extensions should be part of your working knowledge. When we get to using frames, for instance, the focus will be on how to script these elements, not on designing pages with them. Netscape and other sources online provide more detailed explanations of frames.

If you've never programmed before

To someone who has learned HTML from a slim guidebook, the size of this book must be daunting. JavaScript may not be the easiest language in the world to learn, but believe me, it's a far cry from having to learn a full programming language such as Java or C. Unlike developing a full-fledged monolithic application (such as the productivity programs you buy in the stores), JavaScript lets you experiment by writing small snippets of program code to accomplish big things. The JavaScript interpreter built into every scriptable browser does a great deal of the technical work for you.

Programming, at its most basic level, consists of nothing more than writing a series of instructions for the computer to follow. We humans follow instructions all the time, even if we don't realize it. Traveling to a friend's house is a sequence of small instructions: Go three blocks that way; turn left here; turn right there. Amid these instructions are some decisions that we have to make: If the stoplight is red, then stop; if the light is green, then go; if the light is yellow, then floor it. Occasionally, we must repeat some operations several times (kind of like having to go around the block until a parking space opens up). A computer program not only contains the main sequence of steps, but it also anticipates what decisions or repetitions may be needed to accomplish the program's goal (such as how to handle the various states of a stoplight or what to do if someone just stole the parking spot you were aiming for).

The initial hurdle of learning to program is becoming comfortable with the way a programming language wants its words and numbers organized in these instructions. Such rules are called *syntax*, the same as in a living language. Because computers generally are dumb electronic hulks, they aren't very forgiving if you don't communicate with them in the specific language they understand. When speaking to another human, you can flub a sentence's syntax and still have a good chance of the other person understanding you fully. Not so with computer programming languages. If the syntax isn't perfect (or at least within the language's range of knowledge that it can correct), the computer has the brazenness to tell you that *you* have made a syntax error.

The best thing you can do is to just chalk up the syntax errors you receive as learning experiences. Even experienced programmers get them. Every syntax error you get — and every resolution of that error made by rewriting the wayward statement — adds to your knowledge of the language.

If you've done a little programming before

Programming experience in a procedural language such as BASIC or Pascal may almost be a hindrance rather than a help to learning JavaScript. Although you may have an appreciation for precision in syntax, the overall concept of how a program fits into the world is probably radically different from JavaScript. Part of this has to do with the typical tasks a script performs (carrying out a very specific task in response to user action within a Web page), but a large part also has to do with the nature of object-oriented programming.

In a typical procedural program, the programmer is responsible for everything that appears on the screen and everything that happens under the hood. When the program first runs, a great deal of code is dedicated to setting up the visual environment. Perhaps the screen contains several text entry fields or clickable buttons. To determine which button a user clicked, the program examines the coordinates of the click and compares those coordinates against a list of all button coordinates on the screen. Program execution then branches out to perform the instructions reserved for clicking in that space.

Object-oriented programming is almost the inverse of that process. A button is considered an object — something tangible. An object has properties, such as its label, size, alignment, and so on. An object may also contain a script. At the same time, the system software and browser, working together, can send a message to an object — depending on what the user does — to trigger the script. For example, if a user clicks in a text entry field, the system/browser tells the field that somebody has clicked there (that is, has set the *focus* to that field), giving the field the task of deciding what to do about it. That's where the script comes in. The script is connected to the field, and it contains the instructions that the field carries out when the user activates it. Another set of instructions may control what happens when the user types an entry and tabs or clicks out of the field, thereby changing the content of the field.

Some of the scripts you will write may seem to be procedural in construction: They contain a simple list of instructions that are carried out in order. But when dealing with data from form elements, these instructions will be working with the object-based nature of JavaScript. The form is an object; each radio button or text field is an object as well. The script then acts on the properties of those objects to get some work done.

Making the transition from procedural to object-oriented programming may be the most difficult challenge for you. When I was first introduced to object-oriented programming a number of years ago, I didn't get it at first. But when the concept clicked — a long pensive walk helped — so many lightbulbs went on inside my head that I thought I might glow in the dark. From then on, object orientation seemed to be the only sensible way to program.

If you've programmed in C before

By borrowing syntax from Java (which, in turn, is derived from C and C++), JavaScript shares many syntactical characteristics with C. Programmers familiar with C will feel right at home. Operator symbols, conditional structures, and repeat loops follow very much in the C tradition. You will be less concerned about data types in JavaScript than you are in C. In JavaScript, a variable is not restricted to any particular data type.

With so much of JavaScript's syntax familiar to you, you will be able to concentrate on the unique aspects of JavaScript, notably the object hierarchy. You will still need a good grounding in HTML (especially form elements) to put your expertise to work in JavaScript.

If you've programmed in Java before

Despite the similarity in their names, the two languages share only surface aspects: Loop and conditional constructions, C-like "dot" object references, curly braces for grouping statements, several keywords, and a few other attributes. Variable declarations, however, are quite different, because JavaScript is a *loosely typed* language. A variable can contain an integer value in one statement and a string in the next (though I'm not saying that this is good style). What Java refers to as *methods*, JavaScript calls *methods* (when associated with a predefined object) or *functions* (for user-defined actions). JavaScript methods and functions may return values of any type without having to state the data type ahead of time.

Perhaps the most important aspects of Java to suppress when writing JavaScript are the object-oriented notions of classes, inheritance, instantiation, and message passing. These aspects are simply nonissues when scripting. At the same time, however, the language's designers knew that you'd have some hard-to-break habits. For example, although JavaScript does not require a semicolon at the end of each statement, if you type one in your JavaScript source code, the JavaScript interpreter won't balk.

If you've written scripts (or macros) before

Experience with writing scripts in other authoring tools or macros in productivity programs is helpful for grasping a number of JavaScript's concepts. Perhaps the most important concept is the idea of combining a handful of statements to perform a specific task on some data. For example, you can write a macro in Microsoft Excel that performs a data transformation on daily figures that come in from a corporate financial report on another computer. The macro is built into the Macro menu, and you run it by choosing that menu item whenever a new set of figures arrives.

More sophisticated scripting, such as that found in Toolbook or HyperCard, prepares you for the object orientation of JavaScript. In those environments, screen objects contain scripts that are executed when a user interacts with those objects. A great deal of the scripting you will do in JavaScript matches that pattern exactly. In fact, those environments resemble JavaScript in another way: They provide a finite set of predefined objects that have fixed sets of properties and behaviors. This predictability makes learning the entire environment and planning an application easier to accomplish.

Formatting and Naming Conventions

The script listings and words in this book are presented in a `monospace font` to set them apart from the rest of the text. Due to restrictions in page width, lines of script listings may, from time to time, break unnaturally. In such cases, the remainder of the script appears in the following line, flush with the left margin of the listing, just as they would appear in a text editor with word wrapping turned on. If these line breaks cause you problems when you type a script listing into a document yourself, I encourage you to access the corresponding listing on the CD-ROM to see how it should look when you type it.

This book is written coincidentally with the release of Version 4 browsers from Netscape and Microsoft. I frequently refer to these releases collectively as *level 4 browsers*. As for the Netscape product in particular, the company calls its suite of client-side applications Communicator, yet the browser alone is installable as Navigator. To assist in backward compatibility with the names of previous versions of the browser, I refer to Netscape's product exclusively as Navigator. When referring to the latest version, I call it Navigator 4, when, in fact, it may be part of the suite of software you have installed as Communicator. I sometimes use a shortcut method of referring to Microsoft's Internet Explorer by the product's initials and version number: IE3 for Internet Explorer 3 and IE4 for Internet Explorer 4. Unless I specifically mention a subversion of a browser of either brand (for example, a version number such as 4.03), the version description generally applies to the entire generation.

Note and Caution icons occasionally appear in the book to flag important points.

Acknowledgments

Before closing, I would like to acknowledge the contributions of many folks who helped make this edition possible: Norris Boyd, Eric Krock, Tom Pixley, everyone from the DevEdge group whom I've hounded with questions, and especially the ever-patient, all-knowing Brendan Eich (Netscape); Brenda McLaughlin, Walt Bruce, Michael Roney, Sue Pines, Ami Knox, and Michael Welch (IDG Books Worldwide, Inc.); technical reviewers David Wall and Mike Shaver; "cookie man" Bill Dortch (hIdaho Design); fellow scripters and newsgroup kibitzers, who unwittingly advised me as to where scripters were having trouble with the language; and the first-class designers at YO in San Francisco (info@yodesign.com), who brought the art spots of my JavaScript Web site pages to life. Above all, I want to thank the many readers of the first two editions of this book (with both titles, *Danny Goodman's JavaScript Handbook* and the *JavaScript Bible*) for investing in this ongoing effort. I wish I had the space here to acknowledge by name so many who have sent e-mail notes and suggestions: Your input has been most welcome and greatly appreciated. Now it's time to get down to the fun of learning JavaScript. Enjoy!

Contents at a Glance

Contents

Part II: JavaScript Tutorial   27

Chapter 4: Browser and Document Objects 29

Chapter 5: Scripts and HTML Documents 51

Part III: JavaScript Object and Language Reference 141

Part IV: Putting JavaScript to Work 747

Getting Started with JavaScript

JavaScript's Role in the World Wide Web

For the many individuals responsible today for content on the World Wide Web, it wasn't long ago that terms such as *HTML* (Hypertext Markup Language) and *URL* (Universal Resource Locator) seemed like words from a foreign language. Growth in activity on the Web — producing content and surfing it — has been nothing short of phenomenal. Some may even call the hyperactivity "scary." I could quote the estimates of the number of Web sites available on the Internet, but that count would be woefully outdated before these words ever reached a printing press.

Developers of Web software technologies are now in a desperate race to catch up with the enthusiasm that people have for the Internet — and for the Web in particular. Web site authors are constantly seeking tools that will make their sites engaging (if not "cool") with the least amount of effort. This is particularly true when the task is in the hands of people more comfortable with writing, graphic design, and page layout than with hard-core programming. Not every Webmaster has legions of experienced programmers on hand to whip up some special, custom enhancement for the site. Nor does every Web author have control over the Web server that physically houses the collection of HTML and graphics files. JavaScript brings programming power within reach of anyone familiar with HTML, even when the server is a black box at the other end of a telephone line.

Competition on the Web

Web page publishers revel in logging as many visits to their sites as possible. Regardless of the questionable accuracy of Web page *hit* counts, a site consistently logging 10,000 dubious hits per week is clearly far more popular than one with 1,000 dubious hits per week. Even if the precise number is unknown, relative popularity is a valuable measure.

Encouraging people to visit a site frequently is the Holy Grail of Web publishing. Competition for viewers is enormous. Not only is the Web like a million-channel television, but the Web competes for viewers' attention with all kinds of computer-generated information. That includes anything that appears on-screen as interactive multimedia.

Users of entertainment programs, multimedia encyclopedias, and other colorful, engaging, and mouse-finger-numbing actions are accustomed to high-quality presentations. Frequently, these programs sport first-rate graphics, animation, live-action video, and synchronized sound. In contrast, the lowest-common-denominator Web page has little in the way of razzle-dazzle. Even with the help of recent advances in Dynamic HTML, the layout of pictures and text is highly constrained compared to the kinds of desktop publishing documents you see all the time. Regardless of the quality of its content, a vanilla HTML document is flat. At best, interaction is limited to whatever navigation the author offers in the way of hypertext links or forms whose filled-in content magically disappears into the Web site's server.

Stretching the Standards

As an outgrowth of *SGML* (Standard Generalized Markup Language), HTML is generally viewed as nothing more than a document formatting, or *tagging,* language. The tags (inside <> delimiter characters) instruct a viewer program (the *browser* or the *client*) how to display chunks of text or images.

Relegating HTML to the category of tagging language does disservice not only to the effort that goes into fashioning a first-rate Web page, but also to the way users interact with the pages. To my way of thinking, any collection of commands and other syntax that directs the way users interact with digital information is *programming*. With HTML, a Web page author controls the user experience with the content, just as the engineers who program Microsoft Excel craft the way users interact with spreadsheet content and functions.

Unfortunately, the HTML standards agreed to by industry groups leave much to be desired in the way HTML programmers can customize the level of interactivity between document and user. Software companies that develop browsers feel the urgency to move the facilities of HTML forward to meet the demands of Web authors who want more control over the display of various kinds of information. Browser companies are engaged in a constant game of leapfrog as they race ahead of still-emerging standards. Even before an HTML standard version is released to the public, aggressive and creative companies such as Netscape and Microsoft implement their own extensions to stretch the state-of-the-art.

CGI Scripting

One way to enhance the interaction between user and content is to have the page communicate with the Web server that houses the Web pages. Popular Web search sites, such as Yahoo!, Digital's Alta Vista, and Lycos, let users type search criteria and click a button or two to specify the way the search engine should treat the query. When you click the Submit or Search buttons, your browser sends your entries from the form to the server. On the server, a program known as a CGI

(Common Gateway Interface) script formats the data you've entered and sends it to a database or other program running on the server. The CGI script then sends the results to your browser, sometimes in the form of a new page or as information occupying other fields in the form.

Writing customized CGI scripts typically requires considerable programming skill. It definitely requires the Web page author to be in control of the server, including whatever *back-end* programs, such as databases, are needed to supply results or to massage the information coming from the user. Even with the new, server-based, Web site design tools available, CGI scripting often is not a task that a content-oriented HTML author can do without handing it off to a more experienced programmer.

As interesting and useful as CGI scripting is, it burdens the server with the job of processing queries. A busy server may be processing hundreds of CGI scripts at a time, while the client computers — the personal computers running the browsers — are sitting idle as the browser's logo icon dances its little animation. This wastes desktop processing horsepower. That's why some people regard browsing a basic Web page as little more than using a dumb terminal to access some server content.

Of Helpers, Plug-ins, and Applets

Not that long ago, browsers relied on helper applications to make up for their internal deficiencies. For example, browsers typically don't know how to deal with audio that comes in from a Web site. Instead, your browser knows that when it encounters an audio file, it must launch a separate helper program (if available on your hard disk) to do the job of making your particular flavor of computer (Windows 3.*x*, Windows 95, UNIX, or MacOS) convert the digitized sound to audio you can hear through speakers.

A current trend in browsers is to bring as much functionality as possible into the browser itself, so you don't have to run another program to play a movie or audio clip. This integration also helps in giving the overall presentation a cleaner appearance to the user. Instead of having to play in a separate window atop the browser's document window, a movie can appear in the page, perhaps accompanied by label text or a caption.

Plug-ins

First available in Navigator 2, software plug-ins for browsers enable developers to incorporate a variety of capabilities into the browser without having to modify the browser. Unlike a helper application, a plug-in is usually less demanding of client resources and enables external content to be blended into the document seamlessly.

The most common plug-ins are those that facilitate the playback of audio and video from the server. Audio may include music tracks that play in the background while visiting a page or live audio similar to a radio station. Video and animation can operate in a space on the page when played through a plug-in that knows how to process such data.

Java applets

When the interaction required between user and Web page exceeds the capabilities of HTML, experienced programmers may prefer to "roll their own" programs to handle the special needs not available in existing plug-ins. Filling this need is the Java programming language. Developed at Sun Microsystems, the language enables programmers to write small applications (*applets*) that download to the browser (as separate files, such as image files). An applet runs as the user needs it and then is automatically discarded (from memory) when the user moves elsewhere in the Web.

Animation, including animated text whose content can change over time, is a popular application of the Java applet in an HTML page. Because applets can also communicate with the Internet as they run, they are also used for real-time, data streaming applications, displaying up-to-the-minute news, stock market, and sports data as it comes across the wires. All of this activity can be surrounded by standard HTML content as the Web page designer sees fit.

To play a Java applet, a browser company must have licensed the technology from Sun and built it into its browser. Netscape was the first third-party browser supplier to license and produce a browser capable of running Java applets (Navigator 2 under Windows 95 and UNIX). Today, both Netscape Navigator and Microsoft Internet Explorer (IE) can load and run Java applets on almost every operating system platform supported by the browser. The perceived popularity of Java is so strong today that the capability of running Java-based programs is being built or planned not only for browsers (such as Internet Explorer), but for entire operating systems, such as the MacOS and Windows 98/NT.

JavaScript: A Language for All

The Java language is derived from C and C++, but it is a distinct language. Its main audience is the experienced programmer. That leaves out many Web page authors. I was dismayed at this situation when I first read about Java's specifications. I would have preferred a language that casual programmers and scripters who use authoring tools such as ToolBook, HyperCard, and even Visual Basic could adopt quickly. As these accessible development platforms have shown, nonprofessional authors can dream up many creative applications, often for very specific tasks that no programmer would have the inclination to work on. Personal needs often drive development in the classroom, office, den, or garage. But Java was not going to be that kind of inclusive language.

My spirits lifted several months later, in November 1995, when I heard of a scripting language project brewing at Netscape. Initially born under the name LiveScript, this language was developed in parallel with Netscape's Web server software. The language was to serve two purposes with the same syntax. One purpose was as a scripting language that Web server administrators could use to manage the server and connect its pages to other services, such as back-end databases and search engines for users looking up information. Extending the "Live" brand name further, Netscape assigned the name LiveWire to the database connectivity usage of JavaScript on the server.

On the client side — in HTML documents — these scripts could be used to enhance Web pages in a number of ways. For example, an author could use LiveScript to make sure that the information a user entered into a form would be of the proper type. Instead of forcing the server or database to do the data validation (requiring data exchanges between the client browser and the server), the user's computer handles all the calculation work — putting some of that otherwise wasted horsepower to work. In essence, LiveScript could provide HTML-level interaction for the user.

As the intensity of industry interest in Java grew, Netscape saw another opportunity for LiveScript: as a way for HTML documents (and their users) to communicate with Java applets. For example, a user might make some preference selections from checkboxes and pop-up selection lists located at the top of a Web page. Scrolling down to the next screenful, the user sees text in the Java applet scrolling banner on the page that is customized to the settings made above. In this case, the LiveScript script sends the text that is to appear in the scrolling banner to the applet (and perhaps a new color to use for the banner's background and text). While this is happening, the server doesn't have to worry a bit about it, and the user hasn't had to wait for communication between the browser and the server. As great an idea as this was initially, this connectivity feature didn't make it into Navigator 2 when JavaScript first became available.

LiveScript becomes JavaScript

In early December 1995, Netscape and Sun jointly announced that the scripting language would thereafter be known as JavaScript. Though Netscape had several good marketing reasons for adopting this name, the changeover may have contributed more confusion to both the Java and HTML scripting worlds than anyone had expected.

Before the announcement, the language was already related to Java in some ways. Many of the basic syntax elements of the language were reminiscent of the C and C++ style of Java. For client-side scripting, the language was intended for very different purposes than Java — essentially, to function as a programming language integrated into HTML documents, rather than as a language for writing applets that occupy a fixed rectangular area on the page (and that are oblivious to whatever else may be on the page). Instead of Java's full-blown programming language vocabulary (and conceptually difficult object-oriented approach), JavaScript had a small vocabulary and more easily digestible programming model.

The true difficulty, it turned out, was making the distinction between Java and JavaScript clear to the world. Many computer journalists made major blunders when they said or implied that JavaScript was a simpler way of building Java applets. To this day, many programmers believe JavaScript to be synonymous with the Java language: They post Java queries to JavaScript-specific Internet newsgroups and mailing lists.

The fact remains today that Java and JavaScript are more different than they are similar. Java support in a browser or operating system does not automatically imply JavaScript support. The two languages require entirely different interpreter engines to execute their lines of code. Whereas JavaScript support shipped in every platform-specific version of Navigator 2 in February 1996, Java was not available for Windows 3.1 users until late in the life of Navigator 3. (Many squirrelly technical issues make it difficult for this modern language to work in an "ancient" MS-DOS operating system.)

Coming together

Now that I've made such a point of distinguishing JavaScript from Java, I'm here to tell you that the two languages are more complementary than ever since the release of Navigator 3. Detailed at length later in the book, a Netscape technology called *LiveConnect* makes it possible for JavaScript to communicate with Java applets (as well as perform some Java functionality directly). JavaScript writers can treat prewritten Java applets as ready-to-run programs that require very little in the way of coding to modify and control.

By adding scriptability to Java applets (when applets have been written to be scriptable), LiveConnect significantly increases the powers of HTML authors and scripters, without requiring them to trudge up the steep learning curve of the full Java language. Java applets can do their animation and highly powered algorithmic tasks, whereas we scripters control how the applets behave in response to user interaction with HTML elements, such as buttons and select lists. It truly is a win-win-win scenario for scripters, Java applet programmers, and the users of our pages.

The Microsoft world

Anyone who follows the Web software industry knows about the race for market superiority involving players such as Netscape, Microsoft, and Sun Microsystems. Each company has contributed to the user enjoyment of the Internet and will continue to do so in the "Web Weeks" ahead (a measure of time coined by Eric Schmidt while he was at Sun).

As a result of Microsoft being a comparative latecomer to the Internet party, it has embarked on a philosophy that it calls "embrace and extend." This means that even if Microsoft prefers its own technologies to market-leading products developed outside of Microsoft, the company will find ways to enable those outside technologies to work within its products. As solid demonstrations of that philosophy, Microsoft implemented both Java and JavaScript for release 3 of its Internet Explorer browser. The company has greatly enhanced the JavaScript offering in Internet Explorer 4.

In keeping with the competitive nature of the Web browser market, Netscape and Microsoft continue to attract developers to their camps with unique extensions in each new version. If you are developing pages for an audience that uses both browser brands, this creates challenges. I address these issues in the next chapter.

JavaScript: The Right Tool for the Right Job

Knowing how to match an authoring tool to a solution-building task is an important part of being a well-rounded Web page author. A Web page designer who ignores JavaScript is akin to a plumber who bruises his knuckles by using pliers instead of the wrench at the bottom of the toolbox. By the same token, JavaScript won't fulfill every dream.

The more you understand about JavaScript's intentions and limitations, the more likely you will be to turn to it immediately when it is the proper tool. In particular, look to JavaScript for the following kinds of solutions:

✦ You want your Web page to respond or react directly to user interaction with form elements (input fields, text areas, buttons, radio buttons, checkboxes, selection lists) and hypertext links — a class of application I call the *serverless CGI*.

✦ You want to distribute small collections of database-like information and provide a friendly interface to that data.

✦ You need to control multiple-frame navigation, plug-ins, or Java applets based on user choices in the HTML document.

✦ You want data preprocessed on the client before submission to a server.

At the same time, understanding what JavaScript is not capable of doing is vital. Scripters waste many hours looking for ways of carrying out tasks for which JavaScript was not designed. Most of the limitations are designed to protect visitors from invasions of privacy or unauthorized access to their desktop computers. Therefore, unless a visitor is using a modern browser and explicitly gives you permission to access protected parts of his or her computer, JavaScript cannot surreptitiously perform any of the following actions:

✦ Setting or retrieving the browser's preferences settings, main window appearance features, action buttons, and printing

✦ Launching an application on the client computer

✦ Reading or writing files or directories on the client computer

✦ Extracting the text content of HTML pages or their files from the server

✦ Writing files to the server

✦ Reading a server directory

✦ Capturing live data streams from the server

✦ Sending secret e-mails from Web site visitors to you

Beyond the security issues, should you turn to JavaScript and find that it doesn't have the capabilities you need, speak up! Let the JavaScript development team at Netscape know what you'd like it to do in the future. JavaScript will certainly evolve and grow as scripters stretch its powers.

✦   ✦   ✦

Authoring Challenges amid the Browser Wars

If you are learning JavaScript just now in the brief history of scriptable browsers, you have both a distinct advantage and disadvantage. The advantage is that you have the wonderful capabilities of the level 4 browser offerings from Netscape and Microsoft at your bidding. The disadvantage is that you have not experienced the painful history of authoring for older browser versions that were buggy and at times incompatible with each other due to a lack of standards. You have yet to learn the anguish of carefully devising a scripted application for the browser version you use, only to have site visitors sending you voluminous e-mail messages about how the page triggers all kinds of script errors when run on a different browser brand, generation, or operating system platform.

Welcome to the real world of scripting Web pages in JavaScript. Several dynamics are at work to help make an author's life difficult if the audience for the application uses more than a single type of browser. This chapter introduces you to these challenges before you type your first word of JavaScript code. My fear is that the subjects I raise may dissuade you from progressing further into JavaScript and its powers. But as a developer myself — and as someone who has been using JavaScript since the earliest days of its public prerelease availability — I dare not sugarcoat the issues facing scripters today. Instead, I want to make sure you have an appreciation of what lies ahead to assist you in learning the language. I believe if you understand the Big Picture of the browser scripting world as it stands near the beginning of 1998, you will find it easier to target JavaScript usage in your Web application development.

Leapfrog

Browser compatibility has been an issue for authors since the earliest days of rushing to the Web. Despite the fact that browser developers and other interested parties had their voices heard during formative stages of standards development, HTML authoring has rarely been the "write once, run everywhere" phenomenon that Sun Microsystems promises for the Java development environment. It may have been one thing to establish a set of standard tags for defining heading levels and line breaks, but it was rare for the actual rendering of content inside those tags to look identical on two different brands of browsers.

Then, as the competitive world heated up — and Web browser developers transformed themselves from volunteer undertakings into profit-seeking businesses — creative people defined new features and new tags that helped authors create more flexible and interesting-looking pages. As happens a lot in any industry that is computer-related, the pace of commercial development easily outpaced the studied processing of standards. A browser maker would build a new HTML feature into a browser and propose that feature to the relevant standards body. Web authors were using these features (sometimes for prerelease browser versions) before the proposals were published for review.

When the deployment of content depends almost entirely on an interpretive engine on the client computer receiving the data — the HTML engine in a browser, for example — authors face an immediate problem. Unlike a standalone computer program that can extend and even invent functionality across a wide range and have it run on everyone's computer (at least for a given operating system), Web content providers must rely on the functionality built into the browser. If not all browsers coming to my site support a particular HTML feature, then should I apply newfangled HTML features for visitors only at the bleeding edge? And if I do deploy the new features, what do I do for those with older browsers?

Authors who developed pages in the earliest days of the Web wrestled with this question for many HTML features that we today take for granted. Tables and frames come to mind. Eventually the standards caught up with the proposed HTML extensions, but not without a lot of author anguish along the way.

The same game continues today. But the field of players has shrunk to two primary players: Netscape and Microsoft. And for these companies, the stakes are higher than ever before — market share, investor return on investment — pick a business buzzword, and you'll find a reason behind the competition. What had begun years ago as a friendly game of leapfrog (long before Microsoft even acknowledged the Web) has become an out-and-out war: the Browser War.

Ducking for Cover

Sometimes it is difficult to tell from week to week where the battles are being fought. Marketing messages from the combatants turn on a dime. You can't tell if the message is proactive to stress a genuinely new corporate strategy or reactive to match the opponent's latest salvo. The combatants keep touting to each other: "Anything you can do, we can do better."

If it were a case of Netscape and Microsoft pitching their server and browser software to customers for the creation of monolithic intranets, I could understand

and appreciate such efforts. The battle lines would be clearly drawn, and potential customers could base their decisions on unemotional criteria — how well the solution fits the customer's information distribution and connectivity goals. In fact, if your development environment is monolithic, you are in luck, because authoring for a single browser brand and minimum version is a piece of cake. But you are not in the majority.

As happens in war, civilian casualties mount when the big guns start shooting. The guns are going off around the clock with the release of level 4 browsers: Netscape Navigator 4 and Microsoft Internet Explorer 4. While a fair amount of common ground exists between the two browsers that authors can work with, the newest features cause the biggest problems for authors wishing to deploy on both browsers. Trying to determine where the common denominator is may be the toughest part of the authoring job.

Compatibility Issues Today

Allow me to describe the current status of compatibility between Navigator and Internet Explorer. The discussion in the next few sections intentionally does not get into specific scripting technology very deeply — some of you may know very little about programming. In many chapters throughout Parts III and IV, I offer scripting suggestions to accommodate both browsers.

Separating language from objects

Although early JavaScript authors initially treated client-side scripting as one environment that permitted the programming of page elements, the scene has changed a bit as the browsers have matured. Today, a clear distinction exists between specifications for the core JavaScript language and for the elements you script in a document (for example, buttons and fields in a form).

On one level, this separation is a good thing. It means that one specification exists for basic programming concepts and syntax that enables the same language to be applied to environments that may not even exist today. You can think of the core language as basic wiring. Once you know how electric wires work, you can connect them to all kinds of electrical devices, including some that may not yet be invented. Similarly, JavaScript today is used to wire together page elements in an HTML document. Tomorrow, the core language could be used by operating systems to let users wire together desktop applications that need to exchange information automatically.

At the ends of today's JavaScript wires are the elements on the page. In programming jargon, these items are known as *document objects*. By keeping the specifications for document objects separate from the wires that connect them, other kinds of wires (other languages) can be used to connect them. It's like designing telephones that can work with any kind of wire, including a type of wire that hasn't yet been invented. Today the devices can work with copper wire or fiber optic cable. You get a good picture of this separation in Internet Explorer, whose set of document objects can be scripted with JavaScript or VBScript. They're the same objects, just different wiring.

The separation of core language from document objects enables each concept to have its own standards effort and development pace. But even with recommended standards for each factor, each browser maker is free to extend the standards, and authors may have to expend more effort to devise one version of a page or script that plays on both browsers unless the script adheres to a common denominator (or uses some other branching techniques to let each browser run its own way).

Core language standard

Keeping track of JavaScript language versions requires study of history and politics. The history covers the three versions developed by Netscape; politics covers Microsoft's versions and the joint standards effort. The first version of JavaScript (in Navigator 2) was Version 1.0, although that numbering was not part of the language usage. JavaScript was JavaScript. Version numbering became an issue when Navigator 3 came out. The version of JavaScript associated with that Navigator version was JavaScript 1.1. As you will learn later in this book, the version number is sometimes necessary in an attribute of the HTML tags that surround a script. Navigator 4 increased the language version one more notch, with JavaScript 1.2.

Microsoft's scripting effort contributes confusion for scripting newcomers. The first version of Internet Explorer to include scripting was Internet Explorer 3. The timing of Internet Explorer 3 was roughly coincidental to Navigator 3. But as scripters soon discovered, Microsoft's scripting effort was one generation behind. Microsoft apparently did not (and may still not) have a license to the JavaScript name. As a result, the company called its language JScript. Even so, the HTML tag attribute that requires naming the language of the script inside the tags could be either JScript or JavaScript for Internet Explorer. A JavaScript script written for Navigator 2 would be understood by Internet Explorer 3.

During this period of dominance by Navigator 3 and Internet Explorer 3, scripting newcomers were often confused because they expected the scripting languages to be the same. Unfortunately for the scripters, there were language features in JavaScript 1.1 that were not available in the older JavaScript version in Internet Explorer 3. The situation smoothes out for Internet Explorer 4. Its core language is up to the level of JavaScript 1.2 in Navigator 4. Microsoft still officially calls the language JScript. Language features new in Navigator 4 (including the script tag attribute identifying JavaScript 1.2) are understood when the scripts load into Internet Explorer 4.

While all of this jockeying for JavaScript versions was happening, Netscape, Microsoft, and other concerned parties met to establish a core language standard. The standards body is a Switzerland-based organization called the European Computer Manufacturer's Association, or ECMA (commonly pronounced ECK-ma). In mid-1997, the first formal language specification was agreed on and published (ECMA-262). Due to licensing issues with the JavaScript name, the body created a new name for the language: ECMAScript.

With only minor and esoteric differences, this first version of ECMAScript is essentially the same as JavaScript 1.1 found in Navigator 3. Both Navigator 4 and Internet Explorer 4 support the ECMAScript standard. Moreover, as happens so often when commerce meets standards bodies, both browsers have gone beyond the ECMAScript standard. Fortunately, the common denominator of this extended core language is broad, lessening authoring headaches on this front.

Document Object Model

If Navigator 4 and Internet Explorer 4 are close in core JavaScript language compatibility, nothing could be further from the truth when it comes to the document objects. Internet Explorer 3 based its document object model (DOM) on that of Netscape Navigator 2, the same browser level it used as a model for the core language. When Netscape added a couple of new objects to the model in Navigator 3, the addition caused further headaches for neophyte scripters who expected those objects to be in Internet Explorer 3. Probably the most commonly missed object in Internet Explorer 3 was the image object, which lets scripts swap the image when a user rolls the cursor atop a graphic — *mouse rollovers*, they're commonly called.

In the level 4 browsers, however, Internet Explorer's document object model has jumped way ahead of the object model Netscape implemented in Navigator 4. You will see the benefits of this expanded object model in chapters that cover scripting Dynamic HTML (Chapters 41 through 43). Suffice it to say that it is an enviable implementation.

At the same time, a document object model standard is being negotiated under the auspices of the World Wide Web Consortium (W3C). The specification was in an incomplete draft stage in late 1997. An HTML-specific subset of the DOM standard will support object syntax implemented in Navigator 3. If you wish to script to a common denominator, most of the document object model in Navigator 4 is supported in Internet Explorer 4. Even so, scripting for objects that have been defined later than Navigator 3 is touchy business, and requires a good knowledge of compatibility, as described in the object discussions throughout this book.

Cascading Style Sheets

Navigator 4 and Internet Explorer 4 claim compatibility with a W3C recommendation called Cascading Style Sheets, Level 1 (CSS1). This specification for a way to customize content in an organized fashion throughout a document (and thus minimize the HTML in each tag) is an effort to extend the Web's tradition of publishing static content. A Level 2 version is currently in working draft form.

Neither company's implementation is 100 percent compatible with the W3C standard, although Internet Explorer 4 has fewer omissions than Navigator 4. Moreover, each browser has its own mutually incompatible extensions. Netscape's extensions are a completely different way of defining style sheets, using JavaScript syntax, rather than the recommended standard syntax. Internet Explorer 4 does not recognize these so-called JavaScript style sheets.

JavaScript also comes into play on the Internet Explorer side, because its object model embraces the implementation of CSS1 in the browser. Style sheet information is part of the object model, and is therefore accessible and modifiable from JavaScript. This is not the case in Navigator 4.

Dynamic HTML

Perhaps the biggest improvements to the inner workings of the level 4 browsers from both Netscape and Microsoft revolve around a concept called *Dynamic HTML* (DHTML). The ultimate goal of DHTML is to enable scripts in documents to control the content, content position, and content appearance in response to user actions.

To that end, the W3C organization is developing another standard for the precise positioning of HTML elements on a page as an extension of the CSS standards effort. The CSS-Positioning recommendation adds to the CSS1 syntax for specifying an exact location on the page where an element is to appear, whether the item should be visible, and what order it should take among all the items that might overlap it.

Internet Explorer 4 adheres to the CSS-P standard, and makes positionable items subject to script control. Navigator 4 follows the standard and implements an alternative methodology involving an entirely new, albeit unsanctioned, tag for layers. Such positionable items are scriptable in Navigator 4 as well, although some of the script syntax is different from that used in Internet Explorer 4. As a result, three chapters later in this book discuss the individual browser implementations of CSS-P as well as a way to script both versions in one page. This kind of cross-platform scripting can be challenging, yet is certainly possible if you understand the limitations imposed by following a common denominator.

Developing a Scripting Strategy

As you have seen in this chapter, the two level 4 browsers contain a hodgepodge of standards and proprietary extensions. Even if you try to script to a common denominator, it probably won't take into account the earlier versions of both the JavaScript core language and the browser document object models.

The true challenge for authors these days is determining the audience for which scripted pages are intended. You will learn techniques in Chapter 13 that let you redirect users to different paths in your Web site based on their browser capabilities. Each new generation of browser not only brings with it new and exciting features you are probably eager to employ in your pages, it also adds to the fragmentation of the audience visiting a publicly accessible page. With each new upgrade, fewer existing users are ready to download tens of megabytes of browser merely to have the latest and greatest browser version. For many pioneers — and certainly for most nontechie users — there is an increasingly smaller imperative to upgrade browsers, unless that browser comes via a new computer or operating system upgrade.

As you work your way through the early parts of this book, know that many common denominators depend on where you wish to draw the line for browser support. Even if you wish to adhere to the absolutely lowest common denominator of scripting, I've got you covered: The tutorial of Part II focuses on language and object aspects that are compatible with every version of JavaScript.

At the same time, I think it is important for you to understand that the cool application you see running on your level 4 browser may not translate to Navigator 2. Therefore, when you see a technique that you'd like to emulate, be realistic in your expectations of adapting that trick for your widest audience. Only a good working knowledge of JavaScript and an examination of the cool source code will reveal how well it will work for your visitors.

✦   ✦   ✦

Your First JavaScript Script

♦ ♦ ♦ ♦

In This Chapter

Choosing basic
JavaScript authoring
tools

Setting up your
authoring
environment

Entering a simple
script to a Web page

♦ ♦ ♦ ♦

In this chapter, you set up a productive script-writing and previewing environment on your computer — and then write a simple script whose results you will see in your JavaScript-compatible browser.

Because of differences in the way various personal computing operating systems behave, I present details of environments for two popular variants: Windows 95 and the MacOS. For the most part, your JavaScript authoring experience will be the same regardless of the operating system platform you use — including UNIX. Although there may be slight differences in font designs depending on your browser and operating system, the information will be the same. All illustrations of browser output in this book are made from the Windows 95 version of Netscape Navigator 4. If you're running another version of Navigator, don't fret if every pixel doesn't match with the illustrations in this book.

The Software Tools

The best way to learn JavaScript is to type the HTML and scripting code into documents in a text editor. Your choice of editor is up to you, though I provide you with some guidelines for choosing a text editor in the next section. HTML files are raw ASCII text files, and any scripting has to be done in those files. While learning JavaScript, you may be better off using a simple text editor rather than a high-powered word processor with HTML extensions.

Choosing a text editor

For the purposes of learning JavaScript in this book, avoid WYSIWYG (What You See Is What You Get) Web-page authoring tools for now. These tools will certainly come in handy afterward, when you can productively use those facilities for molding the bulk of your content and layout. But the examples in this book focus more on script content (which you must type in anyway), so there won't be much HTML that you have to type. Files for all complete Web page listings are also included on the companion CD-ROM.

An important factor to consider in your choice of editor is how easy it is to save standard text files. In the case of Windows, any program that not only saves the file as text by default but also lets you set the extension to .htm or .html will prevent a great deal of problems. If you were to use Microsoft Word, for example, the program tries to save files as binary Word files — something that no Web browser can load. To save the file initially as a text or .html extension file requires mucking around in the Save As dialog box. This requirement is truly a nuisance.

Nothing's wrong with using bare-essentials text editors. In Windows 95, that includes the WordPad program or a more fully featured product such as the shareware editor called TextPad. For the MacOS, SimpleText is also fine, though the lack of a search-and-replace function may get in the way when you start managing your Web site pages. A favorite among Mac HTML authors and scripters is BBEdit (Bare Bones Software), which includes a number of useful aids for scripters, such as optional line numbers (which help in debugging JavaScript). In Chapter 46, I describe a Windows-based JavaScript authoring tool named Infuse 2.0 by Acadia Software. This product includes a nice text editor window for entering scripts.

Choosing a browser

The other component required for learning JavaScript is the *browser*. You don't have to be connected to the Internet to test your scripts in the browser. You can do all of it offline. This means you can learn JavaScript and create cool-scripted Web pages with a laptop computer, even on a boat in the middle of an ocean.

The only requirement for the browser is that it be compatible with the current release of JavaScript. The instructions and samples in this book are designed for Netscape's Navigator 4. Microsoft's Internet Explorer 4 supports most of the core language of Navigator 4, but you'll still find occasional incompatibilities.

Setting up your authoring environment

To make the job of testing your scripts easier, make sure that you have enough free memory in your computer to let both your text editor and browser run simultaneously. You need to be able to switch quickly between editor and browser as you experiment and repair any errors that may creep into your code. The typical workflow entails the following steps:

1. Enter HTML and script code into the source document.

2. Save the latest version to disk.

3. Switch to the browser.

4. Do one of the following: If this is a new document, open the file via the browser's Open menu. Or if the document is already loaded, reload the file into the browser.

Steps 2 through 4 are the key ones you will follow frequently. I call this three-step sequence the *save-switch-reload sequence*. You will perform this sequence so often as you script that the physical act will quickly become second nature to you. How you arrange your application windows and effect the save-switch-reload sequence varies according to your operating system.

Windows

You don't have to have either the editor or browser window maximized (at full screen) to take advantage of them. In fact, you may find them easier to work with if you adjust the size and location of each window so both windows are as large as they can be while still enabling you to click on a sliver of the other's window. Or, in Windows 95, leave the taskbar visible so you can click the desired program's button to switch to its window (Figure 3-1). A monitor that displays more than 640 × 480 pixels certainly helps in offering more screen real estate for the windows and the taskbar.

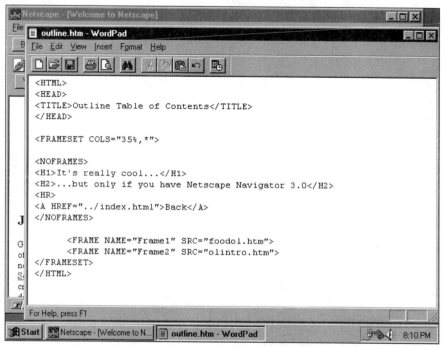

Figure 3-1: Editor and browser window arrangement in Windows 95

In practice, however, the Windows Alt+Tab task-switching keyboard shortcut makes the job of the save-switch-reload steps outlined earlier a snap. If you're running Windows 95 and also using a Windows 95-compatible text editor (which more than likely has a Ctrl+S file-saving keyboard shortcut) and the Netscape Navigator 4 browser (which has a Ctrl+R reload keyboard shortcut), you can effect the save-switch-reload from the keyboard, all with the left hand: Ctrl+S (save the source file); Alt+Tab (switch to the browser); Ctrl+R (reload the saved source file).

As long as you keep switching between the browser and text editor via Alt+Tab task switching, either program is always just an Alt+Tab away.

MacOS

If you expand the windows of your text editor and browser to full screen, you have to use the rather inconvenient Application menu (right-hand icon of the menu bar) to switch between the programs. A better method is to adjust the size and location of the windows of both programs so they overlap, while allowing a portion of the inactive window to remain visible (Figure 3-2). That way, all you have to do is click anywhere on the inactive window to bring its program to the front.

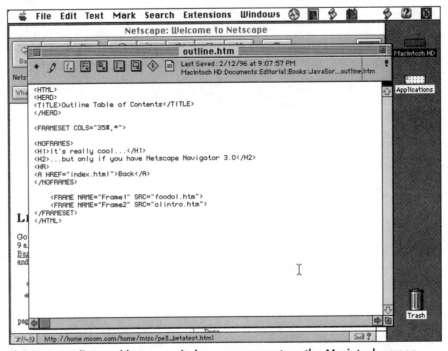

Figure 3-2: Editor and browser window arrangement on the Macintosh screen

With this arrangement, the save-switch-reload sequence is a two-handed affair. Assuming that you have Navigator 4 (which enables you to reload the current URL with a ⌘-R keyboard shortcut), the sequence is as follows:

1. Press ⌘-S (save the source file).

2. Click in the browser window.

3. Press ⌘-R (reload the saved source file).

To return to editing the source file, click on any exposed part of the text editor's window.

A useful utility called Program Switcher (http://www.kamprath.net/claireware) puts the Alt+Tab program switching functionality on the Mac keyboard. It is more convenient than using the Application menu.

What Your First Script Will Do

For the sake of simplicity, the kind of script you will be looking at is the kind that runs automatically when the browser opens the HTML page. Although all scripting and browsing work done here is offline, the behavior of the page would be identical if you placed the source file on a server and someone were to access it via the Web.

Figure 3-3 shows the page as it appears in the browser after you're finished (the exact wording differs slightly if you're running your browser on an operating system platform other than Windows 95 or NT, or if you're using a browser other than Netscape Navigator). The part of the page that is defined in regular HTML contains nothing more than an <H1>-level header with a horizontal rule under it. If someone were not using a JavaScript-equipped browser, all he or she would see is the header and horizontal rule (unless that person had a truly outmoded browser, in which case some of the script words would appear in the page).

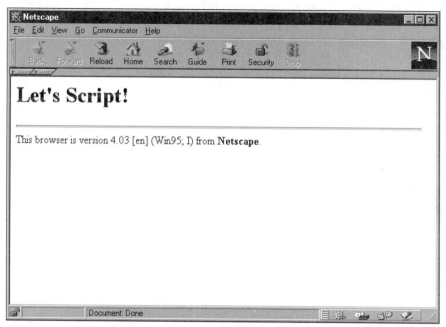

Figure 3-3: The finished page of your first JavaScript script

Below the rule, the script displays plain body text that combines static text with information about the browser you used to load the document. The script writes a stream of HTML information to the browser, including a tag to render a portion of the information in boldface. Even though two lines of code are writing information to the page, the result is rendered as one line, just as it would be if all the text had been hard-coded in HTML.

Entering Your First Script

It's time to start creating your first JavaScript script. Launch your text editor and browser. If your browser offers to dial your Internet service provider (ISP) or begins dialing automatically, cancel or quit the dialing operation. If the browser's Stop button is active, click it to halt any network searching it may be trying to do. You may receive a dialog box message indicating that the URL for your browser's home page (usually the home page of the browser's publisher — unless you've changed the settings) is unavailable. That's fine. You want the browser open, but you shouldn't be connected to your ISP. If you're automatically connected via a local area network in your office or school, that's also fine, but you won't be needing the network connection for now. Next, follow these steps to enter and preview your first JavaScript script:

1. Activate your text editor and create a new blank document.

2. Type the script into the window exactly as shown in Listing 3-1.

Listing 3-1: Source Code for script1.htm

```
<HTML>
<HEAD>
<TITLE>My First Script</TITLE>
</HEAD>

<BODY>
<H1>Let's Script...</H1>
<HR>
<SCRIPT LANGUAGE="JavaScript">
<!-- hide from old browsers
document.write("This browser is version " + navigator.appVersion)
document.write(" of <B>" + navigator.appName + "</B>.")
// end script hiding -->
</SCRIPT>
</BODY>
</HTML>
```

3. Save the document with the name *script1.htm*. (This is the lowest common denominator file-naming convention for Windows 3.1 — feel free to use an .html extension if your operating system allows it.)

4. Switch to your browser.

5. Choose Open File from the File menu and select script1.htm.

If you typed all lines as directed, the document in the browser window should look like the one in Figure 3-3 (with minor differences for your computer's operating system and browser version). If the browser indicates that a mistake exists somewhere as the document loads, don't do anything about it for now (click the OK button in the script error dialog box). Let's first examine the details of the entire document so you understand some of the finer points of what the script is doing.

Examining the Script

You do not need to memorize any of the commands or syntax that I discuss in this section. Instead, relax and watch how the lines of the script become what you see in the browser. In Listing 3-1, all of the lines up to the `<SCRIPT>` tag are very standard HTML. Your JavaScript-enhanced HTML documents should contain the same style of opening tags you normally use.

The `<SCRIPT>` tag

Any time you include JavaScript verbiage in an HTML document, you must enclose those lines inside a `<SCRIPT>...</SCRIPT>` tag pair. These tags alert the browser program to begin interpreting all the text between these tags as a script. Because other scripting languages, such as Microsoft's VBScript, can take advantage of these script tags, you must specify the precise name of the language in which the enclosed code is written. Therefore, when the browser receives this signal that your script uses the JavaScript language, it uses its built-in JavaScript interpreter to handle the code. You can find parallels to this setup in real life: If you have a French interpreter at your side, you need to know that the person with whom you're conversing also knows French. If you encounter someone from Russia, the French interpreter won't be able to help you. Similarly, if your browser has only a JavaScript interpreter inside, it won't be able to understand code written in VBScript.

Now is a good time to instill an aspect of JavaScript that will be important to you throughout all your scripting ventures: JavaScript is case-sensitive. Therefore, any item in your scripts that uses a JavaScript word must be entered with the correct uppercase and lowercase letters. Your HTML tags (including the `<SCRIPT>` tag) can be in the case of your choice, but everything in JavaScript is case-sensitive. When a line of JavaScript doesn't work, wrong case is the first thing to look for. Always compare your typed code against the listings printed in this book and against the various vocabulary entries discussed throughout it.

A script for all browsers

The next line after the `<SCRIPT>` tag in Listing 3-1 appears to be the beginning of an HTML comment tag. It is, but the JavaScript interpreter treats comment tags in a special way. Although JavaScript dutifully ignores a line that begins with an HTML comment start tag, it treats the next line as a full-fledged script line. In other words, the browser begins interpreting the next line after a comment start tag. If you want to put a comment inside JavaScript code, the comment must start with a double slash (`//`). Such a comment may go near the end of a line (such as after a JavaScript statement that is to be interpreted by the browser) or on its own line. In fact, the latter case appears near the end of the script. The comment line starts with two slashes.

Step back for a moment and notice that the entire script (including comments) is contained inside a standard HTML comment tag (`<!--comment-->`). The value of this containment is not clear until you see what happens to your scripted HTML document in a non–JavaScript-compatible browser. Such a browser would blow past the <SCRIPT> tag as being an advanced tag it doesn't understand. But it would treat a line of script as regular text to be displayed in the page. By enclosing script lines between HTML comment tags, most older browsers won't display the script lines. Still, some old browsers can get tripped up and present some ugliness because they interpret any > symbol (not the whole --> symbol) to be an end-of-comment character. Figure 3-4 shows the results of your first script when viewed in a now-obsolete version of the America Online Web browser (version 2.5 for Windows).

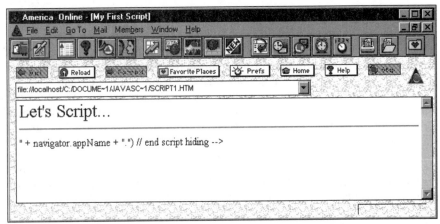

Figure 3-4: By enclosing script lines between HTML comments, the entire script is ignored by most, but not all, non-JavaScript browsers. Here, an old America Online browser shows part of the script anyway.

Remember, too, that some users don't have access to modern browsers or graphical browsers (they use the Lynx text-oriented UNIX Web reader software or Lynx-like browsers in hand-held computers). By embracing your script lines within these comments, your Web pages won't look completely broken in relatively modern non-JavaScript browsers.

Notice that the comment lines that shield older browsers from your scripts go inside the <SCRIPT>...</SCRIPT> tags. Do not put these comment lines above the <SCRIPT> tag or below the </SCRIPT> tag and expect them to work.

One more issue about the script-hiding comment lines in this book. To save space on the page, most examples do not have comment lines inserted in them. But as you can see in the full-fledged application examples on the CD-ROM (in the folder named Bonus Applications Chapters), the comment lines are where they should be. For any pages you produce for public consumption, always encase your script lines inside these comments.

Displaying some text

Both script lines use one of the possible actions a script can ask a document to perform (document.write(), meaning display text in the current document). You learn more about the document object in Chapter 16.

Whenever you ask an object (a document in this case) to perform a task for you, the name of the task is always followed by a set of parentheses. In some cases — the write() task, for example — JavaScript needs to know what information it should act on. That information (called a *parameter*) goes inside parentheses after the name of the task. Thus, if you want to write the name of the first U.S. president to a document, the command to do so is

```
document.write("George Washington")
```

The line of text that the script writes starts with some static text ("This browser is version") and adds some evaluated text (the version of the browser) to it. The writing continues with more static text that includes an HTML tag ("of <B>"), more evaluated text (the name of the browser application), and ends with an HTML closing tag and the sentence's period ("</B>."). JavaScript uses the plus symbol (+) to join (*concatenate*) text components into a larger, single string of text characters to be written by the document. Neither JavaScript nor the + symbol knows anything about words and spaces, so the script is responsible for making sure that the proper spaces are passed along as part of the parameters. Notice, therefore, that an extra space exists after the word "version" in the first document.write() parameter, as well as spaces on both sides of "of" in the second document.write() parameter.

To fetch the information about the browser version and name for your parameters, you call upon JavaScript to extract the corresponding properties from the navigator object. You extract a property by appending the property name to the object name (navigator in this case) and separating the two names with a period. If you're searching for some English to mentally assign to this scheme as you read it, start from the right side and call the right item a property "of" the left side: the appVersion property of the navigator object. This dot syntax looks a great deal like the document.write() task, but a property name does not have parentheses after it. In any case, the reference to the property in the script tells JavaScript to insert the value of that property in the spot where the call is made. For your first attempt at the script, JavaScript substitutes the internal information about the browser as part of the text string that gets written to the document.

Have Some Fun

If you encountered an error in your first attempt at loading this document into your browser, go back to the text editor and check the lines of the script section against Listing 3-1, looking carefully at each line in light of the explanations. There may be a single character out of place, a lowercase letter where an uppercase one belongs, or a quote or parenthesis missing. Make necessary repairs, switch to your browser, and click Reload.

To see how dynamic the script in script1.htm is, go back into the text editor and replace the word "browser" with "client software." Save, switch, and reload to see how the script has changed the text in the document. Feel free to substitute other text for the quoted text in the `document.write()` statement. Or, add more text with additional `document.write()` statements. The parameters to `document.write()` are HTML text, so you can even write a "`<BR>`" to make a line break. Always be sure to save, switch, and reload to see the results of your handiwork.

✦   ✦   ✦

JavaScript Tutorial

Browser and Document Objects

♦ ♦ ♦ ♦

In This Chapter

What client-side scripts do

What happens when a document loads

How the browser creates objects

How scripts refer to objects

How to find out what is scriptable in an object

♦ ♦ ♦ ♦

This chapter marks the first of nine tutorial chapters (which compose Part II) tailored to authors who have at least basic grounding in HTML concepts. You will see several practical applications of JavaScript and begin to see how a JavaScript-enabled browser turns familiar HTML elements into objects that your scripts control.

Scripts Run the Show

If you have authored in plain HTML, you are familiar with how HTML tags influence the way content is rendered on a page when viewed in the browser. As the page loads, the browser recognizes tags (by virtue of their containing angle brackets) as formatting instructions. Instructions are read from the top of the document downward, and elements defined in the HTML document appear on screen in the same order in which they are entered in the document. As an author, you do a little work one time up front — adding the tags — and the browser does a lot more work every time a visitor loads the page into a browser.

Assume for a moment that one of the elements on the page is a text field inside a form. The user is supposed to enter some text in the text field and then click the Submit button to send that information back to the Web server. If that information must be an Internet e-mail address, how do you ensure the user included the "@" symbol in the address?

One way is to have a Common Gateway Interface (CGI) program on the server scan the submitted form data after the user has clicked the Submit button and the form information has been transferred to the server. If the user omitted or forgot the "@" symbol, the CGI program resends the page, but this time with an instruction to include the symbol in the address. Nothing is wrong with this exchange, but it means a significant delay for the user to find out that the address does not contain the crucial symbol. Moreover, the Web server has had to expend some of its resources to perform the validation and communicate back to the visitor. If the Web site is a busy one, the server may be trying to perform hundreds of these validations at any given moment, probably slowing the response time to the user even more.

Now imagine if the document containing that text field had some intelligence built into it that could make sure the text field entry contains the "@" symbol before ever sending one bit (literally!) of data to the server. That kind of intelligence would have to be embedded in the document in some fashion — downloaded with the page's content so it can stand ready to jump into action when called upon. The browser must know how to run that embedded program. Some user action must start the program, perhaps when the user clicks the Submit button. As the program runs, if it detects a lack of the "@" symbol, an alert message should appear to bring the problem to the user's attention; the same program should also be able to decide if the actual submission can proceed, or if it should wait until a valid e-mail address is entered into the field.

This kind of presubmission data entry validation is but one of the practical ways JavaScript adds intelligence to an HTML document. Looking at this example, you might recognize that a script must know how to look into what has been typed in a text field; a script must also know how to let a submission continue or how to abort the submission. A browser capable of running JavaScript programs conveniently treats elements such as the text field as *objects*. A JavaScript script controls the action and behavior of objects — most of which you see on the screen in the browser window.

JavaScript in Action

By adding lines of JavaScript code to your HTML documents, you control on-screen objects as your applications require. To give you an idea of the scope of application you can create with JavaScript, I show you several applications from the CD-ROM (in the folder named Bonus Applications Chapters). I strongly suggest you open the applications and play with them in your browser. Links to the application files from the CD-ROM can be found on the page tutor1.htm in the book listings folder. I also provide URLs to the examples at my Web site.

Interactive user interfaces

HTML hyperlinks do a fine job, but they're not necessarily the most engaging way to present a table of contents to a large site or document. With a bit of JavaScript, it is possible to create an interactive, expandable table of contents listing that displays the hierarchy of a large body of material (see Figure 4-1). Just like the text listings in operating system file management windows, the expandable table of contents lets the user see as much or as little as possible, while providing a shortcut to the Big Picture of the entire data collection.

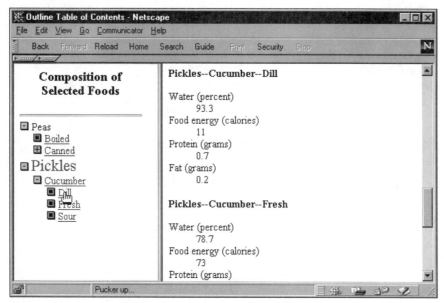

Figure 4-1: An expandable table of contents (http://www.dannyg.com/javascript/ol2/index.htm)

Click on a gray widget icon to expand the items underneath. An endpoint item has an orange and black widget icon. Items in the outline can be links to other pages or descriptive information. You also maintain the same kind of font control over each entry as you would expect from HTML. While such outlines have been created with server CGIs in the past, the response time between clicks is terribly slow. By placing all of the smarts behind the outline inside the page, it downloads once and runs quickly after each click.

As demonstrated in the detailed description of this outline in the application Outline-Style Table of Contents (Chapter 50 of the bonus applications chapters on the CD-ROM), the scriptable workings can be implemented within straight HTML for Navigator 2 and 3 and in Dynamic HTML for Navigator 4 and Internet Explorer 4. Either way you do it, the quick response and action on the screen makes for a more engaging experience for Web surfers who are in a hurry to scout your site.

Small data lookup

A common application on the Web is having a CGI program present a page that visitors use to access large databases on the server. Large data collections are best left on the server, where search engines and other technologies are the best fit. But if your page acts as a "front end" to a small data collection lookup, you can consider embedding that data collection in the document (out of view) and letting JavaScript act as the intermediary between user and data.

I've done just that in a Social Security prefix lookup system shown in Figure 4-2. I converted a printed table of about 55 entries into a JavaScript table that occupies only a few hundred bytes. When the visitor types the three-character prefix of his or her Social Security number into the field and clicks the Search button, a script behind the scenes compares that number against the 55 or so ranges in the table. When the script finds a match, it displays the corresponding state of registration in a second field.

If the application were stored on the server and the data stored in a server database, each click of the Search button would mean a delay of many seconds, as the server processes the request, gets the data from the database, and reformulates the page with the result for the user. Built instead as a JavaScript application, once the page downloads the first time, any number of lookups are instantaneous.

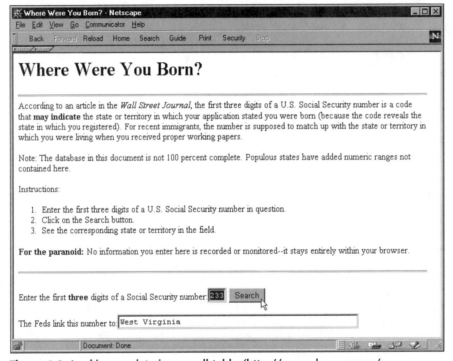

Figure 4-2: Looking up data in a small table (http://www.dannyg.com/javascript/ssn2/ssbirthplace.htm)

Forms validation

I've already used data entry form validation as an example of when JavaScript is a good fit. In fact the data entry field in the Social Security lookup page (see Figure 4-2) includes scripting to check the validity of the entered number. Just as a CGI program for this task would have to verify that the entry was a three-digit number, so, too, must the JavaScript program verify the entered value. If a mistake appears in the entry — perhaps a finger slipped and hit a letter key — the visitor is advised of the problem and directed to try another entry. The validation script even preselects the text in the entry field for the visitor so that typing a new value replaces the old.

Interactive data

JavaScript opens opportunities for turning static information into interactive information. Figure 4-3 shows a graphical calculator for determining the value of an electrical component (called a resistor) whose only markings are colored bars.

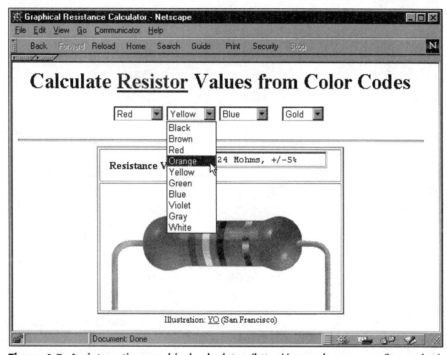

Figure 4-3: An interactive graphical calculator (http://www.dannyg.com/javascript/res2/resistor.htm)

The image in the bottom half of the page is composed of seven images in vertical slices all bunched up against each other. As the visitor selects a color from a pop-up list near the top, the associated image slice changes to the selected color and the resistance value is calculated and displayed.

Again, with the page loaded, response time is instantaneous, whereas a server-based version of this calculator would take many seconds between color changes. Moreover, JavaScript provides the power to preload all possible images while the main page loaded. Therefore, with only a slight extra delay to download all images with the page, no further delay occurs when a visitor chooses a new color. Not only is the application practical (for its intended audience), but it's just plain fun to play with.

Multiple frames

While frames are the domain of HTML, they suddenly become more powerful with some JavaScript behind them. The Decision Helper application shown in Figure 4-4 takes this notion to the extreme.

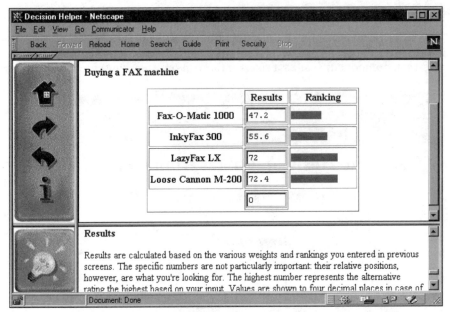

Figure 4-4: The Decision Helper (http://www.dannyg.com/javascript/dh2/)

The Decision Helper is a full-fledged application that includes four input screens and one screen that displays the results of some fairly complex calculations based on the input screens. Results are shown both in numbers and in a bar graph form, as shown in Figure 4-4.

Interaction among three of the four frames requires JavaScript. For example, if the user clicks on one of the directional arrows in the top-left frame, not only does the top-right frame change to another document, but the instructions document in the bottom-right frame shifts to the anchor point that parallels the content of the input screen. Scripting behind the top-right frame documents uses various techniques to preserve entry information as the user navigates through the sequence of input pages. These are the same techniques you might use to build an online product catalog and shopping cart — accumulating the customer's selections from various catalog pages, and then bringing them together in the checkout order form.

Certainly this application could be fashioned out of a CGI program on the server. But the high level of interaction and calculation required would turn this now speedy application into a glacially slow exchange of information between user and server.

Dynamic HTML

Starting with the level 4 browsers from both Netscape and Microsoft, more and more content on the page can be modified with the help of client-side scripts. In Figure 4-5, for example, scripts in the page control the dragging of map pieces in the puzzle. Highlight colors change as you click on the state maps, instruction panels fly in from the edge of the screen, and another item appears when you place all the states in their proper positions.

The browser feature that makes this level of script control possible is *Dynamic HTML*. JavaScript becomes the vital connection between the user and dynamically respositionable elements on the screen. Not even a CGI program could help this application, since you need immediate programmatic control in the page to respond to user mouse motion and instantaneous changes to screen elements.

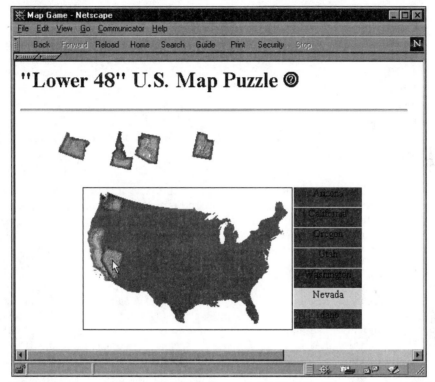

Figure 4-5: A map game in scriptable Dynamic HTML (http://www.dannyg.com/javascript/puzzle/mapgame.htm)

When to use JavaScript

The preceding examples demonstrate a wide range of applications for JavaScript, but by no means do they come close to exhausting JavaScript's possibilities. When faced with a Web application task, I look to client-side JavaScript for help with the following requirements:

✦ **Data entry validation:** If form fields need to be filled out for processing on the server, I let client-side scripts prequalify the data entered by the user.

✦ **Server-less CGIs:** I use this term to describe processes that, were it not for JavaScript, would be programmed as CGIs on the server, yielding slow performance because of the interactivity required between the program and user. This includes tasks such as small data collection lookup, modification of images, and generation of HTML in other frames and windows based on user input.

✦ **Dynamic HTML interactivity:** It's one thing to use DHTML's abilities to precisely position elements on the page — you don't need scripting for that. But if you intend to make the content dance on the page, scripting makes that happen.

✦ **CGI prototyping:** Sometimes you may want a CGI program to be at the root of your application because it reduces the potential incompatibilities among browser brands and versions. It may be easier to create a prototype of the CGI in client-side JavaScript. Use the opportunity to polish the user interface before implementing the application as a CGI.

✦ **Offloading a busy server:** If you have a highly trafficked Web site, it may be beneficial to convert frequently used CGI processes to client-side JavaScript scripts. Once a page is downloaded, the server is freed to serve other visitors. Not only does this lighten server load, but users experience quicker response to the application embedded in the page.

✦ **Adding life to otherwise dead pages:** HTML by itself is pretty "flat." Adding a blinking chunk of text doesn't help much; animated GIF images more often distract from than contribute to the user experience at your site. But if you can dream up ways to add some interactive zip to your page, it may engage the user and encourage a recommendation to friends or repeat visits.

✦ **Creating "Web pages that think":** If you let your imagination soar, you may develop new, intriguing ways to make your pages appear to be smart. For example, in the application Intelligent "Updated" Flags (Chapter 52 on the CD-ROM) you will see how, without a server CGI or database, an HTML page can "remember" when a visitor last came to the page; then any items that have been updated since the last visit — regardless of the number of updatings you've done to the page — are flagged for that visitor. That's the kind of subtle, thinking Web page that best displays JavaScript's powers.

The Document Object Model

Before you can truly start scripting, you should have a good feel for the kinds of objects you will be scripting. A scriptable browser does a lot of the work of creating software objects that generally represent the visible objects you see in an HTML page in the browser window. Obvious objects include images and form elements. However, there may be other objects that aren't so obvious by looking at a page, but make perfect sense when you consider the HTML tags used to generate a page's content.

To help scripts control these objects — and to help authors see some method to the madness of potentially dozens of objects on a page — the browser makers define a *document object model*. A model is like a prototype or plan for the organization of objects in a page. Figure 4-6 shows the document object model that

Netscape has defined for Navigator 4. Internet Explorer contains almost all of the objects in Figure 4-6, but Microsoft's model is more extensive. At this stage of the learning process, it is not important to memorize every last object in the model, but rather to get a general feel for what's going on.

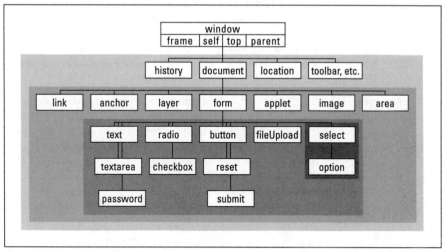

Figure 4-6: Netscape Navigator 4 document object model

One misconception you must avoid at the outset is that the model shown in Figure 4-6 is the model for every document that loads into the browser. On the contrary — it represents an idealized version of a document that includes one of every possible type of object that Navigator 4 knows about. In a moment, I will show you how the document object model stored in the browser at any given instant reflects the HTML in the document. But for now, I want to impress an important aspect of the structure of the idealized model: its hierarchy.

Containment Hierarchy

Notice in Figure 4-6 that objects are grouped together in various levels designated by the density of the gray background. Objects are organized in a hierarchy, not unlike the hierarchy of a company's organization chart of job positions. At the top is the president. Reporting to the president are several vice presidents. One of the vice presidents manages a sales force that is divided into geographical regions. Each region has a manager who reports to the vice president of sales; each region then has several salespeople. If the president wanted to communicate to a salesperson who handles a big account, the protocol would call for the president to route the message through the hierarchy — to the vice president of sales; to the sales manager; to the salesperson. The hierarchy clearly defines each unit's role and relationship to the other units.

This hierarchical structure applies to the organization of objects in a document. Allow me to highlight the key objects and explain their relationships to others.

✦ **Window object:** At the top of the hierarchy is the window. This object represents the content area of the browser window where HTML documents appear. In a multiple-frame environment, each frame is also a window, but don't concern yourself with this just yet. Because all document action takes place inside the window, the window is the outermost element of the object hierarchy. Its physical borders contain the document.

✦ **Document object:** Each HTML document that gets loaded into a window becomes a document object. Its position in the object hierarchy is an important one, as you can see in Figure 4-6. The document object contains by far the most other kinds of objects in the model. This makes perfect sense when you think about it: The document contains the content that you are likely to script.

✦ **Form object:** Users don't see the beginning and ending of forms on a page, only their elements. But a form is a distinct grouping of content inside an HTML document. Everything that is inside the <FORM>...</FORM> tag set is part of the form object. A document might have more than one pair of <FORM> tags if that's what the page design calls for. If so, the map of the objects for that particular document would have two form objects instead of the one that appears in Figure 4-6.

✦ **Form elements:** Just as your HTML defines form elements within the confines of the <FORM>...</FORM> tag pair, so does a form object contain all the elements defined for that object. Each one of those form elements — text fields, buttons, radio buttons, checkboxes, and the like — is a separate object. Unlike the one-of-everything model shown in Figure 4-6, the precise model for any document depends on the HTML tags in the document.

When a Document Loads

Programming languages, such as JavaScript, are convenient intermediaries between your mental image of how a program works and the true inner workings of the computer. Inside the machine, every word of a program code listing influences the storage and movement of bits (the legendary 1s and 0s of the computer's binary universe) from one RAM storage slot to another. Languages and object models are inside the computer (or, in the case of JavaScript, inside the browser's area of the computer) to make it easier for programmers to visualize how a program works and what its results will be. The relationship reminds me a lot of knowing how to drive an automobile from point A to point B without knowing exactly how an internal combustion engine, steering linkages, and all that other internal "stuff" works. By controlling high-level objects such as the ignition key, gear shift, gas pedal, brake, and steering wheel, I can get the results I need.

Of course programming is not exactly like driving a car with an automatic transmission. Even scripting requires the equivalent of opening the hood and perhaps knowing how to check the transmission fluid or change the oil. Therefore, now it's time to open the hood and watch what happens to the document object model as a page loads into the browser.

A simple document

Figure 4-7 shows the HTML and corresponding object model for a very simple document. When this page loads, the browser maintains in its memory a map of the objects generated by the HTML tags in the document. The window object is always there for every document. Every window object also contains an object called the *location* object (it stores information about the URL of the document being loaded). I'll skip that object for now, but acknowledge its presence (as a dimmed box in the diagram) because it is part of the model in the browser memory. Finally, since a document has been loaded, the browser generates a document object in its current map.

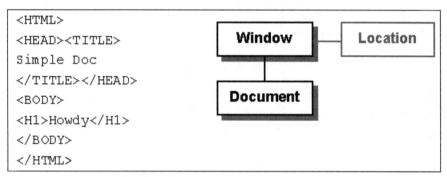

```
<HTML>
<HEAD><TITLE>
Simple Doc
</TITLE></HEAD>
<BODY>
<H1>Howdy</H1>
</BODY>
</HTML>
```

Figure 4-7: A simple document and object map

Add a form

Now I modify the HTML file to include a blank <FORM> tag set and reload the document. Figure 4-8 shows what happens to both the HTML (changes in boldface) and the object map as constructed by the browser. Even though no content appears in the form, the <FORM> tags are enough to tell the browser to create that form object. Also note that the form object is contained by the document in the hierarchy of objects in the current map. This mirrors the structure of the idealized map shown back in Figure 4-6.

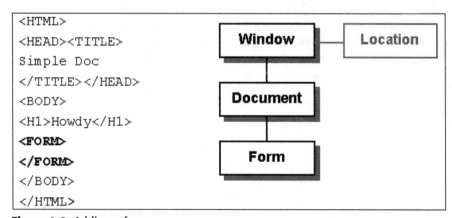

```
<HTML>
<HEAD><TITLE>
Simple Doc
</TITLE></HEAD>
<BODY>
<H1>Howdy</H1>
<FORM>
</FORM>
</BODY>
</HTML>
```

Figure 4-8: Adding a form

Add a text input element

I modify and reload the HTML file again, this time including an `<INPUT>` tag that defines a text field form element, shown in Figure 4-9. As mentioned earlier, the containment structure of the HTML (the `<INPUT>` tag goes inside a `<FORM>` tag set) is reflected in the object map for the revised document. Therefore, the window contains a document; the document contains a form; and the form contains a text input element.

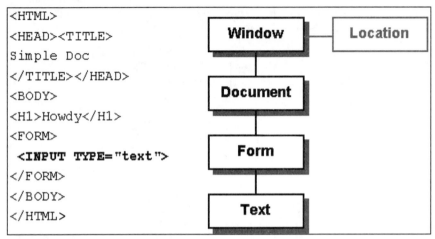

Figure 4-9: Adding a text input element to the form

Add a button element

The last modification I make to the file is to add a button input element to the same form as the text input element earlier (see Figure 4-10). Notice that the HTML for the button is contained by the same `<FORM>` tag set as the text field. As a result, the object map hierarchy shows both the text field and button being contained by the same form object. If the map were a corporate organization chart, the employees represented by the Text and Button boxes would be at the same level, reporting to the same boss.

Now that you see how objects are created in memory in response to HTML tags, the next step is to figure out how scripts can communicate with these objects. After all, scripting is mostly about controlling these objects.

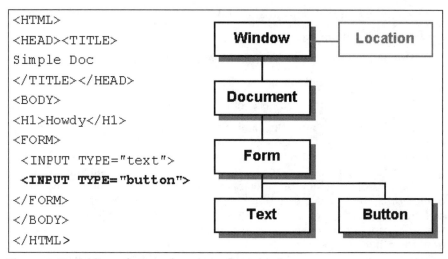

```
<HTML>
<HEAD><TITLE>
Simple Doc
</TITLE></HEAD>
<BODY>
<H1>Howdy</H1>
<FORM>
 <INPUT TYPE="text">
 <INPUT TYPE="button">
</FORM>
</BODY>
</HTML>
```

Figure 4-10: Adding a button element to the same form

Object References

After a document has loaded into the browser, all of its objects are safely stored in memory in the containment hierarchy structure specified by the browser's document object model. For a script to control one of those objects there must be a way to point to an object and find out something about it: "Hey, Mr. Text Field, what has the user typed in there?"

The JavaScript language uses the containment hierarchy structure to let scripts get in touch with any object in a document. For a moment, make believe you are the browser with a document loaded into your memory. You have this road map of objects handy. If a script needs you to locate one of those objects, it would be a big help if the script showed you what route to follow in the map to reach that object. There must be some way for the script to denote which object he means: an *object reference*.

Object naming

The biggest aid in creating script references to objects is assigning names to every scriptable object in your HTML. Scriptable browsers such as modern versions of Navigator and Internet Explorer acknowledge an optional tag attribute called NAME. The attribute lets you assign a unique name to each object. Here are some examples of NAME attributes being added to typical tags:

```
<FORM NAME="dataEntry" METHOD=GET>

<INPUT TYPE="text" NAME="entry">

<FRAME SRC="info.html" NAME="main">
```

The only rules about object names (also called *identifiers*) are that they

✦ May not contain spaces

✦ Should not contain punctuation except for the underscore character

✦ Must be inside quotes when assigned to the `NAME` attribute

✦ Must not start with a numeric character

Think of assigning names the same as sticking name tags on everyone attending a conference meeting. The name of the object, however, is only one part of the actual reference that the browser needs to locate the object. For each object, the reference must include the steps along the object hierarchy starting at the top down to the object, no matter how many levels of containment are involved. In other words, the browser cannot pick out an object by name only. A reference includes the names of each object along the path from the window to the object. In the JavaScript language, each successive object name along the route is separated from the other by a period.

To demonstrate what real references look like within the context of an object model you've already seen, I retrace the same model steps shown earlier in the following sections, but this time show the reference to each object as the document acquires more objects.

A simple document

I start with the model whose only objects are the window (and its location object) and document from the simple HTML file. Figure 4-11 shows the object map and references for the two main objects. Every document resides in a window, so to reference the window object, you start with the object name, `window`. Also fixed in this reference is the document, since there can be only one document per window (or frame). Therefore, a reference to the document object is `window.document`.

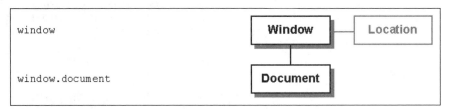

Figure 4-11: References to the window and document

Add a form

Modifying the document to include the empty `<FORM>` tag generates the form object in the map. If I did the job right, the `<FORM>` tag would also include a `NAME` attribute. The reference to the form object, as shown in Figure 4-12, starts with the window, wends through the document, and reaches the form, which I would call by name: `window.document.`*formName* (the italics meaning that in a real script, I would substitute the form's name for *formName*).

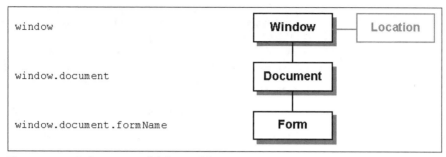

Figure 4-12: Reference to the form object

Add a text input element

As the hierarchy gets deeper, the object reference gets longer. In Figure 4-13, I have added a text input object to the form. The reference to this deeply nested object still starts at the window level, and works its way down to the name I assigned to the object in its `<INPUT>` tag: `window.document.`*`formName.textName`*.

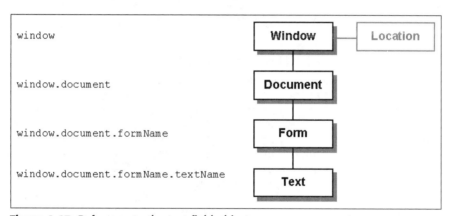

Figure 4-13: Reference to the text field object

Add a button element

When I add a button to the same form as the text object, the reference stays the same length (see Figure 4-14). All that changes is the last part of the reference, where the button name goes in place of the text field name: `window.document.`*`formName.buttonName`*.

About the Dot Syntax

JavaScript uses the period to separate components of a hierarchical reference. This convention is adopted from Java, which, in turn, based this formatting on the C language. Every reference typically starts with the most global scope — the window for client-side JavaScript — and narrows focus with each "dot" (.) delimiter.

If you have not programmed before, don't be put off by the dot syntax. You are probably already using it, such as when you access Usenet newsgroups. The methodology for organizing the thousands of newsgroups is to group them in a hierarchy that makes it relatively easy to both find a newsgroup and visualize where the newsgroup you're currently reading is located in the scheme of things.

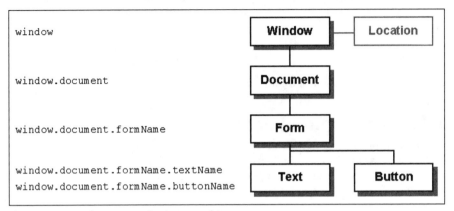

Figure 4-14: Reference to the button object

Newsgroup Organization Model

Let me briefly dissect a typical newsgroup address, to help you understand dot syntax: `rec.sport.skating.inline`. The first entry (at the left edge) defines the basic group — recreation — among all the newsgroup categories. Other group categories, such as `comp.` and `alt.`, have their own sections and do not overlap with what goes on in the `rec` section. Within the `rec` section are dozens of subsections, one of which is `sport`. That distinguishes all the sport-related groups from, say, the automobile or music groups within recreational newsgroups.

Like most broad newsgroup categories, `rec.sport` has many subcategories, each one devoted to a particular sport. In this case, it is skating. Other sport newsgroups include `rec.sport.rugby` and `rec.sport.snowboarding`. Even within the `rec.sport.skating` category, a further subdivision exists to help narrow the subject matter for participants. Therefore, a separate newsgroup just for inline skaters exists, just as a group for roller-skating exists (`rec.sport.skating.roller`). As a narrower definition is needed for a category, a new level is formed by adding a dot and a word to differentiate that subgroup from the thousands of newsgroups on the Net. When you ask your newsgroup software to view messages in the `rec.sport.skating.inline` group, you're giving it a map to follow in the newsgroup hierarchy to go directly to a single newsgroup.

Another benefit of this syntactical method is that names for subcategories can be reused within other categories, if necessary. For example, with this naming scheme, it is possible to have two similarly named subcategories in two separate newsgroup classifications, such as `rec.radio.scanners` and `alt.radio.scanners`. When you ask to visit one, the hierarchical address, starting with the `rec.` or `alt.` classification, ensures you get to the desired place. Neither collection of messages is automatically connected with the other (although subscribers frequently cross-post to both newsgroups).

For complete newbies to the Net, this dot syntax can be intimidating. Because the system was designed to run on UNIX servers (the UNIX operating system is written in C), the application of a C-like syntax for newsgroup addressing is hardly surprising.

What Defines an Object?

When an HTML tag defines an object, the browser creates a slot for it in memory. But an object is far more complex internally than, say, a mere number stored in memory. The purpose of an object is to represent some "thing." Because in JavaScript you deal with items that appear in a browser window, an object may be an input text field, a button, or the whole HTML document. Outside of the pared-down world of a JavaScript browser, an object can also represent abstract entities, such as a calendar program's appointment entry or a paragraph in an object-oriented word processor.

Every object is unique in some way, even if it should look identical to you in the browser. Three very important facets of an object define what it is, what it looks like, how it behaves, and how scripts control it. Those three facets are *properties*, *methods*, and *event handlers*. They play such key roles in your future JavaScript efforts that the Object Road Map in Appendix A summarizes the properties, methods, and event handlers for each object. You might want to take a quick peek at that road map if for no other reason than to gain an appreciation for the size of the scripting vocabulary that consists of these object features.

Properties

Any physical object you hold in your hand has a collection of characteristics that defines it. A coin, for example, has a shape, diameter, thickness, color, weight, embossed images on each side, and any number of other attributes that distinguish a coin from, say, a feather. Each of those features is called a *property*. Each property has a value of some kind attached to it (even if the value is empty or null). For example, the shape property of a coin might be "circle" — in this case, a text value. In contrast, the denomination property is most likely a numeric value.

You may not have known it, but if you've written HTML for use in a scriptable browser, you have been setting object properties all along without writing one iota of JavaScript. Tag attributes are the most common way an HTML object's properties are set. The presence of JavaScript often adds optional attributes whose initial values can be set when the document loads. For example, the following HTML tag defines a button object that assigns two property values:

```
<INPUT TYPE="button" NAME="clicker" VALUE="Hit Me...">
```

In JavaScript parlance, then, the name property holds the word "clicker," while the value property is the text that appears on the button label, "Hit Me...". In truth, a button has more properties than just these, but you don't have to set every property for every object. Most properties have default values that are automatically assigned if nothing special is set in the HTML or later from a script.

The contents of some properties can change while a document is loaded and the user interacts with the page. Consider the following text input tag:

```
<INPUT TYPE="text" NAME="entry" VALUE="User Name?">
```

The name property of this object is the word "entry." When the page loads, the text of the VALUE attribute setting is placed in the text field — the automatic behavior of an HTML text field when the VALUE attribute is specified. But if a user enters some other text into the text field, the value property changes — not in the HTML, but in the memory copy of the object model that the browser maintains. Therefore, if a script queries the text field about the content of the value property, the browser yields the current setting of the property, which may not be the one specified by the HTML if a user changes the text.

To gain access to an object's property, you use the same kind of dot syntax, hierarchical addressing scheme you saw earlier for objects. Since a property is contained by its object, the reference to it consists of the reference to the object plus one more extension naming the property. Therefore, for the button and text object tags just shown, references to various properties would be

```
document.formName.clicker.name
document.formName.clicker.value
document.formName.entry.value
```

You may be wondering what happened to the window part of the reference. It turns out that since there can only be one document contained in a window, references to objects inside the document can omit the window portion and start the reference with document. The document object, however, cannot be omitted from the reference. Notice, too, that the button and text field both have a property named value. These properties represent very different attributes for each object. For the button, the property determines the button label; for the text field, the property reflects the current text in the field. You now see how the (sometimes lengthy) hierarchical referencing scheme helps the browser locate exactly the object and property your script needs. No two items in a document can have identical references.

Methods

If a property is like a descriptive adjective for an object, then a method is a verb. A method is all about action related to the object. A method either does something to the object or with the object that affects other parts of a script or document. They are commands of a sort, but whose behaviors are tied to a particular object.

An object can have any number of methods associated with it (including none at all). Method names are like property names except that the format for methods insists that they end with a pair of parentheses. To set a method into motion, a JavaScript statement must include a reference to it, via its object, as in the following examples:

```
document.orderForm.submit()
document.orderForm.entry.select()
```

The first is a scripted way of clicking on a Submit button to send a form to a server. The second selects the text inside a text field named `entry` (which is contained by a form named `orderForm`).

Sometimes a method requires that additional information be sent along with it so that it can do its job. Each chunk of information passed with the method is called a *parameter* or *argument* (you can use the terms interchangeably). You saw examples of passing a parameter in your first script in Chapter 3. Two script statements invoked the `write()` method of the document object:

```
document.write("This browser is version " + navigator.appVersion)
document.write(" of <B>" + navigator.appName + "</B>.")
```

As the page loaded into the browser, each `document.write()` method sent whatever text is inside the parentheses to the current document. In both cases, the content being sent as a parameter consisted of straight text (inside quotes) and the values of two object properties: the `appVersion` and `appName` properties of the navigator object (the navigator object does not appear in the object hierarchy diagram of Figure 4-6, because in Navigator, this object exists outside of the document object model).

As you learn more about the details of JavaScript and the document objects you can script, pay close attention to the range of methods defined for each object. They reveal a lot about what an object is capable of doing under script control.

Event handlers

One last characteristic of a JavaScript object is the event handler. Events are actions that take place in a document, usually as the result of user activity. Common examples of user actions that trigger events include clicking on a button or typing a character into a text field. Some events, such as the act of loading a document into the browser window or experiencing a network error while an image loads, are not so obvious.

Almost every JavaScript object in a document receives events of one kind or another — summarized for your convenience in the Object Road Map of Appendix A. What determines whether the object will do anything in response to the event is an extra attribute you enter into the object's HTML definition. The attribute consists of the event name, an equals sign (just like any HTML attribute), followed by instructions about what to do when the particular event fires. Listing 4-1 shows a very simple document that displays a single button with one event handler defined for it.

Listing 4-1: **A Simple Button with an Event Handler**

```
<HTML>
<BODY>
<FORM>
<INPUT TYPE="button" VALUE="Click Me" onClick="window.alert ('Ouch!')">
</FORM>
</BODY>
</HTML>
```

The form definition contains what, for the most part, looks like a standard input item. But notice the last attribute, `onClick="window.alert('Ouch!')"`. Button objects, as you see in their complete descriptions in Chapter 23, react to mouse clicks. When a user clicks on the button, the browser sends a click event to the button. In this button's definition, the attribute says that whenever the button receives that message, it should invoke one of the window object's methods, `alert()`. The alert method displays a simple alert dialog box whose content is whatever text is passed as a parameter to the method. Like most arguments to HTML attributes, the attribute setting to the right of the equals sign goes inside quotes. If additional quotes are necessary, as in the case of the text to be passed along with the event handler, those inner quotes can be single quotes. In actuality, JavaScript doesn't distinguish between single or double quotes but does require that each set be of the same type. Therefore, the attribute could have also been written

```
onClick='alert("Ouch!")'
```

Exercises

1. Which of the following applications are well-suited to client-side JavaScript, and why or why not?

   a. Music jukebox

   b. Web-site visit counter

   c. Chat room

   d. Graphical Fahrenheit-to-Celsius temperature calculator

   e. All of the above

   f. None of the above

2. General Motors has five divisions for its automobile brands: Chevrolet, Pontiac, Oldsmobile, Buick, and Cadillac. Each brand has several models of automobile. Following this hierarchy model, write the dot-syntax equivalent reference to the following three vehicle models:

   a. Chevrolet Malibu

   b. Pontiac Firebird

   c. Pontiac Bonneville

3. Which of the following object names are valid in JavaScript? For each one that is not valid, explain why.

   a. lastName

   b. company_name

   c. 1stLineAddress

   d. zip code

   e. today's_date

4. An HTML document contains tags for one image and one form. The form contains tags for three text boxes, one checkbox, a Submit button, and a Reset button. Using the object hierarchy diagram from Figure 4-6 for reference, draw a diagram of the object model that Navigator would create in its memory for these objects. Give names to the image, form, text fields, and checkbox, and write the references to each of those objects.

5. Write the HTML tag for a button input element whose name is "Hi", whose visible label reads "Howdy", and whose onClick= event handler displays an alert dialog box that says "Hello to you, too!"

✦   ✦   ✦

Scripts and HTML Documents

✦ ✦ ✦ ✦

In This Chapter

Where to place
scripts in HTML
documents

What a JavaScript
statement is

What makes a
script run

The difference
between scripting
and programming

✦ ✦ ✦ ✦

In this chapter's tutorial, you begin to see how scripts are embedded within HTML documents and what a script statement consists of. You also see how script statements can run when the document loads or in response to user action.

Where Scripts Go in Documents

In Chapter 4, not much was said about what scripts look like or how you add them to an HTML document. That's where this lesson picks up the story.

The <SCRIPT> tag

To assist the browser in recognizing lines of code in an HTML document as belonging to a script, you surround lines of script code with a `<SCRIPT>...</SCRIPT>` tag set. This is common usage in HTML, where start and end tags encapsulate content controlled by that tag, whether the tag set be for a form or a bold font.

Depending on the browser, the `<SCRIPT>` tag has a variety of attributes you can set that govern the script. One attribute shared by Navigator and Internet Explorer is the `LANGUAGE` attribute. This attribute is essential because each browser brand and version accepts a different set of scripting languages. One setting that all scriptable browsers accept is the JavaScript language, as in

```
<SCRIPT LANGUAGE="JavaScript">
```

Other possibilities include later versions of JavaScript (version numbers are part of the language name), Microsoft's JScript variant, and the separate VBScript language. You don't need to specify any of these other languages unless your script intends to take specific advantage of a particular language version to the exclusion of all others. Until you learn the differences among the language versions, you can safely specify plain JavaScript on all scriptable browsers.

Be sure to include the ending tag for the script. Lines of JavaScript code go between the two tags:

```
<SCRIPT LANGUAGE="JavaScript">
  one or more lines of JavaScript code here
</SCRIPT>
```

If you forget the closing script tag, not only may the script not run properly, but the HTML elsewhere in the page may look strange.

Although you won't be working with it in this tutorial, another attribute works with more recent browsers to blend the contents of an external script file into the current document. A SRC attribute (similar to the SRC attribute of an <IMG> tag) points to the file containing the script code. Such files must end with a .js extension, and the tag set looks like the following:

```
<SCRIPT LANGUAGE="JavaScript" SRC="myscript.js"></SCRIPT>
```

Since all script lines are in the external file, no script lines are included between the start and end script tags in the document.

Tag positions

Where do these tags go within a document? The answer is, Anywhere they're needed in the document. Sometimes it makes sense to include the tags nested within the <HEAD>...</HEAD> tag set; other times it is essential that the script be dropped into a very specific location in the <BODY>...</BODY> section.

In the following four listings, I demonstrate with the help of a skeletal HTML document some of the possibilities of <SCRIPT> tag placement. Later in this lesson, you will see why scripts may need to go in different places within a page depending on the scripting requirements.

Listing 5-1 shows the outline of what may be the most common positioning of a <SCRIPT> tag set in a document: in the <HEAD> tag section. Typically, the Head is a place for tags that influence noncontent settings for the page — items such as <META> tags and the document title. It turns out that this is also a convenient place to plant scripts that are called on in response to user action.

Listing 5-1: **Scripts in the Head**

```
<HTML>
<HEAD>
<TITLE>A Document</TITLE>
<SCRIPT LANGUAGE="JavaScript">
      //statements
</SCRIPT>
</HEAD>
<BODY>
</BODY>
</HTML>
```

On the other hand, if you need a script to run as the page loads so that the script generates content in the page, the script goes in the ⟨BODY⟩ portion of the document, as shown in Listing 5-2. If you check the code listing for your first script in Chapter 3, you see that the script tags are in the Body, because the script needed to fetch information about the browser and write the results to the page as the page loaded.

Listing 5-2: **A Script in the Body**

```
<HTML>
<HEAD>
<TITLE>A Document</TITLE>
</HEAD>
<BODY>
<SCRIPT LANGUAGE="JavaScript">
      //statements
</SCRIPT>
</BODY>
</HTML>
```

It's also good to know that you can place an unlimited number of ⟨SCRIPT⟩ tag sets in a document. For example, Listing 5-3 shows a script in both the Head and Body portions of a document. Perhaps this document needs the Body script to create some dynamic content as the page loads, but the document also contains a button that needs a script to run later. That script is stored in the Head portion.

Listing 5-3: **Scripts in the Head and Body**

```
<HTML>
<HEAD>
<TITLE>A Document</TITLE>
<SCRIPT LANGUAGE="JavaScript">
      //statements
</SCRIPT>
</HEAD>
<BODY>
<SCRIPT LANGUAGE="JavaScript">
      //statements
</SCRIPT>
</BODY>
</HTML>
```

You also are not limited to one ⟨SCRIPT⟩ tag set in either the Head or Body. You can include as many ⟨SCRIPT⟩ tag sets in a document as are needed to complete your application. In Listing 5-4, for example, two ⟨SCRIPT⟩ tag sets are located in the Body portion, with some other HTML between them.

Listing 5-4: **Two Scripts in the Body**

```
<HTML>
<HEAD>
<TITLE>A Document</TITLE>
</HEAD>
<BODY>
<SCRIPT LANGUAGE="JavaScript">
      //statements
</SCRIPT>
<MORE HTML>
<SCRIPT LANGUAGE="JavaScript">
      //statements
</SCRIPT>
</BODY>
</HTML>
```

Handling older browsers

Only browsers that include JavaScript in them know to interpret the lines of code between the `<SCRIPT>` and `</SCRIPT>` tag pair as script statements and not HTML text to be displayed in the browser. This means that a pre-JavaScript browser not only will ignore the tags, but will treat the JavaScript code as page content. As you saw at the end of Chapter 3 in an illustration of your first script running on an old browser, the results can be disastrous to a page.

You can reduce the risk of old browsers displaying the script lines by playing a trick. The trick is to enclose the script lines between HTML comment symbols, as shown in Listing 5-5. Most nonscriptable browsers completely ignore the content between the `<!--` and `-->` comment tags, whereas scriptable browsers ignore those comment symbols when they appear inside a `<SCRIPT>` tag set.

Listing 5-5: **Hiding Scripts from Most Old Browsers**

```
<SCRIPT LANGUAGE="JavaScript">
<!--
      statements
// -->
</SCRIPT>
```

The odd construction right before the ending script tag needs a brief explanation. The two forward slashes are a JavaScript comment symbol. This symbol is necessary, because JavaScript would try to interpret the components of the ending HTML symbol (`-->`). Therefore, the forward slashes tell JavaScript to skip the line entirely; a nonscriptable browser simply treats those slash characters as part of the entire HTML comment to be ignored.

Despite the fact that this technique is often called "hiding scripts," it does not disguise the scripts entirely. All client-side JavaScript scripts are part of the HTML document and download to the browser just like all the other HTML. Do not be fooled into thinking that you can hide your scripts entirely from prying eyes.

JavaScript Statements

Every line of code that sits between a `<SCRIPT>` and `</SCRIPT>` tag is a JavaScript *statement*. To be compatible with habits of experienced programmers, JavaScript accepts a semicolon at the end of every statement. Fortunately for newcomers, this semicolon is optional. The carriage return at the end of a statement is enough for JavaScript to know the statement has ended. A statement must be in the script for a purpose. Therefore, every statement does "something" relevant to the script. The kinds of things that statements do are

✦ Defining or initializing a variable

✦ Assigning a value to a property or variable

✦ Changing the value of a property or variable

✦ Invoking an object's method

✦ Invoking a function routine

✦ Making a decision

If you don't yet know what all of these mean, don't worry — you will by the end of the next lesson. The point I want to stress is that each statement contributes to the scripts you write. The only statement that doesn't perform any explicit action is the comment. A pair of forward slashes (no space between them) is the most common way to include a comment in a script. You add comments to a script for your benefit. Comments usually explain in plain language what a statement or group of statements does. The purpose of including comments is to remind you six months from now how your script works.

When Script Statements Execute

Now that you know where scripts go in a document, it's time to look at when they run. Depending on what you need a script to do, you have four choices for determining when a script runs: while a document loads; immediately after a document loads; in response to user action; and when called upon by other script statements.

A determining factor is how the script statements are positioned in a document.

While a document loads — immediate execution

Your first script in Chapter 3 (reproduced in Listing 5-6) runs while the document loads into the browser. For this application, it is essential that a script inspect some properties of the navigator object and include those property values in the content being rendered for the page as it loads. It makes sense, therefore, to include the `<SCRIPT>` tags and statements in the Body portion of the document. I call the kind of statements that run as the page loads *immediate* statements.

Listing 5-6: HTML Page with Immediate Script Statements

```
<HTML>
<HEAD>
<TITLE>My First Script</TITLE>
</HEAD>

<BODY>
<H1>Let's Script...</H1>
<HR>
<SCRIPT LANGUAGE="JavaScript">
<!-- hide from old browsers
document.write("This browser is version " + navigator.appVersion)
document.write(" of <B>" + navigator.appName + "</B>.")
// end script hiding -->
</SCRIPT>
</BODY>
</HTML>
```

Deferred scripts

The other three ways that script statements run are grouped together as what I called *deferred* scripts. To demonstrate these deferred script situations, I must introduce you briefly to a concept covered in more depth in Chapter 7: the *function*. A function defines a block of script statements summoned to run some time after those statements load into the browser. Functions are clearly visible inside a `<SCRIPT>` tag because each function definition begins with the word function, followed by the function name (and parentheses). Once a function has loaded into the browser (commonly in the Head portion so it loads early), it stands ready to run whenever called upon.

One of the times a function is called upon to run is immediately after a page loads. The window object has an event handler called onLoad=. Unlike most event handlers, which are triggered in response to user action (for example, clicking a button), the onLoad= event handler fires the instant that all of the page's components (including images, Java applets, and embedded multimedia) have loaded into the browser. The onLoad= event handler goes in the `<BODY>` tag, as shown in Listing 5-7. If you recall from Chapter 4 (Listing 4-1), an event handler can run a script statement directly. But if the event handler must run several script statements, it is usually more convenient to put those statements in a function definition, and then have the event handler *invoke* that function. That's what is happening in Listing 5-7: When the page completes loading, the onLoad= event handler triggers the done() function. That function (simplified for this example) displays an alert dialog box.

Listing 5-7: **Running a Script from the onLoad= Event Handler**

```
<HTML>
<HEAD>
<TITLE>An onLoad= script</TITLE>
<SCRIPT LANGUAGE="JavaScript">
<!--
function done() {
        alert("The page has finished loading.")
}
// -->
</SCRIPT>
</HEAD>
<BODY onLoad="done()">
Here is some body text.
</BODY>
</HTML>
```

Don't worry about the curly braces or other oddities in Listing 5-7 that cause you concern at this point. Focus instead on the structure of the document and the flow: The entire page loads without running any script statements (although the page loads the done() function in memory so that it is ready to run at a moment's notice); after the document loads, the browser fires the onLoad= event handler; that causes the done() function to run; the user sees the alert dialog box.

To get a script to execute in response to a user action is very similar to the example you just saw for running a deferred script right after the document loads. Commonly, a script function is defined in the Head portion, and an event handler in, say, a form element calls upon that function to run. Listing 5-8 includes a script that runs when a user clicks on a button.

Listing 5-8: **Running a Script from User Action**

```
<HTML>
<HEAD>
<TITLE>An onClick= script</TITLE>
<SCRIPT LANGUAGE="JavaScript">
<!--
function alertUser() {
        alert("Ouch!")
}
// -->
</SCRIPT>
</HEAD>
<BODY>
Here is some body text.
<FORM>
```

(continued)

Listing 5-8 *(continued)*

```
        <INPUT TYPE="text" NAME="entry">
        <INPUT TYPE="button" NAME="oneButton" VALUE="Press Me!"
onClick="alertUser()">
</FORM>
</BODY>
</HTML>
```

Not every object must have an event handler defined for it in the HTML, as shown in Listing 5-8 — only the ones for which scripting is needed. No script statements execute in Listing 5-8 until the user clicks on the button. The `alertUser()` function is defined as the page loads, and will wait to run as long as the page remains loaded in the browser. If it is never called upon to load, there's no harm done.

The last scenario for when script statements run also involves functions. In this case, a function is called upon to run by another script statement. Before you see how that works, it will help to have been through the next lesson (Chapter 6). Therefore, I will hold off on this example until later in the tutorial.

Scripting versus Programming

It is easy to get the impression that scripting must be somehow easier than programming. "Scripting" simply sounds easier or more friendly than "programming." And in many respects this is true. One of my favorite analogies is the difference between a hobbyist who builds model airplanes from scratch and a hobbyist who builds model airplanes from commercial kits. The "from scratch" hobbyist carefully cuts and shapes each piece of wood and metal according to very detailed plans before the model starts to take shape. The commercial kit builder starts with many prefabricated parts and assembles them into the finished product. When both builders are finished, you may not be able to tell which airplane was built from scratch and which one came out of a box of components. In the end, both builders used many of the same techniques to complete the assembly, and each can take pride in the result.

As you've seen with the document object model, the browser gives scripters many prefabricated components to work with. A programmer might have to write code that builds all of that infrastructure that scripters get for "free" from the browser. In the end, both authors have working applications, each of which looks as professional as the other.

Beyond the document object model, however, "real programming" nibbles its way into the scripting world. That's because scripts (and programs) work with more than just objects. When I said earlier in this lesson that each statement of a JavaScript script does something, that "something" involves *data* of some kind. Data is the information associated with objects or other pieces of information that a script pushes around from place to place with each statement.

Data takes many forms. In JavaScript, the common incarnations of data are as numbers; text (called *strings*), objects (both from the object model and others you can create with scripts); and true and false (called *Boolean* values).

Each programming or scripting language determines numerous structures and limits for each kind of data. Fortunately for newcomers to JavaScript, the universe of knowledge necessary for working with data is smaller than in a language such as Java. At the same time, what you learn about data in JavaScript is immediately applicable to future learning you may undertake in any other programming language — don't believe for an instant that your efforts in learning scripting will be wasted.

Because deep down scripting is programming, you need to have a basic knowledge of fundamental programming concepts to consider yourself a good JavaScript scripter. In the next two lessons, I set aside most discussion about the document object model and focus on the programming principles that will serve you well in JavaScript and future programming endeavors.

Exercises

1. Write the complete script tag set for a script whose lone statement is

```
document.write("Hello, world.")
```

2. Build an HTML document and include the answer to the previous question such that the page executes the script as it loads. Open the document in your browser.

3. Add a comment to the script in the previous answer that explains what the script does.

4. Create an HTML document that displays an alert dialog box immediately after the page loads and displays a different alert dialog box when the user clicks on a form button.

5. Carefully study the document in Listing 5-9. Without entering and loading the document, predict

   a. What the page looks like

   b. How users interact with the page

   c. What the script does

   Then type the listing into a text editor exactly as shown (observe all capitalization and punctuation). Do not type a carriage return after the "-" sign in the upperMe function statement; let the line word-wrap as it does in the listing below. Save the document as an HTML file, and load the file into your browser to see how well you did.

Listing 5-9: **How Does This Page Work?**

```
<HTML>
<HEAD>
<TITLE>Text Object Value</TITLE>
<SCRIPT LANGUAGE="JavaScript">
<!--
function upperMe() {
        document.converter.output.value =
document.converter.input.value.toUpperCase()
}
// -->
</SCRIPT>
</HEAD>

<BODY>
Enter lowercase letters for conversion to uppercase:<BR>
<FORM NAME="converter">
        <INPUT TYPE="text" NAME="input" VALUE="sample"
onChange="upperMe()"><BR>
        <INPUT TYPE="text" NAME="output" VALUE="">
</FORM>
</BODY>
</HTML>
```

✦   ✦   ✦

Programming Fundamentals, Part I

✦ ✦ ✦ ✦

In This Chapter

What variables are
and how to use them

How to evaluate
expressions

How to convert data
from one type to
another

How to use basic
operators

✦ ✦ ✦ ✦

The tutorial breaks away from HTML and documents for a while, as you begin to learn programming fundamentals that apply to practically every scripting and programming language you will encounter. You'll start here learning about variables, expressions, data types, and operators — things that might sound scary if you haven't programmed before. Don't worry. With a little practice, you will become quite comfortable with these terms and concepts.

Working with Information

With rare exception, every JavaScript statement you write does something with a hunk of information — *data*. The chunk of data may be text information displayed on the screen by a JavaScript statement or the on/off setting of a radio button in a form. Each single piece of information in programming is also called a *value*. Outside of programming, the term *value* usually connotes a number of some kind; in the programming world, however, the term is not as restrictive. A string of letters is a value. A number is a value. The setting of a checkbox (the fact of whether it is checked or not) is a value.

In JavaScript, a value can be one of several types. Table 6-1 lists JavaScript's formal data types, with examples of the values you will see displayed from time to time.

A language that contains these few data types simplifies programming tasks, especially those involving what other languages consider to be incompatible types of numbers (integers versus real or floating-point values). In some definitions of syntax and parts of objects later in this book, I make specific reference to the type of value accepted in placeholders. When a string is required, any text inside a set of quotes suffices.

Table 6-1 JavaScript Value (Data) Types		
Type	*Example*	*Description*
String	`"Howdy"`	A series of characters inside quote marks
Number	`4.5`	Any number not inside quote marks
Boolean	`true`	A logical true or false
Null	`null`	Completely devoid of any value
Object		All properties and methods belonging to the object or array
Function		A function definition

You will encounter situations, however, in which the value type may get in the way of a smooth script step. For example, if a user enters a number into a form's input field, JavaScript stores that number as a string value type. If the script is to perform some arithmetic on that number, the string must be converted to a number before the value can be applied to any math operations. You will see examples of this later in this lesson.

Variables

Cooking up a dish according to a recipe in the kitchen has one advantage over cooking up some data in a program. In the kitchen, you follow recipe steps and work with real things: carrots, milk, or a salmon fillet. A computer, on the other hand, follows a list of instructions to work with data. Even if the data represents something that looks real, such as the text entered into a form's input field, once the value gets into the program, you can no longer reach out and touch it.

In truth, the data that a program works with is merely a collection of bits (on and off states) in your computer's memory. More specifically, data in a JavaScript-enhanced Web page occupies parts of the computer's memory set aside for exclusive use by the browser software. In the olden days, programmers had to know the numeric address in memory (RAM) where a value was stored to retrieve a copy of it for, say, some addition. Although the innards of a program have that level of complexity, programming languages such as JavaScript shield you from it.

The most convenient way to work with data in a script is to first assign the data to what is called a *variable*. It's usually easier to think of a variable as a basket that holds information. How long the variable holds the information depends on a number of factors, but the instant a Web page clears the window (or frame), any variables it knows about are immediately discarded.

Creating a variable

You have a couple of ways to create a variable in JavaScript, but one will cover you properly in all cases. Use the `var` keyword, followed by the name you want to give that variable. Therefore, to *declare* a new variable called `myAge`, the JavaScript statement is

```
var myAge
```

That statement lets the browser know that you can use that variable later to hold information or to modify any of the data in that variable.

To assign a value to a variable, use one of the *assignment operators*. The most common one by far is the equals sign. If I want to assign a value to the `myAge` variable at the same time I declare it (a combined process known as *initializing* the variable), I use that operator in the same statement as the `var` keyword:

```
var myAge = 45
```

On the other hand, if I declare a variable in one statement and later want to assign a value to it, the sequence of statements is

```
var myAge
myAge = 45
```

Use the `var` keyword *only for declaration or initialization* — once for the life of any variable name in a document.

A JavaScript variable can hold any value type. Unlike many other languages, you don't have to tell JavaScript during variable declaration what type of value the variable will hold. In fact, the value type of a variable could change during the execution of a program (this flexibility drives experienced programmers crazy because they're accustomed to assigning both a data type and a value to a variable).

Variable names

Choose the names you assign to variables with care. You'll often find scripts that use vague variable names, such as single letters. Other than a few specific times where using letters is a common practice (for example, using `i` as a counting variable in repeat loops in Chapter 7), I recommend using names that truly describe a variable's contents. This practice can help you follow the state of your data through a long series of statements or jumps, especially for complex scripts.

A number of restrictions help instill good practice in assigning names. First, you cannot use any reserved keyword as a variable name. That includes all keywords currently used by the language and all others held in reserve for future versions of JavaScript. The designers of JavaScript, however, cannot foresee every keyword that the language may need in the future. By using the kind of single words that currently appear in the list of reserved keywords (see Appendix B), you always run a risk of a future conflict.

To complicate matters, a variable name cannot contain space characters. Therefore, one-word variable names are fine. Should your description really benefit from more than one word, you can use one of two conventions to join multiple words as one. One convention is to place an underscore character between the words; the other is to start the combination word with a lowercase letter and capitalize the first letter of each subsequent word within the name — I refer to this as the interCap format. Both of the following examples are valid variable names:

```
my_age
myAge
```

My preference is for the second version. I find it easier to type as I write JavaScript code and easier to read later. In fact, because of the potential conflict with future keywords, using multiword combinations for variable names is a good idea. Multiword combinations are less likely to be part of the reserved word list.

Expressions and Evaluation

Another concept closely related to the value and variable is *expression evaluation* — perhaps the most important concept of learning how to program a computer.

We use expressions in our everyday language. Remember the theme song of *The Beverly Hillbillies*?

> *Then one day he was shootin' at some food*
> *And up through the ground came a-bubblin' crude*
> *Oil that is. Black gold. Texas tea.*

At the end of the song, you find four quite different references ("crude," "oil," "black gold," and "Texas tea"). They all mean oil. They're all *expressions* for oil. Say any one of them, and other people know what you mean. In our minds, we *evaluate* those expressions to one thing: Oil.

In programming, a variable always evaluates to its contents, or value. For example, after assigning a value to a variable, such as

```
var myAge = 45
```

any time the variable is used in a statement, its value, 45, is automatically extracted from that variable and applied to whatever operation that statement is calling. Therefore, if you're 15 years my junior, I can assign a value to a variable representing your age based on the evaluated value of `myAge`:

```
var yourAge = myAge - 15
```

The variable, `yourAge`, evaluates to 30 the next time the script uses it. If the `myAge` value changes later in the script, the change has no link to the `yourAge` variable because `myAge` evaluated to 45 when it was used to assign a value to `yourAge`.

Expressions in script1.htm

You probably didn't recognize it at the time, but you saw how expression evaluation can come in handy in your first script of Chapter 3. Recall the second `document.write()` statement:

```
document.write(" of " + navigator.appName + ".")
```

The `document.write()` method (remember, JavaScript uses the term *method* to mean *command*) requires a parameter in parentheses: the text string to be displayed on the Web page. The parameter here consists of one expression that joins three distinct strings:

```
" of "
navigator.appName
"."
```

The plus symbol is one of JavaScript's ways of joining strings. Before JavaScript can display this line, it must perform some quick evaluations. The first evaluation is the value of the `navigator.appName` property. This property evaluates to a string of the name of your browser. With that expression safely evaluated to a string, JavaScript can finish the job of joining the three strings in the final evaluation. That evaluated string expression is what ultimately appears on the Web page.

Expressions and variables

As one more demonstration of the flexibility that expression evaluation offers, in this section I show you a slightly different route to the `document.write()` statement. Rather than join those strings as the direct parameter to the `document.write()` method, I could have gathered the strings together earlier in a variable and then applied the variable to the `document.write()` method. Here's how that method might have looked, as I simultaneously declare a new variable and assign it a value:

```
var textToWrite = " of " + navigator.appName + "."
document.write(textToWrite)
```

This method works because the variable, `textToWrite`, evaluates to the combined string. The `document.write()` method accepts that string value and does its display job. As you read a script or try to work through a bug, pay special attention to how each expression (variable, statement, object property) evaluates. I guarantee that as you're learning JavaScript (or any language), you will end up scratching your head from time to time because you haven't stopped to examine how expressions evaluate when a particular kind of value is required in a script.

Testing evaluation in Navigator

You can begin experimenting with the way JavaScript evaluates expressions with the help of a hidden feature of Navigator. (Note: if you are using the Windows 95/NT version of Navigator 4, make sure you have Version 4.03 or later to use this feature.) The feature is not available in Internet Explorer. Choose Open Location/Open Page from the File menu and enter the following:

```
javascript:
```

Navigator displays a special two-frame window. The bottom frame contains a field where you can type one-line expressions. Press Enter to view the results in the upper frame.

You can assign values to variables, test comparison operators, and even do math here. Following the variable examples earlier in this chapter, type each of the following statements into the type-in field and observe how each expression evaluates. Be sure to observe case-sensitivity in your entries.

```
var myAge = 45
myAge
var yourAge = myAge - 15
myAge - yourAge
myAge > yourAge
```

Figure 6-1 shows the results. To close this display, use the Navigator to open any HTML file or URL.

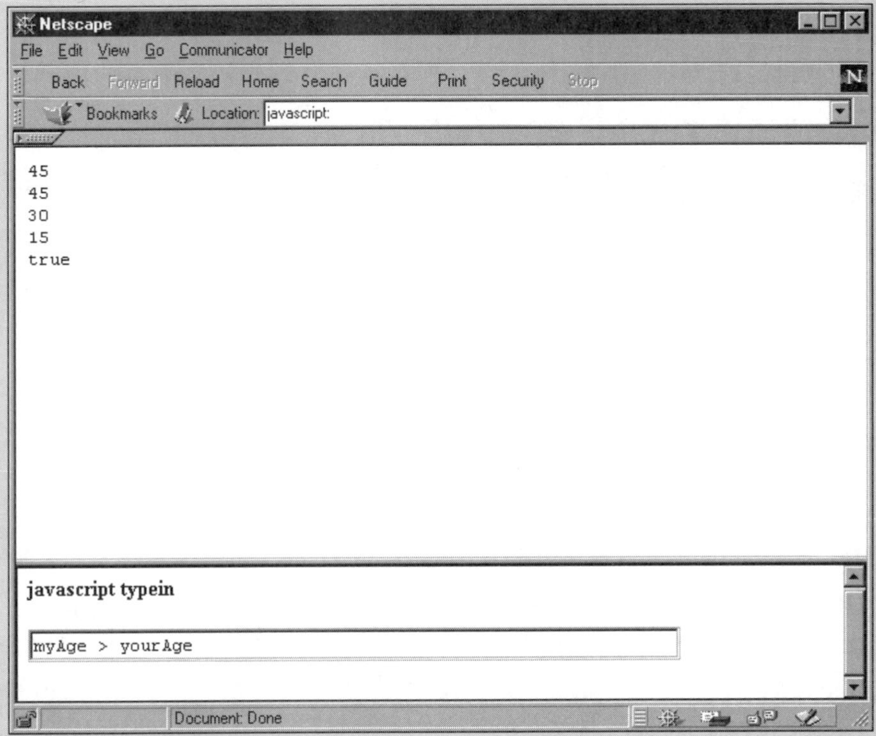

Figure 6-1: Evaluating expressions

Data Type Conversions

I mentioned earlier that the type of data in an expression can trip up some script operations if the expected components of the operation are not of the right type. JavaScript tries its best to perform internal conversions to head off such problems, but JavaScript cannot read your mind. If your intentions are different from the way JavaScript treats the values, you won't get the results you expected.

A case in point is adding numbers that may be in the form of text strings. In a simple arithmetic statement that adds two numbers together, the result is as you'd expect:

```
3 + 3        // result = 6
```

But if one of those numbers is a string, JavaScript leans toward converting the other value to a string, thus turning the plus sign's action from arithmetic addition to joining strings. Therefore, in the statement

```
3 + "3"     // result = "33"
```

the "string-ness" of the second value prevails over the entire operation. The first value is automatically converted to a string, and the result joins the two strings together. Try this yourself in the JavaScript type-in expression evaluator.

If I take this progression one step further, look what happens when another number is added to the statement:

```
3 + 3 + "3"   // result = "63"
```

This might seem totally illogical, but there is logic behind this result. The expression is evaluated from left to right. The first plus operation works on two numbers, yielding a value of 6. But as the 6 is about to be added to the "3," JavaScript lets the "string-ness" of the "3" rule. The 6 is converted to a string, and two string values are joined to yield 63.

Most of your concern about data types will be focused on performing math operations like the ones here. However, some object methods also require one or more parameters that must be particular data types. While JavaScript provides numerous ways to convert data from one type to another, it is appropriate at this stage of the tutorial to introduce you to the two most common data conversions: string to number and number to string.

Converting strings to numbers

As you saw in the last section, if a numeric value is stored as a string — as it is when entered into a form text field — your scripts will have difficulty applying that value to a math operation. The JavaScript language provides two built-in functions to convert string representations of numbers to true numbers: parseInt() and parseFloat().

The difference between an integer and a floating-point number in JavaScript is that integers are always whole numbers, with no decimal point or numbers to the right of a decimal. A floating-point number, on the other hand, can have fractional values to the right of the decimal. By and large, JavaScript math operations don't differentiate between integers and floating-point numbers: A number is a number. The only time you need to be cognizant of the difference is when a method parameter requires an integer, because it can't handle fractional values. For example, parameters to the moveTo() method of a window require integer values of the coordinates where you want to position the window. That's because you can't move an object a fraction of a pixel on the screen.

To use either of these conversion functions, insert the string value you wish to convert as a parameter to the function. For example, look at the results of two different string values when passed through the parseInt() function:

```
parseInt("42")    // result = 42
parseInt("42.33") // result = 42
```

Even though the second expression passes the string version of a floating-point number to the function, the value returned by the function is an integer. No rounding of the value occurs here (although other math functions can help with that if necessary). The decimal and everything to its right are simply stripped off.

The parseFloat() function returns an integer if it can; otherwise, it returns a floating-point number as follows:

```
parseFloat ("42")        // result = 42
parseFloat ("42.33")     // result = 42.33
```

Because these two conversion functions evaluate to their results, you simply insert the entire function wherever you need a string value converted to a string. Therefore, modifying an earlier example in which one of three values was a string, the complete expression can evaluate to the desired result:

```
3 + 3 + parseInt("3")    // result = 9
```

Converting numbers to string

You'll have less need for converting a number to its string equivalent than the other way around. As you saw in the previous section, JavaScript gravitates toward strings when faced with an expression containing mixed data types. Even so, it is good practice to perform data type conversions explicitly in your code to prevent any potential ambiguity. The simplest way to convert a number to a string is to take advantage of JavaScript's string tendencies in addition operations. By adding an empty string to a number, you convert the number to its string equivalent:

```
("" + 2500)                // result = "2500"
("" + 2500).length         // result = 4
```

In the second example, you can see the power of expression evaluation at work. The parentheses force the conversion of the number to a string. A string is a JavaScript object that has properties associated with it. One of those properties is the length property, which evaluates to the number of characters in the string. Therefore, the length of the string "2500" is 4. Note that the length value is a number, not a string.

Operators

You will use lots of *operators* in expressions. Earlier, you used the equal sign (=) as an assignment operator to assign a value to a variable. In the previous examples with strings, you used the plus symbol (+) to join (*concatenate*) two strings. An operator generally performs some kind of calculation (operation) or comparison with two values to reach a third value. In this lesson I briefly describe two categories of operators — arithmetic and comparison. Many more operators are covered in Chapter 32, but once you understand the basics here, the others will be easier to grasp when you're ready for them.

Arithmetic operators

The string concatenation operator doesn't know about words and spaces, so the programmer must make sure that any two strings to be joined have the proper word spacing as part of the strings, even if that means adding a space:

```
firstName = "John"
lastName = "Doe"
fullName = firstName + " " + lastName
```

JavaScript uses the same plus operator for arithmetic addition. When both values on either side of the plus sign are numbers, JavaScript knows to treat the expression as an arithmetic addition rather than a string concatenation. The standard math operators for addition, subtraction, multiplication, and division (+, -, *, /) are built into JavaScript.

Comparison operators

Another category of operator helps you compare values in scripts — whether two values are the same, for example. These kinds of comparisons return a value of the Boolean type — true or false. Table 6-2 lists the comparison operators. The operator that tests whether two items are equal consists of a pair of equals signs to distinguish it from the single equals sign assignment operator.

Table 6-2	
JavaScript Comparison Operators	
Symbol	**Description**
==	Equals
!=	Does not equal
>	Is greater than
>=	Is greater than or equal to
<	Is less than
<=	Is less than or equal to

Where comparison operators come into greatest play is in the construction of scripts that make decisions as they run. A cook does this in the kitchen all the time: If the sauce is too watery, add a bit of flour. You see comparison operators in action in the next chapter.

Exercises

1. Which of the following are valid variable declarations or initializations? Explain why each one is or is not valid. If an item is not valid, how would you fix it so that it is?

   a. my_name = "Cindy"

   b. var how many = 25

   c. var zipCode = document.form1.zip.value

   d. var 1address = document.nameForm.address1.value

2. For each of the statements in the following sequence, write down how the someVal expression evaluates after the statement executes in JavaScript.

   ```
   var someVal = 2
   someVal = someVal + 2
   someVal = someVal * 10
   someVal = someVal + "20"
   someVal = "Robert"
   ```

3. Name the two JavaScript functions that convert strings to numbers. How do you give the function a string value to convert to a number?

4. Type and load the HTML page and script shown in Listing 6-1. Enter a three-digit number into the top two fields and click the Add button. Examine the code and explain what is wrong with the script. How would you fix the script so the proper sum is displayed in the output field?

Listing 6-1: **What's Wrong with This Page?**

```
<HTML>
<HEAD>
<TITLE>Sum Maker</TITLE>
<SCRIPT LANGUAGE="JavaScript">
<!--
function addIt() {
        var value1 = document.adder.inputA.value
        var value2 = document.adder.inputB.value
        document.adder.output.value = value1 + value2
}
// -->
</SCRIPT>
</HEAD>

<BODY>
<FORM NAME="adder">
<INPUT TYPE="text" NAME="inputA" VALUE="0" SIZE=4><BR>
<INPUT TYPE="text" NAME="inputB" VALUE="0" SIZE=4>
<INPUT TYPE="button" VALUE="Add" onClick="addIt()">
<P>_____</P>
<INPUT TYPE="text" NAME="output" SIZE=6> <BR>
</FORM>
</BODY>
</HTML>
```

5. What does the term *concatenate* mean in the context of JavaScript programming?

✦　　✦　　✦

Programming Fundamentals, Part II

✦   ✦   ✦   ✦

In This Chapter

How control
structures make
decisions

How to define
functions

Where to initialize
variables efficiently

What those darned
curly braces are
all about

The basics of data
arrays

✦   ✦   ✦   ✦

Your tour of programming fundamentals continues in this chapter with subjects that have more intriguing possibilities. For example, I show you how programs make decisions and learn why a program must sometimes repeat statements over and over. Before you're finished here, you will learn how to use one of the most powerful information holders in the JavaScript language, the array.

Decisions and Loops

Every waking hour of every day you make decisions of some kind — most of the time you probably don't even realize it. Don't think so? Well, look at the number of decisions you make at the grocery store, from the moment you enter the store to the moment you clear the checkout aisle.

No sooner do you enter the store than you are faced with a decision: Based on the number and size of items you intend to buy, do you pick up a hand-carried basket or attempt to extricate a shopping cart from the metallic conga line near the front of the store? That key decision may have impact later when you see a special offer on an item that is too heavy to put into the hand basket. Now you head for the food aisles. Before entering an aisle, you compare the range of goods stocked in that aisle against items on your shopping list. If an item you need is likely to be found in this aisle, you turn into the aisle and start looking for the item; otherwise, you skip the aisle and move to the head of the next aisle.

Later you reach the produce section, in search of a juicy tomato. Standing in front of the bin of tomatoes, you begin inspecting them, one by one — picking one up, feeling its firmness, checking the color, looking for blemishes or signs of pests. You discard one, pick up another, and continue this process until one matches the criteria you have set in your mind for an acceptable morsel. Your last stop in the store is the checkout aisle. "Paper or plastic?" the clerk asks. One more decision to make. What you choose impacts how you get the groceries from the car to the kitchen as well as your recycling habits.

In your trip to the store, you have gone through the same kinds of decisions and repetitions that your JavaScript programs will also encounter. If you understand these frameworks in real life, you can now look into the JavaScript equivalents and the syntax required to make them work.

Control Structures

In the vernacular of programming, the kinds of statements that make decisions and loop around to repeat themselves are called *control structures*. A control structure directs the execution flow through a sequence of script statements based on simple decisions and other factors.

An important part of a control structure is the *condition*. Just as you may have different routes to work depending on certain conditions (for example, nice weather, nighttime, attending a soccer game), so, too, does a program sometimes have to branch to an execution route if a certain condition exists. Each condition is an expression that evaluates to `true` or `false` — one of those Boolean data types mentioned in the previous lesson. The kinds of expressions commonly used for conditions are expressions that include a comparison operator. You do the same in real life: If it is true that the outdoor temperature is less than freezing, then you put on a coat before going outside. In programming, however, the comparisons are strictly comparisons of number or string values.

JavaScript provides several kinds of control structures for different programming situations. Three of the most common control structures you'll use are `if` constructions; `if...else` constructions; and `for` loops.

Other common control structures you'll want to know, some of which were introduced only in Navigator 4 and Internet Explorer 4, are covered in great detail in Chapter 31. For this tutorial, however, you need to learn about the three common ones just mentioned.

If constructions

The simplest program decision is to follow a special branch or path of the program if a certain condition is true. Formal syntax for this construction follows. Items in italics get replaced in a real script with expressions and statements that fit the situation.

```
if (condition) {
        statement[s] if true
}
```

Don't worry about the curly braces yet. Instead, get a feel for the basic structure. The keyword, `if`, is a must. In parentheses goes an expression that evaluates to a Boolean value. This is the condition being tested as the program runs past this point. If the condition evaluates to `true`, then one or more statements inside the curly braces execute before continuing on with the next statement after the closing brace; if the condition evaluates to `false`, the statements inside the curly brace are ignored, and processing continues with the next statement after the closing brace.

The following example assumes that a variable, myAge, has had its value set earlier in the script (exactly how is not important for this example). The condition expression compares the value myAge against a numeric value of 18.

```
if (myAge < 18) {
     alert("Sorry, you cannot vote.")
}
```

The data type of the value inside myAge must be a number so that the proper comparison (via the < comparison operator) does the right thing. For all instances of myAge being less than 18, the nested statement inside the curly braces runs, displaying the alert to the user. After the user closes the alert dialog box, the script continues with whatever statement follows the entire if construction.

If . . . else constructions

Not all program decisions are as simple as the one shown for the if construction. Rather than specifying one detour for a given condition, you might want the program to follow either of two branches depending on that condition. It is a fine but important distinction. In the plain if construction, no special processing is performed when the condition evaluates to false. But if processing must follow one of two special paths, you need the if...else construction. The formal syntax definition for an if...else construction is as follows:

```
if (condition) {
     statement[s] if true
} else {
     statement[s] if false
}
```

Everything you know about the condition for an if construction applies here. The only difference is the else keyword, which provides an alternate path for execution to follow if the condition evaluates to false.

As an example, the following if...else construction determines how many days are in February for a given year. To simplify the demo, the condition simply tests whether the year divides equally by 4 (true testing for this value includes special treatment of end-of-century dates, but I'm ignoring that for now). The % operator symbol is called the *modulus* operator (covered in more detail in Chapter 32). The result of an operation with this operator yields the remainder of division of the two values. If the remainder is zero, it means the first value divides evenly by the second.

```
var febDays = 0
var theYear = 1993
if (theYear % 4 == 0) {
    febDays = 29
} else {
    febDays = 28
}
```

The important point to see from the example is that by the end of the if...else construction, the febDays variable is set to either 28 or 29. No other value is possible. For years evenly divisible by 4, the first nested statement runs;

for all other cases, the second statement runs. Processing then picks up with the next statement after the `if...else` construction.

About Repeat Loops

Repeat loops in real life generally mean repeating a series of steps until some condition is met, allowing you to break out of that loop. Such was the case earlier in this chapter when you looked through a bushel of tomatoes for the one that came closest to your ideal tomato. The same could be said for driving around the block in a crowded neighborhood until a parking space opens up.

A repeat loop lets a script cycle through a sequence of statements until some condition is met. For example, a JavaScript data validation routine might look at every character that has been entered into a form text field to make sure that every character is a number. Or if you have a collection of data stored in a list, the loop can check whether an entered value is in that list. Once that condition is met, the script can then break out of the loop and continue with the next statement after the loop construction.

The most common repeat loop construction used in JavaScript is called the `for` loop. It gets its name from the keyword that begins the construction. A `for` loop is a powerful device, because you can set it up to keep track of the number of times the loop repeats itself. The formal syntax of the `for` loop is as follows:

```
for ([initial expression]; [condition]; [update expression]) {
     statement[s] inside loop
}
```

The square brackets mean that the item is optional, but until you get to know the `for` loop better, I recommend designing your loops to utilize all three items inside the parentheses. The *initial expression* portion usually sets the starting value of a counter. The *condition* — the same kind of condition you saw for `if` constructions — defines the condition that forces the loop to stop going around and around. Finally, the *update expression* is a statement that executes each time all of the statements nested inside the construction have completed running.

A common implementation initializes a counting variable, `i`, increments the value of `i` by one each time through the loop, and repeats the loop until the value of `i` exceeds some maximum value, as in the following:

```
for (var i = startValue; i <= maxValue; i++) {
     statement[s] inside loop
}
```

Placeholders `startValue` and `maxValue` represent any numeric values, including direct numbers or variables holding numbers. In the update expression is an operator you have not seen yet. The ++ operator adds 1 to the value of `i` each time the update expression runs at the end of the loop. If `startValue` is 1, the value of `i` is 1 the first time through the loop, 2 the second time through, and so on. Therefore, if `maxValue` is 10, the loop will repeat itself 10 times. Generally speaking, the statements inside the loop use the value of the counting variable in their execution. Later in this lesson, I show how the variable can play a key role in the statements inside a loop. At the same time you will see how to break out of a loop prematurely and why you may need to do this in a script.

Functions

In Chapter 5, you saw a preview of the JavaScript function. A function is a definition of a set of deferred actions. Functions are invoked by event handlers or by statements elsewhere in the script. Whenever possible, good functions are designed to be reusable in other documents. They can become building blocks you can use over and over again.

If you have programmed before, you will see parallels between JavaScript functions and other languages' subroutines. But unlike some languages that distinguish between procedures (which carry out actions) and functions (which carry out actions and return values), only one classification of routine exists for JavaScript. A function is capable of returning a value to the statement that invoked it, but this is not a requirement. However, when a function does return a value, the calling statement treats the function call like any expression — plugging in the returned value right where the function call is made. I will show some examples in a moment.

Formal syntax for a function is as follows:

```
function functionName ( [parameter1]...[,parameterN] ) {
        statement[s]
}
```

Names you assign to functions have the same restrictions as names you assign HTML elements and variables. You should devise a name that succinctly describes what the function does. I tend to use multiword names with the interCap (internally capitalized) format that start with a verb, since functions are action items, even if they do nothing more than get or set a value.

Another practice to keep in mind as you start to create functions is to keep the focus of each function as narrow as possible. It is possible to generate functions literally hundreds of lines long. Such functions are usually difficult to maintain and debug. Chances are that the long function can be divided up into smaller, more tightly focused fragments.

Function parameters

In Chapter 5, you saw how an event handler invokes a function by calling the function by name. Any call to a function, including one that comes from another JavaScript statement, works the same way: the function name is followed by a set of parentheses.

Functions can also be defined so they receive parameter values from the calling statement. Listing 7-1 shows a simple document that has a button whose onClick= event handler calls a function while passing text data to the function. The text string in the event handler call is in a nested string — a set of single quotes inside the double quotes required for the entire event handler attribute.

Listing 7-1: **Calling a Function from an Event Handler**

```
<HTML>
<HEAD>
<SCRIPT LANGUAGE="JavaScript">
function showMsg(msg) {
        alert("The button sent: " + msg)
}
</SCRIPT>
</HEAD>
<BODY>
<FORM>
        <INPUT TYPE="button" VALUE="Click Me" onClick="showMsg ('The
button has been clicked!')">
</FORM>
</BODY>
</HTML>
```

Parameters provide a mechanism for "handing off" a value from one statement to another by way of a function call. If no parameters occur in the function definition, both the function definition and call to the function have only empty sets of parentheses, as shown in Chapter 5, Listing 5-8.

When a function receives parameters, it assigns the incoming values to the variable names specified in the function definition's parentheses. Consider the following script segment:

```
function sayHiToFirst(a, b, c) {
        alert("Say hello, " + a)
}
sayHiToFirst("Gracie", "George", "Harry")
sayHiToFirst("Larry", "Moe", "Curly")
```

After the function is defined in the script, the next statement calls that very function, passing three strings as parameters. The function definition automatically assigns the strings to variables a, b, and c. Therefore, before the alert() statement inside the function ever runs, a evaluates to "Gracie", b evaluates to "George", and c evaluates to "Harry". In the alert() statement, only the a value is used, and the alert reads

```
Say hello, Gracie
```

When the user closes the first alert, the next call to the function occurs. This time through, different values are passed to the function and assigned to a, b, and c. The alert dialog reads

```
Say hello, Larry
```

Unlike other variables that you define in your script, function parameters do not use the var keyword to initialize them. They are automatically initialized whenever the function is called.

Variable scope

Speaking of variables, it's time to distinguish between variables that are defined outside and those defined inside of functions. Variables defined outside of functions are called *global* variables; those defined inside functions are called *local* variables.

A global variable has a slightly different connotation in JavaScript than it has in most other languages. For a JavaScript script, the "globe" of a global variable is the current document loaded in a browser window or frame. Therefore, when you initialize a variable as a global variable, it means that all statements in the page, including those inside functions, have direct access to that variable value. Statements can retrieve and modify global variables from anywhere in the page. In programming terminology, this kind of variable is said to have global *scope*, because everything on the page can "see" it.

It is important to remember that the instant a page unloads itself, all global variables defined in that page are erased from memory. If you need a value to persist from one page to another, you must use other techniques to store that value (for example, as a global variable in a framesetting document, as described in Chapter 14, or in a cookie, as described in Chapter 16). While the `var` keyword is usually optional for initializing global variables, I strongly recommend you use it for *all* variable initializations to guard against future changes to the JavaScript language.

In contrast to the global variable, a local variable is defined inside a function. You already saw how parameter variables are defined inside functions (without `var` keyword initializations). But you can also define other variables with the `var` keyword (absolutely required for local variables). The scope of a local variable is only within the statements of the function. No other functions or statements outside of functions have access to a local variable.

Local scope allows for the reuse of variable names within a document. For most variables, I strongly discourage this practice because it leads to confusion and bugs that are difficult to track down. At the same time, it is convenient to reuse certain kinds of variables names, such as `for` loop counters. These are safe because they are always reinitialized with a starting value whenever a `for` loop starts. You cannot, however, nest a `for` loop inside another without specifying a different loop counting variable.

To demonstrate the structure and behavior of global and local variables — and show you why you shouldn't reuse most variable names inside a document — Listing 7-2 defines two global and two local variables. I intentionally use bad form by initializing a local variable that has the same name as a global variable.

Listing 7-2: **Variables Scope Demonstration**

```
<HTML>
<HEAD>
<SCRIPT LANGUAGE="JavaScript">
var aBoy = "Charlie Brown"      // global
var hisDog = "Snoopy"           // global
function sampleFunction() {
```

(continued)

Listing 7-2 *(continued)*

```
        // using improper design to demonstrate a point
        var hisDog = "Gromit"     // local version of hisDog
        var output = hisDog + " does not belong to " + aBoy + ".<BR>"
        document.write(output)
}
</SCRIPT>
<BODY>
<SCRIPT LANGUAGE="JavaScript">
sampleFunction() // runs as document loads
document.write(hisDog + " belongs to " + aBoy + ".")
</SCRIPT>
</BODY>
</HTML>
```

When the page loads, the script in the Head portion initializes the two global variables and defines the function in memory. In the Body, another script begins by invoking the function. Inside the function a local variable is initialized with the same name as one of the global variables — hisDog. In JavaScript such a local initialization overrides the global variable for all statements inside the function. (But note that if the var keyword had been left off of the local initialization, the statement would have reassigned the value of the global version to "Gromit".)

Another local variable, output, is merely a repository for accumulating the text that is to be written to the screen. It begins by evaluating the local version of the hisDog variable. Then it concatenates some hard-wired text (note the extra spaces at the edges of the string segment). Next comes the evaluated value of the aBoy global variable — any global not overridden by a local is available for use inside the function. Since the expression is accumulating HTML to be written to the page, it ends with a period and a <BR> tag. The final statement of the function writes content to the page.

After the function completes its task, the next statement in the Body script writes another string to the page. Because this script statement is executing in global space (that is, not inside any function), it accesses only global variables — including those that were defined in another <SCRIPT> tag set in the document. By the time the complete page finishes loading, it contains the following text lines:

```
Gromit does not belong to Charlie Brown.
Snoopy belongs to Charlie Brown.
```

About Curly Braces

Despite the fact that you probably rarely — if ever — use curly braces ({ }) in your writing, there is no mystery to their usage in JavaScript (and many other languages). Curly braces enclose blocks of statements that belong together. While they do assist humans in reading scripts to know what's going on, the browser also relies on curly braces to know which statements belong together. Curly braces must always be used in matched pairs.

You use curly braces most commonly in function definitions and control structures. For example, in the function definition in Listing 7-2, curly braces enclose four statements that make up the function definition (including the comment line). The closing brace lets the browser know that whatever statement that may come next is a statement outside of the function definition.

Physical placement of curly braces is not critical (nor is the indentation style you see in the code I provide). The following function definitions are treated identically by scriptable browsers:

```
function sayHiToFirst(a, b, c) {
        alert("Say hello, " + a)
}

function sayHiToFirst(a, b, c)
{
        alert("Say hello, " + a)
}

function sayHiToFirst(a, b, c) {alert("Say hello, " + a)}
```

Throughout this book, I use the style shown in the first example because I find it makes lengthy and complex scripts easier to read, including scripts that have many levels of nested control structures.

Arrays

The JavaScript array is one of the most useful data constructions you have available to you. The structure of a basic array resembles that of a single-column spreadsheet. Each row of the column holds a distinct piece of data, and each row is numbered. Numbers assigned to rows are in strict numerical sequence, starting with zero as the first row (programmers always start counting with zero). This row number is called an *index*. To access an item in an array, you need to know the name of the array and the index for the row. Because index values start with zero, the count of items of the array (as determined by the array's length property) is always one more than the highest index value of the array. More advanced array concepts allow you to essentially create arrays with multiple columns (described in Chapter 29), but for this tutorial, I stay with the single column basic array.

Data elements inside JavaScript arrays can be any data type, including objects. And, unlike a lot of other programming languages, different rows of the same JavaScript array can contain different data types.

Creating an array

An array is stored in a variable, so when you create an array, you assign the new array object to the variable (yes, arrays are JavaScript objects, but they belong to the core JavaScript language, rather than the document object model). A special keyword — new — preceding a call to the JavaScript function that generates arrays creates space in memory for the array. An optional parameter to the Array() function lets you specify at the time of creation how many elements (rows) of data will eventually occupy the array. JavaScript is very forgiving about this, because you can change the size of an array at any time. Therefore, if you omit a parameter when generating a new array, no penalty is incurred.

To demonstrate the array creation process, I create an array that holds the names of the 50 States and the District of Columbia. The first task is to create that array and assign it to a variable of any name that helps me remember what this collection of data is about:

```
var USStates = new Array(51)
```

At this point, the USStates array is sitting in memory like a 51-row table with no data in it. To fill the rows, I must assign data to each row. Addressing each row of an array requires a special way of indicating the index value of the row: square brackets after the name of the array. The first row of the USStates array is addressed as

```
USStates[0]
```

And to assign the string name of the first state of the alphabet to that row, I use a simple assignment operator:

```
USStates[0] = "Alabama"
```

To fill in the rest of the rows, I include a statement for each row:

```
USStates[1] = "Alaska"
USStates[2] = "Arizona"
USStates[3] = "Arkansas"
...
USStates[50] = "Wyoming"
```

Therefore, if you want to include a table of information in a document from which a script can look up information without accessing the server, you include the data in the document in the form of an array creation sequence. When the statements run as the document loads, by the time the document has finished loading into the browser, the data collection array is built and ready to go. Despite what appears to be the potential for a lot of statements in a document for such a data collection, the amount of data that must download for typical array collections is small enough not to severely impact page loading, even for dial-up users at 28.8 Kbps.

Accessing array data

The array index is the key to accessing an array element. The name of the array and an index in square brackets evaluates to the content of that array location. For example, after the USStates array has been built, a script could display an alert with Alaska's name in it with the following statement:

```
alert("The largest state is " + USStates[1] + ".")
```

Just as you can retrieve data from an indexed array element, so can you change the element by reassigning a new value to any indexed element in the array.

Although I won't dwell on it in this tutorial, you can also use string names as index values instead of numbers. In essence, this allows you to create an array that has named labels for each row of the array — a definite convenience for certain circumstances. But whichever way you use to assign data to an array element the first time is the way you must access that element thereafter in the page's scripts.

Parallel arrays

Now I show you why the numeric index methodology works well in JavaScript. To help with the demonstration, I will generate another array that is parallel with the USStates array. This new array is also 51 elements long, and it contains the year in which the state in the corresponding row of USStates became a state. That array construction would look like the following:

```
var stateEntered = new Array(51)
stateEntered [0] = 1819
stateEntered [1] = 1959
stateEntered [2] = 1912
stateEntered [3] = 1836
...
stateEntered [50] = 1890
```

In the browsers memory, then, are two tables that you can visualize as looking like the model in Figure 7-1. I could build more arrays that are parallel to these for items such as the postal abbreviation and capital city. The important point is that the zeroth element in each of these tables applies to Alabama, the first state in the USStates array.

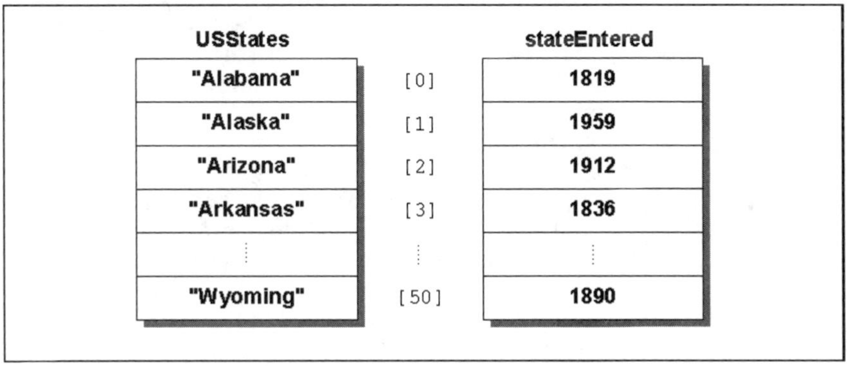

USStates		stateEntered
"Alabama"	[0]	1819
"Alaska"	[1]	1959
"Arizona"	[2]	1912
"Arkansas"	[3]	1836
⋮	⋮	⋮
"Wyoming"	[50]	1890

Figure 7-1: Visualization of two related parallel tables

If a Web page included these tables and a way for a user to look up the entry date for a given state, the page would need a way to look through all of the USStates entries to find the index value of the one that matches the user's entry. Then that index value could be applied to the stateEntered array to find the matching year.

For this demo, the page includes a text entry field in which the user types the name of the state to look up. In a real application, this methodology is fraught with peril, unless the script performs some error checking in case the user makes a mistake. But for now, I assume that the user will always type a valid state name (don't ever make this assumption in your Web site's pages). An event handler from either the text field or a clickable button will call a function that looks up the state name, fetches the corresponding entry year, and displays an alert message with the information. The function is as follows.

```
function getStateDate() {
    var selectedState = document.entryForm.entry.value
    for ( var i = 0; i < USStates.length; i++) {
        if (USStates[i] == selectedState) {
            break
        }
    }
    alert("That state entered the Union in " + stateEntered[i] +
".")
}
```

In the first statement of the function, I grab the value of the text box and assign the value to a variable, `selectedState`. This is mostly for convenience, because I can use the shorter variable name later in the script. In fact, because the usage of that value is inside a `for` loop, the script is marginally more efficient, as the browser doesn't have to evaluate that long reference to the text field each time through the loop.

The key to this function is in the `for` loop. Here is where I combine the natural behavior of incrementing a loop counter with the index values assigned to the two arrays. Specifications for the loop indicate that the counter variable, `i`, is initialized with a value of zero. The loop is directed to continue as long as the value of `i` is less than the length of the `USStates` array. Remember that the length of an array is always one more than the index value of the last item. Therefore, the last time the loop will run is when `i` is 50, which is both less than the length of 51 and equal to the index value of the last element. Each time after the loop runs, the counter increments by one.

Nested inside the `for` loop is an `if` construction. The condition it is testing is the value of an element of the array against the value typed in by the user. Each time through the loop, the condition tests a different row of the array, starting with row zero. In other words, this `if` construction might be performed dozens of times before a match is found, but each time the value of `i` will be one larger than the previous try.

When a match is found, the statement nested inside the `if` construction runs. The `break` statement is designed to help control structures bail out if the program needs it. For this application, it is imperative that the `for` loop stop running when a match for the state name is found. When the `for` loop breaks, the value of the `i` counter is fixed at the row of the `USStates` array containing the entered state. I need that index value to find the corresponding entry in the other array. Even though the counting variable, `i`, is initialized in the `for` loop, it is still "alive" and in the scope of the function for all statements after the initialization. That's why I can use it to extract the value of the row of the `stateEntered` array in the final statement that displays the results in an alert message.

This application of a `for` loop and array indexes is a common one in JavaScript. Study the code carefully and be sure you understand how it works. This way of cycling through arrays plays a role not only in the kinds of arrays you create in your code, but also with the arrays that browsers generate for the document object model.

Document objects in arrays

If you look at the document object portion of the JavaScript Object Road Map in Appendix A, you will see that the properties of some objects are listed with square brackets after them. These are, indeed, the same kind of square brackets you saw above for array indexes. That's because when a document loads, the browser creates arrays of like objects in the document. For example, if your page includes two <FORM> tag sets, then two forms appear in the document. The browser maintains an array of form objects for that document. References to those forms would be

```
document.forms[0]
document.forms[1]
```

Index values for document objects are assigned according to the loading order of the objects. In the case of form objects, the order is dictated by the order of the <FORM> tags in the document. This indexed array syntax is another way to reference forms in an object reference. You can still use a form's name if you prefer — and I heartily recommend using object names wherever possible, because even if you change the physical order of the objects in your HTML, references that use names will still work without modification. But if your page contains only one form, you can use the reference types interchangeably, as in the following examples of equivalent references to a text field's value property in a form:

```
document.entryForm.entry.value
document.forms[0].entry.value
```

In examples throughout this book, you can see that I often use the array type of reference to simple forms in simple documents. But in my production pages, I almost always use named references.

Exercises

1. With your newly acquired knowledge of functions, event handlers, and control structures, use the script fragments from this chapter to complete the page that has the lookup table for all of the states and the years they were entered into the Union. If you do not have a reference book for the dates, then use different year numbers starting with 1800 for each entry. In the page, create a text entry field for the state and a button that triggers the lookup in the arrays.

2. Examine the following function definition. Can you spot any problems with the definition? If so, how would you fix the problems?

```
function format(ohmage) {
       var result
       if ohmage >= 10e6 {
               ohmage = ohmage / 10e5
               result = ohmage + " Mohms"
       } else {
               if (ohmage >= 10e3)
```

```
                              ohmage = ohmage / 10e2
                              result = ohmage + " Kohms"
                    else

                              result = ohmage + " ohms"
          }
          alert(result)
```

3. Devise your own syntax for the scenario of looking for a ripe tomato at the grocery store, and write a `for` loop using that object and property syntax.

4. Modify Listing 7-2 so it does not reuse the `hisDog` variable inside the function.

5. Given the following table of data about several planets of our solar system, create a Web page that lets users enter a planet name and, at the click of a button, have the distance and diameter appear either in an alert box or (as extra credit) in separate fields of the page.

Planet	Distance	Diameter
Mercury	36 million miles	3,100 miles
Venus	67 million miles	7,700 miles
Earth	93 million miles	7,920 miles
Mars	141 million miles	4,200 miles

✦   ✦   ✦

Window and Document Objects

Now that you have exposure to programming fundamentals, it will be easier to demonstrate how to script document objects. Starting with this lesson, the tutorial turns back to the document object model, diving more deeply into each of the objects you will place in many of your documents.

Document Objects

As a refresher, study the Netscape Navigator document object hierarchy in Figure 8-1. This lesson focuses on objects at or near the top of the hierarchy: window, location, history, and document. The goal is not only to equip you with the basics so you can script simple tasks, but also to prepare you for in-depth examinations of each object and its properties, methods, and event handlers in Part III of this book. I introduce only the basic properties, methods, and event handlers for objects in this tutorial — far more are to be found in Part III. Examples in that part of the book assume you know the programming fundamentals covered in previous lessons.

The Window Object

At the very top of the document object hierarchy is the window object. This object gains that exalted spot in the object food chain because it is the master container for all content you view in the Web browser. As long as a browser window is open — even if no document is loaded in the window — the window object is defined in the current model in memory.

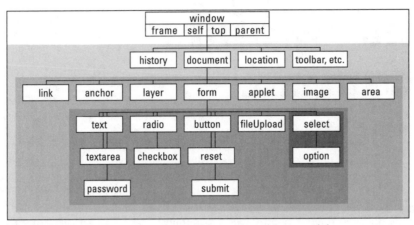

Figure 8-1: The Netscape Navigator 4 document object model

In addition to the content part of the window where documents go, a window's sphere of influence includes the dimensions of the window and all of the "stuff" that surrounds the content area. Netscape calls this area — where scrollbars, toolbars, the status bar, and menu bar on non-Macintosh versions live — a window's *chrome*. Not every browser or every version of Navigator has full scripted control over the chrome of the main browser window, but you can easily script the creation of additional windows sized the way you want and have only the chrome elements you wish to display in that subwindow.

Although the discussion about frames comes in Chapter 11, I can safely say now that each frame is also considered a window object. If you think about it, that makes sense, because each frame can hold a different document. When a script runs in one of those documents, it regards the frame that holds the document as the window object in its view of the object hierarchy.

As you will see here, the window object is a convenient place for the document object model to attach methods that display modal dialog boxes and adjust the text that displays in the status bar at the bottom of the browser window. Another window object method lets you create a separate window that appears on the screen. When you look at all of the properties, methods, and event handlers defined for the window object in Netscape's object model (see Appendix A), it should be clear why they are attached to window objects — visualize their scope and the scope of a browser window.

Accessing window properties and methods

Script references to properties and methods of the window object can be worded in several ways, depending more on whim and style than on specific syntactical requirements. The most logical and common way to compose such references includes the window object in the reference:

```
window.propertyName
window.methodName([parameters])
```

A window object also has a synonym when the script doing the referencing is pointing to the window that houses the document. The synonym is `self`. Reference syntax then becomes

```
self.propertyName
self.methodName([parameters])
```

You can use these initial reference object names interchangeably, but I tend to reserve the use of `self` for more complex scripts that involve multiple frames and windows. The `self` moniker more clearly denotes the current window holding the script's document. To me, it makes the script more readable — by me and by others.

Back in Chapter 4, I indicated that because the window object is always "there" when a script runs, you can omit it from references to any objects inside that window. Therefore, the following syntax models assume properties and methods of the current window:

```
propertyName
methodName([parameters])
```

In fact, as you will see in a few moments, some methods may be more understandable if you omit the window object reference. The methods run just fine either way.

Creating a window

A script does not create the main browser window. A user does that by virtue of launching the browser or by opening a URL or file from the browser's menus (if the window is not already open). But a script can generate any number of subwindows once the main window is open (and contains a document whose script needs to open subwindows).

The method that generates a new window is `window.open()`. This method contains up to three parameters that define window characteristics, such as the URL of the document to load, its name for `TARGET` reference purposes in HTML tags, and physical appearance (size and chrome contingent). I won't go into the details of the parameters here (they're covered in great depth in Chapter 14), but I do want to expose you to an important concept involved with the `window.open()` method.

Consider the following statement that opens a new window to a specific size and with an HTML document from the server:

```
var subWindow =
window.open("definition.html","def","HEIGHT=200,WIDTH=300")
```

The important part of this statement is that it is an assignment statement. Something gets assigned to that variable `subWindow`. What is it? It turns out that when the `window.open()` method runs, it not only opens up that new window according to specifications set as parameters, but it evaluates to a reference to that new window. In programming parlance, the method is said to *return* a value — in this case, a genuine object reference. The value returned by the method is assigned to the variable.

Your script can now use that variable as a valid reference to the second window. If you need to access one of its properties or methods, you must use that reference as part of the complete reference. For example, to close the subwindow from a script in the main window, the reference to the `close()` method for that subwindow would be

```
subWindow.close()
```

If you were to issue `window.close()`, `self.close()`, or just `close()` in the main window's script, the method would close the main window, and not the subwindow. To address another window, then, you must include a reference to that window as part of the complete reference. This will have an impact on your code, because you probably want the variable holding the reference to the subwindow to be valid as long as the main document is loaded into the browser. For that to happen, the variable will have to be initialized as a global variable, rather than inside a function (although its value can be set inside a function). That way, one function can open the window while another closes it.

Listing 8-1 is a page that has a button for opening a blank new window and closing that window from the main window. To view this demonstration, shrink your main browser window to less than full screen. Then when the new window is generated, reposition the windows so you can see the smaller new window when the main window is in front. The key point of Listing 8-1 is that the `newWindow` variable is defined as a global variable so that both functions have access to it. When a variable is declared with no value assignment, its value is null. It turns out that a null value is the same as `false` in a condition, while any value is the same as `true` in a condition. Therefore, in the `closeNewWindow()` function, the condition tests whether the window has been created before issuing the subwindow's `close()` method.

Listing 8-1: **References to Window Objects**

```
<HTML>
<HEAD>
<TITLE>Window Opener and Closer</TITLE>
<SCRIPT LANGUAGE="JavaScript">
var newWindow
function makeNewWindow() {
        newWindow = window.open("","","HEIGHT=300,WIDTH=300")
}
function closeNewWindow() {
        if (newWindow) {
            newWindow.close()
        }
}
</SCRIPT>
</HEAD>

<BODY>
<FORM>
<INPUT TYPE="button" VALUE="Create New Window"
onClick="makeNewWindow()">
<INPUT TYPE="button" VALUE="Close New Window"
onClick="closeNewWindow()">
```

```
</FORM>
</BODY>
</HTML>
```

Window Properties and Methods

The one property and three methods for the window object described in this lesson have an immediate impact on user interaction. They work with all scriptable browsers. Extensive code examples can be found in Part III for each property and method.

window.status property

The status bar at the bottom of the browser window normally displays the URL of a link when you roll the mouse pointer atop it. Other messages also appear in that space during document loading, Java applet initialization, and the like. However, you can use JavaScript to display your own messages in the status bar at times that may be beneficial to your users. For example, rather than display the URL of a link, you can display a friendlier plain-language description of the page at the other end of the link (or a combination of both to accommodate both newbies and geeks).

The `window.status` property can be assigned some other text at any time. To change the text of a link, the action is triggered by an `onMouseOver=` event handler of a link object. A peculiarity of the `onMouseOver=` event handler for setting the status bar is that an additional statement — `return true` — must also be part of the event handler. This is very rare in JavaScript, but required here for the status bar to be successfully overridden by your script.

Due to the simplicity of setting the `window.status` property, it is most common for the script statements to be run as inline scripts in the event handler definition. This is handy for short scripts, because you don't have to specify a separate function or add `<SCRIPT>` tags to your page. You simply add the script statements to the `<A>` tag:

```
<A HREF="http://home.netscape.com" onMouseOver="window.status='Visit
the Netscape Home page (home.netscape.com)'; return true">Netscape</A>
```

Look closely at the script statements assigned to the `onMouseOver=` event handler. The two statements are

```
window.status='Visit the Netscape Home page (home.netscape.com)'
return true
```

When run as inline scripts, the two statements must be separated by a semicolon. Equally important, the entire set of statements is surrounded by double quotes(" . . . "). To nest the string being assigned to the `window.status` property inside the double-quoted script, the string is surrounded by single quotes (' . . . '). You get a lot of return for a little bit of script when you set the status bar. The downside is that scripting this property is how those awful status bar scrolling banners are created. Yech!

window.alert() method

I have already used the `alert()` method many times so far in this tutorial. This window method generates a dialog box that displays whatever text you pass as a parameter (see Figure 8-2). A single OK button (which cannot be changed) lets the user dismiss the alert.

Figure 8-2: A JavaScript alert dialog box

The appearance of this and two other JavaScript dialog boxes (described next) has changed slightly since the first scriptable browsers. In versions prior to Navigator 4 (as shown in Figure 8-2), the browser inserted words clearly indicating that the dialog box was a "JavaScript Alert." This text cannot be altered by script: Only the other message content can be changed.

All three dialog box methods are good cases for using a window object's methods without the reference to the window. Even though the `alert()` method is technically a window object method, no special relationship exists between the dialog box and the window that generates it. In production scripts, I rarely use the full reference:

```
alert("This is a JavaScript alert dialog.")
```

window.confirm() method

The second style of dialog box presents two buttons (Cancel and OK in most versions on most platforms) and is called a confirm dialog (see Figure 8-3). More importantly, this is one of those methods that returns a value: `true` if the user clicks OK, `false` if the user clicks Cancel. You can use this dialog and its returned value as a way to have a user make a decision about how a script will progress.

Figure 8-3: A JavaScript confirm dialog box

Because the method always returns a Boolean value, you can use the evaluated value of the entire method as a condition statement in an `if` or `if...else` construction. For example, in the following code fragment, the user is asked about starting the application over. Doing so causes the default page of the site to be loaded into the browser.

```
if (confirm("Are you sure you want to start over?")) {
     location = "index.html"
}
```

window.prompt() method

The final dialog box of the window object, the prompt dialog box (see Figure 8-4), displays a message that you set and provides a text field for the user to enter a response. Two buttons, Cancel and OK, let the user dismiss the dialog box with two opposite expectations: canceling the entire operation or accepting the input typed into the dialog box.

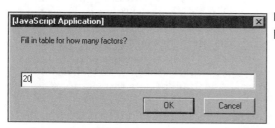

Figure 8-4: A JavaScript prompt dialog box

The `window.prompt()` method has two parameters. The first is the message that acts as a prompt to the user. You can suggest a default answer in the text field by including a string as the second parameter. If you don't want any default answer to appear, then include an empty string (two double quotes without any space between them).

This method returns one value when the user clicks on either button. A click of the Cancel button returns a value of `null`, regardless of what is typed into the field. A click of the OK button returns a string value of the typed entry. Your scripts can use this information in conditions for `if` and `if...else` constructions. A value of `null` is treated as `false` in a condition. It turns out that an empty string is also treated as `false`. Therefore, a condition can easily test for the presence of real characters typed into the field to simplify a condition test, as shown in the following fragment:

```
var answer = prompt("What is your name?","")
if (answer) {
     alert("Hello, " + answer + "!")
}
```

The only time the `alert()` method is called is when the user has entered something into the prompt dialog and clicked the OK button.

onLoad= event handler

The window object reacts to several system and user events, but the one you will probably use most is the event that fires as soon as everything in a page has finished loading. This event waits for images, Java applets, and data files for plug-ins to download fully to the browser. It can be dangerous to script access to elements of a document object while the page loads, because if the object has not yet loaded (perhaps due to a slow network connection or server), a script error will result. The advantage of using the onLoad= event to invoke functions is that you are assured that all document objects are in the browser's document object model. All window event handlers are placed inside the <BODY> tag. Even though you will come to associate the <BODY> tag's attributes with the document object's properties, it is the window object's event handlers that go inside the tag (the document object has no event handlers).

The Location Object

Sometimes an object in the hierarchy represents something that doesn't seem to have a physical presence, like a window or a button. That's the case with the location object. This object represents the URL loaded into the window. This is different from the document object (discussed later in this lesson), because the document is the real content; the location is simply the URL.

Unless you are truly Web-savvy, you may not realize a URL consists of many components that define the address and method of data transfer for a file. Pieces of a URL include the protocol (like http:) and the hostname (like www.giantco.com). All of these items are accessed as properties of the location object. For the most part, though, your scripts will be interested in only one property: the href property, which defines the complete URL.

Setting the location.href property is the primary way your scripts navigate to other pages, either in the current window or another frame. You can generally navigate to a page in your own Web site by specifying a relative URL (that is, relative to the currently loaded page), rather than the complete URL with protocol and host info. For pages outside of your domain, you need to specify the complete URL.

A shortcut that works well in Navigator is to omit the reference to the href property. You can simply set the location object to a URL (relative or absolute), and Navigator will get to the desired page. Therefore, both of the following statements accomplish the same end:

```
location = "http://www.dannyg.com"
location.href = "http://www.dannyg.com"
```

If the page to be loaded is in another window or frame, the window reference must be part of the statement. For example, if your script opens a new window and assigns its reference to a variable named newWindow, the statement that loads a page into that window would be

```
newWindow.location = "http://www.dannyg.com"
```

The History Object

Another object that doesn't have a physical presence on the page is the history object. Each window maintains a list of recent pages that have been visited by the browser. While the history object's list contains the URLs of recently visited pages, those URLs are not generally accessible by script. But methods of the history object allow for navigating backward and forward through the history relative to the currently loaded page.

The Document Object

The document object holds the real content of the page. Properties and methods of the document object generally affect the look and content of the document that occupies the window. Except for some of the advances in Dynamic HTML in Internet Explorer 4, the text contents of a page cannot be accessed or changed once the document has loaded. However, as you saw in your first script of Chapter 3, the `document.write()` method lets a script dynamically create content as the page is loading. A great many of the document object's properties are established by attributes of the `<BODY>` tag. Many other properties are arrays of other objects in the document.

Accessing a document object's properties and methods is straightforward, as shown in the following syntax examples:

```
[window.]document.propertyName
[window.]document.methodName([parameters])
```

The window reference is optional when the script is accessing the document object that contains the script.

document.forms[] property

One of the object types contained by a document is the form object. Because there can conceivably be more than one form in a document, forms are stored as arrays in the `document.forms[]` property. As you recall from the discussion of arrays in Chapter 7, an index number inside the square brackets points to one of the elements in the array. To access the first form in a document, for example, the reference would be

```
document.forms[0]
```

In general, however, I recommend that you access a form by way of a name you assign to the form in its `NAME` attribute, as in

```
document.formName
```

Either methodology reaches the same object. When a script needs to reference elements inside a form, the complete address to that object must include the document and form.

document.title property

Not every property about a document object is set in a `<BODY>` tag attribute. If you assign a title to the page in the `<TITLE>` tag set within the Head portion, that title text is reflected by the `document.title` property. A document's title is mostly a cosmetic setting that gives a plain-language name of the page appearing in the browser's title bar, as well as the user's history listing and bookmark of your page.

document.write() method

The `document.write()` method can be used in both immediate scripts to create content in a page as it loads and in deferred scripts that create new content in the same or different window. The method requires one string parameter, which is the HTML content to write to the window or frame. Such string parameters can be variables or any other expressions that evaluate to a string. Very often, the content being written includes HTML tags.

Bear in mind that after a page loads, the browser's output stream is automatically closed. After that, any `document.write()` method issued to the current page opens a new stream that immediately erases the current page (along with any variables or other values in the original document). Therefore, if you wish to replace the current page with script-generated HTML, you need to accumulate that HTML in a variable and perform the writing with just one `document.write()` method. You don't have to explicitly clear a document and open a new data stream: One `document.write()` call does it all.

One last piece of housekeeping advice about the `document.write()` method involves its companion method, `document.close()`. Your script must close the output stream when it has finished writing its content to the window (either the same window or another). After the last `document.write()` method in a deferred script, be sure to include a `document.close()` method. Failure to do this may cause images and forms not to appear; also, any `document.write()` method invoked later will only append to the page, rather than clear the existing content to write anew. To demonstrate the `document.write()` method, I show two versions of the same application. One writes to the same document that contains the script; the other writes to a separate window. Type in each document, save it, and open it in your browser.

Listing 8-2 creates a button that assembles new HTML content for a document, including HTML tags for a new document title and color attribute for the `<BODY>` tag. One `document.write()` statement blasts the entire new content to the same document, obliterating all vestiges of the content of Listing 8-2. The `document.close()` statement, however, is required to properly close the output stream. When you load this document and click the button, notice that the document title in the browser's title bar changes accordingly. As you click back to the original and try the button again, notice that the dynamically written second page loads much faster than even a reload of the original document.

Listing 8-2: **Using document.write() on the Same Window**

```
<HTML>
<HEAD>
<TITLE>Writing to Same Doc</TITLE>
<SCRIPT LANGUAGE="JavaScript">
function reWrite() {
        // assemble content for new window
        var newContent = "<HTML><HEAD><TITLE>A New Doc</TITLE></HEAD>"
        newContent += "<BODY BGCOLOR='aqua'><H1>This document is brand
new.</H1>"
        newContent += "Click the Back button to see original document."
        newContent += "</BODY></HTML>"
        // write HTML to new window document
        document.write(newContent)
        document.close() // close layout stream
}
```

```
</SCRIPT>
</HEAD>
<BODY>
<FORM>
<INPUT TYPE="button" VALUE="Replace Content" onClick="reWrite()">
</FORM>
</BODY>
</HTML>
```

In Listing 8-3, the situation is a bit more complex because the script generates a subwindow, to which is written an entirely script-generated document. To keep the reference to the new window alive across both functions, the `newWindow` variable is declared as a global variable. As soon as the page loads, the `onLoad=` event handler invokes the `makeNewWindow()` function. This function generates a blank subwindow. I have added a property to the third parameter of the `window.open()` method that instructs the status bar of the subwindow appear.

A button in the page invokes the `subWrite()` method. The first task it performs is to check the `closed` property of the subwindow. This property (which exists only in newer browser versions) returns `true` if the referenced window is closed. If that's the case (in case the user has manually closed the window), the function invokes the `makeNewWindow()` function again to open that window again.

With the window open, new content is assembled as a string variable. As with Listing 8-2, the content is written in one blast (although that isn't necessary for a separate window), followed by a `close()` method. But notice an important difference: both the `open()` and `close()` methods explicitly specify the subwindow.

Listing 8-3: **Using document.write() on Another Window**

```
<HTML>
<HEAD>
<TITLE>Writing to Sub Window</TITLE>
<SCRIPT LANGUAGE="JavaScript">
var newWindow
function makeNewWindow() {
        newWindow = window.open("","","status,height=200,width=300")
}

function subWrite() {
        // make new window if someone has closed it
        if (newWindow.closed) {
            makeNewWindow()
        }
        // assemble content for new window
        var newContent = "<HTML><HEAD><TITLE>A New Doc</TITLE></HEAD>"
        newContent += "<BODY BGCOLOR='coral'><H1>This document is brand
new.</H1>"
```

(continued)

Listing 8-3 *(continued)*

```
            newContent += "</BODY></HTML>"
            // write HTML to new window document
            newWindow.document.write(newContent)
            newWindow.document.close() // close layout stream
    }
</SCRIPT>
</HEAD>
<BODY onLoad="makeNewWindow()">
<FORM>
<INPUT TYPE="button" VALUE="Write to Subwindow" onClick="subWrite()">
</FORM>
</BODY>
</HTML>
```

The Link Object

Belonging to the document object in the hierarchy is the link object. A document can have any number of links, so references to links, if necessary, are usually made via the array index method:

```
document.links[n].propertyName
```

More commonly, though, links are not scripted. However, there is an important JavaScript component to these objects. When you want the click on a link to execute a script rather than navigate directly to another URL, you can redirect the HREF attribute to call a script function. The technique involves a pseudo-URL called the javascript: URL. If you place the name of a function after the javascript: URL, a scriptable browser runs that function. So as not to mess with the minds of users, the function should probably perform some navigation in the end, but the script can do other things as well, such as simultaneously changing the content of two frames within a frameset.

The syntax for this construction in a link is as follows:

```
<A HREF="javascript:void
functionName([parameter1]...[parameterN])">...</A>
```

The void keyword prevents the link from trying to display any value that may be returned from the function. Remember this javascript: URL technique for all tags that include HREF and SRC attributes: If an attribute accepts a URL, it can accept this javascript: URL as well. This can come in handy as a way to script actions for client-side image maps that don't necessarily navigate anywhere, but cause something to happen on the page just the same.

The next logical step past the document level in the object hierarchy is the form. That's where you will spend the next lesson.

Exercises

1. Which of the following references are valid and which are not? Explain what is wrong with the invalid references.

   a. `window.document.form[0]`

   b. `self.entryForm.entryField.value`

   c. `document.forms[2].name`

   d. `entryForm.entryField.value`

   e. `newWindow.document.write("Howdy")`

2. Write the JavaScript statement that displays a message in the status bar welcoming visitors to your Web page.

3. Write the JavaScript statement that displays the same message to the document as an `<H1>`-level headline on the page.

4. Create a page that prompts the user for his or her name as the page loads (via a dialog box) and then welcomes the user by name in the body of the page.

5. Create a page with any content you like, but one that automatically displays a dialog box after the page loads to show the user the URL of the current page.

✦　　✦　　✦

Forms and Form Elements

◆ ◆ ◆ ◆

In This Chapter

What the form object represents

How to access key form object properties and methods

How text, button, and select objects work

How to submit forms from a script

How to pass information from form elements to functions

◆ ◆ ◆ ◆

Most interactivity between a Web page and the user takes place inside a form. That's where a lot of the cool HTML stuff lives: text fields, buttons, checkboxes, option lists, and so on. As you can tell from the by now familiar object hierarchy diagram (refer back to Figure 8-1), a form is always contained by a document. Even so, the document object must be part of the reference to the form and its elements.

The Form Object

A form object can be referenced either by its position in the array of forms contained by a document or by name (if you assign a name to the form in the <FORM> tag). Even if only one form appears in the document, it is a member of a one-element array, and is referenced as follows:

```
document.forms[0]
```

Notice that the array reference uses the plural version of the word, followed by a set of square brackets containing the index number of the element (zero always being first). But if you assign a name to the form, simply plug the form's name into the reference:

```
document.formName
```

Form as object and container

A form has a relatively small set of properties, methods, and event handlers. Almost all of the properties are the same as the attributes for forms. Navigator allows scripts to change these properties under script control (Internet Explorer allows this only starting with Version 4), which gives your scripts potentially significant power to direct the behavior of a form submission in response to user selections on the page.

A form is contained by a document, and it in turn contains any number of elements. All of those interactive elements that let users enter information or make selections belong to the form object. This relationship mirrors the HTML tag organization, where items such as <INPUT> tags are nested between the <FORM> and </FORM> tag "bookends."

Creating a form

Forms are created entirely from standard HTML tags in the page. You can set attributes for NAME, TARGET, ACTION, METHOD, and ENCTYPE. Each of these is a property of a form object, accessed by all lowercase versions of those words, as in

```
document.forms[0].action
document.formName.action
```

To change any of these properties, simply assign new values to them:

```
document.forms[0].action = "http://www.giantco.com"
```

form.elements[] property

In addition to keeping track of each type of element inside a form, the browser also maintains a list of all elements within a form. This list is another array, with items listed according to the order in which their HTML tags appear in the source code. It is generally more efficient to create references to elements directly, using their names. However, there are times when a script needs to look through all of the elements in a form. This would be especially true if the content of a form were to change with each loading of the page because the number of text fields changes based on the user's browser type.

The following code fragment shows the form.elements[] property at work in a for repeat loop that looks at every element in a form to set the contents of text fields to an empty string. The script cannot simply barge through the form and set every element's content to an empty string, because some elements may be buttons, which don't have a property that can be set to an empty string.

```
var form = window.document.forms[0]
for (var i = 0; i < form.elements.length; i++) {
        if (form.elements[i].type = "text") {
            form.elements[i].value = ""
        }
}
```

In the first statement, I create a variable — form — that holds a reference to the first form of the document. I do this so that when I make many references to form elements later in the script, the length of those references will be much shorter (and marginally faster). I can use the form variable as a shortcut to building references to items more deeply nested in the form.

Next I start looping through the items in the elements array for the form. Each form element has a type property, which reveals what kind of form element it is: text, button, radio, checkbox, and so on. I'm interested in finding elements whose type is "text." For each of those, I set the value property to an empty string.

I will come back to forms later in this chapter to show you how to submit a form without a Submit button and how client-side form validation works.

Text Objects

Each of the four text-related HTML form elements — text, textarea, password, and hidden — is an element in the document object hierarchy. All but the hidden object display themselves in the page, allowing users to enter information. These objects are also used to display text information that changes in the course of using a page (although Dynamic HTML in Internet Explorer 4 also allows the scripted change of body text in a document).

To make these objects scriptable in a page, you do nothing special to their normal HTML tags — with the possible exception of assigning a NAME attribute. I strongly recommend assigning unique names to every form element if your scripts will either be getting or setting properties or invoking their methods.

For the visible objects in this category, event handlers are triggered from many user actions, such as giving a field focus (getting the text insertion pointer in the field) and changing text (entering new text and leaving the field). Most of your text field actions will be triggered by the change of text (the onChange= event handler). In the level 4 browsers, new event handlers fire in response to individual keystrokes as well.

Without a doubt, the single most used property of a text element is the value property. This property represents the current contents of the text element. Its content can be retrieved and set by a script at any time. Content of the value property is always a string. This may require conversion to numbers (Chapter 6) if text fields are used to enter values for some math operations.

Text object behavior

Many scripters look to JavaScript to solve what are perceived as shortcomings or behavioral anomalies with text objects in forms. I want to single these out early in your scripting experience so that you are not confused by them later.

First, the font, font size, font style, and text alignment of a text object's content cannot be altered by script, any more than they can be altered by most versions of HTML. This situation will probably change, but for all browsers scriptable in early 1998, these characteristics are not modifiable.

Second, Navigator forms practice a behavior that was recommended as an informal standard by Web pioneers. When a form contains only one text object, a press of the Enter key while the text object has focus automatically submits the form. For two or more fields, another way is needed to submit the form (for example, a Submit button). This one-field submission scheme works well in many cases, such as the search page at most Web search sites. But if you are experimenting with simple forms containing only one field, the form will be submitted with a press of the Enter key. Submitting a form that has no other action or target specified means the page performs an unconditional reload — wiping out any information entered into the form. You can, however, cancel the submission through an onSubmit= event handler in the form, as shown later in this lesson.

To demonstrate how a text field's `value` property can be read and written, Listing 9-1 provides a complete HTML page with a single entry field. Its `onChange=` event handler invokes the `upperMe()` function, which converts the text to uppercase. In the `upperMe()` function, the first statement assigns the text object reference to a more convenient variable, `field`. A lot goes on in the second statement of the function. The right side of the assignment statement performs a couple of key tasks. Working from left to right, the reference to the `value` property of the object (`field.value`) evaluates to whatever content is in the text field at that instant. That string is then handed over to one of JavaScript's string functions, `toUpperCase()`, which converts the value to uppercase. Therefore, the entire right side of the assignment statement evaluates to an uppercase version of the field's content. But that, in and of itself, does not change the field's contents. That's why the uppercase string is assigned to the `value` property of the field.

Listing 9-1: Getting and Setting a Text Object's Value Property

```
<HTML>
<HEAD>
<TITLE>Text Object value Property</TITLE>
<SCRIPT LANGUAGE="JavaScript">
function upperMe() {
        var field = document.forms[0].converter
        field.value = field.value.toUpperCase()
}
</SCRIPT>
</HEAD>
<BODY>
<FORM onSubmit="return false">
<INPUT TYPE="text" NAME="converter" VALUE="sample"
onChange="upperMe()">
</FORM>
</BODY>
</HTML>
```

Later in this chapter, I will show you how to reduce even further the need for explicit references in functions such as `upperMe()` in Listing 9-1. In the meantime, notice for a moment the `onSubmit=` event handler in the `<FORM>` tag. I will get more deeply into this event handler later in this chapter, but I want to point out the construction that prevents a single-field form from being submitted when the Enter key is pressed.

The Button Object

I have used the button form element in many examples up to this point in the tutorial. The button is one of the simplest objects to script. It has only a few properties, which are rarely accessed or modified in day-to-day scripts. Like the text object, the visual aspects of the button are governed not by HTML or scripts, but by the operating system and browser being used by the page visitor. By far the most useful event handler of the button object is the onClick= event handler. It fires whenever the user clicks on the button. Simple enough. No magic here.

The Checkbox Object

A checkbox is also a simple form object, but some of the properties may not be entirely intuitive. Unlike the value property of a plain button object (the text of the button label), the value property of a checkbox is any other text you want associated with the object. This text does not appear on the page in any fashion, but the property (initially set via the VALUE tag attribute) might be important to a script that wants to know more about the checkbox.

The key property of a checkbox object is whether or not the box is checked. The checked property is a Boolean value: true if the box is checked, false if not. When you see that a property is a Boolean, that's a clue that the value might be usable in an if or if...else condition expression. In Listing 9-2, the value of the checked property determines which alert box is shown to the user.

Listing 9-2: **The Checkbox Object's Checked Property**

```
<HTML>
<HEAD>
<TITLE>Checkbox Inspector</TITLE>
<SCRIPT LANGUAGE="JavaScript">
function inspectBox() {
        if (document.forms[0].checkThis.checked) {
            alert("The box is checked.")
        } else {
            alert("The box is not checked at the moment.")
        }
}
</SCRIPT>
</HEAD>
<BODY>
<FORM>
<INPUT TYPE="checkbox" NAME="checkThis">Check here<BR>
<INPUT TYPE="button" VALUE="Inspect Box" onClick="inspectBox()">
</FORM>
</BODY>
</HTML>
```

Checkboxes are generally used as preferences setters, rather than as action inducers. While a checkbox object has an onClick= event handler, a click of a checkbox should never do anything drastic, such as navigate to another page.

The Radio Object

Setting up a group of radio objects for scripting requires a bit more work. To let the browser manage the highlighting and unhighlighting of a related group of buttons, you must assign the same name to each of the buttons in the group. You can have multiple groups within a form, but each member of the same group must have the same name.

Assigning the same name to a form element forces the browser to manage the elements differently than if they each had a unique name. Instead, the browser maintains an array list of objects with the same name. The name assigned to the group becomes the name of the array. Some properties apply to the group as a whole; other properties apply to individual buttons within the group, and must be addressed via array index references. For example, you can find out how many buttons are in a group by reading the length property of the group:

```
document.forms[0].groupName.length
```

But if you want to find out if a particular button is currently highlighted — via the same checked property used for the checkbox — you must access the button element individually:

```
document.forms[0].groupName[0].checked
```

Listing 9-3 demonstrates several aspects of the radio button object, including how to look through a group of buttons to find out which one is checked and how to use the VALUE attribute and corresponding property for meaningful work.

The page includes three radio buttons and a plain button. Each radio button's VALUE attribute contains the full name of one of the Three Stooges. When the user clicks the button, the onClick= event handler invokes the fullName() function. In that function, the first statement creates a shortcut reference to the form. Next, a for repeat loop is set up to look through all of the buttons in the stooges radio button group. An if construction looks at the checked property of each button. When a button is highlighted, the break statement bails out of the for loop, leaving the value of the i loop counter at the number when the loop broke ranks. The alert dialog box then uses a reference to the value property of the i'th button so that the full name can be displayed in the alert.

Listing 9-3: **Scripting a Group of Radio Objects**

```
<HTML>
<HEAD>
<TITLE>Extracting Highlighted Radio Button</TITLE>
<SCRIPT LANGUAGE="JavaScript">
function fullName() {
        var form = document.forms[0]
        for (var i = 0; i < form.stooges.length; i++) {
            if (form.stooges[i].checked) {
                break
            }
        }
        alert("You chose " + form.stooges[i].value + ".")
}
</SCRIPT>
</HEAD>
```

```
<BODY>
<FORM>
<B>Select your favorite Stooge:</B>
<INPUT TYPE="radio" NAME="stooges" VALUE="Moe Howard" CHECKED>Moe
<INPUT TYPE="radio" NAME="stooges" VALUE="Larry Fine" >Larry
<INPUT TYPE="radio" NAME="stooges" VALUE="Curly Howard" >Curly<BR>
<INPUT TYPE="button" NAME="Viewer" VALUE="View Full Name..."
onClick="fullName()">
</FORM>
</BODY>
</HTML>
```

As you will learn about form elements in later chapters of this book, the browser's tendency to create arrays out of identically named objects of the same type (except for Internet Explorer 3) can be a benefit to scripts that work with, say, columns of fields in an HTML order form.

The Select Object

The most complex form element to script is the select object. As you can see from the object hierarchy diagram (Figure 9-1), the select object is really a compound object: an object that contains an array of option objects. Moreover, the object can be established in HTML to display itself as either a pop-up list or a scrolling list, the latter configurable to accept multiple selections by users. For the sake of simplicity at this stage, this lesson focuses on deployment as a pop-up list allowing only single selections.

Some properties belong to the entire select object; others belong to individual options inside the select object. If your goal is to determine which item was selected by the user, you must use properties of both the select object and the selected option.

The most important property of the select object itself is the `selectedIndex` property, accessed as follows:

```
document.form[0].selectName.selectedIndex
```

This value is the index number of the item that is currently selected. As with most index counting schemes in JavaScript, the first item (the one at the top of the list) has an index of zero. The `selectedIndex` value is critical for letting you access properties of the selected item. Two important properties of an option item are `text` and `value`, accessed as follows:

```
document.forms[0].selectName.options[n].text
document.forms[0].selectName.options[n].value
```

The `text` property is the string that appears on screen in the select object. It is unusual for this information to be exposed as a form property, because in the HTML that generates a select object, the text is defined outside of the `<OPTION>` tag. But inside the `<OPTION>` tag you can set a `VALUE` attribute, which, like the radio buttons shown earlier, lets you associate some hidden string information with each visible entry in the list.

To extract the `value` or `text` property of a selected option most efficiently, you can use the select object's `selectedIndex` property as an index value to the option. References for this kind of operation get pretty long, so take the time to understand what's happening here. In the following function, the first statement creates a shortcut reference to the select object. The `selectedIndex` property of the select object is then substituted for the index value of the options array of that same object:

```
function inspect() {
        var list = document.forms[0].choices
        var chosenItem = list.options[list.selectedIndex].text
}
```

To bring a select object to life, use the `onChange=` event handler. As soon as a user makes a new selection in the list, this event handler runs the script associated with that event handler (except for Windows versions of Navigator 2, whose `onChange=` event handler doesn't work for select objects). Listing 9-4 shows a common application for a select object. Its text entries describe places to go in and out of a Web site, while the `VALUE` attributes hold the URLs for those locations. When a user makes a selection in the list, the `onChange=` event handler triggers a script that extracts the `value` property of the selected option, and assigns that value to the location object to effect the navigation. Under JavaScript control, this kind of navigation doesn't need a separate Go button on the page.

Listing 9-4: **Navigating with a Select Object**

```
<HTML>
<HEAD>
<TITLE>Select Navigation</TITLE>
<SCRIPT LANGUAGE="JavaScript">
function goThere() {
        var list = document.forms[0].urlList
        location = list.options[list.selectedIndex].value
}
</SCRIPT>
</HEAD>

<BODY>
<FORM>
Choose a place to go:
<SELECT NAME="urlList" onChange="goThere()">
        <OPTION SELECTED VALUE="index.html">Home Page
        <OPTION VALUE="store.html">Shop Our Store
        <OPTION VALUE="policies">Shipping Policies
        <OPTION VALUE="http://www.yahoo.com">Search the Web
</SELECT>
</FORM>
</BODY>
</HTML>
```

There is much more to the select object, including the ability to change the contents of a list in newer browsers. Chapter 24 covers the object in depth.

Passing Form Data and Elements to Functions

In all of the examples so far in this lesson, when an event handler invoked a function that worked with form elements, the form or form element was explicitly referenced in the function. But valuable shortcuts do exist for transferring information about the form or form element directly to the function without dealing with those typically long references that start with the window or document object level.

JavaScript features a keyword — this — that always refers to whatever object contains the script in which the keyword is used. Thus, in an onChange= event handler for a text field, you can pass a reference to the text object to the function by inserting the this keyword as a parameter to the function:

```
<INPUT TYPE="text" NAME="entry" onChange="upperMe(this)">
```

At the receiving end, the function defines a parameter variable that turns that reference into a variable that the rest of the function can use:

```
function upperMe(field) {
        statement[s]
}
```

The name you assign to the parameter variable is purely arbitrary, but it is helpful to give it a name that expresses what the reference is. Importantly, this reference is a "live" connection back to the object. Therefore, statements in the script can get and set property values at will.

For other functions, you may wish to receive a reference to the entire form, rather than just the object calling the function. This is certainly true if the function is called by a button whose function needs to access other elements of the same form. To pass the entire form, you reference the form property of the object, still using the this keyword:

```
<INPUT TYPE="button" VALUE="Click Here" onClick="inspect(this.form)">
```

The function definition should then have a parameter variable ready to be assigned to the form object reference. Again, the name of the variable is up to you. I tend to use the variable name form as a way to remind me exactly what kind of object is referenced.

```
function inspect(form) {
        statement[s]
}
```

Listing 9-5 demonstrates passing both an individual form element and the entire form in the performance of two separate acts. This page makes believe it is connected to a database of Beatles songs. When you click the Process Data button, it passes the form object, which the processData() function uses to access the group of radio buttons inside a `for` loop. Additional references using the passed form object extract the `value` properties of the selected radio button and the text field.

The text field has its own event handler, which passes just the text field to the `verifySong()` function. Notice how short the reference is to reach the `value` property of the `song` field inside the function.

Listing 9-5: Passing a Form Object and Form Element to Functions

```
<HTML>
<HEAD>
<TITLE>Beatle Picker</TITLE>
<SCRIPT LANGUAGE="JavaScript">
function processData(form) {
        for (var i = 0; i < form.Beatles.length; i++) {
            if (form.Beatles[i].checked) {
                break
            }
        }
        // assign values to variables for convenience
        var beatle = form.Beatles[i].value
        var song = form.song.value
        alert("Checking whether " + song + " features " + beatle +
"...")
}

function verifySong(entry) {
        var song = entry.value
        alert("Checking whether " + song + " is a Beatles tune...")
}
</SCRIPT>
</HEAD>

<BODY>
<FORM onSubmit="return false">
Choose your favorite Beatle:
<INPUT TYPE="radio" NAME="Beatles" VALUE="John Lennon" CHECKED>John
<INPUT TYPE="radio" NAME="Beatles" VALUE="Paul McCartney">Paul
<INPUT TYPE="radio" NAME="Beatles" VALUE="George Harrison">George
<INPUT TYPE="radio" NAME="Beatles" VALUE="Ringo Starr">Ringo<P>

Enter the name of your favorite Beatles song:<BR>
<INPUT TYPE="text" NAME="song" VALUE = "Eleanor Rigby"
onChange="verifySong(this)"><P>
<INPUT TYPE="button" NAME="process" VALUE="Process Request..."
onClick="processData(this.form)">
</FORM>
</BODY>
</HTML>
```

Get to know the usage of the `this` keyword in passing form and form element objects to functions. The technique not only saves you typing in your code, but assures accuracy in references to those objects.

Submitting Forms

If you have worked with Web pages and forms before, you are familiar with how simple it is to add a Submit-style button that sends the form to your server. However, design goals for your page may rule out the use of ugly system buttons. If you'd rather display a pretty image, the link tag surrounding that image should use the `javascript:` URL technique to invoke a script that submits the form.

The scripted equivalent of submitting a form is the form object's `submit()` method. All you need in the statement is a reference to the form and this method, as in

```
document.forms[0].submit()
```

One limitation might inhibit your plans to secretly have a script send you an e-mail message from every visitor who comes to your Web site. If the form's `ACTION` attribute is set to a `mailTo:` URL, JavaScript will not pass along the `submit()` method to the form. Of course, Internet Explorer does not allow e-mailing of forms through any machinations.

Before a form is submitted, you may wish to perform some last-second validation of data in the form or other scripting (for example, changing the form's `action` property based on user choices). This can be done in a function invoked by the form's `onSubmit=` event handler. Specific validation routines are beyond the scope of this tutorial (although explained in substantial detail in Chapter 37), but I want to show you how the `onSubmit=` event handler works.

In all but the first generation of scriptable browsers from Microsoft and Netscape, you can let the results of a validation function cancel a submission if the validation shows some data to be incorrect or a field is empty. To control submission, the `onSubmit=` event handler must evaluate to `return true` (to allow submission to continue) or `return false` (to cancel submission). This is a bit tricky at first, because it involves more than just having the function called by the event handler return `true` or `false`. The `return` keyword must also be part of the final evaluation.

Listing 9-6 shows a page with a simple validation routine that ensures all fields have something in them before allowing submission to continue. Notice how the `onSubmit=` event handler (which passes the form object as a parameter — in this case the `this` keyword points to the form object) includes the `return` keyword before the function name. When the function returns its `true` or `false` value, the event handler evaluates to the requisite `return true` or `return false`.

Listing 9-6: **Last-minute Checking before Form Submission**

```
<HTML>
<HEAD>
<TITLE>Validator</TITLE>
```

(continued)

Listing 9-6 *(continued)*

```
<SCRIPT LANGUAGE="JavaScript">
function checkForm(form) {
        for (var i = 0; i < form.elements.length; i++) {
            if (form.elements[i].value == "") {
                alert("Fill out ALL fields.")
                return false
            }
        }
        return true
}
</SCRIPT>
</HEAD>

<BODY>
<FORM onSubmit="return checkForm(this)">
Please enter all requested information:<BR>
First Name:<INPUT TYPE="text" NAME="firstName" ><BR>
Last Name:<INPUT TYPE="text" NAME="lastName" ><BR>
Rank:<INPUT TYPE="text" NAME="rank" ><BR>
Serial Number:<INPUT TYPE="text" NAME="serialNumber" ><BR>

<INPUT TYPE="submit">
</FORM>
</BODY>
</HTML>
```

One quirky bit of behavior involving the submit() method and onSubmit= event handler needs explanation. While you might think (and logically so, in my opinion) that the submit() method would be exactly the scripted equivalent of a click of a real Submit button, it's not. In Navigator, the submit() method does not cause the form's onSubmit= event handler to fire at all. If you want to perform validation on a form submitted via the submit() method, invoke the validation in the script that calls the submit() method.

So much for the basics of forms and form elements. In the next lesson, you step away from HTML for a moment to look at more advanced JavaScript core language items: strings, math, and dates.

Exercises

1. Rework Listings 9-1, 9-2, 9-3, and 9-4 so that the script functions all receive the most efficient form or form element references from the invoking event handler.

2. Modify Listing 9-6 so that instead of the submission being made by a Submit button, the submission is performed from a hyperlink. Be sure to include the form validation in the process.

3. In the following HTML tag, what kind of information do you think is being passed with the event handler? Write a function that displays in an alert dialog box the information being passed.

```
<INPUT TYPE="text" NAME="phone" onChange="format(this.value)">
```

4. A document contains two forms, named specifications and accessories. In the accessories form is a field named acc1. Write two different statements that set the contents of that field to Leather Carrying Case.

5. Create a page that includes a select object to change the background color of the current page. The property that needs to be set is document.bgColor, and the three values you should offer as options are red, yellow, and green. In the select object, the colors should be displayed as Stop, Caution, and Go. Note: If you are using a Macintosh or UNIX version of Navigator, you must be using Version 4 or later for this exercise.

✦   ✦   ✦

Strings, Math, and Dates

♦ ♦ ♦ ♦

In This Chapter

How to modify strings with common string methods

When and how to use the Math object

How to use the Date object

♦ ♦ ♦ ♦

For most of the lessons in the tutorial so far, the objects at the center of attention were objects belonging to the document object model. But as indicated in Chapter 2, a clear dividing line exists between the document object model and the JavaScript language. The language has some of its own objects that are independent of the document object model. These objects are defined such that if a vendor wished to implement JavaScript as the programming language for an entirely different kind of product, the language would still use these core facilities for handling text, advanced math (beyond simple arithmetic), and dates.

Core Language Objects

It is often difficult for newcomers to programming or even experienced programmers who have not worked in object-oriented worlds before to think about objects, especially when attributed to "things" that don't seem to have a physical presence. For example, it doesn't require lengthy study to grasp the notion of a button on a page being an object. It has several physical properties that make perfect sense. But what about a string of characters? As you learn in this chapter, in an object-based environment such as JavaScript, everything that moves is treated as an object — each piece of data from a Boolean value to a date. Each such object probably has one or more properties that help define the content; such an object may also have methods associated with it to define what the object can do or what can be done to the object.

I call all objects not part of the document object model *global objects*. You can see the full complement of them in the JavaScript Object Road Map in Appendix A. In this lesson the focus is on the String, Math, and Date objects.

String Objects

You have already used string objects many times in earlier lessons. A string is any text inside a quote pair. A quote pair consists of either double quotes or single quotes. This allows one string to be nested inside another, as often happens in event handlers. In the following example, the `alert()` method requires a quoted string as a parameter, but the entire method call must also be inside quotes.

```
onClick="alert('Hello, all')"
```

JavaScript imposes no practical limit on the number of characters that a string can hold. However, most browsers have a limit of 255 characters in length for a script statement. This limit is sometimes exceeded when a script includes a lengthy string that is to become scripted content in a page. Such lines need to be divided into smaller chunks using techniques described in a moment.

You have two ways to assign a string value to a variable. The simplest is a simple assignment statement:

```
var myString = "Howdy"
```

This works perfectly well except in some exceedingly rare instances. Beginning with Navigator 3 and Internet Explorer 4, you can also create a string object using the more formal syntax that involves the `new` keyword and a constructor function (that is, it "constructs" a new object):

```
var myString = new String("Howdy")
```

Whichever way you use to initialize a variable with a string, the variable is able to respond to all string object methods.

Joining strings

Bringing two strings together as a single string is called *concatenating* strings, a term I introduce in Chapter 6. String concatenation requires one of two JavaScript operators. Even in your first script in Chapter 3, you saw how the addition operator linked multiple strings together to produce the text dynamically written to the loading Web page:

```
document.write(" of <B>" + navigator.appName + "</B>.")
```

As valuable as that operator is, another operator can be even more scripter-friendly. The situation that calls for this operator is when you are building large strings. The strings are either so long or cumbersome that you need to divide the building process into multiple statements. Some of the pieces may be string literals (strings inside quotes) or variable values. The clumsy way to do it (perfectly doable in JavaScript) is to use the addition operator to append more text to the existing chunk:

```
var msg = "Four score"
msg = msg + " and seven"
msg = msg + " years ago,"
```

But another operator, called the add-by-value operator, offers a handy shortcut. The symbol for the operator is a plus and equal sign together. The operator means "append the stuff on the right of me to the end of the stuff on the left of me." Therefore, the above sequence would be shortened as follows:

```
var msg = "Four score"
msg += " and seven"
msg += " years ago,"
```

You can also combine the operators if the need arises:

```
var msg = "Four score"
msg += " and seven" + " years ago"
```

I use the add-by-value operator a lot when accumulating HTML text to be written to the current document or another window.

String methods

Of all the JavaScript global objects, the string object has the most diverse collection of methods associated with it. Many methods are designed to help scripts extract segments of a string. Another group, rarely used in my experience, lets methods style text for writing to the page (a scripted equivalent of tags for font size, style, and the like).

To use a string method, the string being acted upon becomes part of the reference, followed by the method name. All methods return a value of some kind. At times, the returned value is a converted version of the string object referred to in the method call. Therefore, if the returned value is not being used directly as a parameter for some method or function call, it is vital that the returned value is caught by a variable:

```
alert(string.methodName())
var result = string.methodName()
```

The following sections introduce you to several important string methods available to all browser brands and versions.

Changing string case

A pair of methods convert a string to all uppercase or lowercase letters:

```
var result = string.toUpperCase()
var result = string.toLowerCase()
```

Not surprisingly, you must observe the case of each letter of the method names if you want them to work. These methods come in handy for times when your scripts need to compare strings that may not have the same case (for example, a string in a lookup table compared to a string typed by a user). Because the methods don't change the original strings attached to the expressions, you can simply compare the evaluated results of the methods:

```
var foundMatch = false
if (stringA.toUpperCase() == stringB.toUpperCase()) {
        foundMatch = true
}
```

String searches

You can use the `string.indexOf()` method to determine if one string is contained by another. Even within JavaScript's own object data this can be useful information. For example, another property of the navigator object you used in Chapter 3 (`navigator.userAgent`) reveals a lot about the browser that has loaded the page. A script can investigate the value of that property for the existence of, say, "Win" to determine that the user has a Windows operating system. That short string might be buried somewhere inside a long string, and all the script needs to know is whether the short string is present in the longer one, wherever it might be.

The `string.indexOf()` method returns a number indicating the index value (zero based) of the character in the larger string where the smaller string begins. The key point about this method is that if no match occurs, the returned value is -1. To find out whether the smaller string is inside, all you need to test is whether the returned value is something other than -1.

Two strings are involved with this method, the shorter one and the longer one. The shorter string is the one that appears in the reference to the left of the method name; the longer string is inserted as a parameter to the `indexOf()` method. To demonstrate the method in action, the following fragment looks to see if the user is running Windows:

```
var isWindows = false
if ("Win".indexOf(navigator.userAgent") != -1) {
        isWindows = true
}
```

The operator in the `if` construction's condition (`!=`) is the inequality operator. You can read it as meaning "is not equal to."

Extracting characters and substrings

To extract a single character at a known position within a string, use the `charAt()` method. The parameter of the method is an index number (zero based) of the character to extract. When I say "extract," I don't mean delete, but rather grab a snapshot of the character. The original string is not modified in any way.

For example, consider a script in a main window that is capable of inspecting a variable, `stringA`, in another window that shows maps of different corporate buildings. When the window has a map of Building C in it, the `stringA` variable contains "Building C". Since the building letter is always at the tenth character position of the string (or number 9 in a zero-based counting world), the script can examine that one character to identify the map currently in that other window:

```
var stringA = "Building C"
var oneChar = stringA.charAt(9)
        // result: oneChar = "C"
```

Another method — `string.substring()` — lets you extract a contiguous sequence of characters, provided you know the starting and ending positions of the substring you want to grab a copy of. Importantly, the character at the ending position value is not part of the extraction: All applicable characters up to *but not including* that character are part of the extraction. The string from which the extraction is made appears to the left of the method name in the reference. Two parameters specify the starting and ending index values (zero based) for the start and end positions:

```
var stringA = "banana daiquiri"
var excerpt = stringA.substring(2,6)
       // result: excerpt = "nana"
```

String manipulation in JavaScript is fairly cumbersome compared to some other scripting languages. Higher level notions of words, sentences, or paragraphs are completely absent. Therefore, sometimes it takes a bit of scripting with string methods to accomplish what would seem like a simple goal. And yet you can put your knowledge of expression evaluation to the test as you assemble expressions that utilize heavily nested constructions. For example, the following fragment needs to create a new string that consists of everything from the larger string except the first word. Assuming the first word of other strings could be of any length, the second statement utilizes the `string.indexOf()` method to look for the first space character and adds 1 to that value to serve as the starting index value for an outer `string.substring()` method. For the second parameter, the `length` property of the string provides a basis for the ending character's index value (one more than the actual character needed).

```
var stringA = "The United States of America"
var excerpt = stringA.substring((stringA.indexOf(" ") + 1,
stringA.length)
       // result: excerpt = "United States of America"
```

Since creating statements like this one is not something you are likely to enjoy over and over again, I show you in Chapter 26 how to create your own library of string functions you can reuse in all of your scripts that need their string-handling facilities.

The Math Object

JavaScript provides ample facilities for math — far more than most scripters who don't have a background in computer science and math will use in a lifetime. But every genuine programming language needs these powers to accommodate clever programmers who can make windows fly in circles on the screen.

All of these powers are contained by the Math object. This object is unlike most of the rest in JavaScript in that you don't generate copies of the object to use. Instead your scripts summon a single Math object's properties and methods (inside Navigator, one Math object actually occurs per window or frame, but this has no impact whatsoever on your scripts). That Math object (with an uppercase M) is part of the reference to the property or method. Properties of the Math object are constant values, such as pi and the square root of two:

```
var piValue = Math.PI
var rootOfTwo = Math.SQRT2
```

Methods cover a wide range of trigonometric functions and other math functions that work on numeric values already defined in your script. For example, you can find which of two numbers is the larger:

```
var larger = Math.max(value1, value2)
```

Or you can raise one number to a power of ten:

```
var result = Math.pow(value1, power1)
```

More common, perhaps, is the method that rounds a value to the nearest integer value:

```
var result = Math.round(value1)
```

Another common request of the Math object is a random number. Although the feature was broken on Windows and Macintosh versions of Navigator 2, it works in all other versions and brands since. The `Math.random()` method returns a floating-point number between 0 and 1. If you are designing a script to act like a card game, you need random integers between 1 and 52; for dice, the range is 1 to 6 per die. To generate a random integer between zero and any top value, use the following formula:

```
Math.round(Math.random() * n)
```

where n is the top number. To generate random numbers between a different range use this formula:

```
Math.round(Math.random() * n) + m
```

where m is the lowest possible integer value of the range and n equals the top number of the range minus m. In other words n+m should add up to the highest number of the range you want. For the dice game, the formula for each die would be

```
newDieValue = Math.round(Math.random() * 5) + 1
```

One bit of help JavaScript doesn't offer is a way to specify a number formatting scheme. Floating-point math can display more than a dozen numbers to the right of the decimal. Moreover, results can be influenced by each operating system's platform-specific floating-point errors, especially in earlier versions of scriptable browsers. Any number formatting — for dollars and cents, for example — must be done through your own scripts. An example is provided in Chapter 27.

The Date Object

Working with dates beyond simple tasks can be difficult business in JavaScript. A lot of the difficulty comes with the fact that dates and times are calculated internally according to Greenwich mean time (GMT) — provided the visitor's own internal PC clock and control panel are set accurately. As a result of this complexity, better left for Chapter 28, this section of the tutorial touches on only the basics of the JavaScript Date object.

A scriptable browser contains one global Date object (in truth one Date object per window) that is always present, ready to be called upon at any moment. When you wish to work with a date, such as displaying today's date, you need to invoke the Date object constructor to obtain an instance of a date object tied to a specific time and date. For example, when you invoke the constructor without any parameters, as in

```
var today = new Date()
```

the Date object takes a snapshot of the PC's internal clock and returns a date object for that instant. The variable, today, contains not a ticking clock, but a value that can be examined, torn apart, and reassembled as needed for your script.

Internally, the value of a date object instance is the time, in milliseconds, from zero o'clock on January 1, 1970, in the Greenwich mean time zone — the world standard reference point for all time conversions. That's how a date object contains both date and time information.

You can also grab a snapshot of the Date object for a particular date and time in the past or future by specifying that information as parameters to the Date object constructor function:

```
var someDate = new Date("Month dd, yyyy hh:mm:ss")
var someDate = new Date("Month dd, yyyy")
var someDate = new Date(yy,mm,dd,hh,mm,ss)
var someDate = new Date(yy,mm,dd)
```

If you attempt to view the contents of a raw date object, JavaScript converts the value to the local time zone string as indicated by your PC's control panel setting. To see this in action, use Navigator to go to the javascript: URL where you can type in an expression to see its value. Enter the following:

```
new Date()
```

The current date and time as your PC's clock calculates it is displayed (even though JavaScript still stores the date object's millisecond count in the GMT zone). You can, however, extract components of the date object via a series of methods that you can apply to the date object instance. Table 10-1 shows an abbreviated listing of these properties and information about their values.

Be careful about values whose ranges start with zero, especially the months. The getMonth() and setMonth() method values are zero-based, so the numbers will be one less than the month numbers you are accustomed to working with (for example, January is 0, December is 11).

Table 10-1
Some Date Object Methods

Method	Value Range	Description
dateObj.getTime()	0-...	Milliseconds since 1/1/70 00:00:00 GMT
dateObj.getYear()	70-...	Specified year minus 1900; 4-digit year for 2000+
dateObj.getMonth()	0-11	Month within the year (January = 0)
dateObj.getDate()	1-31	Date within the month
dateObj.getDay()	0-6	Day of week (Sunday = 0)
dateObj.getHours()	0-23	Hour of the day in 24-hour time
dateObj.getMinutes()	0-59	Minute of the specified hour

(continued)

Table 10-1 (continued)

Method	Value Range	Description
dateObj.getSeconds()	0-59	Second within the specified minute
dateObj.setTime(val)	0-...	Milliseconds since 1/1/70 00:00:00 GMT
dateObj.setYear(val)	70-...	Specified year minus 1900; 4-digit year for 2000+
dateObj.setMonth(val)	0-11	Month within the year (January = 0)
dateObj.setDate(val)	1-31	Date within the month
dateObj.setDay(val)	0-6	Day of week (Sunday = 0)
dateObj.setHours(val)	0-23	Hour of the day in 24-hour time
dateObj.setMinutes(val)	0-59	Minute of the specified hour
dateObj.setSeconds(val)	0-59	Second within the specified minute

You may notice one difference about the methods that set values of a date object. Rather than returning some new value, these methods actually modify the value of the date object referenced in the call to the method.

Date Calculations

Performing calculations with dates requires working with the millisecond values of the date objects. This is the surest way to add, subtract, or compare date values. To demonstrate a few date object machinations, Listing 10-1 displays the current date and time as the page loads. Another script calculates the date and time seven days from the current date and time value.

In the Body portion, the first script runs as the page loads, setting a global variable, today, to the current date and time. The string equivalent is written to the page. In the second Body script, the document.write() method invokes the nextWeek() function to get a value to display. That function utilizes the today global variable, copying its millisecond value to a new variable, todayInMS. To get a date 7 days from now, the next statement simply adds the number of milliseconds in 7 days (60 seconds times 60 minutes times 24 hours times 7 days times 1000 milliseconds) to today's millisecond value. The script now needs a new date object calculated from the total milliseconds. This requires invoking the Date object constructor with the milliseconds as a parameter. The returned value is a date object, which is automatically converted to a string version for writing to the page. Letting JavaScript create the new date with the accumulated number of milliseconds is more accurate than trying to add 7 to the value returned by the date object's getDate() method. JavaScript automatically takes care of figuring out how many days there are in a month and leap years.

Listing 10-1: Date Object Calculations

```
<HTML>
<HEAD>
<TITLE>Date Calculation</TITLE>
<SCRIPT LANGUAGE="JavaScript">
function nextWeek() {
        var todayInMS = today.getTime()
        var nextWeekInMS = todayInMS + (60 * 60 * 24 * 7 * 1000)
        return new Date(nextWeekInMS)
}
</SCRIPT>
</HEAD>

<BODY>
Today is:
<SCRIPT LANGUAGE="JavaScript">
var today = new Date()
document.write(today)
</SCRIPT>
<BR>
Next week will be:
<SCRIPT LANGUAGE="JavaScript">
document.write(nextWeek())
</SCRIPT>
</BODY>
</HTML>
```

Many other quirks and complicated behavior await you if you script dates in your page. As later chapters demonstrate, however, it may be worth the effort.

Exercises

1. Create a Web page that has one form field for entry of the user's e-mail address and a Submit button. Include a presubmission validation routine that verifies that the text field has the @ symbol found in all e-mail addresses before allowing the form to be submitted.

2. Given the string "Netscape Navigator," fill in the blanks of the `string.substring()` method parameters here that yield the results shown to the right of each method call:

```
var myString = "Netscape Navigator"
myString.substring(___,___)   // result = "Net"
myString.substring(___,___)   // result = "gator"
myString.substring(___,___)   // result = "cape Nav"
```

3. Fill in the rest of the function in the listing that follows that would look through every character of the entry field and count how many times the letter "e" appears in the field. (Hint: All that is missing is a `for` repeat loop.)

```
<HTML>
<HEAD>
<TITLE>Wheel o' Fortuna</TITLE>
<SCRIPT LANGUAGE="JavaScript">
function countE(form) {
    var count = 0
    var inputString = form.mainstring.value.toUpperCase()
    missing code
    alert("The string has " + count + " instances of the letter e.")
}
</SCRIPT>
</HEAD>

<BODY>
<FORM>
Enter any string: <INPUT TYPE="text" NAME="mainstring" SIZE=30><BR>
<INPUT TYPE="button" VALUE="Count the Es" onClick="countE(this.form)">
</BODY>
</HTML>
```

4. Create a page that has two fields and one button. The button is to trigger a function that generates two random numbers between 1 and 6, placing each number in one of the fields. (This is used as a substitute for rolling a pair of dice in a board game.)

5. Create a page that displays the number of days between today and next Christmas.

✦   ✦   ✦

Scripting Frames and Multiple Windows

One of the cool aspects of JavaScript on the client is it
allows user actions in one frame or window to
influence what happens in other frames and windows. In this
section of the tutorial, you extend your existing knowledge of
object references to the realm of multiple frames and
windows.

Frames: Parents and Children

You probably noticed that at the top of the Navigator
document object hierarchy diagram (refer back to Figure 8-1)
the window object has some other object references
associated with it. Back in Chapter 8 you learned that self is
synonymous with window when the reference applies to the
same window that contains the script's document. In this
lesson, you'll learn the roles of the other three object
references — frame, top, and parent.

Loading an ordinary HTML document into the browser
creates a model in the browser that starts out with one
window object and the document it contains (the document
likely contains other elements, but I'm not concerned with
that stuff yet). The top rungs of the hierarchy model are as
simple as can be, as shown in Figure 11-1. This is where
references begin with window or self (or with document,
since the current window is assumed).

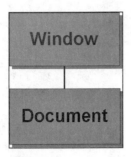

Figure 11-1: Single-frame window and document hierarchy

The instant a framesetting document loads into a browser, the browser starts building a slightly different hierarchy model. The precise structure of that model depends entirely on the structure of the frameset defined in that framesetting document. Consider the following skeletal frameset definition:

```
<HTML>
<FRAMESET COLS="50%,50%">
        <FRAME NAME="leftFrame" SRC="somedoc1.html">
        <FRAME NAME="rightFrame" SRC="somedoc2.html">
</FRAMESET>
</HTML>
```

This HTML splits the browser window into two frames side by side, with a different document loaded into each frame. The model is concerned only with structure — it doesn't care about the relative sizes of the frames or whether they're set up in columns or rows.

Framesets establish relationships among the frames in the collection. Borrowing terminology from the object-oriented programming world, the framesetting document loads into a *parent* window. Each of the frames defined in that parent window document is a *child* frame (although you won't be using the child term in scripting). Figure 11-2 shows the hierarchical model of a two-frame environment. This illustration reveals a lot of subtleties about the relationships among framesets and their frames.

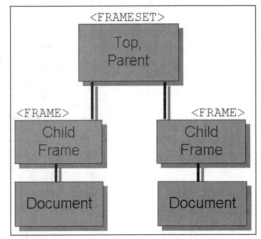

Figure 11-2: Two-frame window and document hierarchy

It is often difficult at first to visualize the frameset as a window object in the hierarchy. After all, with the exception of the URL showing in the Location field, you don't see anything about the frameset in the browser. But that window object exists in the object model. Notice, too, that the framesetting parent window has no document object. This may also seem odd, since the window obviously requires an HTML file containing the specifications for the frameset. But because the HTML of a framesetting file has no <BODY> tag or other document-centric elements, no document object in this portion of the object model is loaded in the browser.

If you were to add a script to the framesetting document that needed to access a property or method of that window object, references would be like any single-frame situation. Think about the point of view of a script located in that window. Its immediate universe is the very same window.

Things get more interesting when you start looking at the child frames. Each of these frames contains a document object whose content you see in the browser window. And the structure is such that each document is entirely independent of the other. It is as if each document lived in its own browser window. Indeed, that's why each child frame is also a window type of object. A frame has all the properties and methods of the window object that occupies the entire browser.

From the point of view of either child window in Figure 11-2, its immediate container is the parent window. When a parent window is at the very top of the hierarchical model loaded in the browser, that window is also referred to as the top object.

References among Family Members

Given the frame structure of Figure 11-2, it's time to look at how a script in any one of those windows would access objects, functions, or variables in the others. An important point to remember about this facility is that if a script has access to an object, function, or global variable in its own window, that same item can be reached by a script from another frame in the hierarchy (provided both documents come from the same Web server).

A script reference may need to take one of three possible routes in the two-generation hierarchy described so far: parent to child; child to parent; or child to child.

Each of the paths between these windows requires a different reference style.

Parent-to-child references

Probably the least common direction taken by references is when a script in the parent document needs to access some element of one of its frames. From the point of view of the parent, it contains two or more frames, which means the frames are also stored in the model as an array of frame objects. You can address a frame by array syntax or by the name you assign to it with the NAME attribute inside the <FRAME> tag. In the following examples of reference syntax, I substitute a placeholder named *ObjFuncVarName* for whatever object, function, or global variable you intend to access in the distant window or frame. Remember that each visible frame contains a document object, which is generally the container of elements you will be scripting — be sure references include the document. With that in mind, a reference from a parent to one of its child frames follows either of the following models:

```
[window.]frames[n].ObjFuncVarName
[window.]frameName.ObjFuncVarName
```

Index values for frames are based on the order in which their <FRAME> tags appear in the framesetting document. You will make your life easier, however, if you assign recognizable names to each frame and use the frame's name in the reference. Some problems also existed in early scriptable browsers with including the window reference at the start of all of the references described in this chapter. I recommend omitting window from all such references.

Child-to-parent references

It is not uncommon to place scripts in the parent (in the Head portion) that multiple child frames or multiple documents in a frame use as a kind of script library. By loading in the frameset, they load only once while the frameset is visible. If other documents load into the frames over time, they can take advantage of the parent's scripts without having to load their own copies into the browser.

From the child's point of view, the next level up the hierarchy is called the parent. Therefore, a reference to items at that level is simply

```
parent.ObjFuncVarName
```

If the item accessed in the parent is a function that returns a value, the returned value transcends the parent-child borders without hesitation.

When the parent window is also at the very top of the object hierarchy currently loaded into the browser, you can optionally refer to it as the top window, as in

```
top.ObjFuncVarName
```

Using the top reference can be hazardous if for some reason your Web page gets displayed in some other Web site's frameset. What is your top window is not the master frameset's top window. Therefore, I recommend using the parent reference whenever possible.

Child-to-child references

The browser needs a bit more assistance when it comes to getting one child window to communicate with one of its siblings. One of the properties of any window or frame is its parent (if a parent exists). A reference must use this property to work its way out of the current frame to a point that both child frames have in common — the parent in this case. Once the reference is at the parent level, the rest of the reference can carry on as if starting at the parent. Thus, from one child to one of its siblings, you can use either of the following reference formats:

```
parent.frames[n].ObjFuncVarName
parent.frameName.ObjFuncVarName
```

A reference from the other sibling back to the first would look the same, but the frames[] array index or frameName part of the reference would be different. Of course, much more complex frame hierarchies are possible in HTML. An example of a three-generation frameset is shown in Chapter 14. Even so, the document object model and referencing scheme provides a solution for the most deeply nested and gnarled frame arrangement you can think of — following the same precepts you just learned.

Frame Scripting Tips

One of the first mistakes that frame scripting newcomers make is writing immediate script statements that call upon other frames while the pages are loading. The problem here is there is no guaranteed document loading sequence. All you know for sure is that the parent document begins loading first. Regardless of the order of <FRAME> tags, child frames can begin loading at any time. Moreover, a frame's loading time depends on other elements in the document, such as images or Java applets.

Fortunately, you can use a certain technique to initiate a script once all of the documents in the frameset have completely loaded. Just as the onLoad= event handler for a document fires when that document has fully loaded, a parent's onLoad= event handler fires after the onLoad= event handlers in its child frames have fired. Therefore, you can specify an onLoad= event handler in the <FRAMESET> tag. That handler might invoke a function in the framesetting document that then has the freedom to tap the objects, functions, or variables of all frames throughout the object hierarchy.

Controlling Multiple Frames — Navigation Bars

If you are enamored of frames as a way to help organize a complex Web page, you may find yourself wanting to control the navigation of one or more frames from a static navigation panel. I demonstrate here scripting concepts for such control using an application called Decision Helper (which can be found in the Bonus Applications Chapters folder on the CD-ROM). The application, consists of four frames (see Figure 11-3). The top-left frame is one image that has four graphical buttons in it. The goal is to turn that image into a client-side image map, and script it so the pages change in the two right-hand frames. In the upper-right frame, the script will load an entirely different document along the sequence of five different documents that go in there; in the lower-right frame, the script will navigate to one of five anchors to display the segment of instructions that applies to the document loaded in the upper-right frame.

Listing 11-1 shows a slightly modified version of the actual file for the Decision Helper application. The listing contains a couple of new objects and concepts not yet covered in this tutorial. But as you will see, they are extensions to what you already know about JavaScript and objects. To help simplify the discussion here, I have removed the scripting and HTML for the top and bottom button of the area map. Only the two navigation arrows are covered here.

Look first at the HTML section for the Body portion. Almost everything there is standard stuff for defining client-side image maps. The coordinates form rectangles around each of the arrows in the larger image. The HREF attributes for the two areas point to JavaScript functions defined in the Head portion of the document.

In the frameset that defines the Decision Helper application, names are assigned to each frame. The upper-right frame is called entryForms; the lower-left frame is called instructions.

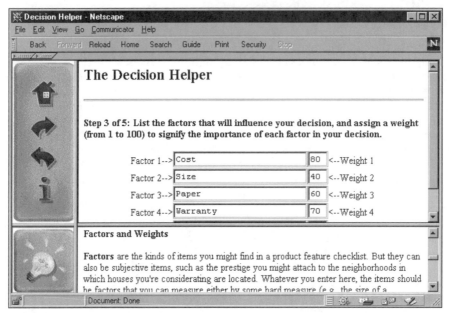

Figure 11-3: The Decision Helper screen

Knowing that navigation from page to page in the upper-right frame would require knowledge of which page is currently loaded there, I built some other scripting into both the parent document and each of the documents that loads into that frame. In the parent document is defined a global variable called `currTitle`. Its value is an integer indicating which page of the sequence (1 through 5) is currently loaded. An `onLoad=` event handler in each of the five documents (named dh1.htm, dh2.htm, dh3.htm, dh4.htm, dh5.htm) assigns its page number to that parent global variable. This arrangement allows that value to be shared easily with all frames in the frameset.

When a user clicks on the right-facing arrow to move to the next page, the `goNext()` function is called. The first statement gets the `currTitle` value from the parent window, and assigns it to a local variable, `currOffset`. An `if...else` construction tests whether the current page number is less than five. If so, the add-by-value operator adds one to the local variable so I can use that value in the next two statements.

In those next two statements, I adjust the content of the two right frames. Using the parent reference to gain access to both frames, I set the location object of the top-right frame to the name of the file next in line (by concatenating the number with the surrounding parts of the filename). The second statement sets the `location.hash` property (a property that controls the anchor being navigated to) to the corresponding anchor in the instructions frame (anchor names `help1`, `help2`, `help3`, `help4`, and `help5`).

A click of the left-facing arrow reverses the process, subtracting 1 from the current page number (using the subtract-by-value operator) and changing the same frames accordingly.

Listing 11-1: A Graphical Navigation Bar

```
<HTML>
<HEAD>
<TITLE>Navigation Bar</TITLE>
<SCRIPT LANGUAGE="JavaScript">
<!-- start
function goNext() {
        var currOffset = parent.currTitle
        if (currOffset <5) {
           currOffset += 1
           parent.entryForms.location = "dh" + currOffset + ".htm"
           parent.instructions.location.hash = "help" + currOffset
        } else {
           alert("This is the last form.")
        }
}
function goPrev() {
        var currOffset = parseInt(parent.currTitle)
        if (currOffset > 1) {
           currOffset -= 1
           parent.entryForms.location = "dh" + currOffset + ".htm"
           parent.instructions.location.hash = "help" + currOffset
        } else {
           alert("This is the first form.")
        }
}
// end -->
</SCRIPT>
</HEAD>
<BODY bgColor="white">
<MAP NAME="navigation">
<AREA SHAPE="RECT" COORDS="25,80,66,116" HREF="javascript:goNext()">
<AREA SHAPE="RECT" COORDS="24,125,67,161" HREF="javascript:goPrev()">
</MAP>
<IMG SRC="dhNav.gif" HEIGHT=240 WIDTH=96 BORDER=0 USEMAP="#navigation">
</BODY>
</HTML>
```

The example shown in Listing 11-1 is one of many ways to script a navigation frame in JavaScript. Whatever methodology you use, there will be much interaction among the frames in the frameset.

More about Window References

Back in Chapter 8, you saw how to create a new window and communicate with it by way of the window object reference returned from the `window.open()` method. In this section, I introduce you to how one of those subwindows can communicate with objects, functions, and variables back in the window or frame that created the subwindow.

In scriptable browsers except for Navigator 2, every window has a property called opener. The property contains a reference to the window or frame that held the script whose window.open() statement generated the subwindow. For the main browser window and frames therein, this value is null. Because the opener property is a valid window reference, you can use it to begin the reference to items back in the original window, just like a script in a child frame would use parent to access items in the parent document. The parent-child terminology doesn't apply to subwindows, however.

Listings 11-2 and 11-3 contain documents that work together in separate windows. Listing 11-2 displays a button that opens a smaller window and loads Listing 11-3 into it. The main window document also contains a text field that gets filled in when you enter text into a corresponding field in the subwindow.

In the main window document, the newWindow() function generates the new window. Because no other statements in the document require the reference to the new window just opened, the statement does not assign its returned value to any variable. This is an acceptable practice in JavaScript if you don't need the returned value of a function or method.

Listing 11-2: **A Main Window Document**

```
<HTML>
<HEAD>
<TITLE>Main Document</TITLE>
<SCRIPT LANGUAGE="JavaScript">
function newWindow() {
        window.open("subwind.htm","sub","HEIGHT=200,WIDTH=200")
}
</SCRIPT>
</HEAD>

<BODY>
<FORM>
<INPUT TYPE="button" VALUE="New Window" onClick="newWindow()">
<BR>
Text incoming from subwindow:
<INPUT TYPE="Text" NAME="entry">
<FORM>
</BODY>
</HTML>
```

All of the action in the subwindow document comes in the onChange= event handler of the text field. It assigns the subwindow field's own value to the value of the field in the opener window's document. Remember that the contents of each window and frame belong to a document. So even after your reference targets a specific window or frame, the reference must continue helping the browser find the ultimate destination, which is generally some element of the document.

Listing 11-3: **A Subwindow Document**

```
<HTML>
<HEAD>
<TITLE>A SubDocument</TITLE>
</HEAD>
<BODY>
<FORM onSubmit="return false">
Enter text to be copied to the main window:
<INPUT TYPE="text" onChange="opener.document.forms[0].entry.value =
this.value">
</FORM>
</HTML>
```

Just one more lesson to go before I let you explore all the details elsewhere in the book. I'll use the final class to show you some fun things you can do with your Web pages, like changing images when the user rolls the mouse atop a picture.

Exercises

Before answering the first three questions, study the structure of the following frameset for a Web site that lists college courses:

```
<FRAMESET ROWS="85%,15%">
    <FRAMESET COLS="20%,80%">
        <FRAME NAME="mechanics" SRC="history101M..html">
        <FRAME NAME="description" SRC="history101D.html">
    </FRAMESET>
    <FRAMESET COLS="100%">
        <FRAME NAME="navigation" SRC="navigator.html">
    </FRAMESET>
</FRAMESET>
</HTML>
```

1. Whenever a document loads into the description frame, it has an `onLoad=` event handler that stores a course identifier in the framesetting document's global variable called `currCourse`. Write the `onLoad=` event handler that sets this value to "history101".

2. Draw a block diagram that describes the hierarchy of the windows and frames represented in the frameset definition.

3. Write the JavaScript statements located in the navigation frame that load the file "french201M.html" into the mechanics frame and the file "french201D.html" into the description frame.

4. While a frameset is still loading, a JavaScript error message suddenly appears saying that "window.document.navigation.form.selector is undefined." What do you think is happening in the application's scripts, and how can the problem be solved?

5. A script in a child frame of the main window uses `window.open()` to generate a second window. How would a script in the second window access the location object (URL) of the parent window in the main browser window?

✦   ✦   ✦

Images and Dynamic HTML

◆ ◆ ◆ ◆

In This Chapter

How to precache
images

How to swap images
for mouse rollovers

What you can do
with Dynamic HTML
and scripting

◆ ◆ ◆ ◆

The previous eight lessons have been intensive, covering a lot of ground for both programming concepts and JavaScript. Now it's time to apply what you've learned to learn some more. I will cover two areas here. First, I show you how to implement the ever-popular mouse rollover, where images swap when the user rolls the cursor around the screen. Finally, I introduce you to concepts surrounding scripted control of Dynamic HTML in the level 4 browsers, and the Netscape <LAYER> tag in particular.

The Image Object

One of the objects contained by the document is the image object. Unfortunately this object is not available in all scriptable browsers. You can script it in Navigator 3 and later or Internet Explorer 4. Therefore, everything you learn here about the image object won't apply to Navigator 2 or Internet Explorer 3 for Windows.

Because a document can have more than one image, image object references are stored in the object model as an array. You can therefore reference an image by array index or image name:

```
document.images[n]
document.imageName
```

Each of the <IMG> tag's attributes is accessible to JavaScript as a property of the image object. No mouse-related event handlers are affiliated with the image object (although they are in Internet Explorer 4). If you want to make an image a clickable item, surround it with a link (and set the image's border to zero) or attach a client-side image map to it. The combination of a link and image is how you make a clickable image button (the image type of form input element is not a scriptable object).

Interchangeable images

When the image became an object with the release of Navigator 3, it did so with a special behavior: a script could change the image occupying the rectangular space already occupied by an image. This was one of the first examples of dynamically changing a page's content after a page has loaded.

The script behind this kind of image change is simple enough. All it entails is assigning a new URL to the image object's `src` property. The size of the image on the page is governed by the `HEIGHT` and `WIDTH` attributes set in the `<IMG>` tag as the page loads and cannot be modified. Therefore, you need to select your images carefully so that all images that supply content to a document image object are the same size. Otherwise the image scales to the original dimensions assigned to the object.

Precaching images

Images often take several extra seconds to download from a Web server. If you are designing your page so an image changes in response to user action, you usually want the same fast response that users are accustomed to in multimedia programs. Making the user wait many seconds for an image to change can severely distract from enjoyment of the page.

To the rescue comes the ability to precache images. The tactic that works best is to preload the image into the browser's image cache when the page initially loads. Users will be less impatient for those few extra seconds during the main page loading than they would be while waiting for an image to change.

Precaching an image requires constructing an image object in memory. An image object created in memory is different in some respects from the document image object that you create with the `<IMG>` tag. Memory-only objects are created by script, and you don't see them on the page at all. But their presence in the document forces the browser to load the images as the page loads. JavaScript provides a constructor function for the memory type of image object as follows:

```
var myImage = new Image(width, height)
```

Parameters to the constructor function are the width and height of the image. These dimensions should match the width and height of the `<IMG>` tag attributes where the new image will eventually go. Once the image object exists in memory, you can then assign a filename or URL to the `src` property of that image object:

```
myImage.src = "someArt.gif"
```

When JavaScript encounters a statement assigning a URL to an image object's `src` property, it instructs the browser to go out and load that image into the image cache. All the user sees is some extra loading information in the status bar, as if another image were in the page. By the time the `onLoad=` event handler fires, all images generated in this way are tucked away in the image cache. You can then assign your cached image's `src` property or the actual image URL to the `src` property of the document image created with the `<IMG>` tag:

```
document.images[0].src = myImage.src
document.images[0].src = someArt.gif
```

The change to the image in the document is instantaneous.

Listing 12-1 shows a simple listing for a page that has one `<IMG>` tag and a select list that lets you replace the document image with any of four precached images (including the original image specified for the tag). If you type this listing — as I strongly recommend — you can obtain copies of the four image files from the companion CD-ROM in the Chapter 18 listings.

As the page loads, it executes several statements immediately. These statements create four new memory image objects and assigns a file name to the src property of each one. These images will be loaded into the image cache as the page loads. Down in the Body portion of the document, an <IMG> tag stakes its turf on the page and loads one of the images as a starting image.

A select object lists user-friendly names for the pictures while housing the names of the image files (without the extension) already precached. When the user makes a selection from the list, the loadCached() function extracts the value of the selected item and assembles the complete name of the desired image. That name is assigned to the src property of the document's image object, and the image changes in a snap.

Listing 12-1: **Precaching Images**

```
<HTML>
<HEAD>
<TITLE>Image Object</TITLE>
<SCRIPT LANGUAGE="JavaScript1.1">
// pre-cache four images
image1 = new Image(120,90)
image1.src = "desk1.gif"
image2 = new Image(120,90)
image2.src = "desk2.gif"
image3 = new Image(120,90)
image3.src = "desk3.gif"
image4 = new Image(120,90)
image4.src = "desk4.gif"

// load an image chosen from select list
function loadCached(list) {
        var img = list.options[list.selectedIndex].value
        document.thumbnail.src = img + ".gif"
}
</SCRIPT>
</HEAD>

<BODY >
<H2>Image Object</H2>
<IMG SRC="desk1.gif" NAME="thumbnail" HEIGHT=90 WIDTH=120>
<FORM>
<SELECT NAME="cached" onChange="loadCached(this)">
<OPTION VALUE="desk1">Bands
<OPTION VALUE="desk2">Clips
<OPTION VALUE="desk3">Lamp
<OPTION VALUE="desk4">Erasers
</SELECT>
</FORM>
</BODY>
</HTML>
```

Creating image rollovers

A favorite technique to add some pseudo-excitement to a page is to swap button images as the user rolls the cursor atop them. The degree of change to the image is largely a matter of taste. The effect can be subtle — a slight highlight or glow around the edge of the original image — or drastic — a radical change of color. Whatever your approach, the scripting is the same.

When several of these graphical buttons occur in a group, I tend to organize the memory image objects as arrays and create naming and numbering schemes that facilitate working with the arrays. Listing 12-2 shows such an arrangement for four buttons that control a jukebox. The code in the listing is confined to the image-swapping portion of the application. This is the most complex and lengthiest listing of the tutorial, so it requires a bit of explanation as it goes along.

Listing 12-2: **Image Rollovers**

```
<HTML>
<HEAD>
<TITLE>Jukebox/Image Rollovers</TITLE>
```

Because the image object was not in Navigator until Version 3, I limit access to the code via the LANGUAGE attribute of the <SCRIPT> tag. Here the language is specified as JavaScript Version 1.1, the version incorporated into Navigator 3. All versions of Navigator beyond that and Version 4 of Internet Explorer will be able to use this script.

```
<SCRIPT LANGUAGE="JavaScript1.1">
```

The first task in the script is to build two arrays of image objects. One array stores information about the images depicting the graphical button's "off" position; the other is for images depicting their "on" position. After creating the array and assigning new blank image objects to the first four elements of the array, I go through the array again, this time assigning file pathnames to the src property of each object stored in the array. Since these lines of code are executing as the page loads, the images load into the image cache along the way.

```
// pre-cache all 'off' button images
var offImgArray = new Array()
offImgArray[0] = new Image(75,33)
offImgArray[1] = new Image(75,33)
offImgArray[2] = new Image(75,33)
offImgArray[3] = new Image(86,33)

// off image array -- set 'off' image path for each button
offImgArray[0].src = "images/playoff.jpg"
offImgArray[1].src = "images/stopoff.jpg"
offImgArray[2].src = "images/pauseoff.jpg"
offImgArray[3].src = "images/rewindoff.jpg"

// pre-cache all 'on' button images
var onImgArray = new Array()
onImgArray[0] = new Image(75,33)
onImgArray[1] = new Image(75,33)
onImgArray[2] = new Image(75,33)
onImgArray[3] = new Image(86,33)
```

```
// on image array -- set 'on' image path for each button
onImgArray[0].src = "images/playon.jpg"
onImgArray[1].src = "images/stopon.jpg"
onImgArray[2].src = "images/pauseon.jpg"
onImgArray[3].src = "images/rewindon.jpg"
```

As you will see in the HTML below, when the user rolls the mouse atop any of the document image objects, the onMouseOver= event handler (from the link object surrounding the document image object) invokes the imageOn() function, passing an index value for the particular image. The index value corresponds to the index values of the image arrays defined above. The imageOn() function uses that index value to assign the URL from the onImgArray entry to the corresponding document image src property.

```
// functions that swap images & status bar
function imageOn(i) {
        document.images[i].src = onImgArray[i].src
}
```

The same goes for the onMouseOut= event handler, which needs to turn the image off by invoking the imageOff() function with the same index value.

```
function imageOff(i) {
        document.images[i].src = offImgArray[i].src
}
```

Both the onMouseOver= and onMouseOut= event handlers set the status bar to prevent the ugly javascript: URL from appearing there as the user rolls the mouse atop the image. The onMouseOut= event handler sets the status bar message to an empty string.

```
function setMsg(msg) {
        window.status = msg
        return true
}
```

For this demonstration, I have disabled the functions that control the jukebox. But I leave the empty function definitions here so they catch the calls made by the clicks of the links associated with the images.

```
// controller functions (disabled)
function playIt() {
}
function stopIt() {
}
function pauseIt(){
}
function rewindIt() {
}
</SCRIPT>
</HEAD>

<BODY>
<CENTER>
<FORM>
Jukebox Controls<BR>
```

(continued)

Listing 12-2 *(continued)*

I surround each document image object with a link because the link object has the event handlers needed to respond to the mouse rolling over the area. Each link's onMouseOver= event handler calls the imageOn() function with the index value of this image's position in both image arrays defined earlier. Because both the onMouseOver= and onMouseOut= event handlers require a return true statement to work, I combined the second function call (to setMsg()) with the return true requirement. The setMsg() function always returns true, which is combined with the return keyword before the call to the setMsg() function. It's just a trick to reduce the amount of code in these event handlers.

```
<A HREF="javascript:playIt()" onMouseOver="imageOn(0); return
setMsg('Play the selected tune')" onMouseOut="imageOff(0); return
setMsg('')">
        <IMG SRC="images/playoff.jpg" NAME="hiliteBtn0" HEIGHT=33
WIDTH=75 BORDER=0></A>
<A HREF="javascript:stopIt()" onMouseOver="imageOn(1); return
setMsg('Stop the playing tune')" onMouseOut="imageOff(1); return
setMsg('')">
        <IMG SRC="images/stopoff.jpg" NAME="hiliteBtn1" HEIGHT=33
WIDTH=75 BORDER=0></A>
<A HREF="javascript:pauseIt()" onMouseOver="imageOn(2); return
setMsg('Pause the playing tune')" onMouseOut="imageOff(2); return
setMsg('')">
        <IMG SRC="images/pauseoff.jpg" NAME="hiliteBtn2" HEIGHT=33
WIDTH=75 BORDER=0></A>
<A HREF="javascript:rewindIt()" onMouseOver="imageOn(3); return
setMsg('Rewind back to the beginning')" onMouseOut="imageOff(3); return
setMsg('')">
        <IMG SRC="images/rewindoff.jpg" NAME="hiliteBtn3" HEIGHT=33
WIDTH=86 BORDER=0></A>
</FORM>
</CENTER>
</BODY>
</HTML>
```

The results of this lengthy script can be seen in Figure 12-1. As the user rolls the mouse atop one of the images, it changes from a light to dark color by swapping the entire image.

More Dynamism in HTML

The image object swapping technique is but a preview of what the newest developments in Dynamic HTML are all about. With each new generation of browser, scripts can change more content on the fly. Navigator's implementation of this involves a new object and tag. The <LAYER> tag identifies an object within a document that can contain its own separate document and can be positioned and sized anywhere in the document. It is kind of like a floating frame. But unlike a frame, a layer is contained by a document, not a parent window.

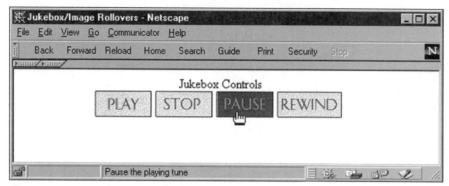

Figure 12-1: Typical mouse rollover image swapping

As described in depth in Chapter 19, the layer object has a large number of properties and methods, most of which are unique to the layer object — new behaviors and facilities for a new kind of object. Most of the methods, for example, concern themselves with the positioning and viewable size of the layer. You can also hide a layer and change the HTML that goes into a layer after the page has loaded.

Internet Explorer 4 treats Dynamic HTML differently, and does not implement a layer object. But as you will discover in Chapter 41, it is possible to create Dynamic HTML pages that work with both systems, thanks to industry standards efforts in this arena.

And so ends the final lesson of the *JavaScript Bible, Third Edition* tutorial. If you have gone through every lesson and tried your hand at the exercises, you are now ready to dive into the rest of the book to learn the fine details and many more features of both the document object model and the JavaScript language.

Exercises

1. Explain the difference between a document image object and the memory type of image object.

2. Write the JavaScript statements needed to precache an image named "jane.jpg" that will later be used to replace the document image defined by the following HTML:

   ```
   <IMG NAME="people" SRC="john.jpg" HEIGHT=120 WIDTH=100>
   ```

3. With the help of the code you wrote for question 2, write the JavaScript statement that replaces the document image with the memory image.

4. Document image objects do not have event handlers for mouse events. How do you trigger scripts needed to swap images for mouse rollovers?

✦   ✦   ✦

JavaScript Object and Language Reference

JavaScript Essentials

◆ ◆ ◆ ◆

In This Chapter

Understanding the document object model

Where scripts go in your documents

How to develop a single application for multiple browser versions

◆ ◆ ◆ ◆

The purpose of most JavaScript scripts is to make a Web page interactive, whether or not a program is running on the server to enhance that interactivity. Making a page interactive means tracking user action and responding with some visible change on the page. The avenues for communication between user and script include familiar on-screen elements, such as fields and buttons, as well as dynamic content in level 4 browsers.

To assist the scripter in working with these elements, the browser and JavaScript implements them as software objects. These objects have *properties* that often define the visual appearance of the object. Objects also have *methods,* which are the actions or commands that an object can carry out. Finally, these objects have *event handlers* that trigger the scripts you write in response to an action in the document (usually instigated by the user). This chapter begins by helping you understand that the realm of possibilities for each JavaScript object is the key to knowing how you can use JavaScript to convert an idea into a useful Web page. From there you see how to add scripts to an HTML page and learn several techniques to develop applications for a wide range of browsers — including nonscriptable browsers.

Language and Document Objects

As described briefly in Chapter 2, the environment you will come to know as JavaScript scripting is composed of two quite separate pieces: the core JavaScript language and the document object models of "things" you script with the language. By separating the core language from the objects it works with, the language's designers created a programming language that can be linked to a variety of object collections for different environments. In fact, even within Web applications, the same core JavaScript language is applied to the browser document object model and the server-side object model for processing requests and communicating with databases. Everything an author knows about the core language can be applied equally to client-side and server-side JavaScript.

Core language standard — ECMAScript

Although the JavaScript language was first developed by Netscape, Microsoft incorporated its version of the language, called JScript, in Internet Explorer 3. The core language part of JScript is essentially identical to that of JavaScript in Netscape Navigator, albeit usually one generation behind. Where the two browsers greatly differ, however, is in their document object models.

As mentioned in Chapter 2, standards efforts are in various stages to address potential incompatibilities among browsers. The core language is the first component to achieve standard status. Through the European standards body called ECMA, a formal standard for the language has been agreed to and published. This language, dubbed ECMAScript, is roughly the same as JavaScript 1.1 in Netscape Navigator 3. The standard defines how various data types are treated, how operators work, what various data-specific syntax looks like, and other language characteristics. You can view the ECMA-262 specification at http://www.ecma.ch. If you are a student of programming languages, you will find the document fascinating; if you simply want to script your pages, you will probably find the minutia mind-boggling.

Both Netscape and Microsoft have pledged to make their browsers compliant with this standard. Because of the fortuitous timing of the completion of the standard and the formal release of Internet Explorer 4, the latest version of the Microsoft browser is the first to comply with ECMAScript (with a couple minor omissions). Navigator 3 and 4 are already very close to the standard.

Document object standard

A recommendation for a document object model standard has yet to be finalized as this book goes to press. A comparison of the object models in Navigator 4 and Internet Explorer 4 reveals what appears to be diverging strategies — at least for now. While Navigator currently adheres to a fairly simple model, as previewed in earlier chapters and discussed in more detail later in this chapter, Internet Explorer 4 defines an object model that is at once extremely flexible and significantly more complicated to work with.

A key beneficiary of the added complexity in Internet Explorer 4's object model is the scripter who wishes to make a lot of changes to content on the fly — beyond the kind of object positioning possible with standard Cascading Style Sheet-Positioning (see Chapter 41). Internet Explorer 4's page rendering engine is fast enough to reflow content when a script changes the text inside a tag or the size of an object. Virtually everything that can be defined in HTML with a tag is an object in Internet Explorer 4. Moreover, properties for each of these objects include the body text that appears in the document and the very HTML for the element itself — all of which can be modified on the fly without reloading the document.

Standards efforts on the document object model are under way under the auspices of the W3C, the same organization that oversees the HTML specification. While both Netscape and Microsoft again pledge to support industry standards, each company is taking its own route until this particular standard is established, and both are not bashful about including their own proprietary extensions.

Later in this chapter, I say more about how to address issues of incompatibility among browser versions and brands. Suffice it to say that because this book focuses on Netscape's implementation of the JavaScript language, it also focuses on its document object model. Throughout the rest of this chapter, when I refer to objects and the object hierarchy, I am talking about document objects, as opposed to core language objects.

The Object Hierarchy

In the tutorial chapters of Part II, I speak of the JavaScript *object hierarchy*. In other object-oriented languages, object hierarchy plays a much greater role than it does in JavaScript (you don't have to worry about related terms, such as classes, inheritance, and instances, in JavaScript). Even so, you cannot ignore the hierarchy concept, because much of your code relies on your ability to write *references* to objects that depend on their position within the hierarchy.

Calling these objects *JavaScript objects* is not entirely accurate either. These are really browser document objects: you just happen to use the JavaScript language to bring them to life. Technically speaking, JavaScript objects are the ones that apply to data types and other core language objects separate from the document. These objects are covered in many chapters, beginning with Chapter 26. The more you can keep document and core language objects separate in your head, the more quickly you'll be able to deal with browser brand compatibility issues.

Hierarchy as road map

For the programmer, the primary role of the document object hierarchy is to provide scripts with a way to reference a particular object among all the objects that a browser window can contain. The hierarchy acts as a road map the script can use to know precisely which object to address.

Consider, for a moment, a scene in which you and your friend Tony are in a high school classroom. It's getting hot and stuffy as the afternoon sun pours in through the wall of windows on the west side of the room. You say to Tony, "Would you please open a window?" and motion your head toward a particular window in the room. In programming terms, you've issued a command to an object (whether or not Tony appreciates the comparison). This human interaction has many advantages over anything you can do in programming. First, by making eye contact with Tony before you spoke, he knew that he was the intended recipient of the command. Second, your body language passed along some parameters with that command, pointing ever so subtly to a particular window on a particular wall.

If, instead, you were in the principal's office using the public address system, and you broadcasted the same command, "Would you please open a window?" no one would know what you meant. Issuing a command without directing it to an object is a waste of time, because every object would think, "That can't be meant for me." To accomplish the same goal as your one-on-one command, the broadcasted command would have to be something like "Would Tony Jeffries in Room 312 please open the middle window on the west wall?"

Let's convert this last command to JavaScript "dot" syntax form (see Chapter 4). Recall from the tutorial that a reference to an object starts with the most global point of view and narrows to the most specific point of view. From the point of view of the principal's office, the location hierarchy of the target object is `room312.Jeffries.Tony`

You could also say that Tony's knowledge about how to open a window is one of Tony's methods. The complete reference to Tony and his method then becomes

`room312.Jeffries.Tony.openWindow()`

Your job isn't complete yet. The method requires a parameter detailing which window to open. In this case, the window you want is the middle window of the west wall of Room 312. Or, from the hierarchical point of view of the principal's office, it becomes

`room312.westWall.middleWindow`

This object road map is the parameter for Tony's `openWindow()` method. Therefore, the entire command that comes over the PA system should be

`room312.Jeffries.Tony.openWindow(room312.westWall.middleWindow)`

If, instead of barking out orders while sitting in the principal's office, you were attempting the same task via radio from an orbiting space shuttle to all the inhabitants on Earth, imagine how laborious your object hierarchy would be. The complete reference to Tony's `openWindow()` method and the window that you want opened would have to be mighty long to distinguish the desired objects from the billions of objects within the space shuttle's view.

The point is that the smaller the scope of the object-oriented world you're programming, the more you can assume about the location of objects. For JavaScript, the scope is no wider than the browser itself. In other words, every object that a JavaScript script can work with is within the browser application. A script does not access anything about your computer hardware, operating system, or desktop, or any other stuff beyond the browser program.

The JavaScript document object road map

Figure 13-1 shows the complete JavaScript document object hierarchy as implemented in Netscape Navigator 4. Notice that the window object is the topmost object in the entire scheme. Everything you script in JavaScript is in the browser's window — whether it be the window itself or a form element.

Of all the objects shown in Figure 13-1, you are likely to work most of the time with the ones that appear in boldface. Objects whose names appear in italics are synonyms for the window object, and are used only in some circumstances.

Pay attention to the shading of the concentric rectangles. Every object in the same shaded area is at the same level relative to the window object. When a link from an object extends to the next darker shaded rectangle, that object contains all the objects in darker areas. There exists at most one of these links between levels. A window object contains a document object; a document object contains a form object; a form object contains many different kinds of form elements.

Study Figure 13-1 to establish a mental model for the scriptable elements of a Web page. After you script these objects a few times, the object hierarchy will become second nature to you — even if you don't necessarily remember every detail (property, method, and event handler) of every object. At least you will know where to look for information.

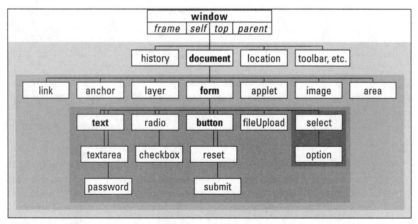

Figure 13-1: The JavaScript document object hierarchy in Navigator 4

Creating JavaScript Objects

Most of the objects that a browser creates for you are established when an HTML document loads into the browser. The same kind of HTML code you've used to create links, anchors, and input elements tells a JavaScript-enhanced browser to create those objects in memory. The objects are there whether or not your scripts call them into action.

The only visible differences to the HTML code for defining those objects are the one or more optional attributes specifically dedicated to JavaScript. By and large, these attributes specify the event you want the user interface element to react to and what JavaScript should do when the user takes that action. By relying on the document's HTML code to perform the object generation, you can spend more time figuring out how to do things with those objects or have them do things for you.

Bear in mind that objects are created *in their load order*, which is why you should put most, if not all, deferred function definitions in the document's Head. And if you're creating a multiframe environment, a script in one frame cannot communicate to another frame's objects until both frames load. This trips up a lot of scripters who are creating multiframe and multiwindow sites (more in Chapter 14).

Object Properties

A property generally defines a particular, current setting of an object. The setting may reflect a visible attribute of an object, such as a document's background color; it may also contain information that is not so obvious, such as the action and method of a form when it is submitted.

Document objects have most of their properties assigned by the attribute settings of the HTML tags that generate the objects. Thus, a property may be a string (for example, a name) or a number (for example, a size). A property can also be an array, such as an array of images contained by a document. If the HTML does not include all attributes, the browser usually fills in a default value for both the attribute and the corresponding JavaScript property.

A note to experienced object-oriented programmers

Although the JavaScript hierarchy appears to have a class-subclass relationship, many of the traditional aspects of a true, object-oriented environment don't apply to the document object model. The JavaScript document object hierarchy is a *containment* hierarchy, not an *inheritance* hierarchy. No object inherits properties or methods of an object higher up the chain. Nor is there any automatic message passing from object to object in any direction. Therefore, you cannot invoke a window's method by sending a message to it via a document or form object. All object references must be explicit.

Predefined document objects are generated only when the HTML code containing their definitions loads into the browser. Many properties, methods, and event handlers cannot be modified once you load the document into the browser. In Chapter 34, you learn how to create your own objects, but those objects cannot be the type that present new visual elements on the page that go beyond what HTML, Java applets, and plug-ins can portray.

Note

When used in script statements, property names are case-sensitive. Therefore, if you see a property name listed as `bgColor`, you must use it in a script statement with that exact combination of lowercase and uppercase letters. But when you are setting an initial value of a property by way of an HTML attribute, the attribute name (like all of HTML) is not case-sensitive. Thus, `<BODY BGCOLOR="white">` and `<body bgcolor="white">` both set the same property value.

Each property determines its own read-write status. Some objects are read-only, whereas others can be changed on the fly by assigning a new value to them. For example, to put some new text into a text object, you assign a string to the object's `value` property:

```
document.forms[0].phone.value = "555-1212"
```

Once an object contained by the document exists (that is, its HTML has loaded into the document), you can also add one or more custom properties to that object. This can be helpful if you wish to associate some additional data with an object for later retrieval. To add such a property, simply specify it in the same statement that assigns a value to it:

```
document.forms[0].phone.delimiter = "-"
```

Any property you set survives as long as the document remains loaded in the window and scripts do not overwrite the object.

Object Methods

An object's method is a command that a script can give to that object. Some methods return values, but that is not a prerequisite for a method. Also, not every object has methods defined for it. In a majority of cases, invoking a method from a script causes some action to take place. It may be an obvious action, such as resizing a window, or something more subtle, such as processing a mouse click.

All methods have parentheses after them and always appear at the end of an object's reference. When a method accepts or requires parameters, their values go inside the parentheses.

While an object has its methods predefined by the object model, you can also assign one or more additional methods to an object that already exists (that is, its HTML has loaded into the document). To do this, a script in the document (or in another window or frame accessible by the document) must define a JavaScript function, then assign that function to a new property name of the object. In the following Navigator 4 script example, the `fullScreen()` function invokes one window object method and adjusts two window object properties. By assigning the function reference to the new `window.maximize` property, I have defined a `maximize()` method for the window object. Thus, a button's event handler can call that method directly.

```
function fullScreen() {
        this.moveTo(0,0)
        this.outerWidth = screen.availWidth
        this.outerHeight = screen.availHeight
}
window.maximize = fullScreen
...
<INPUT TYPE="button" VALUE="Maximize Window"
onClick="window.maximize()">
```

Object Event Handlers

Event handlers specify how an object reacts to an event, whether the event is triggered by a user action (for example, a button click) or a browser action (for example, the completion of a document load). Going back to the earliest JavaScript-enabled browser, event handlers were defined inside HTML tags as extra attributes. They included the name of the attribute, followed by an equals sign (working as an assignment operator) and a string containing the script statement(s) or function(s) to execute when the event occurs. Event handlers also have other forms. In Navigator 3 and later, event handlers have corresponding methods for their objects and every event handler is a property of its object.

Event handlers as methods

Consider a button object whose sole event handler is `onClick=`. This means whenever the button receives a click event, the button triggers the JavaScript expression or function call assigned to that event handler in the button's HTML definition:

```
<INPUT TYPE="button" NAME="clicker" VALUE="Click Me" onClick="doIt()">
```

Normally, that click event is the result of a user physically clicking on the button in the page. You can also trigger the event handler with a script by calling the event handler as if it were a method of the object:

```
document.formName.clicker.onclick()
```

Notice that when summoning an event handler as a method, the method name is all lowercase, regardless of the case used in the event handler attribute within the original HTML tag. This lowercase reference is a requirement.

Invoking an event handler this way is different from using a method to replicate the physical action denoted by the event. For example, imagine a page containing three simple text fields. One of those fields has an `onFocus=` event handler defined for it. Physically tabbing to or clicking in that field brings focus to the field and thereby triggers its `onFocus=` event handler. If the field did not have focus, a button could invoke that field's `onFocus=` event handler by referencing it as a method:

```
document.formName.fieldName.onfocus()
```

This scripted action does not bring physical focus to the field. The field's own `focus()` method, however, does that under script control.

A byproduct of an event handler's capability to act like a method is that you can define the action of an event handler by defining a function with the event handler's name. For example, instead of specifying an `onLoad=` event handler in a document's `<BODY>` tag, you can define a function like this:

```
function onload() {
        statements
}
```

This capability is particularly helpful if you want event handler actions confined to a script running in Navigator 3 or later. Your scripts won't require special traps for Navigator 2 or Internet Explorer 3.

Event handlers as properties

Although event handlers are normally defined in an object's HTML tag, you also have the power to change the event handler from Navigator 3 onward, the reason being that an event handler is treated like any other object property whose value you can both retrieve and modify. The value of an event handler property looks like a function definition. For example, given this HTML definition:

```
<INPUT TYPE="text" NAME="entry" onFocus="doIt()">
```

the value of the object's `onfocus` (all lowercase) property is

```
function onfocus() {
        doIt()
}
```

You can, however, assign an entirely different function to an event handler by assigning a function reference to the property. Such references don't include the parentheses that are part of the function's definition (you see this again much later in Chapter 34, when you assign functions to object properties).

Using the same text field definition you just looked at, assign a different function to the event handler, because based on user input elsewhere in the document, you

want the field to behave differently when it receives the focus. If you define a
function like this:

```
function doSomethingElse() {
        statements
}
```

you can then assign the function to the field with this assignment statement:

```
document.formName.entry.onfocus = doSomethingElse
```

Because the new function reference is written in JavaScript, you must observe
case. In Navigator 3, the handler name must be all lowercase; in Navigator 4, you
can also use the more familiar interCap version (for example,
`document.formName.entry.onFocus = doSomethingElse`).

 Be aware, however, that as with several settable object properties that don't
manifest themselves visually, any change you make to an event handler property
disappears with a document reload. Therefore, I advise you not to make such
changes except as part of a script that also invokes the event handler like a method.

Because every event handler operates as both property and method, I won't list
these properties and methods as part of each object's definition in the next
chapters. You can be assured this feature works for every JavaScript object that
has an event handler from Navigator 3 onward.

Embedding Scripts in Documents

JavaScript offers three ways to include scripts or scripted elements in your
documents — the <SCRIPT> tag, the external library, and the JavaScript entity for
HTML attributes, discussed in the following sections. Not all approaches are
available in all versions of Navigator, but you do have everything at your disposal
for Navigator 3 onward and for some versions of Internet Explorer 3 onward.

<SCRIPT> tags

The simplest and most compatible way to include script statements in a
document is inside a <SCRIPT>...</SCRIPT> tag set. You can have any number of
such tag sets in your document. For example, you can define some functions in the
Head section to be called by event handlers in HTML tags within the Body section.
Another tag set could be within the Body to dynamically write part of the content
of the page. Place only script statements and comments between the start and end
tags of the tag set. Do not place any HTML tags inside unless they are part of a
parameter to a `document.write()` statement that creates content for the page.

Every opening <SCRIPT> tag should specify the LANGUAGE attribute. Because
the <SCRIPT> tag is a generic tag indicating that the contained statements are to
be interpreted as executable script and not renderable HTML, the tag is designed
to accommodate any scripting language the browser knows about.

All scriptable browsers (from Navigator 2 onward and Internet Explorer 3
onward) recognize the LANGUAGE="JavaScript" attribute setting. However, more
recent browsers typically acknowledge additional versions of JavaScript or, in the
case of Internet Explorer, other languages. For example, the JavaScript interpreter
built into Navigator 3 knows the JavaScript 1.1 version of the language; Navigator 4

and Internet Explorer 4 include the JavaScript 1.2 version. For versions beyond the original JavaScript, you specify the language version by appending the version number after the language name, without any spaces, as in

```
<SCRIPT LANGUAGE="JavaScript1.1">
```

```
<SCRIPT LANGUAGE="JavaScript1.2">
```

How you use these later-version attributes depends on the content of the scripts and your intended audience. For example, while Navigator 4 is JavaScript 1.2–compatible, it works with all versions of the JavaScript LANGUAGE attribute. Even features of the language new in JavaScript 1.2 will be executed if the LANGUAGE attribute is set to only "JavaScript". On rare occasions (detailed in the succeeding chapters) the behavior of the language changes in a Navigator 4 browser if you specify the JavaScript 1.2 language instead of an earlier version.

Writing scripts for a variety of browser versions requires a bit of care, especially when the scripts may contain language features available only in newer browsers. As demonstrated in an extensive discussion about browser detection later in this chapter, there may be a need to include multiple versions of a script function, each in its own <SCRIPT> tag with a different LANGUAGE attribute.

JavaScript versus JScript and VBScript

As previously explained, Internet Explorer's version of JavaScript is called JScript. As a result, Internet Explorer's default script language is JScript. While Internet Explorer acknowledges the LANGUAGE="JavaScript" attribute, Netscape Navigator ignores the LANGUAGE="JScript" attribute. Therefore, if you are writing scripts that must work in both Internet Explorer and Netscape Navigator, you can specify one language ("JavaScript") and count on both browsers interpreting the code correctly (assuming you take into account the other compatibility issues).

An entirely different issue is Internet Explorer's other scripting language, VBScript. This language is a derivative of Visual Basic and offers no interoperability with JavaScript scripts (even though both languages work with the same Internet Explorer object model). You can mix scripts from both languages in the same document, but their tag sets must be completely separate, with the LANGUAGE attributes clearly specifying the language for the <SCRIPT> tag.

Hiding script statements from older browsers

As more versions of scriptable browsers spread among the user community, the installed base of older, nonscriptable browsers diminishes. However, public Web sites can still attract a variety of browsers that date back to the World Wide Web Stone Age (before A.D.1996).

Browsers from those olden days do not know about the <SCRIPT> tag. Normally, browsers ignore tags they don't understand. That's fine when a tag is just one line of HTML, but a <SCRIPT> tag sets off any number of script statement lines in a document. Old browsers don't know to expect a closing </SCRIPT> tag. Therefore, their natural inclination is to render any lines they encounter after the opening <SCRIPT> tag. Unfortunately, this places script statements squarely in the document — surely to confuse anyone who sees such gibberish on the page.

You can, however, exercise a technique that tricks most older browsers into ignoring the script statements. The trick is surrounding the script statements — inside the <SCRIPT> tag set — with HTML comment markers. An HTML comment begins with the sequence `<!--` and ends with `-->`. Therefore, you should embed these comment sequences in your scripts according to the following format:

```
<SCRIPT LANGUAGE="JavaScript">
<!--
script statements here
//-->
</SCRIPT>
```

JavaScript interpreters also know to ignore a line that begins with the HTML beginning comment sequence, but the interpreter needs a little help with the ending sequence. The close of the HTML comment starts with a JavaScript comment sequence (`//`). This tells JavaScript to ignore the line; but a nonscriptable browser sees the ending HTML symbols and begins rendering the page with the next HTML tag or other text in the document. Since an older browser won't know what the `</SCRIPT>` tag is, the tag is ignored, and rendering begins after that.

Even with this subterfuge, not all browsers handle HTML comment tags gracefully. Some older America Online browsers will display the script statements no matter what you do. Fortunately, these browsers are disappearing.

If your pages are being designed for public access, include these HTML comment lines in all your `<SCRIPT>` tag sets. Make sure they go *inside* the tags, not outside. Also note that most of the script examples in this part of the book do not include these comments, for the sake of saving space in the listings.

Hiding scripts entirely?

It may be misleading to say that this HTML comment technique hides scripts from older browsers. In truth, the comments hide the scripts from being rendered by the browsers. The tags and script statements, however, are still downloaded to the browser and appear in the source when viewed by the user.

A common wish among authors is to truly hide scripts from visitors to a page. Client-side JavaScript must be downloaded with the page and is, therefore, visible in the source view of pages. There are, of course, some tricks you can implement that may disguise client-side scripts from prying eyes. The most easily implemented technique is to let the downloaded page contain no visible elements, only scripts that assemble the page that the visitor sees. Source code for such a page is simply the HTML for the page. But that page will not be interactive, because no scripting would be attached unless it were written as part of the page — defeating the goal of hiding scripts. If you are worried about your scripts being "stolen" by other scripters, a perfect way to prevent it is to include a copyright notification in your page's source code. Not only are your scripts visible to the world, but so, too, would a thief's scripts be. This way you can easily see if someone has lifted your scripts verbatim.

Script libraries

If you do a lot of scripting or script a lot of pages for a complex Web application, you will certainly develop some functions and techniques that could be used for several pages. Rather than duplicate the code in all of those pages (and go through the nightmare of making changes to all copies for new features or bug fixes), you can create separate script library files and link them to your pages.

Such an external script file contains nothing but JavaScript code — no
⟨SCRIPT⟩ tags, no HTML. The script file you create must be a text-only file, such as
an HTML source file, but its filename must end with the two-character extension
.js. To instruct the browser to load the external file at a particular point in your
regular HTML file, you add a SRC attribute to the ⟨SCRIPT⟩ tag, as follows:

```
<SCRIPT LANGUAGE="JavaScript" SRC="hotscript.js"></SCRIPT>
```

This kind of tag should go at the top of the document so it loads before any
other in-document ⟨SCRIPT⟩ tags load. If you load more than one external library,
include a series of these tag sets at the top of the document.

Note two features about this tag construction: First, the ⟨SCRIPT⟩ ...
⟨/SCRIPT⟩ tag pair is required, even though nothing appears between them. You
can mix ⟨SCRIPT⟩ tag sets that specify external libraries and include in-document
scripts in the same document.

How you reference the source file in the SRC attribute depends on its physical
location and your HTML coding style. In the preceding example, the .js file is in the
same directory as the HTML file containing the tag. But if you want to refer to an
absolute URL, the protocol for the file is http://, just like with an HTML file:

```
<SCRIPT LANGUAGE="JavaScript" SRC="http://www.cool.com/hotscript.js">
</SCRIPT>
```

A very important prerequisite for using script libraries with your documents is
your Web server software must know how to map files with the .js extension to a
MIME type of application/x-javascript. If you plan to deploy JavaScript in this
manner, be sure to test a sample on your Web server beforehand and arrange for
any server adjustments that may be necessary.

When a user chooses Document Source from Navigator's View menu, code from
a .js file does not appear in the window, even though the browser treats the loaded
script as part of the current document. However, the name or URL of the .js file is
plainly visible (displayed exactly as you wrote it for the SRC attribute). Anyone can
then open that file with the browser (using the http:// protocol) and view the .js
file's source code. In other words, an external JavaScript source file is no more
hidden from view than JavaScript embedded directly in an HTML file.

Navigator 3 exhibits a bug if you specify an external .js library file in a tag that
specifies JavaScript 1.2 as the language. Unfortunately, Navigator 3 ignores the
language version and loads the external file no matter what language is specified in
that tag. Therefore, if you don't want those scripts to run in Navigator 3, surround
the scripts in the external file in a version-checking if clause:

```
if (parseInt(navigator.appVersion) > 3) {
    statements to run here
}
```

Compatibility issues

On the Netscape Navigator side, the external capability was new with Navigator
3. Therefore, the SRC attribute is ignored in Navigator 2, and none of the external
scripts become part of the document.

The situation is more clouded on the Internet Explorer side. When Internet
Explorer 3 shipped for Windows, the external script library feature was not

available. By most accounts, Internet Explorer Version 3.02 included support for external libraries, but I have heard reports that this is not the case. I know that the Version 3.02 installed on my Windows 95 computers loads external libraries from .js files. It may be a wise tactic to specify a complete URL for the .js file, as this has been known to assist Internet Explorer 3 in locating the script library file associated with an HTML file.

JavaScript entities

Another feature that started with Navigator 3 was the *JavaScript entity*. The idea behind this technique was to provide a way for the browser to use script expressions to fill in the data for any HTML tag attribute. Netscape entities are strings that allow special characters or symbols to be embedded in HTML. They begin with an ampersand symbol (&) and end with a semicolon (;). For example, the &c; entity is rendered in Netscape browsers as a copyright symbol (©).

To assign a JavaScript expression to an entity, the entity still begins and ends like all entities, but the expression is surrounded by curly braces. For example, consider a document containing a function that returns the current day of the week, as follows:

```
function today() {
        var days = new
Array("Sunday","Monday","Tuesday","Wednesday","Thursday","Friday",
"Saturday")
        var today = new Date()
        return days[today.getDay()]
}
```

This function can be assigned to a JavaScript entity such that the label of a button is created with the returned value of the function:

```
<INPUT TYPE=button VALUE=&{today()}; onCLick="handleToday()">
```

Expressions can be used to fulfill only attribute assignments, not other parts related to a tag, such as the text for a document title or link. Those items can still be dynamically generated via document.write() statements as the document loads.

Browser Version Detection

Without question the biggest challenge facing client-side scripters is how to program an application that accommodates a wide variety of browser versions and brands, each one of which can bring its own quirks and bugs. Happy is the intranet developer who knows for a fact that the company has standardized its computers with a particular brand and version of browser. But that is a rarity, especially in light of the concept of the *extranet* — private corporate networks and applications that open up for access to the company's suppliers and customers.

Having dealt with this problem since the original scripted browser, Navigator 2, had to work alongside a hoard of nonscriptable browsers, I have identified several paths that an application developer can follow. Unless you decide to be autocratic about browser requirements for using your site, you must make compromises in desired functionality or provide multiple paths in your Web site for two or more classes of browsers. Plenty of Web surfers are still using the text-only, server-based browser called Lynx. In this section, I give you several ideas about how to approach development in an increasingly fragmented browser world.

Is JavaScript on?

Very often, the first decision an application must make is whether the client accessing the site is JavaScript-enabled. Non–JavaScript-enabled browsers fall into two categories: a) JavaScript-capable browsers that have JavaScript turned off in the preferences; and b) browsers that have no JavaScript interpreter built in.

Using the <NOSCRIPT> tag

Except for some of the earliest versions of Netscape Navigator, all JavaScript-capable browsers have a preferences setting to turn off JavaScript (and a separate one for Java). You should know that even though JavaScript is turned on by default in Navigator, many institutional deployments have it turned off by default. The reasons behind this MIS deployment decision vary from scares about Java security violations incorrectly associated with JavaScript, valid JavaScript security concerns on some browser versions, and the fact that some firewalls try to filter JavaScript lines from incoming HTML streams.

All JavaScript-capable browsers include a set of <NOSCRIPT>...</NOSCRIPT> tags to balance the <SCRIPT>...</SCRIPT> tag set. If one of these browsers has JavaScript turned off, the <SCRIPT> tag is ignored, but the <NOSCRIPT> tag is observed. As with the <NOFRAMES> tag, you can use the body of a <NOSCRIPT> tag set to display HTML that lets users know JavaScript is turned off and therefore the full benefit of the page won't be available unless JavaScript is turned on. Listing 13-1 shows a skeletal HTML page that uses these tags.

Listing 13-1: **Employing the <NOSCRIPT> Tag**

```
<HEAD>
<TITLE>Some Document</TITLE>
<SCRIPT LANGUAGE="JavaScript">
      // script statements
</SCRIPT>
<NOSCRIPT>
<B>Your browser has JavaScript turned off.</B><BR>
You will experience a more enjoyable time at this Web site if you turn
JavaScript on.<BR>
Open your browser preferences, and enable JavaScript.<BR>
You do not have to restart your browser or your computer after you
enable JavaScript. Simply click the 'Reload' button.
<HR>
</NOSCRIPT>
</HEAD>
<BODY>
<H2>The body of your document.</H2>
</BODY>
</HTML>
```

You can display any standard HTML within the `<NOSCRIPT>` tag set. An icon image might be a colorful way to draw the user's attention to the special advice at the top of the page. If your document is designed to dynamically create content in one or more places in the document, you may have to include a `<NOSCRIPT>` tag set after more than one `<SCRIPT>` tag set to let users know what they're missing. Do not include the HTML comment tags that you use in hiding JavaScript statements from older browsers. Their presence inside the `<NOSCRIPT>` tags prevents the HTML from rendering.

Other nonscriptable browsers

Unfortunately, browsers that don't know about JavaScript also don't know about the `<NOSCRIPT>` tag. They generally do not render the content of those tags.

At this point I must point out that newcomers to scripting frequently want to know what script to write to detect whether JavaScript is turned on. Because scripters are so ready to write a script to work around all situations, it takes some thought to realize that a non-JavaScript browser cannot execute such a script: If no JavaScript interpreter exists in the browser (or it is turned off), the script is ignored. I suppose that the existence of a JavaScript-accessible method for Java detection — the `navigator.javaEnabled()` method — promises a parallel method for JavaScript. But logic fails to deliver on that unspoken promise.

Another desire is to have JavaScript substitute document content when the browser is JavaScript-enabled. But you cannot create a script to write scripted content where normal HTML is destined to appear. All HTML in a document appears in the browser, while scripted content can only be additive.

You can use this additive scripting to create unusual effects when displaying different links and (with a caveat) body text for scriptable and nonscriptable browsers. Listing 13-2 shows a short document that uses HTML comment symbols to trick nonscriptable browsers into displaying a link to Netscape's Web site and two lines of text. A scriptable browser takes advantage of a behavior that allows only the nearest `<A>` tag to be associated with a closing `</A>` tag. Therefore, the Netscape link isn't rendered at all, but the link to my Web site is. For the body text, the script assigns the same text color to a segment of HTML body text as the document's background. While the colored text is camouflaged in a scriptable browser (and some other text written to the document), the "hidden" text is still in the document, but not visible.

Listing 13-2: **Rendering Different Content for Scriptable and Nonscriptable Browsers**

```
<HTML>
<BODY BGCOLOR="yellow">
<A HREF="http://www.yahoo.com">
<SCRIPT>
<!--
document.writeln("<A HREF=\"http://www.excite.com\">")
//-->
</SCRIPT>
Where?</A>
```

(continued)

Listing 13-2 *(continued)*

```
<HR>
<SCRIPT>
<!--
document.write("Howdy from the script!<FONT COLOR='yellow';>")
//-->
</SCRIPT>
<!--
If you can read this, JavaScript is not available.
<SCRIPT>
document.write("</FONT>")
//-->
</SCRIPT>
<BR>
Here's some stuff afterward.
</BODY>
</HTML>
```

Scripting for different browsers

The number of solutions for accommodating different client browsers is large because the specific compatibility need might be as simple as letting a link navigate to a scripted page for script-enabled browsers or as involved as setting up distinct areas of your application for different browser classes. The first step in planning for compatibility is determining what your goal is for various visitor classes.

Establishing goals

Once you have mapped out your application, you must then look at the implementation details to see which browser is required for the most advanced aspect of the application. For example, if the design calls for image swapping on mouse rollovers, that feature requires Navigator 3 or later and Internet Explorer 4 or later. In implementing Dynamic HTML features, you also have to decide if the functionality you specified can be made to work on both Navigator 4 and Internet Explorer 4 through some cross-platform scripting (see Chapter 41).

After you determine the lowest common denominator for the optimum experience, you then must decide how gracefully you want to degrade the application for visitors whose browsers do not meet the common denominator. For example, if you plan a page or site that requires Navigator 4 or Internet Explorer 4 for all the bells and whistles, you could provide an escape path with content in a simple format that every browser from Lynx to Navigator 3 would get. Or perhaps you would provide for users of older scriptable browsers a third offering with limited scriptability that works on all scriptable browsers.

Creating an application or site that has multiple paths for viewing the same content may sound good at the outset, but don't forget that maintenance chores lie ahead as the site evolves. Will you have the time, budget, and inclination to keep all paths up to date? Despite any good intentions a designer of a new Web site may have, in my experience the likelihood that a site will be properly maintained diminishes rapidly with the complexity of the maintenance task.

Implementing a branching index page

If you decide to offer two or more paths into your application or content, one place you can start visitors down their individual paths is at the default page for your site. Numerous techniques are available that can redirect visitors to the appropriate perceived starting point of the site.

One design to avoid is placing the decision about the navigation path in the hands of the visitor. Offering buttons or links that describe the browser requirements may work for users who are HTML and browser geeks, but the average consumers surfing the Web these days likely won't have a clue about what level of HTML their browsers support or whether they are JavaScript-enabled. It is incumbent upon the index page designer to automate the navigation task as much as possible.

A branching index page has almost no content. It is not the "home page" per se of the site, rather merely a portal to the entire Web site. Its job is to redirect users to what appears to be the home page for the site. Listing 13-3 shows what such a branching index page looks like.

Listing 13-3: **A Branching Index Page**

```
<HTML>
<HEAD>
   <TITLE>GiantCo On The Web</TITLE>
   <SCRIPT LANGUAGE="JavaScript">
   <!--
       window.location = "home1.html"
   //-->
   </SCRIPT>
   <META HTTP-EQUIV="REFRESH" CONTENT="1;
URL=http://www.giantco.com/home2.html">
</HEAD>

<BODY>
<CENTER>
   <A HREF="home2.html"><IMG SRC="images/giantcoLogo.gif" HEIGHT=60
WIDTH=120 BORDER=0 ALT="GiantCo Home Page"></A>
</CENTER>
</BODY>
</HTML>
```

Notice that the only visible content is an image surrounded by a standard link. The <BODY> tag contains no background color or art. A single script statement is located in the Head. A <META> tag is also in the Head to automate navigation for some users. To see how a variety of browsers would respond to this page, here are what three different classes of browser would do with Listing 13-3:

A JavaScript-enabled browser. Although the entire page loads momentarily (flashing the company logo for a brief moment), the browser executes the script statement that loads home1.html into the window. This executes within about a second after the page loads. In the meantime, the image has been preloaded into the browser's memory cache. This image should be one that is reused in home1.html so the download time isn't wasted on a one-time image. If your pages require a specific brand or minimum version number, this would be the place to filter out browsers that don't meet the criteria (which may include the installation of a particular plug-in). Use the properties of the navigator object (Chapter 25) to allow only those browsers meeting your design minimum to navigate to the scripted home page. All others fall through to the next execution possibility.

A modern browser with JavaScript turned off or missing. Several modern browsers recognize the special format of the <META> tag as one that loads a URL into the current window after a stated number of seconds. In Listing 13-3 that interval is one second. The <META> tag is executed only if the browser ignores the <SCRIPT> tag. Therefore, any scriptable browser that has JavaScript turned off or browser that knows <META> tags but no scripting will follow the refresh command for the <META> tag. If you utilize this tag, be very careful to observe the tricky formatting of the CONTENT attribute value. The number of seconds is followed by a semicolon and the subattribute URL. A complete URL for your nonscriptable home page version is required for this subattribute. Importantly, the entire CONTENT attribute value is inside one set of quotes.

Older graphical browsers, PDA browsers, and Lynx. The last category includes graphical browsers some would call "brain-dead" as well as intentionally stripped down browsers. Lynx is designed to work in a text-only VT-100 terminal screen; personal digital assistants (PDAs) such as the Apple Newton and Windows CE devices have browsers optimized for usage through slow modems and viewing on small screens. If such browsers do not understand the <META> tag for refreshing content, they will land at this page with no further automatic processing. But by creating an image that acts as a link, the tendency will be to click on it to continue. The link then leads to the nonscriptable home page. Also note that the ALT attribute for the image is supplied. This takes care of Lynx and PDA browsers (with image loading off), because these browsers show the ALT attribute text in lieu of the image. Users click on the text to navigate to the URL referenced in the link tag.

I have a good reason to keep the background of the branching index page plain. For those whose browsers automatically lead them to a content-filled home page, the browser window will flash from a set background color to the browser's default background color before the new home page and its background color appear. By keeping the initial content to only the company logo, less screen flashing and obvious navigation are visible to the user.

One link — alternate destinations

Another filtering technique is available directly from links. With the exceptions of Navigator 2 and Internet Explorer 3, a link can navigate to one destination via a link's onClick= event handler and to another via the HREF attribute if the browser is not scriptable.

The trick is to include an extra return false statement in the onClick= event handler. This statement cancels the link action of the HREF attribute. For example, if a nonscriptable browser is to go to one version of a page at the click of a link and the scriptable browser should go to another, the link tag would be as follows:

```
<A HREF="nonJSCatalog.html" onClick="location='JSCatalog.html';return
false">Product Catalog</A>
```

Only nonscriptable browsers, Navigator 2, and Internet Explorer 3 go to the nonJSCatalog.html page; all others go to the JSCatalog.html page.

Multiple-level scripts

Each new JavaScript level brings more functionality to the language. You can use the LANGUAGE attribute of the <SCRIPT> tag to provide road maps for the execution of functions according to the power available in the browser. For example, consider a button whose event handler invokes a function. That function can be written in such a way that users of each JavaScript version get special treatment with regard to unique features of that version. To make sure all scriptable browsers handle the event handler gracefully, you can create multiple versions of the function, each wrapped inside its own <SCRIPT> tag specifying a particular language version.

Listing 13-4 shows the outline of a page that presents different versions of the same event handler. For this technique to work properly, you must lay out the <SCRIPT> tags in ascending order of JavaScript version. In other words, the last function that the browser knows how to read (according to the LANGUAGE version) is the one that gets executed. In Listing 13-4, for instance, Navigator 3 gets only as far as the middle version and executes only that one.

Listing 13-4: **Multiple Script Versions**

```
<HTML>
<HEAD>
    <SCRIPT LANGUAGE="JavaScript">
    <!--
        function doIt() {
          // statements for JavaScript 1.0 browsers
        }
     //-->
    </SCRIPT>
    <SCRIPT LANGUAGE="JavaScript1.1">
    <!--
        function doIt() {
          // statements for JavaScript 1.1 browsers
        }
     //-->
    </SCRIPT>
    <SCRIPT LANGUAGE="JavaScript1.2">
    <!--
        function doIt() {
          // statements for JavaScript 1.2 browsers
        }
     //-->
    </SCRIPT>
</HEAD>
<BODY>
<FORM>
    <INPUT TYPE=button VALUE="Click Me" onClick="doIt()">
</FORM>
</BODY>
</HTML>
```

If you use this technique, you must define an event handler for each level below the highest version you intend to support. For example, failure to include a version for JavaScript 1.0 in Listing 13-4 would result in a script error for users of Navigator 2 and Internet Explorer 3. If you don't want an older browser to execute a function (because the browser doesn't support the functionality required for the action), include a *dummy function* (a function definition with no statements) in the lower-level <SCRIPT> tag to catch the event handlers of less-capable browsers.

Scripted event handler properties

Along the same lines of Listing 13-4, you can define event handlers for objects within separate language versions. For example, in Listing 13-5, a button is assigned an event handler within the context of a JavaScript 1.1–level script. Navigator 2 and Internet Explorer 3 users won't have their button's event handler set, because the HTML tag doesn't have an event handler. In fact, you could also specify a different function for JavaScript 1.2–level browsers by including another <SCRIPT> tag below the one that currently sets the event handler. The new tag would specify JavaScript 1.2 as the language and assign a different function to the event handler.

Listing 13-5: **Event Handler Assignments**

```
<HTML>
<HEAD>
    <SCRIPT LANGUAGE="JavaScript1.1">
    <!--
        function doIt() {
            // statements for JavaScript 1.1 browsers
        }
    //-->
    </SCRIPT>
</HEAD>
<BODY>
<FORM>
    <INPUT TYPE=button NAME=janeButton VALUE="Click Me">
    <SCRIPT LANGUAGE="JavaScript1.1">
    <!--
        document.forms[0]. janeButton.onclick=doIt
    //-->
    </SCRIPT>
</FORM>
</BODY>
</HTML>
```

Designing for Compatibility

Each new major release of a browser brings compatibility problems for page authors. It's not so much that old scripts break in the new versions (well-written scripts rarely break in new versions). No, the problems center on the new features that attract designers and how to handle visitors who have not yet advanced to the latest and greatest browser version.

Adding to these problems are numerous bugs, particularly in first-generation browsers from both Netscape and Microsoft. Worse still, some of these bugs affect only one operating system platform among the many supported by the browser. Even if you have access to all the browsers for testing, the process of finding the errors, tracking down the bugs, and implementing workarounds that won't break later browsers can be a frustrating process, even when you've scripted pages from the earliest days and have a long memory for ancient bug reports.

Catering only to the lowest common denominator can more than double your development time, due to the expanded testing matrix necessary to ensure a good working page in all operating systems on all versions. Decide how important the scripted functionality you're employing in a page is for every user. If you want some functionality that works only in a later browser, then you may have to be a bit autocratic in defining the minimum browser for scripted access to your page — any lesser browser gets shunted to a simpler presentation of your site's data.

Another possibility is to make a portion of the site accessible to most, if not all, browsers, restricting the scripting to only the occasional enhancement that nonscriptable browser users won't miss. But once the application reaches a certain point in the navigation flow, then a more capable browser is necessary to get to the really good stuff. This kind of design is a carefully planned strategy that lets the site welcome all users up to a point, but then enables the application to shine for users of, say, Navigator 3 or higher.

The ideal page is one that displays useful content on any browser, but whose scripting enhances the experience of the page visitor — perhaps in the way of more efficient site navigation or interactivity with the page's content. That is certainly a worthy goal to aspire to. But even if you can achieve this nirvana on only some pages, you will reduce the need for defining entirely separate, difficult-to-maintain paths for browsers of varying capabilities.

Dealing with beta browsers

If you have crafted a skillfully scripted Web page or site, you may be concerned when a prerelease version of a browser available to the public causes script errors or other compatibility problems to appear on your page. Do yourself a favor — don't overreact to bugs and errors that occur in prerelease browser versions. If your code is well written, it should work with any new generation of browser. If the code doesn't work correctly, consider the browser to be buggy. Report the bug (preferably with a script sample) to the browser maker.

It is often difficult to prevent yourself from getting caught up in browser makers' enthusiasm for a new release. But remember that a prerelease version is not a shipping version. Users who visit your page with prerelease browsers should know that there may be bugs in the browser. That your code does not work with a prerelease version is not a sin, nor is it worth losing sleep over. Just be sure to report the bug so the problem doesn't make it into the release version.

Browser version headaches

As described more fully in Chapter 25's discussion of the navigator object, your scripts can easily determine which browser is the one running the script. However, the properties that reveal the version don't always tell the whole story about Internet Explorer 3.

For one thing, the Windows and Macintosh versions of the same major browser version (3.0x) implement slightly different object models. The Mac version includes the ever-popular image object for mouse rollover image swapping; the Windows version does not, and any attempt to use such code in the Windows version results in script errors.

Next, the first release of Internet Explorer 3 for the Macintosh was not scriptable at all — the JavaScript interpreter was left out. Macintosh Version 3.01 was the first Mac version to be scriptable. Even among minor generation releases of Internet Explorer 3 for Windows, Microsoft implemented some new features here and there.

But probably the most troublesome problem is that an improved JavaScript interpreter (in the JScript.dll file) underwent substantial improvements between Version 1 and Version 2 for Windows. Many copies of browser Version 3.02 for Windows shipped with Version 1 of the .dll. Some users updated their browsers if they knew to download the new .dll from Microsoft. Unfortunately, the interpreter version is not reflected in any navigator object property. A nasty Catch-22 in this regard is that Version 2 of the interpreter includes a new property that lets you examine the interpreter version, but testing for that property in a browser that has Version 1 of the interpreter installed results in an error message.

Due to the insecurity of knowing exactly what will and won't work in a browser that identifies itself as Internet Explorer 3.0x, you might decide to redirect all users of Internet Explorer 3 to pages in your application that include no scripting. But before you think I'm bashing Internet Explorer 3, you should also consider doing the same redirection for Navigator 2 users due to the number of platform-specific bugs that littered that first round of JavaScript. JavaScript Versions 1.1 and 1.2 are much more stable and reliable platforms on which to build scriptable applications. If you have an opportunity to study the access logs of your Web site, analyze the proportion of different browser versions over several days before deciding where you set your lowest common denominator for scripted access.

Compatibility ratings in reference chapters

With the proliferation of scriptable browser versions since Navigator 2, it is important to know up front whether a particular object, property, method, or event handler is supported in the lowest common denominator you are designing for. Therefore, in the rest of the chapters of this reference part of the book, I include frequent compatibility charts, like the following example:

	Nav2	Nav3	Nav4	IE3/J1	IE3/J2	IE4/J3
Compatibility	✓	✓	✓	(✓)	✓	✓

The first three columns represent Navigator Versions 2, 3, and 4, respectively. For Internet Explorer, two columns appear for Version 3. One, marked IE3/J1, represents the combination of Internet Explorer 3 and JScript.dll Version 1; IE3/J2 represents Internet Explorer 3 and JScript.dll Version 2. The first shipping version of Internet Explorer 4 comes with JScript.dll Version 3, which is the latest one available as this book goes to press. A checkmark means the feature is compatible with the designated browser. You will also occasionally see one or more of the checkmarks surrounded in parentheses. This means some bug or partial implementation for that browser is explained in the body text.

I also recommend that you print out the JavaScript Road Map file shown in Appendix A. The map is on the companion CD-ROM in Adobe Acrobat format. This quick reference clearly shows each object's properties, methods, and event handlers, along with keys to the browser version in which each language item is supported. You should find the printout to be as valuable a day-to-day resource.

Object Definitions in This Book

Throughout the rest of Part III, I present detailed descriptions of each document object (and many core language objects). Each object definition begins with a summary listing of its properties, methods, and event handlers, giving you a sense of the scope of everything a particular object has to offer. From there, I go into detailed explanations of when and how to use each term.

Whenever a syntax definition appears, note the few conventions used to designate items, such as the optional parameters and placeholders that describe the kind of data that belongs in those slots. All syntax definitions and code examples are in HTML, so expect to see plenty of HTML tags in the familiar angle brackets (<>). Listing 13-6 shows the button object definition.

Listing 13-6: **Sample Object Definition**

```
<INPUT
        TYPE="button" | "submit" | "reset"
        NAME="buttonName"
        VALUE="labelText"
        [onClick="handlerTextOrFunction"]
        [onMouseDown="handlerTextOrFunction"]
        [onMouseUp="handlerTextOrFunction"] >
```

You should recognize most of this definition as the typical form for an HTML element. The entire definition is surrounded by angle brackets. Some attribute parameters (for NAME=, VALUE=, and the event handlers) let you assign names and other values meaningful to your script: In this case, the attribute parameters represent how you name the button, what text you want to appear on the button's label, and what you want the button to do when someone clicks it. Those placeholders appear in italics to remind you that you need to fill in those blanks with your own names. The placeholders attempt to describe the nature of the parameter. This is nothing more than what you'd find in a good HTML guide.

The last three attributes of the definition in Listing 13-6 appear inside square brackets. This convention means the attributes are optional. In this case, if you omit the event handler attributes, the button is just another HTML button like others you've probably specified before (although it won't do anything when clicked).

In other definitions, especially parameters for methods, the values to be supplied must be a particular data type (string, number, or Boolean). When the value must be of a specific type, the placeholder for that parameter indicates the data type in its name. For example, look at the history object's go() method:

```
go (deltaNumber | "TitleOrURL")
```

In this rare instance of JavaScript accepting either one of two data types (shown on either side of the "|" character), the method can accept either a number or a string (denoted by the quotes) containing a valid title or URL in the window's history list.

Some methods return values after they execute. For example, one window method displays a dialog box that prompts a user to enter text. When the user clicks on the OK button, the text entered into the dialog box is passed back as a value that can be assigned to a variable or used directly as a parameter for another method. Each method listed in the object definitions indicates what kind of value, if any, is returned by that method.

The last item of note about these definitions concerns the way you handle property values. Every property has a value that must be one of the valid JavaScript data types. Whether a property returns a Boolean, a string, or a number can be important for your scripting statements. Therefore, I note the kind of value required for each property.

✦   ✦   ✦

The Window Object

✦   ✦   ✦   ✦

In This Chapter

Scripting
communication
among multiple
frames

Creating and
managing new
windows

Controlling the size,
position, and
appearance of the
browser window

✦   ✦   ✦   ✦

A quick look at the Netscape document object model diagram in Chapter 13 (Figure 13-1) reveals that the window object is the outermost, most global container of all document-related objects in the JavaScript world. All HTML and JavaScript activity takes place inside a window. That window may be a standard Windows, Mac, or Xwindows application-style window, complete with scrollbars, toolbars and other "chrome"; if you have Navigator 4 or Internet Explorer 4 running in certain modes, the window may appear in the guise of the underlying desktop itself. A frame is also a window, even though it doesn't have many accoutrements beyond scrollbars. The window object is where everything begins in JavaScript, and this chapter begins the in-depth investigation of JavaScript objects with the window.

Of all the Navigator document model objects, the window object has by far the most terminology associated with it. This necessitates an abnormally long chapter to keep the discussion in one place. Use the running footers as a navigational aid through this substantial collection of information.

Window Terminology

The window object is often a source of confusion when you first learn about the document object model. A number of synonyms for window objects muck up the works: *top*, *self*, *parent*, and *frame*. Aggravating the situation is that these terms are also properties of a window object. Under some conditions, a window is its own parent, but if you define a frameset with two frames, there is only one parent among a total of three window objects. It doesn't take long before the whole subject can make your head hurt.

If you do not use frames in your Web applications, all of these headaches never appear. But if frames are part of your design plan, you should get to know how frames affect the object model.

Frames

The application of frames has become a religious issue among page authors: some swear by them, while others swear at them. I believe there can be compelling reasons to use frames at times. For example, if you have a document that requires considerable scrolling to get through, you may want to maintain a static set of navigation controls visible at all times. By placing those controls — be they links or image maps — in a separate frame, you have made the controls available for immediate access, regardless of the scrolled condition of the main document.

Creating frames

The task of defining frames in a document remains the same whether or not you're using JavaScript. The simplest framesetting document consists of tags that are devoted to setting up the frameset, as follows:

```
<HTML>
<HEAD>
<TITLE>My Frameset</TITLE>
</HEAD>
<FRAMESET>
        <FRAME NAME="Frame1" SRC="document1.html">
        <FRAME NAME="Frame2" SRC="document2.html">
</FRAMESET>
</HTML>
```

The preceding HTML document, which the user never sees, defines the frameset for the entire browser window. Each frame must have a URL reference (specified by the SRC attribute) for a document to load into that frame. For scripting purposes, assigning a name to each frame with the NAME attribute greatly simplifies scripting frame content.

The frame object model

Perhaps the key to successful frame scripting is understanding that the object model in the browser's memory at any given instant is determined by the HTML tags in the currently loaded documents. All canned object model graphics, such as Figure 13-1 in this book, do not reflect the precise object model for your document or document set.

For a single, frameless document, the object model starts with just one window object, which contains one document, as shown in Figure 14-1. In this simple structure, the window object is the starting point for all references to any loaded object. Because the window is always there — it must be there for a document to load into — a reference to any object in the document can omit a reference to the current window.

Figure 14-1: The simplest window-document relationship

In a simple two-framed frameset model (Figure 14-2), the browser treats the container of the initial, framesetting document as the *parent* window. The only visible evidence that the document exists is that the framesetting document's title appears in the browser window title bar.

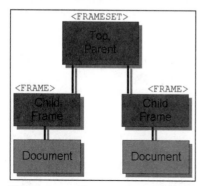

Figure 14-2: The parent and frames are part of the object model.

Each <FRAME> tag inside the <FRAMESET> tag set creates another window object into which a document is loaded. Each of those frames, then, has a document object associated with it. From the point of view of a given document, it has a single window container, just like the model shown in Figure 14-2. And although the parent frame object is not visible to the user, it remains in the object model in memory. The presence of the parent often makes it a convenient repository for variable data that needs to be shared by multiple child frames or must persist between loading of different documents inside a child frame.

In even more complex arrangements, as shown in Figure 14-3, a child frame itself may load a framesetting document. In this situation, the differentiation between the parent and top object starts to come into focus. The top window is the only one in common with all frames in Figure 14-3. As you will see in a moment, when frames need to communicate with other frames (and their documents), you must fashion references to the distant object via the window object they all have in common.

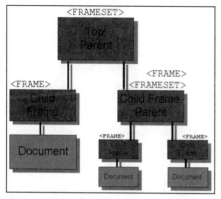

Figure 14-3: Three generations of window objects

Referencing frames

The purpose of an object reference is to help JavaScript locate the desired object in the object model currently held in memory. A reference is a road map for the browser to follow, so that it can track down, say, the value of a particular text field in a particular document. Therefore, when you construct a reference, think about where the script appears in the object model and how the reference can help the browser determine where it should go to find the distant object. In a two-generation scenario such as the one shown in Figure 14-2, three intergenerational references are possible:

✦ Parent-to-child

✦ Child-to-parent

✦ Child-to-child

Assuming that you need to access an object, function, or variable in the relative's frame, the following are the corresponding reference structures: `frameName.objFuncVarName`; `parent.objFuncVarName`; `parent.frameName.objFuncVarName`.

The rule is this: Whenever a reference must point to another frame, begin the reference with the window object that the two destinations have in common. To demonstrate that rule on the complex model in Figure 14-3, if the left-hand child frame's document needs to reference the document at the bottom right of the map, the reference structure is

`top.frameName.frameName.document. ...`

Follow the map from the top window object down through two frames to the final document. JavaScript has to take this route, so your reference must help it along.

Top versus parent

After seeing the previous object maps and reference examples, you may be wondering, Why not use `top` as the leading object in all trans-frame references? From an object model point of view, you'll have no problem doing that: A `parent` in a two-generation scenario is also the `top` window. What you can't count on, however, is your framesetting document always being the top window object in someone's browser. Take the instance where a Web site loads other Web sites into one of its frames. At that instant, the `top` window object belongs to someone else. If you always specify `top` in references intended just for your `parent` window, your references won't work and will probably lead to script errors for the user. My advice, then, is to use `parent` in references whenever you mean one generation above the current document.

Preventing framing

You can use your knowledge of `top` and `parent` references to prevent your pages from being displayed inside another Web site's frameset. Your top-level document must check whether it is loaded into its own top or parent window. When a document is in its own top window, a reference to the `top` property of the current window is equal to a reference to the current window (the window synonym `self` seems most grammatically fitting here). If the two values are not equal, you can script your document to reload itself as a top-level document. When it is critical that your document be a top-level document, include the script in Listing 14-1 in the head portion of your document:

Listing 14-1: **Prevention from Getting "Framed"**

```
<SCRIPT LANGUAGE="JavaScript">
if (top != self) {
    top.location = location
}
</SCRIPT>
```

Your document may appear momentarily inside the other site's frameset, but then the slate is wiped clean, and your top-level document rules the browser window.

Switching from frames to frameless

Some sites load themselves in a frameset by default and offer users the option of getting rid of the frames. You cannot dynamically change the makeup of a frameset once it has loaded, but you can load the content page of the frameset into the main window. Simply include a button or link whose action loads that document into the top window object:

```
top.location = "mainBody.html"
```

A switch back to the frame version entails nothing more complicated than loading the framesetting document.

Inheritance versus containment

Scripters who have experience in object-oriented programming environments probably expect frames to inherit properties, methods, functions, and variables defined in a parent object. That's *not* the case in JavaScript. You can, however, still access those parent items when you make a call to the item with a complete reference to the parent. For example, if you want to define a deferred function in the framesetting parent document that all frames can share, the scripts in the frames would refer to that function with this reference:

```
parent.myFunc()
```

You can pass arguments to such functions and expect returned values.

Navigator 2 bug: Parent variables

Some bugs linger in Navigator 2 that cause problems when accessing variables in a parent window from one of its children. If a document in one of the child frames unloads, a parent variable value that depends on that frame may get scrambled or disappear. Using a temporary document.cookie for global variable values may be a better solution. For Navigator 3 and up, you should declare parent variables that are updated from child frames as first-class string objects (with the new String() constructor) as described in Chapter 27.

Frame synchronization

A pesky problem for some scripters' plans is that including immediate scripts in the framesetting document is dangerous — if not crash-prone in Navigator 2. Such scripts tend to rely on the presence of documents in the frames being created by this framesetting document. But if the frames have not yet been created and their documents loaded, the immediate scripts will likely crash and burn.

One way to guard against this problem is to trigger all such scripts from the frameset's onLoad= event handler. This handler won't trigger until all documents have successfully loaded into the child frames defined by the frameset. At the same time, be careful with onLoad= event handlers in the documents going into a frameset's frames. If one of those scripts relies on the presence of a document in another frame (one of its brothers or sisters), you're doomed to eventual failure. Anything coming from a slow network or server to a slow modem can get in the way of other documents loading into frames in the ideal order.

One way to work around this problem is to create a string variable in the parent document to act as a flag for the successful loading of subsidiary frames. When a document loads into a frame, its onLoad= event handler can set that flag to a word of your choice to indicate that the document has loaded. A better solution, however, is to construct the code so that the parent's onLoad= event handler triggers all the scripts that you want to run after loading. Depending on other frames is a tricky business, but the farther the installed base of Web browsers gets from Navigator 2, the less the associated risk. For example, beginning with Navigator 3, if a user resizes a window, the document does not reload itself, as it used to in Navigator 2. Even so, you still should test your pages thoroughly for any residual effects that may accrue if someone resizes a window or clicks Reload.

Blank frames

Often, you may find it desirable to create a frame in a frameset but not put any document in it until the user has interacted with various controls or other user interface elements in other frames. Navigator has a somewhat empty document in one of its internal URLs (about:blank). But with Navigator 2 and 3 on the Macintosh, an Easter egg–style message appears in that window when it displays. This URL is also not guaranteed to be available on non-Netscape browsers. If you need a blank frame, let your framesetting document write a generic HTML document to the frame directly from the SRC attribute for the frame, as shown in the skeletal code in Listing 14-2. It requires no additional transactions to load an "empty" HTML document.

Listing 14-2: **Creating a Blank Frame**

```
<HTML>
<HEAD>
<SCRIPT LANGUAGE="JavaScript">
<!--
function blank() {
      return "<HTML></HTML>"
}
//-->
```

```
</SCRIPT>
</HEAD>
<FRAMESET>
      <FRAME NAME="Frame1" SRC="someURL.html">
      <FRAME NAME="Frame2" SRC="javascript:'parent.blank()'">
</FRAMESET>
</HTML>
```

Viewing frame source code

Studying other scripters' work is a major learning tool for JavaScript (or any programming language). Beginning with Navigator 3, you can easily view the source code for any frame, including those frames whose content is generated entirely or in part by JavaScript. Click the desired frame to activate it (a subtle border appears just inside the frame on some browser versions, but don't be alarmed if the border doesn't appear). Then select Frame Source from the View menu (or right-click submenu). You can also print or save a selected frame (from the File menu).

Window Object

Properties	Methods	Event Handlers
closed	alert()	onBlur=
defaultStatus	back()	onDragDrop=
document	blur()	onFocus=
frames[]	captureEvents()	onLoad=
history	clearInterval()	onMove=
innerHeight	clearTimeout()	onResize=
innerWidth	close()	onUnload=
location	confirm()	
locationbar	disableExternalCapture()	
menubar	enableExternalCapture()	
name	find()	
onerror	handleEvent()	
opener	forward()	
outerHeight	home()	
outerWidth	moveBy()	
pageXOffset	moveTo()	
pageYOffset	focus()	

Properties	Methods	Event Handlers
parent	open()	
personalbar	print()	
scrollbars	prompt()	
self	releaseEvents()	
status	resizeBy()	
statusbar	resizeTo()	
toolbar	routeEvent()	
top	scroll()	
window	scrollBy()	
	scrollTo()	
	setInterval()	
	setTimeout()	
	stop()	

Syntax

Creating a window:

```
windowObject = window.open([parameters])
```

Accessing window properties or methods:

```
window.property | method([parameters])

self.property | method([parameters])

windowObject.property | method([parameters])
```

About this object

The window object has the unique position of being at the top of the JavaScript object hierarchy. This exalted location gives the window object a number of properties and behaviors unlike those of any other object.

Chief among its unique characteristics is that because everything takes place in a window, you can usually omit the window object from object references. You've seen this behavior in previous chapters when I invoked document methods such as document.write(). The complete reference is window.document.write(). But because the activity was taking place in the window that held the document running the script, that window was assumed to be part of the reference. For single-frame windows, this concept is simple enough to grasp.

As previously stated, among the list of properties for the window object is one called self. This property is synonymous with the window object itself (which is why it shows up in hierarchy diagrams as an object). Having a property of an object that is the same name as the object may sound confusing, but this situation is not that uncommon in object-oriented environments. I discuss the reasons why you may want to use the `self` property as the window's object reference in the `self` property description that follows.

As indicated earlier in the syntax definition, you don't always have to specifically create a window object in JavaScript code. When you start your browser, it usually opens a window. That window is a valid window object, even if the window is blank. Therefore, when a user loads your page into the browser, the window object part of that document is automatically created for your script to access as it pleases.

Your script's control over an existing (already open) window's user interface elements varies widely with the browser and browser version for which your application is intended. With the exception of Navigator 4, the only change you can make to an open window is to the status line at the bottom of the browser window. With Navigator 4, however, you can control such properties as the size, location, and "chrome" elements (toolbars and scrollbars, for example) on the fly. Many of these properties can be changed beyond specific safe limits only if you cryptographically sign the scripts (see Chapter 40) and the user grants permission for your scripts to make those modifications.

Window properties are far more flexible on all browsers when your scripts generate a new window (with the `window.open()` method): You can influence the size, toolbar, or other view options of a window. Navigator 4 provides even more options for new windows, including whether the window should remain at a fixed layer among desktop windows and whether the window should even display a title bar. Again, if an option can conceivably be used to deceive a user (for example, hiding one window that monitors activity in another window), signed scripts and user permission are necessary.

The window object is also the level at which a script asks the browser to display any of three styles of dialog boxes (a plain alert dialog box, an OK/Cancel confirmation dialog box, or a prompt for user text entry). Although dialog boxes are extremely helpful for cobbling together debugging tools for your own use (Chapter 45), they can be very disruptive to visitors who navigate through Web sites. Because JavaScript dialog boxes are *modal* (that is, you cannot do anything else in the browser — or anything at all on a Macintosh — until you dismiss the dialog box), use them sparingly, if at all. Remember that some users may create macros on their computers to visit sites unattended. Should such an automated access of your site encounter a modal dialog box, it would be trapped on your page until a human could intervene.

All dialog boxes generated by JavaScript in Netscape browsers identify themselves as being generated by JavaScript (less egregiously so in Navigator 4). This is primarily a security feature to prevent deceitful, unsigned scripts from creating system- or application-style dialog boxes that convince visitors to enter private information. It should also discourage dialog box usage in Web page design. And that's good, because dialog boxes tend to be disruptive.

Why are dialog boxes window methods?

I find it odd that dialog boxes are generated as window methods rather than as methods of the navigator object. These dialogs don't really belong to any window. In fact, their modality prevents the user from accessing any window.

To my way of thinking, these methods (and the ones that create or close windows) belong to an object level one step above the window object in the hierarchy (which would include the properties of the navigator object described in Chapter 25). I don't lose sleep over this setup, though. If the powers that be insist on making these dialog boxes part of the window object, that's how my code will read.

Netscape's JavaScript dialog boxes are not particularly flexible in letting you fill them with text or graphic elements beyond the basics. In fact, you can't even change the text of the dialog buttons or add a button. With Navigator 4, however, you can use signed scripts to generate a window that looks and behaves very much like a modal dialog box. Into that window you can load any HTML you like. Thus, you can use such a window as an entry form, preferences selector, or whatever else makes user interface sense in your application. Internet Explorer 4, on the other hand, has a separate method and set of properties specifically for generating a modal dialog. The two scripted solutions are not compatible with each other.

Properties

closed

Value: Boolean   **Gettable:** Yes   **Settable:** No

	Nav2	Nav3	Nav4	IE3/J1	IE3/J2	IE4/J3
Compatibility		✔	✔			✔

When you create a subwindow with the `window.open()` method, you may need to access object properties from that subwindow, such as setting the value of a text field. Access to the subwindow is via the window object reference that is returned by the `window.open()` method, as in the following code fragment:

```
var newWind = window.open("someURL.html","subWind")
...
newWind.document.entryForm.ZIP.value = "00000"
```

In this example, the `newWind` variable is not linked "live" to the window, but is only a reference to that window. If the user should close the window, the `newWind` variable still contains the reference to the now missing window. Thus, any script reference to an object in that missing window will likely cause a script error. What you need to know before accessing items in a subwindow is whether the window is still open.

The `closed` property returns true if the window object has been closed either by script or by the user. Any time you have a script statement that can be triggered after the user has an opportunity to close the window, test for the `closed` property before executing that statement.

As a workaround for Navigator 2, any property of a closed window reference returns a null value. Thus, you can test whether, say, the `parent` property of the new window is null: If so, the window has already closed. Internet Explorer 3, on the other hand, triggers a scripting error if you attempt to access a property of a closed window — there is no error-free way to detect whether a window is open or closed in Internet Explorer 3. The `window.closed` property is implemented in Internet Explorer 4.

Example

In Listing 14-3, I have created the ultimate cross-platform window opening and closing sample. It takes into account the lack of the `opener` property in Navigator 2, the missing `closed` property in Navigator 2 and Internet Explorer 3, and even provides an ugly but necessary workaround for Internet Explorer 3's inability to gracefully see if a subwindow is still open.

The script begins by initializing a global variable, `newWind`, which is used to hold the object reference to the second window. This value needs to be global so that other functions can reference the window for tasks such as closing. Another global variable, `isIE3`, is a Boolean flag that will let the window closing routines know whether the visitor is using Internet Explorer 3 (see details about the `navigator.appVersion` property in Chapter 25).

For this example, the new window contains some HTML code written dynamically to it, rather than loading an existing HTML file into it. Therefore, the URL parameter of the `window.open()` method is left as an empty string. It is vital, however, to assign a name in the second parameter to accommodate the Internet Explorer 3 workaround for closing the window. After the new window is opened, the script assigns an `opener` property to the object if one is not already assigned (this is needed only for Navigator 2). After that, the script assembles HTML to be written to the new window via one `document.write()` statement. The `document.close()` method closes writing to the document — a different kind of close than a window close.

A second function is responsible for closing the subwindow. To accommodate Internet Explorer 3, the script appears to create another window with the same characteristics as the one opened earlier in the script. This is the trick: If the earlier window exists (with exactly the same parameters and a name other than an empty string), Internet Explorer does not create a new window even with the `window.open()` method executing in plain sight. To the user, nothing unusual appears on the screen. Only if the user has closed the subwindow do things look weird for Internet Explorer 3 users. The `window.open()` method momentarily creates that subwindow. This is necessary because a "living" window object must be available for the upcoming test of window existence (Internet Explorer 3 displays a script error if you try to address a missing window, while Navigator and Internet Explorer 4 simply return friendly null values).

As a final test, an `if` condition looks at two conditions: 1) if the window object has ever been initialized with a value other than null (in case you click the window closing button before ever having created the new window) and 2) if the window's `closed` property is null or false. If either condition is true, the `close()` method is sent to the second window.

Listing 14-3: **Checking Before Closing a Window**

```
<HTML>
<HEAD>
<TITLE>window.closed Property</TITLE>
<SCRIPT LANGUAGE="JavaScript">
// initialize global var for new window object
// so it can be accessed by all functions on the page
var newWind
// set flag to help out with special handling for window closing
var isIE3 = (navigator.appVersion.indexOf("MSIE 3") != -1) ? true :
false
// make the new window and put some stuff in it
function newWindow() {
        var output = ""
        newWind = window.open("","subwindow","HEIGHT=200,WIDTH=200")
        // take care of Navigator 2
        if (newWind.opener == null) {
            newWind.opener = window
        }
        output += "<HTML><BODY><H1>A Sub-window</H1>"
        output += "<FORM><INPUT TYPE='button' VALUE='Close Main Window'"
        output +="onClick='window.opener.close()'></FORM></BODY></HTML>"
        newWind.document.write(output)
        newWind.document.close()
}
// close subwindow, including ugly workaround for IE3
function closeWindow() {
        if (isIE3) {
            // if window is already open, nothing appears to happen
            // but if not, the subwindow flashes momentarily (yech!)
            newWind = window.open("","subwindow","HEIGHT=200,WIDTH=200")
        }
        if (newWind && !newWind.closed) {
            newWind.close()
        }
}
</SCRIPT>
</HEAD>
<BODY>
<FORM>
<INPUT TYPE="button" VALUE="Open Window" onClick="newWindow()"><BR>
<INPUT TYPE="button" VALUE="Close it if Still Open" onClick="closeWindow()">
</FORM>
</BODY>
</HTML>
```

To complete the example of the window opening and closing, notice that the subwindow is given a button whose onClick= event handler closes the main window. In Navigator 2 and Internet Explorer 3, this occurs without complaint. But in Navigator 3 and up and Internet Explorer 4, the user will likely be presented with an alert asking to confirm the closure of the main browser window.

Related Items: window.open() method; window.close() method.

defaultStatus

Value: String   **Gettable:** Yes   **Settable:** Yes

	Nav2	Nav3	Nav4	IE3/J1	IE3/J2	IE4/J3
Compatibility	✔	✔	✔	✔	✔	✔

After a document is loaded into a window or frame, the statusbar's message field can display a string that is visible any time the mouse pointer is not atop an object that takes precedence over the statusbar (such as a link object or an image map). The window.defaultStatus property is normally an empty string, but you can set this property at any time. Any setting of this property will be temporarily overridden when a user moves the mouse pointer atop a link object (see window.status property for information about customizing this temporary statusbar message).

Probably the most common time to set the window.defaultStatus property is when a document loads into a window. You can do this as an immediate script statement that executes from the Head or Body portion of the document or as part of a document's onLoad= event handler.

Note

The defaultStatus property does not work well in Navigator 2 or Internet Explorer 3, and experiences problems in Navigator 3, especially on the Macintosh (where the property doesn't change even after loading a different document into the window). Many users simply don't see the statusbar change during Web surfing, so don't put mission-critical information in the statusbar.

Example

Unless you plan to change the default statusbar text while a user spends time at your Web page, the best time to set the property is when the document loads. In Listing 14-4, notice how I also extract this property to reset the statusbar in an onMouseOut= event handler. Setting the status property to empty also resets the statusbar to the defaultStatus setting.

Listing 14-4: **Setting the Default Status Message**

```
<HTML>
<HEAD>
<TITLE>window.defaultStatus property</TITLE>
<SCRIPT LANGUAGE="JavaScript">
```

(continued)

Listing 14-4 *(continued)*

```
window.defaultStatus = "Welcome to my Web site."
</SCRIPT>
</HEAD>
<BODY>
<A HREF="http://home.netscape.com" onMouseOver="window.status = 'Go to
your browser Home page.';return true" onMouseOut="window.status =
'';return true">Home</A><P>
<A HREF="http://home.netscape.com" onMouseOver="window.status = 'Visit
Netscape\'s Home page.';return true" onMouseOut="window.status =
window.defaultStatus;return true">Netscape</A>
</BODY>
</HTML>
```

If you need to display single or double quotes in the statusbar (as in the second link in Listing 14-4), use escape characters (\' and \") as part of the strings being assigned to these properties.

Related Items: `window.status` property.

document

Value: Object   **Gettable:** Yes   **Settable:** No

	Nav2	Nav3	Nav4	IE3/J1	IE3/J2	IE4/J3
Compatibility	✔	✔	✔	✔	✔	✔

I list the `document` property here primarily for completeness. A window object contains a single document object (although in Navigator 4, a window may also contain layers, each of which has a document object, as described in Chapter 19). The value of the `document` property is the document object, which is not a displayable value. Instead, you use the `document` property as you build references to properties and methods of the document and to other objects contained by the document, such as a form and its elements. To load a different document into a window, use the location object (see Chapter 15). The document object is described in detail in Chapter 16.

Related Items: document object.

frames

Value: Window object   **Gettable:** Yes   **Settable:** No

	Nav2	Nav3	Nav4	IE3/J1	IE3/J2	IE4/J3
Compatibility	✔	✔	✔	✔	✔	✔

In a multiframe window, the top or parent window contains any number of separate frames, each of which acts like a full-fledged window object. The `frames` property (note the plural use of the word as a property name) plays a role when a statement must reference an object located in a different frame. For example, if a button in one frame is scripted to display a document in another frame, the button's event handler must be able to tell JavaScript precisely where to display the new HTML document. The `frames` property assists in that task.

To use the `frames` property to communicate from one frame to another, it should be part of a reference that begins with the `parent` or `top` property. This lets JavaScript make the proper journey through the hierarchy of all currently loaded objects to reach the desired object. To find out how many frames are currently active in a window, use this expression:

```
parent.frames.length
```

This expression returns a number indicating how many frames are defined by the parent window. This value does not, however, count further nested frames, should a third generation of frame be defined in the environment. In other words, no single property exists that you can use to determine the total number of frames in the browser window if multiple generations of frames are present.

The browser stores information about all visible frames in a numbered (indexed) array, with the first frame (that is, the topmost `<FRAME>` tag defined in the framesetting document) as number 0:

```
parent.frames[0]
```

Therefore, if the window shows three frames (whose indexes would be `frames[0]`, `frames[1]`, and `frames[2]`, respectively), the reference for retrieving the `title` property of the document in the second frame is

```
parent.frames[1].document.title
```

This reference is a road map that starts at the parent window and extends to the second frame's document and its `title` property. Other than the number of frames defined in a parent window and each frame's name (`top.frames[i].name`), no other values from the frame definitions are directly available from the frame object via scripting.

Using index values for frame references is not always the safest tactic, however, because your frameset design may change over time, in which case the index values will also change. Instead, you should take advantage of the NAME attribute of the `<FRAME>` tag, and assign a unique, descriptive name to each frame. Then you can use a frame's name as an alternative to the indexed reference. For example, in Listing 14-5, two frames are assigned with distinctive names. To access the title of a document in the `JustAKid2` frame, the complete object reference is

```
parent.JustAKid2.document.title
```

with the frame name (case-sensitive) substituting for the `frames[1]` array reference. Or, in keeping with JavaScript flexibility, you can use the object name in the array index position:

```
parent.frames["JustAKid2"].document.title
```

The supreme advantage to using frame names in references is that no matter how the frameset may change over time, a reference to a named frame will always find that frame, although its index value (that is, position in the frameset) may change.

Example

Listings 14-5 and 14-6 demonstrate how JavaScript treats values of frame references from objects inside a frame. The same document is loaded into each frame. A script in that document extracts info about the current frame and the entire frameset. Figure 14-4 shows the results after loading the HTML document in Listing 14-3.

Listing 14-5: **Framesetting Document for Listing 14-6**

```
<HTML>
<HEAD>
<TITLE>window.frames property</TITLE>
</HEAD>
<FRAMESET COLS="50%,50%">
        <FRAME NAME="JustAKid1" SRC="lst14-06.htm">
        <FRAME NAME="JustAKid2" SRC="lst14-06.htm">
</FRAMESET>
</HTML>
```

A call to determine the number (length) of frames returns 0 from the point of view of the current frame referenced. That's because each frame here is a window that has no nested frames within it. But add the `parent` property to the reference, and the scope zooms out to take into account all frames generated by the parent window's document.

Listing 14-6: **Showing Various window Properties**

```
<HTML>
<HEAD>
<TITLE>Window Revealer II</TITLE>
<SCRIPT LANGUAGE="JavaScript">
function gatherWindowData() {
        var msg = ""
        msg += "<B>From the point of view of this frame:</B><BR>"
        msg += "window.frames.length: " + window.frames.length + "<BR>"
        msg += "window.name: " + window.name + "<P>"
        msg += "<B>From the point of view of the framesetting
document:</B><BR>"
        msg += "parent.frames.length: " + parent.frames.length + "<BR>"
        msg += "parent.frames[0].name: " + parent.frames[0].name
        return msg
}
</SCRIPT>
</HEAD>
```

```
<BODY>
<SCRIPT LANGUAGE="JavaScript">
document.write(gatherWindowData())
</SCRIPT>
</BODY>
</HTML>
```

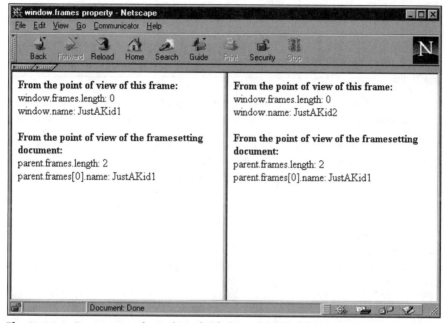

Figure 14-4: Property readouts from both frames loaded from Listing 14-5

The last statement in the example shows how to use the array syntax (brackets) to refer to a specific frame. All array indexes start with 0 for the first entry. Because the document asks for the name of the first frame (`parent.frames[0]`), the response is `JustAKid1` for both frames.

Related Items: `window.parent` property; `window.top` property.

history

Value: Object   **Gettable:** Yes   **Settable:** No

	Nav2	Nav3	Nav4	IE3/J1	IE3/J2	IE4/J3
Compatibility	✔	✔	✔	✔	✔	✔

See the discussion of the history object in Chapter 15.

innerHeight
innerWidth
outerHeight
outerWidth

Value: Integer   **Gettable:** Yes   **Settable:** Yes

	Nav2	Nav3	Nav4	IE3/J1	IE3/J2	IE4/J3
Compatibility			✔			

Navigator 4 lets scripts adjust the height and width of any window, including the main browser window. This can be helpful when your page shows itself best with the browser window sized to a particular height and width. Rather than relying on the user to size the browser window for optimum viewing of your page, you can dictate the size of the window (although the user can always manually resize the main window). And because you can examine the operating system of the visitor via the navigator object (see Chapter 25), you can size a window to adjust for the differences in font and form element rendering on different platforms.

Netscape provides two different points of reference for measuring the height and width of a window: *inner* and *outer*. Both are measured in pixels. The inner measurements are that of the active document area of a window (sometimes known as a window's *content region*). If the optimum display of your document depends on the document display area being a certain number of pixels high and/or wide, the innerHeight and innerWidth properties are the ones to set.

In contrast, the outer measurements are of the outside boundary of the entire window, including whatever "chrome" is showing in the window: scrollbars, statusbar, and so on. Setting the outerHeight and outerWidth is generally done in concert with a reading of screen object properties (Chapter 25). Perhaps the most common usage of the outer properties is to set the browser window to fill the available screen area of the visitor's monitor.

A more efficient way of modifying both outer dimensions of a window is with the window.resizeTo() method. The method takes width and height as parameters, thus accomplishing a window resizing in one statement. Be aware that resizing a window does not adjust the location of a window. Therefore, just because you set the outer dimensions of a window to the available space returned by the screen object doesn't mean that the window will suddenly fill the available space on the monitor. Application of the window.moveTo() method is necessary to ensure the top-left corner of the window is at screen coordinates 0,0.

Despite the freedom that these properties afford the page author, Netscape has built in a minimum size limitation for scripts that are not cryptographically signed. You cannot set these properties such that the outer height and width of the window is smaller than 100 pixels on a side. This is to prevent an unsigned script from setting up a small or nearly invisible window that monitors activity in other windows. With signed scripts, however, windows can be made smaller than 100-by-100 pixels with the user's permission.

Example

In Listing 14-7, a number of buttons let you see the results of setting the innerHeight, innerWidth, outerHeight, and outerWidth properties.

Listing 14-7: **Setting Window Height and Width**

```
<HTML>
<HEAD>
<TITLE>Window Sizer</TITLE>
<SCRIPT LANGUAGE="JavaScript">
// store original outer dimensions as page loads
var originalWidth = window.outerWidth
var originalHeight = window.outerHeight
// generic function to set inner dimensions
function setInner(width, height) {
        window.innerWidth = width
        window.innerHeight = height
}
// generic function to set outer dimensions
function setOuter(width, height) {
        window.outerWidth = width
        window.outerHeight = height
}
// restore window to original dimensions
function restore() {
        window.outerWidth = originalWidth
        window.outerHeight = originalHeight
}
</SCRIPT>
</HEAD>
<BODY>
<FORM>
<B>Setting Inner Sizes</B><BR>
<INPUT TYPE="button" VALUE="600 Pixels Square"
onClick="setInner(600,600)"><BR>
<INPUT TYPE="button" VALUE="300 Pixels Square"
onClick="setInner(300,300)"><BR>
<INPUT TYPE="button" VALUE="Available Screen Space"
onClick="setInner(screen.availWidth, screen.availHeight)"><BR>
<HR>
<B>Setting Outer Sizes</B><BR>
<INPUT TYPE="button" VALUE="600 Pixels Square"
onClick="setOuter(600,600)"><BR>
<INPUT TYPE="button" VALUE="300 Pixels Square"
onClick="setOuter(300,300)"><BR>
<INPUT TYPE="button" VALUE="Available Screen Space"
onClick="setOuter(screen.availWidth, screen.availHeight)"><BR>
```

(continued)

Listing 14-7 *(continued)*

```
<HR>
<INPUT TYPE="button" VALUE="Cinch up for Win95"
onClick="setInner(273,304)"><BR>
<INPUT TYPE="button" VALUE="Cinch up for Mac"
onClick="setInner(273,304)"><BR>
<INPUT TYPE="button" VALUE="Restore Original" onClick="restore()"><BR>
</FORM>
</BODY>
</HTML>
```

As the document loads, it saves the current outer dimensions in global variables. One of the buttons restores the windows to these settings. Two parallel sets of buttons set the inner and outer dimensions to the same pixel values so you can see the effects on the overall window and document area when a script changes the various properties.

Because Navigator 4 displays different-looking buttons in different platforms (as well as other elements), the two buttons contain script instructions to size the window to best display the window contents. Unfortunately, no measure of the active area of a document is available, so the dimension values were determined by trial and error before being hard-wired into the script.

Related Items: `window.resizeTo()` method; `window.moveTo()` method; screen object; navigator object.

location

Value: Object   **Gettable:** Yes   **Settable:** No

	Nav2	Nav3	Nav4	IE3/J1	IE3/J2	IE4/J3
Compatibility	✔	✔	✔	✔	✔	✔

See the discussion of the location object in Chapter 15.

locationbar
menubar
personalbar
scrollbars
statusbar
toolbar

Value: Object   **Gettable:** Yes   **Settable:** Yes (with signed scripts)

	Nav2	Nav3	Nav4	IE3/J1	IE3/J2	IE4/J3
Compatibility	✔	✔	✔	✔	✔	✔

Beyond the rectangle of the content region of a window (where your documents appear), the Netscape browser window displays an amalgam of bars and other features known collectively as *chrome*. All browsers can elect to remove these chrome items when creating a new window (as part of the third parameter of the `window.open()` method), but until signed scripts were available in Navigator 4, these items could not be turned on and off in the main browser window or any existing window.

Navigator 4 promotes these elements to first-class objects contained by the window object. Figure 14-5 points out where each of the six bars appears in a fully chromed window. The only element that is not part of this scheme is the window's title bar. You can create a new window without a title bar (with a signed script), but you cannot hide and show the title bar on an existing window.

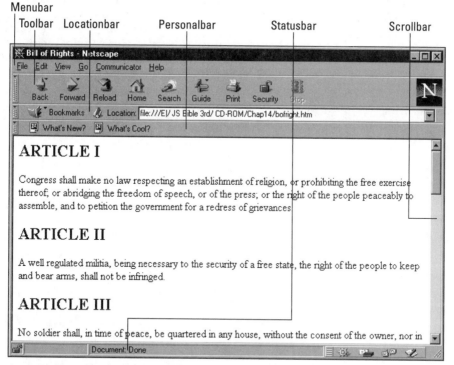

Figure 14-5: Window chrome items

Chrome objects have but one property: `visible`. Reading this Boolean value (possible without signed scripts) lets you inspect the visitor's browser window for the elements currently engaged. There is no intermediate setting or property for the expanded/collapsed state of the toolbar, locationbar, and personalbar.

Changing the visibility of these items on the fly alters the relationship between the inner and outer dimensions of the browser window. If you must carefully size a window to display content, you should adjust the chrome elements before sizing the window. Before you start changing chrome visibility on your page visitors, weigh the decision carefully. Experienced users have fine-tuned the look of their browser windows to just the way they like them. If you mess with that look, you might anger your visitors. Fortunately, changes you make to a chrome element's visibility are not stored to the user's preferences. However, the changes you make survive an unloading of the page. If you change the settings, be sure you first save the initial settings and restore them with an `onUnload=` event handler.

Note

The Macintosh menubar is not part of the browser's window chrome. Therefore, its visibility cannot be adjusted from a script.

Example

In Listing 14-8, you can experiment with the look of a browser window with any of the chrome elements turned on and off. To run this script, you must either sign the scripts or turn on codebase principals (see Chapter 40). Java must also be enabled to use the signed script statements.

As the page loads, it stores the current state of each chrome element. One button for each chrome element triggers the `toggleBar()` function. This function inverts the visible property for the chrome object passed as a parameter to the function. Finally, the Restore button returns visibility to their original settings. Notice that the `restore()` function is also called by the `onUnload=` event handler for the document.

Listing 14-8: **Controlling Window Chrome**

```
<HTML>
<HEAD>
<TITLE>Bars Bars Bars</TITLE>
<SCRIPT LANGUAGE="JavaScript">
// store original outer dimensions as page loads
var originalLocationbar = window.locationbar.visible
var originalMenubar = window.menubar.visible
var originalPersonalbar = window.personalbar.visible
var originalScrollbars = window.scrollbars.visible
var originalStatusbar = window.statusbar.visible
var originalToolbar = window.toolbar.visible

// generic function to set inner dimensions
function toggleBar(bar) {
netscape.security.PrivilegeManager.enablePrivilege("UniversalBrowserWrite")
        bar.visible = !bar.visible

netscape.security.PrivilegeManager.disablePrivilege("UniversalBrowserWrite")
}
// restore settings
function restore() {
netscape.security.PrivilegeManager.enablePrivilege("UniversalBrowserWrite")
```

```
          window.locationbar.visible = originalLocationbar
          window.menubar.visible = originalMenubar
          window.personalbar.visible = originalPersonalbar
          window.scrollbars.visible = originalScrollbars
          window.statusbar.visible = originalStatusbar
          window.toolbar.visible = originalToolbar
netscape.security.PrivilegeManager.disablePrivilege("UniversalBrowserWrite")
}
</SCRIPT>
</HEAD>
<BODY onUnload="restore()">
<FORM>
<B>Toggle Window Bars</B><BR>
<INPUT TYPE="button" VALUE="Location Bar"
onClick="toggleBar(window.locationbar)"><BR>
<INPUT TYPE="button" VALUE="Menu Bar"
onClick="toggleBar(window.menubar)"><BR>
<INPUT TYPE="button" VALUE="Personal Bar"
onClick="toggleBar(window.personalbar)"><BR>
<INPUT TYPE="button" VALUE="Scrollbars"
onClick="toggleBar(window.scrollbars)"><BR>
<INPUT TYPE="button" VALUE="Status Bar"
onClick="toggleBar(window.statusbar)"><BR>
<INPUT TYPE="button" VALUE="Tool Bar"
onClick="toggleBar(window.toolbar)"><BR>
<HR>
<INPUT TYPE="button" VALUE="Restore Original Settings"
onClick="restore()"><BR>
</FORM>
</BODY>
</HTML>
```

Related Items: `window.open()` method.

name

Value: String   **Gettable:** Yes   **Settable:** Yes

	Nav2	Nav3	Nav4	IE3/J1	IE3/J2	IE4/J3
Compatibility	✔	✔	✔	✔	✔	✔

All window objects can have names assigned to them. Names are particularly useful for working with frames, because a good naming scheme for a multiframe environment can help you determine precisely which frame you're working with in references coming from other frames.

The main browser window, however, has no name attached to it by default. Its value is an empty string. There aren't many reasons to assign a name to the window, because JavaScript and HTML provide plenty of other ways to refer to the window object (the `top` property, the `_top` constant for `TARGET` attributes, and the `opener` property from subwindows).

If you want to attach a name to the main window, you can do so by setting the `window.name` property at any time. But be aware that because this is a window property, the life of its value extends beyond the loading and unloading of any given document. Chances are that your scripts would use the reference in only one document or frameset. Unless you restore the default empty string, your programmed window name will be present for any other document that loads later. My suggestion in this regard is to assign a name in a window's or frameset's `onLoad=` event handler and then reset it to empty in a corresponding `onUnload=` event handler:

```
<BODY onLoad="self.name = 'Main'" onUnload="self.name = "">
```

You can see an example of this application in Listing 14-14, where setting a parent window name is helpful for learning the relationships among parent and child windows.

Related Items: `window.open()` method; `top` property.

onerror

Value: Null, Undefined, or Function Object   **Gettable:** Yes   **Settable:** Yes

	Nav2	Nav3	Nav4	IE3/J1	IE3/J2	IE4/J3
Compatibility		✔	✔			✔

Although script error dialog boxes are a scripter's best friend (if you're into debugging, that is), they can be confusing for users who have never seen such dialog boxes. JavaScript lets you turn off the display of script error windows as someone executes a script on your page. The question is: When should you turn off these dialog boxes?

Script errors generally mean that something is wrong with your script. The error may be the result of a coding mistake or, conceivably, a bug in JavaScript (perhaps on a platform version of the browser you haven't been able to test). When such errors occur, often the script won't continue to do what you intended. Hiding the script error from yourself during development would be foolhardy, because you'd never know whether unseen errors are lurking in your code. It can be equally dangerous to turn off error dialog boxes for users who may believe that the page is operating normally, when, in fact, it's not. Some data values may not be calculated or displayed correctly.

That said, I can see some limited instances of when you'd like to keep such dialog windows from appearing. For example, if you know for a fact that a platform-specific bug trips the error message without harming the execution of the script, you may want to prevent that error alert dialog box from appearing in the files posted to your Web site. You should do this only after extensive testing to ensure that the script ultimately behaves correctly, even with the bug or error.

When the browser starts, the `window.onerror` property is <undefined>. In this state, all errors are reported via the normal JavaScript error window. To turn off error dialog boxes, set the `window.onerror` property to null:

```
window.onerror = null
```

You may recognize this syntax as looking like a property version of an event handler described earlier in this chapter. For Netscape browsers, however, no `onError=` event handler exists that you specify in an HTML tag associated with the window object. The error event just happens. (Internet Explorer 4 lets you add an `onError=` event handler to just about every object tag, but these are ignored by Netscape browsers.)

To restore the error dialog boxes, perform a soft or hard reload of the document. Clicking on the Reload button turns them back on.

You can, however, assign a custom function to the `window.onerror` property. This function then handles errors in a more friendly way under your script control. I prefer an even simpler way: Let a global `onerror()` function do the job. Whenever error dialog boxes are turned on (the default behavior), a script error (or Java applet or class exception) invokes the `onerror()` function, passing three parameters:

✦ Error message

✦ URL of document causing the error

✦ Line number of the error

You can essentially trap for all errors and handle them with your own interface (or no user alert dialog box at all). The last line of this function must be `return true` if you do not want the JavaScript script error dialog box to appear.

If you are using LiveConnect to communicate with a Java applet or call up Java class methods directly from your scripts, you can use an `onerror()` function to handle any *exception* that Java may throw. A Java exception is not necessarily a mistake kind of error: some methods assume that the Java code will trap for exceptions to handle special cases (for example, reacting to a user's denial of access when prompted by a signed script dialog). See Chapter 40 for an example of trapping for a specific Java exception via an `onerror()` function.

Example

In Listing 14-9, one button triggers a script that contains an error. I've added an `onerror()` function to process the error so it opens a separate window, filling in a textarea form element (see Figure 14-6). A Submit button is also provided to mail the bug information to a support center e-mail address from Navigator only — an example of how to handle the occurrence of a bug in your scripts. In case you have not yet seen a true JavaScript error dialog box, change the last line of the `onerror()` function to `return false`, then reload the document and trip the error.

Listing 14-9: **Controlling Script Errors**

```
<HTML>
<HEAD>
<TITLE>Error Dialog Control</TITLE>
<SCRIPT LANGUAGE="JavaScript1.1">
// function with invalid variable value
function goWrong() {
       var x = fred
}
// turn off error dialogs
function errOff() {
       window.onerror = null
}
// turn on error dialogs with hard reload
function errOn() {
       location.reload()
}
function onerror(msg, URL, lineNum) {
       var errWind = window.open("","errors","HEIGHT=270,WIDTH=400")
       var wintxt = "<HTML><BODY BGCOLOR=RED>"
       wintxt += "<B>An error has occurred on this page.  Please
report it to Tech Support.</B>"
       wintxt += "<FORM METHOD=POST ENCTYPE='text-plain'
ACTION=mailTo:support3@dannyg.com>"
       wintxt += "<TEXTAREA COLS=45 ROWS=8 WRAP=VIRTUAL>"
       wintxt += "Error: " + msg + "\n"
       wintxt += "URL: " + URL + "\n"
       wintxt += "Line: " + lineNum + "\n"
       wintxt += "Client: " + navigator.userAgent + "\n"
       wintxt += "-----------------------------------------\n"
       wintxt += "Please describe what you were doing when the error
occurred:"
       wintxt += "</TEXTAREA><P>"
       wintxt += "<INPUT TYPE=SUBMIT VALUE='Send Error Report'>"
       wintxt += "<INPUT TYPE=button VALUE='Close'
onClick='self.close()'>"
       wintxt += "</FORM></BODY></HTML>"
       errWind.document.write(wintxt)
       errWind.document.close()
       return true
}
</SCRIPT>
</HEAD>
<BODY>
<FORM NAME="myform">
<INPUT TYPE="button" VALUE="Cause an Error" onClick="goWrong()"><P>
<INPUT TYPE="button" VALUE="Turn Off Error Dialogs" onClick="errOff()">
<INPUT TYPE="button" VALUE="Turn On Error Dialogs" onClick="errOn()">
</FORM>
</BODY>
</HTML>
```

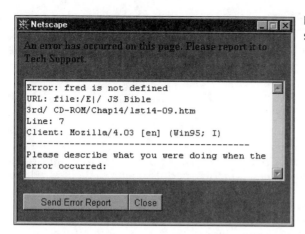

Figure 14-6: An example of a self-reporting error window

Turn off the dialog box by setting the `window.onerror` property to null. I provide a button that performs a hard reload, which, in turn, resets the `window.onerror` property to its default value. With error dialog boxes turned off, the `onerror()` function does not fire.

Related Items: `location.reload()` method; debugging scripts (Chapter 45).

opener

Value: Window object   **Gettable:** Yes   **Settable:** No

	Nav2	Nav3	Nav4	IE3/J1	IE3/J2	IE4/J3
Compatibility		✔	✔	✔	✔	✔

Many scripters make the mistake of thinking that a new browser window created with the `window.open()` method has a child-parent relationship similar to the one that frames have with their parents. That's not the case at all. New browser windows, once created, have a very slim link to the window from whence they came: via the `opener` property. The purpose of the `opener` property is to provide scripts in the new window with valid references back to the original window. For example, the original window may contain some variable values or general-purpose functions that a new window at this Web site will want to use. The original window may also have form elements whose settings either are of value to the new window or get set by user interaction in the new window.

Because the value of the `opener` property is a true window object, you can begin references with the property name. Or, you may use the more complete `window.opener` or `self.opener` reference. But the reference must then include some object or property of that original window, such as a window method or a reference to something contained by that window's document.

Although this property was new for Navigator 3 (and was one of the rare Navigator 3 features to be included in Internet Explorer 3), you can make your scripts backward compatible to Navigator 2. For every new window you create, make sure it has an `opener` property as follows:

```
var newWind = window.open()
if (newWind.opener == null) {
        newWind.opener = self
}
```

For Navigator 2, this step adds the `opener` property to the window object reference. Then, no matter which version of JavaScript-enabled Navigator the user has, the `opener` property in the new window's scripts points to the desired original window.

When a script that generates a new window is within a frame, the `opener` property of the subwindow points to that frame. Therefore, if the subwindow needs to communicate with the main window's parent or another frame in the main window, you have to very carefully build a reference to that distant object. For example, if the subwindow needs to get the `checked` property of a checkbox in a sister frame of the one that created the subwindow, the reference would be

```
opener.parent.sisterFrameName.document.formName.checkboxName.checked
```

It is a long way to go, indeed, but building such a reference is always a case of mapping out the path from where the script is to where the destination is, step by step.

Example

To demonstrate the importance of the `opener` property, let's take a look at how a new window can define itself from settings in the main window (Listing 14-10). The `doNew()` function generates a small subwindow and loads the file in Listing 14-11 into the window. Notice the initial conditional statements in `doNew()` to make sure that if the new window already exists, it comes to the front by invoking the new window's `focus()` method. You can see the results in Figure 14-7. Because the `doNew()` function in Listing 14-10 uses window methods and properties not available in Internet Explorer 3, this example does not work correctly in Internet Explorer 3.

Listing 14-10: Contents of a Main Window Document That Generates a Second Window

```
<HTML>
<HEAD>
<TITLE>Master of all Windows</TITLE>
<SCRIPT LANGUAGE="JavaScript1.1">
var myWind
function doNew() {
        if (!myWind || myWind.closed) {
            myWind = window.open("lst14-
11.htm","subWindow","HEIGHT=200,WIDTH=350")
        } else{
```

```
                    // bring existing subwindow to the front
                    myWind.focus()
                }
        }
    </SCRIPT>
    </HEAD>
    <BODY>
    <FORM NAME="input">
    Select a color for a new window:
    <INPUT TYPE="radio" NAME="color" VALUE="red" CHECKED>Red
    <INPUT TYPE="radio" NAME="color" VALUE="yellow">Yellow
    <INPUT TYPE="radio" NAME="color" VALUE="blue">Blue
    <INPUT TYPE="button" NAME="storage" VALUE="Make a Window"
    onClick="doNew()">
    <HR>
    This field will be filled from an entry in another window:
    <INPUT TYPE="text" NAME="entry" SIZE=25>
    </FORM>
    </BODY>
    </HTML>
```

The window.open() method doesn't provide parameters for setting the new window's background color, so I let the getColor() function in the new window do the job as the document loads. The function uses the opener property to find out which radio button on the main page is selected.

Listing 14-11: **References to the opener Property**

```
<HTML>
<HEAD>
<TITLE>New Window on the Block</TITLE>
<SCRIPT LANGUAGE="JavaScript">
function getColor() {
        // shorten the reference
        colorButtons = self.opener.document.forms[0].color
        // see which radio button is checked
        for (var i = 0; i < colorButtons.length; i++) {
            if (colorButtons[i].checked) {
                return colorButtons[i].value
            }
        }
        return "white"
}
</SCRIPT>
</HEAD>
<SCRIPT LANGUAGE="JavaScript">
document.write("<BODY BGCOLOR='" + getColor() + "'>")
</SCRIPT>
<H1>This is a new window.</H1>
<FORM>
```

(continued)

Listing 14-11 *(continued)*

```
<INPUT TYPE="button" VALUE="Who's in the Main window?"
onClick="alert(self.opener.document.title)"><P>
Type text here for the main window:
<INPUT TYPE="text" SIZE=25
onChange="self.opener.document.forms[0].entry.value = this.value">
</FORM>
</BODY>
</HTML>
```

In the getColor() function, the multiple references to the radio button array would be very long. To simplify the references, the getColor() function starts out by assigning the radio button array to a variable I've arbitrarily called colorButtons. That shorthand now stands in for lengthy references as I loop through the radio buttons to determine which button is checked and retrieve its value property.

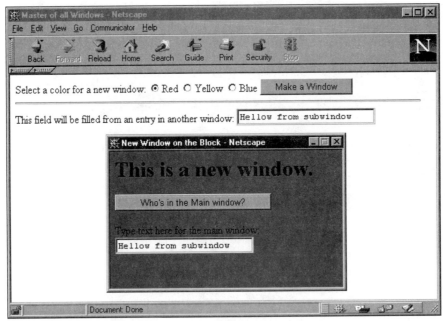

Figure 14-7: The main and subwindows, inextricably linked via the window.opener property

A button in the second window simply fetches the title of the opener window's document. Even if another document loads in the main window in the meantime, the opener reference still points to the main window: Its document object, however, will change.

Finally, the second window contains a text object. Enter any text you like there and either tab or click out of the field. The onChange= event handler updates the field in the opener's document (provided that document is still loaded).

Related Items: window.open() method; window.focus() method.

outerHeight
outerWidth

See innerHeight and innerWidth, earlier.

pageXOffset
pageYOffset

Value: Integer   **Gettable:** Yes   **Settable:** No

	Nav2	Nav3	Nav4	IE3/J1	IE3/J2	IE4/J3
Compatibility			✔			

The top-left corner of the content (inner) region of the browser window is an important geographical point for scrolling documents. When a document is scrolled all the way to the top and flush left in the window (or when a document is small enough to fill the browser window without displaying scrollbars), the document's location is said to be 0,0, meaning zero pixels from the top and zero pixels from the left. If you were to scroll the document, some other coordinate point of the document would be under that top-left corner. That measure is called the *page offset,* and the pageXOffset and pageYOffset properties let you read the pixel value of the document at the inner window's top-left corner: pageXOffset is the horizontal offset, and pageYOffset is the vertical offset.

The value of these measures becomes clear if you design navigation buttons in your pages to carefully control paging of content being displayed in the window. For example, you might have a two-frame page in which one of the frames features navigation controls, while the other displays the primary content. The navigation controls take the place of scrollbars, which, for aesthetic reasons, are turned off in the display frame. Scripts connected to the simulated scrolling buttons can determine the pageYOffset value of the document and then use the window.scrollTo() method to position the document precisely to the next logical division in the document for viewing.

Example

The script in Listing 14-12 is an unusual construction that creates a frameset and creates the content for each of the two frames all within a single HTML document (see "Frame Object" later in this chapter for more details). The purpose of this example is to provide you with a playground to get familiar with the page offset concept and how the values of these properties correspond to physical activity in a scrollable document.

In the left frame of the frameset are two fields that are ready to show the pixel values of the right frame's `pageXOffset` and `pageYOffset` properties. The content of the right frame is a 30-row table of fixed width (800 pixels). Mouse click events are captured by the document level (see Chapter 39), allowing you to click any table or cell border or outside the table to trigger the `showOffsets()` function in the right frame. That function is a simple script that displays the page offset values in their respective fields in the left frame.

Listing 14-12: **Viewing the pageXOffset and pageYOffset Properties**

```
<HTML>
<HEAD>
<TITLE>Master of all Windows</TITLE>
<SCRIPT LANGUAGE="JavaScript">
function leftFrame() {
        var output = "<HTML><BODY><H3>Page Offset Values</H3><HR>\n"
        output += "<FORM>PageXOffset:<INPUT TYPE='text' NAME='xOffset'
SIZE=4><BR>\n"
        output += "PageYOffset:<INPUT TYPE='text' NAME='yOffset'
SIZE=4><BR>\n"
        output += "</FORM></BODY></HTML>"
        return output
}

function rightFrame() {
        var output = "<HTML><HEAD><SCRIPT LANGUAGE='JavaScript'>\n"
        output += "function showOffsets() {\n"
        output += "parent.readout.document.forms[0].xOffset.value =
self.pageXOffset\n"
        output += "parent.readout.document.forms[0].yOffset.value =
self.pageYOffset\n}\n"
        output += "document.captureEvents(Event.CLICK)\n"
        output += "document.onclick = showOffsets\n"
        output += "<\/SCRIPT></HEAD><BODY
onClick='showOffsets()'><H3>Content Page</H3>\n"
        output += "Scroll the page and click on a table border to view
page offset values.<BR><HR>\n"
        output += "<TABLE BORDER=5 WIDTH=800>"
        var oneRow = "<TD>Cell 1</TD><TD>Cell 2</TD><TD>Cell
3</TD><TD>Cell 4</TD><TD>Cell 5</TD>"
        for (var i = 1; i <= 30; i++) {
            output += "<TR><TD><B>Row " + i + "</B></TD>" + oneRow +
"</TR>"
        }
        output += "</TABLE></BODY></HTML>"
        return output
}
</SCRIPT>
```

```
</HEAD>
<FRAMESET COLS="30%,70%">
        <FRAME NAME="readout" SRC="javascript:parent.leftFrame()">
        <FRAME NAME="display" SRC="javascript:parent.rightFrame()">
</FRAMESET>
</HTML>
```

To gain an understanding of how the offset values work, scroll the window slightly in the horizontal direction and notice that the `pageXOffset` value increases; the same goes for the `pageYOffset` value as you scroll down. Remember that these values reflect the coordinate in the document that is currently under the top-left corner of the window (frame) holding the document.

Related Items: `window.innerHeight` property; `window.innerWidth` property; `window.scrollBy()` method; `window.scrollTo()` method.

parent

Value: Window object   **Gettable:** Yes   **Settable:** No

	Nav2	Nav3	Nav4	IE3/J1	IE3/J2	IE4/J3
Compatibility	✔	✔	✔	✔	✔	✔

The `parent` property (and the `top` property that follows) comes into play primarily when a document is to be displayed as part of a multiframe window. The HTML documents that users see in the frames of a multiframe browser window are distinct from the document that specifies the frameset for the entire window. That document, though still in the browser's memory (and appearing as the URL in the location field of the browser), is not otherwise visible to the user (except in the Document Source view).

If scripts in your visible documents need to reference objects or properties of the frameset window, you can reference those frameset window items with the `parent` property (do not, however, expand the reference by preceding it with the window object, as in `window.parent.propertyName`). In a way, the `parent` property seems to violate the object hierarchy because, from a single frame's document, the property points to a level seemingly higher in precedence. If you didn't specify the `parent` property or instead specified the `self` property from one of these framed documents, the object reference is to the frame only, rather than to the outermost framesetting window object.

A nontraditional but perfectly legal way to use the `parent` object is as a means of storing temporary variables. Thus, you could set up a holding area for individual variable values or even an array of data. These values can then be shared among all documents loaded into the frames, including when documents change inside the frames. You have to be careful, however, when storing data in the parent on the fly (that is in response to user action in the frames). Variables can revert to their default values (that is, the values set by the parent's own script) if the user resizes the browser window.

A child window can also call a function defined in the parent window. The reference for such a function is

```
parent.functionName([parameters])
```

At first glance, it may seem as though the `parent` and `top` properties point to the same framesetting window object. In an environment consisting of one frameset window and its immediate children, that's true. But if one of the child windows was, itself, another framesetting window, then you wind up with three generations of windows. From the point of view of the "youngest" child (for example, a window defined by the second frameset), the `parent` property points to its immediate parent, whereas the `top` property points to the first framesetting window in this chain.

On the other hand, a new window created via the `window.open()` method has no parent-child relationship to the original window. The new window's `top` and `parent` point to that new window. You can read more about these relationships in the "Frames" section earlier in this chapter.

Example

To demonstrate how various `window object` properties refer to window levels in a multiframe environment, use your browser to load the Listing 14-13 document. It, in turn, sets each of two equal-size frames to the same document: Listing 14-14. This document extracts the values of several window properties, plus the `document.title` properties of two different window references.

Listing 14-13: **Framesetting Document for Listing 14-14**

```
<HTML>
<HEAD>
<TITLE>The Parent Property Example</TITLE>
<SCRIPT LANGUAGE="JavaScript">
self.name = "Framesetter"
</SCRIPT>
</HEAD>
<FRAMESET COLS="50%,50%" onUnload="self.name = ''">
        <FRAME NAME="JustAKid1" SRC="lst14-14.htm">
        <FRAME NAME="JustAKid2" SRC="lst14-14.htm">
</FRAMESET>
</HTML>
```

Listing 14-14: **Revealing Various Window-Related Properties**

```
<HTML>
<HEAD>
<TITLE>Window Revealer II</TITLE>
<SCRIPT LANGUAGE="JavaScript">
function gatherWindowData() {
        var msg = ""
```

```
        msg = msg + "top name: " + top.name + "<BR>"
        msg = msg + "parent name: " + parent.name + "<BR>"
        msg = msg + "parent.document.title: " + parent.document.title +
"<P>"
        msg = msg + "window name: " + window.name + "<BR>"
        msg = msg + "self name: " + self.name + "<BR>"
        msg = msg + "self.document.title: " + self.document.title
        return msg
}
</SCRIPT>
</HEAD>
<BODY>
<SCRIPT LANGUAGE="JavaScript">
document.write(gatherWindowData())
</SCRIPT>
</BODY>
</HTML>
```

In the two frames (Figure 14-8), the references to the `window` and `self` object names return the name assigned to the frame by the frameset definition (`JustAKid1` for the top frame, `JustAKid2` for the bottom frame). In other words, from each frame's point of view, the window object is its own frame. References to `self.document.x` refer only to the document loaded into that window frame. But references to the top and parent windows (which are one and the same in this example) show that those `object` properties are shared among both frames.

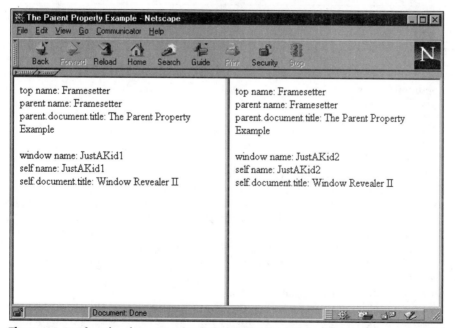

Figure 14-8: After the document in Listing 14-14 loads into the two frames established by Listing 14-13, parent and top properties are shared by both frames.

A couple other fine points are worth highlighting. First, the name of the framesetting window is set as the Listing 14-13 loads, rather than in response to an `onLoad=` event handler in the `<FRAMESET>` tag. The reason for this is that the name must be set in time for the documents loading in the frames to get that value. If I had waited until the frameset's `onLoad=` event handler, the name wouldn't be set until *after* the frame documents had loaded. Second, I restore the parent window's name to an empty string when the framesetting document unloads. This is to prevent future pages from getting confused about the window name.

Related Items: `window.frames` property; `window.self` property; `window.top` property.

personalbar
scrollbar

See locationbar.

self

Value: Window object   **Gettable:** Yes   **Settable:** No

	Nav2	Nav3	Nav4	IE3/J1	IE3/J2	IE4/J3
Compatibility	✔	✔	✔	✔	✔	✔

Just as the window object reference is optional, so too is the `self` property when the object reference points to the same window as the one containing the reference. In what may seem to be an unusual construction, the `self` property represents the same object as the window. For instance, to obtain the title of the document in a single-frame window, you can use any of the following three constructions:

```
window.document.title
self.document.title
document.title
```

Although `self` is a property of a window, you should not combine the references within a single-frame window script (for example, don't begin a reference with `window.self`). Specifying the `self` property, though optional for single-frame windows, can help make an object reference crystal clear to someone reading your code (and to you, for that matter). Multiple-frame windows are where you need to pay particular attention to this property.

JavaScript is pretty smart about references to a statement's own window. Therefore, you can generally omit the `self` part of a reference to a same-window document element. But when you intend to display a document in a multiframe window, complete references (including the `self` prefix) to an object make it much easier on anyone who reads or debugs your code to track who is doing what to whom. You are free to retrieve the `self` property of any window. The value that comes back is an entire window object — a copy of all data that makes up the window (including properties and methods).

Example

Listing 14-15 uses the same operations as Listing 14-4, but substitutes the `self` property for all window object references. The application of this reference is entirely optional, but it can be helpful for reading and debugging scripts if the HTML document is to appear in one frame of a multiframe window — especially if other JavaScript code in this document refers to documents in other frames. The `self` reference helps anyone reading the code know precisely which frame was being addressed.

Listing 14-15: **Using the self Property**

```
<HTML>
<HEAD>
<TITLE>self Property</TITLE>
<SCRIPT LANGUAGE="JavaScript">
self.defaultStatus = "Welcome to my Web site."
</SCRIPT>
</HEAD>
<BODY>
<A HREF="http://home.netscape.com" onMouseOver="self.status = 'Go to
your browser Home page.';return true" onMouseOut="self.status =
'';return true">Home</A><P>
<A HREF="http://home.netscape.com" onMouseOver="self.status = 'Visit
Netscape\'s Home page.';return true" onMouseOut="self.status =
self.defaultStatus;return true">Netscape</A>
</BODY>
</HTML>
```

Related Items: `window.frames` property; `window.parent` property; `window.top` property.

status

Value: String   **Gettable:** No   **Settable:** Yes

	Nav2	Nav3	Nav4	IE3/J1	IE3/J2	IE4/J3
Compatibility	✔	✔	✔	✔	✔	✔

At the bottom of the browser window is a statusbar. Part of that bar includes an area that normally discloses the document loading progress or the URL of a link that the mouse is pointing to at any given instant. You can control the temporary content of that field by assigning a text string to the window object's `status` property (Figure 14-9). You should adjust the `status` property only in response to events that have a temporary effect, such as a link or image map area object's `onMouseOver=` event handler. When the `status` property is set in this situation, it overrides any other setting in the statusbar. If the user then moves the mouse pointer away from the object that changes the statusbar, the bar returns to its default setting (which may be empty on some pages).

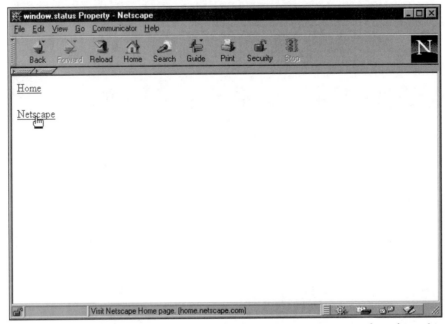

Figure 14-9: The statusbar can be set to display a custom message when the pointer rolls over a link.

Use this window property as a friendlier alternative to displaying the URL of a link as a user rolls the mouse around the page. For example, if you'd rather use the statusbar to explain the nature of the destination of a link, put that text into the statusbar in response to the `onMouseOver=` event handler. But be aware that experienced Web surfers like to see URLs down there. Therefore, consider creating a hybrid message for the statusbar that includes both a friendly description followed by the URL in parentheses. In multiframe environments, you can set the `window.status` property without having to worry about referencing the individual frame.

Example

In Listing 14-16, the `status` property is set in a handler embedded in the `onMouseOver=` attribute of two HTML link tags. Notice that the handler requires a `return true` statement (or any expression that evaluates to `return true`) as the last statement of the handler. This statement is required or the status message will not display.

Listing 14-16: **Links with Custom Statusbar Messages**

```
<HTML>
<HEAD>
<TITLE>window.status Property</TITLE>
</HEAD>
<BODY>
<A HREF="http://www.dannyg.com" onMouseOver="window.status = 'Go to my
Home page. (www.dannyg.com)'; return true">Home</A><P>
<A HREF="http://home.netscape.com" onMouseOver="window.status = 'Visit
Netscape Home page. (home.netscape.com)'; return true">Netscape</A>
</BODY>
</HTML>
```

As a safeguard against platform-specific anomalies that affect the behavior of
onMouseOver= event handlers and the window.status property, you should also
include an onMouseOut= event handler for links and client-side image map area
objects. Such onMouseOut= event handlers should set the status property to an
empty string. This setting ensures that the statusbar message returns to the
defaultStatus setting when the pointer rolls away from these objects. If you
want to write a generalizable function that handles all window status changes, you
can do so, but word the onMouseOver= attribute carefully so that the event
handler evaluates to return true. Listing 14-17 shows such an alternative.

Listing 14-17: **Handling Status Message Changes**

```
<HTML>
<HEAD>
<TITLE>Generalizable window.status Property</TITLE>
<SCRIPT LANGUAGE="JavaScript">
function showStatus(msg) {
        window.status = msg
        return true
}
</SCRIPT>
</HEAD>
<BODY>
<A HREF="http://home.netscape.com" onMouseOver="return showStatus('Go
to my Home page.')" onMouseOut="return showStatus('')">Home</A><P>
<A HREF="http://home.netscape.com" onMouseOver="return
showStatus('Visit Netscape Home page.')" onMouseOut="return
showStatus('')">Netscape</A>
</BODY>
</HTML>
```

Notice how the event handlers return the results of the showStatus() method
to the event handler, allowing the entire handler to evaluate to return true.

One final example of setting the statusbar (shown in Listing 14-18) also demonstrates how to create a scrolling banner in the statusbar.

Listing 14-18: **Creating a Scrolling Banner**

```
<HTML>
<HEAD>
<TITLE>Message Scroller</TITLE>
<SCRIPT LANGUAGE="JavaScript">
<!--
var msg = "Welcome to my world..."
var delay = 150
var timerId
var maxCount = 0
var currCount = 1

function scrollMsg() {
        // set the number of times scrolling message is to run
        if (maxCount == 0) {
            maxCount = 3 * msg.length
        }
        window.status = msg
        // keep track of how many characters have scrolled
        currCount++
        // shift first character of msg to end of msg
        msg = msg.substring (1, msg.length) + msg.substring (0, 1)
        // test whether we've reached maximum character count
        if (currCount >= maxCount) {
            timerID = 0          // zero out the timer
            window.status = ""   // clear the status bar
            return               // break out of function
        } else {
            // recursive call to this function
            timerId = setTimeout("scrollMsg()", delay)
        }
}
// -->
</SCRIPT>
</HEAD>
<BODY onLoad="scrollMsg()">
</BODY>
</HTML>
```

Because the statusbar is being set by a standalone function (rather than by an onMouseOver= event handler), you do not have to append a return true statement to set the status property. The scrollMsg() function uses more advanced JavaScript concepts, such as the window.setTimeout() method (covered later in this chapter) and string methods (covered in Chapter 27). To speed the pace at which the words scroll across the statusbar, reduce the value of delay.

Note

Many Web surfers (myself included) don't care for these scrollers that run forever in the statusbar. They can also crash earlier browsers, because the `setTimeout()` method eats application memory in Navigator 2. Use scrolling bars sparingly or design them to run only a few times after the document loads.

Setting the status property with `onMouseOver=` event handlers has had a checkered career along various implementations in Navigator. A script that sets the statusbar is always in competition against the browser itself, which uses the statusbar to report loading progress. Bugs also prevent the bar from clearing itself, even when an `onMouseOut=` event handler sets it to an empty string. The situation improves with each new browser version, but be prepared for anomalies among visitors using older scriptable browsers.

Related Items: `window.defaultStatus` property; `onMouseOver=` event handler; `onMouseOut=` event handler; link object.

statusbar
toolbar

See locationbar.

top

Value: Window object   **Gettable:** Yes   **Settable:** No

	Nav2	Nav3	Nav4	IE3/J1	IE3/J2	IE4/J3
Compatibility	✔	✔	✔	✔	✔	✔

The window object's `top` property refers to the topmost window in the JavaScript hierarchy. For a single-frame window, the reference is to the same object as the window itself (including the `self` and `parent` property), so do not include `window` as part of the reference. In a multiframe window, the top window is the one that defines the first frameset (in case of nested framesets). Users don't ever really see the top window in a multiframe environment, but the browser stores it as an object in its memory. The reason is that the top window has the road map to the other frames (if one frame should need to reference an object in a different frame), and its children frames can call upon it. Such a reference looks like

```
top.functionName([parameters])
```

For more about the distinction between the `top` and `parent` properties, see the in-depth discussion about scripting frames at the beginning of this chapter. See also the example of the `parent` property for listings that demonstrate the values of the `top` property.

Related Items: `window.frames` property; `window.self` property; `window.parent` property.

window

Value: Window object   **Gettable:** Yes   **Settable:** No

	Nav2	Nav3	Nav4	IE3/J1	IE3/J2	IE4/J3
Compatibility	✔	✔	✔	✔	✔	✔

Listing the window property as a separate property may be more confusing than helpful. The window property is the same object as the window object. You do not need to use a reference that begins with window.window. Although the window object is assumed for many references, you can use window as part of a reference to items in the same window or frame as the script statement that makes that reference. You should not, however, use window as a part of a reference involving items higher up in the hierarchy (top or parent).

Methods

alert(*message*)

Returns: Nothing.

	Nav2	Nav3	Nav4	IE3/J1	IE3/J2	IE4/J3
Compatibility	✔	✔	✔	✔	✔	✔

An alert dialog box is a modal window that presents a message to the user with a single OK button to dismiss the dialog box. As long as the alert dialog box is showing, no other application or window can be made active. The user must dismiss the dialog box before proceeding with any more work in the browser or on the computer.

The single parameter to the alert() method can be a value of any data type, including representations of some unusual data types whose values you don't normally work with in JavaScript (such as complete objects). This makes the alert dialog box a handy tool for debugging JavaScript scripts. Anytime you want to monitor the value of an expression, use that expression as the parameter to a temporary alert() method in your code. The script proceeds to that point and then stops to show you the value. (See Chapter 45 for more tips on debugging scripts.)

What is often disturbing to application designers is that all JavaScript-created modal dialog boxes (via the alert(), confirm(), and prompt() methods) identify themselves as being generated by JavaScript or the browser (Internet Explorer 4). The look is particularly annoying in browsers before Navigator 4 and Internet Explorer 4, because the wording appears directly in the dialog box's content area, rather than in the title bar of the dialog box. The purpose of this identification is to act as a security precaution against unscrupulous scripters who might try to spoof system or browser alert dialog boxes inviting a user to reveal passwords or other private information. These identifying words cannot be overwritten or eliminated by your scripts. If you want more control over a window, generate a separate browser window with `window.open()`. Unless you use signed scripts to create an always raised window, that new window will not be a modal dialog box and could get hidden behind a larger window. Syntax for Internet Explorer 4's special dialog-style window is not part of Navigator 4.

Because the `alert()` method is of a global nature (that is, no particular frame in a multiframe environment derives any benefit from laying claim to the alert dialog box), a common practice is to omit all window object references from the statement that calls the method. Restrict the use of alert dialog boxes in your HTML documents and site designs. The modality of the windows is disruptive to the flow of a user's navigation around your pages. Communicate with users via forms or by writing to separate document window frames.

Example

The parameter for the example in Listing 14-19 is a concatenated string. It joins together two fixed strings and the value of the browser's `appName` property. Loading this document causes the alert dialog box to appear, as shown in several configurations in Figure 14-10. The `JavaScript Alert:` line cannot be deleted from the dialog box in earlier browsers, nor can the title bar be changed in Navigator 4 or Internet Explorer 4.

Listing 14-19: **Displaying an Alert Dialog Box**

```
<HTML>
<HEAD>
<TITLE>window.alert() Method</TITLE>
</HEAD>
<BODY>
<SCRIPT LANGUAGE="JavaScript">
alert("You are running the " + navigator.appName + " browser.")
</SCRIPT>
</BODY>
</HTML>
```

Figure 14-10: Results of the alert() method in Listing 14-19 in Navigator 3 and Navigator 4 for Windows 95

Related Items: `window.confirm()` method; `window.prompt()` method.

back()

Returns: Nothing.

	Nav2	Nav3	Nav4	IE3/J1	IE3/J2	IE4/J3
Compatibility			✔			

The Back button's behavior has gone through transformations since Navigator 2. Some authors like the changes, others do not. In Navigator 2, the history object (and all navigation methods associated with it) assumed the entire browser window would change with a click of the Back or Forward button in the toolbar. With the increased popularity of frames, this mechanism didn't work well if one frame remained static while documents flew in and out of another frame: navigation had to be on a frame-by-frame basis, and that's how the Back and Forward buttons worked in Navigator 3 and now in Navigator 4.

From Navigator 3 onward, each window object (including frames) maintains its own history. Unfortunately, JavaScript doesn't observe this until you get to Navigator 4, and thus for a lot of browsers out there (including Internet Explorer 3 and Internet Explorer 4), the history navigation methods control the global history. The purpose of the window.back() method is to offer a scripted version of the global back and forward navigation buttons, while allowing the history object to control navigation strictly within a particular window or frame — as it should. For more information about version compatibility and the back and forward navigation, see the history object in Chapter 15.

Example

Listing 14-20 is a framesetting document for a back() and forward() method laboratory to help you understand the differences between window and history navigation. All the work is done in the document shown in Listing 14-21.

Listing 14-20: **Navigation Lab Frameset**

```
<HTML>
<HEAD>
<TITLE>Back and Forward</TITLE>
</HEAD>
<FRAMESET COLS="45%,55%">
        <FRAME NAME="controller" SRC="lst14-21.htm">
        <FRAME NAME="display" SRC="lst14-03.htm">
</FRAMESET>
</HTML>
```

The top portion of Listing 14-21 contains simple links to other example files from this chapter. A click on any link loads a different document into the right-hand frame to let you build some history inside the frame.

Listing 14-21: **Navigation Lab Control Panel**

```
<HTML>
<HEAD>
<TITLE>Lab Controls</TITLE>
</HEAD>
<BODY>
<B>Load a series of documents into the right frame by clicking some of
these links (make a note of the sequence you click on):</B><P>
<A HREF="lst14-04.htm" TARGET="display">Listing 14-4</A><BR>
<A HREF="lst14-05.htm" TARGET="display">Listing 14-5</A><BR>
<A HREF="lst14-09.htm" TARGET="display">Listing 14-9</A><BR>
<A HREF="lst14-10.htm" TARGET="display">Listing 14-10</A><BR>
<HR>
<FORM NAME="input">
<B>Click on the various buttons below to see the results in this
frameset:</B><P>
<UL>
<LI>Substitute for toolbar buttons -- <TT>window.back()</TT> and
<TT>window.forward()</TT>:<INPUT TYPE="button" VALUE="Back"
onClick="window.back()"><INPUT TYPE="button" VALUE="Forward"
onClick="window.forward()"><P>

<LI><TT>history.back()</TT> and <TT>history.forward()</TT> for
righthand frame:<INPUT TYPE="button" VALUE="Back"
onClick="parent.display.history.back()"><INPUT TYPE="button"
VALUE="Forward" onClick="parent.display.history.forward()"><P>

<LI><TT>history.back()</TT> for this frame:<INPUT TYPE="button"
VALUE="Back" onClick="history.back()"><P>
</UL>
</FORM>
</BODY>
</HTML>
```

At the bottom are three sets of navigation buttons. All scripting is performed directly in the button event handlers. The button first pair is tied to the `window.back()` and `window.forward()` methods. These work only in Navigator 4. The others are tied to histories of each frame. When you reach the end of a history list (by clicking either of the `history.back()` buttons), navigation ceases, because that frame is out of history. But the `window.back()` button is connected to the browser's global history (the one you see in the Go menu) and can keep going back until the entire frameset of Listing 14-20 is gone. The behavior of the history methods is different outside of Navigator 4.

Related Items: `window.forward()` method; `history.back()` method; `history.forward()` method; `history.go()` method.

blur()

Returns: Nothing.

	Nav2	Nav3	Nav4	IE3/J1	IE3/J2	IE4/J3
Compatibility		✔	✔			✔

The opposite of `window.focus()` is `window.blur()`, which pushes the referenced window to the back of all other open windows. If other Navigator windows, such as the Mail or News windows, are open, the window receiving the `blur()` method is placed behind these windows as well. As with the `window.focus()` method, make sure that your references signify the correct window. See Listing 14-30 for an example of `window.blur()` in action.

Related Items: `window.open()` method; `window.focus()` method; `window.opener` property.

captureEvents(*eventTypeList*)

Returns: Nothing.

	Nav2	Nav3	Nav4	IE3/J1	IE3/J2	IE4/J3
Compatibility			✔			

In Navigator 4, an event filters down from the window object and eventually reaches its intended target. For example, if you click a button, the click event first reaches the window object; then it goes to the document object; and eventually (in a split second) it reaches the button, where an `onClick=` event handler is ready to act on that click.

The Netscape mechanism allows window, document, and layer objects to intercept events and process them prior to reaching their intended targets (or preventing them from reaching their destinations entirely). But for one of these outer containers to grab an event, your script must instruct it to capture the type of event your application is interested in preprocessing. If you want the window object to intercept all events of a particular type, use the `window.captureEvents()` method to turn that facility on.

This method takes one or more *event types* as parameters. An event type is a constant value built inside Navigator 4's event object. One event type exists for every kind of event handler you see in all of Navigator 4's document objects. The syntax is the event object name (`Event`) and the event name in all uppercase letters. For example, if you want the window to intercept all click events, the statement is

```
window.captureEvents(Event.CLICK)
```

For multiple events, add them as parameters, separated by the pipe (|) character:

```
window.captureEvents(Event.MOUSEDOWN | Event.KEYPRESS)
```

Once an event type is captured by the window object, it must have a function ready to deal with the event. For example, perhaps the function looks through all Event.MOUSEDOWN events and looks to see if the right mouse button was the one that triggered the event and what form element (if any) is the intended target. The goal is to perhaps display a pop-up menu (as a separate layer) for a right-click. If the click comes from the left mouse button, the event is routed to its intended target.

To associate a function with a particular event type captured by a window object, assign a function to the event. For example, to assign a custom doClickEvent() function to click events captured by the window object, use the following statement:

```
window.onclick=doClickEvent
```

Note that the function name is assigned only as a reference name (no quotes or parentheses), not like an event handler within a tag. The function itself is like any function, but it has the added benefit of automatically receiving the event object as a parameter. To turn off event capture for one or more event types, use the window.releaseEvent() method. See Chapter 33 for details of working with events in this manner.

Example

The page in Listing 14-22 is an exercise in capturing and releasing click events in the window layer. Whenever the window is capturing click events, the flash() function runs. In that function, the event is examined so that only if the Control key is also being held down and the name of the button starts with "button" does the document background color flash red. For all click events (that is, those directed at objects on the page capable of their own onClick= event handlers), the click is processed with the routeEvent() method to make sure the target buttons execute their own onClick= event handlers.

Listing 14-22: **Capturing Click Events in the Window**

```
<HTML>
<HEAD>
<TITLE>Window Event Capture</TITLE>
<SCRIPT LANGUAGE="JavaScript1.2">
// function to run when window captures a click event
function flash(e) {
        if (e.modifiers == Event.CONTROL_MASK &&
e.target.name.indexOf("button") == 0) {
            document.bgColor = "red"
            setTimeout("document.bgColor = 'white'", 500)
        }
        // let event continue to target
        routeEvent(e)
}
// default setting to capture click events
```

(continued)

Listing 14-22 *(continued)*

```
window.captureEvents(Event.CLICK)
// assign flash() function to click events captured by window
window.onclick = flash
</SCRIPT>
</HEAD>
<BODY BGCOLOR="white">
<FORM NAME="buttons">
<B>Turn window click event capture on or off (Default is "On")</B><P>
<INPUT NAME="captureOn" TYPE="button" VALUE="Capture On"
onClick="window.captureEvents(Event.CLICK)"> 
<INPUT NAME="captureOff" TYPE="button" VALUE="Capture Off"
onClick="window.releaseEvents(Event.CLICK)">
<HR>
<B>Ctrl+Click on a button to see if clicks are being captured by the
window (background color will flash red):</B><P>
<UL>
<LI><INPUT NAME="button1" TYPE="button" VALUE="Informix"
onClick="alert('You clicked on Informix.')">
<LI><INPUT NAME="button2" TYPE="button" VALUE="Oracle"
onClick="alert('You clicked on Oracle.')">
<LI><INPUT NAME="button3" TYPE="button" VALUE="Sybase"
onClick="alert('You clicked on Sybase.')">
</UL>
</FORM>
</BODY>
</HTML>
```

When you try this page, also turn off window event capture. Now only the buttons' onClick= event handlers execute, and the page does not flash red.

Related Items: window.disableExternalCapture() method; window.enableExternalCapture() method; window.handleEvent() method; window.releaseEvents() method; window.routeEvent() method.

clearInterval(*intervalIDnumber*)

Returns: Nothing.

	Nav2	Nav3	Nav4	IE3/J1	IE3/J2	IE4/J3
Compatibility			✔			✔

Use the window.clearInterval() method to turn off an interval loop action started with the window.setInterval() method. The parameter is the ID number returned by the setInterval() method. A common application for the JavaScript interval mechanism is animation of an object on a page. If you have multiple intervals running, each has its own ID value in memory. You can turn off any interval by its ID value. Once an interval loop stops, your script cannot resume that interval: It must start a new one, which will generate a new ID value.

Example

See Listings 14-43 and 14-44 for an example of how `setInterval()` and `clearInterval()` are used together on a page.

Related Items: `window.setInterval()` method; `window.setTimeout()` method; `window.clearTimeout()` method.

clearTimeout(*timeoutIDnumber*)

Returns: Nothing.

	Nav2	Nav3	Nav4	IE3/J1	IE3/J2	IE4/J3
Compatibility	✔	✔	✔	✔	✔	✔

Use the `window.clearTimeout()` method in concert with the `window.setTimeout()` method, as described later in this chapter, when you want your script to cancel a timer that is waiting to run its expression. The parameter for this method is the ID number that the `window.setTimeout()` method returns when the timer starts ticking. The `clearTimeout()` method cancels the specified timeout. A good practice is to check your code for instances where user action may negate the need for a running timer — and to stop that timer before it goes off.

Example

The page in Listing 14-23 features one text field and two buttons (Figure 14-11). One button starts a count-down timer coded to last one minute (easily modifiable); the other button interrupts the timer at any time while it is running. When the minute is up, an alert dialog box lets you know.

Listing 14-23: **A Count-Down Timer**

```
<HTML>
<HEAD>
<TITLE>Count Down Timer</TITLE>
<SCRIPT LANGUAGE="JavaScript">
<!--
var running = false
var endTime = null
var timerID = null

function startTimer() {
        running = true
        now = new Date()
```

(continued)

Listing 14-13 *(continued)*

```
        now = now.getTime()
        // change last multiple for the number of minutes
        endTime = now + (1000 * 60 * 1)
        showCountDown()
}

function showCountDown() {
        var now = new Date()
        now = now.getTime()
        if (endTime - now <= 0) {
           stopTimer()
           alert("Time is up.  Put down your pencils.")
        } else {
           var delta = new Date(endTime - now)
           var theMin = delta.getMinutes()
           var theSec = delta.getSeconds()
           var theTime = theMin
           theTime += ((theSec < 10) ? ":0" : ":") + theSec
           document.forms[0].timerDisplay.value = theTime
           if (running) {
              timerID = setTimeout("showCountDown()",1000)
           }
        }
}

function stopTimer() {
        clearTimeout(timerID)
        running = false
        document.forms[0].timerDisplay.value = "0:00"
}
//-->
</SCRIPT>
</HEAD>

<BODY>
<FORM>
<INPUT TYPE="button" NAME="startTime" VALUE="Start 1 min. Timer"
onClick="startTimer()">
<INPUT TYPE="button" NAME="clearTime" VALUE="Clear Timer"
onClick="stopTimer()"><P>
<INPUT TYPE="text" NAME="timerDisplay" VALUE="">
</FORM>
</BODY>
</HTML>
```

Notice that the script establishes three variables with global scope in the window: running, endTime, and timerID. These values are needed inside multiple functions, so they are initialized outside of the functions.

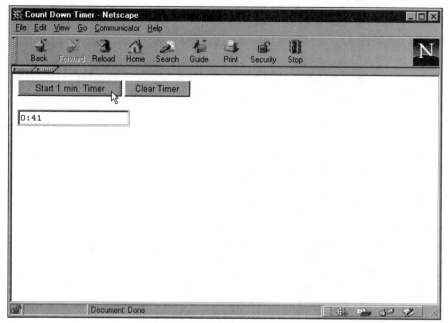

Figure 14-11: The count-down timer page as it displays the time remaining

In the startTimer() function, you switch the running flag on, meaning that the timer should be going. Using some date functions (Chapter 29), you extract the current time in milliseconds and add the number of milliseconds for the next minute (the extra multiplication by one is the place where you can change the amount to the desired number of minutes). With the end time stored in a global variable, the function now calls another function that compares the current and end times and displays the difference in the text field.

Early in the showCountDown() function, check to see if the timer has wound down. If so, you stop the timer and alert the user. Otherwise, the function continues to calculate the difference between the two times and formats the time in mm:ss format. As long as the running flag is set to true, the function sets the one-second timeout timer before repeating itself. To stop the timer before it has run out (in the stopTimer() function), the most important step is to cancel the timeout running inside the browser. The clearTimeout() method uses the global timerID value to do that. Then the function turns off the running switch and zeros out the display.

When you run the timer, you may occasionally notice that the time skips a second. It's not cheating. It just takes slightly more than one second to wait for the timeout and then finish the calculations for the next second's display. What you're seeing is the display catching up with the real time left.

Related Items: window.setTimeout().

close()

Returns: Nothing.

	Nav2	Nav3	Nav4	IE3/J1	IE3/J2	IE4/J3
Compatibility	✔	✔	✔	✔	✔	✔

The `window.close()` method closes the browser window referenced by the window object. Most likely, you will use this method to close subwindows created from a main document window. If the call to close the window comes from a window other than the new subwindow, the original window object *must* maintain a record of the subwindow object. You accomplish this by storing the value returned from the `window.open()` method in a global variable that will be available to other objects later (for example, a variable not initialized inside a function). If, on the other hand, an object inside the new subwindow calls the `window.close()` method, the `window` or `self` reference is sufficient.

Be sure to include a window as part of the reference to this method. Failure to do so causes JavaScript to regard the statement as a `document.close()` method, which has different behavior (see Chapter 16). Only the `window.close()` method can close the window via a script. Closing a window, of course, forces the window to trigger an `onUnload=` event handler before the window disappears from view; but once you've initiated the `window.close()` method, you cannot stop it from completing its task.

While I'm on the subject of closing windows, a special case exists when a subwindow tries to close the main window (via a statement such as `self.opener.close()`) when the main window has more than one entry in its session history. As a safety precaution against scripts closing windows they did not create, Navigator 3 and later ask the user whether he or she wants the main window to close (via a Navigator-generated JavaScript confirm dialog box). This security precaution cannot be overridden except in Navigator 4 via a signed script when the user grants permission to control the browser (Chapter 40).

Example

See Listing 14-3 (for the `window.closed` property), which provides an elaborate, cross-platform, bug-accommodating example of applying the `window.close()` method across multiple windows.

Related Items: `window.open()`; `document.close()`.

confirm(*message*)

Returns: True or false.

	Nav2	Nav3	Nav4	IE3/J1	IE3/J2	IE4/J3
Compatibility	✔	✔	✔	✔	✔	✔

A confirm dialog box presents a message in a modal dialog box along with OK and Cancel buttons. Such a dialog box can be used to ask a question of the user, usually prior to a script performing actions that will not be undoable. Querying a user about proceeding with typical Web navigation in response to user interaction on a form element is generally a disruptive waste of the user's time and attention. But for operations that may reveal a user's identity or send form data to a server, a JavaScript confirm dialog box may make a great deal of sense. Users can also accidentally click buttons, so you should provide avenues for backing out of an operation before it executes.

Because this dialog box returns a Boolean value (OK = `true`; Cancel = `false`), you can use this method as a comparison expression or as an assignment expression. In a comparison expression, you nest the method within any other statement where a Boolean value is required. For example

```
if (confirm("Are you sure?")) {
        alert("OK")
} else {
        alert("Not OK")
}
```

Here, the returned value of the confirm dialog box provides the desired Boolean value type for the `if...else` construction (Chapter 31).

This method can also appear on the right side of an assignment expression, as in

```
var adult = confirm("You certify that you are over 18 years old?")
if (adult) {
        statements for adults
} else {
        statements for children
}
```

You cannot specify other alert icons or labels for the two buttons in JavaScript confirm dialog box windows.

Be careful how you word the question in the confirm dialog box. In Navigator 2 and 3, the buttons are labeled OK and Cancel in Windows browsers; the Mac versions, however, label the buttons Yes and No. If your visitors may be using older Mac Navigators, be sure your questions are logically answered with both sets of button labels. In Navigator 4, all platforms are the same (OK and Cancel).

Example

The example in Listing 14-24 shows the user interface part of how you can use a confirm dialog box to query a user before clearing a table full of user-entered data. The `JavaScript Application` line in the title bar, as shown in Figure 14-12, or the `JavaScript Confirm` legend in earlier browser versions cannot be removed from the dialog box.

Listing 14-24: **The Confirm Dialog Box**

```
<HTML>
<HEAD>
<TITLE>window.confirm() Method</TITLE>
<SCRIPT LANGUAGE="JavaScript">
function clearTable() {
        if (confirm("Are you sure you want to empty the table?")) {
            alert("Emptying the table...") // for demo purposes
            //statements that actually empty the fields
        }
}
</SCRIPT>
</HEAD>
<BODY>
<FORM>
<!-- other statements that display and populate a large table -->
<INPUT TYPE="button" NAME="clear" VALUE="Reset Table"
onClick="clearTable()">
</FORM>
</BODY>
</HTML>
```

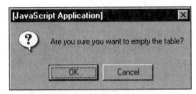

Figure 14-12: A JavaScript confirm dialog box (Navigator 4 Windows 95 format)

Related Items: `window.alert();` `window.prompt();` `form.submit()` method.

disableExternalCapture()

enableExternalCapture()

Returns: Nothing.

	Nav2	Nav3	Nav4	IE3/J1	IE3/J2	IE4/J3
Compatibility			✔			

Security restrictions prevent one frame from monitoring events in another frame (when a different domain is in that second frame) unless the user has granted permission to a signed script. Controlling this cross-frame access requires two special window object methods: `enableExternalCapture()` and `disableExternalCapture()`.

Putting these methods to work is a little trickier than manipulating the regular `window.captureEvents()` method. You have to turn on external capture in the frame doing the capture, but then set `captureEvents()` and the event handler in the frame whose events you want to capture. Moreover, when a new document loads into the second frame, you must set the `captureEvents()` and event handler for that frame again. See Chapter 40 for details about signed scripts.

Example

A framesetting document in Listing 14-25 loads two frames that let you experiment with both local and external event capture. You must either code sign the page or turn on codebase principals (see Chapter 40) to use this example. In the left frame is the control panel (Listing 14-26) for the laboratory. In the right frame I load Netscape's home page to provide a page with a different domain than your local disk or Web server. You can see what this frameset looks like in Figure 14-13.

Listing 14-25: **Frameset for Capture Laboratory**

```
<HTML>
<HEAD>
<TITLE>window.frames property</TITLE>
</HEAD>
<FRAMESET COLS="40%,60%">
        <FRAME NAME="controls" SRC="lst14-26.htm">
        <FRAME NAME="display" SRC="http://home.netscape.com">
</FRAMESET>
</HTML>
```

The control panel is an extension of the one used to demonstrate the `window.captureEvents()` method earlier in this chapter. In addition to the local window event capture, this new version adds a function that toggles external event capture on and off. To help differentiate the results of the local and external click event capture, the local capture flashes the control panel color in red; the external capture flashes in yellow.

Listing 14-26: **Control Panel for Capture Laboratory**

```
<HTML>
<HEAD>
<TITLE>Window Event Capture</TITLE>
<SCRIPT LANGUAGE="JavaScript1.2" ARCHIVE="lst14-26.jar" ID="main">
// function to run when window captures a click event
function flashRed(e) {
        if (e.modifiers == Event.CONTROL_MASK &&
```

(continued)

Listing 14-26 (continued)

```
e.target.name.indexOf("button") == 0) {
        document.bgColor = "red"
        setTimeout("document.bgColor = 'white'", 500)
    }
    // let event continue to target
    routeEvent(e)
}
function flashYellow(e) {
    if (e.target.href) {
        document.bgColor = "yellow"
        setTimeout("document.bgColor = 'white'", 500)
    }
    // let event continue to target
    routeEvent(e)
}
function setExternal(on) {
    if (on) {

netscape.security.PrivilegeManager.enablePrivilege("UniversalBrowserWrite")
        window.enableExternalCapture()
        parent.display.captureEvents(Event.CLICK)
        parent.display.onclick=flashYellow
    } else {

netscape.security.PrivilegeManager.enablePrivilege("UniversalBrowserWrite")
        window.disableExternalCapture()
    }
}

// default setting to capture click events
window.captureEvents(Event.CLICK)
// assign flash() function to click events captured by window
window.onclick = flashRed
</SCRIPT>
</HEAD>
<BODY BGCOLOR="white"
onUnload="netscape.security.PrivilegeManager.disablePrivilege('Universal
BrowserWrite')" ID="handler">
<FORM NAME="buttons">
<B>Turn window click event capture on or off (Default is "On")</B><P>
<INPUT NAME="captureOn" TYPE="button" VALUE="Capture On"
onClick="window.captureEvents(Event.CLICK)"> 
<INPUT NAME="captureOff" TYPE="button" VALUE="Capture Off"
onClick="window.releaseEvents(Event.CLICK)">
<HR>
<B>Turn window click event EXTERNAL capture on or off (Default is
"Off")</B><P>
<INPUT NAME="captureOn" TYPE="button" VALUE="External Capture On"
onClick="setExternal(true)"> 
```

```
<INPUT NAME="captureOff" TYPE="button" VALUE="External Capture Off"
onClick="setExternal(false)">
<HR>
<B>Ctrl+Click on a button to see if clicks are being captured by the
window (background color will flash red):</B><P>
<UL>
<LI><INPUT NAME="button1" TYPE="button" VALUE="Informix"
onClick="alert('You clicked on Informix.')">
<LI><INPUT NAME="button2" TYPE="button" VALUE="Oracle"
onClick="alert('You clicked on Oracle.')">
<LI><INPUT NAME="button3" TYPE="button" VALUE="Sybase"
onClick="alert('You clicked on Sybase.')">
</UL>
</FORM>
</BODY>
</HTML>
```

When the frameset initially loads, only the local window event capture is turned on, as before. The two statements at the end of the `<SCRIPT>` tag take care of that, including the one that directs all click events from the control panel window to the flashRed() function. In the `<SCRIPT>` tag, I put the attributes relating to signed scripts as a reminder that if this page were to be deployed on a server, the `<SCRIPT>` tag and every event handler in the document would require an ID attribute (see Chapter 40 for details). For the sake of readability, I have omitted the ID attributes for most of the event handlers, assuming that you will be trying this example with the help of codebase principals enabled.

The setExternal() function is a single function that toggles the external capture based on the Boolean value it receives as an argument. To turn on external capture, the script first invokes the Java method that requests UniversalBrowserWrite permission from the user (no error handling is built into this example to accommodate permission denial). Next, enableExternalCapture() is set for the control panel window: the one with the scripts that will be doing the processing of events from the second frame.

The remaining two statements are directed at the other frame. They engage event capturing over there for click events and direct those events to the flashYellow() function defined here in the control panel. JavaScript takes care of making the connections that force those external events to run a local function.

When you load this frameset and start clicking around, turn on the external capture, and click any link in the right frame. The control panel should flash yellow momentarily. If that link navigated to another page, you must turn on external capture again; but if the link navigated to an anchor on the same page, the next click will flash the yellow again. All the while, Ctrl+clicking on the lower three control panel buttons causes the background to flash red. Study the code carefully in Listing 14-26 and click around the laboratory frames to see how the two frames are handled.

Related Items: window.captureEvents() method; event object; signed scripts.

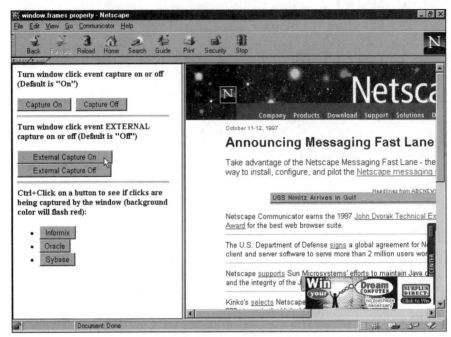

Figure 14-13: The local and external event capture laboratory

find(["*searchString*" [, *matchCaseBoolean,
searchUpBoolean*]])

Returns: Boolean value for nondialog searches.

	Nav2	Nav3	Nav4	IE3/J1	IE3/J2	IE4/J3
Compatibility			✔			

The window.find() method gives you a good amount of control over searching for a text string within a document contained by a window or frame. The action of this method mimics the powers of the browser's Find dialog box, accessible from the Find button in the toolbar.

The easiest way to deploy this command is without any parameters. This displays the browser's Find dialog box, just as if the user had clicked the Find button in the toolbar. If you want a search function available in a window lacking a toolbar, this is the way to go. With no parameters, this function does not return a value.

You can, however, go further to put the search facility more under script control. At the minimum, you can specify a search string as a parameter to the function. The search is based on simple string matching, and is not in any way connected with the regular expression kind of search (see Chapter 30). If the search finds a match, the browser scrolls to that matching word, and highlights the word, just like using the browser's own Find dialog box. The function also returns a Boolean `true` when a match is found. This function does not allow you to bypass the scrolling and physical highlighting of the found string. If no match is found in the document or no more matches occur in the current search direction (the default direction is from top to bottom), the function returns `false`. This lets you control how the lack of a match is alerted to the user or what action the script should take.

Two optional parameters to the scripted find action let you specify whether the search should be case-sensitive and whether the search direction should be upward from the bottom of the document. These choices are identical to the ones that appear in the browser's Find dialog. Default behavior is case-insensitive searches from top to bottom. If you specify any one of these two optional parameters, you must specify both of them.

Internet Explorer 4 also has a text search facility, but it is implemented in an entirely different way (using its TextRange object and `findText()` method). The visual behavior also differs in that it does not highlight and scroll to a matching string in the text.

Example

Listing 14-27 is a framesetting document for an interface that permits experimentation with the `window.find()` method. The top frame is a control panel for searching in a copy of the Bill of Rights that appears in the bottom frame.

Listing 14-27: **Find() Method Frameset**

```
<HTML>
<HEAD>
<TITLE>window.find() method</TITLE>
</HEAD>
<FRAMESET ROWS="25%,75%">
        <FRAME NAME="controls" SRC="lst14-28.htm">
        <FRAME NAME="display" SRC="bofright.htm">
</FRAMESET>
</HTML>
```

All the action takes place in Listing 14-28, which is the control panel for text searches in the lower frame.

Listing 14-28: **Find() Method Control Panel**

```
<HTML>
<HEAD>
<TITLE>Window Event Capture</TITLE>
<SCRIPT LANGUAGE="JavaScript1.2">
// function to run when window captures a click event
function findIt(form) {
        var matchString = form.searchTxt.value
```

(continued)

Listing 14-28 *(continued)*

```
            var showDialog = form.dialog.checked
            var caseSensitive = form.sensitive.checked
            var backward = form.bkward.checked
            var wind = parent.display
            var success = true

            if (showDialog) {
                wind.find()
            } else {
                if (!matchString) {
                    alert("Enter a search string in the field.")
                } else {
                    success = wind.find(matchString,caseSensitive,backward)
                }
            }
            if (!success) {
                alert("No (more) matches found.")
            }
        }
    }
</SCRIPT>
</HEAD>
<BODY>
<FORM NAME="controls">
<INPUT NAME="finder" TYPE="button" VALUE="Find..."
onClick="findIt(this.form)">
<INPUT NAME="searchTxt" TYPE="text"><BR>
<INPUT NAME="dialog" TYPE="checkbox"
onClick="this.form.sensitive.checked = false; this.form.bkward.checked
= false">Show Find dialog<BR>
<INPUT NAME="sensitive" TYPE="checkbox"
onClick="this.form.dialog.checked = false">Match case<BR>
<INPUT NAME="bkward" TYPE="checkbox" onClick="this.form.dialog.checked
= false">Search up<BR>
</FORM>
</BODY>
</HTML>
```

The control panel contains one text field for input of a string to search for. Three checkboxes let you set whether the browser's Find dialog should appear or the search should be entirely under script control with the two optional parameters. The Find button triggers the findIt() function, which assembles find() methods based on the checkbox settings and field input.

In the find() function, I first extract all the settings and assign them to individual variables. This is primarily for readability later in the function (eliminating all the long references in statements). Notice that the window being targeted for the search is the display frame, not the current window where the controls are.

To start playing with this example, enter the word "article" into the text box and click the Find button. Continue clicking as the highlighted instances of found text come into view. When you reach the end of the document, the function's alert dialog box tells you there are no more matches to be found (at least in the current direction). Activate the "Search up" checkbox and then start finding in the opposite direction. If you activate the "Match case" checkbox, no matches will be found, since the word "article" is in all uppercase letters in the document.

Related Items: None.

focus()

Returns: Nothing.

	Nav2	Nav3	Nav4	IE3/J1	IE3/J2	IE4/J3
Compatibility		✔	✔			✔

The minute you create another window for the user in your Web site environment, you must pay attention to window layer management. With browser windows so easily activated by the slightest mouse click, a user can lose a smaller window behind a larger one in a snap. Most inexperienced Navigator users won't think to pull down the Window or Communicator menu to see whether the smaller window is still open and then activate it from the menu. If that subwindow is important to your site design, then you should present a button or other device in each window that enables users to safely switch between windows. The `window.focus()` method brings the referenced window to the front of all the windows.

Rather than supply a separate button on your page to bring a hidden window forward, you should build your window-opening functions in such a way that if the window is already open, the function automatically brings that window forward, as shown in the example that follows. This removes the burden of window management from your visitors.

The key to success with this method is making sure that your references to the desired windows are correct. Therefore, be prepared to use the `window.opener` property to refer to the main window if a subwindow needs to bring the main window back into focus. If your windowing environment consists of three or more windows, you have to make sure that you assign a unique name to each window and then use those names if subwindows need to communicate with other subwindows.

Example

To show how both the `window.focus()` method and its opposite, `window.blur()`, operate, Listing 14-29 creates a two-window environment. From each window, you can bring the other window to the front. The main window uses the object returned by `window.open()` to assemble the reference to the new window. In the subwindow (whose content is created entirely on the fly by JavaScript), `self.opener` is summoned to refer to the original window, while `self` is used to direct the `blur()` method to the subwindow itself. Blurring one window and focusing on another window both have the same result of sending the window to the back of the pile.

Listing 14-29: The window.focus() and window.blur() Methods

```
<HTML>
<HEAD>
<TITLE>Focus() and Blur()</TITLE>
<SCRIPT LANGUAGE="JavaScript1.1">
// declare global variable name
var newWindow = null
function makeNewWindow() {
        // check if window already exists
        if (!newWindow || newWindow.closed) {
                // store new window object in global variable
                newWindow = window.open("","","width=250,height=250")
                // assemble content for new window
                var newContent = "<HTML><HEAD><TITLE>Another Sub
Window</TITLE></HEAD>"
                newContent += "<BODY bgColor='salmon'><H1>A Salmon-Colored
Subwindow.</H1>"
                newContent += "<FORM><INPUT TYPE='button' VALUE='Bring Main
to Front' onClick='self.opener.focus()'>"
                newContent += "<FORM><INPUT TYPE='button' VALUE='Put Me in
Back' onClick='self.blur()'>"
                newContent += "</FORM></BODY></HTML>"
                // write HTML to new window document
                newWindow.document.write(newContent)
                newWindow.document.close()
        } else {
        // window already exists, so bring it forward
        newWindow.focus()
        }
}
</SCRIPT>
</HEAD>
<BODY>
<FORM>
<INPUT TYPE="button" NAME="newOne" VALUE="Show New Window"
onClick="makeNewWindow()">
</FORM>
</BODY>
</HTML>
```

A key ingredient to the success of the `makeNewWindow()` function in Listing 14-29 is the first conditional expression. Because `newWind` is initialized as a null value when the page loads, that is its value the first time through the function. But after the subwindow is opened the first time, `newWind` is assigned a value (the subwindow object) that remains intact even if the user closes the window. Thus, the value doesn't revert to null by itself. To catch the possibility that the user has closed the window, the conditional expression also sees if the window is closed. If it is, a new subwindow is generated, and that new window's reference value is reassigned to the `newWind` variable. On the other hand, if the window reference exists and the window is not closed, that subwindow is brought to the front with the `focus()` method.

Related Items: `window.open()` method; `window.blur()` method; `window.opener` property.

forward()

Returns: Nothing.

	Nav2	Nav3	Nav4	IE3/J1	IE3/J2	IE4/J3
Compatibility			✔			

The Forward button's behavior has followed the same evolution as the Back button's since Navigator 2. In Navigator 2, the history object (and all navigation methods associated with it) assumed the entire browser window would change with a click of the Back or Forward button in the toolbar. With the increased popularity of frames, this mechanism didn't work well if one frame remained static while documents flew in and out of another frame: navigation had to be on a frame-by-frame basis, and that's how the Back and Forward buttons worked in Navigator 3 and now in Navigator 4.

From Navigator 3 onward, each window object (including frames) maintains its own history. Unfortunately, JavaScript doesn't observe this until you get to Navigator 4, and thus for a lot of browsers out there (including Internet Explorer 3 and Internet Explorer 4), the history navigation methods control the global history. The purpose of the `window.forward()` method is to offer a scripted version of the global forward navigation, while allowing the history object to control navigation strictly within a particular window or frame — as it should. For more information about version compatibility and the back and forward navigation, see the history object in Chapter 15.

Example

See the Navigation laboratory example in Listing 14-20 and 14-21 to see the differences among the various navigation methods.

Related Items: `window.back()` method; history object.

handleEvent(*event*)

Returns: Nothing.

	Nav2	Nav3	Nav4	IE3/J1	IE3/J2	IE4/J3
Compatibility			✔			

When you explicitly capture events in the window, document, or layer object (by invoking the captureEvents() method for that object), you can control where the events go after their initial capture. To let an event continue to its original target (for example, a button that was clicked by a user), you use the routeEvent() method. But if you want to redirect an event (or class of events) to a particular event handler elsewhere in the document, use the handleEvent() method.

Every object that has event handlers associated with it also has a handleEvent() method. Thus, if you are capturing click events in a window, you can redirect the events to, say, a particular button or link on the page because both of those objects know what to do with click events. Consider the following code excerpt:

```
<SCRIPT LANGUAGE="JavaScript1.2">
// function to run when window captures a click event
function doClicks(e) {
        // send all clicks to the first link in the document
        document.links[0].handleEvent(e)
}
// set window to capture click events
window.captureEvents(Event.CLICK)
// assign doClick() function to click events captured by window
window.onclick = doClicks
</SCRIPT>
```

The window is set up to capture all click events and invoke the doClicks() function each time the user clicks on a clickable item in the window. In the doClicks() function is a single statement that instructs the first link in the document to handle the click event being passed as a parameter. The link must have an onClick= event handler defined for this to be meaningful. Because the event object is passed along, the link's event handler can examine event properties (for example, location of the click) and perhaps alter some of the link's properties before letting it perform its linking task. The preceding example is really showing how to use handleEvent() with a link object, rather than a window object. There is little opportunity for other objects to capture events that normally go to the window, but this method is part of every event-aware object.

Example

See Chapter 33 for details and in-depth examples of working with the event object.

Related Items: window.captureEvents() method; window.releaseEvents() method; window.routeEvent() method; event object.

home()

Returns: Nothing.

	Nav2	Nav3	Nav4	IE3/J1	IE3/J2	IE4/J3
Compatibility			✔			

Like many of the window methods new to Navigator 4, the `window.home()` method provides a scripted way of replicating the action of a toolbar button: the Home button. The action navigates the browser to whatever URL is set in the browser preferences for home page location. Even if you have the starting page set to a blank page, both the Home button and the `window.home()` method go to the URL. You cannot control the default home page of a visitor's browser. Therefore, I recommend that you use this method only if you provide an alternative interface to the toolbar you have turned off (with a signed script).

Related Items: `window.back()` method; `window.forward()` method; `window.toolbar` property.

moveBy(*deltaX,deltaY*)
moveTo(*x,y*)

Returns: Nothing.

	Nav2	Nav3	Nav4	IE3/J1	IE3/J2	IE4/J3
Compatibility			✔			

JavaScript (starting with Navigator 4) can adjust the location of a browser window on the screen. This applies to the main window or any subwindow generated by script. The only security restriction that applies is moving the window off screen entirely: you need a signed script and the user's permission to hide a window this way.

You can move a window to an absolute position on the screen or adjust it along the horizontal and/or vertical axis by any number of pixels, irrespective of the absolute pixel position. The coordinate space for the x (horizontal) and y (vertical) position is the entire screen, with the top-left corner representing 0,0. The point of the window you set with the `moveBy()` and `moveTo()` methods is the very top-left corner of the outer edge of the browser window. Therefore, when you move the window to point 0,0, that sets the window flush with the top-left corner of the screen.

If you try to adjust the position of the window such that any edge falls beyond the screen area, the window remains at the edge of the screen — unless you are using a signed script and have the user's permission to adjust the window partially or completely offscreen. It is dangerous to move the only visible browser window entirely off screen, because the user has no way to get it back into view without quitting and relaunching Navigator 4.

The difference between the `moveTo()` and `moveBy()` methods is that one is an absolute move, while the other is relative. Parameters you specify for `moveTo()` are the precise horizontal and vertical pixel counts on the screen where you want the upper-left corner of the window to appear. In contrast, the parameters for `moveBy()` indicate how far to adjust the window location in either direction. If you want to move the window 25 pixels to the right, you must still include both parameters, but the y value will be zero:

```
window.moveBy(25,0)
```

To move to the left, the first parameter must be a negative number.

Example

Several examples of using the `window.moveTo()` and `window.moveBy()` methods are shown in Listing 14-30. The page presents four buttons, each of which performs a different kind of browser window movement.

Listing 14-30: **Window Boogie**

```
<HTML>
<HEAD>
<TITLE>Window Gymnastics</TITLE>
<SCRIPT LANGUAGE="JavaScript1.2">
// function to run when window captures a click event
function moveOffScreen() {
netscape.security.PrivilegeManager.enablePrivilege("UniversalBrowserWrite")
        var maxX = screen.width
        var maxY = screen.height
        window.moveTo(maxX+1, maxY+1)
        setTimeout("window.moveTo(0,0)",500)
netscape.security.PrivilegeManager.disablePrivilege("UniversalBrowserWrite")
}
// moves window in a circular motion
function revolve() {
        var winX = (screen.availWidth - window.outerWidth) / 2
        var winY = 50
        window.resizeTo(300,200)
        window.moveTo(winX, winY)

        for (var i = 1; i < 36; i++) {
            winX += Math.cos(i * (Math.PI/18)) * 5
            winY += Math.sin(i * (Math.PI/18)) * 5
            window.moveTo(winX, winY)
        }
}
// moves window in a horizontal zig-zag pattern
function zigzag() {
        window.resizeTo(300,200)
        window.moveTo(0,80)
        var incrementX = 2
        var incrementY = 2
        var floor = screen.availHeight - outerHeight
        var rightEdge = screen.availWidth - outerWidth
        for (var i = 0; i < rightEdge; i += 2) {
            window.moveBy(incrementX, incrementY)
            if (i%60 == 0) {
                incrementY = -incrementY
            }
        }
}
// resizes window to occupy all available screen real estate
function maximize() {
```

```
            window.moveTo(0,0)
            window.outerWidth = screen.availWidth
            window.outerHeight = screen.availHeight
    }
</SCRIPT>
</HEAD>
<BODY>
<FORM NAME="buttons">
<B>Window Gymnastics</B><P>
<UL>
<LI><INPUT NAME="offscreen" TYPE="button" VALUE="Disappear a Second"
onClick="moveOffScreen()">
<LI><INPUT NAME="circles" TYPE="button" VALUE="Circular Motion"
onClick="revolve()">
<LI><INPUT NAME="bouncer" TYPE="button" VALUE="Zig Zag"
onClick="zigzag()">
<LI><INPUT NAME="expander" TYPE="button" VALUE="Maximize"
onClick="maximize()">
</UL>
</FORM>
</BODY>
</HTML>
```

The first button requires that you have codebase principals turned on (see Chapter 40) to take advantage of what would normally be a signed script. The moveOffScreen() function momentarily moves the window entirely out of view. Notice how the script determines the size of the screen before deciding where to move the window. After the journey off screen, the window comes back into view at the upper-left corner of the screen.

If using the Web sometimes seems like going around in circles, then the second function, revolve(), should feel just right. After reducing the size of the window and positioning it near the top center of the screen (notice the calculation to determine the x coordinate for centering the window horizontally), the script uses a bit of math to position the window along 36 places around a perfect circle (at 10-degree increments). This is an example of how to dynamically control a window's position based on math calculations.

To demonstrate the moveBy() method, the third function, zigzag(), uses a for loop to increment the coordinate points to make the window travel in a sawtooth pattern across the screen. The x coordinate continues to increment linearly until the window is at the edge of the screen (also calculated on the fly to accommodate any size monitor). The y coordinate must increase and decrease as that parameter changes direction at various times across the screen.

In the fourth function, you see some practical code (finally) that demonstrates how best to maximize the browser window to fill the entire available screen space on the visitor's monitor. Notice that instead of using the resizeTo() method, I set the outerHeight and outerWidth properties of the window. These settings are less bug prone than the resizeTo() method.

Related Items: window.outerHeight property; window.outerWidth property; window.resizeBy() method; window.resizeTo() method.

open("*URL*", "*windowName*" [, "*windowFeatures*"])

Returns: A window object representing the newly created window; null if method fails.

	Nav2	Nav3	Nav4	IE3/J1	IE3/J2	IE4/J3
Compatibility	✔	✔	✔	✔	✔	✔

With the window.open() method, a script provides a Web site designer with an immense range of options for the way a second or third Web browser window looks on the user's computer screen. Moreover, most of this control can work with all JavaScript-enabled browsers without the need for signed scripts. Because the interface elements of a new window are easier to envision, I cover those aspects of the window.open() method parameters first.

The optional windowFeatures parameter is *one string*, consisting of a comma-separated list of assignment expressions (behaving something like HTML tag attributes). If you omit this third parameter, JavaScript creates the same type of new window you'd get from the New Web Browser menu choice in the File menu. But you can control which window elements appear in the new window with the third parameter. Remember this important rule: If you specify *any* of the method's original set of third parameter values, all of those features are turned off unless the parameters specify the features to be switched on. Table 14-1 lists the attributes you can control for a newly created window in all browsers.

Table 14-1
window.open() Method Attributes Controllable via Script

Attribute	Value	Description
toolbar	Boolean	"Back," "Forward," and other buttons in the row
location	Boolean	Field displaying the current URL
directories	Boolean	"What's New" and other buttons in the row
status	Boolean	Statusbar at bottom of window
menubar*	Boolean	Menubar at top of window
scrollbars	Boolean	Displays scrollbars if document is larger than window
resizable**	Boolean	Interface elements that allow resizing by dragging
copyhistory	Boolean	Duplicates Go menu history for new window
width	pixelCount	Window outer width in pixels
height	pixelCount	Window outer height in pixels

*   Not on Macintosh because the menubar is not in the browser window; when off in Navigator 4, displays an abbreviated Mac menubar.

**   Macintosh windows are always resizable.

Boolean values for true can be either `yes`, `1`, or just the feature name by itself; for false, use a value of `no` or `0`. If you omit any Boolean attributes, they are rendered as false. Therefore, if you want to create a new window that shows only the toolbar and statusbar and is resizable, the method looks like this:

```
window.open("newURL","NewWindow", "toolbar,status,resizable")
```

A new window that does not specify the height and width is set to the default size of the browser window that the browser creates from a File menu's New Web Browser command. In other words, a new window does not automatically inherit the size of the window making the `window.open()` method call. A new window created via a script is positioned somewhat arbitrarily, depending on the operating system platform of the browser. Generally, though, the position is at or near the top-left corner of the screen, just as a new Web browser window would be; window position is not scriptable except in Navigator 4.

Speaking of Navigator 4, this browser version includes a suite of extra features for the `window.open()` method. Those parameters deemed to be security risks require signed scripts and the user's permission before they are recognized. If the user fails to grant permission, the secure parameter is ignored. Table 14-2 shows the extra window features provided by Navigator 4.

Table 14-2
Extra window.open() Method Attributes in Navigator 4

Attribute	Value	Description
alwaysLowered*	Boolean	Always behind other browser windows
alwaysRaised*	Boolean	Always in front of other browser windows
dependent	Boolean	Subwindow closes if the opener window closes
hotkeys	Boolean	If true, disables menu shortcuts (except Quit and Security Info) when menubar is turned off
innerHeight**	pixelCount	Content region height; same as old `height` property
innerWidth**	pixelCount	Content region width; same as old `width` property
outerHeight**	pixelCount	Visible window height
outerWidth**	pixelCount	Visible window width
screenX**	pixelCount	Horizontal position of top-left corner on screen
screenY**	pixelCount	Vertical position of top-left corner on screen
titlebar*	Boolean	Title bar and all other border elements
z-lock*	Boolean	Window layer is fixed below browser windows

*   Requires a signed script

**   Requires a signed script to size or position a window beyond safe threshold

A couple of these new attributes have different behaviors on different operating system platforms, due to the way the systems manage their application windows.

For example, the alwaysLowered, alwaysRaised, and z-locked styles can exist in layers that range behind Navigator 4's own windows in the Windows 95 platform; on the Mac, however, such windows are confined to the levels occupied by Navigator 4. The difference is that Windows 95 allows windows from multiple applications to interleave each other, while the Mac keeps each application's windows in contiguous layers.

To apply signed scripts to opening a new window with the secure window features, you must enable UniversalBrowserWrite privileges like you do for other signed scripts (see Chapter 40). A code fragment that generates an alwaysRaised style window follows:

```
<SCRIPT LANGUAGE="JavaScript" ARCHIVE="myJar.jar" ID="1">
function newRaisedWindow() {
netscape.security.PrivilegeManager.enablePrivilege("UniversalBrowserWrite")
        var newWindow =
window.open("","","HEIGHT=100,WIDTH=300,alwaysRaised")

netscape.security.PrivilegeManager.disablePrivilege("UniversalBrowserWrite")
        var newContent = "<HTML><BODY><B> "On top of spaghetti!"</B>"
        newContent += "<FORM><CENTER><INPUT TYPE='button' VALUE='OK'"
        newContent +=
"onClick='self.close()'></CENTER></FORM></BODY></HTML>"
        newWindow.document.write(newContent)
        newWindow.document.close()
}
</SCRIPT>
```

You can experiment with the look and behavior of new windows with any combination of attributes with the help of the script in Listing 14-31. This page presents a table of all new window Boolean attributes and creates a new 300-by-300 pixel window based on your choices. This page assumes that if you are using Navigator 4 you have codebase principals turned on for signed scripts (see Chapter 40). The interface for this laboratory is shown in Figure 14-14.

Be careful with turning off the title bar and hotkeys. With the title bar off, the content appears to float in space, because absolutely no borders are displayed. With hotkeys still turned on, you can use Ctrl+W to close this borderless window (except on the Mac, for which the hotkeys are always disabled with the title bar off). This is how you can turn a computer into a kiosk by sizing a window to the screen's dimensions and setting the window options to "titlebar=no, hotkeys=no,alwaysRaised=yes".

Listing 14-31: **New Window Laboratory**

```
<HTML>
<HEAD>
<TITLE>window.open() Options</TITLE>
<SCRIPT LANGUAGE="JavaScript">
var isNav4 = (navigator.appName == "Netscape" &&
navigator.appVersion.charAt(0) == 4) ? true : false

function makeNewWind(form) {
```

```
            if (isNav4) {

netscape.security.PrivilegeManager.enablePrivilege("UniversalBrowserWrite")
            }
        var attr = "HEIGHT=300,WIDTH=300"
        for (var i = 0; i < form.elements.length; i++) {
            if (form.elements[i].type == "checkbox") {
                attr += "," + form.elements[i].name + "="
                attr += (form.elements[i].checked) ? "yes" : "no"
            }
        }
        var newWind = window.open("bofright.htm","subwindow",attr)
        if (isNav4) {

netscape.security.PrivilegeManager.disablePrivilege("CanvasAccess")
            }
}
</SCRIPT>
</HEAD>
<BODY>
<FORM>
<B>Select new window options:</B>
<TABLE BORDER=2>
<TR>
        <TD COLSPAN=2 BGCOLOR="yellow" ALIGN="middle">All Browsers
Features:</TD>
</TR>
<TR>
        <TD><INPUT TYPE="checkbox" NAME="toolbar">toolbar</TD>
        <TD><INPUT TYPE="checkbox" NAME="location">location</TD>
</TR>
<TR>
        <TD><INPUT TYPE="checkbox" NAME="directories">directories</TD>
        <TD><INPUT TYPE="checkbox" NAME="status">status</TD>
</TR>
<TR>
        <TD><INPUT TYPE="checkbox" NAME="menubar">menubar</TD>
        <TD><INPUT TYPE="checkbox" NAME="scrollbars">scrollbars</TD>
</TR>
<TR>
        <TD><INPUT TYPE="checkbox" NAME="resizable">resizable</TD>
        <TD><INPUT TYPE="checkbox" NAME="copyhistory">copyhistory</TD>
</TR>
<TR>
        <TD COLSPAN=2 BGCOLOR="yellow" ALIGN="middle">Communicator
Features:</TD>
</TR>
<TR>
        <TD><INPUT TYPE="checkbox"
NAME="alwaysLowered">alwaysLowered</TD>
        <TD><INPUT TYPE="checkbox" NAME="alwaysRaised">alwaysRaised</TD>
</TR>
```

(continued)

Listing 14-31 *(continued)*

```
<TR>
        <TD><INPUT TYPE="checkbox" NAME="dependent">dependent</TD>
        <TD><INPUT TYPE="checkbox" NAME="hotkeys" CHECKED>hotkeys</TD>
</TR>
<TR>
        <TD><INPUT TYPE="checkbox" NAME="titlebar" CHECKED>titlebar</TD>
        <TD><INPUT TYPE="checkbox" NAME="z-lock">z-lock</TD>
</TR>
<TR>
        <TD COLSPAN=2 ALIGN="middle"><INPUT TYPE="button" NAME="forAll"
VALUE="Make New Window" onClick="makeNewWind(this.form)"></TD>
</TR>
</TABLE>
<BR>
</FORM>
</BODY>
</HTML>
```

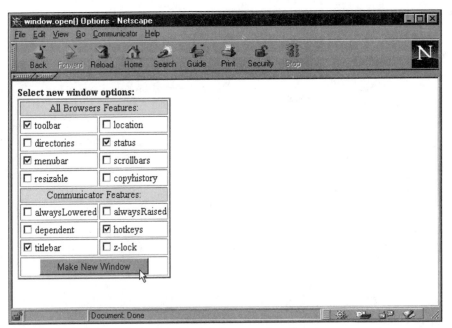

Figure 14-14: A new window attribute laboratory interface

Getting back to the other parameters of window.open(), the middle parameter is the name for the new window. Don't confuse this parameter with the document's title, which would normally be set by whatever HTML text determines the content of the window. A window name must be the same style of one-word identifier you use for other object names and variables. This name is also an entirely different entity than the window object that the open() method returns. You don't use the name in your scripts. At most, the name can be used for TARGET attributes of links and forms.

A script generally populates a window with one of two kinds of information:

✦ An existing HTML document whose URL is known beforehand

✦ An HTML page created on the fly

To create a new window that displays an existing HTML document, supply the full URL as the first parameter of the window.open() method. If your page is having difficulty loading a URL into a new page (except as noted in the sidebar "A Navigator 2 bug workaround"), try specifying the complete URL of the target document (instead of just the filename).

Leaving the first parameter as an empty string forces the window to open with a blank document, ready to have HTML written to it by your script (or loaded separately by another statement that sets that window's location to a specific URL). If you plan to write the content of the window on the fly, assemble your HTML content as one long string value and then use the document.write() method to post that content to the new window. If you plan to append no further writing to the page, also include a document.close() method at the end to tell the browser that you're finished with the layout (so that the Layout:Complete or Document:Done message appears in the statusbar, if your new window has one).

A call to the window.open() method returns a value of the new window's object if the window opens successfully. This value is vitally important if your script needs to address elements of that new window (such as when writing to its document). When a script creates a new window, the default window object (which the script normally points to) still contains the document that holds the script. The new window does not, even though it may be on top. Therefore, to further manipulate items within the new window, you need a reference to that new window object. After the new window is open, however, no parent-child relationship exists between the windows.

To handle references to the subwindow properly, you should always assign the result of a window.open() method to a global variable. Before writing to the new window the first time, test the variable to make sure that it is not a null value — the window may have failed to open because of low memory, for instance. If everything is okay, you can use that variable as the beginning of a reference to any property or object within the new window. For example

```
newWindow = window.open("","")
if (newWindow != null) {

newWindow.document.write("<HTML><HEAD><TITLE>Hi!</TITLE></HEAD>")
}
```

If you initialize the new window's variable as a global variable (see Chapter 34), any value that the variable receives (even if it gets the value while inside a function) remains in effect as long as the original document stays loaded in the first window. You can come back to that value in another script handler (perhaps some button that closes the subwindow) by making the proper reference to the new window.

A Navigator 2 bug workaround

If you're concerned about backward compatibility with Navigator 2, you should be aware of a bug in the Macintosh and UNIX flavors of the browser. In those versions, if you include a URL as a parameter to `window.open()`, Navigator opens the window but does not load the URL. A second call to the `window.open()` method is required. Moreover, the second parameter must be an empty string if you add any third-parameter settings. Here is a sample listing you can adapt for your own usage:

```
<HTML>
<HEAD>
<TITLE>New Window</TITLE>
<SCRIPT LANGUAGE="JavaScript">
// workaround for window.open() bug on X and Mac platforms
function makeNewWindow() {
    var newWindow =
window.open("http://www.dannyg.com","","status,height=200,width=300")
    if (navigator.appVersion.charAt(0) == "2" &&
navigator.appName == "Netscape") {
        newWindow =
window.open("http://www.dannyg.com","","status,height=200,width=300")
    }
}
</SCRIPT>
</HEAD>
<BODY>
<FORM>
<INPUT TYPE="button" NAME="newOne" VALUE="Create New Window"
onClick="makeNewWindow()">
</FORM>
</BODY>
</HTML>
```

This workaround can also be used without penalty in Windows versions of Navigator 2 and Navigator 3.

When scripts in the subwindow need to communicate with objects and scripts in the originating window, you must make sure that the subwindow has an `opener` property if the level of JavaScript in the visitor's browser doesn't automatically supply one. See the discussion about the `window.opener` property earlier in this chapter.

Invoking multiple `window.open()` methods with the same window name parameter (the second parameter) does not create additional copies of that window in Netscape browsers (although it does in Internet Explorer 3). JavaScript prevents you from creating two windows with the same name. Nor does a `window.open()` method bring an existing window of that name to the front of the window layers: Use `window.focus()` for that.

Example

In Listing 14-32, I install a button that generates a new window of a specific size that has only the statusbar turned on. The script here shows all the elements necessary to create a new window that has all the right stuff on most platforms. The new window object reference is assigned to a global variable, newWindow. Before a new window is generated, the script looks to see if the window has never been generated before (in which case newWindow would be null) or, for newer browsers, the window is closed. If either condition is true, the window is created with the open() method. Otherwise, the existing window is brought forward with the focus() method (Navigator 3 and up; Internet Explorer 4).

As a safeguard against older browsers, the script manually adds an opener property to the new window if one is not already assigned by the open() method. The current window object reference is assigned to that property.

To build the string that is eventually written to the document, I use the += (add-by-value) operator, which appends the string on the right side of the operator to the string stored in the variable on the left side. In this example, the new window is handed an <H1>-level line of text to display.

Listing 14-32: **Creating a New Window**

```
<HTML>
<HEAD>
<TITLE>New Window</TITLE>
<SCRIPT LANGUAGE="JavaScript">
var newWindow
function makeNewWindow() {
        if (!newWindow || newWindow.closed) {
            newWindow = window.open("","","status,height=200,width=300")
            if (!newWindow.opener) {
                newWindow.opener = window
            }
            // assemble content for new window
            var newContent = "<HTML><HEAD><TITLE>One Sub
Window</TITLE></HEAD>"
            newContent += "<BODY><H1>This window is brand new.</H1>"
            newContent += "</BODY></HTML>"
            // write HTML to new window document
            newWindow.document.write(newContent)
            newWindow.document.close() // close layout stream
        } else {
            // window's already open; bring to front
            newWindow.focus()
        }
}
</SCRIPT>
</HEAD>
<BODY>
<FORM>
<INPUT TYPE="button" NAME="newOne" VALUE="Create New Window"
  onClick="makeNewWindow()">
```

(continued)

Listing 14-32 *(continued)*

```
</FORM>
</BODY>
</HTML>
```

If you need to create a new window for the lowest common denominator of scriptable browser, you will have to omit the `focus()` method and the `window.closed` property from the script (as well as add the bug workaround described earlier). Or you may prefer to forego a subwindow for all browsers below a certain level. For example, Navigator 3 and up provide a solid foundation for new window features available for Internet Explorer users only from Version 4. But also see Listing 14-3 (in the `window.closed` property discussion) for other ideas about cross-platform authoring for subwindows.

Related Items: `window.close()` method; `window.blur()` method; `window.focus()` method; `window.closed` property.

print()

Returns: Nothing.

	Nav2	Nav3	Nav4	IE3/J1	IE3/J2	IE4/J3
Compatibility			✔			

Like several other new window methods for Navigator 4, `print()` provides a scripted way of invoking the Print button in the toolbar, whether the toolbar is visible or not. Printing, however, is a little different, because a user — and now a script — can specify that the entire browser window be printed or just a particular frame. If you build a reference to the `print()` method with a reference to a frame, then just that frame will be printed. To prevent a rogue `print()` command from tying up a printer without the user's permission, the `print()` method goes only so far as to present the browser's print dialog box. The user must still click the OK or Print button (depending on the operating system) to send the window or frame content to the printer.

Example

Listing 14-33 is a frameset that loads Listing 14-34 into the top frame and a copy of the Bill of Rights into the bottom frame.

Listing 14-33: **Print Frameset**

```
<HTML>
<HEAD>
<TITLE>window.print() method</TITLE>
```

```
</HEAD>
<FRAMESET ROWS="25%,75%">
      <FRAME NAME="controls" SRC="lst14-34.htm">
      <FRAME NAME="display" SRC="bofright.htm">
</FRAMESET>
</HTML>
```

Two buttons in the top control panel (Listing 14-34) let you print the whole frameset or just the lower frame. To print the entire frameset, the reference includes the parent window; to print the lower frame, the reference is directed at the parent.display frame.

Listing 14-34: **Printing Control**

```
<HTML>
<HEAD>
<TITLE>Print()</TITLE>
</HEAD>
<BODY>
<FORM>
<INPUT TYPE="button" NAME="printWhole" VALUE="Print Entire Frameset"
onClick="parent.print()"><P>
<INPUT TYPE="button" NAME="printFrame" VALUE="Print Bottom Frame Only"
onClick="parent.display.print()"><P>
</FORM>
</BODY>
</HTML>
```

If you don't like some facet of the printed output, blame the browser's print engine, and not JavaScript. The print() method merely invokes the browser's regular printing routines. Pages whose content is generated entirely by JavaScript print only in Navigator 3 and later (and Internet Explorer 4). A page containing some HTML and some JavaScript-generated content prints only the HTML portion.

Related Items: window.back() method; window.forward() method; window.home() method; window.find() method.

prompt(*message, defaultReply*)

Returns: String of text entered by user or null.

	Nav2	Nav3	Nav4	IE3/J1	IE3/J2	IE4/J3
Compatibility	✔	✔	✔	✔	✔	✔

The third kind of dialog box that JavaScript can display includes a message from the script author, a field for user entry, and two buttons (OK and Cancel, or Yes and No on Mac versions of Navigator 2 and 3). The script writer can supply a prewritten answer so a user confronted with a prompt dialog box can click OK (or press Enter) to accept that answer without further typing. Supplying both parameters to the `window.prompt()` method is important. Even if you don't want to supply a default answer, enter an empty string as the second parameter:

```
prompt("What is your postal code?","")
```

If you omit the second parameter, JavaScript inserts the string `<undefined>` into the dialog box's field. This will be disconcerting to most Web page visitors.

The value returned by this method is a string in the dialog box's field when the user clicks on the OK button. If you're asking the user to enter a number, remember that the value returned by this method is a string. You may need to perform data-type conversion with the `parseInt()` or `parseFloat()` functions (see Chapter 28) to use the returned values in math calculations.

When the user clicks on the prompt dialog box's OK button without entering any text into a blank field, the returned value is an empty string (" "). Clicking on the Cancel button, however, makes the method return a null value. Therefore, the scripter must test for the type of returned value to make sure that the user entered some data that can be processed later in the script, as in

```
var entry = prompt("Enter a number between 1 and 10:","")
if (entry != null) {
        statements to execute with the value
}
```

This script excerpt assigns the results of the prompt dialog box to a variable and executes the nested statements if the returned value of the dialog box is not null (if the user clicked on the OK button). The rest of the statements then have to include data validation to make sure that the entry was a number within the desired range (see Chapter 37).

It may be tempting to use the prompt dialog box as a handy user input device. But, like the other JavaScript dialog boxes, the modality of the prompt dialog box is disruptive to the user's flow through a document and can also trap automated macros that some users activate to capture Web sites. In forms, HTML fields are better user interface elements for attracting user text entry. Perhaps the safest way to use a prompt dialog box is to have it appear when a user clicks a button element on a page — and then only if the information you require of the user can be provided in a single prompt dialog box. Presenting a sequence of prompt dialog boxes is downright annoying to users.

Example

The function that receives values from the prompt dialog box in Listing 14-35 (see the dialog box in Figure 14-15) does some data-entry validation (but certainly not enough for a commercial site). It first checks to make sure that the returned value is neither null (Cancel) nor an empty string (the user clicked on OK without entering any values). See Chapter 37 for more about data-entry validation.

Listing 14-35: **The Prompt Dialog Box**

```
<HTML>
<HEAD>
<TITLE>window.prompt() Method</TITLE>
<SCRIPT LANGUAGE="JavaScript">
function populateTable() {
        var howMany = prompt("Fill in table for how many factors?","")
        if (howMany != null && howMany != "") {
            alert("Filling the table for " + howMany) // for demo
            //statements that validate the entry and
            //actually populate the fields of the table
        }
}
</SCRIPT>
</HEAD>
<BODY>
<FORM>
<!-- other statements that display and populate a large table -->
<INPUT TYPE="button" NAME="fill" VALUE="Fill Table..."
onClick="populateTable()">
</FORM>
</BODY>
</HTML>
```

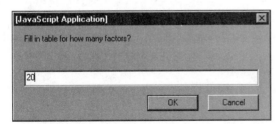

Figure 14-15: The prompt dialog box displayed
from Listing 14-35 (Windows 95 format)

Notice one important user interface element in Listing 14-35. Because clicking on
the button leads to a dialog box that requires more information from the user, the
button's label ends in an ellipsis (or, rather, three periods acting as an ellipsis
character). The ellipsis is a common courtesy to let users know that a user interface
element leads to a dialog box of some sort. As in similar situations in Windows 95
and Macintosh programs, the user should be able to cancel out of that dialog box
and return to the same screen state that existed before the button was clicked.

Related Items: window.alert() method; window.confirm() method.

releaseEvents(*eventTypeList*)

Returns: Nothing.

	Nav2	Nav3	Nav4	IE3/J1	IE3/J2	IE4/J3
Compatibility			✔			

If your scripts have enabled event capture for the window object (or document or layer, for that matter), you can turn off that capture with the releaseEvents() method. This does not inhibit events from reaching their intended target. In fact, by releasing capture from a higher object, released events don't bother stopping at those higher objects anymore. Parameters for the releaseEvents() method are one or more event types. Each event type is its own entity, so if your window captures three event types at one point, you can release some or all of those event types as the visitor interacts with your page. For example, if the page loads and captures three types of events, as in

```
window.captureEvents(Event.CLICK | Event.KEYPRESS | Event.CHANGE)
```

you can later turn off window event capture for all but the click event:

```
window.releaseEvents(Event.KEYPRESS | Event.CHANGE)
```

The window will still capture and process click events, but keyPress and change events go directly to their target objects.

Related Items: window.captureEvents() method; window.routeEvent() method.

resizeBy(*deltaX,deltaY*)

resizeTo(*outerwidth,outerheight*)

Returns: Nothing.

	Nav2	Nav3	Nav4	IE3/J1	IE3/J2	IE4/J3
Compatibility			✔			

Starting with Navigator 4, scripts can control the size of the current browser window on the fly. While you can set the individual inner and outer width and height properties of a window, the resizeBy() and resizeTo() methods let you adjust both axis measurements in one statement. In both instances, all adjustments affect the lower-right corner of the window: To move the top-left corner, use the window.moveBy() or window.moveTo() methods.

Each resize method requires a different kind of parameter. The resizeBy() method adjusts the window *by* a certain number of pixels along one or both axes. Therefore, it is not concerned with the specific size of the window beforehand —

only by how much each axis is to change. For example, to increase the current window size by 100 pixels horizontally and 50 pixels vertically, the statement would be

```
window.resizeBy(100, 50)
```

Both parameters are required, but if you only want to adjust the size in one direction, set the other to zero. This would be the same as adding a value to one of the outer window measurement properties. You may also shrink the window by using negative values for either or both parameters.

There is greater need for the `resizeTo()` method, especially when you know that on a particular platform the window needs adjustment to a specific width and height to best accommodate that platform's display of form elements. Parameters for the `resizeTo()` method are the actual pixel width and height of the outer dimension of the window — the same as the `window.outerWidth` and `window.outerHeight` properties. In practice, I have found that the `resizeTo()` method behaves less accurately than setting the individual properties. If you need to maximize the browser window to the user's monitor, use the script segment shown in the `window.outerHeight` property discussion.

For both methods, you are limited to the viewable area of the screen unless the page uses signed scripts (see Chapter 40). With signed scripts and the users permission, you can adjust windows beyond the available screen borders.

Example

You can experiment with the resize methods with the page in Listing 14-36. Two parts of a form let you enter values for each method. The one for `window.resize()` also lets you enter a number of repetitions to better see the impact of the values. Enter zero and negative values to see how those affect the method.

Listing 14-36: **Window Resize Methods**

```
<HTML>
<HEAD>
<TITLE>Window Resize Methods</TITLE>
<SCRIPT LANGUAGE="JavaScript">
function doResizeBy(form) {
        var x = parseInt(form.resizeByX.value)
        var y = parseInt(form.resizeByY.value)
        var count = parseInt(form.count.value)
        for (var i = 0; i < count; i++) {
            window.resizeBy(x, y)
        }
}
function doResizeTo(form) {
        var x = parseInt(form.resizeToX.value)
        var y = parseInt(form.resizeToY.value)
        window.resizeTo(x, y)
}
</SCRIPT>
</HEAD>
```

(continued)

Listing 14-36 *(continued)*

```
<BODY>
<FORM>
<B>Enter the x and y increment, plus how many times the window should
be resized by these increments:</B><BR>
Horiz:<INPUT TYPE="text" NAME="resizeByX" SIZE=4>
Vert:<INPUT TYPE="text" NAME="resizeByY" SIZE=4>
How Many:<INPUT TYPE="text" NAME="count" SIZE=4>
<INPUT TYPE="button" NAME="ResizeBy" VALUE="Show resizeBy()"
onClick="doResizeBy(this.form)">
<HR>
<B>Enter the desired width and height of the current window:</B><BR>
Width:<INPUT TYPE="text" NAME="resizeToX" SIZE=4>
Height:<INPUT TYPE="text" NAME="resizeToY" SIZE=4>
<INPUT TYPE="button" NAME="ResizeTo" VALUE="Show resizeTo()"
onClick="doResizeTo(this.form)">
</FORM>
</BODY>
</HTML>
```

Related Items: `window.outerHeight` property; `window.outerWidth` property; `window.moveTo()` method.

routeEvent(*event*)

Returns: Nothing.

	Nav2	Nav3	Nav4	IE3/J1	IE3/J2	IE4/J3
Compatibility			✔			

If you turn on event capturing in the window, document, or layer object (via their respective `captureEvents()` methods), the event handler you assign to those events really captures those events, preventing them from ever reaching their intended targets. For some page designs, this is intentional, as it allows the higher-level object to handle all events of a particular type. But if your goal is to perform some preprocessing of events before they reach their destination, you need a way to pass that event along its regular path. That's what the `routeEvent()` method is for.

Perhaps a more common reason for capturing events at the window (or similar) level is to look for special cases, such as when someone Ctrl+clicks on an element. In this case, even though the window event handler receives all click events, it performs further processing only when the `event.modifiers` property indicates the Ctrl key is also pressed and the `event.target` property reveals the item being clicked is a link rather than a button. All other instances of the click event are routed on their way to their destinations. The event object knows where it's going, so your `routeEvent()` method doesn't have to worry about that.

The parameter for the routeEvent() method is the event object that is passed to the function that processes the high-level event, as shown here:

```
function flashRed(e) {
    [statements that filter specific events to flash background color red]
    routeEvent(e)
}
```

The event object, e, comes into the function and is passed unmodified to the object that was clicked.

Example

The window.routeEvent() method is used in the example for window.captureEvents(), Listing 14-22.

Related Items: window.captureEvents() method; window.releaseEvents() method; window.handleEvent() method; event object.

scroll(*horizontalCoord, verticalCoord*)

Returns: Nothing.

	Nav2	Nav3	Nav4	IE3/J1	IE3/J2	IE4/J3
Compatibility		✔	✔			✔

Although you can control precious little about the look of an existing window via JavaScript, you can adjust the way a document scrolls inside a window or frame. On the surface, the window.scroll() method sounds like a practical power within scripts. Due to the way various platforms render fonts and other visual elements on the screen, the window.scroll() method works best when you use absolute positioning of Dynamic HTML. Unless you know the precise pixel location of a desired element to bring into view, the method won't be particularly valuable as an internal navigation device (navigating to anchors with the location object is more precise in this situation).

 Note

If you are designing for Navigator 4 and do not require backward compatibility to Navigator 3 or Internet Explorer 4, use the window.scrollTo() method instead of the window.scroll() method. Both methods perform the same operation, but the new method better fits into the latest direction of the Netscape object model.

The window.scroll() method takes two parameters, the horizontal (x) and vertical (y) coordinates of the document that is to be positioned at the top-left corner of the window or frame. You must realize that the window and document have two similar, but independent, coordinate schemes. From the window's point of view, the top-left pixel (of the active area) is point 0,0. All documents also have a 0,0 point: the very top-left of the document. The window's 0,0 point doesn't move, but the document's 0,0 point can move — via manual or scripted scrolling. Although scroll() is a window method, it seems to behave more like a document method, as the document appears to reposition itself within the window. Conversely, you can also think of the window moving to bring its 0,0 point to the designated coordinate of the document.

Although you can set values to ones that go beyond the maximum size of the document or to negative values, the results vary from platform to platform. For the moment, the best usage of the `window.scroll()` method is as a means of adjusting the scroll to the very top of a document (`window.scroll(0,0)`) when you want the user to be at a base location in the document. For vertical scrolling within a text-heavy document, an HTML anchor may be a better alternative for now (though it doesn't readjust horizontal scrolling).

Example

To demonstrate the `scroll()` method, Listing 14-37 defines a frameset with a document in the top frame (Listing 14-38) and a control panel in the bottom frame (Listing 14-39). A series of buttons and text fields in the control panel frame directs the scrolling of the document. I've selected an arbitrary, large GIF image to use in the example. To see results of some horizontal scrolling values, you may need to shrink the width of the browser window until a horizontal scrollbar appears in the top frame.

Listing 14-37: **A Frameset for the scroll() Demonstration**

```
<HTML>
<HEAD>
<TITLE>window.scroll() Method</TITLE>
</HEAD>

<FRAMESET ROWS="50%,50%">
        <FRAME SRC="lst14-38.htm" NAME="display">
        <FRAME SRC="lst14-39.htm" NAME="control">
</FRAMESET>
</HTML>
```

Listing 14-38: **The Image to Be Scrolled**

```
<HTML>
<HEAD>
<TITLE>Arch</TITLE>
</HEAD>

<BODY>
<H1>A Picture is Worth...</H1>
<HR>
<CENTER>
<TABLE BORDER=3>
<CAPTION ALIGN=bottom>A Splendid Arch</CAPTION>
<TD>
<IMG SRC="arch.gif">
</TD></TABLE></CENTER>
</BODY>
</HTML>
```

Listing 14-39: **Controls to Adjust Scrolling of the Upper Frame**

```html
<HTML>
<HEAD>
<TITLE>Scroll Controller</TITLE>
<SCRIPT LANGUAGE="JavaScript1.1">
function scroll(x,y) {
        parent.frames[0].scroll(x,y)
}
function customScroll(form) {

parent.frames[0].scroll(parseInt(form.x.value),parseInt(form.y.value))
}
</SCRIPT>
</HEAD>
<BODY>
<H2>Scroll Controller</H2>
<HR>
<FORM NAME="fixed">
Click on a scroll coordinate for the upper frame:<P>
<INPUT TYPE="button" VALUE="0,0" onClick="scroll(0,0)">
<INPUT TYPE="button" VALUE="0,100" onClick="scroll(0,100)">
<INPUT TYPE="button" VALUE="100,0" onClick="scroll(100,0)">
<P>
<INPUT TYPE="button" VALUE="-100,100" onClick="scroll(-100,100)">
<INPUT TYPE="button" VALUE="20,200" onClick="scroll(20,200)">
<INPUT TYPE="button" VALUE="1000,3000" onClick="scroll(1000,3000)">
</FORM>
<HR>
<FORM NAME="custom">
Enter an Horizontal
<INPUT TYPE="text" NAME="x" VALUE="0" SIZE=4>
and Vertical
<INPUT TYPE="text" NAME="y" VALUE="0" SIZE=4>
value.  Then
<INPUT TYPE="button" VALUE="click to scroll"
onClick="customScroll(this.form)">
</FORM>
</BODY>
</HTML>
```

Notice that in the `customScroll()` function, JavaScript must convert the string values from the two text boxes to integers (with the `parseInt()` method) for the `scroll()` method to accept them. Nonnumeric data can produce very odd results. Also be aware that although this example shows how to adjust the scroll values in another frame, you can set such values in the same frame or window as the script, as well as in subwindows, provided that you use the correct object references to the window.

Related Items: `window.scrollBy()` method; `window.scrollTo()` method.

scrollBy(*deltaX*,*deltaY*)
scrollTo(*x*,*y*)

Returns: Nothing.

	Nav2	Nav3	Nav4	IE3/J1	IE3/J2	IE4/J3
Compatibility			✔			

Navigator 4 provides a related pair of window scrolling methods. The window.scrollTo() method is the new version of the window.scroll() method. The two work identically to position a specific coordinate point of a document at the top-left corner of the inner window region.

In contrast, the window.scrollBy() method allows for relative positioning of the document. Parameter values indicate by how many pixels the document should scroll in the window (horizontally and vertically). Negative numbers are allowed if you want to scroll to the left and/or upward. The scrollBy() method comes in handy if you elect to hide the scrollbars of a window or frame and offer other types of scrolling controls for your users. For example, to scroll down one screenful of a long document, you can use the window.innerHeight to determine what the offset from the current position would be:

```
window.scrollBy(0, window.innerHeight)
```

To scroll upward, use a negative value for the second parameter:

```
window.scrollBy(0, -window.innerHeight)
```

Note

Scrolling the document in the Macintosh exhibits some buggy behavior. At times it appears as though you are allowed to scroll well beyond the document edges. In truth, the document has stopped at the border, but the window or frame may not have refreshed properly.

Example

To work with the scrollTo() method, you can use Listings 14-37 through 14-39 (the window.scroll() method) but substitute window.scrollTo() for window.scroll(). The results should be the same. For scrollBy(), the example starts with the frameset in Listing 14-40. It loads the same content document as the window.scroll() example (Listing 14-38), but the control panel (Listing 14-41) provides input to experiment with the scrollBy() method.

Listing 14-40: **Frameset for ScrollBy Controller**

```
<HTML>
<HEAD>
<TITLE>window.scrollBy() Method</TITLE>
</HEAD>

<FRAMESET ROWS="50%,50%">
```

```
        <FRAME SRC="lst14-38.htm" NAME="display">
        <FRAME SRC="lst14-41.htm" NAME="control">
</FRAMESET>
</HTML>
```

Notice in Listing 14-41 that all references to window properties and methods are directed to the display frame. String values retrieved from text fields are converted to number with the `parseInt()` global function.

Listing 14-41: **ScrollBy Controller**

```
<HTML>
<HEAD>
<TITLE>ScrollBy Controller</TITLE>
<SCRIPT LANGUAGE="JavaScript1.2">
function page(direction) {
      var deltaY = parent.display.innerHeight
      if (direction == "up") {
          deltaY = -deltaY
      }
      parent.display.scrollBy(0, deltaY)
}
function customScroll(form) {
      parent.display.scrollBy(parseInt(form.x.value),
parseInt(form.y.value))
}
</SCRIPT>
</HEAD>
<BODY>
<B>ScrollBy Controller</B>
<FORM NAME="custom">
Enter an Horizontal increment
<INPUT TYPE="text" NAME="x" VALUE="0" SIZE=4>
and Vertical
<INPUT TYPE="text" NAME="y" VALUE="0" SIZE=4>
value.<BR>Then
<INPUT TYPE="button" VALUE="click to scrollBy()"
onClick="customScroll(this.form)">
<HR>
<INPUT TYPE="button" VALUE="PageDown" onClick="page('down')">
<INPUT TYPE="button" VALUE="PageUp" onClick="page('up')">

</FORM>
</BODY>
</HTML>
```

Related Items: `window.pageXOffset` property; `window.pageYOffset` property; `window.scroll()` method.

setInterval("*functionOrExpr*", *msecDelay* [, *funcarg1*, ..., *funcargn*])

Returns: Interval ID integer.

	Nav2	Nav3	Nav4	IE3/J1	IE3/J2	IE4/J3
Compatibility			✔			✔

It is important to understand the distinction between the setInterval() and setTimeout() methods. Before the setInterval() method was part of JavaScript, authors replicated the behavior with setTimeout(), but the task often required reworking scripts a bit.

Use setInterval() when your script needs to call a function or execute some expression repeatedly with a fixed time delay between calls to that function or expression. The delay is not at all like a wait state in some languages: Other processing does not halt while the delay is in effect. Typical applications include animation by moving an object around the page under controlled speed (instead of letting the JavaScript interpreter whiz the object through its path at CPU-dependent speeds). In a kiosk application, you can use setInterval() to advance "slides" that appear in other frames or as layers, perhaps changing the view every ten seconds. Clock displays and countdown timers would also be suitable usage of this method (even though you see examples in this book that use the old-fashioned setTimeout() way to perform timer and clock functions).

In contrast, setTimeout() is best suited for those times when you need to carry out a function or expression one time in the future — even if that future is only a second or two away. See the discussion of the setTimeout() method for details on this application.

The first parameter of the setInterval() method is the name of the function or expression to run when the interval elapses. This item must be a quoted string. If the parameter is a function, no function arguments are allowed inside the function's parentheses unless the arguments are literal strings. You can, however, include evaluated function arguments as a comma-delimited list, starting with the third parameter.

Putting function arguments in the final parameters of the setInterval() method is unique to Navigator 4. Internet Explorer 4 uses the third parameter to specify the scripting language of the statement or function being invoked in the first parameter. If you are trying to achieve cross-platform compatibility, design a function called by setInterval() so no arguments need to be passed. That way, Navigator 4 will ignore the third parameter required for Internet Explorer 4.

The second parameter of this method is the number of milliseconds (1,000 per second) that JavaScript should use as the interval between invocations of the function or expression. Even though the measure is in extremely small units, don't rely on 100 percent accuracy of the intervals. Various other internal processing delays may throw off the timing just a bit.

Like `setTimeout()`, `setInterval()` returns an integer value that is the ID for the interval process. That ID value lets you turn off the process with the `clearInterval()` method. That method takes the ID value as its sole parameter. This mechanism allows for the setting of multiple interval processes running, while giving your scripts the power to stop individual processes at any time without interrupting the others.

Example

The demonstration of the `setInterval()` method entails a two-framed environment. The framesetting document is shown in Listing 14-42.

Listing 14-42: **SetInterval() Demonstration Frameset**

```
<HTML>
<HEAD>
<TITLE>setInterval() Method</TITLE>
</HEAD>

<FRAMESET ROWS="50%,50%">
      <FRAME SRC="lst14-43.htm" NAME="control">
      <FRAME SRC="bofright.htm" NAME="display">
</FRAMESET>
</HTML>
```

In the top frame is a control panel with several buttons that control the automatic scrolling of the Bill of Rights text document in the bottom frame. Listing 14-43 shows the control panel document. Many functions here control the interval, scrolling jump size, and direction, and they demonstrate several aspects of applying `setInterval()`.

Notice that in the beginning the script establishes a number of global variables. Three of them are parameters that control the scrolling; the last one is for the ID value returned by the `setInterval()` method. The script needs that value to be a global value so a separate function can halt the scrolling with the `clearInterval()` method.

All scrolling is performed by the `autoScroll()` function. Because I want this method ultimately to coexist in a page usable in Internet Explorer 4 (with the help of a JScript segment to handle Internet Explorer 4's different manner of scrolling content), the `autoScroll()` method does not rely on parameters. Instead, all controlling parameters are global variables. In this application, placement of those values in globals helps the page restart autoscrolling with the same parameters as it had when it last ran.

Listing 14-43: **SetInterval() Control Panel**

```
<HTML>
<HEAD>
<TITLE>ScrollBy Controller</TITLE>
```

(continued)

Listing 14-43 *(continued)*

```
<SCRIPT LANGUAGE="JavaScript1.2">
var scrollSpeed = 500
var scrollJump = 1
var scrollDirection = "down"
var intervalID

function autoScroll() {
      if (scrollDirection == "down") {
          scrollJump = Math.abs(scrollJump)
      } else if (scrollDirection == "up" && scrollJump > 0) {
          scrollJump = -scrollJump
      }
      parent.display.scrollBy(0, scrollJump)
      if (parent.display.pageYOffset <= 0) {
          clearInterval(intervalID)
      }
}

function reduceInterval() {
      stopScroll()
      scrollSpeed -= 200
      startScroll()
}
function increaseInterval() {
      stopScroll()
      scrollSpeed += 200
      startScroll()
}
function reduceJump() {
      scrollJump -= 2
}
function increaseJump() {
      scrollJump += 2
}
function swapDirection() {
      scrollDirection = (scrollDirection == "down") ? "up" : "down"
}
function startScroll() {
      parent.display.scrollBy(0, scrollJump)
      intervalID = setInterval("autoScroll()",scrollSpeed)
}
function stopScroll() {
      clearInterval(intervalID)
}
</SCRIPT>
</HEAD>
<BODY onLoad="startScroll()">
<B>AutoScroll by setInterval() Controller</B>
<FORM NAME="custom">
<INPUT TYPE="button" VALUE="Start Scrolling" onClick="startScroll()">
```

```
<INPUT TYPE="button" VALUE="Stop Scrolling" onClick="stopScroll()"><P>
<INPUT TYPE="button" VALUE="Shorter Time Interval"
onClick="reduceInterval()">
<INPUT TYPE="button" VALUE="Longer Time Interval"
onClick="increaseInterval()"><P>
<INPUT TYPE="button" VALUE="Bigger Scroll Jumps"
onClick="increaseJump()">
<INPUT TYPE="button" VALUE="Smaller Scroll Jumps"
onClick="reduceJump()"><P>
<INPUT TYPE="button" VALUE="Change Direction"
onClick="swapDirection()">

</FORM>
</BODY>
</HTML>
```

The setInterval() method is invoked inside the startScroll() function. This function initially "burps" the page by one scrollJump interval so that the test in autoScroll() for the page being scrolled all the way to the top doesn't halt a page from scrolling before it gets started. One of the global variables, scrollSpeed, is used to fill the delay parameter for setInterval(). To change this value on the fly, the script must stop the current interval process, change the scrollSpeed value, and start a new process.

The intensely repetitive nature of this application is nicely handled by the setInterval() method.

Related Items: window.clearInterval() method; window.setTimeout() method.

setTimeout("*functionOrExpr*", *msecDelay* [, *funcarg1*, ..., *funcargn*])

Returns: ID value for use with window.clearTimeout() method.

	Nav2	Nav3	Nav4	IE3/J1	IE3/J2	IE4/J3
Compatibility	✔	✔	✔	✔	✔	✔

The name of this method may be misleading, especially if you have done other kinds of programming involving *timeouts*. In JavaScript, a timeout is an amount of time (in milliseconds) *before a stated expression evaluates*. A timeout is not a wait or script delay, but rather a way to tell JavaScript to hold off executing a statement or function for a desired amount of time.

Say that you have a Web page designed to enable users to interact with a variety of buttons or fields within a time limit (this is a Web page running at a free-standing kiosk). You can turn on the timeout of the window so that if no interaction occurs with specific buttons or fields lower in the document after, say, two minutes (120,000 milliseconds), the window reverts to the top of the document or to a help screen. To tell the window to switch off the timeout when a user does navigate within the allotted time, you need to have any button that the user interacts with call the other side of a setTimeout() method — the clearTimeout() method — to cancel the current timer. (The clearTimeout() method is explained earlier in this chapter.)

The expression that comprises the first parameter of the method window.setTimeout() can be either a call to any function or method or a standalone JavaScript statement. The expression evaluates after the time limit expires.

Understanding that this timeout does not halt script execution is very important. In fact, if you use a setTimeout() method in the middle of a script, the succeeding statements in the script execute immediately; after the delay time, the statement in the setTimeout() method executes. Therefore, I've found that the best way to design a timeout in a script is to plug it in as the *last* statement of a function: Let all other statements execute and then let the setTimeout() method appear to halt further execution until the timer goes off. In truth, however, although the timeout is "holding," the user is not prevented from performing other tasks. And once a timeout timer is ticking, you cannot adjust its time. Instead, clear the timeout and start a new one.

It is not uncommon for a setTimeout() method to invoke the very function in which it lives. For example, if you have written a Java applet to perform some extra work for your page and you need to connect to it via LiveConnect, your scripts must wait for the applet to load and carry out its initializations. While an onLoad= event handler in the document ensures that the applet object is visible to scripts, it doesn't know whether the applet has finished its initializations. A JavaScript function that inspects the applet for a clue might need to poll the applet every 500 milliseconds until the applet sets some internal value indicating all is ready, as shown here:

```
var t
function autoReport() {
    if (!document.myApplet.done) {
        t = setTimeout("autoReport",500)
    } else {
        clearTimeout(t)
        [more statements using applet data]
    }
}
```

JavaScript provides no built-in equivalent for a wait command. The worst alternative is to devise a looping function of your own to trap script execution for a fixed amount of time. In Navigator 3 and up, you can also use LiveConnect (see Chapter 38) to invoke a Java method that freezes the browser's thread for a fixed amount of time. Unfortunately, both of these practices prevent other processes from being carried out, so you should consider reworking your code to rely on a setTimeout() method instead.

Example

When you load the HTML page in Listing 14-44, it triggers the updateTime() function, which displays the time (in *hh:mm am/pm* format) in the statusbar (Figure 14-16). Instead of showing the seconds incrementing one by one (which may be distracting to someone trying to read the page), this function alternates the last character of the display between an asterisk and nothing.

Listing 14-44: **Display the Current Time**

```
<HTML>
<HEAD>
<TITLE>Status Bar Clock</TITLE>
<SCRIPT LANGUAGE="JavaScript">
<!--
var flasher = false
// calculate current time, determine flasher state,
// and insert time into status bar every second
function updateTime() {
        var now = new Date()
        var theHour = now.getHours()
        var theMin = now.getMinutes()
        var theTime = "" + ((theHour > 12) ? theHour - 12 : theHour)
        theTime += ((theMin < 10) ? ":0" : ":") + theMin
        theTime += (theHour >= 12) ? " pm" : " am"
        theTime += ((flasher) ? " " : "*")
        flasher = !flasher
        window.status = theTime
        // recursively call this function every second to keep timer going
        timerID = setTimeout("updateTime()",1000)
}
//-->
</SCRIPT>
</HEAD>

<BODY onLoad="updateTime()">
</BODY>
</HTML>
```

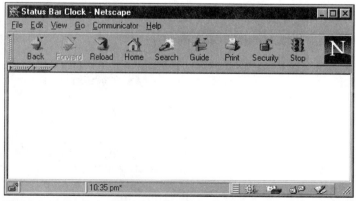

Figure 14-16: A clock ticks in the statusbar.

In this function, the way the setTimeout() method works is that once the current time (including the flasher status) appears in the statusbar, the function waits one second (1,000 milliseconds) before calling the same function again. You don't have to clear the timerID value in this application because JavaScript does it for you every time the 1,000 milliseconds elapse.

A logical question to ask is whether this application should be using setInterval() instead of setTimeout(). This is a case in which either one does the job. To use setInterval() here would require that the interval process start outside of the updateTime() function, because you need only one process running that repeatedly calls updateTime(). It would be a cleaner implementation in that regard, instead of the tons of timeout processes spawned by the above listing. On the other hand, it would not run in any browsers before Navigator 4 or Internet Explorer 4, as Listing 14-44 does.

One warning about setTimeout() functions that dive into themselves as frequently as this one does: Each call eats up a bit more memory for the browser application in Navigator 2. If you let this clock run for a while, some users may encounter memory difficulties, depending on which operating system they're using. But considering the amount of time the typical user spends on Web pages (even if only 10 or 15 minutes), the function shouldn't present a problem. And any reloading invoked by the user (such as by resizing the window in Navigator 2) frees up memory once again.

Related Items: window.clearTimeout() method; window.setInterval() method; window.clearInterval() method.

stop()

Returns: Nothing.

	Nav2	Nav3	Nav4	IE3/J1	IE3/J2	IE4/J3
Compatibility			✔			

Navigator 4's stop() method offers a scripted equivalent of clicking the Stop button in the toolbar. Availability of this method allows you to create your own toolbar on your page and hide the toolbar (in the main window with signed scripts or in a subwindow). For example, if you have an image representing the Stop button in your page, you can surround it with a link whose action stops loading, as in the following:

```
<A HREF="javascript: void stop()"><IMG SRC="myStop.gif" BORDER=0></A>
```

A script cannot stop its own document from loading, but it can stop loading of another frame or window. Similarly, if the current document dynamically loads a new image or a multimedia MIME type file as a separate action, the stop() method can halt that process. Even though the stop() method is a window method, it is not tied to any specific window or frame: Stop means stop.

Related Items: `window.back()` method; `window.find()` method; `window.forward()` method; `window.home()` method; `window.print()` method.

Event handlers

onBlur=
onFocus=

	Nav2	Nav3	Nav4	IE3/J1	IE3/J2	IE4/J3
Compatibility		✔	✔			✔

If knowing when a window or frame has been activated or deactivated is important to your page design, you can set event handlers that fire under those activities. For example, you can track how frequently a user switches between two of your windows over a period of time. By saving timestamps triggered by the `onBlur=` event handler in the subwindow and stamps triggered by the `onFocus=` event handler in the main window, you can create a record of the user's window activity.

You should, however, be aware of some potential side effects of scripting these events. As with their counterparts in text objects of forms, these event handlers, when asked to display JavaScript modal dialog boxes (such as the alert dialog box), can cause a nearly infinite loop, because the alert dialog box interrupts the natural action of window or frame blurring. Therefore, I recommend scripting these event handlers to perform less obvious tasks.

Another issue worth noting is that you should adhere to graphical user interface guidelines when dealing with windows. You may, for example, be tempted to close a subwindow when the user activates the main window. That design is unnatural in most GUI universes. Navigator provides a Window menu (part of the Navigator 4 menu in Navigator 4) to help the user bring forward a hidden window, and you can also script subwindows to gain focus. Regardless of how you decide to include these event handlers in your scripts, be sure to test them for inopportune clicks in the affected windows.

Related Items: `window.blur()`; `window.focus()`.

onDragDrop=

	Nav2	Nav3	Nav4	IE3/J1	IE3/J2	IE4/J3
Compatibility			✔			

With closer integration between the computer desktop and browsers these days, it is increasingly possible that shortcuts (or aliases) to Web URLs will be represented on our desktops and other kinds of documents. Beginning with Navigator 4, you can script awareness of dragging and dropping of such items onto the browser window. The window's dragDrop event fires whenever a user drops a file or other URL-filled object onto the window.

You can add an `onDragDrop=` event handler to the `<BODY>` tag of your document and pass along the event object that has some juicy tidbits about the drop: the object on which the item was dropped and the URL of the item. The function called by the event handler receives the event object information and can process it from there. Because this event is a window event, you don't have to turn on `window.captureEvents()` to get the window to feel the effect of the event.

The juiciest tidbit of the event, the URL of the dropped item, can be retrieved only with a signed script and the user's permission (see Chapter 40). Listing 14-45 shows a simple document that reveals the URL and screen location, as derived from the event objects passed with the dragDrop event. You must have codebase principals turned on to get the full advantage of this listing.

Listing 14-45: **Analyzing a DragDrop Event**

```
<HTML>
<HEAD>
<TITLE>ScrollBy Controller</TITLE>
<SCRIPT LANGUAGE="JavaScript">
function reportDrag(e) {
        var msg = "You dropped the file:\n"

netscape.security.PrivilegeManager.enablePrivilege("UniversalBrowserRead")
        msg += e.data

netscape.security.PrivilegeManager.disablePrivilege("UniversalBrowserRead")
        msg += "\nonto the window object at screen location ("
        msg += e.screenX + "," + e.screenY + ")."
        alert(msg)
        return false
}
</SCRIPT>
</HEAD>
<BODY onDragDrop="reportDrag(event)">
<B>Drag and Drop a file onto this window</B>
</BODY>
</HTML>
```

The dragDrop event is the only one so far that uses the `data` property of the event object. That property contains the URL. The `target` property reveals only the window object, but you can access the event object's `screenX` and `screenY` properties to get the location of the mouse release.

Related Items: event object.

onLoad=

	Nav2	Nav3	Nav4	IE3/J1	IE3/J2	IE4/J3
Compatibility	✔	✔	✔	✔	✔	✔

The load event is sent to the current window at the end of the document loading process (after all text and image elements have been transferred from the source file server to the browser, and after all plug-ins and Java applets have loaded and started running). At that point, the browser's memory contains all the objects and script components in the document that the browser can possibly know about.

The onLoad= handler is an attribute of a <BODY> tag for a single-frame document or of the <FRAMESET> tag for the top window of a multiple-frame document. When the handler is an attribute of a <FRAMESET> tag, the event triggers only after all frames defined by that frameset have completely loaded.

Use either of the following scenarios to insert an onLoad= handler into a document:

```
<HTML>
<HEAD>
</HEAD>
<BODY [other attributes] onLoad="statementOrFunction">
[body content]
</BODY>
</HTML>

<HTML>
<HEAD>
</HEAD>
<FRAMESET [other attributes] onLoad="statementOrFunction">
        <FRAME>frame specifications</FRAME>
</FRAMESET>
</HTML>
```

This handler has a special capability when part of a frameset definition: It won't fire until the onLoad= event handlers of all child frames in the frameset have fired. Therefore, if some initialization scripts depend on components existing in other frames, trigger them from the frameset's onLoad= event handler. This brings up a good general rule of thumb for writing JavaScript: Scripts that execute during a document's loading should contribute to the process of generating the document and its objects. To act immediately on those objects, design additional functions that are called by the onLoad= event handler for that window.

The type of operations suited for an onLoad= event handler are those that can run quickly and without user intervention. Users shouldn't be penalized by having to wait for considerable post-loading activity to finish before they can interact with your pages. At no time should you present a modal dialog box as part of an onLoad= handler. Users who design macros on their machines to visit sites unattended may get hung up on a page that automatically displays an alert, confirm, or prompt dialog box. On the other hand, an operation such as setting the window.defaultStatus property is a perfect candidate for an onLoad= event handler.

As a reminder about a general rule pertaining to JavaScript event handlers, event handlers such as onLoad=, onUnload=, onBlur=, and onFocus= can be set by assignment (window.onload = myfunction) or by creating functions of the same name (function onload()). The majority of your event handlers, however, will likely be defined as HTML tag attributes.

Related Items: onUnload= handler; window.defaultStatus property.

onMove=

	Nav2	Nav3	Nav4	IE3/J1	IE3/J2	IE4/J3
Compatibility			✔			

If a user drags a window around the screen, the action triggers a move event for the window object. When you assign a function to the event (for example, window.onmove = handleMoves), the function receives an event object whose screenX and screenY properties reveal the coordinate point (relative to the entire screen) of the top-left corner of the window after the move.

Related Items: event object.

onLoad= bugs and anomalies

The onLoad= event has changed its behavior over the life of JavaScript in Navigator. In Navigator 2, the onLoad= event handler fired whenever the user resized the window. Many developers considered this a bug because the running of such scripts destroyed carefully gathered data since the document originally loaded. From Navigator 3 onward (and including Internet Explorer 3), a window resize does not trigger a load event.

Two onLoad= bugs haunt Navigator 3 when used in conjunction with framesets. The first bug affects only Windows versions. The problem is that the frameset's onLoad= event handler is not necessarily the last one to fire among all the frames. It is possible that one frame's onLoad= event may still not have processed before the frameset's onLoad= event handler goes. This can cause serious problems if your frameset's onLoad= event handler relies on that final frame being fully loaded.

The second bug affects all versions of Navigator 3, but at least a workaround exists. If a frame contains a Java applet, the frameset's onLoad= event handler will fire before the applet has fully loaded and started. But if you place an onLoad= event handler in the applet's document (even a dummy onLoad="" in the <BODY> tag), the frameset's onLoad= event handler behaves properly.

onResize=

	Nav2	Nav3	Nav4	IE3/J1	IE3/J2	IE4/J3
Compatibility			✔			✔

If a user resizes a window, the action triggers a resize event for the window object. When you assign a function to the event (for example, `window.resize = handleResizes`), the function receives an event object whose `width` and `height` properties reveal the outer width and height of the entire window. A window resize in Navigator 4 does not trigger the `onLoad=` event handler (although the document content is rendered again to fill the inner window size). Therefore, if you want a script to run both when the document loads and when the user resizes the window (this is how Navigator 2 worked), you can use the `onResize=` event handler to help perform those duties.

Related Items: event object.

onUnload=

	Nav2	Nav3	Nav4	IE3/J1	IE3/J2	IE4/J3
Compatibility	✔	✔	✔	✔	✔	✔

An unload event reaches the current window just before a document is cleared from view. The most common ways windows are cleared are when new HTML documents are loaded into them or when a script begins writing new HTML on the fly for the window or frame.

Limit the extent of the `onUnload=` event handler to quick operations that do not inhibit the transition from one document to another. Do not invoke any methods that display dialog boxes. You specify `onUnload=` event handlers in the same places in an HTML document as the `onLoad=` handlers: as a `<BODY>` tag attribute for a single-frame window or as a `<FRAMESET>` tag attribute for a multiframe window. Both `onLoad=` and `onUnload=` event handlers can appear in the same `<BODY>` or `<FRAMESET>` tag without causing problems. The `onUnload=` event handler merely stays safely tucked away in the browser's memory, waiting for the unload event to arrive for processing as the document gets ready to clear the window.

Let me pass along one caution about the `onUnload=` event handler. Even though the event fires before the document goes away, don't burden the event handler with time-consuming tasks, such as generating new objects. The document could possibly go away before the function completes, leaving the function looking for objects and values that no longer exist. The best defense is to keep your `onUnload=` event handler processing to a minimum.

Related Items: `onLoad=` handler; `window.defaultStatus` property.

Frame Object

Properties	Methods	Event Handlers
Same as window object.		

Syntax

Creating a frame:

```
<FRAMESET
        ROWS="ValueList"
        COLS="ValueList"
        [FRAMEBORDER=YES | NO]
        [BORDER=pixelSize]
        [BORDERCOLOR=colorSpecification]
        [onBlur="handlerTextOrFunction"]
        [onDragDrop="handlerTextOrFunction"]
        [onFocus="handlerTextOrFunction"]
        [onLoad="handlerTextOrFunction"]
        [onMove="handlerTextOrFunction"]
        [onResize="handlerTextOrFunction"]
        [onUnload="handlerTextOrFunction"]>
        <FRAME
                SRC="locationOrURL"
                NAME="firstFrameName"
                [FRAMEBORDER= YES | NO]
                [BORDERCOLOR=colorSpecification]
                [MARGINHEIGHT=pixelSize]
                [MARGINWIDTH=pixelSize]
                [NORESIZE]
                [SCROLLING=YES | NO | AUTO]>
        ...
</FRAMESET>
```

Accessing properties or methods of another frame:

```
parent.frameName.property | method([parameters])
parent.frames[i].property | method([parameters])
```

About this object

A frame object behaves exactly like a window object, except that it has been created as part of a frameset by another document. A frame object always has a top and a parent property different from its self property. If you load a document that is normally viewed in a frame into a single browser window, its window is no longer a frame. Consult the earlier discussion about the window object for details on the properties and methods these two objects share.

One other significant difference between a window and frame object occurs in the onLoad= and onUnload= event handlers. Because each document loading into a frame may have its own onLoad= event handler defined in its <BODY> definition, the frame containing that document receives the load event after the individual document (and its components) finishes loading. But the frameset that governs the frame receives a separate load event after all frames have finished loading their documents. That event is captured in the onLoad= event handler of the <FRAMESET> definition (but see specific buggy behavior in the onLoad= event handler discussion, earlier in this chapter). The same applies to the onUnload= event handlers defined in <BODY> and <FRAMESET> definitions. Navigator 3 and later provide an easy way to view the source code for a document loaded in a frame. Click anywhere in the frame to select it (if a border is defined for the frame, it will highlight subtly), and then select Frame Source from the View menu.

✦   ✦   ✦

Location and History Objects

♦   ♦   ♦   ♦

In This Chapter

Loading new pages
and other media
types via the location
object

Security restrictions
across frames

Navigating through
the browser history
under script control

♦   ♦   ♦   ♦

Not all objects in the document object model are "things" you can see in the content area of the browser window. The browser maintains a bunch of other information about the page you are currently visiting and where you have been. The URL of the page you see in the browser is called the *location*, and browsers store this information in the location object. And as you surf the Web, the browser stores the URLs of your past pages in an object called the *history* object. You can manually view what that object contains by looking in the browser menu that lets you jump back to a previously visited page. This chapter is all about these two nearly invisible, but important objects.

Not only are these objects valuable to your browser, but they can also be valuable to snoopers who might want to write scripts to see what URLs you're viewing in another frame or the URLs of other sites you've visited in the last dozen mouse clicks. As a result, there exist security restrictions that limit access to some of these objects' properties unless you use signed scripts in Navigator 4. For older browsers, these properties are simply not available from a script.

Location Object

Properties	Methods	Event Handlers
hash	assign()	(None)
host	reload()	
hostname	replace()	
href		
pathname		
port		
protocol		
search		

Syntax

Loading a new document into the current window:

```
[window.]location = "URL"
```

Accessing location properties or methods:

```
[window.]location.property | method([parameters])
```

About this object

In its place one level below window-style objects in the JavaScript object hierarchy, the location object represents information about the URL of any currently open window or of a specific frame. A multiple-frame window displays the parent window's URL in the Location field. Each frame also has a location associated with it, although no overt reference to the frame's URL can be seen in the browser. To get URL information about a document located in another frame, the reference to the location object must include the window frame reference. For example, if you have a window consisting of two frames, Table 15-1 shows the possible references to the location objects for all frames comprising the Web presentation.

Table 15-1 Location Object References in a Two-Frame Browser Window	
Reference	*Description*
location (or window.location)	URL of frame displaying the document that runs the script statement containing this reference
parent.location	URL info for parent window that defined the <FRAMESET>
parent.frames[0].location	URL info for first visible frame
parent.frames[1].location	URL info for second visible frame
parent.otherFrameName.location	URL info for another named frame in the same frameset

Most properties of a location object deal with network-oriented information. This information includes various data about the physical location of the document on the network, including the host server, the protocol being used, and other components of the URL. Given a complete URL for a typical WWW page, the window.location object assigns property names to various segments of the URL, as shown here:

```
http://www.giantco.com:80/promos/newproducts.html#giantGizmo
```

Property	Value
protocol	"http:"
hostname	"www.giantco.com"
port	"80"
host	"www.giantco.com:80"
pathname	"/promos/newproducts.html"
hash	"#giantGizmo"
href	"http://www.giantco.com:80/promos newproducts. html#giantGizmo"

The `window.location` object can be handy when a script needs to extract information about the URL, perhaps to obtain a base reference on which to build URLs for other documents to be fetched as the result of user action. This object can eliminate a nuisance for Web authors who develop sites on one machine and then upload them to a server (perhaps at an Internet Service Provider) with an entirely different directory structure. By building scripts to construct base references from the directory location of the current document, you can construct the complete URLs for loading documents. You won't have to manually change the base reference data in your documents as you shift the files from computer to computer or from directory to directory. To extract the segment of the URL and place it into the enclosing directory, you can use the following:

```
var baseRef = location.href.substring(0,location.href.lastIndexOf
("/") + 1)
```

Note

Security alert: To allay fears of Internet security breaches and privacy invasions, scriptable browsers prevent your script in one frame from retrieving location object properties from other frames whose domain and server are not your own (unless you are using signed scripts in Navigator 4 — see Chapter 40). This restriction puts a damper on many scripters' well-meaning designs and aids for Web watchers and visitors. If you attempt such property accesses, however, you will receive an "access disallowed" security warning dialog box.

Setting the value of some location properties is the preferred way to control which document gets loaded into a window or frame. Though you may expect to find a method somewhere in JavaScript that contains a plain language "Go" or "Open" word (to simulate what you see in the browser menu bar), the way to "point your browser" to another URL is to set the `window.location` object to that URL, as in

```
window.location.href = "http://www.dannyg.com/"
```

The equals assignment operator (=) in this kind of statement becomes a powerful weapon. In fact, setting the location object to a URL of a different MIME type, such as one of the variety of sound and video formats, causes the browser to load those files into the plug-in or helper application designated in your browser's settings. Internet

Explorer's object model includes a `window.navigate()` method that also loads a document into a window, but this method is not part of Netscape — at least through Navigator 4.

Two methods complement the location object's capability to control navigation: One method is the script equivalent of clicking Reload; the other method enables you to replace the current document's entry in the history with that of the next URL of your script's choice.

Properties

hash

Value: String   **Gettable:** Yes   **Settable:** Yes

	Nav2	Nav3	Nav4	IE3/J1	IE3/J2	IE4/J3
Compatibility	✔	✔	✔	✔	✔	✔

The hash mark (#) is a URL convention that directs the browser to an anchor located in the document. Any name you assign to an anchor (with the `<A NAME="...">` `...</A>` tag pair) becomes part of the URL after the hash mark. A location object's `hash` property is the name of the anchor part of the current URL (which consists of the hash mark and the name).

If you have written HTML documents with anchors and directed links to navigate to those anchors, you have probably noticed that although the destination location shows the anchor as part of the URL (for example, in the Location field), the window's anchor value does not change as the user manually scrolls to positions in the document where other anchors are defined. An anchor appears in the URL only when the window has navigated there as part of a link or in response to a script that adjusts the URL.

Just as you can navigate to any URL by setting the `window.location` property, you can navigate to another hash in the same document by adjusting only the `hash` property of the location, but without the hash mark (as shown in the following example). Such navigation, even within a document, causes Navigator 2 and Internet Explorer 3 to reload the document (and scripted navigation to anchors is incredibly slow in Internet Explorer 3/Windows). No reload occurs in Navigator 3 and up.

Example

When you load the script in Listing 15-1, adjust the size of the browser window so only one section is visible at a time. When you click a button, its script navigates to the next logical section in the progression and eventually takes you back to the top.

Listing 15-1: A Document with Anchors

```
<HTML>
<HEAD>
<TITLE>location.hash Property</TITLE>
<SCRIPT LANGUAGE="JavaScript">
function goNextAnchor(where) {
        window.location.hash = where
}
</SCRIPT>
</HEAD>

<BODY>

<A NAME="start"><H1>Top</H1></A>
<FORM>
<INPUT TYPE="button" NAME="next" VALUE="NEXT"
onClick="goNextAnchor('sec1')">
</FORM>
<HR>
<A NAME="sec1"><H1>Section 1</H1></A>
<FORM>
<INPUT TYPE="button" NAME="next" VALUE="NEXT"
onClick="goNextAnchor('sec2')">
</FORM>
<HR>
<A NAME="sec2"><H1>Section 2</H1></A>
<FORM>
<INPUT TYPE="button" NAME="next" VALUE="NEXT"
onClick="goNextAnchor('sec3')">
</FORM>
<HR>

<A NAME="sec3"><H1>Section 3</H1></A>
<FORM>
<INPUT TYPE="button" NAME="next" VALUE="BACK TO TOP"
onClick="goNextAnchor('start')">
</FORM>

</BODY>
</HTML>
```

Anchor names are passed as parameters with each button's onClick= event handler. Instead of going through the work of assembling a window.location value in the function by appending a literal hash mark and the value for the anchor, here I simply modify the hash property of the current window's location. This is the preferred, cleaner method.

If you attempt to read back the window.location.hash property in an added line of script, however, the window's actual URL will probably not have been updated yet, and the browser will appear to be giving your script false information.

To prevent this problem in subsequent statements of the same function, construct the URLs of those statements from the same variable values you used to set the `window.location.hash` property — don't rely on the browser to give you the values you expect.

Related Items: `location.href` property.

host

Value: String   **Gettable:** Yes   **Settable:** Yes

	Nav2	Nav3	Nav4	IE3/J1	IE3/J2	IE4/J3
Compatibility	✔	✔	✔	✔	✔	✔

The `location.host` property describes both the hostname and port of a URL. The port is included in the value only when the port is an explicit part of the URL. If you navigate to a URL that does not display the port number in the Location field of the browser, the `location.host` property returns the same value as the `location.hostname` property.

Use the `location.host` property to extract the `hostname:port` part of the URL of any document loaded in the browser. This capability may be helpful for building a URL to a specific document that you want your script to access on the fly.

Example

Use the documents in Listings 15-2 through 15-4 as tools to help you learn the values that the various `window.location` properties return. In the browser, open the file for Listing 15-2. This file creates a two-frame window. The left frame contains a temporary placeholder (Listing 15-4) that displays some instructions. The right frame has a document (Listing 15-3) that lets you load URLs into the left frame and get readings on three different windows available: the parent window (which creates the multiframe window), the left frame, and the right frame.

Listing 15-2: **Frameset for the Property Picker**

```
<HTML>
<HEAD>
<TITLE>window.location Properties</TITLE>
</HEAD>
<FRAMESET COLS="50%,50%" BORDER=1 BORDERCOLOR="black">
        <FRAME NAME="Frame1" SRC="lst15-04.htm">
        <FRAME NAME="Frame2" SRC="lst15-03.htm">
</FRAMESET>
</HTML>
```

Listing 15-3: **Property Picker**

```
<HTML>
<HEAD>
<TITLE>Property Picker</TITLE>
<SCRIPT LANGUAGE="JavaScript">
var isNav4 = (navigator.appName == "Netscape" &&
navigator.appVersion.charAt(0) == 4) ? true : false

function fillLeftFrame() {
        newURL = prompt("Enter the URL of a document to show in the
left frame:","")
        if (newURL != null && newURL != "") {
        parent.frames[0].location = newURL
        }
}

function showLocationData(form) {
        for (var i = 0; i <3; i++) {
            if (form.whichFrame[i].checked) {
                var windName = form.whichFrame[i].value
                break
            }
        }
        var theWind = "" + windName + ".location"
        if (isNav4) {

netscape.security.PrivilegeManager.enablePrivilege("UniversalBrowserRea
d")
        }
        var theObj = eval(theWind)
        form.windName.value = windName
        form.windHash.value = theObj.hash
        form.windHost.value = theObj.host
        form.windHostname.value = theObj.hostname
        form.windHref.value = theObj.href
        form.windPath.value = theObj.pathname
        form.windPort.value = theObj.port
        form.windProtocol.value = theObj.protocol
        form.windSearch.value = theObj.search
        if (isNav4) {

netscape.security.PrivilegeManager.disablePrivilege("UniversalBrowserRe
ad")
        }
}
</SCRIPT>
</HEAD>
<BODY>
Click the "Open URL" button to enter the location of an HTML document
to display in the left frame of this window.
<FORM>
```

(continued)

Listing 15-3 *(continued)*

```
<INPUT TYPE="button" NAME="opener" VALUE="Open URL..."
onClick="fillLeftFrame()">
<HR>
<CENTER>
Select a window/frame. Then click the "Show Location Properties" button
to view each window.location property value for the desired window.<P>
<INPUT TYPE="radio" NAME="whichFrame" VALUE="parent" CHECKED>Parent
window
<INPUT TYPE="radio" NAME="whichFrame" VALUE="parent.frames[0]">Left
frame
<INPUT TYPE="radio" NAME="whichFrame" VALUE="parent.frames[1]">This
frame
<P>
<INPUT TYPE="button" NAME="getProperties" VALUE="Show Location
Properties" onClick="showLocationData(this.form)">
<INPUT TYPE="reset" VALUE="Clear"><P>
<TABLE BORDER=2>
<TR><TD ALIGN=right>Window:</TD><TD><INPUT TYPE="text" NAME="windName"
SIZE=30></TD></TR>
<TR><TD ALIGN=right>hash:</TD>
<TD><INPUT TYPE="text" NAME="windHash" SIZE=30></TD></TR>

<TR><TD ALIGN=right>host:</TD>
<TD><INPUT TYPE="text" NAME="windHost" SIZE=30></TD></TR>

<TR><TD ALIGN=right>hostname:</TD>
<TD><INPUT TYPE="text" NAME="windHostname" SIZE=30></TD></TR>

<TR><TD ALIGN=right>href:</TD>
<TD><TEXTAREA NAME="windHref" ROWS=3 COLS=30 WRAP="soft">
</TEXTAREA></TD></TR>

<TR><TD ALIGN=right>pathname:</TD>
<TD><TEXTAREA NAME="windPath" ROWS=3 COLS=30 WRAP="soft">
</TEXTAREA></TD></TR>

<TR><TD ALIGN=right>port:</TD>
<TD><INPUT TYPE="text" NAME="windPort" SIZE=30></TD></TR>

<TR><TD ALIGN=right>protocol:</TD>
<TD><INPUT TYPE="text" NAME="windProtocol" SIZE=30></TD></TR>

<TR><TD ALIGN=right>search:</TD>
<TD><TEXTAREA NAME="windSearch" ROWS=3 COLS=30 WRAP="soft">
</TEXTAREA></TD></TR>
</TABLE>
</CENTER>
</FORM>
</BODY>
</HTML>
```

Listing 15-4: Placeholder Document for Listing 15-2

```
<HTML>
<HEAD>
<TITLE>Opening Placeholder</TITLE>
</HEAD>
<BODY>
Initial place holder. Experiment with other URLs for this frame (see
right).
</BODY>
</HTML>
```

Figure 15-1 shows the dual-frame browser window with the left frame loaded with a page from my Web site.

For the best results, open a URL to a Web document on the network from the same domain and server from which you load the listings (this could be your local hard disk). If possible, load a document that includes anchor points to navigate through a long document. Click the Left frame radio button, and then click the button that shows all properties. This action fills the table in the right frame with all the available location properties for the selected window. Figure 15-2 shows the complete results for a page from my Web site that is set to an anchor point.

Attempts to retrieve these properties from URLs outside of your domain and server will result in a variety of responses based on your browser and browser version. Navigator 2 returns null values for all properties. Navigator 3 presents an "access disallowed" security alert. With codebase principals turned on in Navigator 4 (see Chapter 40), the proper values will appear in their fields. Internet Explorer 3 does not have the same security restrictions that Navigator does, so all values appear in their fields. In Internet Explorer 4, you get a "permission denied" error alert. See the following discussion for the meanings of the other listed properties and instructions on viewing their values.

Related Items: `location.port` property; `location.hostname` property.

hostname

Value: String   **Gettable:** Yes   **Settable:** Yes

	Nav2	Nav3	Nav4	IE3/J1	IE3/J2	IE4/J3
Compatibility	✔	✔	✔	✔	✔	✔

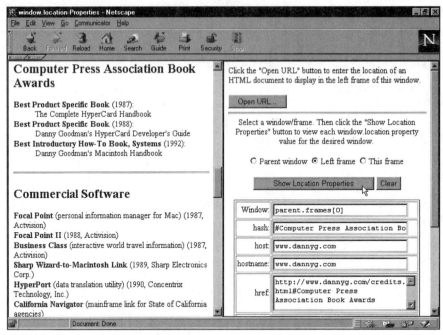

Figure 15-1: Browser window loaded to investigate window.location properties

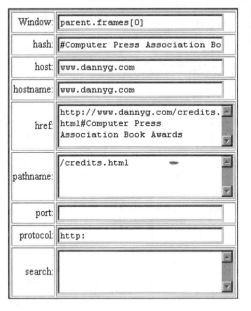

Figure 15-2: Readout of all window.location properties for the left frame

The hostname of a typical URL is the name of the server on the network that stores the document you're viewing in the browser. For most Web sites, the server name includes not only the domain name, but the `www.` prefix as well. The hostname does not, however, include the port number if such a number is specified in the URL.

Example

See Listings 15-2 through 15-4 for a set of related pages to help you view the hostname data for a variety of other pages.

Related Items: `location.host` property; `location.port` property.

href

Value: String   **Gettable:** Yes   **Settable:** Yes

	Nav2	Nav3	Nav4	IE3/J1	IE3/J2	IE4/J3
Compatibility	✔	✔	✔	✔	✔	✔

Of all location object properties, the `href` (hypertext reference) is probably the one most often called upon in scripting. The `location.href` property supplies a string of the entire URL of the specified window object.

Using this property (or just the `window.location` object reference) on the left side of an assignment statement is the JavaScript method of opening a URL for display in a window. Any of the following statements can load my Web site's index page into a single-frame browser window:

```
window.location="http://www.dannyg.com"
window.location.href="http://www.dannyg.com"
```

At times, you may encounter difficulty by omitting a reference to a window. JavaScript may get confused and reference the `document.location` property. To prevent this confusion, the `document.location` property has been deprecated (put on the no-no list) by Netscape, and will eventually be removed from JavaScript. In the meantime, you won't go wrong by always specifying a window in the reference.

Sometimes you must extract the name of the current directory in a script so another statement can append a known document to the URL before loading it into the window. Although the other location object properties yield an assortment of a URL's segments, none of them provides the full URL to the current URL's directory. But you can use JavaScript string manipulation techniques to accomplish this task. Listing 15-5 shows such a possibility.

Depending on your browser, the values for the `location.href` property may be encoded with ASCII equivalents of nonalphanumeric characters. Such an ASCII value includes the % symbol and the ASCII numeric value. The most common encoded character in a URL is the space, %20. If you need to extract a URL and display that value as a string in your documents, the safest way is to pass all such potentially encoded strings through the JavaScript internal `unescape()` function. For example, if a URL to one of Giantco's pages is `http://www.giantco.com/product%20list`, you can convert it by passing it through the function, as in the following example.

```
plainURL = unescape(window.location.href)
        // result = "http://www.giantco.com/product list"
```

Note

The inverse function, escape ( ), is available for sending encoded strings to CGI programs on servers. See Chapter 27 for more details on these functions.

If assigning a URL to location.href is causing difficulty for you in Internet Explorer 3, omit the property and assign the URL to the location object. This shorter statement works fine on all browser versions and platforms. You can also try the complete URL (including protocol).

Example

Listing 15-5 includes the unescape() function in front of the part of the script that captures the URL. This function serves cosmetic purposes by displaying the pathname in alert dialog boxes for browsers that normally display the ASCII-encoded version.

Listing 15-5: **Extracting the Directory of the Current Document**

```
<HTML>
<HEAD>
<TITLE>Extract pathname</TITLE>
<SCRIPT LANGUAGE="JavaScript">
// general purpose function to extract URL of current directory
function getDirPath(URL) {
        var result = unescape(URL.substring(0,(URL.lastIndexOf("/")) +
1))
        return result
}
// handle button event, passing work onto general purpose function
function showDirPath(URL) {
        alert(getDirPath(URL))
}
</SCRIPT>
</HEAD>

<BODY>
<FORM>
<INPUT TYPE="button" VALUE="View directory URL"
onClick="showDirPath(window.location.href)">
</FORM>
</BODY>
</HTML>
```

Related Items: location.pathname property; document.location property; string object (Chapter 27).

pathname

Value: String   **Gettable:** Yes   **Settable:** Yes

	Nav2	Nav3	Nav4	IE3/J1	IE3/J2	IE4/J3
Compatibility	✔	✔	✔	✔	✔	✔

The pathname component of a URL consists of the directory structure relative to the server's *root* volume. In other words, the root (the server name in an `http:` connection) is not part of the pathname. If the URL's path is to a file in the root directory, then the `location.pathname` property is a single slash (/) character. Any other pathname starts with a slash character, indicating a directory nested within the root. The value of the `location.pathname` property also includes the document name.

Example

See Listings 15-2 through 15-4 for a multiple-frame example you can use to view the `location.pathname` property for a variety of URLs of your choice.

Related Items: `location.href` property.

port

Value: String   **Gettable:** Yes   **Settable:** Yes

	Nav2	Nav3	Nav4	IE3/J1	IE3/J2	IE4/J3
Compatibility	✔	✔	✔	✔	✔	✔

These days, few consumer-friendly Web sites need to include the port number as part of their URLs. Port numbers are visible mostly in the less-popular protocols or in URLs to sites used for private development purposes or that have no assigned domain names. You can retrieve the value with the `location.port` property. If you extract the value from one URL and intend to build another URL with that component, be sure to include the colon delimiter between the server's IP address and port number.

Example

If you have access to URLs containing port numbers, use the documents in Listings 15-2 through 15-4 to experiment with the output of the `location.port` property.

Related Items: `location.host` property.

protocol

Value: String   **Gettable:** Yes   **Settable:** Yes

	Nav2	Nav3	Nav4	IE3/J1	IE3/J2	IE4/J3
Compatibility	✔	✔	✔	✔	✔	✔

The first component of any URL is the protocol being used for the particular type of communication. For World Wide Web pages, the Hypertext Transfer Protocol (http) is the standard. Other common protocols you will see in your browser include File Transfer Protocol (ftp), File (file), and Mail (mailto). Values for the location.protocol property include not only the name of the protocol, but the trailing colon delimiter as well. Thus, for a typical Web page URL, the location.protocol property is

```
http:
```

Notice that the usual slashes after the protocol in the URL are not part of the location.protocol value. Of all the location object properties, only the full URL (location.href) reveals the slash delimiters between the protocol and other components.

Example

See Listings 15-2 through 15-4 for a multiple-frame example you can use to view the location.protocol property for a variety of URLs. Also try loading an ftp site to see the location.protocol value for that type of URL.

Related Items: location.href property.

search

Value: String   **Gettable:** Yes   **Settable:** Yes

	Nav2	Nav3	Nav4	IE3/J1	IE3/J2	IE4/J3
Compatibility	✔	✔	✔	✔	✔	✔

Perhaps you've noticed the long, cryptic URL that appears in the Location field of your browser whenever you ask one of the WWW search services to look up matches for items you've entered into the keyword field. The URL starts the regular way — with protocol, host, and pathname values. But following the more traditional URL are search commands that are being submitted to the search engine (a CGI program running on the server). That trailing search query can be retrieved or set by using the location.search property.

Each search engine has its own formula for query submissions based on the designs of the HTML forms that obtain details from users. These search queries come in an encoded format that appears in anything but plain language. If you plan to script a search query, be sure you fully understand the search engine's format before you start assembling a string to assign to the location.search property of a window.

The `location.search` property also applies to any part of a URL after the filename, including parameters being sent to CGI programs on the server.

Example

The same security restrictions apply to retrieving the search property as to most of the location object properties. Because the following example accesses a domain different from yours, you need Navigator 4 with codebase principals turned on (see Chapter 40) to get the desired results. If you don't have Navigator 4 or that feature turned on, just study the code and figures to understand how the property works.

Load Listing 15-6 to view a two-frame window. The upper frame should contain a Yahoo! search engine page that lets you enter search keywords and other specifications (Figure 15-3). The bottom frame (Listing 15-7) contains two buttons.

Listing 15-6: **A Search Frameset**

```
<HTML>
<HEAD>
<TITLE>window.search Property</TITLE>
</HEAD>
<FRAMESET ROWS="50%,50%">
        <FRAME NAME="Frame1" SRC="http://www.yahoo.com/search.html">
        <FRAME NAME="Frame2" SRC="lst15-07.htm">
</FRAMESET>
</HTML>
```

Listing 15-7: **The Search Controller**

```
<HTML>
<HEAD>
<TITLE>Search Viewer/Changer</TITLE>
</HEAD>
<SCRIPT LANGUAGE="JavaScript">
var isNav4 = (navigator.appName == "Netscape" &&
navigator.appVersion.charAt(0) == 4) ? true : false
function scriptedSearch() {
        if (isNav4) {

netscape.security.PrivilegeManager.enablePrivilege("UniversalBrowserRea
d")
        }
        newSearch=prompt("Enter a new search
string:",top.frames[0].location.search)
        if (isNav4) {
netscape.security.PrivilegeManager.revertPrivilege("UniversalBrowserRea
d")
```

(continued)

Listing 15-7 *(continued)*

```
        }
        if (newSearch != null && newSearch != "") {
            if (isNav4) {

netscape.security.PrivilegeManager.enablePrivilege("UniversalBrowserRea
d ")
            }
            top.frames[0].location.search = newSearch
            if (isNav4) {
                netscape.security.PrivilegeManager. revertPrivilege
("UniversalBrowserRead ")
            }
        }
}
function showSearchData() {
        if (isNav4) {

netscape.security.PrivilegeManager.enablePrivilege("UniversalBrowserRea
d")
        }
        var msg = "location.href: " + top.frames[0].location.href +
"\n\n"
        msg += "location.search: " + top.frames[0].location.search
        if (isNav4) {
            netscape.security.PrivilegeManager. revertPrivilege
("UniversalBrowserRead")
        }
        alert(msg)
}
</SCRIPT>
</HEAD>
<BODY>
<FORM>
<B>Perform a search in the Yahoo frame, above.</B> Then click the
 "Show <TT>location.search</TT> Property" button to examine the
<TT>window.location.search</TT> property value for the search.<P>
<INPUT TYPE="button" NAME="getProperties" VALUE="Show location.search
Property" onClick="showSearchData()">
</FORM>
Next, click the "Modify Search..." button to modify the current
search as derived from the upper frame's <TT>location.search</TT>
property. Be sure to follow the codes and conventions for the
 search engine (e.g., a plus sign between terms).
<FORM>
<INPUT TYPE="button" NAME="opener" VALUE="Modify Search..."
onClick="scriptedSearch()">
</FORM>
</BODY>
</HTML>
```

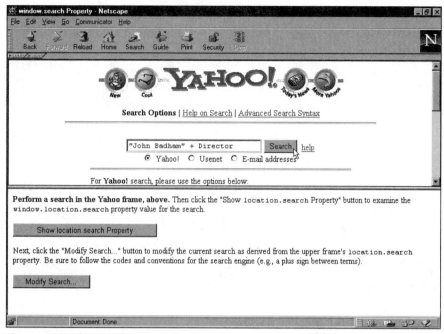

Figure 15-3: The two-frame window used to experiment with the location.search property. Yahoo!'s search page is in the upper frame.

After you perform a search in the upper frame, click the bottom button to view both the complete `location.href` value and the `location.search` portion (shown in Figure 15-4). Click the bottom button to edit the current `location.search` value (Figure 15-5).

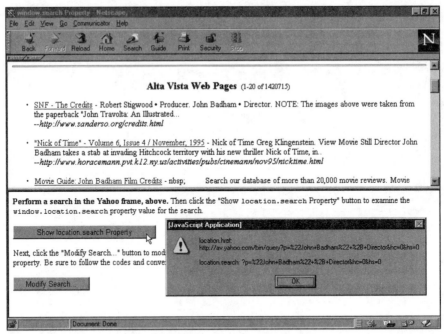

Figure 15-4: The alert dialog box shows both the full URL and the search property.

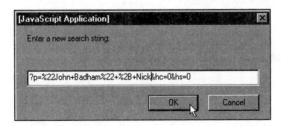

Figure 15-5: Using the existing search property as a model, make small changes to the search property to see how Yahoo! responds.

Although this interface is not as friendly as the one presented in the Yahoo! or other search engine pages, this illustration shows that you can control the search activities of a search engine or CGI parameters from a script. For example, you may prefer to invent a different user interface to search for specific keywords (or to present a limited selection to the user of your page). To do this, your script must gather the user's input in your document's form, construct the appropriate search query (in the search engine's lingo), and construct a URL that performs the search for the user. Because of security issues surrounding access to other sites, such customized interfaces to search engines are best suited to searches performed on intranet servers where all documents share a domain.

Related Items: `location.href` property.

Methods

assign("*URL*")

Returns: Nothing.

	Nav2	Nav3	Nav4	IE3/J1	IE3/J2	IE4/J3
Compatibility	✔	✔	✔	✔	✔	✔

In earlier discussions about the location object, I said that you navigate to another page by assigning a new URL to the location object or location.href property. There also exists a method, location.assign(), that does the same thing. In fact, when you set the location object to a URL, JavaScript silently applies the assign() method. No particular penalty or benefit comes from using the assign() method, except perhaps to make your code more understandable to others. I don't recall the last time I used this method in a production document, but you are free to use it if you like.

Related Items: location.href property.

reload(*unconditionalGETBoolean*)

Returns: Nothing.

	Nav2	Nav3	Nav4	IE3/J1	IE3/J2	IE4/J3
Compatibility		✔	✔			✔

The location.reload() method may be inappropriately named, because it makes you think of the Reload button in the Navigator toolbar. The reload() method is actually more powerful than the Reload button.

Many form elements retain their screen states when you click Reload (except in Internet Explorer 3). Text and textarea objects maintain whatever text is inside them; radio buttons and checkboxes maintain their checked status; select objects remember which item is selected. About the only items the Reload button destroys are global variable values and any settable, but not visible, property (for example, the value of a hidden object). I call this kind of reload a *soft reload*.

A *hard reload,* as initiated by the location.reload() method, pushes aside any document settings the browser may have preserved in memory (in session history) and completely reopens the document as if you had chosen Open Location or Open File from the File menu. This method restores all default settings of form elements and ensures that users (and your scripts) are back at square one with the page.

You can script both types of reloading. For a soft reload, you invoke a window's history.go() method, using 0 as the parameter. For a hard reload, you use the location.reload() method.

By default, the `reload()` method performs what is known as a *conditional-GET,* which means that the file is retrieved from the server or the browser's cache according to the cache preferences in the browser. If your page must perform an *unconditional-GET* to retrieve continually updated server or CGI-based data, then add a `true` parameter to the `reload()` method.

Example

To experience the difference between the two loading styles, load the document in Listing 15-8. Click a radio button, enter some new text, and make a choice in the select object. Clicking the Soft Reload button invokes a method that reloads the document as if you had clicked on the browser's Reload button. It also preserves the visible properties of form elements. The Hard Reload button invokes the `location.reload()` method, which resets all objects to their default settings.

Listing 15-8: **Hard versus Soft Reloading**

```
<HTML>
<HEAD>
<TITLE>Reload Comparisons</TITLE>
<SCRIPT LANGUAGE="JavaScript1.1">
function hardReload() {
        location.reload()
}
function softReload() {
        history.go(0)
}
</SCRIPT>
</HEAD>
<BODY>
<FORM NAME="myForm">
<INPUT TYPE="radio" NAME="rad1" VALUE = 1>Radio 1<BR>
<INPUT TYPE="radio" NAME="rad1" VALUE = 2>Radio 2<BR>
<INPUT TYPE="radio" NAME="rad1" VALUE = 3>Radio 3<P>
<INPUT TYPE="text" NAME="entry" VALUE="Original"><P>
<SELECT NAME="theList">
<OPTION>Red
<OPTION>Green
<OPTION>Blue
</SELECT>
<HR>
<INPUT TYPE="button" VALUE="Soft Reload" onClick="softReload()">
<INPUT TYPE="button" VALUE="Hard Reload" onClick="hardReload()">
</FORM>
</BODY>
</HTML>
```

Related Items: `history.go()` method.

replace("*URL*")

Returns: Nothing.

	Nav2	Nav3	Nav4	IE3/J1	IE3/J2	IE4/J3
Compatibility		✔	✔			✔

In a complex Web site, you may have pages that you do not want to appear in the user's history list. For example, a registration sequence may lead the user to one or more intermediate HTML documents that won't make much sense to the user later: You especially don't want users to see these pages again if they use the Back button to return to a previous URL.

Although you cannot prevent a document from appearing in the history list (visible in the Go menu) while the user is looking at that page, you can instruct the browser to load another document into that window and replace the current history entry with the entry for the new document. This trick does not empty the history list but instead removes the current item from the list before the next URL is loaded. Removing the item from the history list prevents users from seeing the page again by clicking the Back button later.

Example

Calling the `location.replace()` method navigates to another URL, similar to assigning a URL to the location. The difference is that the document doing the calling won't appear in the history list after the new document loads. Check the history listing (in your browser's usual spot for this info) before and after clicking Replace Me in Listing 15-9.

Listing 15-9: **Invoking the location.replace() Method**

```
<HTML>
<HEAD>
<TITLE>location.replace() Demo</TITLE>
<SCRIPT LANGUAGE="JavaScript1.1">
function doReplace() {
      location.replace("lst15-01.htm")
}
</SCRIPT>
</HEAD>
<BODY>
<FORM NAME="myForm">
<INPUT TYPE="button" VALUE="Replace Me" onClick="doReplace()">
</FORM>
</BODY>
</HTML>
```

Related Items: history object.

History Object

Properties	Methods	Event Handlers
current	back()	(None)
length	forward()	
next	go()	
previous		

Syntax

Accessing history properties or methods:

`[window.]history.property | method([parameters])`

About this object

As a user surfs the Web, the browser maintains a list of URLs for the most recent stops. This list is represented in JavaScript by the history object. Actual URLs maintained in that list cannot be surreptitiously extracted by a script unless you are using signed scripts (in Navigator 4 — see Chapter 40) and the user grants permission. Under unsigned conditions, a script can methodically navigate to each URL in the history (by relative number or by stepping back one URL at a time), in which case the user sees the browser navigating on its own, as if possessed by a spirit. Good netiquette dictates that you do not navigate a user outside of your Web site without the user's explicit permission.

One application for the history object and its `back()` or `go()` methods is to provide the equivalent of a Back button in your HTML documents. That button triggers a script that checks for any items in the history list and then goes back one page. Your document doesn't have to know anything about the URL from which the user landed at your page.

The behavior of the Back and Forward buttons in Netscape Navigator underwent a significant change between Versions 2 and 3. In Navigator 2, there was one history list that applied to the entire browser window. You could load a frameset into the window and navigate the contents of each frame individually with wild abandon. But if you then clicked the Back button, Navigator unloaded the frameset and took you back to the page in history prior to that frameset.

In Navigator 3, each frame (window object) maintains its own history list. Thus, if you navigated within a frame, a click of the Back button steps you back out frame by frame. Only after the initial frameset documents appear in the window does the next Back button click unload the frameset. That behavior persists today in Navigator 4 and is the basis for Internet Explorer behavior from Version 3 onward.

How JavaScript reacted to the change of behavior over the generations is a bit murky. In Navigator 2, the `history.back()` and `history.forward()` methods acted like the toolbar buttons, since there was only one kind of history being tracked. In Navigator 3, however, there was a disconnect between JavaScript behavior and what the browser was doing internally with history: JavaScript failed to connect history entries to a particular frame. Therefore, a reference to `history.back()` built with a given frame name did not prevent the method from exceeding the history of that frame. Instead, the behavior was more like a global back operation, rather than frame-specific.

For Navigator 4 there is one more sea change in the relationship between JavaScript and these history object methods. The behavior of the Back and Forward buttons has been shifted to a new pair of window methods: `window.back()` and `window.forward()`. The history object methods are not specific to a frame that is part of the reference. When the `parent.frameName.-history.back()` method reaches the end of history for that frame, further invocations of that method are ignored.

So much for the history of the history object. As the tale of history object method evolution indicates, you must use the history object and its methods with extreme care. Your design must be smart enough to "watch" what the user is doing with your pages (for example, by checking the current URL before navigating with these methods). Otherwise, you run the risk of completely confusing your user by navigating to unexpected places. Your script can also get into trouble because it cannot detect where the current document may be in the Back-Forward sequence in history.

Properties

```
current
next
previous
```

Value: String   **Gettable:** Yes   **Settable:** No

	Nav2	Nav3	Nav4	IE3/J1	IE3/J2	IE4/J3
Compatibility		(✔)	✔			

To know where to go when you click the Back and Forward buttons, the browser maintains a list of URLs visited. To someone trying to invade your privacy and see what sites and pages you frequent, this information is valuable. That's why the three properties that expose the actual URLs in the history list are restricted to pages with signed scripts and whose visitors have given permission to read sensitive browser data (see Chapter 40).

With signed scripts and permission, you can look through the entire array of history entries in any frame or window. Because the list is an array, you can extract individual items by index value. For example, if the array has 10 entries, you can see the fifth item by using normal array indexing methods:

```
var fifthEntry = window.history[4]
```

No property or method exists that directly reveals the index value of the currently loaded URL, but you could script an educated guess by comparing the values of the current, next, and previous properties of the history object against the entire list.

Since I personally don't like some unknown entity watching over my shoulder while I'm on the Net, I respect that same feeling in others and therefore discourage the use of these powers unless the user is given adequate warning in advance. The signed script permission dialog does not offer enough detail about the consequences of revealing this level of information.

Notice that in the compatibility chart these properties were available in some form in Navigator 3. Access to them required a short-lived security scheme called data tainting. That mechanism was never fully implemented and has been replaced by signed scripts.

Related Items: history.length property.

length

Value: Number   **Gettable:** Yes   **Settable:** No

	Nav2	Nav3	Nav4	IE3/J1	IE3/J2	IE4/J3
Compatibility	✔	✔	✔	✔	✔	✔

Use the history.length property to count the items in the history list. Unfortunately, this nugget of information is not particularly helpful in scripting navigation relative to the current location, because your script cannot extract anything from the place in the history queue where the current document is located. If the current document is at the top of the list (the most recently loaded), you can calculate relative to that location. But users can use the Go menu to jump around the history list as they like. The position of a listing in the history list does not change by virtue of navigating back to that document. A history.length of 1, however, indicates that the current document is the first one the user loaded since starting the browser software.

Example

The simple function in Listing 15-10 displays one of two alert messages based on the number of items in the browser's history.

Listing 15-10: A Browser History Count

```
<HTML>
<HEAD>
<TITLE>History Object</TITLE>
<SCRIPT LANGUAGE="JavaScript">
function showCount() {
        var histCount = window.history.length
        if (histCount > 5) {
            alert("My, my, you\'ve been busy. You have visited " +
histCount + " pages so far.")
        } else {
            alert("You have been to " + histCount + " Web pages this
session.")
        }
}
</SCRIPT>
</HEAD>

<BODY>
<FORM>
<INPUT TYPE="button" NAME="activity" VALUE="My Activity"
onClick="showCount()">
</FORM>
</BODY>
</HTML>
```

Related Items: None.

Methods

`back()`

Returns: Nothing.

	Nav2	Nav3	Nav4	IE3/J1	IE3/J2	IE4/J3
Compatibility	✔	✔	✔	✔	✔	✔

The behavior of the `history.back()` method has changed in Netscape's browsers between Versions 3 and 4. Prior to Navigator 4, the method acted identically to clicking the Back button (and even this unscripted behavior changed between Navigator 2 and 3 to better accommodate frame navigation). Internet Explorer 3 and 4 follows this behavior. In Navigator 4, however, the `history.back()` method is window/frame-specific. Therefore, if you direct successive `back()` methods to a frame within a frameset, the method will be ignored once it has reached the first document to be loaded into that frame. The Back button (and the new `window.back()` method) would unload the frameset and continue taking you back through the browser's global history.

If you deliberately lead a user to a dead end in your Web site, you should make sure that the HTML document provides a way to navigate back to a recognizable spot. Because you can easily create a new window that has no toolbar or menu bar (non-Macintosh browsers), you may end up stranding your users, because they have no way to navigate out of a cul-de-sac in such a window. A button in your document should give the user a way back to the last location.

Unless you need to perform some additional processing prior to navigating back to the previous location, you can simply place this method as the parameter to the event handler attribute of a button definition.

Example

For the best demonstration of the differences between history and window object `back()` and `forward()` methods, see Listings 14-20 and 14-21 in the previous chapter.

Related Items: `history.forward()` method; `history.go()` method.

forward()

Returns: Nothing.

	Nav2	Nav3	Nav4	IE3/J1	IE3/J2	IE4/J3
Compatibility	✔	✔	✔	✔	✔	✔

Less likely to be scripted than the `history.back()` action is the method that performs the opposite action: navigating forward one step in the browser's history list. Because the location of the current URL in the history list is impossible for a script to determine if the page is not part of your Web site, your script may not know exactly where it will be going. The only time you can confidently use the `history.forward()` method is to balance the use of the `history.back()` method in the same script — where your script closely keeps track of how many steps the script heads in either direction. Use the `history.forward()` method with extreme caution, and only after performing extensive user testing on your Web pages to make sure that you've covered all user possibilities. The same cautions about differences introduced in Navigator 4 for `history.back()` apply equally to `history.forward()`: Forward progress extends only through the history listing for a given window or frame, not the entire browser history list. See Listings 14-18 and 14-19 for a demonstration.

Related Items: `history.back()` method; `history.go()` method.

go(*relativeNumber* | "*URLOrTitleSubstring*")

Returns: Nothing.

	Nav2	Nav3	Nav4	IE3/J1	IE3/J2	IE4/J3
Compatibility	✔	✔	✔	✔	✔	✔

Use the `history.go()` method if you have enough control over your user that you are confident of the destination before jumping there. This "go" command only accepts items that already exist in the history listing, so you cannot use it in place of setting the `window.location` object to a brand-new URL.

For navigating *n* steps in either direction along the history list, use the *relativeNumber* parameter of the `history.go()` method. This number is an integer value that indicates which item in the list to use, relative to the current location. For example, if the current URL is at the top of the list (that is, the Forward button in the toolbar is dimmed), then you need to use the following method to jump to the URL two items backward in the list:

```
history.go(-2)
```

In other words, the current URL is the equivalent of `history.go(0)` (a method that reloads the window). A positive integer indicates a jump that many items forward in the history list. Thus, `history.go(-1)` is the same as `history.back()`, whereas `history.go(1)` is the same as `history.forward()`.

Alternatively, you can specify one of the URLs or document *titles* stored in the browser's history list (titles are what appear in the Go menu). The method is a bit lenient with the string you specify as a parameter. It compares the string against all listings. The first item in the history list to contain the parameter string will be regarded as the match. But, again, no navigation takes place if the item you specify is not listed in the history.

Like most other history methods, your script will find it difficult to manage the history list or the current URL's spot in the queue. That fact makes it even more difficult for your script to intelligently determine how far to navigate in either direction or to which specific URL or title matches it should jump. Use this method only for situations in which your Web pages are in strict control of the user's activity (or for designing scripts for yourself that automatically crawl around sites according to a fixed regimen). Once you give the user control over navigation, you have no guarantee that the history list will be what you expect, and any scripts you write that depend on a history object will likely break.

In practice, this method is used mostly to perform a soft reload of the current window, using the 0 parameter.

Note

If you are developing a page for all scriptable browsers, be aware that Internet Explorer's `go()` method behaves a little differently than Netscape's. First, a bug in Internet Explorer 3 causes all invocations of `history.go()` with a non-zero value to behave as if the parameter were -1. Second, the string version does not work at all in Internet Explorer 3 (it generates an error alert); for Internet Explorer 4, the matching string must be part of the URL and not part of the document title, as in Navigator. Finally, the reloading of a page with `history.go(0)` takes a long time to complete.

Example

Fill in either the number or text field of the page in Listing 15-11 and then click the associated button. The script passes the appropriate kind of data to the go() method. Be sure to use negative numbers for visiting a page earlier in the history.

Listing 15-11: **Navigating to an Item in History**

```
<HTML>
<HEAD>
<TITLE>Go() Method</TITLE>
<SCRIPT LANGUAGE="JavaScript">
function doGoNum(form) {
        window.history.go(parseInt(form.histNum.value))
}
function doGoTxt(form) {
        window.history.go(form.histWord.value)
}
</SCRIPT>
</HEAD>

<BODY>
<FORM>
<B>Calling the history.go() method:</B>
<HR>
Enter a number (+/-):<INPUT TYPE="text" NAME="histNum" SIZE=3
VALUE="0">
<INPUT TYPE="button" VALUE="Go to Offset"
onClick="doGoNum(this.form)"><P>
Enter a word in a title:<INPUT TYPE="text" NAME="histWord">
<INPUT TYPE="button" VALUE="Go to Match" onClick="doGoTxt(this.form)">
</FORM>
</BODY>
</HTML>
```

Related Items: history.back() method; history.forward() method; location.reload() method.

✦   ✦   ✦

The Document Object

User interaction is a vital aspect of client-side JavaScript
scripting, and most of the communication between
script and user takes place by way of the document object
and its components. Understanding the scope of the
document object is key to knowing how far you can take
JavaScript.

Review the document object's place within the JavaScript
object hierarchy. Figure 16-1 clearly shows that the
document object is a pivotal point for a large percentage of
JavaScript objects.

In fact, the document object and all that it contains is so
big that I have divided its discussion into many chapters,
each focusing on related object groups. This chapter looks
only at the document object, while each of the eight
succeeding chapters details objects contained by the
document object.

I must stress at the outset that many newcomers to
JavaScript have the expectation that they can, on the fly,
modify sections of a loaded page's content with ease: replace
some text here, change a table cell there. It's very important,
however, to understand that except for a limited number of
JavaScript objects, Netscape's document object model does
not allow a lot of content manipulation after a page has
loaded. The items that can be modified on the fly include text
object values, textarea object values, images (starting with
Navigator 3), and select object list contents.

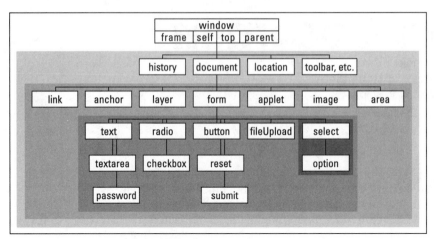

Figure 16-1: The JavaScript object hierarchy

A handful of other invisible properties are modifiable after the fact, but their settings don't survive soft reloads of a document. If your pages need to modify their contents based on user input or timed updates, consider designing your pages so that scripts write the contents; then let the scripts rewrite the entire page with your new settings.

Dynamic HTML and Documents

Navigator 4 and Internet Explorer 4 usher in a new concept called Dynamic HTML (DHTML). I devote Chapters 41 through 43 to the concepts behind DHTML. One of the advantages of this new page construction technique is that more content can, in fact, be altered on the fly after a document has loaded. Many of the roadblocks to creativity in earlier browser versions have been shattered with DHTML. Unfortunately, Netscape and Microsoft are not yet on the same page of the playbook when it comes to implementing scriptable interfaces to DHTML. Some common denominators exist, thanks to the W3C standards body, but both companies have numerous extensions that operate on different principles.

The fundamental difference is in the way each company implements content holders that our scripts can modify. Netscape relies on a new HTML <LAYER> tag and layer object; Microsoft has essentially turned every existing content-related tag into an object in the Internet Explorer 4 document object model.

Both methodologies have their merits. I like the ability to change text or HTML for any given element in an Internet Explorer 4 page. At the same time, Netscape's layer object, despite the HTML tag proliferation it brings, is a convenient container for a number of interesting animation effects. Because the point of view of this book is from that of Navigator, my assumption is you are designing primarily (if not exclusively) for a Netscape user audience, with the need to be compatible with Internet Explorer users. Therefore, if you see that I am glossing over a favorite Internet Explorer–only feature of yours, I do so to keep the discussion focused on Navigator applications, not to denigrate Microsoft's accomplishments.

Document Object

Document Object Properties	Methods	Event Handlers
alinkColor	captureEvents()	(None)
anchors[]	clear()	
applets[]	close()	
bgColor	getSelection()	
cookie	handleEvent()	
cookie	open()	
domain	releaseEvents()	
embeds	routeEvent()	
fgColor	write()	
forms[]	writeln()	
images[]		
lastModified		
layers[]		
linkColor		
links[]		
location		
referrer		
title		
URL		
vlinkColor		

Syntax

Creating a document:

```
<BODY
        [BACKGROUND="backgroundImageURL"]
        [BGCOLOR="#backgroundColor"]
        [TEXT="#foregroundColor"]
        [LINK="#unfollowedLinkColor"]
        [ALINK="#activatedLinkColor"]
        [VLINK="#followedLinkColor"]
        [onClick="handlerTextOrFunction"]
        [onDblClick="handlerTextOrFunction"]
        [onMouseDown="handlerTextOrFunction"]
```

```
            [onMouseUp="handlerTextOrFunction"]
            [onKeyDown="handlerTextOrFunction"]
            [onKeyPress="handlerTextOrFunction"]
            [onKeyUp="handlerTextOrFunction"]
            [onLoad="handlerTextOrFunction"]
            [onUnload="handlerTextOrFunction"]
            [onBlur="handlerTextOrFunction"]
            [onFocus="handlerTextOrFunction"]
            [onMove="handlerTextOrFunction"]
            [onResize="handlerTextOrFunction"]
            [onDragDrop="handlerTextOrFunction"]>
</BODY>
```

Accessing document properties or methods:

```
[window.] document.property | method([parameters])
```

About this object

A document object is the totality of what exists inside the content region of a browser window or window frame (excluding toolbars, status lines, and so on). The document is a combination of the content and interface elements that make the Web page worth visiting.

The officially sanctioned syntax for creating a document object, shown above, may mislead you to think that only elements defined within <BODY> tags comprise a document object. In truth, some <HEAD> tag information, such as <TITLE> and, of course, any scripts inside <SCRIPT> tags, are part of the document as well. So are some other values (properties), including the date on which the disk file of the document was last modified and the URL from which the user reached the current document.

Many event handlers defined in the Body, such as onLoad= and onUnload=, are not document-event handlers but rather window-event handlers. Load and unload events are sent to the window after the document finishes loading and just prior to the document being cleared from the window, respectively. See Chapter 14's discussion about the window object for more details about these and other window events whose event handlers are placed in the <BODY> tag.

Another way to create a document is to use the document.write() method to blast some or all of an HTML page into a window or frame. The window may be the current window running a script, a subwindow created by the script, or another frame in the current frameset. If you are writing the entire document, it is good practice to write a formal HTML page with all the tags you would normally put into an HTML file on your server.

Properties

```
alinkColor
vlinkColor
bgColor
fgColor
linkColor
```

Value: Hexadecimal triplet string   **Gettable:** Yes   **Settable:** Limited

	Nav2	Nav3	Nav4	IE3/J1	IE3/J2	IE4/J3
Compatibility	✔	✔	✔	✔	✔	✔

Netscape began using these `<BODY>` attributes for various color settings with Navigator Version 1.1. Many other browsers now accept these attributes, and they are part of HTML Level 3.2. All five settings can be read via scripting, but the ability to change some or all of these properties varies widely with browser and client platform. Table 16-1 shows a summary of which browsers and platforms can set which of the color properties. Notice that only `document.bgColor` is adjustable on the fly in Navigator browsers.

Table 16-1
Setting Document Colors on the Fly (Browser Versions)

Color Property	Navigator			Internet Explorer		
	Windows	Mac	UNIX	Windows	Mac	UNIX
bgColor	All	4	4	All	All	4
All others	None	None	None	All	All	4

If you experiment with setting `document.bgColor` on Mac or UNIX versions of Navigator 2 and 3, you may be fooled into thinking that the property is being set correctly. While the property value may stick, these platforms do not refresh their windows properly: if you change the color after all content is rendered, the swath of color obscures the content until a reload of the window. The safest, backward-compatible scripted way of setting document color properties is to compose the content of a frame or window and set the `<BODY>` tag color attributes dynamically.

Values for all color properties can be either the common HTML hexadecimal triplet value (for example, `"#00FF00"`) or any of the Netscape color names. Internet Explorer recognizes these plain language color names, as well. But also be aware that some colors work only when the user has the monitor set to 16- or 24-bit color settings.

JavaScript object property names are case-sensitive. This is important for the five property names that begin with lowercase letters and have an uppercase C within them.

Example

I've selected some color values at random to plug into three settings of the ugly colors group for Listing 16-1. The smaller window displays a dummy button so you can see how its display contrasts with color settings. Notice that the script sets the colors of the smaller window by rewriting the entire window's HTML code. After changing colors, the script displays the color values in the original window's textarea. Even though some colors are set with the Netscape color constant values, properties come back in the hexadecimal triplet values. You can experiment to your heart's content by changing color values in the listing. Every time you change the values in the script, save the HTML file and reload it in the browser.

Listing 16-1: **Color Sampler**

```
<HTML>
<HEAD>
<TITLE>Color Me</TITLE>
<SCRIPT LANGUAGE="JavaScript">
function defaultColors() {
        return "BGCOLOR='#c0c0c0' VLINK='#551a8b' LINK='#0000ff'"
}

function uglyColors() {
        return "BGCOLOR='yellow' VLINK='pink' LINK='lawngreen'"
}
function showColorValues() {
        var result = ""
        result += "bgColor: " + newWindow.document.bgColor + "\n"
        result += "vlinkColor: " + newWindow.document.vlinkColor + "\n"
        result += "linkColor: " + newWindow.document.linkColor + "\n"
        document.forms[0].results.value = result
}
// dynamically writes contents of another window
function drawPage(colorStyle) {
        var thePage = ""
        thePage += "<HTML><HEAD><TITLE>Color Sampler</TITLE></HEAD><BODY
"
        if (colorStyle == "default") {
           thePage += defaultColors()
        } else {
           thePage += uglyColors()
        }
        thePage += ">Just so you can see the variety of items and
color, <A "
        thePage += "HREF='http://www.nowhere.com'>here's a link</A>,
and <A HREF='http://home.netscape.com'> here is another link </A> you
can use on-line to visit and see how its color differs from the
standard link."
```

```
        thePage += "<FORM>"
        thePage += "<INPUT TYPE='button' NAME='sample' VALUE='Just a
Button'>"
        thePage += "</FORM></BODY></HTML>"
        newWindow.document.write(thePage)
        newWindow.document.close()
        showColorValues()
}
// the following works properly only in Windows Navigator
function setColors(colorStyle) {
        if (colorStyle == "default") {
            document.bgColor = "#c0c0c0"
        } else {
            document.bgColor = "yellow"
        }
}
var newWindow = window.open("","","height=150,width=300")
</SCRIPT>
</HEAD>

<BODY>
Try the two color schemes on the document in the small window.
<FORM>
<INPUT TYPE="button" NAME="default" VALUE='Default Colors'
onClick="drawPage('default')">
<INPUT TYPE="button" NAME="weird" VALUE="Ugly Colors"
onClick="drawPage('ugly')"><P>
<TEXTAREA NAME="results" ROWS=3 COLS=20></TEXTAREA><P><HR>
These buttons change the current document, but not correctly on all
platforms<P>
<INPUT TYPE="button" NAME="default" VALUE='Default Colors'
onClick="setColors('default')">
<INPUT TYPE="button" NAME="weird" VALUE="Ugly Colors"
onClick="setColors('ugly')"><P>
</FORM>
<SCRIPT LANGUAGE="JavaScript">
drawPage("default")
</SCRIPT>
</BODY>
</HTML>
```

To satisfy the curiosity of those who want to change the color of a loaded document on the fly, the preceding example includes a pair of buttons that set the color properties of the current document. If you're running browsers and versions capable of this power (see Table 16-1), everything will look fine; but in other platforms, you may lose the buttons and other document content behind the color. You can still click and activate these items, but the color obscures them. Unless you know for sure that users of your Web page use only browsers and clients empowered for background color changes, do not change colors by setting properties of an existing document. And if you set the other color properties for Internet Explorer users, the settings are ignored safely by Navigator.

Note

If you are using Internet Explorer 3 for the Macintosh, you will experience some difficulties with Listing 16-1. The script in the main document loses its connection with the subwindow; it does not redraw the second window with other colors. You can, however, change the colors in the main document. The significant flicker you may experience is related to the way the Mac version redraws content after changing colors.

Related Items: `document.links` property.

anchors

Value: Array of anchor objects   **Gettable:** Yes   **Settable:** No

	Nav2	Nav3	Nav4	IE3/J1	IE3/J2	IE4/J3
Compatibility	✔	✔	✔	✔	✔	✔

Anchor objects (described in Chapter 17) are points in an HTML document marked with `<A NAME="">` tags. Anchor objects are referenced in URLs by a trailing hash value. Like other object properties that contain a list of nested objects, the `document.anchors` property (notice the plural) delivers an indexed array of anchors in a document. Use the array references to pinpoint a specific anchor for retrieving any anchor property.

Anchor arrays begin their index counts with 0: The first anchor in a document, then, has the reference `document.anchors[0]`. And, as is true with any built-in array object, you can find out how many entries the array has by checking the `length` property. For example

```
anchorCount = document.anchors.length
```

The `document.anchors` property is read-only (and its array entries come back as null). To script navigation to a particular anchor, assign a value to the `window.location` or `window.location.hash` object, as described in Chapter 15's location object discussion.

Example

In Listing 16-2, I appended an extra script to a listing from Chapter 15 to demonstrate how to extract the number of anchors in the document. The document dynamically writes the number of anchors found in the document. You will not likely ever need to reveal such information to users of your page, and the `document.anchors` property is not one that you will call frequently. The object model defines it automatically as a document property while defining actual anchor objects.

Listing 16-2: **Reading the Number of Anchors**

```
<HTML>
<HEAD>
```

```
<TITLE>document.anchors Property</TITLE>
<SCRIPT LANGUAGE="JavaScript">
function goNextAnchor(where) {
        window.location.hash = where
}
</SCRIPT>
</HEAD>

<BODY>

<A NAME="start"><H1>Top</H1></A>
<FORM>
<INPUT TYPE="button" NAME="next" VALUE="NEXT"
onClick="goNextAnchor('sec1')">
</FORM>
<HR>

<A NAME="sec1"><H1>Section 1</H1></A>
<FORM>
<INPUT TYPE="button" NAME="next" VALUE="NEXT"
onClick="goNextAnchor('sec2')">
</FORM>
<HR>

<A NAME="sec2"><H1>Section 2</H1></A>
<FORM>
<INPUT TYPE="button" NAME="next" VALUE="NEXT"
onClick="goNextAnchor('sec3')">
</FORM>
<HR>

<A NAME="sec3"><H1>Section 3</H1></A>
<FORM>
<INPUT TYPE="button" NAME="next" VALUE="BACK TO TOP"
onClick="goNextAnchor('start')">
</FORM>
<HR><P>
<SCRIPT LANGUAGE="JavaScript">
document.write("<I>There are " + document.anchors.length + " anchors
defined for this document</I>")
</SCRIPT>
</BODY>
</HTML>
```

Related Items: anchor object; location object; `document.links` property.

applets

Value: Array of applet objects   **Gettable:** Yes   **Settable:** No

	Nav2	Nav3	Nav4	IE3/J1	IE3/J2	IE4/J3
Compatibility		✔	✔			✔

The `applets` property refers to Java applets defined in a document by the `<APPLET>` tag. An applet is not officially an object in the document until the applet loads completely.

Most of the work you do with Java applets from JavaScript takes place via the methods and variables defined inside the applet. Although you can reference an applet according to its indexed array position, you will more likely use the applet object's name in the reference to avoid any confusion. For more details, see the discussion of the applet object later in this chapter and the LiveConnect discussion in Chapter 38.

Example

The `document.applets` property is defined automatically as the browser builds the object model for a document that contains applet objects. You will rarely access this property, except to determine how many applet objects a document has.

Related Items: applet object.

cookie

Value: String   **Gettable:** Yes   **Settable:** Yes

	Nav2	Nav3	Nav4	IE3/J1	IE3/J2	IE4/J3
Compatibility	✔	✔	✔	✔	✔	✔

The cookie mechanism in Navigator lets you store small pieces of information on the client computer in a reasonably secure manner. In other words, when you need some tidbit of information to persist at the client level while either loading diverse HTML documents or moving from one session to another, the cookie mechanism saves the day. Netscape's technical documentation (much of which is written from the perspective of a server writing to a cookie) can be found on the Web at `http://www.netscape.com/newsref/std/cookie_spec.html`.

The cookie is commonly used as a means to store the username and password you enter into a password-protected Web site. The first time you enter this information into a CGI-governed form, the CGI program has Navigator write the information back to a cookie on your hard disk (usually after encrypting the password). Rather than bothering you to enter the username and password the next time you access the site, the server searches the cookie data stored for that particular server and extracts the username and password for automatic validation processing behind the scenes.

Note

I cover the technical differences between Navigator and Internet Explorer cookies later in this section. But if you are using Internet Explorer 3, be aware that the browser neither reads nor writes cookies when the document accessing the cookie is on the local hard disk. Internet Explorer 4 works with cookies generated by local files.

The cookie file

Allowing some foreign CGI program to read from and write to your hard disk may give you pause, but Navigator doesn't just open up your drive's directory for the world to see (or corrupt). Instead, the cookie mechanism provides access to just one special text file located in a platform-specific spot on your drive.

In Windows versions of Navigator, the cookie file is named cookies.txt and is located in the Navigator directory; Mac users can find the MagicCookie file inside the Netscape folder, which is located within the System Folder:Preferences folder. The cookie file is a text file (but because the MagicCookie file's type is not TEXT, Mac users can open it only via applications capable of opening any kind of file). Internet Explorer uses a different filing system: Each cookie is saved as its own file inside a Cookies directory within system directories.

Note

If curiosity drives you to open the cookie file, I recommend you do so only with a copy saved in another directory or folder. Any alteration to the existing file can mess up whatever valuable cookies are stored there for sites you regularly visit. Inside the file (after a few comment lines warning you not to manually alter the file) are lines of tab-delimited text. Each return-delimited line contains one cookie's information. The cookie file is just like a text listing of a database.

As you experiment with Navigator cookies, you will be tempted to look into the cookie file after a script writes some data to the cookie. The cookie file will not contain the newly written data, because cookies are transferred to disk only when the user quits Navigator; conversely, the cookie file is read into Navigator's memory when it is launched. While you read, write, and delete cookies during a Navigator session, all activity is performed in memory (to speed up the process) to be saved later.

A cookie record

Among the "fields" of each cookie record are the following:

✦ Domain of the server that created the cookie

✦ Information on whether you need a secure HTTP connection to access the cookie

✦ Pathname of URL(s) capable of accessing the cookie

✦ Expiration date of the cookie

✦ Name of the cookie entry

✦ String data associated with the cookie entry

Notice that cookies are domain-specific. In other words, if one domain creates a cookie, another domain cannot access it through Navigator's cookie mechanism behind your back. That reason is why it's generally safe to store what I call *throwaway passwords* (the username/password pairs required to access some free registration-required sites) in cookies. Moreover, sites that store passwords in a cookie usually do so as encrypted strings, making it more difficult for someone to hijack the cookie file from your unattended PC and figure out what your personal password scheme might be.

Cookies also have expiration dates. Because the Navigator cookie file can hold no more than 300 cookies (as dictated by Navigator), the cookie file can get pretty full over the years. Therefore, if a cookie needs to persist past the current Navigator session, it also has an expiration date established by the cookie writer. Navigator cleans out any expired cookies to keep the file from exploding some years hence.

Not all cookies have to last beyond the current session, however. In fact, a scenario in which you use cookies temporarily while working your way through a Web site is quite typical. Many shopping sites employ one or more temporary cookie records to behave as the shopping cart for recording items you intend to purchase. These items are copied to the order form at check-out time. But once you submit the order form to the server, that client-side data has no particular value. As it turns out, if your script does not specify an expiration date, Navigator keeps the cookie fresh in memory without writing it to the cookie file. When you quit Navigator, that cookie data disappears as expected.

JavaScript access

Scripted access of cookies from JavaScript is limited to setting the cookie (with a number of optional parameters) and getting the cookie data (but with none of the parameters).

The JavaScript object model defines cookies as properties of documents, but this description is somewhat misleading. If you use the default path to set a cookie (that is, the current directory of the document whose script sets the cookie in the first place), then all documents in that same directory have read and write access to the cookie. A benefit of this arrangement is that if you have a scripted application that contains multiple documents, all documents in the same directory can share the cookie data. Netscape Navigator, however, imposes a limit of 20 named cookie entries for any domain; Internet Explorer 3 imposes an even more restrictive limit of one cookie (that is, one name-value pair) per domain. If your cookie requirements are extensive, then you need to fashion ways of concatenating cookie data (I do this in the Decision Helper application on the CD-ROM).

Saving cookies

To write cookie data to the cookie file, you use a simple JavaScript assignment operator with the `document.cookie` property. But the formatting of the data is crucial to achieving success. Here is the syntax for assigning a value to a cookie (optional items are in brackets):

```
document.cookie = "cookieName=cookieData
                [; expires=timeInGMTString]
                [; path=pathName]
                [; domain=domainName]
                [; secure]"
```

Examine each of the properties individually.

Name/Data

Each cookie must have a name and a string value (even if that value is an empty string). Such name-value pairs are fairly common in HTML, but they look odd in an assignment statement. For example, if you want to save the string "Fred" to a cookie named "userName," the JavaScript statement is

```
document.cookie = "userName=Fred"
```

If Navigator sees no existing cookie in the current domain with this name, it automatically creates the cookie entry for you; if the named cookie already exists, Navigator replaces the old data with the new data. Retrieving `document.cookie` at this point yields the following string:

```
userName=Fred
```

You can omit all the other cookie-setting properties, in which case Navigator uses default values, as explained in a following section. For temporary cookies (those that don't have to persist beyond the current Navigator session), the name-value pair is usually all you need.

The entire name-value pair must be a single string with no semicolons, commas, or character spaces. To take care of spaces between words, preprocess the value with the JavaScript `escape()` function, which ASCII-encodes the spaces as `%20` (and then be sure to `unescape()` the value to restore the human-readable spaces when you retrieve the cookie later).

You cannot save a JavaScript array to a cookie. But with the help of the `Array.join()` method, you can convert an array to a string; use `String.split()` to re-create the array after reading the cookie at a later time. These two methods are available in Navigator from Version 3 onward and Internet Explorer 4 onward. If you add extra parameters, notice that all of them are included in the single string assigned to the `document.cookie` property. Also, each of the parameters must be separated by a semicolon and space.

Expires

Expiration dates, when supplied, must be passed as Greenwich mean time (GMT) strings (see Chapter 29 about time data). To calculate an expiration date based on today's date, use the JavaScript Date object as follows:

```
var exp = new Date()
var oneYearFromNow = exp.getTime() + (365 * 24 * 60 * 60 * 1000)
exp.setTime(oneYearFromNow)
```

Then convert the date to the accepted GMT string format:

```
document.cookie = "userName=Fred; expires=" + exp.toGMTString()
```

In the cookie file, the expiration date and time is stored as a numeric value (seconds) but, to set it, you need to supply the time in GMT format. You can delete a cookie before it expires by setting the named cookie's expiration date to a time and date earlier than the current time and date. The safest expiration parameter is

```
expires=Thu, 01-Jan-70 00:00:01 GMT
```

Omitting the expiration date signals Navigator that this cookie is temporary. Navigator never writes it to the cookie file and forgets it the next time you quit Navigator.

Path

For client-side cookies, the default path setting (the current directory) is usually the best choice. You can, of course, create a duplicate copy of a cookie with a separate path (and domain) so the same data is available to a document located in another area of your site (or the Web).

Domain

To help synchronize cookie data with a particular document (or group of documents), Navigator matches the domain of the current document with the domain values of cookie entries in the cookie file. Therefore, if you were to display a list of all cookie data contained in a `document.cookie` property, you would get back all the name-value cookie pairs from the cookie file whose domain parameter matches that of the current document.

Unless you expect the document to be replicated in another server within your domain, you can usually omit the domain parameter when saving a cookie. Navigator automatically supplies the domain of the current document to the cookie file entry. Be aware that a domain setting must have at least two periods, such as

```
.mcom.com
.hotwired.com
```

Or, you can write an entire URL to the domain, including the `http://` protocol (as Navigator does automatically when the domain is not specified).

SECURE

If you omit the `SECURE` parameter when saving a cookie, you imply that the cookie data is accessible to any document or CGI program from your site that meets the other domain- and path-matching properties. For client-side scripting of cookies, you should omit this parameter when saving a cookie.

Retrieving cookie data

Cookie data retrieved via JavaScript is contained in one string, including the whole name-data pair. Even though the cookie file stores other parameters for each cookie, you can only retrieve the name-data pairs via JavaScript. Moreover, in Navigator when two or more (up to a maximum of 20) cookies meet the current domain criteria, these cookies are also lumped into that string, delimited by a semicolon and space. For example, a `document.cookie` string might look like this:

```
userName=Fred; password=NikL2sPacU
```

In other words, you cannot treat named cookies as objects. Instead, you must parse the entire cookie string, extracting the data from the desired name-data pair.

When you know that you're dealing with only one cookie (and that no more will ever be added to the domain), you can customize the extraction based on known data, such as the cookie name. For example, with a cookie name that is seven characters long, you can extract the data with a statement like this:

```
var data =
unescape(document.cookie.substring(7,document.cookie.length))
```

The first parameter of the `substring()` method includes the equals sign to separate the name from the data.

A better approach is to create a general purpose function that can work with single- or multiple-entry cookies. Here is one I use in some of my pages:

```
function getCookieData(label) {
    var labelLen = label.length
    var cLen = document.cookie.length
    var i = 0
    var cEnd
    while (i < cLen) {
        var j = i + labelLen
        if (document.cookie.substring(i,j) == label) {
            cEnd = document.cookie.indexOf(";",j)
            if (cEnd == -1) {
                cEnd = document.cookie.length
            }
            return unescape(document.cookie.substring(j,cEnd))
        }
        i++
    }
    return ""
}
```

Calls to this function pass the name of the desired cookie as a parameter. The function parses the entire cookie string, chipping away any mismatched entries (through the semicolons) until it finds the cookie name.

If all of this cookie code still makes your head hurt, you can turn to a set of functions devised by experienced JavaScripter and Web site designer Bill Dortch of hIdaho Design. His cookie functions provide generic access to cookies that you can use in all of your cookie-related pages. Listing 16-3 shows Bill's cookie functions, which include a variety of safety nets for date calculation bugs that appeared in some versions of Netscape Navigator 2. Don't be put off by the length of the listing: Most of the lines are comments. Updates to Bill's functions can be found at `http://www.hidaho.com/cookies/cookie.txt`.

Listing 16-3: **Bill Dortch's cookie Functions**

```
<html>
<head>
<title>Cookie Functions</title>
</head>
<body>
<script language="javascript">
<!-- begin script
//
//  Cookie Functions -- "Night of the Living Cookie" Version (25-Jul-96)
//
//  Written by:  Bill Dortch, hIdaho Design <bdortch@hidaho.com>
//  The following functions are released to the public domain.
//
```

(continued)

Listing 16-3 *(continued)*

```
//   This version takes a more aggressive approach to deleting
//   cookies.  Previous versions set the expiration date to one
//   millisecond prior to the current time; however, this method
//   did not work in Netscape 2.02 (though it does in earlier and
//   later versions), resulting in "zombie" cookies that would not
//   die.  DeleteCookie now sets the expiration date to the earliest
//   usable date (one second into 1970), and sets the cookie's value
//   to null for good measure.
//
//   Also, this version adds optional path and domain parameters to
//   the DeleteCookie function.  If you specify a path and/or domain
//   when creating (setting) a cookie**, you must specify the same
//   path/domain when deleting it, or deletion will not occur.
//
//   The FixCookieDate function must now be called explicitly to
//   correct for the 2.x Mac date bug.  This function should be
//   called *once* after a Date object is created and before it
//   is passed (as an expiration date) to SetCookie.  Because the
//   Mac date bug affects all dates, not just those passed to
//   SetCookie, you might want to make it a habit to call
//   FixCookieDate any time you create a new Date object:
//
//      var theDate = new Date();
//      FixCookieDate (theDate);
//
//   Calling FixCookieDate has no effect on platforms other than
//   the Mac, so there is no need to determine the user's platform
//   prior to calling it.
//
//   This version also incorporates several minor coding improvements.
//
//   **Note that it is possible to set multiple cookies with the same
//   name but different (nested) paths.  For example:
//
//      SetCookie ("color","red",null,"/outer");
//      SetCookie ("color","blue",null,"/outer/inner");
//
//   However, GetCookie cannot distinguish between these and will return
//   the first cookie that matches a given name.  It is therefore
//   recommended that you *not* use the same name for cookies with
//   different paths.  (Bear in mind that there is *always* a path
//   associated with a cookie; if you don't explicitly specify one,
//   the path of the setting document is used.)
//
//   Revision History:
//
//      "Toss Your Cookies" Version (22-Mar-96)
//        - Added FixCookieDate() function to correct for Mac date bug
//
//      "Second Helping" Version (21-Jan-96)
```

```
//        - Added path, domain and secure parameters to SetCookie
//        - Replaced home-rolled encode/decode functions with Netscape's
//          new (then) escape and unescape functions
//
//    "Free Cookies" Version (December 95)
//
//
//    For information on the significance of cookie parameters,
//    and on cookies in general, please refer to the official cookie
//    spec, at:
//
//        http://www.netscape.com/newsref/std/cookie_spec.html
//
//**********************************************************************
//
// "Internal" function to return the decoded value of a cookie
//
function getCookieVal (offset) {
  var endstr = document.cookie.indexOf (";", offset);
  if (endstr == -1)
    endstr = document.cookie.length;
  return unescape(document.cookie.substring(offset, endstr));
}
//
//   Function to correct for 2.x Mac date bug.  Call this function to
//   fix a date object prior to passing it to SetCookie.
//   IMPORTANT:  This function should only be called *once* for
//   any given date object!  See example at the end of this document.
//
function FixCookieDate (date) {
  var base = new Date(0);
  var skew = base.getTime(); // dawn of (Unix) time - should be 0
  if (skew > 0)  // Except on the Mac - ahead of its time
    date.setTime (date.getTime() - skew);
}
//
//   Function to return the value of the cookie specified by "name".
//     name - String object containing the cookie name.
//     returns - String object containing the cookie value, or null if
//        the cookie does not exist.
//
function GetCookie (name) {
  var arg = name + "=";
  var alen = arg.length;
  var clen = document.cookie.length;
  var i = 0;
  while (i < clen) {
    var j = i + alen;
    if (document.cookie.substring(i, j) == arg)
      return getCookieVal (j);
      i = document.cookie.indexOf(" ", i) + 1;
    if (i == 0) break;
  }
```

(continued)

Listing 16-3 *(continued)*

```
   return null;
}
//
//  Function to create or update a cookie.
//    name - String object containing the cookie name.
//    value - String object containing the cookie value.  May contain
//      any valid string characters.
//    [expires] - Date object containing the expiration data of the cookie.  If
//      omitted or null, expires the cookie at the end of the current session.
//    [path] - String object indicating the path for which the cookie is valid.
//      If omitted or null, uses the path of the calling document.
//    [domain] - String object indicating the domain for which the cookie is
//      valid. If omitted or null, uses the domain of the calling document.
//    [secure] - Boolean (true/false) value indicating whether cookie transmission
//      requires a secure channel (HTTPS).
//
//  The first two parameters are required.  The others, if supplied, must
//  be passed in the order listed above.  To omit an unused optional field,
//  use null as a place holder.  For example, to call SetCookie using name,
//  value and path, you would code:
//
//      SetCookie ("myCookieName", "myCookieValue", null, "/");
//
//  Note that trailing omitted parameters do not require a placeholder.
//
//  To set a secure cookie for path "/myPath", that expires after the
//  current session, you might code:
//
//      SetCookie (myCookieVar, cookieValueVar, null, "/myPath", null, true);
//
function SetCookie (name,value,expires,path,domain,secure) {
  document.cookie = name + "=" + escape (value) +
    ((expires) ? "; expires=" + expires.toGMTString() : "") +
    ((path) ? "; path=" + path : "") +
    ((domain) ? "; domain=" + domain : "") +
    ((secure) ? "; secure" : "");
}


//  Function to delete a cookie. (Sets expiration date to start of epoch)
//    name -     String object containing the cookie name
//    path -     String object containing the path of the cookie to delete.  This MUST
//               be the same as the path used to create the cookie, or null/omitted if
//               no path was specified when creating the cookie.
//    domain - String object containing the domain of the cookie to delete.  This MUST
//               be the same as the domain used to create the cookie, or null/omitted if
//               no domain was specified when creating the cookie.
//
function DeleteCookie (name,path,domain) {
  if (GetCookie(name)) {
    document.cookie = name + "=" +
```

```
        ((path) ? "; path=" + path : "") +
        ((domain) ? "; domain=" + domain : "") +
        "; expires=Thu, 01-Jan-70 00:00:01 GMT";
    }
}

//
//   Examples
//
var expdate = new Date ();
FixCookieDate (expdate); // Correct for Mac date bug - call only once
for given Date object!
expdate.setTime (expdate.getTime() + (24 * 60 * 60 * 1000)); // 24 hrs
from now
SetCookie ("ccpath", "http://www.hidaho.com/colorcenter/", expdate);
SetCookie ("ccname", "hIdaho Design ColorCenter", expdate);
SetCookie ("tempvar", "This is a temporary cookie.");
SetCookie ("ubiquitous", "This cookie will work anywhere in this
domain",null,"/");
SetCookie ("paranoid", "This cookie requires secure
communications",expdate,"/",null,true);
SetCookie ("goner", "This cookie must die!");
document.write (document.cookie + "<br>");
DeleteCookie ("goner");
document.write (document.cookie + "<br>");
document.write ("ccpath = " + GetCookie("ccpath") + "<br>");
document.write ("ccname = " + GetCookie("ccname") + "<br>");
document.write ("tempvar = " + GetCookie("tempvar") + "<br>");
// end script -->
</script>
</body>
</html>
```

Extra batches

You may design a site that needs more than 20 Netscape cookies for a given domain. For example, in a shopping site, you never know how many items a customer might load into the shopping cart cookie.

Because each named cookie stores plain text, you can create your own text-based data structures to accommodate multiple pieces of information per cookie. (Despite Netscape's information that each cookie can contain up to 4,000 characters, the value of one name-value pair cannot exceed 2,000 characters.) The trick is determining a delimiter character that won't be used by any of the data in the cookie. In Decision Helper (on the CD-ROM), for example, I use a period to separate multiple integers stored in a cookie; Netscape uses colons to separate settings in the custom page cookie data.

With the delimiter character established, you must then write functions that concatenate these "subcookies" into single cookie strings and extract them on the other side. It's a bit more work, but well worth the effort to have the power of persistent data on the client.

Example

Experiment with the last group of statements in Listing 16-3 to create, retrieve, and delete cookies.

Related Items: String object methods (Chapter 27).

`domain`

Value: String   **Gettable:** Yes   **Settable:** Yes

	Nav2	Nav3	Nav4	IE3/J1	IE3/J2	IE4/J3
Compatibility		✔	✔			✔

Security restrictions can get in the way of sites that have more than one server at their domain. Because some objects, especially the location object, prevent access to properties of other servers displayed in other frames, legitimate access to those properties are blocked. For example, it's not uncommon for popular sites to have their usual public access site on a server named something like `www.popular.com`. If a page on that server includes a front end to a site search engine located at `search.popular.com`, visitors who use browsers with these security restrictions will be denied access.

To guard against that eventuality, a script in documents from both servers can instruct the browser to think both servers are the same. In the example above, you would set the `document.domain` property in both documents to `popular.com`. Without specifically setting the property, the default value includes the server name as well, thus causing a mismatch between host names.

Before you start thinking you can spoof your way into other servers, be aware that you can set the `document.domain` property only to servers with the same domain (following the "two-dot" rule) as the document doing the setting. Therefore, documents originating only from `xxx.popular.com` can set their `document.domain` properties to `popular.com` server.

Related Items: `window.open()` method; `window.location` object; security (Chapter 40).

`embeds`

Value: Array of plug-ins   **Gettable:** Yes   **Settable:** No

	Nav2	Nav3	Nav4	IE3/J1	IE3/J2	IE4/J3
Compatibility		✔	✔			✔

Whenever you want to load data that requires a plug-in application to play or display, you use the `<EMBED>` tag. The `document.embeds` property is merely one way to determine the number of such tags defined in the document:

```
var count = document.embeds.length
```

For controlling those plug-ins in Navigator, you can use the LiveConnect technology, described in Chapter 38.

forms

Value: Array   **Gettable:** Yes   **Settable:** No

	Nav2	Nav3	Nav4	IE3/J1	IE3/J2	IE4/J3
Compatibility	✔	✔	✔	✔	✔	✔

As I show in Chapter 21, which is dedicated to the form object, an HTML form (anything defined inside a `<FORM>...</FORM>` tag pair) is a JavaScript object unto itself. You can create a valid reference to a form according to its name (assigned via a form's `NAME=` attribute). For example, if a document contains the following form definition

```
<FORM NAME="phoneData">
        input item definitions
</FORM>
```

your scripts can refer to the form object by name:

```
document.phoneData
```

However, a document object also tracks its forms in another way: as a numbered list of forms. This type of list in JavaScript is called an *array,* which means a table consisting of just one column of data. Each row of the table holds a representation of the corresponding form in the document. In the first row of a `document.forms` array, for instance, is the form that loaded first (it was first from the top of the HTML code). If your document defines one form, the `forms` property is an array one entry in length; with three separate forms in the document, the array is three entries long.

To help JavaScript determine which row of the array your script wants to access, you append a pair of brackets to the `forms` property name and insert the row number between the brackets (this is standard JavaScript array notation). This number is formally known as the *index.* JavaScript arrays start their row numbering with 0, so the first entry in the array is referenced as

```
document.forms[0]
```

At that point, you're referencing the equivalent of the first form object. Any of its properties or methods are available by appending the desired property or method name to the reference. For example, to retrieve the value of an input text field named "homePhone" from the second form of a document, the reference you use is

```
document.forms[1].homePhone.value
```

One advantage to using the `document.forms` property for addressing a form object or element instead of the actual form name is that you may be able to generate a library of generalizable scripts that know how to cycle through all available forms in a document and hunt for a form that has some special element and property. The following script fragment (part of a *repeat loop* described more fully in Chapter 31) uses a loop-counting variable (i) to help the script check all forms in a document:

```
for (var i = 0; i < document.forms.length; i++) {
        if (document.forms[i]. ... ) {
            statements
        }
}
```

Each time through the repeat loop, JavaScript substitutes the next higher value for i in the document.forms[i] object reference. Not only does the array counting simplify the task of checking all forms in a document, but this fragment is totally independent of whatever names you assign to forms.

As you saw in the preceding script fragment, there is one more aspect of the document.forms property that you should be aware of. All JavaScript arrays that represent built-in objects have a length property that returns the number of entries in the array. JavaScript counts the length of arrays starting with 1. Therefore, if the document.forms.length property returns a value of 2, the form references for this document would be document.forms[0] and document.forms[1]. If you haven't programmed these kinds of arrays before, the different numbering systems (indexes starting with 0, length counts starting with 1) take some getting used to.

If you use a lot of care in assigning names to objects, you will likely prefer the document.formName style of referencing forms. In this book, you see both indexed array and form name style references. The advantage of using name references is that even if you redesign the page and change the order of forms in the document, references to the named forms will still be valid, whereas the index numbers of the forms will have changed. See also the discussion in Chapter 21 of the form object and how to pass a form's data to a function.

Example

The document in Listing 16-4 is set up to display an alert dialog box that replicates navigation to a particular music site, based on the checked status of the "bluish" checkbox. The user input here is divided into two forms: one form with the checkbox and the other form with the button that does the navigation. A block of copy fills the space in between. Clicking the bottom button (in the second form) triggers the function that fetches the checked property of the "bluish" checkbox, using the document.forms[i] array as part of the address.

Listing 16-4: **Using the document.forms Property**

```
<HTML>
<HEAD>
<TITLE>document.forms example</TITLE>
<SCRIPT LANGUAGE="JavaScript">
function goMusic() {
        if (document.forms[0].bluish.checked) {
            alert("Now going to the Blues music area...")
```

```
            } else {
                alert("Now going to Rock music area...")
            }
}
</SCRIPT>
</HEAD>

<BODY>
<FORM NAME="theBlues">
<INPUT TYPE="checkbox" NAME="bluish">Check here if you've got the
blues.
</FORM>
<HR>
M<BR>
o<BR>
r<BR>
e<BR>
<BR>
C<BR>
o<BR>
p<BR>
y<BR>
<HR>
<FORM NAME="visit">
<INPUT TYPE="button" VALUE="Visit music site" onClick="goMusic()">
</FORM>
</BODY>
</HTML>
```

Related Items: form object.

images

Value: Array of image objects **Gettable:** Yes **Settable:** No

	Nav2	Nav3	Nav4	IE3/J1	IE3/J2	IE4/J3
Compatibility		✔	✔	(✔)		✔

With images treated as first-class objects beginning with Navigator 3 and Internet Explorer 4, it's only natural for a document to maintain an array of all the image tags defined on the page (just as it does for links and anchors). The prime importance of having images as objects is that you can modify their content (the source file associated with the rectangular space of the image) on the fly. You can find details about the image object in Chapter 18.

The lack of an image object in Windows versions of Internet Explorer 3 disappointed many authors who wanted to swap images on mouse rollovers. Little known, however, is that the Macintosh version of Internet Explorer (Version 3.01a) has an image object in its object model, working exactly like Navigator 3's image object. The image object is present on all platforms in Internet Explorer 4.

Use image array references to pinpoint a specific image for retrieval of any image property or for assigning a new image file to its `src` property. Image arrays begin their index counts with 0: The first image in a document has the reference `document.images[0]`. And, as with any array object, you can find out how many images the array contains by checking the `length` property. For example

```
imageCount = document.images.length
```

Images can also have names, so if you prefer, you can refer to the image object by its name, as in

```
imageLoaded = document.imageName.complete
```

Example

The `document.images` property is defined automatically as the browser builds the object model for a document that contains image objects. See the discussion about the `image` object in Chapter 18 for reference examples.

Related Items: image object.

lastModified

Value: DateString   **Gettable:** Yes   **Settable:** No

	Nav2	Nav3	Nav4	IE3/J1	IE3/J2	IE4/J3
Compatibility	✔	✔	✔	✔	✔	✔

Every disk file maintains a modified timestamp, and most servers expose this information to a browser accessing a file. This information is available by reading the `document.lastModified` property (be sure to observe the uppercase M in the property name). If your server supplies this information to the client, you can use the value of this property to present this information for readers of your Web page. The script automatically updates the value for you, rather than requiring you to hand-code the HTML line every time you modify the home page.

The returned value is not a date object (Chapter 29) but rather a straight string consisting of time and date, as recorded by the document's file system. You can, however, convert the date string to a JavaScript date object and use the date object's methods to extract selected elements for recompilation into readable form. Listing 16-5 shows an example.

Even local file systems don't necessarily provide the correct data for every browser to interpret. For example, in Navigator of all generations for the Macintosh, dates from files stored on local disks come back as something from the 1920s (although Internet Explorer manages to reflect the correct date). But put that same file on a UNIX or NT Web server, and the date appears correctly when accessed via the Net.

Example

Experiment with the `document.lastModified` property with Listing 16-5. But also be prepared for inaccurate readings if the file is located on some servers or local hard disks.

Listing 16-5: **document.lastModified Property in Another Format**

```
<HTML>
<HEAD>
<TITLE>Time Stamper</TITLE>
</HEAD>
<BODY>
<CENTER> <H1>GiantCo Home Page</H1></CENTER>
<SCRIPT LANGUAGE="JavaScript">
update = new Date(document.lastModified)
theMonth = update.getMonth() + 1
theDate = update.getDate()
theYear = update.getYear()
document.writeln("<I>Last updated:" + theMonth + "/" + theDate + "/" +
theYear + "</I>")
</SCRIPT>
<HR>
</BODY>
</HTML>
```

As noted at great length in Chapter 29's discussion about the date object, you should be aware that date formats vary greatly from country to country. Some of these formats use a different order for date elements. When you hard-code a date format, it may take a form that is unfamiliar to other users of your page.

Related Items: date object (Chapter 29).

layers

Value: String   **Gettable:** Yes   **Settable:** No

	Nav2	Nav3	Nav4	IE3/J1	IE3/J2	IE4/J3
Compatibility			✔			

The layer object (Chapter 19) is new as of Netscape Navigator 4 and is not part of Internet Explorer 4's object model. Therefore, only the Netscape browser contains a property that reflects the array of layer objects within a document. This is the same kind of array used to refer to other document objects, such as images and applets.

A Netscape layer is a container for content that can be precisely positioned on the page. Layers can be defined with the Netscape-specific <LAYER> tag or with W3C standard style-sheet positioning syntax, as explained in Chapter 19. Each layer contains a document object — the true holder of the content displayed in that layer. Layers can be nested within each other, but a reference to document.layers reveals only the first level of layers defined in the document. Consider the following HTML skeleton.

```
<HTML>
<BODY>
<LAYER NAME="Europe">
        <LAYER NAME="Germany"></LAYER>
        <LAYER NAME="Netherlands"></LAYER>
</LAYER>
</BODY>
</HTML>
```

From the point of view of the primary document, there is one layer (Europe). Therefore, the length of the document.layers array is 1. But the Europe layer has a document, in which two more layers are nested. A reference to the array of those nested layers would be

```
document.layers[1].document.layers
```

or

```
document.Europe.document.layers
```

The length of this nested array is two: The Germany and Netherlands layers. No property exists that reveals the entire set of nested arrays in a document, but you can create a for loop to crawl through all nested layers (shown in Listing 16-6).

Example

Listing 16-6 demonstrates how to use the document.layers property to crawl through the entire set of nested layers in a document. Using recursion (discussed in Chapter 34), the script builds an indented list of layers in the same hierarchy as the objects themselves and displays the results in an alert dialog. After you load this document (the script is triggered by the onLoad= event handler), compare the alert dialog contents against the structure of <LAYER> tags in the document.

Listing 16-6: **A Layer Crawler**

```
<HTML>
<HEAD>
<SCRIPT LANGUAGE="JavaScript1.2">
var output = ""
function crawlLayers(layerArray, indent) {
        for (var i = 0; i < layerArray.length; i++) {
            output += indent + layerArray[i].name + "\n"
            if (layerArray[i].document.layers.length) {
                var newLayerArray = layerArray[i].document.layers
                crawlLayers(newLayerArray, indent + "   ")
            }
        }
        return output
}
function revealLayers() {
        alert(crawlLayers(document.layers, ""))
}
```

```
</SCRIPT>
</HEAD>
<BODY onLoad="revealLayers()">
<LAYER NAME="Europe">
        <LAYER NAME="Germany"></LAYER>
        <LAYER NAME="Netherlands">
            <LAYER NAME="Amsterdam"></LAYER>
            <LAYER NAME="Rotterdam"></LAYER>
        </LAYER>
        <LAYER NAME="France"></LAYER>
</LAYER>
<LAYER NAME="Africa">
        <LAYER NAME="South Africa"></LAYER>
        <LAYER NAME="Ivory Coast"></LAYER>
</LAYER>
</BODY>
</HTML>
```

Related Items: layer object.

links

Value: Array of link objects   **Gettable:** Yes   **Settable:** No

	Nav2	Nav3	Nav4	IE3/J1	IE3/J2	IE4/J3
Compatibility	✔	✔	✔	✔	✔	✔

The `document.links` property is similar to the `document.anchors` property, except that the objects maintained by the array are link objects — items created with `<A HREF="">` tags. Use the array references to pinpoint a specific link for retrieving any link property, such as the target window specified in the link's HTML definition.

Link arrays begin their index counts with 0: The first link in a document has the reference `document.links[0]`. And, as with any array object, you can find out how many entries the array has by checking the length property. For example

```
linkCount = document.links.length
```

Entries in the `document.links` property are full-fledged `location` objects.

Example

The `document.links` property is defined automatically as the browser builds the object model for a document that contains link objects. You will rarely access this property, except to determine the number of link objects in the document.

Related Items: link object; `document.anchors` property.

location
URL

Value: String   **Gettable:** Yes   **Settable:** No (Navigator)

	Nav2	Nav3	Nav4	IE3/J1	IE3/J2	IE4/J3
Compatibility	(✔)	✔	✔	(✔)	(✔)	✔

The fact that JavaScript frequently reuses the same terms in different contexts may be confusing to the language's newcomers. Such is the case with the `document.location` property. You may wonder how it differs from the `location` object (Chapter 15). In practice, many scripts also get the two confused when references don't include the window object. As a result, a new property name, `document.URL`, was introduced in Navigator 3 and Internet Explorer 4 to take the place of `document.location`. You can still use `document.location`, but the term may eventually disappear from the JavaScript vocabulary (or at least from Netscape's object model). To help you get into the future mindset, the rest of this discussion refers to this property as `document.URL`.

The remaining question is how the `window.location` object and `document.URL` property differ. The answer lies in their respective data types.

A location object, you may recall from Chapter 15, consists of a number of properties about the document currently loaded in a window or frame. Assigning a new URL to the object tells the browser to load that URL into the frame. The `document.URL` property, on the other hand, is simply a string (read-only in Navigator) that reveals the URL of the current document. The value may be important to your script, but the property does not have the "object power" of the `window.location` object. You cannot change (assign another value to) this property value because a document has only one URL: its location on the Net (or your hard disk) where the file exists, and what protocol is required to get it.

This may seem like a fine distinction, and it is. The reference you use (`window.location` object or `document.URL` property) depends on what you are trying to accomplish specifically with the script. If the script is changing the content of a window by loading a new URL, you have no choice but to assign a value to the `window.location` object. Similarly, if the script is concerned with the component parts of a URL, the properties of the location object provide the simplest avenue to that information. To retrieve the URL of a document in string form (whether it is in the current window or in another frame), you can use either the `document.URL` property or the `window.location.href` property.

Example

HTML documents in Listing 16-7 through 16-9 create a test lab that enables you to experiment with viewing the `document.URL` property for different windows and frames in a multiframe environment. Results are displayed in a table, with an additional listing of the `document.title` property to help you identify documents being referred to. The same security restrictions that apply to retrieving window.location object properties also apply to retrieving the document.URL property from another window or frame.

Listing 16-7: **Frameset for document.URL Property Reader**

```
<HTML>
<HEAD>
<TITLE>document.URL Reader</TITLE>
</HEAD>
<FRAMESET ROWS="60%,40%">
        <FRAME NAME="Frame1" SRC="lst16-09.htm">
        <FRAME NAME="Frame2" SRC="lst16-08.htm">
</FRAMESET>
</HTML>
```

Listing 16-8: **document.URL Property Reader**

```
<HTML>
<HEAD>
<TITLE>URL Property Reader</TITLE>
<SCRIPT LANGUAGE="JavaScript1.1">
function fillTopFrame() {
        newURL=prompt("Enter the URL of a document to show in the top
frame:","")
        if (newURL != null && newURL != "") {
        top.frames[0].location = newURL
        }
}

function showLoc(form,item) {
        var windName = item.value
        var theRef = windName + ".document"
        form.dLoc.value = unescape(eval(theRef + ".URL"))
        form.dTitle.value = unescape(eval(theRef + ".title"))
}
</SCRIPT>
</HEAD>

<BODY>
Click the "Open URL" button to enter the location of an HTML document
to display in the upper frame of this window.
<FORM>
<INPUT TYPE="button" NAME="opener" VALUE="Open URL..."
onClick="fillTopFrame()">
</FORM>
<HR>
<FORM>
Select a window or frame to view each document property values.<P>
```

(continued)

Listing 16-8 *(continued)*

```
<INPUT TYPE="radio" NAME="whichFrame" VALUE="parent"
onClick="showLoc(this.form,this)">Parent window
<INPUT TYPE="radio" NAME="whichFrame" VALUE="top.frames[0]"
onClick="showLoc(this.form,this)">Upper frame
<INPUT TYPE="radio" NAME="whichFrame" VALUE="top.frames[1]"
onClick="showLoc(this.form,this)">This frame<P>
<TABLE BORDER=2>
<TR><TD ALIGN=RIGHT>document.URL:</TD>
<TD><TEXTAREA NAME="dLoc" ROWS=3 COLS=30
WRAP="soft"></TEXTAREA></TD></TR>

<TR><TD ALIGN=RIGHT>document.title:</TD>
<TD><TEXTAREA NAME="dTitle" ROWS=3 COLS=30
WRAP="soft"></TEXTAREA></TD></TR>
</TABLE>
</FORM>
</BODY>
</HTML>
```

Listing 16-9: **Placeholder for Listing 16-7**

```
<HTML>
<HEAD>
<TITLE>Opening Placeholder</TITLE>
</HEAD>
<BODY>
Initial place holder. Experiment with other URLs for this frame (see
below).
</BODY>
</HTML>
```

Related Items: location object; `location.href` property.

referrer

Value: String   **Gettable:** Yes   **Settable:** No

	Nav2	Nav3	Nav4	IE3/J1	IE3/J2	IE4/J3
Compatibility	✔	✔	✔	✔	✔	✔

When a link from one document leads to another, the second document can, under JavaScript control, reveal the URL of the document containing the link. The `document.referrer` property contains a string of that URL. This feature can be a useful tool for customizing the content of pages based on the previous location the user was visiting within your site. A referrer contains a value only when the user reaches the current page via a link. Any other method of navigation (such as through the history or by manually entering a URL) sets this property to an empty string.

Note

The document.referrer property is broken in Windows versions of Internet Explorer 3 and Internet Explorer 4. In the Windows version, the current document's URL is given as the referrer; the proper value is returned in the Macintosh versions.

Example

This demonstration requires two documents. The first document, in Listing 16-10, simply contains one line of text as a link to the second document. In the second document (Listing 16-11), a script verifies the document from which the user came via a link. If the script knows about that link, it displays a message relevant to the experience the user had at the first document. Also try opening Listing 16-11 from the Open File command in the File menu to see how the script won't recognize the referrer.

Listing 16-10: **A Source Document**

```
<HTML>
<HEAD>
<TITLE>document.referrer Property 1</TITLE>
</HEAD>

<BODY>
<H1><A HREF="lst16-11.htm">Visit my sister document</A>
</BODY>
</HTML>
```

Listing 16-11: **Checking document.referrer**

```
<HTML>
<HEAD>
<TITLE>document.referrer Property 2</TITLE>
</HEAD>

<BODY><H1>
<SCRIPT LANGUAGE="JavaScript">
if(document.referrer.length > 0 && document.referrer.indexOf("16-
10.htm") != -1){
        document.write("How is my brother document?")
        } else {
        document.write("Hello, and thank you for stopping by.")
        }
</SCRIPT>
</H1></BODY>
</HTML>
```

Related Items: link object.

title

Value: String   **Gettable:** Yes   **Settable:** No

	Nav2	Nav3	Nav4	IE3/J1	IE3/J2	IE4/J3
Compatibility	✔	✔	✔	✔	✔	✔

A document's title is the text that appears between the <TITLE>...</TITLE> tag pair in an HTML document's Head portion. The title usually appears in the title bar of the browser window in a single-frame presentation. Only the title of the topmost framesetting document appears as the title of a multiframe window. Even so, the title property for an individual document appearing in a frame is available via scripting. For example, if two frames are available (UpperFrame and LowerFrame), a script in the document occupying the LowerFrame frame could reference the title property of the other frame's document like this:

```
parent.UpperFrame.document.title
```

This property cannot be set by a script except when constructing an entire HTML document via script, including the <TITLE> tags.

UNIX versions of Navigator 2 fail to return the document.title property value. Also, in Navigator 4 for the Macintosh, if a script creates the content of another frame, the document.title property for that dynamically written frame returns the file name of the script that wrote the HTML, even when it writes a valid <TITLE> tag set.

Example

See Listings 16-7 through 16-9 for examples of retrieving the document.title property from a multiframe window.

Related Items: history object.

Methods

captureEvents(*eventTypeList*)

Returns: Nothing.

	Nav2	Nav3	Nav4	IE3/J1	IE3/J2	IE4/J3
Compatibility			✔			

In Navigator 4, an event filters down from the window object, through the document object, and eventually reaches its target. For example, if you click a button, the click event first reaches the window object; then it goes to the document object; if the button is defined within a layer, the event also filters through that layer; eventually (in a split second) it reaches the button, where an onClick= event handler is ready to act on that click.

The Netscape mechanism allows window, document, and layer objects to intercept events and process them prior to reaching their intended targets (or preventing them from reaching their destinations entirely). But for an outer container to grab an event, your script must instruct it to capture the type of event your application is interested in preprocessing. If you want the document object to intercept all events of a particular type, use the document.captureEvents() method to turn that facility on.

The document.captureEvents() method takes one or more event types as parameters. An event type is a constant value built inside Navigator 4's event object. One event type exists for every kind of event handler you see in all of Navigator 4's document objects. The syntax is the event object name (Event) and the event name in all uppercase letters. For example, if you want the document to intercept all click events, the statement is

```
document.captureEvents(Event.CLICK)
```

For multiple events, add them as parameters, separated by the pipe (|) character:

```
document.captureEvents(Event.MOUSEDOWN | Event.KEYPRESS)
```

Once an event type is captured by the document object, it must have a function ready to deal with the event. For example, perhaps the function looks through all Event.MOUSEDOWN events and looks to see if the right mouse button was the one that triggered the event and what form element (if any) is the intended target. The goal is to perhaps display a pop-up menu (as a separate layer) for a right-click. If the click comes from the left mouse button, then the event is routed to its intended target.

To associate a function with a particular event type captured by a document object, assign a function to the event. For example, to assign a custom doClickEvent() function to click events captured by the window object, use the following statement:

```
document.onclick=doClickEvent
```

Notice that the function name is assigned only as a reference name, not like an event handler within a tag. The function, itself, is like any function, but it has the added benefit of automatically receiving the event object as a parameter. To turn off event capture for one or more event types, use the document.releaseEvent() method. See Chapter 33 for details of working with events in this manner.

Example

See the example for the window.captureEvents() method in Chapter 14 (Listing 14-22) to see how to capture events on their way to other objects. You can substitute the document reference for the window reference in that example to see how the document version of the method works just like the window version. If you understand the mechanism for windows, you understand it for documents. The same is true for the other event methods.

Related Items: `document.handleEvent()` method; `document.releaseEvents()` method; `document.routeEvent()` method; parallel window object event methods.

clear()

Returns: Nothing.

	Nav2	Nav3	Nav4	IE3/J1	IE3/J2	IE4/J3
Compatibility	✔	✔	✔	✔	✔	✔

Clearing a document and closing a document are two quite different actions. As described in the following `document.close()` section, closing deals with the layout stream previously opened to a document. Frequently, the stream must be closed before all data specified in the HTML of the document appears correctly.

Clearing a document, on the other hand, removes from the browser whatever HTML is written to the document — as well as the object model for that document. You do not have to clear a document prior to opening or writing to another one (JavaScript clears the old one for you). In fact, the `document.clear()` method does not work correctly, even in Navigator 3, and can cause any number of errors or crash problems in early browsers. To get the same result as the one that you expect to get from `document.clear()`, I recommend loading a blank HTML document (that is, one with the simplest tags and no visible content).

Related Items: `document.close()` method; `document.write()` method; `document.writeln()` method.

close()

Returns: Nothing.

	Nav2	Nav3	Nav4	IE3/J1	IE3/J2	IE4/J3
Compatibility	✔	✔	✔	✔	✔	✔

Whenever a layout stream is opened to a window via the `document.open()` method or either of the document writing methods (which also open the layout stream), you must close the stream once the document has been written. This causes the `Layout:Complete` and `Document:Done` messages to appear in the status line (although you may experience some bugs in the status message on some platforms). The closing step is very important to prepare the window for the next potential round of replenishment with new script-assembled HTML. If you don't close the window, subsequent writing is appended to the bottom of it.

Some or all of the data specified for the window won't display properly until you invoke the `document.close()` method, especially when images are being drawn as part of the document stream. A common symptom is the momentary appearance and then disappearance of the document parts. If you see such behavior, look for a missing `document.close()` method after the last `document.write()` method.

Example

Before you experiment with this method, be sure you understand the `document.write()` method described later in this chapter. After that, make a separate set of the three documents for that method's example (Listing 16-13 through 16-15 in a different directory or folder). In the `takePulse()` function listing, comment out both the `document.open()` and `document.close()` statements, as shown here:

```
msg += "<P>Make it a great day!</BODY></HTML>"
//parent.frames[1].document.open()
parent.frames[1].document.write(msg)
//parent.frames[1].document.close()
```

Now try the pages on your browser. You will see that each click of the upper button appends text to the bottom frame, without first removing the previous text. The reason is that the previous layout stream was never closed. The document thinks that you're still writing to it. Also, without properly closing the stream, the last line of text may not appear in the most recently written batch.

Related Items: `document.open()` method; `document.clear()` method; `document.write()` method; `document.writeln()` method.

getSelection()

Returns: String.

	Nav2	Nav3	Nav4	IE3/J1	IE3/J2	IE4/J3
Compatibility			✔			

It's likely that many Web browser users aren't aware that they can select and copy body text in a document for pasting into other application documents. Even so, Navigator 4 offers a scripted way of capturing the text selected by a user in a page. The `document.getSelection()` method returns the string of text selected by the user. If nothing is selected, an empty string is the result. Returned values consist only of the visible text on the page, and not the underlying HTML or style of the text.

Example

The document in Listing 16-12 combines document event capture and the `getSelection()` method to display in a textarea object the content of any selection you make from the text on the page.

Listing 16-12: **Text Selection**

```
<HTML>
<HEAD>
<TITLE>URL Property Reader</TITLE>
<SCRIPT LANGUAGE="JavaScript1.2">
function showSelection() {
        document.forms[0].selectedText.value = document.getSelection()
}
document.captureEvents(Event.MOUSEUP)
document.onmouseup = showSelection
</SCRIPT>
</HEAD>

<BODY>
<B>Select some text and see how JavaScript can capture the
selection:</B>
<HR>
<H2>ARTICLE I</H2>
<P>
Congress shall make no law respecting an establishment of religion, or
prohibiting the free exercise thereof; or abridging the freedom of
speech, or of the press; or the right of the people peaceably to
assemble, and to petition the government for a redress of grievances.
</P>
</HR>
<FORM>
<TEXTAREA NAME="selectedText" ROWS=3 COLS=40 WRAP="virtual"></TEXTAREA>
</FORM>
</BODY>
</HTML>
```

Related Items: None.

handleEvent(*event*)

Returns: Nothing.

	Nav2	Nav3	Nav4	IE3/J1	IE3/J2	IE4/J3
Compatibility			✔			

When you explicitly capture events in the window, document, or layer object (by invoking the captureEvents() method for that object), you can control where the events go after their initial capture. To let an event continue to its original target (for example, a button that was clicked by a user), you use the routeEvent() method. But if you want to redirect an event (or class of events) to a particular event handler elsewhere in the document, use the `handleEvent()` method.

See the discussion of the `handleEvent()` method for the window object in Chapter 14. The behavior of the `handleEvent()` method for all objects is the same.

Related Items: `document.captureEvents()` method; `document.releaseEvents()` method; `document.routeEvent()` method; event object.

open(["*mimeType*"] [, *replace*])

Returns: Nothing.

	Nav2	Nav3	Nav4	IE3/J1	IE3/J2	IE4/J3
Compatibility	✔	✔	✔	(✔)	(✔)	(✔)

Opening a document is different from opening a window. In the case of a window, you're creating a new object, both on the screen and in the browser's memory. Opening a document, on the other hand, tells the browser to get ready to accept some data for display in the window named or implied in the reference to the `document.open()` method. (For example, `parent.frames[1].document. open()` may refer to a different frame in a frameset, whereas `document.open()` implies the current window or frame.) Therefore, the method name may mislead newcomers because the `document.open()` method has nothing to do with loading documents from the Web server or hard disk. Rather, this method is a prelude to sending data to a window via the `document.write()` or `document.writeln()` methods. In a sense, the `document.open()` method merely opens a door; the other methods send the data, and the `document.close()` method closes that door once the page's data has been sent in full.

The `document.open()` method is optional because a `document.write()` method that attempts to write to a closed document automatically clears the old document and opens a new one. Whether or not you use the `document.open()` method, be sure to use the `document.close()` method after all the writing has taken place.

An optional parameter to the `document.open()` method lets you specify the nature of the data being sent to the window. A MIME (Multipurpose Internet Mail Extension) type is a specification for transferring and representing multimedia data on the Internet (originally for mail transmission, but now applicable to all Internet data exchanges). You've seen MIME depictions in the list of helper applications in your browser's preferences settings. A MIME type is represented by a pair of data type names separated by a slash (such as `text/html` and `image/gif`). When you specify a MIME type as a parameter to the `document.open()` method, you're instructing the browser about the kind of data it is about to receive, so it knows how to render the data. The values that JavaScript accepts are

```
text/html
text/plain
image/gif
image/jpeg
image/xbm
plugIn
```

If you omit the parameter, JavaScript assumes the most popular type, `text/html` — the kind of data you typically assemble in a script prior to writing to the window. The `text/html` type includes any images that the HTML references. Specifying any of the image types means that you have the raw binary representation of the image you want to appear in the new document — possible, but unlikely.

Another possibility is to direct the output of a `write()` method to a Netscape plug-in. For the *mimeType* parameter, specify the plug-in's MIME type (for example, `application/x-director` for Shockwave). Again, the data you write to a plug-in must be in a form that it knows how to handle. The same mechanism also works for writing data directly to a helper application.

Note

Internet Explorer 3 does not accept any parameters for the `document.open()` method. Internet Explorer 4 accepts only the `text/html` MIME type.

Navigator 4 includes a second, optional parameter to the method: `replace`. This parameter does for the `document.open()` method what the `replace()` method does for the location object. For `document.open()`, it means that the new document you are about to write replaces the previous document in the window or frame from being recorded to that window or frame's history.

Finally, be aware that only Navigator 3 or later enables you to use `document.open()` in the same window or frame as the one containing the script that invokes the `document.open()` method. Attempting to reopen the script's own document with this method in Navigator 2 usually leads to a crash of the browser.

Example

You can see an example of where the `document.open()` method fits in the scheme of dynamically creating content for another frame in the discussion of the `document.write()` method, later in this chapter.

Related Items: `document.close()` method; `document.clear()` method; `document.write()` method; `document.writeln()` method.

releaseEvents(*eventTypeList*)

Returns: Nothing.

	Nav2	Nav3	Nav4	IE3/J1	IE3/J2	IE4/J3
Compatibility			✔			

If your scripts have enabled event capture for the document object (or window or layer, for that matter), you can turn off that capture with the `releaseEvents()` method. This does not inhibit events from reaching their intended target. In fact, by releasing capture from a higher object, released events don't bother stopping at those higher objects anymore.

See the discussion of the `releaseEvents()` method for the window object in Chapter 14. The behavior of the `releaseEvents()` method for all objects is the same.

Related Items: `document.captureEvents()` method; `document.routeEvent()` method.

routeEvent(event)

Returns: Nothing.

	Nav2	Nav3	Nav4	IE3/J1	IE3/J2	IE4/J3
Compatibility			✔			

If you turn on event capturing in the window, document, or layer object (via their respective captureEvents() methods), the event handler you assign to those events really captures those events, preventing them from ever reaching their intended targets. For some page designs this is intentional, for it allows the higher-level object to handle all events of a particular type. But if your goal is to perform some preprocessing of events before they reach their destination, you need a way to pass that event along its regular path. That's what the routeEvent() method is for.

See the discussion of the routeEvent () method for the window object in Chapter 14. The behavior of the routeEvent () method for all objects is the same.

```
write("string1" [,"string2" ...
[, "stringn"]])
writeln("string1" [,"string2" ...
[, "stringn"]])
```

Returns: Boolean true if successful.

	Nav2	Nav3	Nav4	IE3/J1	IE3/J2	IE4/J3
Compatibility	✔	✔	✔	✔	✔	✔

Both of these methods send text to a document for display in its window. The only difference between the two methods is that document.writeln() appends a carriage return to the end of the string it sends to the document (but you must still write a <BR> to insert a line break).

A common, incorrect conclusion that many JavaScript newcomers make is that these methods enable a script to modify the contents of an existing document. This is not true. Once a document has loaded into a window (or frame), the only text that you can modify without reloading or rewriting the entire page is the content of text and textarea objects (the exception to this is the manner in which Internet Explorer 4's extended object model allows text and HTML substitutions after document loading). In fact, because of bugs on some versions of Navigator 2, attempting to write to an existing document may cause the browser to crash. The behavior was much improved in Navigator 3, and I have more to say about that in a moment.

The two safest ways to use the `document.write()` and `document.writeln()` methods are to

✦ Embed a script in an HTML document to write some or all of the page's content

✦ Send HTML code to either a new window or to a separate frame in a multiframe window

For the first case, you essentially interlace script segments within your HTML. The scripts run as the document loads, writing whatever scripted HTML content you like. This task is exactly what you did in script1.htm in Chapter 3.

In the latter case, a script can gather input from the user in one frame and then algorithmically determine the layout and content destined for another frame. The script assembles the HTML code for the other frame as a string variable (including all necessary HTML tags). Before the script can write anything to the frame, it can optionally open the layout stream (to close the current document in that frame) with the `parent.frameName.document.open()` method. In the next step, a `parent.frameName.document.write()` method pours the entire string into the other frame. Finally, a `parent.frameName.document.close()` method ensures that the total data stream is written to the window. Such a frame looks just the same as if it were created by a source document on the server rather than on the fly in memory. The document object of that window or frame is a full citizen as a JavaScript document object. You can, therefore, even include scripts as part of the HTML specification for one of these temporary HTML pages.

Starting with Navigator 3 and Internet Explorer 3, you can write to the current window, but you should be prepared for the consequences. Once an HTML document (containing the script that is going to write) is loaded, the page's incoming stream has already closed. If you then attempt to apply a series of `document.write()` statements, the first `document.write()` method completely removes all vestiges of the original document. That includes all of its objects and scripted variable values. Therefore, if you try to assemble a new page with a series of `document.write()` statements, the parameters to the method cannot include any object references or variables from the original document: They will be gone before the second `document.write()` statement executes. To get around this potential problem, assemble the content for the new screenful of content as one variable value and then pass that variable as the parameter to a single `document.write()` statement. Also be sure to include a `document.close()` statement in the next line of script.

Assembling HTML in a script to be written via the `document.write()` method often requires skill in concatenating string values and nesting strings. A number of JavaScript string object shortcuts facilitate the formatting of text with HTML tags (see Chapter 27 for details).

Whether your script should send lots of small strings via multiple `document.write()` methods or assemble a larger string to be sent via one `document.write()` method depends partly on the situation (especially when writing to the current document in Navigator 3) and partly on style. From a performance standpoint, a fairly standard procedure is to do more preliminary work in memory and place as few I/O (input/output) calls as possible. On the other hand, it's easier to make a difficult-to-track mistake in string concatenation when you assemble longer strings. My personal preference is to assemble longer strings, but you should use the system that's most comfortable for you.

You may see another little-known way of passing parameters to these methods. Instead of concatenating string values with the plus operator, you can also bring string values together by separating them with commas. For example, the following two statements produce the same results:

```
document.write("Today is " + new Date())
document.write("Today is ",new Date())
```

Neither form is better than the other, so use the one that feels more comfortable to your existing programming style.

Using the `document.open()`, `document.write()`, and `document.close()` methods to display images in a document requires some small extra steps. First, any URL assignments you write via `document.write()` must be complete (not relative) URL references (especially for users of Navigator 2). Accomplishing this reliably on your HTML authoring computer and the Web server may require you to algorithmically establish the pathname to the current document on the server (see Listing 15-5 in the preceding chapter).

The other image trick is to be sure to specify `HEIGHT` and `WIDTH` attributes for every image, scripted or otherwise. Navigator 2 requires these attributes, and document-rendering performance will be improved on all platforms, because the values help the browser lay out elements even before their details are loaded.

In addition to the `document.write()` example that follows (see Listings 16-13, 16-14, and 16-15), you can find fuller implementations that use this method to assemble images and bar charts in the bonus applications on the CD-ROM. Because you can assemble any valid HTML as a string to be written to a window or frame, a customized, on-the-fly document can be as elaborate as the most complex HTML document you can imagine.

Example

The example in Listings 16-13 through 16-15 demonstrates several important points about using the `document.write()` or `document.writeln()` methods for writing to another frame. First is the fact that you can write any HTML code to a frame, and the browser accepts it as if the source code came from an HTML file somewhere. In the example, I assemble a complete HTML document, including basic HTML tags for completeness.

Listing 16-13: **Frameset for document.write() Example**

```
<HTML>
<HEAD>
<TITLE>Writin' to the doc</TITLE>
</HEAD>
<FRAMESET ROWS="50%,50%">
        <FRAME NAME="Frame1" SRC="lst16-14.htm">
        <FRAME NAME="Frame2" SRC="lst16-15.htm">
</FRAMESET>
</HTML>
```

Listing 16-14: **document.write() Example**

```
<HTML>
<HEAD>
<TITLE>Document Write Controller</TITLE>
<SCRIPT LANGUAGE="JavaScript">
function takePulse(form) {
        var msg = "<HTML><HEAD><TITLE>On The Fly with " +
form.yourName.value + "</TITLE></HEAD>"
        msg += "<BODY BGCOLOR='salmon'><H1>Good Day " +
form.yourName.value + "!</H1><HR>"
        for (var i = 0; i < form.how.length; i++) {
            if (form.how[i].checked) {
                msg += form.how[i].value
                break
            }
        }
        msg += "<P>Make it a great day!</BODY></HTML>"
        parent.Frame2.document.open()
        parent.Frame2.document.write(msg)
        parent.Frame2.document.close()
}
function getTitle() {
        alert("Lower frame document.title is now:" +
parent.Frame2.document.title)
}
</SCRIPT>
</HEAD>

<BODY>
Fill in a name, and select how that person feels today. Then click
"Write To Below" to see the results in the bottom frame.
<FORM>
Enter your first name:<INPUT TYPE="text" NAME="yourName"
VALUE="Dave"><P>
How are you today? <INPUT TYPE="radio" NAME="how" VALUE="I hope that
feeling continues forever." CHECKED>Swell
<INPUT TYPE="radio" NAME="how" VALUE="You may be on your way to
feeling Swell">Pretty Good
<INPUT TYPE="radio" NAME="how" VALUE="Things can only get better from
here.">So-So<P>
<INPUT TYPE="button" NAME="enter" VALUE="Write To Below"
onClick="takePulse(this.form)">
<HR>
<INPUT TYPE="button" NAME="peek" VALUE="Check Lower Frame Title"
onClick="getTitle()">
</BODY>
</HTML>
```

Listing 16-15: Placeholder for Listing 16-13

```
<HTML>
<HEAD>
<TITLE>Placeholder</TITLE>
<BODY>
</BODY>
</HTML>
```

Figure 16-2 shows an example of the frame written by the script.

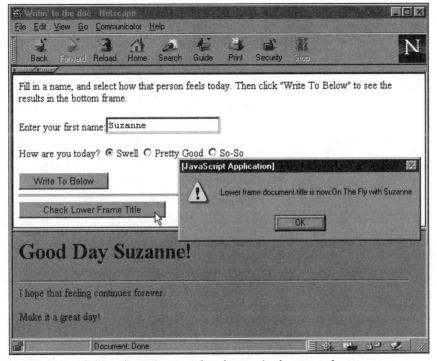

Figure 16-2: Clicking the Write To Below button in the upper frame causes a script to assemble and write HTML for the bottom frame.

A second point to note is that this example customizes the content of the document based on user input. This makes the experience of working with your Web page feel far more interactive to the user — yet you're doing it without any CGI programs running on the server. Although this is a pretty basic computer programming kind of interaction, this capability is relatively new to Web page authoring.

The third point I want to bring home is that the document created in the separate frame by the document.write() method is a real JavaScript document object. In this example, for instance, the <TITLE> tag of the written document changes if you redraw the lower frame after changing the entry of the name field in the upper frame. If you click the lower button after updating the bottom frame, you see that the `document.title` property has, indeed, changed to reflect the `<TITLE>` tag written to the browser in the course of displaying the frame's page (except in Macintosh Navigator 4, which exhibits a bug for this property in a dynamically written document). The fact that you can artificially create full-fledged, JavaScript document objects on the fly represents one of the most important powers of serverless CGI scripting (for information delivery to the user) with JavaScript. You have much to take advantage of here if your imagination is up to the task. To print or view the source of a document written with JavaScript, you must use Navigator 3 or later.

Notice that with Navigator 3, you could easily modify Listing 16-14 to write the results to the same frame as the document containing the field and buttons. Instead of specifying the lower frame

```
parent.frames[1].document.open()
parent.frames[1].document.write(msg)
parent.frames[1].document.close()
```

the code simply could have used

```
document.open()
document.write(msg)
document.close()
```

This code would replace the form document with the results and not require any frames in the first place. Because the code assembles all of the content for the new document into one variable value, that data survives the one `document.write()` method.

The frameset document (Listing 16-13) creates a blank frame by loading a blank document (Listing 16-15). An alternative I highly recommend is to have the framesetting document fill the frame with a blank document of its own creation. See "Blank Frames" in Chapter 14 for further details about this technique for Navigator 3 and later.

Related Items: `document.open()`; `document.close()`; `document.clear()`.

✦   ✦   ✦

Link and Anchor Objects

The Web was based on the notion that the world's information could be strung together by way of the *hyperlink* — the clickable hunk of text or image that navigates an inquisitive reader to a further explanation or related material. Of all the document objects you work with in JavaScript, the link is the one that makes that connection. Anchors also provide guideposts to specific locations within documents.

As scriptable objects, links and anchors are comparatively simple devices. But this simplicity belies their significance in the entire scheme of the Web. And under script control, links can be far more powerful than mere tethers to locations on the Web.

Link Object

Properties	Methods	Event Handlers
target	(None)	onClick=
text		onDblClick=
x		onMouseDown=
y		onMouseOut=
[location object properties]		onMouseOver=
		onMouseUp=

Syntax

Creating a link object:

```
<A HREF="locationOrURL"
     [NAME="anchorName"]
     [TARGET="windowName"]
     [onClick="handlerTextOrFunction"]
     [onDblClick="handlerTextOrFunction"]
     [onMouseDown="handlerTextOrFunction"]
```

```
[onMouseOut="handlerTextOrFunction"]
[onMouseOver="handlerTextOrFunction"]
[onMouseUp="handlerTextOrFunction"]>
linkDisplayTextOrImage
</A>
```

Accessing link object properties:

```
[window.] document.links[index].property
```

About this object

JavaScript treats an HTML document link as a distinct object type. When a document loads, the browser creates and maintains an internal list (in an array) of all links defined in the document.

When working with a link object in your scripts, the JavaScript object world begins to wrap around itself in a way. Despite all the attributes that define a link, JavaScript regards a link as the same as a location object (Chapter 15). In other words, if you need to refer to a link, you can access the same properties of that link the same way you can for any location object (such as href, host, hash, pathname, and so on). This convenience lets your scripts treat all URL-style data the same way.

Defining a link for JavaScript is the same as defining one for straight HTML — with the addition of six possible mouse-related event handlers. In a multiframe or multiwindow environment, it's important to specify the TARGET= attribute with the name of the frame or window in which the content at the URL is to appear. If you don't specify another frame, the browser replaces the frame that contains the link with the new page. Speaking of the TARGET attribute, don't forget the shortcut window references: _top, _parent, _self, and _blank.

As you design your links, consider building onMouseOver= and onMouseOut= event handlers into your link definitions. The most common application for these event handlers is as a means of adjusting the window.status property or swapping images. Thus, as a user rolls the mouse pointer atop a link, a descriptive label (perhaps more detailed or friendly than what the link text or image may indicate) appears in the status line at the bottom of the window. Whether a user notices the change down there is another issue, so don't rely on the status line as a medium for mission-critical communication. Image swaps, however, are more dramatic, letting a user receive visual feedback that the mouse pointer is atop a particular button image. In Navigator 4 and Internet Explorer 4, you can even swap the image when the user presses the mouse button atop the link.

For those times when you want a click of the link (whether the link consists of text or an image) to initiate an action without actually navigating to another URL, you can use a special technique to direct the URL to a JavaScript function. The URL javascript:functionName() is a valid location parameter for the HREF attribute (and not just in the link object). Using the javascript: URL to call a function is also one way you can modify the content of more than one frame at a time. In the function, set the location object of each frame to the desired document.

If you don't want the link to do anything other than change the statusbar in the onMouseOver= event handler, define an empty function and set the URL to that empty JavaScript function (such as `HREF="javascript:doNothing()"`). Starting with Navigator 3, you can also add a special `void` operator that guarantees that the function being called does not trigger any true linking action (`HREF="javascript: void someFunction()"`). Specifying an empty string for the `HREF` attribute yields an ftp-like file listing for the client computer — an undesirable artifact. Don't forget, too, that if the URL leads to a type of file that initiates a browser helper application (for example, to play a RealAudio sound file), then the helper app or plug-in loads and plays without changing the page in the browser window.

One additional technique allows a single link tag to operate for both scriptable and nonscriptable browsers (Navigator 3 and up; Internet Explorer 4). For nonscriptable browsers, establish a genuine URL to navigate from the link. Then make sure that the link's `onClick=` event handler evaluates to return false. At click time, a scriptable browser executes the event handler and ignores the `HREF` attribute; a nonscriptable browser ignores the event handler and follows the link. More about this in the event handler discussions for this object later in this chapter.

If you don't specify an `HREF` attribute in a link tag, the definition becomes an anchor object rather than a link object. The optional `NAME` attribute enables the link object to behave like an anchor object, thus enabling other links to navigate directly to the link.

Properties

target

Value: String   **Gettable:** Yes   **Settable:** No

	Nav2	Nav3	Nav4	IE3/J1	IE3/J2	IE4/J3
Compatibility	✔	✔	✔	✔	✔	✔

The primary property of the link object is the *target*. This value reflects the window name supplied to the `TARGET` attribute in the link's definition. Because link objects are stored as an array of components in a document, you can reference the `target` property of a particular link only via an indexed link reference.

You can temporarily change the target for a link. But, as with most transient object properties, the setting does not survive soft reloads. Rather than altering the target this way, a safer method is to force the target change by letting the `HREF` attribute call a `javascript:functionName()` URL, where the function assigns a document to the desired `window.location`. If you have done extensive HTML authoring before, you will find it hard to break the habit of relying on the `TARGET` attribute.

Example

```
windowName = document.links[3].target
```

Related Items: `document.links` property; anchor object.

text

Value: String   **Gettable:** Yes   **Settable:** No

	Nav2	Nav3	Nav4	IE3/J1	IE3/J2	IE4/J3
Compatibility			✔			

Between the start and end tags for a link goes the text (or image) that is highlighted in the distinguishing link color of the document. Navigator 4 lets you extract that text with the `link.text` property. This property is read-only. Internet Explorer 4 employs a different model and syntax for getting and setting the text and HTML for an object like the link. The two syntaxes are not compatible.

Note

This property was not implemented in releases of Navigator 4 prior to Version 4.02.

Related Items: None.

x
y

Value: Integer   **Gettable:** Yes   **Settable:** No

	Nav2	Nav3	Nav4	IE3/J1	IE3/J2	IE4/J3
Compatibility			✔			

Your Navigator 4 script can retrieve the x and y coordinates of a link object (the top-left corner of the rectangular space occupied by the linked text or image) via the `link.x` and `link.y` properties. These properties are read-only, but you can use Dynamic HTML to change the location of a link if you like (see Chapters 41 to 43). Even without Dynamic HTML, you can use the information from these properties to help scroll a document to a precise position (with the `window.scrollTo()` method) as a navigational aid in your page.

Example

Due to the different ways each operating system platform renders pages and the different sizes of browser windows, you can dynamically locate the position of a link given the current client conditions. For example, if you want to scroll the document so the link is a few pixels below the top of the window, you could use a statement such as this:

```
window.scrollTo(document.links[0].x, (document.links[0].y - 3))
```

Related Items: `window.scrollTo()` method.

Event handlers

`onClick=`
`onDblClick=`

	Nav2	Nav3	Nav4	IE3/J1	IE3/J2	IE4/J3
Compatibility	(✔)	(✔)	(✔)	(✔)	(✔)	✔

By and large, the `HREF` attribute determines the action that a link makes when a user clicks it — which is generally a navigational action. But if you need to execute a script before navigating to a specific link (or to change the contents of more than one frame), you can include an `onClick=` and/or `onDblClick=` event handler in that link's definition. Any statements or functions called by either click event handler execute before any navigation takes place. The `onClick=` event handler is in all versions of all browsers; `onDblClick=` is available only in Navigator 4 (but, alas, not the Macintosh version) and Internet Explorer 4.

You can script entirely different actions for the `onClick=` and `onDblClick=` event handlers, but you must be aware of the interaction between the two events. Moreover, interaction between the single- and double-click events is different in Navigator 4 and Internet Explorer 4. In Navigator 4, each of the two clicks of a dblClick event triggers a single click event; in Internet Explorer 4, only the first of the two clicks registers a click event. In neither case is a single click event cancelled automatically or ignored when the dblClick event occurs. Therefore, if you intend to have single- and double-clicks on a link fire entirely different processes, it is up to your script to delay the action of the single-click until it knows that a double-click has occurred.

Before you get carried away with implementing different actions for single- and double-clicks on the same link, take a cue from the big GUI boys who design our desktops. Many users have difficulty accurately performing a double-click action, based on their computer's mouse control panel setting. Moreover, some users may not be aware that double-clicking a link offers anything, since generic links are all single-click beasts. Therefore, if you require a double-click for a special action, make sure that the single-click action (if any) is mild enough such that the user can see that the desired double-click action did not take place and can try again. On the desktop, double-clicking a document icon opens the file and application, but single-clicking simply selects or highlights the object on the desktop — a pair of complementary actions that works pretty well.

Both click event handlers in a link observe special behavior that enables your scripts to prevent the link from completing its navigation job in Navigator 3 or later and Internet Explorer 4. For example, you may want your scripts to perform some data-entry validation before navigating to another page. If some field isn't filled out correctly, you can alert the user about it and abort the link action at the same time. To make this validation work, the last statement of the handler or the handler itself must evaluate to the word `return` and either `true` or `false`. If `true`, then the navigation completes; if `false`, then all action ceases.

Example

In Listing 17-1, I present a click laboratory that lets you see the behavior of onClick= and onDblClick= event handlers in links. The first link has only an onClick= event handler; the second one has only an onDblClick= event handler.

Things get more interesting in the third link, which has both. You will see from the readout of events in the lab output fields that a double-click user action results in a total of three events firing: two clicks and one dblClick. If you need to segregate single- from double-click user actions, the functions called by the fourth link's event handlers will interest you. They delay the action of the first single-click slightly and then cancel the first click and ignore the second click if a double-click has occurred. All HREF attributes for these links are set to a javascript: URL that goes nowhere.

Listing 17-1: **Single- and Double-Clicks**

```
<HTML>
<HEAD>
<TITLE>Clicking on Links</TITLE>
<SCRIPT LANGUAGE="JavaScript">
var timeoutID
var isDouble = false
function fillSingle() {
        document.lab.singleOut.value = document.lab.singleOut.value +
"Single Click   "
}

function fillDouble() {
        document.lab.doubleOut.value = document.lab.doubleOut.value +
"Double Click   "
}

function smartSingle() {
        clearTimeout(timeoutID)
        if (!isDouble) {
            timeoutID = setTimeout("fillSingle()",300)
        }
        isDouble = false
}

function smartDouble() {
        isDouble = true
        fillDouble()
}</SCRIPT>
</HEAD>
<BODY>
Click <A HREF="javascript:void(0)" onClick="fillSingle()">HERE</A> to
trigger an onClick= event handler.<BR>
Click <A HREF="javascript:void(0)" onDblClick="fillDouble()">HERE</A> to
trigger an onDblClick= event handler.<P>
```

```
Click and Double-Click <A HREF="javascript:void(0)"
onClick="fillSingle()" onDblClick="fillDouble()">HERE</A> to trigger a
dumb version of both event handlers.<P>
Click and Double-Click <A HREF="javascript:void(0)"
onClick="smartSingle()" onDblClick="smartDouble()">HERE</A> to trigger
a smart version of both event handlers.<P>
<FORM NAME="lab">
<INPUT TYPE="Reset"><BR>
<HR>
Single Click Signals:<INPUT TYPE="text" NAME="singleOut" SIZE="50"><BR>
Double Click Signals:<INPUT TYPE="text" NAME="doubleOut" SIZE="50">
</FORM>
</BODY>
</HTML>
```

The second onClick= event handler is associated with the next link. It has a fixed HREF designation, but the onClick= handler returns the Boolean value returned by the verifyMove() function. If you click the confirm dialog's Cancel button, you won't navigate at all, whereas if you click the Yes button (which supplies a true value), you go to the link as if the onClick= event handler did not exist.

onMouseDown=
onMouseUp=

	Nav2	Nav3	Nav4	IE3/J1	IE3/J2	IE4/J3
Compatibility			✔			✔

Additional mouse-related events in Navigator 4 and Internet Explorer 4 are available for links. Events for the mouse being pressed and released supplement the long-standing click event. A click event fires after a matched set of mouseDown and mouseUp events occur on the same link. If the user presses down on the link and slides the mouse pointer off the link to release the mouse button, only the mouseDown event fires on the link.

These events allow authors and designers to add more application-like behavior to images that act as action or icon buttons. If you notice the way most buttons work, the appearance of the button changes while the mouse button is down and reverts to its original style when the mouse button is released (or the cursor is dragged out of the button). These events let you emulate that behavior.

Example

To demonstrate a likely scenario of changing button images in response to rolling atop an image, pressing down on it, releasing the mouse button, and rolling away from the image, Listing 17-2 presents a pair of small navigation buttons (left- and right-arrow buttons). Because the image object is not part of the document object model for Navigator 2 or Internet Explorer 3 (which reports itself as being at

Navigator Version 2), the page is designed to be friendly to all browsers. The duplicate setImage() function is required to accommodate the older browsers. For a browser with an image object, images are preloaded into the browser cache as the page loads so that response to the user is instantaneous the first time the new versions of the images are called upon.

Listing 17-2: **Image Swapping on Mouse Events**

```
<HTML>
<HEAD>
<TITLE>Image Swapping with Links</TITLE>
<SCRIPT LANGUAGE="JavaScript">
function setImage() {}
</SCRIPT>

<SCRIPT LANGUAGE="JavaScript1.1">
if(parseInt(navigator.appVersion) > 2) {
        var RightNormImg = new Image(16,16)
        var RightUpImg = new Image(16,16)
        var RightDownImg = new Image(16,16)
        var LeftNormImg = new Image(16,16)
        var LeftUpImg = new Image(16,16)
        var LeftDownImg = new Image(16,16)

        RightNormImg.src = "RightNorm.gif"
        RightUpImg.src = "RightUp.gif"
        RightDownImg.src = "RightDown.gif"
        LeftNormImg.src = "LeftNorm.gif"
        LeftUpImg.src = "LeftUp.gif"
        LeftDownImg.src = "LeftDown.gif"
}
function setImage(imgName, type) {
        var imgFile = eval(imgName + type + "Img.src")
        document.images[imgName].src = imgFile
        return false
}
</SCRIPT>
</HEAD>
<BODY>
<B>Roll atop and click on the buttons to see how the link event
handlers swap images:</B><P>
<CENTER>
<A HREF="javascript:void(0)"
        onMouseOver="return setImage('Left','Up')"
        onMouseDown="return setImage('Left','Down')"
        onMouseUp="return setImage('Left','Up')"
        onMouseOut="return setImage('Left','Norm')"
>
<IMG NAME="Left" SRC="LeftNorm.gif" HEIGHT=16 WIDTH=16 BORDER=0></A>
  
<A HREF="javascript:void(0)"
        onMouseOver="return setImage('Right','Up')"
```

```
              onMouseDown="return setImage('Right','Down')"
              onMouseUp="return setImage('Right','Up')"
              onMouseOut="return setImage('Right','Norm')"
>
<IMG NAME="Right" SRC="RightNorm.gif" HEIGHT=16 WIDTH=16 BORDER=0></A>
</CENTER>
</BODY>
</HTML>
```

Related Items: `onMouseOver=` event handler; `onMouseOut=` event handler; image object.

onMouseOver=
onMouseOut=

	Nav2	Nav3	Nav4	IE3/J1	IE3/J2	IE4/J3
Compatibility	(✔)	✔	✔	(✔)	(✔)	✔

You've seen it a million times: As you drag the mouse pointer atop a link in a document, the status line at the bottom of the window shows the URL defined in the link's `HREF` attribute. For Net Freaks, URLs are like mother's milk, but for everyday folks, long URLs are more like gibberish. You can override the display of a link's URL by triggering a function with the `onMouseOver=` event handler assigned to a link.

One potentially tricky aspect of this event handler is that no matter what you ask the handler to do, whether it be a statement within the `onMouseOver=` attribute or a call to a JavaScript function, the attribute must end with a `return true` statement. Without this last statement in the `onMouseOver=` attribute, the status bar will not change.

The converse of the `onMouseOver=` event handler is `onMouseOut=`. This handler (not available in Navigator 2 or Internet Explorer 3) fires when the pointer leaves the link's rectangular region. If you use `onMouseOver=` to set the statusbar, you should return the statusbar to its default setting with an `onMouseOut=` event handler (as detailed in Chapter 14's discussion about the `window.status` and `window.defaultStatus` properties).

No conventions exist for the kind of text you put in the status line, but the text should help the user better understand the result of clicking a link. I like to put instructions or a command-like sentence in the status line. For example, for the iconic images of the outline-style table of contents (see the bonus application in Chapter 50 on the CD-ROM), the message advises the user to click to expand or collapse the nested items, depending on which icon is in place; for the text links in the outline, the message gives information about what the user will see upon clicking the link. For experienced Web surfers, displaying the URL in parentheses after the plain language message may be helpful. Web geeks remember and recognize URLs.

Note

The `onMouseOut=` event handler sometimes fails to execute in Navigator 3. This happens most often if the link is near a frame border, and the user quickly moves the mouse from the link to outside the frame.

Example

Listing 17-3 uses the Pledge of Allegiance with four links to demonstrate how to use the `onMouseOver=` and `onMouseOut=` event handlers. Notice that for each link, the handler runs a general-purpose function that sets the window's status message. The function returns a `true` value, which the event handler call evaluates to replicate the required `return true` statement needed for setting the statusbar. In one status message, I supply a URL in parentheses to let you evaluate how helpful you think it may be for users.

Listing 17-3: **Using onMouseOver= and onMouseOut=**

```
<HTML>
<HEAD>
<TITLE>Mousing Over Links</TITLE>
<SCRIPT LANGUAGE="JavaScript">
function setStatus(msg) {
      status = msg
      return true
}
// destination of all link HREFs
function emulate() {
      alert("Not going there in this demo.")
}
</SCRIPT>
</HEAD>
<BODY>
<H1>Pledge of Allegiance</H1>
<HR>
I pledge <A HREF="javascript:emulate()" onMouseOver="return
setStatus('View dictionary definition')" onMouseOut="return
setStatus('')">allegiance</A> to the <A HREF="javascript:emulate()"
onMouseOver="return setStatus('Learn about the U.S. flag
(http://lcweb.loc.gov)')" onMouseOut="return setStatus('')">flag</A> of
the <A HREF="javascript:emulate()" onMouseOver="return setStatus('View
info about the U.S. government')" onMouseOut="return
setStatus('')">United States of America</A>, and to the Republic for
which it stands, one nation <A HREF="javascript:emulate()"
onMouseOver="return setStatus('Read about the history of this phrase in
the Pledge')" onMouseOut="return setStatus('')">under God</A>,
indivisible, with liberty and justice for all.
</BODY>
</HTML>
```

The other technique demonstrated is how to use an internal location (`javascript: emulate()`) as an `HREF` attribute value for each of the links. This technique enables the link to behave like a real link (highlighting the text), but in this case, the link doesn't navigate anywhere. Instead, it invokes the `emulate()` function, defined in the document.

Anchor Object

Properties	Methods	Event Handlers
name	(None)	(None)
text		
x		
y		

Syntax

Creating an anchor object:

```
<A NAME="anchorName">
     anchorDisplayTextOrImage
</A>
```

About this object

As an HTML document loads into a JavaScript-enabled browser, the browser creates and maintains an internal list (as an array) of all the anchors defined in the document. Like link objects, you reference anchor objects according to their indexed value within the `document.anchors[index]` property. New properties in Navigator 4 (one of which is also in Internet Explorer 4) enable your scripts to examine anchors for their names and physical locations in the document.

The preceding syntax shows the simplest way of defining an anchor. You can also turn a link object into an anchor by simply adding a `NAME=` attribute to the link's definition.

Properties

name

Value: String   **Gettable:** Yes   **Settable:** No

	Nav2	Nav3	Nav4	IE3/J1	IE3/J2	IE4/J3
Compatibility			✔			✔

The name property of an anchor object is the string assigned to the NAME attribute of the anchor or link tag. This is a read-only property.

Related Items: None.

text

Value: String   **Gettable:** Yes   **Settable:** No

	Nav2	Nav3	Nav4	IE3/J1	IE3/J2	IE4/J3
Compatibility			✔			

Between the start and end tags for an anchor goes the text (or image) that is associated with the position in the document. Navigator 4 lets you extract that text with the anchor.text property. This property is read-only.

Internet Explorer 4 employs a different model and syntax for getting and setting the text and HTML for an object like the anchor. The two syntaxes are not compatible.

Note

This property was not implemented in releases of Navigator 4 prior to Version 4.02.

Related Items: None.

x
y

Value: Integer   **Gettable:** Yes   **Settable:** No

	Nav2	Nav3	Nav4	IE3/J1	IE3/J2	IE4/J3
Compatibility			✔			

Your Navigator 4 script can retrieve the x and y coordinates of an anchor object (the top-left corner of the rectangular space occupied by the linked text immediately following the opening tag) via the anchor.x and anchor.y properties. These properties are read-only and can be used for the same purposes as the parallel properties of the link object.

Related Items: link.x property; link.y property.

✦   ✦   ✦

Image and Area Objects

For users of Navigator 3, Internet Explorer 4, and later browsers, images and areas — those items created by the ⟨IMG⟩ and ⟨AREA⟩ tags — are first-class objects that can be scripted for enhanced interactivity. The space reserved for an ⟨IMG⟩ tag can be refreshed with other images of the same size, perhaps to show the highlighting of an icon button when the cursor rolls atop it. And with scriptable client-side area maps, pages can be smarter about how users' clicks on image regions respond.

One further benefit afforded scripters is that images can be preloaded into the browser's image cache as the page loads. Therefore, if you intend to swap images in response to user action, no delay occurs in making the first swap: The image is already in the image cache ready to go.

Image Object

Properties	Methods	Event Handlers
border	(None)	onAbort=
complete		onError=
height		onLoad=
hspace		
lowsrc		
name		
src		
vspace		
width		
x		
y		

Syntax

Creating an image:

```
<IMG
     SRC="ImageURL"
     [LOWSRC="LowResImageURL"]
     NAME="ImageName"
     [HEIGHT="PixelCount" | "PercentageValue%"]
     [WIDTH="PixelCount" | "PercentageValue%"]
     [HSPACE="PixelCount"]
     [VSPACE="PixelCount"]
     [BORDER="PixelCount"]
     [ALIGN="left" | "right" | "top" | "absmiddle" | "absbottom" |
            "texttop" | "middle" | "baseline" | "bottom"]
     [ISMAP]
     [USEMAP="#AreaMapName"]
     [onLoad="handlerTextOrFunction"]
     [onAbort="handlerTextOrFunction"]
     [onError="handlerTextOrFunction"]>
</BODY>

imageName = new Image([pixelWidth, pixelHeight])
```

Accessing image properties or methods:

```
[window.] document.imageName. property | method([parameters])

[window.] document.images[index]. property | method([parameters])
```

	Nav2	Nav3	Nav4	IE3/J1	IE3/J2	IE4/J3
Compatibility		✔	✔	(✔)		✔

About this object

Images have been in the HTML vocabulary since the earliest days, but Netscape Navigator 3 was the first to treat them like first-class JavaScript objects. Internet Explorer 3 for the Macintosh includes a partial implementation of the image object (to allow image precaching and swapping), and all flavors of Internet Explorer 4 treat images as true document objects. The primary advantage of this rating is that scripts can read a number of properties from images and, more importantly, change the image that occupies the image object's rectangular space on the page, even after the document has loaded and displayed an initial image. The key to this scriptability is the src property of an image.

In a typical scenario, a page loads with an initial image. That image's tags specify any of the extra attributes, such as HEIGHT and WIDTH (which help speed the rendering of the page), and whether the image uses a client-side image map to make it interactive (see the area object later in this chapter). As the user spends time on the page, the image can then change (perhaps in response to user action or some timed event in the script), replacing the original image with a new one in the same space (the rectangle cannot be modified after the first image loads).

Another benefit of treating images as objects is that a script can create a virtual image to hold a preloaded image (the image gets loaded into the image cache without having to display the image). The hope is that one or more unseen images will load into memory while the user is busy reading the page or waiting for the page to download. Then, in response to user action on the page, an image can change almost instantaneously, rather than forcing the user to wait for the image to load on demand.

To preload an image, begin by generating a new, empty image object as a global variable. You can preload images either in immediate script statements that run as the page loads or in response to the window's onLoad= event handler. An image that is to take the place of an <IMG> tag picture must be the same size as the HEIGHT and WIDTH attributes of the tag. Moreover, you help the virtual image object creation if you specify the width and height in the parameters of new Image() constructor. Then assign an image file URL to its src property:

```
oneImage = new Image(55,68)
oneImage.src = "neatImage.gif"
```

As this image loads, you see the progress in the status bar, just like any image. Later, assign the src property of this stored image to the src property of the image object that appears on the page:

```
document.images[0].src = oneImage.src
```

Depending on the type and size of image, you will be amazed at the speedy response of this kind of loading. With small-palette graphics, the image displays instantaneously.

A popular user interface technique is to change the appearance of an image that represents a clickable button when the user rolls the mouse pointer atop that art. If you surround an image with a link in the latest browser versions, you can even change images when the user presses and releases the mouse button (see Chapter 17).

You can accomplish this many ways, depending on the number of images you need to swap. I employ different methods in relevant listings, such as Listing 17-3 and 18-2. But the barest minimum can be accomplished by preloading both versions of an image as the document loads, and then changing the src property of the image object in the relevant mouse event handler. For example, in a script in the <HEAD> section, you can preload "normal" and "highlighted" versions of some button art in the following manner:

```
var normalButton = new Image(80,20)
var hilitedButton = newImage(80,20)
normalButton.src = "homeNormal.gif"
hilitedButton.src = "homeHilited.gif"
```

Then, in the body of the document, you would create a linked <IMG> tag along these lines:

```
<A HREF="default.html"
       onMouseOver="document.ToHome.src = hilitedButton.src; return
true"
       onMouseOut="documentToHome.scr = normalButton.src; return true"
  >
```

```
<IMG NAME="ToHome" SRC="homeNormal.gif"
      WIDTH=80 HEIGHT=20 BORDER=0
></A>
```

When a user rolls the mouse over the linked image, the `onMouseOver=` event handler changes the URL of the image to the highlighted version loaded into the cache earlier; when the mouse rolls out of the image, the image changes back.

The speed with which this kind of image swapping takes place may lead you to consider using this method for animation. Though this method may be practical for brief bursts of animation, the many other ways of introducing animation to your Web page (such as via GIF89a-standard images, Java applets, and a variety of plug-ins) produce animation that offers better speed control and the like. In fact, swapping preloaded JavaScript image objects for some cartoon-like animations may actually be too fast. You could build a delay mechanism around the `setInterval()` method, but the precise timing between frames would vary with client processor.

If you place an image inside a table cell, Navigator 3 sometimes generates two copies of the image object in its object model. This can disturb the content of the `document.images[]` array for your scripts. Specifying `HEIGHT` and `WIDTH` attributes for the image can sometimes cure the problem. Otherwise you have to craft scripts so they don't rely on the `document.images[]` array.

Properties

```
border
height
hspace
name
vspace
width
```

	Nav2	Nav3	Nav4	IE3/J1	IE3/J2	IE4/J3
Compatibility		✔	✔			✔

Value: Varies   **Gettable:** Yes   **Settable:** No

This long list of properties for the image object provides read-only access to the corresponding `<IMG>` tag attributes that affect the visual appearance of the image. The values that these properties return are the same as those used to initially set the attributes. Once the image is defined by its `<IMG>` tag, you cannot change any of these properties to influence the appearance on the page. More than likely, you will never need to refer to these properties, unless a script that is about to write a new page wants to replicate settings from an existing image object.

If you need to set these attributes with JavaScript writing a page on-the-fly, use the `document.write()` method to write the equivalent of the actual HTML tags and the values you would use in a regular document. Also see Chapters 41 through 43 regarding the use of Cascading Style Sheets for other ways to impact the appearance of a loaded image.

Related Items: None.

complete

Value: Boolean   **Gettable:** Yes   **Settable:** No

	Nav2	Nav3	Nav4	IE3/J1	IE3/J2	IE4/J3
Compatibility		✔	✔			✔

There may be times when you want to make sure that an image object is not still in the process of loading before allowing another process to take place. This situation is different from waiting for an image to load before triggering some other process (which you can do via the image object's `onLoad=` event handler). To verify that the image object displays a completed image, check for the Boolean value of the `complete` property. To verify that a particular image file has loaded, first find out whether the `complete` property is true; then compare the `src` property against the desired filename.

An image's `complete` property switches to true even if only the specified `LOWSRC` image has finished loading. Do not rely on this property alone for determining whether the `SRC` image has loaded if both `SRC=` and `LOWSRC=` attributes are set in the `<IMG>` tag.

This property is not reliable in Navigator 4 and Internet Explorer 4. The value returns `true` in all instances.

Example

To experiment with the `image.complete` property, quit and relaunch Navigator before loading Listing 18-1 (in case the images are in memory cache). As each image loads, click the "Is it loaded yet?" button to see the status of the `complete` property for the image object. The value is false until the loading has finished, at which time the value becomes true. If you experience difficulty with this property in your scripts, try adding an `onLoad=` event handler (even if it is empty, as in Listing 18-1) to your `<IMG>` tag.

Listing 18-1: **Scripting image.complete**

```
<HTML>
<HEAD>
<SCRIPT LANGUAGE="JavaScript1.1">
function loadIt(theImage,form) {
        form.result.value = ""
        document.images[0].src = theImage
}
function checkLoad(form) {
        form.result.value = document.images[0].complete
```

```
    }
    </SCRIPT>
    </HEAD>
    <BODY>
    <IMG SRC="cpu2.gif" WIDTH=120 HEIGHT=90 onLoad="">
    <FORM>
    <INPUT TYPE="button" VALUE="Load keyboard"
    onClick="loadIt('cpu2.gif',this.form)">
    <INPUT TYPE="button" VALUE="Load arch"
    onClick="loadIt('arch.gif',this.form)"><P>
    <INPUT TYPE="button" VALUE="Is it loaded yet?"
    onClick="checkLoad(this.form)">
    <INPUT TYPE="text" NAME="result">
    </FORM>
    </BODY>
    </HTML>
```

Related Items: `img.src` property; `img.lowsrc` property; `onLoad=` event handler.

lowsrc

Value: String   **Gettable:** Yes   **Settable:** No

	Nav2	Nav3	Nav4	IE3/J1	IE3/J2	IE4/J3
Compatibility		✔	✔			✔

For image files that take several seconds to load, recent browsers enable you to specify a lower-resolution image or some other quick-loading placeholder to stand in while the big image crawls to the browser. You assign this alternate image via the `LOWSRC=` attribute in the `<IMG>` tag. The attribute is reflected in the `lowsrc` property of an image object.

Although I list this property as not being settable, you can make a temporary setting safely, provided that you set it in the same script segment as the statement that loads an image to the `src` property. Be aware that if you specify a `LOWSRC` image file, the `complete` property switches to true and the `onLoad=` event handler fires when the alternate file finishes loading: They do not wait for the main `SRC` file to load.

Example

See the example for the image object's `onLoad=` event handler to see how these elements affect each other.

Related Items: `window.open()` method; `window.focus()` method.

src

Value: String   **Gettable:** Yes   **Settable:** Yes

	Nav2	Nav3	Nav4	IE3/J1	IE3/J2	IE4/J3
Compatibility		✔	✔	(✔)		✔

The key to best using the image object from JavaScript is the `src` property, which enables you to assign a URL or preloaded image's `src` property as a way of loading a new image into an existing image's rectangular space. Be aware that the height and width of the image object are defined by the attributes in the `<IMG>` tag. If you simply set the `src` property of an image object to a new image filename, JavaScript scales the image to fit the dimensions defined by the `<IMG>` tag attributes or (if none are provided) by the dimensions of the first image file loaded into that object. JavaScript ignores any discrepancy that exists between these settings and the parameters passed to a `new Image(x,y)` statement.

Example

In the following example (Listing 18-2), you see a few applications of the image object. Of prime importance is a comparison of how precached and regular images feel to the user. As a bonus, I include an example of how to set a timer to automatically change the images displayed in an image object. This feature seems to be a popular request among sites that display advertising banners.

Listing 18-2: **A Scripted Image Object and Rotating Images**

```
<HTML>
<HEAD>
<TITLE>Image Object</TITLE>
<SCRIPT LANGUAGE="JavaScript1.1">

imageDB = new Array(4)
for (var i = 0; i < imageDB.length ; i++) {
        imageDB[i] = new Image(120,90)
        imageDB[i].src = "desk" + (i+1) + ".gif"
}

function loadIndividual(form) {
        var gifName =
form.individual.options[form.individual.selectedIndex].value
        document.thumbnail1.src = gifName
}
function loadCached(form) {
        var gifIndex = form.cached.selectedIndex
        document.thumbnail2.src = imageDB[gifIndex].src
}
function checkTimer() {
        if (document.Timer.timerBox.checked) {
            var newIndex = 0
            var gifName = document.thumbnail2.src
            var gifIndex = (gifName.charAt(gifName.length - 5)) - 1
```

(continued)

Listing 18-2 *(continued)*

```
            if (gifIndex < imageDB.length - 1) {
                newIndex = gifIndex + 1
            }
            document.thumbnail2.src = imageDB[newIndex].src
            document.selections.cached.selectedIndex = newIndex
            var timeoutID = setTimeout("checkTimer()",5000)
        }
    }
}
</SCRIPT>
</HEAD>

<BODY onLoad=checkTimer()>
<CENTER>
<H2>Image Object Demonstration</H2>
<TABLE BORDER=3>
<TR><TH></TH><TH>Individually Loaded</TH><TH>Pre-cached</TH></TR>
<TR><TD ALIGN=RIGHT><B>Image:</B></TD>
<TD><IMG SRC="cpu1.gif" NAME="thumbnail1" HEIGHT=90 WIDTH=120></TD>
<TD><IMG SRC="desk1.gif" NAME="thumbnail2" HEIGHT=90 WIDTH=120></TD>
</TR>
<TR><TD ALIGN=RIGHT><B>Select image:</B></TD>
<FORM NAME="selections">
<TD>
<SELECT NAME="individual" onChange="loadIndividual(this.form)">
<OPTION VALUE="cpu1.gif">Wires
<OPTION VALUE="cpu2.gif">Keyboard
<OPTION VALUE="cpu3.gif">Disks
<OPTION VALUE="cpu4.gif">Cables
</SELECT>
</TD>
<TD>
<SELECT NAME="cached" onChange="loadCached(this.form)">
<OPTION VALUE="desk1.gif">Bands
<OPTION VALUE="desk2.gif">Clips
<OPTION VALUE="desk3.gif">Lamp
<OPTION VALUE="desk4.gif">Erasers
</SELECT></TD>
</FORM>
</TR></TABLE>
<FORM NAME="Timer">
<INPUT TYPE="checkbox" NAME="timerBox" onClick="checkTimer()">Auto-
cycle through pre-cached images
</FORM>
</CENTER>
</BODY>
</HTML>
```

You should notice that because the images being preloaded are in a related sequence, they are conveniently named to make it easy for an array and repeat loop to manage their preloading. The same numbering scheme lets you link the images to select object options for a very compact operation.

To observe the maximum effect of the application in Listing 18-2, quit and relaunch the browser. This clears the image cache for the current session. After you open Listing 18-2, wait until all status bar activity finishes, then choose images from the precached list on the right (Figure 18-1). Unless your browser has its memory cache turned off completely, you should see an instantaneous response to selecting an image.

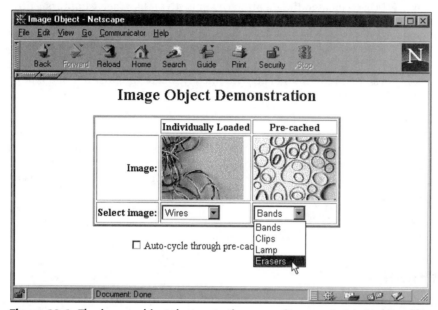

Figure 18-1: The image object demonstration page *(Images © Aris Multimedia Entertainment, Inc. 1994)*

Next, choose an image from the left-hand listing. You should see the image loading individually. The same happens for each new image you load. The images you previously loaded this way are still in the memory cache, so they appear instantaneously thereafter (until you quit again). These images are small images, of course, so the impact on the wait time is not substantial. Imagine the perceived performance improvement for users accessing larger images through the Net.

Finally, check the checkbox to watch the images in the right-hand side of the table cycle through their grouping, changing images every five seconds. This mechanism, too, takes advantage of the array numbering for the images.

Related Items: image.lowsrc property.

x
y

Value: Integer **Gettable:** Yes **Settable:** No

	Nav2	Nav3	Nav4	IE3/J1	IE3/J2	IE4/J3
Compatibility			✔			

Your Navigator 4 script can retrieve the x and y coordinates of an image object (the top-left corner of the rectangular space occupied by the image) via the `image.x` and `image.y` properties. These properties are read-only, but you can use Dynamic HTML to change the location of a link if you like (see Chapters 41 to 43).

Even without Dynamic HTML, you can use the information from these properties to help scroll a document to a precise position (with the `window.scrollTo()` method) as a navigational aid in your page. Due to the different ways each operating system platform renders pages and the different sizes of browser windows, you can dynamically locate the position of a link given the current client conditions.

Example

Due to the different ways each operating system platform renders pages and the different sizes of browser windows, you can dynamically locate the position of a link given the current client conditions. For example, if you want to scroll the document so that the link is a few pixels below the top of the window, you could use a statement such as this:

```
window.scrollTo(document.images[0].x, (document.images[0].y - 3))
```

Related Items: `window.scrollTo()` method.

Event handlers

```
onAbort=
onError=
```

	Nav2	Nav3	Nav4	IE3/J1	IE3/J2	IE4/J3
Compatibility		✔	✔			✔

Your scripts may need to be proactive when a user clicks on the Stop button while an image is loading or when a network or server problem causes the image transfer to fail. Use the `onAbort=` event handler to activate a function in the event of a user clicking on the Stop button; use the `onError=` event handler for the unexpected transfer snafu.

In practice, these event handlers don't supply all the information you may like to have in a script, such as the filename of the image that was loading at the time. If such information is critical to your scripts, then the scripts need to store the name of a currently loading image to a variable before they set the image's `src` property. You also won't know the nature of the error that triggers an error event.

You can treat such problems by forcing a scripted page to reload or by navigating to an entirely different spot in your Web site.

Example

Listing 18-3 includes an `onAbort=` event handler. If the images already exist in the cache, you must quit and relaunch the browser to try to stop the image from loading. In that example, I provide a reload option for the entire page. How you handle the exception depends a great deal on your page design. Do your best to smooth over any difficulties that users may encounter.

onLoad=

	Nav2	Nav3	Nav4	IE3/J1	IE3/J2	IE4/J3
Compatibility	✔	✔				✔

JavaScript sends a load event to an image object when one of three possible conditions occurs: an image's `LOWSRC` image has finished loading; in the absence of a `LOWSRC` image specification, the `SRC` image has finished loading; when each frame of an animated GIF (GIF89a format) appears.

It's important to understand that if you define a `LOWSRC` file inside an `<IMG>` tag, the image object receives no further word about the `SRC` image having completed its loading. If this information is critical to your script, verify the current image file by checking the `src` property of the image object.

Note

This event handler appears to be broken in Navigator 4.

Example

Quit and restart your browser to get the most from Listing 18-3. As the document first loads, the `LOWSRC` image file (the picture of pencil erasers) loads ahead of the computer keyboard image. When the erasers are loaded, the `onLoad=` event handler writes "done" to the text field, even though the main image has not yet loaded. You can experiment further by loading the arch image. This image takes longer to load, so the `LOWSRC` image (set on the fly, in this case) loads way ahead of it.

Listing 18-3: **The Image onLoad= Event Handler**

```
<HTML>
<HEAD>
<SCRIPT LANGUAGE="JavaScript1.1">
function loadIt(theImage,form) {
        form.result.value = ""
        document.images[0].lowsrc = "desk1.gif"
        document.images[0].src = theImage
}
function checkLoad(form) {
        form.result.value = document.images[0].complete
}
```

(continued)

Listing 18-3 *(continued)*

```
function signal() {
        if(confirm("You have stopped the image from loading. Do you want
to try again?")) {
            location.reload()
        }
}
</SCRIPT>
</HEAD>
<BODY>
<IMG SRC="cpu2.gif" LOWSRC="desk4.gif" WIDTH=120 HEIGHT=90
onLoad="document.forms[0].result.value='done'" onAbort="signal()">
<FORM>
<INPUT TYPE="button" VALUE="Load keyboard"
onClick="loadIt('cpu2.gif',this.form)">
<INPUT TYPE="button" VALUE="Load arch"
onClick="loadIt('arch.gif',this.form)"><P>
<INPUT TYPE="button" VALUE="Is it loaded yet?"
onClick="checkLoad(this.form)">
<INPUT TYPE="text" NAME="result">
</FORM>
</BODY>
</HTML>
```

Related Items: `image.src` property; `image.lowsrc` property.

Area Object

Properties	Methods	Event Handlers
target	(None)	onClick=
[location object properties]		onMouseOut=
		onMouseOver=

Syntax

Creating an image map area:

```
<MAP NAME="areaMapName">
      <AREA
          COORDS="x1,y1,x2,y2,..."|"x-center,y-center,radius"
          HREF="locationOrURL"
          [NOHREF]
          [SHAPE="rect" | "poly" | "circle" | "default"]
```

```
                         [TARGET="windowName"]
                         [onMouseOver="handlerTextOrFunction"]
                         [onMouseOut="handlerTextOrFunction"]>
     </MAP>
```

Accessing area object properties:

```
[window.] document.links[index].property
```

About this object

JavaScript treats a map area object as one of the link objects in a document (see the link object in Chapter 17). When you think about it, such treatment is not illogical at all, because clicking on a map area generally leads the user to another document or anchor location in the same document — a hyperlinked reference.

Although the HTML definitions of links and map areas are quite different, both kinds of objects have nearly the same properties and event handlers. Therefore, to read about the details for these items, refer to the discussion about the link object in Chapter 17. The one difference is that a map area object does not have the same full array of mouse event handlers.

Client-side image maps are fun to work with, and they have been well-documented in HTML references since the feature was introduced in Netscape Navigator 2. Essentially, you define any number of areas within the image, based on shape and coordinates. Many graphics tools can help you capture the coordinates of images that you need to enter into the COORDS= attribute of the <AREA> tag.

If one gotcha exists that trips up most HTML authors, it's the link between the <IMG> and <MAP> tags. The reason is that the link is a little tricky. You must assign a name to the <MAP>; in the <IMG> tag, the USEMAP= attribute requires a hash symbol (#) and the map name. If you forget the hash symbol, you won't create a connection between image and map.

The onClick= event handler appears in Netscape's area object beginning with Navigator 4. To be backward compatible with Navigator 3, use a javascript: URL for the HREF attribute if you want a click on the region to navigate to another page.

Example

To demonstrate how to script some area objects atop an image, Listing 18-4 defines six area objects for a space shuttle's view of the Sinai area. Most of the areas are rectangular, except for a path along a snakey Nile River that runs near the bottom of the image. Run the pointer along this path to see how the complex polygon tracks the twists and turns of the river. Can you find Cairo?

Listing 18-4: **A Scripted Image Map**

```
<HTML>
<HEAD>
<SCRIPT LANGUAGE="JavaScript">
function show(msg) {
        window.status = msg
        return true
```

(continued)

Listing 18-4 *(continued)*

```
}
function go(where) {
      alert("We're going to " + where + "!")
}
function clearIt() {
      window.status = ""
      return true
}
</SCRIPT>
</HEAD>
<BODY>
<H1>Sinai and Vicinity</H1>
<IMG SRC="nile.gif" WIDTH=320 HEIGHT=240 USEMAP="#sinai">
<MAP NAME="sinai">
      <AREA HREF="javascript:go('Cairo')" COORDS="12,152,26,161"
SHAPE="rect" onMouseOver="return show('Cairo')" onMouseOut="return
clearIt()">
      <AREA HREF="javascript:go('the Nile River')"
COORDS="1,155,6,162,0,175,3,201,61,232,109,227,167,238,274,239,292,220,
307,220,319,230,319,217,298,213,282,217,267,233,198,228,154,227,107,221
,71,225,21,199,19,165,0,149" SHAPE="poly" onMouseOver="return
show('Nile River')" onMouseOut="return clearIt()">
      <AREA HREF="javascript:go('Israel')" COORDS="95,69,201,91"
SHAPE="rect" onMouseOver="return show('Israel')" onMouseOut="return
clearIt()">
      <AREA HREF="javascript:go('Saudi Arabia')"
COORDS="256,57,319,121" SHAPE="rect" onMouseOver="return show('Saudi
Arabia')" onMouseOut="return clearIt()">
      <AREA HREF="javascript:go('the Mediterranean Sea')"
COORDS="1,55,26,123" SHAPE="rect" onMouseOver="return
show('Mediterranean Sea')" onMouseOut="return clearIt()">
      <AREA HREF="javascript:go('the Mediterranean Sea')"
COORDS="27,56,104,103" SHAPE="rect" onMouseOver="return
show('Mediterranean Sea')" onMouseOut="return clearIt()">
</MAP>
</BODY>
</HTML>
```

Although most maps have HREF attributes that point to URLs on the Web, I use an internal javascript: URL to demonstrate how the window.status messages written by onMouseOver= event handlers override the HREF display in the status bar. For the Mediterranean Sea, I use two adjacent rectangles with identical behaviors to show another way to handle irregular shapes.

✦   ✦   ✦

The Layer Object

One of the hallmarks of the Navigator 4 and Internet Explorer 4 generations of browsers is Dynamic HTML — the ability to alter content on the fly in response to user interaction. Dynamic HTML (DHTML) has two components that often work together: style sheets and positioning. You can read more about these in Chapters 41 through 43.

Netscape Layers

As often happens when browser providers work faster than standards groups, both Microsoft and Netscape have developed supersets of proposed standards of DHTML functionality and implementation. This chapter focuses on Netscape's contribution to DHTML, the layer object. While it may sound as though the layer object is tied directly to Netscape's new <LAYER> tag, the layer object lets you script (primarily for positioning purposes) elements created in a cross-platform, standards-body-approved HTML syntax of Cascading Style Sheets (CSS).

Layer Object

Properties	Methods	Event Handlers
above	load()	onBlur=
background	moveAbove()	onFocus=
below	moveBelow()	onLoad=
bgcolor	moveBy()	onMouseOut=
clip.bottom	moveTo()	onMouseOver=
clip.left	moveToAbsolute()	
clip.right	resizeBy()	
clip.top	resizeTo()	
document		

(continued)

Properties	Methods	Event Handlers
left		
name		
pageX		
pageY		
parentLayer		
siblingAbove		
siblingBelow		
src		
top		
visibility		
zIndex		

Syntax

Creating a layer:

```
<LAYER | ILAYER
        ID="LayerName"
        SRC="DocumentURL"
        [LEFT="PixelCount"]
        [TOP="PixelCount"]
        [PAGEX="PixelCount"]
        [PAGEY="PixelCount"]
        [ABOVE="OtherLayerName"]
        [BELOW="OtherLayerName"]
        [Z-INDEX="LayerIndex"]
        [HEIGHT="PixelCount" | "PercentageValue%"]
        [WIDTH="PixelCount" | "PercentageValue%"]
        [CLIP="LeftPixel, TopPixel, RightPixel, BottomPixel"]
        [BGCOLOR="HexTriplet" | "ColorName"]
        [BACKGROUND="ImageURL"]
        [VISIBILITY="SHOW" | "HIDDEN" | "INHERIT"]
        [onBlur="handlerTextOrFunction"]
        [onFocus="handlerTextOrFunction"]
        [onLoad="handlerTextOrFunction"]
        [onMouseOut="handlerTextOrFunction"]
        [onMouseOver="handlerTextOrFunction"]>
</LAYER | /ILAYER>
<NOLAYER>
        [Content for no layer support]
</NOLAYER>

layerObject = new Layer(pixelWidth [, parentLayerObject])

<STYLE type="text/css">
        #layerName {position:positionType [;attributeLabel1:value1 ...]}
</STYLE>
```

```
<HTMLTag
        ID="layerName"
        STYLE=" position:positionType [;attributeLabel1:value1 ...]>
        LayerContent
</ HTMLTag >
```

Accessing layer properties or methods:

```
[window.] document.layerName.[document.layerName. ...] property |
method([parameters])
```

```
[window.] document.layers[index]. [document.layerName. ...]property |
method([parameters])
```

	Nav2	Nav3	Nav4	IE3/J1	IE3/J2	IE4/J3
Compatibility			✔			

About this object

Perhaps you have seen how animated cartoons were created before computer animation changed the art. Layers of clear acetate sheets were assembled atop a static background. Each sheet contained one character or portion of a character. When all the sheets were carefully positioned atop each other, the view, as captured by a still camera, formed a composite frame of the cartoon. To create the next frame of the cartoon, the artist moved one of the layers a fraction of an inch along its intended path — and then another picture was taken.

If you can visualize how that operation works, you have a good starting point for understanding how layers work in Navigator (from Version 4 onward). In Navigator, each layer contains some kind of HTML content that exists in its own plane above the main document that loads in a window. The content of an individual layer can be changed or replaced on the fly without affecting the other layers; and the entire layer can be repositioned, resized, or hidden under script control.

One aspect of layers that goes beyond the cartoon analogy is that a layer can contain other layers. When that happens, any change that affects the primary layer — such as moving the layer 10 pixels downward — also affects the layers nested inside. It's as if the nested layers are passengers of the outer layer. When the outer layer goes somewhere, the passengers do, too. And yet, within the "vehicle" the passengers may change seats by moving themselves around without regard for what's going on outside.

Layer references

The task of assembling JavaScript references to layers and the objects they contain is very much like doing the same for framesets (in fact, conceptually, a layer is like a dynamically movable and resizable free-floating frame). Therefore, before you start writing the reference, you must know the relationship between the document *containing* the script and the target of the reference.

To demonstrate how this works, I start with a script in the base document loaded into a window that needs to change the background color (bgColor property) of a layer defined in the document. The skeletal HTML is as follows:

```
<HTML>
<HEAD>
</HEAD>
<BODY>
<LAYER NAME="Flintstones" SRC="flintstonesFamily.html">
</LAYER>
</BODY>
</HTML>
```

From a script in the Head section, the statement that changes the layer's bgColor property is

```
document.Flintstones.bgColor = "yellow"
```

This syntax looks like the way you address any object in a document, such as a link or image, but things get tricky in that each layer automatically contains a document object. That document object is what holds the content of the layer. Therefore, if you wanted to inspect the lastModified property of the HTML document loaded into the layer, the statement would be

```
var modDate = document.Flintstones.document.lastModified
```

The situation gets more complex if the layer has another layer nested inside it (one of those "passengers" that goes along for the ride). If the structure changes to

```
<HTML>
<HEAD>
</HEAD>
<BODY>
<LAYER NAME="Flintstones" SRC="flintstonesFamily.html">
        <LAYER NAME="Fred" SRC="fredFlintstone.html">
        <LAYER NAME="Wilma" SRC="wilmaFlintstone.html">
</LAYER>
</BODY>
</HTML>
```

references to items in the second level of frames get even longer. For example, to get the lastModified property of the wilmaFlintstone.html file loaded into the nested Fred layer, the reference from the Head script would be

```
document.Flintstones.document.Fred.document.lastModified
```

The reason for this is Navigator does not have a shortcut access to every layer defined in a top-level document. As stated in the description of the document.layers property in Chapter 16, the property reflects only the first level of layers defined in a document. You must know the way to San Jose if you want to get its lastModified property.

Because each layer has its own document, you cannot spread a form across multiple layers. Each layer's document must define its own <FORM> tags. If you need to submit one form from content located in multiple layers, one of the forms should have an onSubmit= event handler to capture all the related form values and place them in hidden input fields in the document containing the submitted form. In that case, you need to know how to devise references from a nested layer outward.

As a demonstration of reverse-direction references, I'll start with the following skeletal structure containing multiple nested layers:

```
<HTML>
<HEAD>
</HEAD>
<BODY>
<FORM NAME="personal">
        <INPUT TYPE="text" NAME="emailAddr">
</FORM>
<LAYER NAME="product" SRC="ultraGizmoLine.html">
        <LAYER NAME="color" SRC="colorChoice.html">
        <LAYER NAME="size" SRC="sizeChoice.html">
        <LAYER NAME="sendIt" SRC="submission.html"
</LAYER>
</BODY>
</HTML>
```

Each of the HTML files loaded into the layers also has a `<FORM>` tag defining some fields or select lists for relevant user choices, such as which specific model of the UltraGizmo line is selected, what color, and in what size (these last two are defined as separate layers because their positions are animated when they are displayed). The assumption here is that the Submit button is in the `sendIt` layer. That layer's document also includes hidden input fields for data to be pulled from the main document's form and three other layer forms. Two of those layers are at the same nested level as `sendIt`, one is above it, and the main document's form is at the highest level.

To reach the `value` property of a field named `theColor` in the `color` layer, a script in the `sendIt` layer would use the reference

```
parentLayer.document.color.document.forms[0].theColor.value
```

Analogous to working with frames, the reference starts with a reference to the next higher level (`parentLayer`), and then starts working its way down through the parent layer's document, the `color` layer, the `color` layer's document, and finally the form therein.

To reach the `value` property of a field named `modelNum` in the `product` layer, the reference starts the same way, but because the form is at the parent layer level, the reference goes immediately to that layer's document and form:

```
parentLayer.document.forms[0].modelNum.value
```

It may seem odd that a reference to an object at a different layer level is shorter than one at the same level (for example, the `color` layer), but the route to the parent layer is shorter than going via the parent layer to a sibling. Finally, to reach the value of the `emailAddr` field in the base document, the reference must ratchet out one more layer, as follows:

```
parentLayer.parentLayer.document.forms[0].emailAddr.value
```

The two `parentLayer` entries step the reference out two levels, at which point the scope is in the base layer containing the main document and its form.

Cross-platform concerns

Navigator does not rely only on the `<LAYER>` tag or `new Layer()` construction for layer objects. If the document contains Cascading Style Sheet-Positioning (CSS-P) information, as shown in the syntax listing at the start of this section, then Navigator automatically turns each named, positioned item into a layer object. You have the same scripted positioning control over CSS-P-generated layers as over Navigator layer objects.

In the property, method, and event handler listings throughout this chapter, you will see that the syntaxes apply only to Navigator 4. While some Internet Explorer language items are the same, fundamental differences exist in the way positioned objects are references in JScript and JavaScript. Moreover, Internet Explorer 4's object model is much richer in that its positionable objects have more properties that allow such powers as dynamically swapping text without reloading the document in a layer. However, the point of view for this book is from that of Navigator and its implementation of a document object model and JavaScript.

For more details about style sheets and positioning in Navigator and Internet Explorer (separately and in cross-platform scenarios), see Chapters 41 through 43.

Properties

above
below
siblingAbove
siblingBelow

Value: Layer Object   **Gettable:** Yes   **Settable:** No

	Nav2	Nav3	Nav4	IE3/J1	IE3/J2	IE4/J3
Compatibility			✔			

Each layer exists in its own physical layer. Given that width and height are traditionally represented by the variables x and y, the third dimension — the position of a layer relative to the stack of layers — is called the *z-order*. Layer orders are assigned automatically according to the loading order, with the highest number being the topmost layer. That topmost layer is the one closest to you as you view the page on the monitor.

If two layers are on a page, one layer must always be in front of the other, even if they both appear to be transparent and visually overlap each other. Knowing which layer is above the other can be important for scripting purposes, especially if your script needs to re-order the layering in response to user action. Layer objects have four properties to help you determine the layers adjacent to a particular layer.

The first pair of properties, `layer.above` and `layer.below`, takes a global look at all layers defined on the page, regardless of how one layer may contain any number of nested layers separate from other batches on the screen. If a layer lies above the one in question, the property contains a reference to that other layer; if no layer exists in that direction, then the value is null. Attempts to get properties of a nonexistent layer results in runtime scripting errors indicating that the object does have properties (of course not — an object must exist before it can have properties).

To understand these two properties better, consider a document that contains three layers (in any nesting arrangement you like). The first layer to be defined is on the bottom of the stack. It has a layer above it, but none below it. The second layer in the middle has a layer both above and below it. And the topmost layer has a layer only below it, with no more layers above it (that is, coming toward your eye).

Another pair of properties, `layer.siblingAbove` and `layer.siblingBelow`, confine themselves to whatever group of layers are contained by a parent layer. Just as in real family life, siblings are descended from (teens might say "contained by") the same parent. An only child layer has no siblings, so both the `layer.siblingAbove` and `layer.siblingBelow` values are null. For two layers from the same parent, the first one to be defined has a sibling layer above it; the other has a sibling layer below it.

It is important to understand the difference between absolute layering and sibling layering to use these properties correctly. A nested layer might be the fifth layer from the bottom among all layers on the page, but at the same time is the first layer among siblings within its family group. As you can see, these two sets of properties enable your script to be very specific about the relationships under examination.

Example

Listing 19-1 lets you experiment with just one set of these properties: `layer.above` and `layer.below`. The page is almost in the form of a laboratory and quiz that lets you query yourself about the values of these properties for two swappable layers.

Listing 19-1: **A Layer Quiz**

```
<HTML>
<HEAD>
<SCRIPT LANGUAGE="JavaScript">
function checkAbove(oneLayer) {
       document.forms[0].errors.value = ""
       document.forms[0].output.value = oneLayer.above.name
}
function checkBelow(oneLayer) {
       document.forms[0].errors.value = ""
       document.forms[0].output.value = oneLayer.below.name
}
function swapLayers() {
```

(continued)

Listing 19-1 *(continued)*

```
        if (document.yeller.above) {
            document.yeller.moveAbove(document.greeny)
        } else {
            document.greeny.moveAbove(document.yeller)
        }
}
function onerror(msg) {
        document.forms[0].output.value = ""
        document.forms[0].errors.value = msg
        return true
}
</SCRIPT>
</HEAD>
<BODY>
<B>Layer Ordering</B>
<HR>
<FORM>
Results:<INPUT TYPE="text" NAME="output"><P>
<INPUT TYPE="button" VALUE="Who's ABOVE the Yellow layer?"
onClick="checkAbove(document.yeller)"><BR>
<INPUT TYPE="button" VALUE="Who's BELOW the Yellow layer?"
onClick="checkBelow(document.yeller)"><P>
<INPUT TYPE="button" VALUE="Who's ABOVE the Green layer?"
onClick="checkAbove(document.greeny)"><BR>
<INPUT TYPE="button" VALUE="Who's BELOW the Green layer?"
onClick="checkBelow(document.greeny)"><P>
<INPUT TYPE="button" VALUE="Swap Layers" onCLick="swapLayers()"><P>
If there are any errors caused by missing <BR>
properties, they will appear below:<BR>
<TEXTAREA NAME="errors" COLS=30 ROWS=3 WRAP="virtual"></TEXTAREA>
</FORM>
<LAYER NAME="yeller" BGCOLOR="yellow" TOP=60 LEFT=300 WIDTH=200
HEIGHT=200>
<B>This is just a yellow layer.</B>
</LAYER>
<LAYER NAME="greeny" BGCOLOR="lightgreen" TOP=100 LEFT=340 WIDTH=200
HEIGHT=200>
<B>This is just a green layer.</B>
</LAYER>
</BODY>
</HTML>
```

The page contains two layers, one colored yellow, the other light green. Legends on four buttons ask you to guess whether one layer is above or below the other. For example, if you click the button labeled "Who's ABOVE the Yellow layer?" and the green layer is above it, the name of that green layer appears in the Results field. But if layers are oriented such that the returned value is null, the error message (indicating that the nonexistent object doesn't have a name property) appears in the error field at the bottom. Another button lets you swap the order of the layers so you can try your hand at predicting the results based on your knowledge of layers and the `above` and `below` properties.

Related Items: `layer.parentLayer` property; `layer.moveAbove()` method; `layer.moveBelow()` method.

`background`

Value: Image Object   **Gettable:** Yes   **Settable:** Yes

	Nav2	Nav3	Nav4	IE3/J1	IE3/J2	IE4/J3
Compatibility			✔			

You can assign a background image to a layer. The initial image is usually set by the `BACKGROUND` attribute of the `<LAYER>` tag, but you can assign a new image whenever you like via the `layer.background` property.

Layer background images are typically like those used for entire Web pages. They tend to be subtle or at least of such a design and color scheme as to not distract from the primary content of the layer. On the other hand, the background image may in fact be the content. If so, then have a blast with whatever images suit you.

The value of the `layer.background` property is an image object (see Chapter 18). To change the image in that property on the fly, you must set the `layer.background.src` property to the URL of the desired image (just like changing a `document.image` on the fly). You can remove the background image by setting the `layer.background.src` property to `null`. Background images smaller than the rectangle of the layer repeat themselves, just like document background pictures; images larger than the rectangle clip themselves to the rectangle of the layer, rather than scaling to fit.

Example

A simple example (Listing 19-2) defines one layer that features five buttons to change the background image of a second layer. I put the buttons in a layer because I want to make sure the buttons and background layer rectangles align themselves along their top edges on all platforms.

As the second layer loads, I merely assign a gray background color to it and write some reverse (white) text. Most of the images are of the small variety that repeat in the layer. One is a large photograph to demonstrate how images are clipped to the rectangle. Along the way, I hope you also heed the lesson of readability demonstrated by the difficulty of reading text on a wild-looking background.

Listing 19-2: **Setting Layer Backgrounds**

```
<HTML>
<HEAD>
<SCRIPT LANGUAGE="JavaScript">
function setBg(URL) {
        document.bgExpo.background.src = URL
}
</SCRIPT>
</HEAD>
<BODY>
<B>Layer Backgrounds</B>
<HR>
<LAYER NAME="buttons" TOP=50>
        <FORM>
            <INPUT TYPE="button" VALUE="The Usual"
onClick="setBg('cr_kraft.gif')"><BR>
            <INPUT TYPE="button" VALUE="A Big One"
onClick="setBg('arch.gif')"><BR>
            <INPUT TYPE="button" VALUE="Not So Usual"
onClick="setBg('wh86.gif')"><BR>
            <INPUT TYPE="button" VALUE="Decidedly Unusual"
onClick="setBg('sb23.gif')"><BR>
            <INPUT TYPE="button" VALUE="Quick as..."
onClick="setBg('lightnin.gif')"><BR>
        </FORM>
</LAYER>
<LAYER NAME="bgExpo" BGCOLOR="gray" TOP=50 LEFT=250 WIDTH=300
HEIGHT=260>
<B><FONT COLOR="white">Some text, which may or may not read well with
the various backgrounds.</FONT></B>
</LAYER>
</BODY>
</HTML>
```

Related Items: `layer.bgColor` property; image object.

bgColor

Value: String   **Gettable:** Yes   **Settable:** Yes

	Nav2	Nav3	Nav4	IE3/J1	IE3/J2	IE4/J3
Compatibility			✔			

A layer's background color fills the entire rectangle with the color set either in the `<LAYER>` tag or from a script at a later time. Color values are the same as for document-related values, and may be in the hexadecimal triplet format or one of the Netscape plain-language colors. You can turn a layer transparent by setting its bgColor property to null.

Example

You can have some fun with Listing 19-3, which utilizes a number of layer scripting techniques. The page presents a kind of palette of eight colors, each one created as a small layer (see Figure 19-1). Another, larger layer is the one that has its bgColor property changed as you roll the mouse over any color in the palette.

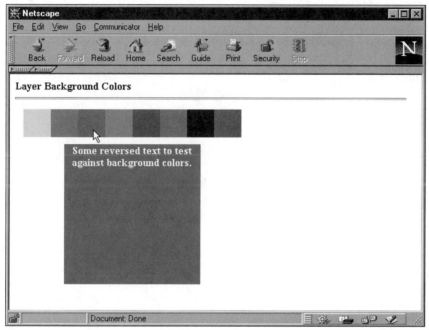

Figure 19-1: Drag the mouse across the palette to change the layer's background color.

To save HTML lines to create those eight color palette layers, I use a script to establish an array of colors, and then document.write() the <LAYER> tags with appropriate attribute settings so the layers all line up in a contiguous row. By predefining a number of variable values for the size of the color layers, I can make all of them larger or smaller with the change of only a few script characters.

The job of capturing the mouseOver events is handed to the document object. I turn on the document's captureEvents() method such that it traps all mouseOver events and hands them to the setColor() function. The setColor() function reads the target object's bgColor and sets the larger layer's bgColor property to the same. If this page had other objects that can receive mouseOver events for other purposes, I would use routeEvents() to let those events pass on to their intended targets. For the purposes of this example, however, the events need go no further.

Listing 19-3: **Layer Background Colors**

```
<HTML>
<HEAD>
<SCRIPT LANGUAGE="JavaScript">
function setColor(e) {
        document.display.bgColor = e.target.bgColor
}
document.captureEvents(Event.MOUSEOVER)
document.onmouseover = setColor
</SCRIPT>
</HEAD>
<BODY>
<B>Layer Background Colors</B>
<HR>
<SCRIPT LANGUAGE="JavaScript">
var oneLayer
var top = 50
var left = 20
var width = 40
var height = 40
var colorPalette = new
Array("aquamarine","coral","forestgreen","goldenrod","red","magenta",
"navy","teal")
for (var i = 0; i < colorPalette.length; i++) {
        oneLayer = "<LAYER NAME=swatch" + i + " TOP=" + top + " LEFT="
+ ((width * i) + 20)
        oneLayer += " WIDTH=" + width + " HEIGHT=" + height
        oneLayer += " BGCOLOR=" + colorPalette[i] + "></LAYER>\n"
        document.write(oneLayer)
}
</SCRIPT>
<LAYER NAME="display" BGCOLOR="gray" TOP=100 LEFT=80 WIDTH=200
HEIGHT=200>
<B><FONT COLOR="white"><CENTER>Some reversed text to test against
background colors.</CENTER></FONT></B>
</LAYER>
</BODY>
</HTML>
```

Related Items: `layer.background` **property;** `layer.onMouseOver=` **event handler.**

clip

Value: String   **Gettable:** Yes   **Settable:** Yes

	Nav2	Nav3	Nav4	IE3/J1	IE3/J2	IE4/J3
Compatibility			✔			

The `layer.clip` property is itself an object (the only one in Netscape 4's document object model that exposes itself as a rectangle object) with six geographical properties defining the position and size of a rectangular area of a layer visible to the user. Those six properties are

```
clip.top
clip.left
clip.bottom
clip.right
clip.width
clip.height
```

The unit of measure is pixels, and the values are relative to the top-left corner of the layer object.

A clip region can be the same size as or smaller than the layer object. If the `CLIP` attribute is not defined in the `<LAYER>` tag, the clipping region is the same size as the layer. In this case, the `clip.left` and `clip.top` values are automatically zero, because the clip region starts at the very top-left corner of the layer's rectangle (measurement is relative to the layer object whose clip property you're dealing with). The height and width of the layer object are not available properties in Navigator 4. Therefore, you may have to use other means to get that information into your scripts if you need it (I do it in Listing 19-4). Also be aware that even if you set the `HEIGHT` and `WIDTH` attributes of a layer tag, the content rules the initial size of the visible layer unless the tag also includes specific clipping instructions. Images, for example, expand a layer to fit the `HEIGHT` and `WIDTH` attributes of the `<IMG>` tag; text (either from an external HTML file or inline in the current file) adheres to the `<LAYER>` tag's `WIDTH` attribute, but flows down as far as necessary to display every character.

Setting a `clip` property does not move the layer or the content of the layer — only the visible area of the layer. Each adjustment has a unique impact on the apparent motion of the visible region. For example, if the `clip.left` value is increased from its original position of 0 to 20, the entire left edge of the rectangle shifts to the right by 20 pixels. No other edge moves. Changes to the `clip.width` property move only the right edge; changes to the `clip.height` property affect only the bottom edge. Unfortunately, no shortcuts exist to adjusting multiple edges at once. JavaScript is fast enough on most client machines to give the impression that multiple sides are moving if you issue assignment statements to different edges in sequence.

Example

Due to the edge movement behavior of adjustments to `layer.clip` properties, I have devised Listing 19-4 to let you experiment with adjustments to each of the six properties. The document loads one layer that is adjustable by entering alternative values into six text fields — one per property. Figure 19-2 shows the page.

As you enter values, all properties are updated to show their current values (via the `showValues()` function). Pay particular attention to the apparent motion of the edge and the effect the change has on at least one other property. For example, a change to the `layer.clip.left` value also affects the `layer.clip.width` property value.

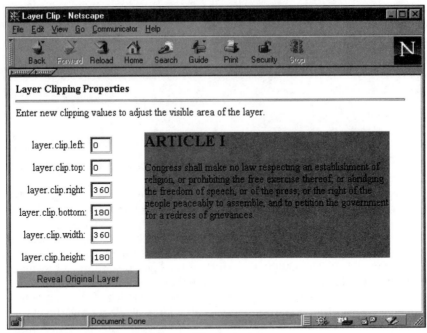

Figure 19-2: Experiment with layer.clip properties

Listing 19-4: **Adjusting layer.clip properties**

```
<HTML>
<HEAD>
<TITLE>Layer Clip</TITLE>
<SCRIPT LANGUAGE="JavaScript">
var origLayerWidth = 0
var origLayerHeight = 0
function initializeXY() {
        origLayerWidth = document.display.clip.width
        origLayerHeight = document.display.clip.height
        showValues()
}

function setClip(field) {
        var clipVal = parseInt(field.value)
        document.display.clip[field.name] = clipVal
        showValues()
}
function showValues() {
        var form = document.layers[0].document.forms[0]
        var propName
        for (var i = 0; i < form.elements.length; i++) {
            propName = form.elements[i].name
            if (form.elements[i].type == "text") {
```

```
                        form.elements[i].value = document.display.clip[propName]
                }
        }
}
var intervalID
function revealClip() {
        var midWidth = Math.round(origLayerWidth /2)
        var midHeight = Math.round(origLayerHeight /2)
        document.display.clip.left = midWidth
        document.display.clip.top = midHeight
        document.display.clip.right = midWidth
        document.display.clip.bottom = midHeight
        intervalID = setInterval("stepClip()",1)
}
function stepClip() {
        var widthDone = false
        var heightDone = false
        if (document.display.clip.left > 0) {
            document.display.clip.left += -2
            document.display.clip.right += 2
        } else {
            widthDone = true
        }
        if (document.display.clip.top > 0) {
            document.display.clip.top += -1
            document.display.clip.bottom += 1
        } else {
            heightDone = true
        }
        showValues()
        if (widthDone && heightDone) {
            clearInterval(intervalID)
        }
}
</SCRIPT>
</HEAD>
<BODY onLoad="initializeXY()">
<B>Layer Clipping Properties</B>
<HR>
Enter new clipping values to adjust the visible area of the layer.<P>
<LAYER TOP=80>
<FORM>
<TABLE>
<TR>
        <TD ALIGN="right">layer.clip.left:</TD>
        <TD><INPUT TYPE="text" NAME="left" SIZE=3
onChange="setClip(this)"></TD>
</TR>
<TR>
        <TD ALIGN="right">layer.clip.top:</TD>
        <TD><INPUT TYPE="text" NAME="top" SIZE=3
onChange="setClip(this)"></TD>
</TR>
```

(continued)

Listing 19-4 *(continued)*

```
<TR>
        <TD ALIGN="right">layer.clip.right:</TD>
        <TD><INPUT TYPE="text" NAME="right" SIZE=3
onChange="setClip(this)"></TD>
</TR>
<TR>
        <TD ALIGN="right">layer.clip.bottom:</TD>
        <TD><INPUT TYPE="text" NAME="bottom" SIZE=3
onChange="setClip(this)"></TD>
</TR>
<TR>
        <TD ALIGN="right">layer.clip.width:</TD>
        <TD><INPUT TYPE="text" NAME="width" SIZE=3
onChange="setClip(this)"></TD>
</TR>
<TR>
        <TD ALIGN="right">layer.clip.height:</TD>
        <TD><INPUT TYPE="text" NAME="height" SIZE=3
onChange="setClip(this)"></TD>
</TR>
</TABLE>
<INPUT TYPE="button" VALUE="Reveal Original Layer"
onClick="revealClip()">
</FORM>
</LAYER>
<LAYER NAME="display" BGCOLOR="coral" TOP=80 LEFT=200 WIDTH=360
HEIGHT=180>
<H2>ARTICLE I</H2>
<P>
Congress shall make no law respecting an establishment of religion, or
prohibiting the free exercise thereof; or abridging the freedom of
speech, or of the press; or the right of the people peaceably to
assemble, and to petition the government for a redress of grievances.
</P>
</LAYER>
</BODY>
</HTML>
```

Listing 19-4 has a lot of other scripting in it to demonstrate a couple other clip area techniques. After the document loads, the onLoad= event handler initializes two global variables that represent the starting height and width of the layer as determined from the clip.height and clip.width properties. Because the <LAYER> tag does not specify any CLIP attributes, the layer.clip region is ensured of being the same as the layer's dimensions at load time.

I preserve the initial values for a somewhat advanced set of functions that act in response to the Reveal Original Layer button. The goal of the button is to temporarily shrink the clipping area to nothing, and then expand the clip rectangle gradually from the very center of the layer. The effect is analogous to a zoom-out visual effect.

The clip region shrinks to practically nothing by setting all four edges to the same point midway along the height and width of the layer. The script then uses `setInterval()` to control the animation in `setClip()`. To make the zoom even on both axes, I first made sure that the initial size of the layer was an even ratio: Twice as wide as it is tall. Each time through the `setClip()` function, the `clip.left` and `clip.right` values are adjusted in their respective directions by two pixels, `clip.top` and `clip.bottom` by one pixel.

To make sure the animation stops when the layer is at its original size, I check whether the `clip.top` and `clip.left` values are their original zero values. If they are, I set a Boolean variable for each side. When both variables indicate that the clip rectangle is its original size, the script cancels the `setInterval()` action.

Related Items: `layer.pageX` property; `layer.pageY` property; `layer.resizeTo()` method.

document

Value: Document Object   **Gettable:** Yes   **Settable:** No

	Nav2	Nav3	Nav4	IE3/J1	IE3/J2	IE4/J3
Compatibility			✔			

Your scripts will practically never have to retrieve the `document` property of a layer. But it is important to remember that it is always there as the actual container of content in the layer. As described at length in the opening section about the layer object, the document object reference plays a large role in assembling addresses to content items and properties in other layers. A document inside a layer has the same powers, properties, and methods of the main document in the browser window or a frame.

Related Items: document object.

left
top

Value: Integer   **Gettable:** Yes   **Settable:** Yes

	Nav2	Nav3	Nav4	IE3/J1	IE3/J2	IE4/J3
Compatibility			✔			

The `layer.left` and `layer.top` properties correspond to the LEFT and TOP attributes of the `<LAYER>` tag. These integer values determine the horizontal and vertical coordinate point of the top-left corner of the layer relative to the browser window, frame, or parent layer in which it lives. The coordinate system of the layer's most immediate container is the one that these properties reflect.

Adjustments to these properties reposition the layer without adjusting its size. Clipping area values are untouched by changes in these properties. Thus, if you are creating a draggable layer object that needs to follow a dragged mouse pointer in a straight line along the x or y axis, it is more convenient to adjust one of these properties than to use the `layer.moveTo()` method.

Example

To let you experiment with manually setting `layer.top` and `layer.left` properties, I present a modified version of the layer.clip example (Listing 19-4) in Listing 19-5. The current example again has the one modifiable layer, but only four text fields in which you can enter values. Two fields are for the `layer.left` and `layer.top` properties; the other two are for the `layer.clip.left` and `layer.clip.top` properties. I present both sets of values here to help reinforce the lack of connection between layer and clip location properties in the same layer object.

Listing 19-5: Comparison of Layer and Clip Location Properties

```
<HTML>
<HEAD>
<TITLE>Layer vs. Clip</TITLE>
<SCRIPT LANGUAGE="JavaScript">
function setClip(field) {
        var clipVal = parseInt(field.value)
        document.display.clip[field.name] = clipVal
        showValues()
}
function setLayer(field) {
        var layerVal = parseInt(field.value)
        document.display[field.name] = layerVal
        showValues()
}
function showValues() {
        var form = document.layers[0].document.forms[0]
        form.elements[0].value = document.display.left
        form.elements[1].value = document.display.top
        form.elements[2].value = document.display.clip.left
        form.elements[3].value = document.display.clip.top
}
</SCRIPT>
</HEAD>
<BODY onLoad="showValues()">
<B>Layer vs. Clip Location Properties</B>
<HR>
Enter new layer and clipping values to adjust the layer.<P>
<LAYER TOP=80>
<FORM>
<TABLE>
<TR>
        <TD ALIGN="right">layer.left:</TD>
```

```
        <TD><INPUT TYPE="text" NAME="left" SIZE=3
onChange="setLayer(this)"></TD>
</TR>
<TR>
        <TD ALIGN="right">layer.top:</TD>
        <TD><INPUT TYPE="text" NAME="top" SIZE=3
onChange="setLayer(this)"></TD>
</TR>
<TR>
        <TD ALIGN="right">layer.clip.left:</TD>
        <TD><INPUT TYPE="text" NAME="left" SIZE=3
onChange="setClip(this)"></TD>
</TR>
<TR>
        <TD ALIGN="right">layer.clip.top:</TD>
        <TD><INPUT TYPE="text" NAME="top" SIZE=3
onChange="setClip(this)"></TD>
</TR>
</TABLE>
</FORM>
</LAYER>
<LAYER NAME="display" BGCOLOR="coral" TOP=80 LEFT=200 WIDTH=360
HEIGHT=180>
<H2>ARTICLE I</H2>
<P>
Congress shall make no law respecting an establishment of religion, or
prohibiting the free exercise thereof; or abridging the freedom of
speech, or of the press; or the right of the people peaceably to
assemble, and to petition the government for a redress of grievances.
</P>
</LAYER>
</BODY>
</HTML>
```

Related Items: `layer.clip` properties; `layer.parentLayer` property.

name

Value: String   **Gettable:** Yes   **Settable:** No

	Nav2	Nav3	Nav4	IE3/J1	IE3/J2	IE4/J3
Compatibility			✔			

The `layer.name` property reflects the NAME attribute of the `<LAYER>` tag or name you assign to a similar CSS-P object. This property is read-only. If you don't assign a name to a layer as it is being created, Navigator generates a name for the layer in the format:

```
js_layer_nn
```

where *nn* is a serial number. That serial number is not the same every time the page loads, so you cannot rely on the automatically generated name to help you script an absolute reference to the layer.

Related Items: None.

pageX
pageY

Value: String   **Gettable:** Yes   **Settable:** Yes

	Nav2	Nav3	Nav4	IE3/J1	IE3/J2	IE4/J3
Compatibility			✔			

In Netscape's coordinate terminology, the page is the content area of a browser window (or frame) object. The top-left corner of the page space is point 0,0, and any layer, including a nested layer, can be positioned on the page relative to this corner. In the `<LAYER>` tag, the attributes that let authors set the position are `PAGEX` and `PAGEY`. These values are retrievable and modifiable as the `layer.pageX` and `layer.pageY` properties. Note the capitalization of the final letters of these property names.

The `layer.pageX` and `layer.pageY` values are identical to `layer.left` and `layer.top` only when the layer in question is at the main document level. That's because the `layer.left` and `layer.top` values are measured by the next higher container's coordinate system — which in this case happens to be the same as the page.

The situation gets more interesting when you're dealing with nested layers. For a nested layer, the `layer.pageX` and `layer.pageY` values are still measured relative to the page, while `layer.left` and `layer.top` are measured relative to the next higher layer. If conceiving of these differences makes your head hurt, the example in Listing 19-6 should help clear things up for you.

Adjusting the `layer.pageX` and `layer.pageY` values of any layer has the same effect as using the `layer.moveToAbsolute()` method, which measures its coordinate system based on the page. If you are creating flying layers on your page, you won't go wrong by setting the `layer.pageX` and `layer.pageY` properties (or using the `moveToAbsolute()` method) in your script. That way, should you add another layer in the hierarchy between the base document and the flying layer, the animation will be in the same coordinate system as before the new layer was added.

Example

Listing 19-6 defines one outer layer and one nested inner layer of different colors (see Figure 19-3). The inner layer contains some text content, while the outer layer is sized initially to present a colorful border by being below the inner layer and 10 pixels wider and taller.

Two sets of fields display (and let you change) the `layer.pageX`, `layer.pageY`, `layer.left`, and `layer.top` properties for each of the nested layers. Each set of fields is color-coded to its corresponding layer.

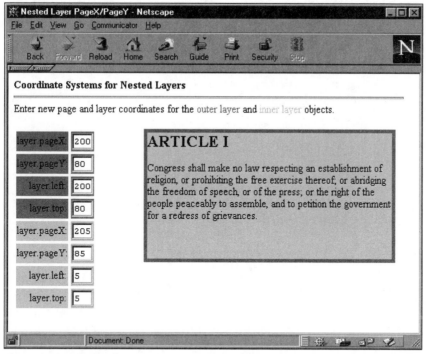

Figure 19-3: Testing the position properties of nested layers

When you change any value, all values are recalculated and displayed in the other fields. For example, the initial pageX position for the outer layer is 200 pixels; for the inner layer the pageX value is 205 pixels (accounting for the five-pixel "border" around the inner layer). If you change the outer layer's pageX value to 220, the outer layer moves to the right by 20 pixels, taking the inner layer along for the ride. The layer.pageX value for the inner layer after the move is 225 pixels.

The outer layer values for the pairs of values are always the same no matter what. But for the inner layer, the page values are significantly different from the layer.left and layer.top values, because these latter values are measured relative to their containing layer, the outer layer. If you move the outer layer, the inner layer values for layer.left and layer.top don't change one iota.

Listing 19-6: **Testing Nested Layer Coordinate Systems**

```
<HTML>
<HEAD>
<TITLE>Nested Layer PageX/PageY</TITLE>
<SCRIPT LANGUAGE="JavaScript">
function setOuterPage(field) {
        var layerVal = parseInt(field.value)
        document.outerDisplay[field.name] = layerVal
        showValues()
```

(continued)

Listing 19-6 *(continued)*

```
}
function setOuterLayer(field) {
        var layerVal = parseInt(field.value)
        document.outerDisplay[field.name] = layerVal
        showValues()
}
function setInnerPage(field) {
        var layerVal = parseInt(field.value)
        document.outerDisplay.document.innerDisplay[field.name] =
layerVal
        showValues()
}
function setInnerLayer(field) {
        var layerVal = parseInt(field.value)
        document.outerDisplay.document.innerDisplay[field.name] =
layerVal
        showValues()
}
function showValues() {
        var form = document.layers[0].document.forms[0]
        form.elements[0].value = document.outerDisplay.pageX
        form.elements[1].value = document.outerDisplay.pageY
        form.elements[2].value = document.outerDisplay.left
        form.elements[3].value = document.outerDisplay.top
        form.elements[4].value =
document.outerDisplay.document.innerDisplay.pageX
        form.elements[5].value =
document.outerDisplay.document.innerDisplay.pageY
        form.elements[6].value =
document.outerDisplay.document.innerDisplay.left
        form.elements[7].value =
document.outerDisplay.document.innerDisplay.top
}
</SCRIPT>
</HEAD>
<BODY onLoad="showValues()">
<B>Coordinate Systems for Nested Layers</B>
<HR>
Enter new page and layer coordinates for the <FONT COLOR="coral">outer
layer</FONT> and <FONT COLOR="aquamarine">inner layer</FONT>
objects.<P>
<LAYER TOP=80>
<FORM>
<TABLE>
<TR>
        <TD ALIGN="right" BGCOLOR="coral">layer.pageX:</TD>
        <TD BGCOLOR="coral"><INPUT TYPE="text" NAME="pageX" SIZE=3
            onChange="setOuterPage(this)"></TD>
</TR>
<TR>
```

```
        <TD ALIGN="right" BGCOLOR="coral">layer.pageY:</TD>
        <TD BGCOLOR="coral"><INPUT TYPE="text" NAME="pageY" SIZE=3
           onChange="setOuterPage(this)"></TD>
</TR>
<TR>
        <TD ALIGN="right" BGCOLOR="coral">layer.left:</TD>
        <TD BGCOLOR="coral"><INPUT TYPE="text" NAME="left" SIZE=3
           onChange="setOuterLayer(this)"></TD>
</TR>
<TR>
        <TD ALIGN="right" BGCOLOR="coral">layer.top:</TD>
        <TD BGCOLOR="coral"><INPUT TYPE="text" NAME="top" SIZE=3
           onChange="setOuterLayer(this)"></TD>
</TR>
<TR>
        <TD ALIGN="right" BGCOLOR="aquamarine">layer.pageX:</TD>
        <TD BGCOLOR="aquamarine"><INPUT TYPE="text" NAME="pageX" SIZE=3
           onChange="setInnerPage(this)"></TD>
</TR>
<TR>
        <TD ALIGN="right" BGCOLOR="aquamarine">layer.pageY:</TD>
        <TD BGCOLOR="aquamarine"><INPUT TYPE="text" NAME="pageY" SIZE=3
           onChange="setInnerPage(this)"></TD>
</TR>
<TR>
        <TD ALIGN="right" BGCOLOR="aquamarine">layer.left:</TD>
        <TD BGCOLOR="aquamarine"><INPUT TYPE="text" NAME="left" SIZE=3
           onChange="setInnerLayer(this)"></TD>
</TR>
<TR>
        <TD ALIGN="right" BGCOLOR="aquamarine">layer.top:</TD>
        <TD BGCOLOR="aquamarine"><INPUT TYPE="text" NAME="top" SIZE=3
           onChange="setInnerLayer(this)"></TD>
</TR>
</TABLE>
</FORM>
</LAYER>
<LAYER NAME="outerDisplay" BGCOLOR="coral" TOP=80 LEFT=200 WIDTH=370
HEIGHT=190>
<LAYER NAME="innerDisplay" BGCOLOR="aquamarine" TOP=5 LEFT=5 WIDTH=360
HEIGHT=180>
<H2>ARTICLE I</H2>
<P>
Congress shall make no law respecting an establishment of religion, or
prohibiting the free exercise thereof; or abridging the freedom of
speech, or of the press; or the right of the people peaceably to
assemble, and to petition the government for a redress of grievances.
</P>
</LAYER>
</LAYER>
</BODY>
</HTML>
```

Related Items: `layer.left` property; `layer.top` property; `layer.moveToAbsolute()` method; `window.innerHeight` property; `window.innerWidth` property.

parentLayer

Value: Object   **Gettable:** Yes   **Settable:** No

	Nav2	Nav3	Nav4	IE3/J1	IE3/J2	IE4/J3
Compatibility			✔			

Every layer has a parent that contains that layer. In the case of a layer defined at the main document level, its parent layer is the window or frame containing that document (the "page"). For this kind of layer, the `layer.parentLayer` property object is a window object. But for any nested layer contained by a layer, the `parentLayer` property is a layer object.

Be aware of the important distinction between `layer.parentLayer` and `layer.below`. As a parent layer can contain multiple layers in the next containment level, each of those layers' `parentLayer` properties evaluate to that same parent layer. But because each layer object is its own physical layer among the stack of layers on a page, the `layer.below` property in each layer points to a different object — the layer next lower in z-order.

Keeping the direction of things straight can get confusing. On the one hand, you have a layer's parent, which, by connotation, is higher up the hierarchical chain of layers. On the other hand, the order of physical layers is such that a parent more than likely has a lower z-order than its children because it is defined earlier in the document.

The `layer.parentLayer` property is used primarily to assemble references to other nested layers. See the discussion about layer references at the beginning of this chapter for several syntax examples.

Related Items: `layer.above` property; `layer.below` property.

siblingAbove

siblingBelow

See `layer.above` and `layer.below` properties earlier in this chapter.

src

Value: String   **Gettable:** Yes   **Settable:** Yes

	Nav2	Nav3	Nav4	IE3/J1	IE3/J2	IE4/J3
Compatibility			✔			

Content for a layer may come from within the document that defines the layer or from an external source, such as an HTML or image file. If defined by a `<LAYER>` tag, an external file is specified by the `SRC` attribute. It is this attribute that is reflected by the `layer.src` property.

The value of this property is a string of the URL of the external file. If no `SRC` property is specified in the `<LAYER>` tag, the value returns `null`. Do not set this property to an empty string in an effort to clear the layer of content: `document.write()` or load an empty page instead. Otherwise, the empty string is treated like a URL and loads the current client directory.

You can, however, change the content of a layer by loading a new source file into the layer. Simply assign a new URL to the `layer.src` property. Again, if a layer has nested layers inside it, those nested layers get blown away by the content that loads into the layer whose `src` property you are changing. The new file, of course, might be an HTML file that defines its own nested layers, which then become part of the page's object model.

Netscape also provides the `layer.load()` method to put new content into a layer. One advantage of the method is that an optional second parameter lets you redefine the width of the layer at the same time as you specify a new document. But if you are simply replacing the content in the same width layer, you can use either way of loading new content.

Be aware that the height and width of a replacement layer is as much governed by its hard-coded content size as by the initial loading of any layer. For example, if your layer is initially sized at a width of 200 pixels and your replacement layer document includes an image whose width is set to 500 pixels, the layer expands its width to accommodate the larger content — unless you also restrict the view of the layer via the `layer.clip` properties. Similarly, longer text content flows beyond the bottom of the previously sized layer unless restricted by clipping properties.

Example

Setting the `layer.src` property of a layer that is a member of a layer family (that is, one with at least one parent and one child) can be tricky business if you're not careful. Listing 19-7 presents a workspace for you to see how changing the `src` property of outer and inner layers affects the scenery.

When you first load the document, one outer layer contains one inner layer (each with a different background color). Control buttons on the page let you set the `layer.src` property of each layer independently. Changes to the inner layer content affect only that layer. Long content forces the inner layer to expand its depth, but its view is automatically clipped by its parent layer.

Changing the outer layer content, however, removes the inner layer completely. Code in the listing shows one way to examine for the presence of a particular layer before attempting to load new content in it. If the inner layer doesn't exist, the script creates a new layer on the fly to replace the original inner layer.

Listing 19-7: **Setting Nested Layer Source Content**

```
<HTML>
<HEAD>
<TITLE>Layer Source</TITLE>
<SCRIPT LANGUAGE="JavaScript">
function loadOuter(doc) {
      document.outerDisplay.src = doc
}
function loadInner(doc) {
      var nested = document.outerDisplay.document.layers
      if (nested.length > 0) {
         // inner layer exists, so load content or restore
         if (doc) {
            nested[0].src = doc
         } else {
            restoreInner(nested[0])
         }
      } else {
         // prompt user about restoring inner layer
         if (confirm("The inner layer has been removed by loading an
outer document. Restore the original layers?")) {
            restoreLayers(doc)
         }
      }
}
function restoreLayers(doc) {
      // reset appearance of outer layer
      document.outerDisplay.bgColor = "coral"
      document.outerDisplay.resizeTo(370,190) // sets clip
      document.outerDisplay.document.write("")
      document.outerDisplay.document.close()
      // generate new inner layer
      var newInner = new Layer(360, document.layers["outerDisplay"])
      newInner.bgColor = "aquamarine"
      newInner.moveTo(5,5)
      if (doc) {
         // user clicked an inner content button
         newInner.src = doc
      } else {
         // return to pristine look
         restoreInner(newInner)
      }
      newInner.visibility = "show"
}
function restoreInner(inner) {
      inner.document.write("<HTML><BODY><P><B>Placeholder text for raw
inner layer.</B></P></BODY></HTML>")
      inner.document.close()
      inner.resizeTo(360,180) // sets clip
}
```

```
</SCRIPT>
</HEAD>
<BODY>
<B>Setting the <TT>layer.src</TT> Property of Nested Layers</B>
<HR>
Click the buttons to see what happens when you load new source
documents into the <FONT COLOR="coral">outer layer</FONT> and <FONT
COLOR="aquamarine">inner layer</FONT> objects.<P>
<LAYER TOP=100 BGCOLOR="coral">
<FORM>
Load into outer layer:<BR>
<INPUT TYPE="button" VALUE="Article I"
onClick="loadOuter('article1.htm')"><BR>
<INPUT TYPE="button" VALUE="Entire Bill of Rights"
onClick="loadOuter('bofright.htm')"><BR>
</FORM>
</LAYER>
<LAYER TOP=220 BGCOLOR="aquamarine">
<FORM>
Load into inner layer:<BR>
<INPUT TYPE="button" VALUE="Article I"
onClick="loadInner('article1.htm')"><BR>
<INPUT TYPE="button" VALUE="Entire Bill of Rights"
onClick="loadInner('bofright.htm')"><BR>
<INPUT TYPE="button" VALUE="Restore Original"
onClick="loadInner()"><BR>
</FORM>
</LAYER>
<LAYER NAME="outerDisplay" BGCOLOR="coral" TOP=100 LEFT=200 WIDTH=370
HEIGHT=190>
        <LAYER NAME="innerDisplay" BGCOLOR="aquamarine" TOP=5 LEFT=5
WIDTH=360 HEIGHT=180>
        <P><B>Placeholder text for raw inner layer.</B></P>
        </LAYER>
</LAYER>
</BODY>
</HTML>
```

The restoration of the original layers via script (as opposed to reloading the document) does not perform a perfect restoration. The key difference is the scripts use the `layer.resizeTo()` method to set the layers to the height and width established by the `<LAYER>` tags that created the layers in the first place. This method, however, sets the clipping rectangle of the layer, not the layer's size. Therefore, if you use the script to restore the layers, loading the longer text file into either layer does not force the layer to expand to display all the content: The clipping region governs the view.

Related Items: `layer.load()` method; `layer.resizeTo()` method.

visibility

Value: String   **Gettable:** Yes   **Settable:** Yes

	Nav2	Nav3	Nav4	IE3/J1	IE3/J2	IE4/J3
Compatibility			✔			

A layer's visibility property can use one of three settings: show, hide, or inherit — the same values you can assign to the VISIBILITY attribute of the <LAYER> tag. But to be compatible with the same property in Internet Explorer 4, Navigator 4 also lets you set the property to hidden and visible.

Unlike many other layer properties, the visibility property can be set such that a layer can either follow the behavior of its parent or strike out on its own. By default, a layer's visibility property is set to inherit, which means the layer's visibility is governed solely by that of its parent (and of *its* parent, if the nesting goes many layers). When the governing parent's property is, say, hide, the child's property remains inherit. Thus, you cannot tell whether an inheriting layer is presently visible or not without checking up the hierarchy (with the help of the layer.parentLayer property). However, you can override the parent's behavior by setting the current layer's property explicitly to show or hide. This action does not alter in any way other parent-child relationships between layers.

Example

Use the page in Listing 19-8 to see how the layer.visibility property settings affect a pair of nested layers. When the page first loads, the default inherit setting is in effect. Changes you make to the outer layer by clicking on the outer layer buttons affect the inner layer, but setting the inner layer's properties to hide or show severs the visibility relationship between parent and child.

Listing 19-8: **Nested Layer Visibility Relationships**

```
<HTML>
<HEAD>
<TITLE>Layer Source</TITLE>
<SCRIPT LANGUAGE="JavaScript">
function setOuterVis(type) {
      document.outerDisplay.visibility = type
}
function setInnerVis(type) {
      document.outerDisplay.document.innerDisplay.visibility = type
}
</SCRIPT>
</HEAD>
<BODY>
<B>Setting the <TT>layer.visibility</TT> Property of Nested Layers</B>
<HR>
```

```
Click the buttons to see what happens when you change the visibility
of the <FONT COLOR="coral">outer layer</FONT> and <FONT
COLOR="aquamarine">inner layer</FONT> objects.<P>
<LAYER TOP=100 BGCOLOR="coral">
<FORM>
Control outer layer property:<BR>
<INPUT TYPE="button" VALUE="Hide Outer Layer"
onClick="setOuterVis('hide')"><BR>
<INPUT TYPE="button" VALUE="Show Outer Layer"
onClick="setOuterVis('show')"><BR>
</FORM>
</LAYER>
<LAYER TOP=220 BGCOLOR="aquamarine">
<FORM>
Control inner layer property:<BR>
<INPUT TYPE="button" VALUE="Hide Inner Layer"
onClick="setInnerVis('hide')"><BR>
<INPUT TYPE="button" VALUE="Show Inner Layer"
onClick="setInnerVis('show')"><BR>
<INPUT TYPE="button" VALUE="Inherit Outer Layer"
onClick="setInnerVis('inherit')"><BR>
</FORM>
</LAYER>
<LAYER NAME="outerDisplay" BGCOLOR="coral" TOP=100 LEFT=200 WIDTH=370
HEIGHT=190>
        <LAYER NAME="innerDisplay" BGCOLOR="aquamarine" TOP=5 LEFT=5
WIDTH=360 HEIGHT=180>
        <P><B>Placeholder text for raw inner layer.</B></P>
        </LAYER>
</LAYER>
</BODY>
</HTML>
```

Related Items: None.

zIndex

Value: Integer   **Gettable:** Yes   **Settable:** Yes

	Nav2	Nav3	Nav4	IE3/J1	IE3/J2	IE4/J3
Compatibility			✔			

Close relationships exist among the `layer.above`, `layer.below`, and `layer.zIndex` properties. When you define a layer in a document with the `<LAYER>` tag, you can supply only one of the three attributes (ABOVE, BELOW, and Z-INDEX). After the layer is generated with any one of those attributes, the document object model automatically assigns values to at least two of those properties (`layer.above` and `layer.below`) unless you specify the Z-INDEX attribute, in which case all three properties are assigned to the layer. If you don't specify any of these properties, the physical stacking order of the layers is the same as in the HTML document. The `layer.above` and `layer.below` properties are set as described in their discussion earlier in this chapter. But the `layer.zIndex` properties for all layers are zero.

The attribute is spelled with a hyphen after the "z". Because a JavaScript property name cannot contain a hyphen, the character has been removed for the property name. The capital "I" is important, because JavaScript properties are case-sensitive.

Changes to `layer.zIndex` values affect the stacking order only of sibling layers. It is possible to assign the same value to two layers, but the last layer to have its `layer.zIndex` property set will be physically above the other one. Therefore, if you want to ensure a stacking order, you should set the `zIndex` values for all layers within a container. Each value should be a unique number.

Stacking order is determined simply by the value of the integer assigned to the property. If you want to stack three sibling layers, the order would be the same if they were assigned the values of 1, 2, 3 or 10, 13, 50. As you modify a `layer.zIndex` value, the `layer.above` and `layer.below` properties for all affected layers change as a result.

Avoid setting `zIndex` property values to negative numbers in Navigator 4. Negative values are treated as their absolute (positive) values for ordering.

Example

The relationships among the three stacking properties can be difficult to visualize. Listing 19-9 offers a way to see the results of changing the `layer.zIndex` properties of three overlapping sibling layers. The beginning organization of layers after the page loads is shown in Figure 19-4.

Original stacking order is governed by the position of the `<LAYER>` tags in the document. Because the attribute is not set in the HTML, the initial values appear as zero for all three layers. But, as the page reveals, the `layer.above` and `layer.below` properties are automatically established. When a layer has no other layer object above it, the page shows "(none)". Also, if the layer below the bottom of the stack is the main window, a strange inner layer name is assigned (something like `_js_layer_21`).

To experiment with this page, first make sure you understand the `layer.above` and `layer.below` readings for the default order of the layers. Then assign different orders to the layers with value sequences such as 3-2-1, 1-3-2, 2-2-2, and so on. Each time you enter one new value, check the actual layers to see if their stacking order changed and how that affected the other properties of all layers.

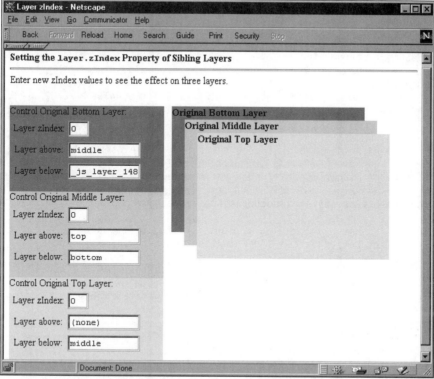

Figure 19-4: A place to play with zIndex property settings

Listing 19-9: **Relationships among zIndex, Above and Below**

```
<HTML>
<HEAD>
<TITLE>Layer zIndex</TITLE>
<SCRIPT LANGUAGE="JavaScript">
function setZ(field) {
      switch (field.name) {
          case "top" :
              document.top.zIndex = parseInt(field.value)
              break
          case "mid" :
              document.middle.zIndex = parseInt(field.value)
              break
          case "bot" :
              document.bottom.zIndex = parseInt(field.value)
      }
      showValues()
}
function showValues() {
```

(continued)

Listing 19-9 *(continued)*

```
        document.layers[0].document.forms[0].bot.value =
document.bottom.zIndex
        document.layers[1].document.forms[0].mid.value =
document.middle.zIndex
        document.layers[2].document.forms[0].top.value =
document.top.zIndex

        document.layers[0].document.forms[0].above.value =
(document.bottom.above) ? document.bottom.above.name : "(none)"
        document.layers[1].document.forms[0].above.value =
(document.middle.above) ? document.middle.above.name : "(none)"
        document.layers[2].document.forms[0].above.value =
(document.top.above) ? document.top.above.name : "(none)"

        document.layers[0].document.forms[0].below.value =
(document.bottom.below) ? document.bottom.below.name : "(none)"
        document.layers[1].document.forms[0].below.value =
(document.middle.below) ? document.middle.below.name : "(none)"
        document.layers[2].document.forms[0].below.value =
(document.top.below) ? document.top.below.name : "(none)"
}
</SCRIPT>
</HEAD>
<BODY onLoad="showValues()">
<B>Setting the <TT>layer.zIndex</TT> Property of Sibling Layers</B>
<HR>
Enter new zIndex values to see the effect on three layers.<P>
<LAYER TOP=90 WIDTH=240 BGCOLOR="coral">
<FORM>
Control Original Bottom Layer:<BR>
<TABLE>
<TR><TD ALIGN="right">Layer zIndex:</TD><TD><INPUT TYPE="text"
NAME="bot" SIZE=3 onChange="setZ(this)"></TD></TR>
<TR><TD ALIGN="right">Layer above:</TD><TD><INPUT TYPE="text"
NAME="above" SIZE=13></TD></TR>
<TR><TD ALIGN="right">Layer below:</TD><TD><INPUT TYPE="text"
NAME="below" SIZE=13></TD></TR>
</TABLE>
</FORM>
</LAYER>
<LAYER TOP=220 WIDTH=240 BGCOLOR="aquamarine">
<FORM>
Control Original Middle Layer:<BR>
<TABLE>
<TR><TD ALIGN="right">Layer zIndex:</TD><TD><INPUT TYPE="text"
NAME="mid" SIZE=3 onChange="setZ(this)"></TD></TR>
<TR><TD ALIGN="right">Layer above:</TD><TD><INPUT TYPE="text"
NAME="above" SIZE=13></TD></TR>
<TR><TD ALIGN="right">Layer below:</TD><TD><INPUT TYPE="text"
NAME="below" SIZE=13></TD></TR>
```

```
</TABLE></FORM>
</LAYER>
<LAYER TOP=350 WIDTH=240 BGCOLOR="yellow">
<FORM>
Control Original Top Layer:<BR>
<TABLE><TR><TD ALIGN="right">Layer zIndex:</TD><TD><INPUT TYPE="text"
NAME="top" SIZE=3 onChange="setZ(this)"></TD></TR>
<TR><TD ALIGN="right">Layer above:</TD><TD><INPUT TYPE="text"
NAME="above" SIZE=13></TD></TR>
<TR><TD ALIGN="right">Layer below:</TD><TD><INPUT TYPE="text"
NAME="below" SIZE=13></TD></TR>
</TABLE>
</FORM>
</LAYER>
<LAYER NAME="bottom" BGCOLOR="coral" TOP=90 LEFT=260 WIDTH=300
HEIGHT=190>
        <P><B>Original Bottom Layer</B></P>
</LAYER>
        <LAYER NAME="middle" BGCOLOR="aquamarine" TOP=110 LEFT=280
WIDTH=300 HEIGHT=190>
        <P><B>Original Middle Layer</B></P>
</LAYER>
<LAYER NAME="top" BGCOLOR="yellow" TOP=130 LEFT=300 WIDTH=300
HEIGHT=190>
        <P><B>Original Top Layer</B></P>
</LAYER>
</LAYER>
</BODY>
</HTML>
```

Related Items: layer.above **property;** layer.below **property;** layer.moveAbove()
method; layer.moveBelow() method.

Methods

load("*URL*", *newLayerWidth*)

Returns: Nothing.

	Nav2	Nav3	Nav4	IE3/J1	IE3/J2	IE4/J3
Compatibility			✔			

One way to change the content of a layer after it has loaded is to use the
layer.load() method. This method has an advantage over setting the layer.src
property, because the second parameter is a new layer width for the content if one
is desired. If you don't specify the second parameter, a small default value is
substituted for you (unless the new document has hard-wired widths to its

elements that must expand the current width). If you are concerned about a new document being too long for the existing height of the layer, use the `layer.resizeTo()` method or set the individual `layer.clip` properties before loading the new document. This keeps the viewable area of the layer at a fixed size.

Example

Buttons in Listing 19-10 let you load short and long documents into a layer. The first two buttons don't change the width (in fact, the second parameter to `layer.load()` is the `layer.clip.left` value). For the second two buttons, a narrower width than the original is specified. Click the Restore button frequently to return to a known state.

Listing 19-10: Loading Documents into Layers

```
<HTML>
<HEAD>
<TITLE>Layer zIndex</TITLE>
<SCRIPT LANGUAGE="JavaScript">
function loadDoc(URL,width) {
        if (!width) {
            width = document.myLayer.clip.width
        }
        document.myLayer.load(URL, width)
}
</SCRIPT>
</HEAD>
<BODY>
<B>Loading New Documents</B>
<HR>
<LAYER TOP=90 WIDTH=240 BGCOLOR="yellow">
<FORM>
Loading new documents:<BR>
<INPUT TYPE="button" VALUE="Small Doc/Existing Width"
onClick="loadDoc('article1.htm')"><BR>
<INPUT TYPE="button" VALUE="Large Doc/Existing Width"
onClick="loadDoc('bofright.htm')"><P>
<INPUT TYPE="button" VALUE="Small Doc/Narrower Width"
onClick="loadDoc('article1.htm',200)"><BR>
<INPUT TYPE="button" VALUE="Large Doc/Narrower Width"
onClick="loadDoc('bofright.htm',200)"><P>
<INPUT TYPE="button" VALUE="Restore"
onClick="location.reload()"></FORM>
</LAYER>
<LAYER NAME="myLayer" BGCOLOR="yellow" TOP=90 LEFT=300 WIDTH=300
HEIGHT=190>
        <P><B>Text loaded in original document.</B></P>
</LAYER>
</BODY>
</HTML>
```

Related Items: `layer.src` property.

moveAbove(*layerObject*)
moveBelow(*layerObject*)

Returns: Nothing.

	Nav2	Nav3	Nav4	IE3/J1	IE3/J2	IE4/J3
Compatibility			✔			

With the exception of the `layer.zIndex` property, the layer object does not let you adjust properties that affect the global stacking order of layers. The `layer.moveAbove()` and `layer.moveBelow()` methods let you adjust a layer in relation to another layer object. Both layers in the transaction must be siblings — they must be in the same container, whether it be the base document window or some other layer. You cannot move existing layers from one container to another, but must delete the layer from the source and create a new layer in the destination. Neither of these methods affects the viewable size or coordinate system location of the layer.

The syntax for these methods is a little strange at first, because the statement that makes these work has two layer object references in it. Named first in the statement (to the left of the method name, separated by a period) is the layer object you want to move. The sole parameter for each method is a reference to the layer object that is the physical reference point for the trip. For example, in the statement

```
document.fred.moveAbove(document.ginger)
```

the instruction is to move the `fred` layer above the `ginger` layer. The `fred` layer can be in any stacking relation to `ginger`, but, again, both must be in the same container.

Obviously, after one of these moves, the `layer.above` and `layer.below` properties of some or all layers in the container feel the ripple effects of the shift in order. If you have several layers that may have gotten out of order due to user interaction with your scripts, you can reorder them using these methods or, more practically, by setting their `layer.zIndex` properties. In the latter case, it is easier to visualize through your code how the ordering is being handled with increasing `zIndex` values for each layer.

Example

You can see the `layer.moveAbove()` method at work in Listing 19-1, earlier in this chapter.

Related Items: `layer.above` property; `layer.below` property; `layer.zIndex` property.

```
moveBy(deltaX,deltaY)
moveTo(x,y)
moveToAbsolute(x,y)
```

Returns: Nothing.

	Nav2	Nav3	Nav4	IE3/J1	IE3/J2	IE4/J3
Compatibility			✔			

Much of what CSS-Positioning is all about is being able to precisely plant an element on a Web page. The unit of measure is the pixel, with the coordinate space starting at an upper-left corner at location 0,0. That coordinate space for a layer is typically the container (parent layer) for that layer. The `layer.moveTo()` and `layer.moveBy()` methods let scripts adjust the location of a layer inside that coordinate space — very much the way `window.moveTo()` and `window.moveBy()` work for window objects.

Moving a layer entails moving it (and its nested layers) without adjusting its size or stacking order. Animation of a layer can be accomplished by issuing a series of `layer.moveTo()` methods if you know the precise points along the path. Or you can nudge the layer by increments in one or both axes with the `layer.moveBy()` method.

In case you need to position a layer with respect to the page's coordinate system (for example, you are moving items from multiple containers to a common point), the `layer.moveToAbsolute()` method bypasses the layer's immediate container. The 0,0 point for this method is the top-left corner of the content window or frame. Be aware, however, that you can move a layer to a position such that some or all of it is out of range of the container's clip rectangle.

Example

A demonstration of the `layer.moveTo()` method is shown in Listing 19-11. It is a simple script that lets you click and drag a layer around the screen. The script employs the coordinate values of the mouseMove event and, after compensating for the offset within the layer at which the click occurs, moves the layer to track the mouse action.

I wanted to present this example for an additional reason: to explain an important user interface difference between Windows and Macintosh versions of Navigator 4. In Windows versions, you can click and hold the mouse button down on an object and let the object receive all the mouseMove events as you drag the cursor around the screen. On the Macintosh, however, Navigator tries to compensate for the lack of a second mouse button by popping up a context-sensitive menu at the cursor position when the user holds the mouse button down for more than just a click. To replicate the action of dragging on the Macintosh, users must Ctrl-click (and release). That action engages a drag mode that remains in effect until the user clicks again. I suspect that fewer than ten percent of Mac Navigator users know this. Therefore, if you script any layer dragging for a cross-platform audience, be sure to include instructions for Mac users about how to effect the drag (you can add this only for Mac users by analyzing the `navigator.userAgent` string, as shown in Listing 19-11).

Notice in the listing how the layer captures a number of mouse events. Each one plays an important role in creating a mode that is essentially like a mouseStillDown event (which doesn't exist in Navigator's event model). The mouseDown event sets a Boolean flag (`engaged`) indicating that the user clicked down in the layer. At the same time, the script records how far away from the layer's top-left corner the mouseDown event occurred. This offset information is needed so that any setting of the layer's location takes this offset into account (otherwise the top-left corner of the layer would jump to the cursor position and be dragged from there).

During the drag (mouseDown events firing with each mouse movement), the `dragIt()` function checks whether the drag mode is engaged. If so, the layer is moved to the page location calculated by subtracting the original downstroke offset from the mouseMove event location on the page. When the user releases the mouse button, the mouseUp event turns off the drag mode Boolean value.

Listing 19-11: **Dragging a Layer**

```
<HTML>
<HEAD>
<TITLE>Layer Dragging</TITLE>
<SCRIPT LANGUAGE="JavaScript">
var engaged = false
var offsetX = 0
var offsetY = 0
function dragIt(e) {
        if (engaged) {
            document.myLayer.moveTo(e.pageX - offsetX, e.pageY -
offsetY)
        }
}
function engage(e) {
        engaged = true
        offsetX = e.pageX - document.myLayer.left
        offsetY = e.pageY - document.myLayer.top
}
function release() {
        engaged = false
}
</SCRIPT>
</HEAD>
<BODY>
<B>Dragging a Layer</B>
<HR>
<LAYER NAME="myLayer" BGCOLOR="lightgreen" TOP=90 LEFT=100 WIDTH=300
HEIGHT=190>
        <P><B>Drag me around the window.</B></P>
        <SCRIPT LANGUAGE="JavaScript">
        if (navigator.userAgent.indexOf("Mac") != -1) {
```

(continued)

Listing 19-11 *(continued)*

```
            document.write(" (Mac users: Ctrl-Click me first; then Click
to stop dragging.) ")
        }
      </SCRIPT>
</LAYER>
<SCRIPT LANGUAGE="JavaScript">
document.myLayer.captureEvents(Event.MOUSEDOWN | Event.MOUSEUP |
Event.MOUSEMOVE)
document.myLayer.onMouseDown = engage
document.myLayer.onMouseUp = release
document.myLayer.onMouseMove = dragIt
</SCRIPT>
</BODY>
</HTML>
```

Related Items: `layer.resizeBy()` method; `layer.resizeTo()` method; `window.moveBy()` method; `window.moveTo()` method.

resizeBy(*deltaX,deltaY*)
resizeTo(*width,height*)

Returns: Nothing.

	Nav2	Nav3	Nav4	IE3/J1	IE3/J2	IE4/J3
Compatibility			✔			

The basic functionality and parameter requirements of the `layer.resizeBy()` and `layer.resizeTo()` methods are similar to the identically named methods of the window object. You should, however, be cognizant of some considerations unique to layers.

Unlike resizing a window, which causes all content to reflow to fit the new size, the layer sizing methods aren't truly adjusting the size of the layer. Instead, the methods control the size of the clipping region of the layer. Therefore, the content of the layer does not automatically reflow when you use these methods — any more than they do when you change individual `layer.clip` values.

Another impact of this clipping region relationship has to do with content that extends beyond the bounds of the layer. For example, if you provide `HEIGHT` and `WIDTH` attributes to a `<LAYER>` tag, content that requires more space to display itself than those attribute settings automatically expands the viewable area of the layer. To rein in such runaway content, you can set the `CLIP` attribute. But because the layer resize methods adjust the clipping rectangle, outsized content won't overflow the `<LAYER>` tag's height and width settings. This may be beneficial for you or not, depending on your design intentions. Adjusting the size of a layer with either method affects only the position of the right and bottom edges of the layer. The top-left location of the layer does not move.

Example

It is important to understand the ramifications of content flow when a layer is resized by these two methods. Listing 19-12 (and companion document Listing 19-13) shows you how to set the lower-right corner of a layer to be dragged by a user for resizing the layer (much like grabbing the resize corner of a document window). Three radio buttons let you choose whether and when the content should be redrawn to the layer: never, after resizing, or during resizing.

Event capture is very much like that in Listing 19-11 for layer dragging. The primary difference is that drag mode is engaged only when the mouse event takes place in the region of the lower-right corner. A different kind of offset value is saved here than for dragging, because for resizing, the script needs to know the mouse event offset from the right and bottom edges of the layer.

Condition statements in the resizeIt() and release() functions check whether a specific radio button is checked to determine when (or if) the content should be redrawn. I design this page with the knowledge that its content might be redrawn. Therefore, I build the content of the layer as a separate HTML document that is loaded in the <LAYER> tag.

Redrawing the content requires reloading the document into the layer. I use the layer.reload() method, because I want to send the current layer.clip.width as a parameter for the width of the clip region to accommodate the content as it loads.

An important point to know about reloading content into a layer is that all property settings for the layer's event capture are erased when the document loads. To overcome this behavior requires setting the layer's onLoad= event handler to set the layer's event capture mechanism. If the layer event capturing had been specified as part of the statements at the end of the document, the layer would ignore some important events needed for the dynamic resizing after the document reloaded the first time.

As you experiment with the different feel for resizing and redrawing behavior, you will see that redrawing during resizing is a slow process due to the repetitive loading (from cache) needed each time. On slower client machines, it is easy for the cursor to outrun the layer region, causing the layer to not get mouseOver events at all. It may not be the best-looking solution, but I prefer to redraw after resizing the layer.

Listing 19-12: **Resizing a Layer**

```
<HTML>
<HEAD>
<TITLE>Layer Resizing</TITLE>
<SCRIPT LANGUAGE="JavaScript">
var engaged = false
var offsetX = 0
var offsetY = 0
function resizeIt(e) {
        if (engaged) {
```

(continued)

Listing 19-12 *(continued)*

```
            document.myLayer.resizeTo(e.pageX + offsetX, e.pageY +
offsetY)
            if (document.forms[0].redraw[2].checked) {
                document.myLayer.load("lst19-13.htm",
document.myLayer.clip.width)
            }
        }
    }
}
function engage(e) {
        if (e.pageX > (document.myLayer.clip.right - 10) && e.pageY >
(document.myLayer.clip.bottom - 10)) {
            engaged = true
            offsetX = document.myLayer.clip.right - e.pageX
            offsetY = document.myLayer.clip.bottom - e.pageY
        }
}
function release() {
        if (engaged && document.forms[0].redraw[1].checked) {
            document.myLayer.load("lst19-13.htm",
document.myLayer.clip.width)
        }
        engaged = false
}
function grabEvents() {
        document.myLayer.captureEvents(Event.MOUSEDOWN | Event.MOUSEUP |
Event.MOUSEMOVE)
}
</SCRIPT>
</HEAD>
<BODY>
<B>Resizing a Layer</B>
<HR>
<FORM>
Redraw layer content:<BR>
<INPUT TYPE="radio" NAME="redraw" CHECKED>Never
<INPUT TYPE="radio" NAME="redraw">After resize
<INPUT TYPE="radio" NAME="redraw">During resize
</FORM>
<LAYER NAME="myLayer" SRC="lst19-13.htm" BGCOLOR="lightblue" TOP=120
LEFT=100 WIDTH=300 HEIGHT=190 onLoad="grabEvents()">
</LAYER>
<SCRIPT LANGUAGE="JavaScript">
document.myLayer.onMouseDown = engage
document.myLayer.onMouseUp = release
document.myLayer.onMouseMove = resizeIt
</SCRIPT>
</BODY>
</HTML>
```

document.*layerObject***.resizeBy()**

Listing 19-13: **Content for the Resizable Layer**

```
<HTML>
<BODY>
     <P><B>Resize me by dragging the lower right corner.</B></P>
     <SCRIPT LANGUAGE="JavaScript">
     if (navigator.userAgent.indexOf("Mac") != -1) {
         document.write("(Mac users: Ctrl-Click me first; then Click
to stop dragging.)")
     }
     </SCRIPT>
</BODY>
</HTML>
```

Related Items: `layer.moveBy()` method; `layer.moveTo()` method; `window.resizeBy()` method; `window.resizeTo()` method.

Event handlers

onBlur=
onFocus=

	Nav2	Nav3	Nav4	IE3/J1	IE3/J2	IE4/J3
Compatibility			✔			

A user gets no visual clue when a layer receives focus. But a click on the clipping region of a layer triggers a focus event that can be handled with an `onFocus=` event handler. Clicking anywhere on the page outside of that layer area fires a blur event. Changing the stacking order of sibling layers does not fire either event unless mouse activity occurs in one of the layers.

If your layer contains elements that have their own focus and blur events (such as text fields), those objects' event handlers still fire, even if you also have the same event handlers defined for the layer. The layer's events fire after the text field's events.

Unlike comparable event handlers in windows, layer events for blur and focus do not have companion methods to bring a layer into focus or to blur it. However, if you use the `focus()` and/or `blur()` methods on applicable form elements in a layer, the layer's corresponding event handlers are triggered as a result.

Related Items: `textbox.blur()` method; `textbox.focus()` method.

onLoad=

	Nav2	Nav3	Nav4	IE3/J1	IE3/J2	IE4/J3
Compatibility			✔			

Scripting layers can sometimes lead to instances of unfortunate sequences of loading. For example, if you want to set some layer object properties via a script (that is, not in the `<LAYER>` tag), you can do so only after the layer object exists in the document object model. One way to make sure the object exists is to place the scripting in `<SCRIPT>` tags at the end of the document. Another is to specify an `onLoad=` event handler in the tag, as shown in Listing 19-12.

Each time you load a document into the layer — either via the SRC attribute in the `<LAYER>` tag or by invoking the `layer.load()` method, the `onLoad=` event handler runs. But also be aware that an interaction occurs between a layer's `onLoad=` event handler and an `onLoad=` event handler in the `<BODY>` tag of a document loaded into a layer. If the document body has an `onLoad=` event handler, then the layer's `onLoad=` event handler does not fire. You get one or the other, but not both.

Related Items: `window.onLoad=` event handler.

onMouseOut=
onMouseOver=

	Nav2	Nav3	Nav4	IE3/J1	IE3/J2	IE4/J3
Compatibility			✔			

A layer knows when the cursor rolls into and out of its clipping region. Like several other objects in the document object model, the layer object has `onMouseOver=` and `onMouseOut=` event handlers to let you perform any number of actions in response to those user activities. Typically, a layer's `onMouseOver=` event handler changes colors, hides or shows pseudo-borders devised of colored layers behind the primary layer, or even changes the text or image content. The status bar is also available to plant plain-language legends about the purpose of the layer or offer other relevant help.

Both events occur only once per entrance and egress from a layer's region by the cursor. If you want to script actions dependent upon the location of the cursor in the layer, you can use `layer.captureEvents()` to grab mouseMove and all types of mouse button events. This kind of event capture generates an event object (see Chapter 33) that includes information about the coordinate position of the cursor at the time of the event.

Related Items: `link.onMouseOut=` event handler; `link.onMouseOver=` event handler; `area.onMouseOut=` event handler; `area.onMouseOver=` event handler.

✦   ✦   ✦

The Applet Object

Java applets let experienced programmers design interactive elements that go way beyond what HTML, the document object model, and JavaScript can do. Applets occupy their segregated rectangular spaces on the page (even if those spaces are each no larger than one pixel square for what I call "faceless" applets) and generally operate only within that rectangle. But JavaScript can interact with the applet, because an applet becomes an object — an *applet object* — when it finishes loading into the browser. The most complete interaction is possible in Navigator (from Version 3 onward), although some connectivity is possible in Internet Explorer 3 and up.

No Java Required

What I like about this connectivity is you don't have to be a Java programmer to let your JavaScript use the applet's powers. In most cases the applet needs to be constructed in anticipation of being accessed from JavaScript, but once the applet has been compiled, we scripters can blend it into our pages as we like without having to learn Java.

Applet Object

Properties	Methods	Event Handlers
name	(Applet methods)	(None)
(Applet variables)		

Syntax

Creating an applet:

```
<APPLET
        CODE="AppletURL"
        NAME="AppletName"
        HEIGHT="PixelCount"
        WIDTH="PixelCount"
        [CODEBASE="classFileDirectory"]
        [ALT="alternateTextDisplay"]
        [ALIGN="alignmentLocation"]
        [HSPACE="marginPixelCount"]
        [VSPACE="marginPixelCount"]>
            <PARAM NAME="appletParameterName" VALUE="parameterValue">
            . . .
            <PARAM NAME="appletParameterName" VALUE="parameterValue">
</APPLET>
```

Accessing applet properties or methods:

```
document.appletName.property | method([parameters])
```

```
document.applets[index].property | method([parameters])
```

About this object

Starting with Navigator 3, Java applets are treated as scriptable objects. The two-way connection between JavaScript and Java in Navigator browsers is called *LiveConnect*. This Netscape technology also encompasses plug-ins and is covered in more detail in Chapter 38. Here I merely introduce you to the capabilities applets have as JavaScript objects. By and large the information in this short chapter also applies to Internet Explorer 3 and later.

Applets typically have what are called *public instance variables* (sort of like JavaScript global variables) and *public methods* (like JavaScript functions). You can access these items using JavaScript just as if they were properties and methods of any JavaScript object. The key, of course, is you must know the variables and methods of the applet to access them. If you're writing your own applets, the task is easy enough; but if you are relying on a ready-made applet, scripting it may be difficult without examining the source code or having some instruction from the applet's author.

The most common way to interact with an applet is via one of its methods. You can pass parameters to methods as you would to a JavaScript function:

```
document.appletName.methodName(parameterValue)
```

Similarly, some methods may return values, which you can capture in JavaScript:

```
var returnValue = document.appletName.methodName()
```

For more about the value types that can be exchanged between applets and JavaScript, see Chapter 38.

Perhaps the most important point to remember about accessing applets is you must have them loaded and running before you can address them as objects. Although you cannot query an applet to find out whether it's loaded (as with an image), you can rely on the `onLoad=` event handler of a window to fire only when all applets in the window are loaded and running (with the occasional version- or platform-specific bug in frames, as described in the `window.onLoad=` event handler discussion in Chapter 14). Therefore, you won't be able to use an applet embedded in a document to help you create the HTML content of that page as it loads, but an applet can provide content for new documents or for those few modifiable elements of a page.

Example

See Chapter 38 for examples of accessing applet objects in documents from JavaScript and how applets can communicate with scripts.

✦   ✦   ✦

The Form Object

T he majority of scripting in an HTML document takes place in and around forms. Because forms tend to be the primary user interface elements of HTML documents, this fact shouldn't be surprising. The challenge of scripting forms and form elements often comes from getting object references just right: The references can get pretty long by the time you start pointing to the property of a form element (which is part of a form, which is part of a document, which is part of a window or frame).

The Form in the Object Hierarchy

Take another look at the JavaScript object hierarchy in Navigator 4 (refer back to Figure 16-1). The form object can contain a wide variety of form element objects, which are covered in Chapters 22 through 24. In this chapter, however, the focus is strictly on the container.

The good news on the compatibility front is that with the exception of differences when submitting forms to CGI programs on the server, much of the client-side scripting works on all scriptable browsers. Where differences exist, I point out the real gotchas.

Form Object

Properties	Methods	Event Handlers
action	handleEvent()	onReset=
elements[]	reset()	onSubmit=
encoding	submit()	
length		
method		
name		
target		

Syntax

Creating a form:

```
<FORM
    [NAME="formName"]
    [TARGET="windowName"]
    [ACTION="serverURL"]
    [METHOD=GET | POST]
    [ENCTYPE="MIMEType"]
    [onReset="handlerTextOrFunction"]
    [onSubmit="handlerTextOrFunction"] >
</FORM>
```

Accessing form properties or methods:

```
[window.] document.formName.property | method([parameters])
```

```
[window.] document.forms[index].property | method([parameters])
```

About this object

Forms and their elements are the primary, two-way gateways between users and JavaScript scripts. A form element provides the only way that users can enter textual information or make a selection from a predetermined set of choices, whether those choices appear in the form of an on/off checkbox, one of a set of mutually exclusive radio buttons, or a selection from a list.

As you have seen in many Web sites, the form is the avenue for the user to enter information that gets sent to the server housing the Web files. Just what the server can do with this information depends on the CGI (Common Gateway Interface) programs running on the server. If your Web site runs on a server directly under your control (that is, it is "in-house" or "hosted" by a service), you have the freedom to set up all kinds of data-gathering or database search programs to interact with the user. But if you rely on an Internet service provider (ISP) to house your HTML files, you're limited to a usually plain set of CGI programs available to all customers of the service. Custom databases or transactional services are rarely provided for this kind of dial-up Internet service — popular with individuals and small businesses who cannot justify the cost of maintaining their own servers.

Regardless of your Internet server status, you can find plenty of uses for JavaScript scripts in documents. For instance, rather than using data exchanges (and Internet bandwidth) to gather raw user input and report any errors, a JavaScript-enhanced document can preprocess the information to make sure that it uses the format that is most easily received by your back-end database or other programs. All corrective interaction takes place in the browser, without one extra bit flowing across the Net. I devote all of Chapter 37 to form data-validation techniques.

How you define a form object (independent of the user interface elements, described later in this chapter) depends a great deal on how you plan to use the information from the form's elements. If you're using the form completely for

JavaScript purposes (that is, no queries or postings will be going to the server), you do not need to use the `ACTION`, `TARGET`, and `METHOD` attributes. But if your Web page will be feeding information or queries back to a server, you need to specify at least the `ACTION` and `METHOD` attribute; you need to also specify the `TARGET` attribute if the resulting data from the server is to be displayed in a window other than the calling window and the `ENCTYPE` attribute if your form's scripts fashion the server-bound data in a MIME type other than a plain ASCII stream.

References to form elements

For most client-side scripting, user interaction comes from the elements within a form; the form object becomes merely a repository for the various elements. If your scripts will be performing any data validation checks on user entries prior to submission or other calculations, many statements will have the form object as part of the reference to the element.

A complex HTML document can have multiple form objects. Each `<FORM>...</FORM>` tag pair defines one form. You won't receive any penalties (except for potential confusion on the part of someone reading your script) if you reuse a name for an element in each of a document's forms. For example, if each of three forms has a grouping of radio buttons with the name "choice," the object reference to each button ensures that JavaScript won't confuse them. The reference to the first button of each of those button groups is as follows:

```
document.forms[0].choice[0]

document.forms[1].choice[0]

document.forms[2].choice[0]
```

Remember, too, that you can create forms (or any HTML object for that matter) on the fly when you assemble HTML strings for writing into other windows or frames. Therefore, you can determine various attributes of a form from settings in an existing document.

Passing forms and elements to functions

When a form or form element contains an event handler that calls a function defined elsewhere in the document, a couple shortcuts are available that you can use to simplify the task of addressing the objects in the function. Failure to grasp this concept not only causes you to write more code than you have to, but also hopelessly loses you when you try to trace somebody else's code in his or her JavaScripted document. The watchword in event handler parameters is

```
this
```

which represents the current object that contains the event handler attribute. For example, consider the function and form definition in Listing 21-1. The entire user interface for this listing consists of form elements, as shown in Figure 21-1.

Listing 21-1: **Passing the Form Object as a Parameter**

```
<HTML>
<HEAD>
<TITLE>Beatle Picker</TITLE>
<SCRIPT LANGUAGE="JavaScript">
function processData(form) {
        for (var i = 0; i < form.Beatles.length; i++) {
            if (form.Beatles[i].checked) {
                break
            }
        }
        var chosenBeatle = form.Beatles[i].value
        var chosenSong = form.song.value
        alert("Looking to see if " + chosenSong + " was written by " +
chosenBeatle + "...")
}

function checkSong(songTitle) {
        var enteredSong = songTitle.value
        alert("Making sure that " + enteredSong + " was recorded by the
Beatles.")
}
</SCRIPT>
</HEAD>

<BODY>
<FORM NAME="Abbey Road">
Choose your favorite Beatle:
<INPUT TYPE="radio" NAME="Beatles" VALUE="John Lennon"
CHECKED="true">John
<INPUT TYPE="radio" NAME="Beatles" VALUE="Paul McCartney">Paul
<INPUT TYPE="radio" NAME="Beatles" VALUE="George Harrison">George
<INPUT TYPE="radio" NAME="Beatles" VALUE="Ringo Starr">Ringo<P>

Enter the name of your favorite Beatles song:<BR>
<INPUT TYPE="text" NAME="song" VALUE="Eleanor Rigby"
onChange="checkSong(this)"><P>
<INPUT TYPE="button" NAME="process" VALUE="Process Request..."
onClick="processData(this.form)">
</FORM>
</BODY>
</HTML>
```

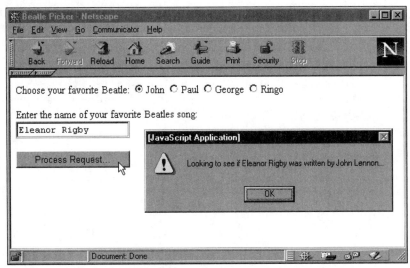

Figure 21-1: A variety of elements compose the form of Listing 21-1.

If you want to summon any properties of the form elements to work on them inside the `processData()` function, you can go about it in two different ways. One is to have the `onClick=` event handler (in the button element at the bottom of the document) call the `processData()` function and not pass any parameters. Inside the function, all references to objects (such as the radio buttons or the song field) must be complete references, such as

```
document.forms[0].song.value
```

to retrieve the value entered into the "song" field.

A more efficient way is to send the form object as a parameter with the call to the function (as shown in Listing 21-1). By specifying `this.form` as the parameter, you tell JavaScript to send along everything it knows about the form from which the function is being called. At the function, that form object is assigned to a variable name (arbitrarily set to `form` here) that appears in parentheses after the function name. I've used the parameter variable name `form` here because it represents an entire form. But you can use any valid variable name you like.

Part of the information that comes along with that form is its address among all JavaScript objects loaded with the document. That means as long as statements refer to that form object (by its variable name) the full address is automatically part of the reference. Thus, here I can use `form` to take the place of `document.forms[0]` in any address. To get the value of the song field, the reference is

```
form.song.value
```

Had I assigned the form object to a parameter variable called `sylvester`, the reference would have been

```
sylvester.song.value
```

This referencing methodology works for retrieving or setting properties and calling an object's methods. Another version of the this parameter passing style is simply to use the word this as the parameter. Unlike this.form, which passes a reference to the entire form connected to a particular element, this passes only a reference to that one element. In Listing 21-1, you could add an event handler to the song field to do some validation of the entry (to make sure that the entry appears in a database array of Beatles' songs created elsewhere in the document). Therefore, you want to send only the field object to the function for analysis:

```
<INPUT TYPE="text" NAME="song" onChange="checkSong(this)"><P>
```

You then have to create a function to catch this call:

```
function checkSong(songTitle) {
    var enteredSong = songTitle.value
    alert("Making sure that " + enteredSong + " was recorded by the
Beatles.")
}
```

Within this function, you can go straight to the heart — the value property of the field element without a long address. The entire field object came along for the ride with its complete address.

One further extension of this methodology is to pass only a single property of a form element as a parameter. In the last example, since the checkSong() function needs only the value property of the field, the event handler could have passed this.value as a parameter. Because this refers to the very object in which the event handler appears, this.*propertyName* syntax lets you extract and pass along a single property:

```
<INPUT TYPE="text" NAME="song" onChange="checkSong(this.value)"><P>
```

A benefit of this way of passing form element data is that the function doesn't have to do as much work:

```
function checkSong(songTitle) {
    alert("Making sure that " + songTitle + " was recorded by the
Beatles.")
}
```

Therefore, I suggest passing the entire form element (this) when the function needs to make multiple accesses to that element (perhaps reading one property and then writing back to that very element's value property, such as converting a text field to all uppercase letters). But if only one property is needed in the function, pass only that one property (this.*propertyName*). Lastly, if the function will access multiple elements in a form (for example, a button click means that the function must retrieve a field's content), pass the entire form (this.form). Also be aware that you can submit multiple parameters (for example, onClick="someFunction (this.form, this.name)") or even an entirely different object from the same form (for example, onClick="someFunction(this.form.emailAddr.value)"). Simply adjust your function's incoming parameters accordingly (see Chapter 34 for more details about custom functions).

E-mailing forms

A common request among scripters is the ability to send a form via e-mail back to the page's author. This includes the occasional desire to send "secret" e-mail back to the author whenever someone visits the Web site. Let me address the privacy issue first.

A site visitor's e-mail address is valuable personal information that should not be retrieved from the user without his or her permission or knowledge. That's one reason why Netscape plugged a privacy hole in Navigator 2 that allowed submitting a form to a `mailto:` URL without requesting permission from the user. Some workarounds for this could be used in Navigator 3, but I do not condone surreptitiously lifting e-mail addresses, so I choose not to publicize those workarounds here.

Microsoft, on the other hand, goes too far in preventing forms e-mailing. While Netscape's browsers reveal to the user in an alert that an e-mail message bearing the user's e-mail address (as stored in the browser's preferences) will be sent upon approval, Internet Explorer 3 does not send form content via e-mail at all; Internet Explorer 4 sends form content as an attachment, but only after displaying a mail composition window to the user. In all cases, the mail composition window appears to the user.

Many ISPs that host Web sites provide standard CGIs for forwarding forms to an e-mail address of your choice. This manner of capturing form data, however, does not also capture the visitor's e-mail address unless your form has a field where the visitor voluntarily enters that information.

Back to Navigator, if you want to have forms submitted as e-mail messages, you must attend to three `<FORM>` tag attributes. The first is the `METHOD` attribute. It must be set to `POST`. Next comes the `ACTION` attribute. Normally the spot for a URL to another file or server CGI, you substitute the special mailto: URL followed by an optional parameter for the subject. Unlike the more fully featured `mailto:` URLs possible with the location and link objects (see Chapters 15 and 17), a form's `mailto:` URL can include at most the subject for the message. Here is a sample:

```
ACTION="mailto:prez@whitehouse.gov?subject=Opinion Poll"
```

The last attribute of note is `ENCTYPE`. If you omit this attribute, Navigator sends the form data as an attachment consisting of escaped name-value pairs, as in this example:

```
name=Danny+Goodman&rank=Scripter+First+Class&serialNumber=042
```

But if you set the `ENCTYPE` attribute to `"text/plain"`, the form name-value pairs are placed in the body of the mail message in a more human-readable format:

```
name=Danny Goodman
rank=Scripter First Class
serialNumber=042
```

To sum up, the following example shows the complete `<FORM>` tag for e-mailing the form in Navigator.

```
<FORM NAME="entry"
      METHOD=POST
      ACTION="mailto:prez@whitehouse.gov?subject=Opinion Poll"
      ENCTYPE="text/plain">
```

Changing form attributes

Navigator exposes all form attributes as modifiable properties. Therefore, you can change, say, the action of a form via a script in response to user interaction on your page. For example, you might have two different CGI programs on your server depending on whether a form's checkbox is checked.

Note

Form attribute properties cannot be changed on the fly in Internet Explorer 3. They can be modified in Internet Explorer 4.

Buttons in forms

A common mistake that newcomers to scripting make is defining all clickable buttons as the submit type of input object (`<INPUT TYPE="submit">`). The submit style of button does exactly what it says: It submits the form. If you don't set any METHOD or ACTION attributes of the `<FORM>` tag, the browser inserts its default values for you: METHOD=GET and ACTION=`<pageURL>`. When a form with these attributes is submitted, the page reloads itself and resets all field values to their initial values.

Use a submit button only when you want the button to actually submit the form. If you want a button for other types of action, use the button style (`<INPUT TYPE="button">`).

Redirection after submission

All of us have submitted a form to a site and seen a "Thank You" page come back from the server to verify that our submission was accepted. This is warm and fuzzy, if not logical, feedback for the submission action. It is not surprising that you would want to re-create that effect even if the submission is to a mailto: URL. Unfortunately, a problem gets in the way.

A commonsense approach to the situation would call for a script to perform the submission (via the form.submit() method) and then navigate to another page that does the "Thank You." Here would be such a scenario from inside a function triggered by a click of a link surrounding a nice graphical Submit button:

```
function doSubmit() {
      document.forms[0].submit()
      location = "thanks.html"
}
```

The problem is that when another statement executes after the form.submit() method, the submission is canceled. In other words, the script does not wait for the submission to complete itself and verify to the browser that all is well (even though the browser appears to know how to track that information, given the status bar feedback during submission). The point is, because JavaScript does not provide an event that is triggered by a successful submission, there is no sure-fire way to display your own "Thank You" page.

Don't be tempted by the `window.setTimeout()` method to change the location after some number of milliseconds following the `form.submit()` method. You cannot predict how fast the network and/or server will be for every visitor. If the submission does not fully complete before the timeout ends, then the submission is still canceled, even if it is partially completed.

It's too bad we don't have this power at our disposal yet. Perhaps a future version of the document object model will provide an event that lets us do something only after a successful submission.

Form element arrays

Since the first implementation of JavaScript in Navigator 2, Netscape's document object model has provided a feature beneficial to a lot of scripters. If you create a series of like-named objects, they automatically become an array of objects accessible via array syntax (see Chapter 7). This is particularly helpful if you are creating forms with columns and rows of fields, such as in an order form. By assigning the same name to all fields in a column, you can use `for` loops to cycle through each row using the loop index as an array index.

As an example, the following code shows a typical function that calculates the total for an order form row (and calls another custom function to format the value):

```
function extendRows(form) {
        for (var i = 0; i < Qty.length; i++) {
            var rowSum = form.Qty[i].value * form.Price[i].value
            form.Total[i].value = formatNum(rowSum,2)
        }
}
```

All fields in the Qty column are named Qty. The item in the first row has the array index value of zero and is addressed as `form.Qty[i]`.

Unfortunately, Internet Explorer 3 does not turn like-named fields into an array of references, although Internet Explorer 4 does. But you can still script repetitive moves through an organized set of fields. The key is to assign names to the fields that include their index numbers: `Qty0, Qty1, Qty2`, and so on. You can even assign these names in a `for` loop that generates the table:

```
for (var i = 0; i <= 10; i++) {
        ...
        document.write("<INPUT TYPE='text' NAME='Qty" + i + "'>")
        ...
}
```

Later, when it comes time to work with the fields, you can use the indexing scheme to address the fields:

```
for (var i = 0; i < Qty.length; i++) {
        var rowSum = form["Qty" + i].value * form["Price" + i].value
        form["Total" + i].value = formatNum(rowSum,2)
}
```

In other words, construct names for each item, and use those names as array index names. This solution is backward and forward compatible.

Properties

action

Value: URL   **Gettable:** Yes   **Settable:** Yes

	Nav2	Nav3	Nav4	IE3/J1	IE3/J2	IE4/J3
Compatibility	✔	✔	✔	✔	✔	✔

The `action` property (along with the `method` and `target` properties) is primarily for HTML authors whose pages communicate with server-based CGI scripts. This property is the same as the value you assign to the `ACTION` attribute of a `<FORM>` definition. The value is typically a URL on the server where queries or postings are sent for submission.

User input may affect how you want your page to access a server. For example, a checked box in your document may set a form's `action` property so that a CGI script on one server handles all the input, whereas an unchecked box means the form data goes to a CGI script on an entirely different server. Or, one setting may direct the action to one `mailto:` address, whereas another setting sets the `action` property to a different `mailto:` address.

Although the specifications for all three related properties indicate that they can be set on the fly, such changes are ephemeral. A soft reload eradicates any settings you make to these properties, so at best you'd make changes only in the same scripts that submit the form (see `form.submit()`).

Note

This value is not modifiable in Internet Explorer 3 but is in Internet Explorer 4.

Example

```
document.forms[0].action = "mailto:jdoe@giantco.com"
```

Related Items: `form.method` property; `form.target` property; `form.encoding` property.

elements

Value: Array of sub-objects   **Gettable:** Yes   **Settable:** No

	Nav2	Nav3	Nav4	IE3/J1	IE3/J2	IE4/J3
Compatibility	✔	✔	✔	✔	✔	✔

Elements include all the user interface elements defined for a form: text fields, buttons, radio buttons, checkboxes, selection lists, and more. Like some other

JavaScript object properties, the `elements` property is an array of all items defined within the current HTML document. For example, if a form defines three `<INPUT>` items, the `elements` property for that form is an array consisting of three entries, one for each item. Each entry is the full object specification for that element; so, to extract properties or call methods for those elements, your script must dig deeper in the reference. Therefore, if the first element of a form is a text field, and you want to extract the string currently showing in the field (a text element's `value` property), the reference looks like this:

```
document.forms[0].elements[0].value
```

Notice that this reference summons two array-oriented properties along the way: one for the document's `forms` property and, subsequently, one for the form's `elements` property.

You can access an element in other ways, too (see discussions of individual element objects later in this chapter). An advantage to using the `elements` property occurs when you have a form with many elements, each with a related or potentially confusing name. In such circumstances, references that point directly to an element's name may be more difficult to trace or read. On the other hand, the order of entries in an elements array depends entirely upon their order in the HTML document — the first `<INPUT>` item in a form is `elements[0]`, the second is `elements[1]`, and so on. If you redesign the physical layout of your form elements after writing scripts for them, the index values you originally had for referencing a specific form may no longer be valid. Referencing an element by name, however, works no matter how you move the form elements around in your HTML document.

To JavaScript, an element is an element, whether it is a radio button or textarea. If your script needs to loop through all elements of a form in search of particular kinds of elements, use the `type` property of every form object (Navigator 3+ and Internet Explorer 4+) to identify which kind of object it is. The `type` property consists of the same string used in the `TYPE=` attribute of an `<INPUT>` tag.

Overall, my personal preference is to generate meaningful names for each form element and use those names in references throughout my scripts. Just the same, if I have a script that must poll every element or contiguous range of elements for a particular property value, the indexed array of elements facilitates using a repeat loop to examine each one efficiently.

Example

The document in Listing 21-2 demonstrates a practical use of the elements property. A form contains four fields and some other elements mixed in between (Figure 21-2). The first part of the function that acts on these items repeats through all the elements in the form to find out which ones are text objects and which text objects are empty. Notice how I use the `type` property to separate objects from the rest, even when radio buttons appear amid the fields. If one field has nothing in it, I alert the user and use that same index value to place the insertion point at the field with the field's `focus()` method.

Listing 21-2: **Using the form.elements[] Array**

```
<HTML>
<HEAD>
<TITLE>Elements Array</TITLE>
<SCRIPT LANGUAGE="JavaScript1.1">
function verifyIt() {
        var form = document.forms[0]
        for (i = 0; i < form.elements.length; i++) {
            if (form.elements[i].type == "text" &&
form.elements[i].value == ""){
                alert("Please fill out all fields.")
                form.elements[i].focus()
                break
            }
            // more tests
        }
        // more statements
}
</SCRIPT>
</HEAD>
<BODY>
<FORM>
Enter your first name:<INPUT TYPE="text" NAME="firstName"><P>
Enter your last name:<INPUT TYPE="text" NAME="lastName"><P>
<INPUT TYPE="radio" NAME="gender">Male
<INPUT TYPE="radio" NAME="gender">Female <P>
Enter your address:<INPUT TYPE="text" NAME="address"><P>
Enter your city:<INPUT TYPE="text" NAME="city"><P>
<INPUT TYPE="checkbox" NAME="retired">I am retired
</FORM>
<FORM>
<INPUT TYPE="button" NAME="act" VALUE="Verify" onClick="verifyIt()">
</FORM>
</BODY>
</HTML>
```

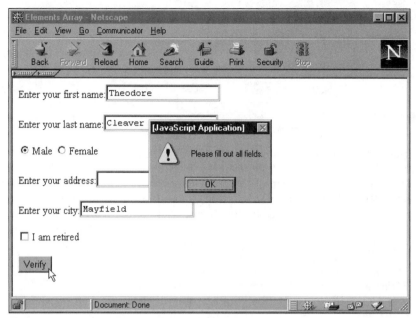

Figure 21-2: A document with mixed elements

Related Items: text, textarea, button, radio, checkbox, and select objects.

encoding

Value: MIMETypeString   **Gettable:** Yes   **Settable:** Yes

	Nav2	Nav3	Nav4	IE3/J1	IE3/J2	IE4/J3
Compatibility	✔	✔	✔	✔	✔	✔

You can define a form to alert a server that the data being submitted is in a MIME type. This property reflects the setting of the ENCTYPE attribute in the form definition. For mailto: URLs, I recommend setting this value (in the tag or via script) to "text/plain" to have the form contents placed in the mail message body. If the definition does not have an ENCTYPE attribute, this property is an empty string.

This value is not modifiable in Internet Explorer 3 but is in Internet Explorer 4.

Example

```
formMIME = document.forms[0].encoding
```

Related Items: form.action method; form.method method.

method

Value: "GET" or "POST"   **Gettable:** Yes   **Settable:** Yes

	Nav2	Nav3	Nav4	IE3/J1	IE3/J2	IE4/J3
Compatibility	✔	✔	✔	✔	✔	✔

A form's method property is either the GET or POST values assigned to the METHOD attribute in a <FORM> definition. Terminology overlaps here a bit, so be careful to distinguish a form's method of transferring its data to a server from the object-oriented method (action or function) that all JavaScript forms have.

Of primary importance to HTML documents that submit a form's data to a server-based CGI script is the method property, which determines the format used to convey this information. For example, to submit a form to a mailto: URL, the method property must be POST. Details of forms posting and CGI processing are beyond the scope of this book. Consult HTML or CGI documentation to determine which is the appropriate setting for this attribute in your Web server environment. If a form does not have a METHOD attribute explicitly defined for it, the default value is GET.

Note

This value is not modifiable in Internet Explorer 3 but is in Internet Explorer 4.

Example

```
formMethod = document.forms[0].method
```

Related Items: form.action property; form.target property; form.encoding property.

name

Value: String   **Gettable:** Yes   **Settable:** Yes

	Nav2	Nav3	Nav4	IE3/J1	IE3/J2	IE4/J3
Compatibility	✔	✔	✔	✔	✔	✔

Assigning a name to a form via the NAME attribute is optional but highly recommended when your scripts need to reference a form or its elements. This attribute's value is retrievable as the name property of a form. You won't have much need to read this property unless you're inspecting another source's document for its form construction, as in

```
var formName = parent.frameName.document.forms[0].name
```

target

Value: WindowNameString   **Gettable:** Yes   **Settable:** Yes

	Nav2	Nav3	Nav4	IE3/J1	IE3/J2	IE4/J3
Compatibility	✔	✔	✔	✔	✔	✔

Whenever an HTML document submits a query to a server for processing, the server typically sends back an HTML page — whether it is a canned response or, more likely, a customized page based on the input provided by the user. You see this situation all the time when you perform a search at Web search sites, such as Yahoo!, Lycos, and AltaVista. In a multiframe or multiwindow environment, you may want to keep the form part of this transaction in view for the user, while leaving the responding page in a separate frame or window for viewing. The purpose of the TARGET attribute of a <FORM> definition is to enable you to specify where the output from the server's query should be displayed.

The value of the target property is the name of the window or frame. For instance, if you define a frameset with three frames and assign the names Frame1, Frame2, and Frame3 to them, you need to supply one of these names (as a quoted string) as the parameter of the TARGET attribute of the <FORM> definition. Navigator and compatible browsers also observe four special window names that you can use in the <FORM> definition: _top, _parent, _self, and _blank. To set the target as a separate subwindow opened via a script, be sure to use the window name from the window.open() method's second parameter, and not the window object reference that the method returns.

This value is not modifiable in Internet Explorer 3 but is in Internet Explorer 4.

Example

```
document.forms[0].target = "resultFrame"
```

Related Items: form.action property; form.method property; form.encoding property.

Methods
handleEvent(*event*)

Returns: Nothing.

	Nav2	Nav3	Nav4	IE3/J1	IE3/J2	IE4/J3
Compatibility			✔			

See the discussion of the `window.handleEvent()` method in Chapter 14 and the event object in Chapter 33 for details on this ubiquitous form element method.

reset()

Returns: Nothing.

	Nav2	Nav3	Nav4	IE3/J1	IE3/J2	IE4/J3
Compatibility		✔	✔			✔

A common practice, especially with a long form, is to provide a button that enables the user to return all the form elements to their default settings. The standard Reset button (a separate object type described in Chapter 23) does that task just fine. But if you want to clear the form using script control, you must do so by invoking the `reset()` method for the form. More than likely, such a call will come from outside the form, perhaps from a function or from a graphical button. In such a case, make sure that the reference to the `reset()` method includes the complete reference to the form you want to reset — even if the page only has one form defined for it.

Example

In Listing 21-3, the act of resetting the form is assigned to the HREF attribute of a link object (that is attached to a graphic called `reset.jpg`). I use the `javascript:` URL to invoke the `reset()` method for the form directly (in other words, without doing it via function).

Listing 21-3: **form.reset() and form.submit() Methods**

```
<HTML>
<HEAD>
<TITLE>Registration Form</TITLE>
</HEAD>
<BODY>
<FORM NAME="entries" METHOD=POST ACTION="http://www.u.edu/pub/cgi-
bin/register">
Enter your first name:<INPUT TYPE="text" NAME="firstName"><P>
Enter your last name:<INPUT TYPE="text" NAME="lastName"><P>
Enter your address:<INPUT TYPE="text" NAME="address"><P>
Enter your city:<INPUT TYPE="text" NAME="city"><P>
<INPUT TYPE="radio" NAME="gender" CHECKED>Male
<INPUT TYPE="radio" NAME="gender">Female <P>
<INPUT TYPE="checkbox" NAME="retired">I am retired
```

```
</FORM>
<P>
<A HREF="javascript:document.forms[0].submit()"><IMG SRC="submit.jpg"
HEIGHT=25 WIDTH=100 BORDER=0></A>
<A HREF="javascript:document.forms[0].reset()"><IMG SRC="reset.jpg"
HEIGHT=25 WIDTH=100 BORDER=0></A>
</BODY>
</HTML>
```

Related Items: `onReset=` event handler; `reset` object.

submit()

Returns: Nothing.

	Nav2	Nav3	Nav4	IE3/J1	IE3/J2	IE4/J3
Compatibility	✔	✔	✔	✔	✔	✔

The most common way to send a form's data to a server's CGI program for processing is to have a user click a Submit button. The standard HTML Submit button is designed to send data from all elements of a form according to the specifications listed in the `<FORM>` definition's attributes. But if you want to submit a form's data to a server automatically for a user, or want to use a graphical button for submission, you can accomplish the submission with the `form.submit()` method.

Invoking this method is almost the same as a user clicking a form's Submit button (except that the `onSubmit=` event handler is not triggered in Navigator). Therefore, you may have an image on your page that is a graphical submission button. If that image is associated with a link object, you can capture a mouse click on that image and trigger a function whose content includes a call to a form's `submit()` method (see Listing 21-3).

In a multiple-form HTML document, however, you must be sure to reference the proper form, either by name or according to its position in a `document.forms[]` array. Always make sure that the reference you specify in your script points to the desired form before submitting any data to a server.

As a security and privacy precaution for people visiting your site, JavaScript ignores all `submit()` methods whose associated form action is set to a `mailto:` URL. Many Web page designers would love to have secret e-mail addresses captured from visitors. Because such a capture could be considered an invasion of privacy, the power has been disabled since Navigator 2.02. You can, however, still use an explicit Submit button object to mail a form to you from Navigator browsers only (see "E-mailing forms" earlier).

Because the `form.submit()` method does not trigger the form's `onSubmit=` event handler, you must perform any presubmission processing and forms validation in the same script that ends with the `form.submit()` statement. You also do not want to interrupt the submission process after the script invokes the

`form.submit()` method. Script statements after one invoking `form.submit()` —
especially those that navigate to other pages or attempt a second submission —
will cause the first submission to cancel itself.

Example

Consult Listing 21-3 for an example of using the `submit()` method from outside
of a form.

Related Items: `onSubmit=` event handler.

Event handlers

onReset=

	Nav2	Nav3	Nav4	IE3/J1	IE3/J2	IE4/J3
Compatibility		✔	✔			✔

Immediately before a Reset button returns a form to its default settings,
JavaScript sends a reset event to the form. By including an `onReset=` event
handler in the form definition, you can trap that event before the reset takes place.

A friendly way of using this feature is to provide a safety net for a user who
accidentally clicks on the Reset button after filling out a form. The event handler
can run a function that asks the user to confirm the action.

The `onReset=` event handler employs a technique that started surfacing with
Navigator 3: The event handler must evaluate to `return true` for the event to
continue to the browser. This may remind you of the way `onMouseOver=` and
`onMouseOut=` event handlers work for links and image areas. This requirement is
far more useful here because your function can control whether the reset
operation ultimately proceeds to conclusion.

Example

Listing 21-4 demonstrates one way to prevent accidental form resets or
submissions. Using standard Reset and Submit buttons as interface elements, the
`<FORM>` object definition includes both event handlers. Each event handler calls its
own function that offers a choice for users. Notice how each event handler
includes the word `return` and takes advantage of the Boolean values that come
back from the `confirm()` method dialog boxes in both functions.

Listing 21-4: **The onReset= and onSubmit= Event Handlers**

```
<HTML>
<HEAD>
<TITLE>Submit and Reset Confirmation</TITLE>
<SCRIPT LANGUAGE="JavaScript">
function allowReset() {
        return window.confirm("Go ahead and clear the form?")
```

```
        }
function allowSend() {
        return window.confirm("Go ahead and mail this info?")
}
</SCRIPT>
</HEAD>
<BODY>
<FORM METHOD=POST ACTION="mailto:trash3@dannyg.com" onReset="return
allowReset()" onSubmit="return allowSend()">
Enter your first name:<INPUT TYPE="text" NAME="firstName"><P>
Enter your last name:<INPUT TYPE="text" NAME="lastName"><P>
Enter your address:<INPUT TYPE="text" NAME="address"><P>
Enter your city:<INPUT TYPE="text" NAME="city"><P>
<INPUT TYPE="radio" NAME="gender" CHECKED>Male
<INPUT TYPE="radio" NAME="gender">Female <P>
<INPUT TYPE="checkbox" NAME="retired">I am retired<P>
<INPUT TYPE="reset">
<INPUT TYPE="submit">
</FORM>
</BODY>
</HTML>
```

onSubmit=

	Nav2	Nav3	Nav4	IE3/J1	IE3/J2	IE4/J3
Compatibility	✔	✔	✔	✔	✔	✔

No matter how a form's data is actually submitted (by a user clicking a Submit button or by a script invoking the form.submit() method), you may want your JavaScript-enabled HTML document to perform some data validation on the user input, especially with text fields, before the submission heads for the server. You have the option of doing such validation while the user enters data (see Chapter 37) or in batch mode before sending the data to the server — or both. The place to trigger this last-ditch data validation is the form's onSubmit= event handler.

When you define an onSubmit= handler as an attribute of a <FORM> definition, JavaScript sends the submit event to the form just before it dashes off the data to the server. Therefore, any script or function that is the parameter of the onSubmit= attribute executes before the data is actually submitted. Note that this event handler fires only in response to a genuine Submit-style button, and not from a form.submit() method.

Any code executed for the onSubmit= event handler must evaluate to an expression consisting of the word return plus a Boolean value. If the Boolean value is true, the submission executes as usual; if the value is false, no submission is made. Therefore, if your script performs some validation prior to submitting data, make sure that the event handler calls that validation function as part of a return statement, as shown in Listing 21-4.

Even after your `onSubmit=` event handler traps a submission, JavaScript's security mechanism can present additional alerts to the user, depending on the server location of the HTML document and the destination of the submission.

Example

See Listing 21-4 for an example of trapping a submission via the `onSubmit=` event handler.

✦   ✦   ✦

Text-Related Objects

◆   ◆   ◆   ◆

In This Chapter

Capturing and
modifying text
field contents

Triggering action
by entering text

Capturing individual
keystroke events

◆   ◆   ◆   ◆

The Netscape document object model for forms includes
four text-related input objects — text, password,
textarea, and hidden. All four of these objects are used for
entry, display, or temporary storage of text data. While all of
these objects can have text placed in them by default as the
page loads, scripts can also modify the contents of these
objects. Importantly, all but the hidden objects retain their
user- or script-modified content during a soft reload (for
example, clicking the Reload button), except in Internet
Explorer 3. Hidden objects revert to their default values on all
reloads in all browsers.

A more obvious difference between the hidden object and
the rest is that its invisibility removes it from the realm of
user events and actions. Therefore, only the text-style object
properties apply to the hidden object.

The persistence of text and textarea object data through
reloads (and window resizes) makes these objects prime
targets for off-screen storage of data that might otherwise be
stored temporarily in a cookie. If you create a frame with no
size (for example, you set the COLS or ROWS values of a
<FRAMESET> tag to let all visible frames occupy 100% of the
space and assign the rest — * — to the hidden frame), you
can populate it with fields that act as shopping cart
information or other data holders. Therefore, if users have
cookies turned off or don't usually respond affirmatively to
cookie requests, your application can still make use of
temporary client storage. The field contents may survive
unloading of the page, but whether this happens and for how
many navigations away from the page the contents last
depends on the visitor's cache settings (or if the browser is
Internet Explorer 3, in which case no values preserve the
unloading of a document). If the user quits Navigator, the
field entry is lost.

Text Object

Properties	Methods	Event Handlers
defaultValue	blur()	onBlur=
form	focus()	onChange=
name	handleEvent()	onFocus=
type	select()	onKeyDown=
value		onKeyPress=
		onKeyUp=
		onSelect=

Syntax

Creating a text object:

```
<FORM>
<INPUT
      TYPE="text"
      NAME="fieldName"
      [VALUE="contents"]
      [SIZE="characterCount"]
      [MAXLENGTH="maxCharactersAllowed"]
      [onBlur="handlerTextOrFunction"]
      [onChange="handlerTextOrFunction"]
      [onFocus="handlerTextOrFunction"]
      [onKeyDown="handlerTextOrFunction"]
      [onKeyPress="handlerTextOrFunction"]
      [onKeyUp="handlerTextOrFunction"]
      [onSelect="handlerTextOrFunction"]>
</FORM>
```

Accessing text object properties or methods:

```
[window.] document.formName.fieldName.property |
      method([parameters])

[window.] document.formName.elements[index].property |

      method([parameters])

[window.] document.forms[index].fieldName.property |
      method([parameters])

[window.]document.forms[index].elements[index].property |
method([parameters])
```

About this object

The text object is the primary medium for capturing user-entered text. Browsers tend to display entered text in a monospaced font (usually Courier or a derivative), so you can easily specify the width (SIZE) of a field based on the anticipated number of characters that a user may put into the field. The font is a fixed size and always is left-aligned in the field. If your design requires multiple lines of text, use the textarea object that follows.

Due to the limitations scripts have in updating information on an existing HTML page (without assembling and rewriting an entire page in JavaScript), a common practice is to use text objects to display results of a script calculation or other processing. Such fields may stand alone on a page or be part of a table.

Unfortunately, these fields are not write-protected, so it's easy to understand how a novice user may become confused when he or she causes the text pointer or selection to activate a field used exclusively for output, simply by tabbing through a page. Of course, if such a script does not have an event handler attached to it, no harm can come in manually changing the contents of a results field — but the user may get mighty confused. A better choice for the scripter may be to attach an onChange= event handler to output fields so that if a user attempts to change the contents of a field, the calculation runs again or the previous result (if stored in the script as a global variable) is automatically reinserted when the user tabs or clicks out of that changed field.

Text object methods and event handlers use terminology that may be known to Windows users but not to Macintosh users. A field is said to have *focus* when the user clicks on or tabs into the field. When a field has focus, either the text insertion pointer flashes, or any text in the field may be selected. Only one text object on a page can have focus at a time. The inverse user action — clicking or tabbing away from a text object — is called a *blur*. Clicking another object, whether it is another field or a button of any kind, causes a field that currently has focus to blur.

If you don't want the contents of a field to be changed by the user, you can force the field to lose focus when a user tabs to or clicks on a field. Use the following event handler in such a field:

```
onFocus="this.blur()"
```

Focus and blur also interact with other possible user actions to a text object: selecting and changing. *Selecting* occurs when the user clicks and drags across any text in the field; *changing* occurs when the user makes any alteration to the content of the field and then either tabs or clicks away from that field.

When you design event handlers for fields, be aware that a user's interaction with a field may trigger more than one event with a single action. For instance, clicking a field to select text may trigger both a focus and select event. If you have conflicting actions in the onFocus= and onSelect= event handlers, your scripts can do some weird things to the user's experience with your page. Displaying alert dialog boxes, for instance, also triggers blur events, so a field that has both an onSelect= handler (which displays the alert) and an onBlur= handler will get a nasty interaction from the two.

As a result, you should be very judicious with the number of event handlers you specify in any text object definition. If possible, pick one user action you want to use to initiate some JavaScript code execution and deploy it consistently on the page. Not all fields require event handlers — only those you want to perform some action as the result of user activity in that field.

Many newcomers also become confused by the behavior of the change event. To prevent this event from being sent to the field for every character the user types, any change to a field is determined only *after* the field loses focus by the user's clicking or tabbing away from it. At that point, instead of a blur event being sent to the field, only a change event is sent, triggering an onChange= event handler if one is defined for the field. This extra burden of having to click or tab away from a field may entice you to shift any onChange= event handler tasks to a separate button that the user must click to initiate action on the field contents.

Many scripters dream of possibilities for text objects that, alas, are simply not possible in the current implementation, including the capabilities to dim the text box to prevent entry, select a portion of the text, and change font and color attributes.

Some of these items may be scriptable in the future, but we will have to wait and see. In the meantime, some new functionality was added to the object in Navigator 4. The biggest news was the addition of keystroke events, making it possible to monitor keystrokes before they register their characters in the field.

Text objects (including the related textarea object) have one unique behavior that can be very important to some document and script designs. Even if a default value is specified for the content of a field (in the VALUE attribute), any text entered into a field by a user or script persists in that field as long as the document is cached in the browser's memory cache (but Internet Explorer 3 has no such persistence). Therefore, if users of your page enter values into some fields, or your scripts display results in a field, all that data will be there later, even if the user performs a soft reload of the page or navigates to dozens of other Web pages or sites. Navigating back via the Go or Bookmarks menu entries causes the browser to retrieve the cached version (with its field entries). To force the page to appear with its default text object values, use the Open Location or Open File selections in the File menu, or script the location.reload() method. These actions cause the browser to load the desired page from scratch, regardless of the content of the cache. When you quit and relaunch the browser, the first time it goes to the desired page, the browser loads the page from scratch — with its default values.

This level of persistence is not as reliable as the document.cookie property because a user can reopen a URL at any time, thus erasing whatever was temporarily stored in a text or textarea object. Still, this method of temporary data storage may suffice for some designs. Unfortunately, you cannot completely hide a text object in case the data you want to store is for use only by your scripts. The TYPE="hidden" form element is not an alternative here because script-induced changes to its value do not persist across soft reloads.

If you prefer to use a text or textarea object as a storage medium but don't want users to see it, design the page to display in a nonresizable frame of height or width zero. Use proper frame references to store or retrieve values from the fields. Carrying out this task requires a great deal of work. The document.cookie may not seem so complicated after all that.

To extract the current content of a text object, summon the property document.formName.fieldName.value. Once you have the string value, you can use JavaScript's string object methods to parse or otherwise massage that text as needed for your script. If the field entry is a number and you need to pass that value to methods requiring numbers, you have to convert the text to a number with the help of the `parseInt()` or `parseFloat()` global functions.

Properties

defaultValue

Value: String   **Gettable:** Yes   **Settable:** No

	Nav2	Nav3	Nav4	IE3/J1	IE3/J2	IE4/J3
Compatibility	✔	✔	✔	✔	✔	✔

Though your users and your scripts are free to muck with the contents of a text object by assigning strings to the `value` property, you can always extract (and thus restore, if necessary) the string assigned to the text object in its `<INPUT>` definition. The `defaultValue` property yields the string parameter of the `VALUE=` attribute.

Example

Listing 22-1 has a simple form with a single field that has a default value set in its tag. A function (`resetField()`) restores the contents of the page's lone field to the value assigned to it in the `<INPUT>` definition. For a single-field page such as this, defining a `TYPE="reset"` button or calling `form.reset()` works the same way because such buttons reestablish default values of all elements of a form. But if you want to reset only a subset of fields in a form, follow the example button and function in Listing 22-1.

Listing 22-1: **Resetting a Text Object to Default Value**

```
<HTML>
<HEAD>
<TITLE>Text Object DefaultValue</TITLE>
<SCRIPT LANGUAGE="JavaScript">
function upperMe(field) {
      field.value = field.value.toUpperCase()
}
function resetField(form) {
      form.converter.value = form.converter.defaultValue
}
</SCRIPT>
</HEAD>

<BODY>
<FORM>
Enter lowercase letters for conversion to uppercase: <INPUT TYPE="text"
NAME="converter" VALUE="sample" onChange="upperMe(this)">
<INPUT TYPE="button" VALUE="Reset Field"
```

(continued)

Listing 22-1 *(continued)*

```
onClick="resetField(this.form)">
</FORM>
</BODY>
</HTML>
```

Related Items: value property.

name

Value: String   **Gettable:** Yes   **Settable:** No

	Nav2	Nav3	Nav4	IE3/J1	IE3/J2	IE4/J3
Compatibility	✔	✔	✔	✔	✔	✔

Text object names are important for two reasons. First, if your HTML page is used to submit information to CGI scripts, the input device passes the name of the text object along with the data to help the server program identify the data being supplied by the form. Second, you can use a text object's name in its reference within JavaScript coding. If you assign distinctive, meaningful names to your fields, these names will help you read and debug your JavaScript listings (and will help others follow your scripting tactics).

Be as descriptive about your text object names as you can. Borrowing text from the field's on-page label also helps you mentally map a scripted reference to a physical field on the page. Like all JavaScript object names, text object names must begin with a letter and be followed by any number of letters or numbers. Avoid punctuation symbols with the exception of the very safe underscore character.

Although I urge you to use distinctive names for all objects you define in a document, you can make a case for assigning the same name to a series of interrelated fields — and JavaScript is ready to help. Within a single form, any reused name for the same object type is placed in an indexed array for that name. For example, if you define three fields with the name entry, the following statements retrieve the value property for each field:

```
data = document.forms[0].entry[0].value
data = document.forms[0].entry[1].value
data = document.forms[0].entry[2].value
```

This construction may be useful if you want to cycle through all of a form's related fields to determine which ones are blank. Elsewhere, your script probably needs to know what kind of information each field is supposed to receive, so it can process the data intelligently. I don't often recommend reusing object names, but you should be aware of how JavaScript handles them in case you need this construction. Unfortunately, Internet Explorer 3 does not turn like-named text input objects into arrays. See "Form Element Arrays" in Chapter 21 for more details.

Example

Consult Listing 22-2, where I use the text object's name, `convertor`, as part of the reference when assigning a value to the field. To extract the name of a text object, you can use the property reference. Therefore, assuming that your script doesn't know the name of the first object in the first form of a document, the statement is

```
objectName = document.forms[0].elements[0].name
```

Related Items: `form.elements` property; all other form element objects' name property.

type

Value: String   **Gettable:** Yes   **Settable:** No

	Nav2	Nav3	Nav4	IE3/J1	IE3/J2	IE4/J3
Compatibility		✔	✔			✔

Use the `type` property to help you identify a text object from an unknown group of form elements. For a text input object, the value is `text`.

Related Items: `form.elements` property.

value

Value: String   **Gettable:** Yes   **Settable:** Yes

	Nav2	Nav3	Nav4	IE3/J1	IE3/J2	IE4/J3
Compatibility	✔	✔	✔	✔	✔	✔

A text object's `value` property is the two-way gateway to the content of the field. A reference to an object's `value` property returns the string currently showing in the field. Note that all values coming from a text object are string values. If your field prompts a user to enter a number, your script may have to perform data conversion to the number-as-string value ("42" instead of plain old 42) before a user can perform any math operations on it. JavaScript tries to be as automatic about this data conversion as possible and follows some rules about it (Chapter 27). If you see an error message that says a value is not a number (for a math operation), the value is still a string.

Your script places text of its own into a field for display to the user by assigning a string to the `value` property of a text object. Use the simple assignment operator. For example

```
document.forms[0].ZIP.value = "90210"
```

JavaScript is more forgiving about data types when assigning values to a text object. JavaScript automatically converts any value to a string on its way to a text object display. Even Boolean values get converted to their string equivalents "true" or "false." Scripts can place numeric values into fields without a hitch. But remember that if a script later retrieves these values from the text object, they will come back as strings.

Storing arrays in a field does require special processing. You need to use the `array.join()` method to convert an array into a string. Each array entry is delimited by a character you establish in the `array.join()` method. Later you can use the `string.split()` method to turn this delimited string into an array.

Example

Important: Listings 22-2 and 22-3 feature a form with only one text input object. The rules of HTML forms say that such a form will submit itself if the user presses the Enter key whenever the field has focus. Such a submission to a form whose action is undefined causes the page to perform a hard reload. Moreover, the form's `onSubmit=` event handler is not triggered with this kind of submission, so you cannot set an event handler to prevent the submission. To see the results of either listing, enter a value and then either press the Tab key or click anywhere outside of the field.

As a demonstration of how to retrieve and assign values to a text object, Listing 22-2 shows how the action in an `onChange=` event handler is triggered. Enter any lowercase letters into the field and click out of the field. I pass a reference to the entire form object as a parameter to the event handler. The function extracts the value, converts it to uppercase (using one of the JavaScript string object methods), and assigns it back to the same field in that form.

Listing 22-2: **Getting and Setting a Text Object's Value**

```
<HTML>
<HEAD>
<TITLE>Text Object Value</TITLE>
<SCRIPT LANGUAGE="JavaScript">
function upperMe(form) {
        inputStr = form.converter.value
        form.converter.value = inputStr.toUpperCase()
}
</SCRIPT>
</HEAD>

<BODY>
<FORM>
Enter lowercase letters for conversion to uppercase: <INPUT TYPE="text"
NAME="converter" VALUE="sample" onChange="upperMe(this.form)">
</FORM>
</BODY>
</HTML>
```

I also show two other ways to accomplish the same task, each one more efficient than the previous example. Both utilize the shortcut object reference to get at the heart of the text object. Listing 22-3 passes the field object — contained in the `this` reference — to the function handler. Because that field object contains a complete reference to it (out of sight, but there just the same), you can access the `value` property of that object and assign a string to that object's `value` property in a simple assignment statement.

Listing 22-3: **Passing a Text Object (as this) to the Function**

```
<HTML>
<HEAD>
<TITLE>Text Object Value</TITLE>
<SCRIPT LANGUAGE="JavaScript">
function upperMe(field) {
        field.value = field.value.toUpperCase()
}
</SCRIPT>
</HEAD>

<BODY>
<FORM>
Enter lowercase letters for conversion to uppercase: <INPUT TYPE="text"
NAME="converter" VALUE="sample" onChange="upperMe(this)">
</FORM>
</BODY>
</HTML>
```

A more efficient way is to deal with the field values directly in an embedded event handler — instead of calling an external function (which might still be useful if other objects need this functionality). With the function removed from the document, the event handler attribute of the `<INPUT>` definition changes to do all the work:

```
<INPUT TYPE="text" NAME="converter" VALUE="sample"
  onChange="this.value = this.value.toUpperCase()">
```

The right-hand side of the assignment expression extracts the current contents of the field and (with the help of the `toUpperCase()` method of the string object) converts the original string to all uppercase letters. The result of this operation is assigned to the `value` property of the field.

The application of the `this` keyword in the previous examples may be confusing at first, but these examples represent the range of ways in which you can use such references effectively. Using `this` by itself as a parameter to an object's event handler refers only to that single object — a text object in Listing 22-3. If you want to pass along a broader scope of objects that contain the current object, use the `this` keyword along with the outer object layer you want. In Listing 22-2, I sent the entire form along by specifying `this.form` — meaning the form that contains "this" object, which is being defined in the line of HTML code.

At the other end of the scale, you can use similar-looking syntax to specify a particular property of the "this" object. Thus, in the last example, I zeroed in on just the `value` property of the current object being defined — `this.value`. Although the formats of `this.form` and `this.value` appear the same, they encompass entirely different ends of the range of focus — simply by virtue of the meaning of the keywords to the right of the period. As long as you know that a form is an object of larger scope than the currently defined object, you will know that `this.form` includes an entire form object (and all its elements); conversely, if you know that a text object has a property named "value," you will know that a reference to `this.value` focuses only on the `value` property of the currently defined object. This is why it's so important for JavaScript authors to be completely familiar with both the object hierarchy and the range of property and method names for those objects.

Related Items: `form.defaultValue` property.

Methods

blur()

Returns: Nothing.

	Nav2	Nav3	Nav4	IE3/J1	IE3/J2	IE4/J3
Compatibility	✔	✔	✔	✔	✔	✔

Just as a camera lens blurs when it goes out of focus, a text object blurs when it loses focus — when someone clicks or tabs out of the field. Under script control, `blur()` deselects whatever may be selected in the field, and the text insertion pointer leaves the field. The pointer does not proceed to the next field in tabbing order, as it does if you perform a blur by tabbing out of the field manually.

Example

    document.forms[0].vanishText.blur()

Related Items: `focus()` method; `onBlur=` event handler.

focus()

Returns: Nothing.

	Nav2	Nav3	Nav4	IE3/J1	IE3/J2	IE4/J3
Compatibility	✔	✔	✔	✔	✔	✔

For a text object, having focus means that the text insertion pointer is flashing in that text object's field (it means something different for buttons in a Windows environment). Giving a field focus is like opening it up for human editing.

Setting the focus of a field containing text does not let you place the cursor at any specified location in the field. The cursor usually appears at the beginning of the text. To prepare a field for entry to remove the existing text, use both the focus() and select() methods.

Note

The focus() method does not work reliably in Navigator 3 for UNIX clients. While the select() method selects the text in the designated field, focus is not handed to the field.

Example

See Listing 22-4 for an example of an application of the focus() method in concert with the select() method.

Related Items: select() method; onFocus= event handler.

handleEvent(*event*)

Returns: Nothing.

	Nav2	Nav3	Nav4	IE3/J1	IE3/J2	IE4/J3
Compatibility			✔			

See the discussion of the window.handleEvent() method in Chapter 14 and the event object in Chapter 33 for details on this ubiquitous form element method.

select()

Returns: Nothing.

	Nav2	Nav3	Nav4	IE3/J1	IE3/J2	IE4/J3
Compatibility	✔	✔	✔	✔	✔	✔

Selecting a field under script control means selecting all text within the text object. A typical application is one in which an entry validation script detects a mistake on the part of the user. After alerting the user to the mistake (via a window.alert() dialog box), the script finishes its task by selecting the text of the field in question. Not only does this action draw the user's eye to the field needing attention (especially important if the validation code is checking multiple fields), but it also keeps the old text there for the user to examine for potential problems. With the text selected, the next key the user presses erases the former entry.

Trying to select a text object's contents with a click of a button is problematic. One problem is that a click of the button brings the document's focus to the button, which disrupts the selection process. For more ensured selection, the script should invoke both the `focus()` and the `select()` methods for the field, in that order. No penalty exists for issuing both methods, and the extra insurance of the second method provides a more consistent user experience with the page.

Selecting a text object via script does *not* trigger the same `onSelect=` event handler for that object as the one that triggers if a user manually selects text in the field. Therefore, no event handler script is executed when a user invokes the `select()` method.

Example

A click of the Verify button in Listing 22-4 sends the text object's contents for validation as all numbers. If the validation returns false, the script preselects the field entry for the user. To make sure the selection takes place, you first set the document's focus to the field and then select its contents. If the focus was on the field immediately before clicking the button, the selection may work without requiring you to set the focus. But you cannot be sure of what the user will do between entering text and clicking the button. Try commenting out (`//`) the `form.numeric.focus()` statement, and then reload the document and see how well the selection works by itself under a variety of circumstances. You will find that setting the focus is a surefire method.

Listing 22-4: **Selecting a Field**

```
<HTML>
<HEAD>
<TITLE>Text Object Select/Focus</TITLE>
<SCRIPT LANGUAGE="JavaScript">
// general purpose function to see if a suspected numeric input is a
number
function isNumber(inputStr) {
        for (var i = 0; i < inputStr.length; i++) {
            var oneChar = inputStr.charAt(i)
            if (oneChar < "0" || oneChar > "9") {
                alert("Please make sure entries are numbers only.")
                return false
            }
        }
        return true
}
function checkIt(form) {
        inputStr = form.numeric.value
        if (isNumber(inputStr)) {
            // statements if true
        } else {
            form.numeric.focus()
            form.numeric.select()
```

```
        }
    }

    </SCRIPT>
    </HEAD>

    <BODY>
    <FORM>
    Enter any positive integer: <INPUT TYPE="text" NAME="numeric"><P>
    <INPUT TYPE="button" VALUE="Verify" onClick="checkIt(this.form)">
    </FORM>
    </BODY>
    </HTML>
```

Related Items: focus() method; onSelect= event handler.

Event handlers

onBlur=

onFocus=

onSelect=

	Nav2	Nav3	Nav4	IE3/J1	IE3/J2	IE4/J3
Compatibility	✔	✔	✔	✔	✔	✔

All three of these event handlers should be used only after you have a firm understanding of the interrelationships of the events that reach text objects. You must use extreme care and conduct lots of user testing before including more than one of these three event handlers in a text object. Because some events cannot occur without triggering others either immediately before or after (for example, an onFocus= occurs immediately before an onSelect= if the field did not have focus before), whatever actions you script for these events should be as distinct as possible to avoid interference or overlap.

In particular, be careful about displaying modal dialog boxes (for example, window.alert() dialog boxes) in response to the onFocus= event handler. Because the text field loses focus when the alert displays and then regains focus when the alert is closed, you can get yourself into a loop that is difficult to break out of. If you should get trapped in this manner, try the keyboard shortcut for reloading the page (Ctrl+R or ⌘-R) repeatedly as you keep closing the dialog window.

A question arises about whether data-entry validation should be triggered by the onBlur= or onChange= event handler. An onBlur= validation cannot be fooled, whereas an onChange= one can be (the user simply doesn't change the bad entry as he or she tabs out of the field). What I don't like about the onBlur= way is it can cause a frustrating experience for a user who wants to tab through a field now and come back to it later (assuming your validation requires data be entered into the field before submission). As in Chapter 37's discussion about form data validation, I recommend using onChange= event handlers to trigger immediate data checking and then using another last-minute check in a function called by the form's onSubmit= event handler.

Example

To demonstrate one of these event handlers, Listing 22-5 shows how you might use the window's status bar as a prompt message area when a user activates any field of a form. When the user tabs to or clicks on a field, the prompt message associated with that field appears in the status bar.

Listing 22-5: **The onFocus= Event Handler**

```
<HTML>
<HEAD>
<TITLE>Elements Array</TITLE>
<SCRIPT LANGUAGE="JavaScript">
function prompt(msg) {
        window.status = "Please enter your " + msg + "."
}
</SCRIPT>
</HEAD>

<BODY>
<FORM>
Enter your first name:<INPUT TYPE="text" NAME="firstName"
onFocus="prompt('first name')"><P>
Enter your last name:<INPUT TYPE="text" NAME="lastName"
onFocus="prompt('last name')"><P>
Enter your address:<INPUT TYPE="text" NAME="address"
onFocus="prompt('address')"><P>
Enter your city:<INPUT TYPE="text" NAME="city"
onFocus="prompt('city')"><P>
</FORM>
</BODY>
</HTML>
```

onChange=

	Nav2	Nav3	Nav4	IE3/J1	IE3/J2	IE4/J3
Compatibility	✔	✔	✔	✔	✔	✔

Of all the event handlers for a text object, you will probably use the `onChange=` handler the most in your forms (see Listing 22-6). This event is the one I prefer for triggering the validation of whatever entry the user just typed in the field. The potential hazard of trying to do only a batch-mode data validation of all entries before submitting an entire form is that the user's mental focus is away from the entry of a given field as well. When you immediately validate an entry, the user is already thinking about the information category in question. See Chapter 37 for more about data-entry validation.

Note

In Navigator 4, if you have both `onChange=` and any keyboard event handlers defined for the same text field tag, the `onChange=` event handlers are ignored. This is not true for Internet Explorer 4, where all events fire.

Example

Whenever a user makes a change to the text in a field in Listing 22-6 and then either tabs or clicks out of the field, the change event is sent to that field, triggering the `onChange=` event handler.

Because the form in Listing 22-6 has only one field, the same warning about the effect of pressing the Enter key applies here as to Listings 22-1 and 22-2 earlier in this chapter. Press Tab or click outside the field to trigger the `onChange=` event handler without submitting the form.

Listing 22-6: **Data Validation via an onChange= Event Handler**

```
<HTML>
<HEAD>
<TITLE>Text Object Select/Focus</TITLE>
<SCRIPT LANGUAGE="JavaScript">
// general purpose function to see if a suspected numeric input is a
number
function isNumber(inputStr) {
        for (var i = 0; i < inputStr.length; i++) {
            var oneChar = inputStr.substring(i, i + 1)
            if (oneChar < "0" || oneChar > "9") {
                alert("Please make sure entries are numbers only.")
                return false
            }
        }
        return true
}
function checkIt(form) {
        inputStr = form.numeric.value
```

(continued)

> **Listing 22-6** *(continued)*
>
> ```
>             if (isNumber(inputStr)) {
>                 // statements if true
>             } else {
>                 form.numeric.focus()
>                 form.numeric.select()
>             }
>     }
>     </SCRIPT>
>     </HEAD>
>
>     <BODY>
>     <FORM>
>     Enter any positive integer: <INPUT TYPE="text" NAME="numeric"
>     onChange="checkIt(this.form)"><P>
>     </FORM>
>     </BODY>
>     </HTML>
> ```

onKeyDown=

onKeyPress=

onKeyUp=

	Nav2	Nav3	Nav4	IE3/J1	IE3/J2	IE4/J3
Compatibility			✔			✔

New text field events for Navigator 4 and Internet Explorer 4 let your scripts capture user activity from the keyboard while the field has focus. The keyDown event occurs the instant the user presses the key far enough to make contact; the keyUp event occurs when electrical contact with the key breaks; and a keyPress event occurs after the keyUp event, signaling the completion of a matched pair of keyDown and keyUp events. No event exists to let you know when a key starts repeating itself.

Whichever event(s) you trap for, you can also extract the ASCII (or UniCode in Internet Explorer 4) value of the key. All of this event activity occurs *before* the typed character ever appears in the field. This allows your scripts a chance to filter out unwanted characters or even convert characters to different ones (for example, turning all letters into their uppercase equivalents for storage in a database).

Navigator and Internet Explorer have different ways of revealing the typed character to a script. But, as you can see in Listing 22-7, they are close enough that you can accommodate both browsers in simple key capture event handlers.

For an event handler to inspect a key character, the event handler must pass the event object that automatically accompanies such an event. The way you do this is to pass the keyword `event` as one of the parameters to the function called by the event handler:

```
onKeyPress="filterKeys(event)"
```

Notice that the `event` keyword is not a string, but rather a reference to the event object generated by the press of the key. You can also assign this kind of event handler in a script statement in the following manner:

```
document.formName.fieldName.onkeypress = filterKeys
```

In this latter format, the event object is automatically passed to the function whose reference is assigned to the event for the field object. Be aware, however, that assignments like the previous one must be lower in the document than the object for which the event hander is being assigned. Otherwise, the field won't yet be defined in the browser's object model for the document, and the statement generates an error during page loading.

You can control whether the keyboard action ever reaches the display area of the text object. Like many of the objects in the document model, if an event handler evaluates to `return false`, the event goes no further than the function invoked by the event handler; but if the handler evaluates to `return true`, then the natural behavior of the event carries on.

Note In Navigator 4, if you have both `onChange=` and any keyboard event handlers defined for the same text field tag, the `onChange=` event handlers are ignored. This is not true for Internet Explorer 4, where all events fire.

Example

Listing 22-7 is a simple script that inspects the key presses in a field expecting only numbers. By checking the value of each key before it reaches the value of the field, the event handler function can alert the user about the correct kind of characters to enter. The `checkIt()` function receives the event object passed by the event handler. To work with both Navigator and Internet Explorer, the function does one differentiation about how to extract the value of the typed character, depending on the browser version. After that, the value is in the `charCode` variable, and the rest of the function works the same for both platforms.

Notice the construction of the event handler such that it evaluates to `return true` or `return false`, depending on the results of the function. When the handler evaluates to `return false`, the typed character does not appear in the field, since in this case, I don't want nonnumbers to show themselves in the field.

Listing 22-7: **Keyboard Filtering for Numbers Only**

```
<HTML>
<HEAD>
<TITLE>Keyboard Capture</TITLE>
<SCRIPT LANGUAGE="JavaScript">
function checkIt(e) {
        var charCode = (navigator.appName == "Netscape") ? e.which :
e.keyCode
        status = charCode // see ASCII character value!
        if (charCode > 31 && (charCode < 48 || charCode > 57)) {
            alert("Please make sure entries are numbers only.")
            return false
        }
        return true
}
</SCRIPT>
</HEAD>

<BODY>
<FORM>
Enter any positive integer: <INPUT TYPE="text" NAME="numeric"
onKeyPress="return checkIt(event)"><P>
</FORM>
</BODY>
</HTML>
```

Learn more about handling events for Navigator 4 and cross-compatibility in Chapter 39.

Related Items: event object.

Password Object

Properties	Methods	Event Handlers
defaultValue	blur()	onBlur=
form	focus()	onChange=
name	handleEvent()	onFocus=
type	select()	onKeyDown=
value		onKeyPress=
		onKeyUp=
		onSelect=

Syntax

Creating a password object:

```
<FORM>
<INPUT
        TYPE="password"
        NAME="fieldName"
        [VALUE="contents"]
        [SIZE="characterCount"]
        [MAXLENGTH="maxCharactersAllowed"]
        [onBlur="handlerTextOrFunction"]
        [onChange="handlerTextOrFunction"]
        [onFocus="handlerTextOrFunction"]
        [onKeyDown="handlerTextOrFunction"]
        [onKeyPress="handlerTextOrFunction"]
        [onKeyUp="handlerTextOrFunction"]
        [onSelect="handlerTextOrFunction"]>
</FORM>
```

About this object

A password-style field looks like a text object, but when the user types something into the field, only asterisks or bullets (depending on your operating system) appear in the field. For the sake of security, any password exchanges should be handled by a server-side CGI program.

Many properties of the password object were blocked from scripted access until Navigator 3. Scripts now can treat a password object exactly like a text object. This might lead a scripter to capture a user's Web site password for storage in the document.cookie of the client machine. A password object value property is returned in plain language, so such a captured password would be stored in the cookie file the same way. Because a client machine's cookie file can be examined on the local computer (perhaps by a snoop during lunch hour), plain-language storage of passwords is a potential security risk. Instead, develop a scripted encryption algorithm for your page for reading and writing the password in the cookie. Most password-protected sites, however, usually have a CGI program on the server encrypt the password prior to sending it back to the cookie.

See the text object discussion for the behavior of password object's properties, methods, and event handlers. The type property for this object returns "password".

Textarea Object

Properties	Methods	Event Handlers
defaultValue	blur()	onBlur=
form	focus()	onChange=
name	handleEvent()	onFocus=

(continued)

Properties	Methods	Event Handlers
type	select()	onKeyDown=
value		onKeyPress=
		onKeyUp=
		onSelect=

Syntax

Creating a textarea object:

```
<TEXTAREA
      NAME="fieldName"
      [ROWS="rowCount"]
      [COLS="columnCount"]
      [WRAP="off" | "virtual" | "physical"]
      [onBlur="handlerTextOrFunction"]
      [onChange="handlerTextOrFunction"]
      [onFocus="handlerTextOrFunction"]
      [onKeyDown="handlerTextOrFunction"]
      [onKeyPress="handlerTextOrFunction"]
      [onKeyUp="handlerTextOrFunction"]
      [onSelect="handlerTextOrFunction"]>
      defaultText
</TEXTAREA>
</FORM>
```

Accessing textarea object properties or methods:

```
[window.] document.formName.fieldName.property |
      method([parameters])
```

```
[window.] document.formName.elements[index].property |
      method([parameters])
```

```
[window.] document.forms[index].fieldName.property |
      method([parameters])
```

```
[window.] document.forms[index].elements[index].property |
      method([parameters])
```

About this object

Although not in the same syntax family as other <INPUT> elements of a form, a textarea object is indeed a form input element. Any definition for a textarea object must be written within the confines of a <FORM>...</FORM> tag pair.

A textarea object closely resembles a text object, except for attributes that define its physical appearance on the page. Because the intended use of a textarea object is for multiple-line text input, the attributes include specifications for height (number of rows) and width (number of columns in the monospaced font). No matter what size you specify, the browser displays a textarea with horizontal and vertical scrollbars. Neither the user nor a script can resize the field, nor does text wrap within the visible rectangle of the field unless you set the WRAP attribute to "virtual" or "physical". Instead, the user is encouraged to press Enter to make manual carriage returns. If the user fails to do so, the text scrolls for a significant distance horizontally (the horizontal scrollbar appears when wrapping has the default off setting). This field is, indeed, a primitive text field by GUI computing standards.

All properties, methods, and event handlers of text objects apply to the textarea object. They all behave exactly the same way (except, of course, for the type property, which is "textarea"). Therefore, refer to the previous listings for the text object for scripting details.

Carriage returns inside textareas

The three classes of operating systems supported by Netscape Navigator — Windows, Macintosh, and UNIX — do not agree about what constitutes a carriage return character in a text string. This discrepancy carries over to the textarea object and its contents on these platforms.

When a user enters text and uses Enter/Return on the keyboard, one or more unseen characters are inserted into the string. In the parlance of JavaScript's literal string characters, the carriage return consists of some combination of the new line (\n) and return (\r) character. The following list shows the characters inserted into the string for each operating system category.

Operating System	Character String
Windows	\r\n
Macintosh	\r
Unix	\n

This tidbit is valuable if you need to remove carriage returns from a textarea for processing in a CGI or local script. The problem is that you obviously need to perform platform-specific operations on each. For the situation in which you must preserve the carriage return locations, but your server-side database cannot accept the carriage return values, I suggest you use the string.escape() method to URL-encode the string. The return character is converted to %0D and the newline character is converted to %0A. Of course these characters occupy extra character spaces in your database, so these additions must be accounted for in your database design.

As far as writing carriage returns into textareas, the situation is a bit easier. From Navigator 3 onward, if you specify any one of the combinations in the preceding list, all platforms know how to automatically convert the data to the form native to the operating system. Therefore, you can set the value of a textarea object to "1\r\n2\r\n3" in all platforms, and a columnar list of the numbers 1, 2, and 3 will appear in those fields. Or, if you URL-encoded the text for saving to a database, you can unescape that character string before setting the textarea value, and no matter what platform the visitor has, the carriage returns are rendered correctly. Upon reading those values again by script, you can see that the carriage returns are in the form of the platform (as shown in the previous table).

Hidden Object

Properties	Methods	Event Handlers
defaultValue	(None)	(None)
form		
name		
type		
value		

Syntax

Creating a hidden object:

```
<FORM>
<INPUT
        TYPE="hidden"
        NAME="fieldName"
        [VALUE="contents"]>
</FORM>
```

Accessing hidden object properties:

```
[window.] document.formName.fieldName.property

[window.] document.formName.elements[index].property

[window.] document.forms[index].fieldName.property

[window.] document.forms[index].elements[index].property
```

About this object

A hidden object is a simple string holder within a form object whose contents are not visible to the user of your Web page. With no methods or event handlers, the hidden object's value to your scripting is as a delivery vehicle for strings that your scripts need for reference values or other hard-wired data.

The hidden object plays a vital role in applications that rely on CGI programs on the server. Very often, the server has data that it needs to convey to itself the next time the client makes a submission (for example, a user ID captured at the application's login page). A CGI program can generate an HTML page with the necessary data hidden from the user but located in a field transmitted to the server at submit time.

Along the same lines, a page for a server application may present a user-friendly interface that makes data entry easy for the user. But on the server end, the database or other application requires that the data be in a more esoteric format. A script located in the page generated for the user can perform the last minute assemblage of user-friendly data into database-friendly data in a hidden field. When the CGI program receives the request from the client, it passes along the hidden field value to the database.

I am not a fan of the hidden object for use on client-side-only JavaScript applications. If I want to deliver with my JavaScript-enabled pages some default data collections or values, I do so in JavaScript variables and arrays as part of the script.

Because scripted changes to the contents of a hidden field are fragile (for example, a soft reload erases the changes), the only place you should consider making such changes is in the same script that submits a form to a CGI program or in a function triggered by an `onSubmit=` event handler. In effect, you're just using the hidden fields as holding pens for the scripted data to be submitted. For more persistent storage, use the `document.cookie` property or genuine text fields in hidden frames, even if just for the duration of the visit to the page.

For information about the properties of the hidden object, consult the earlier listing for the text object.

✦   ✦   ✦

Button Objects

This chapter is devoted to those lovable buttons that invite users to initiate action and make choices with a single click of the mouse button. In this category fall the standard system-looking buttons with labels on them as well as radio buttons and checkboxes. For such workhorses of the HTML form, these objects have a limited vocabulary of properties, methods, and event handlers.

I group together the button, submit, and reset objects for an important reason: they look alike yet they are intended for very different purposes. It is important to know when to use which button — especially in the case of the button and submit objects. Many a newcomer get the two confused and wind up with scripting error headaches. That shouldn't happen to you by the time you've finished this chapter.

The Button Object, Submit Object, and Reset Object

Properties	Methods	Event Handlers
name	click()	onClick=
type	handleEvent()	onMouseDown=
value		onMouseUp=

Syntax

Creating a button:

```
<FORM>
<INPUT
        TYPE="button" | "submit" | "reset"
        NAME="buttonName"
        VALUE="labelText"
        [onClick="handlerTextOrFunction"]
        [onMouseDown="handlerTextOrFunction"]
        [onMouseUp="handlerTextOrFunction"] >
</FORM>
```

Accessing button object properties or methods:

```
[window.] document.formName.buttonName.property |
    method([parameters])

[window.] document.formName.elements[index].property |
    method([parameters])

[window.] document.forms[index].buttonName.property |
    method([parameters])

[window.] document.forms[index].elements[index].property |
    method([parameters])
```

About these objects

Button objects generate standard, pushbutton-style user interface elements on the page, depending on the operating system on which the particular browser runs. Figure 23-1 shows examples of a typical button in both the Windows 95 and Macintosh versions for Navigator 4. The precise look also varies with browser version and supplier. In the early days, the browsers called upon the operating systems to generate these standard interface elements. In more recent versions, the browsers define their own look, albeit still different for each operating system.

Figure 23-1: Comparison of the button object in Navigator 4 for the Windows 95 (left) and Macintosh (right) operating systems

The only visual characteristic of a button controlled by the HTML page author is the text that appears on the button. That label text is the parameter to the VALUE attribute of the button's definition. The width of the button on the screen is calculated for you, based on the width of the button's label text. Always give careful thought to the label you assign to a button. Because a button initiates some action, make sure that the verb in the label clearly defines what happens when you click it. Also take cues from experienced user interface designers who craft operating system and commercial software buttons: Be concise. If you find your button labels going longer than two or three words, reconsider the design of your page so the user can clearly understand the purpose of any button from a shorter label. Like most user interface elements, JavaScript automatically draws buttons left-aligned on the page. For earlier browsers not fitted with element positioning, you can surround a button's <INPUT> definition with the <DIV ALIGN="where">... </DIV> tags to have them align center or right, if you prefer. However, Navigator 4 and Internet Explorer 4 offer the best solution by letting you specify the precise coordinates of the top-left corner of the button. This kind of positioning still does not address the cross-platform problem of laying out form elements with a uniform look on all operating systems, because one may be wider or taller than another — topographical features not under control of style sheets or JavaScript. Therefore, unless you branch the layout properties of your form elements according to operating system (and then test the appearance on the ones you're concerned about), precise positioning of buttons against other objects or images is difficult or impossible to guarantee.

Buttons in the Windows environment follow their normal behavior in that they indicate the focus with highlighted button-label text. You cannot control the focus or blur of a button via JavaScript as you can for a text object. Buttons are also highlighted according to the conventions of the host operating system, and you cannot override these conventions with scripting commands.

The lone button object event handler that works on all browser versions is one that responds to a user clicking the pointer atop the mouse: the onClick= event handler. Virtually all action surrounding a button object comes from this event handler. You will rarely need to extract property values or invoke the click() method (particularly because the method does not work correctly, even in Navigator 3). Navigator 4 and Internet Explorer 4 add events for the components of a click: mouseDown and mouseUp.

Two special variants of the JavaScript button object are the *submit* and *reset* button objects. With their heritages going back to early incarnations of HTML, these two button types perform special operations on their own. The submit-style button automatically sends the data within the same form object to the URL listed in the ACTION attribute of the <FORM> definition. The METHOD attribute dictates the format in which the button sends the data. Therefore, you don't have to script this action if your HTML page is communicating with a CGI program on the server.

If the form's ACTION attribute is set to a mailto: URL, you must provide the page visitor with a Submit button to carry out the action. It is also helpful to set the form's ENCTYPE attribute to text/plain so that the form data arrives in a more readable form than the normal encoded name-value pairs. See "E-Mailing forms" in Chapter 21 for details about submitting form content via e-mail.

The partner of the Submit button is the Reset button. It, too, has special features. A click of this button type restores all elements within the form to their default values. That goes for text objects, radio button groups, checkboxes, and selection lists. The most common application of the button is to clear entry fields of the last data entered by the user.

All that distinguishes these three types of buttons from each other in the <INPUT> element definition is the parameter of the TYPE attribute. For buttons not intended to send data to a server, use the "button" style. Reserve "submit" and "reset" for their special CGI-related powers.

If you want an image to behave like a button, consider either associating a link with an image (see the discussion on the link object in Chapter 17) or creating a client-side image map (see the area object discussion in Chapter 18).

Probably the biggest mistake scripters make with these buttons is using a Submit button to do the work of a plain button. Because they look alike and the submit type of input element has a longer tradition than the button, it is easy to confuse the two. But if all you want is to display a button that initiates client-side script execution, use a plain button. The Submit button will attempt to submit the form. If no ACTION attribute is set, then the page reloads, and all previous processing and field entries are erased. The plain button does its job quietly without reloading the page (unless the script intentionally does so).

Properties

name

Value: String   **Gettable:** Yes   **Settable:** Yes

	Nav2	Nav3	Nav4	IE3/J1	IE3/J2	IE4/J3
Compatibility	✔	✔	✔	✔	✔	✔

A button's name is fixed in the `<INPUT>` definition's `NAME` attribute and cannot be adjusted via scripting except in newer browsers. You may need to retrieve this property in a general-purpose function handler called by multiple buttons in a document. The function can test for a button name and perform the necessary statements for that button. If you change the name of the object, even a soft reload or window resize will restore its original name.

Example

```
buttonName = document.forms[0].elements[3].name // 4th element is a
button
```

Related Items: `name` property of all form elements.

type

Value: String   **Gettable:** Yes   **Settable:** No

	Nav2	Nav3	Nav4	IE3/J1	IE3/J2	IE4/J3
Compatibility		✔	✔			✔

The precise value of the `type` property echoes the setting of the `TYPE` attribute of the `<INPUT>` tag that defined the object: button; submit; or reset.

value

Value: String   **Gettable:** Yes   **Settable:** Yes

	Nav2	Nav3	Nav4	IE3/J1	IE3/J2	IE4/J3
Compatibility	✔	✔	✔	✔	✔	✔

A button's visible label is determined by the VALUE attribute of the <INPUT> element's definition. The value property reveals that text. A strong convention exists that assigns the words "Submit" and "Reset" to their respective button-style labels. As long as the purpose of either button is clear, you can assign whatever label you like to any of the button objects in the <INPUT> definitions. Unlike button (and other object) names, the VALUE attribute can be more than one word.

You can modify this text on the fly in a script, but some cautions apply. Except for Internet Explorer 4's extraordinary redrawing behavior, all other browsers do not resize the width of the button to accommodate a new name that is longer or shorter than the original. Moreover, any soft reload or resize of the window restores the original label. Internet Explorer 4, however, resizes the button and reflows the page to meet the new space needs; the new label survives a window resizing, but not a soft reload of the page.

Example

In the following excerpt, the statement toggles the label of a button from "Play" to "Stop":

```
btn = document.forms[0].controlButton
btn.value = (btn.value == "Play") ? "Stop" : "Play"
```

Related Items: value property of text object.

Methods
click()

Returns: Nothing.

	Nav2	Nav3	Nav4	IE3/J1	IE3/J2	IE4/J3
Compatibility	✔	✔	✔	✔	✔	✔

A button's click() method should replicate, via scripting, the human action of clicking that button. Unfortunately, this method was broken in Navigator 2 and was still unreliable in Navigator 3. Don't bother trying to include it in your repertoire unless you can test the results thoroughly on all platforms that your page visitors will be using.

Example

```
document.forms[0].sender.click()// sender is the name of a Submit-style
button
```

Related Items: onClick= event handler.

handleEvent(*event*)

Returns: Nothing.

	Nav2	Nav3	Nav4	IE3/J1	IE3/J2	IE4/J3
Compatibility			✔			

See the discussion of the window.handleEvent() method in Chapter 14 and the event object in Chapter 33 for details on this ubiquitous form element method.

Event handlers
onClick=

	Nav2	Nav3	Nav4	IE3/J1	IE3/J2	IE4/J3
Compatibility	✔	✔	✔	✔	✔	✔

Virtually all button action takes place in response to the onClick= event handler. A click is defined as a press and release of the mouse button while the screen pointer rests atop the button. The event goes to the button only after the user releases the mouse button, and no events go to the button while the user holds the mouse button down.

For a Submit button, you should probably omit the onClick= event handler and allow the form's onSubmit= event handler to take care of last minute data-entry validation before sending the form. By triggering validation with the onSubmit= event handler, your scripts can cancel the submission if something is not right (see the form object discussion in Chapter 21).

Example

In Listing 23-1, I demonstrate not only the onClick= event handler of a button but also how you may need to extract a particular button's name or value properties from a general-purpose function that services multiple buttons. In this case, each button passes its own object as a parameter to the displayTeam() function. The function then displays the results in an alert dialog box. A production environment would probably use a more complex if...else decision tree to perform more sophisticated actions based on the button clicked (or in Navigator 4 and Internet Explorer 4, it would use a `switch` construction on the `btn.value` expression).

Listing 23-1: **Three Buttons Sharing One Function**

```
<HTML>
<HEAD>
<TITLE>Button Click</TITLE>
<SCRIPT LANGUAGE="JavaScript">
function displayTeam(btn) {
        if (btn.value == "Abbott") {alert("Abbott & Costello")}
        if (btn.value == "Rowan") {alert("Rowan & Martin")}
        if (btn.value == "Martin") {alert("Martin & Lewis")}
}
</SCRIPT>
</HEAD>

<BODY>
Click on your favorite half of a popular comedy team:<P>
<FORM>
<INPUT TYPE="button" VALUE="Abbott" onClick="displayTeam(this)">
<INPUT TYPE="button" VALUE="Rowan" onClick="displayTeam(this)">
<INPUT TYPE="button" VALUE="Martin" onClick="displayTeam(this)">
</FORM>
</BODY>
</HTML>
```

Related Items: `button.onMouseDown=` event handler; `button.onMouseUp=` event handler; `form.submit=` event handler.

onMouseDown=

onMouseUp=

	Nav2	Nav3	Nav4	IE3/J1	IE3/J2	IE4/J3
Compatibility			✔			✔

More recent browsers add event handlers for the components of a click event: the `onMouseDown=` and `onMouseUp=` event handlers. These events fire in addition to the `onClick=` event handler.

The system-level buttons provided by the operating system perform their change of appearance while a button is being pressed. Therefore, trapping for the components of a click action won't help you in changing the button's appearance via scripting. Remember that a user can roll the cursor off the button while the button is still down. When the cursor leaves the region of the button, the button's appearance returns to its unpressed look, but any setting you make with the `onMouseDown=` event handler won't undo itself with an `onMouseUp=` counterpart, even after the user releases the mouse button elsewhere. On the other hand, if you can precache a click-on and click-off sound, you can use these events to fire the respective sounds in response to the mouse button action.

Related Items: `button.onClick=` event handler.

Checkbox Object

Properties	*Methods*	*Event Handlers*
checked	click()	onClick=
defaultChecked	handleEvent()	onMouseDown=
name		onMouseUp=
type		
value		

Syntax

Creating a checkbox:

```
<FORM>
<INPUT
      TYPE="checkbox"
      NAME="boxName"
      VALUE="buttonValue"
      [CHECKED]
      [onClick="handlerTextOrFunction"]
      [onMouseDown="handlerTextOrFunction"]
      [onMouseUp="handlerTextOrFunction"] >
      buttonText
</FORM>
```

Accessing checkbox properties or methods:

```
[window.] document.formName.boxName.property |
      method([parameters])

[window.] document.formName.elements[index].property |
      method([parameters])

[window.] document.forms[index].boxName.property |
      method([parameters])

[window.] document.forms[index].elements[index].property |
      method([parameters])
```

About this object

Checkboxes have a very specific purpose in modern graphical user interfaces: to toggle between "on" and "off" settings. As with a checkbox on a printed form, a mark in the box indicates that the label text is true or should be included for the individual who made that mark. When the box is unchecked or empty, the text is false or should not be included. If two or more checkboxes are physically grouped together, they should have no interaction: Each is an independent setting (see the discussion on the radio object for interrelated buttons).

I make these user interface points at the outset because, in order to present a user interface in your HTML pages consistent with the user's expectations based on exposure to other programs, you must use checkbox objects only for on-off choices that the user makes. Using a checkbox as an action button that, say, navigates to another URL is not good form. Just as they do in a Windows or Mac dialog box, users make settings with checkboxes and radio buttons and initiate action by clicking a standard button or image map.

That's not to say that a checkbox object cannot perform some limited action in response to a user's click, but such actions are typically related to the context of the checkbox button's label text. For example, in some Windows and Macintosh dialog boxes, turning on a checkbox may activate a bunch of otherwise inactive settings elsewhere in the same dialog box. Although Navigator 4 doesn't provide you with such advanced graphical powers for HTML, there may be other ways to turn a click of a checkbox into a meaningful action. For example, in a two-frame window, a checkbox in one frame may control whether the viewer is an advanced user. If so, the content in the other frame may be more detailed. Toggling the checkbox changes the complexity level of a document showing in the other frame (using different URLs for each level). The bottom line, then, is that you should use checkboxes for toggling between on-off settings. Use regular button objects for initiating processing.

In the `<INPUT>` definition for a checkbox, you can preset the checkbox to be checked when the page appears. Add the constant `CHECKED` attribute to the definition. If you omit this attribute, the default, unchecked appearance rules. As for the checkbox label text, its definition lies outside the `<INPUT>` tag. If you look at the way checkboxes behave in HTML browsers, this location makes sense: The label is not an active part of the checkbox (as it typically is in Windows and Macintosh user interfaces, where clicking the label is the same as clicking the box).

Naming a checkbox can be an important part of the object definition, depending on how you plan to use the information in your script or document. For forms whose content goes to a CGI program on the server, you must word the box name as needed for use by the CGI program, so the program can parse the form data and extract the setting of the checkbox. For JavaScript client-side use, you can assign not only a name that describes the button, but also a value useful to your script for making `if...else` decisions or for assembling strings that are eventually displayed in a window or frame.

Properties

checked

Value: Boolean   **Gettable:** Yes   **Settable:** Yes

	Nav2	Nav3	Nav4	IE3/J1	IE3/J2	IE4/J3
Compatibility	✔	✔	✔	✔	✔	✔

The simplest property of a checkbox reveals (or lets you set) whether or not a checkbox is checked. The value is true for a checked box and false for an unchecked box. To check a box via a script, simply assign *true* to the checkbox's checked property:

```
document.forms[0].boxName.checked = true
```

Setting the checked property from a script does not trigger a click event for the checkbox object.

There may be instances in which one checkbox should automatically check another checkbox elsewhere in the same or other form of the document. To accomplish this task, create an onClick= event handler for the one checkbox and build a statement similar to the preceding one to set the other related checkbox to true. Don't get too carried away with this feature, however: For a group of interrelated, mutually exclusive choices, use a group of radio buttons instead.

If your page design requires that a checkbox be checked when the page loads, don't bother trying to script this checking action. Simply add the one-word CHECKED attribute to the <INPUT> definition. Because the checked property is a Boolean value, you can use its results as an argument for an if clause, as shown in the next example.

Example

The simple example in Listing 23-2 passes the entire form object to the JavaScript function. The function, in turn, extracts the checked value of the form's checkbox object (checkThis.checked) and uses its Boolean value as the test result for the if...else construction.

Listing 23-2: **The checked Property as a Conditional**

```
<HTML>
<HEAD>
<TITLE>Checkbox Inspector</TITLE>
<SCRIPT LANGUAGE="JavaScript">
function inspectBox(form) {
        if (form.checkThis.checked) {
           alert("The box is checked.")
        } else {
           alert("The box is not checked at the moment.")
```

```
        }
    }
</SCRIPT>
</HEAD>

<BODY>
<FORM>
<INPUT TYPE="checkbox" NAME="checkThis">Check here<P>
<INPUT TYPE="button" NAME="boxChecker" VALUE="Inspect Box"
onClick="inspectBox(this.form)">
</FORM>
</BODY>
</HTML>
```

Related Items: value property; defaultChecked property.

defaultChecked

Value: Boolean   **Gettable:** Yes   **Settable:** No

	Nav2	Nav3	Nav4	IE3/J1	IE3/J2	IE4/J3
Compatibility	✔	✔	✔	✔	✔	✔

If you add the CHECKED attribute to the <INPUT> definition for a checkbox, the defaultChecked property for that object is true; otherwise, the property is false. Having access to this property enables your scripts to examine checkboxes to see if they have been adjusted (presumably by the user, if your script does not set properties).

Example

The function in Listing 23-3 (this fragment is not in the CD-ROM listings) is designed to compare the current setting of a checkbox against its default value. The if construction compares the current status of the box against its default status. Both are Boolean values, so they can be compared against each other. If the current and default settings don't match, the function goes on to handle the case in which the current setting is other than the default.

Listing 23-3: **Examining the defaultChecked Property**

```
function compareBrowser(thisBox) {
    if (thisBox.checked != thisBox.defaultChecked) {
        // statements about using a different set of HTML pages
    }
}
```

Related Items: `checked` property; `value` property.

name

Value: String   **Gettable:** Yes   **Settable:** No

	Nav2	Nav3	Nav4	IE3/J1	IE3/J2	IE4/J3
Compatibility	✔	✔	✔	✔	✔	✔

Unless a page design submits a form's data to a server for CGI program execution, the primary importance of a checkbox's name is to help you identify it in scripted references to its properties or methods. Be as descriptive as you can with the name, so that the name immediately invokes the vision of the checkbox.

Example

Listing 23-2 shows how a checkbox's name is used in a function's reference to the object. Although the name in this particular listing, `checkThis`, is not exactly a work of fine literature, it's better than generic names such as `myBox`.

Related Items: `name` property of all form elements.

type

Value: "checkbox"   **Gettable:** Yes   **Settable:** No

	Nav2	Nav3	Nav4	IE3/J1	IE3/J2	IE4/J3
Compatibility		✔	✔			✔

Use the `type` property to help you identify a checkbox object from an unknown group of form elements.

Related Items: `form.elements` property.

value

Value: String   **Gettable:** Yes   **Settable:** No

	Nav2	Nav3	Nav4	IE3/J1	IE3/J2	IE4/J3
Compatibility	✔	✔	✔	✔	✔	✔

A checkbox object's `value` property is a string of any text you want to associate with the box. Note that the checkbox's `value` property is not the label, as it is for a regular button, but hidden text associated with the checkbox. For instance, the label you attach to a checkbox may not be worded in a way that is useful to your script. But if you place that useful wording in the `VALUE` attribute of the checkbox definition, you can extract that string via the `value` property.

When a checkbox object's data is submitted to a CGI program, the `value` property is sent as part of the `name=value` pair if the box is checked (nothing about the checkbox is sent if the box is unchecked). If you omit the `VALUE` attribute in your definition, the property always yields the string "on," which is submitted to a CGI program when the box is checked. From the JavaScript side, don't confuse this string with the on and off settings of the checkbox: Use the `checked` property to determine a checkbox's status.

Example

The scenario for the skeleton HTML page in Listing 23-4 is a form with a checkbox whose selection determines which of two actions to follow for submission to the server. When the user clicks the Submit button, a JavaScript function examines the checkbox's `checked` property. If the property is true (the button is checked), the script sets the `action` property for the entire form to the content of the `value` property — thus influencing where the form goes on the server side. If you try this listing on your computer, you will receive error messages about being unable to locate a file with the name `primaryURL` or `alternateURL` because those files don't exist. The names and the error message come from the submission process for this demonstration.

Listing 23-4: **Adjusting a CGI Submission Action**

```
<HTML>
<HEAD>
<TITLE>Checkbox Submission</TITLE>
<SCRIPT LANGUAGE="JavaScript">
function setAction(form) {
        if (form.checkThis.checked) {
            form.action = form.checkThis.value
        } else {
            form.action = "primaryURL"
        }
        return true
}
</SCRIPT>
</HEAD>
```

(continued)

Listing 23-4 *(continued)*

```
<BODY>
<FORM METHOD="POST">
<INPUT TYPE="checkbox" NAME="checkThis" VALUE="alternateURL">Use
alternate<P>
<INPUT TYPE="submit" NAME="boxChecker" onClick="return
setAction(this.form)">
</FORM>
</BODY>
</HTML>
```

Related Items: checked property.

Methods

click()

Returns: Nothing.

	Nav2	Nav3	Nav4	IE3/J1	IE3/J2	IE4/J3
Compatibility	✔	✔	✔	✔	✔	✔

The intention of the click() method is to enact, via script, the physical act of checking a checkbox (but without triggering the onClick= event handler). Unfortunately, this method does not work in Navigator 2 or 3 as expected. Even if it worked flawlessly, your scripts are better served by setting the checked property so that you know exactly what the setting of the box is at any time.

Related Items: onClick= event handler; checked property.

handleEvent(*event*)

Returns: Nothing.

	Nav2	Nav3	Nav4	IE3/J1	IE3/J2	IE4/J3
Compatibility			✔			

See the discussion of the window.handleEvent() method in Chapter 14 and the event object in Chapter 33 for details on this ubiquitous form element method.

Event handlers
onClick=

	Nav2	Nav3	Nav4	IE3/J1	IE3/J2	IE4/J3
Compatibility	✔	✔	✔	✔	✔	✔

Because users click checkboxes, they have an event handler for the click event. Use this event handler only when you want your page (or variable values hidden from view) to respond in some way to the action of clicking a checkbox. Most user actions, as mentioned earlier, are initiated by clicking standard buttons rather than checkboxes, so be careful not to overuse event handlers in checkboxes.

Example

The page in Listing 23-5 shows how to trap the click event in one checkbox to influence the setting in another. Here, the assumption is that if your computer has a mouse, in all likelihood it also has a mouse port. Therefore, an onClick= event handler in the Mouse checkbox calls a function to set the Mouse Port checkbox to true whenever the Mouse checkbox is set to true. But unchecking the Mouse checkbox does not influence the Mouse Port checkbox—perhaps you're using a laptop's touch pad, even though the computer has a mouse port.

Listing 23-5: **A Checkbox and an onClick= Event Handler**

```
<HTML>
<HEAD>
<TITLE>Checkbox Event Handler</TITLE>
<SCRIPT LANGUAGE="JavaScript">
function setPort(form) {
        if (form.mouse.checked) {
            form.mousePort.checked = true
        }
}
</SCRIPT>
</HEAD>

<BODY>
<FORM>
<H3>Check all accessories for your computer:</H3>
<INPUT TYPE="checkbox" NAME="colorMonitor" >Color Monitor<P>
<INPUT TYPE="checkbox" NAME="mouse"
onClick="setPort(this.form)">Mouse<P>
```

(continued)

Listing 23-5 *(continued)*

```
<INPUT TYPE="checkbox" NAME="mousePort" >Mouse Port<P>
<INPUT TYPE="checkbox" NAME="modem" >Modem<P>
<INPUT TYPE="checkbox" NAME="keyboard" >Keyboard<P>
</FORM>
</BODY>
</HTML>
```

onMouseDown=
onMouseUp=

	Nav2	Nav3	Nav4	IE3/J1	IE3/J2	IE4/J3
Compatibility			✔			✔

More recent browsers add event handlers for the components of a click event: the onMouseDown= and onMouseUp= event handlers. These events fire in addition to the onClick= event handler. See the discussion of these events for the button object earlier in this chapter for application ideas.

Related Items: checkbox.onClick= event handler.

Radio Object

Properties	Methods	Event Handlers
checked	click()	onClick=
defaultChecked	handleEvent()	onMouseDown=
length		onMouseUp=
name		
type		
value		

Syntax

Creating a radio object:

```
<FORM>
<INPUT
        TYPE="radio"
        NAME="buttonGroupName"
```

```
        [VALUE="buttonValue"]
        [CHECKED]
        [onClick="handlerTextOrFunction"]>
        buttonText
</FORM>
```

Accessing radio object properties or methods:

```
[window.] document.formName.buttonGroupName[index].property |
        method([parameters])
```

```
[window.] document.forms[index].buttonGroupName.property |
        method([parameters])
```

About this object

A radio button object is an unusual one within the body of JavaScript applications. In every other case of form elements, one object equals one visual element on the screen. But a radio object actually consists of a group of radio buttons. Because of the nature of radio buttons — a mutually exclusive choice among two or more selections — a group always has multiple visual elements. All buttons in the group share the same name — which is how JavaScript knows to group buttons together and to let the clicking of a button deselect any other selected button within the group. Beyond that, however, each button can have unique properties, such as its `value` or `checked` property.

JavaScript uses an array syntax to enable you to access information about an individual button within the button group. Let's look at an example of defining a button group and see how to reference each button. This button group lets the user select a favorite member of the Three Stooges:

```
<FORM>
<B>Select your favorite Stooge:</B><P>
<INPUT TYPE="radio" NAME="stooges" VALUE="Moe Howard" CHECKED>Moe
<INPUT TYPE="radio" NAME="stooges" VALUE="Larry Fine" >Larry
<INPUT TYPE="radio" NAME="stooges" VALUE="Curly Howard" >Curly
<INPUT TYPE="radio" NAME="stooges" VALUE="Shemp Howard" >Shemp
</FORM>
```

When this group displays on the page, the first radio button is preselected for the user (all radio button groups should have one button already selected as a default value). Only one of the six properties contained by a radio button object (length) applies to the entire group. However, the other five properties apply to individual buttons within the group. To access any button, use an array index value as part of the button group name. For example

```
firstBtnValue = document.forms[0].stooges[0].value // "Moe Howard"

secondBtnValue = document.forms[0].stooges[1].value // "Larry Fine"
```

Any time you access the `checked`, `defaultChecked`, `type`, or `value` property, you must point to a specific button within the group according to its order in the array. The order depends on the sequence in which the individual buttons are defined in the HTML document.

Supplying a VALUE attribute to a radio button can be very important in your script. Although the text label for a button is defined outside the <INPUT> tag, the VALUE attribute lets you store any string in the button's hip pocket. In the earlier example, the radio button labels were just first names, whereas the value properties were set in the definition to the full names of the actors. The values could have been anything that the script needed, such as birth dates, shoe sizes, URLs, or the first names again (because a script would have no way to retrieve the labels otherwise). The point is that the VALUE attribute should contain whatever string the script needs to derive from the selection made by the user. The VALUE attribute contents are also what is sent to a CGI program on a server in a submit action for the form.

How you decide to orient a group of buttons on the screen is entirely up to your design and the real estate available within your document. You can string them in a horizontal row (as shown earlier), place <BR> tags after each one to form a column, or do so after every other button to form a double column. Numeric order within the array is determined only by the order in which the buttons are defined in the document, not by where they appear. To determine which radio button of a group is checked before doing processing based on that choice, you need to construct a repeat loop to cycle through the buttons in the group (shown in the next example). For each button, your script examines the checked property.

To be Navigator 2–friendly, be sure to always specify an onClick= event handler to every radio button (even if onClick=""). This action overrides a bug that causes index values to be reversed among buttons in a group.

Properties

checked

Value: Boolean   **Gettable:** Yes   **Settable:** Yes

	Nav2	Nav3	Nav4	IE3/J1	IE3/J2	IE4/J3
Compatibility	✔	✔	✔	✔	✔	✔

Only one radio button in a group can be highlighted (checked) at a time (the browser takes care of highlighting and unhighlighting buttons in a group for you). That one button's checked property is set to true, whereas all others in the group are set to false.

Beginning with Navigator 3, you can safely set the checked property of a radio button. By setting the checked property of one button in a group to true, all other buttons automatically uncheck themselves.

Example

In Listing 23-6, I use a repeat loop in a function to look through all buttons in the Stooges group in search of the checked button. When the loop finds the one whose

checked property is true, it returns the value of the index. In one instance, I use that index value to then extract the value property for display in the alert dialog box; in the other instance, I use the value to help determine which button in the group is next in line to have its checked property set to true.

Listing 23-6: **Finding the Selected Button in a Radio Group**

```
<HTML>
<HEAD>
<TITLE>Extracting Highlighted Radio Button</TITLE>
<SCRIPT LANGUAGE="JavaScript">
function getSelectedButton(buttonGroup){
        for (var i = 0; i < buttonGroup.length; i++) {
            if (buttonGroup[i].checked) {
                return i
            }
        }
        return 0
}
function fullName(form) {
        var i = getSelectedButton(form.stooges)
        alert("You chose " + form.stooges[i].value + ".")
}
function cycle(form) {
        var i = getSelectedButton(form.stooges)
        if (i+1 == form.stooges.length) {
            form.stooges[0].checked = true
        } else {
            form.stooges[i+1].checked = true
        }
}
</SCRIPT>
</HEAD>

<BODY>
<FORM>
<B>Select your favorite Stooge:</B><P>
<INPUT TYPE="radio" NAME="stooges" VALUE="Moe Howard" CHECKED>Moe
<INPUT TYPE="radio" NAME="stooges" VALUE="Larry Fine" >Larry
<INPUT TYPE="radio" NAME="stooges" VALUE="Curly Howard" >Curly
<INPUT TYPE="radio" NAME="stooges" VALUE="Shemp Howard" >Shemp<P>
<INPUT TYPE="button" NAME="Viewer" VALUE="View Full Name..."
onClick="fullName(this.form)"><P>
<INPUT TYPE="button" NAME="Cycler" VALUE="Cycle Buttons"
onClick="cycle(this.form)">
</FORM>
</BODY>
</HTML>
```

Related Items: defaultChecked property.

defaultChecked

Value: Boolean   **Gettable:** Yes   **Settable:** No

	Nav2	Nav3	Nav4	IE3/J1	IE3/J2	IE4/J3
Compatibility	✔	✔	✔	✔	✔	✔

If you add the CHECKED attribute to the <INPUT> definition for a radio button, the defaultChecked property for that object is true; otherwise, the property is false. Having access to this property enables your scripts to examine individual radio buttons to see if they have been adjusted (presumably by the user, if your script does not perform automatic clicking).

Example

In the script fragment of Listing 23-7 (not among the CD-ROM files), a function is passed a form containing the Stooges radio buttons. The goal is to see, in as general a way as possible (supplying the radio group name where needed), if the user changed the default setting. Looping through each of the radio buttons, you look for the one whose CHECKED attribute was set in the <INPUT> definition. With that index value (i) in hand, you then look to see if that entry is still checked. If not (notice the ! negation operator), you display an alert dialog box about the change.

Listing 23-7: **Has a Radio Button Changed?**

```
function groupChanged(form) {
        for (var i = 0; i < form.stooges.length; i++) {
            if (form.stooges[i].defaultChecked) {
                if (!form.stooges[i].checked) {
                    alert("This radio group has been changed.")
                }
            }
        }
}
```

Related Items: checked property; value property.

length

Value: Integer   **Gettable:** Yes   **Settable:** No

	Nav2	Nav3	Nav4	IE3/J1	IE3/J2	IE4/J3
Compatibility	✔	✔	✔	✔	✔	✔

A radio button group has length — the number of individual radio buttons defined for that group. Attempting to retrieve the length of an individual button yields a null value. The `length` property is valuable for establishing the maximum range of values in a repeat loop that must cycle through every button within that group. If you specify the `length` property to fill that value (rather than hardwiring the value), the loop construction will be easier to maintain — as you make changes to the number of buttons in the group during page construction, the loop adjusts to the changes automatically.

Example

See the loop construction within the function of Listing 23-7 for one way to apply the `length` property.

Related Items: None.

name

Value: String   **Gettable:** Yes   **Settable:** No

	Nav2	Nav3	Nav4	IE3/J1	IE3/J2	IE4/J3
Compatibility	✔	✔	✔	✔	✔	✔

The `name` property, while associated with an entire radio button group, can be read only from individual buttons in the group, such as

```
btnGroupName = document.forms[0].groupName[2].name
```

In that sense, each radio button element in a group inherits the name of the group. Your scripts have little need to extract the `name` property of a button or group. More often than not, you will hard-wire a button group's name into your script to extract other properties of individual buttons. Getting the `name` property of an object whose name you know is obviously redundant. But understanding the place of radio button group names in the scheme of JavaScript objects is important for all scripters.

Related Items: `value` property.

type

Value: "radio"   **Gettable:** Yes   **Settable:** No

	Nav2	Nav3	Nav4	IE3/J1	IE3/J2	IE4/J3
Compatibility		✔	✔			✔

Use the `type` property to help identify a radio object from an unknown group of form elements.

Related Items: `form.elements` property.

value

Value: String   **Gettable:** Yes   **Settable:** No

	Nav2	Nav3	Nav4	IE3/J1	IE3/J2	IE4/J3
Compatibility	✔	✔	✔	✔	✔	✔

As described earlier in this chapter for the checkbox object, the `value` property contains arbitrary information that you assign when mapping out the `<INPUT>` definition for an individual radio button. Using this property is a handy shortcut to correlating a radio button label with detailed or related information of interest to your script or CGI program on a server. If you like, the `value` property can contain the same text as the label.

Example

Listing 23-6 demonstrates how a function extracts the `value` property of a radio button to display otherwise hidden information stored with a button. In this case, it lets the alert dialog box show the full name of the selected Stooge.

Related Items: `name` property.

Methods

click()

Returns: Nothing.

	Nav2	Nav3	Nav4	IE3/J1	IE3/J2	IE4/J3
Compatibility	✔	✔	✔	✔	✔	✔

The intention of the `click()` method is to enact, via a script, the physical act of clicking a radio button. Unfortunately, this method does not work in Navigator 2 or 3. Even if it worked flawlessly, you better serve your scripts by setting the `checked` properties of all buttons in a group so that you know exactly what the setting of the group is at any time.

Related Items: `onClick=` event handler; `checked` property.

handleEvent(*event*)

Returns: Nothing.

	Nav2	Nav3	Nav4	IE3/J1	IE3/J2	IE4/J3
Compatibility			✔			

See the discussion of the `window.handleEvent()` method in Chapter 14 and the event object in Chapter 33 for details on this ubiquitous form element method.

Event handlers
onClick=

	Nav2	Nav3	Nav4	IE3/J1	IE3/J2	IE4/J3
Compatibility	✔	✔	✔	✔	✔	✔

Radio buttons, more than any user interface element available in HTML, are intended for use in making choices that other objects, such as submit or standard buttons, act upon later. You may see cases in Windows or Mac programs in which highlighting a radio button — at most — activates or brings into view additional, related settings. Unfortunately, you don't have such dynamic facilities on Web pages with most of today's browsers.

I strongly advise you not to use scripting handlers that perform significant actions at the click of any radio button. At best, you may want to use knowledge about a user's clicking of a radio button to adjust a global variable or `document.cookie` setting that influences subsequent processing. Be aware, however, that if you script such a hidden action for one radio button in a group, you must also script similar actions for others in the same group. That way, if a user changes the setting back to a previous condition, the global variable is reset to the way it was. JavaScript, however, tends to run fast enough so that a batch operation can make such adjustments when the user clicks a more action-oriented button.

Example

Every time a user clicks one of the radio buttons in Listing 23-8, he or she sets a global variable to true or false, depending on whether the person is a Shemp lover. This action is independent of the action taking place when the user clicks on the View Full Name button. An onUnload= event handler in the <BODY> definition triggers a function that displays a message to Shemp lovers just before the page clears (click the browser's Reload button to leave the current page prior to reloading). Here I use an initialize function triggered by onLoad= so that the current radio button selection sets the global value upon a reload.

Listing 23-8: An onClick= Event Handler for Radio Buttons

```
<HTML>
<HEAD>
<TITLE>Radio Button onClick Handler</TITLE>
<SCRIPT LANGUAGE="JavaScript">
var ShempOPhile = false
function initValue() {
        ShempOPhile = document.forms[0].stooges[3].checked
}
 function fullName(form) {
        for (var i = 0; i < form.stooges.length; i++) {
            if (form.stooges[i].checked) {
                break
            }
        }
        alert("You chose " + form.stooges[i].value + ".")
}
function setShemp(setting) {
        ShempOPhile = setting
}
function exitMsg() {
        if (ShempOPhile) {
            alert("You like SHEMP?")
        }
}
</SCRIPT>
</HEAD>

<BODY onLoad="initValue()" onUnload="exitMsg()">
<FORM>
<B>Select your favorite Stooge:</B><P>
<INPUT TYPE="radio" NAME="stooges" VALUE="Moe Howard" CHECKED
onClick="setShemp(false)">Moe
<INPUT TYPE="radio" NAME="stooges" VALUE="Larry Fine"
onClick="setShemp(false)">Larry
```

```
<INPUT TYPE="radio" NAME="stooges" VALUE="Curly Howard"
onClick="setShemp(false)">Curly
<INPUT TYPE="radio" NAME="stooges" VALUE="Shemp Howard"
onClick="setShemp(true)">Shemp<P>
<INPUT TYPE="button" NAME="Viewer" VALUE="View Full Name..."
onClick="fullName(this.form)">
</FORM>
</BODY>
</HTML>
```

✦   ✦   ✦

Select and FileUpload Objects

Selection lists — whether in the form of pop-up menus or scrolling lists — are space-saving form elements in HTML pages. They allow designers to present a lot of information in a comparatively small space. At the same time, users are familiar with the interface elements from working in their own operating systems' preference dialog boxes and application windows.

However, selection lists are more difficult to script, because the objects themselves are complicated entities. As you can see throughout this chapter, the references necessary to extract information from a list can get pretty long. The results, however, are worth the effort.

The other object covered in this chapter, the fileUpload object, is frequently misunderstood as being more powerful than it actually is. It is, alas, not the great file transfer elixir desired by many page authors.

Select Object

Properties	Methods	Event Handlers
length	blur()	onChange=
name	focus()	onFocus=
options[i]	handleEvent()	onBlur=
selectedIndex		
options[i].defaultSelected		
options[i].index		
options[i].selected		

(continued)

Properties	Methods	Event Handlers
options[i].text		
options[i].value		
type		

Syntax

Creating a select object:

```
<FORM>
<SELECT
      NAME="listName"
      [SIZE="number"]
      [MULTIPLE]
      [onBlur="handlerTextOrFunction"]
      [onChange="handlerTextOrFunction"]
      [onFocus="handlerTextOrFunction"]>
      <OPTION [SELECTED] [VALUE="string"]>listItem
      [...<OPTION [VALUE="string"]>listItem]
</SELECT>
</FORM>
```

Accessing select object properties:

```
[window.] document.formName.listName.property
[window.] document.forms[index].listName.property
[window.] document.formName.listName.options[index].property
[window.] document.forms[index].listName.options[index].property
```

About this object

Select objects are perhaps the most visually interesting user interface elements among the standard built-in objects. In one form, they appear on the page as pop-up lists; in another form, they appear as scrolling list boxes. Pop-up lists, in particular, offer efficient use of page real estate for presenting a list of choices for the user. Moreover, only the choice selected by the user shows on the page, minimizing the clutter of unneeded verbiage.

Compared to other JavaScript objects, select objects are difficult to script — mostly because of the complexity of data that goes into a list of items. Some properties of the object apply to the entire object, whereas other properties pertain only to a single item in the list (each item is called an *option*). For example, you can extract the number (index) of the currently selected option in the list — a property of the entire selection object. To get the text of the selected option, however, you must zero in further, extracting the text property of a single option among all options defined for the object.

When you define a select object within a form, the construction of the `<SELECT>...</SELECT>` tag pair is easy to inadvertently mess up. First, most attributes that define the entire object, such as `NAME`, `SIZE`, and event handlers, are attributes of the opening `<SELECT>` tag. Between the end of the opening tag and the closing `</SELECT>` tag are additional tags for each option to be displayed in the list. The following object definition creates a selection pop-up list containing three colors:

```
<FORM>
<SELECT NAME="RGBColors" onChange="changeColor(this)">
      <OPTION SELECTED>Red
      <OPTION>Green
      <OPTION>Blue
</SELECT>
</FORM>
```

The formatting of the tags in the HTML document is not critical. I indented the lines of options merely for the sake of readability.

The `SIZE` attribute determines whether a select object appears as a pop-up list or a list box. If you omit the attribute, the browser automatically assigns the default value of 1. This value forces the browser to display the list as a pop-up menu. Assigning any other integer value to the `SIZE` attribute causes the browser to display the list as a list box. The number indicates how many options will be visible in the list without scrolling—how tall the box will be, measured in lines. Because scrollbars in GUI environments tend to require a fair amount of space to display a minimum set of clickable areas (including sliding "thumbs"), you should set list-box style sizes to no less than 4. If that makes the list box too tall for your page design, consider using a pop-up menu instead. Figure 24-1 shows two versions of a select object: one with a size of 1, the other with a size of 4.

Significant differences exist in the way each GUI platform presents pop-up menus. Because each browser relies on the operating system to display its native pop-up menu style, considerable differences exist among the OS platforms in the size of a given pop-up menu. What fits nicely within a standard window width of one OS may not fit in the window of another OS. In other words, you cannot rely on any select object having a precise dimension on a page (in case you're trying to align a select object with an image). With object positioning in Navigator 4 and Internet Explorer 4, you can align one edge of multiple items, but you cannot control, for example, the precise width of a select list or the size of the text in the list.

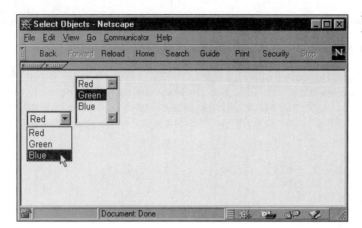

Figure 24-1: Two versions of the select object

In list box form, a select object can be set to accept multiple, noncontiguous selections. Users typically accomplish such selections by holding down a modifier key (Shift, Ctrl, or ⌘ keys, depending on operating system) while clicking additional options. To switch on this capability for a select object, include the MULTIPLE attribute constant in the definition.

For each entry in a list, your <SELECT> definition must include an <OPTION> tag plus the text as you want it to appear in the list. If you want a pop-up list to show a default selection when the page loads, you must attach a SELECTED attribute to that item's <OPTION> tag. Without this attribute, the pop-up list appears empty at first — not a friendly way to greet your page's viewers. You can also assign a string value to each option. As with radio buttons, this value can be text other than the wording displayed in the list; so your script can act on that "hidden" value rather than on the displayed text, such as letting a plain-language select listing actually refer to a complex URL. This string value is also the value sent to a CGI program (as part of the name=value pair) when the user submits the select object's form.

One behavioral aspect of the select object may influence your page design. The onChange= event handler triggers immediately when a user makes a new selection in a pop-up list (except in cases affected by a Navigator 2 bug on Windows versions). If you prefer to delay any action until other settings are made, omit an onChange= event handler in the select object, but be sure to create a button that lets users initiate whatever action requires those settings.

Modifying select options

Script control gives you considerable flexibility for modifying the contents and selection of a select object. These powers are available only in Navigator 3 or later and Internet Explorer 4 or later. Some of this flexibility is rather straightforward, such as changing the selectObj.options[i].text property to alter the display of a single option entry. The situation gets tricky, though, when the number of options in the select object changes. The choices you have include

✦ Removing an individual option (and thus collapsing the list)

✦ Reducing an existing list to a fewer number of options

✦ Removing all options

✦ Adding new options to a select object

To remove an option from the list, set the specific option to null. For example, if a list contains five items, and you want to eliminate the third item altogether (reducing the list to four items), the syntax (from the select object reference) for doing that task is

```
selectObj.options[2] = null
```

After this statement, `selectObj.options.length` equals 4.

In another scenario, suppose that a select object has five options in it, and you want to replace it with one having only three options. You first must hard-code the `length` property to 3:

```
selectObj.options.length = 3
```

Then set individual text properties for index values 0 through 2.

Perhaps you'd rather start building a new list of contents by completely deleting the original list (without harming the select object). To accomplish this, set the length to 0:

```
selectObj.options.length = 0
```

From here, you have to create new options (as you would if you wanted to expand a list from, say, three to seven options). The mechanism for creating a new option involves an object constructor: `new Option()`. This constructor accepts up to four parameters, which let you specify the equivalent of an `<OPTION>` tag's attributes:

✦ Text to be displayed in the option

✦ Contents of the option's `value` property

✦ Whether the item is the `defaultSelected` option (Boolean)

✦ Whether the item is selected (Boolean)

You can set any (or none) of these items as part of the constructor and come back in other statements to set their properties. I suggest setting the first two parameters (leave the others blank); then set the `selected` property separately. The following is an example of a statement that creates a new, fifth entry in a select object, setting both its displayed text and value property:

```
selectObj.options[4] = new Option("Yahoo","http://www.yahoo.com")
```

To demonstrate all of these techniques, Listing 24-1 lets you change the text of a select object: first by adjusting the text properties in the same number of options and then by creating an entirely new set of options. Functions for making these changes are triggered by radio button `onClick=` event handlers — rare examples of when radio buttons can logically initiate visible action.

Listing 24-1: **Modifying Select Options**

```
<HTML>
<HEAD>
<TITLE>Changing Options On The Fly</TITLE>
<SCRIPT LANGUAGE="JavaScript1.1">
// initialize color list arrays
plainList = new Array(6)
hardList = new Array(6)
plainList[0] = "cyan"
hardList[0] = "#00FFFF"
plainList[1] = "magenta"
hardList[1] = "#FF00FF"
plainList[2] = "yellow"
hardList[2] = "#FFFF00"
plainList[3] = "lightgoldenrodyellow"
hardList[3] = "#FAFAD2"
plainList[4] = "salmon"
hardList[4] = "#FA8072"
plainList[5] = "dodgerblue"
hardList[5] = "#1E90FF"

// change color language set
function setLang(which) {
        var listObj = document.forms[0].colors
        // find out if it's 3 or 6 entries
        var listLength = listObj.length
        // replace individual existing entries
        for (var i = 0; i < listLength; i++) {
            if (which == "plain") {
                listObj.options[i].text = plainList[i]
            } else {
                listObj.options[i].text = hardList[i]
            }
        }
        if (navigator.appName == "Netscape") {
            history.go(0)
        }
}

// create entirely new options list
function setCount(choice) {
        var listObj = document.forms[0].colors
        // get language setting
        var lang = (document.forms[0].geekLevel[0].checked) ? "plain" :
"hard"
        // empty options from list
        listObj.length = 0
        // create new option object for each entry
        for (var i = 0; i < choice.value; i++) {
            if (lang == "plain") {
                listObj.options[i] = new Option(plainList[i])
```

```
                } else {
                    listObj.options[i] = new Option(hardList[i])
                }
            }
        }
        listObj.options[0].selected = true
        if (navigator.appName == "Netscape") {
            history.go(0)
        }
    }
}
</SCRIPT>
</HEAD>

<BODY>
<H1>Flying Select Options</H1>
<FORM>
Choose geek level:
<INPUT TYPE="radio" NAME="geekLevel" onClick="setLang('plain')"
CHECKED>Plain-language
<INPUT TYPE="radio" NAME="geekLevel" onClick="setLang('hard')">Gimme
hex-triplets!
<P>
Choose a palette size:
<INPUT TYPE="radio" NAME="paletteSize" VALUE=3 onClick="setCount(this)"
CHECKED>Three
<INPUT TYPE="radio" NAME="paletteSize" VALUE=6
onClick="setCount(this)">Six
<P>
Select a color:
<SELECT NAME="colors">
        <OPTION SELECTED>cyan
        <OPTION>magenta
        <OPTION>yellow
</SELECT>
</FORM>
</BODY>
</HTML>
```

In an effort to make this code easily maintainable, the color choice lists (one in plain language, the other in hexadecimal triplet color specifications) are established as two separate arrays. Repeat loops in both grand functions can work with these arrays no matter how big they get.

The first two radio buttons (see Figure 24-2) trigger the `setLang()` function. Its first task is to extract a reference to the select object so additional references will be shorter (just `listObj`). Then you find out how many items are currently displayed in the list, because you just want to replace as many items as are already there. In the repeat loop, you set the `text` property of the existing select options to corresponding entries in either of the two array listings.

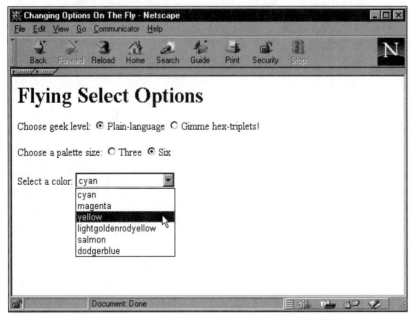

Figure 24-2: Radio button choices alter the contents of the select object on the fly.

In the second pair of radio buttons, each button stores a value indicating how many items should be displayed when the user clicks the button. This number is picked up by the setCount() function and is used in the repeat loop as a maximum counting point. In the meantime, the function finds the selected language radio button and zeros out the select object entirely. Options are rebuilt from scratch using the new Option() constructor for each option. The parameters are the corresponding display text entries from the arrays. Because none of these new options has other properties set (such as which one should be selected by default), the function sets that property of the first item in the list.

Notice that both functions call history.go(0) for Netscape browsers after they have set up their select objects. The purpose of this call is to give Navigator an opportunity to resize the select object to accommodate the contents of the list. The difference in size here is especially noticeable when you switch from the six-color, plain-language list to any other list. Without resizing, some long items would not be fully readable. Internet Explorer 4, on the other hand, automatically redraws the page to the newly sized form element.

The more drastic the differences between select option displays in your page, the more code is required. But at least you have the flexibility to make yet another object come alive with JavaScript.

Properties

length

Value: Integer   **Gettable:** Yes   **Settable:** Yes (Nav 3+/ IE4+)

document.*formObject.selectObject*.length

	Nav2	Nav3	Nav4	IE3/J1	IE3/J2	IE4/J3
Compatibility	✔	✔	✔	✔	✔	✔

Like all arrays of JavaScript's built-in functions, the options array has a `length` property of its own. But rather than having to reference the options array to determine its length, the select object has its own `length` property, which you use to find out how many items are in the list. This value is the number of options in the object (starting with 1). A select object with three choices in it has a `length` property of 3.

In newer browsers you can adjust this value downward after the document has loaded. This is one way to decrease the number of options in a list. Setting the value to 0 causes the select object to empty but not to disappear.

Example

See Listing 24-1 for an illustration of the way you use the `length` property to help determine how often to cycle through the repeat loop in search of selected items. Because the loop counter, `i`, must start at 0, the counting continues until the loop counter is one *less* than the actual length value (which starts its count with 1).

Related Items: `options` property.

name

Value: String   **Gettable:** Yes   **Settable:** No

	Nav2	Nav3	Nav4	IE3/J1	IE3/J2	IE4/J3
Compatibility	✔	✔	✔	✔	✔	✔

A select object's `name` property is the string you assign to the object by way of its `NAME` attribute in the object's `<SELECT>` definition. This reflects the entire select object rather than any individual options that belong to it. You may want to access this property via the `elements[]` style of reference to a form's components.

Example

    objName = document.forms[0].elements[3].name

Related Items: `forms[].elements[]` property.

options[*index*]

Value: Array of options   **Gettable:** Yes   **Settable:** No

	Nav2	Nav3	Nav4	IE3/J1	IE3/J2	IE4/J3
Compatibility	✔	✔	✔	✔	✔	✔

You typically won't summon this property by itself. Rather, it becomes part of a reference to a specific option's properties within the entire select object. In other words, the options property becomes a kind of gateway to more specific properties, such as the value assigned to a single option within the list.

As is true with many JavaScript properties, you can use the options property by itself for debugging purposes. The value it returns in Navigator is the object definition (complete with tags). If you have more than one select object in your page, you can use this property temporarily to review the definitions as JavaScript sees them. I don't recommend using this data for your working scripts, however, because easier ways are available for extracting necessary data.

Example

To enable you to inspect how JavaScript sees the selection object defined in the body, the alert dialog box reveals the definition data. Figure 24-3 shows the alert dialog box's contents in Navigator when the first option of Listing 24-2 is selected. This information should be used for debugging purposes only. Internet Explorer 4 shows only a generic reference to an object in its dialog box.

Listing 24-2: **Options Property Readout**

```
<HTML>
<HEAD>
<TITLE>Select Inspector</TITLE>
<SCRIPT LANGUAGE="JavaScript">
function inspect(form) {
        alert(form.colorsList.options)
}
</SCRIPT>
</HEAD>

<BODY>
<FORM>
<SELECT NAME="colorsList">
        <OPTION SELECTED>Red
        <OPTION VALUE="Plants"><I>Green</I>
        <OPTION>Blue
</SELECT> <P>
<INPUT TYPE="button" VALUE="Show Stuff" onClick="inspect(this.form)">
</FORM>
</BODY>
</HTML>
```

Related Items: All options[index].property items.

options[*index*].defaultSelected

Value: Boolean   **Gettable:** Yes   **Settable:** No

	Nav2	Nav3	Nav4	IE3/J1	IE3/J2	IE4/J3
Compatibility	✔	✔	✔	✔	✔	✔

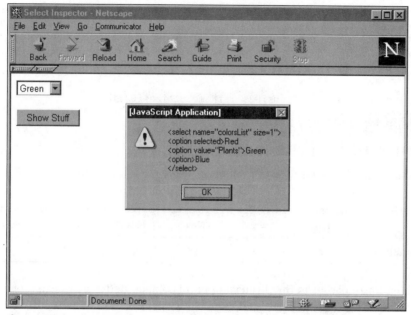

Figure 24-3: A typical readout of the options property in Navigator

If your select object definition includes one option whose SELECTED attribute is included, that option's defaultSelected property is set to true. The defaultSelected property for all other options is false. If you define a select object that allows multiple selections (and whose SIZE attribute is greater than 1), however, you can define the SELECTED attribute for more than one option definition. When the page loads, all items with that attribute will be preselected for the user, even in discontiguous groups.

Example

```
isDefault = document.forms[0].listName.options[0].defaultSelected
```

Related Items: options[index].selected property.

options[*index*].index

Value: Integer   **Gettable:** Yes   **Settable:** No

	Nav2	Nav3	Nav4	IE3/J1	IE3/J2	IE4/J3
Compatibility	✔	✔	✔	✔	✔	✔

The index value of any single option in a select object will likely be a redundant value in your scripting. Because you cannot access the option without knowing the index anyway (in brackets as part of the options[index] array reference), you have little need to extract the index value. The value is a property of the item, just the same.

Example

```
itemIndex = document.forms[0].listName.options[0].index
```

Related Items: options[] property.

options[*index*].selected

Value: Boolean   **Gettable:** Yes   **Settable:** Yes

	Nav2	Nav3	Nav4	IE3/J1	IE3/J2	IE4/J3
Compatibility	✔	✔	✔	✔	✔	✔

As mentioned earlier in the discussion of this object, better ways exist for determining which option a user has selected from a list than looping through all options and examining the selected property. An exception to that "rule" occurs when a list box is set up to enable multiple selections. In this situation, the selectedIndex property returns an integer of only the topmost item selected. Therefore, your script needs to look at the true or false values of the selected property for each option in the list and determine what to do with the text or value data.

Example

To accumulate a list of all items selected by the user, the seeList() function in Listing 24-3 systematically examines the options[index].selected property of each item in the list. The text of each item whose property is true is appended to a list. I added the "\n   " inline carriage returns and spaces to make the list in the alert dialog box look nice and indented. Had other values been assigned to the VALUE attributes of each option, the script could have extracted the options[index].value property to collect those values instead.

Listing 24-3: **Cycling through a Multiple-Selection List**

```
<HTML>
<HEAD>
<TITLE>Accessories List</TITLE>
<SCRIPT LANGUAGE="JavaScript">
function seeList(form) {
      var result = ""
      for (var i = 0; i < form.accList.length; i++) {
         if (form.accList.options[i].selected) {
            result += "\n  " + form.accList.options[i].text
         }
}
      alert("You have selected:" + result)
}
</SCRIPT>
</HEAD>

<BODY>
<FORM>
Control/Command-click on all accessories you use:
<SELECT NAME="accList" SIZE=9 MULTIPLE>
      <OPTION SELECTED>Color Monitor
      <OPTION>Modem
      <OPTION>Scanner
      <OPTION>Laser Printer
      <OPTION>Tape Backup
      <OPTION>MO Drive
      <OPTION>Video Camera
</SELECT> <P>
<INPUT TYPE="button" VALUE="View Summary..."
onClick="seeList(this.form)">
</FORM>
</BODY>
</HTML>
```

Related Items: `options[index].text` property; `options[index].value` property; `selectedIndex` property.

`options[index].text`

Value: String   **Gettable:** Yes   **Settable:** Yes

	Nav2	Nav3	Nav4	IE3/J1	IE3/J2	IE4/J3
Compatibility	✔	✔	✔	✔	✔	✔

The text property of an option is the text of the item as it appears in the list. If you can pass that wording along with your script to perform appropriate tasks, this property is the one you want to extract for further processing. But if your processing requires other strings associated with each option, assign a VALUE attribute in the definition and extract the options[index].value property (see Listing 24-5).

Example

To demonstrate the text property of an option, Listing 24-4 applies the text from a selected option to the background color property of a document in a separate window. The color names are part of the collection built into the Navigator browser.

Listing 24-4: **Extracting the options[index].text Property**

```
<HTML>
<HEAD>
<TITLE>Color Changer 1</TITLE>
<SCRIPT LANGUAGE="JavaScript">
var newWindow = null
function seeColor(form) {
        newColor =
(form.colorsList.options[form.colorsList.selectedIndex].text)
        if (newWindow == null) {
            var newWindow =
window.open("","colors","HEIGHT=200,WIDTH=150")
        }
        newWindow.document.write("<HTML><BODY BGCOLOR=" + newColor +
">")
        newWindow.document.write("<H1>Color Sampler</H1></BODY></HTML>")
        newWindow.document.close()
}
</SCRIPT>
</HEAD>

<BODY>
<FORM>
Choose a background color:
<SELECT NAME="colorsList">
        <OPTION SELECTED>Gray
        <OPTION>Lime
        <OPTION>Ivory
        <OPTION>Red
</SELECT> <P>
<INPUT TYPE="button" VALUE="Change It" onClick="seeColor(this.form)">
</FORM>
```

```
</BODY>
</HTML>
```

Related Items: `options[index].value`.

options[*index*].value

Value: String   **Gettable:** Yes   **Settable:** Yes

	Nav2	Nav3	Nav4	IE3/J1	IE3/J2	IE4/J3
Compatibility	✔	✔	✔	✔	✔	✔

In many instances, the words in the options list appear in a form that is convenient for the document's users but inconvenient for the scripts behind the page. Rather than set up an elaborate lookup routine to match the `selectedIndex` or `options[index].text` values with the values your script needs, an easier technique is to store those values in the `VALUE` attribute of each `<OPTION>` definition of the select object. You can then extract those values as needed and be merrily on your way.

You can store any string expression in the `VALUE` attributes. That includes URLs, object properties, or even entire page descriptions that you want to send to a `parent.frames[index].document.write()` method, if you prefer.

Example

This variation in Listing 24-5 requires the option text that the user sees to be in familiar, multiple-word form. But to set the color using Navigator's built-in color palette, you must use the one-word form. Those one-word values are stored in the `VALUE` attributes of each `<OPTION>` definition. The function then extracts the value property, assigning it to the `bgColor` of the document in the smaller window. Had you preferred to use the hexadecimal triplet form of color specifications, those values would have been assigned to the `VALUE` attributes (`<OPTION VALUE="#e9967a">Dark Salmon`).

Listing 24-5: **Using the options[index].value Property**

```
<HTML>
<HEAD>
<TITLE>Color Changer 2</TITLE>
<SCRIPT LANGUAGE="JavaScript">
var newWindow = null
function seeColor(form) {
     newColor =
(form.colorsList.options[form.colorsList.selectedIndex].value)
     if (newWindow == null) {
          var newWindow =
```

(continued)

Listing 24-5 *(continued)*

```
window.open("","colors","HEIGHT=200,WIDTH=150")
        }
        newWindow.document.write("<HTML><BODY BGCOLOR=" + newColor +
">")
        newWindow.document.write("<H1>Color Sampler</H1></BODY></HTML>")
        newWindow.document.close()
}
</SCRIPT>
</HEAD>

<BODY>
<FORM>
Choose a background color:
<SELECT NAME="colorsList">
        <OPTION SELECTED VALUE="cornflowerblue">Cornflower Blue
        <OPTION VALUE="darksalmon">Dark Salmon
        <OPTION VALUE="lightgoldenrodyellow">Light Goldenrod Yellow
        <OPTION VALUE="seagreen">Sea Green
</SELECT> <P>
<INPUT TYPE="button" VALUE="Change It" onClick="seeColor(this.form)">
</FORM>
</BODY>
</HTML>
```

Related Items: `options[index].text`.

selectedIndex

Value: Integer   **Gettable:** Yes   **Settable:** Yes

	Nav2	Nav3	Nav4	IE3/J1	IE3/J2	IE4/J3
Compatibility	✔	✔	✔	✔	✔	✔

When a user clicks on a choice in a selection list, the `selectedIndex` property changes to a number corresponding to that item in the list. The first item has a value of 0. This information is valuable to a script that needs to extract either the value or text of a selected item for further processing.

You can use this information as a shortcut to getting at a selected option's properties. To examine its `selected` property, rather than cycling through every option in a repeat loop, use the `selectedIndex` property to fill in the index value for the reference to the selected item. The wording gets kind of long, but from an execution standpoint, this methodology is much more efficient. Note, however, that when the select object is a multiple-style, the `selectedIndex` property value reflects the index of the topmost item selected in the list.

Example

In the `inspect()` function of Listing 24-6, notice that the value inside the `options[]` property index brackets is a reference to the object's `selectedIndex` property. Because this property always returns an integer value, it fulfills the needs of the index value for the `options[]` property. Therefore, if Green is selected in the pop-up menu, `form.colorsList.selectedIndex` returns a value of 2; that reduces the rest of the reference to `form.colorsList.options[2].text`, which equals "Green."

Listing 24-6: Using the selectedIndex Property

```
<HTML>
<HEAD>
<TITLE>Select Inspector</TITLE>
<SCRIPT LANGUAGE="JavaScript">
function inspect(form) {

alert(form.colorsList.options[form.colorsList.selectedIndex].text)
}
</SCRIPT>
</HEAD>

<BODY>
<FORM>
<SELECT NAME="colorsList">
        <OPTION SELECTED>Red
        <OPTION VALUE="Plants"><I>Green</I>
        <OPTION>Blue
</SELECT> <P>
<INPUT TYPE="button" VALUE="Show Selection"
onClick="inspect(this.form)">
</FORM>
</BODY>
</HTML>
```

Related Items: `options[]` property.

type

Value: String   **Gettable:** Yes   **Settable:** No

	Nav2	Nav3	Nav4	IE3/J1	IE3/J2	IE4/J3
Compatibility		✔	✔			✔

Use the `type` property to help you identify a select object from an unknown group of form elements. The precise string returned for this property depends on whether the select object is defined as a single- ("`select-one`") or multiple- ("`select-multiple`") style object.

Related Items: `form.elements` property.

Methods

blur()

focus()

	Nav2	Nav3	Nav4	IE3/J1	IE3/J2	IE4/J3
Compatibility		✔	✔			✔

Your scripts can bring focus to a select object by invoking the object's `focus()` method. The method activates the object, but does not, in the case of a pop-up list, pop up the list for the user. To remove focus from an object, invoke its `blur()` method. These methods work identically with their counterparts in the text object.

handleEvent(*event*)

Returns: Nothing.

	Nav2	Nav3	Nav4	IE3/J1	IE3/J2	IE4/J3
Compatibility			✔			

See the discussion of the `window.handleEvent()` method in Chapter 14 and the event object in Chapter 33 for details on this ubiquitous form element method.

Event handlers

onChange=

	Nav2	Nav3	Nav4	IE3/J1	IE3/J2	IE4/J3
Compatibility	✔	✔	✔	✔	✔	✔

As a user clicks on a new choice in a select object, the object receives a change event that can be captured by the `onChange=` event handler. In examples earlier in this section (Listings 24-5 and 24-6, for example), the action was handed over to a separate button. This design may make sense in some circumstances, especially when you use multiple select lists or any list box (typically, clicking a list box item does not trigger any action that the user sees). But for most pop-up menus, triggering the action when the user makes a choice is desirable.

To bring a pop-up menu to life, add an onChange= event handler to the <SELECT> definition. If the user makes the same choice as previously selected, the onChange= event handler is not triggered.

Example

In Listing 24-7, I converted the document from Listing 24-5 so that all action takes place as the result of a user making a selection from the pop-up menu. I removed the action button and placed the onChange= event handler in the <SELECT> object definition. For this application—when you desire a direct response to user input—an appropriate method is to have the action triggered from the pop-up menu rather than by a separate action button. A focus() method brings the smaller window forward in case it's hidden behind the main window.

Listing 24-7: **Triggering a Color Change from a Pop-Up Menu**

```
<HTML>
<HEAD>
<TITLE>Color Changer 2</TITLE>
<SCRIPT LANGUAGE="JavaScript">
var newWindow = null
function seeColor(form) {
        newColor =
(form.colorsList.options[form.colorsList.selectedIndex].value)
        if (newWindow == null) {
            newWindow = window.open("","colors","HEIGHT=200,WIDTH=150")
        }
        newWindow.document.write("<HTML><BODY BGCOLOR=" + newColor +
">")
        newWindow.document.write("<H1>Color Sampler</H1></BODY></HTML>")
        newWindow.document.close()
        if (parseInt(navigator.appVersion.charAt(0)) > 2) {
            newWindow.focus()
        }
}
</SCRIPT>
</HEAD>

<BODY>
<FORM>
Choose a background color:
<SELECT NAME="colorsList" onChange="seeColor(this.form)">
        <OPTION SELECTED VALUE="cornflowerblue">Cornflower Blue
        <OPTION VALUE="darksalmon">Dark Salmon
        <OPTION VALUE="lightgoldenrodyellow">Light Goldenrod Yellow
        <OPTION VALUE="seagreen">Sea Green
</SELECT>
</FORM>
</BODY>
</HTML>
```

Note

A bug in the Windows versions of Navigator 2 causes the `onChange=` event handler in select objects to fail unless the user clicks outside the select object. If your audience includes users of these browsers, then consider including a special routine that uses `document.write()` to include a "do nothing" button next to the select object that entices the user to click out of the select object. The `onChange=` event handler will fire at a click of that button (or any other location on the page).

fileUpload Object

Properties	Methods	Event Handlers
name	blur()	onBlur=
value	focus()	onFocus=
type	select()	onChange=

Syntax

Creating a fileUpload object:

```
<FORM>
<INPUT
        TYPE="file"
        [NAME="fieldName"]
        [SIZE="charCount"]>
</FORM>
```

Accessing fileUpload object properties:

```
[window.] document.formName.fileUploadName[index].property
[window.] document.forms[index].fileUploadName.property
```

About this object

Some Web sites enable you to upload files from the client to the server, typically by using a form-style submission to a CGI program on the server. The fileUpload object (type "file") is merely a user interface that enables users to specify which file on their PC they want to upload.

This object displays a field and a Browse button. The Browse button leads to an open file dialog box (in the local operating system's interface vernacular) where a user can select a file. After making a selection, the filename (or pathname, depending on the operating system) appears in the fileUpload object's field. The filename is the `value` property.

You do not have to script much for this object on the client side. The `value` property, for example, is read-only, although it provides a full pathname in MIME-encoded text. The point is that scripts or CGIs cannot fill this object with a filename or pathname to surreptitiously extract content from a client disk volume.

Note

The fileUpload object is available in Navigator from Version 3 onward. Internet Explorer 4 uses different terminology to talk about this kind of object. But such objects are referenced the same way in both platforms.

Listing 24-8 helps you see what the object looks like. The syntax is compatible in Navigator 3 or later and Internet Explorer 4 or later.

Listing 24-8: **fileUpload Object**

```
<HTML>
<HEAD>
<TITLE>FileUpload Object</TITLE>
</HEAD>
<BODY>
<FORM>
File to be uploaded:
<INPUT TYPE="file" SIZE=40 NAME="fileToGo"><P>
<INPUT TYPE="button" VALUE="View Value"
onClick="alert(this.form.fileToGo.value)">
</FORM>
</BODY>
</HTML>
```

In a true production environment, a Submit button and a CGI would be specified for the ACTION attribute of the <FORM> definition. I list the object in this book, primarily because it is reflected as part of the JavaScript object model, even if scripting it is not a big part of everyday life. Moreover, you may run into difficulty in extracting the value property in Navigator 3 on some platforms without bringing focus to the object after a file has been chosen.

✦   ✦   ✦

Navigator and Other Environment Objects

◆ ◆ ◆ ◆

In This Chapter

Determining which
browser the user has

Branching scripts
according to the
user's operating
system

Verifying that
a specific plug-in
is installed

◆ ◆ ◆ ◆

JavaScript devotes one category of its objects to browser software (also called the client by some users). These objects are not part of any windows or documents that you see, but rather apply to the inner workings of the browser software.

In addition to providing some of the same information that CGI programs on the server extract as environment variables, these browser-level objects also include information about how well-equipped the browser is with regard to plug-ins and Java. And one object newly defined for Navigator 4 reveals information about the user's video monitor, which may influence the way your scripts define information displayed on the page.

The objects in this chapter don't show up on the JavaScript object hierarchy diagrams except as a free-standing group derived from the navigator and screen objects (see Appendix A). Internet Explorer 4's object model, however, places its corresponding objects under the window object. Because the `window` reference is optional, you can omit it for Internet Explorer 4 and wind up with a cross-compatible script. With the added built-in capabilities that each generation of browser introduces, these small independent objects are sure to grow even more in importance.

Navigator Object

Properties	Methods	Event Handlers
appName	javaEnabled()	(None)
appCodeName	preference()	
appVersion	taintEnabled()	
language		
mimeTypes[]		
platform		
plugins[]		
userAgent		

Syntax

Accessing navigator object properties and methods:

`navigator.property | method()`

About this object

In Chapter 14, I repeatedly mentioned that the window object is the top banana of the JavaScript object hierarchy. In other programming environments, you will likely find an application level higher than the window. You may think that an object known as the navigator object would be that all-encompassing object. That is not the case, however.

Although Netscape originally defined the navigator object for the Navigator 2 browser, Microsoft Internet Explorer also supports the object in its object model. Despite the object name seeming to be tied to a specific commercial browser, other software vendors appear to find the object vocabulary an acceptable standard among their JavaScript implementations.

The properties of the navigator object deal with the browser program the user runs to view documents. Properties include those for extracting the version of the browser and the platform of the client running the browser. Because so many properties of the navigator object are similar, I treat four of them together.

Properties

```
appName
appCodeName
appVersion
userAgent
```

Value: String   **Gettable:** Yes   **Settable:** No

	Nav2	Nav3	Nav4	IE3/J1	IE3/J2	IE4/J3
Compatibility	✔	✔	✔	✔	✔	✔

The best way to see what these properties hold is to view them from two different versions of Navigator 4: The Windows 95 version and the Macintosh version (Figure 25-1).

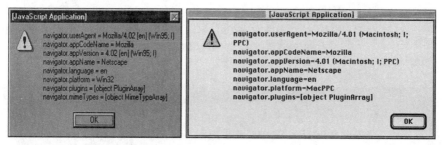

Figure 25-1: Property dumps for the navigator object under Windows 95 (left) and Macintosh (right) versions of Navigator 4

The appName and appCodeName properties are simply the official name and the internal code name for the browser application. For Netscape browsers, the appName value is Netscape; for Internet Explorer, the value is Microsoft Internet Explorer. Both browsers bear the Netscape code name, Mozilla, as the appCodeName property.

The appVersion and userAgent properties provide more meaningful detail. They contain not only the browser's version number, but also data about the platform of the browser and the country for which the browser is released (in Navigator, "I" stands for "international," which has a less rigid encryption feature built into it than the "U" version for the United States). It seems that with each generation of browser, more information is revealed in the userAgent property. For example in Navigator 4, a code for the localized language of the browser is also part of the property. The userAgent property is a string similar to the USER_AGENT header that the browser sends to the server at certain points during the connection process between client and server.

Because the `userAgent` property reveals more information about a visitor's browser than other properties, viewing a selection of such values from many generations and types of browsers will help you learn how it works. Table 25-1 shows some of the values that your scripts are likely to see. This table does not include, of course, the many values that would not be reflected by browsers that do not support JavaScript.

Table 25-1
Typical navigator.userAgent Values

navigator.userAgent	Description
Mozilla/4.02 [en] (Win95; I; Nav)	Navigator-only version of Communicator 4.02, English edition for Windows 95, and export encryption
Mozilla/4.01 [fr] (Win95; I)	Navigator 4.01, French edition for Windows 95, export encryption
Mozilla/4.01 [en] (WinNT; U)	Navigator 4.01, English edition for Windows NT with U.S. encryption
Mozilla/4.01 (Macintosh; I; 68K)	Navigator 4.01 for 68xxx processor on Macintosh
Mozilla/4.0 (compatible; MSIE 4.0b2; Windows NT)	Internet Explorer 4.0b2 (Preview 2) on via proxy gatewayCERN-HTTPD/3.0 libwww/2.17 Windows NT; accessed via a gateway
Mozilla/3.01Gold (Win95; I)	Navigator 3.01 Gold for Windows 95
Mozilla/3.01 (Macintosh; I; PPC)	Navigator 3.01 for PowerPC Macintosh
Mozilla/3.01 (X11; I; HP-UX A.09.05 9000/720)	Navigator 3.01 for HP-UX on RS-9000
Mozilla/3.01 (X11; I; IRIX 6.2 IP22)	Navigator 3.01 for IRIX
Mozilla/3.01 (X11; I; SunOS 5.4 sun4m)	Navigator 3.01 for SunOS 5.4
Mozilla/3.01-C-MACOS8 (Macintosh; I; PPC)	Navigator 3.01 running on a MacOS8-equipped PowerPC Macintosh

navigator.userAgent	Description
Mozilla/3.01Gold [de] (Win16; I)	Navigator 3.01, German edition for Windows 3.0x
Mozilla/3.0 (Win95; I)	Navigator 3 for Windows 95
Mozilla/3.0 WebTV/1.2 (compatible; MSIE 2.0)	IE 2 built into a WebTV box, emulating Navigator 3 (its scripting compatibility with Navigator 3 is in question)
Mozilla/3.0 (compatible; MSIE 3.01; Navigator 3	IE 3.01 on a PowerPC Macintosh, emulating (which it does better than Windows versions) Mac_PowerPC)
Mozilla/2.0 (compatible; MSIE 3.0; AOL 3.0; Windows 3.1)	IE 3 (version for America Online software Version 3) for Windows 3.1, emulating Navigator 2
Mozilla/2.0 (compatible; MSIE 3.02; Update a; Windows 95)	IE 3.02, Update a for Windows 95, emulating Navigator 2
Mozilla/2.0 (compatible; MSIE 3.01; Windows 95)	IE 3.01 for Windows 95, emulating Navigator 2
Mozilla/2.0 (compatible; MSIE 3.0B; Windows NT)	IE 3 (beta) emulating Navigator 2

Because you will mostly call upon these properties to define a special case for a particular browser version or platform, choose the property that most easily provides the information you need to extract. For example, as you can see from Table 25-1, assuming that all userAgent values starting with "Mozilla" are Netscape browsers would be wrong. The appName property is a better choice to examine for this browser distinction.

Be careful about values for navigator.appVersion, especially with regard to what we know as Internet Explorer 3. If you look through Table 25-1, you will see that Internet Explorer 3's userAgent string reveals itself to be a Navigator 2 compatible. The navigator.appVersion string for such versions of Internet Explorer starts with the userAgent string after the Mozilla/designation. Therefore, if your scripts for distinguishing browser versions look only at the first character of the navigator.appVersion value to obtain the browser generation, the script might think it is working with Internet Explorer 2, rather than 3.0x. In truth, the Windows versions of Internet Explorer 3 are closer to the scriptability of Navigator 2 than to Navigator 3, so the value returned from the property is an honest self-appraisal. Still, if your scripts rely on knowing for sure that the version is Internet Explorer 3.0x, you should use the string.indexOf() method to look for the presence of the unique string "MSIE 3" in either the navigator.appVerion or navigator.userAgent values.

Speaking of compatibility and browser versions, the question often arises whether your scripts should distinguish among incremental releases within a browser's generation (for example, 3.0, 3.01, 3.02, and so on). The latest incremental release occasionally contains bug fixes and (rarely) new features that you may rely on. If that is the case, then I suggest looking for this information when the page loads and recommend to the user that he or she download the latest browser version. Beyond that, I suggest scripting for the latest version of a given generation, and don't bother branching for incremental releases.

Even scripting for only the browser generation can get you in trouble if you fail to think ahead. It was common, for example, for scripted pages to look at the first character of the `navigator.appVersion` value to determine if the visitor had the latest browser:

```
if (navigator.appVersion.charAt(0) == "3") {
    do scripted stuff
}
```

What this tactic misses is the inevitable evolution of browser versions. When someone visits with generation 4, the scripting is ignored. It is better to test for the minimum version by turning that character into a number and comparing accordingly:

```
if (parseInt(navigator.appVersion.charAt(0)) >= 3) {
    do scripted stuff
}
```

See Chapter 13 for more information about designing pages for cross-platform deployment.

Example

Listing 25-1 provides a number of reusable functions that your scripts can use to determine a variety of information about the currently running browser. All functions return a Boolean value in line with the pseudo-question presented in the function's name. For example, the `isWindows()` function returns true if the browser is any type of Windows browser and false if it's not (in Internet Explorer 3, the values are zero for false and -1 for true, but those values are perfectly usable in `if` condition phrases). Some functions extract one or more characters from `navigator` properties to determine the browser's version number. If this kind of browser detection occurs frequently in your pages, consider moving these functions into an external .js source library for inclusion in your pages (see Chapter 13).

When you load this page, it presents fields that display the results of each function depending on the type of browser and client operating system you are using at the time.

Listing 25-1: **Functions to Examine Browsers**

```
<HTML>
<HEAD>
<TITLE>UserAgent Property Library</TITLE>
<SCRIPT LANGUAGE="JavaScript">
```

```
function isWindows() {
        return (navigator.appVersion.indexOf("Win") != -1)
}

function isWin95NT() {
        return (isWindows() && (navigator.appVersion.indexOf("Win16")
== -1 && navigator.appVersion.indexOf("Windows 3.1") == -1))
}

function isMac() {
        return (navigator.appVersion.indexOf("Mac") != -1)
}

function isMacPPC() {
        return (isMac() && (navigator.appVersion.indexOf("PPC") != -1
|| navigator.appVersion.indexOf("PowerPC") != -1))
}

function isUnix() {
        return (navigator.appVersion.indexOf("X11") != -1)
}

function isNav() {
        return (navigator.appName == "Netscape")
}

function isGeneration2() {
        return (navigator.appVersion.charAt(0) == "2")
}

function isGeneration3() {
        return (navigator.appVersion.charAt(0) == "3")
}

function isGeneration3Min() {
        return (parseInt(navigator.appVersion.charAt(0)) >= 3)
}
function isNav4_02() {
        return (isNav() && (navigator.appVersion.substring(0,4) ==
"4.02") )
}

function isMSIE3Min() {
        return (navigator.appVersion.indexOf("MSIE") != -1)
}

function checkBrowser() {
        var form = document.forms[0]
        form.brand.value = isNav()
        form.win.value = isWindows()
        form.win32.value = isWin95NT()
        form.mac.value = isMac()
```

(continued)

Listing 25-1 *(continued)*

```
          form.ppc.value = isMacPPC()
          form.unix.value = isUnix()
          form.ver3Only.value = isGeneration3()
          form.ver3Up.value = isGeneration3Min()
          form.Nav4_02.value = isNav4_02()
          form.MSIE3.value = isMSIE3Min()
}
</SCRIPT>
</HEAD>

<BODY onLoad="checkBrowser()">
<H1>About This Browser</H1>
<FORM>
<H2>Brand</H2>
Netscape Navigator:<INPUT TYPE="text" NAME="brand" SIZE=5>
<HR>
<H2>Platform</H2>
Windows:<INPUT TYPE="text" NAME="win" SIZE=5>
Windows 95/NT:<INPUT TYPE="text" NAME="win32" SIZE=5><P>
Macintosh: <INPUT TYPE="text" NAME="mac" SIZE=5>
Mac PPC:<INPUT TYPE="text" NAME="ppc" SIZE=5><P>
Unix:<INPUT TYPE="text" NAME="unix" SIZE=5><P>
<HR>
<H2>Version</H2>
3.0x Only:<INPUT TYPE="text" NAME="ver3Only" SIZE=5><P>
3 or Later: <INPUT TYPE="text" NAME="ver3Up" SIZE=5><P>
Navigator 4.02: <INPUT TYPE="text" NAME="Nav4_02" SIZE=5><P>
MSIE 3 or Later: <INPUT TYPE="text" NAME="MSIE3" SIZE=5><P>
</FORM>
</BODY>
</HTML>
```

Sometimes you may need to use more than one of these functions together. For example, if you want to create a special situation for the `window.open()` bug that afflicts UNIX and Macintosh versions of Navigator 2, then you have to put your Boolean operator logic powers to work to construct a fuller examination of the browser:

```
function isWindowBuggy() {
      return (isGeneration2() && (isMac() || isUnix()))
}
```

Related Items: None.

language

Value: Two-character String   **Gettable:** Yes   **Settable:** No

	Nav2	Nav3	Nav4	IE3/J1	IE3/J2	IE4/J3
Compatibility			✔			

Navigator 4 and later include a navigator property that reflects the identifier for a localized language version of the program (it has nothing to do with scripting or programming language). These short strings resemble but are not identical to the URL suffixes for countries. In the `navigator.userAgent` property value, the language appears inside brackets, but the raw property value is without the brackets. Table 25-2 shows a sampling of languages and their designations.

Table 25-2
Sample navigator.language Values

navigator.language	Language
en	English
de	German
es	Spanish
fr	French
ja	Japanese
da	Danish
it	Italian
ko	Korean
nl	Dutch
pt	Brazilian Portuguese
sv	Swedish

The assumption you can make is that a user of a particular language version of Navigator will also be interested in content in the same language. If your site offers multiple language paths, then you can use this property setting to automate the navigation to the proper section for the user.

Related Items: `navigator.userAgent` property.

mimeTypes[]

Value: Array of MIME types   **Gettable:** Yes   **Settable:** No

	Nav2	Nav3	Nav4	IE3/J1	IE3/J2	IE4/J3
Compatibility		✔	✔			

A MIME (*Multipurpose Internet Mail Extension*) type is a file format for information that travels across the Internet. Browsers usually have a limited capability for displaying or playing information beyond HTML text and one or two image standards (.gif and .jpg are the most common formats). To fill in the gap, browsers maintain an internal list of MIME types with corresponding instructions on what to do when information of a particular MIME type arrives at the client. For example, when a CGI program serves up an audio stream in an audio format, the browser locates that MIME type in its table (the MIME type is among the first chunk of information to reach the browser from the server) and then launches a helper application or activates a plug-in capable of playing that MIME type. Your browser is not equipped to display every MIME type, but it does know how to alert you when you don't have the helper application or plug-in needed to handle an incoming file. For instance, the browser may ask if you want to save the file for later use or switch to a Web page containing more information about the necessary plug-in.

The `mimeTypes[]` property of the navigator object is simply the array of MIME types about which your browser knows (see "MimeType Object" later in this chapter). Navigator 3 and up come with dozens of MIME types already listed in their tables (even if the browser doesn't have the capability to handle all those items automatically). If you have third-party plug-ins in Navigator's plug-ins directory/folder or helper applications registered with Navigator, that array contains these new entries as well.

If your Web pages are media-rich, you likely will want to be sure that each visitor's browser is capable of playing the media your page has to offer. With JavaScript and Navigator, you can cycle through the `mimeTypes[]` array to find a match for the MIME type of your media. Then use the properties of the mimeType object (detailed later in this chapter) to ensure the optimum plug-in is available. If your media still requires a helper application instead of a plug-in, the array only lists the MIME type; thus, you won't be able to determine whether a helper application has been assigned to this MIME type from the array list.

Example

For examples of this property and details about using the mimeType object, see the discussion of the object later in this chapter. A number of simple examples showing how to use this property to see whether the navigator object has a particular MIME type do not go far enough to determine whether a plug-in is installed and enabled to play the incoming data.

Related Items: `navigator.plugin[]` property; `mimeType` object.

platform

Value: String   **Gettable:** Yes   **Settable:** No

	Nav2	Nav3	Nav4	IE3/J1	IE3/J2	IE4/J3
Compatibility			✔			

Another part of the `navigator.userAgent` is retrievable as a separate entity starting with Navigator 4. The `navigator.platform` value reflects the operating system according to the codes established by Netscape for its `userAgent` values. Table 25-3 lists values of the most popular operating systems.

In the long list of browser detection functions in Listing 25-1, I elected not to use the `navigator.platform` property because it is limited to Navigator 4 and later, while the other properties in that listing are available to all scriptable browsers.

Table 25-3
Sample navigator.platform Values

navigator.platform	Operating System
Win95	Windows 95
WinNT	Windows NT
Win16	Windows 3.x
Mac68k	Mac (680x0 CPU)
MacPPC	Mac (PowerPC CPU)
SunOS	Solaris

Notice that the `navigator.platform` property does not go into versioning of the operating system. Only the raw name is provided.

Related Items: `navigator.userAgent` property.

plugins[]

Value: Array of plug-ins   **Gettable:** Yes   **Settable:** No

	Nav2	Nav3	Nav4	IE3/J1	IE3/J2	IE4/J3
Compatibility		✔	✔			

You rarely find users involved with Web page design for Navigator who have not heard about *plug-ins* — the technology that enables you to embed new media types and foreign file formats directly into Web documents. For instance, instead of requiring you to view a video clip in a separate window atop the main browser window, a plug-in enables you to make that viewer as much a part of the page design as a static image. The same goes for audio players, 3-D animation, chat sessions — even the display of Microsoft Office documents, such as PowerPoint and Word.

Whenever you launch Navigator, you probably watch the status of its loading process in the splash screen. One of the messages that appears is "Registering Plug-ins." During that brief moment, Navigator creates its built-in list of available plug-ins to include all the plug-in files contained in a special directory/folder (the name varies with the operating system, but is obvious). The items registered at launch time are the ones listed in the `navigator.plugins[]` array. Each plug-in is, itself, an object with several properties.

Being able to have your scripts investigate the visitor's browser for a particular installed plug-in is a valuable capability if you want to guide the user through the process of downloading and installing a plug-in, if the system does not currently have it.

Example

For examples of this property and for details about using the plugin object, see "Plugin Object" later in this chapter.

Related Items: `navigator.mimeTypes[]` property; plugin object.

Methods
javaEnabled()

Returns: Boolean.

	Nav2	Nav3	Nav4	IE3/J1	IE3/J2	IE4/J3
Compatibility		✔	✔			✔

Although Navigator and Internet Explorer 4 ship with Java support turned on, a user can easily turn it off in a preferences dialog box. Some corporate installations may also turn off Java as the default setting for their users. If your pages specify Java applets, you don't normally have to worry about this property, because the applet tag's alternate text fills the page in the places where the applet would normally go. But if you are scripting applets from JavaScript (via LiveConnect, Chapter 38), you won't want your scripts making calls to applets or Java classes if you have Java support turned off. In a similar vein, if you are creating a page with JavaScript, you can fashion two quite different layouts, depending on whether Java is available.

Navigator's `javaEnabled()` method returns a Boolean value reflecting the Preferences setting. This value does not necessarily reflect Java support in the browser, but rather whether Java is turned on inside a JavaScript 1.1–level or later browser. A script cannot change the `navigator` setting, but its value does change immediately upon toggling the Preference setting.

Related Items: `navigator.preference()` method; LiveConnect (Chapter 38).

preference(*name* [, *val*])

Returns: Preference Value.

	Nav2	Nav3	Nav4	IE3/J1	IE3/J2	IE4/J3
Compatibility			✔			

Browser preferences are normally set by the user. Until Navigator 4 and the advent of signed scripts, almost all of their settings had been completely out of view of scripts, even when it might make sense to expose them. But with signed scripts and the `navigator.preference()` method, many preferences are now viewable and settable with the user's permission. These preferences were exposed to scripting primarily for the purposes of centralized configuration administration for enterprise installations. I don't recommend altering a public Web site visitor's browser preferences, even if given permission to do so — the user may not know how much trouble you can cause.

When you want to read a particular preference setting, you pass only the preference name parameter with the method. Reading a preference requires a signed script with the target of `UniversalPreferencesRead` (see Chapter 40). To change a preference, pass both the preference name and the value (with a signed script target of `UniversalPreferencesWrite`).

Table 25-4 shows a handful of scriptable preferences in Navigator 4 (learn more about these settings at `http://developer.netscape.com/library/documentation/deploymt/jsprefs.htm`). Each item has a corresponding entry in the preferences window in Navigator 4 (shown in parentheses). Notice that the preference name uses dot syntax that mimics the hierarchical structure of the Navigator 3 preferences menu, rather than the Navigator 4 preferences organization. The cookie security level is a single preference value with a matrix of integer values indicating the level.

Table 25-4
navigator.preference Values

navigator.preference	*Value*	*Preference Dialog Listing*
`general.always_load_images`	Boolean	(Advanced) Automatically load images
`security.enable_java`	Boolean	(Advanced) Enable Java
`javascript.enabled`	Boolean	(Advanced) Enable JavaScript
`browser.enable_style_sheets`	Boolean	(Advanced) Enable style sheets
`autoupdate.enabled`	Boolean	(Advanced) Enable AutoInstall

(continued)

navigator.preference	Value	Preference Dialog Listing
network.cookie.cookieBehavior	0	(Advanced) Accept all cookies
network.cookie.cookieBehavior	1	(Advanced) Accept only cookies that get sent back to the originating server
network.cookie.cookieBehavior	2	(Advanced) Disable cookies
network.cookie.warnAboutCookies	Boolean	(Advanced) Warn me before accepting a cookie

Caution

One preference to watch out for is the one that disables JavaScript. If you disable JavaScript, the only way for JavaScript to be reenabled is by the user manually changing the setting in his or her Navigator preferences dialog box.

Example

The page in Listing 25-2 displays checkboxes for each of the preferences listed in Table 25-4. To run this script without signing the scripts, turn on codebase principals, as directed in Chapter 40.

One function reads all the preferences and sets the checkbox values accordingly. Another function sets a preference when you click its checkbox. Because of the interaction among three of the cookie settings, it is easier to have the script rerun the showPreferences() function after each setting, rather than trying to manually control the properties of the three checkboxes. Rerunning that function also helps verify that the preference was set.

Listing 25-2: **Reading and Writing Browser Preferences**

```
<HTML>
<HEAD>
<TITLE>Reading/Writing Browser Preferences</TITLE>
<SCRIPT LANGUAGE="JavaScript1.2">
function setPreference(pref, value) {

netscape.security.PrivilegeManager.enablePrivilege("UniversalPreference
sWrite")
        navigator.preference(pref, value)

netscape.security.PrivilegeManager.disablePrivilege("UniversalPreferenc
esWrite")
        showPreferences()
}

function showPreferences() {
        var form = document.forms[0]

netscape.security.PrivilegeManager.enablePrivilege("UniversalPreference
sRead")
```

```
        form.imgLoad.checked =
navigator.preference("general.always_load_images")
        form.javaEnable.checked =
navigator.preference("security.enable_java")
        form.jsEnable.checked =
navigator.preference("javascript.enabled")
        form.ssEnable.checked =
navigator.preference("browser.enable_style_sheets")
        form.autoIEnable.checked =
navigator.preference("autoupdate.enabled")
        var cookieSetting =
navigator.preference("network.cookie.cookieBehavior")
        for (var i = 0; i < 3; i++) {
            form.elements["cookie" + i].checked = (i == cookieSetting) ?
true : false
        }
        form.cookieWarn.checked =
navigator.preference("network.cookie.warnAboutCookies")

    netscape.security.PrivilegeManager.disablePrivilege("UniversalPreferenc
    esRead")
    }
</SCRIPT>
</HEAD>

<BODY onLoad="showPreferences()">
<B>Browser Preferences Settings</B>
<HR>
<FORM>
<INPUT TYPE="checkbox" NAME="imgLoad"
onClick="setPreference('general.always_load_images',this.checked)">Auto
matically Load Images<BR>
<INPUT TYPE="checkbox" NAME="javaEnable"
onClick="setPreference('security.enable_java',this.checked)">Java
Enabled<BR>
<INPUT TYPE="checkbox" NAME="jsEnable"
onClick="setPreference('javascript.enabled',this.checked)">JavaScript
Enabled<BR>
<INPUT TYPE="checkbox" NAME="ssEnable"
onClick="setPreference('browser.enable_style_sheets',this.checked)">Sty
le Sheets Enabled<BR>
<INPUT TYPE="checkbox" NAME="autoIEnable"
onClick="setPreference('autoupdate.enabled',this.checked)">AutoInstall
Enabled<BR>
<INPUT TYPE="checkbox" NAME="cookie0"
onClick="setPreference('network.cookie.cookieBehavior',0)">Accept All
Cookies<BR>
<INPUT TYPE="checkbox" NAME="cookie1"
onClick="setPreference('network.cookie.cookieBehavior',1)">Accept Only
Cookies Sent Back to Server<BR>
<INPUT TYPE="checkbox" NAME="cookie2"
onClick="setPreference('network.cookie.cookieBehavior',2)">Disable
Cookies<BR>
```

(continued)

Listing 25-2 *(continued)*

```
<INPUT TYPE="checkbox" NAME="cookieWarn"
onClick="setPreference('network.cookie.warnAboutCookies',this.checked)"
>Warn Before Accepting Cookies<BR>
</FORM>
</BODY>
</HTML>
```

Related Items: `navigator.javaEnabled()` method.

taintEnabled()

Returns: Boolean.

	Nav2	Nav3	Nav4	IE3/J1	IE3/J2	IE4/J3
Compatibility		✔	✔			✔

Navigator 3 featured a partially implemented security feature called *data tainting,* which was turned off by default. This feature has been replaced by signed scripts, but for backward compatibility, the `navigator.taintEnabled()` method is available in more modern browsers that don't employ tainting (in which case the method returns false). Do not employ this method in your scripts.

MimeType Object

Properties	Methods	Event Handlers
description	(None)	(None)
enabledPlugin		
type		
suffixes		

Syntax

Accessing `mimeType` properties:

`navigator.mimeTypes[i].property`

About this object

A browser's mimeType object is essentially an entry in the internal array of MIME types about which the browser knows. Navigator 3 and later, for example, ships with an internal list of more than five dozen MIME types. Only a handful of these types are associated with helper applications or plug-ins. But add to that plug-ins and other helpers you've added over time, and the number of MIME types can grow to more than a hundred.

The MIME type for the data is usually among the first bits of information to arrive at a browser from the server. A MIME type consists of two pieces of information: type and subtype. The traditional way of representing these pieces is as a pair separated by a slash, as in

```
text/html

image/gif

audio/wav

audio/x-midi

video/quicktime

application/x-zip-compressed
```

If a file does not contain the MIME type "header" (or a CGI program sending the file does not precede the transmission with the MIME type string), the browser receives the data as a `text/plain` MIME type. When the file is loaded from a local hard drive, the browser looks to the filename's extension (the suffix after the period) to figure out the file's type.

Regardless of the way it determines the MIME type of the incoming data, the browser then acts according to instructions it maintains internally. You can see these settings by looking at the Applications or Helpers preference settings (depending on which version of Navigator you use). In Navigator 4, a click on a file type description reveals the extension and MIME type registered for that type, as well as whether the file is processed by an application or a plug-in.

By having the mimeType object available to JavaScript, your page can query a visitor's browser to discover not only whether it has a particular MIME type listed currently, but ultimately whether the browser has a corresponding plug-in installed and enabled. In such queries, the mimeType and plugin objects work together to help scripts make these determinations.

Because of the close relationships between mimeType and plugin objects, I save the examples of using these objects and their properties for the end of the chapter. There, you can see how to build functions into your scripts that enable you to examine how well a visitor's Netscape browser is equipped for either a MIME type or data that requires a specific plug-in (Internet Explorer's JScript implementation does not provide facilities for examining this information). In the meantime, be sure that you understand the properties of both objects.

Properties

description

Value: String   **Gettable:** Yes   **Settable:** No

	Nav2	Nav3	Nav4	IE3/J1	IE3/J2	IE4/J3
Compatibility		✔	✔			

While registering themselves with the browser at launch time, plug-ins can provide the browser with an extra field of information: a plain-language description of the plug-in. For example, the Microsoft video plug-in, whose MIME types are video/msvideo and video/x-msvideo, supplies the following description field:

```
Video for Windows
```

When you select About Plug-ins from the Help menu, you can see the descriptions of the various installed plug-ins. This information is useful primarily for the kind of display you see in About Plug-ins, rather than as a way for your scripts to compare values.

When a MIME type does not have a plug-in associated with it (either no plug-in is installed or a helper application is used instead), you often see the type property repeated in the description field.

Related Items: None.

enabledPlugin

Value: Plugin object   **Gettable:** Yes   **Settable:** No

	Nav2	Nav3	Nav4	IE3/J1	IE3/J2	IE4/J3
Compatibility		✔	✔			

The descriptions of the mimeType and plugin objects seem to come full circle when you reach the mimeType.enabledPlugin property, the reason being that the property is a vital link between a known MIME type and the plug-in that the browser engages when data of that type arrives.

Knowing which plug-in is associated with a MIME type becomes very important when you have more than one plug-in capable of playing a given MIME type. For example, the Crescendo MIDI audio plug-in can take the place of the default LiveAudio plug-in if you set up your browser that way. Therefore, all MIDI data streams are played through the Crescendo plug-in. If you prefer to have your Web page's MIDI sound played only through LiveAudio, your script needs to know which plug-in is set to receive your data and perhaps alert the user accordingly. These kinds of conflicts are not common (at least at this early stage of plug-in development), because each plug-in developer with a new type of data tries to choose a MIME type that is unique. But you have no guarantee of such uniqueness even today, so a careful check of MIME type and plug-in is highly recommended if you want your page to look professional.

The enabledPlugin property evaluates to a plugin object. Therefore, you can dig a bit deeper with this information to fetch the name or filename properties of a plug-in directly from a mimeType object. Go through the following steps to see how this all works (Windows users with Navigator 4 should use Version 4.02 or later):

1. Choose Open Location or Open Page from the File menu and enter

   ```
   javascript:
   ```

2. In the "javascript typein" field, enter

   ```
   navigator.mimeTypes[0].type
   ```

   You then see the MIME type and subtype for the first entry in your browser's `mimeTypes[]` array (the exact item varies depending on the items registered in your browser).

3. Edit the typein field to read

   ```
   navigator.mimeTypes[0].enabledPlugin
   ```

   This statement returns a plugin object for the first entry in the `mimeTypes[]` array.

4. Add the name property to the end, so that the field reads

   ```
   navigator.mimeTypes[0].enabledPlugin.name
   ```

The result is the name of the plug-in that your browser invokes whenever it receives data of the type shown as the result of step 2.

Example

See "Looking for MIME and Plug-ins" later in this chapter.

Related Items: None.

type

Value: String   **Gettable:** Yes   **Settable:** No

	Nav2	Nav3	Nav4	IE3/J1	IE3/J2	IE4/J3
Compatibility		✔	✔			

A mimeType object's `type` property is the combination of the type and subtype commonly used to identify the kind of data coming from the server. CGI programs, for example, typically precede a data transmission with a special header string in the following format:

```
Content-type: <type>/<subtype>
```

This string prompts a browser to look up how to treat an incoming data stream of this kind. As you see later in this chapter, knowing whether a particular MIME type is listed in the `navigator.mimeTypes[]` array is not enough. A good script must dig deeper to uncover additional information about what is truly available for your data.

Example

See "Looking for MIME and Plug-ins" later in this chapter.

Related Items: description property.

suffixes

Value: String   **Gettable:** Yes   **Settable:** No

	Nav2	Nav3	Nav4	IE3/J1	IE3/J2	IE4/J3
Compatibility		✔	✔			

Every MIME type has one or more filename extensions, or suffixes, associated with it. You can read this information for any mimeType object via the suffixes property. The value of this property is a string. If the MIME type has more than one suffix associated with it, the string contains a comma-delimited listing, as in

```
mpg, mpeg, mpe
```

Multiple versions of a suffix have no distinction between them. Those MIME types that are best described in four or more characters (derived from a meaningful acronym, such as mpeg) have three-character versions to accommodate the "8-dot-3" filename conventions of MS-DOS and its derivatives.

Example

See "Looking for MIME and Plug-ins" later in this chapter.

Related Items: None.

Plugin Object

Properties	Methods	Event Handlers
name	refresh()	(None)
filename		
description		
length		

Syntax

Accessing plug-in properties or method:

```
navigator.plugins[i].property | method()
```

About this object

Understanding the distinction between the data embedded in documents that summon the powers of plug-ins and those items that browsers consider to be plug-ins is important. The former are made part of the document object by way of `<EMBED>` tags. If you want to control the plug-in via LiveConnect, you can gain access through the `document.embedName` object (see Chapter 38).

The concern here, however, deals with the way the plug-ins work from the browser's perspective: The software items registered with the browser at launch time stand ready for any matching MIME type that comes from the Net. One of the main purposes of having these objects scriptable is to let your scripts determine whether a desired plug-in is currently registered with the browser and even to help with installing a plug-in.

The close association between the plugin and mimeType object, demonstrated by the `mimeType.enabledPlugin` property, is equally visible coming from the direction of the plug-in. A plugin object evaluates to an array of MIME types that the plug-in interprets. Let's experiment to make this association clear (Windows users with Navigator 4 should use Version 4.02 or later):

1. Select Open Location from the File menu and enter

```
javascript:
```

2. In the "javascript typein" field, enter

```
navigator.plugins["LiveAudio"].length
```

Instead of the typical index value for the array notation, you use the actual name of the LiveAudio plug-in. This expression evaluates to 7, meaning that the `navigator.plugins["LiveAudio"]` array entry contains an array of seven items—the MIME types it recognizes.

3. Edit the typein field to read

```
navigator.plugins["LiveAudio"][0].type
```

That's not a typo: Because one array evaluates to a different array, the second set of square brackets is not separated from the first set by a period. In other words, this statement evaluates to the `type` property of the first mimeType object contained by the LiveAudio plug-in.

I doubt that you will have to use this kind of construction much, because if you know the name of the desired plug-in, you know what MIME types it already supports. In most cases, you come at the search from the MIME type direction and look for a specific enabled plug-in. See "Looking for MIME and Plug-ins" later for details on how to use the plug-in object in a production setting.

Properties

```
name
filename
description
length
```

Value: String   **Gettable:** Yes   **Settable:** No

	Nav2	Nav3	Nav4	IE3/J1	IE3/J2	IE4/J3
Compatibility		✔	✔			

The first three properties of the plugin object provide descriptive information about the plug-in file. The plug-in developer supplies the name and description. It's unclear whether future versions of plug-ins will differentiate themselves from earlier ones via either of these fields. That may be important if you are transferring data to a plug-in that requires a later version of the software. In the meantime, however, these items can play a role in helping a site visitor understand that a plug-in other than the ideal one (for a given MIME type) currently has an enabled setting.

Be aware that along the way, Netscape forgot to tell plug-in authors in the early days to assign the same name to every platform version of a plug-in. Be prepared for discrepancies across platforms.

Another piece of information available from a script is the plug-in's filename. On some platforms, such as Windows, this data comes in the form of a complete pathname to the plug-in DLL file; on other platforms, only the plug-in file's name appears.

Finally, the `length` property of a plugin object counts the number of MIME types that the plug-in recognizes. Although you could use this information to loop through all possible MIME types for a plug-in, a more instructive way would probably be to have your scripts approach the issue via the MIME type, as discussed later in this chapter.

Example

See "Looking for MIME and Plug-ins" later in this chapter.

Related Items: `mimeType.description` property.

Methods

```
refresh()
```

Returns: Nothing.

	Nav2	Nav3	Nav4	IE3/J1	IE3/J2	IE4/J3
Compatibility		✔	✔			

You may have guessed that Navigator determines its list of installed plug-ins while it launches. If you were to drop a new plug-in file into the plug-ins directory/folder, you would have to quit Navigator and relaunch it before it would see the new plug-in file. But that isn't a very friendly approach if you take pains to guide a user through the downloading and installation of a new plug-in file. The minute the user quits the browser, you have a slim chance of getting that person right back. That's where the `refresh()` method comes in.

The `refresh()` method is directed primarily at the browser, but the syntax of the call reminds the browser to refresh just the plug-ins:

```
navigator.plugins.refresh()
```

Interestingly, this command works only for adding a plug-in to the existing collection. If the user removes a plug-in and invokes this method, the removed one stays in the `navigator.plugins[]` array, although it may not be available for use. Only quitting and relaunching Navigator makes a plug-in removal take full effect.

I think it's a good idea to have a routine ready that leads a user through downloading and installing a plug-in not normally delivered with Navigator. Doing so through a separate window or a branch of your Web site's organization is ideal. Always include a `refresh()` method before returning to the point where the plug-in is required for your special media.

Example

If you want to experiment with this method, follow this sequence:

1. Move one of the plug-in files from the Navigator plug-ins directory/folder (whatever it may be called on your operating system) to another directory/folder.

2. Quit and restart Navigator.

3. Select About Plug-ins from the Help menu and make note of the plug-ins listed in this screen.

4. Move the plug-in file back to the plug-ins directory/folder.

5. Open Location `javascript:`

6. In the "javascript typein" field, type

```
navigator.plugins.refresh()
```

7. Select About Plug-ins again from the Help menu.

The restored plug-in should now appear as part of the list. Starting with Navigator 4, plug-ins can be constructed to take advantage of automatic installation via the SmartUpdate technique. If you are a plug-in developer, consult Netscape's developer Web site (`http://developer.netscape.com`) for details on adding this feature to your plug-in. SmartUpdate obviates the need for MIME type or plug-in checking as well as the `refresh()` method for visitors using Navigator 4.

Related Items: None.

Looking for MIME and Plug-ins

If you go to great lengths to add new media and data types to your Web pages, then you certainly want your visitors to reap the benefits of those additions. But you cannot be guaranteed that they have the requisite plug-ins installed to accommodate that fancy data. Fortunately, if your audience is dependent on Navigator 3 (and not Navigator 4 with its SmartUpdate auto-installation of plug-ins), you can use JavaScript to inspect the browser to find out if the desired software is ready for your data.

The value of this inspection capability is that you can maintain better control of your site visitors who don't yet have the necessary plug-in in Navigator 3. Rather than merely providing a link to the plug-in's download site, you can build a more complete interface around the downloading and installation of the plug-in, without losing your visitor. I have some suggestions about such an interface at the end of this discussion.

How you go about inspecting a visitor's plug-in library depends on what information you have about the data file or stream and how precise you must be in locating a particular plug-in. Some plug-ins may override MIME type settings that you would expect to be in a browser. For example, a new audio plug-in may take over for LiveAudio when it's installed by the user (often without the user's explicit permission). Another issue that complicates matters is that the same plug-in may have a different name (`navigator.plugins[i].name` property) depending on the operating system. Therefore, searching your script for the presence of a plug-in by name is not good enough if the name may be different on the Macintosh version versus the Windows 95 version. With luck, this naming discrepancy will resolve itself over time as plug-in developers understand the scripter's need for consistency across platforms.

To help you jump-start the process in your scripts, I discuss three utility functions you can use without modification in your own scripts. These functions are excerpts from a long listing (Listing 25-3), which is located in its entirety on the book's CD-ROM. The pieces not shown here are merely user interface elements to let you experiment with these functions.

Note

The scripts in Listing 25-3 reveal a bug in the Windows version of Navigator 4 that crashes Navigator when the script attempts to retrieve mimeType objects of certain types too quickly (in a `for` loop). The script does work fine in Windows for Navigator 3. Also, to date I have not found a compatible workaround for any version of Internet Explorer.

Verifying a MIME type

Listing 25-3a is a function whose narrow purpose is to compare any MIME type definition (in the `<type>/<subtype>` format as a string) against the browser's internal list of MIME types. The function does more, however, than simply look for a match. The reason is that the browser can easily list MIME types for which no plug-in is installed (as is the case with dozens of MIME types in the default list provided in Navigator).

Listing 25-3a: **Verifying a MIME type**

```
// Pass "<type>/<subtype>" string to this function to find
// out if the MIME type is registered with this browser
// and that at least some plug-in is enabled for that type.
function mimeIsReady(mime_type) {
        for (var i = 0; i < navigator.mimeTypes.length; i++) {
            if (navigator.mimeTypes[i].type == mime_type) {
                if (navigator.mimeTypes[i].enabledPlugin != null) {
                    return true
                }
            }
        }
        return false
}
```

The real power of this function comes in the most nested `if` statement. For script execution to reach this point, the MIME type in question has been found to be listed in the browser's massive `mimeTypes[]` array. What you really need to know is whether a plug-in is enabled for that particular MIME type. If the script passes that final test, then you can safely report back that the browser supports the MIME type. If, on the other hand, no match has been found after cycling through all listed MIME types, the function returns false.

Verifying a plug-in

Next, in Listing 25-3b, you let JavaScript see if the browser has a specific plug-in registered in the `navigator.plugins[]` array. This method approaches the installation question from a different angle. Instead of coming with a known MIME type, you come with a known plug-in. But because more than one registered plug-in can support a given MIME type, this function explores one step further to see whether at least one of the plug-in's MIME types (of any kind) is enabled in the browser.

Listing 25-3b: **Verifying a Plug-in**

```
// Pass the name of a plug-in for this function to see
// if the plug-in is registered with this browser and
// that it is enabled for at least one MIME type of any kind.
function pluginIsReady(plug_in) {
        for (var i = 0; i < navigator.plugins.length; i++) {
            if (navigator.plugins[i].name.toLowerCase() ==
plug_in.toLowerCase()) {
                for (var j = 0; j < navigator.plugins[i].length; j++) {
                    if (navigator.plugins[i][j].enabledPlugin) {
```

(continued)

Listing 25-3b *(continued)*

```
                    return true
            }
        }
        return false
    }
}
return false
}
```

The parameter for the `pluginIsReady()` function is a string consisting of the plug-in's name as it appears in boldface in the About Plug-ins listing (from the Navigator Help menu). The script loops through all registered plug-ins for a match against this string (converting both strings to all lowercase to help overcome discrepancies in capitalization).

Next comes a second repeat loop, which looks through the MIME types associated with a plug-in (in this case, only a plug-in whose name matches the parameter). Notice the use of the strange, double-array syntax for the most nested `if` statement: For a given plug-in (denoted by the `i` index), you have to loop through all items in the MIME types array (`j`) connected to that plug-in. The conditional phrase for the last `if` statement has an implied comparison against null (see another way of explicitly showing the null comparison in Listing 25-3a). The conditional statement evaluates to either an object or a null, which JavaScript can accept as `true` or `false`, respectively. The point is that if an enabled plug-in is found for the given MIME type of the given plug-in, then this function returns true.

I must emphasize that before using this function, make sure that the plug-in is internally named the same way on all platforms for which a plug-in version exists. Such is not the case with many early plug-ins.

Verifying both plug-in and MIME type

The last utility function (Listing 25-3c) is the safest way of determining whether a visitor's browser is equipped with the "right stuff" to play your media. This function requires both a MIME type and plug-in name as parameters and also makes sure that both items are supported and enabled in the browser before returning a true.

Listing 25-3c: **Verifying Plug-in and MIME type**

```
// Pass "<type>/<subtype>" and plug-in name strings for this
// function to see if both the MIME type and plug-in are
// registered with this browser, and that the plug-in is
// enabled for the desired MIME type.
function mimeAndPluginReady(mimetype,plug_in) {
```

```
        for (var i = 0; i < navigator.plugins.length; i++) {
             if (navigator.plugins[i].name.toLowerCase() ==
plug_in.toLowerCase()) {
                 for (var j = 0; j < navigator.plugins[i].length; j++) {
                     var mimeObj = navigator.plugins[i][j]
                     if (mimeObj.enabledPlugin && (mimeObj.type ==
mimetype)) {
                             return true
                     }
                 }
                 return false
             }
         }
         return false
    }
```

This function resembles the one in Listing 25-3b until you reach the most nested statements. Here, instead of looking for any old MIME type, you insist on the existence of an explicit match between the MIME type passed as a parameter and an enabled MIME type associated with the plug-in. Because this function relies on a plug-in's name, the same cautions about checking for name consistency across platforms applies here. To see how these functions work on your browser, open the complete file (lst25-03.htm) from the CD-ROM.

Managing plug-in installation (Navigator 3)

If your scripts determine that a visitor is using Navigator 3 and does not have the plug-in your data expects, you may want to consider providing an electronic guide to installing the plug-in. One way to do this is to open a new frameset (in the main window). One frame would contain step-by-step instructions with links to the plug-in's download site. The download site's page would appear in the other frame of this temporary window. The steps must take into account all installation requirements for every platform, or, alternatively, you can create a separate installation document for each unique class of platform. Macintosh files, for instance, frequently must be decoded from binhex format and then uncompressed before you move them into the plug-ins folder. Other plug-ins have their own, separate installation program. The final step should include a call to

```
navigator.plugins.refresh()
```

to make sure that the browser updates its internal listings. After that, the script can go back to the `document.referrer`, which should be the page that sent the visitor to the installation pages. All in all, the process is cumbersome — it's not like downloading a Java applet. But if you provide some guidance, you stand a better chance of the user coming back to play your cool media.

Screen Object

Properties	Methods	Event Handlers
availHeight	(None)	(None)
availWidth		
colorDepth		
height		
pixelDepth		
width		

Syntax

Accessing screen properties:

screen.*property*

	Nav2	Nav3	Nav4	IE3/J1	IE3/J2	IE4/J3
Compatibility			✔			(✔)

About this object

Navigator 4 provides a screen object that lets your scripts inquire about the size and color settings of the video monitor used to display a page. Properties are carefully designed to reveal not only the raw width and height of the monitor (in pixels), but what the available width and height are once you take into account the operating system's screen-hogging interface elements (for example, the Windows 95/NT Taskbar and the Mac menubar).

Some of these property values are also accessible in Navigator 3 if you use LiveConnect to access Java classes directly. Example code for this approach is supplied in the individual property listings.

Internet Explorer 4 provides a screen object, although it appears as an element of the window object in the Internet Explorer 4 object model. Only three properties of the Internet Explorer 4 screen object — height, width, and colorDepth — are the same syntax as Navigator 4's screen object.

availHeight
availWidth
height
width

Value: Integer   **Gettable:** Yes   **Settable:** No

	Nav2	Nav3	Nav4	IE3/J1	IE3/J2	IE4/J3
Compatibility			✔			(✔)

With Navigator 4's additional window sizing methods, your scripts may want to know how large the user's monitor is. This is particularly important if you are setting up an application to run in kiosk mode, which occupies the entire screen. Two pairs of properties let scripts extract the dimensions of the screen. All dimensions are in pixels.

The gross height and width of the monitor is available from the `screen.height` and `screen.width` properties. Thus, a monitor rated as an 800×600 monitor returns values of 800 and 600 for width and height, respectively. These properties are available in Internet Explorer 4, as well.

But the gross size is not always completely available as displayable area for a window. To the rescue come the `screen.availWidth` and `screen.availHeight` properties. For example, Windows 95 and NT 4 display the Taskbar. The default location for this bar is at the bottom of the window, but users can reorient it along any edge of the screen. If the default behavior of always showing the Taskbar is in force, the bar takes away from the screen real estate available for window display (unless you intentionally size or position a window so that part of the window extends under the bar). When along the top or bottom edge of the screen, the Taskbar occupies 28 vertical pixels; when positioned along one of the sides, the bar occupies 60 horizontal pixels. On the Macintosh platform, the 20-pixel-deep menubar occupies a top strip of the screen. While windows can be positioned and sized so they are partially covered by the menubar, it is not a good idea to open a window in or move a window into that location.

You can use the available screen size values as settings for window properties. For example, to maximize a window, you must position the window at the top left of the screen and then set the outer window dimensions to the available sizes, as follows:

```
function maximize() {
        window.moveTo(0,0)
        window.outerWidth = screen.availWidth
        window.outerHeight = screen.availHeight
}
```

The above function positions the window appropriately on the Macintosh just below the menubar so that the window is not obscured by the menubar. If, however, the client is Windows 95/NT and the user has positioned the Taskbar at the top of the screen, the window will be partially hidden under the Taskbar (you cannot query the available screen space's coordinates).

For Navigator 3, you can use LiveConnect to access a native Java class that reveals the overall screen size (not the available screen size). If the user is running Navigator 3 and Java is enabled, the following script fragment can be placed in the Head portion of your document to set variables with screen width and height:

```
var toolkit = java.awt.Toolkit.getDefaultToolkit()
var screen = toolkit.getScreenSize()
```

The screen variable is an object whose properties (`width` and `height`) contain the pixel measures of the current screen. This LiveConnect technique also works in Navigator 4 (but not in Internet Explorer 3), so you can use one screen size method for all late-model Navigators. In fact, you can also extract the screen resolution (pixels per inch) in the same manner. The following statement, added after the ones above, sets the variable `resolution` to that value:

```
var resolution = toolkit.getScreenResolution()
```

Related Items: `window.innerHeight` property; `window.innerWidth` property; `window.outerHeight` property; `window.outerWidth` property; `window.moveTo()` method; `window.resizeTo()` method.

colorDepth
pixelDepth

Value: Integer   **Gettable:** Yes   **Settable:** No

	Nav2	Nav3	Nav4	IE3/J1	IE3/J2	IE4/J3
Compatibility			✔			(✔)

You can design a page for Navigator 4 with different color models in mind, because your scripts can query the client to find out how many colors the user has set the monitor to display. This can be helpful if you have more subtle color schemes that require 16-bit color settings or images tailored to specific palette sizes.

Both `screen.colorDepth` and `screen.pixelDepth` properties return the number of bits that the color client computer's video display control panel is set to. The `screen.colorDepth` value may take into account a custom color palette, so in general I prefer to rely only on the `screen.pixelDepth` value (Internet Explorer 4 supports only the `screen.colorDepth` property of this pair). You can use this value to determine which of two image versions to load, as shown in the following script fragment that runs as the document loads.

```
if (screen.colorDepth > 8 ) {
      document.write("<IMG SRC='logoHI.jpg' HEIGHT='60' WIDTH='100'")
} else {
      document.write("<IMG SRC='logoLO.jpg' HEIGHT='60' WIDTH='100'")
}
```

In this example, the logoHI.jpg image is designed for 16-bit displays or better, while the colors in logoLO.jpg have been tuned for 8-bit display.

While LiveConnect in Navigator 3 has a way to extract what appears to be the pixelDepth equivalent, the Java implementation is flawed. You do not always get the correct value, so I don't recommend relying on this tactic for Navigator 3 users.

Related Items: None.

✦   ✦   ✦

The String Object

Chapter 6's tutorial introduced you to the concepts of values and the types of values that JavaScript works with—things such as strings, numbers, and Boolean values. In this chapter, you look more closely at the very important String data type, as well as its relationship to the Number data type. Along the way, you encounter the many ways in which JavaScript enables scripters to manipulate strings.

Much of the syntax you see in this chapter is identical to that of the Java programming language. Because the scope of JavaScript activity is narrower than that of Java, there isn't nearly as much to learn for JavaScript as for Java. At the same time, certain string object language features apply to scripting but not to Java programming. Improvements to the string object's methods in Navigator 4 greatly simplify a number of string manipulation tasks. If you must script for a lower common denominator of browser, however, you may need some of the same kind of string micro-management skills that a C programmer needs. I'll soften the blow by providing some general purpose functions that you can plug into your scripts to make those jobs easier.

String and Number Data Types

Although JavaScript is not what is known as a "strongly typed" language, you still need to be aware of several data types because of their impact on the way you work with the information in those forms. In this section, I focus on strings and two types of numbers.

Simple strings

A string consists of one or more standard text characters between matching quote marks. JavaScript is forgiving in one regard: You can use single or double quotes, as long as you match two single quotes or two double quotes around a string. Another benefit to this scheme becomes apparent when you try to include a quoted string inside a string. For example, say that you're assembling a line of HTML code in a variable that you will eventually write to a new window completely controlled by JavaScript. The line of text you want to assign to a variable is this:

```
<INPUT TYPE="checkbox" NAME="candy">Chocolate
```

To assign this entire line of text to a variable, you have to surround the line in quotes. But because quotes appear inside the string, JavaScript (or any language) has problems deciphering where the string begins or ends. By carefully placing the other kind of quote pairs, however, you can make the assignment work. Here are two equally valid ways:

```
result = '<INPUT TYPE="checkbox" NAME="candy">Chocolate'
result = "<INPUT TYPE='checkbox' NAME='candy'>Chocolate"
```

Notice in both cases, the entire string is surrounded by the same unique pair of quotes. Inside the string, two quoted strings appear that will be treated as such by JavaScript. I recommend that you settle on one form or the other and then use it consistently throughout your scripts.

Building long string variables

The act of joining strings together — *concatenation* — enables you to assemble long strings out of several little pieces. This feature is very important for some of your scripting — for example, when you need to build an HTML page's specifications entirely within a variable before writing the page to another frame with one `document.write()` statement.

One tactic I use keeps the length of each statement in this building process short enough so it's easily readable in your text editor. This method uses the add-by-value assignment operator (+=) that appends the right-hand side of the equation to the left-hand side. Here is a simple example, which begins by initializing a variable as an empty string:

```
var newDocument = ""
newDocument += "<HTML><HEAD><TITLE>Life and Times</TITLE></HEAD>"
newDocument += "<BODY><H1>My Life and Welcome to It</H1>"
newDocument += "by Sidney Finortny<HR>"
```

Starting with the second line, each statement adds more data to the string being stored in `newDocument`. You can continue appending string data until the entire page's specification is contained in the `newDocument` variable.

Joining string literals and variables

In some cases, you need to create a string out of literal strings (characters with quote marks around them) and string variable values. The methodology for concatenating these types of strings is no different from that of multiple string literals. The plus-sign operator does the job. Therefore, in the following example, a variable contains a name. That variable value is made a part of a larger string whose other parts are string literals:

```
yourName = prompt("Please enter your name:","")
var msg = "Good afternoon, " + yourName + "."
alert(msg)
```

Some common problems that you may encounter while attempting this kind of concatenation include the following:

✦ Accidentally omitting one of the quotes around a literal string

✦ Failing to insert blank spaces in the string literals to accommodate word spaces

✦ Forgetting to concatenate punctuation after a variable value

Also, don't forget that what I show here as variable values can be any expression that evaluates to a string, including property references and the results of some methods. For example

```
var msg = "The name of this document is " + document.title + "."
alert(msg)
```

Special inline characters

The way string literals are created in JavaScript makes adding certain characters to strings difficult. I'm talking primarily about adding quotes, carriage returns, apostrophes, and tab characters to strings. Fortunately, JavaScript provides a mechanism for entering such characters into string literals. A backslash symbol, followed by the character you want to appear as inline, makes that task happen. For the "invisible" characters, a special set of letters following the backslash tells JavaScript what to do.

The most common backslash pairs are as follows:

\"	Double quote
\'	Single quote (apostrophe)
\\	Backslash
\b	Backspace
\t	Tab
\n	New line
\r	Carriage return
\f	Form feed

Use these "inline characters" (also known as "escaped characters," but this terminology has a different connotation for Internet strings) inside quoted string literals to make JavaScript recognize them. When assembling a block of text that needs a new paragraph, insert the \n character pair. Here are some examples of syntax using these special characters:

```
msg = "You\'re doing fine."
msg = "This is the first line.\nThis is the second line."
msg = document.title + "\n" + document.links.length + " links present."
```

Technically speaking, a complete carriage return, as known from typewriting days, is both a line feed (advance the line by one) and a carriage return (move the carriage all the way to the left margin). Although JavaScript strings treat a line feed (\n new line) as a full carriage return, you may have to construct \r\n breaks when assembling strings that go back to a CGI script on a server. The format that you use all depends on the string-parsing capabilities of the CGI program. (Also see the special requirements for the textarea object in Chapter 22.)

It's easy to confuse the strings assembled for display in textarea objects or alert boxes with strings to be written as HTML. For HTML strings, make sure that you use the standard HTML tags for line breaks (<BR>) and paragraph breaks (<P>) rather than the inline return or line feed symbols.

String Object

Properties	Methods	Event Handlers
length	anchor()	(None)
prototype	big()	
	blink()	
	bold()	
	charAt()	
	charCodeAt()	
	concat()	
	fixed()	
	fontcolor()	
	fontsize()	
	fromCharCode()	
	indexOf()	
	italics()	
	lastIndexOf()	
	link()	
	match()	
	replace()	
	search()	
	slice()	
	small()	
	split()	
	strike()	
	sub()	
	substr()	
	substring()	

Properties	Methods	Event Handlers
	sup()	
	toLowerCase()	
	toUpperCase()	

Syntax

Creating a string object:

```
var myString = new String("characters")
```

Accessing select object properties and methods:

```
string.property | method
```

About this object

JavaScript draws a fine line between a string value and a string object. Both let you use the same methods on their contents, so by and large, you do not have to create a string object (with the `new String()` constructor) every time you want to assign a string value to a variable. A simple assignment operation (`var myString = "fred"`) is all you need to create a string value that behaves on the surface very much like a full-fledged string object.

Where the difference comes into play is when you wish to exploit the "object-ness" of a genuine string object, which I explain further in the discussion of the `string.prototype` property later in this chapter.

With string data often comes the need to massage that text in scripts. In addition to concatenating strings, you at times need to extract segments of strings, delete parts of strings, and replace one part of a string with some other text. Unlike many plain-language scripting languages, JavaScript is fairly low-level in its built-in facilities for string manipulation. This means that unless you can take advantage of the regular expression powers of Navigator 4, you must fashion your own string handling routines out of very elemental powers built into JavaScript. Later in this chapter, I provide several functions that you can use in your own scripts for common string handling.

As you work with string values, visualize every string value as an object with properties and methods like other JavaScript objects. JavaScript defines one property and a slew of methods for any string value (and one extra property for a true string object). The syntax is the same for string methods as it is for any other object method:

```
stringObject.method()
```

What may seem odd at first is that the `stringObject` part of this reference can be any expression that evaluates to a string, including string literals, variables containing strings, or other object properties. Therefore, the following examples of calling the `toUpperCase()` method are all valid:

```
"george burns".toUpperCase()
yourName.toUpperCase() // yourName is a variable containing a string
```

```
document.forms[0].entry.value.toUpperCase() // entry is a text field
object
```

An important concept to remember is that invoking a string method does not change the string object that is part of the reference. Rather, the method returns a value, which can be used as a parameter to another method or function call, or assigned to a variable value.

Therefore, to change the contents of a string variable to the results of a method, you must use an assignment operator, as in

```
yourName = yourName.toUpperCase() // variable is now all uppercase
```

Note   In Navigator 2, avoid nesting method calls for the same string object when the methods modify the string. The evaluation does not work as you might expect. Instead, break out each call as a separate JavaScript statement.

Properties

length

Value: Integer   **Gettable:** Yes   **Settable:** No

	Nav2	Nav3	Nav4	IE3/J1	IE3/J2	IE4/J3
Compatibility	✔	✔	✔	✔	✔	✔

The most frequently used property of a string is `length`. To derive the length of a string, extract its property as you would extract the `length` property of any object:

```
string.length
```

The `length` value represents an integer count of the number of characters within the string. Spaces and punctuation symbols count as characters. Any backslash special characters embedded in a string count as one character, including such characters as newline and tab. Here are some examples:

```
"Lincoln".length // result = 7
"Four score".length // result = 10
"One\ntwo".length // result = 7
"".length // result = 0
```

The `length` property is commonly summoned when dealing with detailed string manipulation in repeat loops.

prototype

Value: Object   **Gettable:** Yes   **Settable:** Yes

	Nav2	Nav3	Nav4	IE3/J1	IE3/J2	IE4/J3
Compatibility		✔	✔			✔

String objects defined with the `new String("`*`stringValue`*`")` constructor are robust objects compared to plain old variables that are assigned string values. You certainly don't have to create this kind of string object for every string in your scripts, but these objects do come in handy when you find that strings in variables go awry. This happens occasionally while trying to preserve string information as script variables in other frames or windows. By using the string object constructor, you can be relatively assured that the string value will be available in the distant frame when needed.

Another byproduct of true string objects is that you can assign prototype properties and methods to all string objects in the document. A prototype is a property or method that becomes a part of every new object created after the prototype items have been added. For strings, as an example, you may want to define a new method for converting a string into a new type of HTML font tag not already defined by JavaScript's string object. Listing 26-1 shows how to create and use such a prototype.

Listing 26-1: **A String Object Prototype**

```
<HTML>
<HEAD>
<TITLE>String Object Prototype</TITLE>
<SCRIPT LANGUAGE="JavaScript1.1">
function makeItHot() {
        return "<FONT COLOR='red'>" + this.toString() + "</FONT>"
}
String.prototype.hot = makeItHot
</SCRIPT>
<BODY>
<SCRIPT LANGUAGE="JavaScript1.1">
document.write("<H1>This site is on " + "FIRE".hot() + "!!</H1>")
</SCRIPT>
</BODY>
</HTML>
```

A function definition (`makeItHot()`) accumulates string data to be returned to the object when the function is invoked as the object's method. The `this` keyword extracts the object making the call, which you convert to a string for concatenation with the rest of the strings to be returned. In the page's Body, I call upon that prototype method in the same way one calls upon existing String methods that turn strings into HTML tags (discussed later in this chapter).

In the next sections, I divide the string object methods into two distinct categories. The first, parsing methods, focuses on string analysis and character manipulation within strings. The second group, formatting methods, are devoted

entirely to assembling strings in HTML syntax for those scripts that assemble the
text to be written into new documents or other frames.

Parsing methods

string.charAt(*index*)

Returns: Character in *string* at the *index* count.

	Nav2	Nav3	Nav4	IE3/J1	IE3/J2	IE4/J3
Compatibility	✔	✔	✔	✔	✔	✔

Use the `string.charAt()` method to extract a single character from a string
when you know the position of that character. For this method, you specify an
index value in the string as a parameter to the method. The index value of the first
character of the string is 0. To grab the last character of a string, mix string
methods:

```
myString.charAt(myString.length - 1)
```

If your script needs to get a range of characters, use the `string.substring()`
method. It is a common mistake to use `string.substring()` to extract a
character from inside a string, when the `string.charAt()` method is more
efficient.

Examples

```
char = "banana daiquiri".charAt(0) // result = "b"
char = "banana daiquiri".charAt(5) // result = "a" (third "a" in
"banana")
char = "banana daiquiri".charAt(6) // result = " " (a space character)
char = "banana daiquiri".charAt(20) // result = "" (empty string)
```

Related Items: `string.lastIndexOf()` method; `string.IndexOf()` method;
`string.substring()` method.

string.charCodeAt([*index*]) String.fromCharCode(*num1* [, *num2* [, ... numn]])

Returns: Integer code number for a character; concatenated string value of code
numbers supplied as parameters.

	Nav2	Nav3	Nav4	IE3/J1	IE3/J2	IE4/J3
Compatibility			✔			✔

Conversions from plain language characters to their numeric equivalents have a long tradition in computer programming. For a long time, the most common numbering scheme was the ASCII standard, which covers the basic English alphanumeric characters and punctuation within 128 values (numbered 0 through 127). An extended version with a total of 256 characters, with some variations depending on the operating system, accounts for other roman characters in other languages, particularly vowels with umlauts and other pronunciation marks. To bring all languages, including pictographic languages and other nonroman alphabets, into the computer age, a world standard called Unicode provides space for thousands of characters.

In JavaScript, the character conversions are string methods. Acceptable values depend on the browser you are using. Navigator works only with the 256 ISO-Latin-I values; Internet Explorer works with the Unicode system.

The two methods that perform these conversions work in very different ways syntactically. The first, *string*.charCodeAt(), converts a single string character to its numerical equivalent. The string being converted is the one to the left of the method name — and it may be a literal string or any other expression that evaluates to a string value. If no parameter is passed, the character being converted is by default the first character of the string. However, you can also specify a different character as an index value into the string (first character is 0), as demonstrated here:

```
"abc".charCodeAt()   // result = 97
"abc".charCodeAt(0)  // result = 97
"abc".charCodeAt(1)  // result = 98
```

If the string value is an empty string, the result is NaN.

To convert numeric values to their characters, use the String.fromCharCode() method. Notice that the object beginning the method call is the generic string object, not a string value. Then, as parameters, you can include one or more integers separated by commas. In the conversion process, the method combines the characters for all of the parameters into one string, an example of which is shown here:

```
String.fromCharCode(97, 98, 99)  // result "abc"
```

Note

The *string*.charCodeAt() method is broken on the Macintosh version of Navigator 4, and always returns NaN.

Example

Listing 26-2 provides examples of both methods on one page. Moreover, because one of the demonstrations relies on the automatic capture of selected text on the page, the scripts include code to accommodate the different handling of selection events and capture of the selected text in Navigator and Internet Explorer 4.

After you load the page, select part of the body text anywhere on the page. If you start the selection with the lowercase letter "a," the character code displays as 97. If you select no text, the result is NaN.

Try entering numeric values in the three fields at the bottom of the page. Values below 32 are ASCII control characters that most fonts represent as hollow squares. But try all other values to see what you get. Notice that the script passes all three values as a group to the String.fromCharCode() method, and the result is a combined string.

Listing 26-2: Character Conversions

```
<HTML>
<HEAD>
<TITLE>Character Codes</TITLE>
<SCRIPT LANGUAGE="JavaScript">
var isNav = (navigator.appName == "Netscape")
function showProps(objName,obj) {
        var msg = ""
        for (var i in obj) {
            objName + "." + i + "=" + obj[i]
        }
        alert(msg)
}
function showCharCode() {
        if (isNav) {
            var theText = document.getSelection()
        } else {
            var theText = document.selection.createRange().text
        }
        document.forms[0].charCodeDisplay.value = theText.charCodeAt()
}
function showString(form) {
        form.result.value =
String.fromCharCode(form.entry1.value,form.entry2.value,form.entry3.value)
}
if (isNav) {
        document.captureEvents(Event.MOUSEUP)
}
document.onmouseup = showCharCode
</SCRIPT>
</HEAD>
<BODY>
<B>Capturing Character Codes</B>
<FORM>
Select any of this text, and see the character code of the first
character.<P>
Character Code:<INPUT TYPE="text" NAME="charCodeDisplay" SIZE=3><BR>
<HR>
<B>Converting Codes to Characters</B><BR>
Enter a value  0-255:<INPUT TYPE="text" NAME="entry1" SIZE=4><BR>
Enter a value  0-255:<INPUT TYPE="text" NAME="entry2" SIZE=4><BR>
Enter a value  0-255:<INPUT TYPE="text" NAME="entry3" SIZE=4><BR>
<INPUT TYPE="button" VALUE="Show String" onClick="showString(this.form)">
Result:<INPUT TYPE="text" NAME="result" SIZE=5>
</FORM>
</BODY>
</HTML>
```

Related Items: None.

string.concat(*string2*)

Returns: Combined string.

	Nav2	Nav3	Nav4	IE3/J1	IE3/J2	IE4/J3
Compatibility			✔			✔

JavaScript's add-by-value operator (+=) provides a convenient way to concatenate strings. Navigator 4, however, introduces a string object method that performs the same task. The base string to which more text is appended is the object or value to the left of the period. The string to be appended is the parameter of the method, as the following example demonstrates:

```
"abc".concat("def")  // result: "abcdef"
```

Like the add-by-value operator, the concat() method doesn't know about word endings. You are responsible for including the necessary space between words if the two strings require a space between them in the result.

Related Items: Add-by-value (+=) operator.

string.indexOf(*searchString* [, *startIndex*])

Returns: Index value of the character within *string* where *searchString* begins.

	Nav2	Nav3	Nav4	IE3/J1	IE3/J2	IE4/J3
Compatibility	✔	✔	✔	✔	✔	✔

Like some languages' offset string function, JavaScript's indexOf() method enables your script to obtain the number of the character in the main string where a search string begins. Optionally, you can specify where in the main string the search should begin — but the returned value is always relative to the very first character of the main string. Like all string object methods, index values start their count with 0. If no match occurs within the main string, the returned value is -1. Thus, this method is a convenient way to determine whether one string contains another.

A bug exists in some versions of Navigator 2 and 3 that can trip up your scripts if you don't guard against it. If the string being searched is empty, the indexOf() method returns an empty string rather than the expected -1 value. Therefore, you may want to test to make sure the string is not empty before applying this method. A look at the following examples tells you more about this method than a long description. In all examples, you assign the result of the method to a variable named offset.

Examples

```
offset = "bananas".indexOf("b") // result = 0 (index of first letter is
zero)
offset = "bananas".indexOf("a") // result = 1

offset = "bananas".indexOf("a",1) // result = 1 (start from second
letter)

offset = "bananas".indexOf("a",2) // result = 3 (start from third
letter)

offset = "bananas".indexOf("a",4) // result = 5 (start from fifth
letter)

offset = "bananas".indexOf("nan") // result = 2

offset = "bananas".indexOf("nas") // result = 4

offset = "bananas".indexOf("s") // result = 6

offset = "bananas".indexOf("z") // result = -1 (no "z" in string)
```

Related Items: `string.lastIndexOf()`; `string.charAt()`;
`string.substring()`.

string.lastIndexOf(*searchString*
[, *startIndex*])

Returns: Index value of the last character within *string* where *searchString* begins.

	Nav2	Nav3	Nav4	IE3/J1	IE3/J2	IE4/J3
Compatibility	✔	✔	✔	✔	✔	✔

The `string.lastIndexOf()` method is closely related to the method `string.IndexOf()`. The only difference is that this method starts its search for a match from the end of the string (`string.length - 1`) and works its way backward through the string. All index values are still counted, starting with 0, from the front of the string. In the examples that follow, I use the same values as in the examples for `string.IndexOf` so that you can compare the results. In cases where only one instance of the search string is found, the results are the same; but when multiple instances of the search string exist, the results can vary widely — hence the need for this method.

This string method has experienced numerous bugs, particularly in Navigator 2, and in later versions for UNIX. Scripts using this method should be tested exhaustively.

Examples

```
offset = "bananas".lastIndexOf("b") // result = 0 (index of first
letter is zero)
```

```
offset = "bananas".lastIndexOf ("a") // result = 5

offset = "bananas".lastIndexOf ("a",1) // result = 1 (start from
second letter working toward the front)

offset = "bananas".lastIndexOf ("a",2) // result = 1 (start from third
letter working toward front)

offset = "bananas".lastIndexOf ("a",4) // result = 3 (start from fifth
letter)

offset = "bananas".lastIndexOf ("nan") // result = 2 [ except for -1
Nav 2.0 bug]

offset = "bananas".lastIndexOf ("nas") // result = 4

offset = "bananas".lastIndexOf ("s") // result = 6

offset = "bananas".lastIndexOf ("z") // result = -1 (no "z" in string)
```

Related Items: `string.lastIndexOf();` `string.charAt();`
`string.substring().`

`string.match(regExpression)`

Returns: Array of matching strings.

	Nav2	Nav3	Nav4	IE3/J1	IE3/J2	IE4/J3
Compatibility			✔			✔

The `string.match()` method relies on the RegExp (regular expression) object introduced to JavaScript in Navigator 4. The string value under scrutiny is to the left of the dot, while the regular expression to be used by the method is passed as a parameter. The parameter must be a regular expression object, created according to the two ways these objects can be generated.

This method returns an array value when at least one match turns up; otherwise the returned value is null. Each entry in the array is a copy of the string segment that matches the specifications of the regular expression. You can use this method to uncover how many times a substring or sequence of characters appears in a larger string. Finding the offset locations of the matches requires other string parsing.

Example

To help you understand the `string.match()` method, Listing 26-3 provides a workshop area for experimentation. Two fields occur for data entry: the first is for the long string to be examined by the method; the second is for a regular expression. Some default values are provided in case you're not yet familiar with the syntax of regular expressions. A checkbox lets you specify whether the search through the string for matches should be case-sensitive. When you click the "Execute Match()" button, the script creates a regular expression object out of your input, performs the `string.match()` method on the big string, and reports two kinds of results to the page. The primary result is a string version of the array returned by the method; the other is a count of items returned.

Listing 26-3: **Regular Expression Match Workshop**

```
<HTML>
<HEAD>
<TITLE>Regular Expression Match</TITLE>
<SCRIPT LANGUAGE="JavaScript">
function doMatch(form) {
        var str = form.entry.value
        var delim = (form.caseSens.checked) ? "/g" : "/gi"
        var regexp = eval("/" + form.regexp.value + delim)
        var resultArray = str.match(regexp)
        if (resultArray) {
            form.result.value = resultArray.toString()
            form.count.value = resultArray.length
        } else {
            form.result.value = "<no matches>"
            form.count.value = ""
        }
}
</SCRIPT>
</HEAD>
<BODY>
<B>String Match with Regular Expressions</B>
<HR>
<FORM>
Enter a main string:<INPUT TYPE="text" NAME="entry" SIZE=60
   VALUE="Many a maN and womAN have meant to visit GerMAny."><BR>
Enter a regular expression to match:<INPUT TYPE="text" NAME="regexp"
SIZE=25
   VALUE="\wa\w">
<INPUT TYPE="checkbox" NAME="caseSens">Case-sensitive<P>
<INPUT TYPE="button" VALUE="Execute Match()"
onClick="doMatch(this.form)">
<INPUT TYPE="reset"><P>
Result:<INPUT TYPE="text" NAME="result" SIZE=40><BR>
Count:<INPUT TYPE="text" NAME="count" SIZE=3><BR>
</FORM>
</BODY>
</HTML>
```

The default value for the main string has unusual capitalization intentionally. It lets you see more clearly where some of the matches come from. For example, the default regular expression looks for any three-character string that has the letter "a" in the middle. Six string segments match that expression. With the help of capitalization, you can see where each of the four strings containing "man" are extracted from the main string. The following table lists some other regular expressions to try with the default main string.

RegExp	Description
`man`	Both case-sensitive and not
`man\b`	Where "man" is at the end of a word
`\bman`	Where "man" is at the start of a word
`me*an`	Where zero or more "e" letters occur between "m" and "a"
`.a.`	Where "a" is surrounded by any one character (including space)
`\sa\s`	Where "a" is surrounded by a space on both sides
`z`	Where a "z" occurs (none in the default string)

In the scripts for Listing 26-3, if the `string.match()` method returns null, you are informed politely, and the count field is emptied.

Related Items: `window.setTimeout()`.

string.replace(*regExpression, replaceString*)

Returns: Changed string.

	Nav2	Nav3	Nav4	IE3/J1	IE3/J2	IE4/J3
Compatibility			✔			✔

Regular expressions are commonly used to perform search-and-replace operations. JavaScript's `string.replace()` method provides a simple framework in which to perform this kind of operation on any string.

Searching and replacing requires three components. The first is the main string that is the target of the operation. Second is the regular expression to search for. And third is the string to replace each instance of the text found by the operation. For the `string.replace()` method, the main string is the string value or object referenced to the left of the period. This string can also be a literal string (that is, text surrounded by quotes). The regular expression to search for is the first parameter, while the replacement string is the second parameter.

As long as you know how to generate a regular expression, you don't have to be a whiz to use the `string.replace()` method to perform simple replacement operations. But using regular expressions can make the operation more powerful. Consider these soliloquy lines by Hamlet:

```
To be, or not to be: that is the question:
Whether 'tis nobler in the mind to suffer
```

If you wanted to replace both instances of "be" with "exist," you could do it in this case by specifying

```
var regexp = /be/
soliloquy.replace(regexp, "exist")
```

But you can't always be assured that the letters "b" and "e" will be standing alone as a word. What happens if the main string contains the word "being" or "saber"? The above example would replace the "be" letters in them as well.

The regular expression help comes from the special characters to better define what to search for. In the example here, the search is for the word "be." Therefore, the regular expression should surround the search text with word boundaries (the \b special character), as in

```
var regexp = /\bbe\b/
soliloquy.replace(regexp, "exist")
```

This syntax also takes care of the fact that the first two "be" words are followed by punctuation, rather than a space, as you might expect for a free-standing word. For more about regular expression syntax, see Chapter 30.

Example

The page in Listing 26-4 lets you practice with the string.replace() and string.search() methods and regular expressions in a protected environment. The source text is a five-line excerpt from *Hamlet*. You can enter the regular expression to search for as well as the replacement text. Note that the script completes the job of creating the regular expression object, so you can focus on the other special characters used to define the matching string.

Default values in the fields replace the contraction 'tis with it is when you click the Execute Replace() button. As described in the section on the string.search() method, the button connected to that method returns the offset character number of the matching string (or -1 if no match occurs).

Listing 26-4: **Lab for string.replace() and string.search()**

```
<HTML>
<HEAD>
<TITLE>Regular Expression Replace and Search</TITLE>
<SCRIPT LANGUAGE="JavaScript">
var mainString = "To be, or not to be: that is the question:\n"
mainString += "Whether 'tis nobler in the mind to suffer\n"
mainString += "The slings and arrows of outrageous fortune,\n"
mainString += "Or to take arms against a sea of troubles,\n"
mainString += "And by opposing end them."

function doReplace(form) {
        var replaceStr = form.replaceEntry.value
        var delim = (form.caseSens.checked) ? "/g" : "/gi"
        var regexp = eval("/" + form.regexp.value + delim)
        form.result.value = mainString.replace(regexp, replaceStr)
}
function doSearch(form) {
        var replaceStr = form.replaceEntry.value
        var delim = (form.caseSens.checked) ? "/g" : "/gi"
        var regexp = eval("/" + form.regexp.value + delim)
        form.result.value = mainString.search(regexp)
}
```

```
</SCRIPT>
</HEAD>
<BODY>
<B>String Replace and Search with Regular Expressions</B>
<HR>
Text used for string.replace() and string.search() methods:<BR>
<B>To be, or not to be: that is the question:<BR>
Whether 'tis nobler in the mind to suffer<BR>
The slings and arrows of outrageous fortune,<BR>
Or to take arms against a sea of troubles,<BR>
And by opposing end them.</B>

<FORM>
Enter a regular expression to match:<INPUT TYPE="text" NAME="regexp"
SIZE=25 VALUE="\B't">
<INPUT TYPE="checkbox" NAME="caseSens">Case-sensitive<BR>
Enter a string to replace the matching strings:<INPUT TYPE="text"
NAME="replaceEntry" SIZE=30 VALUE="it "><P>
<INPUT TYPE="button" VALUE="Execute Replace()"
onClick="doReplace(this.form)">
<INPUT TYPE="reset">
<INPUT TYPE="button" VALUE="Execute Search()"
onClick="doSearch(this.form)"><P>
Result:<BR>
<TEXTAREA NAME="result" COLS=60 ROWS=5 WRAP="virtual"></TEXTAREA>
</FORM>
</BODY>
</HTML>
```

Related Items: `string.match()` method; regular expression object.

string`.search(`*regExpression*`)`

Returns: Offset Integer.

	Nav2	Nav3	Nav4	IE3/J1	IE3/J2	IE4/J3
Compatibility			✔			✔

The results of the `string.search()` method should remind you of the `string.indexOf()` method. In both cases, the returned value is the character number where the matching string first appears in the main string, or -1 if no match occurs. The big difference, of course, is that the matching string for `string.search()` is a regular expression.

Example

Listing 26-4, in the preceding section, provides a laboratory to experiment with the `string.search()` method.

Related Items: `string.match()` method; regular expression object.

string.slice(*startIndex* [, *endIndex*])

Returns: String.

	Nav2	Nav3	Nav4	IE3/J1	IE3/J2	IE4/J3
Compatibility			✔			✔

The string.slice() method (new in Navigator 4) resembles the method string.substring() in that both let you extract a portion of one string and create a new string as a result (without modifying the original string). A helpful improvement in string.slice(), however, is that it is easier to specify an ending index value relative to the end of the main string.

Using string.substring() to extract a substring that ends before the end of the string requires machinations such as this:

```
string.substring(4, (string.length-2))
```

Instead, you can assign a negative number to the second parameter of string.slice() to indicate an offset from the end of the string:

```
string.slice(4, -2)
```

The second parameter is optional. If you omit it, the returned value is a string from the starting offset to the end of the main string.

Note   In Windows 95, you receive an "out of memory" error if you assign a positive integer to the second parameter that is smaller than the first parameter integer. This is a bug.

Example

With Listing 26-5, you can try several combinations of parameters with the string.slice() method (see Figure 26-1). A base string is provided (along with character measurements). Select from the different choices available for parameters, and study the outcome of the slice.

Listing 26-5: **Slicing a String**

```
<HTML>
<HEAD>
<TITLE>String Slicing and Dicing, Part I</TITLE>
<SCRIPT LANGUAGE="JavaScript">
var mainString = "Electroencephalograph"
function showResults() {
        var form = document.forms[0]
        var param1 =
parseInt(form.param1.options[form.param1.selectedIndex].value)
        var param2 =
parseInt(form.param2.options[form.param2.selectedIndex].value)
```

```
                    if (!param2) {
                        form.result1.value = mainString.slice(param1)
                    } else {
                        form.result1.value = mainString.slice(param1, param2)
                    }
    }
    </SCRIPT>
    </HEAD>
    <BODY onLoad="showResults()">
    <B>String slice() Method</B>
    <HR>
    Text used for the methods:<BR>
    <FONT SIZE=+1><TT><B>Electroencephalograph<BR>
    ----5----5----5----5-</B></TT></FONT>
    <TABLE BORDER=1>
    <FORM>
    <TR><TH>String Method</TH><TH>Method
    Parameters</TH><TH>Results</TH></TR>
    <TR>
    <TD>string.slice()</TD><TD ROWSPAN=3 VALIGN=middle>
    ( <SELECT NAME="param1" onChange="showResults()">
            <OPTION VALUE=0>0
            <OPTION VALUE=1>1
            <OPTION VALUE=2>2
            <OPTION VALUE=3>3
            <OPTION VALUE=5>5
    </SELECT>,
    <SELECT NAME="param2" onChange="showResults()">
            <OPTION >(None)
            <OPTION VALUE=5>5
            <OPTION VALUE=10>10
            <OPTION VALUE=-1>-1
            <OPTION VALUE=-5>-5
            <OPTION VALUE=-10>-10
    </SELECT> ) </TD>
    <TD><INPUT TYPE="text" NAME="result1" SIZE=25></TD>
    </TR>
    </TABLE>
    </FORM>
    </BODY>
    </HTML>
```

Related Items: string.substr() **method;** string.substring() **method.**

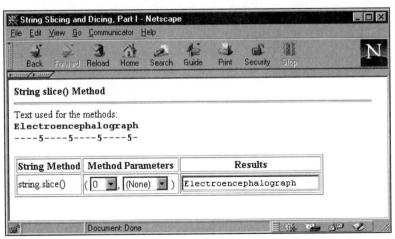

Figure 26-1: Lab for exploring the string.slice() method

string.split("delimiterCharacter" [, limitInteger])

Returns: Array of delimited items.

	Nav2	Nav3	Nav4	IE3/J1	IE3/J2	IE4/J3
Compatibility		✔	✔			✔

The split() method is the functional opposite of the array.join() method (see Chapter 29). From the string object point of view, JavaScript splits a long string into pieces delimited by a specific character and then creates a dense array with those pieces. You do not need to initialize the array via the new Array() constructor. Given the powers of array object methods such as array.sort(), you may want to convert a series of string items to an array to take advantage of those powers. Also, if your goal is to divide a string into an array of single characters, you can still use the split() method, but specify an empty string as a parameter. For Navigator 3 and Internet Explorer 4, only the first parameter is observed.

Navigator 4 loads additional functionality onto the string.split() method. For one, you can use a regular expression object for the first parameter, enhancing the powers of finding delimiters in strings. For example, consider the following string:

```
var nameList = "1.Fred,2.Jane,3.Steve"
```

To convert that string into a three-element array of only the names would take a lot of parsing without regular expressions before you could even use string.split(). However, with a regular expression as a parameter,

```
var regexp = /,*\d.\b/
var newArray = nameList.split(regexp)
      // result = an array "Fred", "Jane", "Steve"
```

the new array entries hold only the names and not the leading numbers or periods. A second addition is an optional second parameter. This integer value allows you to specify a limit to the number of array elements generated by the method.

And finally, if you use the `string.split()` method inside a `<SCRIPT LANGUAGE="JavaScript1.2">` tag, an empty space as a single parameter, such as `string.split(" ")`, is interpreted to mean any white space (spaces, tabs, carriage returns, line feeds) between runs of characters. Even if the number of spaces between elements is not uniform, they are treated all the same.

Examples

```
var myString = "Anderson,Smith,Johnson,Washington"
var myArray = myString.split(",")
var itemCount = myArray.length  // result: 4
```

Related Items: `Array.join()`.

string.substr(*start* [, *length*])

Returns: Nothing.

	Nav2	Nav3	Nav4	IE3/J1	IE3/J2	IE4/J3
Compatibility			✔			✔

Navigator 4's new `string.substr()` method offers a variation of the `string.substring()` method that has been in the language since the beginning. The distinction is that the `string.substr()` method's parameters specify the starting index and a number of characters to be included from that start point. In contrast, the `string.substring()` method parameters specify index points for the start and end characters within the main string.

As with all string methods requiring an index value, the `string.substr()` first parameter is zero-based. If you do not specify a second parameter, the returned substring starts at the indexed point and extends to the end of the string. A second parameter value that exceeds the end point of the string means that the method returns a substring to the end of the string.

Note

Macintosh users should avoid setting the second parameter to a negative number, to prevent a crash.

Example

Listing 26-6 lets you experiment with a variety of values to see how the `string.substr()` method works.

Listing 26-6: **Extracting from a String**

```
<HTML>
<HEAD>
<TITLE>String Slicing and Dicing, Part II</TITLE>
<SCRIPT LANGUAGE="JavaScript">
var mainString = "Electroencephalograph"
function showResults() {
        var form = document.forms[0]
        var param1 =
parseInt(form.param1.options[form.param1.selectedIndex].value)
        var param2 =
parseInt(form.param2.options[form.param2.selectedIndex].value)
        if (!param2) {
            form.result1.value = mainString.substr(param1)
        } else {
            form.result1.value = mainString.substr(param1, param2)
        }
}
</SCRIPT>
</HEAD>
<BODY onLoad="showResults()">
<B>String substr() Method</B>
<HR>
Text used for the methods:<BR>
<FONT SIZE=+1><TT><B>Electroencephalograph<BR>
----5----5----5----5-</B></TT></FONT>
<TABLE BORDER=1>
<FORM>
<TR><TH>String Method</TH><TH>Method
Parameters</TH><TH>Results</TH></TR>
<TR>
<TD>string.substr()</TD><TD ROWSPAN=3 VALIGN=middle>
( <SELECT NAME="param1" onChange="showResults()">
        <OPTION VALUE=0>0
        <OPTION VALUE=1>1
        <OPTION VALUE=2>2
        <OPTION VALUE=3>3
        <OPTION VALUE=5>5
</SELECT>,
<SELECT NAME="param2" onChange="showResults()">
        <OPTION >(None)
        <OPTION VALUE=5>5
        <OPTION VALUE=10>10
        <OPTION VALUE=20>20
</SELECT> ) </TD>
<TD><INPUT TYPE="text" NAME="result1" SIZE=25></TD>
</TR>
</TABLE>
</FORM>
</BODY>
</HTML>
```

Related Items: `string.substring()` method.

string.`substring(`*indexA, indexB*`)`

Returns: Characters of *string* between index values *indexA* and *indexB*.

	Nav2	Nav3	Nav4	IE3/J1	IE3/J2	IE4/J3
Compatibility	✔	✔	✔	✔	✔	✔

The `string.substring()` method enables your scripts to extract a contiguous range of characters from any string. The parameters to this method are the starting and ending index values (first character of the string object is index value 0) of the main string from which the excerpt should be taken. An important item to note is that the excerpt goes up to, *but does not include*, the character pointed to by the higher index value.

It makes no difference which index value in the parameters is larger than the other: The method starts the excerpt from the lowest value and continues to (but does not include) the highest value. If both index values are the same, the method returns an empty string; and if you omit the second parameter, the end of the string is assumed to be the endpoint.

Behavior of this method in Navigator 2 and 3 called for parameter values that were switched around (that is, the second value was smaller than the first) to be automatically reversed by JavaScript. If you use this method in a `<SCRIPT LANGUAGE="JavaScript1.2">` tag, the values are not automatically switched.

Example

Listing 26-7 lets you experiment with a variety of values to see how the `string.substring()` method works. If you are using Navigator 4, try changing the LANGUAGE attribute of the script to `JavaScript1.2` and see the different behavior when you set the parameters to 5 and 3. The parameters switch themselves, essentially letting the second index value become the beginning of the extracted substring.

Listing 26-7: **Extracting from a String**

```
<HTML>
<HEAD>
<TITLE>String Slicing and Dicing, Part II</TITLE>
<SCRIPT LANGUAGE="JavaScript">
var mainString = "Electroencephalograph"
function showResults() {
        var form = document.forms[0]
        var param1 =
parseInt(form.param1.options[form.param1.selectedIndex].value)
        var param2 =
parseInt(form.param2.options[form.param2.selectedIndex].value)
```

(continued)

Listing 26-7 *(continued)*

```
            if (!param2) {
                form.result1.value = mainString.substring(param1)
            } else {
                form.result1.value = mainString.substring(param1, param2)
            }
}
</SCRIPT>
</HEAD>
<BODY onLoad="showResults()">
<B>String substr() Method</B>
<HR>
Text used for the methods:<BR>
<FONT SIZE=+1><TT><B>Electroencephalograph<BR>
----5----5----5----5-</B></TT></FONT>
<TABLE BORDER=1>
<FORM>
<TR><TH>String Method</TH><TH>Method
Parameters</TH><TH>Results</TH></TR>
<TR>
<TD>string.substring()</TD><TD>
( <SELECT NAME="param1" onChange="showResults()">
        <OPTION VALUE=0>0
        <OPTION VALUE=1>1
        <OPTION VALUE=2>2
        <OPTION VALUE=3>3
        <OPTION VALUE=5>5
</SELECT>,
<SELECT NAME="param2" onChange="showResults()">
        <OPTION >(None)
        <OPTION VALUE=3>3
        <OPTION VALUE=5>5
        <OPTION VALUE=10>10
</SELECT> ) </TD>
<TD><INPUT TYPE="text" NAME="result1" SIZE=25></TD>
</TR>
</TABLE></FORM>
</BODY>
</HTML>
```

Related Items: `string.substr()` method; `string.slice()` method.

string.toLowerCase()
string.toUpperCase()

Returns: The string in all lower- or uppercase, depending on which method you invoke.

	Nav2	Nav3	Nav4	IE3/J1	IE3/J2	IE4/J3
Compatibility	✔	✔	✔	✔	✔	✔

A great deal of what takes place on the Internet (and in JavaScript) is case-sensitive. URLs on some servers, for instance, are case-sensitive for directory names and filenames. These two methods, the simplest of the string methods, convert any string to either all lowercase or all uppercase. Any mixed-case strings get converted to a uniform case. If you want to compare user input from a field against some coded string without worrying about matching case, you should convert both strings to the same case for the comparison.

Examples

```
newString = "HTTP://www.Netscape.COM".toLowerCase()
        // result = "http://www.netscape.com"

if (guess.toUpperCase() == answer.toUpperCase()) {...
        // comparing strings without case sensitivity
```

Related Items: None.

String utility functions

Figuring out how to apply the various string object methods to a string manipulation challenge is not always an easy task, especially if you need backward compatibility to older scriptable browsers. I also find it difficult to anticipate every possible way you may need to massage strings in your scripts. But to help you get started, Listing 26-8 contains a library of string functions for inserting, deleting, and replacing chunks of text in a string. If your audience uses browsers capable of including external .js library files, that would be an excellent way to make these functions available to your scripts.

Listing 26-8: **Utility String Handlers**

```
// extract front part of string prior to searchString
function getFront(mainStr,searchStr){
        foundOffset = mainStr.indexOf(searchStr)
        if (foundOffset == -1) {
            return null
        }
        return mainStr.substring(0,foundOffset)
}

// extract back end of string after searchString
function getEnd(mainStr,searchStr) {
        foundOffset = mainStr.indexOf(searchStr)
        if (foundOffset == -1) {
            return null
        }
```

(continued)

Listing 26-8 *(continued)*

```
        return
mainStr.substring(foundOffset+searchStr.length,mainStr.length)
}

// insert insertString immediately before searchString
function insertString(mainStr,searchStr,insertStr) {
        var front = getFront(mainStr,searchStr)
        var end = getEnd(mainStr,searchStr)
        if (front != null && end != null) {
            return front + insertStr + searchStr + end
        }
        return null
}

// remove deleteString
function deleteString(mainStr,deleteStr) {
        return replaceString(mainStr,deleteStr,"")
}

// replace searchString with replaceString
function replaceString(mainStr,searchStr,replaceStr) {
        var front = getFront(mainStr,searchStr)
        var end = getEnd(mainStr,searchStr)
        if (front != null && end != null) {
            return front + replaceStr + end
        }
        return null
}
```

The first two functions extract the front or end components of strings as needed for some of the other functions in this suite. The final three functions are the core of these string-handling functions. If you plan to use these functions in your scripts, be sure to notice the dependence that some functions have on others. Including all five functions as a group ensures that they work as designed.

Formatting methods

Now we come to the other group of string object methods, which ease the process of creating the numerous string display characteristics when you use JavaScript to assemble HTML code. The following is a list of these methods:

```
string.anchor("anchorName")         string.link(locationOrURL)
string.blink()                      string.big()
string.bold()                       string.small()
string.fixed()                      string.strike()
string.fontcolor (colorValue)       string.sub()
string.fontsize(integer1to7)        string.sup()
string.italics()
```

Let's first examine the methods that don't require any parameters. You probably see a pattern: All of these methods are font-style attributes that have settings of on or off. To turn on these attributes in an HTML document, you surround the text in the appropriate tag pairs, such as `<B>. . .</B>` for boldface text. These methods take the string object, attach those tags, and return the resulting text, which is ready to be put into any HTML that your scripts are building. Therefore, the expression

```
"Good morning!".bold()
```

evaluates to

```
<B>Good morning!</B>
```

Of course, nothing is preventing you from building your HTML by embedding real tags instead of by calling the string methods. The choice is up to you. One advantage to the string methods is that they never forget the ending tag of a tag pair. Listing 26-9 shows an example of incorporating a few simple string methods in a string variable that is eventually written to the page as it loads. Internet Explorer does not support the `<BLINK>` tag, and therefore ignores the `string.blink()` method.

Listing 26-9: **Using Simple String Methods**

```
<HTML>
<HEAD>
<TITLE>HTML by JavaScript</TITLE>
</HEAD>

<BODY>
<SCRIPT LANGUAGE="JavaScript">
var page = ""
page += "JavaScript can create HTML on the fly.<P>Numerous string
object methods facilitate creating text that is " + "boldfaced".bold()
+ ", " + "italicized".italics() + ", or even the terribly annoying " +
"blinking text".blink() + "."
document.write(page)
</SCRIPT>
</BODY>
</HTML>
```

Of the remaining string methods, two more (`string.fontsize()` and `string.fontcolor()`) also affect the font characteristics of strings displayed in the HTML page. The parameters for these items are pretty straightforward—an integer between 1 and 7 corresponding to the seven browser font sizes and a color value (as either a hexadecimal triplet or color constant name) for the designated text. Listing 26-10 adds a line of text to the string of Listing 26-9. This line of text not only adjusts the font size of some parts of the string, but also nests multiple attributes inside one another to set the color of one word in a large-font-size string. Because these string methods do not change the content of the string, you can safely nest methods here.

Listing 26-10: Nested String Methods

```
<HTML>
<HEAD>
<TITLE>HTML by JavaScript</TITLE>
</HEAD>

<BODY>
<SCRIPT LANGUAGE="JavaScript">
var page = ""
page += "JavaScript can create HTML on the fly.<P>Numerous string
object methods facilitate creating text that is " + "boldfaced".bold()
+ ", " + "italicized".italics() + ", or even the terribly annoying " +
"blinking text".blink() + ".<P>"
page += "We can make " + "some words big".fontsize(5) + " and some
words both " + ("big and " + "colorful".fontcolor('coral')).fontsize(5)
+ " at the same time."
document.write(page)
</SCRIPT>
</BODY>
</HTML>
```

The final two string methods let you create an anchor and a link out of a string. The `string.anchor()` method uses its parameter to create a name for the anchor. Thus, the following expression

```
"Table of Contents".anchor("toc")
```

evaluates to

```
<A NAME="toc">Table of Contents</A>
```

In a similar fashion, the `string.link()` method expects a valid location or URL as its parameter, creating a genuine HTML link out of the string:

```
"Back to Home".link("index.html")
```

This evaluates to the following:

```
<A HREF="index.html">Back to Home</A>
```

Again, the choice of whether you use string methods to build HTML anchors and links over assembling the actual HTML is up to you. The methods may be a bit easier to work with if the values for the string and the parameters are variables whose content may change based on user input elsewhere in your Web site.

URL String Encoding and Decoding

When browsers and servers communicate, some nonalphanumeric characters that we take for granted (such as a space) cannot make the journey in their native form. Only a narrower set of letters, numbers, and punctuation is allowed. To accommodate the rest, the characters must be encoded with a special symbol (%)

and their hexadecimal ASCII values. For example, the space character is hex 20 (ASCII decimal 32). When encoded, it looks like %20. You may have seen this symbol in browser history lists or URLs.

JavaScript includes two functions, escape() and unescape(), that offer instant conversion of whole strings. To convert a plain string to one with these escape codes, use the escape function, as in

```
escape("Howdy Pardner") // result = "Howdy%20Pardner"
```

The unescape() function converts the escape codes into human-readable form.

✦   ✦   ✦

Math, Number, and Boolean Objects

♦ ♦ ♦ ♦

In This Chapter

Advanced math operations

Number base conversions

Working with integers and floating-point numbers

♦ ♦ ♦ ♦

The introduction to data types and values in Chapter 6's tutorial scratched the surface of JavaScript's numeric and Boolean powers. In this chapter, you look more closely at JavaScript's way of working with numbers and Boolean data.

Math often frightens away budding programmers, but as you've probably seen so far in this book, you don't really have to be a math genius to program in JavaScript. The powers described in this chapter are here when you need them — if you need them. So if math was not your strong suit in school, don't freak out over the terminology here.

An important point to remember about the objects described in this chapter is that like string values and string objects, numbers and Booleans are both values and objects. Fortunately for script writers, the differentiation is rarely, if ever, a factor unless you get into some very sophisticated programming. To those who actually write the JavaScript interpreters inside the browsers we use, the distinctions are vital. As the language evolves, its behavior is increasingly formalized to a point at which the core language attributes (of which strings and numbers are a part) have been documented and published as an industry standard (ECMA-262). That standard serves as a guideline for all organizations that build JavaScript interpreters into their products. These folks, in turn, make the scripter's life easier by generally allowing us to treat a number or Boolean as a value or object as we please.

For most scripters, the information about numeric data types and conversions as well as the Math object are important to know. Other details in this chapter about the number and Boolean objects are presented primarily for completeness, since their direct powers are almost never used in day-to-day scripting of Web applications.

Numbers in JavaScript

More powerful programming languages have many different kinds of numbers, each related to the amount of memory they occupy in the computer. Managing all these different types may be fun for some, but it gets in the way of quick scripting. A JavaScript number has only two possibilities. It can be an integer or a floating-point value. An *integer* is any whole number within a humongous range that does not have any fractional part. Integers never contain a decimal point in their representation. *Floating-point numbers* in JavaScript spread across the same range, but they are represented with a decimal point and some fractional value. If you are an experienced programmer, refer to the discussion about the number object later in this chapter to see how the JavaScript number type lines up with numeric data types you use in other programming environments.

Integers and floating-point numbers

Deep inside a computer, the microprocessor has an easier time performing math on integer values as compared to any number with a decimal value tacked on it, which requires the microprocessor to go through extra work to add even two such floating-point numbers. We, as scripters, are unfortunately saddled with this historical baggage and must therefore be conscious of the type of number used in certain calculations.

Most internal values generated by JavaScript, such as index values and length properties, consist of integers. Floating-point numbers usually come into play as the result of the division of numeric values, special values such as pi, and human-entered values such as dollars and cents. Fortunately, JavaScript is forgiving if you try to perform math operations on mixed numeric data types. Notice how the following examples resolve to the appropriate data type:

```
3 + 4 = 7 // integer result
3 + 4.1 = 7.1 // floating-point result
3.9 + 4.1 = 8 // integer result
```

Of the three examples, perhaps only the last result may be unexpected. When two floating-point numbers yield a whole number, the result is rendered as an integer.

When dealing with floating-point numbers, be aware that not all browser versions return the precise same value down to the last digit to the right of the decimal. For example, the following listing shows the result of 8/9 as calculated by numerous scriptable browsers (all Windows 95) and converted for string display:

Navigator 2	0.88888888888888884
Navigator 3	.8888888888888888
Navigator 4	.8888888888888888
Internet Explorer 3	0.888888888888889
Internet Explorer 4	0.8888888888888888

It is clear from this display that you don't want to use floating-point math in JavaScript browsers to plan spaceflight trajectories. But it also means that for everyday math, you need to be cognizant of floating-point errors that accrue in PC arithmetic.

In Navigator, JavaScript relies on the operating system's floating-point math for its own math. Operating systems that offer accuracy to as many places to the right of the decimal as JavaScript displays are exceedingly rare. As you can detect from the preceding table, the more modern versions of browsers from Netscape and Microsoft are in agreement about how many digits to display and how to perform internal rounding for this display. That's good for the math, but not particularly helpful when you need to display numbers in a specific format.

JavaScript does not currently offer any built-in facilities for formatting the results of floating-point arithmetic. Listing 27-1 demonstrates a generic formatting routine for positive values, plus a specific call that turns a value into a dollar value. Remove the comments, and the routine is fairly compact.

Listing 27-1: **A Generic Number Formatting Routine**

```
<HTML>
<HEAD>
<TITLE>Number Formatting</TITLE>
<SCRIPT LANGUAGE="JavaScript">
// generic positive number decimal formatting function
function format (expr, decplaces) {
      // raise incoming value by power of 10 times the
      // number of decimal places; round to an integer; convert to
string
      var str = "" + Math.round (eval(expr) * Math.pow(10,decplaces))
      // pad small value strings with zeros to the left of rounded
number
      while (str.length <= decplaces) {
          str = "0" + str
      }
      // establish location of decimal point
      var decpoint = str.length - decplaces
      // assemble final result from: (a) the string up to the position of
      // the decimal point; (b) the decimal point; and (c) the balance
      // of the string. Return finished product.
      return str.substring(0,decpoint) + "." +
str.substring(decpoint,str.length);
}
// turn incoming expression into a dollar value
function dollarize (expr) {
      return "$" + format(expr,2)
}
</SCRIPT>
</HEAD>
<BODY>
<H1>How to Make Money</H1>
<FORM>
```

(continued)

Listing 27-1 *(continued)*

```
Enter a positive floating point value or arithmetic expression to be
converted to a currency format:<P>
<INPUT TYPE="text" NAME="entry" VALUE="1/3">
<INPUT TYPE="button" VALUE=">Dollars and Cents>"
onClick="this.form.result.value=dollarize(this.form.entry.value)">
<INPUT TYPE="text" NAME="result">
</FORM>
</BODY>
</HTML>
```

This routine may seem like a great deal of work, but it's essential if your script relies on floating-point values and specific formatting.

Floating-point numbers can also be entered with exponents. An exponent is signified by the letter "e" (upper- or lowercase), followed by a sign (+ or -) and the exponent value. Here are examples of floating-point values expressed as exponents:

```
1e6 // 1,000,000 (the "+" symbol is optional on positive exponents)
1e-4 // 0.0001 (plus some error further to the right of the decimal)
-4e-3 // -0.004
```

For values between 1e-5 and 1e15, JavaScript renders numbers without exponents. All other values outside these bounds come back with exponential notation.

Hexadecimal and octal integers

JavaScript allows you to work with values in decimal (base-10), hexadecimal (base-16), and octal (base-8) formats. You only have a few rules to follow when dealing with any of these values.

Decimal values cannot begin with a leading 0. Therefore, if your page asks users to enter decimal values that may begin with a 0, your script must strip those zeroes from the input string or use the number parsing global functions (described in the next section) before performing any math on the values.

Hexadecimal integer values are expressed with a leading "0x" or "0X". That's a zero, not the letter "o". The A through F values can appear in upper- or lowercase, as you prefer. Here are some hex values:

```
0X2B
0X1a
0xcc
```

Don't confuse the hex values used in arithmetic with the hexadecimal values used in color property specifications for Web documents. Those values are expressed in a special *hexadecimal triplet* format, which begins with a crosshatch symbol followed by the three hex values bunched together (such as #c0c0c0).

Octal values are represented by a leading 0 followed by any digits between 0 and 7. Octal values consist only of integers.

You are free to mix and match base values in arithmetic expressions, but JavaScript renders all results in decimal form. For conversions to other number bases, you have to use a user-defined function in your script. Listing 27-2, for example, is a function that converts any decimal value from 0 to 255 into a JavaScript hexadecimal value.

Listing 27-2: **Decimal-to-Hexadecimal Converter Function**

```
function toHex(dec) {
        hexChars = "0123456789ABCDEF"
        if (dec > 255) {
            return null
        }
        var i = dec % 16
        var j = (dec - i) / 16
        result = "0X"
        result += hexChars.charAt(j)
        result += hexChars.charAt(i)
        return result
}
```

The toHex() conversion function assumes that the value passed to the function is a decimal integer.

Converting strings to numbers

What has been missing so far from this discussion is a way to convert a number represented as a string to a number with which the JavaScript arithmetic operators can work. Before you get too concerned about this, be aware that most JavaScript operators and math methods gladly accept string representations of numbers and handle them without complaint. You will run into the data type incompatibilities most frequently when you are trying to accomplish addition with the + operator, but a string representation gets in the way. Also be aware that if you are performing math operations on values extracted from form text boxes, those object value properties are strings. Therefore, in many cases, those values need to be converted to values of the number type for math operations.

Conversion to numbers requires one of two JavaScript functions:

```
parseInt(string [,radix])
parseFloat(string  [,radix])
```

These functions were inspired by the Java language and are used here for compatibility reasons. The term *parsing* has many implied meanings in programming. One meaning is the same as *extracting*. The parseInt() function returns whatever integer value it can extract from the string passed to it; the parseFloat() function returns the floating-point number that can be extracted from the string. Here are some examples and their resulting values:

```
parseInt("42")           // result = 42
parseInt("42.33")        // result = 42
```

```
parseFloat("42.33")     // result = 42.33
parseFloat("42")        // result = 42
parseFloat("fred")      // result = NaN
```

Because the parseFloat() function can also work with an integer and return an integer value, you may prefer using this function in scripts that have to deal with either kind of number, depending on the string entered into a text field by a user.

An optional second parameter to both functions lets you specify the base of the number represented by the string. This comes in particularly handy when you need a decimal number from a string that starts with one or more zeros. Normally the leading zero indicates an octal value. But if you force the conversion to recognize the string value as a decimal, it is converted the way you'd expect:

```
parseInt("010")    // result = 8
parseInt("010",10)       // result = 10
parseInt("F2")    // result = NaN
parseInt("F2", 16)       // result = 242
```

Use these functions wherever you need the integer or floating-point value. For example

```
var result = 3 + parseInt("3")  // result = 6
var ageVal = parseInt(document.forms[0].age.value)
```

The latter technique ensures that the string value of this property is converted to a number (although I'd probably do more data validation — see Chapter 37 — before trying any math on a user-entered value).

Converting numbers to strings

If you attempt to pass a numeric data type value to many of the string methods discussed in Chapter 26, JavaScript complains. Therefore, you should convert any number to a string before you can, for example, find out how many digits make up a number.

You have two ways to force conversion from any numeric value to a string. The old-fashioned way is to precede the number with an empty string and the concatenation operator. For example, assume that a variable named dollars contains the integer value of 2500. To use the string object's length property (discussed later in this chapter) to find out how many digits the number is, use this construction:

```
("" + dollars).length // result = 4
```

The parentheses force JavaScript to evaluate the concatenation before attempting to extract the length property.

A more elegant way is to use the toString() method. Construct such statements as you would to invoke any object's method. For example, to convert the dollars variable value, shown earlier, to a string, the statement is

```
dollars.toString()       // result = "2500"
```

This method has one added power (new from Navigator 3): You can specify a number base for the string representation of the number. Called the *radix,* the base number is added as a parameter to the method name. Here is an example of creating a numeric value for conversion to its hexadecimal equivalent as a string:

```
var x = 30
var y = x.toString(16)   // result = "1e"
```

Use a parameter of 2 for binary results; 8 for octal. The default is base 10. Be careful not to confuse these conversions with true numeric conversions. Results from the toString() method cannot be used as numeric operands in other statements.

When a number isn't a number

In a couple of examples in the previous section, you probably noticed that the result of some operations was a value named NaN. That value is not a string, but rather a special value that stands for Not a Number. For example, if you try to convert a string "joe" to an integer with parseFloat(), the function cannot possibly complete the operation. It reports back that the source string, when converted, is not a number.

When you design an application that requests user input or retrieves data from a server-side database, you frequently cannot be guaranteed that a value you need to be numeric is, or can be converted to, a number. If that's the case, you need a way to see if the value is a number before performing some math operation on it. JavaScript provides a special global function, isNaN(), that lets you test the "number-ness" of a value. The function returns true if the value is not a number and false if it is a number. For example, you can examine a form field that should be a number:

```
var ageEntry = parseInt(document.forms[0].age.value)
if (isNaN(ageEntry)) {
        alert("Try entering your age again.")
}
```

Note

NaN and isNaN() were implemented in Navigator 2 only on UNIX versions. By Navigator 3, the value and function were on all platforms. Neither item is part of Internet Explorer 3, but are both available in Internet Explorer 4.

Math Object

Whenever you need to perform math that is more demanding than simple arithmetic, look through the list of Math object methods for the solution.

Syntax

Accessing select object properties and methods:

```
Math.property
Math.method(value [, value])
```

About this object

In addition to the typical arithmetic operations (covered in detail in Chapter 32), JavaScript includes more advanced mathematical powers that are accessed in a way that may seem odd to you if you have not programmed in true object-oriented environments before. Although most arithmetic takes place on the fly (such as `var result = 2 + 2`), the rest requires use of the JavaScript internal Math object (that's with a capital "M"). The Math object brings with it several properties (which behave like some other languages' constants) and many methods (which behave like some other languages' math functions).

The way you use the Math object in statements is the same way you use any JavaScript object: You create a reference beginning with the Math object's name (`Math`), a period, and the name of the property or method you need:

```
Math.property | method([parameter]…[,parameter])
```

Property references return the built-in values (things such as pi); method references require one or more values to be sent as parameters of the method and then return the result of the method after it performs its operation on the parameter values.

Properties

JavaScript Math object properties represent a number of valuable constant values in math. Table 27-1 best shows you those methods and their values as displayed to 16 decimal places.

Table 27-1
JavaScript Math Properties

Property	Value	Description
Math.E	2.718281828459045091	Euler's constant
Math.LN2	0.6931471805599452862	Natural log of 2
Math.LN10	2.302585092994045901	Natural log of 10
Math.LOG2E	1.442695040888963387	Log base-2 of E
Math.LOG10E	0.4342944819032518167	Log base-10 of E
Math.PI	3.141592653589793116	p
Math.SQRT1_2	0.7071067811865475727	Square root of 0.5
Math.SQRT2	1.414213562373095145	Square root of 2

Because these property expressions return their constant values, you use them in your regular arithmetic expressions. For example, to obtain the circumference of a circle whose diameter is in variable d, you use this statement:

```
circumference = d * Math.PI
```

Perhaps the most common mistakes scripters make with these properties are failing to capitalize the `Math` object name or observing the case-sensitivity of property names.

Methods

Methods make up the balance of JavaScript Math object powers. With the exception of the `Math.random()` method, all Math object methods take one or more values as parameters. Typical trigonometric methods operate on the single values passed as parameters; others determine which of the numbers passed along are the highest or lowest of the group. The `Math.random()` method takes no parameters but returns a randomized, floating-point value between 0 and 1 (but note that the method does not work on Windows or Macintosh versions of Navigator 2). Table 27-2 lists all the Math object methods with their syntax and descriptions of the values they return.

Table 27-2 Math Object Methods	
Method Syntax	**Returns**
`Math.abs(val)`	Absolute value of *val*
`Math.acos(val)`	Arc cosine (in radians) of *val*
`Math.asin(val)`	Arc sine (in radians) of *val*
`Math.atan(val)`	Arc tangent (in radians) of *val*
`Math.atan2(val1, val2)`	Angle of polar coordinates *x* and *y*
`Math.ceil(val)`	Next integer greater than or equal to *val*
`Math.cos(val)`	Cosine of val
`Math.exp(val)`	Euler's constant to the power of *val*
`Math.floor(val)`	Next integer less than or equal to *val*
`Math.log(val)`	Natural logarithm (base e) of *val*
`Math.max(val1, val2)`	The greater of *val1* or *val2*
`Math.min(val1, val2)`	The lesser of *val1* or *val2*
`Math.pow(val1, val2)`	*Val1* to the *val2* power
`Math.random()`	Random number between 0 and 1
`Math.round(val)`	N+1 when *val* >= n.5; otherwise N
`Math.sin(val)`	Sine (in radians) of *val*
`Math.sqrt(val)`	Square root of *val*
`Math.tan(val)`	Tangent (in radians) of *val*

HTML is not exactly a graphic artist's dream environment, so using trig functions to obtain a series of values for HTML-generated charting is not a hot JavaScript prospect. But in the future, as users communicate with Java applets that are better at graphical tasks, you may want to try JavaScript for some data generation using these advanced functions — sending the results to the Java applet for charting. For scripters who were not trained in programming, math is often a major stumbling block. But as you've seen so far, you can accomplish a great deal with JavaScript by using simple arithmetic and a little bit of logic, leaving the heavy-duty math for those who love it.

Creating random numbers

The `Math.random()` method returns a floating-point value between 0 and 1. If you are designing a script to act like a card game, you need random integers between 1 and 52; for dice, the range is 1 to 6 per die. To generate a random integer between zero and any top value, use the following formula:

```
Math.round(Math.random() * n)
```

where n is the top number. To generate random numbers between a different range use this formula:

```
Math.round(Math.random() * n) + m
```

where m is the lowest possible integer value of the range and n equals the top number of the range minus m. In other words n+m should add up to the highest number of the range you want. For the dice game, the formula for each die would be

```
newDieValue = Math.round(Math.random() * 5) + 1
```

Math object shortcut

In Chapter 31, I show you more details about a JavaScript construction that lets you simplify the way you address Math object properties and methods when you have a bunch of them in statements. The trick is using the `with` statement.

In a nutshell, the `with` statement tells JavaScript that the next group of statements (inside the braces) refer to a particular object. In the case of the Math object, the basic construction looks like this:

```
with (Math) {
        [statements]
}
```

For all intervening statements, you can omit the specific references to the Math object. Compare the long reference way of calculating the area of a circle (with a radius of six units)

```
result = Math.pow(6,2) * Math.PI
```

to the shortcut reference way:

```
with (Math) {
        result = pow(6,2) * PI
}
```

Though the latter occupies more lines of code, the object references are shorter and more natural when you're reading the code. For a longer series of calculations involving Math object properties and methods, the `with` construction saves keystrokes and reduces the likelihood of a case-sensitive mistake with the object name in a reference. You can also include other full-object references within the with construction; JavaScript attempts to attach the object name only to those references lacking an object name.

Number Object

Properties	Methods	Event Handler
MAX_VALUE	toString()	(None)
MIN_VALUE		
NaN		
NEGATIVE_INFINITY		
POSITIVE_INFINITY		
prototype		

Syntax

Creating a number object:

```
var val = new Number(number)
```

Accessing number object properties:

```
Number.property | method
```

	Nav2	Nav3	Nav4	IE3/J1	IE3/J2	IE4/J3
Compatibility	✔	✔			✔	✔

About this object

The number object is rarely used, because for the most part, JavaScript satisfies day-to-day numeric needs with a plain number value. But the number object contains some information and power of value to serious programmers.

First on the docket are properties that define the ranges for numbers in the language. The largest number (in both Navigator and Internet Explorer) is 1.79E+308; the smallest number is 2.22E-308. Any number larger than the maximum is POSITIVE_INFINITY; any number smaller than the minimum is NEGATIVE_INFINITY. It will be a rare day on which you accidentally encounter these values.

More to the point of a JavaScript object, however, is the prototype property. In Chapter 26, I show you how to add a method to a string object's prototype such that every newly created object contains that method. The same goes for the

Number.prototype property. If you have a need to add common functionality to every number object, this is where to do it. This prototype facility is unique to objects and does not apply to plain number values. For experienced programmers who care about such matters, JavaScript number objects and values are defined internally as IEEE double-precision 64-bit values.

Boolean Object

Property	Method	Event Handler
prototype	toString()	(None)

Syntax

Creating a Boolean object:

var val = new Boolean(*BooleanValue*)

Accessing Boolean object properties:

Boolean.*property* | *method*

	Nav2	Nav3	Nav4	IE3/J1	IE3/J2	IE4/J3
Compatibility		✔	✔		✔	✔

About this object

You work with Boolean values a lot in JavaScript — especially as the result of conditional tests. Just as string values benefit from association with string objects and their properties and methods, so, too, do Boolean values receive aid from the Boolean object. For example, when you display a Boolean value in a text box, the "true" or "false" string is provided by the Boolean object's toString() method, even though you don't have to invoke it directly.

The only time you need to even think about a Boolean object is if you wish to attach some property or method to Boolean objects that you create with the new Boolean() constructor. Parameter values for the constructor include the string versions of the values, numbers (0 for false; any other integer for true), and expressions that evaluate to a Boolean value. Any such new Boolean object would be imbued with the new properties or methods you have added to the prototype property of the core Boolean object.

✦   ✦   ✦

The Date Object

Perhaps the most untapped power of JavaScript is its date and time handling. Scripters passed over the Date object with good cause in the early days of JavaScript, because in earlier versions of scriptable browsers, significant bugs and platform-specific anomalies made date and time programming hazardous without significant testing. Even with the improved bug situation, working with dates requires a working knowledge of the world's time zones and their relationships with the standard reference point, Greenwich mean time (GMT).

Now that date- and time-handling has improved in the latest browsers, I hope more scripters look into incorporating these kinds of calculations into their pages. In the bonus applications on the CD-ROM, I show you an application that lets your Web site highlight the areas that have been updated since each visitor's last surf ride through your pages.

Before getting to the JavaScript part of date discussions, however, I summarize key facts about time zones and their impact on scripting date and time on a browser. If you're not sure what GMT and UTC mean, the following section is for you.

Time Zones and GMT

By international agreement, the world is divided into distinct time zones that allow the inhabitants of each zone to say with confidence that when the Sun appears directly overhead, it is roughly noon, squarely in the middle of the day. The current time in the zone is what we set our clocks to — the local time.

That's fine when your entire existence and scope of life go no further than the width of your own time zone. But with instant communication among all parts of the world, your scope reaches well beyond local time. Periodically you must be aware of the local time in other zones. After all, if you live in New York, you don't want to wake up someone in Los Angeles before dawn with a phone call from your office.

Note

From here on I speak of the Sun "moving" as if Earth were the center of the solar system. I do so for the convenience of our daily perception of the Sun arcing across what appears to us as a stationary sky. In point of fact, I believe Copernicus, so delete that e-mail you were about to send me.

From the point of view of the time zone over which the Sun is positioned at any given instant, all time zones to the east have already had their noon, so it is later in the day for them — one hour later per time zone (except for those few time zones offset by fractions of an hour). That's why when U.S. television networks broadcast simultaneously to the eastern and central time zones, the announced schedule for a program is "10 eastern, 9 central."

Many international businesses must coordinate time schedules of far-flung events. Doing so and taking into account the numerous time zone differences (not to mention seasonal national variations such as daylight saving time) would be a nightmare. To help everyone out, a standard reference point was devised: the time zone running through the celestial observatory at Greenwich, England (pronounced GREN-itch). This time zone is called Greenwich mean time, or GMT for short. The "mean" part comes from the fact that on the exact opposite side of the globe (through the Pacific Ocean) is the international date line, another world standard that decrees where the first instance of the next calendar day appears on the planet. Thus, GMT is located at the middle, or mean, of the full circuit of the day. Not that many years ago, GMT was given another abbreviation that is not based on any one language of the planet. The abbreviation is UTC (pronounced as its letters: yu-tee-see), and the English version is Coordinated Universal Time. Whenever you see UTC, it is for all practical purposes the same as GMT.

If your personal computer's system clock is set correctly, the machine ticks away in GMT time. But because you set your local time zone in the appropriate control panel, all file time stamps and clock displays are in your local time. The machine knows what the offset time is between your local time and GMT. For daylight saving time, you may have to check a preference setting so that the offset is adjusted accordingly; in Windows 95, the operating system knows when the changeover occurs and prompts you if it's OK to change the offset. In any case, if you travel across time zones with a laptop, you should change the computer's time zone setting, not its clock.

JavaScript's inner handling of date and time works a lot like the PC clock (on which your programs rely). Date values that you generate in a script are stored internally in GMT time; however, almost all the displays and extracted values are in the local time of the visitor (not the Web site server). And remember that the date values are created on the visitor's machine by virtue of your script generating that value — you don't send "living" Date objects to the client from the server. This is perhaps the most difficult concept to grasp as you work with JavaScript date and time.

Whenever you program time and date in JavaScript for a public Web page, you must take the world view. This requires knowing that the visitor's computer settings determine the accuracy of the conversion between GMT time and local time. It also means you'll have to do some testing by changing your PC's clock to times in other parts of the world and making believe you are temporarily in those remote locations. This isn't always easy to do. It reminds me of the time I was visiting Sydney, Australia. I was turning in for the night and switched on the television in the hotel. This hotel received a live satellite relay of a long-running U.S. television program, *Today*. The program broadcast from New York was for the morning of the same day I was just finishing in Sydney. Yes, this time zone stuff can make your head hurt.

The Date Object

Borrowing heavily from the Java world, JavaScript includes a Date object (with a capital "D") and a large collection of methods to help you extract parts of dates and times, as well as assign dates and times. Understanding the object model for dates is vital to successful scripting of such data.

JavaScript's defining of a Date object should clue in experienced scripters that they're dealing with far more than a bunch of functions that dish out data from their desktop computer's clock and let them transform the values into various formats for calculation and display. By referring to a Date object, JavaScript may mislead you into thinking that you work with just one such object. Not at all. Any time you want to perform calculations or display dates or times, you create a new Date object in the browser's memory. This object is associated only with the current page, just like the array objects described in Chapter 29.

Another important point about the creation of a Date object is that it is not a ticking clock. Instead it is a snapshot of an exact millisecond in time, whether it be for the instant at which you generate the object or for a specific time in the past or future you need for calculations. If you need to have a live clock ticking away, your scripts will repeatedly create new Date objects to grab up-to-the-millisecond snapshots of your computer's clock.

In the process of creating a Date object, you assign that object to a variable name (behind the scenes, the variable is really just a pointer to the spot in memory where the Date object's data is stored). In other words, that variable becomes the Date object for further manipulation in your scripts: The variable becomes part of the dot-syntax-style reference to all possible methods for dates (Date objects have no event handlers).

One important point to remember is that despite its name, every Date object contains information about date and time. Therefore, even if you're concerned only about the date part of an object's data, time data is standing by as well. As you learn in a bit, the time element can catch you off-guard for some operations.

Creating a Date object

The statement that asks JavaScript to make an object for your script includes the special object construction keyword `new`. The basic syntax for generating a new Date object is as follows:

```
var dateObjectName = new Date([parameters])
```

The Date object evaluates to an object rather than to some string or numeric value.

With the Date object's reference safely tucked away in the variable name, you access all date-oriented methods in the dot-syntax fashion with which you're already familiar:

```
var result = dateObjectName.method()
```

With variables such as `result`, your scripts perform calculations or displays of the Date object's data (some methods extract pieces of the date and time data from the object). If you then want to put some new value into the Date object (such as adding a year to the Date object), you assign the new value to the object by way of the method that lets you set the value:

```
dateObjectName.method(newValue)
```

This example doesn't look like the typical JavaScript assignment statement, which has an equals sign operator. But this statement is the way in which methods that set Date object data work.

You cannot get very far into scripting dates without digging into time zone arithmetic. Although JavaScript may render the string equivalent of a Date object in your local time zone, the internal storage is strictly GMT.

Even though I haven't yet introduced you to details of the Date object's methods, I use two of them to demonstrate adding one year to today's date.

```
oneDate = new Date() // creates object with current GMT date
theYear = oneDate.getYear() // theYear is now storing the value 98
theYear = theYear + 1 // theYear now is 99
oneDate.setYear(theYear) // new year value now in the object
```

At the end of this sequence, the `oneDate` object automatically adjusts all the other settings that it knows has today's date for the next year. The day of the week, for example, will be different, and JavaScript takes care of that for you, should you need to extract that data. With next year's data in the `oneDate` object, you may now want to extract that new date as a string value for display in a field on the page or submit it quietly to a CGI program on the server.

The issue of parameters for creating a new Date object is a bit complex, mostly because of the flexibility that JavaScript offers the scripter. Recall that the job of the `new Date()` statement is to create a place in memory for all data that a date needs to store. What is missing from that task is the data — what date and time to enter into that memory spot. That's where the parameters come in.

If you leave the parameters empty, JavaScript takes that to mean you want today's date and the current time to be assigned to that new Date object. JavaScript isn't any smarter, of course, than the setting of the internal clock of your page visitor's personal computer. If the clock isn't correct, JavaScript won't do any better of a job identifying the date and time.

Caution

Remember that when you create a new Date object, it contains the current time as well. The fact that the current date may include a time of 16:03:19 (in 24-hour time) may throw off things such as days-between-dates calculations. Be careful.

To create a Date object for a specific date or time, you have five ways to send values as a parameter to the `new Date()` constructor function:

```
new Date("Month dd, yyyy hh:mm:ss")
new Date("Month dd, yyyy")
new Date(yy,mm,dd,hh,mm,ss)
new Date(yy,mm,dd)

new Date(milliseconds)
```

These five schemes break down into two styles — a long string versus a comma-delimited list of data — each with optional time settings. If you omit time settings, they are set to 0 (midnight) in the Date object for whatever date you entered. You cannot omit date values from the parameters — every Date object must have a real date attached to it, whether you need it or not.

In the long string version, the month is spelled out in full in English. No abbreviations are allowed. The rest of the data is filled with numbers representing the date, year, hours, minutes, and seconds. For single-digit values, you can use either a one- or two-digit version (such as 4:05:00). Hours, minutes, and seconds are separated by colons.

The short version is strictly a nonquoted list of integer values in the order indicated. JavaScript cannot know that a 30 means the date when you accidentally place it in the month slot.

Date prototype property

Like a number of JavaScript objects, the Date object has a `prototype` property, which enables you to apply new properties and methods to every Date object created in the current page. You can see examples of how this works in discussions of the `prototype` property for string and array objects (Chapters 26 and 29, respectively).

Date methods

The bulk of a Date object's methods are for extracting parts of the date and time information and for changing the date and time stored in the object. These two sets of methods are easily identifiable because they all begin with the word "get" or "set." Table 28-1 lists all of the Date object's methods. Your initial focus will be on the first sixteen methods, which deal with components of the Date object's data.

Table 28-1
Date Object Methods

Method	Value Range	Description
dateObj.getTime()	0-…	Milliseconds since 1/1/70 00:00:00 GMT
dateObj.getYear()	70-…	Specified year minus 1900
dateObj.getMonth()	0-11	Month within the year (January = 0)
dateObj.getDate()	1-31	Date within the month
dateObj.getDay()	0-6	Day of week (Sunday = 0)
dateObj.getHours()	0-23	Hour of the day in 24-hour time
dateObj.getMinutes()	0-59	Minute of the specified hour
dateObj.getSeconds()	0-59	Second within the specified minute
dateObj.setTime(val)	0-…	Milliseconds since 1/1/70 00:00:00 GMT
dateObj.setYear(val)	70-…	Specified year minus 1900
dateObj.setMonth(val)	0-11	Month within the year (January = 0)

(continued)

Table 28-1 *(continued)*

Method	Value Range	Description
dateObj.setDate(*val*)	1-31	Date within the month
dateObj.setDay(*val*)	0-6	Day of week (Sunday = 0)
dateObj.setHours(*val*)	0-23	Hour of the day in 24-hour time
dateObj.setMinutes(*val*)	0-59	Minute of the specified hour
dateObj.setSeconds(*val*)	0-59	Second within the specified minute
dateObj.getTimezoneOffset()	0-...	Minutes offset from GMT/UTC
dateObj.toGMTString()		Date string in universal format
dateObj.toLocaleString()		Date string in your system's format
Date.parse("dateString")		Converts string date to milliseconds
Date.UTC(date values)		Generates a date value from GMT values

JavaScript maintains its date information in the form of a count of milliseconds (thousandths of a second) starting from January 1, 1970, in the GMT time zone. Dates before that starting point are stored as negative values (but see the section on bugs and gremlins later in this chapter). Regardless of the country you live in or the date and time formats specified for your computer, the millisecond is the JavaScript universal measure of time. Any calculations that involve adding or subtracting times and dates should be performed in the millisecond values to ensure accuracy. Therefore, though you may never display the milliseconds value in a field or dialog box, your scripts will probably work with them from time to time in variables. To derive the millisecond equivalent for any date and time stored in a Date object, use the dateObj.getTime() method, as in

```
startDate = new Date()
started = startDate.getTime()
```

Although the method has the word "time" in its name, the fact that the value is the total number of milliseconds from January 1, 1970, means the value also conveys a date.

Other Date object get methods extract a specific element of the object. You have to exercise some care here, because some values begin counting with 0 when you may not expect it. For example, January is month 0 in JavaScript's scheme; December is month 11. Hours, minutes, and seconds all begin with 0, which, in the end, is logical. Calendar dates, however, use the actual number that would show up on the wall calendar: The first day of the month is date value 1. For the twentieth century years, the year value is whatever the actual year number is, minus 1900. For 1996, that means the year value is 96. But for years before 1900 and after 1999, JavaScript uses a different formula, showing the full year value. This means you have to check whether a year value is less than 100 and add 1900 to it before displaying that year.

```
var today = new Date()
var thisYear = today.getYear()
if (thisYear < 100) {
        thisYear += 1900
}
```

This assumes, of course, you won't be working with years before A.D. 100. This could cause terrible confusion.

To adjust any one of the elements of a date value, use the corresponding set method in an assignment statement. If the new value forces the adjustment of other elements, JavaScript takes care of that. For example, consider the following sequence and how some values are changed for us:

```
myBirthday = new Date("September 11, 1996")
result = myBirthday.getDay() // result = 3, a Wednesday
myBirthday.setYear(97) // bump up to next year
result = myBirthday.getDay() // result = 4, a Thursday
```

Because the same date in the following year is on a different day, JavaScript tracks that for you.

Accommodating time zones

Understanding the dateObj.getTimezoneOffset() method involves both your operating system's time control panel setting and an internationally recognized (in computerdom, anyway) format for representing dates and times. If you have ignored the control panel stuff about setting your local time zone, the values you get for this property may be off for most dates and times. In the eastern part of North America, for instance, the eastern standard time zone is five hours earlier than Greenwich mean time. With the getTimezoneOffset() method producing a value of minutes' difference between GMT and the PC's time zone, the five hours difference of eastern standard time is rendered as a value of 300 minutes. On the Windows platform, the value automatically changes to reflect changes in daylight saving time in the user's area (if applicable). Offsets to the east of GMT (to the date line) are expressed as negative values.

Dates as strings

When you generate a Date object, JavaScript automatically applies the toString() method to the object if you attempt to display that date either in a page or alert box. The format of this string varies with browser and operating system platform. For example, in Navigator 4 for Windows 95, the string is in the following format:

```
Thu Aug 28 11:43:34 Pacific Daylight Time 1997
```

But in the same version for Macintosh, the string is

```
Thu Aug 28 11:43:34 1997
```

Internet Explorer tends to follow the latter format. The point is not to rely on a specific format and character location of this string for the components of dates. Use the Date object methods to extract Date object components.

JavaScript does, however, provide two methods that return the Date object in more constant string formats. One, `dateObj.toGMTString()`, converts the date and time to the GMT equivalent on the way to the variable you use to store the extracted data. Here is what such data looks like:

```
Wed, 07 Aug 1996 03:25:28 GMT
```

If you're not familiar with the workings of GMT and how such conversions can present unexpected dates, you should exercise great care in testing your application. Eight o'clock on a Friday evening in California in the winter is four o'clock on Saturday morning GMT.

If time zone conversions make your head hurt, you can use the second string method, `dateObj.toLocaleString()`. In Navigator 3 for North American Windows users, the returned value looks like this:

```
08/06/96 20:25:28
```

Friendly date formats

What neither of the two string conversion methods address, however, is a way for the scripter to easily extract string segments to assemble custom date strings. For example, you cannot derive any data directly from a Date object that lets you display the object as

```
Friday, August 9, 1996
```

To accomplish this kind of string generation, you have to create your own functions. Listing 28-1 demonstrates one method of creating this kind of string from a Date object (in a form compatible with Navigator 2 and Internet Explorer 3 arrays).

Listing 28-1: **Creating a Friendly Date String**

```
<HTML>
<HEAD>
<TITLE>Date String Maker</TITLE>
<SCRIPT LANGUAGE="JavaScript">
function MakeArray(n) {
        this.length = n
        return this
}
monthNames = new MakeArray(12)
monthNames[1] = "January"
monthNames[2] = "February"
monthNames[3] = "March"
monthNames[4] = "April"
monthNames[5] = "May"
monthNames[6] = "June"
monthNames[7] = "July"
monthNames[8] = "August"
monthNames[9] = "September"
monthNames[10] = "October"
```

```
monthNames[11] = "November"
monthNames[12] = "December"

dayNames = new MakeArray(7)
dayNames[1] = "Sunday"
dayNames[2] = "Monday"
dayNames[3] = "Tuesday"
dayNames[4] = "Wednesday"
dayNames[5] = "Thursday"
dayNames[6] = "Friday"
dayNames[7] = "Saturday"

function customDateString(oneDate) {
        var theDay = dayNames[oneDate.getDay() + 1]
        var theMonth = monthNames[oneDate.getMonth() + 1]
        var theYear = oneDate.getYear() + 1900
        return theDay + ", " + theMonth + " " + oneDate.getDate() +
", " + theYear
}
</SCRIPT>
</HEAD>

<BODY>
<H1> Welcome!</H1>
<SCRIPT LANGUAGE="JavaScript">
document.write(customDateString(new Date()))
</SCRIPT>

<HR>
</BODY>
</HTML>
```

Assuming the user has the PC's clock set correctly (a big assumption), the date appearing just below the opening headline is the current date — making it appear as though the document had been updated today.

More conversions

The final two methods related to Date objects are in the category known as *static methods*. Unlike all other methods, these two do not act on Date objects. Rather, they convert dates from string or numeric forms into millisecond values of those dates. The primary beneficiary of these actions is the `dateObj.setTime()` method, which requires a millisecond measure of a date as a parameter. This is the method you would use to throw an entirely different date into an existing Date object.

`Date.parse()` accepts date strings similar to the ones you've seen in this section, including the internationally approved version. `Date.UTC()`, on the other hand, requires the comma-delimited list of values (in proper order: yy,mm,dd,hh,mm,ss) in the GMT zone. Because setting all other properties via the Date object's methods interpret those values to mean the computer's local time zone, the `Date.UTC()` method gives you a way to hard-code a GMT time. The following is an example that creates a new Date object for 6 p.m. on March 4, 1996, GMT.

dateObject.UTC()

```
newObj = new Date(Date.UTC(96,2,4,18,0,0))
result = newObj.toString() // result = "Tue, Mar 04 10:00:00 Pacific
Standard Time 1996"
```

Because I then convert the object to a string, the local time is what comes as a result: the Pacific standard time zone equivalent of the GMT time entered.

New methods

The ECMA-262 language standard defines additional Date object methods to make it easier to set and get object components in GMT time. These methods are in Internet Explorer 4, but only in the Windows version of Navigator 4 as this is being written. Eventually all browsers will have the full set.

These new methods are similar to the component-oriented ones in the language since the beginning. The difference is that "UTC" is made part of the method name. For example, to the pair of `dateObj.getTime()` and `dateObj.setTime()` methods are added `dateObj.getUTCTime()` and `dateObj.setUTCTime()`. These UTC versions will be available for getting and setting all components.

Another improvement is the addition of `dateObj.getFullYear()` and `dateObj.setFullYear()`. These two new methods provide a workaround for the messy year situation currently in force — that twentieth-century year values are two-digit values. With the new methods, all years are treated with the proper number of digits for the year's full representation.

Date and time arithmetic

You may need to perform some math with dates for any number of reasons. Perhaps you need to calculate a date at some fixed number of days or weeks in the future or figure out the number of days between two dates. When calculations of these types are required, remember the *lingua franca* of JavaScript date values: the milliseconds.

What you may need to do in your date-intensive scripts is establish some variable values representing the number of milliseconds for minutes, hours, days, or weeks, and then use those variables in your calculations. Here is an example that establishes some practical variable values, building on each other:

```
var oneMinute = 60 * 1000
var oneHour = oneMinute * 60
var oneDay = oneHour * 24
var oneWeek = oneDay * 7
```

With these values established in a script, I can use one to calculate the date one week from today:

```
targetDate = new Date()
dateInMs = targetDate.getTime()
dateInMs += oneWeek
targetDate.setTime(dateInMs)
```

In another example, I use components of a Date object to assist in deciding what kind of greeting message to place in a document, based on the local time of the user's PC clock. Listing 28-2 adds to the scripting from Listing 28-1, bringing some quasi-intelligence to the proceedings. Again, this script uses the older array creation mechanism to be compatible with Navigator 2 and Internet Explorer 3.

Listing 28-2: A Dynamic Welcome Message

```
<HTML>
<HEAD>
<TITLE>Date String Maker</TITLE>
<SCRIPT LANGUAGE="JavaScript">
function MakeArray(n) {
      this.length = n
      return this
}
monthNames = new MakeArray(12)
monthNames[1] = "January"
monthNames[2] = "February"
monthNames[3] = "March"
monthNames[4] = "April"
monthNames[5] = "May"
monthNames[6] = "June"
monthNames[7] = "July"
monthNames[8] = "August"
monthNames[9] = "September"
monthNames[10] = "October"
monthNames[11] = "November"
monthNames[12] = "December"
dayNames = new MakeArray(7)
dayNames[1] = "Sunday"
dayNames[2] = "Monday"
dayNames[3] = "Tuesday"
dayNames[4] = "Wednesday"
dayNames[5] = "Thursday"
dayNames[6] = "Friday"
dayNames[7] = "Saturday"

function customDateString(oneDate) {
      var theDay = dayNames[oneDate.getDay() + 1]
      var theMonth = monthNames[oneDate.getMonth() + 1]
      var theYear = oneDate.getYear() + 1900
      return theDay + ", " + theMonth + " " + oneDate.getDate() +
", " + theYear
}
function dayPart(oneDate) {
      var theHour = oneDate.getHours()
      if (theHour <6 )
          return "wee hours"
      if (theHour < 12)
          return "morning"
      if (theHour < 18)
          return "afternoon"
      return "evening"
}
```

(continued)

Listing 28-2 *(continued)*

```
</SCRIPT>
</HEAD>

<BODY>
<H1> Welcome!</H1>
<SCRIPT LANGUAGE="JavaScript">
today = new Date()
var header = (customDateString(today)).italics()
header += "<BR>We hope you are enjoying the "
header += dayPart(today) + "."
document.write(header)
</SCRIPT>
<HR>
</BODY>
</HTML>
```

I've divided the day into four parts and presented a different greeting for each part of the day. The greeting that plays is based, simply enough, on the hour element of a Date object representing the time the page is loaded into the browser. Because this greeting is embedded in the page, the greeting does not change no matter how long the user stays logged on to the page.

Date bugs and gremlins

Each generation of Navigator improves the stability and reliability of scripted Date objects. Unfortunately, Navigator 2 has enough bugs and crash problems across many platforms to make scripting complex world-time applications for this browser impossible. The Macintosh version also has bugs that throw off dates by as much as a full day. I recommend avoiding Navigator 2 on all platforms for serious date and time scripting.

The situation is much improved for Navigator 3. Still, some bugs persist. One bug in particular affects Macintosh versions of Navigator. Whenever you create a new Date object with daylight saving time engaged in the Date and Time control panel, the browser automatically adds one hour to the object. See the time-based application in Chapter 52 of the bonus applications on the CD-ROM for an example of how to counteract the effects of typical time bugs. Also afflicting the Macintosh in Navigator 3 is a faulty calculation of the time zone offset for all time zones east of GMT. Instead of generating these values as negative numbers (getting lower and lower as you head east), the offset values increase continuously as you head west from Greenwich. While the Western Hemisphere is fine, the values continue to increase past the international date line, rather than switch over to the negative values.

Internet Explorer 3 isn't free of problems. It cannot handle dates before January 1, 1970 (GMT). Attempts to generate a date before that one results in that base date as the value. It also completely miscalculates the time zone offset, following the erroneous pattern of Navigator 2. Even Navigators 3 and 4 have problems with historic dates. You are asking for trouble if the date extends beyond January 1, A.D. 1. Internet Explorer 4, on the other hand, appears to sail very well into ancient history.

You should be aware of one more discrepancy between Mac and Windows versions of Navigator. In Windows, if you generate a Date object for a date in another part of the year, the browser sets the time zone offset for that object according to the time zone setting for that time of year. On the Mac, the current setting of the control panel governs whether the normal or daylight saving time offset is applied to the date, regardless of the actual date within the year. This affects Navigator 3 and 4, and can throw off calculations from other parts of the year by one hour.

It may sound as though the road to Date object scripting is filled with land mines. While date and time scripting is far from hassle free, you can put it to good use with careful planning and a lot of testing. Look to the example application on the CD-ROM for ideas on implementing date and time code into your pages.

Validating Date Entries in Forms

Given the bug horror stories in the previous section, you may wonder how you can ever perform data-entry validation for dates in forms. The problem is not in the calculations as it is in the wide variety of acceptable date formats around the world. No matter how well you instruct users to enter dates in a particular format, many will follow their own habits and conventions. Moreover, how can you know whether an entry of 03/04/98 is the North American March 4, 1998, or the European April 3, 1998? The answer is: You can't.

My recommendation is to divide a date field into three components: month, day, and year. Let the user enter values into each field, and validate each field individually for its valid range. Listing 28-3 shows an example of how this is done. The page includes a form that is to be validated before it is submitted. Each component field does its own range checking on the fly as the user enters values. But because this kind of validation can be defeated, the page includes one further check triggered by the form's onSubmit= event handler. If any field is out of whack, the form submission is canceled.

Listing 28-3: **Date Validation in a Form**

```
<HTML>
<HEAD>
<TITLE>Date Entry Validation</TITLE>
<SCRIPT LANGUAGE="JavaScript">
<!--
// **BEGIN GENERIC VALIDATION FUNCTIONS**
// general purpose function to see if an input value has been entered
at all
function isEmpty(inputStr) {
        if (inputStr == "" || inputStr == null) {
            return true
        }
        return false
}
```

(continued)

Listing 28-3 *(continued)*

```javascript
// function to determine if value is in acceptable range for this
application
function inRange(inputStr, lo, hi) {
      var num = parseInt(inputStr, 10)
      if (num < lo || num > hi) {
          return false
      }
      return true
}
// **END GENERIC VALIDATION FUNCTIONS**

function validateMonth(field, bypassUpdate) {
      var input = parseInt(field.value, 10)
      if (isEmpty(input)) {
          alert("Be sure to enter a month value.")
          select(field)
          return false
      } else {
          if (isNaN(input)) {
              alert("Entries must be numbers only.")
              select(field)
              return false
          } else {
              if (!inRange(input,1,12)) {
                  alert("Enter a number between 1 (January) and 12
(December).")
                  select(field)
                  return false
              }
          }
      }
      if (!bypassUpdate) {
          calcDate()
      }
      return true
}

function validateDate(field) {
      var input = parseInt(field.value, 10)
      if (isEmpty(input)) {
          alert("Be sure to enter a date value.")
          select(field)
          return false
      } else {
          if (isNaN(input)) {
              alert("Entries must be numbers only.")
              select(field)
              return false
          } else {
```

```
                var monthField = document.birthdate.month
                if (!validateMonth(monthField, true)) return false
                var monthVal = parseInt(monthField.value, 10)
                var monthMax = new
Array(31,31,29,31,30,31,30,31,31,30,31,30,31)
                var top = monthMax[monthVal]
                if (!inRange(input,1,top)) {
                    alert("Enter a number between 1 and " + top + ".")
                    select(field)
                    return false
                }
            }
        }
        calcDate()
        return true
}

function validateYear(field) {
        var input = parseInt(field.value, 10)
        if (isEmpty(input)) {
            alert("Be sure to enter a month value.")
            select(field)
            return false
        } else {
            if (isNaN(input)) {
                alert("Entries must be numbers only.")
                select(field)
                return false
            } else {
                if (!inRange(input,1900,2005)) {
                    alert("Enter a number between 1900 and 2005.")
                    select(field)
                    return false
                }
            }
        }
        calcDate()
        return true
}

function select(field) {
        field.focus()
        field.select()
}

function calcDate() {
        var mm = parseInt(document.birthdate.month.value, 10)
        var dd = parseInt(document.birthdate.date.value, 10)
        var yy = parseInt(document.birthdate.year.value, 10)
        document.birthdate.fullDate.value = mm + "/" + dd + "/" + yy
}
```

(continued)

Listing 28-3 *(continued)*

```
function checkForm(form) {
        if (validateMonth(form.month)) {
            if (validateDate(form.date)) {
                if (validateYear(form.year)) {
                    return true
                }
            }
        }
        return false
}
//-->
</SCRIPT>
</HEAD>
<BODY>
<FORM NAME="birthdate" ACTION="mailto:fun@dannyg.com" METHOD=POST
onSubmit="return checkForm(this)">
Please enter your birthdate...<BR>
Month:<INPUT TYPE="text" NAME="month" VALUE=1 SIZE=2
onChange="validateMonth(this)">
Date:<INPUT TYPE="text" NAME="date" VALUE=1 SIZE=2
onChange="validateDate(this)">
Year:<INPUT TYPE="text" NAME="year" VALUE=1900 SIZE=4
onChange="validateYear(this)">
<P>
Thank you for entering:<INPUT TYPE="text" NAME="fullDate" SIZE=10><P>
<INPUT TYPE="submit"> <INPUT TYPE="Reset">
</FORM>
</BODY>
</HTML>
```

The page shows the three entry fields as well as a field that would normally be hidden on a form to be submitted to a CGI program. On the server end, the CGI program would respond only to the hidden field with the complete date, which is in a format for entry into, say, an Informix database. Note that in the above example, the form's action is set to a `mailto:` URL, which means it won't work with Internet Explorer.

Not every date entry validation must be divided in this way. For example, an intranet application can be more demanding in the way users are to enter data. Therefore, you can have a single field for date entry, but the parsing required for such a validation is quite different from that shown in Listing 28-3. See Chapter 37 for an example of such a one-field date validation routine.

✦   ✦   ✦

The Array Object

An array is the sole JavaScript data structure provided for storing and manipulating ordered collections of data. But unlike some other programming languages, JavaScript's arrays are very forgiving as to the kind of data you store in each cell or entry of the array. This allows, for example, an array of arrays, providing the equivalent of multidimensional arrays customized to the kind of data your application needs.

If you have not done a lot of programming in the past, the notion of arrays may seem like an advanced topic. But if you ignore their capabilities, you set yourself up for a harder job when implementing many kinds of tasks. Whenever I approach a script, one of my first thoughts is about the data being controlled by the application and whether handling it as an array will offer some shortcuts for creating the document and handling interactivity with the user.

I hope that by the end of this chapter, you will not only be familiar with the properties and methods of JavaScript arrays, but you will begin to look for ways to make arrays work for you.

Structured Data

In programming, an array is defined as *an ordered collection of data*. You can best visualize an array as a table, not much different from a spreadsheet. In JavaScript, arrays are limited to a table holding one column of data, with as many rows as needed to hold your data. As you have seen in many chapters in Part III, a JavaScript-enabled browser creates a number of internal arrays for the objects in your HTML documents and browser properties. For example, if your document contains five links, the browser maintains a table of those links. You access them by number (with 0 being the first link) in the array syntax: the array name followed by the index number in square brackets, as in `document.links[0]`, which represents the first link in the document.

For many JavaScript applications, you will want to use an array as an organized warehouse for data that users of your page access, depending on their interaction with form elements. In one of the bonus applications (Chapter 48) on the CD-ROM, I show you an extended version of this usage in a page that lets users search a small table of data for a match between the first three digits of their U.S. Social Security numbers and the state in which they registered. Arrays are the way JavaScript-enhanced pages can re-create the behavior of more sophisticated CGI programs on servers. When the collection of data you embed in the script is no larger than a typical .gif image file, the user won't experience significant delays in loading your page; yet he or she will have the full power of your small database collection for instant searching without any calls back to the server. Such database-oriented arrays are important applications of JavaScript for what I call *serverless CGIs*.

As you design an application, look for clues as to potential application of arrays. If you have a number of objects or data points that interact with scripts the same way, you have a good candidate for array structures. For example, with the exception of Internet Explorer 3, you can assign like names to every text field in a column of an order form. In that sequence like-named objects are treated as elements of an array. To perform repetitive row calculations down an order form, your scripts can use array syntax to perform all the extensions within a handful of JavaScript statements, rather than perhaps dozens of statements hard-coded to each field name. Chapter 49 on the CD-ROM shows an example of this application.

You can also create arrays that behave like the Java hash table: a lookup table that gets you to the desired data point instantaneously if you know the name associated with the entry. If you can conceive your data in a table format, an array is in your future.

Creating an Empty Array

Arrays are treated in JavaScript like objects, but the extent to which your scripts can treat them as objects depends on whether you're using the first version of JavaScript (in Navigator 2 and Internet Explorer 3 with the Version 1 JScript DLL) or more recent versions (in Navigator 3 or later and Internet Explorer with JScript DLL Version 2 or later). For the sake of compatibility, I'll begin by showing you how to create arrays that work in all scriptable browsers.

You begin by defining an object *constructor* that assigns a passed parameter integer value to the length property of the object:

```
function makeArray(n) {
        this.length = n
        return this
}
```

Then, to actually initialize an array for your script, use the new keyword to construct the object for you while assigning the array object to a variable of your choice:

```
var myArray = new makeArray(n)
```

where *n* is the number of entries you anticipate for the array. This initialization does not make any array entries or create any placeholders. Such preconditioning of arrays is not necessary in JavaScript.

In one important aspect, an array created in this "old" manner does not exhibit an important characteristic of standard arrays. The length property here is artificial in that it does not change with the size of the array (JavaScript arrays are completely dynamic, letting you add items at any time). The length value here is hardwired by assignment. You can always change the value manually, but it takes a great deal of scripted bookkeeping to manage that task.

Another point to remember about this property scheme is that the value assigned to `this.length` in the constructor actually occupies the first entry (index 0) of the array. Any data you want to add to an array should not overwrite that position in the array if you expect to use the length to help a repeat loop look through an array's contents.

What the full-fledged newer array object gains you is behavior more like that of the arrays you work with elsewhere in JavaScript. You don't need to define a constructor function, because it's built into the JavaScript object mechanism. Instead, you create a new array object like this:

```
var myArray = new Array()
```

An array object automatically has a `length` property (0 for an empty array). Most importantly, this length value does not occupy one of the array entries; the array is entirely for data.

Should you want to presize the array (for example, preload entries with null values), you can specify an initial size as a parameter to the constructor. Here I create a new array to hold information about a 500-item compact disc collection:

```
var myCDCollection = new Array(500)
```

Presizing an array does not give you any particular advantage, because you can assign a value to any slot in an array at any time: The `length` property adjusts itself accordingly. For instance, if you assign a value to `myCDCollection[700]`, the array object adjusts its length upward to meet that slot (with the count starting at 0):

```
myCDCollection [700] = "Gloria Estefan/Destiny"
collectionSize = myCDCollection.length  // result = 701
```

A true array object also features a number of methods and the capability to add prototype properties, described later in this chapter.

Populating an Array

Entering data into an array is as simple as creating a series of assignment statements, one for each element of the array. Listing 29-1 (not on the CD-ROM) assumes that you're using the newer style array object and that your goal is to generate an array containing a list of the nine planets of the solar system.

Listing 29-1: **Generating and Populating a New Array**

```
solarSys = new Array(9)
solarSys[0] = "Mercury"
solarSys[1] = "Venus"
solarSys[2] = "Earth"
solarSys[3] = "Mars"
solarSys[4] = "Jupiter"
solarSys[5] = "Saturn"
```

(continued)

Listing 29-1 (*continued*)

```
solarSys[6] = "Uranus"
solarSys[7] = "Neptune"
solarSys[8] = "Pluto"
```

This way of populating a single array is a bit tedious when you're writing the code, but after the array is set, it makes accessing information collections as easy as any array reference:

```
onePlanet = solarSys[4] // result = "Jupiter"
```

A more compact way to create an array is available when you know that the data will be in the desired order (as the solarSys[] preceding array). Instead of writing a series of assignment statements (as in Listing 29-1), you can create what is called a *dense array* by supplying the data as parameters to the Array() constructor:

```
solarSys = new
Array("Mercury","Venus","Earth","Mars","Jupiter","Saturn",
"Uranus","Neptune","Pluto")
```

The term "dense array" means that data is packed into the array without gaps starting at index position 0.

The example in Listing 29-1 shows what you might call a vertical collection of data. Each data point contains the same type of data as the other data points — the name of a planet — and the data points appear in the relative order of the planets from the Sun.

But not all data collections are vertical. You may, for instance, just want to create an array that holds various pieces of information about one planet. Earth is handy, so let's use some of its astronomical data to build a completely separate array of earthly info in Listing 29-2 (not on the CD-ROM).

Listing 29-2: **Creating a "Horizontal" Array**

```
earth = new Array()
earth.diameter = "7920 miles"
earth.distance = "93 million miles"
earth.year = "365.25 days"
earth.day = "24 hours"
earth.length    // result = 4
```

What you see in Listing 29-2 is an alternative way to populate an array. In a sense, you saw a preview of this method when I created an array in the old style earlier and assigned the length property name to its first entry. If you assign a value to a property name that has not yet been assigned for the array, JavaScript is smart enough to append a new property entry for that value.

In an important change from the old style of array construction, the way you define an array entry impacts how you access that information later. For example, when you populate an array based on index values (Listing 29-1), you can retrieve those array entries only via references that include the index values. Conversely, if you define array entries by property name (Listing 29-2), you cannot access those values via the index way. In Navigator 2, for instance, the array assignments of Listing 29-2 can be retrieved by their corresponding index values:

```
earth.diameter          // result = "7920 miles"
earth["diameter"]       // result = "7920 miles"
earth[0]                // result = "7920 miles"
```

In Navigator 3 or 4, however, because these entries are defined as properties, they must be retrieved as properties, not index values:

```
earth.diameter          // result = "7920 miles"
earth["diameter"]       // result = "7920 miles"
earth[0]                // result = null
```

The impact here on your scripts is that you need to anticipate how you expect to retrieve data from your array. If an indexed repeat loop is in the forecast, populate the array with index values (as in Listing 29-1); if the property names are more important to you, then populate the array that way (as in Listing 29-2). Your choice of index value type for a single-column array is driven by the application, but you will want to focus on the named array entry style for creating what appear to be two-dimensional arrays.

JavaScript 1.2 Array Creation Enhancements

Navigator 4 added one new way to create a dense array and also cleared up a bug in the old way. These features are part of the JavaScript 1.2 specification, and so are also available in Internet Explorer 4.

A new, simpler way to create a dense array does not require the array object constructor. Instead, JavaScript 1.2 accepts what is called *literal notation* to generate an array. To demonstrate the difference, the following statement is the regular dense array constructor that works with Navigator 3:

```
solarSys = new
Array("Mercury","Venus","Earth","Mars","Jupiter","Saturn",
"Uranus","Neptune","Pluto")
```

While JavaScript 1.2 fully accepts the preceding syntax, it also accepts the new literal notation:

```
solarSys = ["Mercury","Venus","Earth","Mars","Jupiter","Saturn",
"Uranus","Neptune","Pluto"]
```

The square brackets stand in for the call to the array constructor. You have to judge which browser types your audience will be using before deploying the JavaScript 1.2 version.

The bug fix has to do with how to treat the earlier dense array constructor if the scripter enters only the numeric value 1 as the parameter—new Array(1). In Navigator 3 and Internet Explorer 4, JavaScript erroneously creates an array of length 1, but that element is undefined. For Navigator 4 (and inside a <SCRIPT LANGUAGE="JavaScript1.2"> tag), the same statement creates that one-element array and places the value in that element.

Deleting Arrays and Array Entries

You can always set the value of an array entry to null or an empty string to wipe out any data that used to occupy that space. But until the `delete` operator in Navigator 4, you could not completely remove the element or the array.

Deleting an array element eliminates the index from the list of accessible index values, but does not reduce the array's length, as in the following sequence of statements:

```
myArray.length// result: 5
delete myArray[2]
myArray.length// result: 5
myArray[2] // result: undefined
```

See the `delete` operator in Chapter 32 for further details.

Simulating Two-Dimensional Arrays

As you may have deduced from my examples in Listings 29-1 and 29-2, what I'm really aiming for in this application is a two-dimensional array. If the data were in a spreadsheet, there would be columns for Name, Diameter, Distance, Year, and Day; also, each row would contain the data for each planet, filling a total of 45 cells or data points (9 planets times 5 data points each). Although JavaScript does not have a mechanism for explicit two-dimensional arrays, you can create an array of objects, which accomplishes the same thing.

The mechanism for the array of objects consists of a primary array object creation (whether created by the old or new way), a separate constructor function that builds objects, and the main, data-stuffing assignment statements you saw for the vertical array style. Listing 29-3 (not on the CD-ROM) shows the constructor and stuffer parts of the solar system application.

Listing 29-3: **Building a Two-Dimensional Array**

```
function planet(name,diameter, distance, year, day){
        this.name = name
        this.diameter = diameter
        this.distance = distance
        this.year = year
        this.day = day
}
solarSys = new Array(9)  // Navigator 3.0 array object constructor
solarSys[0] = new planet("Mercury","3100 miles", "36 million miles",
"88 days", "59 days")
solarSys[1] = new planet("Venus", "7700 miles", "67 million miles",
"225 days", "244 days")
solarSys[2] = new planet("Earth", "7920 miles", "93 million miles",
"365.25 days","24 hours")
solarSys[3] = new planet("Mars", "4200 miles", "141 million miles",
"687 days", "24 hours, 24 minutes")
solarSys[4] = new planet("Jupiter","88,640 miles","483 million miles",
"11.9 years", "9 hours, 50 minutes")
solarSys[5] = new planet("Saturn", "74,500 miles","886 million miles",
"29.5 years", "10 hours, 39 minutes")
```

```
solarSys[6] = new planet("Uranus", "32,000 miles","1.782 billion
miles","84 years", "23 hours")
solarSys[7] = new planet("Neptune","31,000 miles","2.793 billion
miles","165 years", "15 hours, 48 minutes")
solarSys[8] = new planet("Pluto", "1500 miles", "3.67 billion miles",
   "248 years", "6 days, 7 hours")
```

After creating the main, nine-data-element array, `solarSys`, the script uses that `new` keyword again to populate each entry of the `solarSys` array with an object fashioned in the `planet()` constructor function. Each call to that function passes five data points, which, in turn, are assigned to named property entries in the planet object. Thus, each entry of the `solarSys` array contains a five-element object of its own.

The fact that all of these subobjects have the same data structure now makes it easy for your scripts to extract the data from anywhere within this 45-entry, two-dimensional array. For example, to retrieve the name value of the fifth entry of the `solarSys` array, the syntax is this:

```
planetName = solarSys[4].name
```

This statement has the same appearance and behavior as properties of JavaScript's built-in arrays. It is, indeed, the very same model. To understand why you want to create this table, study Listing 29-4. Extracting data from the two-dimensional array is quite simple in the `showData()` function. The array structure even makes it possible to create a pop-up button listing from the same array data.

Listing 29-4: **Two-Dimensional Array Results**

```
<HTML>
<HEAD>
<TITLE>Our Solar System</TITLE>
<SCRIPT LANGUAGE="JavaScript1.1">
<!-- start script
// stuff "rows" of data for our pseudo-two-dimensional array
function planet(name,diameter, distance, year, day){
        this.name = name
        this.diameter = diameter
        this.distance = distance
        this.year = year
        this.day = day
}
// create our pseudo-two-dimensional array
solarSys = new Array(9)
solarSys[0] = new planet("Mercury","3100 miles", "36 million miles",
"88 days", "59 days")
```

(continued)

Listing 29-4 *(continued)*

```
solarSys[1] = new planet("Venus", "7700 miles", "67 million miles",
"225 days", "244 days")
solarSys[2] = new planet("Earth", "7920 miles", "93 million miles",
"365.25 days","24 hours")
solarSys[3] = new planet("Mars", "4200 miles", "141 million miles",
"687 days", "24 hours, 24 minutes")
solarSys[4] = new planet("Jupiter","88,640 miles","483 million miles",
"11.9 years", "9 hours, 50 minutes")
solarSys[5] = new planet("Saturn", "74,500 miles","886 million miles",
"29.5 years", "10 hours, 39 minutes")
solarSys[6] = new planet("Uranus", "32,000 miles","1.782 billion
miles","84 years", "23 hours")
solarSys[7] = new planet("Neptune","31,000 miles","2.793 billion
miles","165 years", "15 hours, 48 minutes")
solarSys[8] = new planet("Pluto", "1500 miles", "3.67 billion miles",
"248 years", "6 days, 7 hours")

// fill text area object with data from selected planet
function showData(form) {
        i = form.planets.selectedIndex
        var result = "The planet " + solarSys[i].name
        result += " has a diameter of " + solarSys[i].diameter + ".\n"
        result += "At a distance of " + solarSys[i].distance + ", "
        result += "it takes " + solarSys[i].year + " to circle the
Sun.\n"
        result += "One day lasts " + solarSys[i].day + " of Earth
time."
        form.output.value = result
}
// end script -->
</SCRIPT>
<BODY onLoad="document.forms[0].planets.onchange()">
<H1>The Daily Planet</H1>
<HR>
<FORM>
<SCRIPT LANGUAGE = "JavaScript">
<!-- start script again
var page = "" // start assembling next part of page and form
page += "Select a planet to view its planetary data: "
page += "<SELECT NAME='planets' onChange='showData(this.form)'> "
// build popup list from array planet names
for (var i = 0; i < solarSys.length; i++) {
        page += "<OPTION" // OPTION tags
        if (i == 0) { // pre-select first item in list
            page += " SELECTED"
        }
        page += ">" + solarSys[i].name
}
page += "</SELECT><P>" // close selection item tag
document.write(page) // lay out this part of the page
```

```
// really end script -->
</SCRIPT>
<TEXTAREA NAME="output" ROWS=5 COLS=75>
</TEXTAREA>
</FORM>
</BODY>
</HTML>
```

The Web page code shown in Listing 29-4 uses two blocks of JavaScript scripts. In the upper block, the scripts create the arrays described earlier and define a function that the page uses to accumulate and display data in response to user action (see Figure 29-1).

The body of the page is constructed partially out of straight HTML, with some JavaScript coding in between. I hard-code the <H1> heading, divider, and start of the form definition. From there, I hand-off page layout to JavaScript. It begins assembling the next chunk of the page in a string variable, page. The start of a select object definition follows a line of instructions. To assign values to the <OPTION> tags of the select object, I use a repeat loop that cycles through each entry of the solarSys array, extracting only the name property for each and plugging it into the accumulated HTML page for the select object. Notice how I applied the SELECTED attribute to the first option. I then close out the select object definition in the page variable and write the entire variable's contents out to the browser. The browser sees this rush of HTML as just more HTML to obey as it fills in the page. After the variable's HTML is loaded, the rest of the hard-wired page is loaded, including an output textarea object and the close of all opened tag pairs.

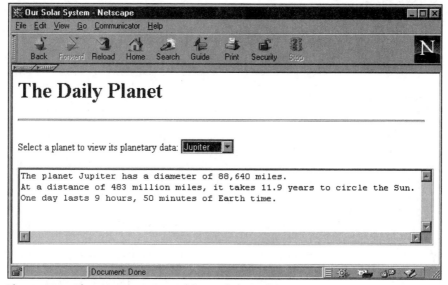

Figure 29-1: The page constructed from Listing 29-4

After the document is loaded into the browser, all activity takes place on the client machine. If the network connection were to drop, the planet data would still be intact. In fact, the user could save the source code on the client computer's hard disk and open it as a file at any time, without reconnecting to the server. Without JavaScript, a CGI program on the server would have to reply to a query from the document, fetch the data, and send it back to the PC — involving two extra network transfers. Another serverless CGI has been born.

Array Object Properties

length

Value: Integer   **Gettable:** Yes   **Settable:** No

	Nav2	Nav3	Nav4	IE3/J1	IE3/J2	IE4/J3
Compatibility		✔	✔		✔	✔

A true array object's length property reflects the number of entries in the array. An entry can be any kind of JavaScript value, including null. If there is an entry in the 10th cell and the rest are null, the length of that array is 10. Note that because array index values are zero-based, the index of the last cell of an array is one less than the length.

prototype

Value: Variable or Function   **Gettable:** Yes   **Settable:** Yes

	Nav2	Nav3	Nav4	IE3/J1	IE3/J2	IE4/J3
Compatibility		✔	✔		✔	✔

Inside JavaScript, an array object has its dictionary definition of methods and length property — items that all array objects have in common. The prototype property enables your scripts to ascribe additional properties or methods that apply to all the arrays you create in the currently loaded documents. You can override this prototype, however, for any individual objects as you want.

To demonstrate how the prototype property works, Listing 29-5 creates a prototype property for all array objects. As the script generates new arrays, the property automatically becomes a part of those arrays. In one array, c, you override the value of the prototype sponsor property. By changing the value for that one object, you don't alter the value of the prototype for the array object. Therefore, another array created afterward, d, still gets the original prototype property value.

Listing 29-5: **Adding a prototype Property**

```
<HTML>
<HEAD>
<TITLE>Array prototypes</TITLE>
<SCRIPT LANGUAGE="JavaScript1.1">
// add prototype to all Array objects
Array.prototype.sponsor = "DG"
a = new Array(5)
b = new Array(5)
c = new Array(5)
// override prototype property for one 'instance'
c.sponsor = "JS"
// this one picks up the original prototype
d = new Array(5)
</SCRIPT>
<BODY><H2>
<SCRIPT LANGUAGE="JavaScript">
document.write("Array a is brought to you by: " + a.sponsor + "<P>")
document.write("Array b is brought to you by: " + b.sponsor + "<P>")
document.write("Array c is brought to you by: " + c.sponsor + "<P>")
document.write("Array d is brought to you by: " + d.sponsor + "<P>")
</SCRIPT>
</H2>
</BODY>
</HTML>
```

You can assign properties and functions to a prototype. To assign a function, define the function as you normally would in JavaScript. Then assign the function by name:

```
function newFunc(param1) {
        // statements
}
Array.prototype.newMethod = newFunc   // omit parentheses in this
reference
```

When you need to call upon that function (which has essentially become a new temporary method for the array object), invoke it as you would any object method. Therefore, if an array named CDCollection has been created and a prototype method showCoverImage() has been attached to the array, the call to invoke the method for a tenth listing in the array is

```
CDCollection[9].showCoverImage(this)
```

where this passes a reference to this particular array entry and all properties and methods associated with it.

Array Object Methods

After you have information stored in an array, JavaScript provides several methods to help you manage that data. These methods have evolved over time, so observe carefully which browser versions a desired method works with.

arrayObject.concat(array2)

Returns: Nothing.

	Nav2	Nav3	Nav4	IE3/J1	IE3/J2	IE4/J3
Compatibility			✔			✔

The `array.concat()` method allows you to join together two array objects into a new, third array object. The action of concatenating the arrays does not alter the contents or behavior of the two original arrays. To join the arrays together, you refer to the first array object to the left of the period before the method; a reference to the second array is the parameter to the method. For example

```
var array1 = new Array(1,2,3)
var array2 = new Array("a","b","c")
var array3 = array1.concat(array2)
        // result: array with values 1,2,3,"a","b","c"
```

If an array element is a string or number value (not a string or number object), the values are copied from the original arrays into the new one. All connection with the original arrays ceases for those items. But if an original array element is a reference to an object of any kind, JavaScript copies a reference from the original array's entry into the new array. This means that if you make a change to either array's entry, the change occurs to the object, and both array entries reflect the change to the object.

Example

Listing 29-6 is a bit complex, but it demonstrates both how arrays can be joined with the `array.concat()` method and how values and objects in the source arrays do or do not propagate based on their data type. The page is shown in Figure 29-2.

When you load the page, you see readouts of three arrays. The first array consists of all string values; the second array has two string values and a reference to a form object on the page (a textbox named "original" in the HTML). In the initialization routine of this page, not only are the two source arrays created, but they are joined together with the `array.concat()` method, and the result is shown in the third box. To show the contents of these arrays in columns, I use the `array.join()` method, which brings the elements of an array together as a string delimited in this case by a return character—giving us an instant column of data.

Two series of fields and buttons let you experiment with the way values and object references are linked across concatenated arrays. In the first group, if you enter a new value to be assigned to `arrayThree[0]`, the new value replaces the string value in the combined array. Because regular values do not maintain a link back to the original array, only the entry in the combined array is changed. A call to `showArrays()` proves that only the third array is affected by the change.

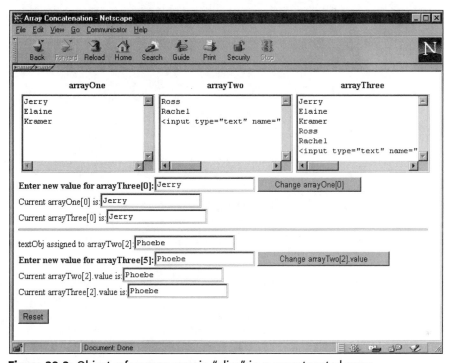

Figure 29-2: Object references remain "alive" in a concatenated array.

More complex is the object relationship for this demonstration. A reference to the first text box of the second grouping has been assigned to the third entry of `arrayTwo`. After concatenation, the same reference is now in the last entry of the combined array. If you enter a new value for a property of the object in the last slot of `arrayThree`, the change goes all the way back to the original object — the first text box in the lower grouping. Thus, the text of the original field changes in response to the change of `arrayThree[5]`. And because all references to that object yield the same result, the reference in `arrayTwo[2]` points to the same text object, yielding the same new answer. The display of the array contents doesn't change, because both arrays still contain a reference to the same object (and the `VALUE` attribute showing in the `<INPUT>` tag of the column listings refers to the default value of the tag, not its current algorithmically retrievable value shown in the last two fields of the page).

Listing 29-6: **Array Concatenation**

```
<HTML>
<HEAD>
<TITLE>Array Concatenation</TITLE>
<SCRIPT LANGUAGE="JavaScript1.1">
// global variables
var arrayOne, arrayTwo, arrayThree, textObj
// initialize after load to access text object in form
function initialize() {
        var form = document.forms[0]
        textObj = form.original
        arrayOne = new Array("Jerry", "Elaine","Kramer")
        arrayTwo = new Array("Ross", "Rachel",textObj)
        arrayThree = arrayOne.concat(arrayTwo)
        update1(form)
        update2(form)
        showArrays()
}
// display current values of all three arrays
function showArrays() {
        var form = document.forms[0]
        form.array1.value = arrayOne.join("\n")
        form.array2.value = arrayTwo.join("\n")
        form.array3.value = arrayThree.join("\n")
}
// change the value of first item in Array Three
function update1(form) {
        arrayThree[0] = form.source1.value
        form.result1.value = arrayOne[0]
        form.result2.value = arrayThree[0]
        showArrays()
}
// change value of object property pointed to in Array Three
function update2(form) {
        arrayThree[5].value = form.source2.value
        form.result3.value = arrayTwo[2].value
        form.result4.value = arrayThree[5].value
        showArrays()
}
</SCRIPT>
</HEAD>
<BODY onLoad="initialize()">
<FORM>
<TABLE>
<TR><TH>arrayOne</TH><TH>arrayTwo</TH><TH>arrayThree</TH></TR>
<TR>
<TD><TEXTAREA NAME="array1" COLS=25 ROWS=6></TEXTAREA></TD>
<TD><TEXTAREA NAME="array2" COLS=25 ROWS=6></TEXTAREA></TD>
<TD><TEXTAREA NAME="array3" COLS=25 ROWS=6></TEXTAREA></TD>
</TR>
</TABLE>
```

```
<B>Enter new value for arrayThree[0]:</B><INPUT TYPE="text"
NAME="source1" VALUE="Jerry">
<INPUT TYPE="button" VALUE="Change arrayOne[0]"
onClick="update1(this.form)"><BR>
Current arrayOne[0] is:<INPUT TYPE="text" NAME="result1"><BR>
Current arrayThree[0] is:<INPUT TYPE="text" NAME="result2"><BR>
<HR>

textObj assigned to arrayTwo[2]:<INPUT TYPE="text" NAME="original"
onFocus="this.blur()"></BR>
<B>Enter new value for arrayThree[5]:</B><INPUT TYPE="text"
NAME="source2" VALUE="Phoebe">
<INPUT TYPE="button" VALUE="Change arrayTwo[2].value"
onClick="update2(this.form)"><BR>
Current arrayTwo[2].value is:<INPUT TYPE="text" NAME="result3"><BR>
Current arrayThree[2].value is:<INPUT TYPE="text" NAME="result4"><P>

<INPUT TYPE="button" VALUE="Reset" onClick="location.reload()">
</FORM>
</BODY>
</HTML>
```

Related Items: `array.join()` method.

arrayObject.`join(`*separatorString*`)`

Returns: String of entries from the array delimited by the *separatorString* value.

	Nav2	Nav3	Nav4	IE3/J1	IE3/J2	IE4/J3
Compatibility		✔	✔		✔	✔

You cannot view data in an array when it's in that form. Nor can you put an array into a form element for transmittal to a server CGI program. To make the transition from discrete array elements to string, the `array.join()` method handles what would otherwise be a nasty string manipulation exercise.

The sole parameter for this method is a string of one or more characters that you want to act as a delimiter between entries. For example, if you want commas between array items in their text version, the statement is

```
var arrayText = myArray.join(",")
```

Invoking this method does not change the original array in any way. Therefore, you need to assign the results of this method to another variable or a `value` property of a form element.

Example

The script in Listing 29-7 converts the now familiar array of planet names into a text string. The page provides you with a field to enter the delimiter string of your choice and shows the results in a textarea.

Listing 29-7: **Using the Array.join() Method**

```
<HTML>
<HEAD>
<TITLE>Array.join()</TITLE>
<SCRIPT LANGUAGE="JavaScript1.1">
solarSys = new Array(9)
solarSys[0] = "Mercury"
solarSys[1] = "Venus"
solarSys[2] = "Earth"
solarSys[3] = "Mars"
solarSys[4] = "Jupiter"
solarSys[5] = "Saturn"
solarSys[6] = "Uranus"
solarSys[7] = "Neptune"
solarSys[8] = "Pluto"

// join array elements into a string
function convert(form) {
        var delimiter = form.delim.value
        form.output.value = unescape(solarSys.join(delimiter))
}
</SCRIPT>
<BODY>
<H2>Converting arrays to strings</H2>
This document contains an array of planets in our solar system.<HR>
<FORM>
Enter a string to act as a delimiter between entries:
<INPUT TYPE="text" NAME="delim" VALUE="," SIZE=5><P>
<INPUT TYPE="button" VALUE="Display as String"
onClick="convert(this.form)">
<INPUT TYPE="reset">
<TEXTAREA NAME="output" ROWS=4 COLS=40 WRAP="virtual">
</TEXTAREA>
</FORM>
</BODY>
</HTML>
```

Notice that this method takes the parameter very literally. If you want to include nonalphanumeric characters, such as a newline or tab, do so with escaped characters ("%0D" for a carriage return; "%09" for a tab) instead of inline string literals. In Listing 29-7, the results of the Array.join() method are subjected to the unescape() function in order to display them in the textarea.

Related Items: String.split() method.

arrayObject.pop()
arrayObject.push(valueOrObject)
arrayObject.shift()
arrayObject.unshift(valueOrObject)

	Nav2	Nav3	Nav4	IE3/J1	IE3/J2	IE4/J3
Compatibility			✔			

The notion of a *stack* is well known to experienced programmers, especially those who know about the inner workings of assembly language at the CPU level. Even if you've never programmed a stack before, you have encountered the concept in real life many times. The classic analogy is the spring-loaded pile of cafeteria trays. If the pile were created one at a time, each tray would be pushed into the stack of trays. When a customer comes along, the topmost tray (the last one to be pushed onto the stack) gets popped off. The last one to be put on the stack is the first one to be taken off.

JavaScript 1.2 in Navigator lets you turn an array into one of these spring-loaded stacks. But instead of placing trays on the pile, you can place any kind of data at either end of the stack, depending on which method you use to do the stacking. Similarly, you can extract an item from either end.

Perhaps the most familiar terminology for this is *push* and *pop*. When you push() a value onto an array, the value is appended as the last entry in the array. When you issue the array.pop() method, the last item in the array is removed from the stack and is returned, plus the array shrinks in length by one. In the following sequence of statements, watch what happens to the value of the array used as a stack:

```
var source = new Array("Homer","Marge","Bart","Lisa","Maggie")
var stack = new Array()
        // stack = <empty>
stack.push(source[0])
        // stack = "Homer"
stack.push(source[2])
        // stack = "Homer","Bart"
var Simpson1 = stack.pop()
        // stack = "Homer" ; Simpson1 = "Bart"
var Simpson2 = stack.pop()
        // stack = <empty> ; Simpson2 = "Homer"
```

While push() and pop() work at the end of an array, another pair of methods work at the front. Their names are not as picturesque as push() and pop(). To insert a value at the front of an array, use the array.unshift() method; to grab the first element and remove it from the array, use array.shift(). Of course you are not required to use these methods in matching pairs. If you push() a series of values onto the back end of an array, you can shift() them off from the front end without complaint. It all depends on how you need the data.

You may readily see existing parallels to some of these operations (especially the `push()` method), but if you need a temporary staging ground for data, the array stacking methods should help out quite a bit.

Related Items: `array.concat()` method; `array.slice()` method.

arrayObject.reverse()

Returns: Array of entries in the opposite order of the original.

	Nav2	Nav3	Nav4	IE3/J1	IE3/J2	IE4/J3
Compatibility		✔	✔		✔	✔

Occasionally, you may find it more convenient to work with an array of data in reverse order. Although you can concoct repeat loops to count backward through index values, a CGI program on the server may prefer the data in a sequence opposite to the way it was most convenient for you to script it.

You can have JavaScript switch the contents of an array for you: Whatever element was last in the array becomes the 0 index item in the array. Bear in mind that when you do this, you're restructuring the original array, not copying it. A reload of the document restores the order as written in the HTML document.

Example

In Listing 29-8, I enhanced Listing 29-7 by including another button and function that reverses the array and displays it as a string in a text area.

Listing 29-8: **Array.reverse() Method**

```
<HTML>
<HEAD>
<TITLE>Array.reverse()</TITLE>
<SCRIPT LANGUAGE="JavaScript1.1">
solarSys = new Array(9)
solarSys[0] = "Mercury"
solarSys[1] = "Venus"
solarSys[2] = "Earth"
solarSys[3] = "Mars"
solarSys[4] = "Jupiter"
solarSys[5] = "Saturn"
solarSys[6] = "Uranus"
solarSys[7] = "Neptune"
solarSys[8] = "Pluto"

// show array as currently in memory
function showAsIs(form) {
        var delimiter = form.delim.value
        form.output.value = unescape(solarSys.join(delimiter))
}
```

```
        // reverse array order, then display as string
        function reverseIt(form) {
                var delimiter = form.delim.value
                solarSys.reverse()    // reverses original array
                form.output.value = unescape(solarSys.join(delimiter))
        }
</SCRIPT>
<BODY>
<H2>Reversing array element order</H2>
This document contains an array of planets in our solar system.<HR>
<FORM>
Enter a string to act as a delimiter between entries:
<INPUT TYPE="text" NAME="delim" VALUE="," SIZE=5><P>
<INPUT TYPE="button" VALUE="Array as-is" onClick="showAsIs(this.form)">
<INPUT TYPE="button" VALUE="Reverse the array"
onClick="reverseIt(this.form)">
<INPUT TYPE="reset">
<INPUT TYPE="button" VALUE="Reload" onClick="self.location.reload()">
<TEXTAREA NAME="output" ROWS=4 COLS=60>
</TEXTAREA>
</FORM>
</BODY>
</HTML>
```

Notice that the `solarSys.reverse()` method stood by itself while the method modified the `solarSys` array. You then run the now inverted `solarSys` array through the `array.join()` method for your text display.

Related Items: `array.sort()` method.

arrayObject.slice(*startIndex* [, *endIndex*])

Returns: Array.

	Nav2	Nav3	Nav4	IE3/J1	IE3/J2	IE4/J3
Compatibility			✔			✔

Behaving like its like-named string method, `array.slice()` lets you extract a contiguous series of items from an array. The extracted segment becomes an entirely new array object. Values and objects from the original array have the same kind of behavior as arrays created with the `array.concat()` method.

One parameter is required — the starting index point for the extraction. If you don't specify a second parameter, the extraction goes all the way to the end of the array; otherwise the extraction goes to *but does not include* the index value supplied as the second parameter. For example, extracting Earth's neighbors from an array of planet names would look like the following.

```
var solarSys = new
Array("Mercury","Venus","Earth","Mars","Jupiter","Saturn","Uranus","Nep
tune","Pluto")
var nearby = solarSys.slice(1,4)
        // result: new array of "Venus", "Earth", "Mars"
```

Related Items: `string.slice()` method.

arrayObject.sort([*compareFunction*])

Returns: Array of entries in the order as determined by the *compareFunction* algorithm.

	Nav2	Nav3	Nav4	IE3/J1	IE3/J2	IE4/J3
Compatibility		✔	✔		✔	✔

JavaScript array sorting is both powerful and a bit complex to script if you haven't had experience with this kind of sorting methodology. The purpose, obviously, is to let your scripts sort entries of an array by almost any kind of criterion that you can associate with an entry. For entries consisting of strings, the criterion may be their alphabetical order or their length; for numeric entries, the criterion may be their numerical order.

Let's look first at the kind of sorting you can do with the `array.sort()` method by itself (for example, without calling a comparison function). When no parameter is specified, JavaScript takes a snapshot of the contents of the array and converts items to strings. From there, it performs a string sort of the values. ASCII values of characters govern the sort, which means that numbers are sorted by their string values, not their numeric values. This fact has strong implications if your array consists of numeric data: The value 201 sorts before 88, because the sorting mechanism compares the first characters of the strings (`"2"` versus `"8"`) to determine the sort order. For simple alphabetical sorting of string values in arrays, the plain `Array.sort()` method should do the trick.

Fortunately, additional intelligence is available that you can add to array sorting. The key tactic is to define a function that helps the `sort()` method compare items in the array. A comparison function is passed two values from the array (what you don't see is that the `Array.sort()` method rapidly sends numerous pairs of values from the array to help it sort through all entries). The comparison function lets the `sort()` method know which of the two items comes before the other based on the value the function returns. Assuming that the function compares two values, a and b, the returned value reveals information to the `sort()` method, as shown in Table 29-1.

Table 29-1
Comparison Function Return Values

Return Value Range	Meaning
< 0	Value b should sort above a
0	The order of a and b should not change
> 0	Value a should sort above b

Consider the following example:

```
myArray = new Array(12, 5, 200, 80)
function compare(a,b) {
      return a - b
}
myArray.sort(compare)
```

The array has four numeric values in it. To sort the items in numerical order, you define a comparison function (arbitrarily named compare()), which is called from the sort() method. Note that unlike invoking other functions, the parameter of the sort() method uses a reference to the function, which lacks parentheses.

When the compare() function is called, JavaScript automatically sends two parameters to the function in rapid succession until each element has been compared against the others. Every time compare() is called, JavaScript assigns two of the array's values to the parameter variables (a and b). In the preceding example, the returned value is the difference between a and b. If a is larger than b, then a positive value goes back to the sort() method, telling it to sort a above b (that is, position a at a lower value index position than b). Therefore, a may end up at myArray[0], whereas b ends up at a higher index-valued location. On the other hand, if b is larger than a, then the returned negative value tells sort() to put b in a lower index value spot than a.

Evaluations within the comparison function can go to great lengths, as long as some data connected with array values can be compared. For example, instead of numerical comparisons, as just shown, you can perform string comparisons. The following function sorts alphabetically by the last character of each array string entry:

```
function compare(a,b) {
      // last character of array strings
      var aComp = a.charAt(a.length - 1)
      var bComp = b.charAt(b.length - 1)
      if (aComp < bComp) {return -1}
      if (aComp > bComp) {return 1}
      return 0
}
```

First, this function extracts the final character from each of the two values passed to it. Then, because strings cannot be added or subtracted like numbers, you compare the ASCII values of the two characters, returning the corresponding values to the `sort()` method to let it know how to treat the two values being checked at that instant.

Array sorting, unlike sorting routines you might find in other scripting languages, is not a stable sort. This means that succeeding sort routines on the same array are not cumulative. Also remember that sorting changes the sort order of the original array. If you don't want the original array harmed, make a copy of it before sorting; or reload the document to restore an array to its original order.

Should an array element be null, the method sorts such elements at the end of the sorted array starting with Navigator 4 (instead of leaving them in their original places as in Navigator 3).

Unfortunately, this powerful method does not work in the Macintosh version of Navigator 3. All platforms have the feature starting with Navigator 4.

Example

You can look to Listing 29-9 for a few examples of sorting an array of string values. Four buttons summon different sorting routines, three of which invoke comparison functions. This listing sorts the planet array alphabetically (forward and backward) by the last character of the planet name and also by the length of the planet name. Each comparison function demonstrates different ways of comparing data sent during a sort.

Listing 29-9: **Array.sort() Possibilities**

```
<HTML>
<HEAD>
<TITLE>Array.sort()</TITLE>
<SCRIPT LANGUAGE="JavaScript1.1">
solarSys = new Array(9)
solarSys[0] = "Mercury"
solarSys[1] = "Venus"
solarSys[2] = "Earth"
solarSys[3] = "Mars"
solarSys[4] = "Jupiter"
solarSys[5] = "Saturn"
solarSys[6] = "Uranus"
solarSys[7] = "Neptune"
solarSys[8] = "Pluto"
// comparison functions
function compare1(a,b) {
        // reverse alphabetical order
        if (a > b) {return -1}
        if (b > a) {return 1}
        return 0
}
function compare2(a,b) {
        // last character of planet names
        var aComp = a.charAt(a.length - 1)
        var bComp = b.charAt(b.length - 1)
        if (aComp < bComp) {return -1}
        if (aComp > bComp) {return 1}
        return 0
```

```
        }
function compare3(a,b) {
        // length of planet names
        return a.length - b.length
}
// sort and display array
function sortIt(form, compFunc) {
        var delimiter = ";"
        if (compFunc == null) {
            solarSys.sort()
        } else {
            solarSys.sort(compFunc)
        }
        // display results in field
        form.output.value = unescape(solarSys.join(delimiter))
}
</SCRIPT>
<BODY onLoad="document.forms[0].output.value =
unescape(solarSys.join(';'))">
<H2>Sorting array elements</H2>
This document contains an array of planets in our solar system.<HR>
<FORM>
Click on a button to sort the array:<P>
<INPUT TYPE="button" VALUE="Alphabetical A-Z"
onClick="sortIt(this.form)">
<INPUT TYPE="button" VALUE="Alphabetical Z-A"
onClick="sortIt(this.form,compare1)">
<INPUT TYPE="button" VALUE="Last Character"
onClick="sortIt(this.form,compare2)">
<INPUT TYPE="button" VALUE="Name Length"
onClick="sortIt(this.form,compare3)">
<INPUT TYPE="button" VALUE="Reload Original"
onClick="self.location.reload()">
<INPUT TYPE="text" NAME="output" SIZE=62>
</TEXTAREA>
</FORM>
</BODY>
</HTML>
```

Related Items: `array.reverse()` method.

Note

As I show you in the next chapter, many regular expression object methods generate arrays as their result (for example, an array of matching values in a string). These special arrays have a custom set of named properties that assist your script in analyzing the findings of the method. Beyond that, these regular expression result arrays behave like all others.

✦   ✦   ✦

Regular Expression and RegExp Objects

Web programmers who have worked in Perl (and other Web application programming languages) know the power of regular expressions for processing incoming data and formatting data for readability in an HTML page or for accurate storage in a server database. Any task that requires extensive search and replacement of text can greatly benefit from the flexibility and conciseness of regular expressions. Navigator 4 and Internet Explorer 4 bring that power to JavaScript.

Most of the benefit of JavaScript regular expressions accrues to those who script their CGI programs with LiveWire on Enterprise Server 3 or later. The JavaScript version in the LiveWire implementation includes the complete set of regular expression facilities described in this chapter. But that's not to exclude the client-side from application of this "language within a language." If your scripts perform client-side data validations or any other extensive text entry parsing, then consider using regular expressions, rather than cobbling together comparatively complex JavaScript functions to perform the same tasks.

Regular Expressions and Patterns

In several chapters earlier in this book, I describe expressions as any sequence of identifiers, keywords, and/or operators that evaluate to some value. A regular expression follows that description, but has much more power behind it. In essence, a regular expression uses a sequence of characters and symbols to define a pattern of text. Such a pattern is used to locate a chunk of text in a string by matching up the pattern against the characters in the string.

An experienced JavaScript writer might point out the availability of the `string.indexOf()` and `string.lastIndexOf()` methods that can instantly reveal whether a string contains a substring and even where in the string that substring begins. These methods work perfectly well when the match is exact, character for character. But if you want to do more sophisticated matching (for example, does the string contain a five-digit ZIP code?), you'd have to cast aside those handy string methods and write some parsing functions. That's the beauty of a regular expression: It lets you define a matching substring that has some intelligence about it and can follow guidelines you set as to what should or should not match.

The simplest kind of regular expression pattern is the same kind you would use in the `string.indexOf()` method. Such a pattern is nothing more than the text you want to match. In JavaScript, one way to create a regular expression is to surround the expression by forward slashes. For example, consider the string

```
Oh, hello, do you want to play Othello in the school play?
```

This string and others may be examined by a script whose job it is to turn formal terms into informal ones. Therefore, one of its tasks is to replace the word "hello" with "hi." A typical brute force search-and-replace function would start with a simple pattern of the search string. In JavaScript, you define a pattern (a regular expression) by surrounding it with forward slashes. For convenience and readability, I usually assign the regular expression to a variable, as in the following example:

```
var myRegExpression = /hello/
```

In concert with some regular expression or string object methods, this pattern matches the string "hello" wherever that series of letters appears. The problem is that this simple pattern causes problems during the loop that searches and replaces the strings in the example string: It finds not only the standalone word "hello," but also the "hello" in "Othello."

Trying to write another brute force routine for this search-and-replace operation that looks only for standalone words would be a nightmare. You can't merely extend the simple pattern to include spaces on either or both sides of "hello," because there could be punctuation — a comma, a dash, a colon, or whatever — before or after the letters. Fortunately, regular expressions provide a shortcut way to specify general characteristics, including something known as a *word boundary*. The symbol for a word boundary is \b (backslash, lowercase b). If you redefine the pattern to include these specifications on both ends of the text to match, the regular expression creation statement looks like

```
var myRegExpression = /\bhello\b/
```

When JavaScript uses this regular expression as a parameter in a special string object method that performs search-and-replace operations, it changes only the standalone word "hello" to "hi," and passes over "Othello" entirely.

If you are still learning JavaScript and don't have experience with regular expressions in other languages, you have a price to pay for this power: Learning the regular expression lingo filled with so many symbols means that expressions sometimes look like cartoon substitutions for swear words. The goal of this chapter is to introduce you to regular expression syntax as implemented in JavaScript rather than engage in lengthy tutorials for this language. Of more importance in the long run is understanding how JavaScript treats regular expressions as objects and distinctions between regular expression objects and the RegExp constructor. I hope the examples in the following sections begin to reveal the powers of regular expressions. An in-depth treatment of the possibilities and idiosyncracies of regular expressions can be found in *Mastering Regular Expressions* by Jeffrey E.F. Friedl. (1997, O'Reilly & Associates, Inc.)

Language Basics

To cover the depth of the regular expression syntax, I divide the subject into three sections. The first covers simple expressions (some of which you've already seen). Then I get into the wide range of special characters used to define specifications for search strings. Last comes an introduction to the usage of parentheses in the language, and how they not only help in grouping expressions for influencing calculation precedence (as they do for regular math expressions), but also how they temporarily store intermediate results of more complex expressions for use in reconstructing strings after their dissection by the regular expression.

Simple patterns

A simple regular expression uses no special characters for defining the string to be used in a search. Therefore, if you wanted to replace every space in a string with an underscore character, the simple pattern to match the space character is

```
var re = / /
```

A space appears between the regular expression start-end forward slashes. The problem with this expression, however, is that it knows only how to find a single instance of a space in a long string. Regular expressions can be instructed to apply the matching string on a global basis by appending the g modifier:

```
var re = / /g
```

When this re value is supplied as a parameter to the replace() method that uses regular expressions (described later in this chapter), the replacement is performed throughout the entire string, rather than just once on the first match found. Notice that the modifier appears *after* the final forward slash of the regular expression creation statement.

Regular expression matching — like a lot of other aspects of JavaScript — is case-sensitive. But you can override this behavior by using one other modifier that lets you specify a case-insensitive match. Therefore, the following expression

```
var re = /web/i
```

finds a match for "web," "Web," or any combination of uppercase and lowercase letters in the word. You can combine the two modifiers together at the end of a regular expression. For example, the following expression is both case-insensitive and global in scope:

```
var re = /web/gi
```

Special characters

The regular expression in JavaScript borrows most of its vocabulary from the Perl regular expression. In a few instances, JavaScript offers alternatives to simplify the syntax, but also accepts the Perl version for those with experience in that arena.

Significant programming power comes from the way regular expressions allow you to include terse specifications about such things as types of characters to accept in a match, how the characters are surrounded within a string, and how often a type of character can appear in the matching string. A series of escaped one-character commands (that is, letters preceded by the backslash) handle most of the character issues; punctuation and grouping symbols help define issues of frequency and range.

You saw an example earlier how \b specified a word boundary on one side of a search string. Table 30-1 lists the escaped character specifiers in JavaScript regular expressions. The vocabulary forms part of what are known as metacharacters — characters in expressions that are not matchable characters themselves, but act more like commands or guidelines of the regular expression language.

Table 30-1
JavaScript Regular Expression Matching Metacharacters

Character	Matches	Example
\b	Word boundary	/\bor/ matches "origami" and "or" but not "normal"
		/or\b/ matches "traitor" and "or" but not "perform"
		/\bor\b/ matches full word "or" and nothing else
\B	Word nonboundary	/\Bor/ matches "normal" but not "origami"
		/or\B/ matches "normal" and "origami" but not "traitor"
		/\Bor\B/ matches "normal" but not "origami" or "traitor"
\d	Numeral 0 through 9	/\d\d\d/ matches "212" and "415" but not "B17"
\D	Nonnumeral	/\D\D\D/ matches "ABC" but not "212" or "B17"
\s	Single white space	/over\sbite/ matches "over bite" but not "overbite" or "over bite"
\S	Single nonwhite space	/over\Sbite/ matches "over-bite" but not "overbite" or "over bite"
\w	Letter, numeral, or underscore	/A\w/ matches "A1" and "AA" but not "A+"

Character	Matches	Example
\W	Not letter, numeral, or underscore	/A\W/ matches "A+" but not "A1" and "AA"
.	Any character except newline	/.../ matches "ABC", "1+3", "A 3", or any three characters
[...]	Character set	/[AN]BC/ matches "ABC" and "NBC" but not "BBC"
[^...]	Negated character set	/[^AN]BC/ matches "BBC" and "CBC" but not "ABC" or "NBC"

Not to be confused with the metacharacters listed in Table 30-1 are the escaped string characters for tab (\t), newline (\n), carriage return (\r), formfeed (\f), and vertical tab (\v).

Let me further clarifiy about the [...] and [^...] metacharacters. You can specify either individual characters between the brackets (as shown in Table 30-1) or a contiguous range of characters or both. For example, the \d metacharacter can also be defined by [0-9], meaning any numeral from zero through nine. If you only want to accept a value of 2 and a range from 6 through 8, the specification would be [26-8]. Similarly, the accommodating \w metacharacter is defined as [A-Za-z0-9_], reminding you of the case-sensitivity of regular expression matches not otherwise modified.

All but the bracketed character set items listed in Table 30-1 apply to a single character in the regular expression. In most cases, however, you cannot predict how incoming data will be formatted — the length of a word or the number of digits in a number. A batch of extra metacharacters lets you set the frequency of the occurrence of either a specific character or a type of character (specified like the ones in Table 30-1). If you have experience in command-line operating systems, you can see some of the same ideas that apply to wildcards apply to regular expressions. Table 30-2 lists the counting metacharacters in JavaScript regular expressions.

Table 30-2
JavaScript Regular Expression Counting Metacharacters

Character	Matches Last Character	Example
*	Zero or more times	/Ja*vaScript/ matches "JvaScript", "JavaScript", and "JaaavaScript" but not "JovaScript"
?	Zero or one time	/Ja?vaScript/ matches "JvaScript" or "JavaScript" but not "JaaavaScript"
+	One or more times	/Ja+vaScript/ matches "JavaScript" or "JaaavaScript" but not "JvaScript"
{n}	Exactly n times	/Ja{2}vaScript/ matches "JaavaScript" but not "JvaScript" or "JavaScript"

(continued)

Table 30-2 *(continued)*

Character	Matches Last Character	Example
{n,}	*n* or more times	/Ja{2,}vaScript/ matches "JaavaScript" or "JaaavaScript" but not "JavaScript"
{n,m}	At least *n*, at most *m* times	/Ja{2,3}vaScript/ matches "JaavaScript" or "JaaavaScript" but not "JavaScript"

Every metacharacter in Table 30-2 applies to the character immediately preceding it in the regular expression. Preceding characters might also be matching metacharacters from Table 30-1. For example, a match occurs for the following expression if the string contains two digits separated by one or more vowels:

```
/\d[aeiouy]+\d/
```

The last major contribution of metacharacters is helping the regular expression search a particular position in a string. By position, I don't mean something like an offset — the matching functionality of regular expressions can tell me that. But, rather, whether the string to look for should be at the beginning or end of a line (if that is important) or whatever string is offered as the main string to search. Table 30-3 shows the positional metacharacters for JavaScript's regular expressions.

Table 30-3
JavaScript Regular Expression Positional Metacharacters

Character	Matches Located	Example
^	At beginning of a string or line	/^Fred/ matches "Fred is OK" but not "I'm with Fred" or "Is Fred here?"
$	At end of a string or line	/Fred$/ matches "I'm with Fred" but not "Fred is OK" or "Is Fred here?"

For example, you might want to make sure that a match for a roman numeral is found only when it is at the start of a line, rather than when it is used inline somewhere else. If the document contains roman numerals in an outline, you can match all the top-level items that are flush left with the document with a regular expression like the following:

```
/^[IVXMDCL]+\./
```

This expression matches any combination of roman numeral characters followed by a period (the period is a special character in regular expressions, as shown in Table 30-1, so you have to escape the period to offer it as a character), provided the roman numeral is at the beginning of a line and has no tabs or spaces before it. There would also not be a match in a line that contains, say, the phrase "see Part IV" because the roman numeral is not at the beginning of a line.

Speaking of lines, a line of text is a contiguous string of characters delimited by a newline and/or carriage return (depending on the operating system platform). Word wrapping in text areas does not affect the starts and ends of true lines of text.

Grouping and backreferencing

Regular expressions obey most of the JavaScript operator precedence laws with regard to grouping by parentheses and the logical Or operator. One difference is that the regular expression Or operator is a single pipe character (|) rather than JavaScript's double pipe.

Parentheses have additional powers that go beyond influencing the precedence of calculation. Any set of parentheses (that is, a matched pair of left and right) stores the results of a found match of the expression within those parentheses. Parentheses can be nested inside one another. Storage is accomplished automatically, with the data stored in an indexed array accessible to your scripts and to your regular expressions (although through different syntax). Access to these storage bins is known as *backreferencing*, because a regular expression can point backward to the result of an expression component earlier in the overall expression. These stored subcomponents come in handy for replace operations, as demonstrated later in this chapter.

Object Relationships

JavaScript has a lot going on behind the scenes when you create a regular expression and perform the simplest operation with it. As important as the regular expression language described earlier in this chapter is to applying regular expressions in your scripts, the JavaScript object interrelationships are perhaps even more important if you want to exploit regular expressions to the fullest.

The first concept to master is that two entities are involved: the *regular expression* object and the *RegExp* constructor. Both objects are core objects of JavaScript and are not part of the document object model. Both objects work together, but have entirely different sets of properties that may be useful to your application.

When you create a regular expression (even via the `/.../` syntax), JavaScript invokes the `new RegExp()` constructor, much the way a `new Date()` constructor creates a date object around one specific date. The regular expression object returned by the constructor is endowed with several properties containing details of its data. At the same time, the RegExp object maintains its own properties that monitor regular expression activity in the current window (or frame).

To help you see the typically unseen operations, I step you through the creation and application of a regular expression. In the process, I show you what happens to all of the related object properties when you use one of the regular expression methods to search for a match. The starting text I'll use to search through is the beginning of Hamlet's soliloquy (assigned to an arbitrary variable named `mainString`):

```
var mainString = "To be, or not to be: That is the question:"
```

If my ultimate goal is to locate each instance of the word "be," I must first create a regular expression that matches the word "be." I set it up to perform a global search when eventually called upon to replace itself (assigning the expression to an arbitrary variable named re):

```
var re = /\bbe\b/g
```

To guarantee that only complete words "be" are matched, I surround the letters with the word boundary metacharacters. The final "g" is the global modifier. The variable to which the expression is assigned, re, represents a regular expression object whose properties and values are as follows:

Object.PropertyName	*Value*
re.source	"\bbe\bg"
re.global	true
re.ignoreCase	false
re.lastIndex	0

A regular expression's source property is the string consisting of the regular expression syntax (less the literal forward slashes). Each of the two possible modifiers, g and i, have their own properties, global and ignoreCase, whose values are Booleans indicating whether the modifiers are part of the source expression. The final property, lastIndex, indicates the index value within the main string at which the next search for a match should start. The default value for this property in a newly hatched regular expression is zero so that the search starts with the first character of the string. This property is read/write, so your scripts may want to adjust the value if they must have special control over the search process. As you will see in a moment, JavaScript modifies this value over time if a global search is indicated for the object.

The RegExp constructor does more than just create regular expression objects. Like the Math object, the RegExp object is always "around" — one RegExp per window or frame — and tracks regular expression activity in a script. Its properties reveal what, if any, regular expression pattern matching has just taken place in the window. At this stage of the regular expression creation process, the RegExp object has only one of its properties set:

Object.PropertyName	*Value*
RexExp.input	
RexExp.multiline	false
RexExp.lastMatch	
RexExp.lastParen	
RexExp.leftContext	

Object.PropertyName	Value
RexExp.rightContext	
RexExp.$1	
...	
RexExp.$9	

The last group of properties ($1 through $9) are for storage of backreferences. But since the regular expression I defined doesn't have any parentheses in it, these properties are empty for the duration of this examination and omitted from future listings in this section.

With the regular expression object ready to go, I invoke the exec() regular expression method, which looks through a string for a match defined by the regular expression. If the method is successful in finding a match, it returns a third object whose properties reveal a great deal about the item it found (I arbitrarily assigned the variable foundArray to this returned object):

```
var foundArray = re.exec(mainString)
```

JavaScript includes a shortcut for the exec() method if you turn the regular expression object into a method:

```
var foundArray = re(mainString)
```

Normally, a script would check whether foundArray is null (meaning that there was no match) before proceeding to inspect the rest of the related objects. Since this is a controlled experiment, I know at least one match exists, so I first look into some other results. Running this simple method has not only generated the foundArray data, but also altered several properties of the RegExp and regular expression objects. The following shows you the current stage of the regular expression object:

Object.PropertyName	Value
re.source	"\bbe\bg"
re.global	true
re.ignoreCase	false
re.lastIndex	5

The only change is an important one: The lastIndex value has bumped up to 5. In other words, this one invocation of the exec() method must have found a match whose offset plus length of matching string shifts the starting point of any successive searches with this regular expression to character index 5. That's exactly where the comma after the first "be" word is in the main string. If the global (g) modifier had not been appended to the regular expression, the lastIndex value would have remained at zero, because no subsequent search would be anticipated.

As the result of the exec() method, the RegExp object has had a number of its properties filled with results of the search:

Object.PropertyName	Value
RexExp.input	
RexExp.multiline	false
RexExp.lastMatch	"be"
RexExp.lastParen	
RexExp.leftContext	"To "
RexExp.rightContext	", or not to be: That is the question:"

From this object you can extract the string segment that was found to match the regular expression definition. The main string segments before and after the matching text are also available individually (in this example, the leftContext property has a space after "To"). Finally, looking into the array returned from the exec() method, some additional data is readily accessible:

Object.PropertyName	Value
foundArray[0]	"be"
foundArray.index	3
foundArray.input	"To be, or not to be: That is the question:"

The first element in the array, indexed as the zeroth element, is the string segment found to match the regular expression, which is the same as the RegExp.lastMatch value. The complete main string value is available as the input property. A potentially valuable piece of information to a script is the index for the start of the matched string found in the main string. From this last bit of data, you can extract from the found data array the same values as RegExp.leftContext (with foundArray.input.substring(0, foundArray.index)) and RegExp.rightContext (with foundArray.input.substring(foundArray.index, foundArray[0].length)).

Since the regular expression suggested a multiple execution sequence to fulfill the global flag, I can run the exec() method again without any change. While the JavaScript statement may not be any different, the search starts from the new re.lastIndex value. The effects of this second time through ripple through the resulting values of all three objects associated with this method:

```
var foundArray = re.exec(mainString)
```

Results of this execution are as follows (changes are in boldface).

Object.PropertyName	*Value*
re.source	"\bbe\bg"
re.global	true
re.ignoreCase	false
re.lastIndex	**19**
RexExp.input	
RexExp.multiline	false
RexExp.lastMatch	"be"
RexExp.lastParen	
RexExp.leftContext	", or not to "
RexExp.rightContext	": That is the question:"
foundArray[0]	"be"
foundArray.index	**17**
foundArray.input	"To be, or not to be: That is the question:"

Because there was a second match, foundArray comes back again with data. Its index property now points to the location of the second instance of the string matching the regular expression definition. The regular expression object's lastIndex value points to where the next search would begin (after the second "be"). And the RegExp properties that store the left and right contexts have adjusted accordingly.

If the regular expression were looking for something less stringent than a hard-coded word, some other properties might also be different. For example, if the regular expression defined a format for a ZIP code, the RegExp.lastMatch and foundArray[0] values would contain the actual found ZIP codes, which would likely be different from one match to the next.

Running the same exec() method once more would not find a third match in my original mainString value, but the impact of that lack of a match is worth noting. First of all, the foundArray value would be null — a signal to our script that no more matches were available. The regular expression object's lastIndex property reverts to zero, ready to start its search from the beginning of another string. Most importantly, however, the RegExp object's properties maintain the same values from the last successful match. Therefore, if you put the exec() method invocations in a repeat loop that exits when no more matches are found, the RegExp object still has the data from the last successful match, ready for further processing by your scripts.

Using Regular Expressions

Despite the seemingly complex hidden workings of regular expressions, JavaScript provides a series of methods that make common tasks involving regular expressions quite simple to use (assuming you figure out the regular expression syntax to create good specifications). In this section, I'll present examples of syntax for specific kinds of tasks for which regular expressions can be beneficial in your pages.

Is there a match?

I said earlier that you can use `string.indexOf()` or `string.lastIndexOf()` to look for the presence of simple substrings within larger strings. But if you need the matching power of regular expression, you have two methods to choose from:

```
regexObject.test(string)
```

```
string.search(regexObject)
```

The first is a regular expression object method, the second a string object method. Both perform the same task and influence the same related objects, but they return different values: a Boolean value for `test()` and a character offset value for `search()` (or -1 if no match is found). Which method you choose depends on whether you need only a true/false verdict on a match or the location within the main string of the start of the substring.

Listing 30-1 demonstrates both methods on a page that lets you get the Boolean and offset values for a match. Some default text and regular expression is provided (it looks for a five-digit number). You can experiment with other strings and regular expressions. Because this script creates a regular expression object with the `new RegExp()` constructor method, you do not include the literal forward slashes around the regular expression.

Listing 30-1: **Looking for a Match**

```
<HTML>
<HEAD>
<TITLE>Got a Match?</TITLE>
<SCRIPT LANGUAGE="JavaScript1.2">
function findIt(form) {
        var re = new RegExp(form.regexp.value)
        var input = form.main.value
        if (input.search(re) != -1) {
            form.output[0].checked = true
        } else {
            form.output[1].checked = true
        }
}
function locateIt(form) {
        var re = new RegExp(form.regexp.value)
        var input = form.main.value
        form.offset.value = input.search(re)
}
```

```
</SCRIPT>
</HEAD>
<BODY>
<B>Use a regular expression to test for the existence of a string:</B>
<HR>
<FORM>
Enter some text to be searched:<BR>
<TEXTAREA NAME="main" COLS=40 ROWS=4 WRAP="virtual">
The most famous ZIP code on Earth may be 90210.
</TEXTAREA><BR>
Enter a regular expression to search:<BR>
<INPUT TYPE="text" NAME="regexp" SIZE=30 VALUE="\b\d\d\d\d\d\b"><P>
<INPUT TYPE="button" VALUE="Is There a Match?"
onClick="findIt(this.form)">
<INPUT TYPE="radio" NAME="output">Yes
<INPUT TYPE="radio" NAME="output">No <P>
<INPUT TYPE="button" VALUE="Where is it?"
onClick="locateIt(this.form)">
<INPUT TYPE="text" NAME="offset" SIZE=4><P>
<INPUT TYPE="reset">
</FORM>
</BODY>
</HTML>
```

Getting information about a match

For the next application example, the task is to not only verify that a one-field date entry is in the desired format, but also extract match components of the entry and use those values to perform further calculations in determining the day of the week. The regular expression in the example that follows is a fairly complex one, because it performs some rudimentary range checking to make sure the user doesn't enter a month over 12 or a date over 31. What it does not take into account is the variety of lengths of each month. But the regular expression and method invoked with it extracts each date object component in such a way that you can perform additional validation on the range to make sure the user doesn't try to give September 31 days. Also be aware that this is not the only way to perform date validations in forms. Chapter 37 offers additional thoughts on the matter that work without regular expressions for backward compatibility.

Listing 30-2 contains a page that has a field for date entry, a button to process the date, and an output field for display of a long version of the date, including the day of the week. At the start of the function that does all the work, I create two arrays (using the JavaScript 1.2 literal array creation syntax) to hold the plain language names of the months and days. These are used only if the user enters a valid date.

Next comes the regular expression to be matched against the user entry. If you can decipher all the symbols, you see that three components are separated by potential hyphen or forward slash entries ([\-\/]). These symbols must be escaped in the regular expression. Importantly, each of the three component definitions is surrounded by parentheses, which are essential for the various objects created with the regular expression to remember their values for extraction later.

Here is a brief rundown of what the regular expression is looking for:

✦ A string beginning after a word break

✦ A string value for the month that contains a 1 plus a 0 through 2; or an optional 0 plus a 1 through 9

✦ A hyphen or forward slash

✦ A string value for the date that starts with a 0 plus a 1 through 9; or starts with a 1 or 2 and ends with a 0 through 9; or starts with a 3 and ends with 0 or 1

✦ Another hyphen or forward slash

✦ A string value for the year that begins with 19 or 20, followed by two digits

An extra pair of parentheses must surround the 19|20 segment to make sure that either one of the matching values is attached to the two succeeding digits. Without the parentheses, the logic of the expression attaches the digits only to 20.

For invoking the regular expression action, I selected the exec() method, assigning the returned object to the variable matchArray. I could have also used the string.match() method here. Only if the match is successful (that is, all conditions of the regular expression specification have been met) does the major processing continue in the script.

The parentheses around the segments of the regular expression instruct JavaScript to assign each found value to a slot in the matchArray object. The month segment is assigned to matchArray[1], the date to matchArray[2], and the year to matchArray[3] (matchArray[0] contains the entire matched string). Therefore, the script can extract each component to build a plain-language date string with the help of the arrays defined at the start of the function. I even use the values to create a new Date object that calculates the day of the week for me. Once I have all pieces, I concatenate them and assign the result to the value of the output field. If the regular expression exec() method doesn't match the typed entry with the expression, the script provides an error message in the field.

Listing 30-2: **Extracting Data from a Match**

```
<HTML>
<HEAD>
<TITLE>Got a Match?</TITLE>
<SCRIPT LANGUAGE="JavaScript1.2">
function extractIt(form) {
        var months =
["January","February","March","April","May","June","July","August","Sep
tember","October","November","December"]
        var days =
["Sunday","Monday","Tuesday","Wednesday","Thursday","Friday","Saturday"
]
        var re = /\b(1[0-2]|0?[1-9])[\-\/](0?[1-9]|[12][0-9]|3[01])[\-
\/]((19|20)\d{2})/
```

```
        var input = form.entry.value
        var matchArray = re.exec(input)
        if (matchArray) {
            var theMonth = months[matchArray[1] - 1] + " "
            var theDate = matchArray[2] + ", "
            var theYear = matchArray[3]
            var dateObj = new Date(matchArray[3],matchArray[1]-
1,matchArray[2])
            var theDay = days[dateObj.getDay()] + " "
            form.output.value = theDay + theMonth + theDate + theYear
        } else {
            form.output.value = "An invalid date."
        }
}
</SCRIPT>
</HEAD>
<BODY>
<B>Use a regular expression to extract data from a string:</B>
<HR>
<FORM>
Enter a date in the format mm/dd/yyyy or mm-dd-yyyy:<BR>
<INPUT TYPE="text" NAME="entry" SIZE=12><P>
<INPUT TYPE="button" VALUE="Extract Date Components"
onClick="extractIt(this.form)"><P>
The date you entered was:<BR>
<INPUT TYPE="text" NAME="output" SIZE=40><P>
<INPUT TYPE="reset">
</FORM>
</BODY>
</HTML>
```

String replacement

To demonstrate using regular expressions for performing search-and-replace operations, I chose an application that may be of value to many page authors who have to display and format large numbers. Databases typically store large integers without commas. After five or six digits, however, such numbers are difficult for users to read. Conversely, if the user needs to enter a large number, commas help ensure accuracy.

Helping the procedure in JavaScript regular expressions is the method `string.replace()` that has been added to the language with JavaScript 1.2 (see Chapter 26). The method requires two parameters, a regular expression to search the string and a string to replace any match found in the string. The replacement string can be properties of the RegExp object as it stands after the most recent `exec()` method.

Listing 30-3 demonstrates how only a handful of script lines can do a lot of work when regular expressions handle the dirty work. The page contains three fields. Enter any number you like in the first one. A click of the Insert Commas button invokes the `commafy()` function in the page. The result is displayed in the second field. You can also enter a comma-filled number in the second field and click the

Remove Commas button to see the inverse operation executed through the `decommafy()` function.

Specifications for the regular expression accept any positive or negative string of numbers. The keys to the action of this script are the parentheses around two segments of the regular expression. One set encompasses all characters not included in the second group: a required set of three digits. In other words, the regular expression is essentially working from the rear of the string, chomping off three-character segments and inserting a comma each time a set is found.

A `while` repeat loop cycles through the string and modifies the string (in truth, the string object is not being modified, but, rather, a new string is generated and assigned to the old variable name). I use the `test()` method because I don't need the returned value of the `exec()` method. The `test()` method impacts the regular expression and RegExp object properties the same way as the `exec()` method, but more efficiently. The first time the `test()` method runs, the part of the string that meets the first segment is assigned to the `RegExp.$1` property; the second segment, if any, is assigned to the `RegExp.$2` property. Notice that I'm not assigning the results of the `exec()` method to any variable, because for this application I don't need the array object generated by that method.

Next comes the tricky part. I invoke the `string.replace()` method, using the current value of the string (num) as the starting string. The pattern to search for is the regular expression defined at the head of the function. But the replacement string might look strange to you. It is replacing whatever the regular expression matches with the value of `RegExp.$1`, a comma, and the value of `RegExp.$2`. The RegExp object should not be part of the references used in the `replace()` method parameter. Since the regular expression matches the entire `num` string, the `replace()` method is essentially rebuilding the string from its components, plus adding a comma before the second component (the last free-standing three-digit section). Each `replace()` method invocation sets the value of `num` for the next time through the while loop and the `test()` method.

Looping continues until no matches occur — meaning that no more free-standing sets of three digits appear in the string. Then the results are written to the second field on the page.

Listing 30-3: **Replacing Strings via Regular Expressions**

```
<HTML>
<HEAD>
<TITLE>Got a Match?</TITLE>
<SCRIPT LANGUAGE="JavaScript1.2">
function commafy(form) {
        var re = /(-?\d+)(\d{3})/
        var num = form.entry.value
        while (re.test(num)) {
            num = num.replace(re, "$1,$2")
        }
        form.commaOutput.value = num
}
function decommafy(form) {
        var re = /,/g
```

```
          form.plainOutput.value = form.commaOutput.value.replace(re,"")
   }
</SCRIPT>
</HEAD>
<BODY>
<B>Use a regular expression to add/delete commas from numbers:</B>
<HR>
<FORM>
Enter a large number without any commas:<BR>
<INPUT TYPE="text" NAME="entry" SIZE=15><P>
<INPUT TYPE="button" VALUE="Insert commas"
onClick="commafy(this.form)"><P>
The comma version is:<BR>
<INPUT TYPE="text" NAME="commaOutput" SIZE=20><P>
<INPUT TYPE="button" VALUE="Remove commas"
onClick="decommafy(this.form)"><P>
The un-comma version is:<BR>
<INPUT TYPE="text" NAME="plainOutput" SIZE=15><P>
<INPUT TYPE="reset">
</FORM>
</BODY>
</HTML>
```

Removing the commas is an even easier process. The regular expression is a comma with the global flag set. The replace() method reacts to the global flag by repeating the process until all matches are replaced. In this case, the replacement string is an empty string. For further examples of using regular expressions with string objects, see the discussions of the string.match(), string.replace(), and string.split() methods in Chapter 26.

Regular Expression Object

Properties	Methods	Event Handlers
global	compile()	(None)
ignoreCase	exec()	
lastIndex	test()	
source		

Syntax

Creating a regular expression:

regularExpressionObject = /*pattern*/ [g | i | gi]

regularExpressionObject = new RegExp([*"pattern"*, [*"g"* | *"i"* | *"gi"*]])

Accessing regular expression properties or methods:

```
regularExpressionObject.property | method([parameters])
```

	Nav2	Nav3	Nav4	IE3/J1	IE3/J2	IE4/J3
Compatibility			✔			✔

About this object

The regular expression object is created on the fly by your scripts. Each regular expression object contains its own pattern and other properties. Deciding which object creation style to use depends on the way the regular expression will be used in your scripts.

When you create a regular expression with the literal notation (that is, with the two forward slashes), the expression is automatically compiled for efficient processing as the assignment statement executes. The same is true when you use the `new RegExp()` constructor and specify a pattern (and optional modifier flags) as a parameter. Whenever the regular expression is fixed in the script, use the literal notation; when some or all of the regular expression is derived from an external source (for example, user input from a text field), assemble the expression as a parameter to the `new RegExp()` constructor. A compiled regular expression should be used at whatever stage the expression is ready to be applied and reused within the script. Compiled regular expressions are not saved to disk or given any more permanence beyond the life of a document's script (that is, it dies when the page unloads).

However, there may be times in which the specification for the regular expression changes with each iteration through a loop construction. For example, if statements in a `while` loop modify the content of a regular expression, you should compile the expression inside the `while` loop, as shown in the following skeletal script fragment:

```
var srchText = form.search.value
var re = new RegExp()  // empty constructor
while (someCondition) {
        re.compile("\\s+" + srchText + "\\s+", "gi")
        statements that change srchText
}
```

Each time through the loop, the regular expression object is both given a new expression (concatenated with metacharacters for one or more white spaces on both sides of some search text whose content changes constantly) and compiled into an efficient object for use with any associated methods.

Properties

`global`

`ignoreCase`

Value: Booleans   **Gettable:** Yes   **Settable:** No

	Nav2	Nav3	Nav4	IE3/J1	IE3/J2	IE4/J3
Compatibility			✔			✔

These two properties reflect the regular expression g and i modifier flags, if any, associated with a regular expression. Settings are read-only and are determined when the object is created. Each property is independent of the other.

Related Items: None.

`lastIndex`

Value: Integer   **Gettable:** Yes   **Settable:** Yes

	Nav2	Nav3	Nav4	IE3/J1	IE3/J2	IE4/J3
Compatibility			✔			✔

The lastIndex property indicates the index counter of the main string to be searched against the current regular expression object. When a regular expression object is created, this value is zero, meaning that there have been no searches with this object, and the default behavior of the first search is to start at the beginning of the string.

If the regular expression has the global modifier specified, the lastIndex property value advances to some higher value after the object is used in a method to match within a main string. The value is the position in the main string immediately after the previous matched string (and not including any character of the matched string). After locating the final match in a string, the method resets the lastIndex property to zero for the next time. You can also influence the behavior of matches by setting this value on the fly. For example, if you want the expression to begin its search at the fourth character of a target string, you would change the setting immediately after creating the object, as follows:

```
var re = /somePattern/
re.lastIndex = 3  // fourth character in zero-based index system
```

Related Items: Match result object index property.

```
source
```

Value: String   **Gettable:** Yes   **Settable:** No

	Nav2	Nav3	Nav4	IE3/J1	IE3/J2	IE4/J3
Compatibility			✔			✔

The source property is simply the string representation of the regular expression used to define the object. This property is read-only.

Related Items: None.

Methods

```
compile("pattern", ["g" | "i" | "gi"])
```

Returns: Regular expression object.

	Nav2	Nav3	Nav4	IE3/J1	IE3/J2	IE4/J3
Compatibility			✔			✔

Use the compile() method to compile on the fly a regular expression whose content changes continually during the execution of a script. See the discussion earlier about this object for an example. Other regular expression creation statements (the literal notation and the new RegExp() constructor that passes a regular expression) automatically compile their expressions.

Related Items: None.

```
exec("string")
```

Returns: Match array object or null.

	Nav2	Nav3	Nav4	IE3/J1	IE3/J2	IE4/J3
Compatibility			✔			✔

The exec() method examines the string passed as its parameter for at least one match of the specification defined for the regular expression object. The behavior of this method is similar to that of the string.match() method (although the match() method is more powerful in completing global matches). Typically, a call to the exec() method is made immediately after the creation of a regular expression object, as in the following example.

regularExpressionObject.exec()

```
var re = /somePattern/
var matchArray = re.exec("someString")
```

Much happens as a result of the exec() method. Properties of both the regular expression object and window's RegExp object are updated based on the success of the match. The method also returns an object that conveys additional data about the operation. Table 30-4 shows the properties of this returned object.

Table 30-4
Match Found Array Object Properties

Property	Description
index	Zero-based index counter of the start of the match inside the string
input	Entire text of original string
[0]	String of most recent matched characters
[1],...[n]	Parenthesized component matches

Some of the properties in this returned object mirror properties in the RegExp object. The value of having them in the regular expression object is that their contents are safely stowed in the object while the RegExp object and its properties may be modified soon by another call to a regular expression method. Items the two objects have in common are the [0] property (mapped to the RegExp.lastMatch property) and the [1],...[n] properties (the first nine of which map to RegExp.$1...RegExp.$9). While the RegExp object stores only nine parenthesized subcomponents, the returned array object stores as many as are needed to accommodate parenthesis pairs in the regular expression.

If no match turns up between the regular expression specification and the string, the returned value is null. See Listing 30-2 for an example of how this method can be applied. An alternate shortcut syntax may be used for the exec() method. Turn the regular expression into a function, as in

```
var re = /somePattern/
var matchArray = re("someString")
```

Related Items: string.match() method.

test("*string*")

Returns: Boolean.

	Nav2	Nav3	Nav4	IE3/J1	IE3/J2	IE4/J3
Compatibility			✔			✔

The most efficient way to find out if a regular expression has a match in a string is to use the `test()` method. Returned values are `true` if a match exists and `false` if not. In case you need more information, a companion method, `string.search()`, returns the starting index value of the matching string. See Listing 30-1 for an example of this method in action.

Related Items: `string.search()` method.

RegExp Object

Properties	Methods	Event Handlers
`input`	(None)	(None)
`lastMatch`		
`lastParen`		
`leftContext`		
`multiline`		
`rightContext`		
`$1, ... $9`		

Syntax

Accessing `RegExp` properties:

`RegExp.property`

	Nav2	Nav3	Nav4	IE3/J1	IE3/J2	IE4/J3
Compatibility			✔			✔

About this object

Beginning with Navigator 4 and Internet Explorer 4, the browser maintains a single instance of a RegExp object for each window or frame. The object oversees the action of all methods that involve regular expressions (including the few related string object methods). Properties of this object are exposed not only to JavaScript in the traditional manner, but also to a parameter of the method `string.replace()` for some shortcut access (see Listing 30-3).

With one RegExp object serving all regular expression-related methods in your document's scripts, you must exercise care in accessing or modifying this object's properties. You must make sure that the RegExp object has not been affected by another method. Most properties are subject to change as the result of any method involving a regular expression. This may be reason enough to use the properties of the array object returned by most regular expression methods instead of the RegExp properties. The former stick with a specific regular expression object even after other regular expression objects are used in the same script. The RegExp properties reflect the most recent activity, irrespective of the regular expression object involved.

In the following listings, I supply the long, JavaScript-like property names. But each property also has an abbreviated, Perl-like manner to refer to the same properties. You can use these shortcut property names in the `string.replace()` method if you need the values.

Properties

input

Value: String   **Gettable:** Yes   **Settable:** Yes

	Nav2	Nav3	Nav4	IE3/J1	IE3/J2	IE4/J3
Compatibility			✔			✔

The `RegExp.input` property is the main string against which a regular expression is compared in search of a match. In all of the example listings earlier in this chapter, the property was null. Such is the case when the main string is supplied as a parameter to the regular expression-related method.

But many text-related document objects have an unseen relationship with the RegExp object. If a text, textarea, select, or link object contains an event handler that invokes a function containing a regular expression, the `RegExp.input` property is set to the relevant textual data from the object. You don't have to specify any parameters for the event handler call or in the function called by the event handler. For text and textarea objects, the `input` property value becomes the content of the object; for the select object, it is the text (not the value) of the selected option; and for a link, it is the text highlighted in the browser associated with the link (and reflected in the link's text property).

Having JavaScript set the `RegExp.input` property for you may simplify your script. You can invoke either of the regular expression methods without having to specify the main string parameter. When that parameter is empty, JavaScript applies the `RegExp.input` property to the task. You can also set this property on the fly if you like. The short version of this property is $_ (dollar sign underscore).

Related Items: Matching array object input property.

multiline

Value: Boolean   **Gettable:** Yes   **Settable:** Yes

	Nav2	Nav3	Nav4	IE3/J1	IE3/J2	IE4/J3
Compatibility			✔			✔

The `RegExp.multiline` property determines whether searches extend across multiple lines of a target string. This property is automatically set to true when an event handler of a textarea triggers a function containing a regular expression. You can also set this property on the fly if you like. The short version of this property is `$*`.

Related Items: None.

lastMatch

Value: String   **Gettable:** Yes   **Settable:** No

	Nav2	Nav3	Nav4	IE3/J1	IE3/J2	IE4/J3
Compatibility			✔			✔

After execution of a regular expression-related method, any text in the main string that matches the regular expression specification is automatically assigned to the `RegExp.lastMatch` property. This value is also assigned to the `[0]` property of the object array returned when a match is found by the `exec()` and `string.match()` methods. The short version of this property is `$&`.

Related Items: Matching array object [0] property.

lastParen

Value: String   **Gettable:** Yes   **Settable:** No

	Nav2	Nav3	Nav4	IE3/J1	IE3/J2	IE4/J3
Compatibility			✔			✔

When a regular expression contains many parenthesized subcomponents, the RegExp object maintains a list of the resulting strings in the `$1,...$9` properties. You can also extract the value of the last matching parenthesized subcomponent with the RegExp.lastParen property, which is a read-only property. The short version of this property is $+.

Related Items: RegExp.$1,...$9 properties.

leftContext
rightContext

Value: String   **Gettable:** Yes   **Settable:** No

	Nav2	Nav3	Nav4	IE3/J1	IE3/J2	IE4/J3
Compatibility			✔			✔

After a match is found in the course of one of the regular expression methods, the RegExp object is informed of some key contextual information about the match. The leftContext property contains the part of the main string to the left of (up to but not including) the matched string. Be aware that the leftContext starts its string from the point at which the most recent search began. Therefore, for second or subsequent times through the same string with the same regular expression, the leftContext substring varies widely from the first time through.

The rightContext consists of a string starting immediately after the current match and extending to the end of the main string. As subsequent method calls work on the same string and regular expression, this value obviously shrinks in length until no more matches are found. At this point, both properties revert to null. The short versions of these properties are $` and $' for leftContext and rightContext, respectively.

Related Items: None.

$1...$9

Value: String   **Gettable:** Yes   **Settable:** No

	Nav2	Nav3	Nav4	IE3/J1	IE3/J2	IE4/J3
Compatibility			✔			✔

As a regular expression method executes, any parenthesized result is stored in RegExp's nine properties reserved for just that purpose (called backreferences). The same values (and any beyond the nine that RegExp has space for) are stored in the array object returned with the exec() and string.match() methods. Values are stored in the order in which the left parenthesis of a pair appears in the regular expression, regardless of nesting of other components.

You can use these backreferences directly in the second parameter of the
`string.replace()` method, without using the RegExp part of their address. The
ideal situation is to encapsulate components that need to be rearranged or
recombined with replacement characters. For example, the following script
function turns a name that is last name first into first name last:

```
function swapEm() {
        var re = /(\w+),\s*(\w+)/
        var input = "Lincoln, Abraham"
        return input.replace(re,"$2 $1")
}
```

In the `replace()` method, the second parenthesized component (just the first
name) is placed first, followed by a space and the first component. The original
comma is discarded. You are free to combine these shortcut references as you like,
including multiple times per replacement, if it makes sense to your application.

Related Items: Matching array object [1]. . .[n] properties.

✦   ✦   ✦

Control Structures

You get up in the morning, go about your day's business, and then turn out the lights at night. That's not much different from what a program does from the time it starts to the time it ends. But along the way, both you and a program take lots of tiny steps, not all of which advance the "processing" in a straight line. At times, you have to control what's going on by making a decision or repeating tasks until the whole job is finished. Control structures are the facilities that make these tasks possible in JavaScript.

JavaScript control structures follow along the same lines of many programming languages, particularly with additions made in Navigator 4 and Internet Explorer 4 (for JavaScript 1.2). Basic decision-making and looping constructions satisfy the needs of just about all programming tasks.

If and If. . .Else Decisions

	Nav2	Nav3	Nav4	IE3/J1	IE3/J2	IE4/J3
Compatibility	✔	✔	✔	✔	✔	✔

JavaScript programs frequently have to make decisions based on the current values of variables or object properties. Such decisions can have only two possible outcomes at a time. The factor that determines the path the program takes at these decision points is the truth of some statement. For example, when you enter a room of your home at night, the statement under test is something like "It is too dark to see without a light." If that statement is true, you switch on the light; if that statement is false, you carry on with your primary task.

Simple decisions

JavaScript syntax for this kind of simple decision always begins with the keyword if, followed by the condition to test, and then the statements that execute if the condition yields a true result. JavaScript uses no "then" keyword (as some other languages do); the keyword is implied by the way the various components of this construction are surrounded by parentheses and braces. The formal syntax is

```
if (condition) {
        statementsIfTrue
}
```

This means that if the condition is true, program execution takes a detour to execute statements inside the braces. No matter what happens, the program continues executing statements beyond the closing brace (}). If household navigation was part of the scripting language, the code would look something like this:

```
if (tooDark == true) {
        feel for light switch
        turn on light switch
}
```

If you're not used to C/C++, the double equals sign may have caught your eye. You learn more about this type of operator in the next chapter, but for now, know that this operator compares the equality of items on either side of it. In other words, the condition statement of an if construction must always yield a Boolean (true or false) value. Some object properties, you may recall, are Booleans, so you can stick a reference to that property into the condition statement by itself. Otherwise, the condition statement consists of two values separated by a comparison operator, such as == (equals) or != (does not equal).

Let's look at some real JavaScript. The following function receives a form object containing a text object called entry:

```
function notTooHigh(form) {
        if (parseInt(form.entry.value) > 100) {
            alert("Sorry, the value you entered is too high. Try
again.")
            return false
        }
        return true
}
```

The condition (in parentheses) tests the contents of the field against a hard-wired value of 100. If the entered value is larger than that, the function alerts you and returns a false value to the calling statement elsewhere in the script. But if the value is less than 100, all intervening code is skipped and the function returns true.

About *(condition)* expressions

A lot of condition testing for control structures compares a value against some very specific condition, such as a string being empty or a value being null. You can use a couple of shortcuts to take care of many circumstances. Table 31-1 details the values that evaluate to a true or false (or equivalent) to satisfy a control structure's *condition* expression.

True	False
Nonempty string	Empty string
Nonzero number	0
Nonnull value	Null
Object exists	Object doesn't exist
Property is defined	Undefined property

Table 31-1
Condition value equivalents

Instead of having to spell out an equivalency expression for a condition involving these kinds of values, you can simply supply the value to be tested. For example, if a variable named myVal might reach an if construction as null, an empty string, or a string value for further processing, you can use the following shortcut:

```
if (myVal) {
        do processing on myVal
}
```

All null or empty string conditions evaluate to false, so only the cases of myVal being a processable value get inside the if construction.

Complex decisions

The simple type of if construction described earlier is fine when the decision is to take a small detour before returning to the main path. But not all decisions — in programming or in life — are like that. To present two alternate paths in a JavaScript decision, you can add a component to the construction. The syntax is

```
if (condition) {
        statementsIfTrue
} else {
        statementsIfFalse
}
```

By appending the else keyword, you give the if construction a path to follow in case the condition evaluates to false. The *statementsIfTrue* and *statementsIfFalse* do not have to be balanced in any way: One statement could be one line of code, the other one hundred lines. But when either one of those branches completes, execution continues after the last closing brace. To demonstrate how this construction can come in handy, the following example is a script fragment that assigns the number of days in February based on whether the year is a leap year (using modulo arithmetic, explained in the next chapter, to determine if the year is evenly divisible by four):

```
var howMany = 0
var theYear = 1993
```

```
if (theYear % 4 == 0) {
        howMany = 29
} else {
        howMany = 28
}
```

Here is a case where execution has to follow only one of two possible paths to assign the number of days to the howMany variable. Had I not used the else portion, as in

```
var howMany = 0
var theYear = 1993
if (theYear % 4 == 0) {
        howMany = 29
}
howMany = 28
```

then the variable would always be set to 28, occasionally after momentarily being set to 29. The else construction is essential in this case.

Nesting if. . .else statements

Designing a complex decision process requires painstaking attention to the logic of the decisions your script must process and the statements that must execute for any given set of conditions. The need for many complex constructions disappears with the advent of Navigator 4's switch construction (described later in this chapter), but there may still be times when you must fashion complex decision behavior out of a series of nested if...else constructions. Without a JavaScript-aware text editor to help keep everything properly indented and properly terminated (with closing braces), you have to monitor the authoring process very carefully. Moreover, the error messages that JavaScript provides when a mistake occurs (see Chapter 45) may not point directly to the problem line, but only to the region of difficulty.

Another important point to remember about nesting if...else statements in JavaScript before Version 1.2 is that the language does not provide a mechanism to break out of a nested part of the construction. For that reason, you have to construct complex assemblies with extreme care to make sure only the desired statement executes for each set of conditions. Extensive testing, of course, is also required (see Chapter 45).

To demonstrate a deeply nested set of if...else constructions, Listing 31-1 presents a simple user interface to a complex problem. A single text object asks the user to enter one of three letters, A, B, or C. The script behind that field processes a different message for each of the following conditions:

✦ The user enters no value.

✦ The user enters A.

✦ The user enters B.

✦ The user enters C.

✦ The user enters something entirely different.

What's with the formatting?

Indentation of the if construction and the further indentation of the statements executed on a true condition are not required by JavaScript. What you see here, however, is a convention that most JavaScript scripters follow. As you write the code in your text editor, you can use the Tab key to make each indentation level. The browser ignores these tab characters when loading the HTML documents containing your scripts. Until HTML editors are available that automatically format JavaScript listings for you, you have to manually make the listings readable and pretty.

Listing 31-1: **Deeply Nested if. . .else Constructions**

```
<HTML>
<HEAD>
<SCRIPT LANGUAGE="JavaScript">
function testLetter(form){
        inpVal = form.entry.value  // assign to shorter variable name
        if (inpVal != "") {  // if entry is not empty then dive in...
            if (inpVal == "A") {  // Is it an "A"?
               alert("Thanks for the A.")
            } else if (inpVal == "B") {  // No.  Is it a "B"?
               alert("Thanks for the B.")
            } else if (inpVal == "C") {  // No.  Is it a "C"?
               alert("Thanks for the C.")
            } else {             // Nope.  None of the above
               alert("Sorry, wrong letter or case.")
            }
        } else {   // value was empty, so skipped all other stuff
above
            alert("You did not enter anything.")
        }
}
</SCRIPT>
</HEAD>
<BODY>
<FORM>
Please enter A, B, or C:
<INPUT TYPE="text" NAME="entry" onChange="testLetter(this.form)">
</FORM>
</BODY>
</HTML>
```

Each condition executes only the statements that apply to that particular condition, even if it takes several queries to find out what the entry is. You do not need to break out of the nested construction because when a true response is found, the relevant statement executes, and no other statements occur in the execution path to run.

Even if you understand how to construct a hair-raising nested construction such as the one in Listing 31-1, the trickiest part is making sure that each left brace has a corresponding right brace. My technique for ensuring this pairing is to enter the right brace immediately after I type the left brace. I typically type the left brace, press Enter twice (once to open a free line for the next statement, once for the line that is to receive the right brace), tab, if necessary, to the same indentation as the line containing the left brace, and then type the right brace. Later, if I have to insert something indented, I just push down the right braces that I entered earlier. If I keep up this methodology throughout the process, the right braces appear at the desired indentation when I'm finished, even if they end up being dozens of lines below their original spot.

Conditional Expressions

	Nav2	Nav3	Nav4	IE3/J1	IE3/J2	IE4/J3
Compatibility	✔	✔	✔	✔	✔	✔

While I'm showing you decision-making constructions in JavaScript, now is a good time to introduce a special type of expression that you can use in place of an `if. . . else` control structure for a common type of decision — the instance where you want to assign one of two values to a variable, depending on the outcome of some condition. The formal definition for the *conditional expression* is as follows:

```
variable = (condition) ? val1 : val2
```

This means that if the Boolean result of the `condition` statement is true, JavaScript assigns *val1* to the variable; otherwise, it assigns *val2* to the variable. Like other instances of `condition` expressions, this one must also be written inside parentheses. The question mark is key here, as is the colon separating the two possible values.

A conditional expression, though not particularly intuitive or easy to read inside code, is very compact. Compare an `if. . .else` version of an assignment decision that follows

```
var collectorStatus
if (CDCount > 500) {
        collectorStatus = "fanatic"
} else {
        collectorStatus = "normal"
}
```

with the conditional expression version:

```
var collectorStatus = (CDCount > 500) ? "fanatic" : "normal"
```

The latter saves a lot of code lines (although the internal processing is the same as an `if...else` construction). Of course, if your decision path contains more statements than just one setting the value of a variable, the `if...else` or `switch` construction is preferable. This shortcut, however, is a handy one to remember when you need to perform very binary actions, such as setting a true-or-false flag in a script.

Repeat (for) Loops

	Nav2	Nav3	Nav4	IE3/J1	IE3/J2	IE4/J3
Compatibility	✔	✔	✔	✔	✔	✔

As you have seen in numerous examples throughout previous chapters, the capability to cycle through every entry in an array or through every item of a form element is vital to many JavaScript scripts. Perhaps the most typical operation is inspecting a property of many similar items in search of a specific value, such as to determine which radio button in a group is selected. One JavaScript structure that allows for these repetitious excursions is the `for` loop, so named after the keyword that begins the structure. Two other structures, called the `while` loop and `do-while` loop, are covered in following sections.

The JavaScript `for` loop lets a script repeat a series of statements any number of times and includes an optional loop counter that can be used in the execution of the statements. The following is the formal syntax definition:

```
for ( [initial expression]; [condition]; [update expression]) {
    statements
}
```

The three statements inside the parentheses (parameters to the `for` statement) play a key role in the way a `for` loop executes.

An *initial expression* in a `for` loop is executed one time, the first time the `for` loop begins to run. The most common application of the initial expression is to assign a name and starting value to a loop counter variable. Thus, it's not uncommon to see a `var` statement that both declares a variable name and assigns an initial value (generally 0 or 1) to it. An example is

```
var i = 0
```

You can use any variable name, but conventional usage calls for the letter `i`, which is short for *index*. If you prefer the word `counter` or something else that reminds you of what the variable represents, that's fine, too. In any case, the important point to remember about this statement is that it executes once at the outset of the `for` loop.

The second statement is a *condition,* precisely like the `condition` statement you saw in `if` constructions earlier in this chapter. When a loop-counting variable is established in the initial expression, the condition statement usually defines how high the loop counter should go before the looping stops. Therefore, the most common statement here is one that compares the loop counter variable against some fixed value — is the loop counter less than the maximum allowed value? If the condition is false at the start, the body of the loop is not executed. But if the loop does execute, then every time execution comes back around to the top of the loop, JavaScript reevaluates the condition to determine the current result of the expression. If the loop counter increases with each loop, eventually the counter value goes beyond the value in the condition statement, causing the condition statement to yield a Boolean value of false. The instant that happens, execution drops out of the `for` loop entirely.

The final statement, the *update expression,* is executed at the end of each loop execution — after all statements nested inside the `for` construction have run. Again, the loop counter variable can be a factor here. If you want the counter value to increase by one the next time through the loop (called *incrementing* the value), you can use the JavaScript operator that makes that happen: the ++ operator appended to the variable name. That task is the reason for the appearance of all those i++ symbols in the `for` loops you've seen already in this book. You're not limited to incrementing by one. You can increment by any multiplier you want or even drive a loop counter backwards by decrementing the value (i--).

Now let's take this knowledge and beef up the formal syntax definition with one that takes into account a typical loop-counting variable, i, and the common ways to use it:

```
//incrementing loop counter
for (var i = minValue; i <= maxValue; i++) {
    statements
}

//decrementing loop counter
for (var i = maxValue; i >= minValue; i--) {
    statements
}
```

In the top format, the variable, i, is initialized at the outset to a value equal to that of *minValue*. Variable i is immediately compared against *maxValue*. If i is less than or equal to *maxValue,* processing continues into the body of the loop. At the end of the loop, the update expression executes. In the top example, the value of i is incremented by 1. Therefore, if i is initialized as 0, then the first time through the loop, the i variable maintains that 0 value during the first execution of statements in the loop. The next time around, the variable has the value of 1.

As you may have noticed in the formal syntax definition, each of the parameters to the `for` statement is optional. For example, the statements that execute inside the loop may control the value of the loop counter based on data that gets manipulated in the process. Therefore, the update statement would probably interfere with the intended running of the loop. But I suggest that you use all three parameters until such time as you feel absolutely comfortable with their roles in the `for` loop. If you omit the condition statement, for instance, and you don't program a way for the loop to exit on its own, your script may end up in an infinite loop — which does your users no good.

Putting the loop counter to work

Despite its diminutive appearance, the i loop counter (or whatever name you want to give it) can be a powerful tool for working with data inside a repeat loop. For example, let's examine a version of the classic JavaScript function that creates a new Navigator 2–compatible array while initializing entries to a value of 0:

```
// initialize array with n entries
function MakeArray(n) {
        this.length = n
        for (var i = 1; i <= n; i++) {
            this[i] = 0
        }
        return this
}
```

The loop counter, i, is initialized to a value of 1, because you want to create an array of empty entries (with value 0) starting with the one whose index value is 1 (the zeroth entry is assigned to the length property) in the previous line. In the condition statement, the loop continues to execute as long as the value of the counter is less than or equal to the number of entries being created (n). After each loop, the counter increments by 1. In the nested statement that executes within the loop, you use the value of the i variable to substitute for the index value of the assignment statement:

```
this[i] = 0
```

The first time the loop executes, the value expression evaluates to

```
this[1] = 0
```

The next time, the expression evaluates to

```
this[2] = 0
```

and so on, until all entries are created and stuffed with 0.

Recall the HTML page in Listing 29-4, where JavaScript extracted the names of planets from a previously constructed array (called solarSys). Here is the section of that listing that uses a for loop to extract the names and plug them into HTML specifications for a selection pop-up menu:

```
var page = "" // start assembling next part of page and form
page += "Select a planet to view its planetary data: "
page += "<SELECT NAME='planets'> "
// build popup list from array planet names
for (var i = 1; i <= solarSys.length; i++) {
        page += "<OPTION"          // OPTION tags
        if (i == 1) {              // pre-select first item in list
            page += " SELECTED"
        }
        page += ">" + solarSys[i].name
}
page += "</SELECT><P>"  // close selection item tag
document.write(page)    // lay out this part of the page
```

Notice one important point about the condition statement of the for loop: JavaScript extracts the length property from the array to be used as the loop counter boundary. From a code maintenance and stylistic point of view, this method is preferable to hard-wiring a value there. If someone discovers a new planet, you would make the addition to the array "database," whereas everything else in the code would adjust automatically to those changes, including creating a longer pop-up menu in this case. More to the point, though, is that you use the loop counter as an index value into the array to extract the name property for each entry in the array. You also use the counter to determine which is the first option, so you can take a short detour (via the if construction) to add the SELECTED tag to the first option's definition.

The utility of the loop counter in for loops often influences the way you design data structures, such as two-dimensional arrays (Chapter 29) for use as databases. Always keep the loop-counter mechanism in the back of your mind when you begin writing JavaScript script that relies on collections of data you embed in your documents (see Chapter 49 on the CD-ROM for examples).

Breaking out of a loop

Some loop constructions perform their job when a certain condition is met, at which point they have no further need to continue looping through the rest of the values in the loop counter's range. A common scenario for this is the cycling of a loop through an entire array in search of a single entry that matches some criterion. That criterion test is set up as an if construction inside the loop. If that criterion is met, you break out of the loop and let the script continue with the more meaningful processing of succeeding statements in the main flow. To accomplish that exit from the loop, use the break statement. The following schematic shows how the break statement may appear in a for loop:

```
for (var i = 0; i < array.length; i++) {
    if (array[i].property == magicValue) {
        statements that act on entry array[i]
        break
    }
}
```

The break statement tells JavaScript to bail out of the nearest for loop (in case you have nested for loops). Script execution then picks up immediately after the closing brace of the for statement. The variable value of i remains whatever it was at the time of the break, so you can use that variable later in the same script to access, say, that same array entry.

I use a construction like this back in Chapter 23's discussion of radio buttons. In Listing 23-8, I show a set of radio buttons whose VALUE attributes contain the full names of four members of the Three Stooges. A function uses a for loop to find out which button was selected and then uses that item's index value—after the for loop broke out of the loop—to alert the user. Listing 31-2 (not on the CD-ROM) shows the relevant function.

Listing 31-2: Breaking Out of a for Loop

```
function fullName(form) {
     for (var i = 0; i < form.stooges.length; i++) {
        if (form.stooges[i].checked) {
           break
        }
     }
     alert("You chose " + form.stooges[i].value + ".")
}
```

In this case, breaking out of the for loop was for more than mere efficiency: I used the value of the loop counter (frozen at the break point) to summon a different property outside of the for loop. In Navigator 4, the break statement assumes additional powers in cooperation with the new label feature of control structures. This subject is covered later in this chapter.

Directing loop traffic with continue

One other possibility in a for loop is that you may want to skip execution of the nested statements for just one condition. In other words, as the loop goes merrily on its way round and round, executing statements for each value of the loop counter, one value of that loop counter may exist for which you don't want those statements to execute. To accomplish this task, the nested statements need to include an if construction to test for the presence of the value to skip. When that value is reached, the continue command tells JavaScript to immediately skip the rest of the body, execute the update statement, and loop back around to the top of the loop (also skipping the condition statement part of the for loop's parameters).

To illustrate this construction, you create an artificial example that skips over execution when the counter variable is the superstitious person's unlucky 13:

```
for (var i = 1; i <= 20; i++) {
     if (i == 13) {
        continue
     }
     statements
}
```

In this example, the statements part of the loop executes for all values of i except 13. The continue statement forces execution to jump to the i++ part of the loop structure, incrementing the value of i for the next time through the loop. In the case of nested for loops, a continue statement affects the for loop in whose immediate scope the if construction falls. The continue statement is enhanced in Navigator 4 in cooperation with the new label feature of control structures. This subject is covered later in this chapter.

The while Loop

	Nav2	Nav3	Nav4	IE3/J1	IE3/J2	IE4/J3
Compatibility	✔	✔	✔	✔	✔	✔

The `for` loop is not the only kind of repeat loop you can construct in JavaScript. Another statement, called a `while` statement, sets up a loop in a slightly different format. Rather than providing a mechanism for modifying a loop counter, a `while` repeat loop assumes that your script statements will reach a condition that forcibly exits the repeat loop.

The basic syntax for a `while` loop is

```
while (condition) {
      statements
}
```

The `condition` statement is the same kind you saw in `if` constructions and in the middle parameter of the `for` loop. You introduce this kind of loop if some condition exists in your code (evaluates to true) before reaching this loop. The loop then performs some action that affects that condition repeatedly until that condition becomes false. At that point, the loop exits, and script execution continues with statements after the closing brace. If the statements inside the `while` loop do not affect the values being tested in `condition`, your script never exits, and it becomes stuck in an infinite loop.

Many loops can be rendered with either the `for` or `while` loops. In fact, Listing 31-3 (not on the CD-ROM) shows a `while` loop version of the `for` loop from Listing 31-2.

Listing 31-3: **A while Loop Version of Listing 31-2**

```
function fullName(form) {
      var i = 0
      while (!form.stooges[i].checked) {
         i++
      }
      alert("You chose " + form.stooges[i].value + ".")
}
```

One point you may notice is that if the condition of a `while` loop depends on the value of a loop counter, the scripter is responsible for initializing the counter prior to the `while` loop construction and managing its value within the `while` loop.

Should you need their powers, the `break` and `continue` control statements work inside `while` loops as they do in `for` loops. But because the two loop styles treat their loop counters and conditions differently, be extra careful (do lots of testing) when applying `break` and `continue` statements to both kinds of loops.

No hard-and-fast rules exist for which type of loop construction to use in a script. I generally use `while` loops only when the data or object I want to loop through is already a part of my script before the loop. In other words, by virtue of previous statements in the script, the values for any condition or loop counting (if needed) are already initialized. But if I need to cycle through a new object's properties or new array to extract some piece of data for use later in the script, I favor the `for` loop.

The do-while Loop

	Nav2	Nav3	Nav4	IE3/J1	IE3/J2	IE4/J3
Compatibility			✔			✔

JavaScript 1.2 brings you one more looping construction, called the `do-while` loop. The formal syntax for this construction is as follows:

```
do {
      statements
} while  (condition)
```

An important difference distinguishes the `do-while` loop from the `while` loop. In the `do-while` loop, the statements in the construction always execute at least one time before the condition can be tested; in a `while` loop, the statements may never execute if the condition tested at the outset evaluates to false.

Use a `do-while` loop when you know for certain that the looped statements are free to run at least one time. If the condition may not be met the first time, use the other `while` loop. For many instances, the two constructions are interchangeable, although the `while` loop is compatible with all scriptable browsers.

Looping through Properties

	Nav2	Nav3	Nav4	IE3/J1	IE3/J2	IE4/J3
Compatibility	✔	✔	✔	✔	✔	✔

JavaScript includes a variation of the `for` loop, called a `for...in` loop, which has special powers of extracting the names and values of any object property currently in the browser's memory. The syntax looks like this:

```
for (var in object) {
      statements
}
```

The *object* parameter is not the string name of an object, but the object itself. JavaScript delivers an object if you provide the name of the object as an unquoted string, such as `window` or `document`. Using the *var* variable, you can create a script that extracts and displays the range of properties for any given object.

Listing 31-4 shows a page containing a utility function you can insert into your HTML documents during the authoring and debugging stages of designing a JavaScript-enhanced page. In the example, the current window object is examined and its properties presented in the page.

Listing 31-4: **Property Inspector Function**

```
<HTML>
<HEAD>
<SCRIPT LANGUAGE="JavaScript">
function showProps(obj,objName) {
        var result = ""
        for (var i in obj) {
            result += objName + "." + i + " = " + obj[i] + "<BR>"
        }
        return result
}
</SCRIPT>
</HEAD>
<BODY>
<B>Here are the properties of the current window:</B><P>
<SCRIPT LANGUAGE="JavaScript">
document.write(showProps(window, "window"))
</SCRIPT>
</BODY>
</HTML>
```

For debugging purposes, you can revise the function slightly to display the results in an alert dialog box. Replace the "<BR>" HTML tag with the "\n" carriage return character for a nicely formatted display in the alert dialog box. You can call this function from anywhere in your script, passing both the object reference and a string to it to help you identify the object when the results appear in an alert dialog box.

The with Statement

	Nav2	Nav3	Nav4	IE3/J1	IE3/J2	IE4/J3
Compatibility	✔	✔	✔	✔	✔	✔

A with statement enables you to preface any number of statements by advising JavaScript on precisely which object your scripts will be talking about, so you don't have to use full, formal addresses to access properties or invoke methods of the same object. The formal syntax definition of the with statement is as follows:

```
with (object) {
      statements
}
```

The *object* reference is any valid object currently in the browser's memory. You saw an example of this in Chapter 27's discussion of the Math object. By embracing several Math-encrusted statements inside a with construction, your scripts can call the properties and methods without having to make the object part of every reference to those properties and methods.

An advantage of the with structure is that it can make heavily object-dependent statements easier to read and understand. Consider this long version of a function that requires multiple calls to the same object (but different properties):

```
function seeColor(form) {
      newColor =
(form.colorsList.options[form.colorsList.selectedIndex].text)
      return newColor
}
```

Using the with structure, you can shorten the long statement:

```
function seeColor(form) {
      with (form.colorsList) {
          newColor = (options[selectedIndex].text)
      }
      return newColor
}
```

When JavaScript encounters an otherwise unknown identifier inside a with statement, it tries to build a reference out of the object specified as its parameter and that unknown identifier. You cannot, however, nest with statements that build in each other (in the preceding example, you cannot have a with (colorsList) nested inside a with (form) statement and expect JavaScript to create a reference to options out of the two object names).

Labeled Statements

	Nav2	Nav3	Nav4	IE3/J1	IE3/J2	IE4/J3
Compatibility			✔			✔

Crafting multiple nested loops can sometimes be difficult when the final condition your script is looking for is met deep inside the nests. The problem is that the `break` or `continue` statement by itself has scope only to the nearest loop level. Therefore, even if you break out of the inner loop, the outer loop(s) continue to execute. If all you want to do is exit the function when the condition is met, a simple `return` statement performs the same job as some other languages' `exit` command. But if you also need some further processing within that function after the condition is met, you're out of luck unless you fashion some rather complex condition testing in all the loop levels.

To the rescue comes a new facility in JavaScript 1.2 that lets you assign labels to blocks of JavaScript statements. Your `break` and `continue` statements can then alter their scope to apply to a labeled block other than the one containing the statement.

A label is any identifier (that is, name starting with a letter and containing no spaces or odd punctuation other than an underscore) followed by a colon preceding a logical block of executing statements, such as an `if...then` or loop construction. The formal syntax looks like the following:

```
label:
        statements
```

For a `break` or `continue` statement to apply itself to a labeled group, the label is added as a kind of parameter to each statement, as in

```
break label
continue label
```

To demonstrate how valuable this can be in the right situation, Listing 31-5 contains two versions of the same nested loop construction. The goal of each version is to loop through two different index variables until both values equal the target values set outside the loop. When those targets are met, the entire nested loop construction should break off and continue processing afterward. To help you visualize the processing that goes on during the execution of the loops, the scripts output intermediate and final results to the Java Console window. Show that window before clicking the button to trigger either script.

In the version without labels, when the targets are met, only the simple `break` statement is issued. This breaks the inner loop at that point, but the outer loop picks up on the next iteration. By the time the entire construction has ended, a lot of wasted processing has gone on. Moreover, the values of the counting variables max themselves out, because the loops execute in their entirety several times after the targets are met.

But in the labeled version, the inner loop breaks out of the outer loop when the targets are met. Far fewer lines of code are executed, and the loop counting variables are equal to the targets, as desired. Experiment with Listing 31-5 by changing the break statements to continue statements. Then closely analyze the two results in the Java Console window to see how the two versions behave.

Listing 31-5: **Labeled Statements**

```
<HTML>
<HEAD>
<SCRIPT LANGUAGE="JavaScript">
var targetA = 2
var targetB = 2
var range = 5
function run1() {
        java.lang.System.out.println("Running WITHOUT labeled break")
        for (var i = 0; i <= range; i++) {
            java.lang.System.out.println("Outer loop #" + i)
            for (var j = 0; j <= range; j++) {
                java.lang.System.out.println("Inner loop #" + j)
                if (i == targetA && j == targetB) {
                    java.lang.System.out.println("BREAKING OUT OF INNER
LOOP")
                    break
                }
            }
        }
        java.lang.System.out.println("After looping, i = " + i + ", j =
" + j + "\n")
}
function run2() {
        java.lang.System.out.println("Running WITH labeled break")
        outerLoop:
        for (var i = 0; i <= range; i++) {
            java.lang.System.out.println("Outer loop #" + i)
            innerLoop:
            for (var j = 0; j <= range; j++) {
                java.lang.System.out.println("Inner loop #" + j)
                if (i == targetA && j == targetB) {
                    java.lang.System.out.println("BREAKING OUT OF OUTER
LOOP")
                    break outerLoop
                }
            }
        }
        java.lang.System.out.println("After looping, i = " + i + ", j =
" + j + "\n")
}
</SCRIPT>
</HEAD>
<BODY>
```

(continued)

label

Listing 31-5 *(continued)*

```
<B>Breaking Out of Nested Labeled Loops</B>
<HR>
Look in the Java Console window for traces of these button scripts:<P>
<FORM>
<INPUT TYPE="button" VALUE="Execute WITHOUT Label" onClick="run1()"><P>
<INPUT TYPE="button" VALUE="Execute WITH Label" onClick="run2()"><P>
</FORM>
</BODY>
</HTML>
```

The switch Statement

	Nav2	Nav3	Nav4	IE3/J1	IE3/J2	IE4/J3
Compatibility			✔			✔

In some circumstances, a binary—true or false—decision path is not enough to handle the processing in your script. An object property or variable value may contain any one of several values, and a separate execution path is required for each one. In the past, the way to accommodate this is with a series of `if...else` constructions. The more conditions you must test, the less efficient the processing is, because each condition must be tested. Moreover, the sequence of clauses and braces can get very confusing.

In JavaScript 1.2, a control structure in use by many languages comes to JavaScript. The implementation is similar to that of Java and C, using the `switch` and `case` keywords. The basic premise is that you can create any number of execution paths based on the value of some expression. At the beginning of the structure, you identify what that expression is, and then for each execution path, assign a label matching a particular value.

The formal syntax for the switch statement is

```
switch (expression) {
        case label1:
            statements
            [break]
        case label2:
            statements
            [break]
        ...
        [default:
            statements]
}
```

The *expression* parameter of the switch statement can evaluate to any string or number value. Labels are not surrounded by quotes, even if the labels represent string values of the expression. Notice that the break statements are optional. A break statement forces the switch expression to bypass all other checks of succeeding labels against the expression value. Another option is the default statement, which provides a catch-all execution path when the expression value does not match any of the case statement labels. If you'd rather not have any execution take place with a nonmatching expression value, omit the default part of the construction.

To demonstrate the syntax of a working switch statement, Listing 31-6 provides the skeleton of a larger application of this control structure. The page contains two separate arrays of different product categories. Each product has its name and price stored in its respective array. A select list displays the product names. When a user chooses a product, the script looks up the product name in the appropriate array and displays the price.

The trick behind this application is the values assigned to each product in the select list. While the displayed text is the product name, the VALUE attribute of each <OPTION> tag is the array category for the product. That value is the expression used to decide which branch to follow. Notice, too, that I assigned a label to the entire switch construction. The purpose of that is to let the deeply nested repeat loops for each case completely bail out of the switch construction (via a labeled break statement) whenever a match is made. You could extend this example to any number of product category arrays with additional case statements to match.

Listing 31-6: **The switch Construction in Action**

```
<HTML>
<HEAD>
<TITLE>Switch Statement and Labeled Break</TITLE>
<SCRIPT LANGUAGE="JavaScript1.2">
// build two product arrays, simulating two database tables
function product(name, price) {
        this.name = name
        this.price = price
}
var ICs = new Array()
ICs[0] = new product("Septium 300MHz","$149")
ICs[1] = new product("Septium Pro 310MHz","$249")
ICs[2] = new product("Octium BFD 350MHz","$329")
var snacks = new Array
snacks[0] = new product("Rays Potato Chips","$1.79")
snacks[1] = new product("Cheezey-ettes","$1.59")
snacks[2] = new product("Tortilla Flats","$2.29")

// lookup in the 'table' associated with the product
function getPrice(selector) {
        var chipName = selector.options[selector.selectedIndex].text
        var outField = document.forms[0].cost
```

(continued)

Listing 31-6 *(continued)*

```
        master:
            switch(selector.options[selector.selectedIndex].value) {
                case "ICs":
                    for (var i = 0; i < ICs.length; i++) {
                        if (ICs[i].name == chipName) {
                            outField.value = ICs[i].price
                            break master
                        }
                    }
                    break
                case "snacks":
                    for (var i = 0; i < snacks.length; i++) {
                        if (snacks[i].name == chipName) {
                            outField.value = snacks[i].price
                            break master
                        }
                    }
                    break
                default:
                    outField.value = "Not Found"
            }
    }
    </SCRIPT>
    </HEAD>
    <BODY>
    <B>Branching with the switch Statement</B>
    <HR>
    Select a chip for lookup in the chip price tables:<P>
    <FORM>
    Chip:<SELECT NAME="chips" onChange="getPrice(this)">
        <OPTION>
        <OPTION VALUE="ICs">Septium 300MHz
        <OPTION VALUE="ICs">Septium Pro 310MHz
        <OPTION VALUE="ICs">Octium BFD 350MHz
        <OPTION VALUE="snacks">Rays Potato Chips
        <OPTION VALUE="snacks">Cheezey-ettes
        <OPTION VALUE="snacks">Tortilla Flats
        <OPTION>Poker Chipset
    </SELECT> 
    Price:<INPUT TYPE="text" NAME="cost" SIZE=10>
    </FORM>
    </BODY>
    </HTML>
```

If you need this kind of functionality in your script but your audience is not all running level 4 or later browsers, see Listing 31-1 for ways to simulate the switch statement with if...else constructions.

✦   ✦   ✦

JavaScript Operators

JavaScript is rich in *operators*: words and symbols in expressions that perform operations on one or two values to arrive at another value. Any value on which an operator performs some action is called an *operand*. An expression may contain one operand and one operator (called a unary operator) or two operands separated by one operator (called a binary operator). Many of the same symbols are used in a variety of operators. The combination and order of those symbols are what distinguish their powers.

Operator Categories

To help you grasp the range of JavaScript operators, I've grouped them into five categories. I have assigned a wholly untraditional name to the second group — but a name that I believe better identifies its purpose in the language. Table 32-1 shows the operator types.

Table 32-1
JavaScript Operator Categories

Type	What It Does
Comparison	Compares the values of two operands, deriving a result of either true or false (used extensively in condition statements for if...else and for loop constructions)
Connubial	Joins together two operands to produce a single value that is a result of an arithmetical or other operation on the two
Assignment	Stuffs the value of the expression of the right-hand operand into a variable name on the left-hand side, sometimes with minor modification, as determined by the operator symbol
Boolean	Performs Boolean arithmetic on one or two Boolean operands
Bitwise	Performs arithmetic or column-shifting actions on the binary (base-2) representations of two operands

Any expression that contains an operator evaluates to a value of some kind. Sometimes the operator changes the value of one of the operands; other times the result is a new value. Even this simple expression

```
5 + 5
```

shows two integer operands joined by the addition operator. This expression evaluates to 10. The operator is what provides the instruction for JavaScript to follow in its never-ending drive to evaluate every expression in a script.

Doing an equality comparison on two operands that, on the surface, look very different is not at all uncommon. JavaScript doesn't care what the operands look like — only how they evaluate. Two very dissimilar-looking values can, in fact, be identical when they are evaluated. Thus, an expression that compares the equality of two values such as

```
fred == 25
```

does, in fact, evaluate to true if the variable `fred` has the number 25 stored in it from an earlier statement.

Comparison Operators

	Nav2	Nav3	Nav4	IE3/J1	IE3/J2	IE4/J3
Compatibility	✔	✔	✔	✔	✔	✔

Any time you compare two values in JavaScript, the result is a Boolean true or false value. You have a wide selection of comparison operators to choose from, depending on the kind of test you want to apply to the two operands. Table 32-2 lists all six comparison operators.

Table 32-2
JavaScript Comparison Operators

Syntax	Name	Operand Types	Results
==	Equals	All	Boolean
!=	Does not equal	All	Boolean
>	Is greater than	All	Boolean
>=	Is greater than or equal to	All	Boolean
<	Is less than	All	Boolean
<=	Is less than or equal to	All	Boolean

For numeric values, the results are the same as those you'd expect from your high school algebra class. Some examples follow, including some that may not be obvious.

```
10 == 10   // true
10 == 10.0 // true
9 != 10// true
9 > 10 // false
9.99 <= 9.98  // false
```

Strings can also be compared on all of these levels:

```
"Fred" == "Fred" // true
"Fred" == "fred"  // false
"Fred" > "fred"   // false
"Fran" < "Fred"   // true
```

To calculate string comparisons, JavaScript converts each character of a string to its ASCII value. Each letter, beginning with the first of the left-hand operator, is compared to the corresponding letter in the right-hand operator. With ASCII values for uppercase letters being less than their lowercase counterparts, an uppercase letter evaluates to being less than its lowercase equivalent. JavaScript takes case-sensitivity very seriously.

Values for comparison can also come from object properties or values passed to functions from event handlers or other functions. A common string comparison used in data-entry validation is the one that sees if the string has anything in it:

```
form.entry.value != ""   // true if something is in the field
```

Equality of Disparate Data Types

For all versions of JavaScript before 1.2, when your script tries to compare string values consisting of numerals and real numbers (for example, `"123" == 123` or `"123" != 123`), JavaScript anticipates that you want to compare apples to apples. Internally it does some data type conversion that does not affect the data type of the original values (for example, if the values are in variables). But the entire situation is more complex, because other data types, such as objects, need to be dealt with. Therefore, prior to JavaScript 1.2, the rules of comparison are as shown in Table 32-3.

Table 32-3
Equality Comparisons for JavaScript 1.0 and 1.1

Operand A	Operand B	Internal Comparison Treatment
Object reference	Object reference	Compare object reference evaluations
Any data type	Null	Convert nonnull to its object type and compare against null
Object reference	String	Convert object to string and compare strings
String	Number	Convert string to number and compare numbers

The logic to what goes on in equality comparisons from Table 32-3 requires a lot of forethought on the scripter's part, because you have to be very conscious of the particular way data types may or may not be converted for equality evaluation (even though the values themselves are not converted). In this situation, it is best to supply the proper conversion where necessary in the comparison statement. This ensures that what you want to compare — say, the string versions of two values or the number versions of two values — is compared, rather than leaving the conversion up to JavaScript.

Backward compatible conversion from a number to string entails concatenating an empty string to a number:

```
var a = "09"
var b = 9
a == "" + b  // result: false, because "09" does not equal "9"
```

For converting strings to numbers, you have numerous possibilities. The simplest is subtracting zero from a numeric string:

```
var a = "09"
var b = 9
a-0 == b  // result: true because number 9 equals number 9
```

You can also use the `parseInt()` and `parseFloat()` functions to convert strings to numbers:

```
var a = "09"
var b = 9
parseInt(a, 10) == b  // result: true because number 9 equals number 9
```

To clear up the ambiguity of JavaScript's equality internal conversions, JavaScript 1.2 in Navigator 4 introduces a different way of evaluating equality. For all scripts encapsulated inside a `<SCRIPT LANGUAGE="JavaScript1.2">` `</SCRIPT>` tag pair, equality operators do *not* perform any automatic type conversion. Therefore no number will ever be automatically equal to a string version of that same number. Data and object types must match before their values are compared.

JavaScript 1.2 provides some convenient global functions for converting strings to numbers and vice versa: `String()` and `Number()`. To demonstrate these methods, the following examples use the `typeof` operator to show the data type of expressions using these functions:

```
typeof 9  // result: number
type of String(9)  // result: string
type of "9"  // result: string
type of Number("9")  // result: number
```

Neither of these functions alters the data type of the value being converted. But the value of the function is what gets compared in an equality comparison:

```
var a = "09"
var b = 9
a == String(b)  // result: false, because "09" does not equal "9"
typeof b // result: still a number
Number(a) == b // result: true, because 9 equals 9
typeof a // result: still a string
```

For forward and backward compatibility, you should always make your equality comparisons compare identical data types.

Connubial Operators

	Nav2	Nav3	Nav4	IE3/J1	IE3/J2	IE4/J3
Compatibility	✔	✔	✔	✔	✔	✔

Connubial operators is my terminology for those operators that join two operands to yield a value related to the operands. Table 32-4 lists the connubial operators in JavaScript.

Table 32-4 JavaScript Connubial Operators			
Syntax	**Name**	**Operand Types**	**Results**
+	Plus	Integer, float, string	Integer, float, string
-	Minus	Integer, float	Integer, float
*	Multiply	Integer, float	Integer, float
/	Divide	Integer, float	Integer, float
%	Modulo	Integer, float	Integer, float
++	Increment	Integer, float	Integer, float
--	Decrement	Integer, float	Integer, float
-val	Negation	Integer, float	Integer, float

The four basic arithmetic operators for numbers should be straightforward. The plus operator also works on strings to join them together, as in

```
"Howdy " + "Doody" // result = "Howdy Doody"
```

In object-oriented programming terminology, the plus sign is said to be *overloaded,* meaning that it performs a different action depending on its context. Remember, too, that string concatenation does not do anything on its own to monitor or insert spaces between words. In the preceding example, the space between the names is part of the first string.

Modulo arithmetic is helpful for those times when you want to know if one number divides evenly into another. You used it in an example in the last chapter to figure out if a particular year was a leap year. Although some other leap year considerations exist for the turn of each century, the math in the example simply checked whether the year was evenly divisible by four. The result of the modulo math is the remainder of division of the two values: When the remainder is 0, one divides evenly into the other. Here are some samples of years evenly divisible by four:

```
1994 % 4   // result = 2
1995 % 4   // result = 3

1996 % 4   // result = 0 --Bingo! Leap and election year!
```

Thus, I used this operator in a condition statement of an if. . .else structure:

```
var howMany = 0
today = new Date()
var theYear = today.getYear()
if (theYear % 4 == 0) {
        howMany = 29
} else {
        howMany = 28
}
```

Some other languages offer an operator that results in the integer part of a division problem solution: integral division, or div. Although JavaScript does not have an explicit operator for this behavior, you can re-create it reliably if you know that your operands are always positive numbers. Use the Math.floor() or Math.ceil() methods with the division operator, as in

```
Math.floor(4/3)// result = 1
```

In this example, Math.floor() works only with values greater than or equal to 0; Math.ceil() works for values less than 0.

The increment operator (++) is a unary operator (only one operand) and displays two different behaviors, depending on the side of the operand on which the symbols lie. Both the increment and decrement (--) operators can be used in conjunction with assignment operators, which I cover next.

As its name implies, the increment operator increases the value of its operand by one. But in an assignment statement, you have to pay close attention to precisely when that increase takes place. An assignment statement stuffs the value of the right operand into a variable on the left. If the ++ operator is located in front of the right operand (prefix), the right operand is incremented before the value is assigned to the variable; if the ++ operator is located after the right operand (postfix), the previous value of the operand is sent to the variable before the value is incremented. Follow this sequence to get a feel for these two behaviors:

```
var a = 10 // initialize a to 10
var z = 0 // initialize z to zero
z = a       // a = 10, so z = 10
z = ++a // a becomes 11 before assignment, so a = 11 and z becomes 11
z = a++ // a is still 11 before assignment, so z = 11; then a becomes
12
z = a++ // a is still 12 before assignment, so z = 12; then a becomes
13
```

The decrement operator behaves the same way, except that the value of the operand decreases by one. Increment and decrement operators are used most often with loop counters in for and while loops. The simpler ++ or -- symbology is more compact than reassigning a value by adding 1 to it (such as, $z = z + 1$ or $z += 1$). Because these are unary operators, you can use the increment and decrement operators without an assignment statement to adjust the value of a counting variable within a loop:

```
function doNothing() {
        var i = 1
        while (i < 20) {
            ++i
        }
        alert(i) // breaks out at i = 20
}
```

The last connubial operator is the negation operator (`-val`). By placing a minus sign in front of any numeric value (no space between the symbol and the value), you instruct JavaScript to evaluate a positive value as its corresponding negative value, and vice versa. The operator does not change the actual value. The following example provides a sequence of statements to demonstrate:

```
x = 2
y = 8
-x     // expression evaluates to -2, but x still equals 2
-(x + y // doesn't change variable values; evaluates to -10
-x + y  // evaluates to 6, but x still equals 2
```

To negate a Boolean value, see the Not (!) operator in the discussion of Boolean operators.

Assignment Operators

	Nav2	Nav3	Nav4	IE3/J1	IE3/J2	IE4/J3
Compatibility	✔	✔	✔	✔	✔	✔

Assignment statements are among the most common statements you write in your JavaScript scripts. These statements are where you copy a value or the results of an expression into a variable for further manipulation of that value.

You assign values to variables for many reasons, even though you could probably use the original values or expressions several times throughout a script. Here is a sampling of reasons why you should assign values to variables:

✦ Variable names are usually shorter

✦ Variable names can be more descriptive

✦ You may need to preserve the original value for later in the script

✦ The original value is a property that cannot be changed

✦ Invoking the same method several times in a script is not efficient

Newcomers to scripting often overlook the last reason. For instance, if a script is writing HTML to a new document, it's more efficient to assemble the string of large chunks of the page into one variable before invoking the `document.writeln()` method to send that text to the document. This method is more efficient than literally sending out one line of HTML at a time with multiple `document.writeln()` method statements. Table 32-5 shows the range of assignment operators in JavaScript.

Table 32-5
JavaScript Assignment Operators

Syntax	Name	Example	Means
=	Equals	x = y	x = y
+=	Add by value	x += y	x = x + y
-=	Subtract by value	x -= y	x = x - y
*=	Multiply by value	x *= y	x = x * y
/=	Divide by value	x /= y	x = x / y
%=	Modulo by value	x %= y	x = x % y
<<=	Left shift by value	x <<= y	x = x << y
>=	Right shift by value	x >= y	x = x > y
>>=	Zero fill by value	x >>= y	x = x >> y
&=	Bitwise AND by value	x &= y	x = x & y
|=	Bitwise OR by value	x |= y	x = x | y
^=	Bitwise XOR by value	x ^= y	x = x ^ y

As clearly demonstrated in the top group (see "Bitwise Operators" later in the chapter for information on the bottom group), assignment operators beyond the simple equal sign can save some characters in your typing, especially when you have a series of values that you're trying to bring together in subsequent statements. You've seen plenty of examples in previous chapters, where you've used the add-by-value operator (+=) to work wonders with strings as you assemble a long string variable that you eventually send to a `document.write()` method. Look at this excerpt from Listing 29-4, where you use JavaScript to create the content of an HTML page on the fly:

```
var page = "" // start assembling next part of page and form
page += "Select a planet to view its planetary data: "
page += "<SELECT NAME='planets'> "
// build popup list from array planet names
for (var i = 0; i < solarSys.length; i++) {
        page += "<OPTION"          // OPTION tags
        if (i == 1) {              // pre-select first item in list
            page += " SELECTED"
```

```
        }
        page += ">" + solarSys[i].name
    }
    page += "</SELECT><P>"    // close selection item tag
    document.write(page)      // lay out this part of the page
```

The script segment starts with a plain equals assignment operator to initialize the page variable as an empty string. In many of the succeeding lines, you use the add-by-value operator to tack additional string values onto whatever is in the `page` variable at the time. Without the add-by-value operator, you'd be forced to use the plain equals assignment operator for each line of code to concatenate new string data to the existing string data. In that case, the first few lines of code would look like this:

```
var page = "" // start assembling next part of page and form
page = page + "Select a planet to view its planetary data: "
page = page + "<SELECT NAME='planets'> "
```

Within the `for` loop, the repetition of `page +` makes the code very difficult to read, trace, and maintain. These enhanced assignment operators are excellent shortcuts that you should use at every turn.

Boolean Operators

	Nav2	Nav3	Nav4	IE3/J1	IE3/J2	IE4/J3
Compatibility	✔	✔	✔	✔	✔	✔

Because a great deal of programming involves logic, it is no accident that the arithmetic of the logic world plays an important role. You've already seen dozens of instances where programs make all kinds of decisions based on whether a statement or expression is the Boolean value of true or false. What you haven't seen much of yet is how to combine multiple Boolean values and expressions — something that scripts with slightly above average complexity may need to have in them.

In the various condition expressions required throughout JavaScript (such as in an `if` construction), the condition that the program must test for may be more complicated than, say, whether a variable value is greater than a certain fixed value or whether a field is not empty. Look at the case of validating a text field entry for whether the entry contains all the numbers that your script may want. Without some magical JavaScript function to tell you whether or not a string consists of all numbers, you have to break apart the entry character by character and examine whether each character falls within the range of 0 through 9. But that examination actually comprises two tests: You can test for any character whose ASCII value is less than 0 or greater than 9. Alternatively, you can test whether the character is greater than or equal to 0 and is less than or equal to 9. What you need is the bottom-line evaluation of both tests.

Boolean math

That's where the wonder of Boolean math comes into play. With just two values — true and false — you can assemble a string of expressions that yield Boolean results and then let Boolean arithmetic figure out whether the bottom line is true or false.

But you don't add or subtract Boolean values like numbers. Instead, in JavaScript, you use one of three Boolean operators at your disposal. Table 32-6 shows the three operator symbols. In case you're unfamiliar with the characters in the table, the symbols for the Or operator are created by typing Shift-backslash.

	Table 32-6		
	JavaScript Boolean Operators		
Syntax	*Name*	*Operands*	*Results*
&&	And	Boolean	Boolean
||	Or	Boolean	Boolean
!	Not	One Boolean	Boolean

Using Boolean operators with Boolean operands gets tricky if you're not used to it, so I have you start with the simplest Boolean operator: Not. This operator requires only one operand. The Not operator precedes any Boolean value to switch it back to the opposite value (from true to false, or from false to true). For instance

```
!true  // result = false
!(10 > 5) // result = false
!(10 < 5) // result = true
!(document.title == "Flintstones")    // result = true
```

As shown here, enclosing the operand of a Not expression inside parentheses is always a good idea. This forces JavaScript to evaluate the expression inside the parentheses before flipping it around with the Not operator.

The And (&&) operator joins two Boolean values to reach a true or false value based on the results of both values. This brings up something called a *truth table,* which helps you visualize all the possible outcomes for each value of an operand. Table 32-7 is a truth table for the And operator.

	Table 32-7		
	Truth Table for the And Operator		
Left Operand	*And Operator*	*Right Operand*	*Result*
True	&&	True	True
True	&&	False	False
False	&&	True	False
False	&&	False	False

Only one condition yields a true result: Both operands must evaluate to true. It doesn't matter on which side of the operator a true or false value lives. Here are examples of each possibility:

```
5 > 1 && 50 > 10 // result = true
5 > 1 && 50 < 10 // result = false
5 < 1 && 50 > 10 // result = false
5 < 1 && 50 < 10 // result = false
```

In contrast, the Or (||) operator is more lenient about what it evaluates to true. The reason is that if one or the other (or both) operands is true, the operation returns true. The Or operator's truth table is shown in Table 32-8.

Table 32-8
Truth Table for the Or Operator

Left Operand	Or Operator	Right Operand	Result
True	||	True	True
True	||	False	True
False	||	True	True
False	||	False	False

Therefore, if a true value exists on either side of the operator, a true value is the result. Let's take the previous examples and swap the And operators with Or operators so you can see the Or operator's impact on the results:

```
5 > 1 || 50 > 10 // result = true
5 > 1 || 50 < 10 // result = true
5 < 1 || 50 > 10 // result = true
5 < 1 || 50 < 10 // result = false
```

Only when both operands are false does the Or operator return `false`.

Boolean operators at work

Applying Boolean operators to JavaScript the first time just takes a little time and some sketches on a pad of paper to help you figure out the logic of the expressions. Earlier I talked about using a Boolean operator to see whether a character fell within a range of ASCII values for data-entry validation. Listing 32-1 (not on the CD-ROM) is a function discussed in more depth in Chapter 37. This function accepts any string and sees whether each character of the string has an ASCII value less than 0 or greater than 9 — meaning that the input string is not a number.

Listing 32-1: **Is the Input String a Number?**

```
function isNumber(inputStr) {
      for (var i = 0; i < inputStr.length; i++) {
          var oneChar = inputStr.substring(i, i + 1)
          if (oneChar < "0" || oneChar > "9") {
              alert("Please make sure entries are numbers only.")
              return false
          }
      }
      return true
}
```

Combining a number of JavaScript powers to extract individual characters (substrings) from a string object within a `for` loop, the statement you're interested in is the condition of the `if` construction:

```
(oneChar < "0" || oneChar > "9")
```

In one condition statement, you use the Or operator to test for both possibilities. If you check the Or truth table (Table 32-8), you see that this expression returns true if either one or both tests returns true. If that happens, the rest of the function alerts the user about the problem and returns a false value to the calling statement. Only if both tests within this condition evaluate to false for all characters of the string does the function return a true value.

From the simple Or operator, I go to the extreme, where the function checks — in one condition statement — whether a number falls within several numeric ranges. The script in Listing 32-2 comes from one of the bonus applications on the CD-ROM (Chapter 49), in which a user enters the first three digits of a U.S. Social Security number.

Listing 32-2: **Is a Number within Discontiguous Ranges?**

```
// function to determine if value is in acceptable range for this
application
function inRange(inputStr) {
      num = parseInt(inputStr)
      if (num < 1 || (num > 586 && num < 596) || (num > 599 && num <
700) ||num > 728) {
          alert("Sorry, the number you entered is not part of our
database.  Try another three-digit number.")
          return false
      }
      return true
}
```

By the time this function is called, the user's data entry has been validated enough for JavaScript to know that the entry is a number. Now the function must check whether the number falls outside of the various ranges for which the application contains matching data. The conditions that the function tests here are whether the number is

✦ Less than 1

✦ Greater than 586 and less than 596 (using the And operator)

✦ Greater than 599 and less than 700 (using the And operator)

✦ Greater than 728

Each of these tests is joined by an Or operator. Therefore, if any one of these conditions proves false, the whole if condition is false, and the user is alerted accordingly.

The alternative to combining so many Boolean expressions in one condition statement would be to nest a series of if constructions. But such a construction requires not only a great deal more code, but much repetition of the alert message for each condition that could possibly fail. The combined Boolean condition was, by far, the best way to go.

Bitwise Operators

	Nav2	Nav3	Nav4	IE3/J1	IE3/J2	IE4/J3
Compatibility	✔	✔	✔	✔	✔	

For scripters, bitwise operations are an advanced subject. Unless you're dealing with external processes on CGIs or the connection to Java applets, it's unlikely that you will use bitwise operators. Experienced programmers who concern themselves with more specific data types (such as long integers) are quite comfortable in this arena, so I simply provide an explanation of JavaScript capabilities. Table 32-9 lists JavaScript bitwise operators.

Table 32-9
JavaScript's Bitwise Operators

Operator	Name	Left Operand	Right Operand
&	Bitwise And	Integer value	Integer value
|	Bitwise Or	Integer value	Integer value
^	Bitwise XOR	Integer value	Integer value
~	Bitwise Not	(None)	Integer value
<<	Left shift	Integer value	Shift amount
>	Right shift	Integer value	Shift amount
>>	Zero fill right shift	Integer value	Shift amount

The numeric value operands can appear in any of the JavaScript language's three numeric literal bases (decimal, octal, or hexadecimal). Once the operator has an operand, the value is converted to binary representation (32 bits long). For the first three bitwise operations, the individual bits of one operand are compared with their counterparts in the other operand. The resulting value for each bit depends on the operator:

✦ **Bitwise And:** 1 if both digits are 1

✦ **Bitwise Or:** 1 if either digit is 1

✦ **Bitwise Exclusive Or:** 1 if only one digit is a 1

Bitwise Not, a unary operator, inverts the value of every bit in the single operand. The bitwise shift operators operate on a single operand. The second operand specifies the number of positions to shift the value's binary digits in the direction of the arrows of the operator symbols. For example, the left shift (<<) operator has the following effect:

```
4 << 2 // result = 16
```

The reason for this is that the binary representation for decimal 4 is 00000100 (to eight digits, anyway). The left shift operator instructs JavaScript to shift all digits two places to the left, giving the binary result 00010000, which converts to 16 in decimal format. If you're interested in experimenting with these operators, use the `javascript:` URL to enable JavaScript to evaluate expressions for you. More advanced books on C and C++ programming are also of help.

The typeof Operator

	Nav2	Nav3	Nav4	IE3/J1	IE3/J2	IE4/J3
Compatibility		✔	✔	✔	✔	✔

A special unary operator doesn't fall into any of the categories set out at the beginning of this chapter. Unlike all the other operators, which are predominantly concerned with arithmetic and logic, the `typeof` operator defines the kind of value and expression to which a variable evaluates. Typically, this operator is used to identify whether a variable value is one of the following types: number, string, boolean, object, or undefined.

Having this investigative capability in JavaScript is helpful because variables cannot only contain any one of those data types but can change their data type on the fly. Your scripts may need to handle a value differently based on the value's type. The most common use of the `typeof` property is as part of a condition. For example

```
if (typeof myVal == "number") {
      myVal = parseInt(myVal)
}
```

The evaluated value of the `typeof` operation is, itself, a string.

The void Operator

	Nav2	Nav3	Nav4	IE3/J1	IE3/J2	IE4/J3
Compatibility		✔	✔			✔

In all scriptable browsers you can use the `javascript:` pseudo-protocol to supply the parameter for `HREF` and `SRC` attributes in HTML tags, such as links. In the process you have to be careful that the function or statement being invoked by the URL does not return or evaluate to any values. If a value comes back from such an expression, then the page content is often replaced by that value or sometimes the directory of the client's hard disk. To avoid this possibility use the `void` operator in front of the function or expression being invoked by the `javascript:` URL.

Different versions of Navigator accept a couple different ways of using this operator, but the one that works best is just placing the operator before the expression or function and separating them by a space, as in

```
javascript: void doSomething()
```

On occasion, you may have to wrap the expression inside parentheses after the `void` operator. This is necessary only when the expression contains operators of a lower precedence than the `void` operator (see "Operator Precedence" later in the chapter). But don't automatically wrap all expressions in parentheses, because Navigator 4 can experience problems with these.

The `void` operator makes sure the function or expression returns no value that the HTML attribute can use. If your audience consists solely of browsers aware of this operator, you can use it in lieu of the link object's `onClick=` event handler, which returns false to inhibit the link action.

The new Operator

	Nav2	Nav3	Nav4	IE3/J1	IE3/J2	IE4/J3
Compatibility	✔	✔	✔	✔	✔	✔

Most JavaScript core objects have constructor functions built into the language. To access those functions, you use the `new` operator along with the name of the constructor. The function returns a reference to the object, which your scripts can then use to get and set properties or invoke object methods. For example, creating a new date object requires invoking the date object's constructor, as follows:

```
var today = new Date()
```

Some object constructor functions require parameters to help define the object. Others, as in the case of the date object, can accept a number of different

new

parameter formats, depending on the format of date information you have to set the initial object. The `new` operator can be used with the following core language objects:

JavaScript 1.0	JavaScript 1.1	JavaScript 1.2
Date	Array	RegExp
Object	Boolean	
(Custom object)	Function	
	Image	
	Number	
	String	

The delete Operator

	Nav2	Nav3	Nav4	IE3/J1	IE3/J2	IE4/J3
Compatibility			✔			✔

Array objects do not contain a method to remove an element from the collection. You can always empty the data in an element by setting that element to an empty string or null, but the element remains in the collection. With the `delete` operator (new in Navigator 4 and Internet Explorer 4), you can completely remove the element (or the entire array, for that matter). In fact this works to such an extent that if your array uses numeric indices, a deletion of a given index removes that index value from the total array but without collapsing the array (which would alter index values of items higher than the deleted item). For example, consider the following simple dense array:

```
var oceans = new Array("Atlantic", "Pacific", "Indian","Arctic")
```

This kind of array automatically assigns numeric indices to its entries for addressing later in constructions such as `for` loops:

```
for (var i = 0; i < oceans.length; i++) {
        if (oceans[i] == form.destination.value) {
            statements
        }
}
```

If you then issue the statement

```
delete oceans[2]
```

the array undergoes significant changes. First, the third element is removed from the array. Importantly, the length of the array does not change. Even so, the index value (2) is removed from the array, such that schematically the array looks like the following:

```
oceans[0] = "Atlantic"
oceans[1] = "Pacific"
oceans[3] = "Arctic"
```

If you try to reference `oceans[2]` in this collection, the result is `undefined`.

The `delete` operator works best on arrays that have named indices. Your scripts will have more control over the remaining entries and their values, because they don't rely on what could be a missing entry of a numeric index sequence.

Also feel free to use the `delete` operator to eliminate any arrays or objects created by your scripts. JavaScript takes care of this anyway when the page unloads, but your scripts may want to delete such objects to reduce some internal ambiguity with your scripted objects.

The this Operator

	Nav2	Nav3	Nav4	IE3/J1	IE3/J2	IE4/J3
Compatibility	✔	✔	✔	✔	✔	✔

JavaScript includes an operator that allows script statements to refer to the very object in which they are located. The self-referential operator is `this`.

The most common application of the `this` operator is in event handlers that pass references of themselves to functions for further processing, as in

```
<INPUT TYPE="text" NAME="entry" onChange="process(this)">
```

A function receiving the value assigns it to a variable that can be used to reference the sender, its properties, and its methods.

Because the `this` operator references an object, that object's properties can be exposed with the aid of the operator. For example, to send the `value` property of a text input object to a function, the `this` operator stands in for the current object reference and appends the proper syntax to reference the `value` property:

```
<INPUT TYPE="text" NAME="entry" onChange="process(this.value)">
```

The `this` operator also works inside other objects, such as custom objects. When you define a constructor function for a custom object, it is common to use the `this` operator to define properties of the object and assign values to those properties. Consider the following example of an object creation sequence:

```
function bottledWater(brand, ozSize, flavor) {
        this.brand = brand
        this.ozSize = ozSize
        this.flavor = flavor
}
var myWater = new bottledWater("Crystal Springs", 16, "original")
```

When the new object is created via the constructor function, the this operators define each property of the object and then assign the corresponding incoming value to that property. Using the same names for the properties and parameter variables is perfectly fine, and makes the constructor easy to maintain.

By extension, if you assign a function as an object property (to behave as a method for the object), the this operator inside that function refers to the object, offering an avenue to the object's properties. For example, if I add the following function definition and statement to the myWater object created just above, the function can directly access the brand property of the object:

```
function adSlogan() {
        return "Drink " + this.brand + ", it's wet and wild!"
}
myWater.getSlogan = adSlogan
```

When a statement invokes the myWater.getSlogan() method, the object invokes the adSlogan() function, but all within the context of the myWater object. Thus, the this operator applies to the surrounding object, making the brand property available via the this operator (this.brand).

Operator Precedence

When you start working with complex expressions that hold a number of operators (for example, Listing 32-2), knowing the order in which JavaScript evaluates those expressions is vital. JavaScript assigns different priorities or weights to types of operators in an effort to achieve uniformity in the way it evaluates complex expressions.

In the following expression

```
10 + 4 * 5 // result = 30
```

JavaScript uses its precedence scheme to perform the multiplication before the addition — regardless of where the operators appear in the statement. In other words, JavaScript first multiplies 4 by 5, and then adds that result to 10 to get a result of 30. That may not be the way you want this expression to evaluate. Perhaps your intention was to add the 10 and 4 first and then to multiply that sum by 5. To make that happen, you have to override JavaScript's natural operator precedence. To do that, you must enclose an operator with lower precedence in parentheses. The following statement shows how you'd adjust the previous expression to make it behave differently:

```
(10 + 4) * 5 // result = 70
```

That one set of parentheses has a great impact on the outcome. Parentheses have the highest precedence in JavaScript, and if you nest parentheses in an expression, the innermost set evaluates first.

For help in constructing complex expressions, refer to Table 32-10 for JavaScript's operator precedence. My general practice: When in doubt about complex precedence issues, I build the expression with lots of parentheses according to the way I want the internal expressions to evaluate.

Table 32-10
JavaScript Operator Precedence

Precedence Level	Operator	Notes
1	( )	From innermost to outermost
	[]	Array index value
	function()	Any remote function call
2	!	Boolean Not
	~	Bitwise Not
	-	Negation
	++	Increment
	--	Decrement
	typeof	
	void	
	delete	Delete array or object entry
3	*	Multiplication
	/	Division
	%	Modulo
4	+	Addition
	-	Subtraction
5	<<	Bitwise shifts
	>	
	>>	
6	<	Comparison operators
	<=	
	>	
	>=	
7	==	Equality
	!=	
8	&	Bitwise And
9	^	Bitwise XOR
10	|	Bitwise Or
11	&&	Boolean And
12	||	Boolean Or

(continued)

Table 32-10 *(continued)*

Precedence Level	Operator	Notes
13	?	Conditional expression
14	=	Assignment operators
	+=	
	-=	
	*=	
	/=	
	%=	
	<<=	
	>=	
	>>=	
	&=	
	^=	
	|=	
15	,	Comma (parameter delimiter)

This precedence scheme is devised to help you avoid being faced with two operators from the same precedence level that often appear in the same expression. When it happens (such as with addition and subtraction), JavaScript begins evaluating the expression from left to right.

One related fact involves a string of Boolean expressions strung together for a condition statement (Listing 32-2). JavaScript follows what is called *short-circuit evaluation*. As the nested expressions are evaluated left to right, the fate of the entire condition can sometimes be determined before all expressions have been evaluated. Anytime JavaScript encounters an And operator, if the left operand evaluates to false, the entire expression evaluates to false without JavaScript even bothering to evaluate the right operand. For an Or operator, if the left operand is true, JavaScript short-circuits that expression to true. This feature can trip you up if you don't perform enough testing on your scripts: If a syntax error or other error exists in a right operand, and you fail to test the expression in a way that forces that right operand to evaluate, you may not know that a bug exists in your code. Users of your page, of course, will find the bug quickly. Do your testing to head off bugs at the pass.

Note

Notice, too, that all math and string concatenation is performed prior to any comparison operators. This enables all expressions that act as operands for comparisons to evaluate fully before they are compared.

The key to working with complex expressions is to isolate individual expressions and try them out by themselves, if you can. See additional debugging tips in Chapter 45.

✦   ✦   ✦

The Event Object

Prior to Navigator 4, user and system actions — events — were captured predominantly by event handlers defined as attributes inside HTML tags. For instance, when a user clicked on a button, the click event triggered the `onClick=` event handler in the tag. That handler might invoke a separate function or perform some inline JavaScript script. Even so, the events themselves were rather dumb: Either an event occurred or it didn't. Where it occurred (that is, the screen coordinates of the pointer when the mouse button was clicked) and other pertinent event tidbits (for example, whether a keyboard modifier key was pressed at the same time) were not part of the equation. Until Navigator 4, that is.

While remaining fully backward compatible with the event handler mechanism of old, the Navigator 4 event model turns events into first-class objects whose properties automatically carry a lot of relevant information about the event when it occurs. These properties are fully exposed to scripts, allowing pages to respond more intelligently about what the user does with the page and its elements.

Another new aspect of Navigator 4's event model is that an event is no longer confined to only the intended object of the event. It is possible to capture events on a more global basis, perform some preprocessing, if necessary, and then dispatch the event either to its original target or some other object under your script control.

Why Events?

Graphical user interfaces are more difficult to program than the "old-fashioned" command-line interface. With a command-line or menu-driven system, users were intentionally restricted in the types of actions they could take at any given moment. The world was very modal, primarily as a convenience to programmers who led users through rigid program structures.

That all changed in a graphical user interface such as Windows, MacOS, Xwindows, and all others derived from the pioneering work of the Xerox Star system. The challenge for programmers is that a good user interface in this realm must make it possible for users to perform all kinds of actions at any given moment: roll the mouse, click a button, type a key, select text, choose a pull-down menu item, and so on. To accommodate this, a program (or, better yet, the operating system) must be on the lookout for any possible activity coming from all input ports, whether it be the mouse, keyboard, or network connection.

A common methodology to accomplish this at the operating system level is to look for any kind of event, whether it comes from user action or some machine-generated activity. The operating system or program then looks up how it should process each kind of event. Such events, however, must have some smarts about them so that the program knows what and where on the screen the event is.

Event handlers

Fortunately for scripters, the JavaScript language and document object model shield us from the dirty work of monitoring events. In a scriptable browser, an event is processed to some degree before it ever reaches anything scriptable. For instance, when a user clicks on a button, the browser takes care of figuring out where on the page the click occurred and what, if any, button object was under the pointer at the time of the click. If it was a button, then the event is sent to that button. That's where your onClick= event handler first gets wind that a user has done something with the button. The physical action has already taken place; now it's time for the script to do something in response to that action. If no event handler is defined for that event in that object, nothing happens beyond whatever the browser does internally (for example, highlighting the button object art).

In Navigator 2 and Internet Explorer 3, event handlers process events in the simplest possible manner. All event actions were scripted via event handler attributes inside regular HTML tags, such as the following:

```
<INPUT TYPE="text" NAME="age" SIZE="3" onChange="isNumber(this)">
```

When a user types into the above field and tabs or clicks outside of the field, the text object receives a change event from the browser, triggering the onChange= event handler. In the example just given, the event handler invokes a custom function that validates the entry in the field to make sure it's a number. Conveniently, a parameter conveying a reference to the text object is passed to the function. Parameters, including references to the object's containing form, are easily passed to functions this way.

Event properties

Navigator 3 brought an additional way to specify an event handler action for an object. In addition to the traditional event handler attribute in the HTML tag, the event handler was also a property of the object. You could assign a function reference to an object's event property outside of the tag, as follows:

```
document.forms[0].age.onchange = isNumber
```

A big difference with this methodology is that you do not pass arguments to the function, as you can with traditional event handler syntax. You can, however, use some advanced function object techniques to create a reference that passes a parameter to the function, provided you also explicitly include the event objects in the definition, as follows:

```
document.forms[0].age.onchange = new Function("event",
"document.forms[0].age")
```

Or, if the script is written in a `<SCRIPT LANGUAGE="JavaScript1.2">` tag set:

```
document.forms[0].age.onchange = function(event)
{isNumber(document.forms[0].age)}
```

No matter which way you use to assign a function to an event handler on the fly, this flexibility allows a script to modify the function invoked by an object's event handler even after the document has loaded — perhaps user selections in a form dictate that the form's `onsubmit` event handler should process a different presubmission function than the one specified in the tag. In Navigator 3, these event properties are all lowercase, while the corresponding event handler attribute is traditionally spelled with a capital letter after the "on" portion of the event handler name (for example, `onLoad=`).

You must exercise some care in positioning scripts in your page to define event handlers in this fashion. The object must have already been loaded in the document before you can set any of its properties. Therefore, you cannot set a form element's event handlers in this way anywhere in the document that executes before the tag that generates the object in the current document object model. A safe place to set these properties is in a function invoked by the window's `onLoad=` event handler. That way you know for sure all objects have completed their loading and rendering.

New Navigator — New Events

Many new events have been defined for objects in Navigator 4. For form elements, there now exist events for the components of a complete mouse click as well as keyboard events for text objects. Drag and drop is supported such that scripts can capture the user action of dragging URL text from outside of the browser to the current page. And events now signal when a user has moved or resized a browser window or frame. Table 33-1 shows the complete matrix of objects and events introduced with each generation of Navigator from 2 through 4.

Table 33-1
Event Handlers through the Navigator Ages

Object	Navigator 2	Navigator 3	Navigator 4
window	onBlur		onDragDrop
	onFocus		onMove
	onLoad		onResize
	onUnload		

(continued)

		Table 33-1 *(continued)*	
Object	*Navigator 2*	*Navigator 3*	*Navigator 4*
layer			onBlur
			onFocus
			onLoad
			onMouseOut
			onMouseOver
			onMouseUp
link	onClick	onMouseOut	onDblClick
	onMouseOver		onMouseDown
			onMouseUp
area		onMouseOut	onClick
		onMouseOver	
image		onAbort	
		onError	
		onLoad	
form	onSubmit	onReset	
text, textarea, password	onBlur	onKeyDown	
	onChange		onKeyPress
	onFocus		onKeyUp
	onSelect		
all buttons	onClick		onMouseDown
			onMouseUp
select	onBlur		
	onChange		
	onFocus		
fileUpload		onBlur	
		onFocus	
		onSelect	

Enhanced mouse events

Most clickable objects — buttons and links in particular — respond to more events in Navigator 4 than in previous browser versions. Whereas in previous versions all you could script was a complete click of the mouse button atop the object, you can now extract the mouse down (button depression) and mouse up (button release) components of the click event. If the user presses and releases the mouse button with the pointer atop the object, the sequence of events is mouseDown, mouseUp, click. Perhaps the biggest potential for these events is in links surrounding images. Rather than perform the mouse rollover image swap, you can swap the image on the press and release of the mouse button, just the same way as most graphical user interface buttons respond in multimedia programs.

Links can also respond to a double-click event (although this is not implemented for the Macintosh version of Navigator 4). Again, for iconic representations that simulate the workings of the desktop, a double-click action may be appropriate for your page design.

Keyboard events

At long last, Navigator provides facilities for capturing keyboard events in text fields in forms. A complete key press consists of keyDown and keyUp events. Be aware that these events are sent to the event handler before the keyboard characters are rendered in the text box. This allows your script to completely intercept keyboard input before the data reaches the box. Therefore, you might want to inspect characters to make sure only letters or only numbers reach the field.

In Navigator 4, the only keys that generate these events are the basic typewriter character keys and the Enter key. None of the navigation or function keys is capturable at this point (although some modifier keys are, as described in the discussion later in this chapter about the `which` property of the event object).

DragDrop events

Many Navigator 3 and 4 users aren't aware that you can drag text from any document from any application onto the browser window. If that text includes a URL, Navigator loads that URL's document into the browser. In Navigator 4, that user action can be monitored to some degree. The DragDrop event is a window event and fires every time the user drags something to the window. However, the URL is visible to your scripts only if the scripts are signed (see Chapter 40). Such URL data is deemed to be private information that requires user permission to capture.

Window modification events

One last set of events applies to the window object (and, by extension, a frame object). Navigator fires the Move and Resize events when the user changes the location or dimension of the entire browser window or frame border. Since a window's `onLoad=` event handler does not fire on a window resize, this user action may be of value to you if you want to reassess the new window or frame size before reinitializing some data or reloading the page.

In addition to supplying these new events, Navigator adds significant power to all events. Whenever an event occurs (whether it's by the user or the system), Navigator creates an event object. In the next section, I take up the formal definitions of this object and its properties. In Chapter 39, I cover advanced event handling in depth, particularly how to capture and redirect events before they reach their intended targets.

Note

While Internet Explorer 4 also defines an event object in response to a user or system event, it works very differently from the Navigator event object. You can, however, share the "old-fashioned" event handler mechanism even with the newer mouse and keyboard events.

Event Object

Properties	Methods	Event Handlers
data	(None)	(None)
layerX		
layerY		
modifiers		
pageX		
pageY		
screenX		
screenY		
target		
type		
which		

Syntax

Accessing event properties:

eventObject.property

	Nav2	Nav3	Nav4	IE3/J1	IE3/J2	IE4/J3
Compatibility			✔			

About this object

An event object is generated automatically whenever Navigator detects any one of numerous user and browser-induced actions (for example, loading a document in the window). You don't see this object, but it is there, and you can pass the object along to functions invoked by any event handler. The function can then examine the properties of the event object and process the event accordingly.

How you pass the event object to a function depends on the syntax you use to associate a function with the event. For a traditional event handler attribute in an HTML tag, the event object is passed as a keyword parameter. For example, the following tag for a text input field shows an `onKeyPress=` event handler and the passing of both the event object and the form containing the field:

```
<INPUT TYPE="text" NAME="entry" onKeyPress="handleKey(event,
this.form)">
```

Just as the `this` keyword conveys a reference to the current object, the `event` keyword conveys a reference to the event object held in memory as a result of the user pressing a keyboard key. Do not place either keyword inside quotes.

At the receiving end, the function treats the parameter like any other:

```
function handleKey(evt, form) {
      statements
}
```

You assign a local variable to the incoming event object reference (in the example I arbitrarily chose `evt`). Use that variable to access the event object's properties. If, instead of specifying the event handler in the HTML tag, I choose to specify event handling by setting the object's `onkeypress` event property, the association is made with the following syntax:

```
document.forms[0].entry.onkeypress = handleKey
```

This syntax is available from Navigator 3 or later (and Internet Explorer 4 or later), and the event property must be all lowercase for compatibility with Navigator 3. Navigator 4 also accepts the capitalized version of the property, as in

```
document.forms[0].entry.onKeyPress = handleKey
```

As mentioned earlier, this format does not allow passing parameters along with the call to the function. But the event object is a special case: It is passed automatically to the referenced function. Therefore, the function would be defined as follows:

```
function handleKey(evt) {
      statements
}
```

Event objects stay in memory only as long as they are needed for their processing. For example, if you create a button that has event handlers defined for `onMouseDown=` and `onMouseUp=` and the user makes a quick click of the button, both event objects are maintained in memory until the functions invoked by their event handlers have finished running. For a brief moment there might be an overlap in the existence of both objects, with the `mouseUp` event object standing in readiness until the `mouseDown=` event handler finishes its processing. JavaScript handles its own garbage collection of expended event objects.

Properties

data

Value: Array of strings   **Gettable:** Yes   **Settable:** No

	Nav2	Nav3	Nav4	IE3/J1	IE3/J2	IE4/J3
Compatibility			✔			

A DragDrop event contains information about the URL string being dragged to the browser window. Because it is possible to drag multiple items to a window (for example, many icons representing URLs on some operating systems), the value of the property is an array of strings, with each string containing a single URL (including `file://` URLs for computer files).

URL information like this is deemed to be private data, so it is exposed only to signed scripts when the user has granted permission to read browser data. If you want your signed script to capture this information without loading the URL into the window, the event handler must evaluate to `return false`.

Example

The page in Listing 33-1 contains little more than a textarea in which the URLs of dragged items are listed. To run this script without signing the scripts, turn on codebase principals, as directed in Chapter 40.

To experiment with this listing, load the page and drag any desktop icons that represent files, applications, or folders to the window. Select multiple items and drag them all at once. Because the `onDragDrop=` event handler evaluates to `return false`, the files are not loaded into the window. If you want merely to look at the URL and allow only some to process, you would generate an `if...else` construction to return `true` or `false` to the event handler as needed. A value of `return true` allows the normal processing of the DragDrop event to take place after your event handler function has completed its processing.

Listing 33-1: Obtaining URLs of a DragDrop Event's data Property

```
<HTML>
<HEAD>
<TITLE>Drag and Drop</TITLE>
<SCRIPT LANGUAGE="JavaScript1.2">
function handleDrag(evt) {

netscape.security.PrivilegeManager.enablePrivilege("UniversalBrowserRead")
        var URLArray = evt.data
```

```
netscape.security.PrivilegeManager.disablePrivilege("UniversalBrowserRead")
        if (URLArray) {
            document.forms[0].output.value = URLArray.join("\n")
        } else {
            document.forms[0].output.value = "Nothing found."
        }
        return false
}
</SCRIPT>
</HEAD>
<BODY onDragDrop="return handleDrag(event)">
<B>Drag a URL to this window.</B>
<HR>
<FORM>
URLs:<BR>
<TEXTAREA NAME="output" COLS=70 ROWS=4></TEXTAREA><BR>
<INPUT TYPE="reset">
</FORM>
</BODY>
</HTML>
```

layerX
layerY
pageX
pageY
screenX
screenY

Value: Integer   **Gettable:** Yes   **Settable:** No

	Nav2	Nav3	Nav4	IE3/J1	IE3/J2	IE4/J3
Compatibility			✔			

For many (but not all) mouse-related events, the event object contains a lot of information about the coordinates of the pointer when the event occurred. In the most complex case, a click in a layer object has three distinct pairs of horizontal and vertical (x and y) coordinate values relative to the layer, the page, and the entire screen. When no layers are specified for a document, the layer and page coordinate systems are identical. Note that these values are merely geographical in nature and do not, by themselves, contain any information about the object being clicked (information held by the event.target property).

These mouse coordinate properties are set only with specific events. In the case of a link object, the click and all four mouse events pack these values into the event object. For buttons, however, only the mouse events (mouseDown and mouseUp) receive these coordinates.

Each of the two window events (move and resize) uses one of these property pairs to convey the results of the user action involved. For example, when the user resizes a window, the resize event stuffs the `event.layerX` and `event.layerY` properties with the inner width and height (that is, the content area) of the browser window (you can also use the optional `event.width` and `event.height` property names if you prefer). When the user moves the window, the `event.screenX` and `event.screenY` properties contain the screen coordinates of the top-left corner of the entire browser application window.

Example

You can see the effects of the coordinate systems and associated properties with the page in Listing 33-2. Part of the page contains a three-field readout of the layer-, page-, and screen-level properties. Two clickable objects are provided so you can see the differences between an object not in any layer and an object residing within a layer. The object not confined by a layer has its layer and page coordinates the same in the event object properties.

Additional readouts display the event object coordinates for resizing and moving a window. If you maximize the window under Windows, the Navigator browser's top-left corner is actually out of sight, four pixels up and to the left. That's why the `screenX` and `screenY` values are both -4.

Listing 33-2: **X and Y Coordinate Properties**

```
<HTML>
<HEAD>
<TITLE>X and Y Event Properties</TITLE>
<SCRIPT LANGUAGE="JavaScript">
function checkCoords(evt) {
        var form = document.forms[0]
        form.layerCoords.value = evt.layerX + "," + evt.layerY
        form.pageCoords.value = evt.pageX + "," + evt.pageY
        form.screenCoords.value = evt.screenX + "," + evt.screenY
        return false
}
function checkSize(evt) {
        document.forms[0].resizeCoords.value = evt.layerX + "," +
evt.layerY
}
function checkLoc(evt) {
        document.forms[0].moveCoords.value = evt.screenX + "," +
evt.screenY
}
</SCRIPT>
</HEAD>
<BODY onResize="checkSize(event)" onMove="checkLoc(event)">
<B>X and Y Event Properties</B>
<HR>
<P>Click on the button and in the layer/image to see the coordinate
values for the event object.</P>
```

```
<FORM NAME="output">
<TABLE>
<TR><TD COLSPAN=2>Mouse Event Coordinates:</TD></TR>
<TR><TD ALIGN="right">layerX, layerY:</TD><TD><INPUT TYPE="text"
NAME="layerCoords" SIZE=10></TD></TR>
<TR><TD ALIGN="right">pageX, pageY:</TD><TD><INPUT TYPE="text"
NAME="pageCoords" SIZE=10></TD></TR>
<TR><TD ALIGN="right">screenX, screenY:</TD><TD><INPUT TYPE="text"
NAME="screenCoords" SIZE=10></TD></TR>
<TR><TD ALIGN="right"><INPUT TYPE="button" VALUE="Click Here"
onMouseDown="checkCoords(event)"></TD></TR>
<TR><TD COLSPAN=2><HR></TD></TR>
<TR><TD COLSPAN=2>Window Resize Coordinates:</TD></TR>
<TR><TD ALIGN="right">layerX, layerY:</TD><TD><INPUT TYPE="text"
NAME="resizeCoords" SIZE=10></TD></TR>
<TR><TD COLSPAN=2><HR></TD></TR>
<TR><TD COLSPAN=2>Window Move Coordinates:</TD></TR>
<TR><TD ALIGN="right">screenX, screenY:</TD><TD><INPUT TYPE="text"
NAME="moveCoords" SIZE=10></TD></TR>
</TABLE>
<LAYER NAME="display" BGCOLOR="coral" TOP=100 LEFT=240 HEIGHT=250
WIDTH=330>
<A HREF="javascript:void(0)" onClick="return checkCoords(event)">
<IMG SRC="nile.gif" WIDTH=320 HEIGHT=240" BORDER=0></A>
</LAYER>
</BODY>
</HTML>
```

Related Items: Window and layer object move and resize methods.

modifiers

Value: Constant   **Gettable:** Yes   **Settable:** No

	Nav2	Nav3	Nav4	IE3/J1	IE3/J2	IE4/J3
Compatibility			✔			

The modifiers property of the event object refers to the modifier keys that can be pressed while clicking or typing. Modifier keys are Alt (also the Option key on the Macintosh keyboard), Ctrl, Shift, and what is known as a meta key (for example, the Command key, ⌘, on the Macintosh keyboard, and the Windows key on the PC keyboard). You can use this property to find out if one or more modifier keys were pressed at the time the event occurred.

Values for these keys are integer values designed in such a way that any combination of keys generates a unique value. Fortunately, you don't have to know anything about these values, because JavaScript supplies some plain-language constants (properties of a global Event object always available behind the scenes) that a script can apply to the property value passed with the object. The constant names consist of the key name (all uppercase), followed by an underscore and the uppercase word MASK. For example, if the Alt key is pressed by itself or in concert with other modifier keys, you can use the bitwise AND operator (&) and the Event.ALT_MASK constant to test for the presence of the Alt key in the property value:

```
function handleEvent(evt) {
        if (evt.modifiers & Event.ALT_MASK) {
            statements for Alt key handling
        }
}
```

Modifiers are not available with every event. You can capture them with mouseDown and mouseUp events in buttons and links. The only click event offering modifiers is with the button objects. Keyboard events in text objects also include these modifiers. But be aware that accelerated keyboard combinations (for example, Ctrl+Q/⌘-Q for Quit) are not trappable by JavaScript event mechanisms.

Example

You see how a variety of object event handlers work with the modifiers property in Listing 33-3. A link, text box, and button have event handlers set up to pass the event object to a function that displays the modifier key(s) being pressed at the time of the event. The script contains examples of trapping for all four modifier keys with their constant values.

Listing 33-3: **Modifiers Property**

```
<HTML>
<HEAD>
<TITLE>Modifiers Event Properties</TITLE>
<SCRIPT LANGUAGE="JavaScript">
function checkMods(evt) {
        var form = document.forms[0]
        form.modifier[0].checked = evt.modifiers & Event.ALT_MASK
        form.modifier[1].checked = evt.modifiers & Event.CONTROL_MASK
        form.modifier[2].checked = evt.modifiers & Event.SHIFT_MASK
        form.modifier[3].checked = evt.modifiers & Event.META_MASK
        return false
}
</SCRIPT>
</HEAD>
<BODY>
<B>Event Modifiers</B>
<HR>
<P>Hold one or more modifier keys and click on
<A HREF="javascript:void(0)" onMouseDown="return checkMods(event)">
this link</A> to see which keys you are holding.</P>
<FORM NAME="output">
Enter some text with uppercase and lowercase letters:
<INPUT TYPE="text" SIZE=40 onKeyPress="checkMods(event)"><P>
<INPUT TYPE="button" VALUE="Click Here" onClick="checkMods(event)"><P>
<INPUT TYPE="checkbox" NAME="modifier">Alt
<INPUT TYPE="checkbox" NAME="modifier">Control
```

```
<INPUT TYPE="checkbox" NAME="modifier">Shift
<INPUT TYPE="checkbox" NAME="modifier">Meta
</FORM>
</BODY>
</HTML>
```

target

Value: Object Reference   **Gettable:** Yes   **Settable:** No

	Nav2	Nav3	Nav4	IE3/J1	IE3/J2	IE4/J3
Compatibility			✔			

Every event has a property containing a reference to the object that was clicked on, typed into, or otherwise acted upon. Most commonly, this property is examined when you set up a page to trap for events at the window, document, or layer level, as described in Chapter 39. The `target` property lets you better identify the intended destination of the event while handling all processing for that type of event in one place. With a reference to the target object at hand in this property, your scripts can extract and/or set properties of the object directly.

type

Value: String   **Gettable:** Yes   **Settable:** No

	Nav2	Nav3	Nav4	IE3/J1	IE3/J2	IE4/J3
Compatibility			✔			

An event object's type is the name of the event that generated the event object. An event name is the same as the event handler's name, less the "on" prefix. Therefore, if a button's `onClick=` event handler is triggered by a user's click, then the event type is `click` (all lowercase). If you create a multipurpose function for handling events, you can extract the `event.type` property to help the function decide how to handle the current event. This sounds like a good job for the `switch` control structure.

which

Value: Integer   **Gettable:** Yes   **Settable:** No

	Nav2	Nav3	Nav4	IE3/J1	IE3/J2	IE4/J3
Compatibility			✔			

The value of the `which` property depends on the event type: a mouse button indicator for mouse events and a character key code for keyboard events.

For a mouse-related event, the `event.which` property contains either a 1 for the left (primary) mouse button or a 3 for the right (secondary) mouse button. Most Macintosh computers have only a one-button mouse, so exercise care in designing pages that rely on the second mouse button. Even on Windows and other platforms, you must program an object's `onMouseDown=` event handler to return false for the secondary button to be registered instead of a browser pop-up menu appearing on screen.

Keyboard events generate the ISO-Latin character code for the key that has been pressed. This value is an integer between 0 and 255. If your script needs to look at the actual character being typed, rather than the key code, use the `String.fromCharCode()` method (see Chapter 26) to make the conversion.

Example

Listing 33-4 provides a readout in the status bar for the `event.which` property for an `onMouseDown=` event handler of a link and an `onKeyPress=` event handler of a textarea. As you click the link (with each mouse button if you have more than one), the value of the `event.which` property appears in the status bar. The same goes for displaying the key character code as you type into the textarea. Notice that carriage returns and spaces have codes. The Enter key is 13; Ctrl+Enter is 10.

Listing 33-4: **Event.which Property**

```
<HTML>
<HEAD>
<TITLE>Event.which Properties</TITLE>
<SCRIPT LANGUAGE="JavaScript">
function checkWhich(evt) {
        status = evt.which
        return false
}
</SCRIPT>
</HEAD>
<BODY>
<B>Event.which Properties</B> (results in the status bar)
<HR>
<P>Click on
<A HREF="javascript:void(0)" onMouseDown="return checkWhich(event)">
this link</A> with either mouse button (if you have more than
one).</P>
<FORM NAME="output">
Enter some text with uppercase and lowercase letters:
<TEXTAREA COLS=40 ROWS=4 onKeyPress="checkWhich(event)"></TEXTAREA><P>
</FORM>
</BODY>
</HTML>
```

✦   ✦   ✦

Functions and Custom Objects

By now, you've seen dozens of JavaScript functions in action and probably have a pretty good feel for the way they work. This chapter provides the function object specification and delves into the fun prospect of creating objects in your JavaScript code. That includes objects that have properties and methods, just like the big boys.

Function Object

Properties	Methods	Event Handlers
arguments	(None)	(None)
arity		
caller		
prototype		

Syntax

Creating a function object:

```
function functionName([arg1,...[,argN]]) {
      statement(s)
}

var funcName = new
Function(["argName1",...[,"argNameN"],
"statement1;...[;statementN]"])

object.eventHandlerName =
function([arg1,...[,argN]]) {statement(s)}
```

Accessing function properties:

```
functionObject.property
```

	Nav2	Nav3	Nav4	IE3/J1	IE3/J2	IE4/J3
Compatibility	(✔)	✔	✔	(✔)	✔	✔

About this object

JavaScript accommodates what other languages might call procedures, subroutines, and functions all in one type of structure: the *custom function*. A function may return a value (if programmed to do so with the `return` keyword), but it does not have to return any value. Except for JavaScript code that executes as the document loads, all deferred processing takes place in functions.

While you can create functions that are hundreds of lines long, it is advantageous to break up longer processes into shorter functions. Among the reasons for doing so: smaller chunks are easier to write and debug; building blocks make it easier to visualize the entire script; you can make functions generalizable and reusable for other scripts; and other parts of the script or other open frames may be able to use the functions.

Learning how to write good, reusable functions takes time and experience, but the earlier you understand the importance of this concept, the more you will be on the lookout for good examples in other people's scripts on the Web.

Creating functions

The standard way of defining a function in your script means following a simple pattern and then filling in the details. The formal syntax definition for a function is

```
function functionName( [arg1] ... [, argN]) {
      statement(s)
}
```

The task of assigning a function name helps you determine the precise scope of activity of the function. If you find that the planned task for the function can't be reduced to a simple one- to three-word name (which is then condensed into one contiguous sequence of characters for the *functionName*), perhaps you're asking the function to do too much. A better idea may be to break the job into two or more functions. As you start to design a function, you should also be on the lookout for functions that you can call from the one you're writing. If you find yourself copying and pasting lines of code from one part of a function to another because you're performing the same operation in different spots within the function, it may be time to break that segment out into its own function.

Starting with Navigator 3 (and Internet Explorer 3 with JScript.dll Version2), you can also create what is called an *anonymous function* using the `new Function()` constructor. It may be called anonymous, but in fact you assign a name to the function, as follows:

```
var funcName = new Function(["argName1",...[,"argNameN"],
   "statement1;...[;statementN]"])
```

It is another way of building a function and is particularly helpful when your scripts need to create a function after a document loads. All the components of a function are present in this definition. Each function parameter name is supplied as a string value, separated from each other by commas. The final parameter string consists of the statements that execute whenever the function is called. Separate each JavaScript statement with a semicolon, and enclose the entire sequence of statements inside quotes, as in the following:

```
var willItFit = new Function("width","height","var sx =
screen.availWidth; var sy = screen.availHeight; return (sx >= width &&
sy >= height)")
```

The `willItFit()` function takes two parameters; the body of the function defines two local variables (`sx` and `sy`) and then returns a Boolean value if the incoming parameters are smaller than the local variables. In traditional form, this function would be defined as follows:

```
function willItFit(width, height) {
        var sx = screen.availWidth
        var sy = screen.availHeight
        return (sx >= width && sy >= height)
}
```

Once this function exists in the browser's memory, you can invoke it like any other function:

```
if (willItFit(400,500)) {
        statements to load image
}
```

One last function creation format is available in Navigator 4 when you enclose the creation statement in a `<SCRIPT LANGUAGE="JavaScript1.2">` tag set. The advanced technique is called a *lambda expression* and provides a shortcut for creating a reference to an anonymous function (truly anonymous, since the function has no name that can be referenced later). The common application of this technique is to assign function references to event handlers when the event object must also be passed:

```
document.forms[0].age.onchange = function(event)
{isNumber(document.forms[0].age)}
```

Nesting functions

Navigator 4 introduced the ability to nest functions inside one another. In all prior scripting, each function definition is defined at the global level, whereby every function is exposed and available to all other scripting. With nested functions, you can encapsulate the exposure of a function inside another and make that nested function private to the enclosing function. In other words, although it is a form I don't recommend, you could create nested functions with the same name inside multiple global level functions, as the following skeletal structure shows:

```
function outerA() {
        statements
        function innerA() {
            statements
        }
```

```
          statements
     }
function outerB() {
     statements
     function innerA() {
         statements
     }
     function innerB() {
         statements
     }
     statements
}
```

A nested function can be accessed only from statements in its containing function. Moreover, all variables defined in the outer function (including parameter variables) are accessible to the inner function; but variables defined in an inner function are not accessible to the outer function. See "Variable Scope: Globals and Locals" later in this chapter for details on how variables are visible to various components of a script.

Function parameters

The function definition requires a set of parentheses after the *functionName*. If the function does not rely on any information arriving with it when invoked, the parentheses can be empty. But when some kind of data will be coming with a call to the function, you need to assign names to each parameter. Virtually any kind of value can be a parameter: strings, numbers, Booleans, and even complete object references, such as a form or form element. Choose names for these variables that help you remember the content of those values; also avoid reusing existing object names as variable names, because it's easy to get confused when objects and variables with the same name appear in the same statements. You must avoid using JavaScript keywords (including the reserved words listed in Appendix B) and any global variable name defined elsewhere in your script (see more about global variables in following sections).

JavaScript is forgiving about matching the number of parameters in the function definition with the number of parameters passed along from the calling statement. If you define a function with three parameters and the calling statement only specifies two, the third parameter variable value in that function is assigned a null value. For example:

```
function oneFunction(a, b, c) {
     statements
}
oneFunction("George","Gracie")
```

In the preceding example, the values of a and b inside the function are "George" and "Gracie," respectively; the value of c is null.

At the opposite end of the spectrum, JavaScript also won't balk if you send more parameters from the calling statement than the number of parameter variables specified in the function definition. In fact, the language includes a mechanism — the arguments property — that you can add to your function to gather any extraneous parameters that should read your function.

Properties

arguments

Value: Array of arguments   **Gettable:** Yes   **Settable:** No

	Nav2	Nav3	Nav4	IE3/J1	IE3/J2	IE4/J3
Compatibility		✔	✔		✔	✔

When a function receives parameter values from the statement that invokes the function, those parameter values are silently assigned to the `arguments` property of the function object. The property is an array of the values, with each parameter value assigned to a zero-based index entry in the array—whether or not parameters are defined for it (and in Navigator 4, the property is a first-class object). You can find out how many parameters were sent by extracting `functionName.arguments.length`. For example, if four parameters were passed, `functionName.arguments.length` returns 4. Then use array notation (`functionName.arguments[i]`) to extract the values of any parameter(s) you want.

Theoretically, you never have to define parameter variables for your functions, extracting the desired `arguments` array entry instead. Well-chosen parameter variable names, however, are much more readable, so I recommend them over the `arguments` property for most cases. But you may run into situations in which a single function definition needs to handle multiple calls to the function when each call may have a different number of parameters. The function knows how to handle any arguments over and above the ones given names as parameter variables.

See Listings 34-1 and 34-2 for a demonstration of both the `arguments` and `caller` properties.

arity

Value: Integer   **Gettable:** Yes   **Settable:** No

	Nav2	Nav3	Nav4	IE3/J1	IE3/J2	IE4/J3
Compatibility			✔			

As the `arguments` property of a function proves, JavaScript is very forgiving about matching the number of parameters passed to a function with the number of parameter variables defined for the function. But a script can examine the `arity` property of a function to see precisely how many parameter variables are defined for a function. A reference to the property starts with the function name representing the object. For example, consider the following function definition shell:

```
function identify(name, rank, serialNum) {
    ...
}
```

A script statement anywhere outside of the function can read the number of parameters with the reference

```
identify.arity
```

The value of the property in the preceding example is 3.

caller

Value: Function   **Gettable:** Yes   **Settable:** No

	Nav2	Nav3	Nav4	IE3/J1	IE3/J2	IE4/J3
Compatibility		✔	✔		✔	✔

When one function invokes another, a chain is established between the two, primarily so that a returned value knows where to go. Therefore, a function invoked by another maintains a reference back to the function that called it. Such information is automatically stored in a function object as the `caller` property. This relationship reminds me a bit of a subwindow's `opener` property, which points back to the window or frame responsible for the subwindow's creation. The value is valid only while the called function is running at the request of another function; when a function isn't running, its `caller` property is null.

Since the value of the `caller` property is a function object, you can inspect its `arguments` and `caller` properties (in case it was called by yet another function). Thus, a function can look back at a calling function to see what values it was passed.

The `functionName.caller` property reveals the contents of an entire function definition if the current function was called from another function (including an event handler). If the call for a function comes from a regular JavaScript statement (such as in the Body as the document loads), the `functionName.caller` property is null.

To help you grasp all that these two properties yield, study Listing 34-1.

Listing 34-1: **A Function's arguments and caller Properties**

```html
<HTML>
<HEAD>
<SCRIPT LANGUAGE="JavaScript">
function hansel(x,y) {
        var args = hansel.arguments
        document.write("hansel.caller is " + hansel.caller + "<BR>")
        document.write("hansel.arguments.length is " +
hansel.arguments.length + "<BR>")
        document.write("formal x is " + hansel.x + "<BR>")
        for (var i = 0; i < args.length; i++) {
            document.write("argument " + i + " is " + args[i] + "<BR>")
        }
        document.write("<P>")
```

```
      }

      function gretel(x,y,z) {
            today = new Date()
            thisYear = today.getYear()
            hansel(x,y,z,thisYear)
      }
</SCRIPT>
</HEAD>
<BODY>
<SCRIPT LANGUAGE="JavaScript">
hansel(1, "two", 3);
gretel(4, "five", 6, "seven");
</SCRIPT>
</BODY>
</HTML>
```

When you load this page, the following results appear in the browser window:

```
hansel.caller is null
hansel.arguments.length is 3
formal x is 1
argument 0 is 1
argument 1 is two
argument 2 is 3

hansel.caller is function gretel(x, y, z) { today = new Date();
thisYear = today.getYear(); hansel(x, y, z, thisYear); }

hansel.arguments.length is 4
formal x is 4
argument 0 is 4
argument 1 is five
argument 2 is 6
argument 3 is 97 (or whatever the current year is)
```

As the document loads, the hansel() function is called directly in the Body script. It passes three arguments, even though the hansel() function defines only two. The hansel.arguments property picks up all three arguments, just the same. The main Body script then invokes the gretel() function, which, in turn, calls hansel() again. But when gretel() makes the call, it passes four parameters. The gretel() function picks up only three of the four arguments sent by the calling statement. It also inserts another value from its own calculations as an extra parameter to be sent to hansel(). The hansel.caller property reveals the entire content of the gretel() function, whereas hansel.arguments picks up all four parameters, including the year value introduced by the gretel() function.

If you have Navigator 4, you should also try Listing 34-2, which better demonstrates the chain of caller properties through a sequence of invoked functions. A click of the button in the page invokes a simple function named first(). The passed parameter is the button object reference. The first() function in turn invokes the middle() function, passing a string identifying its source as the first function. Finally, the middle() function invokes the last() function, passing along the parameter it received from first(), plus two other string parameters. The last() function defines parameter variables for only two of the incoming parameters.

An examination of the properties for the arguments object in last() reveals a total of three elements — the three parameters. The index values for the first two consist of the parameter variable names, while the third parameter is assigned to the slot indexed with 2 (the third slot in the zero-based counting system). From within the last() function, a statement grabs the arguments property of the caller (the middle() function), whose only entry is the one incoming parameter to that function (firstMsg). And finally, an examination of the first function in the chain (via the caller.caller reference) finds that its arguments property consists of the one entry of the button reference passed from the event handler.

Listing 34-2: **Examining Arguments through Three Generations**

```
<HTML>
<HEAD>
<TITLE>Event.which Properties</TITLE>
<SCRIPT LANGUAGE="JavaScript1.2">
function showProps(objName,obj) {
        var msg = ""
        for (var i in obj) {
            msg += objName + "." + i + "=" + obj[i] + "\n"
        }
        return msg
}
function first(btn) {
        middle("1st Function Parameter")
}
function middle(firstMsg) {
        last(firstMsg, "2nd Function Parameter", "Bonus Param")
}
function last(firstMsg, secondMsg) {
        var thirdMsg = "Var in 3rd Function"
        var form = document.output
        form.lastFuncArgs.value = showProps("last.arguments",
last.arguments)
        form.midFuncArgs.value = showProps("caller.arguments",
caller.arguments)
        form.firstFuncArgs.value = showProps("caller.caller.arguments",
caller.caller.arguments)
}
</SCRIPT>
</HEAD>
<BODY>
<B>Function Properties</B>
<HR>
Click on the button to trigger a three-function ripple. The effects
are shown in the fields below</P>
<FORM NAME="output">
```

```
<INPUT TYPE="button" VALUE="Trigger and Show" onClick="first(this)"><BR>
last.arguments:<BR>
<TEXTAREA NAME="lastFuncArgs" COLS=70 ROWS=3></TEXTAREA><BR>
middle.arguments:<BR>
<TEXTAREA NAME="midFuncArgs" COLS=70 ROWS=2></TEXTAREA><BR>
first.arguments:<BR>
<TEXTAREA NAME="firstFuncArgs" COLS=70 ROWS=2
WRAP="virtual"></TEXTAREA><BR>
</FORM>
</BODY>
</HTML>
```

These are powerful and useful properties of functions, but I recommend that you not rely on them for your normal script operations unless you fully understand their inner workings. You should be defining functions that take into account all the possible parameters that could be sent by other calling functions. I do, however, use these properties as debugging aids when working on complex scripts that have many calls to the same function.

prototype

Value: String or Function   **Gettable:** Yes   **Settable:** Yes

	Nav2	Nav3	Nav4	IE3/J1	IE3/J2	IE4/J3
Compatibility		✔	✔		✔	✔

Like a number of JavaScript objects, the function object has a prototype property, which enables you to apply new properties and methods to every function object that is created in the current page. You can see examples of how this works in discussions of the prototype property for string and array objects (Chapters 26 and 29, respectively).

Function Application Notes

Understanding the ins and outs of JavaScript functions is key to successful scripting, especially for complex applications. Additional topics to be covered in this chapter include the ways to invoke functions, variable scope in and around functions, recursion, and designing reusable functions.

Invoking Functions

A function doesn't perform any work until a script calls it by name. Scripts invoke functions (that is, get functions doing something) via three routes: JavaScript object event handlers; javaScript statements; and HREF= attributes pointing to a javascript: URL.

Because you've seen dozens of examples of the first two methods throughout this book so far, let me say a few words about the last item.

Several HTML tags have HREF attributes that normally point to Internet URLs for either navigating to another page or loading a MIME file that requires a helper application or plug-in. These HTML tags are usually tags for clickable objects, such as links and client-side image map areas.

A JavaScript-enabled browser has a special built-in URL pseudo-protocol — javascript: — that lets the HREF attribute point to a JavaScript function or method, rather than to a URL out on the Net. For example, I use the javascript: URL when I want a link to change the contents of two other frames. Because the HREF attribute enables me to specify only a single URL, I'd be out of luck without a convenient way to put multiframe navigation into my hands. I do that by writing a function that sets the location properties of the two frames; then I invoke that function from the HREF attribute. The following example shows what the script may look like:

```
function loadPages() {
        parent.frames[1].location = "page2.html"
        parent.frames[2].location = "instrux2.html"
}
...
<A HREF="javascript:loadPages()">Next</A>
```

Caution

These kinds of function invocations can include parameters, and the functions can do anything you want. One potential side effect to watch out for occurs when the function returns a value (perhaps the function is also invoked from other script locations where a returned value is expected). Because the HREF attribute sets the TARGET window to whatever the attribute evaluates to, the returned value will be assigned to the TARGET window — probably not what you want.

To prevent the assignment of a returned value to the HREF attribute, prefix the function call with the void operator (you can also surround the function call with void()). The placement of this operator is critical. The following are two examples of how to use void:

```
<A HREF="javascript:void loadPages()">
<A HREF="javascript:void(loadPages())">
```

Experienced programmers of many other languages will recognize this operator as a way of indicating that no values are returned from a function or procedure. The operator has precisely that functionality here, but in a nontraditional location.

Variable Scope: Globals and Locals

A variable can have two scopes in JavaScript. As you'd expect, any variable initialized within the main flow of a script (not inside a function) is a *global variable,* in that any statement in the same document's script can access it by name. You can, however, also initialize variables inside a function (in a var statement) so the variable name applies only to statements inside that function. By limiting the scope of the variable to a single function, you can reuse the same variable name in multiple functions, enabling the variables to carry very different information in each function. To demonstrate the various possibilities, I present the script in Listing 34-3.

Listing 34-3: Variable Scope Workbench Page

```
<HTML>
<HEAD>
<TITLE>Variable Scope Trials</TITLE>
<SCRIPT LANGUAGE="JavaScript">
var headGlobal = "Gumby"
function doNothing() {
        var headLocal = "Pokey"
        return headLocal
}
</SCRIPT>
</HEAD>

<BODY>
<SCRIPT LANGUAGE="JavaScript">
// two global variables
var aBoy = "Charlie Brown"
var hisDog = "Snoopy"
function testValues() {
        var hisDog = "Gromit"  // initializes local version of "hisDog"
        var page = ""
        page += "headGlobal is: " + headGlobal + "<BR>"
        // page += "headLocal is: " + headLocal + "<BR>" // won't run:
headLocal not defined
        page += "headLocal value returned from head function is: " +
doNothing() + "<P>"
        page += " aBoy is: " + aBoy + "<BR>" // picks up global
        page += "local version of hisDog is: " + hisDog + "<P>" //
"sees" only local version
        document.write(page)
}
testValues()
document.write("global version of hisDog is intact: " + hisDog)
</SCRIPT>
</BODY>
</HTML>
```

In this page, you define a number of variables — some global, others local — that are spread out in the document's Head and Body sections. When you load this page, it runs the `testValues()` function, which accounts for the current values of all the variable names. The script then follows up with one more value extraction that was masked in the function. The results of the page look like this:

```
headGlobal is: Gumby
headLocal value returned from head function is: Pokey
```

```
aBoy is: Charlie Brown
local version of hisDog is: Gromit

global version of hisDog is intact: Snoopy
```

Examine the variable initialization throughout this script. In the Head, you define the first variable, headGlobal, as a global style — outside of any function definition. The var keyword for the global variable is optional but often helpful for enabling you to see at a glance where you initialize your variables. You then create a short function, which defines a variable (headLocal) that only statements in the function can use.

In the Body, you define two more global variables, aBoy and hisDog. Inside the Body's function, I intentionally (for purposes of demonstration) have you reuse the hisDog variable name. By initializing hisDog with the var statement inside the function, you tell JavaScript to create a separate variable whose scope is only within the function. This initialization does not disturb the global variable of the same name. It can, however, make things confusing for you as script author.

Statements in the script attempt to collect the values of variables scattered around this script. Even from within this script, JavaScript has no problem extracting global variables directly, including the one defined in the Head. But it cannot get the local variable defined in the other function — that headLocal variable is private to its own function. Trying to run a script that gets that variable value results in an error message saying that the variable name is not defined. In the eyes of everyone else outside of the doNothing() function, that's true. If you really need that value, you can have that function return the value to a calling statement, as you do in the testValues() function.

Near the end of the function, you get the aBoy global value without a hitch. But because you initialized a separate version of hisDog inside that function, only the localized version is available to the function. If you reassign a global variable name inside a function, you cannot access the global version from inside that function.

As proof that the global variable, whose name was reused inside the testValues() function, remains untouched, the script writes that value to the end of the page for all to see. Charlie Brown and his dog are reunited.

A benefit of this variable-scoping scheme is that you can reuse "throw-away" variable names in any function you like. For instance, you are free to use, say, the i loop counting variable in every function that uses loops (in fact, you can reuse it in multiple for loops of the same function, because the for loop reinitializes the value at the start of the loop). If you pass parameters to a function, you can assign those parameters the same names to aid in consistency. For example, a common practice is to pass an entire form object reference as a parameter to a function (using a this.form parameter in the event handler). For every function that catches one of these objects, you can use the variable name form in the parameter, as in

```
function doSomething(form) {
        statements
}
...
<INPUT TYPE="button" VALUE="Do Something"
onClick="doSomething(this.form)">
```

If five buttons on your page pass their form objects as parameters to five different functions, each function can assign `form` (or whatever you want to use) to that parameter value.

I recommend reusing variable names only for these "throw-away" variables. In this case, the variables are all local to functions, so the possibility of a mix-up with global variables does not exist. But the thought of reusing a global variable name as, say, a special case inside a function sends shivers up my spine. Such a tactic is doomed to cause confusion and error.

Some programmers devise naming conventions for themselves to avoid reusing global variables as local variables. A popular scheme puts a lowercase "g" in front of any global variable name. In the example from Listing 34-3, the global variables would have been named

```
gHeadGlobal
gABoy
gHisDog
```

Then if you define local variables, don't use the leading "g." Any scheme you use to prevent the reuse of variable names in different scopes is fine as long as it does the job.

In a multiple-frame or multiple-window environment, your scripts can also access global variables from any other document currently loaded into the browser. For details about this level of access, see Chapter 14.

Variable scoping rules apply equally to nested functions in Navigator 4. Any variables defined in an outer function (including parameter variables) are exposed to all functions nested inside. But if you define a new local variable inside a nested function, that variable is not available to the outer function. Instead, you can return a value from the nested function to the statement in the outer function that invokes the nested function.

Parameter variables

When a function receives data in the form of parameters, remember that the values may be merely copies of the data (in the case of run-of-the-mill data values) or references to real objects (such as a form object). In the latter case, you can change the object's modifiable properties in the function when the function receives the object as a parameter, as shown in the following example:

```
function validateCountry (form) {
        if (form.country.value == "") {
            form.country.value = "USA"
        }
}
```

JavaScript knows all about the form object passed to the `validateCountry()` function. Therefore, whenever you pass an object as a function parameter, be aware that the changes you make to that object in its "passed" form affect the real object.

As a matter of style, if my function needs to extract properties or results of methods from passed data (such as object properties or string substrings), I like to do that at the start of the function. I initialize as many variables as needed for each piece of data used later in the function. This task enables me to assign meaningful names to the data chunks, rather than having to rely on potentially long references within the working part of the function (such as using a variable like `inputStr` instead of `form.entry.value`).

Recursion in functions

Functions can call themselves — a process known as *recursion*. The classic example of programmed recursion is the calculation of the factorial (the factorial for a value of 4 is 4 * 3 * 2 * 1), shown in Listing 34-4 (not on the CD-ROM).

In the third line of this function, the statement calls itself, passing along a parameter of the next lower value of `n`. As this function executes, diving ever deeper into itself, JavaScript watches intermediate values and performs the final evaluations of the nested expressions. Be sure to test any recursive function carefully. In particular, make sure that the recursion is finite: That a limit exists for the number of times it can recurse. In the case of Listing 34-4, that limit is the initial value of `n`. Failure to watch out for this limit may cause the recursion to overpower the limits of the browser's memory and even lead to a crash.

Listing 34-4: **A JavaScript Function Utilizing Recursion**

```
function factorial(n) {
    if (n > 0) {
        return n * (factorial(n-1))
    } else {
        return 1
    }
}
```

Turning functions into libraries

As you start writing functions for your scripts, be on the lookout for ways to make functions generalizable (written so that you can reuse the function in other instances, regardless of the object structure of the page). The likeliest candidates for this kind of treatment are functions that perform specific kinds of validation checks (see examples in Chapter 37), data conversions, or iterative math problems.

To make a function generalizable, don't let it make any references to specific objects by name. Object names will probably change from document to document. Instead, write the function so that it accepts a named object as a parameter. For example, if you write a function that accepts a text object as its parameter, the function can extract the object's data or invoke its methods without knowing anything about its enclosing form or name. Look again, for example, at the `factorial()` function in Listing 34-5 — but now as part of an entire document.

Listing 34-5: **Calling a Generalizable Function**

```
<HTML>
<HEAD>
<TITLE>Variable Scope Trials</TITLE>
<SCRIPT LANGUAGE="JavaScript">
function factorial(n) {
        if (n > 0) {
            return n * (factorial(n - 1))
        } else {
            return 1
        }
}
</SCRIPT>
</HEAD>

<BODY>
<FORM>
Enter an input value: <INPUT TYPE="text" NAME="input" VALUE=0><P>
<INPUT TYPE="button" VALUE="Calc Factorial"
        onClick="this.form.output.value =
            factorial(this.form.input.value)"><P>
Results: <INPUT TYPE="text" NAME="output">
</FORM>
</BODY>
</HTML>
```

The function was designed to be generalizable, accepting only the input value (n) as a parameter. In the form, the `onClick=` event handler of the button extracts the input value from one of the form's fields, sending that value to the `factorial()` function. The returned value is assigned to the output field of the form. The `factorial()` function is totally ignorant about forms, fields, or buttons in this document. If I need this function in another script, I can copy and paste it into that script, knowing that it has been pretested. Any generalizable function becomes part of my personal library of scripts — from which I can borrow — and saves me time in future scripting tasks.

You will not always be able to generalize a function. Somewhere along the line in your scripts, you must have references to JavaScript or custom objects. But if you find that you're frequently writing functions that perform the same kind of actions, it's time to see how you can generalize the code and put the results in your library of ready-made functions. And if your audience is using browsers from Navigator 3 onward (and later versions of Internet Explorer 3 onward), consider placing these library functions in an external .js library file. See Chapter 13 for details on this convenient way to share utility functions among many documents.

Custom Objects

In all the previous chapters of this book, you've seen how conveniently the JavaScript document object model organizes all the information about the browser window and its document. What may not be obvious from the scripting you've done so far is that JavaScript enables you to create your own objects in memory — objects with properties and methods. These objects are not user interface elements per se on the page, but rather the kinds of objects that may contain data and script functions (behaving as methods), whose results the user can see displayed in the browser window.

You actually had a preview of this power in Chapter 29's discussion about arrays. An array, you recall, is an ordered collection of data. You can create a JavaScript array in which entries are labeled just like properties that you access via the now-familiar dot syntax (`arrayName[index].propertyName`). An object typically contains different kinds of data. It doesn't have to be an ordered collection of data — although your scripts can use objects in constructions that strongly resemble arrays. Moreover, you can attach any number of custom functions as methods for that object. You are in total control of the object's structure, data, and behavior.

An example — planetary objects

Building on your familiarity with the planetary data array created in Chapter 29, in this chapter I have you use the same information to build objects. The application goals are the same: Present a pop-up list of the nine planets of the solar system and display data about the selected planet. From a user interface perspective (and for more exposure to multiframe environments), the only difference is that the resulting data displays in a separate frame of a two-frame window rather than in a textarea object. This means your object method will be building HTML on the fly and plugging it into the display frame — a pretty typical task in these multiframe, Web-browsing days.

To recap the array style from Chapter 29: You created a two-dimensional array — a nine-row, five-column table of data about the planets. Each row was an entry in the `solarSys[]` array. For a function to extract and display data about a given planet, it needed the index value of the `solarSys[]` array passed as a parameter, so that it could get whatever property it needed for that entry (such as `solarSys[3]. name`).

In this chapter, instead of building arrays, you build objects — one object for each planet. The design of your object has five properties and one method. The properties are the same ones you used in the array version: name, diameter, distance from the sun, year length, and day length. To give these objects more intelligence, you give each of them the capability to display their data in the lower frame of the window. You can conveniently define one function that knows how to behave with any of these planet objects, rather than having to define nine separate functions.

Listing 34-6 shows the source code for the document that creates the frameset for your planetary explorations; Listing 34-7 shows the entire HTML page for the object-oriented planet document, which appears in the top frame.

Listing 34-6: **Framesetting Document for a Two-Frame Window**

```
<HTML>
<HEAD>
<TITLE>Solar System Viewer</TITLE>
<SCRIPT LANGUAGE="JavaScript">
function blank() {
        return "<HTML><BODY></BODY></HTML>"
}
</SCRIPT>
</HEAD>
<FRAMESET ROWS="50%,50%">
        <FRAME NAME="Frame1" SRC="lst34-07.htm">
        <FRAME NAME="Frame2" SRC="javascript:parent.blank()">
</FRAMESET>
</HTML>
```

One item to point out in Listing 34-6 is that because the lower frame doesn't get filled until the upper frame's document loads, you need to assign some kind of URL for the SRC= attribute of the second frame. Rather than add the extra transaction and file burden of a blank HTML document, here you use the javascript: URL to invoke a function. In this instance, I want the value returned from the function (a blank HTML page) to be reflected into the target frame (no void operator here). This method is the most efficient way of creating a blank frame in a frameset.

Listing 34-7: **Object-Oriented Planetary Data Presentation**

```
<HTML>
<HEAD>
<TITLE>Our Solar System</TITLE>
<SCRIPT LANGUAGE="JavaScript">
<!-- start script
// method definition
function showPlanet() {
        var result = "<HTML><BODY><CENTER><TABLE BORDER=2>"
        result += "<CAPTION ALIGN=TOP>Planetary data for: <B>" +
this.name + "</B></CAPTION>"
        result += "<TR><TD ALIGN=RIGHT>Diameter:</TD><TD>" +
this.diameter + "</TD></TR>"
        result += "<TR><TD ALIGN=RIGHT>Distance from Sun:</TD><TD>" +
this.distance + "</TD></TR>"
        result += "<TR><TD ALIGN=RIGHT>One Orbit Around Sun:</TD><TD>"
+ this.year + "</TD></TR>"
        result += "<TR><TD ALIGN=RIGHT>One Revolution (Earth
Time):</TD><TD>" + this.day + "</TD></TR>"
        result += "</TABLE></CENTER></BODY></HTML>"
        // display results in a second frame of the window
```

(continued)

Listing 34-7 *(continued)*

```
            parent.Frame2.document.write(result)
            parent.Frame2.document.close()
    }

    // definition of planet object type;
    // 'new' will create a new instance and stuff parameter data into
    object
    function planet(name, diameter, distance, year, day) {
            this.name = name
            this.diameter = diameter
            this.distance = distance
            this.year = year
            this.day = day
            this.showPlanet = showPlanet  // make showPlanet() function a
    method of
            // planet
    }

    // create new planet objects, and store in a series of variables
    Mercury = new planet("Mercury","3100 miles", "36 million miles", "88
    days", "59 days")
    Venus = new planet("Venus", "7700 miles", "67 million miles", "225
    days", "244 days")
    Earth = new planet("Earth", "7920 miles", "93 million miles", "365.25
    days","24 hours")
    Mars = new planet("Mars", "4200 miles", "141 million miles", "687
    days", "24 hours, 24 minutes")
    Jupiter = new planet("Jupiter","88,640 miles","483 million miles",
    "11.9 years", "9 hours, 50 minutes")
    Saturn = new planet("Saturn", "74,500 miles","886 million miles", "29.5
    years", "10 hours, 39 minutes")
    Uranus = new planet("Uranus", "32,000 miles","1.782 billion miles","84
    years", "23 hours")
    Neptune = new planet("Neptune","31,000 miles","2.793 billion
    miles","165 years", "15 hours, 48 minutes")
    Pluto = new planet("Pluto", "1500 miles", "3.67 billion miles", "248
    years", "6 days, 7 hours")

    // end script -->
    </SCRIPT>
    <BODY>
    <H1>The Daily Planet</H1>
    <HR>
    <FORM>
    <SCRIPT LANGUAGE = "JavaScript">
    <!-- start script again
    var page = "" // start assembling next part of page and form
    page += "Select a planet to view its planetary data: "
    // build popup list from planet object names
    page += "<SELECT NAME='planets' onChange='doDisplay(this)'> "
```

```
page += "<OPTION>Mercury"
page += "<OPTION>Venus"
page += "<OPTION SELECTED>Earth"
page += "<OPTION>Mars"
page += "<OPTION>Jupiter"
page += "<OPTION>Saturn"
page += "<OPTION>Uranus"
page += "<OPTION>Neptune"
page += "<OPTION>Pluto"
page += "</SELECT><P>"    // close selection item tag
document.write(page)      // lay out this part of the page

// called from push button to invoke planet object method
function doDisplay(popup) {
        i = popup.selectedIndex
        eval(popup.options[i].text + ".showPlanet()")
}
doDisplay(document.forms[0].planets)
// really end script -->
</SCRIPT>
</FORM>
</BODY>
</HTML>
```

The first task in the Head is to define the function that becomes a method in each of the objects. You must do this task before scripting any other code that adopts the function as its method. Failure to define the function ahead of time results in an error — the function name is not defined. If you compare the data extraction methodology to the function in the array version, you will notice that not only is the parameter for the index value gone, but the reference to each property begins with this. I come back to the custom method after giving you a look at the rest of the Head code.

Next comes the object constructor function, which performs several important tasks. For one, everything in this function establishes the structure of your custom object: the properties available for data storage and retrieval and any methods that the object can invoke. The name of the function is the name you will use later to create new instances of the object. Therefore, choosing a name that truly reflects the nature of the object is important. And, because you will probably want to stuff some data into the function's properties to get one or more instances of the object loaded and ready for the page's user, the function definition includes parameters for each of the properties defined in this object definition.

Inside the function, you use the this keyword to assign data that comes in as parameters to labeled properties. For this example, I've decided to use the same names for both the incoming parameter variables and the properties. That's primarily for convenience, but you can assign any variable and property names you want and connect them any way you like. In the planet() constructor function, five property slots are reserved for every instance of the object whether or not any data actually gets in every property (if not, its value is null).

The last entry in the `planet()` constructor function is a reference to the `showPlanet()` function defined earlier. Notice that the assignment statement doesn't refer to the function with its parentheses — just to the function name. When JavaScript sees this assignment statement, it looks back through existing definitions (those functions defined ahead of the current location in the script) for a match. If it finds a function (as it does here), it knows to assign the function to the identifier on the left side of the assignment statement. In doing this task with a function, JavaScript automatically sets up the identifier as a method name for this object. As you do in every JavaScript method you've encountered, you must invoke a method by using a reference to the object, a period, and the method name followed by a set of parentheses. You see that syntax in a minute.

The next long block of statements creates the individual objects according to the definition established in the `planet()` constructor. Notice that like an array, an object is created by an assignment statement and the keyword `new`. I've assigned names that are not only the real names of planets (the Mercury object name is the Mercury planet object), but that will also come in handy later when extracting names from the pop-up list in search of a particular object's data.

The act of creating a new object sets aside space in memory (associated with the current document) for this object and its properties. In this script, you're creating nine object spaces, each with a different set of properties. Notice that no parameter is being sent (or expected at the function) that corresponds to the `showPlanet()` method. Omitting that parameter here is fine, because the specification of that method in the object definition means that script automatically attaches the method to every version (instance) of the planet object that the script creates.

In the Body portion of the document and after the page's headline, you use JavaScript to create the rest of the user interface for the top frame of the browser window. I've replaced the array version's `for` loop for the pop-up list content with a hard-wired approach. The task could have been accomplished in fewer statements, but I set it up so that if I modify or borrow this code for another purpose, the hard-wired strings will be easier to locate, select, and change.

After the HTML for the top frame is assembled, it is written for the first time (`document.write()`) to let the user see what's going on. Another function is included (`doDisplay()`) as an intermediary between the select object event handler and the `showPlanet()` method for the selected item.

The `onChange=` event handler in the select list passes a copy of the form's selection object to the `doDisplay()` function. In that function, the select object is assigned to a variable called `popup` to help you visualize that the object is the pop-up list. The first statement extracts the index value of the selected item. Using that index value, the script extracts the text. But things get a little tricky because you need to use that text string as a variable name — the name of the planet — and append it to the call to the `showPlanet()` method. To make the disparate data types come together, you use the `eval()` function. Inside the parentheses, you extract the string for the planet name and concatenate a string that completes the reference to the object's `showPlanet()` method. The `eval()` function evaluates that string, which turns it into a valid method call. Therefore, if the user selects Jupiter from the pop-up list, the method call becomes `Jupiter.showPlanet()`.

Now it's time to look back to the `showPlanet()` function/method definition at the top of the script. By the time this method starts working, JavaScript has already been to the object whose name is selected in the pop-up list — the Jupiter object, for example. That Jupiter object has the showPlanet() method as part of its definition. When that method runs, its only scope is of the Jupiter object. Therefore, all references to this.propertyName in showPlanet() refer to Jupiter only. The only possibility for this.name in the Jupiter object is the value assigned to the name property for Jupiter. The same goes for the rest of the properties extracted in the function/method.

One final note about user interface for this admittedly minimal application (see Figure 34-1). At the bottom of the Body's script is the following statement:

```
doDisplay(document.forms[0].planets)
```

The purpose of this statement is to draw the lower-frame table of data to match the preselected item in the select object when the page initially loads. Without taking this extra step, the user would be faced with a selection showing and no data appearing in the lower frame. If the user selected the preselected item, no change event would register with the select object, and no data would appear in the lower frame. The user may think that the page or script was broken. To avoid this problem, a good practice is to look at your pages with the fresh eye of a new user when scripting new concepts.

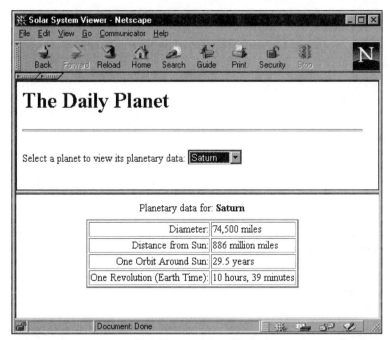

Figure 34-1: An external and internal face-lift for an earlier application

Adding a custom method

You're getting to quite advanced subject matter at this point, so I merely mention and briefly demonstrate an additional power of defining and using custom objects. A custom object can have another custom object as a property. Let's extend the planet example to help you understand the implications.

Say that you want to beef up the planet page with an image of each planet. Each image has a URL for the image file plus other information, such as the copyright notice and a reference number, both of which display on the page for the user. One way to handle this additional information is to create a separate object definition for an image database. Such a definition may look like this:

```
function image(name, URL, copyright, refNum) {
        this.name = name
        this.URL = URL
        this.copyright = copyright
        this.refNum = refNum
}
```

You then need to create individual image objects for each picture. One such definition may look like this:

```
mercuryImage = new image("Planet Mercury", "/images/merc44.gif",
"(c)1990 NASA", 28372)
```

Attaching an image object to a planet object requires modifying the planet constructor function to accommodate one more property. The new planet constructor looks like this:

```
function planet(name, diameter, distance, year, day, image) {
        this.name = name
        this.diameter = diameter
        this.distance = distance
        this.year = year
        this.day = day
        this.showPlanet = showPlanet
        this.image = image // add image property
}
```

Once the image objects are created, you can then create the planet objects, passing one more parameter — an image object you want associated with that object:

```
// create new planet objects, and store in a series of variables
Mercury = new planet("Mercury","3100 miles",  "36 million miles",
"88 days",    "59 days",  mercuryImage)
```

To access a property of an image object, your scripts then have to assemble a reference that works its way through the connection with the planet object:

```
copyrightData = Mercury.image.copyright
```

The potential of custom objects of this type is enormous. For example, you could embed all the copy elements and URL images for an online catalog in a single document. As the user selects items to view (or cycles through them in sequence), a new JavaScript-written page displays the information in an instant, only requiring the image to be downloaded (unless the image was precached, as described in the `document.image` object discussion in Chapter 18, in which case everything works instantaneously — no waiting for page after page of catalog).

If, by now, you think you see a resemblance between this object-within-an-object construction and a relational database, give yourself a gold star. Nothing prevents multiple objects from having the same subobject as their properties — like multiple business contacts having the same company object property.

More ways to create objects

The examples in Listings 34-6 and 34-7 show a way of creating objects that works with all scriptable browsers. If your audience is limited to users with more modern browsers, additional ways of creating custom objects exist.

From Navigator 3 onward and Internet Explorer 4 onward, you can use the `new Object()` constructor to generate a blank object. From that point on, you can define property and method names by simple assignment, as in the following:

```
var Earth = new Object()
Earth.diameter = "7920 miles"
Earth.distance = "93 million miles"
Earth.year = "365.25"
Earth.day = "24 hours"
Earth.showPlanet = showPlanet  // function reference
```

When you are creating a lot of like-structured objects, the custom object constructor shown in Listing 34-7 is more efficient. But for single objects, the `new Object()` constructor is more efficient.

Navigator 4 users can also benefit from a shortcut literal syntax for creating a new object. Pairs of property names and their values can be set inside a set of curly braces, and the whole construction assigned to a variable that becomes the object name. The following script shows how to organize this kind of object constructor:

```
var Earth = {diameter:"7920 miles", distance:"93 million miles",
year:"365.25", day:"24 hours", showPlanet:showPlanet}
```

Name-value pairs are linked together with colons, and multiple name-value pairs are separated by commas. All in all, this is a very compact construction, well suited for single object construction.

Object watcher methods

Navigator 4 includes two special functions for objects that were designed primarily for use with external debugging tools (such as Netscape's JavaScript Debugger, described in Chapter 46). The methods are `watch()` and `unwatch()`. The `watch()` method instructs JavaScript to keep an eye on a particular property in an object (any JavaScript-accessible object) and execute a function when the value of the property changes by assignment (that is, not by user interaction).

You can see how this works in the simplified example of Listing 34-8. Three buttons set the `value` property of a text box. You can turn on the `watch()` method, in which case it calls a handler and passes the name of the property, the old value, and the new value. An alert in the function in the listing demonstrates what those values contain.

Listing 34-8: **Object Watching in Navigator 4**

```
<HTML>
<HEAD>
<TITLE>Our Solar System</TITLE>
<SCRIPT LANGUAGE="JavaScript1.2">
function setIt(msg) {
      document.forms[0].entry.value = msg
}
function watchIt(on) {
      var obj = document.forms[0].entry
      if (on) {
          obj.watch("value",report)
      } else {
          obj.unwatch("value")
      }
}
function report(id, oldval, newval) {
      alert("The field's " + id + " property on its way from \n'" +
oldval + "'\n to \n'" + newval + "'.")
      return newval
}
</SCRIPT>
<BODY>
<B>Watching Over You</B>
<HR>
<FORM>
Enter text here:
<INPUT TYPE="text" NAME="entry" SIZE=50 VALUE="Default Value"><P>
<INPUT TYPE="button" VALUE="Set to Phrase I" onClick="setIt('Four score
and seven years ago...')"><BR>
<INPUT TYPE="button" VALUE="Set to Phrase 2" onClick="setIt('When in
the course of human events...')"><BR>
<INPUT TYPE="reset" onClick="setIt('Default Value')"><P>
<INPUT TYPE="button" VALUE="Watch It" onClick="watchIt(true)">
<INPUT TYPE="button" VALUE="Don't Watch It" onClick="watchIt(false)">
</FORM>
</BODY>
</HTML>
```

Better ways exist to intercept and preprocess user input, but the `watch()` function can be a helpful debugging tool when you want to monitor the hidden workings of scripts.

Using custom objects

There is no magic to knowing when to use a custom object instead of an array in your application. The more you work with and understand the way custom objects work, the more likely you will think about your data-carrying scripts in these terms, especially if an object can benefit from having one or more methods associated with it. This avenue is certainly not one for beginners, but I recommend that you give custom objects more than a casual perusal once you gain some JavaScripting experience.

JavaScript Components

The level 4 browsers from Netscape and Microsoft introduce another twist on the notion of custom objects: external components written in JavaScript. Each company is headed in a different (and mutually exclusive) direction on the authoring and deployment of these components. Netscape is following through on its commitment to the Java environment by fashioning these components after Java Beans, calling them *JavaScript Beans* (or JSBs for short). Microsoft has defined a new term for its components — *scriptlets* — and commonly calls these items *controls*, just as ActiveX components are controls.

What I find most interesting about both approaches is that their goals are identical. In each case, a component author defines in an external file an object that has properties, methods, and event handlers accessible by scripts in a main document. The differences between the two approaches center on how these objects are defined and how each browser handles the objects. For now, neither browser knows what to do with the other browser's JavaScript components.

JavaScript Beans

A JavaScript Bean (JSB) is a separate file (extension .jsb) that defines a new object for inclusion in an HTML document. No HTML content appears in the JSB file, but rather it has an extensive set of tags that let you define constructors, properties, methods, and event handlers for the object. Functions defined inside a JSB file may, however, use `document.write()` to generate content that is displayed in the main document courtesy of the JSB.

If you know Java, you can readily see the Java influence in Netscape's approach to script components. JSB files are treated as classes in packages. A package is nothing more than a directory structure for storing one or more files. The structure is relative to the main HTML document that loads the component. In the Visual JavaScript tool, for example, JavaScript Beans are automatically stored in a directory named peas, which is itself inside a directory named netscape. In Java, such a package would be described as

```
netscape.peas
```

But in JavaScript, which actually accesses these components, the periods are replaced with underscore characters. Therefore, to generate an instance of a JavaScript Bean in a document, you use the new keyword in the following manner:

```
var myJSB = new netscape_peas_BeanObject([params])
```

Parameters to a constructor must be passed in the form of a native JavaScript object. The object defines property names (as named index values to the object properties) and values, as in the following fragment:

```
var params = new Object()
params.name = "Fred"
params.color = "red"
params.birthYear = 1982
var oneMember = new netscape_peas_member(params)
```

Thereafter, you can refer to the object via the variable that holds a reference to its instance. Property and method references are in the same format you use for other objects:

```
JSBRef.propertyName | methodName()
```

If a JavaScript Bean file relies on an external .js or other kind of file, the JSB and supporting files must be encapsulated in a JAR archive file. The archive does not have to be signed (see Chapter 40), but you must use the JAR Packager tool (from Netscape) to join these files together as one entity. It turns out to be a convenience for server management, since there are fewer itsy-bitsy pieces to worry about.

For further details on creating JavaScript Bean components, download the Component Developer's Kit from `http://developer.netscape.com`. Most of Netscape's discussion about JSBs is in relation to the Visual JavaScript tool (see Chapter 46), but you can deploy JSBs without Visual JavaScript if you understand how they work inside your HTML documents (both server- and client-side).

Scriptlets

Technically speaking, scriptlets are not just about JavaScript. In Microsoft's development world, scripting languages are interchangeable. Therefore, you can create scriptlets with JavaScript or VBScript as you like.

A scriptlet definition lives in a file with a standard HTML file extension because this file can also contain HTML content to be displayed within a rectangular space in a main page (much like an ActiveX control does). Inside the scriptlet file are numerous script statements that define the object and its behavior. Many of these scripted items must follow a very specific naming convention and format that allows properties and methods to be exposed to a document that loads the scriptlet.

To load the object into the HTML of the current page requires the `<OBJECT>` tag with a few attributes unique to Internet Explorer (Version 4 or later). For example, the following code loads a calendar scriptlet into a 400 × 300 pixel rectangle:

```
<OBJECT ID="cal" TYPE="text/x-scriptlet" DATA="calendar.html"
HEIGHT="300" WIDTH="400">
```

With an object loaded in the document, you use normal object references to access its values. For example, when the calendar object has its `Value` property retrieved by script, it internally invokes one of its own methods to fetch that value. The document's script to retrieve that value from the calendar object would be

```
var calendarDate = document.cal.Value
```

Scriptlets can also be easily programmed to interact with events on the page. Without much difficulty, you can make the user interaction with the content of a scriptlet and the main document elements completely seamless to the user. For more details on writing scriptlets, download the Component Development section of Microsoft's Internet Client SDK at `http://www.microsoft.com/msdn/sdk/inetsdk/asetup/`.

Deployment

Such divergent approaches to component objects leave developers who desire cross-browser solutions stuck in the middle. Unless you wish to implement the same solution two different ways to support a cross-browser audience, I suggest using scripting components only when the application will be deployed to a single-browser audience, such as on an intranet you control. It is unclear whether the nascent document object model standard will address this aspect of scripted objects. In my examinations and experiments with both component models so far, I don't see a clear advantage for either one over the other. Therefore, until an approach is supported as a standard (if it ever will be), you will have to pick sides in this battle of the browser wars.

✦   ✦   ✦

Global Functions and Statements

In addition to all the objects and other language constructs described in the preceding chapters of this reference part of the book, several language items need to be treated on a global scale. These items apply to no particular objects (or any object) and can be used anywhere in a script. If you've read earlier chapters, you have been introduced to many of these functions and statements. This chapter is presented as a convenient place to highlight these all-important items that are otherwise easily forgotten. This chapter covers the following functions and statements:

Functions	*Statements*
`eval()`	`//` and `/*...*/` (comment)
`escape()`	`var`
`isNaN()`	
`Number()`	
`parseFloat()`	
`parseInt()`	
`String()`	
`unescape()`	
`unwatch()`	
`watch()`	

Very often, the discussions point to examples in earlier chapters that demonstrate the item in context.

Functions

Global functions are not tied to the document object model. Instead they typically let you convert data from one type to another type.

eval(*string*)

Returns: Object reference.

	Nav2	Nav3	Nav4	IE3/J1	IE3/J2	IE4/J3
Compatibility	✔	✔	✔	✔	✔	✔

Expression evaluation, as you are probably well aware by now, is an important concept to grasp in scripting with JavaScript (and programming in general). An expression evaluates to some value. But occasionally you need to force an additional evaluation on an expression to receive the desired results. The eval() function acts on a string value to force an evaluation of that string expression.

Perhaps the most common application of the eval() function is to convert a string version of an object reference to a genuine object reference. For example, in an effort to create a Dynamic HTML script that accommodates the different ways that Microsoft and Netscape reference positionable objects (see Chapter 41), one technique is to assemble references out of the comparable pieces of references. In the following function, the name of a positionable object is passed as a parameter. The example assumes that global variable flags have been set elsewhere for isNav4 and isIE4. The job of the function is to create a valid reference to the object depending on the browser being run by the user:

```
function getReference(objName) {
     if (navigator.appVersion.charAt(0) == "4") {
       if (navigator.appName == "Netscape") {
          var range = ""
          var styleObj = ""
       } else {
          var range = ".all"
          var styleObj = ".style"
       }
       var theObj = eval("document" + range + "." + objName +
styleObj)
       return theObj
     }
     return null
}
```

In the Netscape branch of the preceding example, the variables range and styleObj are assigned empty strings; for the Microsoft branch, each variable assumes the components that must be inserted into an object reference for the Microsoft syntax. If the components are concatenated without the eval() function, the result would simply be a concatenated string, which is not the same as the object reference. By forcing an additional evaluation with the eval() function, the script invokes JavaScript to see if one more level of evaluation is needed. If JavaScript finds that the evaluation of that string is a valid object reference, it returns the reference as the result; otherwise the function returns undefined.

Any JavaScript statement or expression stored as a string can be evaluated with the eval() function. This includes string equivalents of arithmetic expressions, object value assignments, and object method invocation. You may not always need the eval() function. For example, if your script loops through a series of objects whose names include serial numbers, you can use the object names as array indices, rather than using eval() to assemble the object references. The inefficient way to set the value of a series of fields named data0, data1, and so on, is as follows:

```
function fillFields() {
    var theObj
    for (var i = 0; i < 10; i++) {
        theObj = eval("document.forms[0].data" + i)
        theObj.value = i
    }
}
```

A more efficient way is to perform the concatenation within the index brackets for the object reference:

```
function fillFields() {
    for (var i = 0; i < 10; i++) {
        document.forms[0].elements["data" + i].value = i
    }
}
```

Note

A slight change to the eval() function occurred between Navigator 2 and 3. In Navigator 2, the function was considered a built-in function. But in Navigator 3 and onward, eval() was defined internally as a method of all objects. This does not change its basic functionality, but does provide known behavior for all types of objects, including those that would not normally use this method.

escape("*string*" [,1]) unescape("*string*")

Returns: String.

	Nav2	Nav3	Nav4	IE3/J1	IE3/J2	IE4/J3
Compatibility	✔	✔	✔	✔	✔	✔

If you watch the content of the Location field in your browser, you may occasionally see URLs that include a lot of % symbols plus some numbers. The format you see is URL encoding that allows even multiple word strings and nonalphanumeric characters to be sent as one contiguous string of a very low common-denominator character set. This encoding turns a character such as a space into its hexadecimal equivalent value, preceded by a percent symbol. For example, the space character (ASCII value 32) is hexadecimal 20, so the encoded version of a space is %20.

All characters, including tabs and carriage returns, can be encoded in this way and sent as a simple string that can be decoded on the receiving end for reconstruction. This encoding can also be used to preprocess multiple lines of text that must be stored as a character string in databases. To convert a plain-language string to its encoded version, use the escape() method. This function returns a string consisting of the encoded version. For example

```
var theCode = escape("Hello there")
        // result: "Hello%20there"
```

Most, but not all, nonalphanumeric characters are converted to escaped versions with the escape() function. One exception is the plus sign, which URLs use to separate components of search strings. If you must encode the plus symbol, too, then add the optional second parameter to the function, and the plus symbol is converted to its hexadecimal equivalent, 2B:

```
var a = escape("Adding 2+2")
        // result: "Adding%202+2
var a = escape("Adding 2+2",1)
        // result: "Adding%202%2B2
```

To convert an escaped string back into plain language, use the unescape() function. This function returns a string, and converts all URL-encoded strings, including those encoded with the optional parameter.

isNaN(*expression*)

Returns: Boolean.

	Nav2	Nav3	Nav4	IE3/J1	IE3/J2	IE4/J3
Compatibility	(✔)	✔	✔	✔	✔	✔

For those instances in which a calculation relies on data coming from a text field or other string-oriented source, you frequently need to be sure that the value is a number. If the value is not a number, the calculation may result in a script error.

Use the isNaN() function to test whether a value is a number prior to passing the value onto the operation. The most common usage of this function is to test the result of a parseInt() or parseFloat() function. If the strings submitted for conversion to those functions cannot be converted to a number, the resulting value is NaN (a special symbol indicating "not a number"). The isNaN() function returns true if the value is not a number.

A convenient way to use this function is to intercept improper data before it can do damage, as follows:

```
function calc(form) {
        var inputValue = parseInt(form.entry.value)
        if (isNaN(inputValue)) {
           alert("You must enter a number to continue.")
        } else {
```

```
            statements for calculation
        }
    }
```

Probably the biggest mistake scripters make with this function is failing to observe the case of all the letters in the function name. The trailing uppercase "N" is easy to miss.

Note

The isNaN() function works in Navigator 2 only on UNIX platforms. It is available on all platforms in Navigator 3 onward and on Internet Explorer 3 and onward.

Number("*string*")
parseFloat("*string*")
parseInt("*string*" [,*radix*])

Returns: Number.

	Nav2	Nav3	Nav4	IE3/J1	IE3/J2	IE4/J3
Compatibility	(✔)	(✔)	✔	(✔)	(✔)	(✔)

All three of these functions convert string values into a numeric value. The parseInt() and parseFloat() functions are compatible across all versions of all browsers; the Number() function is new with Navigator 4.

Use the Number() function when your script is not concerned with the precision of the value and prefers to let the source string govern whether the returned value is a floating-point number or an integer. The function takes a single parameter, a string to convert to a number value.

The parseFloat() functions also let the string source value determine whether the returned value is a floating-point number or integer. If the source string includes any non-zero value to the right of the decimal, the result is a floating-point number. But if the string value were, say, "3.00", the returned value would be an integer value.

An extra, optional parameter for parseInt() lets you define the number base to be used in the conversion. If you don't specify a radix parameter, JavaScript tries to look out for you, but in so doing may cause some difficulty for you. The primary problem comes when the string parameter for parseInt() starts with a zero, which a text box entry or database field might do. In JavaScript, numbers starting with zero are treated as octal (base 8) numbers. Therefore, parseInt("010") yields the decimal value 8.

When you apply the parseInt() function, you should always specify the radix of 10 if you are working in base 10 numbers. You can, however, specify any radix value from 2 through 36. For example, to convert a binary number string to its decimal equivalent, you would assign a radix of two, as follows:

```
var n = parseInt("011",2)
        // result: 3
```

Similarly, you can convert a hexadecimal string to its decimal equivalent by specifying a radix of 16:

```
var n = parseInt("4F",16)
       // result: 79
```

String(*objectOrValue*)
toString([*radix*])

Returns: String.

	Nav2	Nav3	Nav4	IE3/J1	IE3/J2	IE4/J3
Compatibility	(✔)	(✔)	✔	(✔)	(✔)	(✔)

Every JavaScript language object and document object has a toString() method associated with it. The method is designed to render the contents of the object in as meaningful a way as possible. Table 35-1 shows the result of applying the toString() method on each of the convertible core language object types.

Table 35-1
Object toString() Results

Object Type	Result
String	The same string
Number	String equivalent (but numeric literals cannot be converted)
Boolean	"true" or "false"
Array	Comma-delimited list of array contents (with no spaces after commas)
Function	Decompiled string version of the function definition

Many document objects can also be converted to a string. For example, a location object returns its URL. But when an object has nothing suitable to return for its content as a string, it usually returns a string in the following format:

```
[object objectType]
```

The toString() function is available on all versions of all browsers. New in Navigator 4 is the String() function, which operates like toString(). However, a convenient improvement to toString() for Navigator 3 is the optional radix parameter. By setting this parameter between 2 and 16, you can convert numbers to string equivalents in different number bases. Listing 35-1 calculates and draws a conversion table for decimal, hexadecimal, and binary numbers between 0 and

20. In this case, the values being converted to strings are the index counter of the for loop.

Listing 35-1: **Using toString() with Radix Values**

```
<HTML>
<HEAD>
<TITLE>Number Conversion Table</TITLE>
</HEAD>
<BODY>
<B>Using toString() to convert to other number bases:</B>
<HR>
<TABLE BORDER=1>
<TR>
<TH>Decimal</TH><TH>Hexadecimal</TH><TH>Binary</TH></TR>
<SCRIPT LANGUAGE="JavaScript">
var content = ""
for (var i = 0; i <= 20; i++) {
        content += "<TR>"
        content += "<TD>" + i.toString(10) + "</TD>"
        content += "<TD>" + i.toString(16) + "</TD>"
        content += "<TD>" + i.toString(2) + "</TD></TR>"
}
document.write(content)
</SCRIPT>
</TABLE>
</BODY>
</HTML>
```

User-defined objects do not have a `toString()` method assigned to them, but you can create your own. For example, if you wanted to make your custom object's `toString()` method behave like an array's method, then you define the action of the method and assign that function to a property of the object, as shown in Listing 35-2.

Listing 35-2: **Creating a Custom toString() Function**

```
<HTML>
<HEAD>
<TITLE>Custom toString()</TITLE>
<SCRIPT LANGUAGE="JavaScript1.2">
function customToString() {
        var dataArray = new Array()
        var count = 0
        for (var i in this) {
            dataArray[count++] = this[i]
            if (count > 2) {
                break
            }
```

(continued)

Listing 35-2 *(continued)*

```
        }
        return dataArray.join(",")
}
var book = {title:"The Aeneid", author:"Virgil", pageCount:543}
book.toString = customToString
</SCRIPT>
</HEAD>
<BODY>
<B>A user-defined toString() result:</B>
<HR>
<SCRIPT LANGUAGE="JavaScript">
document.write(book.toString())
</SCRIPT>
</BODY>
</HTML>
```

When you run Listing 35-2, you can see how the custom object's `toString()` handler extracts the values of all elements of the object except for the last one, which is the function handler reference. You can customize how the data should be labeled and/or formatted.

`unwatch(`*`property`*`)`
`watch(`*`property, handler`*`)`

Returns: Nothing.

	Nav2	Nav3	Nav4	IE3/J1	IE3/J2	IE4/J3
Compatibility			✔			

To supply the right kind of information to its own external debugger, JavaScript in Navigator 4 implements two new global functions that belong to every object, including user-defined objects. The `watch()` function keeps an eye on a desired object and property. If that property is set by assignment, the function invokes another user-defined function that receives information about the property name, its old value, and its new value. The `unwatch()` function turns off the watch functionality for a particular property. See Listing 34-8 near the end of Chapter 34 for an example of how to use these functions that can be assigned to any object.

Statements

The final two statements covered here are for setting off comments and defining variables — statements used a lot in JavaScript.

```
//
/*...*/
```

	Nav2	Nav3	Nav4	IE3/J1	IE3/J2	IE4/J3
Compatibility	✔	✔	✔	✔	✔	✔

Comments are statements that are ignored by the JavaScript interpreter (or server-side compiler) but allow authors to leave notes about how things work in their scripts. While lavish comments are useful to authors during a script's creation and maintenance, the full content of a client-side comment is downloaded with the document. Every byte of nonoperational content of the page takes a bit more time to download. Still, I recommend lots of comments, particularly as you create a script.

JavaScript offers two styles of comments. One style consists of two forward slashes (no spaces between them). JavaScript ignores any characters to the right of those slashes, even if they appear in the middle of a line. You can stack as many lines of these single-line comments as is necessary to convey your thoughts. My style typically places a space between the second slash and the beginning of my comment. The following are examples of valid one-line comment formats:

```
// this is a comment line usually about what's to come
var a = "Fred"  // a comment about this line
// You may want to capitalize the first word of a comment
// sentence if it runs across multiple lines.
//
// And you can leave a completely blank line, like the one above.
```

For longer comments, it is usually more convenient to enclose the section in the other style of comment. This one opens with a forward slash and asterisk (/*) and ends with a start and forward slash (*/). All statements in between — including multiple lines — are ignored by JavaScript. If you want to briefly comment out a large segment of your script, it is easiest to bracket the segment with these comment symbols. To make these comment blocks easier to find, I generally place these symbols on their own lines, as follows:

```
/*
some
   commented-out
      statements
*/
```

If you are developing rather complex documents, you might find using comments a convenient way to help you organize segments of your scripts and make each segment easier to find. For example, you could define a comment block above each function and describe what the function is about, as in the following example.

```
/*-------------------------------------------------
   calculate()
   Performs a mortgage calculation based on
   parameters blah, blah, blah.  Called by blah
   blah blah.
-------------------------------------------------*/
function calculate(form) {
      statements
}
```

var

	Nav2	Nav3	Nav4	IE3/J1	IE3/J2	IE4/J3
Compatibility	✔	✔	✔	✔	✔	✔

Before using any variable, you should declare it (and optionally initialize it with a value) via the `var` statement. If you omit the `var` keyword, the variable is automatically assigned as a global variable within the current document. To keep a variable local to a function, you must declare or initialize the variable with the `var` keyword inside the function's braces.

If you assign no value to a variable, it evaluates to null. Because a JavaScript variable is not limited to one variable type during its lifetime, you don't need to initialize a variable to an empty string or zero unless that initial value will help your scripting. For example, if you initialize a variable as an empty string, you can then use the add-by-value operator (+=) to append string values to that variable in a future statement in the document.

To save statement lines, you can declare and/or initialize multiple variables with a single var statement. Each varName=value pair must be separated by a comma, as in

```
var name, age, height   // declare as null
var color="green", temperature=85.6 // initialize
```

Variable names (also known as *identifiers*) must be one contiguous string of characters, but the first character must be a letter. Many punctuation symbols are also banned, but the underscore character is valid and is often used to separate multiple words in a long variable name. All variable names (like most identifiers in JavaScript) are case-sensitive, so your naming of a particular variable must be identical throughout the variable's scope.

✦   ✦   ✦

Server-side JavaScript

Most of this book is devoted to client-side JavaScript, the scripts that execute when their documents are loaded in a browser. But the JavaScript language originally came into existence (under its old name, LiveScript) as a server-side scripting language. Both client-side and server-side JavaScript share a common core language encompassing such items as how to use variables, control structures, data types, and the rest. Where the two scripting environments diverge is in their object models. Client-side JavaScript is concerned with objects that appear in documents; server-side JavaScript is concerned with objects that govern the two-way connection between the user and server applications.

The subject of server-side JavaScript is large enough to fill an entire book. My goal in this chapter is to introduce the concepts and objects of server-side JavaScript to those who are familiar with the client side of things. If you move on to create server-side applications with JavaScript, this chapter should help you reorient yourself to the server way of thinking about applications.

The flavor of server-side JavaScript covered in this chapter is that found in Netscape's SuiteSpot 3 server family. In particular, the Enterprise Server 3 component is where most of the server-side JavaScript action occurs. This is where you can write scripts that act as go-betweens for the user and large server databases.

Adding Server Processing to Documents

A standard HTML page contains tags that instruct the browser about how to render the content of the page. As a page loads, the browser interprets the tags and lays out the words, form elements, and images from the top of the document to the bottom. If the page contains a form, you may want to capture the information entered or selected by the user.

With Navigator you can certainly submit that form and its contents as an e-mail message without any further help from the server, but many applications want to link the form entries with a database (either to save the data to the database or retrieve some data based on a search entry). Before server-side JavaScript, that interactivity with the server was handled exclusively by a Common Gateway Interface (CGI) program on the server commonly written in the Perl language. The ACTION attribute of the form invoked the CGI program by name (as part of the URL). The CGI program would churn on the submitted data and output a full HTML page that comes back in response.

Server-side JavaScript (SSJS) works a little differently. Rather than existing as a separate program on the server, a SSJS script typically resides in an HTML document stored on the server embedded in a compiled program file. A form's ACTION attribute is set to the URL of that HTML file containing the server-side scripts. In response to the submission, the server loads the compiled program while temporarily storing in memory information from the form being submitted. Any HTML content of the associated HTML file is passed on to the client. Some server-side scripts in the document also probably dynamically compose some or all of the content being sent out to the client.

Embedded server scripts

An HTML file on the server contains not only the HTML content, but perhaps some client-side scripts and server-side scripts. Tags distinguish the two types of scripts. Client-side scripts are contained by <SCRIPT>...</SCRIPT> tags (and run only when the document is in the client machine), while server-side script statements are contained by <SERVER>...</SERVER> tag sets. As Enterprise Server starts to respond to a submission from a browser, it runs whatever scripts appear inside these tags. None of the server script statements in these tags or the tags themselves appear in the source code of the document sent to the browser.

Scripts inside the <SERVER> tags work with the same core JavaScript language as you script for the client. But the server doesn't know about document objects. Instead, it knows how to work with server-side objects, such as the object that contains the contents of form elements that arrived with the last submission.

Because server-side scripts can also create content that goes in the HTML page being downloaded to the client, the HTML page can contain basic template content in plain HTML. Custom content created as a result of server processing can be written interspersed in the middle of the page. It's like when you have client-side scripts use document.write() to create a portion of a document as it loads. In the case of the server, it has a write() method that outputs content to the data stream that heads for the client.

At the client end, the only source code it receives is the HTML that defines the page (and perhaps client-side scripts, if that's what the design calls for). Therefore, it is possible to place browser detection on the server (it has access to userAgent data), and let the server dish up the HTML and scripting appropriate for the browser connecting at that instant.

To demonstrate this process, Listing 36-1 shows the server-side HTML file for a simplistic application that does nothing more than display the server version in a document. Then, in Listing 36-2, I show what the source view looks like on the client. (Neither of these listings is on the CD-ROM.)

Listing 36-1: **Server-side HTML File**

```
<HTML>
<HEAD>
<TITLE>Simple Server App</TITLE>
</HEAD>
<BODY>
<B>This application is running on the following Netscape Enterprise
Server version and platform:</B><BR>
<SERVER>
        write(server.httpdjsVersion + ".")
</SERVER>
</BODY>
</HTML>
```

Listing 36-2: **Client-side Source**

```
<HTML>
<HEAD>
<TITLE>Simple Server App</TITLE>
</HEAD>
<BODY>
<B>This application is running on the following Netscape Enterprise
Server version and platform:</B><BR>
3.0 Windows NT.
</BODY>
</HTML>
```

Server-side libraries

The process of creating an Enterprise Server application that uses server-side JavaScript includes a compilation step. Enterprise Server 3 comes with a tool called jsac.exe, which is a JavaScript application compiler. The output of the compiler is a server file (with a .web extension) that is the application as far as the server is concerned (some other application management tools are also provided to install each application into the server). That .web file contains all the HTML files to be used in the application.

In addition to HTML files, which encapsulate their server-side scripting within each document's <SERVER> tag sets, you can add library files of scripts that have global scope among all the HTML files that are part of the application. Not surprisingly (if you know about client-side library files), the server-side libraries are script-only documents whose file names have the .js extension. All HTML and .js files are compiled in the .web application file.

(If the HTML files that are downloaded to the client are to use client-side .js libraries, those .js files are not compiled in the .web application. They simply reside in the same directory as the HTML files that get compiled in the .web application. When Enterprise Server receives a request for one of these client-side source files, it knows where to find the file and sends the library down to the client.)

Essential Server-side Objects

Although the full complement of SSJS objects is beyond the scope of this book, I want to introduce you to the key objects that the server knows how to work with. If for no other reason, this exposure can give you an appreciation of how the core JavaScript language can be applied to different object models (for example, server-side objects versus client-side document objects).

The discussion here focuses on four server-side objects: server, project, client, and request. This order goes from the most "global" in scope to the narrowest. For the most part, all four objects are stored in the server memory (except for some ways of specifying the client object) and don't represent any physical entity. Not every application addresses each object directly, but the objects are almost always present when an application is running.

The server object

Whenever the Enterprise Server software starts up, it automatically generates a server object in the server's memory. The object goes away when the server is stopped (the server software can be started and stopped independently of the server hardware).

Information that the server object stores includes items such as the host, hostname, port, protocol, and server version. All applications running on the server share this information. An application can also create additional custom properties appropriate to the server-level—any information that needs to be shared among all applications running on the server. The syntax for reading or adding a server object property is similar to other JavaScript object properties reading and writing:

```
var hostName = server.hostname

server.adminEMail = "serverdude@giantco.com"
```

Server-side JavaScript offers provisions for maintaining the integrity of changeable data, such as custom server properties. To prevent two applications from simultaneously attempting to change the same property, the server object can be momentarily locked and then unlocked with the `server.lock()` and `server.unlock()` methods.

The project object

The scope of a project object is a single application running on the server. But this also means that all clients that access the application (even simultaneously) have access to project properties.

A project object is created when the application is started on the server. No properties are assigned to the project object by default. It is, rather, a convenient place for an application to store small chunks of data that all users of the application (or the application, itself) can benefit from. Think of it as a global store for all instances of the running application. Perhaps the most common use of the project object is as a place to store the latest unique ID number for new user accounts or database records. If a new record is being added to a database, it is faster to access the project object property that holds the last assigned number, grab a copy, and increment the value in the property for the next time.

For the sake of data integrity, the project object can be locked momentarily while getting and incrementing that value. Other clients wanting access to that property are held in a queue for the next available access (that is, when the property object is unlocked). The simplest example of using the `lock()` method is shown here:

```
project.lock()
var newCustomerID = project.nextID
project.nextID = project.nextID + 1
project.unlock()
```

This sequence locks the project object, copies the current custom property that contains the next customer ID to be issued, increments the property, and unlocks the project object.

The client object

Narrowing the object scope further, the client object is unique to a particular client access of an application. A client object has no predefined properties, so your application is at liberty to assign property names and values that are of interest to a single connection to the application.

You can imagine that a highly trafficked application would drain a server of processing time, memory, and disk space if it had to track the client objects of perhaps hundreds or thousands of simultaneous connections. To counteract the problem, you specify in your application control panel (on the server application manager) whether client object data should be stored on the server or client and how that should be accomplished. From the server's point of view, the most convenient place for such storage is a client cookie. One example of how this works is a server-based shopping cart. When the user clicks to add a product to the cart, the form is submitted to the application. The application extracts pertinent information bits about the product and stores that information in one or more client properties (Enterprise Server writes such a cookie with a special name in the format `NETSCAPE_LIVEWIRE.`*propertyName=value*). With a client object specified as a client cookie, the data is sent to the client and saved in the browser cookie area (the same `document.cookie` described in Chapter 16). At check-out time, the application can retrieve the cookie data from the client and assemble a final order form.

Other client object techniques include client-side URL encoding, server cookies, and server URL encoding. Each approach has its advantages and disadvantages, all of which are detailed in Netscape's documentation for building server-side JavaScript applications.

The request object

The narrowest in scope of all objects is the request object. It contains information about a single submission from a client.

Even before you get to the form data being submitted, the request object has several properties filled automatically. By and large, these preset properties mirror the environment variables that traditional CGI programs extract from submissions. Table 36-1 shows the standard properties for the request object.

Table 36-1
Standard request Object Properties

Property	Description
agent	Browser type and version (the same as client-side `navigator.userAgent`)
auth_type	Authorization type (if any)
auth_user	Remote user (if available)
ip	IP address
method	Form method setting
protocol	Client protocol
query	Query string passed with method=GET
imageX	Area map click horizontal coordinate
imageY	Area map click vertical coordinate
uri	Partial URL of request (after protocol, hostname, and port)

For every named element in the form being submitted, a property is added to the current request object, and the value of the element is assigned to that property. Only one request object is available per client, so these values last only until the next submission (which might be in another frame immediately after the first frame's form is submitted).

Accessing the request object is key to capturing information entered or selected in a form by a user. For example, if you are updating a database with one field's data, you can use the request object's property to fill that column in the database table:

```
database.execute("UPDATE customer phone1 = '" + request.phone1 + "'
WHERE custID = " + request.custID)
```

A form's hidden objects are included among the request object's properties. It is not uncommon to use a hidden object to pass information from one server script execution to the next by writing hidden objects to the page and letting the next request object pick out the data for further processing.

Database Access with LiveWire

LiveWire is Netscape's brand name for the technology that links a server-side application to a database on the server. In the early days of this technology, it was a separate component of the company's server offerings. In SuiteSpot 3, LiveWire is integrated into the offering.

The purpose of LiveWire extends beyond the basic ability to link up a Web application and a database. The goal was to create an application programming interface (API) that lets Web application authors write essentially the same database-related code, regardless of whether the database is IBM's DB2, Oracle, Informix, Sybase, or any ODBC standard database. In these days of competing formats and standards, that is a tall order. Even so, LiveWire comes a long way in establishing a one-code-fits-all implementation, at least for the basic database access tasks (a lot of credit also goes to the Structured Query Language—SQL— standard adopted by many large database makers).

Database access process

Successful database access requires a specific sequence of statements at various places within your code. LiveWire provides a database object, the reference of which you use to open the connection and read or write data to the database.

One page of your application (it might be the home page) contains `<SERVER>` tag code that initiates the connection to the database on behalf of the client accessing the application. The basic format of this statement is as follows:

```
database.connect(databaseType, serverName, username, password,
databaseName)
```

The precise content of the parameters to the `connect()` method vary a great deal with the type of database you are accessing. In my experience, setting up an ODBC database to accept the connection can take a bit of doing, especially in getting the proper ODBC drivers installed.

Accessing records

Before you start writing code to insert or update records in a database, you should be familiar with common SQL commands and syntax for these operations in your database. Using LiveWire, you wrap the SQL expressions inside a `database.exec()` method. The parameter of the method is the precise SQL statement that the database needs for inserting or updating the table.

The real JavaScript fun comes when retrieving data from tables. You use the `database.cursor()` method to send an SQL `SELECT` command to the database, specifying the columns you want to extract and the search criteria to be applied to the table. For example, to extract the name and phone number columns for all records of a customer table whose state column is "FL," the JavaScript code reads

```
var cursor = database.cursor("SELECT name, phone from customer where
state = 'FL'")
```

If any data matches the criteria of the `SELECT` statement, the method `database.cursor()` returns the data in the form of a cursor object. The cursor object is something like a JavaScript array, but not quite. You cannot, for instance, obtain the number of records returned, because you cannot get the length of the object. But you can cycle through each row of returned data with the help of the `cursor.next()` method.

The instant the cursor object is created with the returned data, an internal row pointer is positioned immediately above the first record. One invocation of `cursor.next()` moves the pointer to the first row of data. At that point, you can extract individual column data by using the column name as a property. You continue looping through the cursor until there are no more records, at which point the `cursor.next()` method returns a value of false. The following script fragment extracts the same data as described above and then consolidates the data into an HTML table that is eventually written to the client:

```
var cursor = database.cursor("SELECT name, phone from customer where
state = 'FL'")
var output = "<TABLE><TR><TH>Name</TH><TH>Phone</TH></TR>"
while (cursor.next()) {
        output += "<TR><TD>" + cursor.name + "</TD>"
        output += "<TD>" + cursor.phone + "</TD></TR>"
}
output += "</TABLE>"
write(output)
```

For simple data extractions and table displays, such as the one just given, LiveWire even provides a shortcut statement for creating the HTML table, ready for writing to the client document. Many other cursor and database methods offer sufficient flexibility to build very complex applications atop very complex databases. This includes controlling transaction processes when they are implemented for the database.

Server or Client JavaScript?

When you have the ability to implement an application with server-side and client-side JavaScript, you may wonder how to use both — or if you should use client-side JavaScript at all. A lot depends on the known base of browsers used by application users and the amount of traffic on the site.

One supreme advantage an author has by implementing everything on the server is independence from the JavaScript vagaries from one browser version or brand to the next. Not that it solves the HTML compatibility issues, which you must still face. But when the only concern is HTML compatibility, the testing matrix of browser versions and brands is smaller.

Putting all the processing on the server end, however, may do a disservice to the users of browsers that have the power to do some of that processing locally. For every image change or other adjustment to the HTML page, the user must wait for the transactions with the server, server processing, and another download of data. If you have a high-traffic site, this can also place extra burdens on the server that hinder access to all.

Most commonly, however, authors strike a balance between server-side and client-side scripting to take care of the job. For example, data-entry validation on the client is orders of magnitude more efficient for the user and your server. The server still needs to do validation for non-scriptable browser users, but at least those with scriptable browsers won't be slowed down by server-generated error messages and form redrawing.

As more capabilities are built into modern browsers, such as positionable elements (Chapters 41 through 43), it makes more sense to imbue intelligence into documents that utilize those facilities. The experience will be much crisper for users, as if they're using a local software package, rather than constantly waiting for screen refreshing.

✦   ✦   ✦

Putting JavaScript to Work

Data-Entry Validation

✦ ✦ ✦ ✦

In This Chapter

Validating data as it is being entered

Validating data immediately prior to submission

Organizing complex data validation tasks

✦ ✦ ✦ ✦

Give users a field in which to enter data, and you can be sure that some users will enter the wrong kind of data. Often the "mistake" is accidental — a slip of the pinkie on the keyboard; other times, the incorrect entry is made intentionally to test the robustness of your application. Whether you solicit a user's entry for client-side scripting purposes or for input into a server-based CGI or database, you should use JavaScript on the client to handle validation of the user's entry. Even for a form connected to a CGI script, it's far more efficient from bandwidth, server load, and execution speed perspectives to let client-side JavaScript get the data straight before your server program deals with it.

Real-time versus Batch Validation

You have two opportunities to perform data-entry validation in a form: as the user enters data into a field and just before the form is submitted. I recommend you do both.

Real-time validation triggers

The most convenient time to catch an error is immediately after the user has made it. Especially for a long form that requests a wide variety of information, you can make the user's experience less frustrating if you catch an entry mistake just after the user has entered the information: his or her attention is already focused on the nature of the content (or some paper source material may already be in front of the user). It is much easier for the user to address the same information entry right away.

A valid question for the page author is how to trigger the real-time validation. Text boxes have two potential event handlers for this purpose: onChange= and onBlur=. I personally avoid onBlur= event handlers, especially ones that could display an alert dialog box (as a data-entry validation is likely to do). Because a good validation routine brings focus to the errant text box, you can get some odd behavior with the interaction of the focus() method and the onBlur= event handler. Users who must move on past an invalid field will be locked in a seemingly endless loop.

The problem with using onChange= as the validation trigger is that it can be defeated by a user. A change event occurs only when the text of a field has, indeed, changed when the user tabs or clicks out of the field. If the user is alerted about some bad entry in a field and doesn't fix the error, the change event won't fire again. In some respects, this is good, because a user may have a legitimate reason for passing by a particular form field initially with the intention of coming back to the entry later. Since the onChange= event handler trigger can be defeated, I recommend you also perform batch validation prior to submission.

Batch mode validation

In all scriptable browsers, the onSubmit= event handler cancels the submission if the handler evaluates to return false. You can see an example of this behavior in Listing 21-4 in Chapter 21. That example uses the results of a window.confirm() dialog box to determine the return value of the event handler. But you can use a return value from a series of individual text box validation functions, as well. If any one of the validations fails, the user is alerted, and the submission is canceled.

Before you worry about two versions of validation routines loading down the scripts in your page, you'll be happy to know that you can reuse the same validation routines in both the real-time and batch validations. Later in this chapter, I demonstrate what I call "industrial-strength" data-entry validation adapted from a real intranet application. But before you get there, you should learn about general validation techniques that can be applied to both types of validations.

Designing Filters

The job of writing data validation routines is essentially one of designing filters that weed out characters or entries that don't fit your programming scheme. Whenever your filter detects an incorrect entry, it should alert the user about the nature of the problem and enable the user to correct the entry.

Before you put a text or textarea object into your document that invites users to enter data, you must decide if any kind of entry is possible that will disturb the execution of the rest of your scripts. For example, if your script must have a number from that field to perform calculations, you must filter out any entry that contains letters or punctuation — except for periods if the program can accept floating-point numbers. Your task is to anticipate every possible entry users could make and let through only those your scripts can use.

Not every entry field needs a data validation filter. For example, you may prompt a user for information that is eventually stored as a document.cookie or in a string database field on the server for retrieval later. If no further processing takes place on that information, you may not have to worry about the specific contents of that field.

One other design consideration is whether a text field is even the proper user interface element for the data required of the user. If the range of choices for user entry is small (a dozen or fewer), a more sensible method may be to avoid the data-entry problem altogether by turning that field into a select object. Your HTML attributes for the object ensure that you control the kind of entry made to that object. As long as your script knows how to deal with each of the options defined for that object, you're in the clear.

Building a Library of Filter Functions

A number of basic data validation processes are used repeatedly in form-intensive HTML pages. Filters for integers only, numbers only, empty entries, alphabet letters only, and the like are put to use every day. If you maintain a library of generalizable functions for each of your data validation tasks, you can drop them into your scripts at a moment's notice and be assured that they will work. For Navigator 3 or later and Internet Explorer 4 or later, you can also create the library of validation functions as a separate .js library file and link the scripts into any HTML file that needs them.

Making validation functions generalizable requires careful choice of wording and logic so that they return Boolean values that make syntactical sense when called from elsewhere in your scripts. As you see later in this chapter, when you build a larger framework around smaller functions, each function is usually called as part of an if...else conditional statement. Therefore, assign a name that fits logically as part of an "if" clause in plain language. For example, a function that checks whether an entry is empty might be named isEmpty(). The calling statement for this function would be

```
if (isEmpty(value)) { ...
```

From a plain-language perspective, the expectation is that the function returns true if the passed value is empty. With this design, the statements nested in the if construction handle the case in which the entry field is empty. I come back to this design later in this chapter when I start stacking multiple-function calls together in a larger validation routine.

To get you started with your library of validation functions, I provide a few in this chapter that you can both learn from and use as starting points for more specific filters of your own design. Some of these functions are put to use in the JavaScript application in Chapter 48.

isEmpty()

The first function, shown in Listing 37-1, checks to see if the incoming value is either empty or a null value. Adding a check for a null means that you can use this function for purposes other than just text object validation. For example, if another function defines three parameter variables, but the calling function passes only two, the third variable is set to null. If the script then performs a data validation check on all parameters, the isEmpty() function responds that the null value is devoid of data.

Listing 37-1: Is an Entry Empty or Null?

```
// general purpose function to see if an input value has been
// entered at all
function isEmpty(inputStr) {
        if (inputStr == null || inputStr == "") {
            return true
        }
        return false
}
```

This function uses a Boolean Or operator (||) to test for the existence of a null value or an empty string in the value passed to the function. Because the name of the function implies a `true` response if the entry is empty, that value is the one that goes back to the calling statement if either condition is true. Because a `return` statement halts further processing of a function, the `return false` statement lies outside of the `if` construction. If processing reaches this statement, it means that the `inputStr` value failed the test.

If this seems like convoluted logic — return `true` when the value is empty — you can also define a function that returns the inverse values. You could name it `isNotEmpty()`. As it turns out, however, typical processing of an empty entry is better served when the test returns a true than when the value is empty — aiding the `if` construction that called the function in the first place.

isPosInteger()

The next function examines each character of the value to make sure that only the numbers from 0 through 9 with no punctuation or other symbols exist. The goal of the function in Listing 37-2 is to weed out any value that is not a positive integer.

Listing 37-2: Test for Positive Integers

```
// general purpose function to see if a suspected numeric input
// is a positive integer
function isPosInteger(inputVal) {
        inputStr = inputVal.toString()
        for (var i = 0; i < inputStr.length; i++) {
            var oneChar = inputStr.charAt(i)
            if (oneChar < "0" || oneChar > "9") {
                return false
            }
        }
        return true
}
```

Notice that this function makes no assumption about the data type of the value passed as a parameter. If the value had come directly from a text object, it would already be a string, and the line that forces data conversion to a string would be unnecessary. But to generalize the function, the conversion is included to accommodate the possibility that it may be called from another statement that has a numeric value to check.

The function requires the input value to be converted to a string because it performs a character-by-character analysis of the data. A `for` loop picks apart the value one character at a time. Rather than force the script to invoke the `string.charAt()` method twice for each time through the loop (inside the `if` condition), one statement assigns the results of the method to a variable, which is then used twice in the `if` condition. It makes the `if` condition shorter and easier to read and also is microscopically more efficient.

In the `if` condition, the ASCII value of each character is compared against the range of 0 through 9. This method is safer than comparing numeric values of the single characters because one of the characters could be nonnumeric. You would encounter all kinds of other problems trying to convert that character to a number for numeric comparison. The ASCII value, on the other hand, is neutral about the meaning of a character: If the ASCII value is less than 0 or greater than 9, the character is not valid for a true positive integer. The function bounces the call with a false reply. On the other hand, if the `for` loop completes its traversal of all characters in the value without a hitch, the function returns true.

isInteger()

The next possibility includes the entry of a negative integer value. Listing 37-3 shows that you must add an extra check for a leading negation sign.

Listing 37-3: **Checking for Leading Minus Sign**

```
// general purpose function to see if a suspected numeric input
// is a positive or negative integer
function isInteger(inputVal) {
    inputStr = inputVal.toString()
    for (var i = 0; i < inputStr.length; i++) {
        var oneChar = inputStr.charAt(i)
        if (i == 0 && oneChar == "-") {
            continue
        }
        if (oneChar < "0" || oneChar > "9") {
            return false
        }
    }
    return true
}
```

When a script can accept a negative integer, the filter must enable the leading minus sign to pass unscathed. You cannot just add the minus sign to the `if` condition of Listing 37-2 because you can accept that symbol only when it appears in the first position of the value—anywhere else makes the value an invalid number. To take care of the possibility, you add another if statement whose condition looks for a special combination: the first character of the string (as indexed by the loop counting variable) and the minus character. If both of these conditions are met, execution immediately loops back around to the update expression of the for loop (because of the continue statement) rather than carrying out the second if statement, which would obviously fail. By putting the i == 0 operation at the front of the condition, you ensure the entire condition will short-circuit to false for all subsequent iterations through the loop.

isNumber()

The final numeric filter function in this series enables any integer or floating-point number to pass while filtering out all others (Listing 37-4). All that distinguishes an integer from a floating-point number for data validation purposes is the decimal point.

Listing 37-4: **Testing for a Decimal Point**

```
// general purpose function to see if a suspected numeric input
// is a positive or negative number
function isNumber(inputVal) {
        oneDecimal = false
        inputStr = inputVal.toString()
        for (var i = 0; i < inputStr.length; i++) {
            var oneChar = inputStr.charAt(i)
            if (i == 0 && oneChar == "-") {
                continue
            }
            if (oneChar == "." && !oneDecimal) {
                oneDecimal = true
                continue
            }
            if (oneChar < "0" || oneChar > "9") {
                return false
            }
        }
        return true
}
```

Anticipating the worst, however, the function cannot just add a comparison for a decimal (actually, for *not* a decimal) to the condition that compares ASCII values of each character. Such an act assumes that no one would ever enter more than one decimal point into a text field. Only one decimal point is allowed for this function (as well as for JavaScript math). Therefore, you add a Boolean flag variable (oneDecimal) to the function and a separate if condition that sets that flag to true when the function encounters the first decimal point. Should another decimal point appear in the string, the final if statement has a crack at the character. Because the character falls outside the ASCII range of 0 through 9, it fails the entire function.

If you want to accept only positive floating-point numbers, you can make a new version of this function, removing the statement that lets the leading minus sign through. Be aware that this function works only for values that are not represented in exponential notation.

For validations that don't have to accommodate Navigator 2, you can use an even quicker way to test for a valid number. If you pass the value (whether it be a string or a number) through the parseFloat() global function (see Chapter 35), the returned value is NaN if the conversion is not successful. You can then use the isNaN() function to perform the test, as follows:

```
if (isNaN(parseFloat(inputValue))) {
        alert("The value you entered is not a number.")
        return false
}
return true
```

Custom validation functions

The listings shown so far in this chapter should give you plenty of source material to use in writing customized validation functions for your applications. An example of such an application-specific variation (extracted from the bonus application in Chapter 48 on the CD-ROM) is shown in Listing 37-5.

Listing 37-5: **A Custom Validation Function**

```
// function to determine if value is in acceptable range
// for this application
function inRange(inputStr) {
        num = parseInt(inputStr)
        if (num < 1 || num > 586 && num < 596 || num > 599 && num <
700 || num > 728) {
            return false
        }
        return true
}
```

For this application, you need to see if an entry falls within multiple ranges of acceptable numbers. The value is converted to a number (via the parseInt() function) so it can be numerically compared against maximum and minimum values of several ranges within the database. Following the logic of the previous validation functions, the if condition looks for values that were outside the acceptable range, so it can alert the user and return a false value.

The if condition is quite a long sequence of operators. As you noticed in the list of operator precedence (Chapter 32), the Boolean And operator (&&) has precedence over the Boolean Or operator (||). Therefore, the And expressions evaluate first, followed by the Or expressions. Parentheses may help you better visualize what's going on in that monster condition:

```
if (num < 1 || (num > 586 && num < 596) ||
(num > 599 && num < 700) || num > 728)
```

In other words, you exclude four possible ranges from consideration:

✦ Values less than 1

✦ Values between 586 and 596

✦ Values between 599 and 700

✦ Values greater than 728

Any value for which any one of these tests is true yields a Boolean false from this function. Combining all these tests into a single condition statement eliminates the need to construct an otherwise complex series of nested `if` constructions.

Combining Validation Functions

When you design a page that requests a particular kind of text input from a user, you often need to call more than one data validation function to handle the entire job. For example, if you merely want to test for a positive integer entry, your validation should test for both the presence of any entry and the validation as an integer.

After you know the kind of permissible data that your script will use after validation, you're ready to plot the sequence of data validation. Because each page's validation task is different, I supply some guidelines to follow in this planning rather than prescribe a fixed route for all to take.

My preferred sequence is to start with examinations that require less work and increase the intensity of validation detective work with succeeding functions. I borrow this tactic from real life: When a lamp fails to turn on, I look for a pulled plug or a burned-out lightbulb before tearing the lamp's wiring apart to look for a short.

Using the data validation sequence from the data-entry field (which must be a three-digit number within a specified range) in Chapter 48 on the CD-ROM, I start with the test that requires the least amount of work: Is there an entry at all? After my script is ensured an entry of some kind exists, it next checks whether that entry is "all numbers as requested of the user." If so, the script compares the number against the ranges of numbers in the database.

To make this sequence work together efficiently, I created a master validation function consisting of nested `if...else` statements. Each `if` condition calls one of the generalized data validation functions. Listing 37-6 shows the master validation function.

Listing 37-6: Master Validation Function

```
// Master value validator routine
function isValid(inputStr) {
    if (isEmpty(inputStr)) {
        alert("Please enter a number into the field before clicking
the button.")
        return false
```

```
        } else {
           if (!isNumber(inputStr)) {
              alert("Please make sure entries are numbers only.")
              return false
           } else {
              if (!inRange(inputStr)) {
                  alert("Sorry, the number you entered is not part of
our database.  Try another three-digit number.")
                  return false
              }
           }
        }
        return true
}
```

This function, in turn, is called by the function that controls most of the work in this application. All it wants to know is whether the entered number is valid. The details of validation are handed off to the isValid() function and its special-purpose validation testers.

I constructed the logic in Listing 37-6 so that if the input value fails to be valid, the isValid()function alerts the user of the problem and returns false. That means I have to watch my trues and falses very carefully.

In the first validation test, being empty is a bad thing; thus, when the isEmpty() function returns true, the isValid() function returns false because an empty string is not a valid entry. In the second test, being a number is good; so the logic has to flip 180 degrees. The isValid() function returns false only if the isNumber() function returns false. But because isNumber() returns a true when the value is a number, I switch the condition to test for the *opposite* results of the isNumber() function by negating the function name (preceding the function with the Boolean Not (!) operator). This operator works only with a value that evaluates to a Boolean expression — which the isNumber()function always does. The final test for being within the desired range works on the same basis as isNumber(), using the Boolean Not operator to turn the results of the inRange() function into the method that works best for this sequence.

Finally, if all validation tests fail to find bad or missing data, the entire isValid() function returns true. The statement that called this function can now proceed with processing, ensured that the value entered by the user will work.

One additional point worth reinforcing, especially for newcomers, is that although all these functions seem to be passing around the same input string as a parameter, notice that any changes made to the value (such as converting it to a string or number) are kept private to each function. The original value in the calling function is never touched by these subfunctions — only copies of the original value. Therefore, even after the data validation takes place, the original value is in its original form, ready to go.

Date and Time Validation

You can scarcely open a bigger can of cultural worms than you do when you try to program around the various date and time formats in use around the world. If you have ever looked through the possible settings in your computer's operating system, you can begin to understand the difficulty of the issue.

Trying to write JavaScript that accommodates all of the world's date and time formats for validation would be an enormous, if not wasteful, challenge. My suggestion for querying a user for this kind of information is to either divide the components into individually validated fields (separate text objects for hours and minutes) or, for dates, to make entries select objects.

In the long run, I believe the answer will be a future Java applet or Dynamic HTML component that your scripts will call. The applet will display a clock and calendar on which the user clicks and drags control-panel-style widgets to select dates and times. The values from those settings will then be passed back to your scripts as a valid date object. In the meantime, divide and conquer.

An "Industrial-Strength" Validation Solution

I had the privilege of working on a substantial intranet project that included dozens of forms, often with two or three different kinds of forms being displayed simultaneously within a frameset. Data entry accuracy was essential to the validity of the entire application. My task was to devise a data-entry validation strategy that not only ensured accurate entry of data types for the underlying database, but also intelligently prompted users who made mistakes in their data entry.

Structure

From the start, the validation routines were to be in a client-side library linked in from an external .js file. That would allow the validation functions to be shared by all forms. Because there were multiple forms displayed in a frameset, it would prove too costly in download time and memory requirements to include the validations.js file in every frame's document. Therefore, the page was moved to load in with the frameset. The `<SCRIPT SRC="validations.js"></SCRIPT>` tag set went in the Head portion of the framesetting document.

This logical placement presented a small challenge for the workings of the validations, because there must be two-way conversations between a validation function (in the frameset) and a form element (nested in a frame). As you will see in a moment, the mechanism required that the frame containing the form element had to be passed as part of the validation routine so that corrections, automatic formatting, and erroneous field selections could be made from the frameset document's script (that is, the frameset script needed a path back to the form element making the validation call).

Dispatch mechanism

From the specification drawn up for the application, it was clear that there would be more than two dozen specific types of validations across all the forms. Moreover, multiple programmers would be working on different forms. It would be helpful to standardize the way validations are called, regardless of the validation type (number, string, date, phone number, and so on).

My idea was to create one `validate()` function that would contain parameters for the current frame, the current form element, and the type of validation to perform. This would make it clear to anyone reading the code later that an event handler calling `validate()` was performing validation, and the details of the code would be in the validations.js library file.

To make this idea work meant that in validations.js I had to convert a string name of a validation type into the name of the function that performs the validation. As a bridge between the two, I created what I called a dispatch lookup table for all the primary validation routines that would be called from the forms. Each entry of the lookup table has a label consisting of the name of the validation and a method that invokes the function. Listing 37-7 shows an excerpt of the entire lookup table creation mechanism.

Listing 37-7: **Creating the Dispatch Lookup Table**

```
/*
    Begin validation dispatching mechanism
*/
function dispatcher(validationFunc) {
    this.doValidate = validationFunc
}
var dispatchLookup = new Array()
dispatchLookup["isNotEmpty"] = new dispatcher(isNotEmpty)
dispatchLookup["isPositiveInteger"] = new dispatcher(isPositiveInteger)
dispatchLookup["isDollarsOnly8"] = new dispatcher(isDollarsOnly8)
dispatchLookup["isUSState"] = new dispatcher(isUSState)
dispatchLookup["isZip"] = new dispatcher(isZip)
dispatchLookup["isExpandedZip"] = new dispatcher(isExpandedZip)
dispatchLookup["isPhone"] = new dispatcher(isPhone)
dispatchLookup["isConfirmed"] = new dispatcher(isConfirmed)
dispatchLookup["isNY"] = new dispatcher(isNY)
dispatchLookup["isNum16"] = new dispatcher(isNum16)
dispatchLookup["isM90_M20Date"] = new dispatcher(isM90_M20Date)
dispatchLookup["isM70_0Date"] = new dispatcher(isM70_0Date)
dispatchLookup["isM5_P10Date"] = new dispatcher(isM5_P10Date)
dispatchLookup["isDateFormat"] = new dispatcher(isDateFormat)
```

Each entry of the array is assigned a dispatcher object, whose constructor assigns a function reference to the object's `doValidate()` method. For each of these assignment statements to work, the function must be defined earlier in the document. You will see some of these functions later in this section.

The link between the form elements and the dispatch lookup table is the `validate()` function, shown in Listing 37-8. A call to `validate()` requires a minimum of three parameters, as shown in the following example:

```
<INPUT TYPE="text" NAME="phone" SIZE="10"
onChange="parent.validate(window, this, 'isPhone')">
```

The first is a reference to the frame containing the document that is calling the function (passed as a reference to the current window); second is a reference to the form element itself (using the `this` property); after that come one or more individual validation function names as strings. This last design allows more than one type of validation to take place with each call to `validate()` (for example, in case a field must check both for a datatype and that the datatype is not empty).

Listing 37-8: **Main Validation Function**

```
// main validation function called by form event handlers
function validate(frame, field, method) {
      gFrame = frame
      gField =  eval("window." + frame.name + ".document.forms[0]." +
field.name)
      var args = validate.arguments
      for (i = 2; i < args.length; i++) {
          if (!dispatchLookup[args[i]].doValidate()) {
              return false
          }
      }
      return true
}
```

In the `validate()` function, the frame reference is assigned to a global variable that is declared at the top of the validations.js file. Validation functions will need this information to build a reference back to a companion field required of some validations (explained later in this section). A second global variable contains a reference to the calling form element. Because the form element reference by itself does not contain information about the frame in which it lives, the script must build a reference out of the information passed as parameters. The reference must work from the framesetting document down to the frame, its form, and form element name. Therefore, I use an `eval()` function to derive the object reference and assign it to the `gField` global variable.

Next, the script creates an array of all arguments passed to the `validate()` function. A `for` loop starts with index value 2, the third parameter containing the first validation function name. For each one, the named item's `doValidate()` method is called. If the validation fails, this function returns `false`; but if all validations succeed, then this function returns `true`. Later you will see that this function's returned value is the one that allows or disallows a form submission.

Sample validations

Above the dispatching mechanism in the validations.js are the validation functions themselves. Many of the named validation functions have supporting utility functions that often get reused by other named validation functions. Due to the eventual large size of this library file (the production version was about 40 kilobytes), I organized the functions into two groups: the named functions first, the utility functions below them (but still before the dispatching mechanism at the bottom of the document).

To demonstrate how some of the more common data types were validated for this application, I show several validation functions and, where necessary, their supporting utility functions. As you will see, when you are dealing with critical corporate data, you must go to extreme lengths to ensure valid data. And to help users see their mistakes quickly, you need to build some intelligence into validations where possible.

U.S. state name

The design specification for forms that required entry of a state of the U.S. called for entry of the two-character abbreviation. A companion field to the right would display the entire state name as user feedback verification. The onChange= event handler not only called the validation, but it also fed the focus to the field following the expanded state field so users would be less likely to type into it.

Before the validation can even get to the expansion part, it must first validate that the entry is a valid two-letter abbreviation. Because I would need both the abbreviation and the full expanded state for this validation, I created an array of all the states, using the state abbreviation as the index label for each entry. Listing 37-9 shows that array creation. If the design were only for Navigator 4, I would have used the literal format for creating such an object to save characters (see Chapter 34).

Listing 37-9: **Creating a U.S. States Array**

```
// States array
var USStates = new Array(51)
USStates["AL"] = "ALABAMA"
USStates["AK"] = "ALASKA"
USStates["AZ"] = "ARIZONA"
USStates["AR"] = "ARKANSAS"
USStates["CA"] = "CALIFORNIA"
USStates["CO"] = "COLORADO"
USStates["CT"] = "CONNECTICUT"
USStates["DE"] = "DELAWARE"
USStates["DC"] = "DISTRICT OF COLUMBIA"
USStates["FL"] = "FLORIDA"
USStates["GA"] = "GEORGIA"
USStates["HI"] = "HAWAII"
USStates["ID"] = "IDAHO"
USStates["IL"] = "ILLINOIS"
USStates["IN"] = "INDIANA"
USStates["IA"] = "IOWA"
USStates["KS"] = "KANSAS"
USStates["KY"] = "KENTUCKY"
USStates["LA"] = "LOUISIANA"
USStates["ME"] = "MAINE"
USStates["MD"] = "MARYLAND"
USStates["MA"] = "MASSACHUSETTS"
USStates["MI"] = "MICHIGAN"
USStates["MN"] = "MINNESOTA"
USStates["MS"] = "MISSISSIPPI"
USStates["MO"] = "MISSOURI"
```

(continued)

Listing 37-9 *(continued)*

```
USStates["MT"] = "MONTANA"
USStates["NE"] = "NEBRASKA"
USStates["NV"] = "NEVADA"
USStates["NH"] = "NEW HAMPSHIRE"
USStates["NJ"] = "NEW JERSEY"
USStates["NM"] = "NEW MEXICO"
USStates["NY"] = "NEW YORK"
USStates["NC"] = "NORTH CAROLINA"
USStates["ND"] = "NORTH DAKOTA"
USStates["OH"] = "OHIO"
USStates["OK"] = "OKLAHOMA"
USStates["OR"] = "OREGON"
USStates["PA"] = "PENNSYLVANIA"
USStates["RI"] = "RHODE ISLAND"
USStates["SC"] = "SOUTH CAROLINA"
USStates["SD"] = "SOUTH DAKOTA"
USStates["TN"] = "TENNESSEE"
USStates["TX"] = "TEXAS"
USStates["UT"] = "UTAH"
USStates["VT"] = "VERMONT"
USStates["VA"] = "VIRGINIA"
USStates["WA"] = "WASHINGTON"
USStates["WV"] = "WEST VIRGINIA"
USStates["WI"] = "WISCONSIN"
USStates["WY"] = "WYOMING"
```

The existence of this array comes in handy to determine if the user entered a valid two-state abbreviation. Listing 37-10 shows the actual isUSState() validation function that puts this array to work.

Its first task is to assign an uppercase version of the entered value to a local variable (inputStr), which will be the value being compared throughout the rest of the function. If the user entered something in the field (length > 0) but no entry in the USStates array exists for that value, it means the entry is not a valid state abbreviation. Time to go to work to help out the user.

Listing 37-10: **Validation Function for U.S. States**

```
// input value is a U.S. state abbreviation; set entered value to all
uppercase
// also set companion field (NAME="<xxx>_expand") to full state name
function isUSState() {
        var inputStr = gField.value.toUpperCase()
        if (inputStr.length > 0 && USStates[inputStr] == null) {
           var msg = ""
           var firstChar = inputStr.charAt(0)
           if (firstChar == "A") {
              msg += "\n(Alabama = AL; Alaska = AK; Arizona = AZ;
Arkansas = AR)"
```

```
          }
          if (firstChar == "D") {
              msg += "\n(Delaware = DE; District of Columbia = DC)"
          }
          if (firstChar == "I") {
              msg += "\n(Idaho = ID; Illinois = IL; Indiana = IN; Iowa
   = IA)"
          }
          if (firstChar == "M") {
              msg += "\n(Maine = ME; Maryland = MD; Massachusetts =
   MA; Michigan = MI; Minnesota = MN; Mississippi = MS; Missouri = MO;
   Montana = MT)"
          }
          if (firstChar == "N") {
              msg += "\n(Nebraska = NE; Nevada = NV)"
          }
          alert("Check the spelling of the state abbreviation." + msg)
          gField.focus()
          gField.select()
          return false
       }
       gField.value = inputStr
       var expandField = eval("window." + gFrame.name +
   ".document.forms[0]." + gField.name + "_expand")
       expandField.value = USStates[inputStr]
       return true
   }
```

The function assumes that the user tried to enter a valid state abbreviation, but either had incorrect source material or momentarily forgot a particular state's abbreviation. Therefore, the function examines the first letter of the entry. If that first letter is any one of the five identified as causing the most difficulty, a legend for all states beginning with that letter is assigned to the msg variable (this would be a great place for a Navigator 4 switch construction). An alert message displays the generic alert, plus any special legend if one has been assigned to the msg variable. When the user closes the alert, the field will have focus (except for a Navigator 3 bug in UNIX platforms) and its text selected. The function returns false at this point.

If, on the other hand, the abbreviation entry is a valid one, the field is handed the uppercase version of the entry. The script then uses the two global variables set in validate() to create a reference to the expanded display field (whose name must always be the same as the entry field, plus "_expand"). That expanded display field is then supplied the USStates array entry value corresponding to the abbreviation label. All is well with this validation, so it then returns true.

You can see here that the so-called validation routine is doing far more than simply checking validity of the data. By communicating with the field, converting its contents to uppercase, and talking to another field in the form, a simple call to the validation function yields a lot of mileage.

Date validation

Many of the forms in this application have date fields. In fact dates are an important part of the data being maintained in the database that is behind the forms. Since all users of this application are familiar with standard date formats in use in the United States, I didn't have to worry about the possibility of cultural variations in date formats. Even so, I wanted the date entry to be accommodating to the common date formats, such as mmddyyyy, mm/dd/yyyy, and mm-dd-yyyy (as well as accommodating two-digit year entries spanning 1930 to 2029).

The plan also called for going further in helping users enter dates within certain ranges. For example, a field that is used for a birthdate (the listings were for medical professionals) should recommend dates starting no more than 90 years from the current date and no less than 20. And to keep this application running well into the future, the ranges should be on a sliding scale from the current year, no matter when it might be. Whatever the case, the date range validation would be only a recommendation, and not a transaction stopper.

Rather than create separate validation functions for each date field, I created a system of reusable validation functions for each date range (several fields on different forms required the same date ranges). Each one of these individual functions calls a single generic date validation function that handles the date range checking. Listing 37-11 shows a few examples of these individual range-checking functions.

Listing 37-11: **Date Range Validations**

```
// Date Minus 90/Minus 20
function isM90_M20Date() {
        if (gField.value.length == 0) return true
        var thisYear = getTheYear()
        return isDate((thisYear - 90),(thisYear - 20))
}

// Date Minus 70/Minus 0
function isM70_0Date() {
        if (gField.value.length == 0) return true
        var thisYear = getTheYear()
        return isDate((thisYear - 70),(thisYear))
}

// Date Minus 5/Plus 10
function isM5_P10Date() {
        if (gField.value.length == 0) return true
        var thisYear = getTheYear()
        return isDate((thisYear - 5),(thisYear + 10))
}
```

The naming convention I created for the functions includes the two range components relative to the current date. A letter "M" means the range boundary is minus a number of years from the current date; "P" means the range is plus a number of years. If the boundary should be the current year, a zero is used. Therefore, the isM5_P10Date() function performs range checking for boundaries between five years before and ten years after the current year.

Before performing any range checking, each function makes sure there is some value to validate. If the field entry is empty, the function returns true. This is fine here, because dates are not always required when the data is unknown.

Next, the functions get the current four-digit year. Given the different ways Navigator 3 treats years before and after 2000, I call a separate utility function to return the four-digit version, as shown here:

```
function getTheYear() {
        var thisYear = (new Date()).getYear()
        thisYear = (thisYear < 100)? thisYear + 1900: thisYear
        return thisYear
}
```

The final call from the range validations is to a common isDate() function, which handles not only the date range validation, but also validation for valid dates (for example, making sure that September has only 30 days). Listing 37-12 shows this monster-sized function. Due to the length of this function, I will interlace commentary within the code listing.

Listing 37-12: **Primary Date Validation Function**

```
// date field validation (called by other validation functions that
specify minYear/maxYear)
function isDate(minYear,maxYear,minDays,maxDays) {
        var inputStr = gField.value
```

To make it easier to work with dates supplied with delimiters, I first convert hyphen delimiters to slash delimiters. The replaceString() function is the same one described in Chapter 26 and is located in the utility functions part of the validations.js file.

```
// convert hyphen delimiters to slashes
while (inputStr.indexOf("-") != -1) {
    inputStr = replaceString(inputStr,"-","/")
}
```

For validating whether the gross format is OK, I check whether zero or two delimiters appear. If not, then the overall formatting is not acceptable. The error alert shows models for acceptable date entry formats.

```
var delim1 = inputStr.indexOf("/")
var delim2 = inputStr.lastIndexOf("/")
if (delim1 != -1 && delim1 == delim2) {
        // there is only one delimiter in the string
        alert("The date entry is not in an acceptable format.\n\nYou
can enter dates in the following formats: mmddyyyy, mm/dd/yyyy, or mm-
dd-yyyy.  (If the month or date data is not available, enter \'01\' in
the appropriate location.)")
        gField.focus()
```

(continued)

Listing 37-12 *(continued)*

```
        gField.select()
        return false
    }
```

If there are delimiters, I tear apart the string into components for month, day, and year. Because two-digit entries might begin with zeros, I make sure the `parseInt()` functions specify base 10 conversions.

```
    if (delim1 != -1) {
        // there are delimiters; extract component values
        var mm = parseInt(inputStr.substring(0,delim1),10)
        var dd = parseInt(inputStr.substring(delim1 + 1,delim2),10)
        var yyyy = parseInt(inputStr.substring(delim2 + 1,
inputStr.length),10)
```

For no delimiters, I tear apart the string, assuming two-digit entries for month and year, and either two or four digits for the year.

```
    } else {
        // there are no delimiters; extract component values
        var mm = parseInt(inputStr.substring(0,2),10)
        var dd = parseInt(inputStr.substring(2,4),10)
        var yyyy =
parseInt(inputStr.substring(4,inputStr.length),10)
    }
```

Since the `parseInt()` functions would reveal whether any entry is not a number by returning NaN, I check whether any of the three values is not a number. If so, then an alert signals the formatting problem and supplies acceptable models.

```
    if (isNaN(mm) || isNaN(dd) || isNaN(yyyy)) {
        // there is a non-numeric character in one of the component
values
        alert("The date entry is not in an acceptable format.\n\nYou
can enter dates in the following formats: mmddyyyy, mm/dd/yyyy, or mm-
dd-yyyy.")
        gField.focus()
        gField.select()
        return false
    }
```

Next I perform some gross range validation on the month and date, making sure months are entered from 1 to 12 and dates from 1 to 31. I'll take care of aligning exact month lengths later.

```
    if (mm < 1 || mm > 12) {
        // month value is not 1 thru 12
        alert("Months must be entered between the range of 01
(January) and 12 (December).")
        gField.focus()
        gField.select()
```

```
            return false
      }
      if (dd < 1 || dd > 31) {
            // date value is not 1 thru 31
            alert("Days must be entered between the range of 01 and a
maximum of 31 (depending on the month and year).")
            gField.focus()
            gField.select()
            return false
      }

      // validate year, allowing for checks between year ranges
      // passed as parameters from other validation functions
```

Before getting too deep into the year validation, I convert any two-digit year within the specified range to its four-digit equivalent.

```
      if (yyyy < 100) {
            // entered value is two digits, which we allow for 1930-2029
            if (yyyy >= 30) {
               yyyy += 1900
            } else {
               yyyy += 2000
            }
      }

      var today = new Date()
```

I designed this function to work with either a pair of year ranges or date ranges (so many days before and/or after today). If the function is passed date ranges, then the first two parameters must be passed as null. This first batch of code works with the date ranges (because the `minYear` parameter would be null).

```
      if (!minYear) {
            // function called with specific day range parameters
            var dateStr = new String(monthDayFormat(mm) + "/" +
monthDayFormat(dd) + "/" + yyyy)
            var testDate = new Date(dateStr)
            if (testDate.getTime() < (today.getTime() + (minDays * 24 *
60 * 60 * 1000))) {
                  alert("The most likely range for this entry begins " +
minDays + " days from today.")
            }
            if (testDate.getTime() > today.getTime() + (maxDays * 24 *
60 * 60 * 1000)) {
                  alert("The most likely range for this entry ends " +
maxDays + " days from today.")
            }
```

You can also pass hard-wired four-digit years as parameters. The following branch compares the entered year against the range specified by those passed year values.

(continued)

Listing 37-12 *(continued)*

```
        } else if (minYear && maxYear) {
            // function called with specific year range parameters
            if (yyyy < minYear || yyyy > maxYear) {
                // entered year is outside of range passed from calling
function
                alert("The most likely range for this entry is between
the years " + minYear + " and " + maxYear + ".  If your source data
indicates a date outside this range, then enter that date.")
            }
        } else {
```

For year parameters passed as positive or negative year differences, I begin processing by getting the four-digit year for today's date. Then I compare the entered year against the passed range values. If the entry is outside the desired range, an alert reveals the preferred year range within which the entry should fall. But the function does not return any value here, since an out-of-range value is not critical for this application.

```
            // default year range (now set to (this year - 100) and
(this year + 25))
            var thisYear = today.getYear()
            if (thisYear < 100) {
                thisYear += 1900
            }
            if (yyyy < minYear || yyyy > maxYear) {
                alert("It is unusual for a date entry to be before " +
minYear + " or after " + maxYear + ". Please verify this entry.")
            }
        }
```

One more important validation is to make sure that the entered date is valid for the month and year. Therefore, the various date components are passed to functions to check against month lengths, including the special calculations for the varying length of February. These functions are shown in Listing 37-13. The alert messages they display are smart enough to inform the user what the maximum date is for the entered month and year.

```
        if (!checkMonthLength(mm,dd)) {
            gField.focus()
            gField.select()
            return false
        }
        if (mm == 2) {
            if (!checkLeapMonth(mm,dd,yyyy)) {
                gField.focus()
                gField.select()
                return false
            }
        }
```

The final task is to reassemble the date components into a format that the database wants for its date storage and stuff it into the form field. If the user had entered an all-number or hyphen-delimited date, it is automatically reformatted and displayed as a slash-delimited, four-digit-year date.

```
    // put the Informix-friendly format back into the field
    gField.value = monthDayFormat(mm) + "/" + monthDayFormat(dd) +
"/" + yyyy
    return true
}
```

Listing 37-13: **Functions to Check Month Lengths**

```
// check the entered month for too high a value
function checkMonthLength(mm,dd) {
    var months = new
Array("","January","February","March","April","May","June","July","Augu
st","September","October","November","December")
    if ((mm == 4 || mm == 6 || mm == 9 || mm == 11) && dd > 30) {
        alert(months[mm] + " has only 30 days.")
        return false
    } else if (dd > 31) {
        alert(months[mm] + " has only 31 days.")
        return false
    }
    return true
}

// check the entered February date for too high a value
function checkLeapMonth(mm,dd,yyyy) {
    if (yyyy % 4 > 0 && dd > 28) {
        alert("February of " + yyyy + " has only 28 days.")
        return false
    } else if (dd > 29) {
        alert("February of " + yyyy + " has only 29 days.")
        return false
    }
    return true
}
```

This is a rather extensive date validation routine, but it demonstrates how thorough you must be when a database relies on accurate entries. The more prompting and assistance you can give to a user to ferret out problems with an invalid entry, the happier those users will be.

Cross-confirmation fields

The final validation type that I'll be covering here is probably not a common request, but it demonstrates how the dispatch mechanism created at the outset expanded so easily to accommodate this enhanced client request. The situation was that some fields (mostly dates in this application) were deemed critical pieces of data because these data triggered other processes from the database. As a further check to ensure entry of accurate data, a number of values were set up to be entered twice in separate fields, and the fields had to match exactly. In many ways this mirrors the two passes you are often requested to make when you set a password: enter two copies and let the computer compare them to make sure you typed what you intended to type.

I established a system that placed only one burden on the many programmers working on the forms: while the primary field could be named anything you want (to help alignment with database column names, for example), the secondary field must be named the same plus "_xcfm"— which stands for "cross-confirm." Then, pass the isConfirmed validation name to the validate() function after the date range validation name, as follows:

```
onChange="parent.validate(window, this, 'isM5_P10Date', 'isConfirmed')"
```

In other words, the isConfirmed() validation function will compare the fully vetted, properly formatted date in the current field against its parallel entry.

Listing 37-14 shows the one function in validations.js that handles the confirmation in both directions. After assigning a copy of the entry field value to the inputStr variable, the function next sets a Boolean flag (primary) that lets the rest of the script know if the entry field was the primary or secondary field: If the string "_xcfm" is missing from the field name, then it is the primary.

For the primary field branch, the script assembles the name of the secondary field and compares the content of the secondary field's value against the inputStr value. If they are not the same, it means the user is entering a new value into the primary field, so the script empties the secondary field to force reentry to verify that the user is entering the proper data.

For the secondary field entry branch, the script assembles a reference to the primary field by stripping away the final five characters of the secondary field's name. I could have used the lastIndexOf() string method instead of the longer way involving the string's length, but after experiencing so many platform-specific problems with lastIndexOf() in Navigator, I decided to play it safe. Then the two values are compared, with an appropriate alert displayed if they don't match.

Listing 37-14: **Cross-Confirmation Validation**

```javascript
// checks an entry against a parallel, duplicate entry to
// confirm that correct data has been entered
// Parallel field name must be the main field name plus "_xcfm"
function isConfirmed() {
        var inputStr = gField.value
        // flag for whether field under test is primary (true) or
confirmation field
        var primary = (gField.name.indexOf("_xcfm") == -1)
        if (primary) {
            // clear the confirmation field if primary field is changed
            var xcfmField =  eval("window." + gFrame.name +
".document.forms[0]." + gField.name + "_xcfm")
```

```
            var xcfmValue = xcfmField.value
            if (inputStr != xcfmValue) {
                xcfmField.value = ""
                return true
            }
        } else {
            var xcfmField = eval("window." + gFrame.name +
".document.forms[0]." + gField.name.substring(0,(gField.name.length-
5)))
            var xcfmValue = xcfmField.value
            if (inputStr != xcfmValue) {
                alert("The main and confirmation entry field contents do
not match. Both fields must have EXACTLY the same content to be
accepted by the database.")
                gField.focus()
                gField.select()
                return false
            }
        }
    }
    return true
}
```

Last-minute check

Every validation event handler is designed to return $true$ if the validation is successful. This comes in handy for the batch validation that performs one final check of the entries triggered by the form's onSubmit= event handler. The event handler calls a function called checkForm() and passes the form object as a parameter. That parameter helps create a reference to the form element that is passed to each validation function.

Because successful validations return $true$, you can nest consecutive validation tests so that the most nested statement of the construction is return true, because all validations have succeeded. The form's onSubmit= event handler is as follows:

```
onSubmit="return checkForm(this)"
```

And the following code fragment is an example of a checkForm() function. A separate isDateFormat() validation function called here checks whether the field contains an entry in the proper format, meaning that it has likely survived the range checking and format shifting of the real-time validation check.

```
function checkForm(form) {
    if (parent.validate(window, form.birthdate, "isDateFormat")) {
        if (parent.validate(window, form.phone, "isPhone")) {
            if (parent.validate(window, form.name, "isNotEmpty")) {
                return true
            }
        }
    }
    return false
}
```

If any one validation fails, the field is given focus and its content selected (controlled by the individual validation function), and the `checkForm()` function returns `false`. This, in turn, cancels the form submission.

Plan for Data Validation

I devoted an entire chapter to the subject of data validation because it represents the one area of error checking that almost all JavaScript authors should be concerned with. If your scripts (client-side or server-side) perform processing on user entries, you want to prevent script errors at all costs. Data-entry validation is your last line of defense against user-induced errors.

✦   ✦   ✦

LiveConnect: Scripting Java Applets and Plug-ins

Netscape groups all the features that enable JavaScript
scripts, Java applets, and plug-ins to communicate
with each other under one technology umbrella, called
LiveConnect. Having three avenues of access to LiveConnect
makes it easy to become confused about how LiveConnect
works and how to incorporate these powers into your Web
site presentations. In this chapter, I focus on the scripting
side of LiveConnect: approaching applets and plug-ins from
scripts and accessing scripts from Java applets.

Except for the part about talking to scripts from inside a
Java applet, I don't assume you have any knowledge of Java
programming. The primary goal here is to help you
understand how to control applets and plug-ins from your
scripts. If you're in a position to develop specifications for
applets, you also learn what to ask of your Java
programmers. But if you are also a Java applet programmer,
you learn the necessary skills to get your applets in touch
with HTML pages and scripts.

LiveConnect Overview

The backbone of the LiveConnect facilities in Navigator is
the Java *virtual machine* (VM) you see loading (in the splash
screen) during a Navigator 3 launch (in Navigator 4, the VM
doesn't load until it is needed, sometimes causing a brief
delay in initial execution). This virtual machine (which is
entirely software-based) makes your computer look like every
other computer that has a Java virtual machine running on it
— hence the capability of Java applets (and applications) to
run on Wintel, Macintosh, and UNIX computers without
requiring modification from platform to platform. The Java
virtual machine is not embedded in absolutely every

platform, however. Windows 3.1 users are the last to get Java capabilities for their browsers; also, some LiveConnect communication with plug-ins is not available for non-PowerPC Macintoshes.

For the most part, the underlying Java engine is invisible to the scripter (you) and certainly to the visitors of your sites. At most, visitors see status bar messages about applets loading and running. To applet and plug-in makers, however, Java is the common denominator that enables applets to work with other applets or plug-ins to communicate with applets. In these early stages of LiveConnect history, very little of this cross-applet or applet-to-plug-in communication occurs; but I have little doubt that the situation will change, mostly for controlled intranet installations.

From the point of view of a JavaScript author, LiveConnect extends the object model to include objects and data types that are not a part of the HTML world. HTML, for instance, does not have a form element that displays real-time stock ticker data; nor does HTML have the capability to treat a sound file like anything more than a URL to be handed off to a helper application. With LiveConnect, however, your scripts can treat the applet that displays the stock ticker as an object whose properties and methods can be modified after the applet loads; scripts can also tell the sound when to play or pause by controlling the plug-in that manages the incoming sound file.

Because LiveConnect is a proprietary Netscape technology, not all facilities are available in Internet Explorer. Later versions of Internet Explorer 3 and all versions of Internet Explorer 4 allow scripts to communicate with applets. Internet Explorer 4 has partial support for applet-to-script communication. Neither Internet Explorer 3 nor Internet Explorer 4 supports communication from JavaScript scripts to plug-ins or communication directly accessing Java classes.

Why Control Java Applets?

A question I often hear from experienced Java programmers is, "Why bother controlling an applet via a script when you can build all the interactivity you want into the applet itself?" This question is valid if you come from the Java world, but it takes a viewpoint from the HTML and scripting world to fully answer it.

Java applets exist in their own private rectangles, remaining largely oblivious to the HTML surroundings on the page. Applet designers who don't have extensive Web page experience tend to regard their applets as the center of the universe rather than as components of HTML pages.

As a scripter, on the other hand, you may want to use those applets as powerful components to spiff up the overall presentation. Using applets as prewritten objects enables you to make simple changes to the HTML pages — including the geographic layout of elements and images — at the last minute, without having to rewrite and recompile Java program code. If you want to update the look with an entirely new graphical navigation or control bar, you can do it directly via HTML and scripting.

When it comes to designing or selecting applets for inclusion into my scripted page, I prefer using applet interfaces that confine themselves to data display, putting any control of the data into the hands of the script, rather than using on-screen buttons in the applet rectangle. I believe this setup enables much greater last-minute flexibility in the page design — not to mention consistency with HTML form element interfaces — than putting everything inside the applet rectangle.

A Little Java

If you plan to look at a Java applet's scripted capabilities, you can't escape having to know a little about Java applets and some terminology. The discussion starts to go more deeply into object orientation than you have seen with JavaScript, but I'll try to be gentle.

Java building blocks classes

One part of Java that closely resembles JavaScript is that Java programming deals with objects, much the way JavaScript deals with a page's objects. Java objects, however, are not the familiar HTML objects but rather more basic things, such as tools that draw to the screen and data streams. But both languages also have some non-HTML kinds of objects in common: strings, arrays, numbers, and so on.

Every Java object is known as a *class* — a term from the object-orientation world. When you use a Java compiler to generate an applet, that applet is also a class, which happens to incorporate many Java classes, such as strings, image areas, font objects, and the like. The applet file you see on the disk is called a *class file,* and its file extension is .class. This file is the one you specify for the CODE attribute of an <APPLET> tag.

Java methods

Most JavaScript objects have methods attached to them that define what actions the objects are capable of performing. A string object, for instance, has the toUpperCase() method that converts the string to all uppercase letters. Java classes also have methods. Many methods are predefined in the base Java classes embedded inside the virtual machine. But inside a Java applet, the author can write methods that either override the base method or deal exclusively with a new class created in the program. These methods are, in a way, like the functions you write in JavaScript for a page.

Not all methods, however, are created the same. Java lets authors determine how visible a method is to outsiders. The types of methods that you, as a scripter, are interested in are the ones declared as *public methods.* You can access such methods from JavaScript via a syntax that falls very much in line with what you already know. For example, a common public method in applets stops an applet's main process. Such a Java method may look like this:

```
public void stop() {
        if(thread != null) {
            thread.stop();
            thread = null;
        }
}
```

The void keyword simply means that this method does not return any values (compilers need to know this stuff). Assuming that you have one applet loaded in your page, the JavaScript call to this applet method is

```
document.applets[0].stop()
```

Listing 38-1 shows how all this works with the `<APPLET>` tag for a scriptable digital clock applet example. The script includes calls to two of the applet's methods: to stop and to start the clock.

Listing 38-1: **Stopping and Starting an Applet**

```
<HTML>
<HEAD>
<TITLE>A Script That Could Stop a Clock</TITLE>
<SCRIPT LANGUAGE="JavaScript1.1">
function pauseClock() {
        document.clock1.stop()
}
function restartClock() {
        document.clock1.start()
}
</SCRIPT>
<BODY>
<H1>Simple control over an applet</H1>
<HR>
<APPLET CODE="ScriptableClock.class" NAME="clock1" WIDTH=500 HEIGHT=45>
<PARAM NAME=bgColor VALUE="Green">
<PARAM NAME=fgColor VALUE="Blue">
</APPLET>
<P>
<FORM NAME="widgets1">
<INPUT TYPE="button" VALUE="Pause Clock" onClick="pauseClock()">
<INPUT TYPE="button" VALUE="Restart Clock" onClick="restartClock()">
</FORM>
</BODY>
</HTML>
```

The syntax for accessing the method (in the two functions) is just like JavaScript in that the references to the applet's methods include the applet object (`clock1` in the example), which is contained by the document object.

Java applet "properties"

The Java equivalents of JavaScript object properties are called *public instance variables*. These variables are akin to JavaScript global variables. If you have access to some Java source code, you can recognize a public instance variable by its *public* keyword:

```
public String fontName
```

Java authors must specify a variable's data type when declaring any variable. That's why the `String` data type appears in the preceding example.

Your scripts can access these variables with the same kind of syntax you use to access JavaScript object properties. If the `fontname` variable in ScriptableClock.class had been defined as a public variable (it is not), you could access or set its value directly, as shown in the following example.

```
var theFont = document.applets[0].fontName
document.applets[0].fontName = "Courier"
```

Accessing Java fields

In a bit of confusing lingo, public variables and methods are often referred to as *fields*. These elements are not the kind of text entry fields you see on the screen; rather, they're like *slots* (another term used in Java) where you can slip in your requests and data. Remember these terms, because they may appear from time to time in error messages as you begin scripting applets.

Scripting Applets in Real Life

Because the purpose of scripting an applet is to gain access to the inner sanctum of a compiled program, the program should be designed to handle such rummaging around by scripters. If you can't acquire a copy of the source code or don't have any other documentation about the scriptable parts of the applet, you may have a difficult time knowing what to script and how to do it.

Although the applet's methods are reflected as properties in an applet object, writing a `for...in` loop to examine these methods tells you perhaps too much. Figure 38-1 shows a partial listing of such an examination of the ScriptableClock applet. This applet has only public methods (no variables), but the full listing shows the dozens of fields accessible in the applet. What you probably wouldn't recognize, unless you have programmed in Java, is that within the listing are dozens of fields belonging to the Java classes that automatically become a part of the applet during compilation. From this listing, you have no way to distinguish the fields defined or overridden in the applet code from the base Java fields.

fieldName	fieldValue
	[JavaMethod ScriptableClock.]
getInfo	[JavaMethod ScriptableClock.getInfo]
setColor	[JavaMethod ScriptableClock.setColor]
setFont	[JavaMethod ScriptableClock.setFont]
setTimeZone	[JavaMethod ScriptableClock.setTimeZone]
paint	[JavaMethod ScriptableClock.paint]
run	[JavaMethod ScriptableClock.run]
stop	[JavaMethod ScriptableClock.stop]
start	[JavaMethod ScriptableClock.start]
init	[JavaMethod ScriptableClock.init]
destroy	[JavaMethod ScriptableClock.destroy]
play	[JavaMethod ScriptableClock.play]
getParameterInfo	[JavaMethod ScriptableClock.getParameterInfo]
getAppletInfo	[JavaMethod ScriptableClock.getAppletInfo]
getAudioClip	[JavaMethod ScriptableClock.getAudioClip]

Figure 38-1: Partial listing of fields from ScriptableClock

Getting to scriptable methods

If you write your own applets or are fortunate enough to have the source code for an existing applet, the safest way to modify the applet variable settings or the running processes is through applet methods. Although setting a public variable value may enable you to make a desired change, you don't know how that change may impact other parts of the applet. An applet designed for scriptability should have a number of methods defined that enable you to make scripted changes to variable values.

To view a sample of an applet designed for scriptability, open the Java source code file for Listing 38-2 from the CD-ROM. A portion of that program listing is shown in the following example.

Listing 38-2: **Partial Listing for ScriptableClock.java**

```
/*
        Begin public methods for getting
        and setting data via LiveConnect
*/
public void setTimeZone(String zone) {
        stop();
        timeZone = (zone.startsWith("GMT")) ? true : false;
        start();
}

public void setFont(String newFont, String newStyle, String newSize) {
        stop();
        if (newFont != null && newFont != "")
            fontName = newFont;
        if (newStyle != null && newStyle != "")
            setFontStyle(newStyle);
        if (newSize != null && newSize != "")
            setFontSize(newSize);
        displayFont = new Font(fontName, fontStyle, fontSize);
        start();
}

public void setColor(String newbgColor, String newfgColor) {
        stop();
        bgColor = parseColor(newbgColor);
        fgColor = parseColor(newfgColor);
        start();
}

public String getInfo() {
        String result = "Info about ScriptableClock.class\r\n";
        result += "Version/Date: 1.0d1/2 May 1996\r\n";
        result += "Author: Danny Goodman (dannyg@dannyg.com)\r\n";
        result += "Public Variables:\r\n";
        result += "    (None)\r\n\r\n";
        result += "Public Methods:\r\n";
        result += "    setTimeZone(\"GMT\" | \"Locale\")\r\n";
```

```
        result += "   setFont(\"fontName\",\"Plain\" |\"Bold\" |
\"Italic\", \"fontSize\")\r\n";
        result += "   setColor(\"bgColorName\", \"fgColorName\")\r\n";
        result += "        colors: Black, White, Red, Green, Blue,
Yellow\r\n";
        return result;
    }
    /*
        End public methods for scripted access.
    */
```

The methods shown in Listing 38-2 were defined specifically for scripted access. In this case, they safely stop the applet thread before changing any values. The last method is one I recommend to applet authors. It returns a small bit of documentation containing information about the kind of methods that the applet likes to have scripted and what you can have as the passed parameter values.

Now that you see the amount of scriptable information in this applet, look at Listing 38-3, which takes advantage of that scriptability by providing several HTML form elements as user controls of the clock. The results are shown in Figure 38-2.

Listing 38-3: A More Fully Scripted Clock

```
<HTML>
<HEAD>
<TITLE>Clock with Lots o' Widgets</TITLE>
<SCRIPT LANGUAGE="JavaScript1.1">

function setTimeZone(popup) {
        var choice = popup.options[popup.selectedIndex].value
        document.clock2.setTimeZone(choice)
}

function setColor(form) {
        var bg =
form.backgroundColor.options[form.backgroundColor.selectedIndex].value
        var fg =
form.foregroundColor.options[form.foregroundColor.selectedIndex].value
        document.clock2.setColor(bg, fg)
}

function setFont(form) {
        var fontName =
form.theFont.options[form.theFont.selectedIndex].value
        var fontStyle =
form.theStyle.options[form.theStyle.selectedIndex].value
        var fontSize =
form.theSize.options[form.theSize.selectedIndex].value
        document.clock2.setFont(fontName, fontStyle, fontSize)
}
```

(continued)

Listing 38-3 *(continued)*

```
function getAppletInfo(form) {
        form.details.value = document.clock2.getInfo()
}

function showSource() {
        var newWindow = window.open("ScriptableClock.java","",
"WIDTH=450,HEIGHT=300,RESIZABLE,SCROLLBARS")
}

</SCRIPT>
</HEAD>
<BODY>
<APPLET CODE="ScriptableClock.class" NAME="clock2" WIDTH=500 HEIGHT=45>
<PARAM NAME=bgColor VALUE="Black">
<PARAM NAME=fgColor VALUE="Red">
</APPLET>

<P>
<FORM NAME="widgets2">
Select Time Zone:
<SELECT NAME="zone" onChange="setTimeZone(this)">
        <OPTION SELECTED VALUE="Locale">Local Time
        <OPTION VALUE="GMT">Greenwich Mean Time
</SELECT><P>
Select Background Color:
<SELECT NAME="backgroundColor" onChange="setColor(this.form)">
        <OPTION VALUE="White">White
        <OPTION SELECTED VALUE="Black">Black
        <OPTION VALUE="Red">Red
        <OPTION VALUE="Green">Green
        <OPTION VALUE="Blue">Blue
        <OPTION VALUE="Yellow">Yellow
</SELECT>
Select Color Text Color:
<SELECT NAME="foregroundColor" onChange="setColor(this.form)">
        <OPTION VALUE="White">White
        <OPTION VALUE="Black">Black
        <OPTION SELECTED VALUE="Red">Red
        <OPTION VALUE="Green">Green
        <OPTION VALUE="Blue">Blue
        <OPTION VALUE="Yellow">Yellow
</SELECT><P>
Select Font:
<SELECT NAME="theFont" onChange="setFont(this.form)">
        <OPTION SELECTED VALUE="TimesRoman">Times Roman
        <OPTION VALUE="Helvetica">Helvetica
        <OPTION VALUE="Courier">Courier
        <OPTION VALUE="Arial">Arial
</SELECT><BR>
Select Font Style:
```

```
<SELECT NAME="theStyle" onChange="setFont(this.form)">
       <OPTION SELECTED VALUE="Plain">Plain
       <OPTION VALUE="Bold">Bold
       <OPTION VALUE="Italic">Italic
</SELECT><BR>
Select Font Size:
<SELECT NAME="theSize" onChange="setFont(this.form)">
       <OPTION VALUE="12">12
       <OPTION VALUE="18">18
       <OPTION SELECTED VALUE="24">24
       <OPTION VALUE="30">30
</SELECT><P>
<HR>
<INPUT TYPE="button" NAME="getInfo" VALUE="Applet Info…"
onClick="getAppletInfo(this.form)">
<P>
<TEXTAREA NAME="details" ROWS=11 COLS=70></TEXTAREA>
</FORM>
<HR>
</BODY>
</HTML>
```

Very little of the code here controls the applet — only the handful of functions near the top. The rest of the code makes up the HTML user interface for the form element controls. When you open this document from the CD-ROM, be sure to click the Applet Info button to see the methods that you can script and the way that the parameter values from the JavaScript side match up with the parameters on the Java method side.

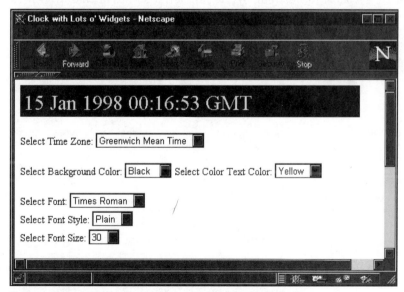

Figure 38-2: Scripting more of the ScriptableClock applet

Applet limitations

Because of concerns about security breaches via LiveConnect, Netscape currently clamps down on some powers that would be nice to have via a scripted applet. The most noticeable barrier is the one that prevents applets from accessing the network under scripted control. Therefore, even though a Java applet has no difficulty reading or writing text files from the server, such capabilities — even if built into an applet of your own design — won't be carried out if triggered by a JavaScript call to the applet.

Some clever hacks used to be posted on the Web, but they were rather cumbersome to implement and may no longer work on more modern browsers. You can also program the Java applet to fetch a text file when it starts up and then script the access of that value from JavaScript (as described in the following section).

Faceless applets

Until LiveConnect came along, Java applets were generally written to show off data and graphics — to play a big role in the presentation on the page. But if you prefer to let an applet do the heavy algorithmic lifting for your pages while the HTML form elements and images do the user interface, you essentially need what I call a *faceless applet*.

The method for embedding a faceless applet into your page is the same as embedding any applet: Use the `<APPLET>` tag. But specify only 1 pixel for both the `HEIGHT` and `WIDTH` attributes (0 has strange side effects). This setting creates a dot on the screen, which, depending on your page's background color, may be completely invisible to page visitors. Place it at the bottom of the page, if you like.

To show how nicely this method can work, Listing 38-4 provides the Java source code for a simple applet that retrieves a specific text file and stores the results in a Java variable available for fetching by the JavaScript shown in Listing 38-5. The HTML even automates the loading process by triggering the retrieval of the Java applet's data from an `onLoad=` event handler.

Listing 38-4: **Java Applet Source Code**

```
import java.net.*;
import java.io.*;

public class FileReader extends java.applet.Applet implements Runnable
{

        Thread thread;
        URL url;
        String output;
        String fileName = "Bill of rights.txt";

        public void getFile(String fileName) throws IOException {
            String result, line;
            InputStream connection;
            DataInputStream dataStream:
            StringBuffer buffer = new StringBuffer();
```

```
        try {
            url = new URL(getDocumentBase(),fileName);
        }
        catch (MalformedURLException e) {
            output = "AppletError " + e;
        }

        try {
            connection = url.openStream();
            dataStream = new DataInputStream(new
BufferedInputStream(connection));

            while ((line = dataStream.readLine()) != null) {
                buffer.append(line + "\n");
            }
            result = buffer.toString();
        }
        catch (IOException e) {
            result = "AppletError: " + e;
        }
        output = result;
    }

    public String fetchText() {
        return output;
    }

    public void init() {
    }

    public void start() {
        if (thread == null) {
            thread = new Thread(this);
            thread.start();
        }
    }
    public void stop() {
        if (thread != null) {
            thread.stop();
            thread = null;
        }
    }

    public void run(){
        try {
            getFile(fileName);
        }
        catch (IOException e) {
            output = "AppletError: " + e;
        }
    }
}
```

All the work of actually retrieving the file is performed in the `getFile()` method (which runs immediately after the applet loads). Notice that the name of the file to be retrieved, Bill of Rights.txt, is stored as a variable near the top of the code, making it easy to change for a recompilation, if necessary. You could also modify the applet to accept the file name as an applet parameter, specified in the HTML code. Meanwhile, the only hook that JavaScript needs is the one public method called `fetchText()`, which merely returns the value of the `output` variable, which in turn holds the file's contents.

This Java source code must be compiled into a Java class file (already compiled and included on the CD-ROM as FileReader.class) and placed in the same directory as the HTML file that loads this applet. Also, no explicit pathname for the text file is supplied in the source code, so the text file is assumed to be in the same directory as the applet.

Listing 38-5: **HTML Asking Applet to Read Text File**

```
<HTML>
<HEAD>
<TITLE>Letting an Applet Do The Work</TITLE>
<SCRIPT LANGUAGE="JavaScript1.1">
function getFile(form) {
        var output = document.readerApplet.fetchText()
        form.fileOutput.value = output
}
function autoFetch() {
        var output = document.readerApplet.fetchText()
        if (output != null) {
            document.forms[0].fileOutput.value = output
            return
        }
        var t = setTimeout("autoFetch()",1000)
}
</SCRIPT>
</HEAD>
<BODY onLoad="autoFetch()">

<H1>Text from a text file...</H1>
<FORM NAME="reader">
<INPUT TYPE="button" VALUE="Get File" onClick="getFile(this.form)">
<P>
<TEXTAREA NAME="fileOutput" ROWS=10 COLS=60 WRAP="hard"></TEXTAREA>
<P>
<INPUT TYPE="Reset" VALUE="Clear">
</FORM>
<APPLET CODE="FileReader.class" NAME="readerApplet" WIDTH=1 HEIGHT=1>
</APPLET>
</BODY>
</HTML>
```

Because an applet is usually the last thing to finish loading in a document, you can't use an applet to generate the page immediately. At best, an HTML document could display a pleasant welcome screen while the applet finishes loading itself and running whatever it does to prepare data for the page's form elements (or for an entirely new page via `document.write()`). Notice, for instance, that in Listing 38-5, the `onLoad=` event handler calls a function that checks whether the applet has supplied the requested data. If not, then the same function is called repeatedly in a timer loop until the data is ready and the textarea can be set. Finally, the `<APPLET>` tag is located at the bottom of the Body, set to 1 pixel square — invisible to the user. No user interface exists for this applet, so you have no need to clutter up the page with any placeholder or bumper sticker.

Figure 38-3 shows the page generated by the HTML and applet working together. The Get File button is merely a manual demonstration of calling the same applet method that the `onLoad=` event handler calls.

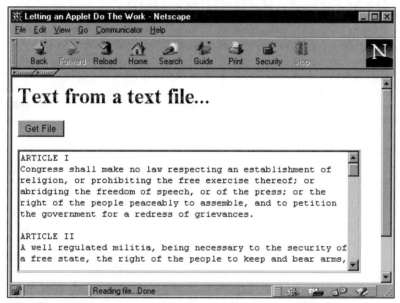

Figure 38-3: The page with text retrieved from a server file

A faceless applet may be one way for Web authors to hide what might otherwise be JavaScript code that is open to any visitor's view. For example, if you want to deliver a small data collection lookup with a document, but don't want the array of data visible in the JavaScript code, you can create the array and lookup functionality inside a faceless applet. Then use form elements and JavaScript to act as query entry and output display devices. Because the parameter values passed between JavaScript and Java applets must be string, numeric, or Boolean values, you won't be able to pass arrays without performing some amount of conversion either within the applet or the JavaScript code (JavaScript's `string.split()` and `array.join()` methods help a great deal here).

Data type conversions

The example in this chapter does not pass any parameters to the applet's methods, but you are free to do so. You need to pay attention to the way in which values are converted to Java data types. JavaScript strings and Boolean values are converted to Java String and Boolean objects. All JavaScript numbers, regardless of their subtype (that is, integer or floating-point number), are converted to Float objects. Therefore, if a method must accept a numeric parameter from a script, the parameter variable in the Java method must be defined as a Float type.

You can also pass objects, such as form elements. Such objects get wrapped with a JSObject type (see discussion about this class later in the chapter). Therefore, parameter variables must be established as type JSObject (and the netscape.javascript.JSObject class must be imported into the applet).

Applet-to-Script Communication

The flip side of scripted applet control is having an applet control script and HTML content in the page. Before you undertake this avenue in a page design, you must bear in mind that any calls made from the applet to the page will be hard-wired for the specific scripts and HTML elements in the page. If this level of tight integration and dependence suits the application, the link up will be successful. The discussion of applet-to-script communication assumes you have experience writing Java applets. I use Java jargon quite freely in this discussion.

What your applet needs

Navigators since Versions 3 come with a zipped set of special class files tailored for use in LiveConnect. In Navigator 3, the file is named java_30 or java_301, the latter one being the latest version; in Navigator 4, the file is named java40.jar. Microsoft versions of these class files are also included in Internet Explorer 4 (in the H3rfb7jn.zip file). The exact location of these files varies with operating system, but for Netscape users they are usually found inside a Java directory within the overall Navigator/Communicator program directory. The browser must see these class files (and have both Java and JavaScript enabled in the preferences screens) for LiveConnect to work.

These zipped class library files contain two vital classes in a netscape package:

```
netscape.javascript.JSObject
netscape.javascript.JSException
```

Both classes must be imported to your applet via the Java import compiler directive:

```
import netscape.javascript.*;
```

When the applet runs, the LiveConnect-aware browser knows how to find the two classes, so the user doesn't have to do anything special as long as the supporting files are in their default locations.

Perhaps the biggest problem applet authors have with LiveConnect is importing these class libraries for applet compilation. Your Java compiler must be able to see these class libraries for compilation to be successful. The prescribed method is to include the path to the zipped class file (either the java_301 or java40.jar file, depending on which Navigator browser version you, as author, have installed in your system) in the class path for the compiler (if you are using Internet Explorer 4 only, add the H3rfb7jn.zip file to your class path).

Problems frequently occur when the Java compiler you use (perhaps inside an integrated development environment, such as Symantec Cafe) doesn't recognize either of the Netscape files as a legitimate zipped class file. You can make your compilation life simpler if you unzip the class file archive and place the netscape package in the same directory in which your compiler looks for the basic Java classes. For example, Symantec Cafe stores the default Java class files inside zipped collections whose class paths (in Windows) are

```
C:\CAFE\BIN\..\JAVA\LIB\CLASSES.ZIP
C:\CAFE\BIN\..\JAVA\LIB\SYMCLASS.ZIP
```

These two class paths are inserted into new projects by default. I then extract the two netscape.javascript class files and store them in the same LIB directory as CLASSES.ZIP and SYMCLASS.ZIP. In other words, in the LIB directory is a directory named netscape; inside the netscape directory is another directory named javascript; inside the javascript directory are the JSObject.class and JSException.class files. Then I add the following class path to the project's class path setting:

```
C:\CAFE\BIN\..JAVA\LIB\
```

This instructs Cafe to start looking for the netscape package (which contains the javascript package, which, in turn, contains the class files) in that directory.

Depending on the unzipping utility and operating system you use, you may have to force the utility to recognize java_301 and java40.jar as zip archive files. If necessary, instruct the utility's file open dialog box to locate all file types in the directory. Both files will open as zipped archives. Sort the long list of files by name. Then select and extract only the two class files into the same directory as your compiler's Java class files. The utility should take care of creating the package directories for you.

What your HTML needs

As a security precaution, an `<APPLET>` tag requires one extra attribute to give the applet permission to access the HTML and scripting inside the document. That attribute is the single word `MAYSCRIPT`, and it can go anywhere inside the `<APPLET>` tag, as follows:

```
<APPLET CODE="myApplet.class" HEIGHT="200" WIDTH="300" MAYSCRIPT>
```

Permission is not required for JavaScript to access an applet's methods or properties, but if the applet initiates contact with the page, this attribute is required.

About JSObject.class

The portal between the applet and the HTML page that contains it is the netscape.javascript.JSObject class. This object's methods let the applet contact document objects and invoke JavaScript statements. Table 38-1 shows the object's methods and one static method.

Table 38-1 JSObject class Methods	
Method	*Description*
`call (String functionName, Object args[])`	Invokes JavaScript function, argument(s) passed as an array
`eval (String expression)`	Invokes a JavaScript statement
`getMember (String elementName)`	Retrieves a named object belonging to a container
`getSlot(Int index)`	Retrieves indexed object belonging to a container
`getWindow (Applet applet)`	Static method retrieves applet's containing window
`removeMember (String elementName)`	Removes a named object belonging to a container
`setMember (String elementName, Object value)`	Sets value of a named object belonging to a container
`setSlot(int index, Object value)`	Sets value of an indexed object belonging to a container
`toString()`	Returns string version of JSObject

Just as the window object is the top of the document object hierarchy for JavaScript references, the window object is the gateway between the applet code and the scripts and document objects. To open that gateway, use the `JSObject.getWindow()` method to retrieve a reference to the document window. Assign that object to a variable that you can use throughout your applet code. The following code fragment shows the start of an applet that assigns the window reference to a variable named `mainwin`:

```
import netscape.javascript.*;

public class myClass extends java.applet.Applet {
    private JSObject mainwin;

    public void init() {
        mainwin = JSObject.getWindow(this);
    }
}
```

If your applet will be making frequent trips to a particular object, you may want to create a variable holding a reference to that object. To accomplish this, the applet needs to make progressively deeper calls into the document object hierarchy with the `getMember()` method. For example, the following sequence assumes `mainwin` is a reference to the applet's document window. Eventually the statements set a form's field object to a variable for use elsewhere in the applet:

```
JSObject doc = (JSObject) mainwin.getMember("document");
JSObject form = (JSObject) doc.getMember("entryForm");
JSObject phonefld = (JSObject) form.getMember("phone");
```

Another option is to use the `eval()` method to execute an expression from the point of view of any object. For example, the following statement gets the same field object from the preceding fragment:

```
JSObject phonefld = mainwin.eval("document.entryForm.phone");
```

Once you have a reference to an object, you can access its properties via the `getMember()` method, as follows:

```
String phoneNum = (String) phonefld.getMember("value");
```

Two JSObject class methods let your applet execute arbitrary JavaScript expressions and invoke object methods: the `eval()` and `call()` methods. Use these methods with any JSObject. If a value is to be returned from the executed statement, you must cast the result into the desired object type. The parameter for the `eval()` method is a string of the expression to be evaluated by JavaScript. Scope of the expression depends on the object attached to the `eval()` method. If you use the window object, the expression would exist as if it were a statement in the document script (not defined inside a function).

Using the `call()` method is convenient for invoking JavaScript functions in the document, although it requires a little more preparation. The first parameter is a string of the function name. The second parameter is an array of arguments for the function. Parameters can be of mixed data types, in which case the array would be of type Object. If you don't need to pass a parameter to the function call, you can define an array of a single empty string value (for example, `String arg[] = {""}`) and pass that array as the second parameter.

Data type conversions

The strongly typed Java language is a mismatch for loosely typed JavaScript. As a result, with the exception of Boolean and string objects (which are converted to their respective JavaScript objects), you should be aware of the way LiveConnect adapts data types to JavaScript.

Any Java object that contains numeric data is converted to a JavaScript number value. Since JavaScript numbers are IEEE doubles, they can accommodate just about everything Java can throw its way.

If the applet extracts an object from the document and then passes that JSObject type back to JavaScript, that passed object is converted to its original JavaScript object type. But objects of other classes are passed as their native objects wrapped in JavaScript "clothing." JavaScript can access the applet object's methods and properties as if the object were a JavaScript object. Finally, Java arrays are converted to the same kind of JavaScript array created via the `new Array()` constructor. Elements can be accessed by integer index values (not named index values). All other JavaScript array properties and methods apply to this object as well.

Example applet-to-script application

To demonstrate several techniques for communicating from an applet to both JavaScript scripts and document objects, I present an applet that displays two simple buttons (see Figure 38-4). One button generates a new window, spawned from the main window, filling the window with dynamically generated content from the applet. The second button communicates from the applet to that second window by invoking a JavaScript function in the document. One last part of the demonstration shows the applet changing the value of a text box when the applet starts up.

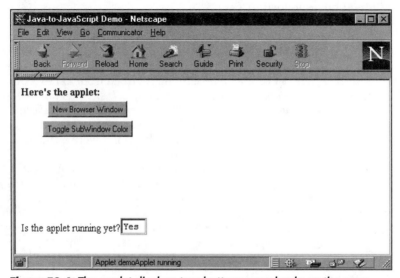

Figure 38-4: The applet displays two buttons seamlessly on the page.

Listing 38-6 shows the source code for the Java applet. For backward compatibility, it uses the JDK 1.02 event handling model.

Because the applet generates two buttons, the code begins by importing the AWT interface builder classes. I also import the netscape.javascript package to get the JSObject class. The name of this sample class is JtoJSDemo. I declare four global variables: Two for the windows, two for the applet button objects.

Listing 38-6: **Java Applet Source Code**

```
import java.awt.*;
import netscape.javascript.*;

public class JtoJSDemo extends java.applet.Applet {
    private JSObject mainwin, subwin;
    private Button newWinButton, toggleButton;
```

The applet's `init()` method establishes the user interface elements for this simple applet. A white background will be matched in the HTML with a white document background color, making the applet appear to blend in with the page. I use this opportunity to set the `mainwin` variable to the browser window that contains the applet.

```
public void init() {
    setBackground(Color.white);
    newWinButton = new Button("New Browser Window");
    toggleButton = new Button("Toggle SubWindow Color");
    this.add(newWinButton);
    this.add(toggleButton);
    mainwin = JSObject.getWindow(this);
}
```

As soon as the applet starts, it changes the `value` property of a text box in the HTML form. Because this is a one-time access to the field, I elected to use the `eval()` method from the point of view of the main window, rather than build successive object references through the object hierarchy with the `getMember()` method.

```
public void start() {
    mainwin.eval("document.indicator.running.value = 'Yes'");
}
```

Event handling is quite simple in this application. A click of the first button invokes `doNewWindow()`; a click of the second invokes `toggleColor()`. Both methods are defined later in the applet.

```
public boolean action(Event evt, Object arg) {
    if (evt.target instanceof Button) {
        if (evt.target == newWinButton) {
            doNewWindow();
        } else if (evt.target == toggleButton) {
            toggleColor();
        }
    }
    return true;
}
```

One of the applet's buttons calls the `doNewWindow()` method defined here. I use the `eval()` method to invoke the JavaScript `window.open()` method. The string parameter of the `eval()` method is exactly like the statement that would appear in the page's JavaScript to open a new window. The `window.open()` method returns a reference to that subwindow, so the statement here captures the returned value, casting it as a JSObject type for the `subwin` variable. That `subwin` variable can then be used as a reference for another `eval()` method that writes to that second window. Notice that the object to the left of the `eval()` method governs the recipient of the `eval()` method's expression. The same is true for closing the writing stream to the subwindow. Unfortunately, Internet Explorer 4's implementation of JSObject does not provide a suitable reference to the external window after it is created. Therefore, the window does not receive its content or respond to color changes in this example.

(continued)

Listing 38-6 *(continued)*

```
     void doNewWindow() {
          subwin = (JSObject)
mainwin.eval("window.open('','fromApplet','HEIGHT=200,WIDTH=200')");
          subwin.eval("document.write('<HTML><BODY BGCOLOR=white>Howdy
from the applet!</BODY></HTML>')");
          subwin.eval("document.close()");
     }
```

The second button in the applet calls the `toggleColor()` method. In the HTML document, a JavaScript function named `toggleSubWindowColor()` takes a window object reference as an argument. Therefore, I first assemble a one-element array of type JSObject consisting of the `subwin` object. That array is the second parameter of the `call()` method, following a string version of the JavaScript function name being called.

```
     void toggleColor() {
          if (subwin != null) {
               JSObject arg[] = {subwin};
               mainwin.call("toggleSubWindowColor", arg);
          }
     }
}
```

Now onto the HTML that loads the above applet class and is the recipient of its calls. The document is shown in Listing 38-7. One function is called by the applet. A text box in the form is initially set to "No," but gets changed to "Yes" by the applet after it has finished its initialization. The only other item of note is that the `<APPLET>` tag includes a `MAYSCRIPT` attribute to allow the applet to communicate with the page.

Listing 38-7: **HTML Document Called by Applet**

```
<HTML>
<HEAD><TITLE>Java-to-JavaScript Demo</TITLE>
<SCRIPT LANGUAGE="JavaScript">
function toggleSubWindowColor(wind) {
     if (wind.closed) {
          alert("The subwindow is closed.  Can't change it's color.")
     } else {
          wind.document.bgColor = (wind.document.bgColor == "#ffffff") ?
"red" : "white"
     }
}
</SCRIPT>
</HEAD>

<BODY BGCOLOR="#FFFFFF">
```

```
<B>Here's the applet:</B><BR>
<APPLET CODE="JtoJSDemo.class" NAME="demoApplet" HEIGHT=150 WIDTH=200
MAYSCRIPT>
</APPLET>

<FORM NAME="indicator">
Is the applet running yet?<INPUT TYPE="text" NAME="running" SIZE="4"
VALUE="No">
</FORM>
</BODY>
</HTML>
```

Scripting Navigator Plug-ins

Controlling a Navigator plug-in from JavaScript is much like controlling a Java applet. In fact, behind the scenes, the Java virtual machine provides the wires connecting JavaScript to plug-ins (although scripting plug-ins is unreliable on the Windows 3.1 or Macintosh 68K platforms). The primary difference between an applet and a plug-in is that a plug-in is initialized from an HTML document via the `<EMBED>` tag, rather than the `<APPLET>` tag.

Before your page loads the foreign MIME type that gets the plug-in functioning, your scripts should make sure that the desired plug-in is installed and set up to accommodate the specific MIME type (if the plug-in handles multiple MIME types). Chapter 25 provides a few examples of how to use JavaScript to verify that a particular MIME type is supported by the desired plug-in on a client's computer.

Once the plug-in (and usually one of its files) is loaded into memory, your scripts can take over, provided that the plug-in is written to be scripted. LiveAudio, for example, is the multiple audio format plug-in that Netscape ships with Navigator 3 and later. LiveAudio is scriptable. Even so, you must know the commands available for a plug-in before you can script it. Third-party scriptable plug-ins should have electronic documentation somewhere to help you script it.

Scripting LiveAudio

Because the LiveAudio plug-in ships with most platforms of Navigator, I want to spend a little time demonstrating how you script it. For up-to-date scripting and relevant `<EMBED>` tag attribute information, consult Netscape's online JavaScript documentation at `http://home.netscape.com/eng/mozilla/3.0/handbook/javascript/index.html`.

Table 38-2 shows the most important LiveAudio methods that you can access from your scripts. The last four methods in the table return values regarding the current state of the plug-in.

Table 38-2
Popular LiveAudio Plug-in Commands

Method	Description
`play('TRUE | FALSE | LoopCount'[,'URL '])`	Plays the currently loaded sound, unless the URL parameter is provided
`stop()`	Stops the currently playing sound
`pause()`	Pauses or restarts the currently playing sound
`start_time(seconds)`	Sets starting time within sound
`end_time(seconds)`	Sets ending time within sound
`start_at_beginning()`	Overrides existing `start_time()` **setting**
`stop_at_end()`	Overrides existing `end_time()` **setting**
`setvol(percent)`	Sets volume percentage (0-100)
`fade_to(percent)`	Gradually adjusts volume-to-volume level
`fade_from_to(startPercent, endPercent)`	Gradually adjusts volume between two fixed levels
`IsReady()`	Returns Boolean of plug-in sound state
`IsPlaying()`	Returns Boolean of playing state
`IsPaused()`	Returns Boolean of paused state
`GetVolume()`	Returns integer (0-100) of volume level percentage

To get a plug-in loaded and ready for action, specify an initial sound file for the SRC attribute of the <EMBED> tag. By default, a LiveAudio sound does not automatically play when it loads (although you can override that with the AUTOSTART attribute inside the tag). You can use scripting to send a different sound file to the loaded plug-in anytime while the page is loaded in the browser.

LiveAudio at work

Listing 38-8 is a sample application showing how to create a kind of jukebox for selecting and controlling multiple sound files with a single <EMBED> tag and scripted calls to the LiveAudio plug-in. Audio files for the example are on the CD-ROM.

Listing 38-8: **A Scripted Jukebox**

```
<HTML>
<HEAD>
<TITLE>Oldies but Goody's</TITLE>
<SCRIPT>
```

```
function showEmbedProps() {
      var obj = document.theme
      var msg = ""
      for (var i in obj) {
          msg += "Embed." + i + "=" + obj[i] + "\n"
      }
      alert(msg)
}
function playIt() {
      var args = playIt.arguments
      var sndFile = ""
      var snd = document.jukebox
      if (args.length == 1) {
          sndFile = args[0][args[0].selectedIndex].value
      }
      var howMany =
document.forms[0].frequency[document.forms[0].frequency.selectedIndex].
value
      howMany = (howMany != "TRUE") ? parseInt(howMany) : true
      if (!snd.IsReady()) {
          alert ("Sorry, still loading the sound.  Try again in a few
seconds.")
          return
      }
      if (sndFile != "") {
          snd.play(howMany,sndFile)
          return
      }
      snd.play(howMany)
}
function stopIt() {
      document.jukebox.stop()
}
function pauseIt(){
      document.jukebox.pause()
}
function rewindIt() {
      document.jukebox.stop()
      document.jukebox.start_at_beginning()
      playIt()
}
function raiseVol() {
      var newLevel = Math.min(currLevel()+10,100)
      setVolumeLevel(newLevel)
}
function lowerVol() {
      var newLevel = Math.max(currLevel()-10,0)
      setVolumeLevel(newLevel)
}
function setVolume(entry) {
      var newLevel = parseInt(entry.value)
      setVolumeLevel(newLevel)
}
```

(continued)

Listing 38-8 *(continued)*

```
function setVolumeLevel(newLevel) {
      var snd = document.jukebox
      snd.setvol(newLevel)
      displayVol()
}
function currLevel() {
      return document.jukebox.GetVolume()
}
function displayVol() {
      document.forms[0].volume.value = currLevel()
}
</SCRIPT>
</HEAD>

<BODY onLoad="displayVol()">
<FORM>
<TABLE BORDER=2><CAPTION ALIGN=top><FONT SIZE=+3>Classical Piano
Jukebox
</FONT></CAPTION>
<TR><TD COLSPAN=2 ALIGN=center>
<SELECT NAME="musicChoice" onChange="playIt(this)">
<OPTION VALUE="Beethoven.aif" SELECTED>Beethoven's Fifth Symphony
(Opening)
<OPTION VALUE="Chopin.aif">Chopin Ballade #1 (Opening)
<OPTION VALUE="Scriabin.aif">Scriabin Etude in D-sharp minor (Finale)
</SELECT></TD></TR>
<TR><TH ROWSPAN=4>Action:</TH>
<TD><INPUT TYPE="button" VALUE="Play" onClick="playIt()">
<SELECT NAME="frequency">
<OPTION VALUE=1 SELECTED>Once
<OPTION VALUE=2>Twice
<OPTION VALUE=3>Three times
<OPTION VALUE=TRUE>Continually
</SELECT></TD></TR>
<TR><TD><INPUT TYPE="button" VALUE="Stop" onClick="stopIt()"></TD></TR>
<TR><TD><INPUT TYPE="button" VALUE="Pause"
onClick="pauseIt()"></TD></TR
<TR><TD><INPUT TYPE="button" VALUE="Rewind" onClick="rewindIt()"></TD>
</TR>
<TR><TH ROWSPAN=3>Volume:</TH>
<TD>Current Setting:<INPUT TYPE="text" SIZE=3 NAME="volume"
onChange="setVolume(this)"></TD></TR>
<TR><TD><INPUT TYPE="button" VALUE="Higher" onClick="raiseVol()"></TD>
</TR>
<TR><TD><INPUT TYPE="button" VALUE="Lower"
onClick="lowerVol()"></TD></TR>
</TABLE>
</FORM>
<EMBED NAME="jukebox" SRC="Beethoven.aif" HIDDEN=TRUE AUTOSTART=FALSE
MASTERSOUND>
</BODY>
</HTML>
```

For this demonstration (shown in Figure 38-5), the <EMBED> tag initially loads one of three audio files. Be sure to include the MASTERSOUND attribute if you want to script the plug-in.

Figure 38-5: The jukebox page

As the user chooses an item from the pop-up listing at the top of the table, the corresponding sound file is loaded and played (there may be a delay if the sound is not cached in the browser). Although the example uses local source files, any valid URL that points to an audio file whose MIME type is readable by LiveAudio will work. Additional choices in this application enable the user to set how many times the selection should play (once, twice, three times, or in a continuous loop). Another group of settings displays and controls the volume level for the plug-in. The scripting is designed to adjust the volume in increments of 10 percent, but on some machines, the default displays may not be so conveniently rendered. Even so, you can manually set the volume to any value between 0 and 100 in the field.

If you decide to run Listing 38-8, you may experience some bugs in LiveConnect's capability to work with LiveAudio on some operating system platforms. I've experienced difficulties with Navigator 3 for Macintosh, especially on 68K Macs (such as those with 68030 and 68040 microprocessors).

Notice that the first function in Listing 38-8 is a property browser for the plug-in object. Although this function is not connected to a button in the listing, feel free to add a button that calls the showEmbedProps() function. The results are similar to the kind of listing you saw earlier in this chapter for Java applets. You see a listing of all methods available to the scripter, plus some Java-level methods that are not usually scripted. As with this kind of exposure to Java methods, you cannot tell from such listings what kind of parameters are required to script the methods. You still need outside documentation.

Scripting Java Classes Directly

Because you need to know your way around Java before programming Java classes directly from JavaScript, I won't get into too much detail in this book. Fortunately, the designers of JavaScript have done a good job of creating JavaScript equivalents for the most common Java language functionality, so there is not a strong need to access Java classes on a daily basis.

To script Java classes, it helps to have a good reference guide to the classes built into Java. Though intended for experienced Java programmers, *Java in a Nutshell* (O'Reilly & Associates, Inc.) offers a condensed view of the classes, their constructors, and their methods.

Java's built-in classes are divided into major groups (called *packages*) to help programmers find the right class and method for any need. Each package focuses on one particular aspect of programming, such as classes for user interface design in application and applet windows, network access, and basic language constructs, such as strings, arrays, and numbers. References to each class (object) defined in Java are "dot" references, just like JavaScript. Each item following a dot helps zero-in on the desired item. As an example, consider one class that is part of the base language class. The base language class is referred to as

```
java.lang
```

One of the objects defined in `java.lang` is the String object, whose full reference is

```
java.lang.String
```

To access one of its methods, you use an invocation syntax with which you are already familiar:

```
java.lang.String.methodName([parameters])
```

To demonstrate accessing Java from JavaScript, I call upon one of Java's String object methods, `java.lang.String.equalsIgnoreCase()`, to compare two strings. Equivalent ways are available for accomplishing the same task in JavaScript (for example, comparing both strings in their `toUpperCase()` or `toLowerCase()` versions), so don't look to this Java demonstration for some great new powers along these lines.

Before you can work with data in Java, you have to construct a new object. Of the many ways to construct a new String object in Java, you will use the one that accepts the actual string as the parameter to the constructor:

```
var mainString = new java.lang.String("TV Guide")
```

At this point, your JavaScript variable, `mainString`, contains a reference to the Java object. From here, you can call this object's Java methods directly:

```
var result = mainString.equalsIgnoreCase("tv Guide")
```

Even from JavaScript, you can use Java classes to create objects that are Java arrays and access them via the same kind of array references (with square brackets) as JavaScript arrays. The more you work with these two languages, the more you will see they have in common.

✦   ✦   ✦

Advanced Event Handling

Once an HTML page loads, virtually nothing happens in the page without events. System and user actions make things happen, especially if those events trigger JavaScript functions. Navigator 4 extends the event mechanism that has been in scriptable browsers since the beginning, providing not only more events, but also a more sophisticated way of trapping and responding to events. This chapter focuses on the details of this new mechanism to help you understand how and when to use it in your pages.

A good deal of the imperative for implementing a deeper event mechanism came from Dynamic HTML. The possibility of hiding and showing any number of positionable elements on the screen — each of which has its own complement of event-driven document elements — is a great advantage to managing event handling across the application on a more global scale. The new event model is very good at helping with this.

The "Other" Event Object

In Chapter 33, you saw the basics of the event object. That was the event object with a lowercase "e," which is generated each time an event fires in response to some action. But an Event object with a capital "E" also exists. This object behaves like the Math object, which is always around and has some handy properties and methods ready for our scripts to use at any time. The Event object provides a series of properties (and no methods) that event handling routines use as constants.

The Event object's properties are divided into two groups. One group consists of four values representing modifier keys on the keyboard (Alt, Ctrl, Shift, Meta). The Meta key is the new Windows key on Windows computers; it's the Command (⌘) key on the Mac. You may recall seeing these constants used to determine whether a mouse event was fired with one or more of those keys pressed at the same time, as in the following example.

```
function doEvent(evt) {
      if (evt.modifiers & Event.ALT_MASK) {
          statements for Alt key handling
      }
}
```

Names for the properties are all uppercase and must be retrieved in a reference with the Event object (`Event.ALT_MASK`, `Event.CONTROL_MASK`, `Event.SHIFT_MASK`, and `Event.META_MASK`). The other group of properties contains a large number of constants that represent event types. There exists one property for each event type used by objects in the document object model (and some events that have not yet been defined for objects, but likely will be in the future). For example, the `Event.CLICK` property is the way a script refers to a generic click event for some event-related methods.

Actual values for these properties are integer values. The integer values are of little use to your scripts, but you are free to substitute the integer values for the constant properties if you like. I won't bother listing the values here, but you can use a `for...in` loop construction with the Event object to obtain a list for yourself.

Capturing Events

The common way of assigning an event handler to an object is to use an event handler attribute in the HTML tag of the intended target of the event. But in Navigator 4, the mouse or keyboard event you assign to be captured by that attribute does not go directly to that object. Instead, the event passes through objects higher up the document object hierarchy. For example, if you define an `onClick=` event handler for a form button and the user clicks on that button, the click event first passes through the window object and the document object before reaching the button. If the button was in a form contained by a document inside a layer, the event passes through the window, main window document, layer object, and the layer's document before finally reaching the button. All of this event traveling occurs in less than a blink of an eye, so events don't seem any slower to react in Navigator 4 than they do in earlier scriptable browsers.

A quick check of the object listings for windows, documents, and layers in Appendix B reveals that these objects don't include event handlers for most of the user interactivity events that come from the user working the mouse or keyboard. But you can assign such an event handler to one of these "higher-up" objects, provided you also specifically instruct one or more of these objects to intercept events on their way to their targets. Moreover, you must instruct these objects to intercept events of a particular type, rather than all events.

Enabling event capture

All three objects just mentioned — window, document, and layer — have a `captureEvents()` method in their definitions. This is the method you use to enable event capture at any of those object levels. The method requires one or more parameters, which are the event types (as supplied by the Event object constants) that the object should capture, while letting all others pass untouched.

For example, if you want the window object to capture all keyPress events, you would include the following statement in a script that executes as the page loads:

```
window.captureEvents(Event.KEYPRESS)
```

If you want the window to capture multiple event types, string the event type constants together, separated by the pipe character:

```
window.captureEvents(Event.KEYPRESS | Event.CLICK)
```

Now you must assign an action to the event at the window's level for each event type. More than likely, you will have defined functions to execute for the event. Assign a function reference to the event handler by setting the handler property of the window object:

```
window.onKeyPress = processKeyEvent
window.onClick = processClickEvent
```

Hereafter, if a user clicks on a button or types into a field inside that window, the events will be processed by their respective window-level event handler functions.

Turning off event capture

Once you have enabled event capture for a particular event type in a document, that capture remains in effect until the page unloads or you specifically disable the capture. You can turn off event capture for each event via the window, document, or layer releaseEvents() method. This method takes the same kind of parameters—Event object type constants—as the captureEvents() method.

The act of releasing an event type simply means that events go directly to their intended targets without stopping elsewhere for processing, even if an event handler for the higher-level object is still defined. And because you can release individual event types based on parameters set for the releaseEvents() method, other events being captured are not affected by the release of others.

To demonstrate not only the captureEvents() and releaseEvents() methods, but other event model techniques, I present a series of several versions of the same document. Each version will implement an added feature to help you experience the numerous interactions among events and event handling methods. The document merely contains a few buttons, plus some switches to enable and disable various methods being demonstrated in the section. A layer object is also thrown into the mixture because a lot of impetus for capturing and modifying event handling comes from application of layers in a document.

Listing 39-1 is the first example, which shows the basic event capture and release from the outermost document level. A checkbox lets you enable or disable the document-level capture of click events (all checkboxes in these examples use onMouseUp= event handlers to avoid getting in the way of tracing click events). Because all click events are being captured by the outermost document, even clicks to the layer's buttons get trapped by the outermost document when captureEvents() is set.

Listing 39-1: **Event Capture and Release**

```
<HTML>
<HEAD>
<SCRIPT LANGUAGE="JavaScript">
function setDocCapture(enable) {
      if (!enable) {
          document.captureEvents(Event.CLICK)
      } else {
          document.releaseEvents(Event.CLICK)
      }
}
function doMainClick(e) {
      if (e.target.type == "button") {
          alert("Captured in top document")
      }
}
document.captureEvents(Event.CLICK)
document.onclick=doMainClick
</SCRIPT>
</HEAD>
<BODY>
<B>Basic document-level capture of Event.CLICK</B>
<HR>
<FORM>
<INPUT TYPE="checkbox" onMouseUp="setDocCapture(this.checked)"
CHECKED>Enable Document Capture
<HR>
<INPUT TYPE="button" VALUE="Button 'main1'" NAME="main1"
      onClick="alert('Event finally reached Button:' + this.name)">
</FORM>

<LAYER ID="layer1" LEFT=200 TOP=150 BGCOLOR="coral">
<HEAD>
</HEAD>
<BODY>
<FORM>
<BR><P><INPUT TYPE="button" VALUE="Button 'layerButton1'"
      NAME="layerButton1"
      onClick="alert('Event finally reached Button:' +
this.name)"></P>
<P><INPUT TYPE="button" VALUE="Button 'layerButton2'"
      NAME="layerButton2"
      onClick="alert('Event finally reached Button:' +
this.name)"></P>
</FORM>
</BODY>
</LAYER>

</BODY>
</HTML>
```

With document-level event capture turned on (the default), all click events are trapped by the document's onclick event handler property, a function that alerts the user that the event was captured by the top document. Because all click events for buttons are trapped there, even click events of the layer's buttons are trapped at the top.

In Listing 39-2, I add some code (shown in boldface) that lets the layer object capture click events whenever the outer document event capture is turned off. Inside the <LAYER> tag, a script sets the layer to capture click events. Therefore, if you disable the outer document capture, the click event goes straight to the main1 button and to the layer event capture. Event capture in the layer object prevents the events from ever reaching the buttons in the layer, unless you disable event capture for both the document and the layer.

Listing 39-2: **Document and Layer Event Capture and Release**

```
<HTML>
<HEAD>
<SCRIPT LANGUAGE="JavaScript">
function setDocCapture(enable) {
        if (!enable) {
            document.captureEvents(Event.CLICK)
        } else {
            document.releaseEvents(Event.CLICK)
        }
}
function setLayerCapture(enable) {
        if (!enable) {
            document.layer1.captureEvents(Event.CLICK)
        } else {
            document.layer1.releaseEvents(Event.CLICK)
        }
}
function doMainClick(e) {
        if (e.target.type == "button") {
            alert("Captured in main.html")
        }
}
document.captureEvents(Event.CLICK)
document.onclick=doMainClick
</SCRIPT>
</HEAD>
<BODY>
<B>Document-level and/or Layer-level capture of Event.CLICK</B>
<HR>
<FORM>
<INPUT TYPE="checkbox" onMouseUp="setDocCapture(this.checked)"
CHECKED>Enable Document Capture
<INPUT TYPE="checkbox" onMouseUp="setLayerCapture(this.checked)"
CHECKED>Enable Layer Capture
<HR>
<INPUT TYPE="button" VALUE="Button 'main1'" NAME="main1"
```

(continued)

Listing 39-2 *(continued)*

```
            onClick="alert('Event finally reached Button:' + this.name)">
</FORM>

<LAYER ID="layer1" LEFT=200 TOP=150 BGCOLOR="coral">
<HEAD>
<SCRIPT LANGUAGE="JavaScript">
function doLayerClick(e) {
        if (e.target.type == "button") {
            alert("Captured in layer1")
        }
}
layer1.captureEvents(Event.CLICK)
layer1.onclick=doLayerClick
</SCRIPT>
</HEAD>
<BODY>
<FORM>
 layer1<BR><P><INPUT TYPE="button" VALUE="Button 'layerButton1'"
        NAME="layerButton1"
        onClick="alert('Event finally reached Button:' +
this.name)"></P>
<P><INPUT TYPE="button" VALUE="Button 'layerButton2'"
        NAME="layerButton2"
        onClick="alert('Event finally reached Button:' +
this.name)"></P>
</FORM>
</BODY>
</LAYER>

</BODY>
</HTML>
```

Passing events toward their targets

If you capture a particular event type, your script may need to perform some limited processing on that event before letting it reach its intended target. For example, perhaps you want to do something special if a user clicks on an element with the Shift metakey pressed. In that case, the function that handles the event at the document level will inspect the event's modifiers property to determine if the Shift key was pressed at the time of the event. If the Shift key was not pressed, you want the event to continue on its way to the element that the user clicked on.

To let an event pass through the object hierarchy to its target, you use the routeEvent() method, passing as a parameter the event object being handled in the current function. A routeEvent() method does not guarantee that the event will reach its intended destination, because another object in between may have event capturing for that event type turned on and will intercept the event. That object, too, can let the event pass through with its own routeEvent() method.

Listing 39-3 demonstrates event routing by adding onto the document being built in previous examples. While the clickable button objects are the same, additional powers are added to the document and layer function handlers that process events that come their way. For each of these event-capturing objects, you have additional checkbox settings to allow or disallow events from passing through once they've been processed by each level.

The default settings for the checkboxes are like the ones in Listing 39-2, where event capture (for the click event) is set for both the document and layer objects. A click on any button causes the document object's event handler to process, and none other. But if you then enable the checkbox that lets the event continue, you find that click events on the layer buttons cause alerts to display from both the document and layer object event handler functions. If you then also let events continue from the layer object, a click on the button displays a third alert, showing that the event has reached the buttons. Because the main1 button is not in the layer, none of the layer object event handling settings affect its behavior.

Listing 39-3: **Capture, Release, and Route Events**

```
<HTML>
<HEAD>
<SCRIPT LANGUAGE="JavaScript">
function setDocCapture(enable) {
        if (!enable) {
            document.captureEvents(Event.CLICK)
        } else {
            document.releaseEvents(Event.CLICK)
            document.forms[0].setDocRte.checked = false
            docRoute = false
        }
}
function setLayerCapture(enable) {
        if (!enable) {
            document.layer1.captureEvents(Event.CLICK)
        } else {
            document.layer1.releaseEvents(Event.CLICK)
            document.forms[0].setLyrRte.checked = false
            layerRoute = false
        }
}
var docRoute = false
var layerRoute = false
function setDocRoute(enable) {
        docRoute = !enable
}
function setLayerRoute(enable) {
        layerRoute = !enable
}
function doMainClick(e) {
        if (e.target.type == "button") {
            alert("Captured in main.html")
```

(continued)

Listing 39-3 *(continued)*

```
            if (docRoute) {
                routeEvent(e)
            }
        }
    }
}
document.captureEvents(Event.CLICK)
document.onclick=doMainClick
</SCRIPT>
</HEAD>
<BODY>
<B>Capture, Release, and Routing of Event.CLICK</B>
<HR>
<FORM>
<INPUT TYPE="checkbox" NAME="setDocCap"
onMouseUp="setDocCapture(this.checked)" CHECKED>Enable Document
Capture 
<INPUT TYPE="checkbox" NAME="setDocRte"
onMouseUp="setDocRoute(this.checked)">And let event continue<P>
<INPUT TYPE="checkbox" NAME="setLyrCap"
onMouseUp="setLayerCapture(this.checked)" CHECKED>Enable Layer
Capture 
<INPUT TYPE="checkbox" NAME="setLyrRte"
onMouseUp="setLayerRoute(this.checked)">And let event continue
<HR>
<INPUT TYPE="button" VALUE="Button 'main1'" NAME="main1"
        onClick="alert('Event finally reached Button:' + this.name)">
</FORM>

<LAYER ID="layer1" LEFT=200 TOP=150 BGCOLOR="coral">
<HEAD>
<SCRIPT LANGUAGE="JavaScript">
function doLayerClick(e) {
        if (e.target.type == "button") {
            alert("Captured in layer1")
            if (layerRoute) {
                routeEvent(e)
            }
        }
}
layer1.captureEvents(Event.CLICK)
layer1.onclick=doLayerClick
</SCRIPT>
</HEAD>
<BODY>
<FORM>
 layer1<BR><P><INPUT TYPE="button" VALUE="Button 'layerButton1'"
        NAME="layerButton1"
        onClick="alert('Event finally reached Button:' +
this.name)"></P>
<P><INPUT TYPE="button" VALUE="Button 'layerButton2'"
```

```
        NAME="layerButton2"
        onClick="alert('Event finally reached Button:' +
this.name)"></P>
</FORM>
</BODY>
</LAYER>

</BODY>
</HTML>
```

In some cases, your scripts need to know if an event passed onward by `routeEvent()` method activated a function that returns a value. This is especially true if your event must return a `true` or `false` value to let an object know if it should proceed with its default behavior (for example, whether a link should activate its `HREF` attribute URL or cancel when the event handler evaluates to `return true` or `return false`). When a function is invoked by the action of a `routeEvent()` method, the return value of the destination function is passed back to the `routeEvent()` method. That value, in turn, can be returned to the object that originally captured the event.

Event traffic cop

The last scenario is one in which a higher-level object captures an event and directs the event to a particular object elsewhere in the hierarchy. For example, you could have a document-level event handler function direct every click event whose modifiers property indicates that the Alt key was pressed to a Help button object whose own `onClick=` event handler displays a help panel (perhaps shows an otherwise hidden layer).

You can redirect an event to any object via the `handleEvent()` method. This method works differently from the others described in this chapter, because the object reference of this method is the reference of the object to handle the event (with the event object being passed as a parameter like the other methods). As long as the target object has an event handler defined for that event, it will process the event as if it had received the event directly from the system (even though the event object's `target` property may be some other object entirely).

To demonstrate how this event redirection works, Listing 39-4 includes the final additions to the document being built in this chapter. It includes mechanisms that allow all click events to be sent directly to the second button in the layer (layerButton2). The previous interaction with document and layer event capture and routing is still intact, although you cannot have event routing and redirection on at the same time.

The best way to see event redirection at work is to enable both document and layer event capture (the default settings). When you click the main1 button, the event reaches only as far as the document-level capture handler. But if you then turn on the Send event to 'layerButton2' checkbox associated with the document level, a click of the main1 button reaches both the document-level event handler and layerButton2, even though the main1 button is not anywhere near the layer button in the document object hierarchy. Click other checkboxes to work with the interaction of event capturing, routing, and redirection.

Listing 39-4: **Redirecting Events**

```
<HTML>
<HEAD>
<SCRIPT LANGUAGE="JavaScript">
function setDocCapture(enable) {
      if (!enable) {
         document.captureEvents(Event.CLICK)
      } else {
         document.releaseEvents(Event.CLICK)
         document.forms[0].setDocRte.checked = false
         docRoute = false
      }

}
function setLayerCapture(enable) {
      if (!enable) {
         document.layer1.captureEvents(Event.CLICK)
      } else {
         document.layer1.releaseEvents(Event.CLICK)
         document.forms[0].setLyrRte.checked = false
         layerRoute = false
      }
}
var docRoute = false
var layerRoute = false
function setDocRoute(enable) {
      docRoute = !enable
      document.forms[0].setDocShortCircuit.checked = false
      docShortCircuit = false
}
function setLayerRoute(enable) {
      layerRoute = !enable
      document.forms[0].setLyrShortCircuit.checked = false
      layerShortCircuit = false
}

var docShortCircuit = false
var layerShortCircuit = false
function setDocShortcut(enable) {
      docShortCircuit = !enable
      if (docShortCircuit) {
         document.forms[0].setDocRte.checked = false
         docRoute = false
      }
}
function setLayerShortcut(enable) {
      layerShortCircuit = !enable
      if (layerShortCircuit) {
         document.forms[0].setLyrRte.checked = false
         layerRoute = false
      }
```

```
      }

function doMainClick(e) {
        if (e.target.type == "button") {
            alert("Captured in main.html")
            if (docRoute) {
                routeEvent(e)
            } else if (docShortCircuit) {

document.layer1.document.forms[0].layerButton2.handleEvent(e)
            }
        }
}
document.captureEvents(Event.CLICK)
document.onclick=doMainClick
</SCRIPT>
</HEAD>
<BODY>
<B>Redirecting Event.CLICK</B>
<HR>
<FORM>
<INPUT TYPE="checkbox" NAME="setDocCap"
onMouseUp="setDocCapture(this.checked)" CHECKED>Enable Document
Capture 
<INPUT TYPE="checkbox" NAME="setDocRte"
onMouseUp="setDocRoute(this.checked)">And let event continue
<INPUT TYPE="checkbox" NAME="setDocShortCircuit"
onMouseUp="setDocShortcut(this.checked)">Send event to
'layerButton2'<P>
<INPUT TYPE="checkbox" NAME="setLyrCap"
onMouseUp="setLayerCapture(this.checked)" CHECKED>Enable Layer
Capture 
<INPUT TYPE="checkbox" NAME="setLyrRte"
onMouseUp="setLayerRoute(this.checked)">And let event continue
<INPUT TYPE="checkbox" NAME="setLyrShortCircuit"
onMouseUp="setLayerShortcut(this.checked)">Send event to
'layerButton2'<P>
<HR>
<INPUT TYPE="button" VALUE="Button 'main1'" NAME="main1"
        onClick="alert('Event finally reached Button:' + this.name)">
</FORM>

<LAYER ID="layer1" LEFT=200 TOP=200 BGCOLOR="coral">
<HEAD>
<SCRIPT LANGUAGE="JavaScript">
function doLayerClick(e) {
        if (e.target.type == "button") {
            alert("Captured in layer1")
            if (layerRoute) {
                routeEvent(e)
            } else if (layerShortCircuit) {
                document.forms[0].layerButton2.handleEvent(e)
```

(continued)

Listing 39-4 *(continued)*

```
            }
        }
}
layer1.captureEvents(Event.CLICK)
layer1.onclick=doLayerClick
</SCRIPT>
</HEAD>
<BODY>
<FORM>
 layer1<BR><P><INPUT TYPE="button" VALUE="Button 'layerButton1'"
        NAME="layerButton1"
        onClick="alert('Event finally reached Button:' +
this.name)"></P>
<P><INPUT TYPE="button" VALUE="Button 'layerButton2'"
        NAME="layerButton2"
        onClick="alert('Event finally reached Button:' +
this.name)"></P>
</FORM>
</BODY>
</LAYER>

</BODY>
</HTML>
```

Modifying events

A desirable capability in some scenarios would be to modify events while they are on their way to their intended targets. For example, you could capture the keyPress event for a text box, and make sure that all letters are converted to uppercase before the characters appear in the box.

Unfortunately, Netscape's event model in Navigator 4 does not support this possibility. This feature may be available in the future, but it will also probably require signed scripts. Changing an event's data could be construed as a security risk. Internet Explorer 4, however, does allow for modifying such items as a keyboard event's character without any added security.

Dueling Event Models

For their level 4 browsers, Netscape and Microsoft have gone their separate ways in expanding an event model to support requirements of flexible Dynamic HTML. While both support the standard event handler mechanism for virtually all objects in the Netscape document object model (except the Netscape-specific layer object), that is where their similarity ends.

Microsoft's document object model turns practically anything that has HTML tags around it into an object capable of supporting one or more events. In other words, you can assign an onClick= event handler to an <H1>-tagged object.

Another significant discrepancy is in the way events can ripple through the document object hierarchy. Navigator 4 has events trickling down from the window object; Internet Explorer 4 has events bubbling up from the object to the window. As a result of these differing event approaches, it is not an easy task to create a single document that meets the event programming needs of both browsers. For some applications, however, your scripts can perform a bit of browser-specific branching to achieve the same goal. I show you two examples for working with click and keyPress events.

Cross-platform modifier key check

Listing 39-5 is an enhanced version of a listing from Chapter 33's discussion of the event object's modifiers property. User interaction is unchanged: You can click a link, type into a text box, and click a button while holding down any combination of modifier keys. A series of four checkboxes representing the four modifier keys is at the bottom. As you click or type, the checkbox(es) of the pressed modifier key(s) become checked.

Listing 39-5: **Checking Events for Modifier Keys**

```
<HTML>
<HEAD>
<TITLE>Modifiers Event Properties</TITLE>
<SCRIPT LANGUAGE="JavaScript">
var isNav4, isIE4
if (parseInt(navigator.appVersion.charAt(0)) >= 4) {
        var isNav4 = (navigator.appName == "Netscape") ? true : false
        var isIE4 = (navigator.appName.indexOf("Microsoft" != -1)) ?
true : false
}

function checkMods(evt) {
        var form = document.forms[0]
        if (isNav4) {
            form.modifier[0].checked = evt.modifiers & Event.ALT_MASK
            form.modifier[1].checked = evt.modifiers & Event.CONTROL_MASK
            form.modifier[2].checked = evt.modifiers & Event.SHIFT_MASK
            form.modifier[3].checked = evt.modifiers & Event.META_MASK
        } else if (isIE4) {
            form.modifier[0].checked = window.event.altKey
            form.modifier[1].checked = window.event.ctrlKey
            form.modifier[2].checked = window.event.shiftKey
            form.modifier[3].checked = false
        }
        return false
}
</SCRIPT>
</HEAD>
<BODY>
<B>Event Modifiers</B>
<HR>
```

(continued)

Listing 39-5 *(continued)*

```
<P>Hold one or more modifier keys and click on
<A HREF="javascript:void(0)" onMouseDown="return checkMods(event)">
this link</A> to see which keys you are holding.</P>
<FORM NAME="output">
Enter some text with uppercase and lowercase letters:
<INPUT TYPE="text" SIZE=40 onKeyPress="checkMods(event)"><P>
<INPUT TYPE="button" VALUE="Click Here" onClick="checkMods(event)"><P>
<INPUT TYPE="checkbox" NAME="modifier">Alt
<INPUT TYPE="checkbox" NAME="modifier">Control
<INPUT TYPE="checkbox" NAME="modifier">Shift
<INPUT TYPE="checkbox" NAME="modifier">Meta
</FORM>
</BODY>
</HTML>
```

The concern in this chapter's listing is that Internet Explorer 4 handles the modifier notification and event object differently from Navigator 4. To start the script, I define two variables to act as flags for Navigator 4 and Internet Explorer 4. If neither browser is running the script, both flags remain null.

Since all event handlers call the same checkMods() function, branching is needed only in this function. For Navigator 4, the event object is passed as a parameter (evt) whose modifiers property is Bitwise ANDed with an Event object constant for each modifier key. For Internet Explorer 4, the script checks the window.event object property for each of three modifiers (Internet Explorer 4 does not have a metakey property). The window.event object is automatically set when the event occurs, so the script can simply query its properties as needed.

Cross-platform key capture

To demonstrate keyboard events in both browsers, Listing 39-6 captures the key character being typed into a text box, as well as the mouse button used to click a link or button. As with the modifiers property example in Listing 39-5, Navigator 4 and Internet Explorer 4 have quite different property references to reach these values. In fact, whereas Netscape combines the features of key character code and mouse button into one event object property (depending upon the event type), Internet Explorer 4 has entirely separate properties for these values.

Listing 39-6: **Checking Events for Key and Mouse Button Pressed**

```
<HTML>
<HEAD>
<TITLE>Event.which Properties</TITLE>
<SCRIPT LANGUAGE="JavaScript">
var isNav4, isIE4
if (parseInt(navigator.appVersion.charAt(0)) >= 4) {
```

```
        var isNav4 = (navigator.appName == "Netscape") ? true : false
        var isIE4 = (navigator.appName.indexOf("Microsoft" != -1)) ?
true : false
}
function checkWhich(evt) {
      var theKey
      if (isNav4) {
         theKey = evt.which
      } else if (isIE4) {
          if (window.event.srcElement.type == "textarea") {
             status = window.event.keyCode
          } else if (window.event.srcElement.type == "button") {
             theKey = window.event.button
          }
      }
      status = theKey
      return false
}
</SCRIPT>
</HEAD>
<BODY>
<B>Event.which Properties</B> (results in the status bar)
<HR>
<FORM NAME="output">
<P>Click on
<A HREF="javascript:void(0)" onMouseDown="return checkWhich(event)">
this link</A> or this
<INPUT TYPE="button" VALUE="Button" onClick="checkWhich(event)">
with either mouse button (if you have more than one).</P>
Enter some text with uppercase and lowercase letters:
<TEXTAREA COLS=40 ROWS=4 onKeyPress="checkWhich(event)"
WRAP="virtual"></TEXTAREA><P>
</FORM>
</BODY>
</HTML>
```

The listing starts as Listing 39-5 does by setting flags for the browser type. All event processing is handled in the checkWhich() function. Navigator 4 extracts the value of the which property. No special processing is needed for object or event type, since all I'm interested in here is the value of the which property. But for Internet Explorer 4, the window.event object has different properties for the typed key and mouse button. Therefore, the script examines the type of element that initiated the event (via the window.event.srcElement property). I fashioned the demonstration to show how you can use both branches of the function to dump the key code value into a single variable (theKey) and then treat the variable independent of the browser that generated its value.

Note

Notice one other point about the event handler processing in Listing 39-6. The event handler function returns false. This lets the link use the returned value to cancel action on the link. But because both the button and textarea event handlers don't utilize the returned value (that is, they don't evaluate to return true or `return false`), the default behavior is to carry out the event after the event handler function has done its processing.

Future events

It is conceivable that the Document Object Model standard or recommendation will establish a common denominator that will enable a single script to handle more complex event management in future versions of the two browsers. In the meantime, it takes a fair amount of thought and planning to minimize the effect of the two largely incompatible models.

✦   ✦   ✦

Security and Signed Scripts

✦ ✦ ✦ ✦

In This Chapter

Why security is so important in Web programming

Navigator security mechanisms affecting JavaScript

How to use signed scripts

✦ ✦ ✦ ✦

The paranoia levels about potential threats to security and privacy on the Internet are at an all-time high. As more people rely on e-mail and Web site content for their daily lives and transactions, the fears will only increase for the foreseeable future (an indeterminate number of *Web Weeks*). As a jokester might say, though, "I may be paranoid, but how do I know someone really isn't out to get me?" The answer to that question is that you don't know, and such a person may be out there.

But Web software developers are doing their darnedest to put up roadblocks to those persons out to get you — hence, the many levels of security that pervade browsers such as Navigator. Unfortunately, these roadblocks also get in the way of scripters who have completely honest intentions. Designing a Web site around these barriers is one of the greatest challenges that many scripters face.

Battening Down the Hatches

When Navigator 2 first shipped to the world (way back in February 1996), it was the first browser released to include support for Java applets and scripting — two entirely different but often confused technologies. It didn't take long for clever programmers in the Internet community to find the ways in which one or the other technology provided inadvertent access to client computer information (such as reading file directories) and Web surfer activities (such as histories of where you've been on the Net and even the passwords you may have entered to access secure sites).

JavaScript, in particular, was the avenue that many of these programmers used to steal such information from Web site visitors' browsers. The sad part is that the same features that provide the access to the information were intentionally made a part of the initial language to aid scripters who would put those features to beneficial use in controlled environments, such as intranets. But out in the Wild Wide Web, a scripter could capture a visitor's e-mail address by having the site's home page surreptitiously send a message to the site's author without the visitor even knowing it.

Word of security breaches of this magnitude not only circulated throughout the Internet, but also reached both the trade and mainstream press. As if the security issues weren't bad enough on their own, the public relations nightmare compounded the sense of urgency to fix the problem. To that end, Netscape released two revised editions of Navigator 2. The final release of that generation of browser, Navigator 2.02, took care of the scriptable security issues by turning off some of the scripted capabilities that had been put into the original 2.0 version. No more capturing visitors' browser histories; no more local file directory listings; no more silent e-mail. Users could even turn off JavaScript support entirely if they so desired.

The bottom line on security is that scripts are prevented from performing automated processes that invade the private property of a Web author's page or a client's browser. Thus, any action that may be suspect, such as sending an e-mail message, requires an explicit action on the part of the user—clicking a Submit button, in this case—to carry it out. Security restrictions must also prevent a Web site from tracking your activity beyond the boundaries of that Web site.

When Worlds Collide

If a script tries to do something that is not allowed or is a potential personal security breach, Navigator reports the situation to the user. Figure 40-1, for instance, shows the warning a user gets from clicking a Submit button located in a form whose `ACTION` is set to a `mailto:` URL.

Another security error message often confuses scripters who don't understand the possible privacy invasions that can accrue from one window or frame having access to the URL information in another window or frame. Figure 40-2 shows the somewhat cryptic JavaScript error message that warns users of an attempt to access URL information from another frame when that URL is from a different Web site.

Despite the fact that a scripted Web site may have even loaded the foreign URL into the other frame, the security restrictions guard against unscrupulous usage of the ability to snoop in other windows and frames.

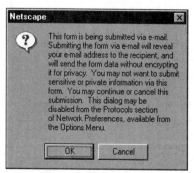

Figure 40-1: Navigator 3 e-mail warning

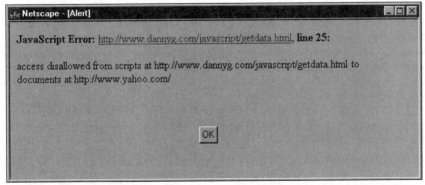

Figure 40-2: Attempting to retrieve a secure property from another server's document yields a script error showing the URLs of the documents containing your script and the secure information.

The Java Sandbox

Much of the security model for JavaScript is similar to that originally defined for Java applets. Applets had a potentially dangerous facility of executing Java code on the client machine. That is a far cry from the original deployment of the World Wide Web as a read-only publishing medium on the Internet. Here were mini-programs downloaded into a client computer that, if unchecked, could have the same access to the system as a local software program.

Access of this type would clearly be unacceptable. Imagine the dismay caused by someone clicking a link that said "Free Money," only to have the linked page download an applet that read or damaged local disk files unbeknownst to the user. In anticipation of pranksters, the designers of Java and the Java virtual machine built in a number of safeguards to prevent applets from gaining access to local machines. This mechanism is collectively referred to as the *sandbox*, a restricted area in which applets can operate. Applets cannot extend their reach outside of the sandbox to access local file systems and many sensitive system preferences. Any applet runs only while its containing page is still loaded in the browser. When the page goes away, so does the applet, without being saved to the local disk cache.

JavaScript adopted similar restrictions. The language provided no read or write access to local files beyond the highly regulated cookie file. Moreover, because JavaScript worked closer with the browser and its documents than applets typically do, the language had to build in extra restrictions to prevent browser-specific privacy invasions. For example, it was not possible for a script in one window to monitor the user's activity in another window, including the URL of the other window, if the page didn't come from the same server as the first window. Sometimes the restrictions on the JavaScript side are even more severe than in Java. For example, while a Java applet is permitted to access the network anytime after the applet is loaded, an applet is prevented from reaching out to the Net if the trigger for that transaction comes from JavaScript via LiveConnect (see Chapter 38). Only partial workarounds are available.

Neither the Java nor JavaScript security blankets were fully bug-free at the outset. Some holes were uncovered by the languages' creators and others in the community. To their credit, Sun and Netscape (and Microsoft for that matter) are quick to plug any holes that are discovered. While the plugs don't necessarily fix existing copies of insecure browsers out there, it means that a Bad Guy can't count on every browser to offer the same security hole for exploitation. That generally makes the effort not worth the bother.

Security Policies

Netscape has defined security mechanism under the term *policies*. This usage of the word mirrors that of institutions and governments: A policy defines the way potentially insecure or invasive requests are handled by the browser or scripting language. Navigator 4 includes two different security policies: *same origin* and *signed script* policies. The same origin policy dates back to Navigator 2, although there have been some additional rules added to that policy as Navigator has matured. The signed script policy is new with Navigator 4 and utilizes the state of the art in cryptographic signatures of executable code inside a browser, whether that code is a plug-in, a Java applet, or a JavaScript script. Navigator 3 included a partially implemented prototype of another policy known as data tainting. Signed scripts supersede data tainting, so if you encounter any writings about data tainting, you can ignore them since the technology is not being further developed.

By and large, the same origin policy is in force inside Internet Explorer 3 and after. Precise details may not match up with Navigator one-for-one, but the most common features are identical. The signed script policy is implemented entirely differently in Navigator 4 versus Internet Explorer 4. In fact, everything you read in this chapter about signed scripts applies only to Navigator 4. If the technology should become part of a future standard, both browsers will likely support it. But for now, no cross-platform implementation of signed scripts exists.

The Same Origin Policy

The "origin" of the same origin policy means the protocol and domain of a source document. If all of the source files currently loaded in the browser come from the same server and domain, scripts in any one part of the environment can poke around the other documents. Restrictions come into play when the script doing the poking and of the document being poked come from different origins. The potential security and privacy breaches this kind of access can cause put this access out of bounds within the same origin policy.

An origin is not the complete URL of a document. Consider the two popular URLs for Netscape's Web sites:

```
http://home.netscape.com
http://developer.netscape.com
```

The protocol for both sites is `http:`. And both sites share the same domain name: `netscape.com`. But the sites run on two different servers: `home` and `developer` (at least this is how the sites appear to browsers accessing them; the physical server arrangement may be quite different).

If a frameset contains documents from the same server at netscape.com, and all frames are using the same protocol, then they have the same origin. Completely open and free access to information, such as the location object properties, is available to scripts in any frame's document. But if one of those frames contains a document from the other server, their origins don't match. A script in a document from one server would display an "access disallowed" error alert message to a user if it tried to get the location property of that other document.

A similar problem occurs if you were creating a Web-based shopping service that displayed the product catalog in one window and displayed the order form from a secure server in another window. The order form, whose protocol might be `https:`, would not be granted access to the location object properties in a catalog page whose protocol is `http:`, even though both share the same server and domain name. In this latter case, however, a workaround lets you store the required data in a JavaScript global variable, which would be accessible to a script whose document doesn't share the same origin. This isn't a security hole, because you, as author of the catalog page, are intentionally exposing the data in a variable in anticipation of it being lifted by an external source.

Setting the document.domain

When both pages in an origin-protected transaction are from the same domain (but different servers or protocols), you can instruct JavaScript to set the `document.domain` properties of both pages to the domain that they share. When this property is set to that domain, the pages are treated as if from the same origin. Making this adjustment is safe, because JavaScript doesn't allow setting the `document.domain` property to any domain other than the origin of the document making the setting. See the `document.domain` property entry in Chapter 16 for further details.

Origin checks

Scattered throughout the language reference chapters are notes about items that undergo origin checks. For the sake of convenience, I list them all here to help you get a better feeling for the kind of information that is protected. The general rule is that any object property or method that exposes a local file in a user's system or can trace Web surfing activity in another window or frame undergoes an origin check. Failure to satisfy the same origin rule yields an "access disallowed" error message on the client's machine.

Window object checks

Navigator 4's `window.find()` method can extract information about the text content in another page. Such text could yield hints about the content or source of material in a foreign page. This method works only on pages from the same origin.

Location object checks

All location object properties are restricted to same origin access. Of all same origin policy restrictions, this one seems to interfere with well-meaning page authors' plans when they wish to provide a frame for users to navigate around the Web. Such access, however, would allow spying on your users.

Document object checks

A document object's properties are by necessity loaded with information about the content of that document. Just about every property other than the ones that specify color properties are off-limits if the origin of the target document is different from the one making the request:

```
anchors[]    lastModified
applets[]    length
cookie       links[]
domain       referrer
embeds       title
forms[]      URL
```

In addition, no normally modifiable document property can be modified if the origin check fails. This, of course, does not prevent you from using `document.write()` to write an entirely new page of content to the frame to replace a document from a different origin.

Layer object checks

While most of a layer's content is protected by the restrictions that apply to the document object inside, a layer object also has a potentially revealing `src` property. This is essentially similar to the `location.href` property of a frame. Thus the `src` property requires an origin check before yielding its information.

Form object checks

Form data is generally protected by the restriction to a document's `forms[]` array. But should a script in another window or frame also know the name of the form, that, too, won't enable access unless both documents come from the same origin. This restriction to a named form was added in Navigator 4.

Applet object checks

The same goes for named Java applets. A script cannot retrieve information about the class file name unless both documents are from the same origin (although the applet can be from anywhere).

LiveConnect access from a Java applet to JavaScript is not an avenue to other windows and frames from other origins. Any calls from the applet to the objects and protected properties described here undergo origin checks when those objects are in other frames and windows. The applet assumes the origin of the document that contains the applet, not the applet codebase.

Image object checks

While image objects are accessible from other origins, their `src` and `lowsrc` properties are not. These URLs could reveal some or all the URL info about the document containing them.

Linked script library checks

To prevent a network-based script from hijacking a local script library file, Navigator 4 prevents a page from loading a `file:` protocol library in the `SRC` attribute of a `<SCRIPT>` tag unless the main document also comes from a `file:` protocol source. If you are beginning to think that security engineers are a suspicious and paranoid lot, you are starting to get the idea. It's not easy to curb potential abuses of Bad Guys in a networked environment initially established for openness and free exchange of information among trusted individuals.

The Signed Script Policy

Just as there are excellent reasons to keep Web pages from poking around your computer and browser, there are equally good reasons to allow such access to a Web site you trust not to be a Bad Guy. To permit trusted access to the client machine and browser, Sun Microsystems and Netscape (in cooperation with other sources) have developed a way for Web application authors to identify themselves officially as authors of the pages and to request permission of the user to access well-defined parts of the computer system and browser.

The technology is called *object signing*. In broad terms, it means that an author can electronically lock down a chunk of computer code (whether it be a Java applet, a plug-in, or a script) with the electronic equivalent of a wax seal stamped by the author's signet ring. At the receiving end, a user is informed that a sealed chunk of code is requesting some normally protected access to the computer or browser. The user can examine the "seal" to see who authored the code and the nature of access being requested. If the user trusts the author not to be a Bad Guy, the user grants permission for that code to execute; otherwise the code does not run at all. Additional checks take place before the code actually runs. That electronic "seal" contains an encrypted, reduced representation of the code as it was locked by the author. If the encrypted representation cannot be re-created at the client end (it takes only a fraction of a second to check), it means the code has been modified in transit and will not run.

In truth, nothing prevents an author from being a Bad Guy, including someone you might normally trust. The point of the object signing system, however, is that a trail leads back to the Bad Guy. An author cannot sneak into your computer or browser without your explicit knowledge and permission.

Signed objects and scripts

A special version of the signed object technology is the one that lets scripts be locked down by their author and electronically signed. Virtually any kind of script in a document can be signed: a linked .js library, scripts in the document, event handlers, and JavaScript entities. As described later in this chapter, you must prepare your scripts for being signed, and then run the entire page through a special tool that attaches your electronic signature to the scripts within that page.

What you get with signed scripts

If you sign your scripts and the user grants your page permission to do its job, signed scripts open up your application to a long list of capabilities, some of which border on acting like genuine local applications. Many of the new capabilities come with the new language and object features of Navigator 4. Since the designers of this version knew that signed scripts would be available to authors, many more properties and actions have been exposed to authors.

The most obvious power you get with signed scripts is freedom from the restrictions of the origin policy. All object properties and methods that perform origin checks for access in other frames and windows become available to your scripts without any special interaction with the user beyond the dialog box that requests the one-time permission for the page.

Some operations that normally display warnings about impending actions — sending a form to a `mailto:` URL or closing the main browser window under script control — lose those warning dialog boxes if the user grants the appropriate permission to a signed script. Object properties considered private information, such as individual URLs stored in the history object and browser preferences, are opened up, including the possibility of altering browser preferences. Existing windows can have their chrome elements hidden. New windows can be set to be always raised or lowered, sized to very small sizes, or positioned offscreen. The dragDrop event of a window reveals its URL. All of these are powerful points of access, provided the user grants permission.

Again, however, I emphasize that these capabilities are accessible via Netscape's signed script policy only in Navigator 4 or later. Internet Explorer, at least through Version 4, does not support Netscape's signed script policy.

The Digital Certificate

Before you can sign a script or other object, you must apply for a *digital certificate*. A digital certificate (also called a *digital ID*) is a small piece of software that gets downloaded and bound to the Navigator 4 (or later) browser on a particular computer. Each downloaded digital certificate appears in the list of certificates under the "Yours" category in Navigator 4's Security Info preferences dialog window. If you have not yet applied for a certificate, the list is empty. When you sign a page with the certificate, information about the certificate is included in the file generated by the signing tool. This is how a user knows you are the author of the page — your identity appears in the security dialog box that requests permission of the user (see Figure 40-3).

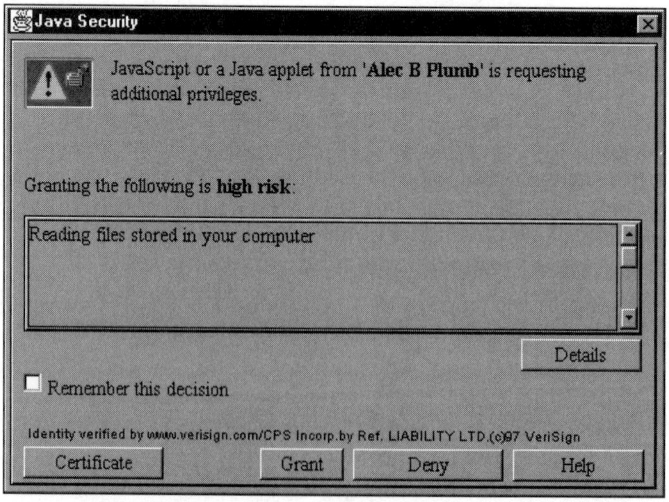

Figure 40-3: The security alert requesting permission of the user

A certificate makes you what is known as a *principal*. When a user loads a page that has signed "stuff" in it, a security alert displays a lot of information about the access being requested, including the principal who signed the script.

Certificates are issued by organizations established as *certificate authorities*. A certificate authority (known as a *CA* for short), or a certificate server authorized by a CA, registers applicants and issues certificates to individuals and software developers. When you register for a certificate, the CA queries you for identification information, which it verifies as best it can. The certificate that is issued to you identifies you as the holder of the certificate. Under the "Signers" category of the Security Info window are the certificate authorities loaded into the browser when you installed the browser. These are organizations that issue certificates. The CA of the organization that issues your certificate must be listed for you to sign scripts.

How to get a certificate

Navigator provides a first-level pointer to certificate authorities when you click Get a Certificate at the bottom of the "Yours" listing in the Security Info window. That button takes you to a help page at Netscape's Web site. On that page are several links to certificate authorities, most of which are outside of the United States. The primary CA, however, is a company named VeriSign, the first company to declare itself a certificate authority. While I do not endorse VeriSign as a CA over any other CA, it is the company I used for my signing certificate.

Working your way through the VeriSign Web site may be a confusing experience, because the company issues many different types of digital certificates that sound alike unless you pay close attention to their names. The kind of certificate you want to get is a Netscape Object Signing certificate (don't confuse this with a Microsoft Authenticode certificate). As of this writing, information for this kind of certificate could be found at `http://digitalid.verisign.com/nosintro.htm`.

The Netscape Object Signing certificate comes in two types. One, called a Class 2 Netscape Object Signing certificate, is for individual software authors and costs $20 per year; the other (Class 3) is for commercial software developers and costs $400 per year. Again, be certain you are signing up for the Netscape Object Signing certificate—the company offers other types of Class 2 and Class 3 certificates for software developers.

As an individual, you will be asked to fill out a form with some personal information, such as driver's license number and the usual name and address info. Payment for the individual certificate is made by credit card through a secure transaction at VeriSign's Web site. After VeriSign processes your application (sometimes in a matter of only a few minutes), the company sends you an e-mail message with a code number to enter into a special page at the VeriSign Web site to pick up your certificate. The act of picking up the certificate is actually downloading the certificate into your browser. Therefore, be sure you are using the Navigator 4 (or later) browser on the computer you will use to sign your pages with.

Verifying your certificate

After the download of the certificate, you can check the "Yours" listing in Navigator's Security Info dialog box. Your certificate should be listed there. Click View to see the details of the certificate, much of which will be gobbledygook if you're not a security guru. If you click the Verify button, the results will likely show you the certificate is not valid. In most versions of Navigator 4, this is bogus information.

You can, however, verify your certificate with VeriSign. Before you do this, you need to have your certificate's serial number handy. This number is a long hexadecimal number visible in the descriptive panel you see when you view the certificate. Unfortunately for the purpose of verifying the certificate, Netscape divides the number into individual hexadecimal pairs, separated by colons. You need to reduce that sequence to a contiguous string of hex characters with no colons (and I recommend turning the uppercase letters, if any, to lowercase).

Next, visit VeriSign's Digital ID center (`http://digitalid.verisign.com /status.htm`). Copy and paste (or type) the serial number into the field, and select the VeriSign Object Signing certificate authority for your class. Click Submit. If the certificate verifies, you will see a message indicating success. If not, double-check the serial number, or even use VeriSign's ID database search facility (linked from the same page) to locate your certificate in the company's database.

Activating the codebase principal

If you want to try out the capabilities available to signed scripts without purchasing a certificate (or without going through the signing process described later in this chapter during script development and debugging), you can set up your copy of Navigator to accept what is called a *codebase principal* in place of a genuine certificate. A codebase principal means that the browser accepts the source file as a legitimate principal, although it contains no identification as to the owner or certificate.

Depending on which version of Navigator 4 you are running, if you set up your browser for codebase principals, you may not be able to verify a certificate that is presented to you when accessing someone else's Web site — even if it is a valid cryptographic certificate. Therefore, even though secure requests won't slip past you silently, your Navigator won't necessarily have the protective shield it normally does to identify certificate holders beyond the URL of the code. Enable codebase principals only on a copy of Navigator that doesn't venture beyond your development environment. To activate codebase principals for your copy of Navigator 4, follow these steps:

1. Quit Navigator.

2. Search your hard disk for a Netscape support file named prefs.js.

3. Open the file in a text editor, and add the following line to the end of the file:

```
user_pref("signed.applets.codebase_principal_support", true);
```

4. Save the file.

To deactivate codebase principals, quit Navigator and remove the line from the file. Because Navigator rebuilds the preference file upon quitting, the entry will be in alphabetical order rather than at the end of the file where you first entered it. This preferences setting does not affect your ability to sign scripts with your certificate as described in the rest of this article. I also emphasize that this setting affects only *your* copy of Navigator.

Signing Scripts

The process of signing scripts entails some new concepts for even experienced JavaScript authors. An entirely new tool and Perl script are part of the process. You must also prepare the page that bears scripts so that the tool and the object signing facilities of the browser can do their jobs.

Signing tools

If you make your way through the Security section of Netscape's DevEdge Web site for developers (`http://developer.netscape.com`), you will eventually come upon a utility program called a JAR Packager. A JAR file is a special kind of zipped file collection that has been designed to work with the Navigator security infrastructure. The letters of the name stand for Java ARchive, which is a file format standard developed primarily by Sun Microsystems in cooperation with Netscape and others.

A JAR file's extension is .jar, and when it contains signed script information, it holds at least one file, known as the *manifest*, or list of items zipped together in the file. Among the items in the manifest is certificate information and data (a hash value code) about the content of the signed items at the instant they were signed. In the case of a single page containing signed scripts, the JAR file contains only the certificate and hash values of the signed scripts within the document. If the document links in an external .js script library file, that library file is also packaged in the JAR file. Thus, a page with signed scripts occupies space on the server for the HTML file and its companion JAR file.

Netscape offers the JAR Packager tool to assist with object signing. While it is a great tool for signing objects such as Java class files, at the time Navigator 4 first shipped, the JAR Packager was not yet capable of signing script-enabled pages.

To fill the gap, Netscape provided a separate utility named zigbert.exe. This program must be run from a command line (that is, from an MS-DOS window in Windows 95). But page signing is even more complex than simply running zigbert on related files. Netscape also provides a Perl script that automates the process of passing the requisite materials though zigbert and creating the JAR file. The bottom line, then, is that to sign a page, you need a Perl interpreter on your computer as well. I show you how to set this up and run it later in this section.

Preparing scripts for signing

It is up to the page author to signify which items in a page are script items that require signing. It is important to remember that if you want to sign even one script in a document, every script in the document must be signed. By "document," I mean an object model document. Since the content of a `<LAYER>` tag exists in its own document, you don't have to sign its scripts if they don't require it nor communicate with the signed scripts in the main document.

The first concept you have to master is recognizing what a script is. For signing purposes, a script is more than just the set of statements between a `<SCRIPT>` and `</SCRIPT>` tag boundary. An event handler—even one that calls a function living in a `<SCRIPT>` tag—is also a script that needs signing. So, too, is a JavaScript entity used to supply a value to an HTML tag attribute. Each one of these items is a script as far as script signing is concerned.

Your job is to mark up the file with special tag attributes that do two things: a) help zigbert know what items to sign in a file; and b) help the browser loading the signed document know what items to run through the hash routine again to compare against the values stored in the JAR file.

The ARCHIVE attribute

The first attribute goes in the first `<SCRIPT>` tag of the file, preferably near the very top of the document in the `<HEAD>` portion. This attribute is the `ARCHIVE` attribute, and its value is the name of the JAR file associated with the HTML file. For example

```
<SCRIPT LANGUAGE="JavaScript" ARCHIVE="myArchive.jar" ID="1">
```

You can add script statements to this tag, or immediately end it with a `</SCRIPT>` tag.

The zigbert utility uses the `ARCHIVE` attribute to assign a name to its archive output file. When the signed page loads into the visitor's browser, the attribute points to the file containing signed script information. It is possible to have more than one JAR archive file associated with a signed page. Typically, such a situation calls for a second JAR archive overseeing a confined portion of the page. That second archive file may even be embedded in the primary archive file, allowing a script segment signed by one principal to be combined with scripts signed by a different principal.

The ID attribute

More perplexing to scripters coming to script signing for the first time is the `ID` attribute. The `ID` attribute is merely a label for each script. Each script must have a label that is unique among all labels specified for a JAR archive file.

Like the `ARCHIVE` attribute, the `ID` plays a dual role. When you run your page through zigbert to sign the page, zigbert (with the help of the Perl script) scans the page for these `ID` attributes. When zigbert encounters one, it calculates a hash value (something like a checksum) on the content of the script. For a `<SCRIPT>` tag set, it is for the entire content of the tag set; for an event handler, it is for the event handler text. The hash value is associated with the `ID` attribute label and stored inside the JAR file. When the document loads into the client's browser, the browser also scans for the `ID` attributes and performs the same hash calculations on the script items. Then the browser can compare the ID/hash value pairs against the list in the JAR file. If they match, then the file has arrived without being modified by a Bad Guy (or a dropped bit in the network).

Most examples show ID attribute values to be numbers, but the attributes are actually strings. No sequence or relationship exists among `ID` attribute values: you can use the names of your favorite cartoon show characters, as long as no two `ID` attributes are given the same name. The only time the same ID attribute value might appear in a document is if another JAR file is embedded within the main JAR file. Even so, I recommend avoiding reusing names inside the same HTML file, no matter how many JAR files are embedded.

With one exception, each script item in a document must have its own ID attribute. The exception is a <SCRIPT> tag that specifies a SRC attribute for an external .js file. That file is part of the JAR file, so the browser knows it's a signed script.

For other <SCRIPT> tags, include the ID attribute anywhere within the opening tag, as follows:

```
<SCRIPT LANGUAGE="JavaScript" ID="3">
     statements
</SCRIPT>
```

For a function handler, the ID attribute comes after the event handler inside the object tag, as follows:

```
<INPUT TYPE="button" VALUE="Calculate" onClick="doCalc(this.form)"
ID="bart">
```

And for a JavaScript entity, the ID attribute must be specified in an empty <SCRIPT> tag immediately before the tag that includes the entity for an attribute value, as follows:

```
<SCRIPT ID="20">
<INPUT TYPE="text" NAME="date" VALUE=&{getToday()};>
```

Listing 40-1 shows a skeletal structure of a document that references a single JAR file and includes five signed scripts: One external .js file and four script items in the document itself. The fetchFile() function invokes a function imported from access.js. Notice that the ARCHIVE attribute appears in the very first <SCRIPT> tag in the document. This also happens to be a tag that imports an external .js file, so no ID attribute is required. If there were no external library file for this page, the ARCHIVE attribute would be located in the main <SCRIPT> tag, which also has the ID attribute. I arbitrarily assigned increasing numbers as the ID attribute values, but I could have used any identifiers. Notice, too, that each script has its own ID value. Just because an event handler invokes a function in a <SCRIPT> tag that has an ID value doesn't mean a relationship exists between the ID attribute values in the <SCRIPT> tag and in the event handler that invokes a function there.

Listing 40-1: **Basic Signed Script Structure**

```
<HTML>
<HEAD>
<TITLE>Signed Scripts Testing</TITLE>
<SCRIPT LANGUAGE="JavaScript" ARCHIVE="myArchive.jar"
SRC="access.js"></SCRIPT>
<SCRIPT LANGUAGE="JavaScript" ID="1">
function fetchFile(form) {
    form.output.value = getFile()
}
function newRaisedWindow() {
    // statements for this function
}
```

(continued)

Listing 40-1 *(continued)*

```
</SCRIPT>
</HEAD>
<BODY>
<FORM>
<TEXTAREA NAME="output" COLS=60 ROWS=10 WRAP="virtual"></TEXTAREA><BR>
<INPUT TYPE="button" VALUE="Read File" onClick="this.form.output.value
= '';
fetchFile(this.form);" ID="2"><BR>

<TEXTAREA NAME="input" COLS=60 ROWS=10 WRAP="virtual"> </TEXTAREA><BR>
<INPUT TYPE="button" VALUE="Save File"
onClick="setFile(this.form.input.value);" ID="3"><P>
<INPUT TYPE="button" VALUE="New Window…" onClick="newRaisedWindow();"
ID="4">
</FORM>
</BODY>
</HTML>
```

Running the page signer

The page signing Perl script relies on the zigbert command-line object signing tool (not available for the Macintosh). Getting all the programs, scripts, and files in their right places may be the hardest part of getting the page signer to work.

Because the page signer script requires a Perl interpreter, you will need to install Perl on your local machine if it is not already installed. You can download a freeware version of Perl from http://www.activeware.com/. Install it as you would any application, but be sure you modify your environment variable to include a path to the directory containing the perl.exe program (that is, in Windows, add the path of the Perl directory to the PATH command line in autoexec.bat).

Next, you must install zigbert and its supporting files. Download the installer at http://developer.netscape.com/library/documentation/signedobj/zigbert/index.htm. Place the expanded contents of the installer in a separate directory. If you also download the JAR Packager (not needed for signing scripts), you will probably want to keep all of these tools together. The zigbert utility comes with a special zipping and unzipping tool, which work well with zigbert. The page signing script is named signpages.pl. To help zigbert find its companion files, you should also add the path to zigbert's directory to your system's environment variables, like you did for Perl.

Before you run the script, you should have some key information handy, since it will be needed for parameters to the command you type to get the script going:

✦ Complete path to your certificate database (usually in a directory called Users/<yourname> in the Netscape directory). It is the directory containing the files Cert7.db and Key3.db.

✦ The complete name of your certificate as it appears in the "Yours" listing in Navigator 4's Security Info dialog box.

✦ Complete path names of the HTML file(s) you want to sign. I often copy the HTML files (and any supporting .js files) into the same directory as zigbert, thus alleviating the need to type the paths.

In Windows, you must open the MS-DOS window to run the script. For convenience, use the `CD` command to change the default directory to the one containing zigbert:

```
C:\>cd "Program Files\Netscape\JAR Packager\zigbert"
```

To run the script, type the command to launch the Perl interpreter with the signpages.pl file and parameters for the certificate directory (the `-d` switch) and certificate name (`-k`) in the following format:

```
perl signpages.pl -dcertDirectory -k"certName" somefile.html
```

The following example plugs in sample data for the placeholders:

```
perl signpages.pl -d"c:\Program Files\Netscape\Users\Dannyg" -k"Danny's
VeriSign Signer" testFile.html
```

When you run this script, you will see many lines of progress code, especially after zigbert starts working on the individual script items. After a successful run of the script, the JAR file named in the topmost `ARCHIVE` attribute of your HTML file will be in the directory with your HTML file. These two files can then be copied to your server for deployment.

Editing and moving signed scripts

The nature of the script signing process requires that even the slightest modification you make to a signed script source code requires re-signing the page. For this reason, enabling codebase principals while you create and debug your early code is a convenient alternative.

The rigid link between the hash value of a script element at both the signing and visitor loading times means that you must exercise care when shifting an HTML file that contains signed script elements between servers of differing operating systems. Windows, UNIX, and Macintosh have different ways of treating carriage returns. If you change the representation of an HTML source file when you move the source from, say, a Windows machine to a UNIX server, then the signature no longer works. However, if you perform a purely binary transfer of the HTML files, every byte is the same, and the signature should work. This operating system-specific text representation affects only how files are stored on servers, not how various client platforms interpret the source code.

Accessing Protected Properties and Methods

For the browser to allow access to protected properties or methods, it must have its privileges enabled. Only the user can grant permission to enable privileges, but it is up to your code to request those privileges of the user.

Gaining privileges

Navigator 4 comes with some Java classes that allow signed scripts and other signed objects to display the privilege request alert windows, and then turn on the privileges if the user clicks the "Grant" button. A lot of these classes show up in the `netscape.security` package, but scripters only work directly with one class and three of its methods:

```
netscape.security.PrivilegeManager.enablePrivilege(["targetName"])
netscape.security.PrivilegeManager.revertPrivilege(["targetName"])
netscape.security.PrivilegeManager.disablePrivilege(["targetName"])
```

The `enablePrivilege()` method is the one that displays the security alert for the user. Depending on the target submitted as a parameter to the method (discussed next), the alert displays relevant details about what kind of access the script is requesting.

If the user grants the privilege, script processing continues with the next statement. But if the user denies access, then processing stops, and the PrivilegeManager class throws a Java exception that gets displayed as a JavaScript error message. Later in this chapter I show you how to gracefully handle the user's denial of access.

Enabling a privilege in JavaScript is generally not as risky as enabling a Java applet. The latter can be more easily hijacked by an alien class to piggyback on the trusted applet's privileges. Even though the likelihood of such activity taking place in JavaScript is very low, it is always a good idea to turn privileges off after the statement that requires privileges. Use the `revertPrivilege()` method to temporarily turn off the privilege; another statement that enables the same privilege target will go right ahead without asking the user again. Disable privileges only when the script requiring privileged access won't be run again until the page reloads.

Specifying a target

Rather than opening blanket access to all protected capabilities in one blow, the Netscape security model defines narrow capabilities that are opened up when privileges are granted. Each set of capabilities is called a *target*. Netscape defines dozens of different targets, but not all of them are needed to access the kinds of methods and properties available to JavaScript. You will likely confine your targets to the nine discussed here.

Each target has associated with it a risk level (low, medium, or high) and two plain-language descriptions about the kinds of actions the target exposes to code. This information appears in the security privilege dialog box that faces a user the first time a particular signature requests privileges. All of the targets related to scripted access are medium or high risk, since they tend to open up local hard disk files and browser settings.

Netscape has produced two categories of targets: *primitive* and *macro*. A primitive target is the most limited target type. It usually confines itself to either reading or writing of a particular kind of data, such as a local file or browser preference. A macro target usually combines two or more primitive targets into a single target to simplify the user experience when your scripts require multiple kinds of access. For example, if your script must both read and write a local file, it could request privileges for each direction, but the user would be presented with a quick succession of two similar-looking security dialog boxes. Instead, you can use a macro target that combines both reading and writing into the privilege. The user sees one security dialog, which explains that the request is for both read and write access to the local hard disk.

Likely targets for scripted access include a combination of primitive and macro targets. Table 40-1 shows the most common script-related targets and the information that appears in the security dialog.

For each call to `netscape.security.PrivilegeManager.enablePrivilege()`, you specify a single target name as a string, as in

```
netscape.security.PrivilegeManager.enablePrivilege
("UniversalBrowserRead")
```

This allows you to enable, revert, and disable individual privileges as required in your script.

Table 40-1
Scripting-related Privilege Targets

Target Name Risk	Short Description	Long Description
Universal BrowserAccess High	Reading or modifying browser data	Reading or modifying browser data that may be considered private, such as a list of Web sites visited or the contents of Web forms you may have filled in. Modifications may also include creating windows that look like they belong to another program or positioning windows anywhere on the screen.
Universal BrowserRead Medium	Reading browser data	Access to browser data that may be considered private, such as a list of Web sites visited or the contents of Web page forms you may have filled in.
Universal BrowserWrite High	Modifying the browser	Modifying the browser in a potentially dangerous way, such as creating windows that may look like they belong to another program or positioning windows anywhere on the screen.

(continued)

Table 40-1 *(continued)*		
Target Name **Risk**	**Short Description**	**Long Description**
Universal FileAccess High	Reading, modifying, or deleting any of your files	This form of access is typically required by a program such as a word processor or a debugger that needs to create, read, modify, or delete files on hard disks or other storage media connected to your computer.
Universal FileRead High	Reading files stored in your computer	Reading any files stored on hard disks or other storage media connected to your computer.
Universal FileWrite High	Modifying files stored in your computer	Modifying any files stored on hard disks or other storage media connected to your computer.
Universal PreferencesRead Medium	Reading preferences settings	Access to read the current settings of your preferences.
Universal PreferencesWrite High	Modifying preferences settings	Modifying the current settings of your preferences.
Universal SendMail Medium	Sending e-mail messages on your behalf	

Blending Privileges into Scripts

The implementation of signed scripts in Navigator 4 protects scripters from many of the potential hazards that Java applet and plug-in developers must watch for. The chance that a privilege enabled in a script can be hijacked by code from a Bad Guy is very small. Still, it is good practice to exercise safe practices in case you someday work with other kinds of signed objects.

Keep the window small

Privilege safety is predicated on limiting exposure. The first technique is to enable only the level of privilege required for the protected access your scripts need. For example, if your script only needs to read a normally protected document object property, then enable the UniversalBrowserRead target rather than the wider UniversalBrowserAccess macro target.

The second is to keep privileges enabled only as long as the scripts need them enabled. If a statement calls a function that invokes a protected property, enable the privilege for that property in the called function, not at the level of the calling statement. If a privilege is enabled inside a function, the browser automatically reverts the privilege at the end of the function. Even so, if the privilege isn't needed all the way to the end of the function, I recommend manually reverting it once you are through with the privilege.

Think of the users

One other deployment concern focuses more on the user's experience with your signed page. You should recognize that the call to the Java PrivilegeManager class is a LiveConnect call from JavaScript. Because the Java virtual machine does not start up automatically when Navigator 4 does (as it did in Navigator 3), a brief delay occurs the first time a LiveConnect call is made in a session (the status bar displays "Starting Java..."). Such a delay might interrupt the user flow through your page if, for example, a click of a button needs access to a privileged property. Therefore, consider gaining permission for protected access as the page loads. Execute an `enablePrivilege()` and `revertPrivilege()` method in the very beginning. If Java isn't yet loaded into the browser, the delay will be added to the other loading delays for images and the rest of the page. Thereafter, when privileges are enabled again for a specific action, neither the security dialog nor the startup delay will get in the way for the user.

Also remember that users don't care for security dialog boxes to interrupt their navigation. If your page utilizes a couple of related primitive targets, enable at the outset the macro target that encompasses those primitive targets. The user gets one security dialog box covering all potential actions in the page. Then let your script enable and revert each primitive target as needed.

Examples

To demonstrate signed scripts in action, I show two pages that access different kinds of targets. One opens an always raised new window; the other reads and writes to a local file. In these two examples, no error checking occurs for the user's denial of privilege. Therefore, if you experiment with these pages (either with codebase principals turned on or signing them yourself), you will see the JavaScript error alert that displays the Java exception.

Accessing a protected window property

Listing 40-2 is a small document that contains one button. The button calls a function that opens a new window with the `alwaysRaised` parameter turned on. Setting protected `window.open()` parameters in Navigator 4 requires the UniversalBrowserWrite privilege target. Inside the function, the privilege is enabled only for the creation of the new window. For this simple example, I do not enable the privilege when the document loads.

Listing 40-2: Creating an AlwaysRaised Window

```
<HTML>
<HEAD>
<TITLE>Simple Signed Script</TITLE>
<SCRIPT LANGUAGE="JavaScript" ARCHIVE="myJar.jar" ID="1">
function newRaisedWindow() {

netscape.security.PrivilegeManager.enablePrivilege("UniversalBrowser
Write")
        var newWindow =
window.open("","","HEIGHT=100,WIDTH=300,alwaysRaised")

netscape.security.PrivilegeManager.disablePrivilege("UniversalBrowser
Write")
        var newContent = "<HTML><BODY><B>It\'s good to be the
King!</B>"
        newContent += "<FORM><CENTER><INPUT TYPE='button' VALUE='OK'"
        newContent +=
"onClick='self.close()'></CENTER></FORM></BODY></HTML>"
        newWindow.document.write(newContent)
        newWindow.document.close()
}
</SCRIPT>
</HEAD>
<BODY>
<B>This button generates an always-raised new window.</B>
<FORM>
<INPUT TYPE="button" VALUE="New 'Always Raised' Window"
onClick="newRaisedWindow()" ID="2">
</BODY>
</HTML>
```

Listing 40-2 has two script items that need signing: the `<SCRIPT>` tag and the event handler for the button. Also, the `ARCHIVE` attribute points to the JAR file that contains the script signature.

Accessing local files

For the second example, shown in Listings 40-3 and 40-4, I demonstrate how to structure an HTML file that also loads a client-side library from a .js file. The page provides two textareas and two buttons. One button invokes the `setFile()` function from the .js file to save the contents of one textarea to a file that the user assigns in a standard Save As file dialog box. The other button displays a File Open dialog to let the user select a text file for display in the other textarea.

Listing 40-3: **HTML File for File Reading and Writing**

```
<HTML>
<HEAD>
<TITLE>Local File Reading and Writing</TITLE>
<SCRIPT LANGUAGE="JavaScript" ARCHIVE="fileExample.jar" SRC="filelib.js">
</SCRIPT>
<SCRIPT LANGUAGE="JavaScript1.2" ID="1">
netscape.security.PrivilegeManager.enablePrivilege("UniversalFileAccess
")
netscape.security.PrivilegeManager.revertPrivilege("UniversalFileAccess
")
</SCRIPT>
</HEAD>
<BODY>
<B>Reading and writing a text file on the client machine with signed
scripts.</B>
<HR>
<FORM>
Enter text to be saved to a local file:<BR>
<TEXTAREA NAME="toSave" COLS=40 ROWS=4 WRAP="virtual">
Mares eat oats and does eat oats.</TEXTAREA><BR>
<INPUT TYPE="button" NAME="Save" VALUE="Save As…"
onClick="setFile(this.form.toSave.value)" ID="2"><P>
<HR>
Open a text file to be viewed in the textarea:
<INPUT TYPE="button" NAME="Open" VALUE="Open File…"
onClick="this.form.fromOpen.value = getFile()" ID="3"><P>
<TEXTAREA NAME="fromOpen" COLS=40 ROWS=4 WRAP="virtual"></TEXTAREA>
</FORM>
</BODY>
</HTML>
```

The first <SCRIPT> tag is used to both specify the JAR file for the page and load in the external script library file (filelib.js). <SCRIPT> tags that load external files do not need an ID attribute, so none is added here. But in the next <SCRIPT> tag, I assign the ID of "1." Other ID attributes are assigned to the two button event handlers in the form.

This listing shows how to enable a macro target when the page loads. Because the functions in the external library rely on UniversalFileWrite and UniversalFileRead, I gain initial privilege from the user for both targets by requesting UniversalFileAccess privileges as the page loads.

Listing 40-4: **External Script Library (filelib.js)**

```
// filelib.js library file
function getFile() {
        // create frame for file dialog
        var frame = new java.awt.Frame()
        // create load-type dialog in frame, labeled "Open"
        var dlog = new java.awt.FileDialog(frame, "Open",
java.awt.FileDialog.LOAD)
        // bring the still invisible frame to the front, then show it
        dlog.toFront()
        dlog.show()
        // capture both path and file selected by user; assemble into
one file pathname
        var filename = dlog.getDirectory() + dlog.getFile()
        // we're about to read; enable privileges

netscape.security.PrivilegeManager.enablePrivilege("UniversalFileRead")
        // make Java calls to open stream for selected file;
        // load lines of the file into a text buffer
        var inputStream = new java.io.FileInputStream(filename)
        var reader = new java.io.BufferedReader(new
java.io.InputStreamReader(inputStream))
        var buffer = new java.lang.StringBuffer()
        while ((line = reader.readLine()) != null) {
            buffer.append(line + "\n")
        }
        // close up loose ends
        inputStream.close()

netscape.security.PrivilegeManager.disablePrivilege("UniversalFileRead"
)
        // send text read from file back to calling function
        return buffer
}
function setFile(str) {
        // create frame and dialog
        var frame = new java.awt.Frame()
        var dlog = new java.awt.FileDialog(frame, "Save As…",
java.awt.FileDialog.SAVE)
        // bring dialog to front and show it
        dlog.toFront()
        dlog.show()
        // capture path selected by user and file name entered into
dialog field
        var filename = dlog.getDirectory() + dlog.getFile()
        // turn on privileges for writing

netscape.security.PrivilegeManager.enablePrivilege("UniversalFileWrite"
)
        // do the Java stuff for writing the data to that file
        var outputStream = new java.io.FileOutputStream(filename)
```

```
        var writer = new java.io.BufferedWriter(new
java.io.OutputStreamWriter(outputStream))
        writer.write(str)
        // flush the queue and close everything up
        writer.flush()
        writer.close()
        outputStream.close()

netscape.security.PrivilegeManager.disablePrivilege("UniversalFileWrite
")
    }
```

Scripts for the two file access functions are considerably more complex, but that is only because they rely on LiveConnect to invoke many Java classes and methods for displaying file dialog boxes and opening and closing file streams. JavaScript offers no such capabilities, so it is convenient here to leverage off Java's capabilities. Of course you need to know a bit of Java to write such scripts. I've written two important functions for you, so you can use these as-is in your scripts.

It is important to study how the access privileges must be open for a longer time than the example in Listing 40-2. The scripts here rely on much more protected access to Java classes. At the same time, however, the privileges are turned on only when needed: Displaying the file dialog boxes is not, in and of itself, a protected action. But doing something with the file names and reaching out to the file system are protected actions and must have privileges enabled for them to work.

Handling Java Class Errors

Java's primary error mechanism is different from JavaScript's. Many Java class methods intentionally generate error messages so that other parts of the code can capture them and handle them gracefully. This approach is called *throwing an exception*. Not every exception is an error, per se. For example, if a user clicks the Deny button in a Navigator 4 security alert, the `netscape.security.Privilege.enablePrivilege()` method throws an error (named ForbiddenTargetException, because the user forbids access to the requested target). Because your script is calling this Java method through LiveConnect, no applet code intercepts the exception. You must do it in JavaScript.

The secret to catching Java exceptions is to define the global `onerror()` function in your script. Since a Java exception (or a JavaScript script error, for that matter) passes a description of the error as one of three parameters to the `onerror()` function, your scripts can look for unique words that the Java classes use to describe their exceptions. Then your function can treat individual exception types differently. If you fail to process these errors in a user-friendly way, users who perform perfectly acceptable operations, such as denying privileges, will see rather terrifying script errors.

Listing 40-5 shows an `onerror()` function that would be an excellent addition to the external code library shown in Listing 40-4 (in fact, this function is already included in the filelib.js file on the CD-ROM in this chapter's directory). The function handles all errors, including JavaScript errors. It assigns the incoming error message to a local variable (`errorMsg`). If the message contains the string "ForbiddenTargetException," the function knows that the user has denied access when presented with the security alert. Another kind of Java exception can also occur in accessing a disk for either the read or write operations in the script library of Listing 40-4. Therefore, this `onerror()` function treats the IOException with a special user-friendly message. In the end, all errors have a message to display, and they are shown in an alert. The function ends in a `return true` statement so that JavaScript will not show its regular error alert window.

Listing 40-5: **Error Handling**

```
function onerror(msg, URL, lineNum) {
      var errorMsg = msg
      if (msg.indexOf("ForbiddenTargetException") != -1) {
          errorMsg = "You have elected not to grant privileges to this
script."
      } else if (msg.indexOf("IOException") != -1) {
          errorMsg = "There was a problem accessing the disk."
      }
      alert(errorMsg)
      return true
}
```

Signed Script Miscellany

In this last section of the chapter, I list some of the more esoteric issues surrounding signed scripts. Three in particular are 1) how to allow unsigned scripts in other frames, windows, or layers to access signed scripts; 2) how to make sure your signed scripts are not stolen and reused; and 3) special notes about international text characters.

Exporting and importing signed scripts

JavaScript provides an escape route that lets you intentionally expose functions from signed scripts for access by unsigned pages. If such a function contains a trusted privilege without careful controls on how that privilege is used, the trust could be hijacked by a page that is not as well intentioned as yours.

The command for exposing this function is `export`. The following example exports a function named `fileAccess()`:

```
export fileAccess
```

A script in another window, frame, or layer can use the `import` command to bring that function into its own set of scripts:

```
import fileAccess
```

Even though the function is now also a part of the second document, it executes within the context of the original document, whose signed script governs the privilege. For example, if you exported a function that did nothing but enable a file access privilege, a Bad Guy who studies your source code could write a page that imports that function into a page that now has unbridled file access.

If you wish to share functions from signed scripts in unsigned pages loaded into your own frames or layers, avoid exporting functions that enable privileges. Other kinds of functions, if hijacked, can't do the same kind of damage as a privileged function can.

Locking down your signed pages

Speaking of hijacking scripts, it would normally be possible for someone to download your HTML and JAR archive files and copy them to another site. When a visitor comes to that other site and loads your copied page and JAR file, your signature is still attached to the scripts. While this may sound good from a copyright point of view, you may not want your signature to appear as coming from someone else's Web server. You can, however, employ a quick trick to ensure that your signed scripts work only on your server. By embedding the domain of the document in the code, you can branch execution so scripts work only when the file comes from your server.

The following script segment demonstrates one way to employ this technique:

```
<SCRIPT LANGUAGE="JavaScript1.2" ARCHIVE="myPage.jar" ID="1">
if (document.URL.match(/^http:\/\/www.myDomain.com\//)) {
        privileges statements execute only from my server
}
</SCRIPT>
```

This technique works only if you specify JavaScript 1.2 as the script language. Even though this branching code is visible in the HTML file, the hash value of your code is saved and signed in the archive. If someone modifies the HTML, the hash value that is recalculated when a visitor loads the page won't match the JAR file manifest, and the script signature fails.

International characters

While international characters are fine for HTML content, they should not be used in signed scripts. The problem is that international characters are often converted to other character sets for display. This conversion invalidates the signature, because the signed and recalculated hash values don't match. Therefore, do not put international characters in any signable script item. If you must include such a character, you can escape it, or put such scripts in unsigned layers.

✦   ✦   ✦

Scripting Cross-Platform Dynamic HTML

✦ ✦ ✦ ✦

In This Chapter

Introduction to
Dynamic HTML

The common
denominator of
DHTML functionality
across browsers

An interactive map
puzzle written for
cross-platform
deployment

✦ ✦ ✦ ✦

Level 4 browsers—Navigator 4 and Internet Explorer 4—
incorporate some of the latest World Wide Web
technologies for display and control over Web page content.
Lumped together under the heading of Dynamic HTML
(DHTML), these technologies dramatically extend the simple
formatting of standard HTML that page authors have used for
years. As the installed base of level 4 browsers grows, the
competition among application authors will drive the desire
to provide more engaging and satisfying applications with
little added cost in download time for the user.

A lot of what the user gets with DHTML has previously
been accomplished only via Java applets and plug-ins, such
as ShockWave. Not that DHTML will eliminate these
technologies from the Web author's arsenal (DHTML doesn't
do sound or video, for example), but because DHTML can
accomplish much more of what authors look for in
assembling page content and layout without the long
downloads of applets or plug-in content, it becomes an
attractive way for nonprogrammers to spice up Web
applications.

Perhaps categorizing DHTML authors as
"nonprogrammers" is not quite right. DHTML also adds
significantly to the vocabulary required to incorporate
dynamic content into pages. Suddenly HTML becomes a lot
more programming than simply adding tags to existing
content. And if you want to do dynamic positioning of
elements, be prepared to put your JavaScript skills to use.

What is DHTML?

You can practically find as many definitions of Dynamic
HTML as there are people to ask. This is especially true if you
ask Netscape and Microsoft. Each company defines DHTML in
terms of the support its browser has for a variety of
technologies. My definition covers a broad range, because

DHTML is not really any one "thing." Instead it is an amalgam of several technologies, each of which has a standards effort in varying stages of readiness. The key technologies are as follows: Cascading Style Sheets (CSS1); Cascading Style Sheets-Positioning (CSS-P); Document Object Model (DOM); and client-side scripting.

To this list I also admit recent advances in downloadable font technology and Extensible Markup Language (XML), the latter opening the door to author-generated, page-specific HTML extensions that don't rely on standards bodies or browser support. Both of these are currently beyond the scope of a JavaScript-centered book.

Cascading Style Sheets (CSS1)

The "1" in the acronym for Cascading Style Sheets stands for "Level 1." As this book goes to press, a working draft for Level 2 (CSS2) has been released for public comment.

A style sheet defines a display characteristic for a document element. Any element contained by an HTML tag can be directed to adhere to one or more settings pertaining to the display of that content. For example, a paragraph of text (delimited by a <P>...</P> tag pair) might have a style sheet attached to it such that the right margin is wider than normal, its text color is blue, and a colorful border surrounds the entire chunk of text.

The combination of an HTML tag identifier and its style setting is called a *rule*. Components of a rule are the *selector* (the tag identifier, such as H1) and the *declaration*. A declaration itself has two components: A *property* name and a *value*, separated by a colon. For example, a common way to define a style sheet is inside a <STYLE> tag, as follows:

```
<STYLE TYPE="text/css">
      P {color:red}
</STYLE>
```

In this definition, the type of style sheet is specified as a Cascading Style Sheet type whose style specification is straight text. The rule establishes that all blocks surrounded by <P>...</P> tag pairs (the P selector) will have their text colored red. Here, the property being specified is color, and its value red. Notice that the definition is inside curly braces and that the property and its value are separated by a colon. This may take some getting used to after defining attribute-value pairs in HTML as separated by an equals sign. If you want to add another declaration to the same rule, you separate the first from the second by a semicolon, as follows:

```
<STYLE TYPE="text/css">
      P {color:red; font-size:14pt}
</STYLE>
```

The above style sheet tells the browser that every <P>-tagged block of text in the document (below this style definition in the document) is to be displayed in red at 14 points.

The CSS1 recommendation offers several ways to incorporate style sheets into a document, including linking in external documents that contain style sheet rules (very much like linking in an external .js script library). Other parts of the specification detail how you override a blanket rule with a tag-specific rule. For example, if a document were governed by the preceding paragraph rule, an individual paragraph in the document can have its own color with the following beginning tag:

```
<P STYLE="color:blue">
```

By changing only one property, the prevailing font size from the earlier rule applies to this paragraph as well.

Even more sophisticated parts of the CSS1 specification allow for creating subsets (classes) of each style. For example, if your document required several instances of two paragraph styles, you can define P-level rules for each, assigning each style a class name. Then, in the actual <P> tag where each document exists, specify the CLASS attribute so the browser knows which P-level rule to apply to the ensuing paragraph.

As mentioned earlier in the book, industry standards for Cascading Style Sheets is under the aegis of the W3C organization. As of this writing, CSS1 is a published recommendation, available at http://www.w3.org/pub/WWW/TR/REC-CSS1.

Both Navigator 4 and Internet Explorer 4 support CSS1 (Internet Explorer 3 also had some support for CSS), although neither implementation is flawless. While CSS1 is not necessarily dynamic (that is, once you lay out a page according to a style, that's as far as the specification goes), Internet Explorer 4 makes it truly dynamic. As explained in detail in Chapter 43, the content and style of each HTML tag can be changed on the fly from a script. Changes to the page that require rerendering of the page are handled well, with very fast reflowing of content. In this regard, the rendering engine of Internet Explorer 4 is superior to that of Navigator 4 (at least as of Navigator Version 4.04).

Netscape added another type of style sheet system to Navigator 4. Called JavaScript Style Sheets (JSS), this style sheet methodology's syntax more closely resembles JavaScript. It is covered in detail in Chapter 42.

Cascading Style Sheets-Positioning (CSS-P)

An entirely separate standards effort is assigned to the positioning of HTML elements on a page. The goal is to extend the syntactical framework of CSS1 so that items can be precisely positioned on a page. Without precise positioning of content, Web publishing is extremely crude compared to the current state of the art, desktop publishing (DTP). For content providers with experience in DTP, adapting carefully designed content to the Web is often a frustrating—and certainly limiting—experience.

Positioning encompasses more than simply defining a point on the page where an element is to start rendering itself. Built into the specification are properties for whether an element is visible or hidden and whether one element that overlaps another is visibly closer to the user's eye than elements behind it. With a syntax in place for setting these properties as the page loads, it is a small extension to making these properties visible to JavaScript. When that happens, the properties become truly dynamic, allowing for moving an element across the screen like an animation, and hiding or showing elements as needed.

Although the CSS-P recommendation is only at the working draft stage at the time of release of Navigator 4 and Internet Explorer 4, both browsers implement CSS-P, albeit not in exactly the same way. You can view the W3C draft at

`http://www.w3.org/pub/WWW/TR/WD-positioning-970131.html`. By the time
you read this, it is possible that a more recent draft or final recommendation will
have been published by W3C.

The truly dynamic nature of CSS-P will likely attract scripters. Most of the
discussion in this and the next two chapters focuses on CSS-P, rather than the less-
dynamic CSS1. Both, however, have a lot in common with basic property and value
pair syntax and structure.

Document Object Model (DOM)

Perhaps the most important piece of the DHTML puzzle is a specification for the
Document Object Model. I assign more weight to the DOM than to, say, CSS-P,
because it is the definition of a standard DOM that scripters will rely on for cross-
platform consistency in their scripts. An inconsistency among document object
models for Internet Explorer 3 and Navigator 3—particularly the lack of an Image
object in Internet Explorer 3—caused no little grief among scripters who
developed mouse rollover scripts in Navigator 3, only to have them cause script
errors for Internet Explorer 3 users.

Given the split evolution of document object models in Navigator and Internet
Explorer (especially with their divergence in level 4 versions), a recognized DOM
standard for scriptable objects will be difficult to achieve. The more each platform
has invested in the installed base of its existing document object model, the more
difficult it will be to reach a consensus, which may require rolling back features to
reach a scriptable common denominator.

Of all the standards efforts described in this chapter, the Document Object
Model is the least far along in its development. As of this writing, the most recent
document is a working draft of HTML-specific syntax. The W3C has assumed
responsibility for this standard. The earliest its results will reach browsers is
perhaps the level 5 versions of Navigator and Internet Explorer.

Client-side scripting

Scripting languages such as JavaScript provide the bridge between an author's
ideas for interactivity and the controllable elements on the page. I specify the
broader "client-side scripting" rather than JavaScript here, because future HTML
standards that accommodate scripting are leaving room for any language that a
browser wishes to support. Navigator, of course, supports only JavaScript. Internet
Explorer, on the other hand, supports its own version of JavaScript (JScript) and
VBScript (a derivative of Visual Basic). Because of its cross-platform support,
JavaScript is the predominant client-side scripting language today.

As discussed in Chapter 2, the core language aspects of JavaScript have been
standardized into a language called ECMAScript (after the ECMA standards body
that oversaw the effort). This specification (ECMA-262) is for the core language
that does not involve document objects, but rather language definitions for
constructs such as variables, data types, operators, and so on. Because Dynamic
HTML is all about scripting page elements (document objects), the core language
serves primarily as essential support for the entirety of JavaScript that deals with
the object model as well.

Cross-Platform DHTML Challenges

Despite all the standards efforts for DHTML technologies, both Netscape and Microsoft develop their own, frequently mutually exclusive, extensions to the standards. In the case of CSS-P, both browsers let scripts control identical positioning characteristics, but differences in the document object models render any chance of writing one script that works in both browsers virtually impossible unless you are familiar with the idiosyncracies of each implementation.

To help you understand the challenges that you'll face in creating DHTML pages for both browsers, I will introduce you to the implementation of positionable elements — I like to call them *positionable thingies*, or *PTs* for short — in both Navigator and Internet Explorer. Until you know how to create JavaScript references to PTs in both platforms, you will never be able to write one script for all browsers.

Netscape extensions — the layer

Due to the timing of the release of Navigator 4, some of the standards built into the later-shipping Internet Explorer 4 were not finalized in time to be in Navigator 4. Moreover, Netscape had proposed a new HTML tag to account for positionable thingies. That tag is the <LAYER> tag. The W3C organization that oversees the HTML specification and many of the DHTML specifications did not adopt the <LAYER> tag, but Netscape had already built its flavor of DHTML around this object (see Chapter 19). In the ever-changing political climate of the browser wars, Netscape (as of this writing, anyway) is downplaying the term "layer," even though it is plainly part of the tag and scripted object vocabulary. Where this current thinking will lead is anyone's guess.

In the meantime, if you want to script a PT in Navigator, you must use the layer object vocabulary, even if you don't use a <LAYER> tag to create a PT. As discussed in detail in Chapter 19, the layer object features a rich set of properties and methods that let you adjust the position, visibility, and z-order of objects on a page. In the HTML for a page containing a layer, the content of a layer can be embedded in the same document or loaded from an external HTML file. Once the page is loaded, the base document contains its own content, plus any documents loaded via the <LAYER> tag.

Object references to layers mimic the same hierarchical approach that you use for frames in a frameset. The more deeply nested an object, the longer the reference. You must also pay attention to the layer containing the script that needs to communicate with another layer (or one of its elements) and traverse the layer hierarchy in the reference (for example, when using the parentLayer property).

An important point to remember about a layer is that its content is associated with a document object contained by that layer. Therefore, the layer itself has properties and methods that affect its "layer-ness"; but if you want scripted access to the content of the layer (for example, a form element value), you must refer to the layer's document when you assemble your scripted reference.

Because of the hierarchical nature of layers in Navigator, a reference to a layer and its content must represent the hierarchy. No global view of all layer objects in the document exists. Therefore, even if you assign unique names to each layer object (as you should anyway), that won't help the browser locate the object without the complete hierarchical map to the object in the reference.

If you are comfortable with the frame referencing mechanism in JavaScript (in both Navigator and Internet Explorer), you may well feel comfortable applying the same methodology to layer objects in Navigator 4. It is also often convenient to drop in an external HTML document at a location within the main document. As a result, Netscape's layer object provides a good mental model for many scripters.

Microsoft extensions — style objects

Internet Explorer 4 ignores the `<LAYER>` tag, so nothing you define in a document with that tag will become a PT in Internet Explorer. Instead, Microsoft turns the PT concept on its side. You create a PT in Internet Explorer by virtue of including one special property-value pair in a style definition (either in a `<STYLE>` tag or in the `STYLE` attribute of any container tag). That property is the `position` property, and it has two possible values: `relative` and `absolute`. This is not specifically an Internet Explorer invention, but rather is spelled out in the CSS-P specification.

Microsoft's spin on the matter comes in the way scripts reference these thingies. Rather than referring to them as physical layers you can move around, hide, show, and stack in different orders, Internet Explorer refers to these objects as `styles`. A style is an extremely powerful object in the Internet Explorer 4 document object model. It has dozens of properties, each reflecting the properties that can be set according to the CSS1 and CSS-P recommendations. A style also contains content in the form of HTML that can be modified on the fly after the document has loaded.

All of a style object's controls for adjusting positioning characteristics are properties. Unlike the Navigator layer, a style object has no methods for positioning.

Finding the Common Denominator

If you intend to deploy a Dynamic HTML page that works with both Navigator and Internet Explorer, you need to know how to create a common denominator of objects that both browsers recognize. Citing its adherence to the CSS1 and CSS-P recommendations, Microsoft recognizes only one kind of positionable object: its style object.

Netscape, however, has one extra trick up its sleeve. While Navigator only recognizes layers, it is more lenient about how you define a layer object. In addition to observing the `<LAYER>` tag as a layer object maker (and the `new Layer()` constructor), any object defined as a CSS-P object is automatically recognized as a layer and can be referenced with the Navigator layer syntax.

Creating PTs

The common denominator for creating a PT is the CSS-P syntax that defines a style with the `position` property. Therefore, you can use the `<STYLE>` tag that created named items, as follows:

```
<HTML>
```

```
<HEAD>
<STYLE TYPE="text/css">
        #thingy1Name {position:absolute}
        #thingy2Name {position:absolute}
</STYLE>
</HEAD>
```

Later in the document, you assign the item name to the ID attribute of a container tag:

```
<DIV ID="thingy1Name">...</DIV>
```

All position properties are applied to the content of the container before it is rendered on the page. As an alternate syntax, you define a STYLE attribute for a container tag as follows:

```
<DIV ID="thingy1Name" STYLE="position:absolute">...</DIV>
```

For either approach, you can specify additional positioning properties as you like. For example, a positionable thingy named controlPanel would be positioned at a top-left location of 100, 20 and initially hidden as the page loads, from the following specification:

```
#controlPanel {position:absolute; top:20; left:100; visibility:hidden}
```

Table 41-1 shows the positionable object properties you can use on both platforms. Because this is part of the CSS-P recommendation, the syntax is identical for both platforms.

Table 41-1 CSS-P Rule Properties and Values	
Property	**Values**
position	Absolute | relative
left	Pixels relative to the containing element
top	Pixels relative to the containing element
visibility	Visible | hidden | inherit
z-index	Layer position in stack (integer)

Note

In Navigator 4, you may encounter a problem with a PT defined in the CSS-P syntax and later shown, moved, and hidden by script control. For unknown reasons (that is, bugs), after scripts move and hide the object, events are prevented from reaching existing objects. To work around the problem, you can use JavaScript to document.write() the portion of the document affected by the problem. For Navigator users, document.write() a <LAYER> tag; for Internet Explorer 4 users, document.write() the CSS-P syntax. Later in this chapter I demonstrate how to execute this methodology.

References to positionable thingies

Once a PT is created, your script may need to read or modify one of its properties. You need to watch for two factors. The first is the way you reference the thingy; the other is the property or method you use to extract or adjust a setting.

Referencing the object is the first cross-platform hurdle. Recall that Navigator uses the layer object as its PT, while Internet Explorer uses the style object. References to layer objects must also take into account the hierarchy of nested layers, if any. Styles, on the other hand, can be accessed globally in a window or frame.

Navigator layer references

Consider a script in the main document that wants to adjust a position property of a layer created at that document level. The reference format would be

```
document.layerName
```

Layers are also stored as arrays of the document object, so you can use array indexing and naming techniques to access that layer object:

```
document.layers[0]
document.layers["\"]
```

To access content of that layer, the reference must include the document inside the layer that contains the content. For example, to access the value of a text box in a form in a layer would require a reference with the following format:

```
document.layerName.document.formName.textBoxName.value
```

When a layer is nested inside another layer, the reference gets even longer. The traversal of the object hierarchy always goes through a document and a layer, because only a document can contain a layer, and every layer contains a document. Therefore, it would not be unfeasible to see a reference format such as the following:

```
document.layerName1.document.layerName2.document.formName.textBoxName.
value
```

For more details on referencing layer objects from a variety of locations in a layer hierarchy see Chapter 19.

Internet Explorer style references

Internet Explorer 4's document object model provides a way to transcend any hierarchical structure of nested style objects with a document property called all. A reference to document.all exposes all named objects in the document. To that reference beginning, you add the name of the object defined in the document, plus a further reference to the style property, according to the following format:

```
document.all.objectName.style
```

This document.all property exposes all kinds of objects. Therefore, to access the same text box value described previously in Internet Explorer syntax, the reference format would be

```
document.all.formName.textBoxName.value
```

Of course this means that you need to assign unique names to each addressable object, but you should be doing that anyway. This format also simplifies writing generalizable functions that need to work with style objects.

Property name incompatibilities

While the names for position properties are the same in both platforms, scripted access to them varies in a couple of key instances. Table 41-2 shows the corresponding scripted position-related property names for Navigator and Internet Explorer.

Table 41-2	
CSS-P Scripted Object Properties Names	
Navigator Layer Property	*Internet Explorer Style Property*
left	pixelLeft
top	pixelTop
visibility	visibility
zIndex	zIndex

The Internet Explorer style object does have left and top properties, but these values return the unit along with the coordinate value (for example, 20px) bundled together as a string value. If you want to shift the position along the horizontal or vertical axis by adding or subtracting some number of pixels from the current position, you need the pixelLeft and pixelTop properties, which return integer values for the coordinates.

Also note in Table 41-2 that the property name for setting the stacking order of objects is zIndex, while the HTML style property is named z-index. Many CSS property names are hyphenated words. Unfortunately for compatibility, JavaScript does not allow hyphens in identifiers. Therefore, property names usually include the components of the CSS property names, but assembled in interCap format. This is true throughout Microsoft's extensive object properties that reflect CSS1 style properties. Navigator 4 does not have as thorough support for such properties. In some cases, Navigator even diverges from the CSS convention, instead following the scripting and HTML convention. For example, setting the background color of a positionable thingy requires setting the background-color property. Internet Explorer 4's scripted access to that property is backgroundColor. But Navigator follows the convention from its object model by using the bgColor property (the same as in document.bgColor).

About methods

Navigator defines a number of methods for its layer object (see Chapter 19). Several of these facilitate repositioning an object to a specific coordinate location or shifting an object by a number of pixels along each axis. Internet Explorer offers no equivalent methods for the style object. Instead, you set the pixelLeft and pixelTop properties.

These properties, as mentioned previously, have analogs in Navigator (`left` and `top`), so no matter how you plan to reposition an object in a cross-platform page, you will have to create branches in your code to accommodate each browser type. I personally find the Navigator methods convenient, since a single method call handles both axes.

Working Around Incompatibilities

The bottom line on incompatibilities is that you have to accommodate incompatible object references and occasionally incompatible property names. Scripting gives you several alternatives to working your way around these potential problems.

Of course, you are not obligated to create one page that works on both platforms. You are free to create a version that is optimized for each browser, and let some of the redirection techniques discussed in Chapter 13 automatically navigate users to the page for their browsers. To give you an idea of what such optimized designs might look like, the primary application examples in Chapters 42 and 43 are browser-specific versions of the cross-platform application assembled in this chapter.

In the rest of this section, I present several code examples of ways to accommodate both browsers in a single document. The three basic techniques are inline script branching, something I call *platform equivalency*, and custom APIs (application program interfaces).

Inline branching

Before you can begin to write code that creates branches for each browser, you should define two global variables at the top of the page that act as Boolean flags for your `if...else` constructions later. Therefore, at the first opportunity for a `<SCRIPT>` tag in a page, include the following code fragment to set flags named `isNav4` and `isIE4`:

```
var isNav4, isIE4
if (navigator.appVersion.charAt(0) == "4") {
        if (navigator.appName == "Netscape") {
            isNav4 = true
        } else if (navigator.appVersion.indexOf("MSIE") != -1) {
            isIE4 = true
        }
}
```

Version checking here is quite specific. First of all, it intentionally limits access to browsers whose versions come back as Version 4. Elsewhere in this book, I recommend making such conditions based on whether an integer representation of the version is the same or greater than a minimum level. This would accommodate the next generation of browser without having to modify the code. In this instance, however, I decided to limit the access only to Version 4. I would hope that future versions would be backward compatible to the code written for level 4 browsers, but DHTML is volatile enough that I limit access to level 4 browsers until I get a peek at the next generation.

Another aspect of the flag-setting script I should mention is that the example provides no escape route for browsers that aren't level 4 or aren't either Navigator or Internet Explorer (should there be a level 4 browser from another brand). In a production environment, I would either prefilter access to the page or redirect ill-equipped users to a page that explains why they can't view the page. In the structure of the above script, redirection would have to be made in two places, as follows:

```
var isNav4, isIE4
if (navigator.appVersion.charAt(0) == "4") {
        if (navigator.appName == "Netscape") {
           isNav4 = true
        } else if (navigator.appVersion.indexOf("MSIE") != -1) {
           isIE4 = true
        } else {
           location = "sorry.html"
        }
} else {
        location = sorry.html"
}
```

Later in this chapter, I discuss the issue of designing DHTML pages that degrade gracefully in pre-DHTML browsers.

With the global variables defined in the document, you can use them as condition values in branching statements that address an object according to the reference appropriate for each platform. For example, to change the visibility property of an object named instructions, you would use the flags as follows:

```
if (isNav4) {
        document.instructions.visibility = "hidden"
} else {
        document.all.instructions.style.visibility = "hidden"
}
```

Platform equivalency

Another technique attempts to limit the concern for the different ways each platform refers to a PT. If you examine the formats for each platform's object references, you see that both formats contain a reference to the document and to the object name. Internet Explorer 4's syntax also includes property words such as all and style. If you assign these extra property names to variables for Internet Explorer 4 and leave those variables as empty strings for Navigator 4, you can assemble an object reference for both platforms in one statement.

To begin using this technique, set two global variables that store reference components for the scope (all in Internet Explorer 4) and the style object (style in Internet Explorer 4):

```
var range = ""
var styleObj = ""
if (navigator.appVersion.charAt(0) == "4") {
        if (navigator.appVersion.indexOf("MSIE") != -1) {
           range = "all."
           styleObj = ".style"
        }
}
```

From this point, you can assemble an object reference with the help of the JavaScript eval() function, as follows:

```
var instrux = eval("document." + range + "instructions" + styleObj)
instrux.visibility = "hidden"
```

Or, you can use the eval() function to handle the entire property assignment in one statement, as follows:

```
eval("document." + range + "instructions" + styleObj + ".visibility =
'hidden'")
```

If your page does not have a lot of objects that your scripts will be adjusting, you can use this platform equivalency approach to create global variables holding references to your positionable objects at load time (triggered by the onLoad= event handler so that all objects exist and can be referenced by the eval() function). Then use those variables for object references throughout the scripts.

Unfortunately, the platform equivalency methodology breaks down when a Navigator layer object is nested inside another layer. The platform equivalency formulas assume that each object is directly addressable from the outermost document object. If your objects have a variety of nested locations, you can use either the inline branching method described earlier, or batch-assign objects to global variables at load time using platform branching techniques along the lines of the following example:

```
var instrux
function initObjectVars() {
        if (isNav4) {
            instrux = document.outerLayer.document.instructions
        } else {
            instrux = document.all.instructions.style
        }
}
```

Once the variable contains a valid reference to the object for the current platform, your scripts can treat the object without further concern for platform when addressing properties that have the same name in both platforms:

```
instrux.visibility = "hidden"
```

But when properties are different for each platform, you might want to examine the custom API approach.

Custom APIs

A JavaScript custom API is a function you design that acts as an intermediary between your scripts and other scriptable entities. Ideally, an API simplifies access to or control of other entities. In the context of designing a cross-platform CSS-P page, an API can offer a single function that smooths over the differences in object references and/or property names between platforms. Your custom function provides a single access point that is consistent across both platforms. In essence, you are creating your own metavocabulary for methods and property settings.

Let me begin with an example that needs to handle only the differences in object referencing. The example assumes that some of the global variables described earlier in other techniques (the browser version flags at the minimum) have been defined in the document's scripts. This API provides a function for setting the zIndex property of an object whose name is passed as a parameter:

```
function setZIndex(objectName, zOrder) {
      var theObj
      if (isNav4) {
          theObj = eval("document." + objectName)
      } else {
          theObj = eval("document.all." + objectName + ".style")
      }
      if (theObj) {
          theObj.zIndex = zOrder
      }
}
```

With this function in place, a script can invoke the setZIndex() function and not have to worry about platform. Since this API can be reused in all your documents (or, better yet, linked in as an external library), you can make it part of your DHTML scripting vocabulary.

The preceding example works only for PTs that are not nested in Navigator. If the page uses nested layers, you can reconfigure the API to accept either an object name — which assumes the object is not nested — or a positionable element object reference — which assumes nothing about its location:

```
function setZIndex(obj, zOrder) {
      var theObj
      if (typeof obj == "string") {
          theObj = eval("document." + range + obj + styleObj)
      } else {
          theObj = obj
      }
      theObj.zIndex = zOrder
}
```

In the reconfigured API, the parameters are the same, but the function takes advantage of JavaScript's loose data typing by accepting either a string or object reference as the first parameter. If the parameter is a string, then a valid object reference is built with the help of the platform equivalency methodology. Otherwise, the object reference parameter is processed as-is. When the function is passed an object reference, this API assumes that the script invoking this function has already assigned a valid positionable element object reference to the parameter being passed.

As one more example, the next API function offers an interface to incompatible ways of adjusting the location of a positionable thingy. For Navigator, it uses the layer.moveTo() method; for Internet Explorer, it sets the pixelLeft and pixelTop properties:

```
function shiftTo(obj, x, y) {
      var theObj
      if (typeof obj == "string") {
          theObj = eval("document." + range + obj + styleObj)
      } else {
```

```
        theObj = obj
    }
    if (isNav4) {
        theObj.moveTo(x,y)
    }
    if (isIE4) {
        theObj.style.pixelLeft = x
        theObj.style.pixelTop = y
    }
}
```

Both ways of setting an object's location require x and y coordinates, but the values are applied differently. Therefore, the script invoking this API still doesn't concern itself with the platform.

Handling Non-DHTML Browsers

An important question to ask yourself as you embark on a DHTML-enhanced page is how you intend to treat visitors whose browsers aren't up to the task. In many respects the problem is similar to the problem of treating nonscriptable browsers when your page relies on scripting (see Chapter 13).

The moment your page uses DHTML to position an element, you must remember that non-DHTML browsers display the content according to the traditional HTML rendering rules. No elements are allowed to overlap. Any block-level tag is rendered at the left margin of the page, unless some other non-DHTML alignment tag is at work. This goes for elements that are DHTML-positioned to sit off screen (perhaps with a clickable tab) until called by the user. An element defined as being hidden in DHTML will be visible. In most cases, your carefully designed DHTML page will look terrible.

However, a page that does not use too radical a layout strategy may still be usable in non-DHTML browsers. You should always check your DHTML-enabled page in an older browser to see how it looks. Perhaps there isn't too much you need to do to degrade the DHTML such that the page is acceptable in older browsers.

The ultimate responsibility for deciding your compatibility strategy with older browsers rests with you and your perceptions about your page visitors. If they are in need of vital information from your site and it is readable in non-DHTML browsers, then that may be enough. Otherwise, you must provide a separate content path for both levels of browsers, much as you may be doing for scriptable versus nonscriptable browsers.

A DHTML Application Example

I have created three versions of the same application to demonstrate scripting DHTML in a cross-platform environment (this chapter), in Navigator 4 (Chapter 42), and in Internet Explorer 4 (Chapter 43). The goal is to let those readers who are interested in any one or more of these deployment scenarios see how scripting is done in each. Rather than custom-fit an application that best fits each scenario, I would rather demonstrate the thrills and pitfalls of implementing the same idea under all circumstances.

The application is a jigsaw puzzle game using pieces of a map of the "lower 48" U.S. states (I think everyone would guess where Alaska and Hawaii go on a larger map of North America). I chose this application because it allows me to demonstrate several typical tasks you might want to script in DHTML: hiding and showing elements; handling events for multiple elements; tracking the position of an element with the mouse cursor; absolute positioning of elements; changing the z-order of elements; changing element colors; and animating movement of elements.

As with virtually any programming task, the example code here is not laid out as the quintessential way to accomplish any given task. Each author brings his or her own scripting style, experience, and implementation ideas to a design. Very often, you have available several ways to accomplish the same end. If you find other strategies or tactics for the operations performed in these examples, it means you are gaining a good grasp of both JavaScript and Dynamic HTML.

The puzzle design

Figure 41-1 shows the finished map puzzle with the game in progress. To keep the code to a reasonable length, the example provides positionable state maps for only seven western states. Also, the overall design is intentionally spartan so as to place more emphasis on the PTs and their scripting, rather than on fancy design.

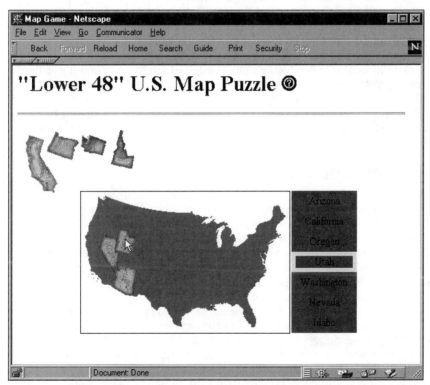

Figure 41-1: The puzzle map game DHTML example (Image courtesy Cartesia Software — www.map-art.com)

When the page initially loads, all the state maps are presented across the top of the puzzle area. The state labels all have a red background, and the silhouette of the continental United States has no features in it. To the right of the title is a question mark icon. A click of this icon causes a panel of instructions to glide to the center of the screen from the right edge of the browser window. That panel has a button that hides the panel.

To play the game (there is no scoring or time keeping in this simplified version), a user clicks once on a state map to "pick it up." While a state map is picked up, its label background to the right of the main map turns yellow to highlight the name of the state being worked on. When it is picked up, the state map tracks the position of the mouse cursor. The user then tries to position each state where it belongs on the map, just like a jigsaw puzzle. To release the state in its trial position, the user clicks the mouse again. If the state is within a four-pixel square region around its true location, the state snaps into its correct position and the corresponding label background color turns green. If the map is not dropped close enough to its destination, the label background reverts to red, meaning that the state still needs to be placed.

After the last state map is dropped into its proper place, all the label backgrounds will be green, and a congratulatory message is displayed where the state map pieces originally lay. Should a user then pick up a state and drop it out of position, the congratulatory message disappears.

I had hoped that all versions of the application would look the same on all platforms. They do, with one exception. The cross-platform version shown in this chapter displays one idiosyncrasy on Navigator 4 browsers. I'll have more to say about it later, but suffice it to say that the background color property of the labels is treated differently in Navigator than in Internet Explorer. When implemented as Netscape layers, however, the look is exactly as intended. Therefore, if you try this chapter's version on both Navigator and Internet Explorer, you will see minor differences in the way the labels are colored (red, yellow, and green) during game play. And yet the platform-specific versions in Chapters 42 and 43 look identical to each other.

Implementation details

Due to the number of different scripted properties being changed in this application, I decided to implement a lot of the cross-platform scripting as a custom API loaded from an external .js file library. The library contains functions for most of the scriptable items you can access in DHTML. Having these functions available simplified what would have been more complex functions in the main part of the application. Since the library requires the platform Boolean flags described earlier in this chapter, all functions in the document can use them if needed for some small platform-specific branch detail.

Although I frown on using global variables except where absolutely necessary (like for the platform-specific flags used throughout the application), I needed to assign a few more globals for this application. All of them store information about the state map and state currently picked up by the user. This information needs to survive the invocations of many functions between the time the state is picked up until it is dropped and checked against the "database" of state data.

That database is another global object. Constructed as a multidimensional array, each "record" in the database stores several fields about the state, including its destination coordinates inside the outline map and a Boolean field to store whether the state has been correctly placed in position.

One final point about the overall structure covers the different ways Navigator and Internet Explorer handle events. Rather than define event handlers for each state map object, I wanted the scripts to use a more generic approach. For Navigator that means capturing events at the document level and figuring out which object has been clicked on; for Internet Explorer, it means letting the event object reveal which item has been clicked on. More importantly, I had to make sure that the different ways of handling events didn't step on each other. In some cases, events are handled the same way in both platforms.

The custom API

To begin the analysis of the code, I start with the external .js library file that contains the custom API. Listing 41-1 contains that code. It begins with declaration and initialization of key global variables used throughout the API code. As you can tell from the code and the discussions earlier in this chapter, the API functions use both the platform branching style for some operations and the platform equivalency approach for others. For your convenience, I interlace further commentary amid the long listing.

Listing 41-1: **The Custom API (DHTMLapi.js)**

```
// Global variables
var isNav4, isIE4
var range = ""
var styleObj = ""
if (navigator.appVersion.charAt(0) == "4") {
        if (navigator.appName == "Netscape") {
            isNav4 = true
            insideWindowWidth = window.innerWidth
        } else {
            isIE4 = true
            range = "all."
            styleObj = ".style"
        }
}
```

Many of the functions in this API accept either an object name or object reference as a parameter. The following function processes the first parameter such that object name strings are converted to object references (using the platform equivalency approach), while object references are passed through. This function is called by many functions in the API.

```
// Convert object name string or object reference
// into a valid object reference
function getObject(obj) {
        var theObj
        if (typeof obj == "string") {
```

(continued)

Listing 41-1 *(continued)*

```
        theObj = eval("document." + range + obj + styleObj)
    } else {
        theObj = obj
    }
    return theObj
}
```

The next function, `shiftTo()`, is analogous to Navigator's `layer.moveTo()` method. In fact, for Navigator browsers, that is the method invoked here. But for Internet Explorer, the same action requires adjusting two positional properties, `pixelLeft` and `pixelTop`. Even though the adjustments are made in separate statements, the action on the screen does not follow the action statement-by-statement. Internet Explorer appears to buffer the statements so that the repositioning appears as a single shift.

This `shiftTo()` function accepts either an object name (string) or object reference. As you will see in the main program code, when a user clicks on a state map, the positionable thingy containing the map image becomes the selected object. It is that object that is usually passed to this function.

```
// Positioning an object at a specific pixel coordinate
function shiftTo(obj, x, y) {
    var theObj = getObject(obj)
    if (isNav4) {
        theObj.moveTo(x,y)
    } else {
        theObj.pixelLeft = x
        theObj.pixelTop = y
    }
}
```

The `shiftBy()` function mimics Navigator's `layer.moveBy()` method. The second and third parameters represent the number of pixels that the object should be moved on the page. A positive number means to the right or down; a negative number means to the left or up; a value of zero means no change to the axis. For Navigator, the script uses the `layer.moveBy()` method. But for Internet Explorer, the script uses the add by value operator to change the current value of the style object's `pixelLeft` and `pixelTop` properties.

```
// Moving an object by x and/or y pixels
function shiftBy(obj, deltaX, deltaY) {
    var theObj = getObject(obj)
    if (isNav4) {
        theObj.moveBy(deltaX, deltaY)
    } else {
        theObj.pixelLeft += deltaX
        theObj.pixelTop += deltaY
    }
}
```

Both platforms use the same property name for setting the stacking order of positionable thingies. Therefore, most of the `setZIndex()` function is devoted to handling the string and object versions of the first parameter.

```
// Setting the z-order of an object
function setZIndex(obj, zOrder) {
      var theObj = getObject(obj)
      theObj.zIndex = zOrder
}
```

Each platform has its own way of referring to the background color. The `setBGColor()` function applies the correct syntax for the current platform.

```
// Setting the background color of an object
function setBGColor(obj, color) {
      var theObj = getObject(obj)
      if (isNav4) {
         theObj.bgColor = color
      } else {
         theObj.backgroundColor = color
      }
}
```

I find the allowable values for the `visibility` property very unprogrammatic (I expect a Boolean value). Therefore, to make the process of showing and hiding elements more logical to me, I created API functions called `show()` and `hide()`.

```
// Setting the visibility of an object to visible
function show(obj) {
      var theObj = getObject(obj)
      theObj.visibility = "visible"
}
```

```
// Setting the visibility of an object to hidden
function hide(obj) {
      var theObj = getObject(obj)
      theObj.visibility = "hidden"
}
```

Because of the different property names for coordinate locations in each platform, I created two functions that extract the left and top positions for any object. The API takes care of the platform specifics, while code in the main program merely calls for the coordinates.

```
// Retrieving the x coordinate of a positionable object
function getObjectLeft(obj)  {
      var theObj = getObject(obj)
      if (isNav4) {
         return theObj.left
      } else {
         return theObj.pixelLeft
      }
}
```

(continued)

Listing 41-1 *(continued)*

```
// Retrieving the y coordinate of a positionable object
function getObjectTop(obj)  {
        var theObj = getObject(obj)
        if (isNav4) {
            return theObj.top
        } else {
            return theObj.pixelTop
        }
}
```

The above API is generalizable enough to be used as a library with any cross-platform DHTML application. It could even be used with a platform-specific page. It is more efficient, however, to use a browser's native objects, properties, and methods if you know for sure that users will have only one brand of browser.

The main program

Code for the main program is shown in Listing 41-2. It is a comparatively lengthy document, so I will interlace commentary throughout the listing. Before diving into the code, however, allow me to present a preview of the structure of the document. With one exception (the instructions panel), all PTs are defined as CSS-P items. For such a batch generation of items, I usually set the properties for all items within a <STYLE> tag set at the very beginning of the HTML page. After that come the scripts for the page. All of this material is inside the <HEAD> tag section. I leave the <BODY> section to contain the visible content of the page. This is an organization style that works well for me, but you can adopt any style you like, provided various elements that support others on the page are loaded before the dependent items (for example, define a style before assigning its name to the corresponding content tag's ID attributes).

Listing 41-2: **The Main Program (mapgame.htm)**

```
<HTML>
<HEAD><TITLE>Map Game</TITLE>
```

Most of the positionable elements have their CSS-P properties established in the <STYLE> tag at the top of the document. The TYPE attribute points to the cross-platform compatible version. As you will learn in Chapter 42, Navigator offers another type as well but does accept the standard type.

PTs for this application include a background map, a text label for each state, a map for each state, and a congratulatory message. Notice that the names of the label and state map objects begin with a two-letter abbreviation of the state. This comes in handy in the scripts when synchronizing the selected map and its label.

The label objects will be nested inside the background map object. Therefore, the coordinates for the labels are relative to the coordinate system of the background map, not the page. That's why the first label has a top property of zero.

```
<STYLE TYPE="text/css">
        #bgmap {position:absolute; left:100; top:180; width:406;}

        #azlabel {position:absolute; left:310; top:0; background-
color:red;
                width:100; height:28; border:none; text-align:center;}
        #calabel {position:absolute; left:310; top:29; background-
color:red;
                width:100; height:28; border:none; text-align:center;}
        #orlabel {position:absolute; left:310; top:58; background-
color:red;
                width:100; height:28; border:none; text-align:center;}
        #utlabel {position:absolute; left:310; top:87; background-
color:red;
                width:100; height:28; border:none; text-align:center;}
        #walabel {position:absolute; left:310; top:116; background-
color:red;
                width:100; height:28; border:none; text-align:center;}
        #nvlabel {position:absolute; left:310; top:145; background-
color:red;
                width:100; height:28; border:none; text-align:center;}
        #idlabel {position:absolute; left:310; top:174; background-
color:red;
                width:100; height:28; border:none; text-align:center;}

        #camap {position:absolute; left:20; top:100; width:1;}
        #ormap {position:absolute; left:60; top:100; width:1;}
        #wamap {position:absolute; left:100; top:100; width:1;}
        #idmap {position:absolute; left:140; top:100; width:1;}
        #nvmap {position:absolute; left:180; top:100; width:1;}
        #azmap {position:absolute; left:220; top:100; width:1;}
        #utmap {position:absolute; left:260; top:100; width:1;}

        #congrats {position:absolute; visibility:hidden; left:20;
top:100; width:1;}
</STYLE>
```

The next statement loads the external .js library file that contains the API described in Listing 41-1. I tend to load external library files before listing any other JavaScript code in the page, just in case the main page code relies on global variables or functions in its initializations.

```
<SCRIPT LANGUAGE="JavaScript" SRC="DHTMLapi.js"></SCRIPT>
```

Now comes the main script, which contains all the document-specific functions and global variables. Global variables here are ready to hold information about the selected state object (and associated details), as well as the offset between the position of a click inside a map object and the top-left corner of that map object. You will see that this offset is important to allow the map to track the cursor at the same offset position within the map. And since the tracking is done by repeated calls to a function (triggered by numerous mouse events), these offset values must have global scope.

(continued)

Listing 41-2 *(continued)*

```
<SCRIPT LANGUAGE="JavaScript">
// Global variables
var offsetX = 0
var offsetY = 0
var selectedObj
var selectedState = ""
var selectedStateIndex
```

As the page loads, it executes the following chunk of script to build a database (multidimensional array) of information about each state. The fields for each record are for the two-letter state abbreviation, the full name (not used in this application, but included for use in a future version), the x and y coordinates (within the coordinate system of the background map) for the exact position of the state, and a Boolean flag to be set to true whenever a user correctly places a state.

Getting the data for the x and y coordinates required some legwork. Once I had the pieces of art for each state and the code for dragging them around the screen, I disengaged the part of the script that tested for accuracy. Instead, I added a statement to the code that revealed the x and y position of the dragged item in the status bar (rather than being bothered by alerts). When I carefully positioned a state in its destination, I copied the coordinates from the status bar into the statement that created that state record. Sure, it was tedious, but once I had that info in the database, I could adjust the location of the background map and not have to worry about the destination coordinates, because they were based on the coordinate system inside the background map.

```
// Create 'database' of state information
function state(abbrev, fullName, x, y) {
        this.abbrev = abbrev
        this.fullName = fullName
        this.x = x
        this.y = y
        this.done = false
}
var states = new Array()
states[0] = new state("ca", "California", 7, 54)
states[1] = new state("or", "Oregon", 7, 24)
states[2] = new state("wa", "Washington", 23, 8)
states[3] = new state("id", "Idaho", 48, 17)
states[4] = new state("az", "Arizona", 45, 105)
states[5] = new state("nv", "Nevada", 27, 61)
states[6] = new state("ut", "Utah", 55, 69)
```

The following function, getSelectedMap(), is the most complex of the entire application and runs into the most incompatibility between the Navigator layer object and the Internet Explorer style object. The purpose of this function (invoked by the engage() function) is to determine which map object has been clicked on by the user and to set key global variables that other functions will use to accomplish the dragging and release of the object.

As happens with several functions in this application, this function defines one parameter (e) to accommodate the Navigator event object. Because the parameter is not used in the Internet Explorer 4 branch, no conflict occurs there.

For Navigator processing, the event object plays a key role. The behavior of layer objects and events does not let the event object's target property reveal the specific layer being clicked on (unless I had also defined layer events for every map — not a happy prospect). Therefore, I compare the coordinate of the click against the areas occupied by each state map layer. A for loop cycles through the state layers in reverse order (so that if the first layout of loose state maps displays maps overlapped with each other, the comparison is done with the map closest to the user's eye). Testing whether a click is within a rectangular region takes a bit of calculation, as you can see from the lengthy conditions in the if construction.

Once a coordinate match is found, the selectedObj global is set to the layer object occupying that space. Next, two other global values are established: One for the layer containing the label object, and one for the index value in the state "database" for the current state. Notice that the label objects are nested, which means that the Navigator layer reference must traverse the object hierarchy to reach the actual label layer. Also, to bring the selected map to the top of the heap (so it always floats above other states while selected), I set its zIndex property to 100 (via one of the API functions).

For Internet Explorer 4 processing, the image inside the positionable thingy is the item that receives the event. Using Internet Explorer's event object, the script extracts that object (via the srcElement property). The actual style object is part of the image's parent element, so the selectedObj global is set to that object.

The script still needs to set the other global variables for Internet Explorer 4, so it first extracts the state abbreviation from the image object's parentElement ID. Then a for loop cycles through the database to see if a match occurs for the state abbreviation. If so, the script assembles the reference to the label's style object with the help of that information. Then it saves the index of the record in the database for that state. Finally, the zIndex property is set to 100. It is essential to set the selectedStateLabel object inside the for loop, because that object must be set only when a state map is clicked on.

Every event (of the mouseDown variety, as explained later) on the page is examined by this function. Therefore, if no match is found in the database for the item being clicked on, it must mean that the item is not a map. All the key global variables must be set to null so that no other functions act on those objects.

```
// Set global values related to the selected state map
function getSelectedMap(e) {
    if (isNav4) {
        var clickX = e.pageX
        var clickY = e.pageY
        var testObj
```

(continued)

Listing 41-2 *(continued)*

```
                    for (var i = states.length - 1; i >= 0; i--) {
                        testObj = document.layers[states[i].abbrev + "map"]
                        if ((clickX > testObj.left) && (clickX < testObj.left +
testObj.clip.width) && (clickY > testObj.top) && (clickY < testObj.top
+ testObj.clip.height)) {
                            selectedObj = testObj
                            if (selectedObj) {
                                selectedStateLabel =
document.bgmap.document.layers[states[i].abbrev + "label"]
                                selectedStateIndex = i
                                setZIndex(selectedObj, 100)
                                return
                            }
                        }
                    }
                } else {
                    var imgObj = window.event.srcElement
                    selectedObj = imgObj.parentElement.style
                    if (selectedObj) {
                        var stateName = imgObj.parentElement.id.substring(0,2)
                        for (var i = 0; i < states.length; i++) {
                            if (states[i].abbrev == stateName ) {
                                selectedStateLabel = document.all(stateName +
"label").style
                                selectedStateIndex = i
                                setZIndex(selectedObj,100)
                                return
                            }
                        }
                    }
                }
                selectedObj = null
                selectedStateLabel = null
                selectedStateIndex = null
                return
}
```

The `dragIt()` function, compact as it is, provides the main action in the application by keeping a picked-up state object under the cursor as the user moves the mouse. This function is called repeatedly by the mouseMove event, although the actual event handling methodology varies with platform. In Navigator, the event object is passed as a parameter and used to help calculate the position where the map should be in relation to the event coordinates. Internet Explorer coordinates are extracted from its event object, which is accessible as a window property. Both branches call the same API function to adjust the position of the map object.

```
// Position the map where the cursor is
function dragIt(e) {
        if (selectedObj) {
            if (isNav4) {
                shiftTo(selectedObj, (e.pageX - offsetX), (e.pageY -
offsetY))
```

```
        } else {
            shiftTo(selectedObj, (window.event.clientX - offsetX),
(window.event.clientY - offsetY))
        }
    }
}
```

When a user clicks anywhere on the page of this application, the mouseDown event invokes the `toggleEngage()` function. This function acts primarily as a dispatcher to two branches. If `selectedObj` is a value other than null, then it means that the user has previously picked up a state map, and the mouse action is meant to release the map. But if `selectedObj` is null, then it's time to select a map (if one was clicked).

```
function toggleEngage(e) {
    if (selectedObj) {
        release(e)
    } else {
        engage(e)
    }
}
```

The following function contains the code that "picks up" a state map for the user. This only happens if the call to `getSelectedMap()` passes the tests that indicate a state map has been clicked. If that test succeeds, then the offset coordinates of the click relative to the selected object's location are saved in two global variables (`offsetX` and `offsetY`).

Measuring this offset in each platform requires very different syntax due to the different ways each browser refers to its coordinate space. For Navigator, the offset within an object is the difference between the point in the page minus the location of the object. In Navigator, the page coordinates are not affected by scrolling: The top-left of the page is the top-left of the page, no matter where the page is scrolled. At the same time, the object coordinates are measured with respect to the page. But in Internet Explorer, even though you can get the offset coordinate of the event directly from the event object, the value is measured only within the visible area of the document. Therefore, you must also adjust for any possible scrolling of the page.

```
// select a map, set the global offset values, and turn label color to
yellow
function engage(e) {
    getSelectedMap(e)
    if (selectedObj) {
        if (isNav4) {
            offsetX = e.pageX - selectedObj.left
            offsetY = e.pageY - selectedObj.top
        } else {
            offsetX = window.event.offsetX - document.body.scrollLeft
            offsetY = window.event.offsetY - document.body.scrollTop
        }
        setBGColor(selectedStateLabel,"yellow")
    }
}
```

(continued)

Listing 41-2 *(continued)*

When a user drops the currently selected map object, the release() function invokes the onTarget() function to find out if the current location of the map is within range of the desired destination. If it is in range, the background color of the state label object is set to green, and the done property of the selected state database entry is set to true. One additional test looks to see if all the done properties are true in the database. If so, the congrats object is shown. But if the object is not in the right place, the label reverts to its original red color. In case the user moves a state that was previously okay, its database entry is also adjusted. No matter what the outcome, however, the user has dropped the map, so key global variables are set to null and the layer order for the item is set to zero (bottom of the heap) so it doesn't interfere with the next selected map.

```
// Drop map object and see if it's in range
function release(e) {
        if (onTarget(e)) {
            setBGColor(selectedStateLabel, "green")
            states[selectedStateIndex].done = true
            if (isDone()) {
                show("congrats")
            }
        } else {
            setBGColor(selectedStateLabel, "red")
            states[selectedStateIndex].done = false
            hide("congrats")
        }
        setZIndex(selectedObj, 0)
        selectedObj = null
        selectedState = null
}
```

To find out if a dropped map is in its correct position, the onTarget() function first calculates the target spot on the page by adding the location of the bgmap object to the coordinate positions stored in the states database. Since the bgmap object doesn't come into play in other parts of this script, it is convenient to pass merely the object name to the two API functions that get the object's left and top coordinate points.

Next, the script uses platform-specific properties to get the object's current location. The Navigator version is relative to the entire page, while the Internet Explorer version is relative to the visible portion of the page showing in the browser.

A large if condition checks whether the object's coordinate point is within a 4-pixel square region around the destination point. If you wanted to make the game easier, you could increase the cushion values from 2 to 3 or 4.

If the map is within the range, the script calls the shiftTo() API function to snap the map into the exact destination position, and reports back to the release() function the appropriate Boolean value.

```
// See if item is in range of desired location
function onTarget(e) {
        var x = states[selectedStateIndex].x + getObjectLeft("bgmap")
        var y = states[selectedStateIndex].y + getObjectTop("bgmap")
        if (isNav4) {
            var objX = selectedObj.pageX
            var objY = selectedObj.pageY
        } else {
            var objX = selectedObj.pixelLeft
            var objY = selectedObj.pixelTop
        }
        if ((objX >= x-2 && objX <= x+2) && (objY >= y-2 && objY <=
y+2)) {
            shiftTo(selectedObj, x, y)
            return true
        }
        return false
}
```

A simple `for` loop cycles through the states database to see if all of the `done` properties are set to true. When they are, the `release()` function (which calls this `isDone()` function) displays the congratulatory object.

```
// See if all states are "done"
function isDone() {
        for (var i = 0; i < states.length; i++) {
            if (!states[i].done) {
                return false
            }
        }
        return true
}
```

The `help` PT is created differently on this page, as discussed later in the chapter. When the user clicks on the Help button at the top of the page, the instructions panel flies in from the right edge of the window. The `showHelp()` function begins the process by setting its location to the current right window edge, bringing its layer to the very front of the heap, showing the object, and then initiating an interval mechanism that repeatedly calls `moveHelp()`.

```
// Show the help object and start the animation
function showHelp() {
        var objName = "help"
        shiftTo(objName, insideWindowWidth, 80)
        setZIndex(objName,1000)
        show(objName)
        intervalID = setInterval("moveHelp()", 1)
}
```

In the `moveHelp()` function, the `help` object is shifted in 5-pixel increments to the left. The ultimate destination is the spot where the object is in the middle of the browser window. That midpoint must be calculated each time, because the window may have been resized. Unfortunately, Navigator does not provide a mechanism for extracting the width of a layer, so the calculation for the union of the window and layer midpoints is hard-wired to the pixel measure of the layer object.

(continued)

Listing 41-2 *(continued)*

This function is called repeatedly under the control of a `setInterval()` method in `showHelp()`. But when the object reaches the middle of the browser window, the interval ID is canceled, which stops the animation.

The `help` object processes a mouse event to hide the object. An extra `clearInterval()` method is called here in case the user clicks on the object's Close button before the object has reached midwindow (where `moveHelp()` cancels the interval). The script also shifts the position to the right edge of the window, but it isn't absolutely necessary, since the `showHelp()` method positions the window there.

```
// Fly to the left until reaching mid-window
function moveHelp() {
        shiftBy("help",-5,0)
        var objectLeft = getObjectLeft("help")
        if (objectLeft <= (insideWindowWidth/2) - 150) {
            clearInterval(intervalID)
        }
}
// Hide the help window
function hideMe() {
        clearInterval(intervalID)
        hide("help")
        shiftTo("help", insideWindowWidth, 80)
}
```

The document's `onLoad=` event handler calls two functions. The first is `setNSEvents()`, which turns on event capturing for the document and the help layer. Because the help layer is defined so late in the document, it is safest to initialize its events after the page has loaded.

Each object captures different events. The document captures mouseDown and mouseMove events (for picking up, moving, and dropping state maps); the help layer object captures only click events (for hiding the layer).

The second function called at load time is a general-purpose `init()` function. It processes miscellaneous housekeeping items for each platform. Netscape's implementation of CSS1 exhibits odd behavior for setting the background color, as is needed for the labels. While it sets the background color initially, the color does not extend to the edge of the specified height and width of the object. If you then set the layer's `bgColor` property to a color, the gaps between the originally colored space and the edges take on the new color — but the original color stays in the center. To fill out the edge space with the red color at startup time, the `init()` function cycles through all the label objects and sets their background colors to red.

For convenience in moving the help window in Internet Explorer 4, I set a global variable (`insideWindowWidth`) to hold the width of the browser window. I establish this value at load time and also whenever a user resizes a window (as set in the `setWidth()` function that is called by the document's resize event).

```
// Initialize event capturing for Navigator
function setNSEvents() {
```

```
            if (isNav4) {
                document.captureEvents(Event.MOUSEDOWN | Event.MOUSEMOVE)
                document.onMouseDown = toggleEngage
                document.onMouseMove = dragIt
                document.help.captureEvents(Event.CLICK)
                document.help.onClick = hideMe
            }
}
// Miscellaneous inits
function init() {
            if (isNav4) {
                for (var i = 0; i< states.length; i++) {

setBGColor((document.bgmap.document.layers[states[i].abbrev +
"label"]),"red")
                }
            } else if (isIE4) {
                insideWindowWidth = document.body.scrollWidth
            }
}
// Reset window width variable upon resize
function setWidth() {
            if (isIE4) {
                insideWindowWidth = document.body.scrollWidth
            }
}
</SCRIPT>
</HEAD>
```

Now comes the part of the document that generates the visible content.
Several event handlers are defined in the <BODY> tag. Only the onLoad= and
onResize= event handlers are observed by both browsers. Document-level
event capture of the mouseDown and mouseMove events for Navigator were
handled in the preceding scripts. But Internet Explorer 4 provides these event
handlers for the document object, so they can be defined in the traditional
event handler format. Navigator simply ignores them.

```
<BODY onLoad="init(); setNSEvents()" onResize="setWidth()"
onMouseDown="toggleEngage()" onMouseMove="dragIt()">
<H1>"Lower 48" U.S. Map Puzzle <A HREF="javascript:void
showHelp()" onMouseOver="status='Show help panel...';return true"
onMouseOut="status='';return true"><IMG SRC="info.gif" HEIGHT=22
WIDTH=22 BORDER=0></A></H1>
<HR>
```

To be CSS-P friendly, the styles defined early in the document are assigned to
block HTML tags. The positionable object for the background map is set up to
be a container for all the label objects. Thus, all position coordinates are
relative to the coordinate space of the bgmap object.

```
<DIV ID=bgmap><IMG SRC="us11.gif" WIDTH=306 HEIGHT=202
BORDER=1> </IMG>
```

(continued)

Listing 41-2 *(continued)*

```
<DIV ID=azlabel>Arizona</DIV>
<DIV ID=calabel>California</DIV>
<DIV ID=orlabel>Oregon</DIV>
<DIV ID=utlabel>Utah</DIV>
<DIV ID=walabel>Washington</DIV>
<DIV ID=nvlabel>Nevada</DIV>
<DIV ID=idlabel>Idaho</DIV>
</DIV>
```

HTML block tags for the map objects appear later in the document than the background map and labels, even though the state maps are positioned higher in the document. In DHTML, it is not the tag location that determines where objects are placed, but rather the position attributes assigned to the style or layer.

```
<DIV ID=camap><IMG SRC="ca.gif" WIDTH=47 HEIGHT=82 BORDER=0></DIV>
<DIV ID=ormap><IMG SRC="or.gif" WIDTH=57 HEIGHT=45 BORDER=0></DIV>
<DIV ID=wamap><IMG SRC="wa.gif" WIDTH=38 HEIGHT=29 BORDER=0></DIV>
<DIV ID=idmap><IMG SRC="id.gif" WIDTH=34 HEIGHT=55 BORDER=0></DIV>
<DIV ID=azmap><IMG SRC="az.gif" WIDTH=38 HEIGHT=45 BORDER=0></DIV>
<DIV ID=nvmap><IMG SRC="nv.gif" WIDTH=35 HEIGHT=56 BORDER=0></DIV>
<DIV ID=utmap><IMG SRC="ut.gif" WIDTH=33 HEIGHT=41 BORDER=0></DIV>

<DIV ID=congrats><FONT
COLOR="red"><H1>Congratulations!</H1></FONT></DIV>
```

In developing this application, I encountered what surely seems like a bug to me. When using CSS-P to define the instructions panel, Navigator 4 exhibited unwanted behavior after the instruction panel was shown and flown into place under script control. Even after hiding the help object, the page no longer received mouse events, making it impossible to pick up a state map once the instructions appeared. The problem did not surface, however, if the help object was defined in the document with a `<LAYER>` tag.

Therefore, I did what I don't like to do unless absolutely necessary: I created branches in the content that used `document.write()` to create the same content with different HTML syntax depending on the browser. For Internet Explorer, the page creates the same kind of block (with the `<DIV>` tag pair) used elsewhere in the document. Positioning properties are assigned to this block via a `STYLE` attribute in the `<DIV>` tag. You cannot assign a style in the `<STYLE>` tag that is visible to the entire document, because that specification and a like-named `<LAYER>` tag get confused.

For Navigator, the page uses the `<LAYER>` tag and loads the content of the object from a separate HTML file (instrux.htm). One advantage I had with the `<LAYER>` tag was that I could assign an initial horizontal position of the help object with a JavaScript entity. The entity reaches into the `window.innerWidth` property to set the `LEFT` attribute of the layer.

```
<SCRIPT LANGUAGE="JavaScript">
if (isIE4) {
```

```
        var output = "<DIV ID='help' onClick='hideMe()'
STYLE='position:absolute; visibility:hidden; top:80; width:300;
border:none; background-color:#98FB98;'>\n"
        output += "<P STYLE='margin-
top:5'><CENTER><B>Instructions</B></CENTER></P>\n"
        output += "<HR COLOR='seagreen'>\n<OL STYLE='margin-right:20'>"
        output += "<LI>Click on a state map to pick it up. The label
color turns yellow.\n"
        output += "<LI>Move the mouse and map into position, and click
the mouse to drop the state map.\n"
        output += "<LI>If you are close to the actual location, the
state snaps into place and the label color turns green.\n"
        output += "</OL>\n<FORM>\n<CENTER><INPUT TYPE='button'
VALUE='Close'>\n</FORM></DIV>"
        document.write(output)
} else if (isNav4) {
        var output = "<LAYER ID='help' TOP=80
LEFT=&{window.innerWidth}; WIDTH=300 VISIBILITY='HIDDEN'
SRC='instrux.htm'></LAYER>"
        document.write(output)
}
</SCRIPT>
</BODY>
</HTML>
```

Lessons learned

Once the external cross-platform API was in place, it helped frame a lot of the other code in the main program. The APIs provided great comfort in that they encouraged me to reference a complex object fully in the main code as a platform-shared value (for example, the selectedObj and selectedState global variables). At the same time, I could reference top-level thingies (that is, nonnested objects) simply by their names when passing them to API functions.

In many respects, the harder task was defining the CSS-P properties and syntax that both browsers would treat similarly. In the case of the label objects, I couldn't reach complete parity in a cross-platform environment (the labels look different in Navigator), and in the case of the help object, I had to code the HTML separately for each platform. Therefore, when approaching this kind of project, work first with the HTML and CSS-P syntax to build the look that works best for both platforms. Then start connecting the scripted wires. You may have to adjust the CSS-P code if you find odd behavior in one platform or the other with your scripting, but it is still easier to work from a good layout.

But without a doubt the biggest lesson you learn from working on a project like this is how important it still is to test an application on Navigator and Internet Explorer. It would be nearly impossible to design a cross-platform application on one browser and have it run flawlessly on the other the first time. Be prepared to go back and forth between browsers, breaking existing working code along the way until you eventually reach a version that works on both.

✦   ✦   ✦

Netscape Dynamic HTML and JavaScript Extensions

While Netscape Navigator 4 provides support for the Cascading Style Sheets, Level 1 recommendation by W3C, the company created its own implementation of style sheets, sometimes called JavaScript Style Sheets, or JSSs. It's not that these style sheets become part of the scripts in your document, but rather they adopt many of the syntactical traditions of JavaScript. This is in contrast to the new syntax (characterized by the property-value pair) of CSS1. In the arena of dynamically positionable objects, Navigator 4 adheres in part to the CSS-P recommendation and also offers a new HTML tag, the <LAYER> tag, to create such objects.

This chapter introduces the JavaScript language extensions employed by JavaScript Style Sheets. Because this is not the same kind of scripting that you've been reading about in this book, the coverage is intended merely to acquaint you with the syntax in case you are not aware of it. More coverage is accorded the positioning aspects of the <LAYER> tag because these items are scriptable from your regular scripts. At the end of the chapter, I provide a Navigator-specific version of the map puzzle game demonstrated in cross-platform format in Chapter 41.

JavaScript Styles

As with Cascading Style Sheets, JavaScript Style Sheets define layout characteristics for the content of an HTML tag. A style defines how the browser renders the page as it loads. Any adjustment to the content after the page loads requires scripting beyond the scope of style sheets.

If you are familiar with Cascading Style Sheets (as defined in the published W3C specification available at `http://www.w3.org/pub/WWW/TR/REC-CSS1`), you know that a typical way for a style sheet to be defined is with the `<STYLE>` tag whose TYPE attribute is "text/css", as follows:

```
<STYLE TYPE="text/css">
        H1 {color:red}
</STYLE>
```

Rules inside the style tag specify the tag type and declarations of properties and values that override default browser rendering settings.

Navigator provides an alternate syntax that follows the dot syntax model of JavaScript. Its style type is "text/javascript", as follows:

```
<STYLE TYPE="text/javascript">
        tags.H1.color="red"
</STYLE>
```

Within the context of the `<STYLE>` tag, Navigator recognizes a tags object, which can contain any known tag name and one of that tag's properties. Internet Explorer 4 does not recognize the "text/javascript" style type, nor the JavaScript-like syntax within a `<STYLE>` tag set. Moreover, while Netscape's JavaScript objects used in `<STYLE>` tags are exposed to scripts written inside `<SCRIPT>` tag sets, their values cannot be modified to change the rendering of the object on the fly.

Netscape has defined several objects for style definitions. Many of them assist in creating groups of styles and exceptions to the rules defined by other styles.

The tags object

Every document object has a tags object. But since the tags object is always at the document level, the `document` reference is not needed inside the `<STYLE>` tag (although it is required if you intend to read a style property from inside a `<SCRIPT>` tag).

The tags object represents all the tags in the current document. To assign a style to a tag, you must build a reference to that tag and its property according to the following format:

```
tags.tagName.propertyName = value
```

You can assign only one property per statement.

The `tagName` part of the statement is the text you normally find between the angle brackets of a tag, such as P for the `<P>` tag or BODY for the `<BODY>` tag. Unlike the usually case-sensitive JavaScript, these tag names can be in upper- or lowercase. Tags you can use for this purpose are only those that come in a pair of opening and closing tags. These pairs delimit the range of content affected by a particular style. You can, however, apply some of your scripting knowledge to JavaScript inside the `<STYLE>` tag. For example, if you have many properties you wish to set for a single tag, the long way to do it would be

```
<STYLE TYPE="text/javascript">
        tags.p.color = "green"
        tags.p.borderColor = "blue"
        tags.p.borderStyle = "3D"
        tags.p.borderWidths("2px","2px","2px","2px")
</STYLE>
```

However, you can use the `with` operator to shorten the references:

```
<STYLE TYPE="text/javascript">
with(tags.p) {
        color = "green"
        borderColor = "blue"
        borderStyle = "3D"
        borderWidths("2px","2px","2px","2px")
}
</STYLE>
```

The classes object

Defining style properties for a given tag could be limiting if you intend to reuse that tag with a different style. For example, consider a page that contains many text paragraphs designed with a specific margin and font color. You decide you want to insert in a few places paragraphs that follow a style that increases the left and right margins and sets the text to a bold font in a different color. The cumbersome way to accomplish this would be to keep changing the style definitions throughout the document. A better way is to define different classes of the same tag. To define a class, you use the classes object in a style rule. The format for this kind of statement is as follows:

```
classes.className.tagName.propertyName = value
```

For example, to define two different classes for the <P> tag, you would use a construction like the following:

```
<STYLE TYPE="text/javascript">
        classes.normal.p.margins("2em","3em","2em","3em")
        classes.normal.p.textAlign = "justify"
        classes.inset.p.margins("2em","10em","2em","10em")
        classes.inset.p.textAlign = "center"
        classes.inset.p.fontWeight = "bold"
</STYLE>
```

To apply a class to a tag, use the CLASS attribute for the tag:

```
<P CLASS="normal">...</P>
<P CLASS="inset">...</P>
```

In an abstract way, the classes object lets you define new versions of tags, although the tag name stays the same. Importantly, it means you can define multiple styles for a given tag, and then deploy each style where needed throughout the document.

The ids object

One more object, the ids object, lets you assign a single style property to an identifier to make it easy to make exceptions to other styles. This works best when a tag is assigned a group of style properties, but your document needs two versions of the same style that differ by only one or two style properties. To create an ids object, use the following syntax format:

```
ids.idName.propertyName = value
```

As an example of the ids object in use, consider the two paragraph classes defined in the preceding section. If I also want an inset class that looks just like the insert class except the fontWeight property is normal and a fontStyle property italic, the entire definition would be as follows:

```
<STYLE TYPE="text/javascript">
        classes.normal.p.margins("2em","3em","2em","3em")
        classes.normal.p.textAlign = "justify"
        classes.inset.p.margins("2em","10em","2em","10em")
        classes.inset.p.textAlign = "center"
        classes.inset.p.fontWeight = "bold"
        ids.altInset.fontWeight = "normal"
        ids.altInset.fontStyle = "italic"
</STYLE>
```

To deploy the inset paragraph with the alternate properties, the container tag specifies both the CLASS and ID attributes:

```
<P CLASS="inset" ID="altInset">...</P>
```

The all keyword

For one more slice on the organization of styles, you can specify that a given style class is applicable to any tag in the document. In contrast, under normal circumstances, a class is restricted to the tags specified in the classes object definition. The all keyword defines a class that can be used for all tags in a document. For example, consider the following style definition:

```
<STYLE TYPE="text/javascript">
        classes.hotStuff.all.color = "red"
        classes.normal.p.margins("2em","3em","2em","3em")
        classes.normal.p.textAlign = "justify"
        classes.inset.p.margins("2em","10em","2em","10em")
        classes.inset.p.textAlign = "center"
        classes.inset.p.fontWeight = "bold"
</STYLE>
```

With this definition, the hotStuff class could be applied to any tag to turn its content red. But if I wanted to make the content of a <DIV> tag bold and center-aligned, I could not use the inset class, because that class is defined to be applied only to a <P> tag.

Be sure to separate in your mind Navigator's all keyword from Internet Explorer's all keyword. The former applies to style classes; the latter applies to document objects in general (in the context of the Internet Explorer 4 document object model).

Contextual styles

One final entry in Navigator's JavaScript Style Sheet vocabulary is the contextual() method. It provides yet another way to specify the application of a specific style. In this case, it defines what outer block tag surrounds a tag with a special style. For example, if I want all <B> tags inside <P> tags (but nowhere else) to display its text in red, I would define a contextual connection between the <P> and <B> tags as follows.

```
<STYLE TYPE="text/javascript">
        contextual(tags.p, tags.b).color = "red"
</STYLE>
```

Given the above style, a `<B>` tag set in a `<DIV>` or `<H1>` block would be displayed in the default color; but inside any `<P>` block, the color would be red.

Style Properties

If you use JavaScript Style Sheets, you must use the JavaScript syntax for setting style properties. For the most part, the property names are interCap versions of the CSS property names (which often include hyphens that JavaScript can't handle in identifiers). In-depth coverage of these properties and how to use them are within the scope of a volume dedicated to Dynamic HTML, not a JavaScript book, but I would be remiss if this book did not include at least a quick reference to the terminology. If the day should come that more of these properties are modifiable on the fly, then all of these properties (and the tags, classes, and ids objects) will become part of Navigator's document object model and move into the mainstream of JavaScript programming on Navigator.

Properties listed in this section are properties of the tags, classes, and ids objects. Many properties rely on specific settings, rather than numeric values. As a result, these items have a default value that governs the property if the property is not explicitly set in the style sheet.

In the property listings that follow, you will see several property value types listed as *size*. This usually means that the property must be set to a particular length that can be specified in several different units. When the content is designed for display on computer screen (as opposed to designed exclusively for printing), the unit is usually the pixel, abbreviated "px." Thus, a value to be set to 20 pixels would be entered as `20px`. Other supported unit measures are points, ems, picas, and x-height, entered as `pt`, `em`, `pi`, and `ex`, respectively.

As with HTML attributes that specify color, style properties for colors accept either Netscape color names or the standard RGB hexadecimal-triplet color designation. Note, however, that in Navigator 4, if you retrieve a color value, it may be returned as a decimal equivalent of the hexadecimal value. This makes it difficult to test for the current color of an object.

Block-level formatting properties

A block-level element is one that is normally rendered as a self-contained item, beginning its display on a new line and ending its display such that the next element appears on a new line after the block. For example, all the heading tags (for example, `<H1>`) are block-level elements, because the content between the start and end tags always starts on a new line, and forces a pseudo line break after the end. Properties that affect block-level rendering are shown in Table 42-1.

Block-level elements lend themselves to being surrounded by borders. They also can have margins, padding between borders and content, and other properties that befit a rectangular space on the page. When a block-level element property is one of a matched set, such as the top, left, bottom, and right edges of a block, JavaScript style sheets usually provide a single method that lets you set all four properties in one statement. For example, you can set the `borderWidth` property for any single side with the specific property name (such as borderWidthTop), but to set all four at once, use the borderWidths() method, and fill in four parameters to set a block's complete border width specification:

```
classes.special.div.borderWidths("2px","3px","2px","3px")
```

Before using these methods, be sure you understand which parameter treats which side of the block. In the case of borders, the parameter sequence starts on the top edge and progresses clockwise around the rectangle.

Table 42-1
Block-level Style Properties

Property	Default	Values
align	none	left | right | none
backgroundColor	*browser default*	*colorName* | *RGB*
backgroundImage	*empty*	*URL*
borderBottomWidth	0	*size*
borderLeftWidth	0	*size*
borderRightWidth	0	*size*
borderTopWidth	0	*size*
borderWidths()	0,0,0,0	*valueTop, valueRight, valueBottom, valueLeft*
borderColor	none	*colorValue* | none
borderStyle	none	none | solid | 3D
clear	none	left | right | both | none
color	*browser default*	*colorName* | *RGB*
height	auto	*size* | auto
marginBottom	0	*size* | *percentage* | auto
marginLeft	0	*size* | *percentage* | auto
marginRight	0	*size* | *percentage* | auto
marginTop	0	*size* | *percentage* | auto
margins()	0,0,0,0	*valueTop, valueRight, valueBottom, valueLeft*
paddingBottom	0	*size* | *percentage*
paddingLeft	0	*size* | *percentage*
paddingRight	0	*size* | *percentage*
paddingTop	0	*size* | *percentage*
paddings()	0,0,0,0	*valueTop, valueRight, valueBottom, valueLeft*
width	auto	*size* | auto

Font and text properties

The next grouping, shown in Table 42-2, encompasses properties that control the look of fonts and text. These properties can be assigned to block-level and in-line elements.

To specify a value for the `fontFamily` property, you can name specific fonts or classes of fonts, each separated by a comma. The browser attempts to find a match for the font name on the user's system (the list of available fonts may be smaller than installed fonts, however). If no match occurs, the browser tries to use the next font specification in the font family list. For example, if you want to define Arial as the primary font and a generic serif font from the built-in list of generic font families (`serif`, `sans-serif`, `cursive`, `monospace`, and `fantasy`), define a tag style property like the following:

```
tags.p.fontFamily = "Arial, serif"
```

When a text property in Table 42-2 includes choices for a size or a percentage, the property may be influenced by related settings of a parent container. For example, if a paragraph tag has its `fontSize` property set to `large`, a style for an in-line tag inside that paragraph uses the parent container's settings as a starting point. Therefore, to increase the font size for an in-line item (say, a `<DIV>` tag) to 150 percent of the parent, define the style as follows:

```
tags.div.fontSize *= 1.5
```

With the multiply-by-value operator at work here, the property value acts as a percentage value over the value inherited from the parent. You can read more about the fine points of style inheritance at Netscape's online documentation for Dynamic HTML (`http://developer.netscape.com/library/documentation/-communicator/dynhtml/`).

Table 42-2
Font and Text Style Properties

Property	Default	Values
fontFamily	*browser default*	*fontFamilyList*
fontSize	medium	x-small	small	medium	large	x-large	xx-large	larger	smaller	[+/-] *integer*	*percentage*
fontStyle	normal	normal	italic	italic small-caps	oblique	oblique small-caps	small-caps
fontWeight	normal	normal	bold	bolder	lighter	100 - 900
lineHeight	*browser default*	*number*	*size*	*percentage*
textAlign	*browser default*	left	right	center	justify
textDecoration	none	none	underline	overline	line-through	blink

(continued)

	Table 42-2 *(continued)*	
Property	*Default*	*Values*
textIndent	0	*size* | *percentage*
textTransform	none	none | capitalize | lowercase | uppercase
verticalAlign	baseline	baseline | sub | super | top | text-top | middle | bottom | text-bottom | percentage

Classification properties

One last group of properties, shown in Table 42-3, works more in the plumbing of style sheets, rather than impacting visual elements on a page. The first property, display, defines whether a tag should be treated as a block, inline, or list-item element. All HTML tags have default settings for this property, but you can override the default behavior, which may come in handy as you deploy generic tags such as <DIV> and <SPAN> for special purposes in your document.

The second property, listStyleType, gives you control over the way unordered and ordered lists display leading characters for their items. You assign this property to any tag whose display property is set to list-item (such as the <UL> and <OL> tags). And the third property, whiteSpace, defines how white space in the HTML source should be treated by the browser rendering engine. Normal processing collapses white space, but setting the property to pre is the same as surrounding a source in a <PRE> tag set.

	Table 42-3 Classification Properties	
Property	*Default*	*Values*
display	*HTML default*	block | inline | list-item | none
listStyleType	disc	disc | circle | square | decimal | lower-roman | upper-roman | lower-alpha | upper-alpha | none
whiteSpace	normal	normal | pre

Dynamic Positioning

In addition to supporting the Cascading Style Sheets-Positioning (CSS-P) standard, Navigator 4 also features its own implementation of a Dynamic HTML positioning system. This system is built around the layer object — generally created via the <LAYER> tag — which is so far unique to Navigator. Chapter 19 goes into great detail about the layer object and provides several example pages that help you learn how the object's properties, methods, and event handlers work.

In this chapter, I apply the <LAYER> object to the Dynamic HTML example shown for the first time as a cross-platform DHTML application in Chapter 41. Because the version in this chapter deals with only one platform, the amount of code is substantially less.

Navigator puzzle game overview

The Navigator-only version of the game relies on two HTML files and numerous image files. The main HTML file loads to reveal the play area (Figure 42-1). Content and HTML rendering instructions for a normally hidden panel of instructions are in the second HTML file. That second file is loaded as the source for a <LAYER> object defined in the main document. But, as you will see, even the secondary document contains JavaScript Style Sheets to help format the content as desired. Image files for this and the other two versions of the game are completely identical.

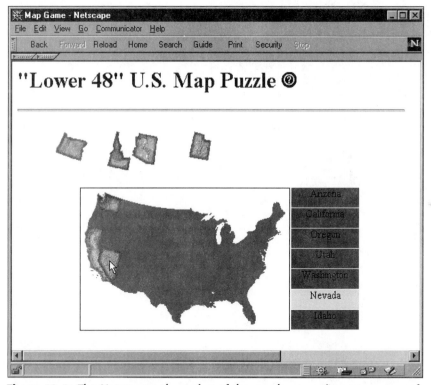

Figure 42-1: The Netscape-only version of the puzzle game (Image courtesy of Cartesia Software — www.map-art.com)

Structure of the main HTML document is straightforward. A large <SCRIPT> tag segment in the Head portion contains all the scripting for the main document (the instructions file has its own scripting). Document-level event capture is set for the main document to control the picking up, dragging, and release of state maps.

The main document

Listing 42-1 contains the entire source code for the main document. In most cases, the scripting code is identical to the Navigator portion of scripts in the cross-platform version. One large exception is that there is no external library of DHTML APIs, because the scripts can take direct advantage of Navigator's own vocabulary for layer properties and methods.

A big divergence between the versions appears in the usage of the <LAYER> tag throughout the Body portion of this chapter's version. Each positionable element is defined as a layer. Layer object properties that have the same names as JavaScript style properties are not the same items. For example, you cannot set the height and width of a layer object via the style sheet syntax in a <STYLE> tag elsewhere in the document.

For in-depth descriptions of the functions in the script and the structure of the layer objects, see the commentary associated with Listing 41-2.

Listing 42-1: **The Main Document (NSmapgam.htm)**

```
<HTML>
<HEAD><TITLE>Map Game</TITLE>
<SCRIPT LANGUAGE="JavaScript">
// global variables
// click offsets
var offsetX = 0
var offsetY = 0
// info about clicked state map
var selectedObj
var selectedState = ""
var selectedStateIndex
var intervalID

// state object constructor
function state(abbrev, fullName, x, y) {
        this.abbrev = abbrev
        this.fullName = fullName
        // correct destination position
        this.x = x
        this.y = y
        this.done = false
}
// build states objects
var states = new Array()
states[0] = new state("ca", "California", 107, 234)
states[1] = new state("or", "Oregon", 107, 204)
states[2] = new state("wa", "Washington", 123, 188)
states[3] = new state("id", "Idaho", 148, 197)
states[4] = new state("az", "Arizona", 145, 285)
states[5] = new state("nv", "Nevada", 127, 241)
states[6] = new state("ut", "Utah", 155, 249)
```

```
// find out which state map layer is clicked on
function getSelectedMap(clickX, clickY) {
      var obj
      var testObj
      for (var i = states.length - 1; i >= 0; i--) {
            testObj = document.layers[states[i].abbrev + "map"]
            if ((clickX > testObj.left) && (clickX < testObj.left +
testObj.clip.width) && (clickY > testObj.top) && (clickY < testObj.top
+ testObj.clip.height)) {
                  obj = testObj
                  break
            }
      }
      selectedObj = obj
      if (selectedObj) {
            selectedStateLabel =
document.bgmap.document.layers[states[i].abbrev + "label"]
            selectedStateIndex = i
            // zoom the selected map to the frontmost layer
            selectedObj.zIndex = 100
      }
}
// handle drag
function dragIt(e) {
      if (selectedObj) {
            selectedObj.moveTo(e.pageX - offsetX, e.pageY - offsetY)
      }
}
// turn click mode on and off
function toggleEngage(e) {
      if (selectedObj) {
            release(e)
      } else {
            engage(e)
      }
}
// turn click mode on
function engage(e) {
      // set global selected values
      getSelectedMap(e.pageX, e.pageY)
      if (selectedObj) {
            // store click offsets within layer and save to globals
            offsetX = e.pageX - selectedObj.left
            offsetY = e.pageY - selectedObj.top
            // turn corresponding label background to yellow
            selectedStateLabel.bgColor = "yellow"
      }
}
// handle mouse button release
function release(e) {
      if (selectedObj) {
            // see if state has been dragged to within 4 pixels of
destination
```

(continued)

Listing 42-1 *(continued)*

```
            if (onTarget(e)) {
                // set label to green
                selectedStateLabel.bgColor = "green"
                // and state object's done property to true
                states[selectedStateIndex].done = true
                // see if you're done and flash the labels
                if (isDone()) {
                    document.congrats.visibility="visible"
                }
            } else {
                // otherwise revert label to red
                selectedStateLabel.bgColor = "red"
                states[selectedStateIndex].done = false
                document.congrats.visibility="hidden"
            }
            // set object z-order to bottom
            selectedObj.zIndex = 0
            selectedObj = null
            selectedState = ""
        }
}
// test whether dragged map is near destination
function onTarget(e) {
        // get destination coords from states object
        var x = states[selectedStateIndex].x
        var y = states[selectedStateIndex].y
        // get current location
        var objX = selectedObj.pageX
        var objY = selectedObj.pageY
        // see if object is within 4 pixels of destination
        if ((objX >= x-2 && objX <= x+2) && (objY >= y-2 && objY <=
y+2)) {
            // snap object to destination
            selectedObj.moveTo(x,y)
            return true
        }
        return false
}
// test if all states have been placed
function isDone() {
        for (var i = 0; i < states.length; i++) {
            if (!states[i].done) {
                return false
            }
        }
        return true
}
function showHelp() {
        var help = document.help
        help.visibility = "show"
```

```
            help.zIndex = 1000
            intervalID = setInterval(moveHelp,1)
}
function moveHelp(obj) {
            var help = document.help
            help.moveBy(-5,0)
            if (help.pageX <= (window.innerWidth/2) - 150) {
                clearInterval(intervalID)
            }
}
function setEvents() {
            document.captureEvents(Event.MOUSEDOWN | Event.MOUSEMOVE)
            document.onMouseDown = toggleEngage
            document.onMouseMove = dragIt
}
</SCRIPT>
</HEAD>
<BODY onLoad="setEvents()">
<H1>"Lower 48" U.S. Map Puzzle <A HREF="javascript:void
showHelp()" onMouseOver="status='Show help panel....';return true"
onMouseOut="status='';return true"><IMG SRC="info.gif" HEIGHT=22
WIDTH=22 BORDER=0></A></H1>
<HR>
<LAYER ID="help" TOP=80 LEFT=&{window.innerWidth}; WIDTH=300
VISIBILITY="HIDDEN" SRC="instrux.htm"></LAYER>

<LAYER ID="bgmap" TOP=180 LEFT=100><IMG SRC="us11.gif" WIDTH=306
HEIGHT=202 BORDER=1>
<LAYER ID="azlabel" TOP=0 LEFT=310 BGCOLOR="red" WIDTH=100
HEIGHT=28><CENTER>Arizona</CENTER></LAYER>
<LAYER ID="calabel" TOP=29 LEFT=310 BGCOLOR="red" WIDTH=100
HEIGHT=28><CENTER>California</CENTER></LAYER>
<LAYER ID="orlabel" TOP=58 LEFT=310 BGCOLOR="red" WIDTH=100
HEIGHT=28><CENTER>Oregon</CENTER></LAYER>
<LAYER ID="utlabel" TOP=87 LEFT=310 BGCOLOR="red" WIDTH=100
HEIGHT=28><CENTER>Utah</CENTER></LAYER>
<LAYER ID="walabel" TOP=116 LEFT=310 BGCOLOR="red" WIDTH=100
HEIGHT=28><CENTER>Washington</CENTER></LAYER>
<LAYER ID="nvlabel" TOP=145 LEFT=310 BGCOLOR="red" WIDTH=100
HEIGHT=28><CENTER>Nevada</CENTER></LAYER>
<LAYER ID="idlabel" TOP=174 LEFT=310 BGCOLOR="red" WIDTH=100
HEIGHT=28><CENTER>Idaho</CENTER></LAYER>
</LAYER>

<LAYER ID="congrats" TOP=100 LEFT=20 VISIBILITY="HIDDEN"><H1><FONT
COLOR="red">Congratulations!</FONT></H1></LAYER>
<LAYER ID="camap" TOP=100 LEFT=20><IMG SRC="ca.gif" WIDTH=47 HEIGHT=82
BORDER=0></LAYER>
<LAYER ID="ormap" TOP=100 LEFT=60><IMG SRC="or.gif" WIDTH=57 HEIGHT=45
BORDER=0></LAYER>
<LAYER ID="wamap" TOP=100 LEFT=100><IMG SRC="wa.gif" WIDTH=38 HEIGHT=29
BORDER=0></LAYER>
```

(continued)

Listing 42-1 *(continued)*

```
<LAYER ID="idmap" TOP=100 LEFT=140><IMG SRC="id.gif" WIDTH=34 HEIGHT=55
BORDER=0></LAYER>
<LAYER ID="azmap" TOP=100 LEFT=180><IMG SRC="az.gif" WIDTH=38 HEIGHT=45
BORDER=0></LAYER>
<LAYER ID="nvmap" TOP=100 LEFT=220><IMG SRC="nv.gif" WIDTH=35 HEIGHT=56
BORDER=0></LAYER>
<LAYER ID="utmap" TOP=100 LEFT=260><IMG SRC="ut.gif" WIDTH=33 HEIGHT=41
BORDER=0></LAYER>

<SCRIPT LANGUAGE="JavaScript">
</SCRIPT>
</BODY>
</HTML>
```

The help panel

Content for the flying help panel comes from the second file, instrux.htm. The source for that document is shown in Listing 42-2. Although quite simple as HTML goes, this document benefits from a couple style rules. Without setting the `marginTop` property of the first paragraph or the `marginRight` property of the ordered list entries, the text would be positioned too close to the edges of the panel. Other style properties could also be used to make the same adjustments. You can see the results in Figure 42-2.

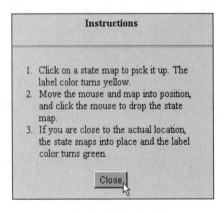

Figure 42-2: The help panel at rest

An advantage of having a layer's content loaded as a separate HTML document comes home in this example. All event handling and scripting related to this positionable element is encapsulated in the external document. Nothing from this document clutters the source code of the main document, except for the animation routine. Moreover, the content can be reused in another document by having another `<LAYER>` tag load it in.

Listing 42-2: **The Help Panel Document (instrux.htm)**

```
<HTML>
<HEAD>
<STYLE TYPE="text/javascript">
tags.P.marginTop = 5
tags.OL.marginRight = 20
</STYLE>
<SCRIPT LANGUAGE="JavaScript">
window.captureEvents(Event.CLICK)
window.onclick = hideMe
function hideMe() {
        window.document.help.visibility = "hidden"
        window.document.help.moveTo(window.innerWidth,120)
}
</SCRIPT>
</HEAD>
<BODY BGCOLOR="#98FB98">
<P><CENTER><B>Instructions</B></CENTER></P>
<HR COLOR="seagreen">
<OL>
<LI>Click on a state map to pick it up. The label color turns yellow.
<LI>Move the mouse and map into position, and click the mouse to drop
the state map.
<LI>If you are close to the actual location, the state snaps into
place and the label color turns green.
</OL>
<FORM>
<CENTER>
<INPUT TYPE="button" VALUE="Close" onClick="">
</CENTER>
</FORM>
</BODY>
</HTML>
```

Lessons learned

Because I am comfortable with Netscape's document object model and the hierarchy of nested objects such as frames, the experience of building this page with the <LAYER> tag and its scriptable pieces seemed like a natural extension to my previous knowledge. Using separate HTML files as building blocks to a complex document also has its appeal in a number of application scenarios. At the same time, it becomes clear that JavaScript Style Sheets and positionable elements are two distinct components of Navigator Dynamic HTML. There is very little overlap in the syntax or objects in the implementation of Navigator 4. Even so, if my deployment environment were guaranteed to be Navigator 4 only, I would build the application with the Netscape-specific extensions.

✦   ✦   ✦

Microsoft Dynamic HTML

When comparing the implementation of Dynamic HTML in Navigator 4 and Internet Explorer 4, you get the impression that Internet Explorer 4's DHTML is more flexible and better integrated into the whole of authoring for the browser. Some of this advantage comes from being a more recent product in the game of leapfrog that Microsoft and Netscape play with browser and technology releases. Internet Explorer 4's style sheets use the Cascading Style Sheets (CSS) recommendation as a basis for its extensions. The same is true for the CSS-Positioning (CSS-P) capabilities in the browser.

Authors, however, pay a price for the flexibility built into Internet Explorer 4. The extensive object model and its large complement of properties, methods, and event handlers creates an enormous vocabulary to get to know and work with. Experienced scripters may not have a problem with this, because knowing where to look for information is almost second nature. But newcomers, or those upgrading their skills from HTML to DHTML and scripting, have much to become acquainted with before feeling comfortable in the environment.

Internet Explorer 4 Document Object Model

At the core of Internet Explorer's DHTML and scripting functionality is an impressive document object model. In addition to the typical object containment hierarchy in use since the earliest days of JavaScript, Internet Explorer 4 also turns every document element that can be contained within a tag pair into a scriptable object. This includes style tags (such as `<B>...</B>`) as well as the more obvious block tags (such as `<P>...</P>`). Each of these objects has a set of properties, methods, and event handlers.

A typical object

To give you an idea of the kinds of properties, methods, and event handlers assigned to a tag as simple as the bold tag, Table 43-1 lists the scriptable support for the <B> tag.

Table 43-1
Internet Explorer 4 B Object (<B>)
Properties, Methods, and Events

Property	Description
className	Value assigned to a CLASS attribute of the tag
document	Reference to the containing document
id	Value assigned to an ID attribute of the tag
innerHTML	Text of HTML between the start and end tags
innerText	Text between the start and end tags
isTextEdit	Boolean flag whether the object can be used to create a text range
lang	ISO language to use in rendering tag content
language	Scripting language of the current script
offsetHeight	Element height within the parent coordinate system
offsetLeft	Element left position within the parent coordinate system
offsetParent	Reference to the container element
offsetTop	Element top position within the parent coordinate system
offsetWidth	Element width within the parent coordinate system
outerHTML	Text of HTML including tags
outerText	Text between tags
parentElement	Reference to parent element
parentTextEdit	Reference to next higher element that can be used to create a text range
sourceIndex	Index of item within the all collection (array) of document elements
style	Reference to the style object associated with the element
tagName	Name of the tag (without angle brackets)
title	Text of tooltip assigned to the TITLE attribute of the tag

Method	Description
click()	Scripted click of the element
contains()	Whether the current element is in the parent hierarchy above another element
getAttribute()	Value of a particular tag attribute
insertAdjacentHTML()	Insert text and/or HTML into the element
insertAdjacentText()	Insert text into the element
removeAttribute()	Delete an attribute and value from the tag
scrollIntoView()	Scroll the page to bring the element into view
setAttribute()	Set a tag attribute's value

Event Handler	Description
onclick	Mouse click
ondblclick	Mouse double-click
ondragstart	Beginning of dragging an object or selection
onfilterchange	Change of filter or end of a transition
onhelp	Press of F1 key
onkeydown	Key down
onkeypress	Complete key press
onkeyup	Key up
onmousedown	Mouse down
onmousemove	Moving the mouse
onmouseout	Moving the cursor out of the element
onmouseover	Moving the cursor into the element
onmouseup	Mouse up
onselectStart	Beginning to select text of the element

The properties and methods that intrigue me the most are the ones that let scripts modify the content of a tag — or the tag itself — after the document has loaded. The rendering engine in Internet Explorer 4 automatically and quickly reflows a page's content in response to a script-driven change in a tag's content. For many scripters, this represents a breakthrough from the design shackles of having to put all script-modifiable text inside text and textarea input objects. That's what I call truly *dynamic* HTML.

The text range

To facilitate working with modifiable content, Internet Explorer 4 defines an object called textRange. The full description of its inner workings is beyond the scope of this book, but I mention it here as a way to fill what may be a gap in understanding how portions of text can be manipulated inside a document or tag.

A text range is a temporary object that defines the start and end point of a chunk of text inside a document. I call it a temporary object because, after you create a text range in a script, it lives only as long as the script function (and any function it calls) is running. Once the function completes its task, the text range goes away.

The textRange object contains many methods that enable a script to move the start and end points of a selection within a text range, find text, remove a chunk of text, and insert text at a specific point in the document. As one simple example of how to use the object, the following code fragment performs a search and replace throughout an entire document.

```
// define the whole body as a text range
var range = document.body.createTextRange()
// loop through range as often as it finds the match word
// and set start/end points to found text
for (var i = 0; range.findText("today") != -1; i++) {
        // scroll document to bring matching word into view
        range.scrollIntoView()
        // select it for visual feedback
        range.select()
        // change the found text
        range.text = "tomorrow"
}
```

The style object

Almost every object in the Internet Explorer 4 object model contains a style object. This is the object that manages the properties for DHTML appearance and positioning settings. Initial values for the object property are established in the <STYLE> tag set, in a STYLE attribute of a tag, or are imported from an external style sheet specification file. The list of properties of the style object is based on the CSS1 recommendation, plus many extensions that are available only in Internet Explorer 4. When a property name contains a hyphen, the scripted property name is generally converted to an interCap format (identifiers in JavaScript cannot contain hyphens).

The range of properties for the style object is quite extensive. Twenty properties alone influence borders around blocks. Later in this chapter you will see a list of properties of the style object.

Referencing objects — the all collection

Internet Explorer 4 objects that are defined in the document by HTML tags become what Internet Explorer 4 calls *element* objects. The main document object has a property that exposes every element object in the document, even when objects are deeply nested within each other. The document property is the all collection (*collection* is a term Internet Explorer 4 uses to represent an array of document objects). A reference that begins with

```
document.all
```

can "see" every element object in the document. Therefore, if you have a tag whose ID attribute is "fred", then you can create a reference to that object with

```
document.all.fred
```

From that point, you can access the style object associated with the object

```
document.all.fred.style.propertyName
```

or any of the element's own properties (such as the properties shown previously in Table 43-1).

You can also use the all collection to reach all instances of the same tag in a document. The tags property lets you specify a particular tag type, from which your script can retrieve an array (collection) of objects with that tag, as shown in the following excerpt:

```
var allBs = document.all.tags("B")
for (var i = 0; i < allBs.length; i++) {
        allBs[i].style.color = "red"
}
```

After the preceding script runs, all contents set to bold via the <B> tag will have its text color appear in red.

Do not confuse the all and tags keywords in Internet Explorer's DHTML vocabulary with the same words in the Navigator DHTML vocabulary. The keywords are used entirely differently in the two environments.

Style Object Properties

This section presents all of the properties of the Internet Explorer 4 style object. The list is long, so I have divided the properties into logical groups (Tables 43-2 through 43-6), based as much as possible on the functionality provided by the property or area of interest. One column of the table also indicates which items are reflected in the Cascading Style Sheets recommendations of the W3C. All other items are unique to Internet Explorer.

If you examine Microsoft's documentation for these properties, you see frequent references to properties being related to Cascading Style Sheets. This is certainly true as far as Microsoft's extended implementation of CSS goes, but not all of these properties are part of the W3C CSS1 recommendation.

Table 43-2
Internet Explorer 4 Style Object
Background and Color Properties

Property	CSS1	Description
background	✔	Shortcut to numerous background properties
backgroundAttachment	✔	Whether the background should scroll or be fixed
backgroundColor	✔	Background color
backgroundImage	✔	URL of image
backgroundPosition	✔	Top-left position of background image
backgroundPositionX		Left position of background image
backgroundPositionY		Top position of background image
backgroundRepeat	✔	Whether the background image should repeat and how often
color	✔	Text (foreground) color

Table 43-3
Internet Explorer 4 Style Object Box Properties

Property	CSS1	Description
border	✔	Shortcut to border width, style, and color properties
borderBottom	✔	Shortcut to bottom border width, style, and color properties
borderBottomColor		Color of bottom border
borderBottomStyle		Style of bottom border
borderBottomWidth	✔	Width of bottom border
borderColor	✔	Color for all border edges of a box
borderLeft	✔	Shortcut to left border width, style, and color properties
borderLeftColor		Color of left border
borderLeftStyle		Style of left border
borderLeftWidth	✔	Width of left border
borderRight	✔	Shortcut to right border width, style, and color properties
borderRightColor		Color of right border

Property	CSS1	Description
borderRightStyle		Style of right border
borderRightWidth	✔	Width of right border
borderStyle	✔	Style of all border edges of a box
borderTop	✔	Shortcut to top border width, style, and color properties
borderTopColor		Color of top border
borderTopStyle		Style of top border
borderTopWidth	✔	Width of top border
borderWidth	✔	Width of all border edges of a box
clear	✔	Side(s) on which floating elements cannot appear
height	✔	Element height (with units)
paddingBottom	✔	Bottom padding
paddingLeft	✔	Left padding
paddingRight	✔	Right padding
paddingTop	✔	Top padding
styleFloat	✔	How text wraps around an element
width	✔	Element width measure (with units)

Table 43-4
Internet Explorer 4 Style Font and Text Properties

Property	CSS1	Description
font	✔	Shortcut to font properties in one statement
fontFamily	✔	Font family name
fontSize	✔	Font size
fontStyle	✔	Font style
fontVariant	✔	Font variant style
fontWeight	✔	Font weight
letterSpacing	✔	Text letter spacing
lineHeight	✔	Text line height
margin	✔	Shortcut to four margin settings

(continued)

	Table 43-4 *(continued)*	
Property	**CSS1**	**Description**
marginBottom	✔	Bottom margin
marginLeft	✔	Left margin
marginRight	✔	Right margin
marginTop	✔	Top margin
pageBreakAfter		Break page after the element when printing
pageBreakBefore		Break page before the element when printing
pixelHeight		Integer height measure
pixelWidth		Integer width measure
textAlign	✔	Text alignment in the element
textDecoration		Text decoration setting
textDecorationBlink		Blinking text (not supported)
textDecorationLineThrough		Strikethrough text
textDecorationNone		Remove decoration
textDecorationOverline		Overline decoration
textDecorationUnderline		Underline decoration
textIndent	✔	Size of indentation of the first line of a block
textTransform	✔	Initial capital, uppercase, lowercase, none
verticalAlign	✔	Vertical positioning relative to the parent

	Table 43-5	
	Internet Explorer 4 Classification and Housekeeping Properties	
Property	**CSS1**	**Description**
cssText		String representation of the CSS rule
cursor		Cursor while pointer is atop an element (for example, "hand," "wait")
display	✔	How or if an element should be rendered
filter		Name of a filter effect

Property	CSS1	Description
listStyle	✔	Shortcut to setting list style properties
listStyleImage	✔	List item image URL
listStylePosition	✔	List item indent/outdent style
listStyleType	✔	List item enumeration character type

Table 43-6
Internet Explorer 4 Style Positioning Properties

Property	CSS-P	Description
clip	✔	Rectangle of viewing region of a style
left	✔	Element left position (with units)
overflow	✔	How to handle overflow content
pixelLeft		Integer left coordinate
pixelTop		Integer top coordinate
posHeight		Floating-point height measure
position	✔	Absolute or relative positioning
posLeft		Floating-point left measure
posTop		Floating-point top measure
posWidth		Floating-point width measure
top	✔	Element top coordinate (with units)
visibility	✔	Whether item can be seen
zIndex	✔	Z-order of element among peers

Dynamic Positioning

Internet Explorer blends the CSS1 and CSS-P recommendations into the document object model and especially the style object. All positioning properties for elements are reflected through the style object, as shown in Table 43-6.

To demonstrate dynamic positioning in action in Internet Explorer, I present the third and final version of the map puzzle game that is implemented earlier in this book in a cross-platform version (Chapter 41) and Navigator-only version (Chapter 42). In this chapter's version, the implementation uses Internet Explorer 4's Cascading Style Sheets for positioning and document object model for scripting the elements. The version shown here will not run successfully in Navigator 4.

Navigator puzzle game overview

The Explorer-only version of the game consists of one HTML file and numerous image files. The document loads to reveal the play area (Figure 43-1). The HTML for the normally hidden panel is integrated into the main document, but as a distinct block-level element. This element specifies a couple of styles for some of the nested elements to help format the content as desired. Image files for this and the other two versions of the game are completely identical.

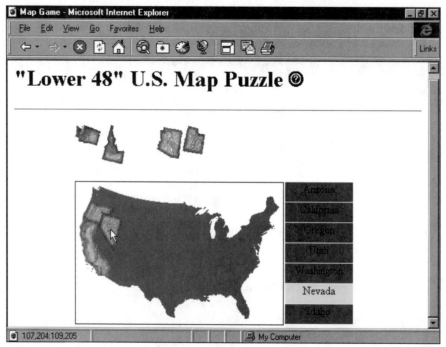

Figure 43-1: The Internet Explorer–only version of the puzzle game (Image courtesy Cartesia Software — www.map-art.com)

Structure of the HTML document is straightforward. A large <SCRIPT> tag segment in the Head portion contains all the scripting for the document (including the dynamic help panel). Document-level event capture is set in the <BODY> tag for the main document to control the picking up, dragging, and release of state maps.

The document

Listing 43-1 contains the entire source code for the document. In most cases, the scripting code is identical to the Internet Explorer portion of scripts in the cross-platform version. No external DHTML API file is needed because the scripts can take direct advantage of Explorer's own vocabulary for style properties. Another small difference is that you have no need for a link surrounding the help image in this version. Internet Explorer 4's document object model defines numerous event handlers for the image object directly.

Positionable elements are defined as CSS-P items, with the style for each element defined in a `<STYLE>` tag at the beginning of the document. `<DIV>` tags in the HTML associate the styles with content blocks. The block for the help panel includes CSS1 styles for a couple of the tags to assist in text formatting.

For in-depth descriptions of the functions in the script and the structure of the positionable objects, see the commentary associated with Listing 41-2.

Listing 43-1: **The Internet Explorer Puzzle Document (IEmapgm.htm)**

```
<HTML>
<HEAD><TITLE>Map Game</TITLE>
<STYLE TYPE="text/css">

        #help {position:absolute; visibility:hidden; top:80; width:300;
background-color:"#98FB98";}
        #bgmap {position:absolute; left:100; top:180; width:1;}

        #azlabel {position:absolute; left:310; top:0; background-
color:red; width:100; height:28; text-align:center;}
        #calabel {position:absolute; left:310; top:29; background-
color:red; width:100; height:28; text-align:center;}
        #orlabel {position:absolute; left:310; top:58; background-
color:red; width:100; height:28; text-align:center;}
        #utlabel {position:absolute; left:310; top:87; background-
color:red; width:100; height:28; text-align:center;}
        #walabel {position:absolute; left:310; top:116; background-
color:red; width:100; height:28; text-align:center;}
        #nvlabel {position:absolute; left:310; top:145; background-
color:red; width:100; height:28; text-align:center;}
        #idlabel {position:absolute; left:310; top:174; background-
color:red; width:100; height:28; text-align:center;}

        #camap {position:absolute; left:20; top:100; width:1;}
        #ormap {position:absolute; left:60; top:100; width:1;}
        #wamap {position:absolute; left:100; top:100; width:1;}
        #idmap {position:absolute; left:140; top:100; width:1;}
        #nvmap {position:absolute; left:180; top:100; width:1;}
        #azmap {position:absolute; left:220; top:100; width:1;}
        #utmap {position:absolute; left:260; top:100; width:1;}

        #congrats {position:absolute; visibility:hidden; left:20;
top:100; width:1;}

</STYLE>

<SCRIPT LANGUAGE="JavaScript">
//var engaged = false
var offsetX = 0
var offsetY = 0
```

(continued)

Listing 43-1 *(continued)*

```
var selectedObj
var selectedState = ""
var selectedStateIndex

function state(abbrev, fullName, x, y) {
      this.abbrev = abbrev
      this.fullName = fullName
      this.x = x
      this.y = y
      this.done = false
}
var states = new Array()
states[0] = new state("ca", "California", 107, 234)
states[1] = new state("or", "Oregon", 107, 204)
states[2] = new state("wa", "Washington", 123, 188)
states[3] = new state("id", "Idaho", 148, 197)
states[4] = new state("az", "Arizona", 145, 285)
states[5] = new state("nv", "Nevada", 127, 241)
states[6] = new state("ut", "Utah", 155, 249)
function showProps(obj, objName) {
      var result = ""
      count = 0
      for (var i in obj) {
          result += objName + "." + i + "=" + obj[i] + "\n"
          count++
          if (count == 25) {
              alert(result)
              result = ""
              count = 0
          }
      }
      alert(result)
}
function getSelectedMap() {
      selectedObj = (window.event.srcElement).parentElement
      if (selectedObj) {
          var stateName = selectedObj.id.substring(0,2)
          selectedObj = selectedObj.style
          for (var i = 0; i < states.length; i++) {
              if (states[i].abbrev == stateName ) {
                  selectedStateLabel = document.all(stateName +
"label")
                  selectedStateIndex = i
                  selectedObj.zIndex = 100
                  return
              }
          }
          selectedObj = null
          selectedStateLabel = null
          selectedStateIndex = null
      }
```

```
            return
    }
    function dragIt() {
            if (selectedObj) {
                selectedObj.pixelLeft = (window.event.clientX - offsetX)
                selectedObj.pixelTop = (window.event.clientY - offsetY)
            }
    }
    function toggleEngage() {
            if (selectedObj) {
                release()
            } else {
                engage()
            }
    }
    function engage() {
            getSelectedMap()
            if (selectedObj) {
                offsetX = window.event.offsetX - document.body.scrollLeft
                offsetY = window.event.offsetY - document.body.scrollTop
                selectedStateLabel.style.backgroundColor = "yellow"
            }
    }
    function release() {
            if (selectedObj) {
                if (onTarget()) {
                    selectedStateLabel.style.backgroundColor = "green"
                    states[selectedStateIndex].done = true
                    if (isDone()) {
                        document.all.congrats.style.visibility = "visible"
                    }
                } else {
                    selectedStateLabel.style.backgroundColor = "red"
                    states[selectedStateIndex].done = false
                    document.all.congrats.style.visibility = "hidden"
                }
                selectedObj.zIndex = 0
                selectedObj = null
                selectedState = ""
            }
    }
    function onTarget() {
            var x = states[selectedStateIndex].x
            var y = states[selectedStateIndex].y
            var objX = selectedObj.pixelLeft
            var objY = selectedObj.pixelTop
            if ((objX >= x-2 && objX <= x+2) && (objY >= y-2 && objY <=
    y+2)) {
                selectedObj.pixelLeft = x
                selectedObj.pixelTop = y
                return true
            }
            return false
```

(continued)

Listing 43-1 *(continued)*

```
}
function isDone() {
        for (var i = 0; i < states.length; i++) {
            if (!states[i].done) {
                return false
            }
        }
        return true
}
function showHelp() {
        var help = document.all.help.style
        help.pixelLeft = document.body.scrollWidth
        help.visibility = "visible"
        help.zIndex = 1000
        intervalID = setInterval("moveHelp()",1)
}
function moveHelp() {
        var help = document.all.help.style
        help.pixelLeft -= 5
        if (help.pixelLeft <= (document.body.scrollWidth/2) -
(help.pixelWidth/2)) {
            clearInterval(intervalID)
        }
}
function hideMe() {
        clearInterval(intervalID)
        document.all.help.style.visibility = "hidden"
        document.all.help.style.pixelLeft = document.body.scrollWidth
}
</SCRIPT>
</HEAD>
<BODY onMouseDown="toggleEngage()" onMouseMove="dragIt()">
<H1>"Lower 48" U.S. Map Puzzle <IMG onClick="showHelp()"
onMouseOver="status='Show help panel...';return true"
onMouseOut="status=''" SRC="info.gif" HEIGHT=22 WIDTH=22 BORDER=0></H1>
<HR>
<DIV ID="bgmap"><IMG SRC="us11.gif" WIDTH=306 HEIGHT=202
BORDER=1> </IMG>
<DIV ID="azlabel">Arizona</DIV>
<DIV ID="calabel">California</DIV>
<DIV ID="orlabel">Oregon</DIV>
<DIV ID="utlabel">Utah</DIV>
<DIV ID="walabel">Washington</DIV>
<DIV ID="nvlabel">Nevada</DIV>
<DIV ID="idlabel">Idaho</DIV>
</DIV>

<DIV ID="camap"><IMG SRC="ca.gif" WIDTH=47 HEIGHT=82 BORDER=0></DIV>
<DIV ID="ormap"><IMG SRC="or.gif" WIDTH=57 HEIGHT=45 BORDER=0></DIV>
<DIV ID="wamap"><IMG SRC="wa.gif" WIDTH=38 HEIGHT=29 BORDER=0></DIV>
```

```
<DIV ID="idmap"><IMG SRC="id.gif" WIDTH=34 HEIGHT=55 BORDER=0></DIV>
<DIV ID="azmap"><IMG SRC="az.gif" WIDTH=38 HEIGHT=45 BORDER=0></DIV>
<DIV ID="nvmap"><IMG SRC="nv.gif" WIDTH=35 HEIGHT=56 BORDER=0></DIV>
<DIV ID="utmap"><IMG SRC="ut.gif" WIDTH=33 HEIGHT=41 BORDER=0></DIV>

<DIV ID="congrats" STYLE="color:red"><H1>Congratulations!</H1></DIV>

<DIV ID="help" onClick="hideMe()">
<P STYLE="margin-top:5"><CENTER><B>Instructions</B></CENTER></P>
<HR COLOR="seagreen">
<OL STYLE="margin-right:20">
<LI>Click on a state map to pick it up. The label color turns yellow.
<LI>Move the mouse and map into position, and click the mouse to drop
the state map.
<LI>If you are close to the actual location, the state snaps into
place and the label color turns green.
</OL>
<FORM>
<CENTER>
<INPUT TYPE="button" VALUE="Close">
</FORM>
</DIV>
</BODY>
</HTML>
```

Lessons learned

The tight integration of dynamic positioning into Internet Explorer 4's CSS implementation provides a fairly logical framework for page design and scripting. Certainly the scriptable access to style properties on virtually any tag is a plus. Perhaps the addition of some higher-level methods for styles (for example, to be able to move an element in one method statement, instead of setting x and y pixel coordinates individually) would make the scripting more enjoyable, but the current way is not intolerable. With commitments by both Netscape and Microsoft to support standards, I wouldn't be surprised if a future version of Navigator supported the same kind of object and style access that Internet Explorer 4 provides now.

✦   ✦   ✦

Internet Explorer 4 JScript and Object Model

Diversity is often a good thing. But when you are trying to develop scripted Web applications that work on all browsers, diversity can become a hurdle to overcome. That's the case when authors learn scripting in one browser environment only to discover too late that some object, property, method, or event is not supported or is supported differently in the other browser.

By including "JavaScript" in the title of this book, I signal that the focus of the book is Netscape's implementation of the language in Navigator. But I cannot ignore Internet Explorer and its JScript language, which is derived from JavaScript. The purpose of this chapter is not to teach you everything you need to know about scripting in JScript for Internet Explorer–only applications. Instead, I want to provide an overview of the pieces in Internet Explorer 4 that differ. Some of what you read about here may eventually come to Navigator in a future version.

Core Language

Internet Explorer's internal architecture clearly distinguishes the core scripting language from the document object model. This is necessary in Internet Explorer because the browser supports two scripting languages: VBScript and JScript. While it is unlikely that a document would contain scripts in both languages, nothing prevents such a situation. Each `<SCRIPT>` tag set can be assigned a different language name in the `LANGUAGE` attribute, and the interpreter of only the named language is invoked for the script.

The core language consists of the normal kinds of programming constructs: how variables work; conditional constructions; data types; and similar items that any programming language needs, regardless of the object environment. Microsoft, Netscape, and other participants established a common denominator standard in 1997 under the auspices of the European Computer Manufacturer's Association (ECMA), a Switzerland-based standards body (http://www.ecma.ch). As mentioned in earlier chapters, the result is a core language description called ECMAScript.

ECMAScript is based on JavaScript Version 1.1, which was built into Navigator 3. Only a few minor differences exist between ECMAScript and JavaScript 1.1. The JScript implementation in Internet Explorer 4 is compatible with the ECMAScript standard (and with the Navigator JavaScript 1.2 core language, as well). But, because most standards define a common denominator, they don't preclude a supporter of the standard from adding proprietary extensions for a single platform. JScript includes some Internet Explorer 4–only extensions, including access to ActiveX constructs and language version checking.

Document Object Model

Figure 44-1 is a diagram of the document object model and containment hierarchy for Internet Explorer 4. Many elements are the same as Navigator, but I should point out the differences that may lead to confusion in terminology. I recommend that you also keep your finger in Appendix B's Navigator Object Road map to examine compatibility of properties, methods, and event handlers for the objects discussed in this section.

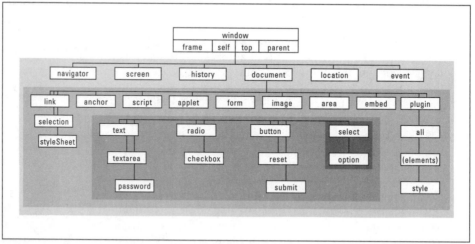

Figure 44-1: Internet Explorer 4 object containment hierarchy

Starting at the top of the hierarchy, Internet Explorer 4 encapsulates the navigator and screen objects inside the window object. Navigator, on the other hand, treats these objects independently of the document object model. Even with this apparent discrepancy, if you reference these objects without the window reference (as is often the case when referring to objects contained by a window), the same statements work in both browsers. Not all properties of these two objects are the same, however.

Diving one level inward to the document object and its components, you may recognize that Internet Explorer 4 has several more objects defined at this level than Navigator 4. The new items consist of the following objects: all; embed; plugin; script; selection; and styleSheet.

You met the all keyword in Chapters 41 and 43 in working with style sheets. This keyword is the gateway to objects defined by HTML tags that are not otherwise part of the object hierarchy. The embed and plugin objects are the same thing: objects reflecting items loaded into the document via the `<EMBED>` tag. Don't confuse this plugin object with Navigator's navigator.plugin object, which looks into the browser at the plug-ins installed in the browser.

A script object reflects the item created by a `<SCRIPT>` tag set. You can literally change the content of a script tag after the page loads. A select object is created whenever the user selects text in the body of the document. And a styleSheet object is added to a document for each `<STYLE>` tag set or each style sheet imported via the `<LINK>` tag.

Element objects

The most intriguing aspect of the Internet Explorer 4 document object model is that virtually every HTML tag in a document becomes an object, called an *element*. The name of each element is the name of the tag (without angle brackets), but for scripting purposes, you probably want to assign an ID attribute to tags you intend to address via scripts. This lets you build a convenient reference to the element through the document.all object. For example, you can define a paragraph tag with an ID as follows:

```
<P ID="quotation">...</P>
```

The ID attribute may be the same as a style defined earlier in the document to be applied to the paragraph block. Either way, you can access the object through a reference that begins

```
document.all.quotation
```

Every element has a number of properties, although most, by virtue of being element objects, have a wide range of properties in common. Among those properties are items such as offsetLeft, offsetTop, outerHTML, outerText, and style. Elements that are block elements (that is, they have start and end tag pairs) also have properties for innerHTML and innerText, which allow retrieval and modification of the text inside the block or the entire block itself (including the tags).

Table 44-1 lists all the element object names. Consult the Internet Explorer 4 SDK documentation for details about the properties, methods, and events for each object.

Table 44-1
Internet Explorer 4 Element Objects

A	COLGROUP	H4	MENU	SUB
ACRONYM	COMMENT	H5	META	SUP
ADDRESS	DD	H6	NEXTID	TABLE
APPLET	DEL	HEAD	OBJECT	TBODY
AREA	DFN	HR	OL	TD
B	DIR	HTML	OPTION	TEXTAREA
BASE	DIV	I	P	TFOOT
BASEFONT	DL	IFRAME	PLAINTEXT	TH
BGSOUND	DT	IMG	PRE	THEAD
BIG	EM	INPUT	Q	TITLE
BLOCKQUOTE	EMBED	INS	S	TR
BODY	FIELDSET	KBD	SAMP	TT
BR	FONT	LABEL	SCRIPT	U
BUTTON	FORM	LEGEND	SELECT	UL
CAPTION	FRAME	LI	SMALL	VAR
CENTER	FRAMESET	LINK	SPAN	XMP
CITE	H1	LISTING	STRIKE	
CODE	H2	MAP	STRONG	
COL	H3	MARQUEE	STYLE	

Collections

Microsoft uses a new term to refer to multiple objects of the same kind in a document: the *collection*. In Navigator terms, a collection is the same as an array of similar objects. For example, when a document contains one or more images, you can refer to one of them using array syntax, as follows:

```
document.images[0]
```

In Internet Explorer terminology, the document contains an images collection. Such a collection may consist of zero or more objects of a particular type, and every collection has a length property your scripts can use to determine the number of objects of that type in the document.

While you can refer to these objects in cross-compatible array syntax, Internet Explorer 4 lets you replace the brackets with parentheses. Arguments for the parentheses can be an index value or a name assigned to the object via the object's ID attribute. Therefore, to access the first image of a document, Internet Explorer 4 accepts the following syntax.

```
document.images(0)
```

For named index references, you have your choice of two formats in Internet Explorer 4. One that is compatible with Navigator (all versions) lets you place the name inside brackets, as in

```
document.images["myCat"].src   // Navigator and Internet Explorer 4
format
```

In Internet Explorer 4, however, named references may also go inside parentheses, not brackets, as follows:

```
document.image("myCat").src   // IE4 format
```

The cross-compatible way is to address objects by numeric index (in array syntax) or by directly naming the object in the reference:

```
document.myCat.src
```

Sometimes, however, a script must assemble the name of an object from other values. For example, the following loops set the URLs of state map image objects. Each image object is named with the state abbreviation plus the word "map." The statement inside the loop assembles the map name from an entry in a lookup table. Due to differences in bracket and parenthesis syntax for each browser, the assembly must be done differently in Navigator and Internet Explorer 4:

```
// Navigator syntax
for (var i = 0; i < stateDB.length; i++) {
      document.images[stateDB[i].abbrev + "map"].src = stateDB[i].URL
}
// IE4 syntax
for (var i = 0; i < stateDB.length; i++) {
      document.images(stateDB[i].abbrev + "map").src = stateDB[i].URL
}
```

Brackets are okay for numeric index values in both browsers, but named index values must be treated differently. You can, however, script around this incompatibility by having the eval() function create an object reference that works with both browsers:

```
// Compatible syntax
var obj
for (var i = 0; i < stateDB.length; i++) {
      obj = eval("document." + stateDB[i].abbrev + "map")
      obj.src = stateDB[i].URL
}
```

It requires a little more effort, but at least a compatible solution exists that works with both browsers — and is even compatible with older versions of all browsers back to Navigator 2 and Internet Explorer 3.

Table 44-2 lists all of the collections in the Internet Explorer 4 document object model. Most collections are properties of the document object. Some, however, are specific to other objects within a document, such as the cells collection, which belongs to a TR (table row) object.

	Table 44-2 Internet Explorer 4 Collections	
Collection	**Description**	
all	Exposes all element objects in the document	
anchors	All document anchors	
applets	All document applets	
areas	All areas defined for client-side image maps	
cells	All cells of a row in a table (collection of a TR object)	
children	All direct descendants of an object	
elements	All elements in a form (collection of a form object)	
embeds	All document embeds	
filters	All filters associated with an element	
forms	All document forms	
frames	All window or document frames	
images	All document images	
imports	All imported style sheets (collection of a styleSheet object)	
links	All document links	
options	All options of a select object	
plugins	All embeds of a document (same as embeds collection)	
rows	All rows of a table (collection of a table object)	
rules	All rules in a styleSheet object	
scripts	All document scripts	
styleSheets	All document style sheets	
tbodies	All TBODY elements of a table object	

Events

Chapter 39 describes the basic difference between Navigator's object capture and Internet Explorer 4's object bubbling mechanisms. The difference in document object models also plays a role in the event model differences. When you consider that all of those element objects have event handlers associated with them, you see that Internet Explorer tightly binds events to objects. In addition to specifying event handlers within a tag in the traditional way via a tag attribute, Internet Explorer offers another way to bind an event handler to an object. You can create a

`<SCRIPT>` tag set whose contents are executed when a particular event for a particular object fires. The syntax for this construction is as follows:

```
<SCRIPT FOR=objectReference EVENT="eventHandlerName([params...])"
LANGUAGE="JavaScript">
        statements to execute (no function name needed)
</SCRIPT>
```

Notice that no function definitions exist in the code within the script. Raw statements are entered inside the tag but they are executed only when the referenced object receives the event named in the `EVENT` attribute. Beware that this construction works only for Internet Explorer 4. If you attempt to include one of these `<SCRIPT>` tags in documents for other browsers, the script statements will execute as the page loads, because the extra attributes are ignored, and the tag is treated like any `<SCRIPT>` tag.

Few system event handlers pass parameters, but some, such as `onError`, do. These parameters are passed along with the event, as if passed with a function call. Given Internet Explorer 4's window-based event object, additional information about the event is available from inside the script by accessing the `window.event` object properties without needing an event object passed, as it is in Navigator 4.

Importantly, the kind of event binding using the special `<SCRIPT>` tag occurs only after the document has loaded. Therefore, if you believe users may try to activate form elements (for example, click a button) before the page has completed loading, then you should define the event handler as an inline event handler inside the tag, even if it must call a function defined earlier in the document.

Internet Explorer 4 also supports setting object event handlers as properties of the object, offering two syntaxes for setting such properties. This is made compatible with Navigator by assigning a function reference to the event property, as in the following example:

```
document.forms[0].clicker.onclick = processClick
```

Internet Explorer also offers a variation on this theme, combining the syntax of object assignment with the syntax of inline event handler assignments, as in the following example:

```
document.forms[0].clicker.onclick = "processClick()"
```

This latter approach requires that the function include its parentheses and that the entire name be in quotes. You can also pass parameters with this method, but if you intend to pass form-related values (for example, the form object or a property of the object), you are better off doing this in an inline event handler, which is also compatible with all browsers.

Scripting Engine Versions

Internet Explorer is structured in such a way that the scripting engine is a separate component of the browser. As happened during the lifetime of Internet Explorer 3 for Windows, the company released two versions of the JScript language. In Windows, the component is a .dll file named jscript.dll. Each major version of the .dll adds to the functionality of the language in the browser, independent of the document object model.

Starting with jscript.dll Version 2, the JScript language comes with its own global functions that reveal the .dll version as well as the default scripting engine. Table 44-3 shows the relevant functions you can use to determine which JScript version is installed in the visitor's browser. Because it is possible that a visitor may be running jscript.dll Version 1, I recommend not using these functions with Internet Explorer 3. An attempt to run these functions with the original .dll file will yield a script error.

Table 44-3
Internet Explorer 4 JScript Versioning Functions

Function	Description
ScriptEngine()	Returns a string of the engine ("JScript")
ScriptEngineBuildVersion()	Integer of the build number of the engine's .dll file
ScriptEngineMajorVersion()	Integer of the value to the left of the decimal of the version number (3 for first release of jscript.dll in Internet Explorer 4)
ScriptEngineMinorVersion()	Integer of the value to the right of the decimal of the version number (0 for the first release of jscript.dll in Internet Explorer 4)

The JScript versioning information is useful only if you are using language constructs that became part of the language after a certain version. For general browser versioning, you should use the navigator object properties, such as navigator.appVersion and navigator.userAgent.

✦　　✦　　✦

Debugging Scripts

◆ ◆ ◆ ◆

In This Chapter

Identifying the
type of error
plaguing a script

Interpreting error
messages

Preventing problems
before they occur

◆ ◆ ◆ ◆

One of the first questions that an experienced
programmer asks about a programming environment is
what support is there for debugging code. Even the best
coders in the world make mistakes when they draft programs.
Sometimes, the mistakes are a mere slip of a finger on the
keyboard; other times, they result from not being careful with
expression evaluation or object references. The cause of the
mistake is not the issue: finding the mistake and getting help
to fix it is.

Some debugging tools are now available for the latest
browsers. Because the debuggers must work so closely with
the internal workings of the browser, the tools so far have
come from the browser makers themselves. While this
chapter shows how Netscape's script debugger works, most of
the discussion is of value even if you debug your scripts the
"old-fashioned" way — by understanding the error messages.

Syntax versus Runtime Errors

As a page loads into a JavaScript-enabled browser, the
browser attempts to create an object model out of the HTML
and JavaScript code in the document. Some types of errors
crop up at this point. These are mostly *syntax errors*, such as
failing to include a closing brace around a function's
statements. Such errors are structural in nature, rather than
about values or object references.

Runtime errors involve failed connections between
function calls and their functions, mismatched data types,
and undeclared variables located on the wrong side of
assignment operators. Such runtime errors can occur as the
page loads if the script lines run immediately as the page
loads. Runtime errors located in functions won't crop up until
the functions are called — either as the page loads or in
response to user action.

Because of the interpreted nature of JavaScript, the
distinction between syntax and runtime errors blurs. But as
you work through whatever problem halts a page from

loading or a script from running, you have to be aware of differences between true errors in language and your errors in logic or evaluation.

Error Message Alerts

Navigator produces a large error dialog box whenever it detects even the slightest problem (Figure 45-1). At the top of the box is the URL of the document causing the problem and a line number. Below that is a (somewhat) plain-language description of the nature of the problem, followed by an extract of the code on which JavaScript is choking.

The line number provided in the error message is a valiant effort to help draw your attention to the problem line of code. The line number, however, may not accurately point to the true source of the problem.

Normally, the first line of such a count is the opening `<SCRIPT>` tag line in the HTML document. If you have more than one set of `<SCRIPT>` tags in your document, the line number is counted from the opening `<SCRIPT>` tag of the group that contains the line with the error. The capability of Navigator to focus on the truly erroneous line has improved substantially with each new release, but you cannot rely on the line number accurately pointing to the problem. This is especially true if your page loads an external .js script library file.

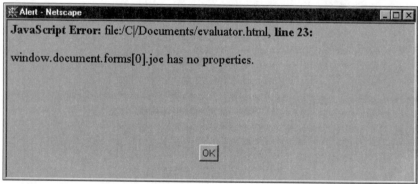

Figure 45-1: A typical error message window

More revealing at times is the code extract in the error dialog. For some syntax errors (such as missing halves of brace, parenthesis, and quote pairs), the extract comes from the line of code truly affected by the problem. The extract won't help at all, unfortunately, on some missing items, such as a missing right brace in a function definition. At best, the error message "missing } after function body" lets you know that an imbalance exists in one of your function definitions. The blank line of code it shows you isn't of much help, and the line number may be off by several lines.

While I'm on the subject of a missing closing brace, worse still is that the missing item doesn't trouble JavaScript until it encounters something later in the code that causes it to scratch its head. For example, if you have two function definitions and forget to insert the closing brace for the first definition, the error message shows as a plain "syntax error" pointing to the completely error-free second function. In truth, the problem is in the function immediately above that, but the JavaScript error detection can't figure that out.

In Navigator 3 and later, whenever a function, property, or method is causing a problem, the error message often includes clues about where in the object model the reference is being directed. For example, if a script attempts to retrieve a color value from a button form input element (a button named "hello"), the error message says

```
Window.Document.Form.Input.hello has no property named 'color'.
```

You can see from this message precisely which object is being examined by the script, and that information should send you to Appendix B of this book to see what properties exist for a button. This error message assistance is especially valuable when working with multiple-frame environments.

Multiple error message windows

It is not uncommon for multiple error windows to appear when a script trips over a mistake. But you need to understand how to treat these multiple errors to get to the root of the problem. The usual reaction is to look at the error message that is displayed once the script stops running. That, however, is usually the error message least likely to lead you to the true problem. Error messages display their windows in the time order in which an error is found. This means that the first window to appear — the bottom error window of the stack of error windows — is the most important error message of them all. More than likely, the error in that window points to a problem that throws off the rest of the script, thus triggering all of the other error message windows that cover the original blooper.

When you encounter multiple windows (you have to watch, because each window is positioned exactly atop the one underneath it), you should look briefly at the message of each window as you work your way down to the first one. To know whether a window is the last one or has others underneath it, drag the error message window's title bar to show what, if anything, is underneath it. Some of those extra error messages may correctly point out an error, so examine them briefly to see if something obvious (for example, a missing close parenthesis) caused the window to show up. But don't start any serious debugging until you get down to the first error message. You must tackle this one before any others. And the solution may cause the other errors to go away.

Error messages

Because so many permutations exist of the potential errors you can make in scripts and the ways the JavaScript interpreter regards these errors, presenting hard-and-fast solutions to every JavaScript error message is impossible. What I can do, however, is list the most common and head-scratch-inducing error messages and relate the kinds of nonobvious problems that can trigger such messages.

"Something is not defined"

This message is fairly easy to understand, yet at times difficult to diagnose. For variable names, the message usually means that you have an uninitialized variable name sitting in the position of a right-hand operand or a unary operand. This variable name has not been declared or assigned with any value prior to this erroneous statement. Perhaps you're attempting to use a variable name that has been initialized only as a local variable in another function. You may also have intended the word to be a string, but you forgot to enclose it in quotes. Another possibility is that you misspelled the name of a previously declared variable. JavaScript rightly regards this item as a new, undeclared variable. Misspellings, you will recall, include errors in upper- and lowercase in the very case-sensitive JavaScript world.

If the item is a function name, you may have to perform a bit of detective work. Though the function may be defined properly, a problem in the script above the function (for example, imbalanced braces) makes JavaScript fail to see the function. In other cases, you may be trying to invoke a function in another window or frame but forgot to include the reference to that distant spot in the call to the function.

Users of Internet Explorer 3 will see this message referencing an image object. This is a case in which the browser does not support that kind of object, and thus any reference to a nonexistent object yields an error. The more each browser brand diverges from the other with its document object model, the more likely these kinds of messages will appear if you implement browser-specific features for deployment across all browsers.

"*Something* is not a function"

Like the preceding one, this error message can be one of the most frustrating, because when you look at the script, it appears as though you have clearly defined a function by that name, and you're simply having an event handler or other running statement call that function. The first problems to look for are mismatched case of letters in the calling statement and function, and the reuse of a variable or HTML object name by the function name.

This latter item is a no-no — it confuses JavaScript into thinking that the function doesn't exist, even though the object name doesn't have parentheses appended to it and the function does. I've also seen this error appear when other problems existed in the script above the function named in the error message, and the named function was the last one in a script.

"Unterminated string literal"

In the code fragment displayed in the error window, the pointer usually appears at the first quote of a string it thinks is unterminated. If you simply forgot to close a string quote pair, the error most frequently appears when you try to concatenate strings or nest quoted strings. Despite the claim that you can nest alternating double and single quotes, I often have difficulties using this nesting method beyond the second nested level (single quotes inside a double-quoted string). At different times, I've gotten away with using a pair of \" inline quote symbols for a third layer. If that syntax fails, I break up the string so that nesting goes no deeper than two layers. If necessary, I even back out the most nested string and assign it to a variable in the preceding line — concatenating it into the more complex string in the next line. You can see an example of this method in bonus application Chapter 50 on the CD-ROM.

In the Windows 3.1 versions of Navigator, you may also see this error if a string value is longer than about 250 characters. But you can divide such a string into smaller segments and concatenate these strings later in the script with the add-by-value (+=) operator.

And in all versions of Navigator, avoid statements in scripts that extend for more than 255 characters. If you use a text editor that counts the column number as you type, use this measure as a guide for long statements. Break up long statements into shorter lines.

"Missing } after function body"

This error usually is easy to recognize in a simple function definition because the closing brace is missing at the end of the function. But when the function includes additional nested items, such as if...else or for loop constructions, you begin dealing with multiple pairs of braces within the function. The JavaScript interpreter doesn't always determine exactly where the missing brace belongs, and thus it simply defaults to the end of the function. This location is a natural choice, I guess, because from a global perspective of the function, one or more of the right braces that ripple down to the end of the function usually are missing.

In any case, this error message means that a brace is missing somewhere in the function, although not necessarily at the end. Do an inventory count for left and right braces and see whether a discrepancy occurs in the counts. One of those nested constructions is probably missing a closing brace. Some programmer-oriented text editors also include tools for finding balanced pairs of braces and parentheses.

"*Something* is not a number"

The variable name singled out in this error message is most likely a string value, a null value, or no value at all (the variable has been declared with the var statement, but not initialized with any value). The line of JavaScript that trips it up has an operator that demands a number. When in doubt about the data type of a variable destined for a math operation, use the parseInt() or parseFloat() functions to convert strings to numbers.

I have also encountered this error when it provides no clue about what isn't a number—the error message simply says, "is not a number." The root of the problem ended up having nothing to do with numbers. A structural imbalance in the script triggered this bogus error message.

"*Something* has no property named . . ."

When a statement trips this error message, an object reference has usually gone awry. You've probably attempted to reference a property of a JavaScript object, but something is wrong with the object reference, or you're trying to retrieve a property that doesn't exist for that object. The error often has to do with the kinds of objects stored as arrays inside the browser (forms or links). If you're trying to retrieve the value property of a button named calcMe, for example, the following incorrect reference triggers the "has no property named" error:

```
document.forms.calcMe.value
```

The error here would read "Window.Document.FormArray.calcMe has no property named 'value'." Notice that the reference in the error message includes something called FormArray (without any array index value in square brackets). You cannot have an entire array in a reference, just a single form. What this error message is very subtly telling you is that you forgot to single out a specific form:

```
document.forms[0].calcMe.value
```

JavaScript has many of these kinds of references that include arrays (radio buttons in a radio object, options in a select object, and so on). Always look very closely at the error message to see if a reference erroneously includes an entire array rather than just one of its elements.

"*Something* has no property indexed by [*i*]"

Look carefully at the object reference in this error message. The last item has an array index in the script, but the item is not an array value type. Users commonly make this mistake within the complex references necessary for radio buttons and select options. Make sure that you know which items in those lengthy references are arrays and which are simply object names that don't require array values.

"*Something* can't be set by assignment"

This error message tells you either that the property shown is read-only or that the reference points to an object, which must be created via a constructor function rather than by simple assignment.

"Test for equality (==) mistyped as assignment (=)? Assuming equality test."

The first time I received this error, I was amazed by JavaScript's intelligence. I had, indeed, meant to use the equality comparison function (==) but had entered only a single equal sign. JavaScript is good at picking out these situations where Boolean values are required.

"Function does not always return a value"

Often while designing deeply nested if...else constructions, your mind follows a single logic path to make sure that a particular series of conditions is met, and that the function returns the desired values under those conditions. What is easy to overlook is that there may be cases in which the decision process may "fall through" all the way to the bottom without returning any value, at which point the function must indicate a value that it returns, even if it is a 0 or empty (but most likely a Boolean value). JavaScript checks the organization of functions to make sure that each condition has a value returned to the calling statement. The error message doesn't tell you where you're missing the return statement, so you will have to do a bit of logic digging yourself.

"Access disallowed from scripts at *URL* to documents at *URL*"

Cross-domain security, which was beefed up during the reign of Navigator 2.0*x*, got even tighter in Navigator 3. This message indicates that a script in one frame is trying to access information in another frame that has been deemed a potential security threat. Such threats include any location object property or other information about the content of the other frame when the other frame's document comes from a protocol, server, or host that is different from the one serving up the document doing the fetching.

Even the best of intentions can be thwarted by these security restrictions. For example, you might be developing an application that blends data in cooperation with another site. Security restrictions, of course, don't know that you have a cooperative agreement with the other Web site, and there is no workaround for accessing a completely different domain unless you use signed scripts (see Chapter 40).

Another possibility is that you are using two different servers in the same domain or different protocols (for example, using https: for the secure part of your commerce site, while all catalog info uses the http: protocol). If the two sites have the same domain (for example, giantco.com) but different server names or protocols, you can set the document.domain properties of documents so that they recognize each other as equals. See Chapter 40 for details on these issues and the restrictions placed on scripts that mean well, but that could be used for evil purposes.

"Lengthy JavaScript still running. Continue?"

Although not a genuine error message (it appears in a JavaScript confirm dialog box), this alert dialog box provides a safeguard against inadvertent infinite loops and intentional ones triggered by JavaScript tricksters. Instead of permanently locking up the browser, Navigator — after processing a large number of rapidly executing script cycles — asks the user whether the scripts should continue.

"Syntax error"

JavaScript is best at detecting true syntax errors and showing you the location of the problem. Even if the line counter is off, the chance that the error dialog box accurately shows the problem-causing code fragment and pointer is still good.

The errors you've seen here aren't the only error messages that you will encounter in your scripts. Other error messages are pretty smart (for example, a message alerting you that you have only one equal sign when you meant to use two for a conditional test on the equality of two values). The real headaches occur when the error message and your code don't seem to mesh.

"Too many JavaScript errors"

You see this after several error message windows appear on the screen. Navigator limits the number of error windows it opens before getting out of control. This error usually crops up when the error appears inside a repeat loop and generates more error windows than Navigator allows. Close error windows to work your way back to the first window, and start your bug hunt with that window's message.

Sniffing Out Problems

It doesn't take many error-tracking sessions to get you in the save-switch-reload mode quickly. Assuming that you know this routine (described in Chapter 3), the following are some techniques I use to find errors in my scripts when the error messages aren't being helpful in directing me right to the problem.

Check the HTML tags

Before I look into the JavaScript code, I review the document carefully to make sure that I've written all my HTML tags properly. That includes making sure that all tags have closing angle brackets and that all tag pairs have balanced opening and closing tags. Digging deeper, especially in tags near the beginning of scripts, I make sure that all tag attributes that must be enclosed in quotes have the quote pairs in place. A browser may be forgiving about sloppy HTML as far as layout goes, but the JavaScript interpreter isn't as accommodating. Finally, I ensure that the `<SCRIPT>` tag pairs are in place (they may be in multiple locations throughout my document) and that the `LANGUAGE="JavaScript"` attribute has both of its quotes.

View the source

Before Navigator 3, debugging HTML that was generated by script (via `document.write()` statements) was difficult. Scripted HTML may be embedded amid regular HTML, or it may make up an entire page itself, usually inside another frame or window. Navigator 3 and later, however, simplify access to scripts in frames — you just click in a frame to select it and then choose Frame Source from the View menu or (if available) right-click the pop-up menu. The displayed result includes any HTML that the script generates. You can see how your expressions evaluate on their way to the page you see in the regular browser window.

This feature, incidentally, is what enables JavaScript-written HTML to be printed, previewed, and saved. Notice the special protocol that such frames have: `wysiwyg://`.

This statement is an internal protocol to the Navigator memory cache. Whenever you see the `wysiwyg://` protocol in a source window title bar, you know that some or all of the page was created with `document.write()` statements.

Intermittent scripts

Without question, the most common bug in Navigator 2.0*x* is the one that makes scripts behave intermittently. Buttons, for example, won't fire `onClick=` event handlers unless the page is reloaded. Or, as a result of the same bug, sometimes a script runs and sometimes it doesn't. The problem here is that Navigator requires all `<IMG>` tags to include `HEIGHT` and `WIDTH` attributes, even when the images are not scripted. Because doing so is good HTML practice anyway (it helps the browser's layout performance), and you will certainly have visitors running Navigator 2 versions for some time to come, if you include these attributes without fail throughout your HTML documents, you won't be plagued by intermittent behavior.

Scripts not working in tables

Tables have been a problem for scripts through Navigator 3. The browser has difficulty when a `<SCRIPT>` tag is included inside a `<TD>` tag pair for a table cell. The workaround for this is to put the `<SCRIPT>` tag outside the table cell tag and use `document.write()` to generate the `<TD>` tag and its contents. I usually go one step further, and use `document.write()` to generate the entire table's HTML. This is necessary only when executable statements are needed in cells (for example, to generate content for the cell). If a cell contains a form element whose event handler calls a function, you don't have to worry about this problem.

Reopen the file

If I make changes to the document that I truly believe should fix a problem, but the same problem persists after a reload, I reopen the file via the File menu. Sometimes, when you run an error-filled script more than once, the browser's internals get a bit confused. Reloading does not clear the bad stuff, although sometimes an unconditional reload (clicking Reload while holding Shift) does the job. Reopening the file, however, clears the old file entirely from the browser's memory and loads the most recently fixed version of the source file. I find this situation to be especially true with documents involving multiple frames and tables and those that load external .js script library files. In severe cases, you may even have to restart the browser to clear its cobwebs.

Find out what works

When an error message gives you no clue about the true location of a runtime problem, or when you're faced with crashes at an unknown point (even during document loading), you need to figure out which part of the script execution works properly.

If you have added a lot of scripting to the page without doing much testing, I suggest removing all scripts except the one(s) that might get called by the document's `onLoad=` event handler. This is primarily to make sure that the HTML is not way out of whack. Browsers tend to be quite lenient with bad HTML, so this tactic won't necessarily tell the whole story. Next, add back the scripts in batches. Eventually, you want to find where the problem really is, regardless of the line number indicated by the error message alert.

To narrow down the problem spot, insert one or more alert dialog boxes into the script with a unique, brief message that you will recognize as reaching various stages (such as `alert("HERE-1")`). Start placing alert dialog boxes at the beginning of any groups of statements that execute and try the script again. Keep moving these dialog boxes deeper into the script (perhaps into other functions called by outer statements) until the error or crash occurs. You now know where to look for problems. See also an advanced tracing mechanism described later in this chapter.

Comment out statements

If the errors appear to be syntactical (as opposed to errors of evaluation), the error message may point to a code fragment several lines away from the problem. More often than not, the problem exists in a line somewhere *above* the one quoted in the error message. To find the offending line, begin commenting out lines one at a time (between reloading tests), starting with the line indicated in the error message. Keep doing this until the error message clears the area you're working on and points to some other problem below the original line (with the lines commented out, some value is likely to fail below). The most recent line you commented out is the one that has the beginning of your problem. Start looking there.

Check expression evaluation

I've said many times throughout this book that one of the two most common problems scripters face is an expression that evaluates to something you don't expect. The best tool for checking evaluation expression is the JavaScript Debugger. See "Using the JavaScript Debugger" later for details.

In lieu of using the debugger, you have a few alternatives to displaying expression values while a script runs. The simplest approaches to implement are an alert box and the statusbar. Both the alert dialog box and statusbar show you almost any kind of value, even if it is not a string or number. An alert box can even display multiple-line values.

Because most expression evaluation problems come within function definitions, start such explorations from the top of the function. Every time you assign an object property to a variable or invoke a string, math, or date method, insert a line below that line with an `alert()` method or `window.status` assignment statement (`window.status = someValue`) that shows the contents of the new variable value. Do this one statement at a time, save, switch, and reload. Study the value that appears in the output device of choice to see if it's what you expect. If not, something is amiss in the previous line involving the expression(s) you used to achieve that value.

This process is excruciatingly tedious for debugging a long function, but it's absolutely essential to track down where a bum object reference or expression evaluation is tripping up your script. When a value comes back as being undefined or null, more than likely the problem is an object reference that is incomplete (for example, trying to access a frame without the parent.frames[i] reference), using the wrong name for an existing object (check case), or accessing a property or method that doesn't exist for that object.

When you need to check the value of an expression through a long sequence of script statements or over the lifetime of a repeat loop's execution, you would be better off with a listing of values along the way. In "Writing Your Own Trace Utility" later in this chapter, I show you how to use Navigator's Java Console window and LiveConnect to provide you with quick trails of values through a script.

Check object references and properties

Another tool to keep in your back pocket is the object property inspector. Using the special for...in loop construction of JavaScript (Chapter 31), you can call the function in Listing 45-1 from anywhere within your scripts to view the values of all properties of an object. You may find, for instance, that your script inadvertently changes the property of an object when you aren't looking. I also find that with more complex object relationships in newer browsers (for example, nested layers and their parent objects), it is not inconceivable to have a reference to the wrong object assigned to a variable. By showing the properties of the object, you can see exactly what object your script is pointing to. The function in Listing 45-1 is designed to accommodate objects that have dozens of properties by showing 25 at a time in an alert dialog. Pass as parameters to this function both the actual object (as an unquoted name) and the name of the object (as a quoted string) so that the resulting alert dialog box explains what's what.

Listing 45-1: **Property Inspector Function**

```
function showProps(obj,objName) {
    var result = ""
    var count = 0
    for (var i in obj) {
        result += objName + "." + i + " = " + obj[i] + "\n"
        count++
        if (count == 25) {
            alert(result)
            result = ""
            count = 0
        }
    }
    alert(result)
}
```

Using the JavaScript Debugger

Still in preview release form as of this writing, the JavaScript Debugger from Netscape is a byproduct of the Visual JavaScript tool (see Chapter 46). The debugger is a Java applet that lives in a separate window. With the debugger on, you can single-step through JavaScript code execution and observe the values of variables or expressions with each step. You can even modify the value of a variable or form element on the fly to test other outcomes. I provide here an overview of how to use the debugger in your authoring.

Installing the debugger

You can download the JavaScript Debugger from Netscape's DevEdge Web site (`http://developer.netscape.com`). The precise URL may change over time, so I suggest you start at the DevEdge home page and look for developer downloads (the debugger may also be listed on the home page). Visit the site with Navigator 4 so that the installation process can properly connect the debugger to your copy of Navigator. The debugger is a signed applet and will ask for your permission to modify the browser. Grant that permission to complete the installation.

The debugger installs in a directory inside the Navigator/Communicator Program directory. While all of the code is stashed in a .jar file, the access to it is via an HTML file, called jsdebugger.html.

Starting the debugger

To get the debugger going, open the jsdebugger.html file in Navigator. I highly recommend adding a bookmark to this file so you can start it up easily during debugging sessions. The file generates a small browser window, which is the window that loads the applet. This frees the main browser window for your own pages. If you close this small window, you quit the debugger.

It takes several seconds for the debugger applet to load, but while it is doing that, you can navigate in the main browser window to the HTML page you want to debug. When the debugger is loaded, its default window appears on screen (see Figure 45-2). If you are using Windows with a taskbar, the JavaScript Debugger appears as a taskbar item with a Java icon (and the small HTML stub window is also shown in the taskbar).

Debugger layout

The main window of the debugger contains three subwindows. The large one at the top is for the current document source code. If you start the debugger normally, this area will be blank until you either open a document or let the debugger interrupt code execution (described in a moment).

At the lower left is a call stack, which lists the current line number and function name when you are stepping through code. If a function calls another function, the stack list starts to grow. The function currently being stepped through is at the top of the stack; immediately below it is the name of the function that called the current function, along with the line number where the call to the current function was made.

The lower-right window (Console) has two elements in it. At the top is where you can view the values of variables or expressions as a script steps through statements. The one-line text field at the bottom is where you can type an expression to see what its value is. You can also use this field to assign a new value to an existing variable or object property.

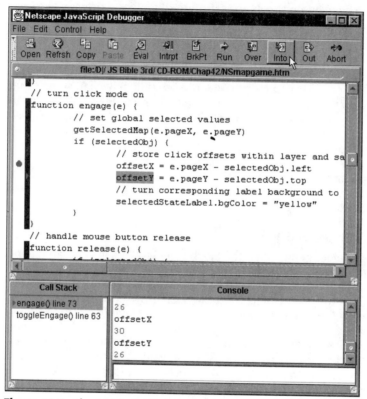

Figure 45-2: The JavaScript Debugger window

All windows are resizable, although you have to do a bit of manual work to get it done. To enlarge the work area, drag an edge or corner of the entire debugger window. This opens up blank space in the window. Then you can drag the individual window title bars to move the windows and/or drag the lower-right corners to resize the windows. In the prerelease version, the windows do not remember their sizes for the next session.

You will encounter some windows in the debugger that appear to float atop the others. But because all of the activity here is within the context of an applet, the view to the debugger area is clipped to the outer edge of the debugger window. Don't be alarmed if you try to drag a window out of the debugger window only to have it slip out of view.

Getting the debugger to single-step

You have two ways to instruct the JavaScript Debugger to pause script execution while the display switches to the debugger for single-stepping through the code. The easiest way is to click the BreakPoint (BrkPt) button in the toolbar. When you switch back to the browser window, the next script that runs (whether it be a script that runs during a document reload or in response to user action) will switch the view to the debugger window, with the page's source code appearing in the top window.

An alternate method is more useful if you know where in a document you want to start watching the script details. In the debugger window, click Open and select the document you wish to debug. When the source code window opens, scroll to the desired script statement where you want to begin stepping through the code. Set a breakpoint by clicking along the left margin of the desired line. A red dot appears where the breakpoint is. You can set more than one breakpoint in a document. Then return to the browser window, and work with the page until the script statement with the breakpoint executes. At that point, the view changes to the debugger window, and you can begin stepping through code while examining values.

Stepping through code

When the debugger is running, the source document window displays vertical yellow bars where the script statement is as well as a blue arrow pointing to the line that is the *next one* to execute. To execute that statement, click the Into or Over buttons in the toolbar. The difference between the buttons becomes apparent if the statement about to be executed contains a call to a custom function in your application. If you click the Into button, the debugger scrolls to that subroutine function in the document (or opens a new source document window if it is in a different document). This allows you to follow the execution logic through nested functions. In the Call Stack window, you see the nested function at the top of the stack.

While stepping through the nested function, you can continue to click the Into or Over buttons, with the Into button leading to any further nested function. When the stepping reaches the end of the nested function, the view returns to the statement of the calling function (and the nested function name pops off the stack). From inside a nested function you can also zoom back out to the calling function by clicking the Out button. If you don't want to step through nested functions at all, click only the Over button.

Occasionally, you may need to inspect only a few places within your script, even though they may be separated by a lot of executing lines (for example, you want to step through lines above and below a repeat loop, but not through dozens of loop iterations). By setting multiple breakpoints in a document, you can single-step where you want and then let processing continue at normal speed until the next breakpoint. Click the Run button to exit single-stepping while letting the script continue its normal course. Or if you want to bail out of the script entirely, click Abort.

Observing values manually

As the debugger single-steps through your code, you can inspect the current value of any expression in the code. This is a manual way of observing variables and expressions, and is convenient when you don't need continued views to certain values. To observe a value, select a variable or expression in the source code, and then click the Eval button in the toolbar (or right-click the selection with a two-button mouse). Appearing in the Console window is the item you selected and (in red) its current value. If a variable has not yet been initialized its value displays as `null`.

As a second manual method, you can also type an expression in the type-in field at the bottom of the Console window. This expression can be any valid JavaScript expression, including one that uses variables and document objects from the document currently being stepped through. When you press Enter, the value appears in the upper area of the Console window.

Observing values automatically — watches

A more efficient way of keeping tabs on expression values while stepping through code is to set up what are called *watches*. These are values that evaluate for each step through the program (even if the value is not directly affected by the code in the step) and display their results in the Console window.

You can set up watches two ways. The easy way is to select an expression in the code (while the debugger is stepping or is at rest) and choose Copy to Watch from the Edit menu. To view the expressions being watched, choose Watches from the Edit menu. The window that appears lists each item. You can also click the New button in the Watches window to type in an expression to watch.

If expressions rely on each other, you may want to control the order in which expressions are evaluated at each step. You can select an item in the Watches window and click the Move Up or Move Down buttons to adjust the item's position in the list of watched items.

As the debugger steps through a script, all items in the Watches window are evaluated, and their results are displayed in the Console window. This lets you keep an eye on several items all at the same time without any extra clicking or selecting beyond the buttons that control the stepping.

Writing Your Own Trace Utility

Single-stepping through running code with the JavaScript Debugger is a valuable aid when you know where the problem is. But when the bug location eludes you, especially in a complex script, you may find it more efficient to follow a rapid trace of execution with intermediate values along the way. The kinds of questions that this debugging technique addresses include

✦ How many times is that loop executing?

✦ What are the values being retrieved each time through the loop?

✦ Why won't the `while` loop exit?

✦ Are comparison operators behaving as I'd planned in if...else constructions?

✦ What kind of value is a function returning?

With thoughtfully placed calls to the trace() method of the external library shown next, the resulting report you get after running your script can answer questions like these and many more.

The trace.js library

Listing 45-2 is the listing for the debug.js library file. It consists of one global variable and one function.

Listing 45-2: **trace.js library**

```
var timestamp = 0
function trace(flag, label, value) {
    if (flag) {
        var funcName = debug.caller.toString()
        funcName = funcName.substring(10, funcName.indexOf(")")) + 1)
        var msg = "In " + funcName + ": " + label + "=" + value
        var now = new Date()
        var elapsed = now - timestamp
        if (elapsed < 10000) {
            msg += " (" + elapsed + " msec)"
        }
        timestamp = now
        java.lang.System.out.println(msg)
    }
}
```

When this file loads into a document, the timestamp variable becomes a global variable in the document. This variable is used to maintain the last time the trace() function is called. The value must persist so that subsequent calls to trace() permit calculations of the time differences between the previous and current invocations. The timestamping is optional, but it can be useful for performing some benchmark tests of alternate ways of processing data.

The trace() function takes three parameters. The first, flag, is a Boolean value that determines whether the trace should proceed (I'll show you a shortcut for setting this flag later). The second parameter is a string used as a plain-language way for you to identify the value being traced. The value to be displayed is passed as the third parameter. Virtually any type of value or expression can be passed as the third parameter — which is precisely what you want in a debugging aid.

Only if the flag parameter is true does the bulk of the trace() function execute. The first task is to extract the name of the function from which the trace() function was called. By retrieving the rarely used caller property of a function (see Chapter 34), the script grabs a string copy of the entire function that has just called trace(). A quick extraction of a substring from the first line yields the name of the function. That information becomes part of the message text that records each trace. The message identifies the calling function followed by a colon;

after that comes the label text passed as the second parameter plus an equals sign and the `value` parameter. The format of the output message adheres to the following syntax:

```
In <funcName>: <label>=<value>
```

Beyond this trace data, the script subtracts the value of the `timestamp` variable from the current time to achieve an elapsed time. If that elapsed time is less than ten seconds, the time value is appended to the message (in parentheses).

The final statement in the function is a LiveConnect call to a native Java class method. Experienced Java programmers will recognize the `System.out.println()` method as the one that writes a value to the Java Console window. If you haven't done any Java programming, you may not even know that Navigator has a Java Console window available under the Options/Communicator menu. Java applet errors automatically appear in this window (even if the window is hidden). LiveConnect gives you the power to make a direct call to the built-in Java method, `java.lang.System.out.println()`, to write anything you like to the window. Anything written to that window is appended to the end of whatever text is already in the window. Therefore, you can write to that window as many trace messages as you like, and they'll all be there for you to see after the script runs.

Loading the trace.js library

To include this debugging library in your document, add the following `<SCRIPT>` tag set at the start of the document's head section:

```
<SCRIPT LANGUAGE="JavaScript" SRC="trace.js"></SCRIPT>
```

The syntax assumes that you have saved trace.js in the same directory as your HTML file.

Preparing documents for trace.js

As you build your document and its scripts, you need to decide how granular you'd like tracing to be: global or function-by-function. This decision affects at what level you place the Boolean "switch" that turns tracing on and off.

You can place one such switch as the first statement in the first script of the page. For example, specify a clearly named variable and assign either false or zero to it so that its initial setting is off:

```
var TRACE = 0
```

To turn debugging on at a later time, simply edit the value assigned to `TRACE` from zero to one:

```
var TRACE = 1
```

Be sure to reload the page each time you edit this global value.

Alternatively, you can define a local `TRACE` Boolean variable in each function for which you intend to employ tracing. One advantage of using function-specific tracing is that the list of items to appear in the Java Console window will be limited to those of immediate interest to you, rather than all tracing calls throughout the document. You can turn each function's tracing facility on and off by editing the values assigned to the local TRACE variables.

Invoking trace()

All that's left now is to insert the one-line calls to trace() according to the following syntax:

```
trace(TRACE,<"label">,<value>)
```

By passing the current value of TRACE as a parameter, you let the library function handle the decision to accumulate and print the trace. The impact on your running code is kept to a one-line statement that is easy to remember. To demonstrate how to make the calls to trace(), Listing 45-3 shows a pair of related functions that convert a time in milliseconds to the string format "hh:mm". To help verify that values are being massaged correctly, the script inserts a few calls to trace().

Listing 45-3: **Calling trace()**

```
function timeToString(input) {
    var TRACE = 1
    trace(TRACE,"input",input)
    var rawTime = new Date(eval(input))
    trace(TRACE,"rawTime",rawTime)
    var hrs = twoDigitString(rawTime.getHours())
    var mins = twoDigitString(rawTime.getMinutes())
    trace(TRACE,"result", hrs + ":" + mins)
    return hrs + ":" + mins
}

function twoDigitString(val) {
    var TRACE = 1
    trace(TRACE,"val",val)
    return (val < 10) ? "0" + val : "" + val
}
```

After running the script, the Java Console window in Navigator shows the following trace:

```
In timeToString(input): input=869854500000
In timeToString(input): rawTime=Fri Jul 25 11:15:00 Pacific Daylight
Time 1997 (60 msec)
In twoDigitString(val): val=11 (0 msec)
In twoDigitString(val): val=15 (0 msec)
In timeToString(input): result=11:15 (220 msec)
```

Having the name of the function in the trace is helpful in cases in which you might justifiably reuse variable names (for example, i loop counters). You can also see more clearly when one function in your script calls another.

About the timer

In the trace results of Listing 45-3 you might wonder how some statements appear to execute literally "in no time." You have to take the timing values of this tracing scheme with a grain of salt. For one thing, these are not intended to be world-class standard benchmarks. Some of the processing in the `trace()` function itself occupies CPU cycles. And with rapid-fire execution in the small scripts of Listing 45-3, the timings are not very meaningful. But in a more complex script, especially one involving numerous calls to subroutines and nested loops, you can place the `trace()` function calls in statements not so deeply nested that the intervals are too small to be of any value. In any case, regard the values as relative, rather than absolute, values. And always run the script several times to help you see a pattern of performance.

Navigator Crashes

Navigator, though seemingly reliable in its browser role, is not so stable when it comes to trying JavaScript statements that would normally be considered illegal. Fortunately, each Navigator generation significantly improves robustness over its previous version.

The seriousness of the crash depends partly on the internal error and the operating system. For instance, I've seen crashes on the Macintosh that range from just "unexpectedly quitting" Navigator (leaving everything else intact) to taking down the entire computer (necessitating a hard restart). Windows 95, on the other hand, protects the rest of the applications running when Navigator takes a dive.

As you develop scripts in a modern version of Navigator, you should be aware that improved robustness makes it all the more dangerous, as some methods could crash earlier Navigator versions. This is particularly true when invoking document-modifying methods, such as `document.write()` and `document.open()`. In Navigator 2, for example, such methods directed to the current document frequently lead to crashes. If you're developing scripts for a production-quality Web site that invites visitors of all browser types, be sure to test your scripts on Navigator 2.02.

Preventing Problems

Even with help of authoring tools and debuggers, you probably want to avoid errors in the first place. I offer a number of suggestions that can help in this regard.

Getting structure right

Early problems in developing a page with scripts tend to be structural: knowing that your objects are displayed correctly on the page; making sure that your `<SCRIPT>` tags are complete; completing brace, parenthesis, and quoted pairs. I start writing my page by first getting down the HTML parts — including all form definitions. Because so much of a scripted page tends to rely on the placement and naming of interface elements, you will find it much easier to work with these items once you lay them out on the page. At that point, you can start filling in the JavaScript.

When you begin defining a function, repeat loop, or `if` construction, fill out the entire structure before entering any details. For example, when I define a function named `verifyData()`, I enter the entire structure for it:

```
function verifyData() {

}
```

I leave a blank line between the beginning of the function and the closing brace in anticipation of entering at least one line of code.

After I decide on a parameter to be passed and assign a variable to it, I may want to insert an `if` construction. Again, I fill in the basic structure:

```
function verifyData(form) {
        if (form.checkbox.checked) {

        }
}
```

This method automatically pushes the closing brace of the function lower, which is what I want — putting it securely at the end of the function where it belongs. It also ensures that I line up the closing brace of the `if` statement with that grouping. Additional statements in the `if` construction push down the two closing braces.

If you don't like typing or don't trust yourself to maintain this kind of discipline when you're in a hurry to test an idea, you should prepare a separate document that has templates for the common constructions: `<SCRIPT>` tags, function, `if`, `if...else`, `for` loop, `while` loop, and conditional expressions. Then if your editor and operating system support it, drag and drop the necessary segments into your working script.

Build incrementally

The worst development tactic you can follow is to write tons of code before trying any of it. Error messages may point to so many lines away from the source of the problem that it could take hours to find the true source of difficulty. The save-switch-reload sequence is not painful like the process of compiling code, so the better strategy is to try your code every time you have written a complete thought — or even enough to test an intermediate result in an alert dialog box — to make sure that you're on the right track.

Test expression evaluation

Especially while you are learning the ins and outs of JavaScript, you may feel unsure about the results that a particular string, math, or date method yields on a value. The longer your scripted document gets, the more difficult it will be to test the evaluation of a statement. You're better off trying the expression in a more controlled, isolated environment, such as in a separate evaluation tester document you write with a couple text or textarea objects in it. Navigator users can use the internal `javascript:` URL to test expressions. By doing this kind of testing in the browser, you save a great deal of time experimenting by going back and forth between the source document and the browser.

Build function workbenches

A similar situation exists for building and testing functions, especially generalizable ones. Rather than test a function inside a complex scripted document, drop it into a skeletal document that contains the minimum number of user interface elements that you need to test the function. This task gets difficult when the function is closely tied to numerous objects in the real document, but it works wonders for making you think about generalizing functions for possible use in the future. Display the output of the function in a text or textarea object or include it in an alert dialog box.

Testing Your Masterpiece

If your background strictly involves designing HTML pages, you probably think of testing as determining your user's ability to navigate successfully around your site. But a JavaScript-enhanced page — especially if the user enters input into fields — requires a substantially greater amount of testing before you unleash it to the online masses.

A large part of good programming is anticipating what a user can do at any point and then being sure that your code covers that eventuality. With multiframe windows, for example, you need to see how unexpected reloading of a document affects the relationships between all the frames — especially if they depend on each other. Users will be able to click Reload at any time or suspend document loading in the middle of a download from the server. How do these activities affect your scripting? Do they cause script errors based on your current script organization?

The minute you enable a user to type an entry into a form, you also invite the user to enter the wrong kind of information into that form. If your script expects only a numeric value from a field, and the user (accidentally or intentionally) types a letter, is your script ready to handle that "bad" data? Or no data? Or a negative floating-point number?

Just because you, as author of the page, know the "proper" sequence to follow and the "right" kind of data to enter into forms, your users will not necessarily follow your instructions. In days gone by, such mistakes were relegated to "user error." Today, with an increasingly consumer-oriented Web audience, any such faults rest solely on the programmer — you.

If I sound as though I'm trying to scare you, I have succeeded. I was serious in the early chapters of this book when I said that writing JavaScript is programming. Users of your pages are expecting the same polish and smooth operation (no script errors and certainly no crashes) from your site as from the most professional software publisher on the planet. Don't let them or yourself down. Test your pages extensively on as many Navigator hardware platforms and JavaScript-enabled browsers as you can and with as wide an audience as possible before putting the pages on the server for all to see.

✦   ✦   ✦

Authoring Tools

Tools to assist JavaScript development have lagged way behind tools for HTML page authoring, but the scripting world is the beneficiary of recent efforts by both browser makers and third parties. As you will see in this chapter, the bulk of tool activity is for development of enterprise-based scripting, either because of tool focus or pricing strategy — both of which limit the audience to serious Web application developers.

With the significant exception of Acadia's Infuse, most of the tools available so far are designed not so much to assist the serious scripter as to put the power of scripting into the hands of the nonprogrammer. This is tricky business. HTML authoring tools can hide well the ugliness of HTML tags because the metaphor of a document is widely accepted by authors who publish content. But a script is a different situation. What is the metaphor for a script? And how well does one script fit all application scenarios? If these questions could be answered easily, there would be dozens of programming tools for nonprogrammers in all languages. But that is not the case.

In the rapidly changing environment of Web authoring tools, I can't guarantee that information I provide here will be current by the time you read it. Therefore, for every tool I mention, I suggest also checking the associated URL for the latest developments.

Acadia's Infuse 2.0

Although only in a prerelease version (PR2) as I write this, Acadia's Infuse 2.0 for Windows 95 shows great potential as a helpful authoring tool for serious scripters of client- or server-side JavaScript. The product includes a source code editor that has scripters in mind, offering shortcuts for inserting both HTML and scripting construct skeletons that authors can fill in. An excellent example is the keystrokes Infuse saves when adding a `for` loop to a script. Type the word "for" and a space, and Infuse automatically enters the entire basic structure of a `for` loop, assigning the `i` variable and preselecting the placeholder where you enter the value of the condition to be tested at the beginning of each loop (see Figure 46-1).

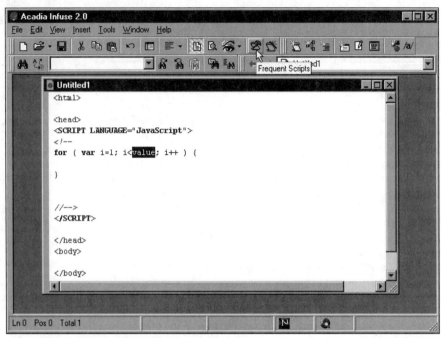

Figure 46-1: Acadia's Infuse 2.0 (prerelease)

Infuse 2.0 comes with a library of frequently used scripts. You can, of course, add your own scripts to the library and insert them into your code with a couple of clicks (and preview the code to each script before you use it).

Even experienced scripters should appreciate one of the tools built into the product that scans a page for language words and objects that may not be supported by all browsers. You can ask Infuse to examine the scripts for Navigator and Internet Explorer compatibility back to the earliest versions of the scriptable browsers. Right up to the current technologies, Infuse 2.0 supports development of Internet Explorer scriptlets. A separate tool by Acadia, BeanBuilder, assists in the creation of Navigator 4 JavaScript Bean (JSB) components. Acadia Software is at `http://www.acadians.com`.

Netscape Visual JavaScript

The name of this authoring tool may mislead the scripting community into thinking that this is a separate version of JavaScript, much like Visual Basic is its own incarnation of Basic. But Visual JavaScript is an authoring tool for creating the same JavaScript code that you would create by hand or with a tool such as Acadia's Infuse 2.0. Visual JavaScript can be used for both client- and server-side JavaScript development. The tool itself is a Java application and will be available for all operating system platforms.

In many ways Visual JavaScript (VJS) resembles an integrated development environment (IDE). Each application you work on is assembled as a project. A project may contain any number of HTML files, Java applets, JavaScript files, images, and server data sources—all managed inside a VJS project.

Each HTML document (called a page) can be viewed and edited in three different views. The Layout view is how you usually assemble the basic content and layout of a page by positioning elements on a dummy page. The plan for the final release indicates that you will have the same level of layout composition tools as is provided in Netscape Composer (part of Communicator). Even so, this view does not purport to be a WYSIWYG (what you see is what you get) display. Many elements that let you connect things like form elements and database connections to forms aren't really seen when displayed in the browser, but must be shown here to let authors make those connections. The two other views are a hierarchical Structure view of the entire document and a Source view that shows the HTML source code generated by the tool.

One of the most powerful parts of Visual JavaScript is the Component Palette (see Figure 46-2). Components consist primarily of Java Beans or JavaScript Beans (JSBs). As a result, they all reflect the introspection feature of beans. When you drop a component onto a page under construction, you double-click on the item to reveal an Inspector window for that component. In that window you can set default properties and assign scripts to event handlers (if the component supports events). For items that are normally HTML objects (for example, form elements), setting these properties instructs VJS to write the HTML tag and attributes for that object. Some of the property settings are quite useful. One of my favorites is the one for setting a color (see Figure 46-3). A pop-up list of the color names with the actual color sample makes it easy to find a suitable color for the object's attribute.

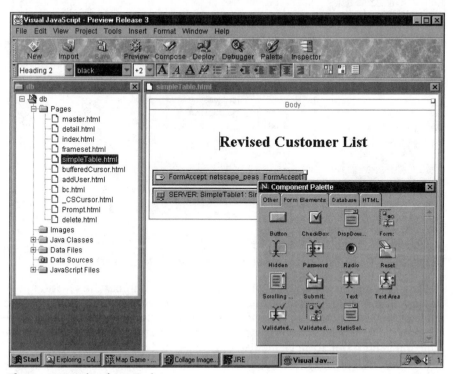

Figure 46-2: Visual JavaScript

HTML generated by VJS includes a lot of commented statements and tag attributes that you may not recognize. All of this extraneous material is used by VJS to display and manage the elements and component connections inside that environment. The browser does not need this information. By the same token, you can import an existing application into VJS, but not all of the connections you've made manually in your page will be converted to the VJS format for further editing visually (although you can continue to edit the source code as you wish).

Despite the ease with which Visual JavaScript lets authors work with preassembled script components, authors are not prevented from adding or enhancing scripts manually. For example, if you wish to create a function executed by a button's `onClick=` event handler, you can add the script statements of that function in the inspector for the button object. You don't have to assign names to the functions, because VJS automatically assigns names to such functions based on the name of the object.

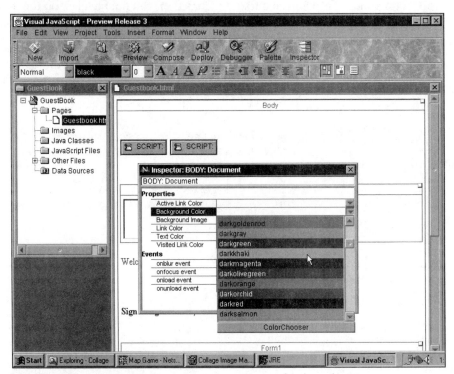

Figure 46-3: Visual JavaScript property inspector and color selector

Visual JavaScript is also endowed with powers to simplify the creation of server-side applications for Enterprise Server 3 and the LiveWire connection between applications and databases. As you work with an application under development in VJS, the tool connects with the database to let you generate connections between table data and HTML form elements with click-and-drag ease.

You can get more information about Visual JavaScript at `http://developer. netscape.com`.

Other Server-side Tools

Assisting in development of server-side applications—especially making the connection between HTML documents and databases via LiveWire in Enterprise Server 3—has attracted at least two other tools developers. Elemental Software (http://www. elementalsoftware.com) has been shipping Drumbeat since early 1997. A more recent entrant is NetObjects (http://www.netobjects.com) with its JavaScript Components add-on to the popular Fusion Web site authoring toolset. Both tools are designed to simplify the writing of server-side JavaScript code to allow nonprogrammers to hook up databases to Web pages.

I expect the JavaScript authoring tools race to heat up as the adoption of level 4 browsers increases. So much more of Web authoring—from Dynamic HTML to server-side CGIs—is relying on JavaScript (or at least the common denominator ECMAScript) that tools vendors will be attracted to solving the problem of increasing complexity of HTML and scripted pages.

✦　　✦　　✦

JavaScript Applications

C H A P T E R S

47
through
53

◆ ◆ ◆ ◆

Chapter 47:
Application: Tables
and Calendars

Chapter 48:
Application: A
Lookup Table

Chapter 49:
Application: An
Order Form

Chapter 50:
Application: Outline-
Style Table of
Contents

Chapter 51:
Application:
Calculations and
Graphics

Chapter 52:
Application:
Intelligent "Updated"
Flags

Chapter 53:
Application: Decision
Helper

◆ ◆ ◆ ◆

Bonus Application Chapters on CD-ROM

Seven full-fledged, JavaScript-enhanced applications can be found on the accompanying CD-ROM in the Bonus Applications Chapters folder. The folder contains a .pdf file with seven bonus chapters that you can read and search through after installing Adobe Acrobat Reader (also on the CD-ROM).

Here are the highlights of these bonus chapters, so you know what to expect when you look for them on the CD-ROM.

Each application demonstrates important concepts that you will likely want to take into consideration when designing your applications. You will read about each segment of JavaScript code and learn about the implementation decisions I made in designing these applications — the same kinds of decisions you will have to make for your site. Most of these examples also run on my Web site (`http://www.dannyg.com/javascript/`), so you can use them from the CD-ROM or see how well they work online from a server.

✦ Chapter 47 on the CD-ROM covers tables and calendars. The chapter traces the implementation of a monthly calendar in both static and dynamic formats in a single frame window.

✦ Chapter 48 presents one way to implement small data collection lookups.

✦ One example of how to script an order form appears in Chapter 49. This example is written so the order form is easy to maintain and involves a small amount of scripting and HTML code for the amount of work it does.

✦ Chapter 50 creates an expandable, outline-type table of contents. Implementing the outline interface as a client-side JavaScript script solves the usual processing delays and makes the outline a more viable interface for a site's table of contents.

✦ Calculations and graphics take center stage in Chapter 51, as you see how I create a graphical calculator.

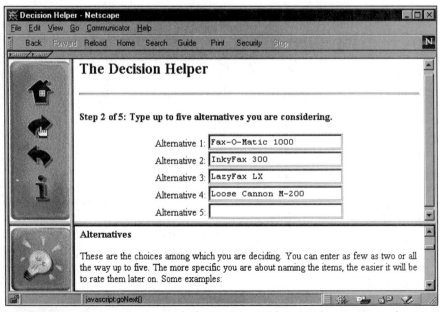

Learn how to create an easy-to-use order form in Chapter 49 on the CD-ROM.

✦ In Chapter 52, I create intelligent "updated" flags that tell visitors what's new or updated on your site since their last visit.

✦ Finally, in Chapter 53 I show you how to build a Decision Helper that could be a practical interactive application on a Web site lacking control over the server.

Develop a practical application with the Decision Helper in Chapter 53 on the CD-ROM.

Appendixes

Netscape Navigator Object Road Map and Compatibility Guide

The following pages contain the text of a handy pamphlet whose Adobe Acrobat (.pdf) file you'll find on the companion CD-ROM. The arrangement of the following material has been modified for printing in this appendix. The .pdf file on the CD-ROM, which you can print it out for quick reference, offers a more compact arrangement. With this compact guide, you can see at a glance the breadth of each object's properties, methods, and event handlers. You can also see which language's words are compatible with each scriptable browser through the level 4 browsers. For instructions on printing and assembling this pamphlet, see the howtoprt.txt readme file on the CD-ROM.

Netscape Navigator 4 Object Road Map

Netscape Navigator 4 Document Object Model Containment Hierarchy

window

closed[N3,M4]	alert("msg")
defaultStatus	back()[N4]
document	blur()[N3,M4]
frames[i]	captureEvents(type)[N4]
history	clearInterval(ID)[N4,M4]
innerHeight[N4,(S)]	clearTimeout(ID)
innerWidth[N4,(S)]	close()
location	confirm("msg")
locationbar[N4,(S)]	disableExternalCapture()[N4,(S)]
menubar[N4,(S)]	enableExternalCapture()[N4,(S)]
name	find([("str")][,case, bkwd])[N4]
onerror[N3,M4]	focus()[N3,M4]
opener[N3,M3]	forward()[N4]
outerHeight[N4,(S)]	handleEvent(event)[N4]
outerWidth[N4,(S)]	home()[N4]
pageXOffset[N4]	moveBy(Δx,Δy)[N4,(S)]
pageYOffset[N4]	moveTo(x,y)[N4,(S)]
parent	open(URL, "name","specs")[(1),(S)]
personalbar[N4,(S)]	print()[N4]
scrollbars[N4,(S)]	prompt("msg","reply")[N4]
self	releaseEvents(type)[N4]
status	resizeBy(Δx,Δy)[N4,(S)]
statusbar[N4,(S)]	resizeTo(width,height)[N4,(S)]
toolbar[N4,(S)]	routeEvent(event)[N4]
top	scroll(x,y)[N3,M4]
window	scrollBy(Δx,Δy)[N4]
	scrollTo(x,y)[N4]
	setInterval(func, msec [,args])[N4,M4,(2)]
	setTimeout(func, msec [,args])[N4,M4,(3)]
	stop()[N4]

onBlur=[N3,M4]
onDragDrop=[N4,(S)]
onFocus=[N3,M4]
onLoad=
onMove=[N4]
onResize=[N4,M4]
onUnload=

(1)New window specs for all browsers: height, width, toolbar, location, directories, status, menubar, scrollbars, resizable, copyhistory. Additional specs for Navigator 4: alwaysLowered(S), alwaysRaised(S), dependent, hotkeys, innerHeight, innerWidth, outerHeight, outerWidth, screenX, screenY; titlebar(S), z-lock(S).
(2)Optional args parameter added to N4; 3rd parameter in M4 is for scripting language.
(3)Third parameter in N4 for args; in M4 for scripting language.

locationbar[N4], menubar[N4], personalbar[N4], scrollbars[N4], statusbar[N4], toolbar[N4]

visible	(None)

history

length	back()
current[(S),(1)]	forward()
next[(S),(1)]	go(int | "URL")
previous[(S),(1)]	

(None)   (None)

(1)Introduced in Navigator 3.0 for use with a trial security method no longer in use. Available in Navigator 4 with signed scripts.

document

alinkColor	captureEvents(type)[N4]
anchors[i]	clear()
applets[i][N3,M4]	close()
bgColor	getSelection()[N4,(2)]
cookie	handleEvent(event)[N4]
domain[N3,M4]	open("mimetype" [,replace])[(3)]
embeds[i][N3,M4]	releaseEvents(type)[N4]
fgColor	routeEvent(event)[N4]
forms[i]	write("string")
images[i][N3,M4]	writeln("string")
lastModified	
layers[i][N4]	
linkColor	
links[i]	
location[(1)]	
referrer	
title	
URL[N3,M4]	
vlinkColor	

(None)

(1)Replaced by the URL property in Navigator 3.
(2)M4 has a document.selection property to retrieve the currently selected text.
(3)mimetype parameter new in M4, but only "text/html" type supported.

location

hash	assign("URL")
host	reload([unconditional])[N3,M4]
hostname	replace("URL")[N3,M4]
href	
pathname	
port	
protocol	
search	

(None)

layer[N4]

above	load("filename",y)
background	moveAbove(layerObj)
below	moveBelow(layerObj)
bgColor	moveBy(Δx, Δy)
clip.top	moveTo(x, y)
clip.left	moveToAbsolute(x, y)
clip.right	resizeBy(Δx, Δy)
clip.bottom	resizeTo(width, height)
clip.width	
clip.height	
document	
left	
name	
pageX	
pageY	
parentLayer	
siblingAbove	
siblingBelow	
src	
top	
visibility	
zIndex	

onBlur=
onFocus=
onLoad=
onMouseOut=
onMouseOver=
onMouseUp=

How to Use This Map

The hierarchy diagram shows the relationships among various HTML-generated objects in Netscape Navigator 4. Follow the dark lines to create references to objects:

`window.document.formName.textName.value`

The three columns in the individual object listings show the properties, methods, and event handlers for the object.

Netscape Navigator 4 Object Road Map

image$^{N3,(1),M4}$

(None)	onAbort= onError= onLoad=

border
complete
height
hspace
lowsrc
name
src
vspace
width
x^{N4}
y^{N4}

(1)Implemented in MSIE 3 for Macintosh, but not Windows.

link (<A HREF=...></A>)

(None)	onClick= onDblClick=$^{N4,(1),M4}$ onMouseDown=^{N4,M4} onMouseOut=^{N3,M4} onMouseOver= onMouseUp=^{N4,M4}

hash
host
hostname
href
pathname
port
protocol
search
target
text^{N4}
x^{N4}
y^{N4}

(1)Not implemented for Macintosh Navigator 4.

area^{N3,M4}

(None)	onClick=^{N4} onMouseOut= onMouseOver=

hash
host
hostname
href
pathname
port
protocol
search
target

applet^{N3,M3}

(Java vars) (Java methods) (None)

anchor (<A NAME=...></A>)

(None) (None)

name^{N4,M4}
text^{N4}
x^{N4}
y^{N4}

form

handleEvent(evt)^{N4} reset()^{N3,M4} submit()	onReset=^{N3,M4} onSubmit=

action
elements[i]
encoding
length
method
name
target

text, textarea, password, hidden

blur() focus() handleEvent(event)^{N4} select()	onBlur= onChange= onFocus= onKeyDown=^{N4,M4} onKeyPress=^{N4,M4} onKeyUp=^{N4,M4} onSelect=

defaultValue
form
name
type^{N3,M4}
value(1)

(1)Password value returns empty string in Navigator 2.

checkbox

click() handleEvent(evt)^{N4}	onClick= onMouseDown=^{N4,M4} onMouseUp=^{N4,M4}

checked
defaultChecked
name
type^{N3,M4}
value

radio

click() handleEvent(evt)^{N4}	onClick= onMouseDown=^{N4,M4} onMouseUp=^{N4,M4}

checked
defaultChecked
length
name
type^{N3,M4}
value

fileUpload$^{N3,M4,(1)}$

blur() focus() handleEvent(evt)^{N4} select()	onBlur= onFocus= onSelect=

name
value

(1)IE4 does not use Netscape's "fileUpload" terminology, but both objects refer to the same kind of <INPUT type="file"> tag.

JavaScript Levels

JavaScript has gone through three versions. The following browsers support features from the corresponding JavaScript level:

Browser	JavaScript Level
Netscape Navigator 2.0x	1.0
MS Internet Explorer 3.0x	1.0
Netscape Navigator 3.0x	1.1
Netscape Navigator 4.0x	1.2
MS Internet Explorer 4.0x	1.2

No other mainstream browsers support JavaScript.

Browser Compatibility Guide

This map is a Netscape-centric view of JavaScript. No items unique to Microsoft Internet Explorer (MSIE) are listed, but Netscape-only items are. Items that have no superscript notation are available to all JavaScript-enabled browsers, including Navigator 2 and MSIE 3. Superscript notations are keyed as follows:

N3 — New in Netscape 3

N4 — New in Netscape Navigator 4

M3 — New in Netscape 3 and MSIE 3

M4 — New in MSIE 4

J2 — New in MSIE 3, JScript.dll Version 2

(S) — Requires Netscape Navigator 4 Signed Scripts

If an item shows N3 or N4 but not M3 or M4, it means that the feature is Netscape-only, and is not available in MSIE.

select

blur()^{N3,M4} focus()^{N3,M4} handleEvent(evt)^{N4}	onBlur= onChange= onFocus=

length
name
options[]
options[i].defaultSelected
options[i].index
options[i].selected
options[i].text
options[i].value
selectedIndex
type^{N3,M4}

button, reset, submit

click() handleEvent(evt)^{N4}	onClick= onMouseDown=^{N4,M4} onMouseUp=^{N4,M4}

name
type^{N3,M4}
value

Netscape Navigator 4 Global Objects

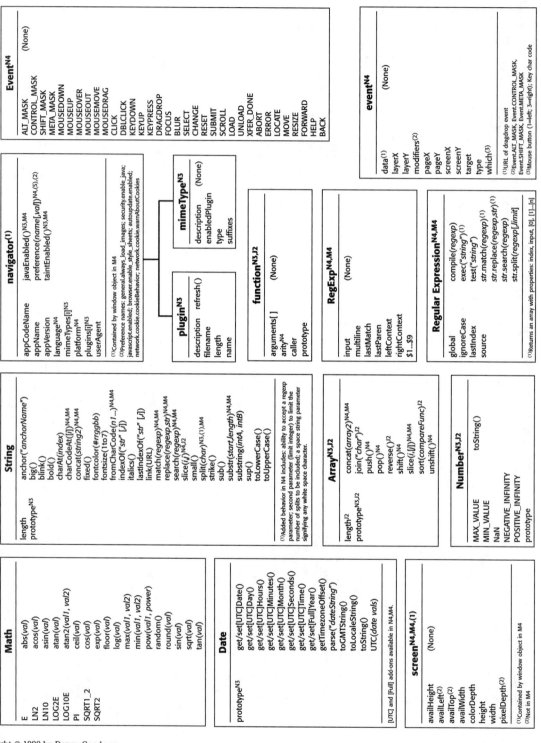

Event[N4]

	(None)
ALT_MASK	
CONTROL_MASK	
SHIFT_MASK	
META_MASK	
MOUSEDOWN	
MOUSEUP	
MOUSEOVER	
MOUSEOUT	
MOUSEMOVE	
MOUSEDRAG	
CLICK	
DBLCLICK	
KEYDOWN	
KEYUP	
KEYPRESS	
DRAGDROP	
FOCUS	
BLUR	
SELECT	
CHANGE	
RESET	
SUBMIT	
SCROLL	
LOAD	
UNLOAD	
XFER_DONE	
ABORT	
ERROR	
LOCATE	
MOVE	
RESIZE	
FORWARD	
HELP	
BACK	

event[N4]

	(None)
data[(1)]	
layerX	
layerY	
modifiers[(2)]	
pageX	
pageY	
screenX	
screenY	
target	
type	
which[(3)]	

(1)URL of dragdrop event
(2)Event.ALT_MASK, Event.CONTROL_MASK, Event.SHIFT_MASK, Event.META_MASK
(3)Mouse button (1=left; 3=right); Key char code

navigator[(1)]

appCodeName	javaEnabled()[N3,M4]
appName	preference(name[,val])[N4,(5),(2)]
appVersion	taintEnabled()[N3,M4]
language[N4]	
mimeTypes[i][N3]	
platform[N4]	
plugins[i][N3]	
userAgent	

(1)Contained by window object in M4
(2)Preference names: general.always_load_images; security.enable_java; javascript.enabled; browser.enable_style_sheets; autoupdate.enabled; network.cookie.cookieBehavior; network.cookie.warnAboutCookies

mimeType[N3]

	(None)
description	
enabledPlugin	
type	
suffixes	

plugin[N3]

description	refresh()
filename	
length	
name	

function[N3,J2]

	(None)
arguments[ ]	
arity[N4]	
caller	
prototype	

RegExp[N4,M4]

	(None)
input	
multiline	
lastMatch	
lastParen	
leftContext	
rightContext	
$1...$9	

Regular Expression[N4,M4]

global	compile(regexp)
ignoreCase	exec("string")[(1)]
lastIndex	test("string")
source	str.match(regexp)[(1)]
	str.replace(regexp,str)[(1)]
	str.search(regexp)
	str.split(regexp[,limit]

(1)Returns an array with properties: index, input, [0], [1]...[n]

String

length	anchor("anchorName")
prototype[N3]	big()
	blink()
	bold()
	charAt(index)
	charCodeAt([i])[N4,M4]
	concat(string2)[N4,M4]
	fixed()
	fontcolor(#rrggbb)
	fontsize(1to7)
	fromCharCode(n1...)[N4,M4]
	indexOf("str" [,i])
	italics()
	lastIndexOf("str" [,i])
	link(URL)
	match(regexp)[N4,M4]
	replace(regexp,str)[N4,M4]
	search(regexp)[N4,M4]
	slice(i,j)[N4,J2]
	small()
	split(char)[N3,(1),M4]
	strike()
	sub()
	substr(start,length)[N4,M4]
	substring(intA, intB)
	sup()
	toLowerCase()
	toUpperCase()

(1)Added behavior in N4 includes: ability to accept a regexp parameter; second parameter (limit integer) to limit the number of splits to be included; a space string parameter signifying any white space character.

Array[N3,J2]

length[J2]	concat(array2)[N4,M4]
prototype[N3,J2]	join("char")[J2]
	push()[N4]
	pop()[N4]
	reverse()[J2]
	shift()[N4]
	slice(i,[j])[N4,M4]
	sort(compareFunc)[J2]
	unshift()[N4]

Number[N3,J2]

MAX_VALUE	toString()
MIN_VALUE	
NaN	
NEGATIVE_INFINITY	
POSITIVE_INFINITY	
prototype	

Math

E	abs(val)
LN2	acos(val)
LN10	asin(val)
LOG2E	atan(val)
LOG10E	atan2(val1, val2)
PI	ceil(val)
SQRT1_2	cos(val)
SQRT2	exp(val)
	floor(val)
	log(val)
	max(val1, val2)
	min(val1, val2)
	pow(val1, power)
	random()
	round(val)
	sin(val)
	sqrt(val)
	tan(val)

Date

prototype[N3]	get/set[UTC]Date()
	get/set[UTC]Day()
	get/set[UTC]Hours()
	get/set[UTC]Minutes()
	get/set[UTC]Month()
	get/set[UTC]Seconds()
	get/set[UTC]Time()
	get/set[UTC]FullYear()
	getTimezoneOffset()
	parse("dateString")
	toGMTString()
	toLocaleString()
	toString()
	UTC(date vals)

[UTC] and [Full] add-ons available in N4,M4.

screen[N4,M4,(1)]

	(None)
availHeight	
availLeft[(2)]	
availTop[(2)]	
availWidth	
colorDepth	
height	
width	
pixelDepth[(2)]	

(1)Contained by window object in M4
(2)Not in M4

Operators

Comparison

==	Equals
!=	Does not equal
>	Is greater than
>=	Is greater than or equal to
<	Is less than
<=	Is less than or equal to

Arithmetic

+	Plus (and string concat.)
–	Minus
*	Multiply
/	Divide
%	Modulo
++	Increment
--	Decrement
–val	Negation

Assignment

=	Equals
+=	Add by value
–=	Subtract by value
*=	Multiply by value
/=	Divide by value
%=	Modulo by value
<<=	Left shift by value
>=	Right shift by value
>>=	Zero fill by value
&=	Bitwise AND by value
|=	Bitwise OR by value
^=	Bitwise XOR by value

Boolean

&&	AND
||	OR
!	NOT

Bitwise

&	Bitwise AND
		Bitwise OR
^	Bitwise XOR
~	Bitwise NOT
<<	Left shift
>>	Right shift
>>>	Zero fill right shift

Miscellaneous

delete[N4,M4]	Property destroyer
new	Object creator
this	Object self-reference
typeof[N3,M3]	Value type
void[N3,M3]	Return no value

Functions of All Objects

watch(id, handler)[N4]	toString()
unwatch(id)[N4]	

Control Statements

```
if (condition) {
    statementsIfTrue
}

if (condition) {
    statementsIfTrue
} else {
    statementsIfFalse
}

result = condition ? expression1 : expression2

for ([init expr]; [condition]; [update expr]) {
    statements
}

for (var in object) {
    statements
}

while (condition) {
    statements
}

with (object) {
    statements
}

do {
    statements
} while (condition)
```
[N4,M4]

```
switch (expression) {
    case label1 :
        statements
        [break]
    case label2 :
        statements
        [break]

    ...

    [default :
        statements]
}
```
[N4,M4]

```
label :
```
[N4,M4]
```
continue [label]
```
[N4,M4]
```
break [label]
```
[N4,M4]

Global Functions

escape("str" [,1])	eval(expression)
unescape("str")	isNaN(expression)
Boolean(value)[N4]	parseFloat("string")
Number("str")[N4]	parseInt("string")
String(value)[N4]	

JavaScript Reserved Words

Every programming language has a built-in vocabulary of keywords that cannot be used for the names of variables and the like. For JavaScript, the restrictions also include any names assigned to functions or objects. Netscape's list of reserved words closely mirrors that of the Java language, thus many of the keywords in the list do not — at least yet — apply to JavaScript. In addition to the reserved words specified for Netscape's JavaScript, the ECMA standards group has identified current and future reserved keywords. The list here is a composite of the Netscape and ECMAScript reserved words. Remember that JavaScript keywords are case-sensitive, so while you may get away with using these words in other cases, it may lead to unnecessary confusion for someone reading your scripts.

abstract	boolean	break	byte
case	catch	char	class
const	continue	debugger	default
delete	do	double	else
enum	export	extends	false
final	finally	float	for
function	goto	if	implements
import	in	instanceof	int
interface	long	native	new
null	package	private	protected
public	return	short	static
super	switch	synchronized	this
throw	throws	transient	true
try	typeof	var	void
while	with		

Answers to Tutorial Exercises

This appendix provides answers to the tutorial exercises that appear in Part II of this book (Chapters 4 through 12).

Chapter 4 Answers

1. The music jukebox (a) and temperature calculator (d) are good client-side JavaScript applications. Even though the jukebox relies on server storage of the music files, you can create a more engaging and responsive user interface of buttons, swappable images, and information from a plug-in, such as LiveAudio. The temperature calculator is a natural, because all processing is done instantaneously on the client, rather than having to access the server for each conversion.

    The Web site visit counter (b) that accumulates the number of different visitors to a Web site is a server-side CGI application, because the count must be updated and maintained on the server. At best, a client-side counter could keep track of the number of visits the user has made to a site and report to the user how many times he or she has been to the site. The storage would require scripting the cookie (Chapter 16). A chat room application (c) done properly requires server facilities to open up communication channels among all users connected simultaneously. Client-side scripting by itself cannot create a live chat environment.

2. The first task is to determine a valid identifier for the General Motors location in the hierarchy. Then "connect the dots":

   a. General_Motors.Chevrolet.Malibu

   b. General_Motors.Pontiac.Firebird

   c. General_Motors.Pontiac.Bonneville

3.   a. Valid, because it is one contiguous word. InterCap spelling is fine.

   b. Valid, because an underscore character is acceptable between words.

   c. Not valid, because an identifier cannot begin with a numeral.

   d. Not valid, because no spaces are allowed.

   e. Not valid, because apostrophes and most other punctuation are not allowed.

4. The names I assign here are arbitrary, but the paths are not.

```
document.myPicture
document.entryForm
document.entryForm.nameField
document.entryForm.addressField
document.entryForm.phoneField
document.entryForm.noArchiveBox
```

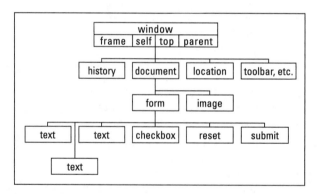

5. `<INPUT TYPE="button" NAME="Hi" VALUE="Howdy" onClick="alert('Hello to you, too!')">`

Chapter 5 Answers

1.
```
<SCRIPT LANGUAGE="JavaScript">
<!--
document.write("Hello, world.")
// -->
</SCRIPT>
```

2.
```
<HTML>
<BODY>
<SCRIPT LANGUAGE="JavaScript">
<!--
document.write("Hello, world.")
// -->
</SCRIPT>
</BODY>
</HTML>
```

3.
```
<HTML>
<BODY>
<SCRIPT LANGUAGE="JavaScript">
<!--
// write a welcome message to the world
document.write("Hello, world.")
// -->
</SCRIPT>
</BODY>
</HTML>
```

4. My answer is written so that both event handlers call separate functions. You can also have each event handler invoke the `alert()` method inline.
```
<HTML>
<HEAD>
<TITLE>An onLoad= script</TITLE>
<SCRIPT LANGUAGE="JavaScript">
<!--
function done() {
    alert("The page has finished loading.")
}
function alertUser() {
    alert("Ouch!")
}
// -->
</SCRIPT>
</HEAD>
<BODY onLoad="done()">
Here is some body text.
<FORM>
    <INPUT TYPE="button" NAME="oneButton" VALUE="Press Me!"
    onClick="alertUser()">
</FORM>
</BODY>
</HTML>
```

5. a. The page displays two text fields.

    b. The user enters text into the first field and either clicks or tabs out of the field to trigger the onChange= event handler.

    c. The function displays an all-uppercase version of one field into the other.

Chapter 6 Answers

1. a. Valid.

   b. Not valid. The variable needs to be a single word, such as `howMany` or `how_many`.

   c. Valid.

   d. Not valid. The variable name cannot begin with a numeral. If the variable needs a number to help distinguish it from other similar variables, then put the numeral at the end: `address1`.

2. a. 4

   b. 40

   c. "4020"

   d. "Robert"

3. The functions are `parseInt()` and `parseFloat()`. Strings to be converted are passed as parameters to the functions: `parseInt(document.forms[0].entry.value)`.

4. Both text field values are strings that must be converted to numbers before they can be arithmetically added together. You can use the `parseFloat()` functions either on the variable assignment expressions (for example, `var value1 = parseFloat(document.adder.inputA.value)`) or in the addition expression (`document.adder.output.value = parseFloat(value1) + parseFloat(value2)`).

5. Concatenate means to join together two strings to become one string.

Chapter 7 Answers

1. Because the references in the function point to a text field named `entry` inside a form named `entryForm`, be sure to assign those names to the `NAME` attributes in the respective HTML tags.

```
<HTML>
<HEAD>
<SCRIPT LANGUAGE="JavaScript">
var USStates = new Array(51)
USStates[0] = "Alabama"
USStates[1] = "Alaska"
USStates[2] = "Arizona"
USStates[3] = "Arkansas"
USStates[4] = "California"
USStates[5] = "Colorado"
USStates[6] = "Connecticut"
USStates[7] = "Delaware"
USStates[8] = "District of Columbia"
```

```
USStates[9] = "Florida"
USStates[10] = "Georgia"
USStates[11] = "Hawaii"
USStates[12] = "Idaho"
USStates[13] = "Illinois"
USStates[14] = "Indiana"
USStates[15] = "Iowa"
USStates[16] = "Kansas"
USStates[17] = "Kentucky"
USStates[18] = "Louisiana"
USStates[19] = "Maine"
USStates[20] = "Maryland"
USStates[21] = "Massachusetts"
USStates[22] = "Michigan"
USStates[23] = "Minnesota"
USStates[24] = "Mississippi"
USStates[25] = "Missouri"
USStates[26] = "Montana"
USStates[27] = "Nebraska"
USStates[28] = "Nevada"
USStates[29] = "New Hampshire"
USStates[30] = "New Jersey"
USStates[31] = "New Mexico"
USStates[32] = "New York"
USStates[33] = "North Carolina"
USStates[34] = "North Dakota"
USStates[35] = "Ohio"
USStates[36] = "Oklahoma"
USStates[37] = "Oregon"
USStates[38] = "Pennsylvania"
USStates[39] = "Rhode Island"
USStates[40] = "South Carolina"
USStates[41] = "South Dakota"
USStates[42] = "Tennessee"
USStates[43] = "Texas"
USStates[44] = "Utah"
USStates[45] = "Vermont"
USStates[46] = "Virginia"
USStates[47] = "Washington"
USStates[48] = "West Virginia"
USStates[49] = "Wisconsin"
USStates[50] = "Wyoming"

var stateEntered = new Array(51)
stateEntered[0] = 1819
stateEntered[1] = 1959
stateEntered[2] = 1912
stateEntered[3] = 1836
stateEntered[4] = 1850
stateEntered[5] = 1876
stateEntered[6] = 1788
stateEntered[7] = 1787
stateEntered[8] = 0000
```

```
stateEntered[9] = 1845
stateEntered[10] = 1788
stateEntered[11] = 1959
stateEntered[12] = 1890
stateEntered[13] = 1818
stateEntered[14] = 1816
stateEntered[15] = 1846
stateEntered[16] = 1861
stateEntered[17] = 1792
stateEntered[18] = 1812
stateEntered[19] = 1820
stateEntered[20] = 1788
stateEntered[21] = 1788
stateEntered[22] = 1837
stateEntered[23] = 1858
stateEntered[24] = 1817
stateEntered[25] = 1821
stateEntered[26] = 1889
stateEntered[27] = 1867
stateEntered[28] = 1864
stateEntered[29] = 1788
stateEntered[30] = 1787
stateEntered[31] = 1912
stateEntered[32] = 1788
stateEntered[33] = 1789
stateEntered[34] = 1889
stateEntered[35] = 1803
stateEntered[36] = 1907
stateEntered[37] = 1859
stateEntered[38] = 1787
stateEntered[39] = 1790
stateEntered[40] = 1788
stateEntered[41] = 1889
stateEntered[42] = 1796
stateEntered[43] = 1845
stateEntered[44] = 1896
stateEntered[45] = 1791
stateEntered[46] = 1788
stateEntered[47] = 1889
stateEntered[48] = 1863
stateEntered[49] = 1848
stateEntered[50] = 1890

function getStateDate() {
    var selectedState = document.entryForm.entry.value
    for ( var i = 0; i < USStates.length; i++) {
        if (USStates[i] == selectedState) {
            break
        }
    }
    alert("That state entered the Union in " + stateEntered[i] +
".")
}
```

```
</SCRIPT>
</HEAD>
<BODY>
<FORM NAME="entryForm">
Enter the name of a state:
<INPUT TYPE="text" NAME="entry">
<INPUT TYPE="button" VALUE="Look Up Entry Date"
onClick="getStateDate()">
</BODY>
</HTML>
```

2. Several problems plague this function definition. Parentheses are missing from the first `if` construction's condition statement. Curly braces are missing from the second nested `if...else` construction. A mismatch of curly braces also exists for the entire function. The following is the correct form (changes and additions in boldface):

```
function format(ohmage) {
    var result
    if (ohmage >= 10e6) {
        ohmage = ohmage / 10e5
        result = ohmage + " Mohms"
    } else {
        if (ohmage >= 10e3) {
            ohmage = ohmage / 10e2
            result = ohmage + " Kohms"
        } else {
            result = ohmage + " ohms"
        }
    }
    alert(result)
}
```

3. Here is one possibility:

```
for (var i = 1; i < tomatoes.length; i++) {
    if (tomatoes[i].looks == "mighty tasty") {
        break
    }
}
var myTomato = tomatoes[i]
```

4. The new version defines a different local variable name for the dog.

```
<HTML>
<HEAD>
<SCRIPT LANGUAGE="JavaScript">
var aBoy = "Charlie Brown"    // global
var hisDog = "Snoopy"         // global
function sampleFunction() {
    // using improper design to demonstrate a point
    var WallacesDog = "Gromit"        // local version of hisDog
    var output = WallacesDog + " does not belong to " + aBoy +
".<BR>"
    document.write(output)
```

```
}
</SCRIPT>
<BODY>
<SCRIPT LANGUAGE="JavaScript">
sampleFunction()        // runs as document loads
document.write(hisDog + " belongs to " + aBoy + ".")
</SCRIPT>
</BODY>
</HTML>
```

5. The application uses three parallel arrays and is structured very much like the solution to question 1. Learn to reuse code whenever you can.

```
<HTML>
<HEAD>
<SCRIPT LANGUAGE="JavaScript">
var planets = new Array(4)
planets[0] = "Mercury"
planets[1] = "Venus"
planets[2] = "Earth"
planets[3] = "Mars"

var distance = new Array(4)
distance[0] = "36 million miles"
distance[1] = "67 million miles"
distance[2] = "93 million miles"
distance[3] = "141 million miles"

var diameter = new Array(4)
diameter[0] = "3100 miles"
diameter[1] = "7700 miles"
diameter[2] = "7920 miles"
diameter[3] = "4200 miles"

function getPlanetData() {
    var selectedPlanet = document.entryForm.entry.value
    for ( var i = 0; i < planets.length; i++) {
        if (planets[i] == selectedPlanet) {
            break
        }
    }
    var msg = planets[i] + " is " + distance[i] + " from the Sun
and "
    msg += diameter[i] + " in diameter."
    document.entryForm.output.value = msg
}
</SCRIPT>
</HEAD>
<BODY>
<FORM NAME="entryForm">
Enter the name of a planet:
<INPUT TYPE="text" NAME="entry">
<INPUT TYPE="button" VALUE="Look Up a Planet"
onClick="getPlanetData()">
```

```
<BR>
<INPUT TYPE="text" SIZE=70 NAME="output">
</BODY>
</HTML>
```

Chapter 8 Answers

1. a. Close, but no cigar. Array references are always plural: `window.document.forms[0]`.

   b. Not valid: `self` refers to a window and `entryForm` must refer to a form. Where's the `document`? It should be `self.document.entryForm.entryField.value`.

   c. Valid.

   d. Not valid. The `document` reference is missing from this one.

   e. Valid, assuming that `newWindow` is a variable holding a reference to a subwindow.

2. `window.status = "Welcome to my Web page."`

3. `document.write("<H1>Welcome to my Web page.</H1>")`

4. A script in the Body portion invokes a function that returns the text entered in a `prompt()` dialog box.

```
<HTML>
<HEAD>
<SCRIPT LANGUAGE="JavaScript">
function askName() {
    var name = prompt("What is your name, please?","")
    return name
}
</SCRIPT>
</HEAD>
<BODY>
<SCRIPT LANGUAGE="JavaScript">
document.write("Welcome to my web page, " + askName() + ".")
</SCRIPT>
</BODY>
</HTML>
```

5. The URL can be derived from the location object.

```
<HTML>
<HEAD>
<SCRIPT LANGUAGE="JavaScript">
function showLocation() {
    alert("This page is at: " + location.href)
}
</SCRIPT>
</HEAD>
<BODY onLoad="showLocation()">
```

```
Blah, blah, blah.
</BODY>
</HTML>
```

Chapter 9 Answers

1. For Listing 9-1, pass the text object because that's the only object involved in the entire transaction.

```
<HTML>
<HEAD>
<TITLE>Text Object value Property</TITLE>
<SCRIPT LANGUAGE="JavaScript">
function upperMe(field) {
    field.value = field.value.toUpperCase()
}
</SCRIPT>
</HEAD>
<BODY>
<FORM onSubmit="return false">
<INPUT TYPE="text" NAME="convertor" VALUE="sample"
onChange="upperMe(this)">
</FORM>
</BODY>
</HTML>
```

For Listing 9-2, the button invokes a function that communicates with a different element in the form. Pass the form object.

```
<HTML>
<HEAD>
<TITLE>Checkbox Inspector</TITLE>
<SCRIPT LANGUAGE="JavaScript">
function inspectBox(form) {
    if (form.checkThis.checked) {
        alert("The box is checked.")
    } else {
        alert("The box is not checked at the moment.")
    }
}
</SCRIPT>
</HEAD>
<BODY>
<FORM>
<INPUT TYPE="checkbox" NAME="checkThis">Check here<BR>
<INPUT TYPE="button" VALUE="Inspect Box"
onClick="inspectBox(this.form)">
</FORM>
</BODY>
</HTML>
```

For Listing 9-3, again the button invokes a function that looks at other elements in the form. Pass the form object.

```
<HTML>
<HEAD>
<TITLE>Extracting Highlighted Radio Button</TITLE>
<SCRIPT LANGUAGE="JavaScript">
function fullName(form) {
    for (var i = 0; i < form.stooges.length; i++) {
        if (form.stooges[i].checked) {
            break
        }
    }
    alert("You chose " + form.stooges[i].value + ".")
}
</SCRIPT>
</HEAD>

<BODY>
<FORM>
<B>Select your favorite Stooge:</B>
<INPUT TYPE="radio" NAME="stooges" VALUE="Moe Howard" CHECKED>Moe
<INPUT TYPE="radio" NAME="stooges" VALUE="Larry Fine" >Larry
<INPUT TYPE="radio" NAME="stooges" VALUE="Curly Howard" >Curly<BR>
<INPUT TYPE="button" NAME="Viewer" VALUE="View Full Name..."
onClick="fullName(this.form)">
</FORM>
</BODY>
</HTML>
```

For Listing 9-4, all action is triggered by and confined to the select object. Pass only that object to the function.

```
<HTML>
<HEAD>
<TITLE>Select Navigation</TITLE>
<SCRIPT LANGUAGE="JavaScript">
function goThere(list) {
    location = list.options[list.selectedIndex].value
}
</SCRIPT>
</HEAD>

<BODY>
<FORM>
Choose a place to go:
<SELECT NAME="urlList" onChange="goThere(this)">
    <OPTION SELECTED VALUE="index.html">Home Page
    <OPTION VALUE="store.html">Shop Our Store
    <OPTION VALUE="policies">Shipping Policies
    <OPTION VALUE="http://www.yahoo.com">Search the Web
</SELECT>
</FORM>
</BODY>
</HTML>
```

2. This requires a bit of surgery. The Submit button is replaced with a standard button whose VALUE attribute is set to "Submit." The button's onClick= event handler calls the checkForm() function, which performs the validation. If an empty field exists, the function must return to bail out of the loop. Because the event handler is not expecting any returned value, you can simply issue the return statement to stop the function altogether. If all the tests pass, then the form is submitted with the submit() method. Functions that have a return statement inside an if construction must also have a return statement outside the construction so it always returns a value (including the null value used here). The other change is that the onSubmit= event handler has been removed from the <FORM> tag, because it is no longer needed (the submit() method does not trigger an onSubmit= event handler).

```
<HTML>
<HEAD>
<TITLE>Validator</TITLE>
<SCRIPT LANGUAGE="JavaScript">
function checkForm(form) {
    for (var i = 0; i < form.elements.length; i++) {
        if (form.elements[i].value == "") {
            alert("Fill out ALL fields.")
            return
        }
    }
    form.submit()
    return
}
</SCRIPT>
</HEAD>

<BODY>
<FORM>
Please enter all requested information:<BR>
First Name:<INPUT TYPE="text" NAME="firstName" ><BR>
Last Name:<INPUT TYPE="text" NAME="lastName" ><BR>
Rank:<INPUT TYPE="text" NAME="rank" ><BR>
Serial Number:<INPUT TYPE="text" NAME="serialNumber" ><BR>

<INPUT TYPE="button" VALUE="Submit" onClick="checkForm(this.form)">
</FORM>
</BODY>
</HTML>
```

3. The this keyword refers to the text field object, so this.value refers to the value property of that object.

```
function showText(txt) {
    alert(txt)
}
```

4.
```
document.accessories.acc1.value = "Leather Carrying Case"
document.forms[1].acc.value = "Leather Carrying Case"
```

5. The select object invokes a function that does the job.

```
<HTML>
<HEAD>
<TITLE>Color Changer</TITLE>
<SCRIPT LANGUAGE="JavaScript">
function setColor(list) {
    var newColor = list.options[list.selectedIndex].value
    document.bgColor = newColor
}
</SCRIPT>
</HEAD>

<BODY>
<FORM>
Select a background color:
<SELECT onChange="setColor(this)">
<OPTION VALUE="red">Stop
<OPTION VALUE="yellow">Caution
<OPTION VALUE="green">Go
</SELECT>
</FORM>
</BODY>
</HTML>
```

Chapter 10 Answers

1. Use `string.indexOf()` to see if the field contains the "@" symbol.

```
<HTML>
<HEAD>
<TITLE>E-mail Validator</TITLE>
<SCRIPT LANGUAGE="JavaScript">
function checkAddress(form) {
    if (form.email.value.indexOf("@") == -1) {
        alert("Check the e-mail address for accuracy.")
        return false
    }
    return true
}
</SCRIPT>
</HEAD>

<BODY>
<FORM onSubmit="return checkAddress(this)">
Enter your e-mail address:
<INPUT TYPE="text" NAME="email" SIZE=30><BR>
<INPUT TYPE="submit">
</FORM>
</BODY>
</HTML>
```

2. Remember that the substring goes up to, but does not include, the index of the second parameter. Spaces count as characters.

```
myString.substring(0,3)      // result = "Net"
myString.substring(13,18)    // result = "gator"
myString.substring(4,12)     // result = "cape Nav"
```

3. The missing for loop is in boldface. You could also use the increment operator on the count variable (++count) to add 1 to it for each letter "e."

```
function countE(form) {
    var count = 0
    var inputString = form.mainstring.value.toUpperCase()
    for (var i = 0; i < inputString.length; i++) {
        if (inputStr.charAt(i) == "e") {
            count += 1
        }
    }
    alert("The string has " + count + " instances of the letter
e.")
}
```

4. The formula for the random throw of one die is in the chapter.

```
<HTML>
<HEAD>
<TITLE>E-mail Validator</TITLE>
<SCRIPT LANGUAGE="JavaScript">
function roll(form) {
    form.die1.value = Math.round(Math.random() * 5) + 1
    form.die2.value = Math.round(Math.random() * 5) + 1
}
</SCRIPT>
</HEAD>

<BODY>
<FORM>
<INPUT TYPE="text" NAME="die1" SIZE=2>
<INPUT TYPE="text" NAME="die2" SIZE=2><BR>
<INPUT TYPE="button" VALUE="Roll the Dice"
onClick="roll(this.form)">
</FORM>
</BODY>
</HTML>
```

5. If you used the Math.round() method in your calculations, that is fine for your current exposure to the Math object. Another method, Math.ceil(), may be more valuable because it rounds up any fractional value.

```
<HTML>
<HEAD>
<TITLE>Waiting for Santa</TITLE>
<SCRIPT LANGUAGE="JavaScript">
function daysToXMAS() {
    var oneDay = 1000 * 60 * 60 * 24
```

```
        var today = new Date()
        var XMAS = new Date("December 25, 1998")
        var diff = XMAS.getTime() - today.getTime()
        return Math.ceil(diff/oneDay)
    }
    </SCRIPT>
    </HEAD>

    <BODY>
    <SCRIPT LANGUAGE="JavaScript">
    document.write(daysToXMAS() + " days until next Christmas.")
    </SCRIPT>
    </BODY>
    </HTML>
```

Chapter 11 Answers

1. `onLoad="parent.currCourse = 'history101'"`

2.

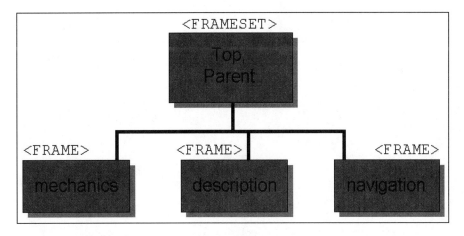

3. All three frames are siblings, so references include the parent.

```
parent.mechanics.location.href = "french201M.html"
parent.description.location.href = "french201D.html"
```

4. A script in one of the documents is attempting to reference the selector object in one of the frames but the document has not fully loaded, causing the object to not yet be in the browser's object model. Rearrange the script so that it fires in response to the `onLoad=` event handler of the framesetting document.

5. From the subwindow, the `opener` property refers back to the frame containing the `window.open()` method. To extend the reference to the frame's parent, the reference includes both pieces:
`opener.parent.ObjVarFuncName`.

Chapter 12 Answers

1. A document image object is created by the `<IMG>` tag as the document loads. A memory image object is created with the `new Image()` constructor. Both objects have the same properties, and assigning a URL to the `src` property of a memory object loads the image into the browser's image cache.

2. ```
var janeImg = new Image(100,120)
janeImg.src = "jane.jpg"
```

**3.** ```
document.images["people"].src = janeImg.src
```

4. Surround `<IMG>` tags with link tags, and use the link's `onClick=`, `onMouseOver=`, and `onMouseOut=` event handlers. Set the image's `BORDER` attribute to zero if you don't want the link highlight to appear around the image.

✦   ✦   ✦

JavaScript Internet Resources

As an online technology, JavaScript has plenty of support online for scripters. Items recommended here were taken as a snapshot of Internet offerings in late 1997. But beware! Sites change. URLs change. Be prepared to hunt around for these items if the information provided here becomes out-of-date by the time you read this.

Newsgroups

A secure newsgroup is available at Netscape for developers. The newsgroup address is `netscape.devs-javascript` on the `secnews.netscape.com` server. Another newsgroup is open to the public. Use your newsreader to access `comp.lang.javascript`. You can expect to get quick answers from a wide audience of experienced scripters here.

Listserv

Currently, two listservs support JavaScript discussions, but traffic has been light. Most of the day-to-day action takes place in the `comp.lang.javascript` newsgroup.

Online Documentation

Netscape and Microsoft maintain sites for the latest official documentation for their respective versions of JavaScript. The URLs change, but here are the sites I recommend you explore.

Current JavaScript docs (for Netscape) are available at

```
http://home.netscape.com/eng/mozilla/3.0/handbook/ja
vascript/index.html
```

A zipped set of Netscape's HTML documents is at

`http://developer.netscape.com/library/documentation/jshtm.zip`

New JavaScript features in Netscape Navigator 4 are detailed at

`http://developer.netscape.com/library/documentation/communicator/jsguide/js1_2.htm`

Documentation for Microsoft's implementation of its core language (called JScript) is at

`http://www.microsoft.com/JScript/us/techinfo/jsdocs.htm`

Also be sure to download Microsoft's document object model description. You can find a link from

`http://www.microsoft.com/JScript/`

Documentation for JScript in Internet Explorer 4 is part of Microsoft's Internet Client SDK documentation

`http://www.microsoft.com/msdn/sdk/inetsdk/asetup/`

World Wide Web

You can obtain updated information about this book and JavaScript developments from the Support Center at my Web site: `http://www.dannyg.com`. Follow the links from the home page to the Support Center.

Because most of the bonus applications on the CD-ROM are subject to upgrades and tweaking, you can not only see the latest versions at the public JavaScript area of my site but can also download the files easily from the Support Center area. You will also find a list of errata and recent ramblings based on reader feedback. If you're experiencing difficulty with any scripts or discussions in this book, use the mail link on my site to ask me. But for general scripting questions, you will get a much faster response (sometimes from me) by going to the `comp.lang` newsgroup.

Additional Web sources for JavaScript information are growing rapidly. Check the Netscape site at `http://developer.netscape.com` for the latest information about bug lists, new releases, and beta version documentation. You will also find a number of JavaScript pointers there. And don't overlook the popular Gamelan site `http://www.gamelan.com` for links to Java and JavaScript items of interest.

✦   ✦   ✦

Using the CD-ROM

The accompanying Windows–Macintosh CD-ROM contains more than 150 HTML documents from the book, an electronic version of the Object Roadmap shown in Appendix A, a complete, searchable version of the book, seven bonus chapters, trial software, and the Adobe Acrobat Reader.

System Requirements

To run the JavaScripts on the CD-ROM, you should have a copy of Netscape Navigator 4 (part of Netscape Communicator), although most scripts will also run with Microsoft Internet Explorer 4. JavaScripts can be written with a simple text editor, word processor, or dedicated HTML editor.

To use the Adobe Acrobat Reader, you need the following:

✦ For Windows 3.1, Windows 95, or Windows NT, you should be using a 486 or Pentium computer with 16MB of RAM and 10MB of hard disk space.

✦ Macintosh users require System 7.0 or later, at least 8MB of RAM, and a 68030, 68040, or PowerPC.

Disc Contents

Platform-specific software is located in the appropriate Windows and Macintosh directories on the CD-ROM. The contents include the following items.

JavaScript listings for Macintosh and Windows text editors

These listings are complete HTML documents that serve as examples of most of the JavaScript vocabulary words in Parts III and IV of the book and include the full-blown application examples from Part V of the book. In a few instances, numbered listings in the book may be too small to have their own listing files on the CD-ROM. In addition, no listings are provided for the tutorial chapters of Part II, because you are encouraged to enter HTML and scripting code manually.

The Macintosh and Windows Listings folders have many nested folders for specific chapters' listings. You can run these files with Netscape Navigator 4 or later.

For your convenience, an index.html file in the JavaScript Bible listings folder provides a front-end table of contents to the HTML files for the book's program listings. Open that file from Navigator whenever you want to access the program listing files. You may also access individual files directly from the browser. For example, to open the file containing Listing 19-1 from Chapter 19, choose Open from Navigator's File menu (the Open Page in Navigator choice in the Macintosh version) and use the file dialog box to locate the file named lst19-01.htm inside the Chap19 directory. To examine and modify the HTML source files, open them from your favorite text editor program.

You can access and use the JavaScript files on the CD-ROM from both Windows and Macintosh environments. For Windows 95, access the software with My Computer or Windows Explorer; for Windows 3.x, use the File Manager. Mac users can access files by using the Finder.

You can open all example files directly from the CD-ROM, but if you copy them to your hard drive, access is faster and you will be able to experiment with modifying the files more readily. Copy the folder named Scripts from the CD-ROM to any location on your hard drive.

JavaScript Object Road Map from Appendix A (Adobe Acrobat format)

If you like the roadmap illustration in Appendix A, you can print it out on two sides of two sheets of paper with the help of the Adobe Acrobat Reader, included with the CD-ROM. The file NS4_Obj.pdf contains this illustration in .pdf format. Start Acrobat Reader on your computer, and open the file from either the CD-ROM or from a copy made to your hard drive. Before printing out the document, be sure to choose landscape orientation in the Page Setup dialog box of Acrobat Reader. You can find full assembly and collating instructions in a companion text file, howtoprt.txt.

Adobe Acrobat Reader

The Adobe Acrobat Reader is a helpful program that enables you to view the JavaScript Object Road Map and the searchable version of this book (including seven bonus application chapters), all of which are in .pdf format on the CD-ROM. It is important that you install the Search edition of Acrobat Reader to use this function. To install and run Adobe Acrobat Reader, follow these steps:

For Windows

1. Start Windows Explorer, Windows NT Explorer, or File Manager and then open the Acrobat folder on the CD-ROM.

2. In the Acrobat folder, double-click RS32e301.exe and follow the instructions presented on-screen for installing Adobe Acrobat Reader.

For Macintosh

1. Open the Acrobat and Search folders on the CD-ROM.

2. In the Acrobat folder, double-click the Search Installer icon and follow the instructions presented on-screen for installing Adobe Acrobat Reader.

Searchable version of the book

This is a complete, searchable version of the book, provided in Adobe Acrobat .pdf format. Access it from the JSB3 folder after installing Adobe Acrobat Reader. The first time you open a .pdf file in Acrobat Reader, click on the Search icon (binoculars in front of a sheet of paper); then click the Index button and select index.pdx from the JSB3 folder. This flags the proper index for each use of the searchable version of the book.

Bonus JavaScript application chapters

Seven full-fledged, JavaScript-enhanced applications can be found in the Bonus folder. These are provided as .pdf files that you can read and search through after installing Adobe Acrobat Reader. Each chapter demonstrates important concepts that you will likely want to include in your applications. See the text on the bonus application chapters at the end of Part IV for details.

Trial software

We've also included the following 30-day trial software for your review:

Macromedia Dreamweaver and Flash

Try out these two leading Web site creation tools from Macromedia. Installation instructions: Double-click on setup.exe (for Windows) or the Demo Install icon (for Mac) in the appropriate application folder under the Macromedia folder.

Marketwave HitList (Windows only)

Collect hit data and other statistics with these three versions of the software: HitList Pro Evaluation, HitList Standard Evaluation, and HitList Enterprise Evaluation. Installation instructions: Double-click on Setup.exe in the Marketwave folder.

✦   ✦   ✦

Index

Note: Italic page numbers reference tables, figures, and listings.

(continued)

(continued)

(continued)

(continued)

(continued)

(continued)

(continued)

(continued)

IDG BOOKS WORLDWIDE, INC.
END-USER LICENSE AGREEMENT

READ THIS. You should carefully read these terms and conditions before opening the software packet(s) included with this book ("Book"). This is a license agreement ("Agreement") between you and IDG Books Worldwide, Inc. ("IDGB"). By opening the accompanying software packet(s), you acknowledge that you have read and accept the following terms and conditions. If you do not agree and do not want to be bound by such terms and conditions, promptly return the Book and the unopened software packet(s) to the place you obtained them for a full refund.

1. **License Grant.** IDGB grants to you (either an individual or entity) a nonexclusive license to use one copy of the enclosed software program(s) (collectively, the "Software") solely for your own personal or business purposes on a single computer (whether a standard computer or a workstation component of a multiuser network). The Software is in use on a computer when it is loaded into temporary memory (RAM) or installed into permanent memory (hard disk, CD-ROM, or other storage device). IDGB reserves all rights not expressly granted herein.

2. **Ownership.** IDGB is the owner of all right, title, and interest, including copyright, in and to the compilation of the Software recorded on the disk(s) or CD-ROM ("Software Media"). Copyright to the individual programs recorded on the Software Media is owned by the author or other authorized copyright owner of each program. Ownership of the Software and all proprietary rights relating thereto remain with IDGB and its licensers.

3. **Restrictions on Use and Transfer.**

    (a) You may only (i) make one copy of the Software for backup or archival purposes, or (ii) transfer the Software to a single hard disk, provided that you keep the original for backup or archival purposes. You may not (i) rent or lease the Software, (ii) copy or reproduce the Software through a LAN or other network system or through any computer subscriber system or bulletin-board system, or (iii) modify, adapt, or create derivative works based on the Software.

    (b) You may not reverse engineer, decompile, or disassemble the Software. You may transfer the Software and user documentation on a permanent basis, provided that the transferee agrees to accept the terms and conditions of this Agreement and you retain no copies. If the Software is an update or has been updated, any transfer must include the most recent update and all prior versions.

4. **Restrictions on Use of Individual Programs.** You must follow the individual requirements and restrictions detailed for each individual program in Appendix E, "Using the CD-ROM," of this Book. These limitations are also

contained in the individual license agreements recorded on the Software Media. These limitations may include a requirement that after using the program for a specified period of time, the user must pay a registration fee or discontinue use. By opening the Software packet(s), you will be agreeing to abide by the licenses and restrictions for these individual programs that are detailed in Appendix E, "Using the CD-ROM," and on the Software Media. None of the material on this Software Media or listed in this Book may ever be redistributed, in original or modified form, for commercial purposes.

5. **Limited Warranty**.

   (a) IDGB warrants that the Software and Software Media are free from defects in materials and workmanship under normal use for a period of sixty (60) days from the date of purchase of this Book. If IDGB receives notification within the warranty period of defects in materials or workmanship, IDGB will replace the defective Software Media.

   (b) **IDGB AND THE AUTHOR OF THE BOOK DISCLAIM ALL OTHER WARRANTIES, EXPRESS OR IMPLIED, INCLUDING WITHOUT LIMITATION IMPLIED WARRANTIES OF MERCHANTABILITY AND FITNESS FOR A PARTICULAR PURPOSE, WITH RESPECT TO THE SOFTWARE, THE PROGRAMS, THE SOURCE CODE CONTAINED THEREIN, AND/OR THE TECHNIQUES DESCRIBED IN THIS BOOK. IDGB DOES NOT WARRANT THAT THE FUNCTIONS CONTAINED IN THE SOFTWARE WILL MEET YOUR REQUIREMENTS OR THAT THE OPERATION OF THE SOFTWARE WILL BE ERROR FREE.**

   (c) This limited warranty gives you specific legal rights, and you may have other rights that vary from jurisdiction to jurisdiction.

6. **Remedies**.

   (a) IDGB's entire liability and your exclusive remedy for defects in materials and workmanship shall be limited to replacement of the Software Media, which may be returned to IDGB with a copy of your receipt at the following address: Software Media Fulfillment Department, Attn.: *JavaScript Bible, 3rd Edition*, IDG Books Worldwide, Inc., 7260 Shadeland Station, Ste. 100, Indianapolis, IN 46256, or call 1-800-762-2974. Please allow three to four weeks for delivery. This Limited Warranty is void if failure of the Software Media has resulted from accident, abuse, or misapplication. Any replacement Software Media will be warranted for the remainder of the original warranty period or thirty (30) days, whichever is longer.

   (b) In no event shall IDGB or the author be liable for any damages whatsoever (including without limitation damages for loss of business profits, business interruption, loss of business information, or any other pecuniary loss) arising from the use of or inability to use the Book or the Software, even if IDGB has been advised of the possibility of such damages.

(c) Because some jurisdictions do not allow the exclusion or limitation of liability for consequential or incidental damages, the above limitation or exclusion may not apply to you.

7. **U.S. Government Restricted Rights.** Use, duplication, or disclosure of the Software by the U.S. Government is subject to restrictions stated in paragraph (c)(1)(ii) of the Rights in Technical Data and Computer Software clause of DFARS 252.227-7013, and in subparagraphs (a) through (d) of the Commercial Computer — Restricted Rights clause at FAR 52.227-19, and in similar clauses in the NASA FAR supplement, when applicable.

8. **General.** This Agreement constitutes the entire understanding of the parties and revokes and supersedes all prior agreements, oral or written, between them and may not be modified or amended except in a writing signed by both parties hereto that specifically refers to this Agreement. This Agreement shall take precedence over any other documents that may be in conflict herewith. If any one or more provisions contained in this Agreement are held by any court or tribunal to be invalid, illegal, or otherwise unenforceable, each and every other provision shall remain in full force and effect.